A Selecti

Leading Cases in Equity

With notes

(Volume I)

Frederick Thomas White,

Owen Davies Tudor

Alpha Editions

This edition published in 2019

ISBN : 9789353953409

Design and Setting By
Alpha Editions
email - alphaedis@gmail.com

A SELECTION

OF

LEADING CASES IN EQUITY,

With Notes.

BY

FREDERICK THOMAS WHITE

AND

OWEN DAVIES TUDOR,

OF THE MIDDLE TEMPLE, ESQRS., BARRISTERS-AT-LAW.

With Annotations,

CONTAINING REFERENCES TO AMERICAN CASES,

BY J. I. CLARK HARE AND H. B. WALLACE.

WITH ADDITIONAL NOTES AND REFERENCES TO AMERICAN DECISIONS,

BY J. I. CLARK HARE.

Fourth American, from the Fourth London Edition.

IN TWO VOLUMES.

VOL. I.

PHILADELPHIA:

T. & J. W. JOHNSON & CO.,

LAW BOOKSELLERS AND PUBLISHERS,

No. 535 CHESTNUT STREET.

1876.

PREFACE

TO THE FIRST EDITION OF VOL. I.

THE plan of this work was suggested by the very able volumes of the late Mr. John William Smith, which contain a selection of Leading Cases principally taken from the Common Law Reports; and it was thought that it might be useful to the profession to have, within a small compass, a selection of Leading Cases decided in Courts of Equity.

Each of the cases chosen will, it is believed, be found either to be frequently referred to in practice, or to enunciate clearly, for the first time, some important principle of equity.

A chronological arrangement of the cases has not been observed, because it has been in the present, and may be in a subsequent volume, found useful to print together cases on the same subject, decided at different periods.

The notes, or abstracts prefixed to the cases, have occasionally, when inaccurate or defective, been altered; and, in some instances, the arguments and judgment in the same case are taken from different reports. Thus, in the well-known case of *Fox* v. *Mackreth*, the arguments are taken from Brown's Chancery Cases, and the judgment from Cox's Reports; and in the celebrated case of *Garth* v. *Cotton*, (a complete report of which is not to be found elsewhere,) the arguments are taken from two different places in Vesey Senior's Reports, the judgment from Dicken's Reports, and the decree from Atkyn's Reports.

In the notes, an attempt has been made to develop the principles laid down or acted upon in the cases, and to collect the recent authorities; but as the nature of the work would not permit that the notes should be complete essays upon the different subjects treated of, they have been principally confined to the points decided in the cases, to which, in fact, they are only intended to be subsidiary.

It will be seen, that, in the notes, some cases of importance are stated at considerable length, and that when it was convenient or practicable, the very words of the Judges have been preserved.

Of imperfections and deficiencies in the notes, the Editors are by no means unconscious, but they venture to hope that the cases (the selection of which, from the great mass of the Equity Reports, was a matter of no small difficulty) will prove useful both to students and to those in actual practice.

July, 1849.

ADVERTISEMENT

TO THE FOURTH LONDON EDITION.

In preparing this Edition, about two hundred pages of new matter have been added to the Notes. A very large number has also been added to the cases cited, which are brought down by the Addenda to the 19th of October, 1872.

November, 1872.

PREFACE

TO THE AMERICAN EDITION.

In the American notes to this work, the range of discussion marked out by the English annotations, has usually been followed, as far as was practicable. In some instances, it will, perhaps, be found, that the field of investigation is more extensive than in the original work. It is narrower, in those cases, only, in which illustrations were not supplied by the American reports.

It will be seen, upon the whole, that the jurisprudence of this country has developed an equity system, scarcely less comprehensive, or less complete, than that which has been established in England: and it is a conclusive testimony to the wisdom and practicable usefulness of the English Chancery, that, at the suggestions of experience, its scheme has been adopted, substantially, throughout a country, not influenced by considerations of authority, but proceeding freely, in quest of essential justice, and under the guidance of a reason proud of its independence.

The doctrine of *Subrogation*, in the learning of Principal and Surety, may be referred to, as an example, in which, among us, a more expanded and consistent application has been given to a settled and valuable principle of equity, and in which the sense of American Judges seems to have gained au advantage, even, over England's greatest Chancellor. Our rule, as to a feme covert's power over her separate estate, is more reasonable and satisfactory, than that prevailing in England ; where, the provision against anticipation admits, without fully controlling, the danger of the original principle. A few titles—such as *Vendor's Lien, Equitable Mortgages, the Tacking of Incumbrances,* and a *Purchaser's duty to see to the application of purchase-money,*—have not been received with much favor here, chiefly in consequence of the policy connected with our registration laws. There are some other subjects—such, for example as the *Purchase of reversionary and expectant interests,* illustrated in the great case of *Chesterfield* v. *Janssen*—which, perhaps, from the rarity of settlements giving rise to such interests, have not often come before our courts for adjudication, though the principles belonging to them, are perfectly well established in this country.

In this edition some three hundred pages have been added to the American notes, and the authorities for the most part brought down to the present time.

PHILADELPHIA, *April,* 1875.

LIST OF CASES REPORTED.

INDEX

TO THE

CASES CITED IN THE ENGLISH NOTES.

THE PAGES REFERRED TO ARE THOSE BETWEEN BRACKETS [   ].

XXX TABLE OF CASES.

INDEX

CASES CITED IN THE AMERICAN NOTES.

THE NUMBERS REFER TO THE PAGING OF THE AMERICAN EDITION.

A SELECTION

OF

LEADING CASES IN EQUITY,

With Notes.

BY

F. T. WHITE AND O. D. TUDOR,

OF THE MIDDLE TEMPLE, ESQRS., BARRISTERS AT-LAW.

With Annotations,

CONTAINING REFERENCES TO AMERICAN CASES,

BY

J. I. CLARK HARE AND H. B. WALLACE.

Fourth American, from the Fourth London Edition.

WITH

ADDITIONAL NOTES AND REFERENCES TO AMERICAN DECISIONS,

BY

J. I. CLARK HARE.

IN TWO VOLUMES.

VOL. I.
Part First.

PHILADELPHIA:
T. & J. W. JOHNSON & CO.,
LAW BOOKSELLERS AND PUBLISHERS,
No. 535 CHESTNUT STREET.
1876.

KING & BAIRD, PRINTERS,
607 Sansom Street, Philadelphia.

LIST OF CASES REPORTED

IN

VOLUME I. PART I.

LEADING CASES IN EQUITY.

LORD GLENORCHY *v.* BOSVILLE.

DE TERM. S. MICH. 1733.

REPORTED CAS. TEMP. TALBOT, 3.

EXECUTED AND EXECUTORY TRUSTS.]—*A. devises real estate to his sister B. and C., and their heirs and assigns, upon trust, until his grand-daughter D. should marry or die, to receive the profits, and thereout to pay her £100 a year for her maintenance; the residue to pay debts and legacies; and after payment thereof, in trust for the said D.; and upon further trust, that, if she lived to marry a Protestant of the Church of England, and at the time of such marriage be at the age of twenty-one or upwards, or, if under that age, such marriage be with the consent of the said B., then to convey the said estate, with all convenient speed after such marriage, to the use of the said D. for life, without impeachment of waste, voluntary waste in houses excepted; remainder to her husband for life; remainder to the issue of her body; with remainders over:—Held, that though D. would have taken an estate tail had it been the case of an immediate devise, yet that the trust being executory, was to be executed in a more careful and more accurate manner; and that a conveyance to D. for life, remainder to her husband for life, with remainder to their first and every other son, with remainder to the daughters, would best serve the testator's intent.*

SIR THOMAS PERSHALL devises all his real estate to his sister, Anne Pershall, and Robert Bosville, and their *heirs and assigns, upon trust, till his grand-daughter, Arabella Pershall, marry or die, to receive the rents and profits thereof, and out of it to pay her 100*l.* a year for her maintenance; and, as to the residue, to pay his debts and legacies; and, after the payment thereof, then in trust for his said grand-daughter; and, upon further trust, that if she lived to marry a Protestant of the Church of England, and at the time of such marriage be of the age of twenty-one or upwards, or if under the age of twenty-one, and [*2] such marriage be with the consent of her aunt, the said Anne Pershall, *then to convey the said estate* with all convenient speed after such marriage, *to the use of the said Arabella for her life, without impeachment of waste, voluntary waste in houses excepted;* remainder, after her death, to her husband for life; *remainder to the issue of her body;* with several remainders over; and, upon further trust, that if the said Arabella Pershall die unmarried, then to the use of the said Anne Pershall for life; remainder to the son of his other grand-daughter, Frances Ireland, in tail; remainder to Mr. Bosville, the defendant, for life; remainder to his first and other sons; remainder to the testator's right heirs; and, upon further trust, if his grand-daughter marry not according to the directions of his will, then upon such marriage, to convey the said estate to trustees; as to one moiety thereof, to the use of the said Arabella for life; remainder to trustees to preserve contingent remainders; remainder to her first and every other son, being a Protestant; with several remainders over; and, as to the other moiety, to his daughter Ireland's son in like manner.

Sir Thomas Pershall died in the year 1722, and Mrs. Arabella Pershall in 1723 attained her full age; and upon a treaty of marriage in 1729, she applies to the trustees for a conveyance of the estate to herself for life; remainder to her intended husband for life; remainder to the issue of her body; and such conveyance was executed by one of the trustees. But Mr. Bosville, the other trustee, who was also a remainder-man, refused to convey. However, she having by this conveyance a legal estate tail in *one [*3] moiety, and an equitable estate tail in the other moiety, suffered a recovery to the use of herself in fee, and in 1730 married the plaintiff, the Lord Glenorchy, who made a considerable settlement upon her; and as to her own estate, she covenanted to settle it upon the Lord Glenorchy and herself for life; remainder to the first and every other son of the marriage, in tail male; and upon failure of such issue, to the survivor of the said husband and wife in fee.

The bill was to have a conveyance of the moiety of the said trust estate from Mr. Bosville to such uses as are limited in the said covenant; and the principal question was whether, under the said will, the Lady Glenorchy was tenant for life or in tail? upon which two other questions arose, viz., first, whether the words in the will, in an immediate devise of a legal estate, would have carried an estate tail? secondly, if so, whether the Court will make any difference between a legal title and a trust estate executory?

[*Lord Chancellor King.*—I should upon the first question make no difficulty of determining it an estate tail, had this been an immediate devise; but when you apply to this court for the carrying a trust estate into execution, the doubt is, whether we shall not vary from the rules of law to follow the testator's intent; which will also bring on another question,—What is the testator's intent in the present case?]

Upon the second question, it was argued for the plaintiffs, that the Lady Glenorchy was, under this will, entitled to an estate tail in equity; for this Court puts the same construction upon limitations of trusts in equity as the law does upon legal estates, and that to prevent confusion. This doctrine is laid down with the strongest reasons by the Earl of Nottingham in the *Duke of Norfolk's Case;*[1] and the authority of *Baile* v. *Coleman*, 2 Vern. 670,[2] where a trust to one for life, remainder to the heirs male of his body, is held an estate tail, has never yet been questioned. So it is held in *Legatt* v. *Sewell*, 2 Vern. 551 (but more fully reported in 1 Abr. Eq. Ca. *394)[3] where money was given to be laid out in land [*4] to one for life, and after his decease to his heirs male, and the heirs male of the body of every such heir male, severally and successively one after another; and a case being made for the opinion of the judges, as of a legal estate, they certified it to be an estate tail. So, in the case of *Bagshaw* v. *Downes*, or *Bagshaw* v. *Spencer*, at the Rolls, Hil. 6 Geo. 2,[4] an executory trust was directed to the judges for their opinion as a legal estate. Upon the same reason do cestuis que trust levy fines and suffer recoveries which are held good in this Court. Indeed, in marriage articles, if they covenant to settle to the husband for life, remainder to the heirs of their two bodies, this Court will decree a conveyance in strict settlement, if any of the parties apply here, because the children are looked upon as purchasers. But in a will it is otherwise; they take through the bounty of the testator, and in such words as he gives it.

It was further insisted for the plaintiffs, that the words *issue of her body* would make a difference from all other cases; for, in the Statute De Donis, which created entails, it is said to be a proper word for that purpose, and is used no less than ten times in that statute; for this the authority of *King* v. *Melling*, 1 Vent. 214, 225,[5] and the reason there given, cannot be contested, which is also an authority in the principal case; for there it is held that a devise to one for life, with a power to make a jointure, is much stronger to show the intent of the testator than the words *without impeachment of waste*. To A. for life, remainder to the issue of her body, and, for want of such issue, remainder over, was held an estate tail in the Court of Exchequer, in the case of *Williams* v. *Tompson*, about three or four years ago. Anders. 86. To one for life, remainder to the children of his body, is an entail. So in *Wild's Case*, 6 Co. 16 (L. Cas. R. Prop. 581, 2nd ed.), and *Sweetapple* v. *Bindon*, 2 Vern. 536.

It was further argued, that, if the remainder in this case to the issue be construed to be words of purchase, they must be attended with the greatest absurdity; for in *what manner [*5] can the issue take? All the sons, daughters and grand-

---

[1] 3 Ch. Ca. 26—47; and 2 Swanst. 454.   [2] S. C., 1 P. Wms. 142; 1 Ves. 151.
[3] S. C., 1 P. Wms. 87; see 2 Ves, 657.
[4] Bagshaw v. Spencer, 2 Atk. 246, 570; on appeal, Id. 577.
[5] S. C., 2 Lev. 58, 61.

children are issue; and if they take as purchasers, they must be joint-tenants, or tenants in common, and that for life only,[1] 2 Vern. 545; which construction can never be agreeable to the testator's intent; and whatever estate was given in the first part of the will, yet the words, "*and for want of such issue, then,*" &c., will give the plaintiff an estate tail, according to the cases of *Langley* v. *Baldwin*, and *Shaw* and *Weigh*, 1 Abr. Eq. Ca. 184, 185, Fitzg. 7. It was also further urged, that from the space of the whole will, and by comparing this clause with the other, it appears that the testator intended the plaintiff, the Lady Glenorchy, should take an estate tail, and that the several clauses in a will are to be taken together, and make but one conveyance; and that it was a proper argument to prove the intention of the party from the different penning of the several clauses. The person who drew the will knew how to convey, either by words of limitation or purchase, where there was occasion for it; for where he limits the estate to Mrs. Ireland, it is in strict settlement by proper words of purchase; and so where he limits it to the Lady Glenorchy, in case she had married a Papist. But further, to shew he well understood the doctrine of conveyances, when he limits by words of purchase to sons not in esse, he has put in trustees to preserve contingent remainders, which he would certainly have done in this case had he intended the Lady Glenorchy an estate for life only.

For the defendant, it was argued, that though in the construction of wills in this Court, uses and trusts are to be governed by the same rules as legal estates, and that there is but little difference between uses and trusts executed and legal estates; yet trusts executory are by no means under the same consideration. In the cases of *Legatt* v. *Sewell*, and *Baile* v. *Coleman*, the Judges were divided in their opinions, and since that time there is an express authority for the defendant. In the case of *Papillon* v. *Voice*, Hil. 5 Geo. 2;[2] so likewise in the *case of the Attorney-General* v. *Young*, in the Court of Exchequer; and the case of *Leonard* v. *Earl of Sussex*, 2 Vern. 526; as also in the case of *Bramston* v. *Kinaston*, heard at the Rolls in June, 1728, where an estate was given by the testator to be settled upon his grandchild for her life, remainder to the issue of her body; and, when she applied to have an estate tail conveyed to her, she was decreed an estate for life only. And to show that this Court is not tied up to the rules of law in cases of executory trusts, the case of the *Earl of Stamford* v. *Sir John Hobart*, concerning Serjeant Maynard's will, was cited, where an estate was given to trustees to convey one moiety to Sir John Hobart, for ninety-nine years, in case he should so long live, with several remainders over; and this Court decreed the Master should settle the conveyance according to the letter of the will; but upon exceptions to the Master's Report, Nov. 19, 1709, it was ordered that proper estates should be made

[*6]

---

[1] Cook v. Cook.　　　　　　　　[2] 2 P. Wms. 471.

to support the remainders, that the testator's intent might not be frustrated; and this resolution was affirmed in the House of Lords.[1] So, in all matters executory, this Court endeavours to find the intent of the parties, and lets it prevail against the rules of law. In marriage settlements it was never doubted but that this Court would carry any words into strict settlement, if the intent of the parties was such; and so held in the case of *West* v. *Erisey*, in the House of Lords;[2] and in that of *Trevor* v. *Trevor*, 1 Abr. Eq. Ca. 387;[3] and the same rules will prevail in cases executory, whether wills or articles. Besides, the present case is very much like that of marriage articles. The testator had all along the marriage of his grand-daughter in view, and intended this will as no more than heads or directions for the trustees in what manner he would have it settled; and so it remains to be carried into execution by the aid of this Court.

Then as to the word *issue*, it is sometimes a word of limitation, sometimes of purchase. There is a case mentioned in *Wild's Case*, 6 Co. 16, where to one and his children is held to be an estate tail; yet had it been to *one for life, remainder to his children, there can be no doubt but that it had been a bare [*7] estate for life. And as to the objection, that the issue, if purchasers, are to take jointly and for life only, why shall it not be as in cases where the limitation is to the first and every other son, and wherever heirs of the body are held to be words of purchase, they are construed to the first and every other son.

To make an estate tail arise by implication upon the words "*and for want of such issue*," has been cited the case of *Langley* v. *Baldwin*, 1 Abr. Eq. Ca. 185. But there is the case of *Bamfield* v. *Popham*, 2 Vern. 427, 449, for the defendant, so the case of *Loddington* v. *Kime*, 3 Lev. 431, and that of *Backhouse* v. *Wells*, 1 Abr. Eq. Ca. 184; besides, it is a general rule, that where an estate is to be raised by implication, it must be a necessary and inevitable implication, and such as that the words can have no other construction whatsoever; and in the present case, there is the word "*issue*" mentioned before; so that these last words must relate to the issue before mentioned. Whereas in the case of *Langley* v. *Baldwin*, the limitation is to six sons only; then come the words "*and for want of issue*," which words could not have relation to anything before mentioned.

LORD CHANCELLOR TALBOT had taken time to advise, and to have the opinion of the judges upon this case: And the same coming now again to be argued upon the same points that had been before the late Lord Chancellor (Lord King).

It was insisted by the plaintiffs' counsel, that the Lady Glenorchy's marrying a Protestant of the Church of England at or

---

[1] 3 Bro. P. C. 31 Toml. ed., 30th Mar. 1710.
[2] 1 Bro. P. C. 225, Toml. ed., overruling the decision of the Barons of the Exchequer, reported 2 P. Wms. 349.
[3] *S. C.*, 1 P. Wms. 622; 5 Bro. P. C. 122, Toml. ed.

after the age of twenty-one, or, if under that age, marrying such an one with her aunt's, or in case she was dead, with the other trustees' consent, was a condition precedent; which, when performed, would give her an estate tail. That this intent appeared from the different penning of the several clauses in this will; for it provides, in case she should not marry such a person as is before described, that she should have but a moiety for *life, [*8] and trustees are appointed to preserve contingent remainders; none of which are injoined in case she should marry a Protestant of the Church of England; which shows a difference was intended in case of performance and non-performance of the condition. Then considering it as a legal devise, no doubt but that a devise to one and the issue of his body will make an estate tail; and so it was held in the case of *King* v. *Melling*, 1 Vent. 214, 225, notwithstanding the proviso there, empowering the devisee to make a jointure; so if in this case the land itself had been devised to the Lady Glenorchy, it would have made an entail at law; and there is no difference between an entail of a legal estate and of an equitable one. *Wild's Case*, 6 Co. 16, devise to a man and his children, who had then two children alive, the devisee took but for life; but in *King* v. *Melling*, 1 Vent. 214, 225, Lord Hale said, that had there been no children living in that case of *Wild*, it would have been an estate tail; though children be not so strong a word as issue; which in many statutes, particularly the Statute de Donis, takes in all the children. In *Shelley's Case*, 1 Co. 88 b (L. Cas. R. Prop. 507, 2nd ed.), it is said, that if there be a gift to one for life, be it by deed or will, and afterwards comes a gift to the heirs of his body, it is an entail; otherwise indeed, if the limitation be to the heirs male of such heir male, as in *Archer's Case*, 1 Co. 66, there it would make but an estate for life; because the limitation there is grafted upon the word "heirs." So, in the case of *Backhouse* v. *Wells*, in B. R. 1712, 1 Abr. Eq. Ca. 184, the devisee took but for life, the limitation being there grafted upon the word "issue;" which for that reason was taken to be only a description of the person in that case; but in *Cosen's Case*, Owen, 29, and in *Langley* v. *Baldwin*, 1 Abr. Eq. Ca. 185, the estate tail was raised by implication; which shews that an estate tail may pass not only by express words but by implication also. In *King* v. *Melling*, the Lord Hale said upon *Wild's Case*, "That had it been to the children of the body, it would have passed an entail;" and yet none of those cases seem so strong as the present. So, in the *case of Cook [*9] v. Cook*, 2 Vern. 545, it is said, "That a devise to one and his children, if there be no children living, will be an estate tail."

The exception of waste is next to be considered; and had it not been for that, this would clearly have passed an entail; but this exception varies not the case, for here the estates must disjoin according to *Lewis Bowle's Case*. 11 Co. 79 b (L. Cas. R. Prop. 27, 2nd ed.), to let in the husband's estate, which must intervene between her estate and that of her issue; and the power of committing waste (*voluntary waste in houses excepted*), was given only to make her dispunishable of waste during the time she should be tenant for life only; which she must be until her husband's death, by reason of the remainder to him, but not at all to restrain the estate, which the words of the will give her, which is plainly an estate tail. The adding the words "*without impeachment of waste*," can alter nothing; for if she was tenant in tail, she had already in her that power which these words would give her; and the expressing the power which was already in her could no more abridge her estate (according to the maxim of *Expressio corom quæ tacitè insunt nil operatur*), than the power of making the jointure did in *King* and *Melling's Case*. In *Langley* v. *Baldwin* there were the same words as here; and that of *Shaw* and *Weigh*, or *Sparrow* v. *Shaw*,[1] 1 Abr. Eq. Ca. 184, which went up to the House of Lords, the prohibition went not only to voluntary but to all manner of waste, and yet there it was decreed to be an estate tail; which was a much stronger implication to make the sister to be but tenant for life than any in the present case. And in *Baile* v. *Coleman*, 2 Vern. 670, an estate tail was decreed by the Lord Harcourt, notwithstanding the power of leasing given to Christopher Baile. Nor can the other words *voluntary waste in houses excepted*, carry the implication further than the former; since this Court will often restrain a tenant for life without impeachment of waste, from committing waste, notwithstanding his power, as was declared by the Earl of Nottingham in *Williams* v. *Day*, 2 Ch. Ca. 32, who there said, that he would stop the pulling *down of houses or defacing a seat by tenant in tail after [*10] possibility of issue extinct, or by tenant for life, though dispunishable of waste by express grant or by trust; and the like has been since done in the case of *Vane* v. *Lord Barnard*, 2 Vern. 733. By comparing this with the other clauses of this will, it appears plainly that the testator did not intend the Lady Glenorchy a less estate than to the other devisees; but that his design was to prefer her and her issue to that of Mrs. Frances Ireland, though Frances was dead at the time of the will; and that her son, who could expect no more favour than his mother could, had she been living, should not have an immediate estate tail, and so a greater estate than she who was intended to be most preferred. It is plain the testator well knew the difference between giving an estate for life and an estate tail, by the different wording of the clauses of this will. In that, whereby he devises the remainder to Mr. Bosville, these words are purposely omitted; and in others he gives the Lady Glenorchy several estates, according to her marrying such or such persons, Protestants or Papists; and, consequently, he must be thought to have intended her a greater estate upon her performing than upon her not performing the condition. If, therefore, these words would create an estate tail at law, the construction will be the same here, since a Court of equity

---

[1] 3 Bro. P. C. 120, Toml. ed.

ought not to go further than the Courts of law; as was held by
Lord Cowper in the case of *Legatt* v. *Sewell*, 2 Vern. 551, 1 Abr.
Eq. Ca. 394, and was also held by Lord Harcourt in the case of
Baile v. *Coleman*, 2 Vern. 670, where he takes a difference between
cases arising upon wills and cases arising upon marriage articles,
where the persons being all purchasers, the agreement is to be
carried into stricter execution than in the case of a will, where
the parties being but volunteers, the words must be taken as you
find them.   The same is held totidem verbis in the case of *Sweetapple* v. *Bindon*, 2 Vern. 536, where it is said " That in a devise,
all being volunteers, the devisee's estate is not to be restrained,
nor is there any argument to be drawn from this being an execu-
[*11] tory trust, since the case *of *Baile* v. *Coleman* was such,
        and looked upon as such by the Lords Cowper and Har-
court; and the case of *Leonard* v. *Earl of Sussex*, 2 Vern. 526, is
widely different from ours, for there was an express injunction
that it should be settled in such manner as that the sons should
never have it in their power to bar the issue.

It was argued for the defendant by Mr. Attorney-General, Mr.
Verney, and Mr. Fazakerley, that the Lady Glenorchy could take
but an estate for life; and they took a difference between the
present case, being of an executory trust, and those of *Cosen's*,
and of *Cook* v. *Cook*, which were legal estates and executed.   The
resolution in *Sonday's Case*, 9 Co. 127 b (which was likewise of
a legal estate) was chiefly founded upon the proviso, restraining
the son or his issue from aliening, which made the argument that
he was intended by the testator to be tenant in tail, since, if he
had been but tenant for life, the restraint had been vain and
needless.   In the case of *Langley* v. *Baldwin*, an estate tail was
raised by implication upon the words, " if he die without issue
male; " because the devise extending no further than the sixth
son, no son born after could have taken ; but the heir-at-law must
have been preferred ; whereas his intent was to provide equally
for all his sons, and, therefore, the raising an estate tail by implication (besides that it was in the case of a legal estate) was carrying the testator's intent into execution.   The case of *King* v.
Melling has, indeed, gone very far, but has always been looked
upon as the ne plus ultra, beyond which no Court would ever go.
This appears from the resolution in the case of *Backhouse* v.
Wells, where the parties intent prevailed against the doctrine now
insisted on.   But it is said, the word *issue* is always a word of
limitation.   In that of *Sweetapple* v. *Bindon*, the words did of
themselves carry an estate tail, and there was no intent appearing to the contrary.   And in. *Legatt* v. *Sewell*, one judge was
of opinion it was but an estate for life, and that case was afterwards agreed.

The difference which was insisted on in the former argument,
[*12] and is still strongly relied on for the defendant, *between
        legal estates and trusts executed, and trusts executory, is
evident, and appears plainly from the case of *Leonard* v. *Earl of*

Sussex, where the words were much stronger to create an estate
tail than they are here; but yet, in that case, the Court declared,
that, it being a trust executory, the provision should be looked
upon as strong for the benefit of the issue, as if it had been in
marriage articles; and that the testator's intent (appearing by the
subsequent words), " *that none should have power to dock the entail* "
should be observed, therefore decreed but an estate for life. This
difference appears likewise from the cases of *White* v. *Thornborough,*
2 Vern. 702, and *Trevor* v. *Trevor,* Eq. Ca. Ab. 387, and from that
of *Papillon* v. *Voice,* Hil. 5 Geo. 2, which is not distinguishable
from our case, except that there were trustees appointed in that
case to preserve contingent remainders, which are not in this.
But notwithstanding that provision, the late Lord Chancellor[1]
declared, in that case, that the limitation, had it been by act executed, would have created an estate tail; but that the trust being
executory, and to be carried into execution by the assistance of
this Court, he would keep the parties to the observance of the
testator's intent, which plainly governs the present case; and by
all those it appears that the testator's intent is as much to be observed in cases of executory trusts as of marriage articles. If,
therefore, the testator's intent is to be observed, and that no
words which may have any operation are to be rejected, it plainly
appears from this and the other clauses of this will, that Sir
Thomas Pershall intended this lady only an estate for life. It is
true, indeed, that the word " *issue* " in a will is generally a word
of limitation, and creates an estate tail; but that is only where no
intent appears to control it. And in every clause of this will,
where he intends only an estate for life, he mentions the words
" *for life;* " and where he intends an estate tail, there is not a
word mentioned of impeachment of waste, which shews he knew
what he was doing when he inserted this exception, and was not
ignorant of the operation these words would have on the
*several estates. And these words were, in the case of [*13]
Loddington v. *Kime,* 3 Lev. 431, taken to be a strong implication of the testator's meaning to give but an estate for life, notwithstanding the other words, which seemed to carry an entail.
Nor is there any colour for what has been insisted on for the
plaintiff, that the power of committing waste, with the restraint
of voluntary waste in houses, was designed only to attend on
her estate for life, till, by her husband's death, she should come
to be tenant in tail, since no more could be meant by it than to
restrain her from defacing or pulling down houses while she was
in her husband's power, the testator not knowing who her husband might be. This power of committing waste has been compared to the power of leasing in the case of *Baile* v. *Coleman,*
though they are widely different; nor can it be compared to that
of making a jointure in *King* v. *Melling;* for, since tenant in tail
cannot make a jointure without a recovery, the power was as

---

[1] King.

proper to be annexed to an estate tail as to an estate for life,
which was one of the reasons of Lord Hale's opinion in that case.
In our case, to serve the intent of restraint of waste in houses, she
must be decreed but an estate for life; if it be an estate tail, she
will be enabled to commit waste in houses as well as in all the
other parts of the estate, notwithstanding any restraint to the
contrary. Nor will the answer that has been given to this, that
she might be restrained in this Court, avail; since no instance
can be shewn where a tenant in tail has been restrained from
committing waste by injunction of this Court.

[*Lord Chancellor.*—That was refused in Mr. *Saville's Case*,[1] of
Yorkshire, who, being an infant, and tenant in tail in possession,
in a very bad state of health, and not likely to live to full age,
cut down by his guardian a great quantity of timber just before
his death, to a very great value; the remainder-man applied here
for an injunction to restrain him, but could not prevail.]

The other objection, that Sir Thomas Pershall could never intend the Lady Glenorchy a less estate than the children of his
[*14] other grand-daughter, Frances Ireland, *turns rather against
the plaintiff; for the testator's intent was to provide for
the Lady Glenorchy's children preferably to those of Frances Ireland, and therefore he makes the lady herself but tenant for life,
and her children tenants in tail. Nor is anything more common
than to limit an estate for life only to the first taker, by which
the intent of providing for children is better answered than if the
first taker was made tenant in tail. Nor will there in this case
follow the inconvenience that has been mentioned, by making the
issue to be purchasers, viz., that the issue must take jointly, and
take estates for life only; for if issue be nomen collectivum, as
has been insisted for the plaintiffs, why may it not be so as well
where they take by purchase, as where they take by limitation?
especially where the testator's intent, that they should take successively, and by seniority of birth, is as well served by their taking one way as the other. And if the word *issue* be tantamount
to the word *heirs*, as it has been agreed to be, they have answered
themselves. In the case of *Burchett* v. *Durdant*, 2 Vent. 311, and
in 2 Lev. 232, by the name of *James* v. *Richardson*, the words,
" *heirs of the body*," were held to be words of purchase, by reason
of the words " *now living*," which came just after, and yet were
at the same time determined to carry an estate tail, the word
" *heirs* " being nomen collectivum; and if so, in case of a legal
estate executed, much more ought this construction to hold here;
this will being meant by the testator only as heads of a settlement to be made, and so may well be thought not to have been
so accurate in the wording as if the conveyance were then to have
been drawn up with advice of counsel, and all other assistances
to make it formal.

Lord Chancellor Talbot.—Several observations have been

[1] See Mos. 224.

made on the different penning of the several clauses of this will, from which I think no inference can be drawn ; the testator having expressed himself variously in many, if not in all of them. It is plain, that by the first part of this will he intended her but an estate for *life till marriage ; then comes the clause upon which the question depends. But before I give my opinion of that, I must observe, that the trustee has not done right ; for nothing was to vest till after her marrying a Protestant. The trustee therefore by conveying, and enabling her to suffer a recovery before marriage, which has been done accordingly, has done wrong. [*15]

But the great question is, what estate she shall take ? And *first*, considering it as a legal devise executed, it is plain that the first limitation, with the power and restriction, carries an estate for life only ; so likewise of the remainder to the husband : But then come the words " *remainder to the issue of her body*," upon which the question arises. The word " *issue* " does, ex vi termini, comprehend all the issue; but sometimes a testator may not intend it in so large a sense, as where there are children alive, &c. That it may be a word of purchase is clear. from the case of *Backhouse* v. *Wells*, and of limitation, by that of *King* v. *Melling;* but that it may be both in the same will has not nor can be proved. The word " *heirs* " is naturally a word of limitation ; and when some other words expressing the testator's intent are added, it may be looked on as a word both of limitation and purchase in the same will ; but should the word " *issue* " be looked upon as both, in the same will, what a confusion would it breed ; for the moment any issue was born, or any issue of that issue, they would all take. The question then will be, whether Sir Thomas Pershall intended the Lady Glenorchy's issue to take by descent or by purchase ? If by purchase, they can take but for life, and so every issue of that issue will take for life; which will make a succession ad infinitum, a perpetuity of estates for life. This inconvenience was the reason of Lord Hale's opinion in *King* v. *Melling*, that the limitation there created an estate tail. It may be, the testator's intent is by this construction rendered a little precarious ; but that is from the power of the law over men's estates, and to prevent confusion. Restraint from waste has been annexed to estates for life, which have *been afterwards construed to be estates tail. I do not say that where an express estate tail is devised, that the annexing a power inconsistent with it, will defeat the estate : No, the power shall be void. But there the power is annexed to the estate for life, which she took first ; and therefore I am rather inclined to think it stronger than *King* v. *Melling*, where there was no mediate estate, as there is here to the husband ; there, there was an immediate devise, here a mediate one ; so the applying this power to the estate for life, carries no incongruity with it. As the estate of *King* v. *Melling*, has never been shaken, and that of *Shaw* v. *Weigh*, or *Sparrow* v. *Shaw*, which went up to the House of Lords, was stronger, I do not [*16]

think that Courts of equity ought to go otherwise than the
Courts of law ; and therefore am inclinable to think it an estate
tail as it would be at law.

But there is another question, viz., How far in cases of trusts
executory, as this is, the testator's estate is to prevail over the
strength and legal signification of the words ? I repeat it, I think,
*in cases of trusts executed or immediate devises, the construction of the
Courts of law and equity ought to be the same; for, there the testator
does not suppose any other conveyance will be made; But in executory
trusts he leaves somewhat to be done; the trusts to be executed in a
more careful and more accurate manner.* The case of *Leonard* v.
The Earl of Sussex, had it been by act executed, would have been
an estate tail, and the restraint had been void ; but *being an executory trust, the Court decreed according to the intent as it was found
expressed in the will, which must now govern our construction.* And
though all parties claiming under this will are volunteers, yet are
they entitled to the aid of this Court to direct their trustees. I
have already said what I should incline to, if this was an immediate devise ; but as it is executory, and that such construction
may be made as that the issue may take without any of the incon-
veniences which were the foundation of the resolution in *King* v.
[*17] *Melling's Case*, and that as the *testator's intent is plain
that the issue should take, the conveyance, by being in the
common form, viz., to the Lady Glenorchy for life, remainder to
her husband the Lord Glenorchy for life, remainder to their first
and every other son, with a remainder to the daughters, will best
serve the testator's intent. In the case of *Earl of Stamford* v.
Sir John Hobart, Dec. 19, 1709, it appeared that, for want of trustees to preserve the contingent remainders, all the uses intended
in the will and in the Act of Parliament to take effect, might
have been avoided ; and therefore the Lord Cowper did, notwithstanding the words of the Act, upon great deliberation, insert
trustees. In the case of *Legatt* v. *Sewell*, the words, if in a settlement, would have made an estate tail; and in that of *Baile* v.
Coleman, the execution was to be of the same estate as he had in
the trust, which in construction of law was an estate tail. Nor
is the rule generally true, that in articles and executory trusts
different constructions are to be admitted ; the late case of *Papillon* v. *Voice* is directly against this ; and it seems to me a very
strong authority for executing the intent in the one case as well
as the other.

And so decreed the Lady Glenorchy but an estate for life, with
remainder, &c.

LEGG v. GOLDWIRE.

NOVEMBER 10, 1736.

REPORTED CAS. TEMP. TALBOT, 20.

N.B. By Lord Chancellor Talbot.—Where articles are entered into before marriage, and a settlement is made *after* marriage different from those articles (as if by articles the estate was to be in strict settlement, and by the settlement the husband is made tenant in tail, whereby he hath it in his power to bar the issue), this Court will set up the articles against the settlement; but where both articles and settlement are *previous* to the marriage, at a time when all parties are at liberty, the *settlement differing from the articles will be taken as a new agreement [*18] between them, and shall control the articles.[1] And although, in the case of *West* v. *Errissey*,[2] Mich. 1726, in the Court of Exchequer, and afterwards in the House of Lords, in 1727, the articles were made to control the settlement made before marriage, yet that resolution no way contradicts the general rule; for in that case the settlement was expressly mentioned to be made in *pursuance and performance of the said marriage articles*, whereby the intent appeared to be still the same as it was at the making of the articles.

" *Lord Glenorchy* v. *Bosville*, in Lord Talbot's time," observes Lord Hardwicke, " has established the distinction between trusts executed and executory : " *Bagshaw* v. *Spencer*, 2 Atk. 582 : His Lordship, however, in the same case, almost denied that any such distinction existed, although he afterwards fully admitted it (see *Exel* v. *Wallace*, 2 Ves. 323 ; *Bastard* v. *Proby*, 2 Cox, 8) ; and it has since been recognized by a long series of decisions. See *Austen* v. *Taylor*, 1 Eden, 367, 368 ; *Countess of Lincoln* v. *Duke of Newcastle*, 12 Ves. 227 ; *Jervoise* v. *Duke of Northumberland*, 1 J. & W. 570 ; *Blackburn* v. *Stables*, 2 V. & B. 369 ; *Lord Deerhurst* v. *Duke of St. Albans*, 5 Madd. 233 ; S. C., nom. *Tollemache* v. *Coventry*, 2 C. & F. 611 ; *Douglas* v. *Congreve*, 1 Beav. 59 ; S. C., 4 Bing. N. C. 1, 5 Bing. N. C. 318 ; *Boswell* v. *Dillon*, 1 Dru. 297. See also *Earl of Stamford* v. *Sir John Hobart*, 3 Bro. P. C. 33 ; Toml. ed. *Papillon* v. *Voice*, 2 P. Wms. 471 ; *Dillon* v. *Blake*, 16 Ir. Ch. Rep. 24.

It is proposed in this note to consider the distinction between trusts

---

[1] See, however, Bold v. Hutchinson, 5 De G. Mac. & G. 558, 567.
[2] 2 P. Wms. 349 ; 3 Bro. P. C. 327 ; Collectanea. Jur. 463.

executed and *executory*, and the consequences which result from it with reference to the limitation of estates.

A trust is said to be *executed* when no act is necessary to be done to give effect to it, the limitation being originally complete, as where an estate is conveyed or devised unto and to the use of A. and his heirs in trust for B. and the heirs of his body.

A trust is said to be *executory* where some further act is necessary to be done by the author of the trust or the trustees, to give effect to it, as in the case of marriage articles, and as in the case of a will where property is vested in trustees in trust to *settle* or *convey* in a more perfect and [*19] *accurate manner; in both of which cases a further act, viz., a settlement or conveyance, is contemplated.

It is now clearly established, as laid down by Lord Talbot in *Lord Glenorchy* v. *Bosville*, that a Court of equity in cases of *executed trusts* will construe the limitation in the same manner as similar legal limitations. If, for instance, an estate is vested in trustees and their heirs in trust for A. for life, without impeachment of waste, with remainder to trustees to preserve contingent remainders, with remainder in trust for the heirs of A.'s body, the trust being an executed trust, A., according to the rule in *Shelley's case*, which is a rule of law, will be held to take an estate tail; See *Wright* v. *Pearson*, 1 Eden, 119; *Austen* v. *Taylor*, 1 Eden, 361; *Jones* v. *Morgan*, 1 Bro. C. C. 206; *Jervoise* v. *Duke of Northumberland*, 1 J. & W. 559, (see *Price* v. *Sesson*, 2 Beasley, 168, 174; *Davison* v. *Goehring*, 7 Barr, 175;) clearly overruling the opinion expressed by Lord *Hardwicke* in *Bagshaw* v. *Spencer*, 2 Atk. 577, when he erroneously reversed the decision of Sir *Joseph Jekyll*, M. R. See also *Boswell* v. *Dillon*, 1 Dru. 291.

In cases, however, of *executory trusts*, where, according to Lord Talbot's observation in *Lord Glenorchy* v. *Bosville*, *something is left to be done, viz., the trusts are left to be executed in a more careful and a more accurate manner*, a Court of equity is not, as in cases of *executed trusts*, bound to construe technical expressions with legal strictness, but will mould the trusts according to the intent of those who create them.

A mere direction, however, *to convey*, upon certain trusts, will not render those trusts executory, in the sense in which the word is used in this note, if the author of the trust has, as it were, taken upon himself to be his own conveyancer, and, instead of leaving anything to be done beyond the mere execution of a conveyance, has defined what the trusts or limitations are to be in accurate and technical terms. " All trusts," observes Lord St. Leonards, " are in a sense executory, because a trust cannot be executed except by conveyance, and therefore, there is something always to be done. But that is not the sense which a court of equity puts upon the term 'executory trust.' A Court of equity considers an executory trust as distinguished from a trust executing itself, and distinguishes the two in this manner :—Has the testator been what is called, and very properly called, his own conveyancer? Has he left it to the Court to make out, from *general expressions*, what his intention is, or has he so defined that intention that you have nothing to do but to take the limitations he has given to you, and to convert them into legal estates ? " *Egerton* v. *Earl of Brownlow*, 4 Ho. L. Cas. 210, and see Ib. p. 49, 60, 61, 181, 88, 209 ; *Austen* v. *Taylor*, 1 *Eden, Rep. 368 367, 368 ; *Wight* v. *Leigh*, 15 Ves. 564, 568 ; *Graham* v. *Stewart*, [*20] 2 Macq. Ho. L. Cas. 295, 325 ; *Herbert* v. *Blunden*, 1 Dru. & Walsh, 78, 89, 91 ; *East* v. *Twyford*, 9 Hare, 713, 733, 4 Ho. L. Ca. 517 ; *Doncaster* v. *Doncaster*, 3 K. & J. 26 ; *Tatham* v. *Vernon*, 29 Beav. 604, 614 ; *Osborn* v. *Bellman*, 2 Giff. 593 ; *Fullerton* v. *Martin*, 1 Drew. & Sm. 31 ; *De Haviland* v. *De Saumarez*, 14 W. R. (L. J.) 118 ; *Lees* v. *Lees*, 5 I. R. Eq. 549 ; and though there is a direction by the testator to the trustees to correct any defect or incorrect expression in his will, and to form a settlement from what appears to them to be his meaning, it will not authorize any change in the limitations, *Stanley* v. *Stanley*, 16 Ves. 491, 511.

It is observed by Lord Talbot, in *Lord Glenorchy* v. *Bosville*, that the rule is not generally true, that in articles and executory trusts (meaning executory trusts in wills) different constructions are to be admitted. This is correct with the qualification or distinction that, in executory trusts under marriage articles, the intention of the parties may fairly be presumed *à priori* from the nature of the transaction ; in executory trusts in wills, it must be gathered from the words of the will alone. Lord Eldon seems to have denied this distinction in *Countess of Lincoln* v. *Duke of Newcastle*, 12 Ves. 227, 230 ; but see his explanation in the case of *Jervoise* v. *Duke of Northumberland*, 1 J. & W. 574. The distinction has been well put by Sir William Grant, M. R., in *Blackburn* v. *Stables*, 2 V. & B. 369 ; " I know," observes his Honor, " of no difference between an executory trust in marriage articles and in a will, *except* that the object and purpose of the former furnish an indication of intention which must be wanting in the latter. When the object is to make a provision, by the settlement of an estate, for the issue of a marriage, it is not to be presumed that the parties meant to put it in the power of the father to defeat that purpose, and appropriate the estate to himself. If, therefore, the agreement is to limit an estate for life, with remainder to the heirs of the body, the Court decrees a strict settlement in conformity to the presumable intention ; but if a will directs a limitation for life, with remainder to the heirs of the body, the Court has no such ground for decreeing a strict settlement. A testator gives arbitrarily what estate he thinks fit ; there is no presumption that he means one quantity of interest rather than another,—an estate for life rather than in tail or in fee. The subject being mere bounty, the intended extent of that bounty can be known only from the words in which it is given ; but, if

[*21] it is clearly to be *ascertained from anything in the will, that the testator did not mean to use the expressions which he has employed, in their strict proper technical sense, the Court, in decreeing such settlement as he has directed, will depart from his words, in order to execute his intention." In *Lord Deerhurst* v. *Duke of St. Albans*, 5 Madd. 260, Sir J. Leach, V. C., observes, as to the distinction between marriage articles and a will, " you are guided to the meaning of articles by the plain object of consideration in them, the issue of the marriage ; but you know nothing of the motive and object of a will, but what you collect from the language of it." See also *Maguire* v. *Scully*, 2 Hog. 113 ; *Stratford* v. *Powell*, 1 Ball & B. 25 ; *Sackville West* v. *Viscount Holmesdale*, 4 L. R. Ho. L. 543 ; *Viscount Holmesdale* v. *West*, 3 L. R. Eq. 474 ; *Magrath* v. *Morehead*, 12 L. R. Eq. 491.

In consequence of the distinction adverted to, it will be most convenient to consider the executory trusts under marriage articles, and executory trusts under wills, separately.

1. *As to Executory Trusts under Marriage Articles.*]—If in articles before marriage, for making a settlement of real estate of either the intended husband or wife, it is agreed that the same shall be settled upon the *heirs of the body* of them or either of them, in such terms as would, if construed with legal strictness, according to the rule in *Shelley's case*, give *either* of them an estate tail, and enable either of them to defeat the provision for their issue, Courts of equity, considering the object of the articles, viz.: to make a provision for the issue of the marriage, will, in conformity with the presumed intention of the parties, decree a settlement to be made upon the husband or wife for life only, with remainder to the issue of the marriage in tail, as purchasers. Thus, in *Trevor* v. *Trevor* (1 Eq. Ca. Abr. 387 ; S. C., 1 P. Wms. 622), A., in consideration of an intended marriage, covenanted with trustees to settle an estate to the use of himself for life, without impeachment of waste, remainder to his intended wife for life, remainder to the use of the heirs males of him on her body to be begotten, and the heirs males of such heirs males issuing, remainder to the right heirs of the said A. for ever, Lord Macclesfield said, that upon articles the case was stronger than on a will ; that articles were only minutes or heads of the agreement of the parties, and ought to be so modelled, when they came to be carried into execution, as to make them effectual ; that the intention was to give A. only an estate for life ; that, if it had been otherwise, the settlement would have been [*22] vain and ineffectual, and it would have been in A.'s power, as *soon as the articles were made, to have destroyed them. And his Lordship therefore held, that A. was entitled to an estate for life only, and that his eldest son took by purchase as tenant in tail. This decision was affirmed on appeal in the House of Lords : 5 Bro, P. C., Toml. ed., 122. In *Streatfield* v. *Streatfield*, Ca. t. Talb. 176 (selected as a leading case on another point), T. S., by articles, agreed to settle lands to

the use of himself and M. his intended wife, for their lives and the life of the survivor; and after the survivor's decease, to the use of the heirs of the body of him the said T. S., on his wife begotten, with other remainders over. After marriage, by a deed reciting the articles, he settled the lands to the use of himself and his wife for their lives and the life of the longest liver of them, without impeachment of waste during the life of T. S.; and after their decease, to the use of the heirs of the body of the said T. S. on the said M. to be begotten; and for want of such issue, to the right heirs of T. S. Lord Talbot held, that the settlement was not a proper execution of the articles, and said that it could not be doubted, but that, upon application to the Court for carrying the articles into execution, it would have decreed it to be done in the strictest manner, and would never leave it in the husband's power to defeat and annul everything he had been doing; and that the nature of the provision was strong enough without express words.

See also *Jones* v. *Laughton*, 1 Eq. Ca. Abr. 392; *Cusack* v. *Cusack*, 5 Bro. P. C., Toml. ed., 116; *Giffith* v. *Buckle*, 2 Vern. 13; *Stonor* v. *Curwen*, 5 Sim. 268, 269; *Davies* v. *Davies*, 4 Beav. 54; *Lambert* v. *Peyton*, 8 Ho. Lo. Ca. 1.

Where in marriage articles the words "heirs of the body," or "issue," are held to indicate an intention that the issue of the marriage should take as purchasers, a settlement will be decreed in favour of daughters as well as sons, viz. on first and other sons successively in tail, with remainder to the daughters as tenants in common in tail, with cross remainders between them: *Nandick* v. *Wilkes*, Gilb. Eq. Rep. 114; S. C., 1 Eq. Ca. Abr. 393, c. 5; *Burton* v. *Hastings*, Gilb. Eq. Rep. 113, S. C., 1 Eq. Ca. Abr. 393; *Hart* v. *Middlehurst*, 3 Atk. 371; *Maguire* v. *Scully*, 2 Hog. 113; S. C., 1 Beat. 370; *Burnaby* v. *Griffin*, 3 Ves. 206; *Horne* v. *Barton*, 19 Ves. 398, Coop. 257, S. C., on an application for a rehearing, 26 L. J. N. S. (Ch.) 225; *Phillips* v. *James*, 2 D. & Sm. 404, 408, 13 W. R. (L. J.) 934. *In re Grier's estate*, 6 I. R. Eq. 1, 11.

In *Rossiter* v. *Rossiter*, 14 Ir. Ch. Rep. 247, the husband agreed to convey to trustees for himself for life, and if his wife survived, to the use of the "wife and children," if no child, to the wife in *fee. A settlement upon the wife for life, with remainder to the children, [*23] was decreed, *Wild's Case*, (6 Co. 16) being held inapplicable to marriage articles.

Where it is agreed to settle real estate to the use of the intended husband for life, remainder to the heirs male of his body, remainder to the *heirs female* of his body, the words "heirs female" will be held to mean daughters of the marriage, and a settlement will be made upon them as tenants in common in tail, with cross remainders between them: *West* v. *Errissey*, 2 P. Wms. 349, Comyn's Rep. 412, 1 Bro. P. C. Toml. ed., 225.

A limitation, however, to the heirs of the body, following after a remainder to the first and other sons of the marriage in tail male, and a remainder to heirs male generally, will not, it seems, be so construed in favour of the daughters of the marriage, especially where portions are by the articles expressly provided for them: *Powell* v. *Price*, 2 P. Wms. 535.

The principle upon which Courts of equity, in such cases as have been considered, decree a strict settlement, seems to be this, viz. to give effect to the presumed intention of the parties to the articles, to make such a provision for the issue of the marriage as it would not be in the power of *either* parent to defeat; where, however, articles are so framed that the concurrence of *both* parents is requisite, in order to defeat the provision for the issue, the same principle does not apply, as it might have been the intention of the parties to the articles, that the husband and wife should *jointly* have such power. Thus where the husband has by articles agreed to settle *his own property* upon himself for life, remainder to his wife for life, with remainder to the heirs of the body of the wife by him, as she would in this case be tenant in tail *ex provisione viri*, and consequently could not, if the property were settled upon her previous to 3 & 4 Will. 4, c. 74, bar the entail without the concurrence of her husband, a settlement making the issue take by purchase would not be decreed: *Whately* v. *Kemp*, cited in *Howel* v. *Howel*, 2 Ves. 358; *Honor* v. *Honor*, 1 P. Wms. 123; *Green* v. *Elkins*, 2 Atk. 477; *Highway* v. *Banner*, 1 Bro. C. C. 584. As, however, the statute 11 Hen. 7, c. 20, has been repealed as to estates *ex provisione viri* by 3 & 4 Will. c. 74, s. 16, this exception from the general rule will cease to be part of the law: *Rochfort* v. *Fitzmaurice*, 2 D. & W. 19.

So, also, where it appears on the face of the articles that the parties themselves knew and made a distinction between limitations in strict settlement, and limitations leaving it in the power of *one* of the parents [*24] to bar the issue, a strict settlement will not be *decreed. Thus, where by articles part of an estate was limited to the husband for life, remainder to the wife for life, remainder to the first and every other son and daughters in tail, and another part to the husband for life and the heirs male of his body by that wife, Lord Macclesfield said, that if the latter had been the sole limitation, he should without scruple decree in strict settlement, according to the common rule; but where the parties had shown they knew the distinction when to put it out of the power of the father, and when to leave it in his power, he would not vary the last limitation decreeing to the father in tail as to the last, though not as to the first: *Anon.*, cited 2 Ves. 359; *Howel* v. *Howel*, 2 Ves. 358; *Powell* v. *Price*, 2 P. Wms. 535; *Chambers* v. *Chambers*, Fitzg. Rep. 127; S. C., Mos. 333, 2 Eq. Ca. Abr. 35, c. 4; *Highway* v. *Banner*, 1 Bro. C. C. 584.

Where words in articles for a settlement would, if interpreted in their strict legal sense, create a joint-tenancy among the children of the marriage, equity will decree a settlement upon them as tenants in common ; for a joint tenancy as a provision for the children of a marriage is an inconvenient mode of settlement, because during their minorities no use can be made of their portions for their advancement, as the joint-tenancy cannot be severed : *Taggart* v. *Taggart*, 1 S. & L. 88 ; *Mayn* v. *Mayn*, 5 L. R. Eq. 150 ; *Liddard* v. *Liddard*, 28 Beav. 266 ; but see *In re Bellasis' trust*, 12 L. R. Eq. 218.

It may be here mentioned, that although, properly speaking, a marriage settlement ought to be executed, in order to carry the executory provisions of marriage articles into effect, the Court has, where the property was personal, at the request of the parties, in order to save expense, made a declaration as to the true meaning of the articles, upon which the parties were able to act, without causing a formal instrument to be prepared and executed : *Byam* v. *Byam*, 19 Beav. 58, 63.

Where, by a postnuptial agreement, a settlement is directed to be made upon a son of the marriage and his issue, the same considerations do not apply as in the case of a similar limitation to an intended husband and his issue by articles before marriage, so as to cut down the interest of the son to a life interest. See *Dillon* v. *Blake*, 16 Ir. Ch. Rep. 24, there by executory articles for valuable consideration, made between H. Blake and his wife and sons, it was agreed that after the death of H. Blake, his estates should be limited to and settled upon B., his eldest son *and his issue*, with remainder, in the *event of B. dying in the lifetime* of H. Blake, without lawful issue, to each of the other sons of H. Blake, in succession, according to their seniority, with an ultimate remainder *to the right heirs of H. Blake. And power was given to the trustees to lease any part of the lands, with the concurrence of H. [*25] Blake. B. survived H. Blake, and had issue. It was held by the Lord Chancellor of Ireland (Blackburne), in a suit to carry these articles into execution, that B. was entitled to an estate tail in possession, with remainder to him in fee.

Covenant to settle chattels on the same trusts as realty.] Where chattels are settled *immediately* or by a *trust executed* upon the same trusts as have been declared of real estate in strict settlement, viz. upon first and other sons successively in tail, if there is no restriction as to the attainment of twenty-one years or the fulfilment of any other condition, such chattels will vest absolutely in the first tenant in tail at his birth, whether the limitation of the chattels be expressed in extenso, or created by reference to the limitations of the realty (*Doncaster* v. *Doncaster*, 3 K. & J. 26), and such reference may be effectually made either by declaring that the chattels are to go upon the limitations of the realty or by saying that they are to be treated as heir looms : *Lord Scarsdale* v. *Curzon*, 1 J. & H. 40. See *In re Johnson*, L. R. 2 Eq. 716.

This result is prevented in well-drawn settlements by a clause in clear words suspending the vesting of the chattels in the first tenant " unless he should attain the age of twenty-one years," or " unless he should die under twenty-one years leaving issue." (And see other forms suggested in Davidson by Waley, vol. iii. p. 497, and the note vol. iv. p. 379, with reference to *Gosling* v. *Gosling*, 1 De G. J. & S. 1, S. C. nom. *Christie* v. *Gosling*, 1 L. R. Ho. Lo. 279.)

In cases, however, of *executed trusts*, doubtful words tending to restrict the interests of chattels to those who come into the possession of the realty, will not overrule the operation of the general canons of construction, nor suspend the interest until possession of the realty is acquired: *Lord Scarsdale* v. *Curzon*, 1 J. & H. 40. *Johnson's trusts*, 2 L. R. Eq. 716.

In the case of an *executory trust* by settlement, as where a person has agreed or covenanted to settle chattels upon similar trusts to real estate in strict settlement, a Court of equity, upon the principle of carrying into effect the intent of the parties as far as possible, will order a clause to be inserted in the settlement of the chattels—that the tenant in tail should not under the limitations be entitled to the absolute property in the chattels " unless he should attain the age of twenty-one years," or " unless he should die under twenty-one, leaving issue." See *Duke of Newcastle* v. *Countess of Lincoln*, 3 Ves. 387, in which case there was [*26] a covenant in a marriage settlement *to settle leaseholds in trust for such persons and for such or the like ends, intents and purposes, *as far as the law in that case would allow and permit*, as were declared concerning certain real estates which were limited to A. for life, remainder to his first and other sons in tail male, remainder to B. for life, remainder to B.'s first and other sons in tail male, remainders over. A. died, leaving a son who lived only nine months. Lord *Loughborough* stated it to be his decided opinion, that in cases of marriage articles, where leasehold property was covenanted to be settled upon the same limitations as freehold estate and the limitations of the freehold estate were to all the sons successively in tail, the settlement to be made of the leaseholds ought to be analogous to that of the freeholds, so that no child born and not attaining twenty-one should by his birth attain a vested interest to transmit to his representatives, and thereby defeat the ulterior object of the articles, which were not in favour of one son, but equally extended to every son; and his Lordship (admitting the law as laid down in *Vaughan* v. *Burslem*, 3 Bro. C. C. 101, to be applicable to wills) observes that " it is not true that you are to do for the testator all that can be done by law. You are to do for the testator no more than what he has intended to be done, and according to the common acceptation of the words. But," said his Lordship, " I wish to put it to you, whether in the nature of things there is not a radical and essential difference between marriage settlements and wills? The parties contract upon a settlement for all the remainders. They are not voluntary, but within the consideration. The issue, then, are all purchasers. Suppose, then, a settlement to be made of freehold estate, and as to the leasehold there is only this article, that the settlement shall be analogous to that of the freehold ; do I execute it and make a like settlement by giving an interest which cuts off all the issue ? Suppose the whole subject was leasehold estate, and stood upon an article that it should be conveyed according to the limitations of an honour, and a bill was brought to carry that settlement into effect after a child had lived a day, should I permit the father to say it was his property ? It is utterly impossible to make the identical settlement of the leasehold estate as of the freehold ; but if I am to make it in analogy to the settlement of the freehold, shall I not carry it on to all the near events ? and shall they fail because I cannot embrace all the remote events ? " And his Lordship thought there was no objection to a proviso that no person should be entitled to the absolute property unless he should attain the age of twenty-one years, or die under that age leaving issue male. *Upon an appeal to the House of Lords (reported 12 Ves. 218), a son of B.'s having in the meantime attained his majority, [*27] it was decreed that the leasehold estate vested absolutely in him ; Lord Ellenborough and Lord Erskine, then Lord Chancellor, to this extent approving of the decree of Lord Loughborough, that the absolute interest did not vest in the first tenant in tail, A.'s son, on his birth ; but it was unnecessary to decide what was the proper limitation to have been inserted in the settlement, whether a limitation over on "dying under twenty-one," or on "dying under twenty-one without issue male." Lord Eldon, however, denying the distinction between wills and marriage articles, expressed some dissatisfaction with the decree, and stated that he could not reconcile the decision with *Vaughan v. Burslem*, (3 Bro. C. C. 101 and *Foley* v. *Burnell*, 1 Bro. C. C. 274), decided by Lord Thurlow, although he did not move an amendment. The cases, however, of *Vaughan* v. *Bruslem* and *Foley* v. *Burnell* are cases of wills ; and Lord Eldon himself afterwards, in *Jervoise* v. *Duke of Northumberland*, fully admitted the distinction between executory trusts in marriage articles and wills ; see 1 J. & W. 574.

2. *As to Executory Trusts in Wills.*]—The intention of the testator must appear from the will itself, that he meant " heirs of the body," or words of similar legal import, to be words of purchase ; otherwise Courts of equity will direct a settlement to be made according to the strict legal construction of those words. Suppose, for instance, a devise to trustees in trust to convey to A. for life, and after his decease to the heirs of his body, or words tantamount to heirs of the body ; as no indication of intention appears that the issue of A. should take as purchasers, the rule of law will prevail, and A. will take an estate tail, although, as we have already seen in the case of marriage articles similarly worded, he would take only as tenant for life. Thus, in *Sweetapple* v. *Bindon*, 2 Vern. 536, B. by will gave 300l. to her daughter Mary, to be

laid out by her executrix in lands and settled to the only use of her daughter Mary and her children, and if she died without issue the land to be equally divided between her brothers and sisters then living; Lord Cowper said, that, had it been an immediate devise of land, Mary, the daughter, would have been, by the words of the will, tenant in tail : and in the case of a voluntary devise the Court must take it as they found it, and not lessen the estate or benefit of the legatee : although upon the like words in marriage articles it might be otherwise. See also *Legatt* v. *Sewell*, 2 Vern. 551 ; *Seale* v. *Seale*, 1 P. Wms. 290 ; *Harrison* v. *Naylor*, 2 Cox, 247 ; *Marshall* v. *Bousfield*, 2 Madd. 166 ; *Blackburn* v. *Stables*, 2 V. & B. 370 ; *Meure* v. *Meure*, 2 Atk. 266.

[*28]

In the following cases, however, it has been held that there has been a sufficient indication of the testator's intention, that the words " heirs of the body," or words of similar import, should be considered as words of purchase and not of limitation, viz., where trustees were directed to settle an estate upon A. and the heirs of his body, taking *special care in such settlement that it should not be in the power of A. to dock the entail of the estate given to him during his life :* Leonard v. Earl of Sussex, 2 Vern. 526.

So, directions in a will that heirs of the body or issue shall take, " in *succession and priority* of birth," or that the settlement shall be made " *as counsel shall advise,*" or " *as executors shall think fit,*" have been held strongly to indicate an intention that an estate should be settled strictly : see *White* v. *Carter*, 2 Eden, 368 ; *Bastard* v. *Proby*, 2 Cox, 6 ; *Rochford* v. *Fitzmaurice*, 2 D. & W. 1 ; *Read* v. *Snell*, 2 Atk. 642 ; *Haddelsey* v. *Adams*, 22 Beav. 276.

So, where a testator directed trustees to convey an estate to his daughter for her life, and so as she alone, or such person as she should appoint, should take or receive the rents and profits thereof, and so that her husband should not intermeddle therewith, and from and after her decease in trust for the heirs of her body for ever ; Lord Hardwicke, considering that it was plainly the intention of the testator that the husband should have no manner of benefit from the estate, either in the lifetime of his wife or after her decease, held, that the words " heirs of her body " were words of purchase, and that the wife was entitled to a life estate only ; for had they been construed as words of limitation, and the wife had taken as tenant in tail, the husband, contrary to the intention of the testator, would have had considerable benefit from the estate as tenant by the curtesy : *Roberts* v. *Dixwell*, 1 Atk. 607 ; S. C. West's Rep. temp. Lord Hardwicke, 536 ; see also *Stonor* v. *Curwen*, 5 Sim. 264 ; *Parker* v. *Bolton*, 5 L. J. N. S. (Ch.) 98 ; *Shelton* v. *Watson*, 16 Sim. 542 ; sed vide *Samuel* v. *Samuel*, 14 L. J. N. S. (Ch.) 222 ; *Young* v. *Macintosh*, 13 Sim. 445 ; *Head* v. *Randall*, 2 Y. & C. C. C. 231. At the present day, under such words, a clause *against anticipation* would probably be added. See *Turner* v. *Sargent*, 17 Beav. 515, in which case a testator having directed that property should be settled upon his daughter, to the exclusion of her present or any future husband, that the same might belong to her during her life, " a settlement was directed in trust for the daughter for her life, to her separate use, without power of anticipation." *Stanley v. Jackman, 23 Beav. 450; In re Dunnell's Trusts, 6 Ir. Eq. 322. [*29]

Where a testator directed that his daughter's share under his will should be "settled upon themselves strictly," it was held by Lord Romilly, M. R., that the income of each daughter's share should, during the joint lives of herself and her husband, be paid to her for life, to her separate use, without power of anticipation ; and if she died in the life of her husband, then her share should go as she should by will appoint, and in default of appointment, to her next of kin, exclusively of her husband ; and if she survived her husband, then to her absolutely : Loch v. Bagley, 4 L. R. Eq. 122.

So, where a testator, as in Lord Glenorchy v. Bosville, directs an estate to be conveyed to a person for life "without impeachment of waste," or to a person for life with a limitation to trustees " to preserve contingent remainders," he will be held sufficiently to have indicated his intention, that in a subsequent limitation to the issue or heirs of the body of the person to whom the life interest is given, such issue or heirs should take as purchasers, and a strict settlement will accordingly be directed : see Papillon v. Voice, 2 P. Wms. 471, in which case the distinction between executed and executory trusts in wills is most strikingly illustrated. There A. bequeathed a sum of money to trustees, in trust, to be laid out in a purchase of lands and to be settled on B. for life, without impeachment of waste, remainder to trustees and their heirs during the life of B. to preserve contingent remainders, remainder to the heirs of the body of B., remainder over, with power to B. to make a jointure ; and by the same will A. devised lands to B. for his life, without impeachment of waste, remainder to trustees and their heirs during the life of B. to support contingent remainders, remainder to the heirs of the body of B., remainder over: though it was decreed at the Rolls that an estate for life only passed to B., with remainder to the heirs of his body by purchase, as well in the lands devised as in those directed to be purchased, yet, upon an appeal from this decree Lord Chancellor King declared as to that part of the case where lands were devised to B. for life, though said to be without impeachment of waste, with remainder to trustees to support contingent remainders, remainder to the heirs of the body of B., this last remainder was within the general rule, and must operate as words of limitation, and consequently create a vested estate tail in B., and that the breaking into this rule would occasion the utmost uncertainty ; but, as to the other point, he declared the Court had a power over the money directed by the will to be invested in land, and that the

[*30] diversity was where the *will passed a legal estate and where it was only executory, and the party must come to the Court in order to have the benefit of the will; that in the latter case the intention should take place and not the rules of law, so that as to the lands to be purchased they should be limited to B. for life, with power to B. to make a jointure, remainder to trustees during his life to preserve contingent remainders, remainder to his first and every other son in tail male successively, remainder over.

So, where a testator directed his estates and house property to be *settled* on his son, T. F. D., and his heirs male; and if he should have no heirs male, on his grandson, J. B., on his taking the name of D. in addition to his own, within twelve months after his succession; and in the event of his having no heirs male, then the estate to go to his brother, G. A. B., and his heirs male, he taking the name of D. It was held by the Master of the Rolls of Ireland that an executory trust was created which the Court directed to be carried out by a settlement with limitations to the several devisees for life, and with remainders to their sons in tail male successively: *Duncan* v. *Bluett*, 4 L. R. Eq. 469, see also *Parker* v. *Bolton*, 5 L. J. (N. S.) Ch. 98.

Where, however, the trusts and limitations of land to be purchased by trustees are expressly declared by the testator, it has been decided that the Court has no authority to make them different from what they would be at law. Thus, in *Austen* v. *Taylor*, 1 Eden, 361, land was devised to trustees in trust to pay an annuity; and subject thereto in trust for A. for life, without impeachment of waste, remainder to trustees to preserve contingent remainders, remainder to the heirs of the body of A., remainder to the testator's right heirs; and the residue of the testator's personal estate was to be laid out in the purchase of lands which should thereafter remain, continue, and be, to, for, and upon such and the like estate or estates, uses, trusts, intents, and purposes, and under and subject to the like charges, restrictions, and limitations, as were by him before devised, limited, and declared of and concerning his lands and premises last before devised, or as near thereto as might be and the deaths of persons would admit. Lord Northington distinguished the case from *Papillon* v. *Voice*, on the ground that the testator refers no settlement to his trustees to complete, but declares his own uses and trusts, which being declared, he knew no instance where the Court had proceeded so far as to alter or change them; and he therefore held, that A. was entitled to an estate tail in the lands to be purchased: and see *East* v. *Twyford*, 9 Hare, 713, 733; 4 Ho. Lo. 517; *Franks* v. *Price*, 3 [*31] Beav. 182; *Rochford* v. *Fitzmaurice*, 1 *C. & L. 172, 2 Dru. & Warr. 21; *Doncaster* v. *Doncaster*, 3 K. & J. 26. See, however, *Meure* v. *Meure*, 2 Atk. 265; *Harrison* v. *Naylor*, 2 Cox, 247; *Green* v. *Stephens*, 17 Ves. 76; *Jervoise* v. *Duke of Northumberland*, 1 J. & W. 572.

The word "issue," as observed by Lord Talbot in *Lord Glenorchy* v. *Bosville*, is both a word of purchase and of limitation; but the word "heirs" is naturally a word of limitation. In executory trusts in wills, therefore, it will be seen, upon examining the cases, that where the word "issue" is made use of, Courts of equity will more readily decree a strict settlement, than where the words "heirs of the body" have been used. See *Meure* v. *Meure*, 2 Atk. 265; *Ashton* v. *Ashton* (cited in *Bagshaw* v. *Spencer*), 1 Coll. Jur. 402; *Horne* v. *Barton*, Coop. 257; *Dodson* v. *Hay*, 3 Bro. C. C. 405; *Stonor* v. *Curwen*, 5 Sim. 264.

Wherever in executory trusts, in wills, the words "heirs of the body," or "issue," are construed as words of purchase, they will be held to include daughters as well as sons, and the settlement, as in *Lord Glenorchy* v. *Bosville*, will be decreed to be made in default of sons and their issue upon daughters, as tenants in common in tail general, with cross remainders between them: *Bastard* v. *Proby*, 2 Cox, 6. In *Trevor* v. *Trevor*, 13 Sim. 108, where a testator devised his estates to trustees, in trust, to settle and convey the same to the use of or in trust for G. R., who had then no issue, for life, without impeachment of waste, with remainder *to his issue in tail male in strict settlement*, Sir L. Shadwell, V. C., held, that the estates ought to be settled upon G. R. for life, without impeachment of waste, with remainder to his sons successively in tail male, with remainder to his daughters as tenants in common in tail male with cross remainders in tail male. This decision was affirmed in the House of Lords: 1 H. L. Cas. 239. See also *Skelton* v. *Watson*, 16 Sim. 543; *Coape* v. *Arnold*, 2 Sm. & Giff. 311, 4 De G. Mac. & G. 574.

In *Turner* v. *Sargent*, 17 Beav. 515, the testator, after directing a settlement to be made of real and personal property upon his daughter for life, added, that it was "to be *secured* for the benefit of her children, if more than one, equally, after her death, so that the issue of any such child dying in his daughter's lifetime might take his or her parent's share, and in default of such children or other issue, then to his son W. absolutely." Sir J. Romilly, M. R., directed a settlement to be made according to which, after the decease of the daughter, the property was to be in trust for her children; but if any child died in her lifetime, leaving children or remoter issue who should be living at her death, such children or remoter issue should take the *share of the child of the testator's daughter so dying, *per stirpes*, but *inter se*, as tenants in common, [*32] with limitations in the nature of cross remainders in favour of the children and issue who should survive the testator's daughter, as respected the share of any child dying in her lifetime without leaving issue, and as respected the share of any issue dying in her lifetime. And if no child of the testator's daughter or issue of any deceased child should be living at her decease, there was to be an ultimate trust for W., so that the death of the testator's daughter was the period or event at which the vesting of the property in the children's issue, or in the legatee and devisee over, was to be ascertained.

In *Thompson* v. *Fisher*, 10 L. R. Eq., 207, a testator subject to the life interest of his widow, devised freehold property to trustees " upon trust to convey, assign and assure " the same " unto and to the use of his son, T. Fisher, and the heirs of his body lawfully issuing, but in such manner and form nevertheless, and subject to such limitations and restrictions, as that if T. Fisher shall happen to die without leaving lawful issue, then that the property may after his death descend unincumbered unto and belong to his daughter, Ruth Fisher, her heirs, executors, administrators and assigns." Sir W. M. James, V. C., held that the devise was an executory trust to be executed by a conveyance to the use of T. Fisher during his life, with remainder to his first and other sons and daughters as purchasers in tail, with remainder to the testator's daughter Ruth, in fee.

Whenever a strict settlement is decreed, limitations to trustees to preserve contingent remainders will, if necessary, be inserted : *Stamford* v. *Hobart*, 3 Bro. P. C. 31, Toml. ed., 1 Atk. 593 ; *Baskerville* v. *Baskerville*, 2 Atk. 279 ; *Harrison* v. *Naylor*, 2 Cox, 247 ; but since the passing of 8 & 9 Vict. c. 106, such limitations are in some cases unnecessary, see sect. 8 ; and sometimes the freehold will be vested in trustees, during the life of the tenant for life : *Woolmore* v. *Burrows*, 1 Sim. 512.

For the manner in which a direction to *entail* real and personal estate will be carried into effect, see *Tennent* v. *Tennent*, 1 Dru. 161 ; *Jervoise* v. *Duke of Northumberland*, 1 J. & W. 559 ; *Randall* v. *Daniel*, 24 Beav. 193 ; and see *Sealy* v. *Stawell*, 2 I. R. Eq. 326 ; as to an entail directed to be made of land in Scotland, *Graham* v. *Stewart*, 2 Macq. H. L. Cas. 295 ; and as to the settlement to be made when estates are directed, as far as the law will permit, to be strictly settled so as to go with an ancient barony, see *Banks* v. *Le Despencer*, 10 Sim. 577, 11 Sim. 508 ; [*33] or to go in a course of entail to correspond as nearly as *may be with the limitations of a modern barony, the patent conferring which contained a shifting clause upon the holder of the barony becoming entitled to an earldom : *Sackville West* v. *Viscount Holmesdale*, 4 L. R. Ho. Lo. 543, reversing *Viscount Holmesdale* v. *West*, 3 L. R. Eq. 474 ; and see *Viscount Holmesdale* v. *West*, 12 L. R. Eq. 280.

Where real and personal property were by will directed to be settled upon the same trusts, the Court did not think itself authorized, through the medium of a trust for sale, to settle the real estate as personalty : *Turner* v. *Sargent*, 17 Beav. 515, 520.

As to the construction which will be put upon the word " family," in case of executory trusts in a will, see *White* v. *Briggs*, 2 Ph. 583. There a testator directed that after the death of his wife (to whom he gave a life interest in all his property both real and personal), his nephew, C. W., should " be considered heir to all his property not otherwise disposed of," and added, that " having had little intercourse with him, and being apprehensive that his habits required some control, he directed that whatever portion of his property might thereafter be possessed by him, should be *secured by his executors for the benefit of his family;* " and he " urged upon his executors to consider it an indispensable obligation to secure his estate in the nature of a trusteeship for the parties who might be interested thereafter." It was held, by Lord Cottenham, C., that the real estate should be settled on the nephew for life, with remainder to his sons successively in tail male, with remainder to his daughters as tenants in common in fee; and that the personal estate should be settled upon the nephew for life, with remainder to all his children as joint tenants, with a proviso that, in the event of all the children dying under twenty-one, and in the case of daughters unmarried, and in the case of sons without lawful issue, the personalty should be held in trust for the nephew absolutely.

A direction to trustees to settle property upon a wife of the testator's son, should he marry, has been held in the absence of words indicating an intention to restrict the jointure to the wife of a first marriage, to authorize the settlement of a jointure upon the wife of a second marriage: *Mason* v. *Mason*, 5 I. R. Eq. 288.

Chattels directed by will to go in strict settlement.]—Where chattels are given by will, and are directed, to go by reference to limitations of real estate in strict settlement, or to go as heirlooms, either simply or " as far as the rules of law and equity will permit," Courts of equity, even although the legal estate may be in executors, will not construe the trusts of the will *as executory, and prevent the chattels vesting [*34] absolutely in the first tenant in tail upon his birth, as we have seen would be done in the case of marriage articles, by the insertion in the settlement of a clause, which would prevent the chattels vesting absolutely, unless the tenant in tail attained twenty-one years of age, or died under that age leaving issue. See *Foley* v. *Burnell*, 1 Bro. C. C. 274; *Vaughan* v. *Burslem*, 2 Bro. C. C. 101; *Duke of Newcastle* v. *Countess of Lincoln*, 3 Ves. 387; *Carr* v. *Lord Erroll*, 14 Ves. 228; *Rowland* v. *Morgan*, 6 Hare, 463; affirmed on appeal, 2 Ph. 764, overruling *Gower* v. *Grosvenor*, Barn. Ch. Rep. 54; S. C., 5 Madd. 337; *Trafford* v. *Trafford*, 3 Atk. 347. See also *Doncaster* v. *Doncaster*, 3 K. & J. 26; *Evans* v. *Evans*, 17 Sim. 108; *Stapleton* v. *Stapleton*, 2 Sim. N. S. 212; and *Tollemache* v. *Coventry*, 2 C. & F. 611; S. C., 8 Bligh, N. S., 547; overruling *Lord Deerhurst* v. *Duke of St. Albans*, 5 Madd. 232; *Gosling* v. *Gosling*, 1 De G. J. & S. 1; 1 L. R. Ho. Lo. 279, nom. *Christie* v. *Gosling; In re Johnson's Trusts*, 2 L. R. Eq. 716; *Countess of Harrington* v. *Earl of Harrington*, 5 L. R. Ho. Lo. 87.

But if a plain intention be expressed that no person shall take the chattels absolutely, who does not live to become entitled to the possession of the real estate, the Court must execute that intention: (*Potts* v.

Potts, 3 J. & L. 353, 1 H. L. Cas. 671. See also *Trafford* v. *Trafford,*
3 Atk. 347); *Foley* v. *Burnell,* 1 Bro. C. C. 101; *Lord Scarsdale* v.
Curzon, 1 J. & H. 40. And the execution of a disentailing deed of the
real estate by a tenant in tail who does not live to become entitled to
the chattels, will not prevent their vesting in the person who would have
been entitled to the real estate in possession if such disentailing deed
had not been executed. Thus, in *Hogg* v. *Jones,* 32 Beav. 45, a testator
devised his freeholds to the first and other sons of A. (who was living
and unmarried) successively in tail, with remainder to B. for life, with
remainder to B.'s first and other sons successively in tail. And he bequeathed his plate to B. for life, and after his decease, he gave the same
" in the nature of an heir-loom to the person who, for the time being,
should be in the actual possession and enjoyment of his freehold estates
under the limitations of his will." In the lifetime of A., B. and her
eldest son executed a disentailing deed. A. survived both B. and her
eldest son, and he died without having been married. At A.'s death,
C. was the issue in tail of B., but was not in possession of the freehold.
It was held by Sir John Romilly, M. R., that there had been no failure
of the gift of the plate, and that C., and not the representatives of B.,
[*35] were entitled to it. " The testator," *said his Honour, " in the
events which have occurred, has expressed his intention, in plain
words, that C. should take the estate and the plate. A disentailing deed,
which the testator could not prevent, has enabled two persons, now
deceased, to defeat this intention, as far as regards the estate; the intention of the testator, as regards the plate, could not be defeated by them,
no deed would affect it; then why is that intention not to take effect?"

   Although it has been doubted whether the Court would limit a sum
of money in the same way as real estate, where there was no real estate
to guide the limitations (*Green* v. *Ekins,* 2 Atk. 473), the objection, if
tenable, does not apply to the case of family jewels, limited by executory
trust as heir-looms. See *Shelley* v. *Shelley,* 6 L. R. Eq. 540. There
jewels were bequeathed to the testatrix's nephew John Shelley, "to and
be held as heir-looms by him, and by his eldest son on his decease, and
to go and descend to the eldest son of such eldest son, and so on to the
eldest son of his descendants, as *far as the rules of law or equity will
permit. And I request my said nephew to do all in his power, by his
will or otherwise, to give effect to this my wish as to these things so
directed to go as heir-looms as aforesaid.*" It was held by Sir W. Page
Wood, V. C., that a valid executory trust was created for John Shelley
for life, with remainder to Edward Shelley, his eldest son, for life; and
upon the death of Edward Shelley, in trust for Edward Shelley's eldest
son, to be a vested interest in him when he should attain twenty-one;
but if he should die in his, Edward Shelley's life-time, or after Edward
Shelley's death, without having attained twenty-one, leaving an eldest
son born before Edward Shelley's death, in trust, for such last-mentioned

eldest son to be a vested interest when he should attain twenty-one ; and in case the jewels should not become vested in any persons under the limitations aforesaid, then (subject to the life interest of Edward Shelley) in trust for John Shelley absolutely.

Doctrine of cy-pres, as applicable to executory trusts.]—Where an executory trust, if carried literally into effect, would be void for illegality, as where it would infringe the rule against perpetuities, the Court, in order to carry the testator's intention into effect as far as possible, or, as it is termed, cy-pres, will direct a settlement to be made as strictly as the law will permit. Thus, in *Humberston* v. *Humberston* (1 P. Wms. 332; S. C., 2 Vern. 737: Prec. Ch. 455), where there was a devise to a corporation in trust to *convey* to A. for life, and afterwards, upon the death of A., to his first son for life, and so to the first son of that first son for life, with *remainder, in default of issue male of A., [*36] to B. for life, and to his sons and their sons in the same manner ; Lord Cowper said that though the attempt to create a perpetuity was vain, yet, so far as was consistent with the rules of law, it ought to be complied with ; and he directed that all the sons already born should take estates for life, with limitations to their unborn sons in tail. See *Williams* v. *Teale*, 6 Hare, 239, and cases there cited ; *Lyddon* v. *Ellison*, 19 Beav. 565, 573 ; *Peard* v. *Kekewich*, 15 Beav. 173 ; see, however, *Blagrove* v. *Hancock*, 16 Sim. 378.

As to what powers or provisions will be inserted in settlements directed to be made by the Court.]—Where in marriage articles or a will, a settlement is directed to be made with the *usual powers* or *proper* powers, a Court of equity will order to be inserted in the settlement powers of leasing for twenty-one years (*Hill* v. *Hill*, 6 Sim. 145 ; *Duke of Bedford* v. *Marquis of Abercorn*, 1 My. & Cr. 12) ; powers to grant building or mining leases where the property is fit for those purposes (*Hill* v. *Hill*, 6 Sim. 145) ; powers of sale and exchange (*Hill* v. *Hill*, 6 Sim. 136 ; *Peake* v. *Penlington*, 2 V. & B. 311 ; *Williams* v. *Carter*, Sug. Pow. App. 22, 7th edit. See, however, *Brewster* v *Angell*, 1 J. & W. 625 ; *Horne* v. *Barton*, Jac. 439) ; powers of partition where there is any joint property (*Hill* v. *Hill*, 6 Sim. 145) ; powers of appointing new trustees (*Lindow* v. *Fleetwood*, 6 Sim. 152 ; *Sampayo* v. *Gould*, 12 Sim. 426) ; but not a power to raise portions (*Higginson* v. *Barneby*, 2 S. & S. 518, and see *In re Grier's Estate*, 4 I. R. Eq. 1, 11, 12) ; nor to jointure a future wife (*Duke of Bedford* v. *Marquis of Abercorn*, 1 My. & C. 312).

In considering these cases, it ought to be remembered that there is a palpable distinction between powers for the management and better enjoyment of the settled estates which are beneficial to all parties, and powers which confer personal privileges on particular parties, such as powers to jointure, or to raise money for any particular purpose. But powers of leasing, of sale, and exchange, and (where there is any joint property, or there are any mines or any land fit for building purposes) powers of partition, of leasing mines, and of granting building leases, are powers for the general management and better enjoyment of the estates, and such powers are beneficial to all parties: *Hill* v. *Hill*, 6 Sim. 145.

But where certain powers are specifically mentioned, the expression *usual powers*, coming afterwards will be considerably narrowed: *Pearse* v. *Baron*, Jac. 158; *Hill* v. *Hill*, 6 Sim. 141; *Brewster* v. *Angell*, 1 J. & W. 625; *Horne* v. *Barton*, Jac. 439; *Higginson* v. *Barneby*, 2 S. & S. 516; unless *it is contained in a separate and distinct sentence: *Lindow* v. *Fleetwood*, 6 Sim. 152.

[*37]

A power of varying securities is analogous to a power of sale and exchange; so that where real estate was covenanted to be settled upon the same trusts, and with the like powers, as stock settled upon trusts, with power of varying securities, a power of sale and exchange of the real estate was inserted in the settlement: *Williams* v. *Carter*, 2 Sug. Pow., App. 22, 7th ed.; *Horne* v. *Barton*, Jac. 440; *Elton* v. *Elton*, 27 Beav. 634.

In the absence of express words, if in the instrument directing a settlement an intention that certain powers should be inserted in the settlement may be implied, the Court will direct the introduction of such powers. Thus, if in a will directing a settlement to be made, powers of jointuring and charging with portions are to be given to tenants for life; and in a codicil directing a different settlement the will is in other respects referred to as the example or model to be followed; the introduction of powers of jointuring and charging, at any rate where there is full discretion given to the trustees as to the insertion of powers, provisoes, declarations, and agreements, will be authorised: *Sackville West* v. *Viscount Holmesdale*, 4 L. R. Ho. Lo. 543, 569, reversing S. S. nom.; *Viscount Holmesdale* v. *West*, 3 L. R. Eq. 474.

But where no direction as to the insertion of powers is given, a Court of equity will not, in the absence of any expression from which the intention to include any powers may be inferred, authorise their introduction into a settlement: *Wheate* v. *Hall*, 17 Ves. 85; *Brewster* v. *Angell*, 1 J. & W. 628; except perhaps a power of leasing. See *Woolmore* v. *Burrows*, 1 Sim. 518; but in that case the property was in *Ireland*.

In a recent case, however, where a testator by his will directed a settlement of real and personal property to be made, but gave no direction as to powers, Sir John Romilly, M. R., was of opinion that the testator by simply directing a settlement, ought to be held to have intended all the *usual* powers to be included. That the settlement, therefore, ought to contain the usual powers of leasing, sale and exchange, and for the appointment of new trustees, together with a receipt clause, and provisions for maintenance, education, and advancement for the children or issue living at the death of the tenant for life, during their minority: *Turner* v. *Sargent*, 17 Beav. 515; *Byam* v. *Byam*, 19 Beav. 58; and see *Scott* v. *Steward*, 27 Beav. 367, where under a covenant to settle after-acquired property upon the same trusts as personalty was settled, or as near thereto as the nature of the property would admit, power to grant mining as well as agricultural leases was ordered by *the [*38] Court to be inserted in the settlement, the prior owner having granted such leases.

Where a testator had directed, that in the event of the marriage of his daughter, a certain portion of his property should be secured to her, and the issue of her marriage, by a settlement or some other good assurance, in such manner as his trustees or trustee for the time being might think fit, the Court on an application to which the surviving trustee was a party, approved of a power in the settlement made on the marriage of the daughter, enabling her to appoint by will a life estate in the property to her husband : *Charlton* v. *Rendall*, 11 Hare, 296.

So in *Stanley* v. *Jackman*, 23 Beav. 450, a father by will directed a fund, given to his daughter, to be settled "upon her and her issue," so that "the same might not be liable or subject to the debts, control, or engagements of any husband" whom she might happen to marry during her lifetime. It was held by Sir John Romilly, M. R., that the settlement ought to give the daughter a power of appointment by will in default of issue.

Where by marriage articles personalty is settled upon the issue of the marriage, it seems that the Court would not direct the insertion of a hotch-pot clause in a settlement, in the absence of any words in the articles indicating the intention of the parties to introduce such clause : *Lees* v. *Lees*, 5 I. R. Eq. 549.

Under an executory agreement to grant a lease of an hotel, with general and usual covenants, clauses, and provisions, it was held, under the circumstances, that the lease ought to contain a power of re-entry on the lessee's becoming bankrupt, or taking the benefit of the Insolvent Act : *Haines* v. *Burnett*, 27 Beav. 500.

In carrying into effect executory trusts, the question sometimes arises whether tenants for life are or are not to be made dispunishable for waste. It seems, however, to be now settled that where, in order to give effect to the general intention, an estate of inheritance is cut down to an estate for life, the Court, in order to give the holder of such life estate the utmost power over the property consistent with his estate, makes him dispunishable for waste (*Leonard* v. *Earl of Sussex*, 2 Vern. 526 ; *Bankes* v. *Le Despencer*, 10 Sim. 576 ; 11 Sim. 508 ; *White* v. *Briggs*, 15 Sim. 17 ; 2 Ph. 583). Where, however, a settlement has been directed to be made upon persons in succession, expressly for life, with remainders over in tail, the Court will not insert a clause rendering the successive tenants for life dispunishable for waste, although the insertion of usual and proper provisions for giving effect to the intentions of the per-

[*39] son directing the settlement be authorised. *Davenport* v. *Davenport*, 1 Hem. & M. 775. Nor will it do so where an executory trust for the settlement of freehold estates " in strict settlement " directs, either expressly or by reference to the trusts of other property, that certain persons shall take life estates : *Stanley* v. *Coulthurst*, 10 L. R. Eq. 250, where the cases are fully explained in the judgment of Sir R. Malins, V. C. And where a settlement of land has been directed to be made upon a woman on marriage for her life with a restraint upon anticipation, it has been held that no clause should be added to the settlement, making her unimpeachable for waste, inasmuch as a life estate without impeachment of waste would be inconsistent with the restraint on anticipation : *Clive* v. *Clive*, 7 L. R. Ch. App., 433, 20 W. R. 477.

But even in the absence of an express direction, an intention that successive tenants for life should be made dispunishable for waste, may be implied. Thus, if in a will, directing a settlement to be made, the tenants for life are made dispunishable for waste, although, by a codicil, a different settlement is directed to be made, if the will is in other respects referred to as the model or example to be followed, its provisions will not be disregarded, and will, at any rate, where there is full discretion given to the trustees as to the insertion of powers, provisoes, declarations, and agreements, justify the limitation of life estates in the settlement directed by the codicil, with the same provisions as to waste as were given by the will : *Sackville West* v. *Viscount Holmesdale*, 4 L. R. Ho. Lo. 543, 576.

It should be remembered that the Court of Chancery can now, under 19 & 20 Vict. c. 120, and 21 & 22 Vict. c. 77, authorise leases and sales of settled estates, and give general powers of leasing to trustees of settlements in cases in which formerly it would have been necessary to have made an application to parliament. And under Lord Cranworth's Act (23 & 24 Vict. c. 145), certain powers now commonly inserted in settlements, mortgages, and wills, are, in the absence of any directions to the contrary, given to trustees, mortgagees, and others.

Rectification of settlement.]—If a settlement directed to be made by a testator is improperly framed, it may, as in *Lord Glenorchy* v. *Bosville*, be rectified by the will ; but, with regard to a settlement agreed to be made by articles, if both articles and settlement are made *before* marriage, the settlement will not in general be controlled by the articles, because, as observed by Lord Talbot in the principal case of *Legg* v. *Goldwire*, " when all parties are at liberty, the settlement will be taken as a new agreement."

Evidence is however admissible, to show that the articles constituted the final agreement between the parties, and that the discrepancy [*40] *between the articles and settlement arose from mistake, and upon this being proved the Court will rectify the settlement, and make it conformable to the real intention of the parties : *Bold* v. *Hutch-*

inson, 5 De G. Mac. & G. 558, 568; but " in order to justify the Court in taking such a course, it is obvious that a *clear* intention must be proved ; it must be shown that the settlement does not carry into effect the intention of the parties. If there be merely evidence of doubtful or ambiguous words having been used, the settlement itself is the construction which the parties have put upon those doubtful or ambiguous words : " per Lord Cottenham, C., in *The Marquess of Breadalbane* v. *The Marquess of Chandos*, 2 My. & Cr. 739.

The Court will only rectify a marriage settlement when the mistake is shown to be common to both parties (*The Earl of Bradford* v. *The Earl of Romney*, 30 Beav. 471 ; *Bentley* v. *Mackay*, 31 Beav. 143 ; *Sells* v. *Sells*, 1 Drew. & Sm. 42 ; *Thompson* v. *Whitmore*, 1 J. & H. 268), and it is essential that the extent of the rectification should be clearly ascertained and defined by evidence cotemporaneous with or anterior to the deed : *The Earl of Bradford* v. *The Earl of Romney*, 30 Beav. 431. And the Court will be guided by what was the intention of the parties at the time when the deed was executed, and not by what would have been their intention if, when they executed it, the result of what they did had been present to their minds : *Wilkinson* v. *Nelson*, 9 W. R. (M. R.) 393. See *Hunt* v. *Rousmanier*, 8 Wheaton, 174 ; 1 Peters, 1, post vol. 2 notes to *Woollam* v. *Hearn*.

The Court acts with this caution in rectifying marriage settlements, and in requiring proof of the exact contract which the parties intended to enter into, because it is impossible to undo the marriage or to remit the parties to the same positions they were in before the marriage. See *Harris* v. *Pepperell*, 5 L. R. Eq. 4, and the remarks of Lord Romilly, M. R.

But the same rule does not apply in cases arising between lessors and lessees, or vendors and purchasers. In such cases where a deed is not actually executed, the Court will not enforce specific performance of a contract which *one* party has entered into by a mistake, and where, as in *Garrard* v. *Frankel*, 30 Beav. 445, a person supposes he has entered into a contract for a lease at one rent, and then it turns out that the rent specified is of a different amount, then, as it is in the power of the Court to put the parties in the same position as if the contract had not been executed, the Court will interfere, provided the party aggrieved comes speedily for redress. See also *Bloomer* v. *Spittle*, 13 L. R. Eq. 427.

Upon the same principle, in *Harris* v. *Pepperell*, 5 L. R. Eq. 1, where in a conveyance of messuages, the plan on the deed comprised *a piece of land not intended by the vendor to be included, Lord [*41] Romilly, M. R., made a decree to rectify the deed, an option being given to the purchaser to have his contract annulled. See also *Mortimer* v. *Shortall*, 2 D. & War. 363 ; *Harryman* v. *Collins*, 18 Beav. 11 ; *Sells* v. *Sells*, 1 Dr. & Sm. 42 ; *Bloomer* v. *Spittle*, 13 L. R. Eq. 427.

As to cases where the Court has rectified settlements, see *Hamil* v. *White*, 3 J. & L. 695; *Wilson* v. *Wilson*, 15 Sim. 487, 1 H. L. Ca. 538; *Walsh* v. *Trevannion*, 16 Sim. 178; *Murray* v. *Parker*, 19 Beav. 305; *in re Morse's Settlement*, 21 Beav. 174; *Torre* v. *Torre*, 1 Sm. & G. 518; *Walker* v. *Armstrong*, 21 Beav. 284, 8 De G. Mac. & G. 531; *Naylor* v. *Wright*, 5 W. R. 770, V. C. S.; *Wolterbeek* v. *Barrow*, 23 Beav. 423; *Tomlinson* v. *Leigh*, 14 W. R. (M. R.) 121; and see *The Earl of Malmesbury* v. *The Countess of Malmesbury*, 31 Beav. 407, where a power of sale in a settlement was rectified, on proof that it was not conformable with the contract. Where it has refused to do so, see *Howkins* v. *Jackson*, 2 Mac. & G. 372; *White* v. *Anderson*, 1 Ir. Ch. Rep. 419; *Brougham* v. *Squire*, 1 Drew. 151; *Lloyd* v. *Cocker*, 19 Beav. 140; *Fyfe* v. *Arbuthnot*, 1 De G. & Jo. 406; *Elwes* v. *Elwes*, 2 Giff. 545, 9 W. R. (L. J.) 820; *Sells* v. *Sells*, 1 Drew. & Sm. 42; *Fowler* v. *Fowler*, 4 De G. & Jo. 250; *Jenner* v. *Jenner*, 6 Jur. (N. S.) 668; 8 W. R. (V. C. S.) 537.

Where, however, the settlement, *though made before* marriage, is expressly mentioned to be made *in pursuance* or *in performance of the marriage articles*, the settlement will be rectified by them, and it will not be necessary to resort to evidence: *West* v. *Errissey*, 2 P. Wms. 349, 3 Bro. P. C. 327; *Bold* v. *Hutchinson*, 5 De G. Mac. & G. 568.

Where the settlement is made *after* marriage, it will in all cases, whether it is mentioned to be made in pursuance or performance of articles or not, be controlled and rectified by them. These distinctions as to rectifying settlements by articles (subject to the qualifications laid down by Lord Cranworth, C., in *Bold* v. *Hutchinson*, 5 De G. Mac. & G. 558, 568), are well stated by Lord Talbot in *Legg* v. *Goldwire*: see also *Honor* v. *Honor*, 2 P. Wms. 123; *Roberts* v. *Kingsley*, 1 Ves. 238; *Streatfield* v. *Streatfield*, Ca. t. Talb. 176; *Warwick* v. *Warwick*, 3 Atk. 293.

A postnuptial settlement, however, professing to be made in pursuance of articles before marriage, especially after the settlement has been acted upon for a long time, will not be reformed so as to make it accord with a mere general recital of the articles contained in the settlement, the articles themselves not being produced: *Mignan* v. *Parry*, 31 Beav. 211.

Courts of Equity will not reform a voluntary deed as against the [*42] *grantor (*Phillipson* v. *Kerry*, 32 Beav. 628; *Broun* v. *Kennedy*, 33 Beav. 133; *Lister* v. *Hodgson*, 4 L. R. Eq. 30, 34, but see *Thompson* v. *Whitmore*, 1 J. & H. 268), nor will they decree a settlement as against purchasers for valuable consideration (amongst whom mortgagees are included), without notice of the articles: *West* v. *Errissey*, 2 P. Wms. 349; *Powell* v. *Price*, 2 P. Wms. 535; *Warwick* v. *Warwick*, 3 Atk. 291.

A settlement, however, will be decreed against purchasers with

notice of the articles. Thus, in *Davies* v. *Davies*, 4 Beav. 54, J. D. by
marriage articles, covenanted to settle an estate to the only proper use
and behoof of himself, and after his decease to the use and behoof of
the heirs of the said J. D. begotten or to be lawfully begotten on the
body of E. D., and for want of such issue to the right heirs and assigns
of the said J. D. for ever. J. D. afterwards, without having executed
any settlement, mortgaged the estate by demise, and he and his wife
levied a fine. The articles were handed over to the mortgagee. It was
contended for the mortgagee, upon the authority of Lord Northington,
in *Cordwell* v. *Mackrill*, 2 Eden, 344, that he was not bound to take
notice of an equity arising out of the mere construction of words which
were uncertain, and that the mortgagee might well suppose that the
mortgagor was entitled to charge the estate. *Cusack* v. *Cusack* (5 Bro.
P. C. 116, Toml. ed.) and *White* v. *Thornborough* (2 Vern. 702) were
also cited. However, Lord Laugdale, M.R., held, that the possession
of the articles gave to the mortgagee a sufficient notice of the title of
the plaintiff, the eldest son of the marriage, as the articles showed a
clear and distinct intention of benefiting the issue of the marriage,
which could not have misled an unprofessional person, and decreed the
estate to be conveyed to the son as tenant in tail, discharged of the
mortgage with costs. *Cordwell* v. *Mackrill* may, therefore, be considered as overruled by *Davies* v. *Davies :* see also *Thompson* v. *Simpson*,
1 D. & W. 491, where Sir Edward Sugden, L. C. of Ireland, observes,
" *Cordwell* v. *Mackrill* is a case of no great authority, though decided
by a great judge. . . It seems to me that where, upon the whole of
the articles, it is plain what construction the Court would have put
upon them, had it been called to execute them about the time they were
made, they should be inforced, however difficult the construction may
be, even as against a purchaser with notice; but not after a lapse of
time, where there is anything so equivocal or ambiguous in them as to
render it doubtful how they ought to be effectuated." See also *Abbot*
v. *Geraghty*, 4 Ir. Ch. Rep. 15, 24, 25.

It may here be mentioned, that in some cases of rectification, in order
to get the legal estate, a re-conveyance *is directed by decree [*43]
(*Malmesbury* v. *Malmesbury*, 31 Beav. 407, 419), but a settlement will sometimes be rectified by a decree merely, without the parties
being put to the expense of a fresh deed (*Tebbitt* v. *Tebbitt*, 1 De G. &
Sm. 506; *Stock* v. *Vining*, 25 Beav. 235). It seems the Court will now
rectify a settlement upon a petition. *In re Morse's Settlement*, 21 Beav.
174; *In re Hoare's Trusts*, 4 Giff. 254; *Lewis* v. *Hillman*, 3 Ho. Lo.
607. And see *In re De La Touche's Settlement*, 10 L. R. Eq. 599.
There, although the fact of the mistake was not admitted by all parties,
the Court, upon the evidence on a Petition, filed under the Trustee
Relief Act, did not order the Petition to be rectified, but prefacing the
order with a declaration, that it appeared the words in question were

inserted by mistake, made an order for distribution of the funds as if the clause had not been inserted. See however *In re Malet*, 30 Beav. 407.

The distinction illustrated in the principal case, between executed and executory trusts, is well settled in this country, in its connexion with the rule in *Shelley's case.* The American courts, however, have never undertaken to decree a strict settlement, upon a mere general intention, in marriage articles or executory trusts, to make provision for children. But the distinction between executed and executory trusts, here, has gone to the extent of arresting the application of the rule in *Shelley's case,* in regard to executory trusts, and causing the person answering the description of issue, heirs of the body, or heirs, to take as purchasers, according to the language of the instrument as it stands. For this purpose, a trust will, in the American courts, be considered as executory, whenever a conveyance is to be made by the trustees, or, in case of personal property, whenever a delivery is to be made by the trustees at successive periods of time to the persons respectively entitled under the will or articles : and the rule in regard to such executory trusts is, that wherever the intention appears to be that the first taker should have only an estate for life, the remaindermen will take as purchasers, unless there be something else in the instrument to control that construction. *Saunders* v. *Edwards*, 2 Jones' Eq. 134.

And upon this point, the obser-vation in the preceding note, after the title *As to executory trusts in Wills*, that under " a devise to trustees in trust to convey to A. for life, and *after his decease* to the heirs of his body, or words tantamount to heirs of the body," A. will take an estate tail, does not appear to be consistent with the views prevailing in the courts of this country, nor is it indeed a quite accurate expression of the result of the English cases immediately thereafter referred to. In all those cases, there was in the will a specific intent to give an estate tail to the first taker ; at least, the directions of the testator were in language which, according to ordinary legal construction, made an estate tail, and there was nothing to indicate another intention. The difference between executory trusts in wills and in marriage articles, as far as it is shown by those cases, is, that in the latter, the *purpose* of the settlement, which principally is to secure an independent estate to the children, will control language in the articles, which else would be construed to give an estate tail to the parents; but in wills, if the language according to its legal construction, import an estate tail in the parents, this cannot be over-borne by any presumed design to benefit the children. In *Sweetapple* v. *Bindon*, 2 Vern. 536, money was by will directed to be laid out in land and settled to the only use of the testatrix's " daughter M. and her children," and if she died without issue, then over : this of course was a direction to create an estate tail in the daughter : but the court said, that upon marriage articles, where it appeared that the estate was intended to be preserved for the benefit of the issue, it might have been otherwise. *Legatt* v. *Sewell*, reported 2 Vern. 551 ; 1 P. Wms. 87 ; but more accurately and intelligibly in 1 Eq. Ca. Abr. 394, pl. 7 ; was not a construction upon an executory but upon an executed trust. The first taker under the will, had upon a bill to which the ultimate remainderman was not a party, obtained a decree that the estate should be settled according to the direction in the will ; the construction afterwards again coming in question, the Lord Keeper said, " There having been a Decree already in this case, it must depend on what it is at Law ;" and he referred it to the Judges of the C. B. as a question upon an executed settlement, and three of them certified that an estate tail had been created ; See *Trevor* v. *Trevor*, 1 Eq. Ca. Abr. 387, 390. In *Seale* v. *Seale*, 1 P. Wms. 290, money was directed to be laid out in lands and settled on " A. and the heirs male of his body," which of course was a direction for an estate tail in A.: and upon its being contended that it was like marriage articles under which a strict settlement would be decreed, the Lord Chancellor said " this case differed ; for that in marriage articles the children are considered as purchasers ; but in the case of

a will (as this was), *where the testator expressed his intent to give an estate tail*, a Court of Equity ought not to abridge the bounty directed by the testator." In *Harrison* v. *Naylor*, 2 Cox, 247, a testator directed lands to be bought, and then devised the lands when purchased " to his son T. N. to him and the heirs male of his body forever ; " which was creating an estate tail as clearly as possible. In *Marshall* v. *Bousfield*, 2 Madd. 166, the testator directed that his estate " should be settled by able counsel, and go to and amongst his grandchildren of the male kind, and their issue in tail male ; " and the Vice Chancellor said that as there was no language used in the will which indicated an intention to give only an estate for life to the grandchildren, and as there was no way of giving an estate in tail male to the issue of the grandchildren (one of the latter having been born after the testator's death), but by giving an estate tail male to the grandchildren which unless barred would descend on their issue, such an estate in the grandchildren was a plain construction of the will, and was the only way in which that executory trust could be carried into execution. In *Blackburn* v. *Stables*, 2 V. & B. 367, a testator devised all his property to his executors in trust for his great nephew, but directed that they should not give up their trust, " till a proper entail be made to the male heir by him : " here the great nephew was the specific object of the testator's bounty, and the direction was to entail the estate given to him, upon his heir male; the Master of the Rolls said, that as no express estate for life was given to the first taker, no clause that his estate should be without impeachment of waste, no direction to frame the limitation so as to deprive him of the power of barring the entail, nothing in the context of the will to show that the words were not to be taken in their legal acceptation, the great nephew was entitled to have a conveyance made to him in tail male. *Meure* v. *Meure*, 2 Atk. 265, was a case in which a trust was to be settled on one for life " and after his decease, then in trust for the use of the issue of the body of the plaintiff lawfully begotten : " and the Master of the Rolls said, " Where lands are to be settled to one for life, and to the heirs of his body, there is no case where such a limitation has not been held to be an estate tail ; on the other hand, there is no case where it is to be settled to one for life, and after his death to the issue of his body, that such a limitation has been construed an estate tail ; " now, although a principal part of this distinction is between " heirs " and " issue," yet a substantive part of it also consists in the presence of the clause " after his death " in the latter case ; and so far, the case of *Meure* v. *Meure* is opposed to the observation above cited from the preceding note. — Upon the whole, there does not appear to be authority in the English cases for inferring that a devise " in trust to convey to A. for life, *and after his decease* to the heirs of his

body," does not indicate an intention that the issue of A. should take as purchasers, and does not prevent an estate tail from vesting in A. In this country, it is believed, that an executory trust in those words or equivalent words, or in any words that limit an estate to the first taker for life only, with a remainder to heirs or heirs of the body, will not be an estate of inheritance in the first taker, but an estate for life only, with a remainder to heirs or heirs of the body as purchasers.

In New York, where, previously to the operation of the Revised Statutes, (1 R. S. 725, § 28,) viz. to January 1, 1830, the rule in *Shelley's case* was recognized as a binding rule of law, in regard both to wills and deeds; (*Brant* v. *Gelston*, 2 Jo. Ca. 384; *Kingsland* v. *Rapelye*, 3 Edwards, 2; *Schoonmaker* v. *Sheeley*, 3 Hill's N. Y. 165; subject to the qualifications settled by the English cases; *Rogers* v. *Rogers*, 3 Wendell, 503; *Tanner* v. *Livingston*, 12 Id. 83;) the distinction between executory trusts and executed trusts had been established in *Wood* v. *Burnham*, 6 Paige, 514: S. C. on appeal, 26 Wendell, 9. This case came before the Chancellor upon appeal from a decree of the Vice-Chancellor which adjudged that the children of the testator, living at the time appointed for the division of his residuary estate, took only estates for life, and that the remainders in fee belonged to those persons, who at the death of the first takers, respectively answered the description of their heirs at law. The trust declared by the will, as to this residuary estate, was, among other things, to receive the rents, profits, and income thereof for the first six years after the testator's death, and divide the same among his children and the issue of such of them as should have died leaving issue, *per stirpes;* and upon the further trust, at the expiration of the six years, to convert the personal estate, and the real estate which had been sold, into stocks; and thereupon to divide such stocks and the real estate remaining unsold into so many shares as there should be children of the testator then alive, and as should have died leaving lawful issue then living. And after having made such division, the executors or trustees were directed to convey by a fit and competent deed or instrument in writing, one share to each of the surviving children and one other share to the lawful issue of each child so deceased leaving issue then living. This executory clause then concluded as follows: " And in each deed or writing executed to any of my children shall be inserted and expressed a clause limiting such grant or interest conveyed to the grantee for life, with remainder over to the right heirs of such grantee, their heirs and assigns forever." The testator died previously to the abrogation of the rule in *Shelley's case,* by the Revised Statutes. The Chancellor declared that the rule in *Shelley's case,* was unquestionably the law of the state before those statutes took effect; but that

" the devise to the executors in this case being an executory and not an executed trust, or, in the language of one of the English Chancellors, the testator having directed his executors to make conveyances of the estate to the *cestuis que trust* instead of being his own conveyancer by vesting either a legal or equitable estate in his children and their heirs directly, it forms an exception to the rule in *Shelley's case:* And this court will direct the conveyances to be made in such a manner as to carry into effect the intention of the testator, notwithstanding the rule." He then reviewed the English cases which established this difference between executed and executory trusts, and concluded as follows. " The principle therefore must be considered as settled, that wherever there is an executory trust to be carried into effect by a conveyance from the trustees, if it is apparent from the instrument creating the trust that the testator or donor intended that the first taker should have a life estate only, and that his heirs should take the remainder in fee as purchasers, this court will direct such a conveyance to be made as will most effectually carry into effect such intention, so far as it can be done consistently with legal rules. In the present case, from an examination of the provisions of the will, I think there cannot be any doubt that it was the intention of the testator that his children who should be living at the expiration of the six years should take an estate for life only in their respective shares, and that their heirs should take the remainder in fee as purchasers. It is impossible to conceive what other object the testator could have had in giving such a positive direction to his executors to insert a clause in the deed limiting the estate in terms to the children of the testator for their respective lives. The decision of the Vice Chancellor was therefore correct.'' Upon appeal to the Court of Errors, this decree of the Chancellor was unanimously affirmed; *Tallman* v. *Wood*, 26 Wendell, 9.

The same principles and distinctions have been accurately defined and established, after great discussion in Georgia. It is there settled, that the rule in *Shelley's case* is a permanent and inflexible rule of property; *Choice* v. *Marshall*, 1 Kelly, 97 ; but that it does not apply to executory trusts, though it does to executed trusts; *Edmondson and Wife* v. *Dyson*, 2 Id. 307 ; *Wiley, Parish & Co. and others* v. *Smith and another*, 3 Id. 551, 559, 560 : and the distinction between the two classes of trust is, in the two latter decisions, stated with great clearness. In *Edmondson and Wife* v. *Dyson*, Mrs. R. by will devised and bequeathed her whole estate to D. in trust, for the sole and exclusive use of her husband during his natural life, and directed that at his death the trustee should convey the property so bequeathed in trust, to such person absolutely as the husband should by will appoint, and if he should die intestate, then, that the trustee should

convey all the property to the heir or heirs at law of the husband absolutely ; and the trustee was further authorized with the husband's consent to sell all or any part of the property, at such time and on such terms as he might think best, and to invest the proceeds in such manner as he might think most to the interest of the husband, first having the latter's consent. The husband died intestate, and the question arose in this case, whether the child of the husband took as a purchaser under Mrs. R.'s will, or whether the whole estate vested in the husband, and his child took as his heir in the regular course of law. The case was admitted to depend entirely upon the question whether the trust was executory or executed. The judge of the Superior Court, below, held it to be executed, and within the rule in *Shelley's case ;* but upon appeal to the Supreme Court, it was adjudged to be executory, on the ground that a conveyance was to be made by the trustee, and therefore without the rule. Mr. Justice Nisbet, in an able opinion, in giving judgment on the appeal, declared the rule in *Shelley's case* to be an established principle of law in that state, and explained the grounds of it; and that it applies equally to real and to personal property; but that it " applies to *legal estates*, and to *executed trusts*, and does not apply to *trusts executory*, where the testator plainly intimates an intention that it shall not apply ;" that the inference of equity in case of marriage articles and *executory trusts* proceeds upon the same ground ; and that executory trusts are where something is left to be done, some conveyance thereafter to be made. " This *something to be done*," said Mr. Justice Nisbet, " is the grand criterion for a correct determination whether a trust is, or is not, executory. What those things are which the testator leaves to be done and the effect of them, are the pivots upon which this discussion turns. It is argued with great force, that if the *limitations are perfect*, if the *character of the estates is ascertained*, the trust is executed. That the something *left to be done* has no reference to any mere act of conveyancing which might be necessary to effectuate limitations which the testator has fully declared, but that the trust is executory only where the limitations themselves are not defined, where the estates are not ascertained, and in cases where the testator only leaves loose statements, or notes of his intention, requiring careful and responsible deeds, or other instruments, to be by the trustee executed, which in themselves create and define estates, or which require a decree of chancery to mould the estates according to such loose memoranda. That it is immaterial whether the limitations are legal or equitable ; that is, whether the estate in the devisee may be asserted at law, or a decree in chancery be necessary to its perfect enjoyment, if the limitations are complete, and there is no doubt about the quantity or quality of the estate. I do not deny, but

upon principle, it is hard to escape from the conclusiveness of this reasoning. It is difficult to see any reason why an estate to A. in trust for B. for life, with remainder to the heirs of B. is an *executed trust*, and an estate to A. in trust for B. for life with remainder in fee, *to be conveyed* to the heirs of B. is an *executory trust*. In both cases the intention of the testator is the same, the estates limited are the same. The only difference is found in the fact that in the first case the testator is his own conveyancer, and the heirs take directly, and in the second he makes his trustee his conveyancer, and the heirs take through his deed. The thing to be done in the last case, to wit, convey, neither restricts nor enlarges the estate to the heirs. And yet the authorities, as we shall see, make this very act of *conveying*, the test, or one of the principal tests, of an executory trust. . . . I should remark as explanatory of some of the authorities, that the rule settled is the same, whether the act to be done is directed to be done by the trustee, or is left to a court of Chancery. To this intent, the agency of the court and of the trustee is the same. And this is a convenient place to remark, that if the property in this case had been left in trust to D. to the husband for life, and remainder in fee to his heirs at law, there could be no doubt about its then being an *executed* trust, and the rule in *Shelley's case*, would apply to and control it. But such are not the terms of limitation ; the property is left in trust with D. *to be conveyed* to the heirs at law of the husband. Now here is something left to be done by the trustee, and *that something is a conveyance,* which brings the case to that direct test to which I have before referred, to wit, the rule in *Shelley's case* not being applicable to executory trusts; and whether a trust be executed or executory, depending upon something being left to be done by the trustee, and that thing to be done, being in this case, *a conveyance; does the direction to convey make this an executory trust?* I have not found in the laborious investigation which I have been compelled to give this subject, a single case where a conveyance was required to be made, however merely formal it might appear to be, which has been determined to be an executed trust." He then reviews the English cases on executory trusts, and concludes; "From all of which it appears to me manifest, that courts of equity, whether with or without sufficient foundation for the act in principle, will take to themselves jurisdiction in case of wills, from the fact that the testator has directed a conveyance to be made by a trustee; will from that fact declare a trust *executory* in contradistinction to *executed;* will defeat in such a case the rule in *Shelley's case* in favor of the intention of the testator, by decreeing a conveyance in pursuance of his intention." In the case of *Wiley, Parish & Co.* v. *Smith and another,* 3 Kelly, 551, 560, the same distinction is explained; and

it is decided that a devise to one in trust for another and his children without any conveyance being required to be made or act to be done by the trustee, is an executed trust.

The same distinctions are established under the decisions of Tennessee. In that State the rule in *Shelly's case,* after great discussion and consideration, was deliberately approved, as a principle of law to which full effect should be given; *Polk and others* v. *Faris,* 9 Yerger, 210: though it is subject to the qualification that if the remainder is limited by will to " children," or to " heirs," obviously in the sense of children, the remaindermen may take as purchasers; *Hughes* v. *Cannon,* 2 Humphreys, 589; *Evans* v. *Wells,* 7 Id. 559; but that executory trusts are not within the rule, had been decided in *Loving and others* v. *Hunter,* 8 Yerger, 4, 30. In that case, the testator directed that his " land be sold for the best price that can be got, and the money arising therefrom, to be laid out in young negroes, at the discretion of my executors; " and " *lent* " two-thirds of the estate " unto his three daughters, to them, during their natural lives, and then giving to the lawfully begotten heirs of their bodies; " and the other third, which he had previously " lent " to his wife, " I desire (he said) may be equally divided, after her decease, among my three daughters, to them lent, during their lives, and then given to the lawfully begotten heirs of their bodies forever." The Court held, in the first place, that "lent" for life, and "given" to the heirs of the body, made the former limitation a trust only, and the latter a legal estate, so that the rule did not apply; and in the next place, that the direction that the land should be sold and laid out in young negroes at the discretion of his executors, contemplated the title to the negroes to be vested in the executors, and subject to trusts to be executed by them. "The idea conveyed by this language (above cited) is," said the court, "that the executors, in whom is vested the title to the negroes, are so to provide, that the daughters of the testator are to enjoy the use of the property during their natural lives, and then, at their death, the executors are to give the estate to those who may then be heirs of the bodies of his daughters. . . He uses the words (in regard to one of the thirds) "to them lent," to express his wish and desire, that the executors, when the event contemplated may occur, shall lend to the daughters during their lives; and when they die, "then," the executors are to give to the heirs. In this view of the case, the word "then," has its full meaning and significancy, as referring to a gift then to be made by the executors. Thus understood, we see why the word "given" was used instead of the word give. The language used is equivalent to the phrase, and "then to be given;" not giving directly himself, but vesting the estate in the executor, who is empowered to lend, and

give, as directed in the will. If this be the meaning of the will, and we think it is, it will be at once perceived, that the rule in *Shelly's case* can have no application here (it being merely an executory trust) and that a daughter took only an interest for life; and after her death her children were entitled to the property."—But executed trusts are completely within the operation of the rule in *Shelly's case*; and where marriage articles are excepted out of the rule, it is only on the ground of the settlement being executory; and therefore, if the trusts in such articles or contracts are executed, a contract in contemplation of marriage is as much within the rule in *Shelly's case* as any other instrument is; as was decided in *Carroll* v. *Renick et al.*, 7 Smedes & Marshall, 799, a case upon a marriage contract executed in Tennessee by residents there, and determined under the decisions in that State. There, by a contract before marriage, personal property had been conveyed to a trustee, to hold subject to the following limitations and trusts, viz., "from and after the solemnization of said marriage to the use and behoof of said (intended wife,) for and during the term of her natural life, and at her death to the heirs of her body and their heirs forever, and if she should die without such heirs, or having such heirs, and they should die before they arrived at mature age, then to her brothers by her mother's side, their heirs and assigns forever. To the application of the rule in *Shelley's case*, upon the authority of *Polk and others* v. *Faris*, for the purpose of vesting the absolute property in the wife, it was objected that the case was under a marriage agreement. " The answer to this," said Mr. Justice Clayton, in pronouncing judgment, " is, that marriage agreements already *executed*, are subject to the same rules, with limitations contained in these instruments. It is only in cases of marriage articles, where the settlement is thereafter to be made, and the trusts are *executory*, that an exception to the general rule is permitted. In the case before us, the settlement was executed before the marriage, and there is no room for the exception."

The rule in *Shelley's case*, with its usual limitations, is received in South Carolina; *Dott* v. *Cunnington*, 1 Bay, 453; *Carr* v. *Porter*, 1 M'Cord's Chancery, 60, 81; *Williams* v. *Caston*, 1 Strobhart, 130; *Williams* v. *Foster*, 3 Hill's So. Car. 193: and where a testator bequeathed personal property in these words, "I lend my daughters P. S. and A. H., each four negroes during their natural lives, and then to the heirs of their bodies," and appointed two persons executors of his will " in trust for the intents and purposes therein contained," it was held that this was not such an executory trust as prevented the operation of the rule in *Shelley's case ;* and therefore that the daughter took the absolute property in the negroes; *Hinson and Wife* v. *Pickett*, 1 Hill's Chancery, 35. But in *Garner* v. *Executors of Garner*, 1 Dessaussure, 437, the distinction between executory and executed trusts in the case of a marriage settlement was fully established. In that case it was agreed by a settlement before marriage that trustees should hold certain negroes in trust, that the husband should receive for life the rents and profits of their hire and labor, and then that the wife should receive the profits during her life, and then, upon the trust that the trustees would deliver up the said negroes and their increase, to the heirs of the body of the wife. It was contended that if this had been a settlement of real estate, the remainder to the heirs of the body would have united with the estate for life and given the husband an estate tail, but being of personal estate, that he took the absolute property. The Court, however, said, that marriage settlements were different from trusts under wills, because the former were on valuable consideration, and were to be carried into execution even against the parents, and if they were to put the children completely in the power of the parents, there would be no object at all in the marriage settlements; provision for the issue being the immediate object of settlement, and intended as an effectual provision. " The intent is plain," said the Court: " The trust is executed as to the husband and wife; executory as to the children. The act to be done by the trustees was to deliver them to the children of the wife. This shows clearly that the husband and wife were to have only an usufructuary interest, and the property to be absolutely secured to the children." It was held accordingly, that the husband took an estate for life, with remainder to the wife for life, and that the limitation over to the heirs of the body of the wife, vested the property in them at her death. " Cases of marriage settlements," said the Court, " are different from estates at law, or mere trust estates, which follow the law." The principle that executory trusts are not within the rule in *Shelley's case*, was again enforced in *Porter* v. *Doby*, 2 Richardson's Equity, 49; where real and personal property was by will directed to be placed in the hands of a trustee, upon trust to apply the proceeds to the maintenance of the testator's children, during their natural lives, and after the death of one of them, to his heirs forever; and if the other should survive, the trustee was to keep a sufficiency for that one's support, and dispose of the rest as before mentioned. " The test of an executory trust," said Johnson, Ch., " is, that the trustee has some duty to perform, for the performance of which, it is necessary that the title be regarded as abiding in him. Here, nothing can be plainer than that the trustee could not perform the trusts conferred on him without retaining the title and property."

In some other states, there are dicta recognizing the distinction between executory trusts in marriage articles and wills, and executed trusts; *Horner* v. *Lyeth*, 4 Harris & Johnson, 431, 434; *Lessee of Findlay* v. *Riddle*, 3 Binney, 139, 152; *Dennison* v. *Goehing*, 7 Barr, 175; *Price* v. *Sisson*, 2 Beasley, 168, 174.

It might be a question, said Ames, C. J., in *Tillinghast* v. *Coggeshall*, 7 Rhode Island, 383, under the distinction laid down by Lord Talbot in *Glenorchy* v. *Bosville*, Cas. Tem. Talb. 8, and the English cases following, which have illustrated the distinction, whether the trust for the heirs, here raised, is, in the sense of a court of equity, an *executory* or an *executed* trust. No doubt, " another conveyance was to be made," and in that respect, " somewhat was to be done;" but that is the case with every trust, since none can be executed without a conveyance. The true test seems to be,— has the creator of the trust been his own conveyancer? has he left it to the court to make out, from *general expressions*, what his intention is, or has he so defined his intention, that you have nothing to do but to take the limitations he has given to you, and to convert them into legal estates? See *Lord Glenorchy* v. *Bosville*, 1 White & Tudor's Lead. Cas. in Equity, 13–36, notes, (4th Am. ed.), and cases cited. It would be difficult to find in the trust here created for the heirs of Mrs. Coggeshall, any discretion left in the trustees or the court as to what or how, in the event contemplated, the heirs were to take!

The distinction, however, is important only so far as it affects the right of the court to apply, or to refuse to apply, the rule in Shelley's case to the limitations of a trust. If an executed trust, the limitations must be construed by that rule of law, precisely as if they were legal limitations; if executory, the court will look at the general purpose and particular intent of the creator of the trust, as expressed in the instrument, and construe the limitations as these may require. Ibid.

In the case before us, the trust is raised neither by a will nor by an agreement before marriage for a marriage settlement, but by a deed of the wife's estate executed by the husband and wife after marriage, for the purpose of directing how, in the contemplated events, the estate should go. In default of an appointment by the will of Mrs. Coggeshall, no other deed or instrument was intended to be executed by her, or by her and husband, by way of completing this settlement. The direction to the trustees to convey the remainder to the heirs at law of Mrs. Coggeshall is certain and explicit; and both upon principle and the decided weight of authority, the trust thus created for her heirs was not executory, but executed in the only sense in which a trust can be. The usual definition of an executory trust, that it is one where something additional is to be done by the trustee, is plainly an imperfect one, as pointed out by Lord St. Leonards, in the case of *Egerton* v. *Lord Brownlow*, in 4 House of Lords Cas. 1 ; for, as he observes, in every trust, even in those called executed, there is still something

additional to be done by the trustees, before the *cestuis que trust* can obtain the full benefit of the trusts created for their advantage. A trust " for B. in fee," and a trust " to convey to B. in fee," cannot be substantially distinguished ; since the latter merely expresses what the former implies, and both are quite distinct from a direction to trustees, to make such a settlement of an estate upon B. as would best ensure the continuance of the estate in him and his children. In the former case, the limitations are perfect, and nothing is left for the trustee but to execute them as directed ; in the latter case, they are yet to be made, and the trustee is to make them, so as best to fulfil the intent and carry out the purpose of the settlor. In the former case, the trusts are said to be executed, in the sense of being definite or completely marked out; in the latter case, executory, since no mode of settlement is prescribed, but merely the *intent or purpose*, of the creator of the trust, to be carried out, as best it may, by a settlement to be made by the trustee. See *Halliday* v. *Overton*, 15 Beavan, 480 ; *Lassence* v. *Tierney*, 1 Mac. & Gor. 551 ; *Tatham* v. *Vernon*, 4 Law Times Rep. (N. S.) 531, 533 ; *Neves et al.* v. *Scott et al.*, 9 Howard, R. 196, 211 ; 2 Story's Eq. Jurisp. § 983, and n. 1 ; 1 Hill on Trustees, 328, side paging; Adams' Equity, 40, 41, side paging.

Construing the trusts under consideration as executed trusts, we do not feel at liberty to depart from the long settled rule, that as a court of equity, we must construe them in the same way as legal estates of the like nature would be construed at law, upon the same language. 2 Story's Eq. Jurisp. § 983, and cases cited. As the estate for life reserved by Mrs. Coggeshall for herself, and the estate given by her to her heirs at law, are both equitable estates, there seems to be nothing wanting to warrant the enlargement of her estate, under the rule in Shelley's case, into an equitable fee. Fearne on Conting. Rem. 52–57 ; *Eaton* v. *Tillinghast, Trustee, and others,* 4 R. I. Rep. 276, 280–2."

The reader desirous to follow the views prevailing in the different courts in this country, upon the application of the rule in *Shelley's case,* may consult the following cases, in addition to those above cited ; *Bishop* v. *Selleck,* 1 Day, 299 ; *Goodrick* v. *Lambert,* 10 Connecticut, 448 ; *M'Feely's Lessee* v. *Moore's Heirs,* 5 Ohio, 464 ; *King's Heirs* v. *King's Administrator,* 12 Id. 390 ; reversed on Bill of Review, in *King* v. *Beck,* 15 Id. 559 ; *Roy and others* v. *Garnett,* 2 Washington, 9 ; *Smith* v. *Chapman,* 1 Hening & Munford, 240 ; *Warners* v. *Mason and wife,* 5 Munford, 242 ; *Bradley* v. *Mosby,* 3 Call, 50 ; *Bramble* v. *Billups,* 4 Leigh, 90 ; *Pryor* v. *Duncan et .als.,* 6 Grattan, 27 ; *Den d. Stith's Heirs* v. *Barnes,* 1 Carolina Law Repository, 484 ; *Williams and wife* v. *Holly,* 2 Id. 286 ; *Swain* v. *Roscoe,* 3 Iredell's Law, 200 ; *Jourdan et al.* v. *Green et al.,* 1 Devereux's Equity, 270 ; *Cutlar's Adm'rs* v. *Cutlar's Executors,* 2 Haywood,

154 ; *Jarvis et al.* v. *Wyatt,* 4 Hawks, 227 ; *M'Graw* v. *Davenport and wife,* 6 Porter, 320, 329 ; *Woodley* v. *Findlay et al.,* 9 Alabama, 716 ; *Machen Ex'r* v. *Machen,* 15 Id. 373, 375 ; *James' claim,* 1 Dallas, 47 ; *Miller* v. *Lynn,* 7 Barr, 443 ; *In the matter of Sanders,* 4 Paige, 293 ; *Cushney* v. *Henry,* Id. 345.

As a general rule, it is well settled, that in the construction of marriage articles, the controlling principle is to give effect to the intention of the parties ; and in seeking to attain this end, the Court is not restrained by the technical rules which prevail in limitations of legal estates and executed trusts, but indulges in a liberal interpretation, so as to secure the protection and support of those interests, which, from the nature of the instrument, it must be presumed, were intended to be secured ; and if a settlement is made in the very words of the articles, yet if the legal effect of those words is not according to the intention, the settlement will be reformed. *Gaillard* v. *Porcher et al.,* 1 M'Mullan's Equity, 358 ; *Smith* v. *Maxwell's Ex'r,* 1 Hill's Chancery, 101 ; *Ex'r of Allen* v. *Rumph and others,* 2 Id. 1, 3 ; *Gause* v. *Hale,* 2 Iredell's Equity, 241, 243 ; *Neves et al.* v. *Scott et al.,* 9 Howard's S. Ct. 197, 212.

With regard to the persons in whose favor equity will decree execution of marriage articles, or other executory trusts, see *Bleeker* v. *Bingham,* 3 Paige, 246, 249 ; *King* v. *Whitely,* 10 Id. 465, 468 ; *Dennison* v. *Goehring,* 7 Barr,

175; *Neves et al.* v. *Scott et al.*, 9 Howard's S. Ct. 197, 208; and in respect to the certainty required in the trusts, see *Sledge's Adm'rs et al.* v. *Clopton*, 6 Alabama, 589, 603. In regard to the provisions which the court will order to be inserted in a settlement upon a married woman, see *Temple* v. *Hawley*, 1 Sandford, 154, 178; *Grout* v. *Van Schoonhoven*, Id. 337, 343.

[*44]   *KEECH v. SANDFORD.

OCTOBER 31, 1726.

REPORTED SELECT CASES IN CHANCERY, 61.

RENEWAL OF A LEASE BY A TRUSTEE.]—*A. being possessed of a Lease of a Market bequeathed it to B. in trust for an infant. B., before the expiration of the term, applied to the Lessor for a renewal for the benefit of the Infant. The Lessor refused to grant such renewal, whereupon B. got a Lease made to himself. Held that B. was Trustee of the Lease for the Infant, and must assign the same to him and account for the profits, but that he was entitled to be indemnified from the Covenants contained in the Lease.*

A PERSON being possessed of a lease of the profits of a market, devised his estate to a trustee in trust for the infant. *Before* the expiration of the term the trustee applied to the lessor for a renewal, for the benefit of the infant, which he refused, in regard that, it being only of the profits of a market, there could be no distress, and must rest singly in covenant, which the infant could not do.

There was clear proof of the refusal to renew for the benefit of the infant, on which the trustee gets a lease made to himself.

Bill is now brought [by the infant] to have the lease assigned to him, and for an account of the profits on this principle, that wherever a lease is renewed by a trustee or executor, it shall be for the benefit of cestui que use, which principle was agreed on the other side, though endeavoured to be differenced on account of the express proof of refusal to renew to the infant.

LORD CHANCELLOR KING.—I must consider this as a trust for the infant, for I very well see, if a trustee, on *the refusal to renew, might have a lease to himself, few trust estates would be renewed to cestui que use. Though I do not say there is a fraud in this case, yet he [the trustee] should rather have let it run out than to have had the lease to himself. This may seem hard, that the trustee is the only person of all mankind who might not have the lease; but it is very proper that rule should be strictly pursued, and not in the least relaxed; for it is very

[*45]

obvious what would be the consequences of letting trustees have
the lease on refusal to renew to cestui que use.

So decreed, that the lease should be assigned to the infant, and
that the trustee should be indemnified from any covenants comprised in the lease, and an account of the profits made since the
renewal.

Keech v. *Sandford*, sometimes called the *Rumford Market Case*, is
usually cited as the leading authority on the doctrine of constructive
,trusts arising upon the renewal of a lease by a trustee or executor in his
own name and for his own benefit. The rule here inflexibly laid down
by Lord King has ever since been invariably followed; viz. that a lease
renewed by a trustee or executor, in his own name, even in the absence
of fraud and upon the refusal of the lessor to grant a new lease to the
cestui que trust, shall be held upon trust for the person entitled to the
old lease: see *Fitzgibbon* v. *Scanlan*, 1 Dow, 261, 269; *Rawe* v. *Chichester*, Amb. 715; *S. C.*, 1 Bro. C. C. 198 n.; 2 Dick, 480; *Pickering*
v. *Vowles*, 1 Bro. C. C. 198; *Pierson* v. *Shore*, 1 Atk. 480; *Nesbitt* v.
Tredennick, 1 Ball & B. 46; *Abney* v. *Miller*, 2 Atk. 597; *Edwards* v.
Lewis, 3 Atk. 538; *Killick* v. *Flexney*, 4 Bro. C. C. 161; *Moody* v.
Matthews, 7 Ves. 174; *James* v. *Dean*, 11 Ves. 383; *Parker* v. *Brooke*,
9 Ves. 583; *Lovatt* v. *Knipe*, 12 Ir. Eq. Rep. 124; *Kendall* v. *Marsters*.
2 De G. F. & Jo. 200; see also *Walley* v. *Walley*, 1 Vern. 484; and
Holt v. *Holt*, 1 Ch. Ca. 190, which seems to be the oldest case upon the
subject.

The same rule applies also to an executor de son tort renewing in his
own name: *Mulvany* v. *Dillon*, 1 Ball & B. 409; *Griffin* v. *Griffin*, 1
S. & L. 352. But where a trustee obtains a new lease, which comprises,
not only the premises in the original lease, but also additional lands, the
trusts will not attach upon the additional lands: *Acheson* v. *Fair*, 3 D.
& W. 512; 2 C. & L. 208.

*In *Foord* v. *Baker*, 27 Beav. 193, a scheme made in 1855 pro- [*46]
vided, that no person should act as trustee of the charity, who
should hold or occupy any part of the charity property. At that time
one of the trustees held a small piece of charity land under a twenty-one
years' lease granted in 1847 by public tender. It was held by Sir John
Romilly, M. R., that he must either give up the lease or the trusteeship.

The ground of decreeing renewals by trustees and executors to enure
to the benefit of cestui que trusts is public policy to prevent persons in
such situations from acting so as to take a benefit to themselves: *Griffin* v. *Griffin*, 1 S. & L. 354, per Lord Redesdale; and see *Blewett* v.
Millett, 7 Bro. P. C. 367, Toml. ed.

So, if a person having a limited interest in a renewable lease, as a
tenant for life, renews it in his own name, he will be held a trustee for

those entitled in remainder to the old lease: (*Rawe* v. *Chichester*, Amb. 715; *S. C.*, 5 Dick. 480; 1 Bro. C. C. 198, n.; *Taster* v. *Marriott*, Amb. 668; *Owen* v. *Williams*, Amb. 734; *Coppin* v. *Fernyhough*, 2 Bro. C. C. 291; *Bowles* v. *Stewart*, 1 S. & L. 209; *Randall* v. *Russell*, 3 Mer. 190; *Giddings* v. *Giddings*, 3 Russ. 241; *Nesbitt* v. *Tredennick*, 1 Ball & B. 46; *Eyre* v. *Dolphin*, 2 Ball & B. 290; *Tanner* v. *Elworthy*, 4 Beav. 487; *Waters* v. *Bailey*, 2 You. & Coll. C. C. 224; *Buckley* v *Lanauze*, L. & G., t. Plunk. 327; *Hill* v. *Mill*, 12 Ir. Eq. Rep. 107; *Mill* v. *Hill*, 3 H. L. Cas. 828); and in the case of a tenant for life under a will, even although the original lease may have expired during the life of the testator, who had continued to hold merely as tenant from year to year. See *James* v. *Dean*, 11 Ves. 383; *S. C.*, 15 Ves. 236, where a testator bequeathed leaseholds for years determinable upon lives to his widow (who was his residuary legatee and executrix) for life, with remainder over; the term expired during the testator's life, who continued to hold as tenant from year to year; a subsequent lease, obtained by his widow, was held to be subject to the trusts of the will, as the residue of the term at his death, if any, however short, would have been. " The question," said Lord Eldon (see 11 Ves. 395), " is, as the interest which passed at the testator's death was an interest he could bequeath by a will antecedent to his acquiring it, and that interest, though but a tenancy from year to year being bequeathed to one for life, with the remainder to another, if, during the tenancy of the person who took for life, acting upon the goodwill that accompanies the possession, she gets a more durable term, whether the persons who are to take against her, are or are not entitled to say, that term is acquired for their benefit as well as her own. If she had died in his lifetime, his [*47] term *from year to year would have passed to the remainderman, who would have been specifically entitled to it. The consequence is, the term, though short, is bequeathed in these particular estates; and it cannot depend upon the question, whether the interest is long or short. Suppose only a quarter of a year subsisted at the death of the testator, if the tenant for life did renew, it must have been as well for the benefit of the persons to take afterwards as herself." If, however, the testator in *James* v. *Dean*, had only been tenant at will or at sufferance, the widow upon renewal of the lease would not have been a trustee for the persons to whom the leaseholds were bequeathed in remainder, for as a tenancy at will or at sufferance would have determined upon the death of the testator, no interest would have passed to them by the will; but Lord Eldon was inclined to think, that, had the widow not been residuary legatee, she would, in such a case, have been a trustee for the residuary legatee. " The question," observed his lordship (see 11 Ves. 393), " is new, whether an executrix, dealing with the opportunities which she derives by her succession without title to the estate a tenant by sufferance or at will had held, is a trustee for the person, who cannot say he took an interest under the will, or whether it is to be said against her only, that the advantage she made of those opportunities should be for the general estate. The result is this: I think it is impossible she could hold it for herself. Not applying it to this case, but supposing another person, not the wife, was residuary legatee, the question, I should think, would be in favour of that other residuary legatee, being a casual advantage from the dealing of the executrix." See also *Randall* v. *Russell*, 3 Mer. 190; *Mill* v. *Hill*, 3 H. L. Cas. 866; *Archbold* v. *Scully*, 9 Ho. Lo. Ca. 360. *In re Tottenham's Estate*, 16 Ir. Ch. Rep. 115.

Although a tenant for life of a lease under a settlement be himself the author of it, if he renew the lease in his own name, he will be a trustee for the parties interested under the settlement: *Pickering* v. *Vowles*, 1 Bro. C. C. 197; *Colgrave* v. *Manby*, 6 Madd. 72; *S. C.*, 2 Russ. 238. And the fact of the settlement containing a special provision that a particular renewal shall enure for the benefit of the trust, will not prevent the application of the general rule: *Tanner* v. *Elworthy*, 4 Beav. 487.

By analogy to these cases, if not under the 73rd section of the Lands Clauses Consolidation Act (8 Vict. c. 18), when a tenant for life receives a sum of money for withdrawing opposition to a bill, and the act then passes authorising the taking of the land in settlement, whether the land is taken or not, and whether the act is proceeded upon or not, the money *so received must be held for the benefit of all the [*48] parties interested: *Pole* v. *Pole*, 2 D. & Sm. 420; *Re Duke of Marlborough's Estates*, 13 Jur. 738; *Earl of Shrewsbury* v. *North Staffordshire Railway Company*, 1 L. R. Eq. 593, 608, *sed vide ex parte Lockwood*, 14 Beav. 158; *Ex parte The Rector of Little Steeping*, 5 Railway Ca. 207.

In *Brookman* v. *Hales*, 2 V. & B. 45, a tenant for life of renewable leaseholds had a general power of appointment, which she did not exercise; it was held that a renewal in her own name, not being an execution of the power, enured over at her death for the benefit of the remainderman.

And where a person who is trustee of property for himself and others, acquires, under an Act of Parliament, upon the representation that he was solely entitled, an absolute interest therein, he will, nevertheless, be held a trustee for all the parties beneficially interested, of whatever estate or right he may have so acquired. Thus: in *Cooper* v. *Phibbs*, 2 L. R. Ho. Lo. 149, E. J. Cooper, being in possession of certain estates and a fishery, which, by a settlement in 1827, he had covenanted to settle, after previous limitations to himself and his issue male, on his brother, R. W. Cooper, for life, with remainder to his issue male, obtained an Act of Parliament, which, after reciting (among other things) that the estates and fishery had descended to and were then vested in the said E. J. Cooper, and that the said E. J. Cooper was desirous of constructing canals or water cuts, at his own expense, in consideration of the exclusive right of fishery being vested in him, his heirs and assigns, it was therefore enacted that the said powers to make the canals and cuts should be granted to him, provided that the cuts "shall be altogether situated on the estates and property of the said E. J. Cooper." There were various other provisions, in all of which E. J. Cooper was spoken of as the owner of the estate. E. J. Cooper having died without issue male, it was held by the House of Lords that E. J. Cooper, under the Act of Parliament, took the fishery bound by the trusts of the settlement of 1827. "I must," said Lord Westbury, " of necessity assume that E. J. Cooper had the intention of stating the truth and the fact to the legislature. When, therefore, I find in this Act of Parliament a recital that this fishery, together with the other hereditaments, on the death of the lunatic, descended to E. J. Cooper, in fee, that must be taken to represent to Parliament that the trust estate did so descend. Your lordships are bound to assume E. J. Cooper's honesty and integrity of purpose, and therefore you cannot [*49] for a moment impute to him that he intended to *conceal from the legislature the fact of the property being bound by the trusts of the settlement. You must take the recital contained in the Act of Parliament as a recital intended to denote the descent of the legal estate in fee held by him upon trust, and you cannot impute to him an intention of representing to Parliament that it was his own property, because you cannot for a moment suppose that he was ignorant of the agreement or contract contained in that deed, or that he intended to repudiate the obligation which he had contracted under that deed. Then, if it be taken that he stood before Parliament as a trustee, the powers and authorities conferred upon him by that Act of Parliament are conferred upon him in his character of trustee. They are attached to the ownership in fee, which he represents himself to have had; and as that ownership was subject to the trust, the powers and authorities attached to the ownership are in like manner subject to the obligation of that trust, and the things acquired by virtue of those powers and authorities would also be subject to the trusts which affected the individual who becomes the parliamentary donee of those powers. There can be no doubt for a moment, therefore, with regard to the settled principles of equity, that what was given to him in the character of owner in trust for the other persons, and what was acquired by him in virtue of those powers, became also subject to that trust. The result, therefore, is, that all he acquired by virtue of the parliamentary powers would become subject to the trusts of the settlement of 1827, subject only to the repayment to him by the parties entitled under those trusts of the moneys properly expended by him in acquiring additional rights of fishery, and improving the whole."

Upon the same principle where the tenant for life, under a devise, of an encroachment upon the property of the Crown in the Forest of Dean, took under an Act of Parliament (1 & 2 Vict. c. 42) for confirming the titles to the encroachments, a conveyance to herself in fee, it was held that as the act was intended only to provide for disputes between parties claiming adversely the legal right (speaking without regard to the Crown's title) to be in possession and treated as holders, the devisee had acquired the fee, not only for her own benefit, but also for the benefit of those in remainder: *Yem* v. *Edwards*, 3 K. & J. 564, 1 De G. & Jo. 598. On the subject of encroachments by tenants, see *Andrews* v. *Hailes*, 2 Ell. & B. 349 ; *Kingsmill* v. *Millard*, 11 Exch. 313.

If one of several persons jointly interested in a lease renew it in his own name, he will hold in trust for the others, according to their respective shares. Thus in *Palmer* *v. *Young*, 1 Vern. 276, one of three who held a lease under a dean and chapter, surrendered [*50] the old lease, and took a new one to himself: the Court said it should be a trust for all. See also *Hamilton* v. *Denny*, 1 Ball & B. 199 ; *Jackson* v. *Welsh*, L. & G., t. Plunk. 346.

And if a person jointly interested with an infant, renew, and the renewed lease turn out not to be beneficial, the person renewing must sustain the loss; if beneficial, the infant can claim his share of the benefit to be derived from it. This is the peculiar privilege of the unprotected situation of the infant. But to any sums which may have been paid for the renewal of the lease, or in consequence of it, the infant must contribute his due proportion, before he can claim any advantage: *Ex parte Grace*, 1 B. & P. 376.

So, likewise, if a partner renew a lease of the partnership premises on his own account, he will as a general rule, be held a trustee of it for the firm: *Lacey* v. *Hall*, 1 Wright, 360, 365. " It is clear," observed an eminent judge, that one partner cannot treat privately, and behind the backs of his copartners, for a lease of the premises where the joint trade is carried on, for his own individual benefit: if he does so treat, and obtains a lease in his own name, it is a trust for the partnership. In this respect there can be no distinction, whether the partnership is for a definite or indefinite period. If one partner might so act in the latter case, he might equally in the former. Supposing the lease and the partnership to have different terms of duration, he might, having clandestinely obtained a renewal of the lease, say to the other partners, ' The premises on which we carried on our trade have become mine exclusively; and I am entitled to demand from you whatever terms I think fit, as the condition for permitting you to carry on that trade here:' " per Sir William Grant, M. R., in *Featherstonhaugh* v. *Fenwick*, 17 Ves. 311. See also *Alder* v. *Fouracre*, 3 Swanst. 489 ; *Fawcett* v. *Whitehouse*, 1 Russ. & My. 132 ; *Glegg* v. *Edmonson*, 22 Beav. 125 ; 8 De G. Mac. & G. 787 ; *Clements* v. *Hall*, 2 De G. & Jo. 173 ;

reversing *S. C.* 24 Beav. 333 ; *Gordon* v. *Scott,* 12 Moo. P. C. C. 1. In
Clegg v. *Fishwick,* 1 Mac. & G. 294, the plaintiff's husband being
engaged in partnership with other persons, they took a lease in 1828 of
certain coal mines, for the purposes of the partnership. He died in
1836, and the plaintiff took out letters of administration. There was
no provision made for the continuance of the partnership with the
administratrix ; but it was in fact carried on between her and the other
partners up to the year 1849, the same partnership property being used
for the purposes of the partnership. In that year the old lease having
[*51] expired a new lease was taken by *some of the other partners,
without the privity of the plaintiffs. It was held by Lord
Cottenham, C., that the administratrix was entitled to a Receiver in
respect of the intestate's share of the partnership including the renewed lease.

The rule, however, to be deduced from the last-mentioned class of
cases has been to some extent departed from where the trade or business carried on in connection with a lease, is one of a speculative character, requiring great outlay with uncertain returns. Thus, if in such
a business, for instance, a mining concern, the surviving partner
renews the lease in his own sole name and carries on the business
with his own capital and in his own name, the Court will not in general
assist the representative of the deceased partner unless he comes forward promptly, and is ready to contribute a due proportion of money
for the purpose of the business, for it would be unjust to permit the
executor of the deceased partner to lie by and remain passive while the
survivor is incurring all the risk of loss, and only to claim to participate after the affairs have turned out to be prosperous (per Lord Cranworth, C., 2 De G. & Jo. 186) ; but this exception to the rule does not
apply where the surviving partner who renews the lease keeps the representative of the deceased partner in ignorance of the real state of the
concern, for he is bound to disclose *uberrimâ fide* every fact which may
enable the representative to exercise a sound discretion as to the course
he ought to pursue : *Clements* v. *Hall,* 2 De G. & Jo. 173, 188.

[Whether a partner who obtains a conveyance of the reversion of a
lease which has been made for partnership purposes, for his own benefit, will be regarded as a trustee for the firm, seems to be doubtful,
but such a trust will arise if he represents himself to be buying for
the common good, and thus obtains a grant which might otherwise
have been refused : *Anderson* v. *Lemon,* 4 Sandford, 552 ; 4 Selden,
236. The point arose in *Anderson* v. *Lemon,* where Gardiner, J., held
the following language in delivering the opinion of the Court : " In a
note to *Moody* v. *Matthews,* (7 Ves. 185, Sumner's Ed.,) it is said, as a
deduction from adjudged cases, that with a possible exception in favor
of a bona fide purchaser, it seems to be an universal rule that no one
who is in possession of a lease, or a particular interest in a lease, which

lease is affected with any sort of equity in behalf of third persons, can renew the same for his own use only, but such renewal must be construed as a graft upon the old stock. In *Featherstonhaugh* v. *Fenwick*, (17 Ves. 298,) it was held that a renewal obtained one month before the expiration of the lease, by two of three partners, for their own benefit, enured to the partnership and must be accounted for as partnership property. But it has been held in several cases, that during the continuance of the lease, any one, even a trustee of the leasehold interest, may purchase the reversion in fee on his sole account, for although the *cestui que trust* will be deprived of all claim of renewal, yet it has been thought impossible to consider the purchase of the inheritance as a graft upon leasehold or life interests : (7 Ves. 186, note, Sumner's Ed.; 3 Meriv. 197, 352; 3 Atk. 38.) The learned Judge who delivered the opinion of the Superior Court, was therefore correct in saying that a co-partner was at liberty to make the purchase stated in this case, under circumstances free from deception and fraud, and consequently to retain it." But it was notwithstanding decided, that although the defendant would have been entitled to the benefit of his purchase, if his conduct had been fair and open, yet, as he had been guilty of misrepresentation to the vendor, and concealment from his co-partners, equity would redress the wrong by raising a trust for their benefit. In *Lacey* v. *Hall*, 1 Wright, 360, the court cited and relied upon *Featherstonhaugh* v. *Fenwick*, and it was said to follow from that decision, that if a partner purchases the reversion in land which has been leased to the firm, and on which they have made valuable improvements, it will be affected with a trust for their benefit. In this instance, however, the defendant had abused the confidence of his co-partners by leading them to believe that the purchase was made on joint account. In like manner, where it appears from written evidence, or from facts and circumstances, that two or more persons have agreed to purchase land jointly, one of them cannot buy for himself alone : *Flagg* v. *Mann*, 2 Sumner 486, 521. The principle applies to a purchase by a partner in the course of the partnership business, or in pursuance of an agreement to that effect, with the other members of the firm, and he will not be allowed to evade it by dissolving the partnership : *Ib.*]

If a mortgagee renew a lease, the renewal shall be for the benefit of the mortgagor, paying the mortgagee his charges ; and per Lord Chancellor Nottingham, " The mortgagee here doth but graft upon his stock, and it shall be for the mortgagor's benefit :" *Rushworth's Case*, Freem. 12 ; *Luckin* v. *Rushworth*, Finch, 392 ; *S. C.*, 2 Ch. Rep. 113 ; *Darrell* v. *Whitchot*, 2 Ch. Rep. 59 ; nor will the case be altered by the expiration of the lease before renewal: *Rakestraw* v. *Brewer*, 2 P. Wms. 510. See *Nesbitt* v. *Treddennick*, 1 Ball & B. 29. On the other hand, if a lessee mortgage leaseholds, and afterwards obtain a new lease, the new lease will be held a graft on the old one, for the benefit of the mortgagee: *Smith* v. *Chichester*, 1 C. & L. 486.

Upon the same principle, if a person entitled to a lease, subject to debts, legacies, or annuities, renews, either in his own name or in the name of a trustee, the incumbrances will remain a charge upon the renewed lease: *Seabourne* v. *Powel*, 2 Vern. 11; *Jackson* v. *Welsh*, L. & G., t. Plunk. 346; *Winslow* v. *Tighe*, 2 Ball. & B. 195; *Stubbs* v. *Roth*, 2 Ball. & B. 548; *Webb* v. *Lugar*, 2 You. & Coll. Exch. Ca. 247; *Jones* [*52] v. *Kearney*, *1 C. & L. 34; *Otter* v. *Vaux*, 6 De G. Mac. & G. 638.

And a lessee will not be allowed to evade the operation of the rule laid down in the principal case by fraudulently incurring a forfeiture of the lease which he induces the landlord to take advantage of, and afterwards obtains for him a new lease: *Hughes* v. *Howard*, 25 Beav. 575; *Stratton* v. *Murphy*, 1 I. R. Eq. 345.

If a person, having the right of renewal, sells such right, the money produced by the sale will be affected by the same trusts as the leaseholds, if renewed, would have been. Thus, in *Owen* v. *Williams*, Amb. 734, where a tenant for life of a Crown lease applied for a further term, but a powerful opponent having applied for a grant, the tenant for life gave up her pretentions for a sum of money, Lord Apsley, upon the authority of the principal case, held that the money ought to be settled upon the same trusts as the lease. And in *Lombard* v. *Hickson*, 13 Ir. Ch. Rep. 98, an execution creditor of the lessee of a share, of renewable leaseholds, of which he had obtained possession by ejectment, and who bought the superior lease, was held bound by a jointure rent created by the lessee, and of which he had notice.

A person acting as agent, or in any similar capacity, for a person having an interest in a lease, cannot renew for his own benefit. See *Edwards* v. *Lewis*, 3 Atk. 538; *Griffin* v. *Griffin*, 1 S. & L. 352; *Mulvany* v. *Dillon*, 1 Ball & B. 417; and *Mulhallen* v. *Marum*, 3 D. & W. 317, in which case a lease was obtained by a person standing, by delegation, in the place of guardians, and who, at the same time, filled the characters of agent, receiver, and tenant; it was set aside by Sir Edward Sugden, L. C., upon the equity arising out of those relations and upon public policy.

A trustee who has renewed will be directed to assign the lease, free from incumbrances, except it seems, any lease made by him bonâ fide at the best rent; (*Bowles* v. *Stewart*, 1 S. & L. 230); and he must account also for the mesne rents and profits and fines which he may have received; (*Mulvany* v. *Dillon*, 1 Ball & B. 409; *Walley* v. *Walley*, 1 Vern. 484; *Luckin* v. *Rushworth*, Finch, 392; *Blewett* v. *Millett*, 7 Bro. P. C. 367, Toml. ed.; *Rawe* v. *Chichester*, Amb. 715); even although the lease had expired before the bill was filed: *Eyre* v. *Dolphin*, 2 Ball & B. 290. But where a tenant for life has renewed, the account will commence only from his decease : *Giddings* v. *Giddings*, 3 Russ. 241. On the other hand, the person who has renewed the lease will be entitled, as in the principal case, to be indemnified against the covenants he may have entered into with the lessor ; (*Giddings* v. *Giddings*, 3 Russ. *241) ; and he will also have a lien upon the estate [*53] for the costs and expenses of renewing the lease, with interest ; (*Rawe* v. *Chichester*, Amb. 715, 720 ; *Coppin* v. *Fernyhough*, 2 Bro. C. C. 291 ; *Lawrence* v. *Maggs*, 1 Eden, 453, and note ; *James* v. *Dean*, 11 Ves. 383 ; *Kempton* v. *Packman*, cited 7 Ves. 176) ; and for the expenses of lasting improvements ; (*Holt* v. *Holt*, 1 Ch. Ca. 190 ; and see *Lawrence* v. *Maggs*, and note ; *Mill* v. *Hill*, 3 H. L. Cas. 828, 869) ; even though incurred after the institution of the suit ; (*Walley* v. *Walley*, 1 Vern. 487) ; but not for any improvements adopted as a mere matter of taste, or as a matter of personal convenience ; (*Mill* v. *Hill*, 3 H. L. Cas. 869) ; at the same time there may be many charges in the nature of waste, and as to deterioration, which must be set off against anything found due in respect of improvements. (*Ib.*) So, also, will a tenant for life have a lien for such proportion of the fine upon renewal as ought to be borne by the remainderman : *Lawrence* v. *Maggs*, and note by Eden.

As to contribution towards payment of fines upon renewals, see *White* v. *White*, 9 Ves. 554 ; *Playters* v. *Abbott*, 2 My. & K. 97 ; *Earl of Shaftesbury* v. *Duke of Marlborough*, 2 My. & K. 111 , *Reeves* v. *Creswick*, 3 You. & Coll. Exch. Ca. 715 ; *Jones* v. *Jones*, 5 Hare, 440 ; *Giddings* v. *Giddings*, 3 Russ. 241, 259. Tudor's Lead. Cas. Real. Prop. 76—82, 2nd ed.

The same remedies which, as we have before seen, may be had against trustees, executors, and persons with limited interests, renewing leases in their own names, may also be had against volunteers claiming through them ; (*Bowles* v. *Stewart*, 1 S. & L. 209 ; *Eyre* v. *Dolphin*, 2 Ball & B. 290 ; *Blewet* v. *Millett*, 7 Bro. P. C. Toml. ed., 367) ; and against purchasers from them, with notice express or implied : *Walley* v. *Walley*, 1 Vern. 484 ; *Eyre* v. *Dolphin*, 2 Ball & B. 290 ; *Parker* v. *Brooke*, 9 Ves. 583 ; *Stratton* v. *Murphy*, 1 I. R. Eq. 345. In *Coppin* v. *Fernyhough*, 2 Bro. C. C. 291, a recital, in a lease assigned to a mortgagee, of the surrender of a former lease, in which mention was made of the settlement under which the cestui que trust claimed, was held to be constructive notice.

And where a deed by which the lease is settled is registered under the Irish Registry Act (6 Ann. c. 2), a purchaser, although without notice from a person having a limited interest, who has renewed the lease in his own name, will be held to be a trustee for the parties interested under the settlement : *Hill* v. *Mill*, 12 Ir. Eq. Rep. 107 ; *S. C.*, nom. *Mill* v. *Hill*, 3 H. L. Cas. 828.

But the cestui que trust may be bound by acquiescence and lapse of

[*54] time. (See *Isald* v. *Fitzgerald*, *cited in *Owen* v. *Williams*, Amb. 735, 737; *Norris* v. *Le Neve*, 3 Atk. 38, 39; *Jackson* v. *Welsh*, L. & G. Ca. temp. Plunk. 346.) Especially where the property sought to be affected with a trust, is, as in the case of mines, subject to extraordinary contingencies, and is capable of being rendered productive only by a large and uncertain outlay: *Clegg* v. *Edmondson*, 8 De G. Mac. & G. 787.

A tenant for life, under a settlement of leaseholds, procuring a renewal to himself, does not take the renewal as an express trustee upon the trusts of the settlement, the Statute of Limitations (3 & 4 Will. 4, c. 27) therefore will run as against other persons claiming under the settlement, *In re Dane's Estate*, 5 I. R. Eq. 498.

When it is impossible to obtain the renewal of a lease, the tenant for life will, it seems, be entitled to the sum accumulated by the direction of the settlor for that purpose. See *Morres* v. *Hodges*, 27 Beav. 625; there by a settlement, the trustees were to use their utmost endeavours to renew an ecclesiastical lease upon reasonable terms, and to raise the fines out of the rents or by mortgage. A renewal became impracticable. It was held by Sir John Romilly, with evident reluctance, upon the authority of *Tardiff* v. *Robinson*, 27 Beav. 629, n.—a decision of Lord Eldon's,—that the fund reserved by the trustees out of the rents for the purpose of renewal belonged absolutely to the tenant for life; and see *In re Money's Trusts*, 2 D. & Sm. 94.

Where renewable leaseholds are taken by a Railway Company under its compulsory powers, a tenant for life will only be entitled to the interest arising from the purchase-money, although the custom to renew may not have ceased until after the premises were taken by the Railway Company; at any rate where the primary intention of the settlor of the leaseholds, appears to have been to create a perpetual estate. Thus, in *Re Wood's Estate*, 10 L. R. Eq. 572, leaseholds under a Dean and Chapter, renewable by custom, were held by trustees upon trust for a tenant for life, with remainder over; and the trustees were directed, "two years, or sooner, before the time for renewal," to bring a part of the rental into a fund until a sufficient sum was raised for the renewal, " so that the estates may be always kept renewed . . for ever." In June, 1865, and February, 1866, notices to treat for parts of the leaseholds, then having about thirteen, and five, years respectively to run, were given by a Railway Company. At Lady-day, 1866, the Dean and Chapter ceased to renew leases; and about the same date their property was taken over by the Ecclesiastical Commissioners.

[*55] —The values of the two properties *having been assessed at amounts which, when paid, and invested in £3 per cent. stock, gave a diminished income, it was argued that as the renewal had become impossible, all trust for renewal had ceased, and that the property ought to be dealt with as if it were a mere leasehold for a term of years, to

which the tenant for life was entitled *in specie;* and that, therefore, the tenant for life was entitled to have the whole fund treated as converted into an annuity of duration equivalent to the term, and to have each year one year's payment of the annuity. It was, however, held by Sir W. W. James, L. J., that the tenant for life was only entitled to the dividends of the fund arising from the sale of the leaseholds to the Railway Company. "I am of opinion," said his lordship, "that I am not in the present case bound by those cases of *Morres* v. *Hodges,* (27 Beav. 625), and *Tardiff* v. *Robinson,* (27 Beav. 629, n.). In those cases the conclusion arrived at by the Court was, that the tenant for life was entitled *in specie* to the whole rents and profits, charged only with the payment of such a sum as might be required for the renewal, and as no renewal was practicable, there was nothing by which the charge could be maintained, and no means by which any substituted benefit could be ascertained by the Court to be given to the remainderman. In this case, however, the primary and paramount intention was 'that the estates may be always kept renewed, and that the younger children may have an equal benefit of time, and so continue to be provided for, for ever.' . . . The testator intended to create, and was creating as he thought, a perpetual estate, out of which he was carving successive interest. . . . The result, in my opinion, of the purchase by the Railway Company is, that one property in perpetuity is substituted for another property in perpetuity; and that as between the tenant for life and the remainderman, I cannot take away any part of the corpus belonging to the latter, in order to make good the diminished income of the former."

Although trustees with power to renew, have power to purchase the reversion in leaseholds, under 23 & 24 Vict. c. 124, the Court will not give its sanction to such purchase, if it will have the effect of throwing a burthen unduly upon any particular person. See *Hayward* v. *Pile,* 5 L. R. Ch. App. 214. There a testatrix bequeathed leaseholds under a Dean and Chapter, to trustees on trust for a tenant for life, with remainders over, and with power to raise money for renewing the leases. The property became vested in the Ecclesiastical Commissioners, with whom the trustees of the will agreed for the purchase of the reversion in part of the leaseholds *in consideration of the surrender of the other part, and the payment of a sum of money. The estate of the [*56] testatrix was administered by the Court, and the agreement was made subject to the approval of the Court. It was held by Lord Hatherley, L. C., affirming the decision of Lord Romilly, M. R., that the Court would not approve of the agreement against the wish of the tenant for life, if his income would be considerably reduced by the purchase. See *Jones* v. *Jones,* 5 Hare, 440, 460, 462.

It is undetermined whether the purchase of the reversion from the lessor by trustees or a tenant for life of a lease comes within the rule which precludes them from renewing such lease for their own benefit, although such a purchase may be made from a stranger. In *Randall v. Russell*, 3 Mer. 190, where a tenant for life of leaseholds held of a college, purchased the reversion in fee from a stranger, to whom the college had sold it; upon a bill filed by the remaindermen, contending that the situation of the tenant for life gave her an opportunity to make the purchase, and that she ought to be turned into a trustee of the reversion for them, Sir William Grant, M. R., said that no case was mentioned in which this sort of equity had been carried to such a length. The College had aliened the property to an individual. The benefit attending the tenant right of renewal with a public body was gone, and a lease at rack-rent was all that was to be expected from the private proprietor. His Honour, therefore, held, that the reversion was not subject to the trusts of the will. With respect to the question, whether the tenant for life could have become a purchaser of the reversion, not from a mere stranger, but from the college, his Honour observed, that it might be said that she thereby intercepted and cut off the chance of future renewals, and consequently made use of her situation to prejudice the interests of those who stood behind her; and that there might be some sort of equity in their claim to have the reversion considered as a substitution for those interests, although he was not aware of any decision to that effect. See *Hardman v. Johnson*, 3 Mer. 347; *Norris v. Le Neve*, 3 Atk. 37; *Lesley's Case*, Freem. 52.

Where, however, the executor of a mortgagee purchased the equity of redemption of the mortgaged estate in his own name, with the money due on the mortgage and a small advance beyond it, he was held to be a trustee of the purchased property for the benefit of the testator's estate: *Fosbrooke v. Balguy*, 1 My. & K. 226.

A quasi tenant in tail or leaseholds, being the absolute owner of them, is not bound by the same *equities as persons having [*57] merely limited interests; thus, where a testator devised leaseholds for lives to trustees for A. and the heirs of his body, and if he should die without issue, remainder to B. A. surrendered the old lease, and took a new one to himself and his heirs for three new lives, and died without issue, having devised the leaseholds to his widow for life, remainders over. A bill, filed by B., to have the benefit of the new lease, insisting that the surrender of the old lease and taking the new one, was not sufficient to bar the limitation to him, and that those claiming under A. ought to be held trustees of the new lease, was dismissed: *Blake v. Blake*, 1 Cox, 266.

Where a stranger obtains a renewal of a lease, or a reversionary lease, the old tenant has no equity against him: *Lee v. Lord Vernon*, 5 Bro. P. C. 10, Toml. ed.; *Earl of Sandwich v. Earl of Lichfield*, Colles, P. C. 104; *Stokes v. Clarke*, Colles, P. C. 192; *Nesbitt v. Tredennick*, 1 Ball. & B. 29; *Lesley's Case*, Freem. 52. *The Attor-*

ney-General v. *Gains*, 11 Beav. 63. Nor, it seems, has a lessee any equity against his sub-lessee, who obtains a renewal from the head landlord without consulting him : *Maunsell* v. *O'Brien*, 1 Jones, 176, Exch. Rep. (Ireland).

A lessee, however, obtaining a renewal of a lease at an increased rent, or purchasing the reversion, is somewhat in the position of a partner or fiduciary with respect to a sub-lessee with whom he has entered into a *toties quoties* covenant to renew at a fixed rent or fine, and is bound either to renew upon the old terms or to convey the property to the sub-lessee upon proper terms. In *Evans* v. *Walshe*, 2 S. & L. 519, A., the defendant, the lessee of a corporation, underlet to the plaintiff at a certain rent, with a covenant to renew to him at the same rent, as often as the corporation should renew to him. The corporation raised the rent payable by A. Lord Redesdale granted an injunction to restrain the defendant from proceeding in ejectment, observing, " that he considered the defendant as bound to renew on the old terms, unless he chose to abandon the property, and allow the plaintiff to stand in his place for the renewal which he had obtained, which, as he had not covenanted to renew with the corporation, he might perhaps be at liberty tó do. But if he thought fit to retain the benefit which he had obtained, he was bound specifically to execute his covenant for renewal."

Upon the same principle, in *Postlethwaite* v. *Lewthwaite*, 2 J. & H. 237, the defendants, lessees for lives from a dean and chapter, without a covenant for perpetual renewal, granted an underlease to the plaintiff for the same lives, of part of the premises, and covenanted that so often as they renewed *their lease, they would add the same life [*58] to the plaintiff's lease, on the payment of a fixed fine, such new lease to contain such or the like rents, covenants, and provisoes as the former lease. The reversion having become vested in the Ecclesiastical Commissioners, they refused to renew, but offered to sell, and the lessee purchased the reversion. Sir W. Page Wood, V. C., acting upon the principles laid down by Lord Redesdale in *Evans* v. *Walshe*, made the following decree : " The defendants offering to convey the reversion in fee simple of the premises comprised in the plaintiff's lease, in preference to granting a new lease of the premises with a covenant for perpetual renewal and otherwise on the terms of the present lease, declare that the plaintiff is entitled to have such reversion conveyed to him on the terms of paying the defendants a due proportion of the consideration paid or given by them, and of the expenses incurred by them, in purchasing the fee simple of so much of the property comprised in their original lease as they did purchase, regard being had to the existing interest of the plaintiff under his lease, and to the extent of the property therein comprised. Then there must be an inquiry what this interest is worth." See *Pilkington* v. *Gore*, 8 Ir. Ch. Rep. 589; *Trumper* v. *Trumper*, 41 L. J. Ch. (N. S.) 673.

A lessee, moreover, cannot, by obtaining a new lease, omitting provisions contained in the former lease, and upon the faith of which he induced another person to take a sub-lease, act in contravention of such provisions to the injury of the sub-lessee. See *Piggott* v. *Stratton*, Johns. 341.

It is a principle firmly maintained in the equity jurisprudence of this country, that a trustee is not at liberty to act or contract for his own benefit in regard to the subject of the trust, and that the advantage of all that he does about the trust property shall accrue to the *cestui que trust*, if the latter desire it: *Staats* v. *Bergen*, 2 C. E. Green, 297, 308, 554, 559. An independent interest in a trustee, in the subject of the trust, would, in its very nature, be an interest hostile to the *cestui que trust;* and that is repugnant to the relation which the trustee has assumed. So far as he acts about the property for himself, distinctly, he divests himself of the character of trustee for another; and this by his own act he cannot do. The *cestui que trust* has a claim to his entire services about the subject which has been confided to him; and equity, therefore, affects with a trust all his transactions and agreements in respect to it; at least it does so at the option of the *cestui que trust*. This claim extends as well to the knowledge, as to the influence and power, which the trustee obtains from his situation: *Coffee* v. *Ruffin*, 4 Caldwell, 487; *Gardner* v. *Ogden*, 22 New York, 327; and if

a person, from being placed in a relation of confidence towards another, or being employed in any fiduciary capacity about property, acquires peculiar information about its value, or circumstances, or condition, he is disabled from exercising this information for his own benefit, in opposition to him by whose confidence he obtained it: *Ringo* v. *Binns*, 10 Peters, 269; *Michaud* v. *Girod*, 4 Howard, 503; *Noel* v. *White*, 1 Wright, 514; *Worm* v. *Dillon*, 27 Mississippi, 494. And this is not confined to cases of express and formal trusts; the rule is applied as far as the principle and morality and policy, upon which it is founded, extend. Wherever a confidence is permitted, a duty is assumed, and a trust is the medium by which chancery enforces mere duties in respect to property. Wherever one person is placed in such relation to another, by the act or consent of that other, or the act of a third person, or of the law, that he becomes interested for him, or interested with him, in any subject of property or business, he is prohibited from acquiring rights in that subject antagonistic to the person with whose interests he has become associated. If one comes into an interest, by the permission of another, or accepts an interest with another by the act of a third person, or of the law, as in the case of tenants in common under the same will or descent, an implied obligation arises to sustain the common interest into which he has been admitted; and equity vindicates it in the form of a trust. A fiduciary obligation sufficient to lead to the enforcement of the prohibitory principle considered in *Keech* v. *Sandford*, is recognized as resting upon executors and administrators, guardians, agents, mortgagees, tenants for life, joint-tenants and co-parceners, tenants in common coming in under the same purchase or descent, and vendees up to the time of the completion of the conveyance.

That the renewal of a lease by a trustee enures to the benefit of the *cestui que trust*, is universally admitted in this country. "If we go through all the cases," said Chancellor Kent, in *Davoue* v. *Fanning*, 2 Johnson's Chancery, 252, 258, "I doubt whether we shall find the rule and the policy of it, laid down with more clearness, strictness and good sense (than in *Keech* v. *Sandford*). This decision has never been questioned; and that a trust results on the renewal of an infant's lease, has since been regarded as a familiar point." The authority of *Keech* v. *Sandford*, and the principle established by it, are also acknowledged in *M'Clanachan's Heirs* v. *Henderson's*, 2 Marshall's Kentucky, 388, 389; *Cox's Heirs* v. *Cox & Talbert*, Peck, 443, 450;

Wallington's Estate, 1 Ashmead, 307, 310; and per Rogers, J., in *Fisk* v. *Sarber*, 6 Watts & Sergeant, 18, 31, 35. "In chancery," said Duncan, J., in *The Case of Heager's Executors*, 15 Sergeant & Rawle, 65, 66, "the principle is one never departed from, and is as binding as any axiom of the common law; *that he who takes upon him a trust takes it for the benefit of him for whom he is intrusted, but not to take any advantage for himself.* A trustee shall never be permitted to raise in himself an interest opposite to that of his *cestui que trust.* . . . If a trustee or executor obtain the renewal of a term in trust, such renewal shall be for the benefit of the trust: *Holt* v. *Holt*, 1 Chan. Cas. 191. Nor will the circumstance of the lessor having refused to renew to the *cestui que trust*, he being an infant, differ the case: Chan. Cas. 61. There cannot well be a stronger proof of the inflexibility of the rule than this: he may decline to accept the lease; but if he does, though the lessor would not grant the benefit to the infant, if his trustee chooses to take it, it enures to the benefit of the infant." "Where an executor or guardian," said Kennedy, J., in *Galbraith* v. *Elder*, 8 Watts, 81, 94, 95, "renews a lease, though with his own money, such renewal shall be deemed to be in trust for the person beneficially interested in the old lease." The same principle, in its application as between mortgagor and mortgagee, was established in *Holdridge* v. *Gillespie*, 2 Johnson's Chancery, 30.

There, the mortgagee of a lease had surrendered up the old lease, and taken a new one in his own name; and the mortgagor sought relief in equity by a bill in the nature of a bill to redeem. "The plaintiff," said Chancellor Kent, "is entitled to redeem the whole of the premises contained in the lease, and to have the *entire* advantage of the new lease, on such redemption. The renewed lease ,enures for the benefit of the mortgagor. According to the cases of *Manlove* v. *Bale*, and of *Rakestraw* v. *Brewer*, (2 Vern. 84; 2 P. Wms. 511,) the additional term comes from the same old root, and is subject to the same equity of redemption, otherwise hardship and oppression might be practised upon the mortgagor. It is analogous, in principle, to the case of a trustee holding a lease for the benefit of the *cestui que trust.* Courts of equity have said, that if he makes use of the influence which his situation enables him to exercise, to get a new lease, he shall hold it for the benefit of the *cestui que trust.* (1 Dow. 269; 1 Ch. Cas. 191; 1 Bro. Ch. Cas. 198.) So, if a guardian takes a renewed lease for lives, the trust follows the actual interest of the infant, and goes to his heir, or executor, as the case may be. (18 Ves. 274.) Indeed, it is a general principle, pervading the cases, that if a mortgagee, executor, trustee, tenant for life, &c., who has a limited interest, gets an advantage by being in possession, 'or behind the back' of the party interested in the subject, or by some contrivance in fraud, he shall not retain the same for his own benefit, but hold it in trust. (Lord Manners, in 1 Ball & Beatty, 46, 47; 2 Ball & Beatty, 290, 298.) The doctrine has been uniform from the decision of Lord Keeper Bridgman, above referred to in 1 Ch. Cas. 191, down to the most recent decisions." The rule was enforced in an analogous case, in *Huson* v. *Wallace*, 1 Richardson's Equity, 2, 4, 7, where an intestate had contracted for the purchase of a tract of land to which a ferry was attached, and his wife becoming administratrix, had obtained after his death a recharter of the ferry in her own name. "From analogy to the doctrine of renewing leases by trustees or tenants," said Harper, C., "I am of opinion that she must be considered a trustee" for the children. He then reviewed the cases from *Keech* v. *Sandford*, down; and added, "It is to be observed, that in most of these cases there was no covenant for renewal, so that it was at the option of the lessors to renew or not; but, as it is said, there is a goodwill in favor of the former tenant, which gives him an interest in the renewal. . . . (The children) had that interest in the renewal of the charter, of which the cases speak, and that claim on the goodwill and preference of the legislature, which we know, in point of fact, to be almost always shown to the former grantees, and owners of the adjoining land; and was it not plainly against equity that, disregarding this claim, she should procure the entire benefit to herself?"

Upon a similar ground, it is a
settled rule in equity, that if a
trustee purchases claims or incumbrances against the trust estate,
at a discount, the purchase shall
enure to the benefit of the interest
which it is his duty to protect.
In *Green* v. *Winter*, 1 Johnson's
Chancery, 27, 36, a trustee had
bought in, at a discount, a mortgage on the trust property. "This
purchase," said the Chancellor,
"ought justly, and upon all sound
principles of equitable policy, to
enure to the benefit of the trust,
and not to the benefit of the trustee. A trustee is not permitted to
use the information he gains as
trustee, by purchasing in for himself. A court of equity watches
the conduct of a trustee with jealousy; and if he compounds debts
or mortgages, or purchases them
in, at a discount, he shall not be
suffered to turn the speculation
to his own advantage." See also
Van Horne v. *Fonda*, 5 Id. 388,
409; *Hawley* v. *Mancius*, 7 Id.
175, 188; *Giddings* v. *Eastman*,
5 Paige, 561; *Steele* v. *Babcock*,
1 Hill's N. Y. 528, 530; *The case
of Heager's Executors*, 15 Sergeant & Rawle, 65; *Boyd* v. *Hawkins*, 2 Iredell's Equity, 304, 306;
Prevost v. *Gratz et al.*, 1 Peters'
C. C. 365, 373; *Calvert* v. *Holland*,
9 B. Monroe, 458, 463. The trustee, however, is entitled to be
reimbursed the amount he has expended, with interest; *Quacken-
bush* v. *Leonard*, 9 Paige, 334,
344; *Mathews & Wife* v. *Dragaud
and others*, 3 Dessaussure, 25, 28.
The same principle is applied where
a trustee buys in an adverse claim

to the trust estate: the purchase
accrues to the benefit of the *cestui
que trust*, who, however, must reimburse the trustee to the extent of
his outlay; *M'Clanachan's Heirs*
v. *Henderson's*, 2 Marshall, 388,
389; *Morrison's Ex'or* v. *Caldwell*, 5 Monroe, 426, 435; *Kellogg*
v. *Wood*, 4 Paige, 578, 621; *King* v.
Cushman, 41 Illinois, 31; *Brantly*
v. *Ker*, 5 Jones, Eq. 352.

[The directors of a railway,
bank, or other body corporate or
joint stock association act in a
fiduciary capacity, and are consequently disabled from dealing with
the interests confided to their care
with a view to their own advantage,
and any purchase made, or act
done in the prosecution of such a
design, may be set aside by the
stockholders and those claiming
under them as creditors; *James* v.
The Railroad Company, 6 Wallace, 752; *Dreery* v. *Cross*, 7 Id.
299. For a like reason, a director
cannot vote as such in favor of a
resolution in which he is interested,
and if his presence is necessary to
a quorum, the resolution will be
invalid; *Betts* v. *Wood*, 37 New
York, 317. In the case last cited
judgment was delivered in the following terms:

"The bill of the defendant, Daniel Wood, was presented, audited
and ordered to be paid at a meeting of the board of directors of
the company, on the 5th day of
July, 1859, when but three of the
five directors who composed the
board were present; the defendant,
Daniel Wood, being one of those
present, and his father, William
Wood, and John Cornwall, another

kinsman, being the other two. This board, as thus constituted, had no authority to entertain the bill in question, or to do anything in relation to it. Daniel Wood being the claimant, was disqualified from acting, because he could not deal with himself, and without him there was no quorum of the directors, and they had no authority to transact business. The relation existing between Daniel Wood and the corporation, was that of trustee and *cestui que trust.* (*Robinson* v. *Smith*, 3 Paige, 322 ; *Angell* and *Ames*, 258, 260 ; *Cumberland Coal Company* v. *Sherman*, 1 Macq. 461 ; *Aberdeen Railway Company* v. *Blaikie Bros.*, 30 Barb. 571.) This being the case, I am disposed on this ground alone, to think that the action of these directors was void."

It will make no difference in the application of the rule that the party is acting for himself, if he also stands in a fiduciary relation to others, and should care for their safety as well as his own ; *Penman* v. *Slocum*, 41 New York, 53. Partners are in this category as being at once principals and agents, and each severally authorized to represent the firm. Hence a partner who sells the property of the firm, or procures it to be sold, and buys it in, will hold it in trust for the partnership. For a like reason a partner will not be allowed to make a profit by selling to the partnership at an advance, unless the transaction is out of the usual course of business of the firm, and it may be said in general, that a man who buys or represents

himself to have bought for others, or for an object in which they are jointly interested with him, will not be permitted to dispose of the property to them at a higher rate, nor to a third person without accounting to them ; *Hecker* v. *Cosgrove*, 4 Russell, 562 ; *Fawcett* v. *Whitehouse*, 1 Russell & Mylne, 132 ; *Beck* v. *Kantarowicz*, 3 Kay & Johnson, 230 ; *McElhenny* v. *The Hubert Oil Co.*, 11 P. F. Smith, 188 ; *Simons* v. *The Vulcan Oil Co.*, Ib. 202.

It follows that the promoters of a business or industrial enterprise, or joint stock company, cannot purchase at one price, and charge the property to their associates at another ; *The Oil Co.* v. *Simons* ; *The Dinsmore Oil Co.* v. *Dinsmore.* Accordingly, if a man buys land with a view to the formation of a company or partnership, and invites others to unite with him on that basis, they will be entitled to assume that they are brought in on an equal footing as it regards price and all other material particulars, unless the contrary is distinctly stated ; *Hecker* v. *Cosgrove* ; *Beck* v. *Kantarowicz* ; *Foss* v. *Harbottle*, 2 Hare, 401, 489 ; *Bank* v. *Tyrrell*, 5 Jurist, N. S. 527 ; *Kent* v. *The Freehold Land and Brickmaking Co.*, 4 Law R. Eq. 588. Any prospectus that may be issued should be sufficiently explicit not to mislead, and a want of candor and frankness in the statement of any material fact, is a fraud against which equity will relieve. *The New Brunswick* v. *Canada Railway Co.* and *Muggeridge*, 1 Drewry & Smale, 363,

367 ; *Kent* v. *The Freehold Land and Brickmaking Co.*, 4 Law R. Eq. 588 ; *The Oil Co.* v. *Simons.*

But the disability does not attach until the fiduciary relation is established, or preclude the right to dispose of prior acquisitions to the best advantage, and there is nothing to prevent a proprietor of a mine or patent, from selling it to a company of which he is to be one, on any terms that he may suggest, and which are acceptable to them. *McElhenny* v. *The Hubert Oil Co.*, 11 P. F. Smith, 188 ; *The Dinsmore Oil Co.* v. *Dinsmore*, 14 Id. 43, 50. The distinction was drawn by Sharswood, J., in *The Dinsmore Oil Co.* v. *Dinsmore*, 14 P. F. Smith, 43, 49, in the following terms :

" There are two principles applicable to all partnerships or associations for a common purpose of trade or business, which appear to be well settled on reason and authority.

The first is, that any man or number of men, who are the owners of any kind of property, real or personal, may form a partnership or association with others, and sell that property to the association at any price which may be agreed upon between them, no matter what it may have originally cost, provided there be no fraudulent misrepresentation made by the vendors to their associates. They are not bound to disclose the profit which they may realize by the transaction. They were in no sense agents or trustees in the original purchase, and it follows, that there is no confidential rela-

tion between the parties, which affects them with any trust. It is like any other case of vendor and vendee. They deal at arm's length. Their partners are in no better position than strangers. They must exercise their own judgment as to the value of what they buy. As it is succinctly and well stated in *Foss* v. *Harbottle*, 2 Hare, 489, " A party may have a clear right to say, I begin the transaction at this time. I have purchased land, no matter how or from whom, or at what price. I am willing to sell it at a certain price for a given purpose." This principle was recognised and applied by this court in the recent case of *McElhenny's Administrators* v. *The Hubert Oil Co.*, decided May 11th, 1869 (11 P. F. Smith, 188). " It nowhere appears," said the present Chief Justice, " that McElhenny, the purchaser from Hubert, the original owner, did it as the agent of Messrs. Baird, Boyd & Co. and others, though he bought it to sell again, no doubt ; he had a perfect right, therefore, to deal with them at arm's length, as it seems he did." And again : " If the property was not purchased by McElhenny for the use, and as agent for the company, but for his own use, he might sell it at a profit, most assuredly. No subsequent purchasers from his vendees would have any right to call upon him to account for the profits made on his sale." In that case, McElhenny, being the owner of property which had cost him only $4,000, sold it to Baird, Boyd & Co., and others, who associated with him to form an oil company, for $12,000, and it was decided that the company could not call him in equity to account for the profit he had made.

The second principle is, that where persons form such an association, or begin or start the project of one, from that time they do stand in confidential relation to each other, and to all others who may subsequently become members or subscribers, and it is not competent for any of them to purchase property for the purposes of such a company, and then sell it at an advance without a full disclosure of the facts. They must account to the company for the profit, because it legitimately is theirs. It is a familiar principle of the law of partnership, one partner cannot buy and sell to the partnership at a profit; nor if a partnership is in contemplation merely, can he purchase with a view to a future sale, without accounting for the profit. Within the scope of the partnership business, each associate is the general agent of the others, and he cannot divest himself of that character without their knowledge and consent. This is the principle of *Hichens* v. *Congrove*, 4 Russ. 562, *Fawcett* v. *Whitehouse*, 1 Russ. & M. 132, and the other cases which have been relied on by the appellants. It was recognised in *McElhenny's Administrators* v. *The Hubert Oil Co.*, just cited; and also in *Simons* v. *The Vulcan Oil Co.*, decided by this court, May 11th, 1869 (11 P. F. Smith, 202). Both of these cases were complicated with evidence of actual mis

representations as to the original cost of the property to the vendors. In the opinion of the court in the last case, delivered by Thompson, C. J., it is said: " If the defendants in fact, acted as the agents of the company in acquiring the property, they could not charge a profit as against their principal. Nor was their position any better if they assumed so to act without precedent authority, if their doings were accepted as the acts of agents by the association or company. If, in order to get up a company, they represented themselves as having acted for the association to be formed, and proposed to sell at the same prices they paid, and their purchases were taken on these representations, and stockholders invested in a reliance upon them, it would be a fraud on the company, and all those interested, to allow them to retain the large profits paid them by the company in ignorance of the true sums actually advanced." The defendants in that case were subscribers with others, to the stock of a projected oil company, and after the plan had been formed, secured to themselves by contract, the refusal of the property which they afterwards sold to the company at a greatly advanced price."]

Joint-tenants and co-parceners stand in such confidential relations in regard to one another's interest, that one of them is not permitted in equity to acquire an interest in the property hostile to that of the other: and, therefore, a purchase, by a joint-tenant or co-parcener, of an incumbrance on the joint estate, or an outstanding title to it, is held, at the election of his co-tenants within a reasonable time, to enure to the equal benefit of all the tenants, upon condition that they will contribute their respective ratios of the consideration actually given ; *Lee & Graham* v. *Fox, &c.*, 6 Dana, 171, 176. The same equity is considered as subsisting between tenants in common claiming under the same ancestor, or through the same will or deed ; *Lloyd* v. *Lynch*, 4 Casey, 419; *Gibson* v. *Winslow*, 10 Wright, 380 ; and was enforced in *Van Horne* v. *Fonda*, 5 Johnson's Chancery, 388, 407, a case of two devisees of an imperfect title under a will. " I will not say," observed the Chancellor in that case, " that one tenant in common may not, in any case, purchase in an outstanding title for his exclusive benefit. But when two devisees are in possession, under an imperfect title, derived from their common ancestor, there would seem naturally and equitably, to arise an obligation between them, resulting from their joint claim and community of interests, that one of them should not affect the claim, to the prejudice of the other. It is like an expense laid out upon a common subject, by one of the owners, in which case all are entitled to the common benefit, on bearing a due proportion of the expense. It is not consistent with good faith, nor with the duty which the connection of the parties, as claimants of a common subject, created, that one of them should be able, without the consent of the other, to buy in an outstanding title, and appropriate the whole subject to himself, and thus undermine, and oust his companion. It would be repugnant to a sense of refined and accurate justice. It would be immoral, because it would be against the reciprocal obligation to do nothing to the prejudice of each other's equal claim, which the relationship of the parties, as joint devisees, created. Community of interest produces a community of duty, and there is no real difference, on the ground of policy and justice, whether one co-tenant buys up an outstanding incumbrance, or an adverse title, to disseise and expel his co-tenant. It cannot be tolerated, when applied to a common subject, in which the parties had equal concern, and which created a mutual obligation, to deal candidly and benevolently with each other, and to cause no harm to their joint interest." This language was cited in *Flagg* v. *Mann*, 2 Sumner, 486, 522, and *Weaver* v. *Wible*, 1 Casey, 270, and said to be equally consonant with authority and principle. The co-tenant, however, upon availing himself of the purchase, becomes subject to an equal contribution to the expense. *Van Horne* v. *Fonda*, 5 Johnson, Ch., 408. In *Ligget* v. *Bechtol*, it is said to have been decided " that two tenants in common, who had heard of an adverse title, and agreed to join in defending against it, or in purchasing, were bound to deal fairly with each other ; and that one of them who purchased the adverse title for a small sum, must hold it in trust for the other, upon that other paying his proportion of the purchase-money : and the law (said Huston, J.,) is clearly as decided in *Van Horne* v. *Fonda* and this case ; nay, it goes further ; and wherever two have a joint estate, it raises a duty in each to deal fairly with the other ; and one who purchases an adverse title, will not be allowed to sweep all from his co-tenant ; unless there is some special circumstance ;" *Smiley* v. *Dixon,* 1 Penrose & Watts, 439, 441.

[The same view was taken in *Lloyd* v. *Lynch,* 4 Casey, 419, and the purchase of an outstanding title, by one of several tenants in common, said to enure for the benefit of all ; and in *Weaver* v. *Wible,* a widow who came into the possession of land under her deceased husband, was held to fall within the operation of a like principle, and to be precluded from buying in an outstanding title to the prejudice of his heirs. (See *Galbraith* v. *Elder,* 8 Watts, 81, 95 ; *Morey* v. *Herrick,* 6 Harris, 123, 128 ; *Myer's Appeal,* 2 Barr, 463, 466 ; *Lafferty* v. *Gurley,* 3 Sneed, 157, 181 ; *Burrill* v. *Bull,* 3 Sanford's Ch. 151 ; *Leisenring* v. *Black,* 5 Watts, 303. In *Leisenring* v. *Black,* the Court held, that if an execution be issued by two jointly, and the land bought in by one of them, for less than the amount of the judgment, he will hold it in trust for both. In like manner one co-tenant cannot defeat the title of another by buying under an execution issued against both ; *Gibson* v. *Winslow,* 10 Wright, 380. So the renewal of a lease by one of the lessees will enure to the use of all ; *Burrill* v. *Bull.*]

In South Carolina also, it is said to have been held that a tenant in common in possession is a trustee to preserve the estate for the rest; *Goulding* v. *Goulding,* cited in *Huson* v. *Wallace,* 1 Richardson's Equity, 9. But tenants in common, probably, are subject to this mutual obligation, only when their interest accrues under the same instrument, or act of the parties or of the law, or where they have entered into some engagement or understanding with one another : for persons acquiring unconnected interests in the same subject, by distinct purchases, though it may be under the same title, are probably not bound to any greater protection of one another's interests, than would be required between strangers. See *Matthews* v. *Bliss,* 22 Pickering, 48 ; where it was held that tenants in common of a vessel do not stand in such a confidential relation that one may not purchase the share of the other, without communicating a circumstance that would materially affect the price.

[However, this may be, it seems that one co-tenant will be presumed to have acted for all, unless he manifested a contrary intention by acts sufficiently notorious to put the others on their guard ; *Baker* v. *Whiting,* 3 Sumner, 475, 495 ; and there can be no doubt that where a promise or agency is superadded to the obligation arising from community of title, its performance will be enforced by equity. Hence a tenant in common who attends a sale made by the State for the non-payment of taxes under a promise to buy for himself and his co-tenant, will not be permitted to appropriate the purchase solely to his own benefit, and will be made a trustee for the share of the co-tenant; *Stewart* v. *Brown*, 2 S. & R. 461.

It is established under the recent decisions in Pennsylvania, that a purchase by one of several co-tenants in common of the common property at a tax sale, or under an execution issued against all, gives rise to a resulting trust, although he is not acting as their agent, and intends to acquire the land for himself; *Gibson* v. *Winslow*, 10 Wright, 380; *Maul* v. *Rider*, 1 P. F. Smith, 377; 9 Id. 167.]

A tenant for life is bound to the same consideration of the interests of those in remainder and reversion, as is required between joint-tenants; and if he purchases an incumbrance or outstanding title, it becomes in his hands a trust for their benefit; *Bowling's Reps.* v. *Dobyn's Adm'r*, 5 Dana, 434, 446; *Stump and others* v. *Findlay and others*, 2 Rawle, 168, 174. In *Dickinson and wife* v. *Codwise and others*, 1 Sandford, 214, 225, it was held that a husband purchasing a gore of land which controlled the access to stores built upon his wife's land, and which could not be used separately for any valuable purpose, must be considered as purchasing in trust for the wife's interest. " As hus-band," said the Asst. V. Chancellor, " in the possession of a life estate in her lands, *jure mariti*, he had a duty to perform, which was incompatible with the purchase of this gore for his own exclusive benefit. He used the means given to him by his position as husband, and obtained this grant. The general principle of equity which prohibits a purchase by parties placed in a situation of trust or confidence with respect to the subject of the purchase, has been steadily and uniformly enforced from the time of Lord Keeper Bridgman in 1670 (*Holt* v. *Holt*, 1 Cha. Cas. 190,) to the present day.

A vendee of lands, entering before the conveyance is perfected, is affected with the same equity in favor of his vendor; and if he purchases an adverse title he cannot set it up against the vendor, but the vendor is entitled to have it, upon reimbursing the purchaser; *Morgan's Heirs* v. *Boone's Heirs*, 4 Monroe, 291, 298; *Harper* v. *Reno et al.*, 1 Freeman's Chancery, 323, 333; *Wood* v. *Perry*, 1 Barbour, 115, 134; see 2 Smith's Leading Cases, 745, 7th Am. ed.

[A like rule prevails between mortgagor and mortgagee, and neither can do any act to defeat the purpose for which the security was given and received. The purchase of an outstanding title by the mortgagor will go to strengthen the security of the mortgagee, and a mortgagee who enters as such, cannot show title in himself, as a reason for holding the premises after the debt has been paid, although he may withdraw, and then re-enter or bring ejectment.

The rule which entitles the landlord to the benefit of acquisitions made by his tenant, from the adjacent waste during the term, may, perhaps, be referred to the same principle; *Kingswell* v. *Willard*, 11 Exchequer, 313, as well as the estoppel by which a tenant is precluded from disputing the landlord's title; 2 Smith's Leading Cases, 749, 7th Am. ed.

The principle applies *a fortiori* as between partners. Obviously a partner ought not to do anything tending to benefit himself at the expense of the other members of the firm in a matter affecting the common interest. If he does, equity will redress the wrong by turning him into a trustee; *Coder* v. *Huling*, 3 Casey, 84; *Lacy* v. *Hall*, 1 Wright, 360. In the case last cited, a firm had a leasehold in a tract of land. One of the partners bought the reversion and took the deed in his own name. The price was paid out of the assets of the firm, but charged to his account on the books as so much withdrawn from capital. It was held that a constructive trust arose for the partnership. Strong, J., said that the condition of the defendant was less favorable than that of a tenant in common who bought an outstanding title. "He was more than a a tenant in common. A partner in a firm who takes a renewal of a lease to the firm in his own name, holds it for the firm, and that even though the lessor has refused to renew the lease with the old lessees;

Featherstonaugh v. *Fenwick*, 17 Vesey, 298. See also, notes to *Moody* v. *Matthews*, 7 Vesey, 186, Sumner's Ed. Yet the consideration for the new lease is the covenant of the partner who obtains it. But his relation to his co-partner forbids him treating for it for his own individual benefit; and if he does so treat, and obtains a lease in his own name, he holds in trust for the partnership.

This is not the case of a resulting trust growing out of the payment of the purchase money. It is rather a constructive trust which equity declares to arise from the relative situation and conduct of the parties. Hall had the firm's funds, at least their credit, in hands. He was not restricted in its use. Good faith required that he should use those funds rather than his own in the purchase of the McLeod tract; and if he employed his own, then equity enforces good faith by regarding him as having lent his funds to the firm, and treats him as a trustee. He may recover his advances in account with his co-partner, but he can claim only one moiety of the land; *Lacy* v. *Hall et al.,* 1 Wright, 360, 366."]

An agent undertaking any business for another, is disabled in equity from dealing in the matter of the agency upon his own account or for his own benefit. If an agent employed to procure a lease, or to purchase lands, for another, take a lease or conveyance in his own name, he will be considered as holding it in trust for his principal; *Parkist* v. *Alexander*, 1 Johnson's Chancery, 394;

Howell v. *Baker*, 4 Id. 118, 120;
Sweet v. *Jacocks*, 6 Paige, 355,
359, 364; *Heacock and others* v.
Coatesworth and others, 1 Clarke,
84, 86; *Massie* v. *Watts*, 6 Cranch,
148, 170; *Ringo et al.* v. *Binns et
al.*, 10 Peters, 270; *Rankin* v.
Porter, 7 Watts, 387; *Church* v.
Sterling, 16 Connecticut, 389, 400;
Segar v. *Edwards and Wife*, 11
Leigh, 213; *Wellford et als.* v.
Chancellor, 5 Grattan, 39; *Switzer
et al.* v. *Skiles et al.*, 3 Gilman, 529;
Baker v. *Whiting*, 3 Sumner, 475;
post, note to *Fox* v. *Mackreth.*

[An·agent employed to obtain
information with a view to the
purchase of real or personal property, cannot buy for himself to the
exclusion of his principal; *Wenn*
v. *Dillon*, 27 Mississippi, 494. For
a stronger reason one who by professing friendship for another, and
promising to aid him in perfecting
his title, ascertains wherein the
defect consists, will not be allowed
to use this knowledge for his own
purposes, by purchasing the legal
or outstanding title, and if he does,
a trust will arise in favor of the
principal; *Noel* v. *White*, 1 Wright,
814.

The rule is broad enough to
include one who has access to
the papers of the principal, or obtains a knowledge of his affairs,
while acting in a subordinate
capacity under an agent whom he
has employed; and hence a pur-

chase by the clerk of an attorney
or broker of the property which
has been placed in the hands of
his employer for sale, may be set
aside although there is no actual
fraud; *Poillon* v. *Martin*, 1 Sandford Ch. 569; *Gardner* v. *Ogden*,
22 New York, 327.]

An attorney or counsellor at
law, who has been consulted professionally in regard to a title,
cannot afterwards purchase an outstanding adverse title to the land,
for himself; his purchase will
enure to the benefit of his client;
Galbraith v. *Elder*, 8 Watts, 81,
94, 100; *Clevinger* v. *Reimar*, 3
Watts & Sergeant, 487, 493;
Hockenbury v. *Carlisle*, 5 Id. 348,
350. In like manner, an attorney
who buys at a sale under a judgment or decree against his client,
will hold in trust for him; *Moore*
v. *Brecken*, 27 Illinois, 23. [And
it has been said that this fidelity
of counsel must be forever observed, and that equity will look
with the same disfavor on the purchase of an adverse title after the
relation of client and attorney has
ceased, as while it continues; *Galbraith* v. *Elder*; *Henry* v. *Raiman*,
1 Casey, 354, 360.]

The cases relating to the inability of a trustee to be a purchaser
of the trust property on his own
account, at a sale of it, will be
found in the note to *Fox* v. *Mackreth, post.*

*ELLIOT *v.* MERRYMAN.

JULY 1, 1740, AT THE ROLLS.

REPORTED BARNISTON'S CHANCERY REPORTS, 78.[1]

LIABILITY OF PURCHASER TO SEE TO THE APPLICATION OF HIS PUR-
CHASE-MONEY.]—*A purchaser of personalty from an executor will
not be held liable to see to the application of the purchase-money,
except in cases of fraud.*

*It is a general rule, that, where real estate is devised to trustees, upon
trust to sell for payment of debts generally, the purchaser is not
bound to see that the money is rightly applied. The same rule applies where real estate is not devised to be sold for the payment of
debts, but is only charged with such payment.*

*If real estate is devised upon trust to be sold for the payment of cer-
tain debts, mentioning to whom in particular those debts are owing,
the purchaser is bound to see that the money is applied for the payment of those debts.*

THOMAS SMITH became indebted to several persons by bond,
and likewise by simple contract. In three of those bonds Goodwin was bound with him as surety; and afterwards Goodwin
gave his own bond alone to one of the creditors, to whom Smith
was bound in a single bond. Smith, being thus indebted, made
his will, and, in the beginning of it, says, " *my will is, that all my
debts be paid ; and I do charge all my lands with the payment
thereof.*" Then came the clause, upon which, together with the
other circumstances of the case, the present question principally
determines. " *Item*—I give all my real and personal estate to
—— Goodwin, to hold to him, his heirs, executors, administrators, and assigns, *chargeable, nevertheless, with the payment of all my
debts and legacies.*" Of this will he made Goodwin his executor.

[*60] *The testator died in 1724; Goodwin proved the will,
and in that same year sold a freehold estate of the testator's to Hunt; in the year following sold a leasehold estate of
the testator's to Wright; and, in 1727, sold another estate of the
testator's, consisting of both freehold and leasehold, to Merryman.

In the several deeds by which these estates were conveyed
from Goodwin to the purchasers, the will of Smith was recited;
and to one of those deeds Elliot, a creditor of Smith's, was a subscribing witness. These lands were sold in the neighbourhood
by outcry. At the time of these sales, the creditors, all of them,
either lived in the town where Goodwin lived, or within three
or four miles of it. During all this time, and till the year 1730,

[1] 1 S. C., Atk. 4.

the creditors went on regularly receiving their interest, which was at 5*l.* per cent., of Goodwin. Goodwin was a solvent man till 1732, and then he became a bankrupt.

In 1734 the present bill was brought by the creditors of Smith against the purchasers of these lands that have been mentioned, against Goodwin, and against the assignees under his commission, in order to have a satisfaction of their debts out of those lands which were sold by Goodwin.

Mr. *Chute* argued on the part of the plaintiffs, and for authority cited 2 Vern. 528,[1] 616,[2] *Pagett* v. *Hoskins*, in Precedents in Chancery,[3] and the case of *Morley* v. *Webb*, determined by the present Chancellor [Lord Hardwick].

Mr. *Idle*, on the same side, cited 2 Vern. 444;[4] and on the same side Mr. *Murray* cited the case of *Nugent* v. *Gifford*,[5] determined by the present Chancellor.

Mr. *Brown* argued as counsel for Hunt and Wright, and for authority cited 2 Cha. Ca. 115,[6] and the case of *Abbott* v. *Gibbs*,[7]

Mr. *Noel* argued on the same side, and cited 1 Vern. 45,[8] 411,[9] and Williams, 430.[10]

Mr. *Hoskins* argued as counsel for Merryman, and cited 1 Vern. 303.[11]

*THE HON. JOHN VERNEY. M. R.—His Honor said, his [*61] opiuion was that the plaintiffs were not entitled to the relief they sought by the bill. He said it was very true, that it was almost impossible to make a determination in the present case, but that it must fall out unfortunately on the one party or the other. The dispute arising between creditors on the one side, and purchasers on the other, both these sorts of persons are entitled to the favour of this Court; and in the present case a misfortune must fall upon one of them. On whom it is to fall is the question. And this is a question that must so frequently have happened, that it is extraordinary to find no determination directly in point.

The case is this:—Thomas Smith being possessed of a real and personal estate, was indebted to several persons by bond, in three of which bonds Goodwin was bound with him as surety; and he had contracted likewise some other debts, and being thus indebted, he makes his will to the following effect. The will begins with this introduction:—"My will is, that all my debts be paid; and I do charge all my lands with the payment thereof. *Item.*—I give all my real and personal estate to ―――― Goodwin, to hold to him, his heirs executors, administrators, and assigns, chargeable, nevertheless, with the payment of my debts and legacies." 'Tis indeed true that these words do not amount to a

[1] Chadwick v. Doleman. [2] Crane v. Drake, [3] Prec. Ch. 431.
[4] Hamble v. Bill. [5] 1 Atk. 463. [6] Culpepper v. Aston.
[7] 1 Eq Ca. Abr. 358. [8] Newman v. Johnson. [9] Clowdsley v. Pelham.
[10] Freemoult v. Dedire, 1 P. Wms. 430. [11] Spalding v. Shalmer.

devise of the lands to be sold for the payment of the debts; and they only import a charge upon them for that purpose. However, this is such a devise as is within the meaning of the proviso of the Statute of Fraudulent Devises,[1] and does interrupt the descent to the heir-at-law. By this will the devisee was made executor.

The testator died in 1724. Goodwin paid interest for the debts at 5*l.* per cent. regularly till 1730. After the testator's death, three sales of this estate were made by Goodwin; one, of an estate which was entirely freehold; the other, of an estate leasehold; and a third, consisting of freehold and leasehold both.

The bill in general is brought by the creditors of Smith [*62] *against the purchasers, in order to have a payment of their debts out of the lands of Smith, which were sold to them by Goodwin.

With regard to the leasehold estate, the case is so extremely plain, that the sale of that must stand, and that the creditors cannot have a satisfaction out of it, that his Honor said it would be monstrous to call it in question. The excutors are the proper persons that, by law, have a power to dispose of a testator's personal estate. 'Tis indeed true that personal estate may be clothed with such a *particular trust,*[2] that it is possible the Court in some cases may require a purchaser of it to see the money rightly applied. But unless there is some such *particular trust,* or a *fraud* in the case, it is impossible to say but the sale of a personal estate, when made by an executor, must stand; and that after the sale is made, the creditors cannot break in upon it.

His Honor said, he would now consider the other sales that have been made, and would examine those, first, upon the general rules of the Court, and in the next place upon the particular circumstances which this case is attended with.

With regard to the first of these matters, the general rule is, that *if a trust directs that land should be sold for the payment of debts generally, the purchaser is not bound to see that the money be rightly applied.* On the other hand, *if the trust directs that lands should be sold for the payment of certain debts, mentioning, in particular, to whom those debts were owing, the purchaser is bound to see that the money be applied for the payment of those debts.*

The present case, indeed, does not fall within either of these rules, because here lands are *not given to be sold for* the payment of debts, but *are only charged with such payment. However, the question is, whether that circumstance makes any difference. And his Honor was of opinion that it did not.* And if such a distinction was to be made, the consequence would be, that whenever lands are charged with the payment of debts generally, they could never be discharged of that trust without a suit in this [*63] *Court which would be extremely inconvenient. *No instances have been produced to show that in any other respect the*

---

[1] 3 W. & M. c. 14.
[2] See Bonney v. Ridgard, 4 Bro. C. C. 130; 1 Cox, 145.

charging lands with the payment of debts differs from the directing
them to be sold for such a purpose; and therefore there is no reason
that there should be a difference established in this respect. The only
objection that seemed to be of weight with regard to this matter
is, that where lands are appointed to be sold for the payment of
debts generally, the trusts may be said to be performed as soon
as those lands are sold; but where they are only charged with
the payment of debts, it may be said that the trust is not performed till those debts are discharged. And so far, indeed, is
true, that where lands are charged with the payment of annuities
those lands will be charged in the hands of the purchaser,[1] because it was the very purpose of making the lands a fund for
that payment, that it should be a constant and subsisting fund ;
but where lands are not burdened with such a subsisting charge,
the purchaser ought not to be bound to look to the application of
the money ; and that seems to be the true distinction.

Having thus considered the case under the general rule, his
Honor said he would now consider it under the particular circumstances that attend it; and the particular circumstances are
such as are far from strengthening the plaintiffs' case, but rather
the contrary.

One of those circumstances is the length of time the plaintiffs
have lain by, without at all insisting on any charge upon these
estates. Goodwin was a solvent man till his bankruptcy, in
1732. Here have been three purchases of these estates, made at
different times—the one in 1727, the other two in 1725 and 1724.
The first of them was made by Hunt, the second by Wright, and
the third by Merryman. During all these transactions the plaintiffs do not mention one word of their charge upon this estate ;
but, on the contrary, regularly received their interest of Goodwin
till the year 1730. It is indeed true, that there is no express
proof that the plaintiffs knew of these purchases, but there is
reason to imagine *that they did. The purchases were [*64]
made in the neighbourhood by outcry ; some of the creditors lived in the same town that Goodwin did ; and all of them
lived within three or four miles of him ; and Elliot, one of the
creditors, was a subscribing witness to one of the purchase-
deeds. The want of notice, too, on the part of the purchasers is,
a considerable circumstance in their favour. It is indeed true,
that they had notice that there were debts chargeable upon this
estate ; but it does not appear they knew to whom those debts
were owing. Another circumstance is, that Goodwin was a co-
obligor in three of these bonds, and to another of the obligees he
afterwards gave his bond alone, which may well be considered as
a satisfaction for that bond. By this it appears that the creditors
greatly relied upon Goodwin for their paymaster ; and there is
not much reason therefore that they should now be allowed to
resort to the testator's estate.

---

[1] Not, it seems, if there is also a charge of debts. See Page v. Adam, 4 Beav.
269.

Upon the whole his Honor's opinion was, that the plaintiffs' bill must be dismissed ; and even with costs, as against Wright, there being no manner of pretence for the plaintiffs to come upon that estate, it being all leasehold and sold to Wright by the executor, who by law is the proper person entrusted to dispose of the testator's personal estate. However, with regard to the rest of the defendants, his honor said he would only dismiss the bill generally, without costs ; and so he was pleased to decree accordingly.

· *Elliot* v. *Merryman* is always cited as a leading case, wherever the question arises as to the liability of a purchaser to see to the application of his purchase-money. See *Bonney* v. *Ridgard*, 1 Cox, 147; *M'Leod* v. *Drummond*, 17 Ves. 162; *Shaw* v. *Borrer*, 1 Keen, 547; and *Colyer* v. *Finch*, 5 H. L. Cas. 923 ; where the rules laid down in that case were approved of and adopted.

It will be seen, on perusing the judgment of the Master of the Rolls, that, in determining this question, the rules applicable to sales of real estate and to sales of personal estate are not identical. It will be convenient, therefore, to consider these rules as applied *to the two [*65] species of property separately.

Before doing so it may be useful to refer, in the first instance, to those statutes by which the law upon this subject has been altered or modified. It was enacted by 7 & 8 Vict. c. 76, s. 10 (taking effect from December 31, 1844), that the bonâ fide payment to, and the receipt of, any person to whom *any money* should be payable upon any express or implied trust, or for any limited purpose, should effectually discharge the person paying the same from seeing to the application or being answerable for the misapplication thereof, unless the contrary should be expressly declared by the instrument creating the trust or security. This Act has, however, been repealed by the 8 & 9 Vict. c. 106, which takes effect, as to this section of the repealed Act, from October 1st, 1845. With regard to wills executed whilst the Act 7 & 8 Vict. was in force, such wills must be construed as having annexed to the trusts the incidents resulting from the then existing state of the law, and that the incidents of the trusts, as so defined, were not altered by the change in the law. 3 Dav. Conv. by Waley, 164.

By 22 & 23 Vict. c. 35 (Property and Trustees Relief Amendment Act), it is enacted that " The bonâ fide payment to, and the receipt of any person to whom any *purchase or mortgage money* shall be payable upon any express or implied trust, shall effectually discharge the person paying the same from seeing to the application, or being answerable for the misapplication thereof, unless the contrary shall be expressly declared by the instrument creating the trust or security " (sect. 23). The operation of this clause would seem to extend to trusts created before it was passed, the future tense used being applicable to the payment of the trustee, not to the creation of the trust. See *Bennett* v. *Lytton*, 2 J. & H. 158; *Dodson* v. *Sammell*, 8 Jur. (N. S.) 584, on a rehearing; and 2 David. 986, 3rd ed.; but see 2 Dart, 546, and Lewin on Trusts, 332, 5th ed., where it is considered not to be retrospective.

It will be observed that the 23rd section applies only to payments made by or to purchasers and mortgagees. A more comprehensive power is given by 23 & 24 Vict. c. 145 (Lord Cranworth's Act), which enacts, that " the receipts in writing of any trustees or trustee, for any money payable to them or him, by reason or in the exercise of any trusts or powers reposed or vested in them or him, shall be sufficient discharges for the money therein expressed to be received, and shall effectually exonerate the persons paying such money from seeing to the application thereof, or from being answerable for any *loss or misapplication thereof" (sect. 29). [*66]

A subsequent section, however, enacts, that " the provisions contained in this Act shall, except as hereinbefore otherwise provided, extend only to persons entitled or acting under a deed, will, codicil, or other instrument executed after the passing of this act (28th August, 1860), or under a will or codicil confirmed or revived by a codicil executed after that date (sect 36).

In this note it is proposed to consider the cases where these Acts have no application.

First as to Purchasers of Real Estate.] It is clear that trustees in whom real property is vested, upon trust for sale, can *at law* give a valid discharge for the purchase-money, because they are at law the owners. *In equity*, however, the persons amongst whom the produce of the sale is to be distributed are considered the owners; and Courts of equity have therefore held that a purchaser must obtain a discharge from them unless the power of giving receipts is either expressly or by implication given to the trustees. If no such discharge is given, and the trustees have no power to give receipts, the estate upon a misapplication of the purchase-money, will remain chargeable in the hands of the purchaser.

Where a power of giving receipts is in expressed terms conferred upon trustees, the purchaser will not, in cases free from fraud and collusion, be bound to see to the application of the purchase-money. Where, however, no such power is in *express* terms given, much difficulty arises in ascertaining the liability of the purchaser, which depends upon the question whether a power of giving receipts can be *implied*.

One of the rules laid down in the principal case, and which is invariably followed, is, *that, if the trust directs lands to be sold for payment of certain debts, mentioning in particular to whom those debts are owing, the purchaser is bound to see that the money is applied for the payment of those debts.* See *Dunch* v. *Kent,* 1 Vern. 261; *Culpepper* v. *Aston,* 2 Ch. Ca. 223; *Cotterell* v. *Hampson,* 2 Vern. 5; *Lloyd* v. *Baldwin,* 1 Ves. 173; *Ithell v. Beane,* 1 Ves. 215; *Doran v. Wiltshire,* 3 Swanst. 701; *Smith v. Guyon,* 1 Bro. C. C. 186; *Rogers* v. *Skillicorne,* Amb. 189; *Binks* v. *Rokeby,* 2 Madd. 238. The same rule is applicable also where there is a trust for payment of legacies or annuities, which, from their nature must be considered as specified or scheduled debts: *Johnson* v. *Kennett,* 3 My. & K. 630; *Horn* v. *Horn,* 2 S. & S. 448.

In cases coming within this rule, as the trusts are of a limited and definite nature, and such as a purchaser might without inconvenience [*67] see properly performed, *a power to give receipts cannot be implied.

Another rule laid down in the principal case is, "*that, if a trust directs the land to be sold for the payment of debts generally, the purchaser is not bound to see that the money be rightly applied;*" and it was, for the first time, decided, *that it makes no difference whether lands are given to be sold for the payment of debts or are only charged with such payment.*

The principle upon which this rule proceeds appears to be this: that, as it cannot be presumed that the settlor or testator could expect a trust of so general and unlimited a nature to be undertaken by a purchaser, it is implied that it was intended that the purchaser should be exempt from the necessity of seeing to the application of the purchase-money: *Williamson* v. *Curtis,* 3 Bro. C. C. 96; *Smith* v. *Guyon,* 1 Bro. C. C. 186, and Mr. Belt's note; *Balfour* v. *Welland,* 16 Ves. 151; *Shaw* v. *Borrer,* 1 Kee. 559; *Hardwicke* v. *Mynd,* 1 Anst. 109; *Barker* v. *Duke of Devon,* 3 Mer. 310; *Robinson* v. *Lowater,* 17 Beav. 592, 5 De G. Mac. & G. 272; *Dundas* v. *Blake,* 11 Ir. Eq. Rep. 138, 156; *Dowling* v. *Hudson,* 17 Beav. 248; *Storry* v. *Walsh,* 18 Beav. 559; *Glynn* v. *Locke,* 3 Dru. & W. 11, 22.

So, also, where there is a trust or charge for the general payment of debts, as well as for the payment of legacies or annuities, the purchaser will not be obliged to see to the application of the purchase-money; for, as Lord Thurlow observed, in *Jebb* v. *Abbott* (cited by Mr. Butler in his note on Co. Litt. 290, b), he cannot be expected to see to the discharge of legacies, which cannot be paid till after the debts. In *Beynon* v. *Gollins* (cited also by Mr. Butler in the same note), the testator had charged his estate with the payment of his debts generally, and with a legacy of £800 for his daughter for life, and after her death for her children. The trustee had joined in a conveyance of part of the estate to a purchaser, and permitted the £800 to come into the hands of the daughter's husband, and it was wasted. The bill was brought by the wife and children, to have the legacy made good by the purchasers of the estate, and against the trustee. It was dismissed against the purchasers. Upon the hearing for further directions, it was pressed by Mr. Ambler, that the trustee should pay the costs of the purchasers. But Lord Thurlow refused this, saying that, as there was a general charge of debts, the purchasers were not liable to see to the application of the purchase-money in payment of the £800, and that, if the plaintiff thought fit to make unnecessary parties, the trustees ought not to pay the costs of such parties, but that they must receive them from the plaintiff. See also *Rogers* v. *Skillicorne*, Amb. 188; *Walker* v. *Flamstead*, 2 Ld. Ken., 2nd part, 57; *Dowling* v. *Hudson*, 17 [*68] Beav. 248.

In *Page* v. *Adam*, 4 Beav. 269, where a testator gave his real and personal estate to A., subject to the payment of his debts and certain annuities, it was argued, upon the authority of a dictum in the principal case, that annuity legacies charged upon land were different from other legacies, inasmuch as it was intended that they should continue a charge upon the land. However, Lord Langdale, M. R., held that A. could make good title to the real estate without the concurrence of the annuitants, and that a purchaser from A. was not bound to see to the application of the purchase-money. "When," observes his Lordship, "an annuity is charged on land, and there *is no devise for the payment of debts, and no general charge of debts*, it must be deemed that the land was intended to be a constant and subsisting security for the payment of the annuity. But in the case of *Elliot* v. *Merryman*, where an expression to that effect is used, it was not considered, and the case did not require it to be considered, whether, in a case in which *both debts and annuities were charged*, the lands would be charged with the annuities in the hands of a purchaser from the person whose duty it was to sell for payment of debts; and the opinion of Lord Eldon, as stated in the note to *Jenkins* v. *Hiles*, 6 Ves. 654, n., is, ' that where a man by deed or will charges or orders an estate to be sold for payment of debts generally, and then makes specific dispositions, the purchaser is not bound to see to the application of the purchase-money. It is just the same as if the specific bequests were out of the will.' Seeing no reason to differ from this opinion, and conceiving that an annuity legacy charged on the estate is, in the sense here used, a specific disposition, subject to the payment of debts, I do not think that the rule ought to be departed from by reason of the nature of the legacy. The reason on which the rule is founded operates precisely in the same manner, whether the legacies are of annuities, or of sums of money: and it would occasion very great inconvenience, if no sale of estates for payment of debts charged thereon could take place without the authority of a Court of equity, if the author of the charge for payment of debts had also charged the estate with the payment of legacies in the form of annuities. There are one or two cases (*Johnson* v. *Kennett*, 3 My. & K. 264; *Eland* v. *Eland*, 1 Beav. 235), in which legacies of annuities have not been distinguished from other legacies; but, as the point was not raised in those cases, I think they are not to be relied on as authorities on the present occasion. But it [*69] appears *to me that, on principle, and for this purpose, there is no substantial difference between the two kinds of legacy. The charge of debts is general, the amount is indefinite, and may exceed the whole value of the estate. It is the first duty of the executor, and of the devisee of the estate which is subject to the charge, to pay the debts; and for that purpose he is entitled to sell: if he sells, something or nothing may be left to secure payment of the annuities. The purchaser seems to have nothing to do with this; he cannot know or ascertain the amount of debts, and cannot, if he would, protect the annuitant. His title is derived under an authority or right to sell for payment of debts—a purpose which is paramount to the payment of annuities: and in respect of debts he is not bound to inquire." See *Johnson* v. *Kennett*, 3 My. & K. 624; *Eland* v. *Eland*, 1 Beav. 235; *S. C.*, 4 My. & Cr. 420.

And where there is a general charge of debts, it is immaterial that a particular debt is mentioned: *Robinson* v. *Lowater*, 17 Beav. 592, 5 De G. Mac. & G. 272.

Upon the same principle, in a recent case, where upon a dissolution of partnership the retiring partner by deed agreed to assign the partnership stock and effects to the partner continuing in the business, who covenanted to pay the debts and indemnify the retiring partner against them, it was held, by Sir John Romilly, M. R., that although the latter and his executors were entitled to pursue and specifically to apply towards the payment of the debts of the partnership any portion of the partnership property in the *possession of the former*, yet, as the case could not be put higher than one of an express trust to sell the property and apply the proceeds in payment of the debts of the partnership, they would not be entitled to do so while in the possession of a purchaser, even with notice of the deed, for he would not be bound to see to the application of the purchase-money. *In re Langmead's Trusts*, 20 Beav. 20, 7 De G. Mac. & G. 353. See *Jones* v. *Williams*, 24 Beav. 47.

Where there is a trust or charge for payments of debts generally and legacies, a purchaser, *even after the debts have been paid*, will not be liable to see to the application of the purchase-money in payment of the legacies: *Johnson* v. *Kennett*, 3 My. & K. 624; in this case the testator, subject to his debts and legacies, gave all his real and personal estate to his son absolutely, and the son thus became trustee for payment of debts and legacies, but, subject to the charge, he was owner. The estate was then settled by the son, who afterwards sold it: Lord Lyndhurst, in reversing the decision of Sir L. Shadwell, V.-C., observed,

that it was said that *the debts having been paid, and paid out
of the personal estate, and nothing remaining but the legacies, [*70]
the case fell within the general rule applicable to cases where legacies
alone were charged upon the real estate. He found no authority for
such a proposition; the rule applied *to the state of things at the death
of the testator;* and if the debts were afterwards paid, and the legacies
alone left as a charge, that circumstances did not vary the general rule.
In *Eland* v. *Eland*, 4 My. & Cr. 429, Lord Cottenham, speaking of the
rule, as laid down by Lord Lyndhurst, says, " I entirely concur in that
opinion, otherwise the mortgagee must in every case, in which there is
a charge of legacies, ascertain whether the debts have been paid or
not." See also *Page* v. *Adam*, 4 Beav. 269 ; and *Forbes* v. *Peacock*,
1 Ph. 717 ; in which case the testator charged his real estate with the
payment of his debts, and directed it to be sold (but without saying by
whom) upon the death of his wife, who was tenant for life, if not sooner
disposed of, and the proceeds, with the residue of his personal estate,
to be divided among certain of his relations. The executors being thus
empowered to sell the real estate, the surviving executor entered into a
contract for that purpose with the defendant. Soon after the death of
the widow (twenty-five years having elapsed since the testator's death),
the defendant, by his solicitor, inquired whether there were any debts
due from the estate which remained unsatisfied; and, if not, whether
the cestuis que trust would give authority to sell. To this question no
answer was returned. Sir L. Shadwell, V.-C., was of opinion that this,
under the circumstances, amounted to notice to the purchaser that the
debts were paid, and that he was therefore bound to see that the purchase-money was properly applied. See 12 Sim. 528. It followed, that
the concurrence of the cestuis que trust was necessary to enable the
purchaser to make a good title. Lord Lyndhurst reversed the decision
of the Vice-Chancellor. " The estate," said his Lordship, " being
charged in the first instance with the payment of debts, the defendant
was not bound, according to the general rule, to see to the application
of the purchase-money. If, indeed, he had notice that the vendor
intended to commit a breach of trust, and was selling the estate for
that purpose, he would, by purchasing under such circumstances, be
concurring in the breach of trust, and thereby become responsible:
Watkins v. *Cheek*, 2 S. &. S. 599 ; *Balfour* v. *Welland*, 16 Ves. 151 ;
Eland v. *Eland*, 4 My. & Cr. 420. But assuming that the facts
relied upon in this case amount to notice that the debts had been paid,
yet, as the executor had authority to *sell, not only for the payment of debts, but also for the purpose of distribution among [*71]
the residuary legatees, this would not afford any inference that the
executor was committing a breach of trust in selling the estate, or that
he was not performing what his duty required. The case, then, comes
to this: if authority is given to sell for the payment of debts and lega-

cies, and the purchaser knows that the debts are paid, is he bound to see to the application of the purchase-money? I apprehend not. In the case of *Johnson* v. *Kennett*, where it was contended that the rule did not apply, because the debts had been paid before the sale took place, I held that the *rule had reference to the death of the testator;* and, therefore, that even supposing the debts were paid before the sale took place, and that the legacies alone remained as a charge, that circumstance would not vary the general rule."

In a note by the learned reporter appended to *Forbes* v. *Peacock*, he says, " If notwithstanding this decision, it should still be inferred from the terms of the dictum in *Johnson* v. *Kennett*, that the rule would not apply to a case in which it should happen that there were no debts due at the testator's death, and that the purchaser knew it, I have the authority of Lord Lyndhurst for stating that he did not intend, on that occasion, to lay down any rule which should govern such a case; and that the guarded and somewhat qualified terms in which the dictum is referred to and adopted in this case, were used for the express purpose of excluding that inference." See 1 Ph. 722, n. Lord St. Leonards, however, in *Stroughill* v. *Anstey*, 1 De G. Mac. & G. 635, 654 (after commenting upon *Watkins* v. *Cheek*, 2 S. & S. 199 ; *Johnson* v. *Kennett*, 6 Sim. 384, 3 My. & K. 624 ; *Page* v. *Adams*, 4 Beav. 269 ; and *Forbes* v. *Peacock*, 11 Sim. 152, 1 Ph. 717, 721), with reference to what fell from Lord Lyndhurst in *Johnson* v. *Kennett* and *Forbes* v. *Peacock*, and the note of the reporter, makes the following useful observations: " I cannot think that, a satisfactory settlement of this important point. The difference is this :—Lord Lyndhurst represents the Vice-Chancellor as saying that if there be a general charge of debts and legacies, the purchaser is absolved from seeing to the payment of the legacies on account of the charge of debts, but if the charge of debts has been satisfied, and the purchaser knows it has been satisfied, he is then in the same situation as if there was only an original charge of legacies, and he is bound to see to the application of the purchase-money; but to this Lord Lyndhurst answers, that the rule is different, and that if there is a general charge of debts, the case must be taken as it stood at [*72] the *death of the testator, and if there were debts then, although they were afterwards satisfied, the purchaser is not liable. Then he says, as I understand by the note, that he did not mean to decide that if there were no debts at the death of the testator, the purchaser was not bound. I cannot, however, follow that distinction. The case must stand upon one of two grounds : either that there are no debts within the knowledge of the purchaser (and then it is indifferent whether there were no debts at the death of the testator or no debts at the time of the purchase) or (which is more satisfactory and open to no ambiguity), on the ground that when a testator by his will charges his estate with debts and legacies, he shows that he means to entrust his trustees with the power of receiving the money, anticipating that there will be debts, and thus providing for the payment of them. It is by implication a declaration by the testator that he intends to entrust the trustees with the receipt and application of the money, and not to throw any obligation at all upon the purchaser or mortgagee. That intention does not cease because there are no debts; it remains just as much if there are no debts, as if there are debts, because the power arises from the circumstance that the debts are provided for, there being in the very creation of the trust a clear indication amounting to a declaration by the testator that he means, and the nature of the trust shows that he means, that the trustees are alone to receive the money and apply it. In that way all the cases are reconcilable, and all stand upon one footing, viz., that if a trust be created for the payment of debts and legacies, the purchaser or mortgagee shall in no case be bound to see to the application of the money raised. This would be a consistent rule, on which everybody would be able to act, authorised, too, by the words of the testator, and drawing none of those fine distinctions which embarrass Courts and counsel, and lead to litigation; and it is one to which I shall adhere as long as I sit in this Court." 1 De G. Mac. & G. 652.

With reference to the ground upon which Lord Lyndhurst decided the case of *Johnson* v. *Kennett*, Lord St. Leonards said that it was not altogether satisfactory. "The son," said his Lordship, "being absolute owner of the estate, subject to the debts and legacies, was at liberty to settle it to uses for himself just as he thought proper, and when he sold he sold as owner as well as trustee, and a sale was no breach of trust: it was a sale by him in his proper character, but still subject in equity to the payment of the debts and legacies. He stood in the same situation as an heir-at-law, who, being liable to the testator's* debts, has power to dispose of the estate by sale, if he thinks proper, but is bound to apply the money that he receives [*73] from the sale in payment and satisfaction of the debts, and this Court will compel him to do so, and will not allow him to divert the money to other purposes." See *Stroughill* v. *Anstey*, 1 De G. Mac. & G. 650.

In *Horn* v. *Horn*, 2 S. & S. 448, where a trader devised his estates, subject to the payment of legacies, it was contended, that as the real estate of a trader was by 47 Geo. 3, c. 74 [repealed and re-enacted by 1 Will. 4, c. 47], subject to debts generally, the purchaser was discharged from the obligation to see that his money was applied in payment of the legacies, as he would have been if the estate had been charged by the testator with payment of his debts. However Sir J. Leach, V. C., held, that the statute made no difference in this respect. The principle of this decision applies to 3 & 4 Will. 4, c. 104, which makes the real estates of all persons who die after the 29th of August, 1833, liable to simple contract debts. See *Shaw* v. *Borrer*, 1 Kee. 566, 577; *Ball* v. *Harris*, 4 My. & Cr. 268; *Jones* v. *Noyes*, 4 Jur. N. S. 1033.

Although there is no trust for the general payment of debts, it will be implied that it was the intention of the settlor or testator to confer upon the trustees a power to give receipts, where they are directed to sell at a time when the persons amongst whom they are to distribute the proceeds of the sale are either not ascertainable or not of age: thus, in *Balfour* v. *Welland*, 16 Ves. 151, where a general assignment for the benefit of certain scheduled creditors, and all other creditors executing the deed, was made to E. and F., upon trust *as soon as conveniently might be*, to sell the assigned property, and *with all convenient speed* to make such dividends out of the proceeds among the creditors as therein mentioned; and the deed contained a provision limiting the time for creditors to execute the deed—*six months* for creditors in India, and *eighteen months* for those in Europe, unless they were disabled by minority, in which cases the same periods were to be allowed respectively *after the disability had ceased*—upon an objection being taken by a purchaser from the trustees to the title of a leasehold house, on the ground that he was bound to see to the application of the money in satisfaction of the scheduled creditors and others coming within a limited time after the date of the deed, Sir William Grant, M. R., overruled the objection, upon the ground that the deed clearly conferred an *immediate* power of sale for a purpose that *could not be immediately defined*, viz., *to pay debts which could not be ascertained until a future and distant period.* [*74] *"It is impossible," observed his Honor, "to contend, that the trustees might not have sold the whole property at any time they thought fit after the execution of the deed; and yet it could not be ascertained until the end of eighteen months who were the persons among whom the produce of the sale was to be distributed. If the sale might take place at a time when the distribution could not possibly be made, it must have been intended that the trustees should of themselves be able to give a discharge for the produce, for the money could not be paid to any other person than the trustees. It is not material, that the objects of the trust may have been actually ascertained before the sale. The deed must receive its construction as from the moment of its execution. According to the frame of the deed, the purchasers, were or were not liable to see to the application of the money; and their liability cannot depend upon any subsequent event." See also *Groom* v. *Booth*, 1 Drew. 548.

So, likewise, in *Sowarsby* v. *Lacy*, 4 Madd. 142, where A. devised certain lands to his children, the same to be sold when the executors and trustees of his will should see proper, and the purchase-money to be equally and severally divided amongst his children, some of whom were then infants, Sir J. Leach said, "It is plain the testator intended that the trustees should have an immediate power of sale. Some of the children were infants, and not capable of signing receipts. I must, therefore, infer, that the testator meant to give to the trustees the power to sign receipts, being an authority necessary for the execution of his declared purpose." See also *Lavender* v. *Stanton*, 6 Madd. 46; *Breedon* v. *Breedon*, 1 Russ. & My. 413; *Keon* v. *Magawly*, 1 D. & W. 401.

If, however, an estate is charged with a sum of money payable to an infant on his attaining his majority, the purchaser will be bound to see the money duly paid: *Dickenson* v. *Dickenson*, 3 Bro. C. C. 19.

Where money to arise from a sale is not merely to be paid to certain persons, but is to be applied by the trustees upon trusts requiring care and discretion, the presumption arises that the settlor intended to confide the execution of the trust to the trustees solely, and the purchaser will not be bound to see to the application of the purchase-money. Thus, in *Doran* v. *Wiltshire*, 3 Swanst. 699, the trustees were to receive the purchase-money, and to lay it out in lands to the uses of the settlement, and till that was done to invest it in the Government funds. Scott, Solicitor-General, urged that no good title could be made, because there was no clause in the settlement making the receipt of the trustees a good discharge to *the purchaser. But Lord Thurlow said, [*75] " As to the power which the trustees have of giving a discharge, it is true, that, when land is to be sold, and a particular debt is to be paid with it, the purchaser is bound to see to the application of the purchase money. But in cases where the application is to a payment of debts generally, or to a general laying out of the money, he knew of no case which lays down, or any reasoning in any case which goes the length of saying that a purchaser is so bound; and, therefore, he conceived that the receipt of the trustees would be a good discharge in this case." See also *Balfour* v. *Welland*, 16 Ves. 151; *Tait* v. *Lathbury*, 35 Beav. 112.

An authority given by a testator to trustees to lay out and invest money upon good security is an authority to do all acts essential to that trust, and necessarily, therefore, to give sufficient discharges to borrowers of that money. *Wood* v. *Harman*, 5 Madd. 368.

Upon the same principle, where the trusts of a term were to raise a sum of money, but there was no express authority to give a receipt for such sum, it was implied by the Court, from authority having been given to invest the money, and vary the investment. For " it is not reasonable," as observed by Sir J. Parker, V. C., to suppose that the testator, giving the trustees authority to change the investments, and to convert them from time to time, had denied to them authority to receive the money." *Locke* v. *Lomas*, 5 De G. & Sm. 326, 329. See *Pell* v. *De Winton*, 2 De G. & J. 13.

Where, however, a testator gives a person like powers of sale and exchange as are contained in the will of another person, in which there are also powers to give receipts, the Court will not hold that such person has by implication a power to give receipts: *Cox* v. *Cox*, 1 K. & J. 251.

Where there is a charge for payment of debts generally, or a charge followed by specific dispositions of real estate, the purchaser is not bound to see to the application of his purchase-money; for, as before observed, the charge is equivalent to a trust, and the same effect will be given to it by a court of equity, as if a direct devise had been made to trustees for payment of debts. See *Walker* v. *Smallwood*, Amb. 676; *Jenkins* v. *Hiles*, 6 Ves. 654, note; *Bailey* v. *Ekins*, 7 Ves. 323; *Dolton* v. *Hewen*, 6 Madd. 9. In *Shaw* v. *Borrer*, 1 Kee. 559, a testator, after commencing his will with words amounting to a charge of his real estate with payment of his debts, devised an advowson to trustees, upon trust to present his youngest son to the living when vacant, and subject thereto, in trust to sell and apply the produce of the sale [*76] for the special purposes therein mentioned; *and he devised his residuary real estate, upon certain trusts, to other trustees, and appointed three executors (who proved his will), one of whom was his youngest son, and another, one of the trustees of the advowson. The personal estate being insufficient for the payment of debts, the trustees of the advowson, one of whom was an executor, at the instance of the other executors, contracted to sell the advowson, before any vacancy had occurred in the living. In a suit for specific performance by the plaintiffs, the trustees of the advowson, and the executors, against the purchaser, it was held by Lord Langdale, M. R., that, the charge being in effect a devise of the real estate in trust for the payment of debts, a good title could be made by the plaintiffs, without the institution of a suit to ascertain the deficiency of the personal estate, and that the purchaser was not bound either to inquire whether other sufficient property ought first to be applied in payment of debts, or to see to the application of the purchase-money. " In discussing an authority," observed his Lordship, " cited in *Jenkins* v. *Hiles*, Lord Eldon is reported to have said, that if a man by deed or will charges or orders an estate to be sold for payment of his debts, and then makes specific dispositions, the purchaser is not bound to see to the application; it is just the same as if the specific bequests were out of the will. It seems, therefore, clear that a charge of this nature has been and ought to be treated as a trust, which gives the creditors a priority over the special purposes of the devise; and no doubt is raised but that, on the application of the creditors, the Court would, in a suit to which the executors were parties, compel the trustees for special purposes to raise the money requisite for payment of the debts. If so, is there any good reason to doubt, but that the trustees and executors may themselves do that which the Court would compel them to do on the application of the creditors? Though the advowson is devised to trustees for special purposes, the testator has, in the first instance, charged all his estate with payment of his debts. The charge affects the equitable, but not the legal estate; and, upon the construction, the trusts of the will affect this estate, first, in common with the testator's other property for the payment of debts, and next, separately, for the special purposes mentioned in his will." In *Ball* v. *Harris*, 4 My. & Cr. 264, Lord Cottenham held, that a charge by will of real estates with the payment of debts, generally, authorised a trustee, who was also executor, to whom, after imposing that charge, the testator had devised the estate, upon trusts for other persons, to make a mortgage (being a conditional sale) of lands purchased under a power and conveyed to him upon the trusts of the *will, and exempted the mortgagee from liability to see to the application of the mortgage money. "The [*77] real question," observed his Lordship, "is, whether the decision in *Shaw* v. *Borrer* is right. I have carefully considered the judgment of the Master of the Rolls upon this point, and I entirely concur with him upon it; the point, indeed, has been long established. It arose directly in *Elliot* v. *Merryman*, and, as there laid down, has been recognised in the several cases referred to by the Master of the Rolls; to which may be added the opinion of Lord Eldon in *Bailey* v. *Ekins*, and *Dolton* v. *Ewen*; for, although the point in some of those cases was, whether the purchaser was bound to see to the application of purchase-money, the decision that he was not assumes that the sale was authorised by the charge in the will of the debts upon the estate; that is, that the charge of the debts upon the estate was equivalent to a trust to sell for payment of them." See also *Johnson* v. *Kennett*, 3 My. & K. 624; *Eland* v. *Eland*, 1 Beav. 235, 4 My. & Cr. 430; *Page* v. *Adam*, 4 Beav. 269; *Forbes* v. *Peacock*, 1 Ph. 717.

A purchaser is not bound to ascertain how much land it is necessary to sell for payment of debts, for, as observed by the Lord Keeper in *Spalding* v. *Shalmer*, 1 Vern. 303, "if more be sold than is sufficient to pay the debts, that shall not turn to the prejudice of the purchaser, for he is not obliged to enter into the account; and the trustees cannot sell just so much as is sufficient to pay the debts."

Where lands are devised to trustees upon *trust* to raise so much money as the personal estate shall fall deficient in paying the testator's debts and legacies, the purchaser is not bound to inquire whether the real estate is wanted or not. Secus if the trustees have a *power* merely to raise money upon the deficiency of the personal estate, for unless there was a deficiency the power never arose, and consequently the purchaser would take no estate by the supposed execution of it. See *Culpepper* v. *Aston*, 2 Ch. C. 115, 223; *Dike* v. *Ricks*, Cro. Car. 335; *Pierce* v. *Scott*, 1 Y. & C. Exch. Ca. 257; Butler's note to Co. Litt. 290, b.; *Bird* v. *Fox*, 11 Hare, 40.

In a recent case, where a testator "in case his personal estate should be insufficient for the payment of his debts," charged them upon his real estate; it was held by Lord Romilly, M. R., that the executor had an implied power to sell and give valid receipts for the purchase-money, without showing the insufficiency of the personal estate, although thirteen years had elapsed since the testator's death. *Greetham* v. *Collon*, 34 Beav. 615.

Where a trustee for the sale of real estate with power to give receipts [*78] and being entitled beneficially to a share of the proceeds *of the sale, has judgments registered against him; it seems that a purchaser with notice of the judgments, may be bound to see to the application of the purchase-money in payment of the judgments. See *Drummond* v. *Tracy*, Johns. 610.

Where, however, a testator gave all his *real and personal* estate to his daughter upon trusts for sale and conversion, and to hold the proceeds for herself and two others equally, with the usual receipt clause, and appointed her executrix; it was held by Sir W. Page Wood, V. C., that the daughter having married and afterwards sold the land, could, with her husband's concurrence, effectually discharge the purchaser, notwithstanding judgments registered against the husband between the date of the sale, and the completion. *Drummond* v. *Tracy*, Johns. 608.

The rule, that a purchaser is not bound, where the debts are charged generally, to see to the application of the purchase-money, "is," as observed by Lord Cottenham, "subject to this obvious exception; that, if a purchaser or mortgagee is a party to a breach of trust, it can afford him no protection." One obvious example is where a devisee has a right to sell, but he sells to pay his own debt, which is a manifest breach of trust, and the party who concurs in the sale is aware or has notice of the fact that such is its object; *Eland* v. *Eland*, 4 My. & Cr. 427. See also *Rogers* v. *Skillicorne*, Ambr. 189; *Watkins* v. *Cheek*, 2 S. & S. 199; *Burt* v. *Trueman*, 8 W. R. (V. C. K.) 635; *Howard* v. *Chaffer*, 11 W. R. (V. C. K.) 1057; 9 Jur. N. S. 767. The fact, however, that an executor, who is also devisee, has mortgaged his private property together with the property devised to him charged with payment of debts, will not raise a presumption against him, that he was not acting in the ordinary discharge of his duty as executor. *Barrow* v. *Griffith*, 13 W. R. (V. C. S.) 41; 11 Jur. N. S. 6.

So, where trustees, instead of selling under a power in a will, raise money by mortgage in a manner not authorised by the power, many years after the death of the testator, the mortgagee being party to a breach of trust, his security will be invalid. Thus, in *Stroughill* v. *Anstey*, 1 De G. Mac. & G. 635, where a testator by his will, after appointing three persons his executors, gave to them the residue of his personal estate, and directed them, or the other trustees to be appointed under the provisions contained in his will, to stand possessed of his residuary personal estate, upon trust at such time or times as to them should seem meet, to sell and convert into money all such part thereof as should not consist of money, and invest the produce in securities, and to stand possessed of the same, upon *trust thereout to pay [*79] his funeral expenses and debts, and certain large legacies which he specified, and to stand possessed of the residue for his two sons equally; and the will contained a clause which, according to the construction put upon it by the Court, empowered the trustees to give receipts. *Sixteen* years after the death of the testator, the then acting trustees of the will, who were not the executors, raised money *upon a deposit of the title-deeds* of two leasehold houses, part of the testator's residuary estate. It was held by Lord St. Leonards, C., dismissing a claim filed by the mortgagees to enforce their securities, that inasmuch as the trusts of the will showed a conversion, out and out, of the testator's property, to be absolutely necessary, the trustees were not authorised in raising money by mortgage. In giving judgment, his Lordship made the following important observations upon the subject, whether a power of sale authorises a mortgage :—" The first question," said his Lordship, " is, whether a mortgage was or was not authorised by the trusts of this will. And in addressing myself to this point, it ought, I think, to be considered, that in a case where trustees have a legal estate, and are to perform a particular trust through the medium of a sale, although a direction for a sale does not properly authorise a mortgage, yet where the circumstances would justify the raising of the particular charge by a mortgage, it must be in some measure in the discretion of the Court whether it will sanction that particular mode or not. It may be the saving of an estate, and the most discreet thing that can be done ; and as the legal estate would go, and as the purposes of the trust would be satisfied, I think it impossible for the Court to lay down, that in every case of a trust for sale to raise particular sums, a mortgage might not, under circumstances, be justified. As a general rule, however, there can be no difficulty in saying, that a mortgage under a mere trust for conversion, out and out, is not a due execution of that trust ; and looking at the nature of the property in the present case, which was leasehold, and which, as being varying property, would, as a matter of course, be directed to be converted into money, where, under a general gift, it was to go to different parties, having different interests, it is impossible to say that this Court could allow the property to remain unconverted under an absolute trust for conversion out and out ; and the trustees to deal with it, as if it were property that was to be enjoyed in specie. In the present instance, the trustees went on, receiving the rents, and accounting to the persons who were entitled to the benefit of the purchase-money of the property producing the rents ; and *this was done where the will contained a trust that, [*80] with all convenient speed after the testator's death, the property should be converted out and out, not simply for the purpose of paying a charge, which might be more conveniently raised by a mortgage, but for the pnrpose of conversion. One of the objects of conversion was to pay debts ; but there were other and final objects which rendered a conversion out and out absolutely necessary; namely, the dedication of the trust-monies to raise particular sums according to the testator's will; and, therefore, to continue the property unconverted was to set aside the testator's will instead of executing the trusts of it ; and if the trusts had been properly executed, the fraud which has been perpetrated could not have taken place." See also, *M'Neillie* v. *Acton*, 4 De G. Mac. & G. 744 ; *Haldenby* v. *Spofforth*, 1 Beav. 390 ; *Raikes* v. *Hall, cited* 1 De G. Mac. & G. 646 ; *Mather* v. *Norton*, 16 Jur. 309, 21 L. J. Ch. 15 ; *Devaynes* v. *Noble*, 24 Beav. 87 ; *Colyer* v. *Finch*, 5 Ho. Lo. Ca. 923.

But the mortgagee in such case will be entitled to stand as a creditor on the produce of the estates, to the extent to which the mortgage money has been properly applied. *Devaynes* v. *Robinson*, 24 Beav. 86.

With reference to the distance *of time* that had elapsed from the death of the testator to the deposit of the deeds, his Lordship observed, " That people who deal with trustees raising money at a considerable distance of time, and without any apparent reason for so doing, must be considered as under some obligation to inquire and look fairly at what they are about. I do not mean to encumber or to lessen the security of purchasers or mortgagees under trusts; but if for a great number of years a trust, such as that here, remains unperformed, and parties are found in possession and receipt of the rents of the trust-property, and then an application is made of it without their concurrence by the trustees, it may place those who deal with the trustees in a situation of having it established that there was a breach of trust, of which they ought to have taken notice." *Stroughill* v. *Anstey*, 1 De G. Mac. & G. 654. See and consider, *Charlton* v. *Earl of Durham*, 4 L. R. Ch. App. 433.

Another exception is, where the purchaser has notice of a suit having been instituted, which takes the administration of the estate out of the hands of the trustee: *Lloyd* v. *Baldwin*, 1 Ves. 173 ; *Walker* v. *Smalwood*, Amb. 676.

It may be here mentioned, that a question may arise of this nature: assuming that trustees for sale have no power to give receipts, can they, by conditions of sale, compel a purchaser to be satisfied with [*81] their receipts alone? It seems *that they can (*Groom* v. *Booth*, 1 Drew. 548), unless the conditions are framed so as to mislead the purchaser (*Ib.* p. 565); or the Court would, by enforcing specific performance, cause a breach of trust (*Ib.*); at all events, it would be too late to take an objection to such a condition on exceptions, after a decree for specific performance, and the usual reference as to title. *Wilkinson* v. *Hartley*, 15 Beav. 183.

The difficulty arising from the absence of a receipt clause may sometimes be got rid of by payment of money into Court under the Trustee
Relief Acts (see *Cox* v. *Cox*, 1 K. & J. 251); but the application of this
relief to the cases under consideration is doubtful; and it has been
decided that the purchaser of an estate subject to a pecuniary charge
cannot avail himself of these Acts. *In re Buckley's Trust*, 17 Beav. 110.

2. *As to Purchasers of Personal Estate from Executors or Administrators.*]—However personal estate may be bequeathed, it must be
applied, in the first place, by the executors for payment of the debts
of the testator, in a due course of administration. Upon the same
principles, therefore, by which a purchaser of real estate, devised for
the general payment of debts, is exempted from seeing to the application of the purchase-money, it is a general rule that a person who purchases or takes a mortgage of leaseholds or other personalty from an
executor or administrator is not bound to see to the application of the
purchase-money. "After the sale is made, the creditors cannot," as
observed by the Master of the Rolls in the principal case, "break in
upon it." See *Bonney* v. *Ridgard*, 1 Cox, 145; *Scott* v. *Tyler*, 2 Dick.
725; *Mead* v. *Orrery*, 3 Atk. 240; *Andrew* v. *Wrigley*, 4 Bro. C. C. 125;
M'Leod v. *Drummond*, 17 Ves. 154; *Keane* v. *Robarts*, 4 Madd. 357;
Ward v. *Ward*, 4 Ir. Ch. Rep. 215; *Humble* v. *Bill*, 2 Vern. 444. The
last-mentioned case, however, was reversed in the House of Lords,
under the name of *Savage* v. *Humble*, 3 Bro. P. C. 5, Toml. ed., in the
opinion of subsequent judges erroneously: *Ewer* v. *Corbet*, 2 P. Wms.
148; *Andrew* v. *Wrigley*, 4 Bro. C. C. 136.

The sale or mortgage of a chattel by an executor will be good against
both the residuary pecuniary and specific legatees, as well as the creditors of the testator, whose remedy, in case of the misapplication of the
money by the executor, will be not against the purchaser or mortgagee,
but against the executor; nor will notice of the will or of the bequest
contained in it be prejudicial to the purchaser or mortgagee. See
Burting v. *Stonard*, 2 P. Wms. 150; *M'Leod* v. *Drummond*, 17 Ves.
163, 169; *Andrew* v. *Wrigley*, 4 Bro. C. C. 125; *Keane* v. *Robarts*,
*4 Madd. 332, 357; *Gray* v. *Johnston*, 3 Law R. Ho. Lo. 1. [*82]

In *Ewer* v. *Corbett*, 2 P. Wms. 148, one possessed of a term
for years devised it to A., and died indebted, having made B. his
executor. The executor sold the term, upon which the legatee of the
term brought a bill against the purchaser, insisting that, the term being
bequeathed to the plaintiff, the executor was but a trustee, and that
the purchaser must have notice of this trust, the term having been
bought of the executor, and consequently must be taken subject to the
trust. However, Sir J. Jekyll, M. R., observed, "I take it to have
been resolved, and with great reason, that an executor, where there
are debts, may sell a term, and the devisee of the term has no other
remedy but against the executor to recover the value thereof, if there

be sufficient assets for the payment of debts. As for the notice of the will and of the devise of the term to a third person, that is nothing; for every person buying of an executor, where he is named executor, must, of necessity, have notice; so that if notice were to be an hindrance, then, of consequence, no executor might sell. It is not reasonable to put every purchaser of a lease from an executor to take an account of the testator's debts, nor has he any means to discover them. On the contrary, as the whole personal estate of the testator is liable to the debts, this lease must (inter alia) of necessity be liable, and therefore may be sold by the executor. If equity were otherwise, it would be a great hindrance to the payment of debts and legacies, and would lay an embargo upon all personal estates in the hands of executors and administrators, which would be attended with great inconvenience." See also *Humble* v. *Bill*, 2 Vern. 445; *Watts* v. *Kancie*, Toth. 77.

The fact that a mortgage of part of the assets has been made to secure a debt originally contracted on the personal security of an executor, and without reference to the assets, is immaterial. See *Miles* v. *Durnford*, 2 De G. Mac. & G. 641, in which the Lords Justices differed as to this point from Sir R. T. Kindersley, V. C. (See 2 Sim. N. S. 234.) "The only evidence," said Lord Justice Knight Bruce, "is that the advances were originally made without security, and that security was afterwards added. That is a circumstance deserving attention, but it does not go far. It is not inconsistent with probability that the advances were made for *a purpose for which the executor might properly borrow* as executor. I think the presumption is in favour of the propriety of the transaction, and that the plaintiff wholly fails." See also *Haynes* v. *Forshaw*, 11 Hare, 93.

[*83]   An executor or administrator *may not only pledge or mortgage the assets, but may also give to the mortgagee of leaseholds a power to sell and give receipts for the purchase-money. See *Russell* v. *Plaice*, 18 Beav. 21. "The power of sale," said Sir John Romilly, M. R., in that case, "given to a mortgagee must, I think, be considered, not as the delegation of a power entrusted to the executor, which is a power to sell for the benefit of his cestui que trust, but as the creation of a new power to sell, not for the benefit of the person interested in the testator's estate, but for the benefit of the person interested in the mortgage; that is, a power to render the mortgage effectual; and I think that the right to create this power is incidental to the authority of the executor to mortgage. If this were withheld, the persons interested in the assets would be injured, because in that case, a mortgage could not be effected, unless on terms less advantageous than could be obtained, if the person advancing the money obtained the same security as if he was dealing with the absolute owner of the estate. For the purpose of selling the estate of the testator, the executor is considered

as the absolute owner, and has all the power incidental to that character. On what principle can it be maintained that he is not to be regarded in the same light, and to have the same power, for the purpose of effecting a mortgage, which may be the most beneficial course to be adopted for his cestui que trust, and of which benefit the executor is constituted the sole judge?" And see *Cruikshank* v. *Duffin*, 13 L. R. Eq. 555; 20 W. R. (V. C. M.) 354, where a mortgage with a power of sale by an executor to a Building Society was held good.

It has been held by the same learned judge that, where there is an express power to mortgage, the donee, as incident to such power, has authority to give a power of sale to the mortgagee. *Bridges* v. *Longman*, 24 Beav. 27; *Cook* v. *Dawson*, 29 Beav. 123, 128, 3 De G. F. & J. 127; *Leigh* v. *Lloyd*, 2 De G. J. & S. 330. *In re Chawner's will*, 8 L. R. Eq. 569; on this point overruling *Clarke* v. *The Royal Panopticon*, 4 Drew, 26, and *Sanders* v. *Richards*, 2 Coll. 568. And now, by Lord Cranworth's Act, 23 & 24 Vict c. 145, s. 11, powers of sale are rendered incident to mortgages.

But where an absolute purchase is held, in consequence of the relation between the parties, to be available as a security only, the Court will not import into the transaction a power of sale. *Pearson* v. *Benson*, 28 Beav. 598; and see *Darke* v. *Williamson*, 25 Beav. 622.

Where money was ordered by the Court to be raised by mortgage of an infant's estate for payment of debts and costs, the Court will, it seems, if the mortgagee requires it, authorise the insertion *of [*84] a power of sale in the mortgage deed. *Selby* v. *Cooling*, 23 Beav. 418.

So likewise an executor may give to a person to whom he has assigned the book debts of the testator by way of mortgage, a power of attorney to collect the debts in his name. *Earl of Vane* v. *Rigden*, 5 L. R. Ch., App. 663.

If there be a specific legatee of a chattel, it is desirable to have his concurrence to a sale of it, as the executor may have done some act amounting to an assent (*Tomlinson* v. *Smith*, Rep. temp. Finch, 378), but the difficulty does not not arise when he is also executor. *Cole* v. *Miles*, 10 Hare, 179; *Taylor* v. *Hawkins*, 8 Ves. 209; *Attorney-General* v. *Potter*, 5 Beav. 164.

If the executor or other person who by reason of a charge of debts and legacies could make a good title, convey to the devisee or other person entitled to the property subject to the charge by deed, reciting the payment of the charge, out of the personal estate, a purchaser from such devisee or other person will not be bound to see to the application of the purchase-money. *Storry* v. *Walsh*, 18 Beav. 559. See also *Forshaw* v. *Higginson*, 26 L. J. N. S. Ch. 174, 8 De G. Mac. & G. 827.

Although an executor has power to give a person advancing money to him a lien on specific assets, he cannot enable a person from whom he obtains a loan to stand as a creditor upon or to prove against the estate in competition with the creditors of the testator. See *Farhall* v. *Farhall*, 7 L. R. Ch. App. 123, reversing S. C. 12, L. R. Eq. 98.

The Master of the Rolls, in the principal case, mentions two exceptions from the rule. As to the first, he observes, " that personal estate may be clothed with such a particular trust, that it is possible the Court, in some cases, may require a purchaser of it to see the money rightly applied." This observation has been approved of by Lord Kenyon, M. R., in *Bonney* v. *Ridgard*, 4 Bro. C. C. 130; 1 Cox, 145. See *M'Leod* v *Drummond*, 17 Ves. 161, 162; *In re Johnston's Estate*, 15 Ir. Ch. Rep. 260.

The second exception from the rule, mentioned by the Master of the Rolls, is, where there is a fraud in the case on the part of a purchaser or mortgagee, which fraud will be inferred in many instances. Thus, where an executor disposes of or pledges his testator's assets in payment of or as a security for a debt of his *own*, the person to whom they are disposed of or pledged will take them subject to the claims of the creditors, specific and general legatees, of the testator: thus in *Hill* v. *Simpson*, 7 Ves. 152, Simpson, an executor, immediately after the death of his testatrix, Mrs. Smith, transferred certain funds *standing in [*85] the name of John Smith, her deceased husband, to whom she was executrix, and other funds standing in her name, and in the name of her co-executor, to Moffat & Co., his bankers, as a security for such sums as he then owed, or might afterwards owe them. Moffat & Co. denied that they knew, or suspected, that the funds were not at the time of the transfer the absolute property of Simpson, as executor or devisee of Mrs. Smith; or that they were part of the personal estate of John Smith; on the contrary, they believed they were Simpson's own property; and he represented to them that he was absolutely entitled thereto subject only to an annuity of 20*l.* to Elizabeth Smith's sister during her life, and to a few very small legacies; that he had full right to dispose thereof, and would have disposed thereof but for the low price of the funds, which he expected would rise. They also stated that they did not know any of the legacies of John Smith to the plaintiffs, or any other person, were unpaid. However, Sir W. Grant, M. R., held that the general legatees could follow the funds transferred to the bankers. " In this instance," observed his Honour, " the assignment was made in less than a month after the death of Mrs. Smith. There is not, therefore, the least ground for the presumption of right acquired to the assets of Mr. or Mrs. Smith by payments made in that short interval on account of either estate. It is not pretended it was to satisfy any claim on either estate; for the express purpose appears to have been to secure a debt of his own, which he already owed to the bankers, and other advances they were to make by taking up bills of his then actually outstanding. They had distinct notice, therefore, that the money was not to be applied to any demand upon either estate; but the assets were to be wholly applied to the private purpose of the executor. Allowing every case to remain undisturbed, does it follow from any that an executor in the first month after the testator's death can apply the assets in payment of his own debt; and that a creditor is perfectly safe in so receiving and applying them, provided he abstains from looking at the will, which would show the existence of unsatisfied demands? I am for the moment keeping out of sight the representation made by Simpson, and supposing the question to be, whether an executor may thus deal and be dealt with; and it is clear, no rule of justice permits, or of convenience requires, that he should have this unbounded power. Though it may be dangerous at all to restrain the power of purchasing from him, what inconvenience can there be in holding, that the *assets, known to be such, should not be applied in any case for the executor's debt, unless the creditor could be first satisfied [*86] of his right? It may be essential that the executor should have the power to sell the assets; but it is not essential that he should have the power to pay his own creditor, and it is not just that one man's property should be applied to the payment of another man's debt. . . . It was gross negligence not to look at the will, under which alone a title could be given to them. It was not necessary to use any exertion to obtain information, but merely not to shut their eyes against the information which, without extraordinary neglect, they could not avoid receiving. No transaction with executors can be rendered unsafe, by holding that assets transferred under such circumstances may be followed." See also *Haynes* v. *Forshaw*, 11 Hare, 93; *Wilson* v. *Moore*, 1 My. & K. 337; *Wilson* v. *Leslie*, 5 W. R. (V. C. K.) 815; *Rolfe* v. *Gregory*, 11 W. R. (V. C. K.) 1016; *Farhall* v. *Farhall*, 7 L. R. Eq. 286.

A different doctrine appears to have formerly prevailed in *Mead* v. *Orrery*, 3 Atk. 235, and *Nugent* v. *Gifford*, 1 Atk. 463. The authority of these cases, however, is weakened, if they are not completely overruled, by *Hill* v. *Simpson;* and see *Bonney* v. *Ridgard*, 1 Cox, 145, where Sir Lloyd Kenyon, M. R., in commenting on *Mead* v. *Lord Orrery*, says that if it had come before him, he should have decided it in direct opposition to that authority. It may be remarked, however, that in *Nugent* v. *Gifford* the executor was the sole residuary legatee; and in *Mead* v. *Lord Orrery* he was one of the residuary legatees, and his co-executors joined with him in the assignment. If, therefore, these cases are rightly decided, they seem to establish that where an executor is also residuary legatee, fraud or collusion will not necessarily be inferred as against the person to whom he sells or mortgages a chattel of the testator's in payment of or as a security for his own debt. See *M'Leod* v. *Drummond*, 17 Ves. 163, 164; *Bedford* v. *Woodham*, 4 Ves. 40, note; *Williams* v. *Massey*, 15 Ir. Ch. Rep. 47.

It is clear, that, in the absence of fraud or collusion, the assignment by an executor, as a security for his own debt, of a chattel specifically bequeathed to him, will be good : *Taylor* v. *Hawkins*, 8 Ves. 209.

A purchaser, however, with notice of the testator's debts being unpaid, will not be allowed to retain a chattel obtained from an executor as a security for his own debt, although the executor is also specific or residuary legatee; thus in *Crane* v. *Drake*, 2 Vern. 616, where the purchaser, with notice of the plaintiff's debt, bought a lease from the executor and devisee, upon an arrangement *that part of the [*87] purchase-money was to go in payment of a debt due to him from the executor, it was held that the sale was not binding upon the plaintiff, the Lord Chancellor saying, " The defendant was a party, and consenting to and contriving a devastavit." In commenting on this case, in *Andrew* v. *Wrigley*, 4 Bro. C. C. 139, Lord Alvanley, M. R., observes, " Can there be a stronger case of a devastavit, than an executor aliening the property of his testator to pay his own debts, and the alienee then knew that the plaintiff's debt was due ? " See also *Nugent* v. *Gifford*, 1 Atk. 464; *M'Leod* v. *Drummond*, 17 Ves. 163.

So, where the executor has sold for an under-value, or to one who has notice that the testator had left no debts, or that all debts had been paid, a sale or mortgage of the personal estate by the executor will not be valid. *Ewer* v. *Corbett*, 2 P. Wms. 148; *Scott* v. *Tyler*, 2 Dick. 725; *Drohan* v. *Drohan*, 1 Ball & B. 185; *Rice* v. *Gordon*, 11 Beav. 265; and see *Stroughill* v. *Anstey*, 1 De G. Mac. & G. 635; *M'Mullen* v. *O'Reilly*, 5 Ir. Ch. Rep. 251; *Hall* v. *Andrews*, 27 L. T. R. (N. S.) 195, 2 W. R. (V. C. W.) 799.

The exceptions from the general rule, that a purchaser from an executor is not bound to see to the application of the purchase-money, have been well summed up by Lord Thurlow in *Scott* v. *Tyler*, 2 Dick, 725. " If," observes his Lordship, " one concerts with an executor, by obtaining the testator's effects at a nominal price, or at a fraudulent under-value, or by applying the real value to the purchase of other subjects for his own behoof, or in extinguishing the private debt of the executor, *or in any other manner*, contrary to the duty of the office of executor, such concert will involve the seeming purchaser, or his pawnee, and make him liable for the full value."

Length of time and acquiescence, as in the principal case, will prevent creditors and legatees from asserting their claims against purchasers, although the sale by the executor was attended with suspicious circumstances of fraud, and a fortiori against mesne purchasers: *Bonney* v. *Ridgard*, 4 Bro. C. C. 138, cited in *M'Leod* v. *Drummond*, 17 Ves. 165; S. C., 1 Cox, 145.

And the fact of the legacies being contingent will be no sufficient excuse for the legatees lying by when they have such an interest as will entitle them to know what debts the testator owed, and what part of his estate had been applied in payment of them: *Andrew* v. *Wrigley*, 4 Bro. C. C. 135; *Rolfe* v. *Gregory*, 11 W. R. (V. C. K.) 1016.

In *Mead* v. *Lord Orrery*, 3 Atk. 235, Lord Hardwicke seems to think that residuary legatees are never permitted in any case to question the disposition which the executors have made of the assets—that creditors or specific legatees *could only do so. However, in *Hill* v. *Simpson*, 7 Ves. 152, Sir William Grant decided that a mere pecuniary legatee could follow the assets into the hands of a third person. In *M'Leod* v. *Drummond*, 17 Ves. 169, Lord Eldon concurred in the principle laid down by Sir William Grant. "I cannot conceive," said his Lordship, "why a creditor or specific legatee should be able to follow the assets, and not a pecuniary or residuary legatee." [*88]

Upon the same principle as that applicable to the cases of sales by executors, a banker will not be liable for paying the cheque of his customer, being an executor, who misapplies the money, unless a misapplication thereof was intended by the executor amounting to a breach of trust of which the banker was cognisant. See *Gray* v. *Johnston*, 3 L. R. Ho. Lo. 1. There R. Gray & Co. acted as bankers to T. Johnston, who carried on business with his son-in-law under the style of Johnston & Mayston, but whose accounts with them were kept in his own name alone, and were unsettled at his death. He left a will, bequeathing all his property to the use of his wife for life, and after her death to be divided among their children as she might think fit. Part of the property consisted of life-policies, which were put into the hands of the bankers, together with the probate of T. Johnston's will, and they received the amount of the policies, made up their accounts, and, after deducting their own unsettled claims, declared a certain sum to remain due from themselves to the executrix. She continued her husband's business with his late partner, under the style of "Johnston & Mayston," and a new account was opened with the bankers in the name of the new firm, and she as executrix drew a cheque for the amount stated to be due to her, and paid it to the bankers to be credited to the firm of "Johnston & Mayston," and it was so credited and paid out, with other money on account of cheques drawn by the new firm. It was held by the House of Lords, reversing the decision of the Lord Chancellor of Ireland (Brady), that these circumstances were not in themselves sufficient to show that a breach of trust had been committed, and that the bankers knew the intention to commit it, so as to render them liable (in a suit by the children of the testator) to replace the money. "The relation," said Lord Westbury, "between banker and customer is somewhat peculiar, and it is most important that the rules which regulate it should be well known and carefully observed. A banker is bound to honour an order of his customer with respect to the money belonging to that customer *which is in the hands of the banker; and it is impossible for the banker to set up a jus [*89] tertii against the order of his customer, or to refuse to honour his draft, on any other ground than some sufficient one resulting from an act of the customer himself. Supposing, therefore, that the banker becomes incidentally aware that the customer, being in a fiduciary or a representative capacity, meditates a breach of trust, and draws a cheque for that purpose, the banker, not being interested in the transaction, has no right to refuse the payment of the cheque; for if he did so he would be making himself a party to an inquiry as between his customer and third persons. He would be setting up a supposed jus tertii, as a reason why he should not perform his own distinct obligation to his customer. But then it has been very well settled, that if an executor or a trustee who is indebted to a banker, or to another person having the legal custody of the assets of a trust estate, applies a portion of them in the payment of his own debt to the individual having that custody, the individual receiving the debt has at once not only abundant proof of this breach of trust, but participates in it for his own personal benefit . . . . . The question then resolves itself into one of fact. Can the payment of that money to the credit of the account of the new firm be properly treated as a payment for the benefit of the bankers, designed and intended to be the means of payment to the bankers of the debt that might be due to them on the new account? It would be impossible to say that any such thing was either designed or intended; and it would be equally impossible to say that any such thing was at once accomplished by means of the payment of the money to the credit of the new account. If it had been so accomplished, if a balance had been immediately struck, and the sum of money so paid in had been appropriated at once to the payment of the balance due on that account to the bankers, or if any other transaction had been made by which you might follow the money, and say that it was applied according to the agreement of the parties, directly and expressly in discharge of a debt due from the new firm to the bankers, then we should want no more to compel restitution from the bankers, and the case would fall within the ambit of well settled and firmly fixed authorities. But it is impossible, I think, to credit the statement that this was a payment intended to be for the benefit of bankers, or that it was made by any collusion or fraudulent agreement between the bankers and the executrix in order that the bankers might derive a personal benefit therefrom." See also *Farhall* v. *Farhall*, 7 L. R. Eq. 286.

[*90]   *Whether a Charge of Debts authorises a Sale of Real Estate by Executors.]—The question has of late been much discussed, whether a general charge of debts upon real estate authorises a sale by the executors. It is laid down broadly by Sir L. Shadwell, V. C., in *Forbes* v. *Peacock* (12 Sim. 541; overruled upon another point, 1 Ph. 717), that "if a testator charges his real estate with pay-

ment of his debts, that, *prima facie*, gives his executor *power to sell* the estate, and to give a good discharge for the purchase-money."

If the learned Vice-Chancellor meant, that such a charge gave a *legal* power to the executors to sell, the subsequent authorities render it necessary that his proposition should to some extent be modified.

The first case which it is important to notice is that of *Shaw* v. *Borrer*, 1 Keen, 559—there the will contained a general direction to pay debts, so expressed as to constitute a charge on all the testator's real estates; followed by a devise of a particular portion of the real estate to trustees for a special purpose, and a residuary devise of real estates for other special purposes. No suit had been instituted in equity to ascertain the deficiency of the personal estate to pay the debts; and the question was, whether the trustees and executors together could make a title to the purchaser of that part of the real estate which was devised to trustees for special purposes. It was argued, that such a sale could only be effected under the decree of a Court of equity for the administration of the testator's estate; but Lord Langdale, M. R., held that a good title could be made. "It seems to be clear," said his Lordship, "that a charge of this nature has been, and ought to be, treated as a trust, which gives the creditors a priority over the special purposes of the devise; and no doubt is raised but that, on the application of the creditors, the Court would, in a suit to which the executors were parties, compel the trustees, for special purposes, to raise the money requisite for the payment of the debts. If so, is there any good reason to doubt but that the trustees and executors may themselves do that which the court would compel them to do on the application of the creditors?"

Shaw v. *Borrer* was approved of by Lord Cottenham in the case of *Ball* v. *Harris* (4 My. & Cr. 264), where he held that an executor, who was also trustee of the real estate for other persons, there being a general charge of debts, had power to sell or mortgage the estate. "I have," said his Lordship, "carefully considered the judgment of the Master of the Rolls in *Shaw* v. *Borrer* upon this point, and I entirely concur with him upon it. The point, indeed, has been long established. It arose directly in *Elliot* v. *Merryman*, and as there laid down, has *been recognised in the several cases referred to by the Master of the Rolls; to which may be added the opinions of Lord [*91] Thurlow and Lord Eldon in *Bailey* v. *Ekins* (7 Ves. 319, 323), and *Dolton* v. *Hewen* (6 Madd. 9); for although the point in some of those cases was, whether the purchaser was bound to see to the application of the purchase-money, the decision that he was not, assumes that the sale was authorised by the charge in the will of the debts upon the estate; that is, that the charge of the debts upon the estate was equivalent to a trust to sell for the payment of them."

Now in the first of these cases, it will be observed that the trus-

tees joined with the executors in the sale; and, in the second, that the
executor was also trustee, so that, as no difficulty arose with respect to
the conveyance of the legal estate, a good title could be made; in the
first case, by the trustees and executors; and in the second case, by the
executor acting in a double capacity alone.

In the case of *Gosling* v. *Carter*, 1 Coll. 644, the testator, after giving
a *general direction* for payment of his debts, gave and bequeathed all
his real and personal estate to his wife for life, with a direction to sell
the same, and divide the proceeds after her decease; and he made his
wife and another person executrix and executor. The executrix and
executor sold the real estate by auction; and upon a bill filed by them
against the purchaser, it was held by Sir. J. L. Knight Bruce, V. C.,
that they had an implied power to sell the estate for payment of debts,
but that the defendant ought not to be compelled to complete the purchase without a conveyance from the heir-at-law. "There is," said his
Honor, "an implied power of sale, because the life interest of the wife
is subject to the general charge for payment of debts; therefore, in a
sense, and in a manner, there does exists a power of selling during the
lifetime of the wife, there being debts, which fact is proved. And I
am of opinion, that there is upon this will an intention exhibited, that
a sale, if made, should be made by the executors, or one of them, and
not otherwise. The next question is, whether this intention is expressed
so as to create a legal power? in which case, the concurrence of the
heir-at-law would not be necessary. I am of opinion this question is
one of too great nicety and difficulty to decide against the purchaser.
If he wishes the concurrence of the heir, he must pay, or not pay, for
the discovery of the heir, according to his contract. Upon that I give
no opinion. But I think that in this suit he is not to be compelled to
take the title from the executor and executrix without the concurrence
of the heir. I decide, therefore, without prejudice to the question,
[*92]   whether *the heir is, or is not, a necessary party to the conveyance, that the executor and executrix, as debts are admitted to
have existed at the time of the sale, had power to sell." And see
Curtis v. *Fulbrook*, 8 Hare, 25, 278.

The question was next considered at law in the case of *Doe* d. *Jones*
v. *Hughes*, 6 Exch. 223; there a testator, after charging all his real and
personal estate with his debts, funeral and testamentary expenses, and
a legacy therein mentioned, subject thereto, gave and devised the rents
and profits of all his messuages, farms, and lands *except his Bala
Houses* to his wife for life, with remainder over to another person in
fee. And he also bequeathed to his wife the whole of his personal
estates, and appointed her sole executrix. It was held by the Court of
Exchequer that the executrix had no implied power to sell or mortgage
the Bala Houses (which descended to the heir) for the payment either
of the debts or of the funeral or testamentary expenses or legacy.

" Upon the argument of this case," said Parke, B., " the several authorities upon the subject were brought before us; and it was contended on behalf of the defendant, that the effect of a charge of the real estates with debts was to give to the executrix an implied power of sale. But upon a due consideration of all the cases, it is perfectly clear that not one of them bears out that proposition. One class of cases shows, that by a devise to trustees of the real estate charged with the testator's debts, the trustees have thereby imposed upon them the duty of raising money to pay those debts; for, as the estate is given to them, they can, through the means of the estate, raise money for the payment of those debts. Another class of cases decides, that if from the whole purview of the will it appears to have been the intention of the testator that his real estate should be sold, and the proceeds of that real estate are to be distributed for the purpose for which it is given, which the executors alone by law could perform, then there is an implied power given them by the will to sell the estate; and that the executor who is to distribute the money is to sell the estate. Several cases were cited which confirm this proposition, and amongst them is that of *Forbes* v. *Peacock*. But upon looking through the cases, not a single authority is to be found which says, that *a simple charge of* the estate with the payment of the debts does more than make a charge upon the estate in the hands of the devisee, if the estate is devised, or upon the estate in the hands of the heir-at-law, if the estate devolves upon him by the law of inheritance. . . . . . The estate is only subjected in the hands of the heir-at-law to a charge for funeral and testamentary expenses, and the charges attending *the proof of the will, which the executrix [*93] must enforce through the medium of a Court of Equity; and we therefore think the executrix had no power to sell or mortgage the estate. It is not within the principle of any of the cases in which it has been held there is an implied power of sale or mortgage." See also *Kenrick* v. *Lord Beauclerk*, 3 B. & P. 175; *Doe* v. *Claridge*, 6 C. B. 641.

The next case to be noticed (apparently conflicting with *Doe* d. *Jones* v. *Hughes*), is the case of *Robinson* v. *Lowater* (17 Beav. 532): there a testator devised some messuages in Rutland Place to his daughter Elizabeth (since deceased) for life, with remainder to all her children living at her decease, and two closes in Sandfield to his son Richard for life, with remainder to the use of his children who should be living at his decease, as tenants in common, with a limitation over in the event of that remainder not taking effect. And he devised his estate at Arnold to his son Richard in fee charged with the payment of the sum of 200*l.* due on mortgage of his messuages devised to his daughter Elizabeth, and of the legacies therein mentioned, and with and to the payment *of his debts*, and funeral and testamentary expenses. But if his premises at Arnold should not be sufficient for that purpose, then he charged his closes at Sandfield with the payment of such deficiency; and he appointed his son Richard sole executor of his will. The testator by a codicil revoked the devise of the Arnold property to his son Richard. The will was proved by the executor, who exhausted the personal estates in payment of debts, except the mortgage debt charged on Rutland Place. He also sold the two closes in Sandfield to Nathaniel Sulley (in whom the legal estate in fee simple was vested as a trustee for the testator and his heirs). The purchaser had notice of the will. The defendant Lowater derived his title to Sandfield from Nathaniel Sulley. The plaintiffs, the children of the testator's daughter Elizabeth, filed a bill, insisting that the Sandfield property was still liable in the hands of the defendant Lowater to pay off the mortgage on the Rutland Place property, which still remained unpaid. The bill however was dismissed by Sir John Romilly, M. R., with costs. " The case of *Doe* d. *Jones* v. *Hughes* (6 Exch. 223)," said his Honor, " is relied upon to show, that the executor could not make a good title to sell, and had no authority to sell vested in him. I find it difficult to reconcile the decision in that case with the numerous authorities to be found on this subject in Chancery; amongst which I may refer to *Ball* v. *Harris* (4 My. & Cr. 264), where Lord Cottenham observes, that a charge of debts [*94] is equivalent to a trust to sell so much as *may be sufficient to pay them; *Forbes* v. *Peacock* (12 Sim. 541), which, on this point, is not affected by the reversal of the decision (1 Ph. 717), and to the case of *Gosling* v. *Carter* (1 Coll. 644).

" Before the case in the Exchequer, I had considered the law to be, that a charge of debts on an estate devised, gave the executors an implied power of sale, because, to use the expression of Sir J. Leach, in *Bentham* v. *Wiltshire*, (4 Madd. 49,) the power to sell is ' implied, from the produce having to pass through their hands in the execution of their office, as in the payment of debts or legacies.' I am of opinion, therefore, that a good title was made to the purchaser Nathaniel Sulley, and that the defendants claiming under him are entitled to hold it, discharged from all claims in favour of the plaintiffs." This decision upon appeal was affirmed by the Lords Justices (5 De G. Mac. & G. 272). During the argument the Lord Justice Knight Bruce, with reference to *Doe* d. *Jones* v. *Hughes*, put the following pertinent question; " Does that case deal with anything beyond the question of *the legal estate*? Can it govern the present, which is an application to a Court of equity to give effect to a charge?" Again, Lord Justice Turner asked; " Does a charge of debts amount to a direction to institute a Chancery suit? Would not that consequence follow from holding that the executor could not sell?" In giving judgment, Lord Justice Turner made the following observations: " The question is, how and by whom the money was to be raised. The purpose for which it was to be raised being to pay debts, it must

have been in the contemplation of the testator that it would have to be
raised *immediately*, but no power is given to the devisees to raise it;
and the will, containing a devise of a life estate, with contingent remainders over, it is impossible that, during the subsistence of those
contingent remainders, the devisees could themselves raise it. On the
face of this will, therefore, it was not the intention of the testator that
the money should be raised by the devisees. Then who was to raise it?
Surely the persons who would have to apply the fund. It seems to me,
therefore, upon the whole scope of this will, without reference to the
cases decided upon the subject, that in this case, at least, it was the intention of the testator that the money should be raised by the executor;
and if by the executor, then the executor must be considered as invested
with all the powers necessary to raise it. I think there is abundant
reason for the conclusion at which the Master of the Rolls has arrived
in this case." See also *Eidsforth* v. *Armstead*, 2 K. & J. 333; *Ogden*
v. *Lowry*, 25 L. J. (Ch.) N. S. 198.

In *Wrigley* v. *Sykes*, 21 Beav. *337, a testator ordered all his [*95]
debts, funeral and testamentary expenses, and legacies "to be
paid and discharged out of his real and personal estate." He then devised certain freehold messuages to trustees for a term of 500 years,
upon the trusts thereinafter mentioned, and subject thereto to his five
sons in fee, as tenants in common, *upon condition* that they should pay,
in equal shares, certain specified legacies and annuities, and also all his
mortgage and *other debts*. The *trusts* of the *term* of 500 years were
declared to be, that if any of the sons should, thirty days after demand,
refuse to pay his proportion of the legacies, annuities, mortgage, and
other debts, the trustees should, out of the rents, of the share of such
son levy such sums unpaid, and all costs; and he appointed his five
sons executors. Thirty-three years after the death of the testator, the
surviving executors sold the estate, as they alleged, to pay the debts.
Sir John Romilly, M. R., held that they had power to sell, and decreed
a specific performance against the purchaser. " I do not think," said
his Honor, "that the creation of the term, which has a distinct and
specified object, supersedes the general charge for payment of debts;
which, in my opinion, gives the executors a power of selling the estate
for payment of debts. And in that view of the case, I am of opinion,
that this is a valid contract. It is very true that the Court will not
compel a person to take a doubtful title; but if the Court is of opinion,
upon due consideration of the question of law, that the title is good,
the Court is bound so to hold, and it cannot, in my opinion, decline to
do so, because it is impossible, that when the case arises between the
parties, some other Court may come to an opposite or contrary conclusion; and, therefore, I am of opinion, that I am right, in this case, in
compelling the purchaser to take what, in my opinion, is not a doubtful
title. I shall certainly secure to the purchaser, as far as it is competent

for the Court to do so, a good legal estate when the conveyance is made;
but as I am of opinion that the executors had power to enter into the
contract which is not disputed, and as, in my opinion, the title is good,
I must decree specific performance." See also *Sabin* v. *Heape*, 27 Beav.
553; *Bolton* v. *Stannard*, 6 W. R. (M. R.) 570; *Greetham* v. *Colton*,
34 Beav. 615, 11 Jur. N. S. 848.

The conclusion which may be drawn from these cases, seems to be
this, that where there is a general charge of debts upon real estate, the
executors have in *equity* an implied power to sell it, and they alone can
give a valid receipt for the purchase money, but as they do not take by
implication a legal power to sell, and cannot therefore convey the legal
[*96] estate, (*Doe* d. *Jones* v. *Hughes*, 6 Exch. *223,) the persons in
whom it is vested (if it be not already in the executors by devise
or otherwise) must concur with them in the conveyance. This conclusion reconciles all the cases in equity with the apparently conflicting
authority of *Doe* d. *Jones* v. *Hughes*. See also *Hodkinson* v. *Quinn*, 1
J. & H. 303, 309; *Hooper* v. *Strutton*, 12 W. R. (V. C. S.) 367.

Real estate in the hands of an alienee of a devisee, or heir-at-law,
where there has been *no charge* of debts by a testator, is discharged
from the debts, and the heir or devisee only remains personally liable
(*Richardson* v. *Horton*, 7 Beav. 112; *Spackman* v. *Timbrell*, 8 Sim.
253; *Pimm* v. *Insall*, 1 Mac. & G. 449; *Kinderley* v. *Jervis*, 22 Beav.
1; *Jones* v. *Noyes*, 4 Jur., N. S. 1033; *Dilkes* v. *Broadmead*, 2 De G.,
F. & Jo. 566; *Hines* v. *Redington*, 13 T. Ch. R. 206). But though
there be no charge of debts, a conveyance to new trustees is not such
an alienation under 3 Will. & M. c. 14, s. 7, as would prevent the
interests so aliened from being affected by an execution at the suit of
the creditors of the devisor (*Coope* v. *Cresswell*, 2 L. R. Ch. App. 112,
122); nor would a mortgage by an equitable tenant for life under the
will be such an alienation, though it seems a Court of equity would
protect the interest of the mortgagee from execution. *Ibid.*

Where, however, there *is a charge of debts* upon real estate, a purchaser from the heir or devisee, or their alienee, cannot safely complete
without either the concurrence of the executors, or without being satisfied that all the debts have been paid. See *Storry* v. *Walsh*, 18 Beav.
559; *Hope* v. *Liddell*, 21 Beav. 183. In *Austin* v. *Martin*, 29 Beav.
523, real estate was devised to A. B. and his heirs in trust to sell, with
power to the trustee or trustees to give receipts for the purchase-money.
A. B. was to pay the debts and hold the surplus on certain trusts, and
he was appointed sole executor. A. B. having renounced and disclaimed, it was held by Sir J. Romilly, M. R., that the heir-at-law, who
had taken out administration, could sell the estate and give valid
receipts.

The opinion among conveyancers, nevertheless, appears to be, that
where, subject to a charge of debts, an estate is devised to persons

either beneficially or as trustees for special purposes, a sale can be affected by them alone; and Lord St.'Leonards, in the last edition of his work on Vendors and Purchasers, with reference to the cases of *Robinson* v. *Lowater*, and *Wrigley* v. *Sykes*, says, " They have introduced considerable difficulty upon titles, by implying a power of sale in executors from a charge of debts, although the estate is devised to others. This is *contrary to the received opinion. It would not [*97] be safe to rely on the authority of these cases." See an article in the " Jurist," vol. ii., N. S. 68. Sugd. V. & P., 13 ed. p. 545, n. (1). See also, " Dart's V. & P." 567, 568, 569, 4th ed.

We must remember, however, that *Robinson* v. *Lowater* is stamped with the high authority of the Lords Justices of the Court of Appeal. See also *Hamilton* v. *Buckmaster*, 3 L. R. Eq. 323.

Where there is an express trust for sale, at a particular period which has arrived, the trustees can sell, without the concurrence of the executors, who might previously have sold under the implied power arising from a general charge of debts. See *Hodkinson* v. *Quinn*, 1 J. & H. 303; there a testator, after a charge of debts, devised certain real estates, subject to the payment of his said debts, to trustees upon trusts for his daughters and their families, and after the death of the surviving daughter, upon trust to sell with power to give receipts, and to apply the proceeds after satisfying all incumbrances affecting the said real estates, upon certain trusts. The daughters being both dead, it was held on demurrer by Sir W. Page Wood, V. C., that the trustees could make a good title without the executors. " It would," said his Honor, " be a very serious conclusion to hold that this decision of *Robinson* v. *Lowater*, has rendered it possible for executors to sell after an actual alienation by devisees. None of the authorities have gone that length. They decide only that the executors have that power . . . . Irrespectively of the reasons afforded by this particular will, I should be inclined to hold generally, that any sale by trustees under a power, prior to an actual sale by executors, would be effectual. But in this will, even assuming that the executors have a complete legal power, when you find it prescribed as the duty of the trustees to exercise another power at a given period, for the express purpose (among others) of doing what the executors' power is intended to effect, it follows that a sale by the trustees must be completely effectual, and no executor could afterwards insist on the right under his implied power to disturb that sale."

The law upon this subject has been partially altered by 22 & 23 Vict. c. 35 (Property and Trustees Relief Amendment Act), passed 13th August, 1859, by which it is enacted, that " where by any will which shall come into operation after the passing of this Act, the testator shall have charged his real estate, or any specific portion thereof, with the payments of his debts, or with the payment of any legacy or other specific sum of money, and shall have devised the estate so charged to any trustee or trustees for the whole of his estate or interest therein, and [*98] *shall not have made any express provision for the raising of such debt, legacy, or sum of money out of such estate, it shall be lawful for the said devisee or devisees in trust, notwithstanding any trusts actually declared by the testator, to raise such debts, legacy, or money as aforesaid, by a sale and absolute disposition by public auction or private contract of the said hereditaments or any part thereof, or by a mortgage of the same, or partly in one mode and partly in the other, and any deed or deeds of mortgage so executed may reserve such rate of interest, and fix such period or periods of repayment, as the person or persons executing the same shall think proper" (sect. 14).

The powers conferred by the last section shall extend to all and every person or persons in whom the estate devised shall for the time being be vested by survivorship, descent, or devise, or to any person or persons who may be appointed under any power in the will, or by the Court of Chancery, to succeed to the trusteeship vested in such devisee or devisees in trust as aforesaid (sect. 15).

If any testator who shall have created such a charge as is described in the fourteenth section, shall not have devised the hereditaments charged as aforesaid in such terms as that his whole estate and interest therein shall become vested in any trustee or trustees, the executor or executors for the time being named in such will (if any) shall have the same or the like power of raising the said monies as is hereinbefore vested in the devisee or devisees in trust of the said hereditaments, and such power shall from time to time devolve to and become vested in the person or persons (if any) in whom the executorship shall for the time being be vested; but any sale or mortgage under this Act shall operate only on the estate and interest, whether legal or equitable, of the testator, and shall not render it unnecessary to get in any outstanding subsisting legal estate (sect. 16).

Purchasers or mortgagees shall not be bound to inquire whether the powers conferred by sections fourteen, fifteen, and sixteen of this Act, or either of them, shall have been duly and correctly exercised by the person or persons acting in virtue thereof (sect. 17).

The provisions contained in sections fourteen, fifteen, and sixteen, shall not in any way prejudice or affect any sale or mortgage already made or hereafter to be made, under or in pursuance of any will coming into operation before the passing of this Act; but the validity of any such sale or mortgage shall be ascertained and determined in all respects as if this Act had not passed; and the said several sections shall not extend to a devise to any person or persons in fee or in tail, or for the [*99] *testator's whole estate and interest charged with debts, or legacies, nor shall they affect the power of any such devisee or devisees to sell or mortgage as he or they may by law now do (sect. 18).

By this Act, says a learned writer, the difficulty created by the decisions has been removed in two cases; 1st, by giving a devisee of the fee, who is a trustee for totally foreign purposes, a power to sell or mortgage for the satisfaction of the charge of debts; and, 2ndly, by giving the executor a power to sell or mortgage when the estate is cut up by successive limitations without the intervention of a trustee of the legal fee. But in cases where the testator died before the 13th August, 1859, or where there is a devise, subject to a charge of debts, to a beneficial owner in fee or in tail, or for all other the testator's interest in the estate, the Act leaves this question in the same doubt and perplexity as before. No testator, then, ought to create a charge of debts upon his real estate, without at the same time expressly creating a trust or power for giving effect to the charge, and without distinctly pointing out the persons by whom the trust or power is to be exercised: Hayes and Jarm. Conc. Forms of Wills, by Eastwood, p. 467.

As to what constitutes a charge of debts, see note to *Silk* v. *Prime*, vol. 2, post.

The cases in this country on the foregoing subject, which are not numerous, may be distinguished into three classes: 1. Relating to sales of personal property by executors, guardians, and other trustees; 2. To sales of real estate under a power in a deed or will to sell for the payment of debts, legacies, or other charges; 3. To sales of real estate by trustees, in a settlement, in pursuance of a power to sell and re-invest. In regard to all of these, it may be considered as the prevailing doctrine in the American courts, that a purchaser from a trustee is not bound to see to the application of the purchase-money, except where the sale is a breach of trust on the part of the trustee, and the purchaser has, either from the face of the transaction itself, or *aliunde*, notice or knowledge of the trustee's violation of duty: but if he has such knowledge or notice as makes him a party or privy to the trustee's misconduct, the property will be affected in his hands with the trusts which previously attached to it: *Nicholls* v. *Peak*, 1 Beasley, 69, 73. This may be considered as established in respect to sales for the payment of debts generally, and sales for payment of debts and legacies, and to sales for reinvestment; *Rutledge* v. *Smith*, 1 Busbee's Eq. 127; *Lening* v. *Peyton*, 2 Dessaussure, 378; *Sims* v. *Lively*, 14 B. Monroe, 433; and though perhaps not expressly decided in the case of sales under a charge for certain specified debts, yet the principles acted upon by the courts seem to cover that ground; *Tillinghast* v. *Champlin*, 4 Rhode Island, 173, 213. See the subject discussed at length in *Garnett, &c.,* v. *Macon et al.,* 6 Call. 309, 354; S. C., 1 Brock. 185, &c.; and see also *Jackson et al.* v. *Updegraffe et al.,* 1 Robinson's Virginia, 107, 120; *Duncan* v. *Jaudon,* 15 Wallace, 365.

1. *In regard to sales of personal property by an executor, guardian, or other trustee.*]—The liability of a purchaser of a testator's assets from his executor was carefully examined by Chancellor Kent in *Field* v. *Schieffelin*, 7 Johnson's Chancery, 150, 160. After a review of the English cases, he concludes as follows: — "They all agree in this, that the purchaser is safe, if he is no party to any fraud in the executor, and has no knowledge or proof that the executor intended to misapply the proceeds, or was in fact by the very transaction, applying them to the extinguishing of his own private debt. The great difficulty has been, to determine how far the purchaser dealt at his peril, when he knew from the very face of the proceeding, that the executor was applying the assets to his own private purposes, as the payment of his own debt. The later and the better doctrine is, that in such a case, he does buy at his peril; but that, if he has no such proof or knowledge, he is not bound to inquire into the state of the trust, because he has no means to support the inquiry, and he may safely repose on the general presumption that the executor is in the due exercise of his trust." And this principle was applied in that case to a purchase from a guardian. It is well settled in accordance with this decision that a bona fide purchaser from an executor, administrator or guardian is not bound to see to the application of the purchase-money; *Hertell* v. *Bogert*, 9 Paige, 57; *Yerger* v. *Jones*, 16 Howard, 57; *Davis* v. *Christian*, 15 Grattan, 9; *Tyrrell* v. *Morris*, 1 Dev. & Batt. 559; *Bond* v. *Zeigler*, 1 Kelly, 324. In like manner, in *Petrie* v. *Clark and others*, 11 Sergeant and Rawle, 377, 385, where the right of creditors and legatees, to follow assets that have been collusively parted with by an executor, was examined by Gibson, J., the principle was declared, that such a right did not exist at law, for the executor is the owner of the legal title to the goods, and may dispose of them by any species of voluntary alienation by which he may dispose of his own, but that equity gives relief on the ground that the executor, though complete owner of the legal title, is *quasi*, a trustee for creditors and legatees, and that it will follow assets into the hands of any one who is not a purchaser for *valuable consideration*, or who having paid a *valuable consideration, has been guilty of fraud and collusion with the executor;* and that an executor's applying the assets in payment of his own debt, is of itself a circumstance of suspicion, which ought to put the purchasing creditor upon inquiry as to the propriety of the transaction.

[The purchase must be in good faith, and for value, and the purchaser will be answerable if there is a want of valuable consideration, or sufficient ground for inferring *mala fides*. Hence, a sale or pledge as security or payment for the antecedent debt of an executor will be invalid, if the party to whom it is made knows that the property belongs to the estate; *Williamson* v. *The Branch Bank*, 7 Alabama, 906; *Austin* v. *Wilson*, 21 Indiana, 252; *Stronach* v. *Stronach*, 20 Wisconsin, 129; *Dodson* v. *Simpson*, 2 Randolph, 294; *Williamson* v. *Morton*, 2 Maryland, Ch. 94; *Wilson* v. *Doster*, 7 Iredell's Eq. 231; *Miller* v. *Williamson*, 5 Maryland, 219; while a pledge for a pre-existing debt will fail for want of a sufficient consideration, although he buys in good faith, (*Petrie* v. *Clark*,) under a mistaken belief that it belongs to the executor; *Hertell* v. *Bogert*, 11 Paige, 57; *Garrard* v. *The Railroad*, 5 Casey, 154: a precedent debt not being in itself a valuable consideration, although such a consideration may, as it would seem, grow out of its suspension or extinguishment; 2 Am. Lead. Cases, 226, 5th ed.; *post*, notes to *Bassett* v. *Nosworthy.* But a pledge for a contemporaneous advance will, as it seems, be good, if free from fraud; *Tyrrell* v. *Morris*, 1 Dev. & Bat. Eq. 559; *Williamson* v. *Morton*, 2 Maryland, Ch. 94, 100; *Mills* v. *Durnford*, 13 English Law & Equity, 123, 124; *Ashton* v. *The Atlantic Bank*, 3 Allen, 217; 2 American Lead. Cases, 235, 5th ed. Fraud will be presumed in equity, if not at law, wherever the purchaser knows, or has such notice as is equivalent to knowledge, that the property belongs to the estate, and that the executor is applying, or means to apply, the proceeds of the sale to his own use; *Sacia* v. *Borthoud*, 17 Barbour, 15; *Swink* v. *Snodgrass*, 17 Alabama, 653; *Parker* v.

Gilliam, 10 Yerger, 394; *Rhame* v. *Lewis*, 13 Richardson's Eq. 269; *Miller* v. *Williamson; Williamson* v. *Morton.* Entire good faith and the payment of value are consequently requisite to give validity to a purchase from an executor or trustee who is acting in fraud of the trust, and equity will follow the assets into the hands of any one who acquires them *mala fide* or without paying a valuable consideration; *Rhame* v. *Lewis; Champlin* v. *Haught*, 10 Paige, 275; *Nicholls* v. *Peak*, 1 Beasley, 69; *Garrard* v. *The Rail Road*, 5 Casey, 154; *The Rail Road* v. *Barker*, Ib. 160. But the bad faith of an executor or his misappropriation of the purchase-money, will not invalidate the title of the purchaser, unless it is in some way brought home to the purchaser at or before the final completion of the sale by delivery and payment; *Hortell* v. *Boyert* 9 Paige, 59; *Bond* v. *Ziegler*, 1 Kelly, 324; *Wilson* v. *Doster*, 7 Iredell, Eq. 231; *Polk* v. *Robinson*, Id. 235; *Pipkin* v. *Casey*, 13 Missouri, 347; *Williamson* v. *Morton*, 2 Maryland, Ch. 94, 103. In like manner, the purchase of partnership property from one or more of the partners, without the concurrence of the rest, does not render it necessary to see that the purchase-money is applied to the use of the firm, even when the purchase is made from a surviving partner, and consists of real estate belonging to the partnership, and consequently charged with a trust for the estate of the deceased partner, and through him for the joint creditors of the partnership; *Tillinghast* v. *Champlin*, 4 Rhode Island, 173, 213. But if the purchaser is, or ought to be, aware that the sale is made in fraud of the duty of the surviving partner to administer the assets fairly for the benefit of all concerned, or with a view to a fraudulent use of the proceeds for his private purposes, he will become *particeps criminis*, and be liable to those whom he has aided to injure; *Hoxie* v. *Carr*, 1 Sumner, 193; *Dyer* v. *Clark*, 5 Metcalf, 580; *Tillinghast* v. *Champlin:* and it would seem that such participation will be implied from the mere fact of accepting a conveyance from a surviving partner of his legal title, as tenant in common, with notice that the land is partnership property, and that the partnership is insolvent; because, under these circumstances, the vendor has nothing which he can properly convey as his own, and ought to dispose of the property as a whole, to the best advantage and apply the proceeds to the payment of the debts of the firm : *Champlin* v. *Tillinghast ; Hoxie* v. *Carr ; Tapley* v. *Butterfield*, 1 Metcalf, 515; 1 American Leading Cases, 609, 5th ed.]

2. *In regard to sales of real estate under a power to sell for payment of debts or legacies.*]—It is universally agreed, that upon a sale of lands under a charge or trust for the payment of debts generally, the purchaser is not bound to see to the application of the purchase-money; *Gardner et al.* v. *Gardner et al.*, 3 Mason, 178, 218; *Potter* v. *Gardner*, 12 Wheaton, 498; *Laurens* v. *Lucas*, 6 Richardson, Eq. 217; *Williams* v. *Otey*, 8 Humphreys, 568; *Hauser* v. *Shore*, 5 Iredell, Eq. 357 ; *Goodrich* v. *Proctor*, 1 Gray, 567; *Davis* v. *Christian*, 15 Grattan, 11, 40 ; *Garnet* v. *Macon*, 2 Brockenborough, 185; *Dalsell* v. *Crawford*, 1 Parson, Eq. 57 ; *Redheimer* v. *Byron*, 1 Spear, Eq. 134. See *Stall* v. *Cincinnati*, 16 Ohio, N. S. 169. The rule and the reason of it were concisely given by Lord Cranworth in *Colyer* v. *Finch*, 5 House of Lord's Cases, 923. " Where the devisee of real estate charged with payment of debts sells, the purchaser has no need to inquire at all whether the money is applied in payment of debts, or even whether it is a sale for the purpose of enabling debts to be paid. The old case of *Elliot* v. *Merryman*, which is always referred to before Lord Hardwicke, makes no such distinction as to whether it was expressed to be made for payment of debts or not. If there is a charge on the devisee in fee; if he takes the estate charged with the payment of debts alone, or debts and legacies, and if he sells, the great convenience of mankind requires that it should be just as if an executor sells when property comes to him, unless it can be shown that the purchaser knew that the purchase-money was not going to be so employed, and he was ancillary to something like a fraud, because he may presume that the sale has taken place in the ordinary administration of the duties which were imposed upon the executor by the will."

It seems to be equally clear, that where the trust is for the payment of debts generally, and also for the payment of legacies, the purchaser is not bound to see the money applied, upon a sale made for the payment of legacies ; because, to hold that he is bound to see the legacies paid, would in fact involve him in the account of the debts, which must first be paid ; *Grant* v. *Hook*, 13 Sergeant & Rawle, 259, 262 ; *Cadbury* v. *Duval*, 10 Barr, 265 ; *Andrews* v. *Sparhawk*, 13 Pickering, 393, 401 ; *Sims* v. *Lively*, 14 B. Monroe, 435 ; see also *Bruch* v. *Ihrie*, 2 Rawle, 392, 417. And it would seem also, that under a devise for the payment of legacies, the purchaser is not bound to see to the application of the purchase money, because, by the law, the debts, generally, must be first paid ; though there is a dictum to the contrary in *Grant* v. *Hook:* and in *Hannum et al.* v. *Spear*, 1 Yeates, 553 ; S. C., 2 Dallas, 291, it was held that when land was sold under a devise for the payment of legacies, it was subject in the purchaser's hands to the lien of debts. With regard to the case of a trust or charge for the payment of certain specified or scheduled debts, there are *dicta*, indeed, recognizing a distinction between it and the case where the devise is for the payment of debts generally ; *Gardner et al.* v. *Gardner et al.*, 3 Mason, 178, 218 ; *Duffy* v. *Calvert*, 6 Gill, 48 ; *St. Mary's Church* v. *Stockton*, 4 Halsted, Ch. 520 ; *Wormly* v. *Wormly*, 8 Wheaton, 422. But though such a distinction is reasonable in England, where, without a

power or charge created by will, lands are not a trust in the hands of executors for the payment of debts, yet in this country, where, generally, if not universally, the law affects the lands of a decedent, with a charge or trust for the satisfaction of his debts, which is paramount to any specific charge in his will, this distinction appears to be inapplicable. In principle, it would seem, that in those states in which lands are subject to be sold by an executor, under an order of court, for the payment of a testator's general debts, a charge or appropriation, by will, of lands to certain specified debts, is without operation or effect in regard to the present purpose ; because, it must be subordinate to the charge and appropriation which the law makes, independently of the devise, and in all cases alike the money must be disposed of, not according to the will of the testator, but according to law : and see the remarks of Wilson, P., in *Cryder's Appeal*, 1 Jones, 72, 74. Under such a system, the purchase money is not to be paid directly to the creditor specified by the testator, but must come into the accounts of the executor, and be disposed of under the direction of the court having jurisdiction of the accounts ; and, of course, the purchaser is not to follow it through the court. Wherever the law creates a general trust of lands for the payment of debts, collateral and paramount to the special appropriation made by the testator, the case becomes similar to that considered in the preceding note, of a general charge by will for payment of debts followed by a specific disposition, as in the cases *Jenkins* v. *Hiles*, 6 Vesey, 654, n., and *Shaw* v. *Borrer*, 1 Keen, 559. These views are sustained by the reasoning in *Grant* v. *Hook*, and the conclusion seems to be inevitable, that upon a sale under a testamentary charge or trust for the payment of specific or scheduled debts, in those states in which the lands are by law subject to be sold by executors for the payment of debts, the purchaser is not bound to see to the application of the money, because the application is not to be according to the schedule or specification fixed by the testator, and under the direct intervention of the purchaser, but according to the law which regulates the priority of debts, and under the control and supervision of the court. It is well settled that a purchaser under a decree of a court has no concern with the disposition which the court may make of the purchase-money, nor can his right as a purchaser be affected by any misapplication which he may make of it; *Coombs* v. *Jordan*, 3 Bland, 284, 329; *Wilson, &c.*, v. *Davisson*, 2 Robinson's Virginia, 385, 412. The case is not materially different where the power is given to a testamentary trustee, and not to the executor; a purchaser, if he undertook to see to the application of the purchase money, would still be involved in the accounts of the estate. A trust for payment of particular debts, is much less specific and immediate than in the instance of a sale of trust property for re-investment; and the cases, under the next head, which hold the purchaser, there, to be liable only where there is collusion, appear, *a fortiori*, to determine this point.

But though, under a devise for the payment of debts generally, the purchaser who pays the purchase-money to the person authorized to sell, is not bound to look to its application, yet if the purchase-money is misapplied with the co-operation of the purchaser, or if he become directly or indirectly *particeps criminis*, by buying with intent to misapply the proceeds, he will remain liable to the creditors for the sum so misapplied; *Potter* v. *Gardner*, 12 Wheaton, 499, 502; *Clyde* v. *Simpson*, 4 Ohio, N. S., 445, 464; *Chaplin* v. *Haight*, 10 Paige, 275; *Nicholls* v. *Peak*, 1 Beasley, 69, 73.

In Pennsylvania, by statute of Feb. 24, 1834, s. 19, in case of sales of a decedent's estate by an executor for any purpose, the purchaser may pay his money into the Orphans' Court, or with leave of that court, to the executor, and the payment shall be valid against all persons.

[Whatever the rule may be where land is sold by an executor, or trustee for the benefit of creditors, and where the proceeds are consequently primarily applicable to the payment of debts, although the sale may be made professedly for a different purpose, there can be little doubt that where the trust is exclusively for the payment of legacies, scheduled debts, or other definite and ascertained charge, it is the duty of the purchaser to see to the application of the purchase-money, unless the intention of the donor clearly was to exonerate him, and throw the whole responsibility on the trustee; *Duffy* v. *Calvert*, 6 Gill, 487; *Downman* v. *Rust*, 6 Randolph, 527. Thus, where land which had been devised to one Simpson, subject to, and charged with, certain legacies, was sold by Simpson with the view of paying a debt for which he had mortgaged the land to Clyde, the Court said, that the purchaser, Miller, was bound to see to the application of the purchase money, and that he consequently would have been answerable to the legatees, even if he had not been aware of the intended misappropriation of the proceeds of the sale by Simpson; and the case may, consequently, be considered as an authority for the former point, although it might have been rested solely on the latter; *Clyde* v. *Simpson*, 4 Ohio, N. S., 445. "It is certain," said Ranney, J., in delivering the opinion of the court, "that Simpson was invested with a power to sell the property devised, (8 Sim. R. 485; Myl. & Cro. R. 264; 1 Kee. 559;) and that no distinction is to be taken between estates devised in trust, or those only charged with the payment of debts or legacies; 2 Sug. on Vend. 38; 2 Story's Eq. sec. 1127; 7 Ves. jr. 323. But, in either case, the general rule undoubtedly is, that wherever the trust or charge is of a defined or limited nature, the purchaser must himself see that the purchase-money is applied to the proper discharge of the trust; but wherever the trust is of a general and unlimited nature, he need not see to it; 2 Story's Eq. sec. 1129; 2 Sug. on Vend. 32; *Murray* v. *Ballou*, 1 Johns. Ch. R. 556.

"In the application of this rule, it has been generally held, that where the trust is created, or the charge imposed, for the payment of a portion, a mortgage, legacies, or scheduled debts, which are definitely ascertained and to be paid over immediately to the person entitled, the purchaser, in the view of a Court of equity, is bound to see that the money is actually applied to their discharge before the estate is relieved from the burden. But where the trust is created, or the charge exists, for the payment of debts generally, or for the payment of debts and legacies, when an account of the debts necessarily precedes the payment of the legacies; or, where the money is to be reinvested or otherwise applied by the trustee to the purposes which require time, deliberation, and discretion on his part, the purchaser is relieved from such responsibility, and *cestuis que trust* must look alone to the trustee.

"I am aware, that several eminent judges have been of opinion, that a purchaser is in no case bound to see to the application of purchase-money, where the deed or will has designated the person to receive it; and that a power to sell necessarily includes the incidental power to give a valid discharge for the purchase-money;

and Mr. Powell has defended the same opinion, with much ingenuity and force; 1 Pow. on Mort. 312. But the general course of decision has clearly been otherwise.

" In this case, the amount of the legacies, and the persons to receive them, are distinctly defined in the will; and they were entitled to payment as soon as the time fixed in the will arrived. There is probably nothing to relieve it from the operation of the general principle; but it does not need the aid of that principle. There never has been any difference of opinion that if the purchaser knew that the sale involved a breach of trust, or that the money was not to be applied in payment of the debts or legacies charged upon the estate, he would be compelled to hold the property subject to the charge: 2 Sug. on Vend. 39; *Watkins* v. *Cheek*, 2 Sim. & Stu. 199; *Wormley* v. *Wormley*, 8 Wheat. 421; *Gardner* v. *Gardner*, 3 Mason, 178.

" Now, at the time Miller made his purchase, he was fully aware, not only in fact, but from the notice furnished by the *lis pendens*, that the legacies were not paid, and that no part of the money received from Clyde had been applied to that purpose; while he advanced his money to pay off Clyde, and denied the existence of any lien in favor of the legatees. He participated in the breach of trust, and after finding himself mistaken as to the lien, he stands upon no ground to insist that it has been discharged."

When, however, the interests of the beneficiaries under a trust, growing out of a devise of land to be sold, or subject to a power of sale, are left uncertain by the testator, and depend for certainty, either as to amount or time of payment, on the choice or discretion of the devisee, the purchasers will not be answerable for the execution of a trust which he has no express or implied power to superintend or control; *Steele* v. *Livesay*, 11 Grattan, 454; *Carrington* v. *Gaden*, 13 Id. 587.]

3. *Where a sale is made by a trustee under a power to sell and re-invest upon the same trust.*]—In *Lining* v. *Peyton*, 2 Dessaussure, 375, a marriage settlement authorized the *cestuis que trust* to sell the lands to any person they pleased, provided the proceeds should be immediately laid out and vested in the purchase of some other estate of equal value, to be secured upon the same trusts; and a purchaser under this power submitted to the court whether it was his duty to see to the appropriation of the consideration-money to the purposes of the trust estate. " Whatever may be the law in Great Britain on this subject," said Chancellor Rutledge in delivering the decree, "there are a variety of local circumstances which render it not only highly improper, but almost impracticable that it should be adopted in this country. The case before us proves the position, for scarcely would a purchaser be found of trust estates who would be inclined to be saddled with the inconvenience and embarrassment of

seeing that the purchase-money was applied to the purposes of the trust. It has never heretofore been determined that he should, and we will not now establish a precedent, for it might tend exceedingly to embarrass, if not shake to the foundation, the titles of very many persons who have heretofore purchased at the sales of the trust estates without the remotest idea of responsibility, as to the application of the purchase-money. We do not say that where property has been conveyed in trust for the payment of debts, or other specific purposes, that it is not the duty as well as the interest of purchasers at such sales to attend to the right appropriation of the money; but in cases like the present, and others that may be assimilated to it, purchasers are not, and ought not to be considered in the same light as trustees, and intrude themselves on the parties to see that the purchase-money is applied as the trust deed directs, because the *cestui que trust* joining in the conveyance with the trustee, it is his particular duty as well as his interest to see the trust money properly applied, and if he finds the trustee disposed to misapply it, he can immediately apply to this court for redress. The court are therefore of opinion and decree, that in this case the complainant is not obliged to attend to the disposition of the purchase-money of the estate, conceiving that the *cestuis que trust*, who are parties to the conveyance, are fully competent, and the only persons who ought

to interest themselves in the business." Notwithstanding the narrow ground of this decision, the case is referred to in *Redheimer* ads. *Pyron*, 1 Spear's Equity, 135, 141, as establishing that, in general, purchasers from a trustee are not bound to see to the application of the purchase-money. "It might be a question, however," said the court in the latter case, "if the purchasers know that the trustee intends to misapply the money, and pay it to him with that knowledge, they might not, in the event of his insolvency, be compelled to make good any deficiency of the fund." And *Wormley* v. *Wormley*, 8 Wheaton, 422, 442, establishes the principle, that if a trustee in a marriage settlement under a power to sell and re-invest, sells under circumstances that constitute a breach of trust, namely not for the purpose of re-investment, but for the purpose of paying his own debts, and the purchaser has notice of this, the land in his hands is affected with the trusts which previously attached to it.

In New York the Revised Statutes (vol. 1, p. 730, ss. 65, 66,) provide, that, " where the trust shall be expressed in the instrument creating the estate, every sale, conveyance or other act of the trustees, in contravention of the trust, shall be absolutely void," but that "no person who shall actually and in good faith pay a sum of money to a trustee, which the trustee as such is authorized to receive, shall be responsible for the proper application of such money, according to the trust;

nor shall any right or title, derived by him from such trustee, in consideration of such payment, be impeached or called in question, in consequence of any misapplication, by the trustee, of the moneys paid." Since these provisions, it has been held, that if a purchaser under a power in a will to trustees to sell and invest the proceeds, for the purposes of the trust, has express notice, at the time of sale, that the sale was not made for the purpose of investing the proceeds in conformity with the trust created in the will, but for a different purpose, he is not protected; *Champlin* v. *Haight*, 10 Paige, 275; reversed on another point, on appeal, 7 Hill, 245.

[All the cases seem to agree, that where the disposition of the proceeds depends in any material particular, upon the discretion of the trustee, or where an interval must or may properly elapse between the sale and the application of the purchase-money, the purchaser will be freed from liability by a payment to the trustee, and will not be responsible for a subsequent misappropriation by the latter; *Wormley* v. *Wormley*, 8 Wheaton, 422; *Davis* v. *Christian*, 15 Grattan, 411; *Sims* v. *Lively*, 14 B. Monroe, 433, 449; *Coonrod* v. *Coonrod*, 6 Hammond, 114; *Hauser* v. *Shore*, 5 Iredell, Eq. 357. Trusts for sale and reinvestment, are emphatically within the operation of this principle, because every investment requires the exercise of discretion in the selection and choice of the security, and must necessarily be delayed until a suita-

ble opportunity is found for investing; and the rule has consequently been said to be, that where a trustee is required or authorized to sell and reinvest for the same trusts or purposes, the purchaser will be discharged from responsibility for the application of the money paid by him to the trustee; *Dalzell* v. *Crawford*, 1 Peason's Eq. 37, 50; *Lanning* v. *Peyton*, 12 Dessaussure, 375; *Redheimer* v. *Peyron*, 1 Spear, Eq. 141; *Sims* v. *Lively*; *Nicholls* v. *Peak*, 1 Beasley, 69, 72; *Coonrod* v. *Coonrod*, 6 Hammond, 114.

In general, one who deals with an executor or trustee, is entitled to presume that he is acting in good faith, and in the due discharge of the duties of his office: *Urban* v. *Hopkins*, 17 Iowa, 105; and hence the title of a purchaser from a trustee who is authorized to sell for the payment of debts, will, in general, be equally good, whether there are, in point of fact, any debts or not; *Garnett* v. *Macon*, 6 Call; 2 Brockenborough, 185; *Williamson* v. *Morton*, 2 Maryland, Ch. 94, 103; *Davis* v. *Christian*, 15 Grattan, 9, 40. The purchaser is not to judge at his peril as to the necessity for a sale. That question is one which the purchaser has ordinarily no means of determining, and which he may, therefore, properly refer to the judgment of the trustee.

The principle is a general one, and applies wherever the founder of the trust vests a discretionary power in the executor or trustee, and leaves him to determine when and how it shall be exercised; *Carrington* v. *Gadden*, 13 Grattan, 587.

But the purchaser will unquestionably be liable to the *cestui que trust*, if he knows that the trustee is acting in violation of his trust, or even, that he entertains such a design and sells as a means of accomplishing it; *Garnett* v. *Macon; Williamson* v. *Morton; Clyde* v. *Simpson*, 4 Ohio, N. S. 445; *Graff* v. *Castleman*, 5 Randolph, 195; *Jackson* v. *Updegraff*, 1 Robinson, 107; *Peackard* v. *Woods*, 8 Grattan, 140. One who buys from an agent, executor, or trustee, knowing that he intends to misappropriate the purchase-money is *particeps criminis.*

For a like reason, one who accepts a bond or other security, from an officer of a bank or railway for a private debt, with notice that it is the property of the corporation may be compelled to refund; *Garrard* v. *The Railroad Company*, 5 Casey, 154, *ante.* 110.

It was held in *Duncan* v. *Jaudon*, 15 Wallace, 165, that one who lends money to a trustee on a pledge of stock which is held in trust, and sells the stock for the repayment of the loan, must account to the *cestui que trusts* if he had either actual or constructive notice that the trustee was abusing his trust, and applying the money to his own use. Such notice will be implied where the certificates disclose the trust, and it would have appeared on inquiry that the loan was for a private purpose of the trustee. Davis, J., said, "In *Lowry* v. *The Commercial and Farmers' Bank of Maryland*, Taney's Circuit Court Decisions,

310, which was a case of misappropriation of corporate stock by an executor, Chief Justice Taney held, " that if a party dealing with an executor has, at the time, reasonable ground for believing that he intends to misapply the money, or is in the very transaction applying it to his own private use, the party so dealing is responsible to the persons injured." And the Supreme Court of Massachusetts, in a recent case, *Shaw* v. *Spencer and others*, 100 Massachusetts, 389, in its essential features, like the case at bar, decides that if a certificate of stock, expressed in the name of " A. B., Trustee," is by him pledged to secure his own debt, the pledgee is by the terms of the certificate put on inquiry as to the character and limitations of the trust, and if he accepts the pledge without inquiry, does so at his peril. In that case the *cestui que trust* was not named in the certificate, and the Court remarked that, if he had been, the duty of inquiry would hardly be controverted. If these propositions are sound, and we entertain no doubt on the point, the liability of the appellants for the conversion of the stock belonging to Mrs. Jaudon, cannot be an open question. They either knew or ought to have known that Jaudon was operating on his own account, and are chargeable with constructive notice of everything which upon inquiry they could have ascertained from the *cestui que trust.*

If this inquiry had been pursued, they could not have failed to discover the nature and foundation of the trust, and that the trustee had no right to pledge the stock for any purpose.

The bank in its dealings with Jaudon was guilty of gross negligence, and in consequence of this inflicted serious injury upon an innocent person. It may be that the cashier never inquired of Jaudon what he wanted with the money; but nine successive loans to him in one year, each time on the pledge of the same trust security, was evidence enough to satisfy any reasonable man that the money was wanted for private uses, and not for any honest purpose connected with the administration of the trust.]

[*100]   *DERING v. EARL OF WINCHELSEA.

IN THE EXCHEQUER. FEBRUARY 8, 1787.

REPORTED 1 COX, 318.[1]

CONTRIBUTION BETWEEN CO-SURETIES.]—*The doctrine of contribution amongst sureties is not founded in contract, but is the result of general equity, on the ground of equality of burthen and benefit. Therefore, where three sureties are bound by different instruments, but for the same principal and the same engagement, they shall contribute.*

THOMAS DERING, ESQ., having been appointed collector of some of the duties belonging to the customs, it became necessary, upon such appointment, for him to enter into bonds to the Crown with three securities for the due performance of this office. Sir Edward Dering his brother, the Earl of Winchelsea, and Sir John Rous having agreed to become sureties for him, a joint and several bond was executed by Thomas Dering and Sir Edward Dering to the Crown in the penalty of £4000; another joint and several bond by Thomas Dering and the Earl of Winchelsea, and a third by Thomas Dering and Sir John Rous, in the same penalty of £4000; all conditioned alike for the due performance of Thomas Dering's duty as collector, Mr. Dering being in arrear to the Crown to the amount of 3883*l*. 14*s*., the Crown put the first bond in suit against Sir Edward Dering, and judgment was obtained thereon for that sum; whereupon Sir Edward filed this bill against the Earl of Winchelsea and Sir John Rous, claiming from them a contribution towards the sum so recovered against him.

The cause has been argued at length in *Michaelmas* Term last, and now stood for judgment.

[*101]   *LORD CHIEF BARON EYRE.—This bill is brought by one surety against his two co-sureties, under the circumstances

[1] S. C., 2. B. & P. 270.

(above mentioned). Mr. Dering's appointment, the three bonds, and the judgment against the plaintiff are in proof in the cause; the original balance due, and the present state of it, are admitted.

The demand is resisted on two grounds: first, that there is no foundation for the demand in the nature of the contract; and, secondly, that the conduct of Sir Edward Dering has been such as to disable him from claiming the benefit of the contract, though it did otherwise exist. There is also a formal objection, which I shall take notice of hereafter.

I shall consider the second ground of objection first, in order to lay it out of the case. The misconduct imputed to Sir Edward is, that he encouraged his brother in gaming and other irregularities; that he knew his brother had no fortune of his own, and must necessarily be making use of the public money; and that Sir Edward was privy to his brother's breaking the orders of the Lords of the Treasury, to keep the money in a particular box, and in a particular manner, &c. This may all be true, and such a representation of Sir Edward's conduct certainly places him in a bad point of view; and perhaps it is not a very decorous proceeding in Sir Edward to come into this court under these circumstances. He might possibly have involved his brother in some measure, but yet it is not made out to the satisfaction of the Court that these facts will constitute a defence. It is argued that the author of the loss shall not have the benefit of a contribution; but no cases have been cited to this point, nor any principle which applies to this case. It is not laying down any principle to say, that his ill conduct disables him from having any relief in this court. If this can be founded on any principle, it must be that a man must come into a court of equity with clean hands: but when this is said, it does not mean a general depravity; it must have an immediate and necessary relation to the equity sued for; it must be a depravity in a legal, as well *as in a moral sense. In a moral sense, the companion, [*102] and perhaps, the conductor of Mr. Dering may be said to be the author of the loss, but, to legal purposes, Mr. Dering himself is the author of it; and if the evil example of Sir Edward led him on, this is not what the Court can take cognizance of. Cases, indeed, might be put, in which the proposition would be true. If a contribution were demanded from a ship and cargo for goods thrown overboard to save the ship, if the plaintiff had actually bored a hole in the ship, he would in that case be certainly the author of the loss, and would not be entitled to any contribution. But speaking of the author of the loss is a mere figure of speech, as applied to Sir Edward Dering in this case.

The real point is, whether a contribution can be demanded between the obligors of distinct and separate obligations under the circumstances of this case. It is admitted, that, if there had been only one bond in which the three sureties had joined for 12,000l., there must have been a contribution amongst them to the extent of any loss sustained; but it is said that that case proceeds on the contract and privity subsisting amongst the sureties, which this case excludes ; that this case admits of the supposition that the three sureties are perfect strangers to each other, and each of them might be ignorant of the other sureties, and that it would be strange to imply any contract as 'amongst the sureties in this situation; that these are perfectly distinct undertakings without connexion with each other, and it is added, that the contribution can never be eodem modo as in the three joining in one bond for 12,000*l.;* for there, if one of them become insolvent, the two others would be liable to contribute in moieties to the amount of 6000*l.* each, whereas here it is impossible to make them contribute beyond the penalty of the bond. Mr Madocks has stated what is decisive, if true, that nobody is liable to contribute who does not appear on the face of the bond. If this means only that there is no contract, then it comes back to the question whether the right of contribution is founded on contract.

[*103]　　*If we take a view of the cases, both in law and equity, we shall find that *contribution is bottomed and fixed on general principles of justice, and does not spring from contract ; though contract may qualify it,* as in *Swain* v. *Wall,* 1 Ch. Rep. 149. In the register 176 b, there are two writs of contribution—one inter co-hæredes, the other inter co-feoffatos ; these are founded on the Statute of Marlbridge. The great object of the statute is, to protect the inheritance from more suits than are necessary. Though contribution is a part of the provision of the statute, yet in Fitzh. N. B. 338, there is a writ of contribution at common law amongst tenants in common, as for a mill falling to decay. In the same page, Fitzherbert takes notice of contribution between co-heirs and co-feoffees ; and as between co-feoffees, he supposes there shall be no contribution without an agreement, and the words of the writ countenance such an idea, for the words are " ex eorum assensu;" and yet this seems to contravene the express provision of the statute. As to co-heirs, the statute is express ; it does not say so as to feoffees, but gives contribution in the same manner. In *Sir William Harbert's case,* 3 Co. 11 b, many cases of contribution are put ; and the reason given in the books is, that in æquali jure the law requires equality : one shall not bear the burthen in ease of the rest, and the law is grounded in great equity. *Contract* is never mentioned. Now, the doctrine of equality operates more effectually in this court than in a court of law. The difficulty in *Coke's Cases* was, how to make them contribute ; they were put to their auditâ quarelâ, or scire facias. In equity there is a string of cases in 1 Eq. Ca. Ab., tit. " Contribution and Average." Another case occurs in Hargr. Law Tracts,[1] on the right of the King on the prisage of wine. The King is entitled to one ton before the mast, and one ton behind ; and in that case a right of contribution accrues, for the King may take by his prerogative

---

[1] P. 120.

any two tons of wine he thinks fit, by which one man might suffer solely. But the contribution is given of course on general principles, which govern all these cases.

*Now, to come to the particular case of sureties. It is [*104] clear that one surety may compel a contribution from another towards payment of a debt for which they are jointly bound. On what principle? Can it be necessary to resort to the circumstance of a joint bond? What if they are jointly and severally bound? What difference will it make if they are severally bound, and by *different* instruments, but for the *same* principal, and the *same* engagement? In all these cases the sureties have a common interest and a common burthen; they are joined by the common end and purpose of their several obligations as much as if they were joined in one instrument, with this difference only, that the penalties will ascertain the proportion in which they are to contribute; whereas if they had joined in one bond, it must have depended on other circumstances.

In this case, the three sureties are all bound that Mr. Dering shall account for the monies he receives. This is a common burthen. All the bonds are forfeited at law and in this court, as far as the balance due. The balance might have been so great as to have exhausted all the penalties, and then the obligee forces them all to pay; but here the balance is something less than one of the penalties. Now, who ought to pay this? The one who is sued must pay it to the Crown, as in the case of prisage; but, as between themselves, there shall be a contribution, for they are in æquali jure. This principle is carried a great way where they are joined in one obligation; for if one should pay the whole 12,000*l.*, and the second were insolvent, the third shall contribute a moiety, though he certainly never meant to be liable for more than a third. This circumstance, and the possibility of one being liable for the whole if the other two should prove insolvent, suggested the mode of entering into separate bonds; but this does not vary the reason for contribution, for there is the *same* principal and the *same* engagement; all are equally liable to the obligee to the extent of the penalty of the bonds when they are not all exhausted. If, in the common case of a joint bond, no distinction is to be *made, why shall not the same rule [*105] govern here? As in the case of average of cargo in a court of law, qui sentit commodum sentire debet et onus. This principle has a direct application here; for the charging one surety discharges the other, and each therefore ought to contribute to the onus. In questions of average, there is no contract or privity in ordinary cases; but it is the result of general justice, from the equality of burthen and benefit. Then there is no difficulty or absurdity in making a contribution take place in this case, if not founded on contract, nor any difficulty in adjusting the proportions in which they are to contribute, for the penalties will necessarily determine this.

The object in point of form, which I before mentioned, is, that the bill cannot be sustained, inasmuch as it has not charged the insolvency of the principal debtor, and that such a charge is absolutely necessary. As a question of form it ought to have been brought on by demurrer; but, in substance, the insolvency of Mr. Dering may be collected from the whole proceedings, which strongly imply it; for the plaintiff appears to have submitted to the judgment, and the defendants have made their defence on other grounds.

On the whole, therefore, we think that the plaintiff is entitled to the relief he prays, and declare that the balance due from Thomas Dering being admitted on all hands to amount to the sum of 3883*l*. 14*s*. 8½*d*., the plaintiff, Sir Edward Dering, and the two defendants, the Earl of Winchelsea and Sir John Rous, ought to contribute in equal shares to the payment of that sum, and direct that the plaintiff and defendants do pay in discharge thereof, each of them, the sum of 1294*l*. 11*s*. 7*d*.; and that on payment thereof, the Attorney-General shall acknowledge satisfaction on the record of the said judgment, and that the two bonds entered into by the Earl of Winchelsea and Sir John Rous be delivered up to them respectively. But this not being a very favourable case to the plaintiff, and the equity he asks being doubtful, we do not think it a case for costs.

[*106] *" The principle," observed Lord Redesdale, " established in the case of *Dering* v. *Lord Winchelsea*, is universal, that the right and duty of contribution is founded in doctrines of equity; it does not depend upon contract. If several persons are indebted, and one makes the payment, the creditor is bound in conscience, if not by contract, to give to the party paying the debt all his remedies against the other debtors. The cases of average in equity rest upon the same principle. It would be against equity for the creditor to exact or receive payment from one, and to permit, or by his conduct to cause, the other debtors to be exempt from payment. He is bound, seldom by contract, but always in conscience, as far as he is able, to put the party paying the debt upon the same footing with those who are equally bound. That was the principle of the decision in *Dering* v. *Lord Winchelsea;* and in that case there was no evidence of contract;" *Stirling* v. *Forrester*, 2 Bligh. 59. See also *Craythorne* v. *Swinburne*, 14 Ves. 160, 165, 169; *Hartly* v. *O'Flaherty*, 1 Beat. 77, 78; *Ware* v. *Horwood*, 14 Ves. 31; *Mayhew* v. *Crickett*, and note, 2 Swanst. 189, 192: *Spottiswood's Case*, 6 De G. Mac. & G. 345, 371, 375; *Whiting* v. *Burke*, 10 L. R. Eq. 539; 6 L. R. Ch. App. 342; where the doctrine laid down in *Dering* v. *Lord Winchelsea*, has been recognised and approved of.

Courts of common law, in modern times, have assumed a jurisdiction to compel contribution between sureties, in the absence of positive contract, on the ground of implied assumpsit; inasmuch as the principle of contribution being in its operation established, a contract may be inferred, upon the implied knowledge of that principle by all persons. This jurisdiction is convenient enough, in a case simple and uncomplicated, but attended with great difficulty where the sureties are numerous; especially since it has been held, that separate actions may be brought against the different sureties for their respective quotas and proportions. It is easy to foresee the multiplicity of suits to which that leads: *Craythorne* v. *Swinburne*, 14 Ves. 164; *Cowell* v. *Edwards*, 2 B. & P. 268; see also 1 Saund. R. 264, n. (*a*), Williams's note (*b*).

In other respects, as will be hereafter seen, the jurisdiction at common law is much more confined and less beneficial than in equity. Thus where there are several sureties, and one becomes insolvent, the surety who pays the entire debt can in equity compel the solvent sureties to contribute towards payment of the entire debt (*Peter* v. *Rich*, 1 Ch. Rep. 34; *Hole* v. *Harrison*, 1 Ch. Ca. *246; S. C., Finch, Rep. 15, 203; *Hitchman* v. *Stewart*, 3 Drew. 271; and see *The Mayor* [*107] *of Berwick* v. *Murray*, 25 L. J., N. S. (Ch.) 201; 7 De G. Mac. & G. 497); but at law he can recover no more than an aliquot part of the whole, regard being had to the number of co-securities: *Cowell* v. *Edwards*, 2 B. & P. 268; *Browne* v. *Lee*, 6 B. & C. 697; S. C., 9 D. & R. 700. See also *Rogers* v. *Mackenzie*, 4 Ves. 752; *Wright* v. *Hunter*, 5 Ves. 927; *Batard* v. *Hawes*, 2 E. & B. 287. So, also, if one of the sureties dies, in equity contribution can be enforced as against his representatives; but at law an action lies only against the surviving sureties: *Primrose* v. *Bromley*, 1 Atk. 90; *Batard* v. *Hawes*, 2 E. & B. 287.

It may here be observed that in all cases of contribution, the jurisdiction assumed by courts of law does not effect the original jurisdiction of courts of equity; *Wright* v. *Hunter*, 5 Ves. 794, where Lord Alvanley, M. R., says, " I would not lay down, nor have it understood, that, because courts of law may entertain actions upon such subjects, a party may not file a bill for contribution."

It is clear, as laid down by the Lord Chief Baron, in *Dering* v. *The Earl of Winchelsea*, that a surety may compel contribution from another for payment of a debt for which they are jointly or severally, or jointly and severally, bound by the same instrument: *Fleetwood* v. *Charnock*, Nels. 10; *Underhill* v. *Horwood*, 10 Ves. 226; *Craythorne* v. *Swinburne*, 14 Ves. 164. It was, however, decided for the first time in *Dering* v. *The Earl of Winchelsea* that there is no difference whether the parties are bound in the same or by different instruments, provided they are co-securities for the *same* principal and in the *same* engagement; and further, that there is no difference if they are bound in different sums, except that contribution could not be required beyond the sum for which they had become bound. In *Craythorne* v. *Swinburne*, 14 Ves. 169, Lord Eldon said that he argued *Dering* v. *The Earl of*

Winchelsea, and that he was much dissatisfied with the whole proceeding and with the judgment; but he had been since convinced that the decision was upon right principles. "Lord Chief Baron Eyre," observed his Lordship, "in that case decided that this obligation of co-securities is not founded in contract, but stands upon a principle of equity." See also *Ware* v. *Horwood*, 14 Ves. 31; *Mayhew* v. *Crickett*, 2 Swanst. 192; *Stirling* v. *Forrester*, 3 Bligh. 596.

And it seems that the right of a surety to enforce contribution against co-sureties will not be affected by his ignorance at the time he became surety that they were also co-sureties; *Craythorne* v. *Swinburne*, 14 Ves. 163, 165.

[*108] *Where, however, sureties are bound by different instruments for distinct portions of a debt due from the same principal, if the suretyship of each is a *separate* and *distinct* transaction, the doctrine laid down in *Dering* v. *Lord Winchelsea* will not apply, and there will be no right of contribution among the sureties: *Coope* v. *Twynam*, 1 T. & R. 426; *Arcedeckne* v. *Lord Howard*, 27 L. T. R. (N. S.) 194; 20 W. R. 879, reversing the decision of Sir R. Malins, V. C., reported Ib. 571.

A surety will in equity be entitled to interest from his co-sureties for the money which he has paid: *Lawson* v. *Wright*, 1 Cox, 275, 277; *Hitchman* v. *Stewart*, 3 Drew. 271; *Swain* v. *Wall*, 1 Ch. Rep. 149; *Petre* v. *Duncombe*, 15 Jur. 86. See, however, *Onge* v. *Truelock*, 2 Moll. 31, 42; *Bell* v. *Free*, 1 Swanst. 90; *Rigby* v. *M'Namara*, 2 Cox, 415.

And it has been held recently in Ireland, overruling the cases of *Onge* v. *Truelock*, 2 Moll. 42, and *Salkeld* v. *Abbott*, Hayes and Jones, 110, that where one of two sureties had paid the full amount of a receiver's recognizance, he was entitled to use the recognizance for the purpose of recovering out of the estate of his co-surety, not only one half of the sum so paid by him, but also interest thereon from the date of payment. *In re Swan's Estate*, 4 I. R. Eq. 209.

Although the principle of contribution is not founded upon contract still a person may by contract qualify, or take himself out of the reach of, the principle or the implied contract. Thus, where three persons became bound for the principal debtor in an obligation, and agreed among themselves that, if the principal debtor failed to pay the debt, they would pay their respective parts; two became insolvent, and the third paid the money, and one of the insolvent sureties afterwards becoming solvent, he was held liable to contribute one-third only: *Swain* v. *Wall*, 1 Ch. Rep. 149; see also *Craythorne* v. *Swinburne*, 14 Ves. 165; *Coope* v. *Twynam*, 1 T. & R. 426; *Collins* v. *Prosser*, 1 B. & C. 682. So also a person may take himself entirely out of the principle, as where he becomes merely a collateral surety, by limiting his liability to payment of the debt upon the default of the principal and other sureties; and on a bill in such a case, filed for contribution, parol evidence is admissible to show what the real contract was, and to rebut the implied contract which equity raises in cases of contribution: *Craythorne* v. *Swinburne*, 14 Ves. 160, overruling *Cooke* v. ———, 2 Frem. 97; S. C., 2 Eq. Ca. Ab. 223, pl. 1; see also *Hartley* v. *O'Flaherty*, L. & G., temp. Plunk. 217, where Lord Plunkett says, "In the case of A. undertaking that if the principal does not pay, and if B., who has already become security, does not pay, he, A., will pay, it seems perfectly clear that B., in that case paying the whole, *would have no claim of contribution against A." [*109]

Sureties who have paid the debt are not only entitled to contribution from the other sureties, but also in the absence of any contract for a particular indemnity (*Cooper* v. *Jenkins*, 32 Beav. 337), to the benefit of any security which any of them may have taken from the principal debtor by way of indemnity: *Swain* v. *Wall*, 1 Ch. Rep. 149: and it is a general rule (subject, however, to some few qualifications) that *a surety is entitled to the benefit of all the securities which the creditor has against the principal.* Thus, if a surety join with the principal in a promissory note or bond, and the surety pays the debt, he will be entitled to have a transfer of any mortgage which the creditor may have taken for his debt. "I take it," says Lord Eldon, "to be exceedingly clear, if at the time a bond is given a mortgage is also made for securing the debt, the surety, if he pays the bond, has a right to stand in the place of the mortgagee; and, as the mortgagor cannot get back his estate again without a conveyance, that security remains a valid and effectual security, notwithstanding the bond debt is paid:" *Copis* v. *Middleton*, T. & R. 231; see also *Hodgson* v. *Shaw*, 3 My. & K. 195; *Gayner* v. *Royner*, cited in *Robinson* v. *Wilson*, 2 Madd. 434; *Yonge* v. *Reynell*, 9 Hare, 809; *Goddard* v. *Whyte*, 2 Giff. 449; *Brandon* v. *Brandon*, 3 De. G. & Jo. 524; and it is immaterial that the surety is not aware of the existence of the mortgage: *Mayhew* v. *Crickett*, 2 Swanst. 191; *Scott* v. *Knox*, 2 Jones, 778.

Where a surety for a mortgagor pays off part of the mortgage debt, he is entitled as against the mortgagor to a charge on the estate, for the amount he has so paid: *Gedye* v. *Matison*, 25 Beav. 310.

A surety who pays off a debt for which he became answerable is entitled not only to all the equities which the creditor could have enforced against the principal debtor, but also against all persons claiming under him. Thus in *Drew* v. *Lockett*, 32 Beav. 499, A. mortgaged his estate to C. and B. became A.'s surety for the debt. Afterwards A. mortgaged the estate to D. who had notice of the first mortgage. The first mortgage was afterwards paid off, partly by B. the surety, but D. got the transfer of the legal estate. It was held by Sir John Romilly, M. R., that the sureties still had priority over D. for the amount paid by him under the first mortgage as surety for A.

And if through neglect on the part of a creditor a security to the benefit of which a surety is entitled is lost, or not properly perfected, the surety will be discharged so far as regards the amount of the security so lost: *Strange* v. *Fooks*, 4 Giff. 408.

But where the creditor advances a further sum upon the security [*110] *of the mortgage, the surety cannot compel the creditor to assign it to him, unless he pays off the further sum, as well as the sum for the payment of which he became surety: *William* v. *Owen*, 13 Sim. 597; but see *Bowker* v. *Bull*, 1 Sim. N. S. 29, and the remarks thereon in *Farebrother* v. *Wodehouse*, 23 Beav. 28.

And where separate debts are due upon distinct securities from the principal debtor to the creditor, the latter will not lose his right to tack, by the fact that a third party who has become surety for one of the debts, has either voluntarily or upon proceedings taken against him by the creditor, paid off such debt: see *Farebrother* v. *Wodehouse*, 23 Beav. 18. There the defendants lent A. B. at the same time two sums of 2000*l.* and 3000*l.* on distinct securities, and the plaintiff was surety for the first sum. It was held by Sir John Romilly, M. R., that the plaintiff, on paying the 2000*l.* was not entitled to have a transfer of the securities held for that sum, until the defendants had also been paid the 3000*l.*

But the right of the mortgagee in such cases to tack as against the surety may be affected by contract between the parties, or by concealment or misrepresentation on the part of the mortgagee; see the remarks of Sir John Romilly, M. R., in *Farebrother* v. *Wodehouse*, 23 Beav. 22, 23, 25, 28; and *Bowker* v. *Bull*, 1 Sim. N. S. 29.

The right of the surety to have the benefit of the securities held by the creditor is derived from the obligation on the part of the principal to indemnify the surety: *Yonge* v. *Reynell*, 9 Hare, 818.

Courts of equity, it seems, would, at a very early period, compel assignments of securities to a surety to a much greater extent than in later times they took upon themselves to do. There is a very strong instance of the application of that equity in *Parsons* v. *Briddock*, 2 Vern. 608. In that case the principal had given bail in an action; judgment was recovered against the bail; afterwards the surety was called upon and paid; and it was held, that he was entitled to an assignment of the judgment against the bail. So that, though the bail were themselves but sureties as between them and the principal debtor, yet, coming in the room of the principal debtor as to the creditor, it was held, that they likewise came in the room of the principal debtor as to the surety. Consequently that decision established that the surety had precisely the same right that the creditor had, and was to stand in his place. The surety had no direct contract or engagement by which the bail were bound to him, but only a claim against them through the medium of the creditor, and was entitled only to all his rights. See, however, *Hodgson* v. *Shaw*, 3 My. & K. 189, and *Armitage* v. *Baldwin*, 5 Beav. 278, where a creditor sued *his principal debtor and [*111] recovered a judgment against him and the bail in the action. The surety thereupon " paid and satisfied " to the creditor the amount of the judgments, with interest and costs, and took an assignment thereof. Lord Langdale, M. R., held, that the judgment was discharged, and that the surety could not recover on the judgment against the bail. See also *Dowbiggin* v. *Bourne*, 2 Y. & C. Exch. Ca. 462.

Upon the same principle, although it was at one time thought that a surety paying off the debt of the principal, secured by their bond, was entitled to have from the creditor an assignment of the debt and of the bond by which it was evidenced or secured, the contrary, was fully established in two cases decided by Lord Eldon, C. and Lord Brougham, C., where the whole subject was examined in a most elaborate manner. In *Copis* v. *Middleton*, 1 T. & R. 229, Lord Eldon said : —" It is a general rule, that, in equity, a surety is entitled to the benefit of all the securities which the creditor has against the principal ; but then the nature of those securities must be considered. Where there is a bond merely, if an action was brought upon the bond, it would appear upon oyer of the bond that the debt was extinguished. The general rule, therefore, must be qualified by considering it to apply to such securities as continue to exist, and do not get back upon payment to the person of the principal debtor. In the case, for instance, where, in addition to the bond, there is a mortgage, with a covenant on the part of the principal debtor to pay the money, the surety paying the money would be entitled to say, ' I have lost the benefit of the bond ; but the creditor has a mortgage, and I have a right to the benefit of the mortgaged estate which has not got back to the debtor.' " So also Lord Brougham, in *Hodgson* v. *Shaw*, 3 My. & K. 190, observes :—" The rule here is undoubted, and it is one founded on the plainest principles of natural reason and justice, that the surety paying off a debt shall stand in the place of the creditor, and have all the rights which he has for the purpose of obtaining his reimbursement. It is hardly possible to put this right of substitution too high ; and the right results more from equity than from contract or *quasi* contract, unless in so far as the known equity may be supposed to be imported into any transaction, and so to raise a contract by implication. The doctrine of the Court in this respect was luminously expounded in the argument of Sir Samuel Romilly in *Craythorne* v. *Swinburne ;* and Lord Eldon, in giving judgment in that case, sanctioned the exposition by his full approval. ' A surety,' to use the language of Sir S. Romilly's reply, ' will be entitled to every remedy which *the creditor has [*112] against the principal debtor ; to enforce every security and all means of payment ; to stand in the place of the creditor, not only through the medium of contract, but even by means of securities entered into without the knowledge of the surety; having a right to have those securities transferred to him, though there was no stipulation for that: and to avail himself of all those securities against the debtor.' I have purposely taken this statement of the right, because it is there placed as high as it ever can be placed, and yet it is quite consistent with the principle of *Copis* v. *Middleton*. Thus the surety paying is entitled to every remedy which the creditor has. But can the creditor be said to have any specialty, or any remedy on any specialty, after the bond is gone by payment? The surety may enforce any security against the debtor which the creditor has; but, by the supposition, there is no security to enforce, for the payment has extinguished it. He has a right to have all the securities transferred to him; but there are, in the case supposed, none to transfer—they are absolutely gone. He may avail himself of all those securities against the debtor, but his own act of payment has left none of which he can take advantage."

[Technically speaking, payment cannot take place after breach, without a new agreement. Payment at the day is performance, payment after the day, another name for accord and satisfaction. The tender must not only be made, but accepted with an intent to extinguish the obligation, and if it be not, the liability will survive although the money comes from the pocket of the debtor and goes into that of the creditor: *Thomas* v. *Cross*, 7 Exchequer, 728; *Buck* v. *Blanchard*, 2 Foster, 303; *The Kingston Bank* v. *Gay*, 19 Barb. 459; *Kington* v. *Kington*, 11 M. & W. 233. Hence a payment by one of several joint debtors will not preclude a recovery for his benefit against all, if the circumstances indicate that the intention was to purchase the demand and not to satisfy it. In *McIntyre* v. *Miller*, 13 M. & W. 472, the demand in suit was a deposit note of a joint stock bank. The defendants, Miller, Harwood and Spence, were shareholders in the bank, and therefore jointly and severally liable on the note. It appeared in evidence that the note had been paid by the London and Westminster Bank, with the funds of Walker, another shareholder, and assigned to one Richards for his use. The suit was confessedly brought for Walker's benefit. It was contended on behalf of the defence, that the note was clearly paid. The cases as between principal and surety were not in point. There the contest was between the party who ought to have paid the debt, but had not, and him who ought not to have paid it, but had, and it was regarded as still in being to give the surety the benefit of the securities held by the creditor. This argument was overruled by the Court. Parke, Baron, said, " If the debt be expressly kept alive at the time, it cannot be satisfied by the very act that keeps it alive. To construe that as payment which was meant to be an assignment, is a contradiction in terms. Unless an act can be made to operate exactly the reverse of what the parties intended, the note is not paid. If the defendants have an equity, and it was a wrong thing for one partner to buy up a debt due from the firm—and so endeavour to recover it without taking the accounts, they must go into equity; but such considerations have no place in a Court of law." So in *Taylor* v. *Van Deusen*, 3 Gray, 498, the Court refused to set aside an execution against the surety, although the debt had been purchased by a third person with the money of the principal and on his behalf. It would notwithstanding appear, that in determining whether a debt has been extinguished, regard should be had to what the parties ought to have done, and not merely to what they designed. As between ordinary co-contractors it may not be inequitable that one should advance the whole amount, and have the demand assigned as a means of compelling the rest to contribute their respective quotas. And it may well be, that where a judgment for a partnership debt binds the real estate of a member of the firm, another partner may take an assignment of the judgment in the name of a third person, as security for the amount that may be due on a settlement of the partnership accounts. But it is very clear that as a principal debtor cannot throw the burden of the debt on the surety by direct means, he should not be allowed to do so by using a third person as an instrument: *Irick* v. *Black*, 2 C. E. Greene. As payment by a surety is treated as a purchase in furtherance of equity, so payment by the principal will operate as an extinguishment, if construing it as a purchase would oppress the surety. It is a familiar principle, that where an act is consistent with a rightful purpose, the doer shall not allege that his intent was wrongful if the effect will be injurious. In *Kinley* v. *Hill*, 4 W. & S. 426, where a surety paid the amount of a mortgage out of trust funds in his hands belonging to the principal, and then sold the instrument, it was held that the purchaser acquired no title. The same principle was applied in *Bartlett* v. *Lang*, 4 Alabama, 689; and *Logan* v. *Reynolds*, 21 Id. 56. In the case last cited, a third person paid a judgment against a firm with money belonging to one of the partners, had it marked to his use, and issued an execution which was levied on the partnership goods. Dargen, C. J., said, that where a judgment is paid by one who is a principal in the debt, and as such bound to pay, he cannot by obtaining an assignment of the judgment, keep it alive in order to coerce payment from his co-principals, and he will not be permitted to do that in the name of another which he would not be entitled to do in his own. So the case of *Jones* v. *Davids*, 4 Russell, 277, shows that an obligor cannot rebut the presumption of payment by taking an assignment of the bond. It seems that payment by a guarantor does not extinguish the debt even at law, at all events where he insured the obligation subsequently at the request of the creditor. Where a man does that which he agreed to do, the contract is fulfilled; but if he fails, the breach is not less complete because a stranger pays the money or furnishes the goods. Such a substituted performance will not preclude the right of suit, although it may entitle the guarantor to subrogation. To operate as payment irrespectively of intention, the tender must be made at the day and by the debtor, or on his behalf. Payment after the day may take effect as satisfaction when such is the design, which may be inferred when the money comes from one who is equally bound. But such an inference cannot be drawn when the payment is made by a third person in pursuance of a collateral obligation. See *Kington* v. *Kington*, 11 M. & W. 233; 1 Smith's Leading Cases, 634, 7 Am. ed.]

It was decided in *Copis* v. *Middleton*, contrary to what was formerly considered to be the law, that a surety, paying off the bond debt of the principal, was in the administration of his assets merely a simple contract, and not a specialty creditor. See also *Jones* v. *Davids*, 4 Russ. 277.

Where, however, a surety paid the debt due from a defaulter to the Crown, the Court of Exchequer would allow him to stand in the place of the Crown: *Regina* v. *Salter*, 1 H. & N. 274; *Regina* v. *Robinson*, Ib. 275, n.

According to the law of Scotland the surety has always been entitled to call upon the creditor for a surrender or assignment of all separate and collateral securities obtained by him for the debt, his right not being limited by the exception introduced or approved of by *Copis* v. *Middleton* and *Hodgson* v. *Shaw.* " The equity and propriety of the Scottish rule" are by the Mercantile Law Commissioners stated to be " obvious, inasmuch as the surety obtains much aid in operating his relief from the hardship of having been compelled to pay another party's debt, and yet no detriment is thereby inflicted on any other party." (Mercantile Commission, Second Report, 1855, p. 13.) And, in accordance with their recommendation, the law of England upon this subject has been assimilated to that of Scotland by the Mercantile Law Amendment Act, 1856 (19 & 20 Vict. c. 97), which enacts, that " Every person who, being surety for the debt or duty of another, or being [*113] *liable with another for any debt or duty, shall pay such debt or perform such duty, shall be entitled to have assigned to him, or to a trustee for him, every judgment, specialty, or other security which shall be held by the creditor in respect of such debt or duty, whether such judgment, specialty, or other security shall, or shall not be deemed at law to have been satisfied by the payment of the debt or performance of the duty; and such person shall be entitled to stand in the place of the creditor, and to use all the remedies, and, if need be, and upon a proper indemnity, to use the name of the creditor, in any action or other proceeding at law or equity, in order to obtain from the principal debtor, or any co-security, co-contractor, or co-debtor, as the case may be, indemnification for the advances made and loss sustained by the person who shall have so paid such debt or performed such duty; and such payment or performance so made by such surety shall not be pleadable in bar of any such action or other proceeding by him : Provided always, that no co-surety, co-contractor, or co-debtor, shall be entitled to recover from any other co-surety, co-contractor, or co-debtor, by the means aforesaid, more than the just proportion to which, as between those parties themselves, such last-mentioned person shall be justly liable." Sect. 5.   See *Allen* v. *De Lisle*, 5 W. R. 158, V. C. S.

A debtor who has paid the whole debt, recovered under a judgment against himself and his co-debtors, has a right to an assignment of such judgment. See *Batchelor* v. *Lawrence*, 9 C. B. (N. S.) 543, where, in an action by a co-debtor against the judgment creditor, refusing to make such assignment, it was held by the Court of Common Pleas, that a plea that the plaintiff was taken in execution on the judgment, and the judgment was satisfied, by the payment of the plaintiff, was a bad plea.

The act is applicable to a contract made before the passing of the act, where a breach of it has taken place and a payment has been made by a surety or co-debtor under such contract after the passing of the act: *Lockhart* v. *Reilly*, 1 De G. & Jo. 464 ; *In re Cochran's Estate*, 5 Law Rep. Eq. 209.

Where, however, a surety upon a second bond, given by him as a collateral security for a debt secured by the original bond of his principal, paid off the debt, he would, even under the old law, have been entitled to an assignment from the creditor of the original bond ; for the original bond still remained as an existing security ; and the surety, therefore, upon an assignment of it, ranked as a specialty creditor against the assets of the principal debtor.   Thus, in *Hodgson* v. *Shaw*, 3 My. & K. 183, " A. and B. executed a joint and several *bond, to secure [*114] a sum of money with interest to W.   Subsequently to the deaths of A. and W., the executors of W. obtained from B. as principal, and from C. as surety, another bond, to secure a part of the money then due on the original bond, with interest.   No payments were ever made in respect of the first bond ; but after C.'s death the second bond was paid off out of C.'s estate, and his representatives thereupon procured the original bond to be assigned to them : it was held, in a suit to administer the estate of A., that C.'s representatives were entitled, by virtue of the assignment, to rank as specialty creditors of A.'s estate, in respect of the payments made by C. or his estate on the second bond, to the extent of the penalty in the assigned bond:" and see *Done* v. *Walley*, 2 Exch. 198.

In many other cases, the surety paying the debt will have a right to stand in the place of the creditor.   Thus, where the creditor has proved the debt against the estate of the principal, and the surety afterwards pays him the debt, the creditor will be held a trustee of the dividends for the surety : *Ex parte Rushworth*, 10 Ves. 409 ; *Wright* v. *Morley*, 11 Ves. 12 ; *Watkins* v. *Flanagan*, 3 Russ. 421.   So also it is now the settled law that a surety may compel the creditor to go in and prove the debt under the bankruptcy of the principal debtor, and if the surety pays the whole, the creditor will be a trustee of the dividends for him: *Ex parte Rushworth*, 10 Ves. 414. "A surety, moreover, as soon as his obligation to pay becomes absolute, has a right in equity to be exonerated by his principal. Thus, in an action by the payee of a joint and several promissory note against one who, to the knowledge of the payee, joined in it as a surety only, it is competent to the surety, by way of equitable defence, to plead a special plea of a set-off due from the payee to the principal, arising out of the same transaction out of which the liability of the surety arose: *Bechervaise* v. *Lewis*, 7 L. R. C. P. 372; and see and consider *In re Jeffery's Policy*, 20 W. R. (V. C. M.) 857."

As to the rights of sureties under successive Bankruptcy Acts, 49 Geo. 2, c. 121, s 8; 6 Geo. 4, c. 168, s. 8; The Bankruptcy Act, 1849, s. 173; and the Bankruptcy Act, 1869, s. 173. See Robson on Bankruptcy, p. 215.

So, where executors pay a debt for which the testator was liable as surety for a legatee, they will have a lien upon the legacy for the sum so paid, in priority to a mortgagee of the legacy: *Willes* v. *Greenhill*, 29 Beav. 376.

It may be here mentioned that when an executor, who has joined as surety with his testator, pays the amount of the debt after the testator's death, he is entitled to retain the amount out of the testator's assets as against all creditors of equal degree: *Ex parte Boyd*, 13 W. R. (L. C.) 419.

A surety for a part of a debt is not entitled to the benefit of a security given by the debtor to the creditor at a different time, in a distinct transaction for another part of the debt: *Wade* v. *Coope*, 2 Sim. 155.

Where a surety gets rid of and discharges an obligation at a less sum than its full amount, he cannot, as against his principal, make himself a creditor for the whole amount, but can only claim what he has actually paid in discharge of the common obligation: *Reed* v. *Norris*, 2 My. & Cr. 361, 375.

It has been uniformly declared, and fully acted upon, in the Courts of Chancery in this country, that the claim for contribution among co-sureties, as well as the claim for indemnity on the part of the surety against the principal, is founded, not upon contract, but upon a principle of natural equity and justice; the maxim adopted in regard to co-sureties being, that equality is equity among persons standing in the same situation: *M'Mahon, &c.* v. *Fawcett, &c.*, 2 Randolph, 514, 529; *Moore* v. *Moore*, 4 Hawks, 358, 360; *Moore* v. *Isley*, 2 Devereux & Battle's Equity, 372, 373; *Allen* v. *Wood*, 3 Iredell's Equity, 386; *Screven* v. *Joyner, Ex'r, and others*, 1 Hill's

Chancery, 252, 260, 261; *M'Kenna* v. *George*, 2 Richardson's Equity, 15, 17; *Breckenridge* v. *Taylor*, 5 Dana, 110, 112; *Mills* v. *Hyde*, 19 Vermont, 60, 64; *Strong et al.* v. *Mitchell et al.*, Id. 644, 647; *Craig & Angle* v. *Ankeney*, 4 Gill, 225, 231 : " and the solidity and necessity of this doctrine," said Chancellor Kent, in *Campbell* v. *Mesier*, 4 Johnson's Chancery, 334, 338, " were forcibly and learnedly illustrated by Lord Ch. Baron Eyre in the case of *Dering* v. *Earl of Winchelsea;*" and the same principle now prevails at law : *Harris* v. *Ferguson*, 2 Bailey, 397, 400; *Norton* v. *Coons*, 3 Denio, 130, 132. This equity springs up at the time the relation is entered into, and is consummated when the surety has paid the debt : *Wayland* v. *Tucker et als.*, 4 Grattan, 268. The practice of subrogation, or substitution, or the cession of remedies, is borrowed from the civil law ; and, under the guidance of Chancellor Kent, has probably gone further in this country than in England. It is the creature of equity, and is administered so as to secure real, essential justice, without regard to form : *Enders, &c.*, v. *Brune*, 4 Randolph, 438, 447; *Douglass* v. *Fagg*, 8 Leigh, 588, 598.

It may be convenient to consider, first, the claim of a surety for indemnity from his principal, and afterwards, the claim for contribution among co-sureties ; and to speak of these, first, in equity, and then at law.

At law, a surety has no remedy until he has paid the debt : *Bonham* v. *Galloway*, 13 Illinois, 68;

Ponder v. *Carter*, 12 Iredell, 32; but in equity, as soon as the debt has become payable, he may file a bill, under certain conditions, to compel payment of it by the principal, in order that he may be relieved from responsibility ; 2 American Lead. Cases, 412, 5 ed. : *Ranelaugh* v. *Hayes*, 1 Vernon, 189; *Nisbet* v. *Smith*, 2 Bro. C. C. 579, 582; *Pride* v. *Boyce*, Rice's Eq. 276, 287; *Bishop* v. *Day*, 13 Vermont, 81, 88; *Hoffman* v. *Johnson*, 1 Bland, 103, 105; *Stevenson* v. *Taverners*, 9 Grattan, 398; *Rice* v. *Downing*, 12 B. Monroe, 44; *Wetzel* v. *Sponsler*, 6 Harris, 460; *Whitridge* v. *Durkee*, 2 Maryland, Ch. 442; *Purviance* v. *Sutherland*, 2 Ohio, N. S. 478; *Irick* v. *Black*, 2 C. E. Greene, 189; although it seems to have been thought in *Lee* v. *Griffin*, 31 Mississippi, 632, that this equity cannot be enforced without paying the debt or bringing the money into court. It has also been held, that where judgment has been obtained against the principal and the surety, and the former is insolvent, the latter, before payment, may file a bill to compel the discharge of the debt out of the principal's estate in the hands of third persons : *Stump* v. *Rogers*, 1 Ohio, 553; *M'Connell* v. *Scott and others*, 15 Id. 401 ; see, also, *Green et al.* v. *Crochett et al.*, 2 Devereux & Battle's Equity, 390, 393. There are also special cases, in which the surety may compel the creditor to resort to the securities and liens which he holds, before coming upon the surety; *Hayes* v. *Ward*, 4 Johnson's Chancery, 123, 132;

Schroeppel v. *Shaw*, 5 Barbour's S. Ct. 580, 589; *Vartie* v. *Underwood*, 18 Id. 561; *Kent* v. *Matthews et al.*, 12 Leigh, 574, 585; *Railroad Co. et al.* v. *Claghorn et al.*; *Irick* v. *Black*, 2 C. E. Greene, 189; 1 Spear's Equity, 547, 561; but this is where speedy, direct and certain redress can be had upon the security, and, then, only under peculiar circumstances; 2 American Lead. Cas, 412, 418, 5th ed.; *Gary* v. *Cannon*, 3 Iredell's Equity, 64, 68; *Morris* v. *M'Anally*, 43 Cald. 304: see *post*, vol. 2, note to *Aldrich* v. *Cooper*.

When the surety has paid the debt, equity has original jurisdiction to compel the principal to reimburse him; *Moore, &c.* v. *Young*, 1 Dana, 516, 517; *Thomas* v. *Beckman*, 1 B. Monroe, 29, 30; *Partlow* v. *Lane*, 3 Id. 424, 425; *Baxter* v. *Moore*, 5 Leigh, 219, 221; *The Wesley Church* v. *Moore*, 10 Barr, 273. So, also, where the land of the surety is taken in execution and sold after his decease, his heirs may file a bill for indemnity, or, perhaps, maintain assumpsit for money paid; *The Wesley Church* v. *Moore.*

Moreover, as soon as the surety has paid the debt, an equity arises in his favor to have all the securities, original and collateral, which the creditor holds against the person or property of the principal debtor, transferred to him, and to avail himself of them as fully as the creditor could have done: for the purpose of obtaining indemnity from the principal, he is considered as at once subrogated to all the rights, remedies and securities of the creditor; as substituted in the place of the creditor, and entitled to enforce all his liens, priorities, and means of payment, as against the principal, and to have the benefit even of securities that were given without his knowledge; see *Lidderdale* v. *Robinson*, 2 Brockenbrough, 160, 167; S. C. 12 Wheaton, 594, 596; *M'Mahon* v. *Fawcett*, 2 Randolph, 514, 530; *Hampton* v. *Levy*, 1 M'Cord's Chancery, 107, 117; *Perkins* v. *Kershaw*, 1 Hill's Chancery, 344, 351; *Railroad Co. et al.* v. *Claghorn et al.*, 1 Spear's Equity, 547, 561; *Loud* v. *Sergeant*, 1 Edwards, 164, 168; *Elwood* v. *Deifendorf*, 5 Barbour, 399, 413; *Lathrop's Appeal*, 1 Barr, 512, 517; *Atwood* v. *Vincent*, 17 Connecticut, 576, 583; *Hardcastle* v. *Commercial Bank of Delaware*, 1 Harrington, 374, 377; note, *Cino* v. *Vance*, 4 Clarke, 434, 441; *York* v. *Landis*, 65 North Carolina, 557; *Burk et al.* v. *Chrisman et al.*, 3 B. Monroe, 50; *Cullem* v. *Emanuel*, 1 Alabama, 23, 28; *Brown* v. *Lang*, 4 Id. 50, 53; *Commercial Bank of Lake Erie* v. *Western Reserve Bank*, 11 Ohio, 444, 449; *Miller* v. *Woodward & Thornton, Adm'rs*, 8 Missouri, 169, 175; *Buthald* v. *Buthald*, 46 Missouri, 557; *Hill* v. *Manner*, 11 Grattan, 522; *Dechard* v. *Edwards*, 2 Sneed, 93; *Dodier* v. *Lewis*, 27 Mississippi, 679; *Lewis* v. *Palmer*, 28 New York, 271; *Klopp* v. *The Lebanon Bank*, 10 Wright, 88. "This right of the surety," says Chancellor Kent, in *Hays* v. *Ward*, 4 Johnson's Chancery, 123, 130, "stands not upon contract, but upon the same principle of natural justice, upon which one surety is entitled to contribution from another:" and the same thing is said in 1 Comstock, 599, 600. Payment by one who stands in the relation of a surety, although it may extinguish the remedy, or discharge the security, as respects the creditor, has not that effect as between the principal debtor and the surety. As between them, it is in the nature of a purchase by the surety from the debtor; it operates an assignment in equity of the debt and of all legal proceedings upon it, and gives a right in equity to call for an assignment of all securities; and, in favor of the surety, the debt and all its obligations and incidents, are considered as still subsisting.

[Every one is a surety within these principles, who incurs a liability in person or estate at the request and for the benefit of another, without sharing in the consideration; *Lewis* v. *Palmer*, 28 New York, 271; see the *Wesley Church* v. *Moore*, 10 Barr, 2 American Leading Cases, 451, 5th ed. A man who makes himself answerable for, or guaranties a debt subsequently, is, therefore, as much entitled to the subrogation as if his liability arose from, or was cotemporaneous with the original obligation; *Cottrell's Appeal*, 11 Harris, 294; because it is an implied condition that the guarantor shall be entitled to the remedies of the creditor on payment.]

These principles may be illustrated, in respect to (1) Bonds, (2) Judgments, (3) Liens upon land, (4) Mortgages and other real securities in which the title passes; and apply equally to securities in which the surety is jointly bound with the principal, and to those which are cumulative and collateral to the original debt. The distinction adopted in *Copis* v. *Middleton*, that equity will not subrogate the surety, in those cases in which payment discharges or extinguishes the security at law, which reaches the case of bonds and judgments binding the surety jointly with the principal, and probably the case of bonds and judgments constituting or merging the debt, though the surety be not bound by them, and also the case of mere liens upon land, where the title does not pass, has, in general, not been adopted in this country; on the contrary, with the exception of the Courts of Alabama, Vermont, and North Carolina, it appears to be universally and firmly settled, that although the security or lien be extinguished at law, yet for the benefit of the surety by whose money or property the creditor has been satisfied, it continues equitably in full force.

1. *In regard to Bond debts.*]—It is not a principle of equity, in this country, that a surety, discharging a bond debt, is in all cases considered as in the position merely of a simple contract creditor of his principal; wherever the distinction is of any benefit to the surety,— wherever a bond has any priority over a simple contract,—as, where the payment is after the principal's death, the surety, upon payment, will be regarded as holding the place of the bond creditor, and en-

titled to all the advantages which such a claimant has over simple contract creditors; *Smith* v. *Swain*, 7 Richardson's Eq. 112. This has been repeatedly decided in Virginia. At law, no doubt, a surety paying off a bond debt becomes only a simple contract creditor; *Dupuy et al.* v. *Southgates*, 11 Leigh, 92, 97; see also *U. S.* v. *Preston & Bunker*, 4 Washington's C. C. 446, 452; *Carroll* v. *Bowie*, 7 Gill, 34; and where the bond is paid off by the surety, while the principal is alive and solvent, in which case the distinction is of no importance, as there is then no superior dignity in bond debts, the surety will be considered in equity, as what he is at law, only a simple contract creditor; per Tucker, P., in *Powell's Ex'ors* v. *White and others*, 11 Leigh, 309, 324; but after the principal's death, a bond creditor has, in Virginia, certain rights beyond a simple contract creditor; a right to charge the heir, and a right of priority in the administration of personal assets; and to these rights, a surety, upon payment of the debt, has an equity to be subrogated. The proper statement of the doctrine appears to be, that the surety is in equity what he is at law, merely a simple contract creditor, but entitled to the security of the bond, as a means of reaching a class of assets upon which otherwise he would have no claim, viz., those appropriated to bond debts. Accordingly, when a surety pays off a bond debt, after the principal obligor's death, he has a right in equity to stand in the place of the

obligee, and to insist on all his claims and advantages; *Eppes and others* v. *Randolph*, 2 Call, 125, 188; *Tinsley* v. *Anderson*, 3 Id. 329; *West* v. *Belches*, 5 Munford, 187, 194; *M'Mahon, &c.* v. *Fawcett, &c.*, 2 Randolph, 514, 533. And the ground of this principle is forcibly and satisfactorily illustrated by Tucker, P., in *Watts et al* v. *Kinney et ux.*, 3 Leigh, 272, 294. "The whole train of authorities on this subject," he remarks, "is founded upon the principle of the superior equity of the sureties, to be paid out of that fund to which their creditor might have resorted, for their relief. The surety in a bond, for the payment of which the principal has bound particular property, has a preference over all other persons, to have the debt charged upon that fund. If the principal dies, and after his death the surety pays off the bond, he has a right to demand the payment of the bond out of the assets, before the simple contract creditors, and thus to be placed in the shoes of the obligee; because at the instant of the principal's death, the obligee had a right to demand payment out of the assets, in preference to any simple contract creditor; in good faith, he should have demanded such payment, instead of putting the burden on the innocent surety; in good faith, the executor should have so applied the assets. An adequate portion should have been set apart and appropriated for that debt. No simple contract creditor had, or could have by law, any claim thereto. If the executor were sued by simple contract creditors, he might plead the outstanding bond in bar of the demand. He might fence around an adequate portion of assets against all their assaults. Nor is the state of things changed by payment being forced from the surety, or being voluntarily made by him. If forced from him, a court of equity will give him redress; it will consider him as standing in the shoes of the creditor, who ought to have looked to the estate of the principal, instead of drawing money from the pocket of the surety; it will consider the executor as holding a certain portion of the assets, as trustee for the payment of this very debt, and hold him to the discharge of the trust in its spirit, when it can no longer be performed to the letter: and it will deny to the simple contract creditor, who has no right to these funds, the application of them to the payment of his debt. And why? If the surety discharge the bond, or a judgment and execution upon it, is he not a simple contract creditor only? and has not any other simple contract creditor a legal right to resort to this fund, as there is now no longer any bond or judgment to be charged upon it? and has he not equal equity? The answer is, No: he not only has not equal equity, but he has no equity whatever to charge a fund which in equity, and justice, belongs to another. He has no equity to demand that money, which by law ought to have been applied to pay my debt, shall be applied to pay his. The case is the same, if the payment is made voluntarily by the surety. In making that payment, he is governed by the law of this court. Even on entering into his engagement as surety, he looks to its well established principles. He knows, if he pays the debt to the obligee, he will stand in the obligee's shoes. He knows he will be subrogated to all the rights of the obligee, as they subsist at the time he makes his payment. He knows that a court of equity looks not to form but to substance; that it looks to the *debt* which is to be paid, not to the *hand* which may happen to hold it; that the fund charged with its payment, shall be so applied, whosoever may be the person entitled; and that it considers a debt as never discharged, until it is discharged by payment to the proper person, and by the proper person. He knows, that that court, which permits no act of a trustee to prejudice a *cestui que trust*, will not permit one who stands in the relation of the creditor or obligee to the surety, to bar him of those rights which the principles of equity have secured to him. He is conscious that his rights do not depend upon the caprice of the creditor, or the whim of an executor, or the sense of right of other creditors, but rest upon the immutable principles of justice and equity; and, in making his payment, he does it in the confidence, that he will be entitled to be indemnified to the full amount, to which his creditor could have charged the assets of the principal." In the more recent case of *Powell's Ex'ors* v. *White and others*, 11 Leigh, 309, the decisions in *Copis* v. *Middleton*, and *Jones* v. *Davids*, were thoroughly examined in the Court of Appeals, and the Virginia practice was vindicated against the authority of Lord Eldon, with distinguished and convincing ability. See also *Wheatley's Heirs* v. *Calhoun*, 12 Id. 265, 274. The principle of these Virginia cases has been fully sustained by the Circuit and Supreme Courts of the United States; *Lidderdale* v. *Robinson*, 2 Brockenbrough, 160; S. C. 12 Wheaton, 594. In South Carolina, the same practice is established. In *Pride* v. *Boyce*, Rice's Equity, 276, the doctrine of *Copis* v. *Middleton* was discussed, not indeed where the surety had paid the debt, but where upon the bonds being due he had filed a bill to compel its payment by the principal's administrator; and it was decided that he was entitled to have it paid according to its priority as a bond debt. In *Schultz* v. *Carter et al.*, 1 Spear's Equity, 534, 543, the point was expressly determined. There, a surety in two joint and several bonds, secured by mortgage, both of which were due and unpaid at the principal's death, had, after his decease, been compelled to pay one, and was sued upon the other: he insisted that he was entitled to reimbursement as a bond creditor out of the assets of the principal's estate, and also to have the benefit of the mortgage; and the court held that he was entitled to both of these advantages. "The result of the cases," said Dunkin, Ch., "is, that a surety who pays a debt of a superior dignity, due by the estate of his deceased principal, is suffered to rank, in the application of assets, according to the dignity of the debt satisfied; or, in other words, is substituted for the creditor who holds the prior debt, and is entitled to the benefit of any security which that creditor may have taken from the principal debtor." In New York and Pennsylvania, also, the right of subrogation to bonds, has been recognized; see *Cheesebrough* v. *Millard*, 1 Johnson's Chancery, 409, 413; *Croft* v. *Moore*, 9 Watts, 451; *Himes* v. *Keller*, 3 Watts and Sergeant, 401, 404; *Lathrop and Dale's Appeal*, 1 Barr, 512.

If a surety in a bond to the United States, pays the debt, he is entitled to the same preference over the other creditors, as the United States had; Act of 1799, c. 128, s. 65; *United States* v. *Hunter*, 5 Mason, 62, 65; S. C. 5 Peters, 174; *Dias* v. *Bouchaud*, 3 Edwards, 485; and see *U. S.* v. *Preston and Bunker*, 4 Washington, 446. And this has been recognized as a general equity; thus where one gave his bond to the United States, for the importer of goods, and afterwards paid it, he was held to be entitled to the same priority as the United States had, in his claim upon the estate of the importer; because, it was said, equity in the matter of subrogation, considers the substance of the relation, and not its mere form; *Enders, &c.* v. *Brune*, 4 Randolph, 438, 447; see also *Grider* v. *Payne*, 9 Dana, 188,

192. In one case, however, it was held that a surety in a bond to the United States, was not entitled to the creditor's priority in his claim for contribution against his co-surety, but came in only as an ordinary creditor; *Bank* v. *Adger*, 2 Hill's Chancery, 262, 266: but as this was grounded on *Copis* v. *Middleton*, which has been since rejected in that state, the decision is probably no longer sound. And if the debt of the principal were a preferred debt, by statute, in the administration of his estate, the surety paying the debt will be entitled to the same preferences; *Schoolfield's Adm'r* v. *Rudd, &c.*, 9 B. Monroe, 291.

2. *Judgments and Decrees.*]—It is generally settled in this country, that a surety paying the debt, is entitled to be subrogated to a judgment or decree against the principal, and to have the benefit of its lien upon his land in preference to subsequent judgment creditors, and of its priority in the distribution of personal assets, and of being permitted to file a creditor's bill in his own name to obtain satisfaction out of assets which could not be reached by execution; and this whether the judgment or decree is against the principal and surety jointly; *Watts et al.* v. *Kinney et ux.*, 3 Leigh, 272, 293; *Speiglemyer* v. *Crawford*, 6 Paige, 254, 257; and see *Clayson* v. *Morris*, 10 Johnson, 524; *Thompson* v. *Palmer*, 3 Richardson's Eq. 139; *Dempsey* v. *Bush*, 18 Ohio, N. S. 566; *Connely* v. *Bourg*, 16 Louisiana Ann. 292; or whether the instrument upon which the surety's obligation arises, is collateral to the judgment against the principal; *Rodgers* v. *Mc Cluer's Adm'rs et als.*, 4 Grattan, 81; *Cottrell's Appeal*, 11 Harris, 294; *McClung* v. *Beirne*, 10 Leigh, 395, 400; in which latter case, Tucker, P., declared that it made no difference that the surety was not a party to the judgment.—The doctrine of *Copis* v. *Middleton*, will not in most of the states, be applied to deprive a surety of the benefit of a judgment against the principal, and though extinguished in law, such a judgment will be kept alive for the indemnity of a surety who has paid the debt. This is established in Virginia; *Tinsley* v. *Anderson*, 3 Call, 329; in New York, *Goodyear* v. *Watson*, 14 Barbour, 481; in Georgia, *M'Dougal* v. *Dougherty*, 14 Georgia, 674; and in South Carolina, *Burrows and Brown* v. *M'Whann and Campbell*, 1 Dessaussure, 409; *Perkins and others* v. *Kershaw and others*. 1 Hill's Chancery, 344, 351; and though the former of these cases was a subrogation against a co-surety, the latter was against a principal debtor. In *Perkins and others* v. *Kershaw and others*, judgments had been obtained against the principal's administrators, and against the surety, for the debt, and executions issued: the surety paid, and the sheriff entered satisfaction on both executions: "In equity," said the Court, "the sureties, upon showing that they and not the administrator, paid the money, would be allowed to vacate the entry of satisfaction on the execution by the sheriff as made by

mistake, and to set up the judgment as a subsisting lien on the real estate of the deceased debtor." In Maryland and Delaware also, it is settled not only that a surety paying the debt, has a claim to be subrogated to the right of the creditor and to all his liens and securities, but that a payment by the surety operates, in itself, as an assignment, in equity, of the debt and of a judgment upon it, so as to authorize him to sue, or issue execution in the creditor's name, for his use: and though as between the surety and creditor this equitable assignment cannot take place till the whole debt is paid, yet when it is fully paid, a partial payment by the surety will, as between him and the principal debtor, entitle him to an assignment *pro tanto; Norwood* v. *Norwood*, 2 Harris & Johnson, 238; *Sotheren* v. *Reed*, 4 Id. 307, 309; *Merryman* v. *The State*, 5 Id. 423, 427; *Hollingsworth* v. *Floyd*, 2 Harris & Gil. 88, 91; *Watkins* v. *Worthington*, 2 Bland, 509, 529; *Hardcastle* v. *Commercial Bank of Delaware*, 1 Harrington, 374, 377, 378, *note*. In Pennsylvania, the subrogation of a surety to a judgment against the principal is well established, and of every day occurrence; *Cottrell's Appeal*, 11 Harris, 294. The decisions in that state were reviewed by Kennedy, J., in *Lathrop and Dale's Appeal*, 1 Barr, 512, with especial reference to the doctrine in *Copis* v. *Middleton*. "From the cases it would appear," he concludes, "that we have adopted the general rule, that a surety by paying the debt of his principal becomes entitled to be subrogated to all the rights of the creditor, so as to have the benefit of all the securities which the creditor had for the payment of the debt, without any exception, as well those which became extinct, at law at least, by the act of the surety's paying the debt, as all collateral securities which the creditor held for the payment of it, which have not been considered as directly extinguished by the surety's paying the debt. . . . These decisions have been made upon a supposed principle of equity, which, for the purpose of doing justice to the surety who has paid the debt, interposes to prevent the judgment, or security, which has been so extinguished at law, from being so considered as between the surety and the principal, or his subsequent lien creditors." When, moreover, the nature of the payment and the circumstances, are such as to entitle the creditor to subrogation, his right cannot be defeated by the creditor, nor satisfaction entered without his consent or approbation; *Baily* v. *Brownfield*, 8 Harris, 48.

3. *Liens upon the lands of the Principal.*]—If a surety for the purchase-money, upon a sale of land which has been executed by a conveyance of the legal title, pays the debt, he is entitled to be subrogated to the vendor's lien for unpaid purchase-money, as against the vendee and purchasers from him with notice; *Kleiser, &c.* v. *Scott, &c.*, 6 Dana, 137; *Burk et al.* v. *Chrisman et al.*, 3 B. Mon-

roe, 50 ; *Ghiselin and Worthington* v. *Ferguson*, 4 Harris & Johnson, 522 ; *Hagruder* v. *Peter*, 11 Gill & Johnson, 219, 228, 245 ; *Welch* v. *Parran et al.*, 2 Gill, 320, 329 ; *Davidson* v. *Carroll*, 29 Louisiana Ann. 199. In like manner, the surety of a vendor who is compelled to repay the purchase-money in consequence of the failure of the principal to execute a conveyance, will succeed to the right of the vendee to a specific performance, and have an equitable lien on the land, which he may enforce against purchasers, with notice of its existence; *Freeman* v. *Mebane*, 2 Jones' Eq. 44 ; while a similar equity will arise when the purchase-money is paid by the surety for the purchaser ; *Jordan* v. *Hudson*, 11 Texas, 82 ; and entitle him either to enforce the contract specifically, or aver the legal title of the seller as an heir for indemnification. *Sute* v. *Shneider*, 23 Missouri, 447. In *Eddy* v. *Traver*, 6 Paige, 521, the heir of an intestate had conveyed with warranty a part of the descended lands, and the administrator, afterwards, having obtained a surrogate's order for the sale of lands for the payment of debts, sold the land which had been thus conveyed ; and the vendee was held entitled to the benefit of the lien of the debts upon lands remaining unsold in the possession of the heir. "It is an established principle of equity," said the Chancellor, " that sureties, or those who stand in the situation of sureties for those for whom they pay a debt, are entitled to stand in the place of the creditor, or to be subrogated to all his rights as to any fund, lien or equity which he may have against any other person or property on account of the debt. . . In cases depending upon this equitable principle, as between the debtor and his sureties, it makes no difference, except as against *bona fide* purchasers or mortgagees, that the debt has been actually paid by the sureties, or out of their property, so that the creditor's lien upon the property of the principal debtor is extinguished at law." See also *Schermerhorn* v. *Barhydt*, 9 Paige, 30, 43 ; *Kinney's Ex'ors, &c.* v. *Harvey, &c.*, 2 Leigh, 70 ; *Haffey's Heirs* v. *Birchett's, &c.*, 11 Id. 83, 89 ; *In re M'Gill*, 6 Barr, 504.

4. *Mortgages, and other conveyances for the security of a debt.*]— A surety paying a debt secured by mortgage is entitled to be substituted to the creditor's interest and lien under the mortgage, both where the surety is a joint-mortgagor with the principal, and where the mortgage is against the principal's property only, and the surety's obligation is collateral ; *Loud* v. *Sergeant*, 1 Edwards, 164, 168 ; *Marsh* v. *Pike*, 1 Sandford, 211 ; S. C. 10 Paige, 595 ; *M'Lean* v. *Towle*, 3 Sandford, 117 ; *Loomer* v. *Wheelright*, Id. 136, 261 ; *Lowndes* v. *Chisolm*, 2 M'Cord's Chancery, 455 ; *Bank* v. *Campbell*, 2 Richardson's Equity, 180, 185 ; *Atwood* v. Vincent, 17 Connecticut, 576, 583 ; *Norton* v. *Soule*, 2 Greenleaf, 341 ; *Dearborn* v. *Taylor*, 18 New Hampshire, 153 ; *Storms* v. *Storms*, 5 Bush. 77 ;

and the same principle applies where lands have been conveyed by a deed of trust for the payment of the debt; *Wheatley's Heirs* v. *Calhoun*, 12 Leigh, 265, 274; *Walker* v. *Crowder*, 2 Iredell's Eq. 479, 486; *Miller* v. *Ord*, 2 Binney, 382.

Alabama, North Carolina and Vermont appear to be the only states in which the doctrine of *Copis* v. *Middleton* has been adopted. In the first, it has been decided that the surety cannot avail himself of the instrument on which he is surety, after payment of it, because it is extinguished; *Houston* v. *The Bank*, 25 Alabama, 250; and this has been applied to instruments under seal; *Foster* v. *The Trustees of the Athenæum*, 3 Alabama, 302, 310; to executions on a judgment against principal and sureties; *Morrison and Givhan et al.* v. *Marvin*, 6 Id. 797; *Saunders and M'Laughlin* v. *Watson et al.*, 14 Id. 199; and apparently with less reason to deeds of trust given as security for the payment of the debt paid by the surety, and to which he would be subrogated even in England; *Houston* v. *The Bank*, 25 Alabama, 250. In North Carolina it was decided that a surety who had paid off a judgment against the principal and himself, became only a simple contract creditor of the principal, the judgment being, by payment, extinguished both at law and in equity; but it was said, that if at the time of payment he had taken an assignment of the judgment to a stranger, and had not intended

satisfaction of it, it would have been kept alive as a judgment, for his benefit; *Briley* v. *Sugg*, 1 Devereux & Battle's Equity, 366. In Vermont, there are dicta to the effect that a surety paying a judgment can be subrogated only to collateral securities and not to the judgment itself; *Pierson* v. *Catlin*, 18 Vermont, 77, 85.

[It is a controverted question whether subrogation is an equity which the surety may waive or assert at pleasure, or a lien attaching at the time of payment, irrespectively of intention. The former seems to be the preferable opinion; *The Harrisburg Bank* v. *Germon*, 3 Barr, 300; although the surety will not be allowed to exercise his discretion in a way to prejudice third persons; *Huston's Appeal*, 19 P. F. Smith, 485. Where, for instance a judgment against a principal and surety is paid by the surety, or out of the proceeds of his real estate, he may by satisfying the judgment, or refusing to issue an execution on it against the principal, preclude those claiming under him as volunteers. But the holder of a subseqent judgment against the surety has an interest in the surety's equity, which no act on his part can defeat. The law was so held in *Huston's Appeal*, overruling *The Harrisburg Bank* v *Germon*. In *Huston's Appeal*, a judgment was obtained against a principal and surety, which bound their real estate. The appellants then obtained a judgment against the surety. He paid the judgment against the principal, and assigned it to the appellees, who were creditors at large. The court held that the equity of the appellants was anterior to the assignment. It was the equity of a creditor who had but one fund to be subrogated to the remedies of him who had two; and as their right was higher than the surety's, it was necessarily superior to that of any one claiming under him as assignee. The rule no doubt is that payment by a surety with an intent to extinguish the debt will preclude the right of subrogation as it regards him, but not where the effect would be injurious to lien creditors, or purchasers.

A question nearly akin to this is also a subject of dispute. The legal remedy of the surety grows out of the implied promise of the principal to save him harmless. He must proceed in assumpsit, although the original obligation be under seal. The statute of limitations will therefore attach to, and may be pleaded in bar of such a demand, if more than six years have elapsed from the time of payment. And it has been contended, that as equity follows the law, such a defence is a sufficient answer to a claim for subrogation. This view is sustained by *Fink* v. *Mahaffy*, 8 Watts, 384; and *Rittenhouse* v. *Levering*, 6 Watts & Sergeant, 190; but the decision was influenced in both instances by other considerations.

In *Smith* v. *Swain*, 7 Richardson's Eq. 112, the court was notwithstanding of opinion that the payment of a debt secured by a bond or other instrument under seal, puts the surety virtually in

the position of a creditor by specialty, and beyond the reach of the statute of limitations. Such it was said would be the effect if the bond were assigned or handed over to a third person for his benefit, and the principle was the same when the assignment was implied.

The better opinion seems to be that expressed by Rogers, J., in *Rittenhouse* v. *Levering*, that the remedy of the surety is primarily for money paid, and the right of subrogation to the bond or judgment a mere collateral, which will fail if the principal demand is barred by the statute of limitations, or by any other cause.

A guarantor who intervenes at the request of the principal debtor, is within the rule laid down in *Rittenhouse* v. *Levering*, unless the case can be distinguished on the ground that payment by one who is not directly responsible is not satisfaction, unless it is shown to have been so designed. See *Jones* v. *Broadhurst*, 9 C. B., 173, Hess' Estate, 19 P. F. Smith, 272, *ante*, 139. But the payment of a bond by one who has assigned it with a guarantee, is *ipso facto* a purchase, entitling him to sue in the name of the obligee without regard to the lapse of time. For as such a payment is not made on behalf of the obligor, or at his request, it does not confer a right of action against him, and there is nothing on which the statute of limitations can operate. In *Elkinton* v. *Newman*, 8 Harris, 281, Huston assigned a ground rent to Newman, which he guarantied. The tenant made default, and Huston was compelled to pay the arrears. He subsequently brought covenant in the name of Newman and recovered, although more than six years had elapsed since the payment.

Whatever doubt may exist on these points, it is well settled, that where the jurisdiction is concurrent, a controversy which has been adjudicated at law, cannot be revived in equity: *Fink* v. *Mahaffy*, 8 Watts, 384. In *Fink* v. *Mahaffy*, Fink was the surety in a judgment, and Mahaffy the principal. He satisfied the judgment, and sued Mahaffy for money paid, laid out and expended. The case was tried, and a verdict and judgment rendered for the defendant. The court held that this debarred Fink from subrogation to the original judgment against Mahaffy. A party could not have relief in equity on a ground which had been determined adversely at law. This decision was cited, and approved in *Rittenhouse* v. *Levering*, 6 W. & S. 190. There can be no doubt that if payment or a release is pleaded or given in evidence by the principal, and found in his favor, it will be a good answer to a bill for subrogation. But a judgment at law does not preclude a recourse to chancery, unless the equity alleged by the complainant is one of which the legal tribunal could have taken cognizance; and not even then, unless the course of procedure at law is adequate to the ends of justice: *King* v. *Baldwin*, 2 Johnson's Ch. 554; 17 Johnson, 384; Notes to the Earl of Oxford's Case, *post*, vol. 2. A judgment for the principal on a plea of the statute of limitations, is not, therefore, necessarily a reason why the surety should not be subrogated to the remedies and securities of the creditor.

To give birth to the relation of principal and surety as between themselves, and entitle the one to proceed against the other for indemnity, the liability for the debt must have been assumed at the request of the principal, or result from a course of dealing to which both are parties : *Lavalette* v. *Thompson*, 2 Beasley, 274.

It may, notwithstanding, be inferred from *McIntyre* v. *Miller*, 13 M. & W. 724, that a third person who pays the amount of a judgment with funds derived from one of the defendants, may take an assignment of the judgment, and use it as a means of compelling the other to contribute, *ante*, 139. The legal right is indisputable, and equity will not intervene unless it is abused. In this instance the debtor paid through another, with the intent to keep the debt alive; and a payment made by him in person or professedly on his behalf, is satisfaction, although the money is advanced by a third person, on the faith of an express or implied understanding that the debt shall survive for his benefit, unless this is disclosed to the creditor and assented to by him: *Eastman* v. *Plumer*, 32 N. Hamp. 238.

The payment of a note, at or after maturity, by the maker, or by one of several makers, extinguishes the obligation under the doctrine of the commercial law. If he is a surety he may be subrogated to the remedy of the payee; but he cannot put the instrument again in circulation as against the other makers; at all events where one is a surety: *Hopkins* v. *Scott*, New Hamp. 425.

The right to subrogation does not ordinarily exist between joint debtors, because they are equally liable not only to the creditor, but as between themselves: *Mahaffy* v. *Share*, 2 Penna. 361; *McCormick* v. *Irwin*, 11 Casey, 111, 117; *Bailly* v. *Brownfield*, 8 Harris, 41; *Hogan* v. *Reynolds*, 21 Alabama, 56. One co-obligor, maker, or indorser, cannot therefore enforce it against another: *The Bank* v. *Armstrong*, 4 Wright, 278. It may, however, arise from a change of circumstances, throwing the burden primarily on one, and rendering it incumbent on him to exonerate the rest: *Warren* v. *Sennett*, 4 Barr, 114; *The Bank of Penna.* v. *Wenger*, 1 Rawle, 303. An outgoing partner who takes a covenant from the remaining members of the firm to pay the partnership debts and save him harmless stands in the position of a surety: *Afflalo* v. *Foudrineir*, 6 Bing. 306; *Wood* v. *Dodgson*, 2 M. & S. 195; *Butler* v. *Birkey*, 13 Ohio, N. S. 514; and may be subrogated to the remedies of the creditors if the covenant is not fulfilled: *The Ætna Ins. Co.* v. *Wires*, 2 Williams, 93; *Morris* v. *Oakford*; *Fleming* v. *Beaver*, 2 Rawle, 128; *Butler* v. *Birkey*, 13 Ohio, N. S. 134.

The principle is the same where one of several joint purchasers parts with his interest to the others, in consideration of an agreement on their part to be answerable for the amount due to the vendor: *Warren* v. *Sennett*, 4 Barr, 114. When, said Gibson, C. J., "Williams took Sennett's place in the purchase, he took not only his property, but his responsibilities, and he consequently ceased to be a surety; for that a surety may in the course of events become a principal, is shown by *The Bank of Penna.* v. *Winger*, 1 Rawle, 303." Conversely, a principal contractor may be turned into a surety through the operation of a subsequent grant or contract: *McCormick* v. *Irwin*, 11 Casey, 111.

In *McCormick* v. *Irwin*, Pyle, Whittaker & Irwin were in partnership. Pyle died, and Irwin transferred his share to Whittaker, subject to the debts of the firm. Pyle's administrator, Smythe, filed a bill against Irwin & Whittaker, and obtained a decree for $4,000. This was satisfied by Irwin, who thereupon asked and obtained subrogation against Whittaker and the sureties in a bond which Whittaker had given during the proceedings in equity, to prevent the appointment of a receiver. Strong, J., said: "The familiar doctrine of subrogation is, that where one has been compelled to pay a debt which ought to have been paid by another, he is entitled to a cession of all the remedies which the creditor possessed against that other. To the creditor, both may have been equally liable; but if, as between themselves, there is a superior obligation resting on one to pay the debt, the other, after paying it, may use the creditor's security to obtain reimbursement. The reason why subrogation is not allowed to one partner as against his co-partner, or to one merely a joint debtor, as against his co-debtor, is because that as between them, there is no obligation to pay the debt resting upon one, superior to that which rests upon the other. The doctrine does not depend upon privity, nor is it confined to cases of strict suretyship. It is a mode which equity adopts to compel the ultimate discharge of the debt by him who in good conscience ought to pay it, and to relieve him whom none but the creditor could ask to pay. To effect this, the latter is allowed to take the place of the creditor, and make use of all the creditor's securities, as if they were his own."

" In the light of these principles, we discover no error in the charge of the Court below. It was a substantial answer to all the points propounded by the plaintiff in error, which arose out of the cause, and it was correct. Smythe, it is true, obtained his decree against both Irwin and Whittaker; but the agreements between them, given in evidence, established that long before the decree, as between them, the primary or superior obligation to pay the sum decreed, lay upon the latter. He had covenanted with Irwin to pay it, and the effect of the covenant was to make himself the principal. Of course, Irwin, after having paid the debt, became entitled in equity to the use of Smythe's decree, obtained

against the principal, and not only to that, but to every remedy to enforce its payment which Smythe had against Whittaker's sureties, who became such after he assumed the superior obligation to pay."

The rule is broad enough to include every instance where one pays a debt for which another is primarily answerable, and that should in equity and good conscience have been discharged by him: *Stevens* v. *Goodenough*, 26 Vermont, 676; *Lewis* v. *Palmer*, 28 New York, 271; see *post*, vol. 2, part 1st, notes to *Aldrich* v. *Cooper*. Which of the parties to a sale is entitled to subrogation to a judgment or other lien on the property sold, consequently depends on whether the sale was made subject to, or free from encumbrances; the vendor being entitled to resort to the judgment as an indemnity in the former case, and the vendee in the latter; *post*, vol. 2, notes to *Aldrich v. Cooper; Johnson* v. *White*, 11 Barb. 194. A purchaser who takes subject to a mortgage which is deducted from the consideration, is primarily liable for the mortgage debt, and bound to indemnify the seller against it. He consequently becomes the principal debtor, and the vendor a surety; *Marsh* v. *Pike*, 10 Paige, 595; *Cornell* v. *Prescott*, 2 Barbour, 17; *Thompson* v. *Thompson*, 4 Ohio, N. S. 333, 349; *Klapworth* v. *Dressler*, 2 Beasley, 62; while the opposite result will follow, where the price is paid in full, and the covenants in the deed make it the duty of the vendor to discharge the encumbrance.

It results from what has been said, that where nothing has occurred to vary the obligation of the parties, one co-contractor is not entitled to subrogation against another, unless he is a surety as it regards the latter. It is therefore important to determine who are sureties within this principle.

The relation of suretyship grows out of the assumption of a liability at the request of another, and for his benefit. It may consequently arise, although the name of the principal does not appear in the instrument which constitutes the evidence of the debt: *Moore* v. *The Wesley Church*, 10 Barr, 273; *Metzner* v. *Baldwin*, 11 Minnesota, 150; *Gray* v. *McDonald*, 19 Wisconsin, 213; or where the principal appears in the contract as the surety, and the surety as the principal; *Hull* v. *Peer*, 27 Illinois, 312. The execution of a note for the accommodation of the payee, renders it incumbent on him to indemnify the maker, and if judgment is obtained against the payee as an indorser, the maker may be subrogated to the judgment: See *Davies* v. *Stainbank*, 6 DeGex, M. & G. 679; *Pooley* v. *Harradine*, 7 E. & Bl. 431. If the equity may be disregarded by the creditor, it is clearly good between the parties: *The Bank* v. *Walker*, 9 S. & R. 229, 12 Id. 382; 2 American Leading Cases, 454, 5th ed. So one who gives a pledge or mortgage as a security for a loan to a third person, may file a bill to compel the latter to pay the debt: *Lea* v. *Rook*, Moseley, 318; *Rowan* v. *Sharp*, 33 Connecticut, 11; and if he dies the equity may be enforced by his heirs: *Moore* v. *The Wesley Church*. See *Wharton* v. *Woodburn*, 4 Dev. & Bat. Law, 507. Though the money be advanced on the mortgage, and not on the credit of the person to whose use it is applied, it is still his duty to save the mortgagor harmless. Hence, a wife who mortgages her estate for the benefit of her husband, becomes a surety, and will be discharged if the creditor does any act tending to prejudice the right of subrogation: *Gahn* v. *Neimcewicz*, 3 Paige, 641; 11 Wend. 312; *Sheidle* v. *Weishlee*, 4 Harris, 134; *Vartie* v. *Underwood*, 18 Barb. 561; *The Earl* v. *The Countess of Huntington, notes, post*, vol. 2.

In like manner, if A. and B. unite in a promise or agreement on behalf of B. and C., or to save C.'s property from execution, A. will have all the rights of a surety against C., although the name of the latter does not appear in the instrument, or it is not legally binding on him; *Purviance* v. *Sutherland*, 2 Ohio, N. S. 478; *Wharton* v. *Woodburn*, 4 Dev. & Bat. Eq. 507. See *Betsonier* v. *Baldwin*, 11 Minnesota, 150. In *Purviance* v. *Sutherland*, and *Wharton* v. *Woodburn*, a partner gave a bond in the firm name for money which was applied to the use of the partnership, and it was held that the other partners were liable to indemnify the plaintiff who had put his name to the instrument as a surety, although the obligee could not have recovered against them at law.

Strictly speaking, a surety is not entitled as such, unless he intervenes at the express or implied request of the principal: *Lavalette* v. *Thompson*, 2 Beasley, 274. But it is also true, that the creditor has all the rights of an owner, and may dispose of the demand to any one whom he thinks proper. He may consequently ask for and obtain a guaranty from a third person, on the express or implied condition that the latter shall stand in his shoes on payment, and be subrogated to every lien, remedy, or security that can in anywise be made effectual for the payment of the debt. This equity is incident to the contract of insurance, and therefore belongs of right to a guarantor. See *Hughes* v. *Littlefield*, 18 Maine, 400; *Powers* v. *Nash*, 36 Id. 322; *Carter* v. *Jones*, 5 Iredell Eq. 196; *Talmadge* v. *Burlingame*, 9 Barr, 210; *Elkinton* v. *Newman*, *Peake* v. *Dorwin*, 25 Vermont, 28; *Keath* v. *Goodwin*, 31 Id. 268; 2 American Ldg. Cases, 835, 5th ed. Under these circumstances, there is no privity of contract between the principal contractor and the guarantor, and he cannot maintain debt or assumpsit against them, but he may, notwithstanding, treat the payment as a purchase, entitling him to proceed in the name of the creditor: *Elkinton* v. *Newman*. In like manner, where a surety takes the bond of a third person as a counter security, payment by the latter will entitle him to subrogation to the remedy of the surety against the principal: *Labeaume* v. *Sweeny*, 17 Missouri, 153.]

A surety, who compounds the debt, has no right at law to recover from the principal more than he has actually paid, or the value of property which he has given up; *Bonney* v. *Seely*, 2 Wendell, 481; and, in equity, his claim is to be subrogated to the rights of the creditor, only so far as to indemnify him; and, therefore, even if he should take a formal assignment of the security, he will be entitled to no more than he has paid to the creditor; *Lawrence* v. *Blow*, 2 Leigh, 30; see also *Hall's Adm'r* v. *Creswell et al.*, 72 Gill & Johnson, 37, 52. "A surety stands in such a relation to his principal," said Rogers, J., in *Wynn, Adm'r*, v. *Brooke et al.*, 5 Rawle, 106, 110, "that he cannot be permitted to speculate upon him." And the rule is the same in relation to contribution between co-sureties; *Hickman, &c.*, v. *M'Curdy*, 7 J. J. Marshall, 555, 560.

The equity of a surety to be subrogated to the rights which the creditor has against the principal debtor or his estate, exists as well where the surety's property only is pledged, as where he came under a personal responsibility; *Niemcewiez* v. *Gahn*, 3 Paige, 614, 642, 648; 11 Wend. 312; *Moore* v. *The Wesley Church*, 10 Barr. And the creditors of a surety have the same right of subrogation which he has; *Neff* v. *Miller*, 9 Barr, 348, 350.

It is only in cases where the

person paying the debt stands in the situation of a surety, or is compelled to pay, in order to protect his own interests, that a court of equity substitutes him in the place of the creditor, as a matter of course, without any special agreement; *Janny* v. *Stephen*, 2 Patton & Heath, 11. A stranger paying the debt of another will not be subrogated to the creditor's rights, without an agreement to that effect; *Swan* v. *Patterson*, 7 Maryland, 164; *The Bank of the United States* v. *Marston*, 2 Brockenbrough, 254; *Burr* v. *Smith*, 21 Barbour, 262; such a payment absolutely extinguishes the debt and security; *Sandford* v. *M'Lean*, 3 Paige, 117, 122; *Banta* v. *Garmo and others*, 1 Sandford, 384; *Wilkes* v. *Harper*, 1 Comstock, 586; *The Bank of the United States et al.* v. *Winston's Executors et al.*, 2 Brockenbrough, 252, 254; *Douglass* v. *Fagg*, 8 Leigh, 588, 602.

[This statement of the law must be taken with these qualifications: First, that a payment by a third person will not extinguish the debt, unless it is made on behalf of the debtor, and authorized or ratified by him; *Belshaw* v. *Bush*, 11 C. B. 191; *Kemp* v. *Balls*, 10 Exchequer, 107; *Simpson* v. *Egginton*, Ib. 845, 1 Smith's Ldg. Cases; *Merriman* v. *The State*, 5 Harris, 602, 633, 7th ed.; 1 Johnson, 423; *Whitney* v. *The Independence M. Ins. Co.*, 15 Maryland, 297, 314; and next, that it may operate as a purchase of the debt, if such is the design with

which the money is given and received; *Carter* v. *Jones*, 5 Iredell, 193. A man cannot acquire a right to sue me by paying my creditor, but he may be entitled to proceed in the name of the creditor. The consent of the debtor is not necessary to the validity of such a transfer, because the right of property is in the creditor, who may deal with it as he thinks fit. It follows that a man who guarantees a debt at the instance of the obligee, and for a consideration moving from him, will have all the rights of a surety, including that of subrogation against the obligor, although he assumed the obligation without his knowledge or assent; *Matthews* v. *Aiken*, 505, 1 Comstock, 595; *Peake* v. *Dorwin*, 25 Vermont, 28; *Talmadge* v. *Burlingame*, 9 Barr, 212; 2 Am. Ldg. Cases, 452, 5th ed. So, where the vendor of a rent charge guarantees the purchaser, and is subsequently compelled to pay the rent, the payment will operate as a purchase, entitling him to proceed in the name of the vendee against the owner of the land; *Elkinton* v. *Newman*, 8 Harris, 281. In this case, Huston conveyed a ground rent to Newman, with a guaranty. Elkinton, the terretenant, made default, and a judgment was obtained on the guaranty against Huston, and paid by him, and it was held that he might sue Elkinton on the covenants in the ground rent deed.

The question whether a payment by a surety operates as a purchase, is, however, one of intention; and although the natural presumption is that he means to keep the debt alive; *Neilson* v. *Fry*, 16 Ohio, N. S., 552, no such inference is possible in the face of an explicit declaration to the contrary; See *Brown* v. *Lang*, 4 Ala. 50; *Houston* v. *The Bank*, 25 Id. 250; *Rittenhouse* v. *Levering*, 6 W. & S. 190, 199; *Kuhn* v. *North*, 10 S. & R. 399. The question should therefore be left to the jury, with instructions to find in favor of the right to subrogation, unless it appears unequivocally that the surety meant to satisfy the demand, not only as it regarded himself but in its bearing on the principal debtor; *Croft* v. *Moore*, 9 Watts, 451, 455; *The Rockingham Bank* v. *Claggett*, 9 Foster, 292. It was, notwithstanding, held in *Moore* v. *Campbell*, 36 Vermont, 361, that if the surety pay the debt without stipulating that it shall be kept alive, the presumption is in favor of extinguishment. The court said that where the surety pays through a third person to whom the debt is assigned, the transaction will be construed as a purchase; *The Ætna Ins. Co.* v. *Wires*, 28 Vermont, 95. And so, perhaps, where he pays himself and takes an assignment; *Edgerly* v. *Emerson*, 3 Foster, 555. But that if he pays in person, and nothing is said, it is satisfaction. This opinion is not tenable because subrogation, like contribution, is an equity which does not depend on contract, although it may be rebutted by evidence that such was not the design.

Where, however, the surety in a bond paid the debt, and tore off the seal, the court held that as the instrument was gone at law, there was nothing to which the surety could be subrogated; *Rittenhouse* v. *Levering*, 6 W. & S. 190, 199.]

In general, a surety is not entitled to subrogation until he pays the debt in full; and if such payment has not been made, the creditor will be left in the full control and possession of the debt and of the remedies for its recovery; *The Bank of England* v. *Tarleton*, 23 Mississippi, 182; *Lee* v. *Griffin*, 31 Id. 632; *Grove* v. *Brien*, 1 Maryland, 438; *The Neptune Ins. Co.* v. *Dorsey*, 3 Maryland, Ch. 334, 433; *Swan* v. *Patterson*, 7 Maryland, 164; *Hollingsworth* v. *Floyd*, 2 Harris & Gill, 87; *Cottrell's Appeal*, 11 Id. 294.]

[It should be observed, that as subrogation is the creature of equity, it will never be enforced against the superior equities of third persons; *Patterson* v. *Pope*, 5 Dana, 241; *Erb's Appeal*, 2 Penrose & Watts, 296; *Goswiler's Estate*, 3 Id. 200; *Himes* v. *Keller*, 3 Watts & Sergeant, 401, 404; *Houston* v. *The Bank*, 25 Alabama, 260; *Kyner* v. *Kyner*, 6 Watts, 221, 227; *Bank of Pennsylvania* v. *Potius*, 10 Id. 148, 152; *Crump et al.* v. *M'Murtry*, 8 Missouri, 408, 413; *Union Bank of Maryland* v. *Edwards*, 1 Gill & Johnson, 346, 365; *Hardcastle* v. *Commercial Bank of Delaware*, 1 Harrington, 374, 378, *note;* nor to the prejudice or injury of the creditor, and therefore not until the creditor is fully paid and satisfied; *Hollingsworth* v. *Floyd*, 2 Harris & Gill, 87; *Swan* v. *Patterson*, 7 Maryland, 164, *ante*. In *Lee* v. *Griffin*, 31 Mississippi, 632, where the creditor held a mortgage as security, the court refused to decree a foreclosure at the instance of the surety, because payment was essential to the right of subrogation. The right of the surety to insist that the obligation shall be paid when due, is notwithstanding recognized in England and the United States; and some of the courts hold that the creditor may be compelled to collect the debt, or lose the power of recourse against the surety: *Pain* v. *Packard*, 13 Johnson, 174; *King* v. *Baldwin*, 2 Johnson, Ch. 554; 17 Johnson, 384; 2 American Leading Cases, 414, 5th ed. It was accordingly said in *Rice* v. *Downing*, 12 B. Monroe, 44, that the surety might, on making a payment on account, or partial payment, or although nothing had been paid, require the creditor to proceed forthwith against the principal, *ante*, 135; and it is plain that the distinction between this and subrogation is extremely thin: the one being a right to sue in the name of the creditor, the other to compel the creditor to proceed by suit, and the object in both cases being to protect or indemnify the surety.]

The principles, and practice in chancery, in regard to contribution among co-sureties, are similar in their nature to those relating to the indemnity of the sureties by the principal.

One surety who has paid the debt, or has paid more than his ratable share, is entitled to recover contribution, in equity, from his co-sureties; and where all are solvent, each is liable for his proportionate share; *Preston* v *Preston et als.*, 4 Gratton, 89, 90; and contribution may be recovered in equity from the estate of a deceased surety, for a payment made after his death: *M'Kenna* v. *George*, 2 Richardson's Equity, 15, 17; *Wood* v. *Leland and others*, 1 Metcalf, 387, 389; though the contrary was held, Archer, J., dissenting, in *Waters* v. *Riley*, 2 Harris & Gill, 306, 311, 314. If one surety is insolvent, his share will in equity be apportioned amongst the solvent sureties; *Burrows and Brown* v. *M'Whann and Campbell*, 1 Desaussure, 409, 424; *Breckinridge* v. *Taylor*, 5 Dana, 110, 111; *Hilton* v. *Crist*, Id. 384; except where the surety, seeking contribution, has himself been the cause of the insolvent surety's share not being made out of his estate; *Preston* v. *Preston et als.;* and the departure of a surety from the state is, in respect to the liability of the other co-sureties for his share, equivalent to his insolvency: *M'Kenna* v. *George*, 2 Richardson's Equity, 15, 18; *Bosley* v. *Taylor, &c.*, 5 Dana, 157. But a surety cannot compel a contribution from his co-sureties until he has paid the debt; *Wood* v. *Leland and others;* nor unless the principal be insolvent, or at least unless it appear that due diligence has been used, unsuccessfully, to obtain from him the sum claimed; *M'Cormack's*

Administrator v. *Obannon's Exe-cutor and Devisees*, 3 Munford, 484, 487; *Daniel* v. *Ballard*, 2 Dana, 296, 297; *Morrison* v. *Poyntz*, 7 Id. 307; *Rainey* v. *Yar-borough*, 2 Iredell's Equity, 249, 251; *Allen* v. *Wood*, 3 Id. 386, 388: "the co-surety," said the court, in the last of these cases, "is bound to answer only in the place of his principal, and, if he is able, it is the duty of the surety, who has paid the debt, to look to him; if he is not able, he then, and only then, has a right to seek his redress from his co-surety. Nor can a co-surety speculate in the debt to the disadvantage of his co-sureties, their liability de-pending, in every instance, on what he has actually paid, and not on the amount of the debt or obli-gation; *Tarr* v. *Ravenscraft*, 12 Grattan, 642; *Edgerly* v. *Emer-son*, 3 Foster, 555; *The Bank of Mobile* v. *Robertson*, 19 Alabama, 798.

But this right of mutual contri-bution exists only among those who are *co-sureties;* that is, are sureties for the same thing, and are bound for the discharge of the same duty. And in determining whether different sets of sureties, are, in reality, co-sureties, and en-titled to contribution among one another, equity has respect to sub-stance and not to form—to the en-gagements which the sureties have entered into, and not to the instru-ments by which their engagements are manifested. If several per-sons, or several sets of persons, enter into engagements of surety-ship, which are the same in their legal operation and character; that is, if they become sureties for the same duty, or debt, of, to, and for the same persons, though by differ-ent instruments, at different times, and without a knowledge of the obligations of each other, they will be bound to mutual contribution in equity; *Breckinridge* v. *Tay-lor*, 5 Dana, 110, 112; *Daniel* v. *M'Rae*, 2 Hawks, 590, 604; *dicta* in *Harrison* v. *Lane et al.*, 5 Leigh, 414, 417; in *Langford's Ex'or* v. *Perrin*, Id. 552, 558; and in *Screven* v. *Joyner, Ex'r, and others*, 1 Hill's Chancery, 252, 260, 261; *Craig & Angle* v. *An-keney*, 4 Gill, 226, 232; *Butler* v. *Birkey*, 13 Ohio, N. S. 514; *Armitage* v. *Pulver*, 37 New York, 494. Thus, if there be several sureties in an official bond for the conduct of a sheriff, guar-dian, or cashier, and, at a subse-quent time, another bond with sureties for the general conduct of the person, in the same form with the previous one, be given, all the sureties in both bonds are liable to contribution among one another; *Bell* v. *Jasper*, 2 Ire-dell's Equity, 597; *M'Kenna* v. *George*, 2 Richardson's Equity, 15, 17, 18; *Breckinridge* v. *Tay-lor*, 5 Dana, 110; *Bosley* v. *Tay-lor, &c.*, Id. 157; *Harris* v. *Fer-guson*, 2 Bailey, 397, 401. And where a note with the names of certain persons upon it, who stood in the relation of co-sureties for the maker, has been offered for discount, and not been satisfac-tory, the name of another person has been procured, who also be-comes a surety for the maker, all these persons are co-sureties with one another, and subject to mutual contribution, though the earliest sureties had no knowledge of the last's becoming a surety; *Stout* v. *Vause, &c.*, 1 Robinson's Virginia, 169; *Warner* v. *Price*, 3 Wendell, 397; *Norton* v. *Coons*, 3 Denio, 130; 2 Selden, 33; *Woodworth* v. *Bowers*, 5 Indiana, 277; *Sisson* v. *Barrett*, 6 Barb. 99; 2 Comstock, 406; see also *M'Neil* v. *Sandford*, 3 B. Monroe, 11, 12. "If the suretyship," said Stanard, J., in *Stout* v. *Vause, &c.*, "be substantially and in its nature that of one of several original sureties, on the payment under its obligation, the duty of contribution attaches to the other sureties." It was said in like manner in *Neil* v. *Sandford*, that the mere circumstance that the last obligor did not sign until three months after the other, was altogether insufficient to qualify the legal import of the contract, or show that he was a collateral guarantor instead of a co-surety. And whatever form the relation of the several sureties may bear upon the face of the instrument, parol evidence is admissible in equity to show that they were in fact co-sureties for the same thing. Where successive endorsers all endorse for accommodation of the maker, though at different times, and without communication or mutual understanding, they are in equity co-sureties, subject to common contribution; *Daniel* v. *M'Rae*, 2 Hawks, 590; and evidence is admissible to show that successive endorsers sign for accommodation, and thus to render

them subject to contribution; *Love* v. *Wall*, 1 Id. 313. It has, notwithstanding, been held, that accommodation endorsers, like endorsers for value, are answerable in the inverse order of their signatures, unless they sign at the same time, or in pursuance of a mutual agreement; *M'Neily* v. *Patchin*, 23 Missouri, 40, 43; *Dunn* v. *Wade*, Ib. 207; *Williams* v. *Bosson*, 11 Ohio, 67; *M'Donald* v. *Magruder*, 3 Peters, 474. The question is one of intention, and open to the whole range of parol evidence. When co-sureties become bound in different bonds for the same duty, and the bonds are for different amounts, contribution between them is to be in the proportion of the penalties of the several bonds; *Bell* v. *Jasper*, 2 Iredell's Equity, 597, 601; *Armitage* v. *Pulver*, 37 New York, 494.

But if several, or successive, obligations of suretyship be not, in substance and nature, those of original sureties for the same thing, then, according to the circumstances, *either* there will be no recourse whatever, of contribution or indemnity, among the several sets of sureties, *or*, the original surety will be exempt from contribution to the latter surety, and entitled to full indemnity from him, *or*, he may be bound to make full indemnity to the new surety, and of course not entitled to call on him for contribution. Each of these cases may be considered separately.

(1.) If the obligations of the different classes of sureties, are for wholly distinct things, and have no relation to, nor operation upon, one another, though they may arise out of the same principal indebtedness, there is no claim, from one class upon the other, either for contribution or indemnity; *Langford's Ex'or* v. *Perrin*, 5 Leigh, 552, 558. In like manner, one set of sureties may be substituted for another, in the same duty, whose liability ceases, and then the latter set have no recourse against their predecessors; as in *Hutchins et al.* v. *M'Cauley*, 2 Devereux & Battle's Equity, 399, and *Longley* v. *Griggs*, 10 Pickering, 121. See also *Field* v. *Pelot*, 1 M'Mullan's Equity, 370, and *U. S.* v. *Wardwell et al.*, 5 Mason, 82, 85.

(2.) If one be bound either personally or in his property, as original surety for a debtor, and the creditor bring suit against the principal, and the latter in the course of the legal proceedings, give a bail-bond, or prison-bounds bond, or appeal bond, or injunction bond, with a surety, this latter surety, upon paying the debt, has has no recourse whatever against the original surety or his property; *Douglass* v. *Fagg*, 8 Leigh, 588; *Givens et al.* v. *Nelson's Ex'or et al.*, 10 Id. 382; *Langford's Ex'or* v. *Perrin*, 5 Id. 555, 557; *Stout* v. *Vause, &c.*, 1 Robinson's Virginia, 169, 180; *Patterson* v. *Pope*, 5 Dana, 241; *Smith* v. *Bing*, 3 Ohio, 33; *Daniel* v. *Joyner*, 3 Iredell's Equity, 513; *Burns and others* v. *The Huntingdon Bank*, 1 Penrose & Watts, 395; *Pott* v. *Nathans*, 1 W. & S. 155; *Knox* v. *Vallandingham*, 13 Smedes & Marshall, 526; *Hammock* v. *Baker*, 3 Bush.

208; *Schnitzel's Appeal*, 13 Wright, 23; *Chaffin* v. *Campbell*, 4 Sneed. 184; And the converse proposition established in *Parsons* v. *Briddock*, 2 Vernon, 608, and approved by Sir William Grant, in *Wright* v. *Morley*, 11 Vesey, 12, 22, that the original surety, if he pays, has a right to enforce the obligation of the bail for his own full indemnity, is enforced in some of the preceding cases; *Potts* v. *Nathan*; *Burns* v. *The Huntingdon Bank*; *Chiffin* v. *Campbell*, 4 Sneed. 184, 191; and nothing can be more certain or obvious than the justice of that principle; *Hammock* v. *Baker*; *Mitchell* v. *De Witt*, 25 Texas, 180. The suit against the principal debtor was brought for the equal benefit of the creditor and of the original surety, who, in fact, has a right in equity to compel such a suit to be brought, or to institute it himself; the bail then engages for the sufficiency of the principal in the matter of that suit, which is for the benefit of the creditor and the original surety, and thus places himself in the position of the principal debtor in relation to them; and he becomes equitably answerable to them, because it was by his intervention that they were deprived of the power of making satisfaction from the principal. [Thus in *Brandenburg* v. *Flynn*, 12 B. M. 397, the court said they knew of no principle on which a subsequent surety who came to the aid of the debtor solely at his instance, and without the request or concurrence of the other sureties, could make them liable for indemnity or contribution, and that the cases had on the contrary, established, that the prior sureties were under these circumstances entitled to be substituted to the remedies of the creditor against the subsequent surety. It follows that the surety in a bond given in the course of an application to chancery to stay proceedings at law, will have no right of recourse against a prior surety, whose obligation reaches back to the acquisition of the debt, or has been assumed at an intermediate period; *Bohanon* v. *Combs*, 12 B. M. 563; *Brandenburgh* v. *Flynn*. In *Schnitzel's Appeal*, 13 Wright, 23, judgment was entered by confession on a joint bond, one obligor being a principal the other a surety; and one Mast, became bail for stay of execution at the request of the principal. It was contended that this enured to the benefit of the surety by postponing the levy, which might otherwise have been made on his goods. He could not, therefore, be entitled to subrogation against Mast. The record showed that the latter intervened on behalf of both obligors, and the presumption was that the request came from both. The court were, however, of opinion that if such was the natural inference, it might be explained by parol. It appeared from the testimony that the bail had been entered exclusively at the instance of the principal. "It is, therefore," said Woodward, J., "the case of a prior surety who has paid the debt of the principal seeking satisfaction out of a subsequent surety, who, by his interposition, got time

for the principal debtor to the prejudice of the prior surety." The principle applies where a surety intervenes, at the request of a party who is primarily liable for the debt, and thereby postpones the remedy of another whose liability is secondary, although the latter may not be a surety in the ordinary sense of the term. In *McCormick* v. *Irwin*, 11 Casey, 111, a bill in equity was filed against Irwin and Whittaker, to enforce the payment of a debt which they owed as co-partners, although Whittaker had covenanted with Irwin to pay the whole. Whittaker thereupon gave a bond with sureties to prevent the appointment of a receiver. A decree was finally rendered against both, which Irwin satisfied, and proceeded on the bond. The court held, that on the execution of the covenant he became a surety, and Whittaker the principal. He was consequently entitled to subrogation against the defendant, who had intervened at Whittaker's request.

The question is, however, primarily one of fact, and if a principal and surety join in taking a writ of error, a third person, who becomes bail, in error, at the instance of the principal, with the knowledge and assent of the surety, may have a right of recovery against the latter; *Hartwell* v. *Smith*, 15 Ohio, N. S. 200. The material inquiry under these circumstances is, at whose instance the subsequent surety assumed the liability, and a request is in this, as in most instances, evidence from which the law will imply a promise.

In *Hartwell* v. *Smith*, the court held the following language in delivering judgment: "It is well settled, that if the interposition of the second surety is for the benefit of the principal alone, without the sanction or assent of the first surety, who may be prejudiced thereby—as when the effect of the second bond to prevent the enforcement of present payment from the principal, and thus to prolong the responsibility of the first surety—in such a case the equity of the first surety is superior, and he is entitled to be subrogated to the rights of the creditor as against the second. * * But the rule is otherwise where the surety in the second bond becomes bound for a purpose in which both the principal and the prior surety concur, in which they both have an interest, and where the assent of the prior surety is expressly given, or is clearly to be inferred from the circumstances of the case. In such a case, the last surety has a right to look for his indemnity, not only to his principal, but to such fixed securities as had been given to the creditor when his engagement was entered into, and on the faith of which he may be presumed to have incurred his obligations; *Howe* v. *Frazer*, 2 Robinson, La. 424."

"It is settled law, that if a creditor, by valid contract with his principal debtor, without the consent of the surety, extend the time of payment, by thus tying up his own hands, and suspending his right of action on the original contract against the principal, he discharges the surety. But if the contract for extending the time be made with the assent of the surety, his liability remains unaffected. Upon a principle quite analogous to this do the conflicting equities of prior and subsequent sureties, in cases like the present, depend. If, without the consent of the first surety, the creditor is arrested in the collection of his debt from the principal, by the interposition of a second surety, the former will be allowed, for his indemnity, to be subrogated to the rights of the creditor against the latter. But this equitable right can have no place where the first surety assents to the second contract of suretyship, and especially where it is entered into at his instance, or for his benefit."]

In Maryland, it has been decided that bail is not liable to the surety for *contribution*; see *Semmes, use of Baden,* v. *Naylor,* 12 Gill & Johnson, 358: but the courts of that State seem to have overlooked the true ground of the decision in *Parsons* v. *Briddock*.

(3.) If one set of sureties be bound for a debt, and then the obligee takes another bond, as supplemental security upon which the obligors are to be liable, only in case the principal and sureties in the former bond fail to pay the sureties in the former bond, stand in the relation of principals to the new sureties, who are not bound with them, but for them; they have no claim for contribution against the new sureties, and are bound to them for full indemnity: and the secondary or supplemental nature of the second bond may be shown by a memorandum upon it, or by parol ; *Craythorne* v. *Swinburne*, 14 Vesey, 160 ; *Harrison* v. *Lane et al.*, 5 Leigh, 414 ; *dicta* in *Langford's Ex'or* v. *Perrin*, Id. 552, 558, and in *Stout* v. *Vause, &c.*, 1 Robinson's Virginia, 169, 181. See the subject at large in *Field* v. *Pelot*, 1 M'Mullan's Equity, 370, where it is held that the question whether the second set of sureties are substituted in the place of the first, or are supplemental to them, or are joint sureties with them, depends upon the evidence of intention afforded by circumstances. Many instances of this supplemental suretyship occur. Thus, where the plaintiff became surety in an appeal from the County Court to the Circuit Court, and upon the affirmance of that decision, the defendant became surety on appeal to the Supreme Court, and judgment was again given against the appellant, and the plaintiff paid the debt, it was held that he was not entitled to recover contribution from the defendant, because they never were co-sureties ; and the defendant was the surety of the plaintiff as much as of his principals ; and if he had paid, would have been entitled to full indemnity from the plaintiff; *Cowan* v. *Duncan*, Meigs, 470, 472. See also, *La Grange* v. *Merrill*, 3 Barbour's Chancery, 625. So, where A. as surety, signs with B. a note payable to C., and C. endorses it for accommodation, C. is a supplemental surety to A., and A. has no right to contribution from him ; this, at least, is the relation of A. and C. on the face of

the paper, but it might be shown by parol evidence that A. and C. agreed to be common sureties for B. ; *Smith* v. *Smith*, 1 Devereux's Equity, 173. So, where a note was signed by A. as principal and B. as surety, and then by C. as " surety for the above names," C. was held to be a supplemental surety, not liable to contribute to B. ; *Harris* v. *Warner*, 13 Wendell, 400 ; *Thompson* v. *Sanders*, 4 Dev. & Bat. 404. And where a note was made by A. as principal, and B. and C. as sureties, and afterwards guarantied by a fourth person, the guarantor was held not to be liable to contribute to one of the sureties who had paid. " The sureties," said the Court, " were in effect principals, so far as regards the guarantor : the law raises no implied promise on the part of the guarantor to contribute in the case of a surety's paying the note, as it does on the part of a co-surety :" *Longley* v. *Griggs*, 10 Pickering, 121.

[In these instances there was a note or memorandum appended to the signature of the party claiming to be exempt from contribution, which indicated that he executed the instrument as a surety for the other signers, and not with them ; and it has been a disputed question whether such a result will follow from a collateral agreement, which does not appear in writing. It is conceded that if A., B. and C. unite in a bond or note, and the consideration is shown to have moved to A., he will be a principal, and the rest sureties, for a reason like that which prevails where one man pays the price, and the conveyance is made to another. This does not affect B. and C., or show that they should not contribute equally to the liquidation of the debt. C. may however offer to prove that he executed the instrument on the faith of a promise by B. to save him harmless, and it will then be requisite to determine whether the case is one for the admission of parol evidence. The weight of authority is, that it should be received, because the note defines the obligation of the makers to the payee, and not their relations to each other. As between the obligees and the obligors, it cannot be shown that some of the obligors were not to be called on in the first instance, nor unless default was made by the person who received and benefited by the consideration. As between the obligors there is no written agreement; there is merely a natural inference or presumption that each is to bear his share of the common burden; *Barry* v. *Ransom*, 12 N. Y. 462.

The law was held the other way in *Norton* v. *Coons*, 3 Denio, 130; 6 N. York, 33; but this decision has been overruled, and it is now established that a co-contractor who gives a promise of indemnity as a means of inducing another to affix his signature, is a principal relatively to him, although both are strangers to the consideration, and sign for the benefit of the party to whom it moves; *Melms* v. *Werdehoff*, 14 Wisconsin, 18; *Barry* v. *Ransom*; *Keith* v. *Good-*

win, 31 Vermont, 268, 275; *Adams* v. *Flanegan*, 36 Id. 400; *Apgar* v. *Hiler*, 4 Zabriskie, 808. Such a promise is not within the statute of frauds, because the parties are liable independently of the promise which merely regulates the order of payment among themselves; *Barry* v. *Ransom*, 2 Kernan, 462; *Apgar* v. *Hiler*; *Batson* v. *King*, 4 Hurlstone & Norman, 739; 1 Smith's Lead. Cases, 512, 7th Am. ed. The principle is the same whether the contract with the creditor is by parol or under seal; *Thomas* v. *Cook*, 8 B. & C. 728.

It is established under these decisions that one of several sureties may show that he became answerable on the faith of an express or implied promise that he should be entitled to look to the other sureties for indemnity.

The right of a surety to contribution is an equity, which may, like most other equities, be rebutted by oral testimony, although the contract out of which it grows is in writing; and hence a parol agreement between the sureties to a bond or other written instrument that one shall be saved harmless by the others, or shall not be liable to them for contribution, will preclude a suit in derogation of the agreement; *Barry* v. *Ransom*, 2 Kernan, 462; *Apgar* v. *Hiler*, 4 Zabriskie, 808.

There is another point about which there has been much difference of opinion. It has been contended that as the right to contribution grows out of the assumption of a common burden, it cannot be taken away without the consent of the parties interested in enforcing it. It is not enough that the surety who seeks to be exonerated, stipulated with the creditor, or with the principal debtor, that the other sureties should be primarily liable. It should appear that the condition was made known to them, and that they agreed to it. The argument was clearly stated by the counsel for the defendant in *Norton* v. *Coons*, 6 N. Y. 33, 38. "When several persons are about to become sureties for a debtor, they either regulate their rights and duties as between themselves by agreement, or leaving them to be determined by law, they enter into the contract with the creditor without any such agreement. If they make no agreement between themselves, equity determines their duty to each other. Their agreement, however, if they make one, forms the law of their rights and duties as between themselves; *Craythorne* v. *Swinburne*, 14 Ves. 160; *Harris* v. *Warner*, 13 Wend. 400. But an agreement affecting the rights and duties of all the sureties, must be made by all. A part of them cannot make an agreement which shall control the rights and duties of all, or have the effect to throw upon one not a party to it, a greater burden than the law would oblige him to bear, had no agreement been made. Still less can a part of the sureties make an agreement with the debtor, which shall have the effect of casting a greater burden upon the other co-sureties, and of exonerating themselves from liability to contribution. As the debtor is

not a party to the obligation to contribute, so it follows that he has no power over that obligation to modify or release it."

This view of the law is sustained by *Warner* v. *Price*, 3 Wend. 397, *Flint* v. *Day*, 9 Wend., and *Norton* v. *Coons*, 3 Denio, 132; 6 New York, 33; although the judgment of the Court of Appeals in the latter case seems to have been based on the idea that parol evidence was inadmissible, as tending to vary the import of a written instrument.

There can be no doubt that the principle on which these decisions proceeds is just. The fallacy lies in applying it to cases where there is no evidence of a common purpose. If two or more persons agree to be sureties for a third, they impliedly agree to be equally liable for the debt. But this presumption may be rebutted by proof that they contracted severally without any common understanding or design. If A. unites with B. in the execution of a promissory note for the accommodation of the latter, without requiring or expecting C. to affix his signature, and C. is subsequently asked to sign by B., he may obviously make any terms that he thinks fit. He may buy the note, or he make an advance and take the note as a security, or he may sign it as a co-promissor or indorser. In the former case, he is entitled to proceed directly on the instrument against A. and B.; and his right to call upon them for indemnity, is not less plain in the latter. It is accordingly well settled under the recent course of decision, that a subsequent surety may make any contract for his own protection, which does not disappoint the legitimate expectations of those who have previously become answerable for the debt; *Adams* v. *Flanagan*, 36 Vermont, 400; *Apgar* v. *Hiler* ; *Keith* v. *Goodwin* ; *Briggs* v. *Boyd*, 37 Vermont, 534; *Melms* v. *Werdehoff*, 14 Wisconsin, 18.

The problem is more complicated where a party who appears on the face of a negotiable instrument as a maker or acceptor, asks for subrogation against another, whose liability is secondary as compared with his own. It is conceded, that in the case of bills and notes, as of other contracts, one who does not receive and profit by the consideration, is a surety, as it regards one who does. Here the form of the contract is controlled by the equity arising out of a collateral fact. But the question which of two or more parties to a commercial instrument, who are alike strangers to the consideration, is a principal relatively to the other, depends in the first instance on the terms of the writing and the order in which they sign; although this presumption is not conclusive, and may be rebutted by parol. Such at least, is the general rule, although there is much doubt whether it applies as between an accommodation drawer and acceptor of a bill. If A. and B. unite in asking C. to make an advance, he may proceed against both, though B. alone receives the money. The case is so far varied where the request is put in the form of a bill of exchange, that the acceptor is liable to the drawer on the face of the instrument, not the drawer to the acceptor. But this rule does not apply in a suit brought dehors the bill, and the acceptor may maintain assumpsit against the drawer for money expended for his use. But the presumption is still in favor of the latter, and a recovery cannot be had in such a suit, unless it appears that the bill was accepted and paid without consideration to accommodate the defendant. And the better opinion seems to be that where the acceptor and drawer are both strangers to the consideration, the liability of the acceptor is primary as the terms of the instrument import, and that he cannot require the drawer to indemnify him in the absence of an agreement to that effect.

In *Griffith* v. *Reed*, 21 Wend. 300. Dickson drew on the plaintiff, Griffith, for $4,000. The draft was also signed by the defendant as "surety." The plaintiff accepted and paid the draft with his own funds, for Dickson's accommodation, and now declared against Dickson and Reed for money paid, &c. The plaintiff contended, that when an advance is made, or an act of any kind performed at the request of two persons, both are answerable, although the consideration moves exclusively to one. Such a request appeared on the face of the bill, and was sufficient to sustain the suit. It is as immaterial that Reed described himself as a surety. This defined his obligation as it regarded Dickson, but did not affect the plaintiff.

Bronson, J., said, "that the plaintiff could not recover on the bill as such. Taking the instrument as it stood, his obligation was primary, that of the defendants secondary, to pay if he made default. It was, therefore, requisite to go outside of the writing, and rely on a collateral and implied agreement. And here the evidence negatived the liability of Reed, by showing that the bill was paid for Dickson's use, and at his instance. That Reed signed the draft as a surety, would not be a defence against any one who was a holder for value and could proceed as such under the law merchant. But it was conclusive, that he, like the plaintiff, became answerable without consideration, and for Dickson's benefit. As between an accommodation drawer and acceptor, the liability of the latter was primary. It was his duty to indemnify the drawer; and as this was a legal inference from the order in which the names appeared on the instrument, it could not be varied by parol." So where there were three drawers, two of whom were sureties for the third, and the drawee accepted and paid with notice of their equity, although it did not appear from the instrument, it was held on the authority of *Phelps* v. *Garrow*, 8 Paige, 322, and *Griffith* v. *Reed*, that he could not look to them for reimbursement, and that his only recourse was against the principal; *Wing* v. *Terry*, 5 Hill, 160.

When, however, the question arose in *Suydam* v. *Woodfall*, 4 Hill, 211; 2 Denio, 205; a different view was taken by the court of appeals, and one who unites with another in drawing on a third person without giving him the means of meeting the draft, said to be under an obligation to indemnify the drawee, although he signs as surety and for the accommodation of the other drawer; See *Wright* v. *Garlinghouse*, 27 Barb. 474; *Batson* v. *King*, 4 Hurlstone & Norman, 739; *Apgar* v. *Hiler*, 4 Zabriskie, 704.

In these instances the drawer who signed as surety, had notice that the bill was accepted for the accommodation of the other drawer, and in the absence of such knowledge would not have been answerable to the acceptor. It is a general rule, that where there is no controlling equity the legal right shall prevail. The promise of the drawer is contingent to pay if the acceptor makes default. *Prima facie* the latter is the principal, the former a guarantor. If both share in, or both are strangers to the consideration, the form of the contract must govern; *Clapp* v. *Rice*, 13 Gray, 403. Where a bill drawn, indorsed, or accepted for the accommodation of a third person, is taken up by the endorser, he may recover on the bill against the drawer, and the latter has a like remedy against the acceptor. Under these circumstances, they are all sureties, as it regards him for whose use the instrument is made or discounted; but the indorser is not a surety with the drawer, nor the drawer with the acceptor. Such is clearly the relation between an accommodation endorser and a drawee who accepts without consideration to accommodate the drawer. See *Sweet* v. *McAllister*, 4 Allen, 353. In *Cooper* v. *Platt*, 3 Wright, 528, the defendant indorsed various bills for the accommodation of the drawer. The plaintiff accepted one of them, which he was subsequently compelled to pay. It appeared in evidence that the acceptance was without consideration, although this was not known to the indorser, and the court held that the latter might appropriate the indemnity which he had received from the drawer to the payment of the other drafts, to the exclusion of that held by the plaintiff. Lowrie, C. J., said that the plaintiff and defendant were both sureties, but the latter, by the terms of the instrument, was liable only in case the plaintiff made default. He might, therefore, stipulate for an indemnity, without being obliged to share it with the plaintiff, unless the fund was large enough to cover both. See *Eastman* v. *Foster*, 8 Metcalf, 19, and *Moore* v. *Moberly*, 7 B. Monroe, 299.

It was held in like manner in *Sweet* v. *McAllister*, 4 Allen, 353, that in the absence of an express agreement to the contrary, effect will be given to the legal tenor of the instrument. If A. makes and B. indorses a promissory note for the accommodation of the payee, A. must indemnify B., unless he can show affirmatively that B. is a surety with, and not, as the indorsement imports, a surety for him. It makes no difference in the application of this principle that B. knew that A. was a surety, or even that the latter appended the word surety to his signature : *Sweet* v. *McAllister*.

It results from what has been said, that, which of the parties to a bill or note should bear the burden of the debt and acquit the rest, is a question of fact which does not necessarily depend on the tenor of the instrument, and admits of parol and extrinsic evidence. Such evidence is not admissible, unless the person who relies on it as a defence or cause of action, was a stranger to the consideration. If the payee gives value, it is immaterial that the maker does not receive it; and a maker who receives value cannot allege that the payee did give it. But it may always be shown as between an acceptor or maker on the one hand, and a drawer or payee on the other, or of two successive indorsers, that one put his name to the instrument without consideration at the request of the other to accommodate a third person, and on the faith of an express or implied promise of indemnity. So either of them may prove a mutual understanding or agreement that they should contribute equally to the discharge of the obligation. Thus an acceptor may show that he became answerable at the request of the indorser to accommodate the drawer, or of the drawer to accommodate the indorser, or of one drawer to accommodate another. In like manner, as between successive accommodation endorsers, it may be shown that the second is a surety for the first, the first for the second; or that they are co-sureties, *ante; Phillips* v. *Preston*, 5 Howard, 278, 291; *Weston* v. *Chamberlin*, 7 Cushing, 43. And as the right of indemnity carries with it that of subrogation, an accommodation acceptor may proceed against the drawer of the bill as such, in the name of the holder, although he could not on his own, or may issue execution on a judgment which the holder has already obtained.

It has been held in Massachusetts in accordance with these principles, that although an indorser for value cannot qualify or limit his liability by parol, an oral agreement by two or more accommodation indorsers to contribute equally to the payment of the note, is valid and upheld by a sufficient consideration: *Weston* v. *Chamberlin*, 7 Cushing, 403; and the decision of the Supreme Court of the United States in *Phillips* v. *Preston* is to the same effect.

It should be remembered, that while a maker or acceptor may recover in indebitatus assumpsit against the payee or drawer, on proof that he incurred the liability at his request, such evidence is not admissible under a count on the instrument itself. But the defendant in a suit on a note or bill may always, to prevent circuity of action, show that if the plain-tiff went to judgment and execution, he would be liable to refund the money as having been laid out for his use: See *Griffith* v. *Reid*, 21 Wend. 502.

The effect of a stipulation by one of several co-sureties that he is not to be called on for contribution, or that he is not to be a surety with the others, but for them, has been much discussed, and is still doubtful under the au-authorities.

It was said in *Norton* v. *Coons*, 3 Denio, 130; 6 New York, 33, that "if a surety refuses to take the burden of a co-surety, he renounces the benefit of that relation. If he will not contribute when the other surety pays the debt, he shall not have contribution when he pays it himself." And this dictum seems to have been approved in *Adams* v. *Flanagan*, 36 Vermont, 400.

This is an inaccurate statement of the question which is not whether both sureties should contribute, but whether one is not as between themselves liable for the the whole. It is no doubt true, that as contribution springs from the maxim that equality is equity, it cannot be enforced unless there is a common burden. But there may obviously be a right to indemnity when there is none to contribution. Such is the rule as between principal and surety; and one who signs as "surety for the above signers," may treat them as principals, whether they are principals or sureties as between themselves. This is generally conceded where he becomes answerable at their request, and not less true where he executes the instrument on the faith of an express or implied agreement with the creditor that he shall be entitled to subrogation on the payment of the debt. If a joint note were tendered for the price of goods, and the vendor refused to accept it without further security, a third person who guaranteed the debt, might obviously proceed in the name of the vendor against the makers, although one of them was a surety, and did not know of the guaranty: *Keith* v. *Goodwin*, 31 Vermont, 169. And as equity regards the substance of such transactions, parol evidence is admissible, that one who appears on the face of the instrument as a joint maker, is in fact a guarantor: *Melms* v. *Werdehoff*, 14 Wisconsin, 18. And the better opinion would seem to be that one who signs a joint and several promissory note, in the belief that the persons whose signatures have been already affixed to the instrument are principals, may claim indemnity from both, although one is in fact a surety: *Melms* v. *Werdehoff*, 14 Wisconsin, 18. See *Adams* v. *Flanagan*, 36 Vermont, 400, 410; *Keith* v. *Goodwin*, 31 Id. 218.

The rule in cases of this description was laid down in *Adams* v. *Flanagan*, 36 Vermont, 400, 408, in the following terms: " Is parol evidence admissible to show that the defendants signed not as co-sureties with the plaintiff, but with the intent to be sureties for him? As between the makers and the payee the note excludes

all parol evidence. It was made for the very purpose of being the proof, the sole and exclusive proof of the contract."

" But as between the signers to it, it was not made or intended to be the exclusive proof of their agreement and relations. It is well settled, that it is open to parol evidence to show the true relations of the signers, and the real nature of the contract between them."

" The makers, though all appearing to be joint principals, may be shown to be some principals and some sureties. An apparent principal may be shown to be a surety, an apparent surety a principal: *Harris* v. *Brooks*, 21 Pick. 195; 23 Maine, 156; *Lapham* v. *Barnes*, 2 Vermont, 220; *Flint* v. *Day*, 9 Vermont, 345; *Keith* v. *Goodwin*, 31 Vermont, 268; *Robinson* v. *Lyle*, 10 Barb. 512."

" In *Keith* v. *Goodwin*, the question underwent a careful examination, and the following conclusions were arrived at by the court: " If one sign a note as surety, and entrusts it to the principal, he thereby gives the latter an implied authority to obtain either additional sureties or guarantors, indefinitely, until the note is fairly launched in the market as a security, having two distinct parties."

" One who signs as surety may so stipulate at the time of entering into the obligation, as not to be liable to contribution with other sureties who have signed before him. And when one guarantees the payment of a note, on which sureties have already signed, it seems that *prima facie* his legal relation to those who have signed before him is such that he is surety for them jointly, not jointly with them." Redfield, C. J., said: "Where there is anything in the form of the contract or the nature of the transaction, to show that the subsequent sureties did not expect to be holden as co-sureties with the others, but to stand merely as sureties for all the former signers, they are entitled to full indemnity from each of the others, or all jointly. As if the surety sign expressly as surety for all the above signers, or when he signs, saying he is willing to be responsible for all of them. In such case, he is not liable to contribution: 1 Story's Eq. Jur. 498; Chitty on Con. 598; 1 Lead. Cases in Eq. 126, and notes; *Pendebury* v. *Walker*, 4 Y. & C. 424; *Moore* v. *Isley*, 2 Dev. & Bat. 372.

This very point is expressly decided in *Craythorne* v. *Swinburne*, 14 Vesey, 160. The facts of this last case seem to us very analogous to those of the present case, so far as the liability of the plaintiff to share the burden of paying this note with the defendant is concerned. In that case, as well as in this, the undertaking of the last surety was without the knowledge, expectation or privity of the former ones; it was done, too, in both cases, to induce the advance of money upon the first contract, and because it could not be obtained without such additional indemnity or guaranty. And in the case of *Craythorne* v. *Swinburne*, it was clearly held, that there was

no duty of contribution among the two classes of sureties. It is held, that in the case of *Craythorne* v. *Swinburne*, the indemnity was by a separate instrument, and here it is upon the same paper, but by a distinct contract, referring to the other for brevity, as written above. We cannot suppose it could have made any difference in the present case if the plaintiff had given his guaranty upon a separate piece of paper, writing the note or describing it, instead of referring to it as written above.

"In the case of *Craythorne* v. *Swinburne*, the question was determined upon the circumstances and oral evidence in the case, as a matter of fact, and made dependent upon the intention of the last surety."

It has accordingly been held, that one who signs as surety for the above sureties, may have recourse to them for indemnity, although his signature is affixed in that form without their knowledge or consent, unless there is some understanding or agreement to the contrary, of which he is cognizant; *Wright* v. *Garlinghouse*, 27 Barb. 474. In *Darrach* v. *Osborne*, 2 Halstead, 71, A. as principal, and B. as surety, executed a joint and several promissory note to C., who subsequently wrote his name under theirs, and transferred the instrument for value. He subsequently took up the note, and it was held that he might recover the whole amount from B.

So one who signs his name as a co-obligor or maker, in the belief that those who have already affixed their signatures are principals, may treat them as such, although they are in fact sureties, *ante;* *Melms* v. *Wirdehoff*, 14 Wisconsin, 18. In this instance the defendants executed a joint and several note, and delivered it to the payee. The latter subsequently procured the signature of the plaintiff, who put his name to the instrument in the belief that it had been given for value in the ordinary course of business, and it was held that the defendants could not allege as against him, that they had made the note without consideration for the accommodation of the payee. The principle was applied in another form in *Darrach* v. *Osborne*, 2 Halstead, 71. There is, notwithstanding, a strong presumption that those who unite in a common obligation should contribute equally to its fulfilment, and as the burden of proof is on him who maintains the contrary, he must make out his case by sufficient evidence. Proof that one of several sureties signed at the request of the others, will not, therefore, exonerate him from contribution; *Warner* v. *Price*, 3 Wend. 397; it should at least appear that they promised to save him harmless in any event; *Woodworth* v. *Bowers*, 5 Id. 277; *Bagott* v. *Muller*, 32 Indiana, 332.

It is equally true that a surety who knows that another signs in the well-founded belief that both are to be equally answerable, cannot disappoint this expectation by a secret stipulation for his own benefit. Such a course would be contrary to the good faith that should prevail in all common undertakings, and especially where the parties are volunteers. It cannot, therefore, be adopted where the sureties sign in each other's presence, nor where the tenor of the writing indicates that they are all to sign, nor where the surety who seeks to be exonerated knew that the contract would be presented to the other sureties for their signatures, nor where he had notice that a prior signer put his name to the instrument on the faith of an assurance that he also would affix his signature. But this argument does not apply where the sureties do not act in concert, nor as against a surety who has no reason to believe that the other sureties are influenced by or rely on his signature; and under these circumstances each may prescribe the terms on which he is willing to be bound; *Melms* v. *Wordshoff*, 14 Wisconsin, 18. This is conceded where the condition is appended to the signature, though not made known to the co-sureties: *Harris* v. *Warner*, 13 Wend. 405; and equally true where it appears from oral and extrinsic evidence; *Adams* v. *Flanagan*, 36 Vermont, 400, *ante,* 161.

We have seen that a joint promisor or obligor, who shows that he does not mean to assume a common burden by adding the words " surety for the above " to his signature, is not liable to contribution; *Harris* v. *Warner*, 13 Wend. 400; *Thompson* v. *Sanders*, 4 Dev. & Bat. 404, and is on the contrary entitled to indemnity if compelled to pay the debt; and it has been contended that the same result should follow where one of several sureties signs as such, while the others affix their signatures without qualification. See *Nichols* v. *Parsons*, 6 New Hampshire, 301; *Wing* v. *Terry*, 5 Hill, 160. It is, however, obvious that such a designation is affirmative, not negative. It may define the character of him who thus describes himself, but will not preclude the other signers from disclosing theirs. A recital does not operate as an estoppel, unless it is certain and leaves no doubt of the intent. That the word surety is added to the name of one joint maker, will, therefore, neither exonerate him from contribution, nor entitle him to indemnity as it regards another whose signature has no such qualification; *Sisson* v. *Barrett*, 6 Barb. 199; 2 Comstock, 406; *Lathrop* v. *Wilson*, 3 Vermont, 604; *McGee* v. *Prouty*, 9 Metcalf, 457; *Apgar* v. *Hiler*, 4 Zabriskie, 704; *Robinson* v. *Lyle*, 10 Barb. 512.]

Co-sureties, otherwise entitled to contribution, may, by agreement among themselves, so far sever their unity of interest and obligation, as to terminate the right of contribution. Thus, where three sureties agreed that the common liability should be divided, and that each should secure to the creditor the payment of one-third of the debt, and receive from him a discharge as to the residue, and this was executed on the part of one, and he obtained, with the assent of the other, a covenant from the creditor not to sue, it was held that one of the remaining sureties paying more than his share, could not call upon this one for contribution; *Moore* v. *Isley*, 2 Devereux & Battle's Equity, 372, 374. And, in some of the courts, it has been held, that wherever one surety is released by the creditor, under circumstances not to discharge the other, this other has no claim for contribution against the released surety; *Waggener* v. *Dyer*, 11 Leigh, 384, 391; *Bouchaud* v. *Dias*, 3 Denio, 238; though, of course, the remaining surety would be discharged from so much of the debt as would properly have fallen upon the one who was released; *Waggener* v. *Dyer*. But in *Boardman* v. *Paige*, 11 New Hampshire, 432, 435, it was held that a release of one surety will not discharge him from liability to contribute to another, who from the insolvency of one of the remaining sureties may pay beyond his share: and this seems to be the necessary result, unless it be considered that the discharge of one surety, without the consent of the others, releases the remaining ones from the obligation to pay more than their share in relation to the whole number originally bound. See 1 American Leading Cases, 400, 5th ed.

For the purpose of enforcing contribution among co-sureties, one surety who pays the debt is entitled to be subrogated to all the rights and remedies of the creditor, as against his co-sureties, in precisely the same manner as against the principal debtor, and though payment may have discharged the security at law, equity will keep it alive for this purpose: and this applies to bonds, judgments, decrees, mortgages, and all other securities whatsoever. See *Cuyler* v. *Ensworth*, 6 Paige, 32, 33; *Cheeseborough* v. *Millard*, 1 Johnson's Chancery, 409, 413; *Scribner* v. *Hickok*, 4 Id. 531, 532; *Lawrence* v. *Cornell*, Id. 545; *Himes* v. *Keller*, 3 Watts & Sergeant, 401, 404; *Croft* v. *Moore*, 9 Watts, 451. "In America, and certainly in Pennsylvania, a surety paying the debt of his principal, is entitled to be subrogated to all the rights and remedies of the creditors, as against his co-sureties, in precisely the same manner as against the principal debtor, and as substituted in the place of the creditor, and entitled to enforce all his liens, priorities and means of payment, and by the act of 19 & 20 Vict. c. 97, § 5, this is now the law of England;" *Hess' Estate*, 19 P. F. Smith, 275. Thus, where a judgment had been recovered against several sureties and their principal jointly, and, the principal being insolvent, two sureties had paid a considerable part of the judgment, and the administrator of another surety having paid a small balance upon it, had procured satisfaction of the judgment to be entered of record, it was held that the sureties who had paid more than their share, were entitled to be subrogated in the original judgment as against the estate of the surety who had paid

less, and for that purpose to have the judgment considered in equity as subsisting and in force; *Burrows & Brown* v. *M'Whann & Campbell*, 1 Dessaussure, 409. In *Cuyler* v. *Ensworth*, a surety, who had paid a joint judgment against himself and other sureties, sought to reach, through its medium, equitable assets of a co-surety; and, as by the practice of the court, that cannot be done until execution has been issued, and returned unsatisfied, it was objected that this was impracticable, as the judgment was satisfied at law; but the Chancellor said, that a court of equity looked to the substantial rights of parties, without regard to mere matters of form, and that, if it had been necessary, he would have restrained the defendant, by injunction, from contesting the validity of the execution at law; and it was decided that the sureties who had paid were to be regarded as assignees in equity of the judgment, and might file a creditor's bill in their own names. And the general principle that a surety paying the debt, stands precisely in the situation of the creditor in relation to the other sureties, for the purposes of contribution, is settled in *Lidderdale* v. *Robinson*, 2 Brockenbrough, 160; 12 Wheaton, 594. A statute of Virginia had provided that debts on bills of exchange should have the rank of judgment debts in the distribution of assets; and, in that case, it was decided that the claim of an indorser, a surety, who had paid the bill, against the estate of another indorser, a co-surety, for contribution, was entitled to the same rank of a judgment debt. " The principle which the case decide," said Chief Justice Marshall in the court below, " is this : where a person has paid money for which others were responsible, the equitable claim which such payment gives him on those who were so responsible, shall be clothed with the legal garb with which the contract he has discharged was invested, and he shall be substituted, to every equitable intent and purpose, in the place of the creditor whose claim he has discharged. The cases suppose the surety to stand in the place of the creditor, as completely as if the instrument had been transferred to him, or to a trustee for his use. Under this supposition; he would be at full liberty to proceed against every person bound by the instrument. Equity would undoubtedly restrain him from obtaining more from any individual than the just proportion of that individual; but to that extent, his claim upon his co-surety is precisely as valid as upon his principal." And this was fully sustained in the Supreme Court.

It has also been said, that subrogation will not be enforced in the face of a legal right; and that if the law has decided against a surety's claim, equity will not give him that claim through the medium of subrogation; *Fink* v. *Mahaffy*, 8 Watts, 384.

[It has been a disputed question whether a surety who has paid the debt is entitled to a dividend for the whole against the estate of an insolvent co-surety, or only for so much as exceeds his just proportion. The former alternative was adopted in *Hess' Estate*, 19 P. F. Smith, 272. The court said that the creditor might clearly have proved the whole debt; *Patten's Appeal*, 9 Wright, 151, and that the surety was subrogated by the mere act of payment.]

It is a settled principle of equity, that if one of several co-sureties subsequently take a security from the principal, for his own indemnity, it enures to the common benefit of all the sureties. If, therefore, the principal convey property, by a deed of trust, expressly for the benefit of one of the sureties only, the others have an equity to come upon it to the same extent that he can ; *West* v. *Belches*, 5 Munford, 187 ; *M'Mahon, &c.* v. *Fawcett, &c.*, 2 Randolph, 514 ; *Fagan* v. *Jacocks*, 4 Devereux, 263 ; *Gregory* v. *Murrell*, 2 Iredell's Equity, 233, 236 ; *Field* v. *Pelot*, 1 M'Mullen's Equity, 370 ; *Hinsdill* v. *Murray et al.*, 6 Vermont, 136, 150 ; *Elwood* v. *Diefendorf*, 5 Barbour's S. Ct. 399, 405 ; *Rice* v. *Morton*, 19 Missouri, 261 ; *Steele* v. *Mealing*, 24 Alabama, 285 ; *Tyus* v. *De Jarnette*, 26 Id. 280 ; *Silvay* v. *Dowell*, 53 Illinois ; *Aldrich* v. *Hapgood*, 30 Vermont, 617 ; *Browne* v. *Ray*, 10 New Hampshire, 702 ; *Hartwell* v. *Whitman*, 36 Alabama, 712 ; *M'Cune* v. *Bell*, 45 Missouri, 174 ; *Parham* v. *Green*, 46 North Carolina, 436 ; *Arnott* v. *Woodburn*, 36 Missouri, 99. A surety who has the means of indemnity in his hands cannot,

therefore, pay the debt and proceed against a co-surety for contribution; and if such an attempt
is made directly or through a
third person, who is used as a
tool or cover, a chancelor will stay
the suit by an injunction; *Silvay
v. Dowell*, 53 Illinois, 260. It is
immaterial whether they became
sureties at the same time or at
different periods; in either case
there is a common burden, and all
are bound to assist in bearing
it. And as each has an equal
equity against the principal, so no
one can engross the funds supplied by him to the exclusion of
the others; *Burton v. Bradly*, 13
Ohio, N. S. 514, 523. " Sureties,"
said Kennedy, J., " are bound to
observe good faith towards each
other; and when funds are placed
by the principal in the hands of
one surety to be applied either to
the payment of the debt, or for
the purpose of indemnifying him
against any loss that may arise
from the suretyship, he must be
considered as holding them for
the common benefit of all concerned. The giving of the funds
was the act of the principal, who
was equally bound to indemnify
all his sureties alike; and upon
him, as well as to all his means for
that purpose, each of them had an
equal and just claim; it is unjust
and inequitable that one surety,
without the consent of his co-sureties, should derive any exclusive
benefit from the act of the principal in giving up what he might
and ought to have applied for the
common benefit of all;" *Agnew v.
Bell*, 4 Watts, 31, 33. " The in-

demuity, which one surety takes,"
says Henderson, J., in *Moore v.
Moore*, 4 Hawks, 358, 360, " is
reached in favor of his co-surety,
upon the ground, either that it
was intended for the benefit of all,
or that the taking it was a fraud
upon the others. In such cases,
courts of equity convert him into
a trustee, not permitting him to
allege his own turpitude or selfish-
ness as a protection; for they
enter into the agreement under a
belief of perfect equality, trusting
apparently to the same laws of indemnity, and to the united exer-
tions of each other, to avoid harm
severally; therefore, to take an indemnity is a fraud upon the rest,
and more especially, as it lessens
the ability of the principal to indemnify the others, and is taken
without such secrecy, it is presumed to be designed for the
benefit of all." See also, *Hall v.
Robinson*, 8 Iredell, 56. But this
equity which arises upon the simple relation of co-sureties, may be
removed by the agreement of the
parties, either before the obligation is assumed, or afterwards.
An agreement for a separate indemnity, entered into, before one
becomes surety, with the knowledge and consent of the other, will
be good, and the latter will be entitled only to the surplus after the
former is satisfied; *Moore v.
Moore;* see also *Thompson et al.,
v. Adams et al.*, 1 Freeman's
Chancery, 225, 228: and it has
been held, also, that after two
persons have become sureties for
a common principal, they may, by
agreement, renounce their right to

take equal benefit from any securities either may obtain, and each may undertake to look out for himself, exclusively, for indemnity from the principal or for contribution from another co-surety; *Tyus* v. *De Jarnette*, 26 Alabama, 280; but such an agreement must be distinctly proved; *Long* v. *Barnett*, 3 Iredell's Equity, 631, 634; *Tyus* v. *De Jarnette*. In *Gould* v. *Fuller*, 18 Maine, 364, 367, where the general principle was admitted, that securities received by one surety before payment, enure in equity to the equal benefit of all, it was yet held that if, after one surety has paid the debt, he receives from the principal, money expressly to indemnify him for his share of the payment, he may sue his co-surety for his contributory share: but this seems to be carrying too far the exception to a settled and salutary principle of equity. If the principal has given securities to one surety, the latter cannot in chancery recover contribution from his co-surety, without accounting for the property, and either showing how much he received upon it, and making a ratable allowance of the proceeds, or showing that he could not by reasonable diligence realize from it; *Goodloe* v. *Clay*, 6 B. Munroe, 236; *Morrison* v. *Poyntz*, 7 Dana, 307, 310; *Dennis* v. *Gillespie*, 24 Mississippi, 58; *Steele* v. *Mealing*, 24 Alabama, 285; *Morrison* v. *Taylor*, 21 Id. 779; and any loss which may arise from his neglect or misconduct, will be a defence to the extent of the loss; *Taylor* v. *Morrison*, 26 Alabama, 728; *Steele* v. *Mealing; The State Bank* v. *Boseman*, 8 English, 631; *Steele* v. *Brown*, 18 Alabama, 700; *Zeiter* v. *Pierce*, 11 B. Munroe, 379; *Crow* v. *Murphy*, 12 Id. 444; *Chilton* v. *Chapman*, 13 Missouri, 470; *Silvay* v. *Dowell*, 53 Illinois, 260; 2 American Leading Cases, 403, 5th ed.; *Hilton* v. *Crist*, 5 Dana, 384, 389. The surety receiving securities, is a trustee for his co-sureties, and is bound to such discreet and reasonable use of them as would be required from a trustee, but no greater: *Carpenter* v. *Kelly*, 9 Ohio, 106; see *Pool* v. *Williams*, 8 Iredell, 286.

In like manner, the principal creditor is in equity entitled to the full benefit of any security given by the debtor to a surety for his indemnity and for the discharge of the debt; and it makes no difference that such principal creditor did not act upon the credit of such security in the first instance, or even know of its existence; *Maure* v. *Harrison*, 1 Equity Cases Abr. 93, pl. 5; *Wright* v. *Morley*, 11 Vesey, 12, 22; *Owens* v. *Miller*, 29 Maryland, 144; *Kirkman* v. *The Bank of North America*, 2 Caldwell, 397; *Moses* v. *Murgatroyd*, 1 Johnson's Chancery, 119, 129; *Phillips* v. *Thompson*, 2 Id. 418, 422; *Pratt* v. *Adams*, 7 Paige, 617, 627; *Curtis* v. *Tyler*, 9 Id. 432, 435; *Ten Eyck* v. *Holmes*, 3 Sandford, 428, 429; *Van Orden* v. *Durham*, 35 Cal. 136; *Roberts* v. *Colvin*, 3 Grattan, 359, 363; *Toulmin et al.* v. *Hamilton et al.*, 7 Alabama, 362, 367; *Ohio Life Ins. Co.* v. *Ledyard, &c.*, 8 Id. 866, 872; *Paris* v. *Hu-*

let, 26 Vermont, 308 ; *Riddle* v. *Bowman*, 7 Foster, 236 ; *Haven* v. *Foley*, 19 Missouri, 632 ; *Aldrick* v. *Martin*, 4 Rhode Island, 520 ; *Cine* v. *Vance*, 4 Clarke, 434, 441. In fact, a court of equity, under the title of subrogation, exercises a paramount control, for purposes of justice and convenience, in respect to the relation of principal and sureties. " If property is pledged to either the creditor or a surety, though not to the person seeking to charge it, it may be reached by substitution in a court of equity, without regard to the intention of the contracting parties;" per Parker, J., in *Hopewell et al.* v. *Bank of Cumberland*, 10 Leigh, 206, 226 ; see also *M'Collum* v. *Hinckley & others*, 9 Vermont, 143, 149. " This," says Parker, J., (p. 221,) " arises not from any notion of mutual contract between the parties, that in providing for the surety, the creditor shall be equally provided, but from a principle of natural equity independent of contract ; namely, that to prevent the surety from being first harassed for the debt or liability, and then turning him round to seek redress from a collateral security given by the principal, a court of equity will authorize, and even encourage, the creditor to claim through the *medium* of the surety, all the rights he has thus acquired, to be exercised for his benefit, and in discharge of his obligations." This equity of the creditor's rests upon the doctrine of subrogation or substitution ; and therefore the creditor cannot claim the security,

unless the surety had a right to come upon it. *Bibb* v. *Martin*, 14 S. & M. 87 ; *Bush* v. *Schups*, 4 Cushman, 463. If, therefore, security be given to a contingent surety, such as an indorser of negotiable paper, to indemnify him, and his liability never becomes absolute, but is discharged from default in giving notice, the payee cannot claim the benefit of the security, because being appropriated only for the case of the indorser's becoming liable, the appropriation, in truth, never took effect at all ; *Hopewell et al.* v. *Bank of Cumberland ; Bank of Virginia* v. *Boisseau et al.*, 12 Leigh, 387 ; see, also, *Ohio Life Ins. & Tr. Co.* v. *Reeder et al.*, 18 Ohio, 35, 46.

[It has been laid down broadly in some instances that the securities received by a surety from the principal, will enure to the benefit of the creditor, and cannot be withheld from him, or diverted to any other use ; *Haggarty* v. *Peterman*, 1 Paige, 299 ; *Keyes* v. *Bush*, 2 Id. 311 ; *Pratt* v. *Adams*, 7 Id. 627 ; *Curtis* v. *Tyler*, 9 Id. 432 ; *The Bank of Auburn* v. *Throppe*, 18 Johnson, 505 ; *Maure* v. *Hanson*, 1 Eq. Cases, 93 ; *Moses* v. *Murgatroyd*, 7 Johnson, Ch. 219 ; *Ten Eyck* v. *Holmes*, 3 Sandford, Ch. 428. If, said Chancellor Walworth, in *Pratt* v. *Adams*, a person standing in the situation of indorser or surety is furnished or provided by the principal debtor with a fund, or with collateral security for such a purpose, the creditor is in equity entitled to have it applied in satisfaction of the debt. It was said in like manner in *The New London Bank* v. *Lee*, 11 Conn. 112, 118, "that it had long been settled, that a surety who has paid the debt may well claim all the funds appropriated for its payment remaining in the hands of the creditors. The plaintiffs insist that the same reasons and equities apply with equal strength to their case, wherein they, as creditors, seek to apply the funds in the hands of the surety to the payment of the debts. And so we think. In both cases the security or fund is created for the payment of the debt, and is a trust existing for that specific purpose ; and whether the creditor, as in the former case, or the surety, as in this, be the trustee, is immaterial."

The rule is, notwithstanding, subject to qualifications which have been variously stated, and are not well defined. Where the principal executes a mortgage, assigns a bond, or transfers property of any kind to the surety to pay or secure the debt, a right will accrue to the creditor, which cannot be defeated by the surety and principal acting severally or in concert. Such an indemnity, is also a trust which equity will enforce notwithstanding any attempt to misappropriate the assets, or return them to the source from whence they came ; *Homer* v. *The Savings Bank*, 7 Conn. 484 ; *The New London Bank, La.*, 11 Id. 112 ; *Miller* v. *Ord*, 2 Binney, 382 ; *Ross* v. *Wilson*, 7 Smedes & Marshall, 766 ; *Dick* v. *Maury*, 9 Id. 456 ; *Paris* v. *Hulet*, 26 Vermont, 308 ;

Eastman v. *Foster*, 8 Metcalf, 19 ; *Collier* v. *Calvin*, 3 Grattan, 353. " These collateral securities," said Chancellor Kent, in *Moses* v. *Murgatroyd*, 1 Johns Ch. 119, 129, " are, in fact, trusts created for the better protection of the debt ; and it is the duty of this court to see that they fulfil their design, and whether the plaintiffs were apprised at the time of the creation of this security, is not material. The trust was created for their benefit, or for the better security of their debt, and when it came to their knowledge, they were entitled to affirm the trust, and to enforce its performance. See *Neilson* v. *Blight*, 1 Johns, Ch. Rep. 205." It was said in like manner in *Kinsey* v. *Dearmon*, 5 Caldwell, 392, that the ignorance of the creditor will not preclude him from enforcing such a trust.

On the other hand, where the security is given solely for the protection of the surety, he may waive a privilege created for his benefit, and the creditor has no interest in the grant that can supply the want of privity of contract. His right can rise no higher than that of the surety, through whom he claims, and will be subject to any defence that would have been valid against the latter : *Dempsey* v. *Bush*, 18 Ohio, N. S. 37 ; *Hunter* v. *Richardson*, 1 Duvall, 247. Whether the surety shall retain or surrender such an indemnity is a question for him alone to consider, and if he elects to give it up, and rely solely on the credit of the principal, a court of equity will not overrule his determination at the instance of the creditor, unless some further and controlling equity has supervened: *Jones* v. *The Quenipiack Bank*, 29 Conn. 35. It is therefore a good answer to such a bill that the surety has not been damnified, or that the securities were appropriated to another purpose by virtue of an agreement with the principal: *Homer* v. *The Savings Bank*; *The Ohio Life & Trust Ins. Co.*, 18 Ohio, 35; *Robb* v. *Martin*, 14 Smedes & Marshall; *Bush* v. *Stamps*, 26 Mississipi; *Osborn* v. *Noble*, 46 Id. 449; *Pratt* v. *Adams*, 7 Paige, 615; *Daniel* v. *Joyner*, 3 Iredell, Eq. 913; *Hopewell* v. *The Bank*, 10 Leigh, 206; *Finney* v. *Finney*, 4 Harris, 380. It results from these principles that the holder of a note will not be subrogated to the securities in the hands of an accommodation indorser who has been discharged by a want of notice, because the indorser is not damnified, and the right of the holder cannot rise higher than his: *Hopewell* v. *The Bank*. The rule is the same between an indorser who is not notified, and a subsequent indorser who is liable for the debt: *The Bank* v. *Boissan*, 11 Leigh, 387.

The subject was carefully examined in *Homer* v. *The Savings Bank*, 7 Conn. 483; where Bissell, J., held the following language in delivering judgment: "In *Maure* v. *Harrison*, 1 Eq. La. Abr. 93, it was adjudged that a bond creditor "shall in chancery have the benefit of all the counter bonds or collateral securities given by the princi-

pal to the surety;" "as if A. owes B. money, and he and C. are bound for it, and A. gives C. a mortgage or bond to indemnify him, B. shall have the benefit of it to recover his debt."

In *Russell* v. *Clark's Executors*, 7 Cranch, 69, 94, 97, the same doctrine was admitted. The Court, in that case, declare that the person for whose benefit a trust is created, who is ultimately to recover the money, may sustain a suit in equity to have it paid directly to himself. In *Phelps* v. *Thompson*, 2 Johns. Ch. Rep. 418. The holder of a promissory note was held entitled to the benefit of a collateral security of the debt given by the maker to the indorser, for his indemnity.

The principle to be extracted from these cases is this, that when collateral security is given, or property assigned, for the better protection or payment of a debt, it shall be made effectual for that purpose,—and that not only to the immediate party to the security, but to others who are entitled to the debt, and to make them thus effectual, a court of chancery will lend its aid. And the reason is, that such is the intent of the transaction.

"They are trusts," says the late Chancellor Kent, in the case already cited, "executed for the better protection of the debt; and a court of chancery will see, that they fulfil their design." Beyond this principle, however, it is believed, no case has gone."

It is notwithstanding obvious, that a surety who has received an indemnity cannot apply it to any other purpose than the payment of the debt, without the consent of the principal debtor. Such an attempt on his part will give rise to an equity in favor of the principal, which may be enforced by the creditor, as the party beneficially interested. It was on this ground, that the surety was endeavoring to withhold the securities in his hands, both from the creditor and principal, and convert them to his own use, that the judgments in *The New London Bank* v. *Lee*, 11 Conn. 112; and *Lewis* v. *DeForest*, 20 Id. 440, can be reconciled with the doctrine of *Homer* v. *The Savings Bank*. See *Jones* v. *The Quinipiack Bank*.

It should moreover be remembered that the insolvency of the surety may vary the case by bringing it within the rule, that one who is unable to fulfil his pecuniary obligations, is not entitled to release or forego any right or interest that can be made available as a means of payment. Under these circumstances, the securities held by the surety cannot be applied to any debt which the principal does not owe, without a breach of faith towards the latter, nor to any debt which he does, unless it is also due by the surety. The principle only applies to a transfer without consideration, or for a consideration in which the surety does not share, and will not preclude the principal and surety from using a collateral given as an indemnity against one liability, for the discharge of another, or as a

means of raising money for their joint account.

The failure of the surety will not invalidate an appropriation made while he is still solvent and able to fulfil his obligations; *Thrall* v. *Spencer*, 16 Conn. 139; *Jones* v. *The Quinipiack Bank*, 29 Id. 25. This is equally true, whether the surety disposes of his own assets, or of those which he has received from the principal. In the case last cited, the condition of the mortgage which gave rise to the controversy, was that the Jerome Manufacturing Company, who were the mortgagors, would "pay at maturity" certain bills drawn on Barnum, the mortgagee, and which he had accepted for their accommodation, and "would save him harmless from all loss or damage by reason of the same." Subsequently, and before the bills matured, the mortgagors and mortgagee joined in a deed of the premises to the Quinipiack Bank, as a security for certain advances to the mortgagee. The Manufacturing Company and Barnum failed, and a bill was filed by the holders of the drafts to set up the mortgage against the deed. It was held that they had no equity that could override the legal title of the grantee. The Court were clearly of opinion that the mortgage was both in effect and form merely an indemnity. It was intended to secure the acceptor, and not to secure the payment of the bills. The stipulation that these should be paid at maturity, merely indicated the mode in which the obligation to save him harmless was to be fulfilled. The mortgage was not therefore an inseparable incident of the debt. It might have acquired that character through the insolvency of the drawers and acceptor. But when the deed to the bank was executed they were in good credit, and able to meet their engagements. Their subsequent failure could not affect the title which had already vested in the defendants. It was held in like manner in *Thrall* v. *Spencer*, that an accommodation indorser, who had received goods from the maker of the note as an indemnity, might return them to the maker, and that the title of the defendant, who had taken the goods subsequently as a pledge, was superior to that of the payee. It seems to have been thought in these instances that the equity of the creditor to the assets in the hands of the surety does not become fixed on the insolvency of the latter, nor until the actual filing of the bill. But the better opinion seems to be that it dates from the period when the inability of the surety to meet his engagements, renders it incumbent on him to take no step that can hinder or delay his creditors. It is, nevertheless, a mere equity, which cannot be enforced against a bona fide purchaser, and this was the main ground of the judgment in *Thrall* v. *Spencer*.

It would seem, that the surety may surrender the securities which he has received from the principal, notwithstanding the insolvency of the latter. In *Homer* v. *The Savings Fund*, 7 Conn. 483, *ante*, the Eagle Bank had conveyed a large amount of property to trustees to indemnify one Homer against the liability which he had incurred by endorsing certain notes at the request of the bank. A bill was filed alleging the insolvency of Homer, and praying that the assets in the hands of the trustees might be applied to the payment of the notes. The Court refused the prayer, on the ground that as the trust was exclusively for the Homer's benefit, neither he nor those claiming under him could assert any right until he had actually paid the notes. This decision seems to have gone too far, because the principal is equitably bound to pay the debt at maturity, and a failure to comply with this obligation is an injury for which relief may be had in chancery. Homer was exposed to a suit by the default of the bank, and as this was enough to entitle him to the benefit of the trust, so the complainants should have been substituted in his place. An endorser who has been discharged by a want of notice, stands on a different footing, and cannot justly ask to be indemnified at the expense of the maker, *ante ;* and this may also be said of a guarantor or surety who is freed from liability by the laches of the creditor or unauthorised variation of the contract. See *Hunter* v. *Richardson*, 1 Duvall, 247 ; *Havens* v. *Fondry*, 4 Metcalf, Ky. 247.

There is another consideration which should not be overlooked. The equitable principle which entitles the surety to the remedies of the creditor gives the creditor an equal claim on the surety: *The New London Bank* v. *Lee,* 11 Conn. 112, 118. It is well settled, that as soon as the debt becomes due, the surety may file a bill against the principal for indemnity, and to have the securities which are in his hands applied to the payment of the debt. It is not essential to such relief that the surety should have been actually damnified in person or estate. It is enough that he is exposed to liability in consequence of the default made by the principal; 2 American Lead. Cases, 412, 5 ed., *ante.* An express or implied agreement to indemnify may be specifically enforced, although the promisee has not paid the whole or any portion of the debt. Otherwise, there would be a circuity of action to attain an end which might be reached at once: *Miller* v. *Lanaster*, 5 Caldwell, 514, 522. The surety is, therefore, entitled to require that the securities which he holds shall be so used as to fulfil the obligation of the principal, whether they were given to indemnify him or secure the creditor. And as he may exercise this right, so he must do so if required by the other parties to the obligation: *Miller* v. *Lanaster; Havens* v. *Fondry,* 4 Metcalf, Ky. 249; *Hopewell* v. *The Bank*, 10 Leigh, 206, 221. This equity arises not "from any notion of mutual contract between the parties, that in providing for the surety the creditor shall be equally provided for, but from a principle of natural equity, independent of

contract, namely, that to prevent the surety from being first harassed for the debt, and then turning him round to seek redress from the collateral security given by the principal, a court of equity will authorize and even encourage the creditor to claim, through the medium of the surety, all the rights he has thus acquired, to be exercised for his benefit, and in discharge of his obligations."

It is, notwithstanding, necessary to remember, that this equity can have no place before the maturity of the debt. Until the principal is in default, there is no right of recourse on the part of the surety, and consequently none to which the creditor can be subrogated. The better opinion, therefore, seems to be, that during the interval between the execution of the obligation and the period appointed for its fulfilment, the creditor has no interest in a security given solely for the protection of the surety, and cannot object to any appropriation of it that may be agreed upon by the surety and principal. But this cannot be said where the surety is insolvent, or where the principal has violated his obligation to the creditor, and thereby entitled the latter to subrogation to the equity of the surety.]

Formerly, no action at law could be maintained against the principal by a surety who had paid the debt, the remedy being only in equity; but in modern times, when many equitable claims are enforced at law, through the medium of implying promises to do what the party is bound in justice and equity to do, it is settled, that when a surety becomes bound for a principal, and at his request, the law implies a promise of indemnity, and an action of assumpsit may be brought. The surety, therefore, may pay the debt at any time after it becomes due, without waiting to be sued, and may then maintain an action for money paid: *Mauri* v. *Heffernan*, 13 Johnson, 58, 75; *Odlin* v. *Greenleaf*, 3 New Hampshire, 270; *Goodall* v. *Wentworth*, 20 Maine, 322, 325; *Frazer* v. *Goode*, 3 Richardson, 199; *Stinson* v. *Brennan*, Cheve's Law, 15; *Williams's Adm'rs* v. *Williams's Adm'rs*, 5 Ohio, 444, 445; or may sue on the implied promise to indemnify; *Babcock* v. *Hubbard*, 2 Connecticut, 536, 539; *Ward* v. *Henry*, 5 Id. 596. And when the debt is satisfied by an extent or sale of the surety's land, he may recover either at law or in equity, although his remedy once lay solely in the latter jurisdiction: *Hulet* v. *Soulard*, 26 Vermont, 295; *The Wesley Church* v. *Moore*, Barr, 273; *Lord* v. *Staples*, 3 Foster, 448; *Randall* v. *Rich*, 11 Mass. 498; and may even declare in general or *indebitatus assumpsit*, and give a satisfaction produced by or resulting from a sale or conveyance of land, in evidence under a bill of particulars setting forth a payment in money, without resorting to a special count; *Bonney* v. *Seeley*, 2 Wend. 481. The implied promise or obligation to indemnify arises as soon as the suretyship is entered into; *Howe* v. *Ward*, 4 Greenleaf,

195; *Appleton & another* v. *Bascom & others*, 3 Metcalf, 169: but no action at law can be brought by the surety until after he has paid or extinguished the debt; *Powell* v. *Smith*, 8 Johnson, 249, 252; *Pigou* v. *French*, 1 Washington's C. C. 278; *Miller* v. *Howry*, 3 Penrose & Watts, 374, 380; *Ingalls* v. *Dennet*, 6 Greenleaf, 79; *Hall and others* v. *Thayer*, 12 Metcalf, 131, 135; *Shepherd* v. *Ogden*, 2 Scammon, 257, 260: see also *Jones and another* v. *Trimble*, 3 Rawle, 381, 388; *Williams's Adm'rs* v. *Williams's Adm'rs*, 5 Ohio, 444, 446; *Elwood* v. *Deifendorf*, 5 Barbour's S. Ct. 399, 410, *ante*, 143. In assumpsit, the surety may recover what he has paid, with interest and costs; *Wynn, Adm.* v. *Brooke et al.*, 5 Rawle, 106, 108; *Hayden* v. *Cabot*, 7 Massachusetts, 169; *Cleveland* v. *Covington*, 3 Strobhart, 184; and even as it has been said, counsel fees and other incidental expenses; *Fletcher* v. *Jackson*, 23 Vermont, 581; *Marsh* v. *Hamington*, 18 Id. 150; although this would seem to be somewhat doubtful, *post*. The surety of a surety, upon paying the principal's debt, may also maintain assumpsit; *Hall* v. *Smith*, 5 Howard, 96, 102. If the sureties pay separately, their legal demands against the principal, are in their nature several, and the sureties cannot join in suing the principal; *Messer* v. *Swan*, 4 New Hampshire, 482, 488; *Lombard* v. *Cobb*, 14 Maine, 222; *Gould* v. *Gould*, 8 Cowen, 168; but if the debt is paid by their joint negotiable note, and also, it seems, if money paid is owned by them jointly, or raised on their joint credit, their proper remedy is by joint action; *Peterson et al.* v. *Parker*, 3 New Hampshire, 366; *Day* v. *Swann*, 13 Maine, 165; *Doolittle* v. *Dwight and another, Admr.*, 2 Metcalf, 561; *Appleton & another* v. *Bascom & others*, 3 Id. 169, 172; see *Lowry* v. *Lumbermen's Bank*, 2 Watts & Sergeant, 210, 215. But a joint action will not lie by one surety against the principal and other sureties; *Lapham* v. *Barnes et al.*, 2 Vermont, 213, 218; *Elwendorph* v. *Tappen & others*, 5 Johnson, 176; even when the plaintiff signed expressly as surety, while the defendants affixed their signatures without any such qualification; *M'Gee* v. *Prouty*, 9 Metcalf, 347. If a surety is bound for two joint° principals, he may sue them jointly for indemnity, unless some agreement has been made inconsistent with this implied liability; *Duncan* v. *Keiffer*, 3 Binney, 126, 129.

[There are two grounds on which a recovery may be had in assumpsit for money paid, laid out and expended; one where the plaintiff pays at the request of the defendant; the other where the payment is made under an obligation, which, though legally incumbent on both, should as between themselves be discharged by the defendant. In the latter case, the existence of the obligation must be proved; in the former it is immaterial that the defendant did not owe the money; *Shaw* v. *Lloyd*, 12 Massachusetts, 447; *Peaslee* v. *Breed*, 10 New Hampshire, 48; *Stevenson*

v. *Burman*, Chevis, 15; *Lempheir* v. *Ferguson*, 10 Richardson, 424.

A man who requests another to be his surety, impliedly asks him to pay the amount when due, and cannot resist an action for indemnity, on the ground that the principal contract was oral and within the statute of frauds, unless he also shows that the request was countermanded; *Alexander* v. *Vance*, 1 M. & W. 571. The principle is the same where the original contract is invalid for want of a stamp, or in consequence of any other defect that can be waived. In like manner, the surety may recover, although he went on to pay after learning that the debt was usurious; unless the information came from the principal debtor in such a shape, as to be an express or implied revocation of the authority which the law infers where an obligation is incurred for the accommodation of another person; *Brittain* v. *Lloyd*, 14 M. & W. 762, 773. So a recovery may be had although the debt was barred by the lapse of time, unless the principal gave notice of his intention to rely on the statute as a defence; *Elkinton* v. *Nichols*, 7 Gill, 85; *Alexander* v. *Vance*. The point was, notwithstanding, decided differently in *Hachett* v. *Pegram*, 21 Louisiana Ann. 722. In *Whitehead* v. *Peck*, 1 Kelly, 141, 151, the payment of a usurious obligation, with notice of its true nature, was said to be essentially invalid, and to give the surety no right to indemnity or re-imbursement.

The indemnity of the surety

should, as it would seem, extend beyond the debt itself, and embrace the costs, which have been recovered against him by the creditor; *Baker* v. *Martin*, 3 Barbour, 634; *Elwood* v. *Deifenderf*, 5 Id. 112; *Wynn* v. *Brooke*, 5 Rawle, 106; *Hayden* v. *Cabot*, 17 Mass. 167; at all events, when the promise to indemnify is express, and not merely implied by the law; *Bonney* v. *Seeley*, 2 Wendell, 481; unless the costs have been incurred needlessly or vexatiously by the surety, without the wish or assent of the principal; *Whitworth* v. *Tillman*, 40 Mississippi, 176: and some of the cases hold that the surety is entitled to reimbursement for counsel fees and other incidental expenses of the same nature; *Marsh* v. *Harrington*, 18 Vermont, 150; *Fletcher* v. *Jackson*, 23 Id. 581. But costs inflicted *in invitum*, by the act of the law, obviously stand on a different footing from payments made voluntarily as a matter of choice, and the better opinion seems to be that counsel fees cannot be included in the recovery against the principal, as not being a necessary or legal consequence of his default, and being merely so much money laid out for the benefit of the surety; *Wynn* v. *Brooke :* and there are several decisions which tend to throw a doubt on the right of the surety even to costs; *Walker* v. *Hatton*, 10 M. & W. 249; *Penley* v. *Watts*, 7 Id. 610; *Tindall* v. *Bell*, 11 Id. 228; *Short* v. *Halloway*, 11 A. & E. 31; *Lowell* v. *The Boston & Lowell R. R. Co.*, 23 Pick. 24; *Greely* v. *Dow*, 2 Met-

calf, 179. "No man," said Lord Denman, in *Short* v. *Halloway*, "is entitled to inflame his account against another by incurring additional expense in an unrighteous resistance to an action which he cannot defend;" 1 Smith's Leading Cases, 287, 7 ed.; and although this language was held in a suit brought to recover compensation for damages which had been recovered against the plaintiff, in consequence of the failure of the defendant to fulfil a covenant to repair, it would seem applicable to the costs of a suit against a surety. But there is quite as much truth in the remark of Gibson, C. J., in *Wynn* v. *Brooke*, that the surety may be unable to prevent or anticipate the infliction of costs by payment, and that the loss should consequently fall upon the principal, whose laches are the cause of the injury. The principle is clear, but there is some difficulty in its application. The surety is entitled to compensation for the costs inflicted by the act of the creditor, in instituting the suit and obtaining judgment by default. These are the legal and natural consequences of the failure of the principal debtor to pay the debt at maturity. But it does not follow that he may resist a clear and unliquidated demand from a spirit of litigation, or for the purpose of gaining time, and if he adopts such a course he ought to bear the loss which it occasions; *Holmes* v. *Friend*, 24 Barb. 540. Nor will the court, as it seems, award damages for the injury resulting from the interruption of the surety's business, or the sacrifice of his goods through a forced sale, under an execution issued by the creditor; *Hayden* v. *Cabot*, 17 Mass. 167.]

It is equally well settled, at the present day, that *indebitatus assumpsit* will lie by one surety who has paid more than his share, to recover contribution from his co-surety; see *Johnson* v. *Johnson*, 11 Massachusetts, 359, 361; *Norton* v. *Soule*, 2 Greenleaf, 341, 343, 344. This implied obligation is founded upon an equitable duty, which the sureties are supposed to be cognizant of, and assenting to, at the time they enter into the contract of suretyship; and, according to the modern and better opinion, the legal rights and duties being founded upon equity, are co-extensive with the equitable claims subsisting among the parties, and are in all respects similar to them. See *Moore* v. *Moore*, 4 Hawks, 358, 360; *Sherrod* v. *Woodard*, 4 Devereux, 360, 361; *Morrison* v. *Poyntz*, 7 Dana, 307; *Bezzell, Ad'mr*, v. *White*, 13 Alabama, 422; *Fletcher* v. *Grover*, 11 New Hampshire, 369, 374; *Boardman* v. *Paige*, Id. 432, 439; *Agnew* v. *Bell*, 4 Watts, 31, 32; *Taylor* v. *Savage*, 12 Massachusetts, 98, 102; *Mason* v. *Lord*, 20 Pickering, 447, 449. "The action of assumpsit for contribution," says C. J. Shaw, in the last case, "is founded purely on equitable principles. It proceeds upon the broad ground, that when two or more are subject to a loss or burden common to all, and one bears the whole or a disproportionate part, it lays

an equitable claim for contribution, from those who are thereby proportionably relieved." The principle, that contribution may be enforced, whether the sureties are bound jointly, or severally, whether by the same or different instruments, and whether with or without mutual knowledge of one another's suretyship, is settled in relation to assumpsit at law, as well as in regard to proceedings in equity; *Norton* v. *Coons*, 3 Denio, 130; *Harris* v. *Ferguson*, 2 Bailey, 397, 400. Assumpsit to recover contribution will lie, also, as well where there are several sureties, as where there are only two; *Foster* v. *Johnson*, 5 Vermont, 60, 63; and it will lie against the representatives of a deceased surety, for a payment after his death, because the implied obligation arose at the time the common suretyship was entered into; *Bachelder* v. *Fiske et al., Ex'rs*, 17 Massachusetts, 464; *Bradley* v. *Burwell*, 3 Denio, 62, 66; *Malin and another* v. *Bull*, 13 Sergeant & Rawle, 441; *M'Kenna* v. *George*, 2 Richardson's Equity, 15, 18; *Aiken* v. *Peay*, 5 Strobhart, 15; see also, *Stothoff* v. *Dunham's Executors*, 4 Harrison, 182; and according to the weight of authority, if one of several sureties be insolvent, contribution at law, as well as in equity, will be according to the number of those who are solvent; *Harris* v. *Ferguson*, 2 Bailey, 397, 401; *Mills* v. *Hyde*, 19 Vt. 60, 63; *Strong et al.* v. *Mitchell et al.*, Id. 644, 647; and removal from the state is for this purpose equivalent to insolvency; *Boardman* v.

Paige, 11 New Hampshire, 432, 440; but in some other courts it has been said that there is in this particular a difference between law and equity, and that a surety who has paid the debt, can at law recover only a proportional contribution, according to the whole original number of sureties; *Stothoff* v. *Dunham's Ex'rs; Parker* v. *Ellis*, 2 Sandford's S. Ct. 224; see *Powell* v. *Edwards*, 2 B. & P. 268; *Dodd* v. *Niven*, 27 Missouri, 501, while equity will apportion the debt equally among the solvent sureties; *Dodd* v. *Niven*, 1 Story Equity, sect. 498; see dictum in *Croft* v. *Moore*, 9 Watts, 451, 453, and see *Hall* v. *Robinson*, 8 Iredell, 56, 59. A surety need not wait to be sued, but as soon as the debt is due, he may pay it, and bring an action of contribution; *Bradley* v. *Burwell*, 3 Denio, 62, 69; and it has been held that he may pay or compromise the debt before it is due, and as soon as it is due may sue for contribution; *Craig* v. *Craig*, 5 Rawle, 91, 98; but he cannot recover unless it appear that he was bound for payment, for if he pay a debt which he was not legally compellable to do, he cannot recover contribution; *Skillin* v. *Merrill*, 16 Massachusetts, 40; see *Cave, use of Wallace* v. *Burns*, 6 Alabama, 780, 782; *Landers* v. *Tuggle*, 22 Louisiana Ann. 443, *ante*. And as this right of action rests upon an equitable claim to be compensated for a disproportionate suffering from a common burden, it will not exist, except for the excess which the surety has paid beyond his just share; *Fletcher* v. *Grover*, 11 New Hampshire, 369; nor will it lie where the party claiming has in fact been reimbursed and has sustained no loss; *Mason* v. *Lord*, 20 Pickering, 447, 449; nor where the surety who has paid is indebted to the principal in more than the amount of the debt; *Bezzell, Adm'r*, v. *White*, 13 Alabama, 422, 423: and if one surety has received any property from the principal for the purpose of indemnifying him, he must account for the proceeds of it, as for so much received on common account; *Bachelder* v. *Fiske et al. Ex'rs*, 17 Massachusetts, 464, 470; *Fletcher* v. *Grover; Agnew* v. *Bell*, 4 Watts, 31, 34; *Selvey* v. *Dowell*, 53 Illinois, 260. A surety who has resisted an action brought by the creditor, cannot, it has been said, recover from his co-surety contribution for the costs, unless he defended at the co-surety's request; *John, Adm'r* v. *Jones*, 16 Alabama, 454, 462; but in *Fletcher* v. *Johnson*, 23 Vermont, 581, co-sureties were held to be entitled to contribution, not only for costs, but for counsel fees and other incidental expenses. In equity, as has been seen, one surety does not recover contribution from his co-surety, without showing that the principal is insolvent, or unable to pay; and the Kentucky courts have held that the same rule must prevail at law, since the legal and equitable liability should be the same; *Pearson & Co.* v. *Duckham*, 3 Littell, 385, 386; *Poignard* v. *Vernon, &c.*, 1 Monroe, 45, 47; *Morrison* v. *Poyntz*, 7 Dana, 307; *Atkinson* v. *Stewart*,

&c., 2 B. Monroe, 348, 350; *Crow
v. Murphy*, 12 Id. 444; but in
other courts, it has been held, that,
at law, a surety has a right of action against his co-surety for contribution, immediately upon payment of the debt, and may recover
without showing the insolvency of
the principal; *Roberts* v. *Adams*,
6 Porter, 361; *Couch* v. *Terry's
Adm'rs*, 12 Alabama, 225, 227;
Odlin v. *Greenleaf*, 3 New Hampshire, 270, 271; *Goodall* v. *Wentworth*, 20 Maine, 322, 324; *Judah*
v. *Mieure*, 5 Blackford, 171; *Sloo*
v. *Pool*, 14 Illinois, 46; and see
Powell v. *Edwards*, 2 B. & P. 268.
And it would seem that these latter cases are correct, and that there
is a distinction between law and
equity, not in principle, but growing out of the difference in the
modes of proceeding. Probably
the obligation of co-sureties, both
at law and in equity, is to make
ratable contribution, without regard to the ability of the principal: but in equity, as the pricipal
debtor is made a party to the bill
for contribution, and as the surety,
sought to be made liable, would
have an immediate claim against
him, the court, to prevent circuity
of action, will require the principal to be charged, unless it appear
that he is insolvent; but, at law,
where the parties must be sued in
successive actions, it would often
be mischievous to prevent the paying surety from bringing action
against his co-surety until he has
pursued the principal to insolvency; and this seems to be admitted in *Caldwell* v. *Roberts*, 1
Dana, 355, 357.

Though relief is now freely
given at law, the jurisdiction of
Chancery on these subjects remains
unimpaired. " The right to afford
contribution originally belonged
to a Court of Equity, and the
jurisdiction now assumed by courts
of law to enforce contribution in
some cases, does not affect the
jurisdiction originally belonging to
a court of equity;" *Wayland* v.
Tucker et als., 4 Grattan, 268,
269; *Couch* v. *Terry's Adm'rs*, 12
Alabama, 225, 228. The jurisdiction of the two tribunals are declared to be concurrent, in *Mitchell's and Davis's Adm'rs* v.
Sproul, 5 J. J. Marshall, 264, 270,
and *Hickman, &c.*, v. *McCurdy*, 7
Id. 555, 559. Indeed the principle is general, that where a court
of equity has had jurisdiction of a
subject, it will retain it, although
the original ground of jurisdiction,
the suitor's inability to recover at
law, no longer exist; *King* v.
Baldwin, 17 Johnson, 384, 388;
Hawley v. *Cramer*, 4 Cowen, 719,
727.

[The relation of principal and
surety, and that which exists between co-sureties, lie in a great
measure without the contract with
the creditor, although founded
upon and growing out of it, and
may consequently be proved or
negatived by extrinsic and unwritten evidence, even when the
contract itself is under seal; *Wharton* v. *Woodburn*, 4 Dev. & Bat.
507.

The motive for reducing an
agreement to writing is to set forth
the obligation of the parties of the
one part towards the parties of the

other part, and not to define the duties of the parties of the same part to each other. Hence, it may be shown that the consideration moved to one of several makers or obligors, and that he consequently ought to indemnify the rest, or even that of several persons who put their names to such an instrument without consideration, one signed on the faith of a promise by the others to save him harmless, *ante; Carpenter* v. *King*, 9 Metcalf, 511; *Austin* v. *Boyd*, 24 Pick. 64, *post*, vol. 2, notes to *Rees* v. *Barrington.*

This may be done not only where the alleged surety is a co-contractor, but where he is primarily or solely liable to the creditor. An accommodation maker may accordingly show that the payee is in fact the principal debtor, where the question arises between themselves; *Pooley* v. *Harradin*, 7 E. & Bl. 431; *Greenough* v. *McClelland*, 2 E. & E. 424; *The Grafton Bank* v. *Woodward*, 4 New Hamp. 221; *Griffith* v. *Reed*, 21 Wend., if not where the interests of the creditor are involved; 2 American Leading Cases, 455, 5th ed. The principle is the same where a bill is accepted for the accommodation of the drawer, or of one or two joint drawers, *ante*, 163. For a like reason, one who gives a bond and mortgage at the request of another, and for his use, has all the rights of a surety against the latter, and may require him to pay the debt, although his name does not appear on the bond, and he is not directly answerable to the obligee; *Purviance* v. *Strickland*, 2 Ohio, N. S.

478; *Wharton* v. *Woodburn*, 4 Dev. & Bat. 507; *The Wesley Church* v. *Moore*, 10 Barr, *ante*, 273. Under these circumstances, however, it must appear that the engagement of the alleged principal was in writing, or that the consideration moved to him, for if it went in any other direction, his promise is collateral to that of the person who received it, and within the statute of frauds; 1 Smith's L. C. 512, 7 Am. Ed.; Notes to *Birkmire* v. *Darnell*. A promise to indemnify a co-obligor is not within the statute, because the liability of the promisor is established by the bond, and the promise merely regulates the order in which the parties are to pay as between themselves; *Apgar* v. *Hiler*, 4 Zabriskie, 704; *Barry* v. *Ransom*, 12 New York, 462; but the case is obviously different where the name of the defendant does not appear in the instrument, and he is charged solely on the promise.

The right of co-sureties to contribution is governed by the same principles, and may, like most other equities, be rebutted by parol evidence, even when it is founded upon a written obligation. It is accordingly a good defense to a suit by a surety for indemnity or contribution, that the defendant became answerable at his request, and on the faith of an assurance that he should not be called on to pay the debt; *Barry* v. *Ransom*, *Apgar* v. *Hiler;* while a co-contractor may be answerable to another as a principal, on proof that such is their relation to each other, although both executed the instrument as "sureties." But the mere circumstance that one of the makers of a note adds the word surety to his signature, will not make him the superior of another surety who signs without qualification, if he knew of the equity of the latter at the time of executing the instrument; and both must contribute equally to the debt; *Sisson* v. *Barrett*, 6 Barb. 199; 2 Comstock, 406. In *M'Gee* v. *Prouty*, 9 Metcalf, 455, one of the makers of a joint and several note who had added the word " surety " to his signature was compelled to pay it at maturity. He brought a suit against the other makers for indemnity. It was alleged that one of the defendants was also a surety. Although this did not appear on the face of the instrument, it was held to be a good defence, as showing that he might be liable for contribution, but was not answerable as a principal debtor. The action should have been several for his share, and not to charge him jointly with the whole amount of the debt.

A promise or agreement will not exempt a surety from liability for contribution, or entitle him to treat his co-sureties as principals, unless it is made with their knowledge and assent. One who enters into a joint undertaking cannot make a secret stipulation in derogation of his duty to bear an equal share of the burden. In *Norton* v. *Coons*, 3 Denio, 130; 2 Selden, 33; an assurance by the first of three makers of a joint and several note, that the third would incur no responsibility by his sig-

nature; and that in the event of a default in payment, the " whole burden should fall on the second, who was well able to bear it," was held to be no defence to a suit for contribution brought by the second against the third, although the latter signed on the faith of the assurance and some time after the execution of the note by the other makers. Sureties who do not sign in pursuance of a common understanding or agreement, are not within this principle. A surety may, therefore, stipulate that he shall not be liable to a prior surety, and shall, on the contrary, be entitled to an indemnity from him if compelled to pay the debt; and hence, a maker of a joint and several promissory note, who appends the words " surety for the above names," to his signature, does not owe contribution to those whose names are prior to his own, even when they have signed expressly as " sureties;" *Harris* v. *Warner*, 13 Wend. 400; *Thompson* v. *Sanders*, 4 Dev. & Bat. 404; *Wright* v. *Garlinghouse*, 27 Barb. 474. But the mere addition of the word " surety" to the signature of one of the makers of a note, is not seemingly, enough to subvert the relation of equality between himself and other sureties, whose signatures have been affixed to the instrument without qualification, or to defeat a claim on their part for contribution; *Sisson* v. *Barrett*, 6 Barbour, 199; 2 Comstock, 406; although he signs after them, and in consequence of the refusal of the creditor to take the instrument unless his name is added; *Woodworth* v. *Bowers*, 5 Indiana, 277; but the defendant may, under these circumstances, resort to parol evidence, to show the nature of his undertaking, and that he is entitled to treat the other parties to the instrument as principals, without regard to their relations as between themselves; *Robison* v. *Lyle*, 10 Barbour, 512; *Darragh* v. *Osborne*, 2 Halsted, 71; *Barry* v. *Ransom*, 12 New York, 462.

[*115]   *FOX v. MACKRETH.

PITT v. MACKRETH.

12 MAY, AND 10, 12, 13, 23, 24, 26 NOVEMBER, 1787, AND 7, 8, AND 11 DECEMBER, 1788, LINC. INN HALL.

THE CASE AND ARGUMENTS ARE TAKEN FROM 2 BRO, C. C. 400. THE JUDGMENT FROM 2 COX, 320 [1]

PURCHASE BY A TRUSTEE FOR SALE.]—*A trustee for the sale of estates for payment of debts, who purchased them himself, by taking an undue advantage of the confidence reposed in him by the settlor, and previous to the completion of the contract, sold them at a highly advanced price, decreed to be a trustee, as to the sums produced by the second sale, for the settlor.*

THIS cause came on by appeal from the Rolls.

The original bill was filed in June, 1781, by the plaintiff, James Fox, Esq., against Robert Mackreth, John Dawes, and John Bayne Garforth, Esqrs. The supplemental bill was by William Morton Pitt, Esq., and James Farrer, trustees of the estate and effects of James Fox, against the same defendants, to have the benefit of the former suit.

The material part of the prayer of the original bill was that the sale of the plaintiff's estates in the county of Surrey, made to Thomas Page, Esq., might be declared to have been made in trust for the plaintiff, and that Mackreth and Dawes might be declared to be accountable to the plaintiff for what the estates were sold for to Page, and also for accounts of what was due to the defendants Mackreth and Dawes, and upon what securities; and that they might be decreed to deliver up the securities, the plaintiff offering that they should be at liberty to retain respectively, out of the purchase-monies of the estates, what should [*116] be found justly due to them from the *plaintiff, and an account of monies due to the defendants, on account of annuities granted by the plaintiff to the defendants, the plaintiff

---

[1] S. C., 4 Bro. P. C., Toml. ed. 258. See Hargreave, Jur. Arg. 453, 526; Reg. Lib. 1788, A. fol. 64.

offering that the defendants should be at liberty to retain the sum found due out of the said purchase-monies.

The circumstances of the case made against the principal defendants, Mackreth and Dawes, as taken from the bill, answer, and evidence, appear to be these:—

That the plaintiff Fox, being seised in tail of an estate at Horseley and elsewhere, in the county of Surrey, subject to an estate for life, in some parts thereof, to his mother for her jointure in lieu of dower, and likewise seised or possessed of copyhold and leasehold estates in the same county, and also entitled to several other estates in expectancy or for life only, had, before he came of age, embarked in a very expensive course of life, and was reduced to great distress, and under these circumstances, had procured money by granting annuities, and engaging his friends who were of age, in bonds and judgments, for securing the payment of them; that his friends, being acquainted with his situation, proposed, that as soon as might be after he should attain his age of twenty-one years, he should suffer a recovery of the Surrey estate, which, or a competent part thereof, should be conveyed to trustees, to be sold for the payment of his debts, and redeeming the annuities for which he, and his friends on his behalf, had engaged; that he attained his age of twenty-one in the month of August, 1777, and was very soon afterwards (in the latter end of that or beginning of the next month) introduced to the defendant Mackreth (who usually supplied young men of fortune with money in their distresses), and, on account of the plaintiff's inability to make a security by mortgage, as a recovery could not be suffered till Michaelmas Term, it was agreed that the defendants, Mackreth and Dawes, should supply the plaintiff with the sum of 5100l., upon the plaintiff's granting two annuities of 500l. and 350l. each for his life; that Dawes, on the 23rd of September, advanced the 5100l., for which the following securities were executed:—A bond of that *date by the plaintiff, in the penal sum of 6000l., for se- [*117] curing to the defendant Dawes an annuity of 500l., for the life of the plaintiff; a warrant of attorney of even date to confess judgment on the said bond; and an indenture tripartite, between the plaintiff of the first part, Dawes of the second part, and Garforth of the third part, whereby lands in the county of York, of which the plaintiff was seised for life, were conveyed to Garforth, for securing the payment of the annuity of 500l. to Dawes. The annuity of 350l. was secured by a similar bond of the same date, warrant of attorney to confess judgment thereon, and a similar conveyance of the same lands to Garforth, for better securing the same. In the annuity of 500l., Mackreth, in his answer, admitted he was interested with Dawes, but denied that he was so in that of 350l.

In Michaelmas Term, 1777, a recovery was suffered of the freehold part of the Surrey estates, by which they were vested (subject to the mother's estate for life in a part thereof) in Oliver

Farrer, in trust to convey the same in such manner as the plaintiff should direct, Mr. Farrer having agreed to act.as a trustee for the purpose of selling the same and discharging the debts, together with and under the direction of two of the plaintiff's friends (who appear to have been Lord Ligonier and Lord Grantley), if they could be prevailed upon to accept the trust. In December, 1777, the plaintiff, being threatened with an arrest for the sum of 2000*l.* by the holder of bills of exchange drawn by the plaintiff while at Paris, applied to the defendant Mackreth, who agreed to lend the plaintiff 3000*l.*, on mortgage of the Surrey estates; upon which mortgage-deeds, dated 22nd and 23rd of this month, were accordingly prepared and executed. At the time of the execution of these deeds, it was proposed that the defendant Mackreth should be a trustee with Farrer for payment of the debts and redeeming the annuities, when the defendant Mackreth proposed the defendant Dawes for that purpose, as being from the course of his business, well acquainted with many of the persons who had purchased the plaintiff's [*118] other annuities, and could *assist in purchasing them at a cheaper rate than Mr. Farrer; which was assented to by the plaintiff, upon an assurance that nothing should be done without Mr. Farrer being consulted and approving thereof.

In the same month the plaintiff delivered to the defendant Mackreth a particular or rental of the estate in Surrey, made by Thomas Jackman, by which it appeared that the rents of the houses and cottages on the premises amounted to 283*l.* 1*s.*, and those of the lands to 979*l.* 14*s.* (subject to the mother's jointure, which was stated at 240*l.* a year), and the timber was valued in the rental at 4000*l.*, and the whole was valued at 45,000*l.* It was also in evidence, that Mackreth sent down a man of the name of Hampton to view the estate, who was there a week, but what valuation he made, or whether the same was communicated to Mackreth, did not appear.

A trust deed was prepared by Garforth, reciting the mortgage, by which the estates were conveyed to Mackreth and Dawes (subject to Mackreth's mortgage and the annuity to Dawes), in trust to sell or mortgage the same, and to pay the debts and redeem the annuities granted by the plaintiff. These deeds being sent to Mr. Farrer, he made some objections thereto, on account of the sums advanced, as the prices of the annuities, not being scheduled as gross sums carrying interest at 5*l.* per cent., and also on account of the trustees being empowered to sell or mortgage the estates without the intervention of Mr. Fox. And it being afterwards agreed, that Mackreth should pay off Dawes, and advance some further sums, a deed poll was prepared, calculated for execution on the 16th January, 1778, and indorsed on the mortgage deed, to secure such further sum of 7000*l.*, consisting of 5100*l.*, the consideration money for the annuities granted by the plaintiff to Dawes, with 212*l.* 10*s.* interest thereon, for the quarter's arrear due 23rd December, 1777 (but which was not paid by Mackreth to Dawes until the 16th July, 1788), and 51*l.* 14*s.* 9½*d.*, twenty-three days' arrear of the said annuities, from 23rd December to said 16th January, and 1635*l.* 15*s.* 2½*d.* paid to the plaintiff on the *16th January, 1778. A new trust- [*119] deed was also prepared, in which this deed poll was re- cited, and the 3000*l.* and 7000*l.* made the first charges on the estate.

On the 16th January, 1778, the plaintiff Fox and the de- fendant Mackreth dined together at the house of the defendant Garforth, for the purpose of executing these deeds, and after din- ner, and before the plaintiff had executed the deeds, a conversa- tion arose in which it was proposed that the defendant Mackreth should become the purchaser of the estate, and Jackman's valua- tion of 45,000*l.* was mentioned by the plaintiff as a fair price which was objected to by Mackreth, considering the value put thereby upon the houses and lands; upon which the defendant made a calculation of the houses at fourteen years' purchase, and the lands at thirty, together with the household furniture, valued at 500*l.*, and the timber at 4000*l.* (on which last two articles they agreed), amounting to 37,853*l.* 14*s.* The plaintiff afterwards offered to sell the estates to the defendant for 42,000*l.*, upon which the defendant said he would split the difference, and give 39,500*l.* for the same, but would not give more, and the plaintiff not agreeing to accept the terms, the trust-deeds were then executed by the plaintiff.

After the deeds were executed, the conversation was renewed, and the plaintiff expressing some concern with respect to his mother's jointure, in case he should accept the defendant's terms, the defendant offered the 39,500*l.*, and to subject himself to the payment of the plaintiff's mother's jointure, in case she should survive him; upon which the parties agreed, and the defendant Garforth (who had been absent during the greatest part of the treaty) was called in, and drew up a memorandum of such agree- ment, by which the money was to paid on or before the 25th of March next, till which time the plaintiff was to receive the rents and profits, and then convey the estate to the defendant Mack- reth; and about twelve o'clock at night this memorandum was signed by the plaintiff, upon which the trust-deed was cancelled.

On the 28th of the same month, articles for the purchase *were executed by both parties. On the 24th April fol- [*120] lowing, the plaintiff, and Anna Fox, his mother, on the 2nd of May, executed conveyances of the estate to the defendant, in consideration of 39,500*l.*, 11,097*l.* of which was retained by the defendant, in payment of the above mortgage of 3000*l.*, the 7000*l.* secured by the deed-poll, and some other sums charged by the defendant, as advanced to the plaintiff; and the defendant gave the plaintiff, as a security for the residue (being 28,403*l.*), a common accountable receipt; and afterwards, on the objection of the plaintiff to this as the only security for the money, the de- fendant wrote, on the same piece of paper which contained the accountable receipt, the following charge:—" 25th April, 1778. I do hereby charge all my estates in the county of Surrey with the payment of the above sum of 28,403*l.* and interest." At the time of signing the above, the defendant had no estates in the county of Surrey but those purchased by him of the plaintiff; and the defendant gave to the plaintiff no other security for the residue of the money than the receipt and charge.

In the interval between the execution of the articles and that of the conveyances, Mackreth had treated with Thomas Page, Esq., for the sale of the whole of the said estate; and on the 21st March, Mr. Page agreed to give 50,500*l.*, for the same, but no article was entered into between him and the defendant till the 30th of April following. Immediately after, Page was let into possession and was to receive the rents and profits from Lady-day then last. The treaty with Page was totally unknown to the plaintiff, when he executed the conveyance to the defendant.

The plaintiff drew upon the defendant for several sums on account of the purchase-money; and in October, 1778, having sent for an account, the defendant drew one out, by which he made a balance remaining in his hands of 773*l.* 18*s.* 9*d.*; but admitted in his answer that he had therein charged monies unpaid, as the supposed amount of two annuities and the arrears thereof then unredeemed; and afterwards, in May, 1779, having then [*121] settled the *said annuities, he sent the plaintiff another account, in which he made the balance 616*l.* 17*s.* above the other balance of 773*l.* 18*s.* 9*d.* In June, 1779, the plaintiff, being again in distress, applied to the defendant, when he advanced him 2100*l.* upon an annuity of 350*l.* a year for plaintiff's life, secured by a bond in the penal sum of 4200*l.*, and warrant of attorney to enter up judgment on the same.

Upon discovery of the sale to Page, under the circumstances as stated above, the plaintiff filed his bill,[1] insisting that the defendant Mackreth, being a trustee for him under the trust-deed for payment of debts, it was his duty to sell the same for the advantage of the plaintiff: and if he purchased for himself (which the plaintiff was advised he could not) it should be for a fair and adequate consideration; that the plaintiff, having been imposed upon, ought to have the benefit of the sale; and that the sum of 7000*l.*, mentioned in the articles as due to Mackreth, on mortgage, or the part thereof estimated to be due to the defendant as the value of the annuities granted to Dawes, was a much greater sum than they were really worth on a fair valuation; that no greater allowance ought to be made out of the purchase-money than the sums really advanced, with interest from the time of advancing the same; that Mackreth had not discharged the annuities granted by the plaintiff, but the plaintiff continued liable to the same; and that at the time he granted the last annuity of 350*l.*, there was money in the defendant's hands, or the defendant

---

[1] In 1781.

was accountable to the plaintiff for larger sums, as he then had in his hands the sums for which he sold the plaintiff's estate, beyond the sum of 39,500*l*., and therefore prayed as is before stated.

The defendant Mackreth, by his answer, insisted on the fairness of the transaction, and that the price at which he bought the estate was an adequate price, though he expected to have some benefit by selling it out in parcels; but that the purchaser, Mr. Page, having an estate in the neighbourhood, gave a larger price than it was worth to other persons. He admitted that he had in his hands a *balance of 617*l*. 13*s*. of the purchase- [*122] money, which he claimed to retain, on account of the plaintiff being only tenant for life in a small part of the estate conveyed to the defendant, and 773*l*. 18*s*. 9*d*. the balance of the accounts sent to the plaintiff in October, 1778; and the defendant Mackreth further said, that on the 30th of August, 1779, part of the estate being discovered to be copyhold, the defendant applied to the plaintiff to execute a letter of attorney, to surrender such copyhold premises to the defendant, which he readily agreed to, and signed such letter of attorney; and that Mr. Page, the purchaser, in November, 1779, having raised a sum of money by mortgage of part of the said estates, and afterwards having occasion to raise money by mortgage of other parts of the said estates, and the solicitor for the person advancing the money requiring to have the original deeds of the 22nd and 23rd December, 1777, and the conveyance from the plaintiff to the defendant or duplicates thereof, the defendant applied to the plaintiff to execute other parts of the deeds, which he agreed to, and, together with his mother, executed the same without expressing himself dissatisfied with the purchase made by the defendant (but it was in evidence that Mr. Farrer only consented to the plaintiff's executing the same under a proviso that the same should not be considered as a confirmation), which acts of the plaintiff the defendant insisted would operate as confirmations of the transactions.

The cause was heard at the Rolls, before his Honor Sir Lloyd Kenyon, the then Master of the Rolls, on the 26th, 27th, and 29th of June, and on the [4th], 13th, 14th, and 26th of July, 1786, on which last day his Honor was pleased to make his decree, whereby he declared that undue advantage was taken by the defendant Mackreth of the confidence reposed in him by the plaintiff Fox, and that therefore the defendant Mackreth ought to be considered as a trustee as to all the estates and interest, comprised in the conveyance of the 23rd and 24th days of April, 1778, for the said plaintiff Fox, after the execution of the said deeds; and ordered it to be referred to the *Master to [*123] take an account of the money received by the defendant Mackreth from Page, and to compute interest thereon, at 5*l*. per cent., from the time of receiving the same, and to take an account of the money paid by defendant Mackreth to Dawes on account of the annuities of 500*l*. and 300*l*.; and also an account of the money advanced by Mackreth on account of the annuity of 350*l.* in 1779 ;[1] and an account of money received by Mackreth an account of the mortgage in 1778, and under the contract for the purchase of the estate,[2] and compute interest on the same ; and that the defendant Mackreth should pay the plaintiff the costs of the suit in respect of his insisting on the conveyance of the 23rd and 24th of April, 1778, as a conveyance for his own benefit: and granted an injunction against the defendant Mackreth, to restrain him from proceeding at law touching any matter in question in the cause ;[3] and reserved further consideration.

From this decree there was an appeal, by the defendant Mackreth only, to the Lord Chancellor, which came on to be heard in Michaelmas term, 1787.

Mr. *Mansfield*, Mr. *Scott*, Mr. *Lloyd*, and Mr. *Mitford* were heard for the respondent in support of his Honor's decree. His Honor declared, as the foundation of his decree, that an undue advantage had been taken of the confidence placed in Mackreth by Fox, and upon that ground directed the proper accounts to be taken. In that decree, Dawes and Garforth have acquiesced. Mackreth, the principal defendant, only disputes the justice of it ; nor is it to be wondered at that he does so, for, whilst the decree stands in force, his character stands materially affected. The parties on the other side are anxious to maintain the decree, not merely on account of the largeness of the property, but as a useful precedent. (The counsel enumerated the facts of the case, as before stated.) Upon the facts as stated, His Honor thought Mackreth had abused the confidence reposed in him by Fox, and ought with respect to the purchase, to be considered as a trustee for him, and that Fox ought to have the advantage of the transaction with Page. The circumstances are *certainly such [*124] as to shew an implicit confidence placed by Fox in Mackreth and Garforth, who appears to have been attorney for Mackreth. Wherever the transaction would bear the light, the deeds were sent to Farrer, the plaintiff's trustee ; where it would not, it was kept a profound secret from him, although Mackreth had promised that nothing should be done without the latter being consulted. That Garforth was the agent of Mackreth, not of Fox, is apparent: he was privy to the whole transaction with Page. If he was the agent of Fox, he should have given him notice of that transaction ; if he was not, the utmost confidence is given to Mackreth ; Fox takes his word in everything ; he gives up to his opinion Jackman's valuation and his own judg-

[1] "And the particular times when, and in what manner, such sums were advanced " Reg. Lib.
[2] " Or the conveyance thereof, and to state the particular times when, and to whom such sums were paid, and the account in which the same were included respectively." Reg. Lib.
[3] This injunction was dissolved by Lord Thurlow, but, as he afterwards confessed, by mistake, see Ex parte Lacey, 6 Ves. 627.

ment; and at twelve o'clock at night sells him the estate at his own price, which was 10,000*l.* below Jackman's valuation. So with respect to the furniture; it is sold at Mackreth's valuation, though it included five hundred pounds' worth added by Fox himself to the furniture left by Lord Bingley. Mackreth through the transaction affected to be the friend of Fox, and, by his con-versation with Farrer, admitted himself to be a trustee for Fox; for that conversation cannot be explained by Mackreth's being to have the purchase-money to pay debts, as that agreement did not subsist at the time, the agreement did not subsist at the time, the agreement at that time only being that the purchase-money should pay the debts charged on the estate. Enough has been stated to show that Fox was in the situation to be the object of fraud, that a trust was reposed in Mackreth, and that fraud has been practised upon him; and, therefore sufficient to maintain the declaration in the decree. But it has been, and will be again endeavoured to protect Mackreth, by arguing that the case does not fall under any of the heads of fraud. To this it has been answered by his Honor, that it was such a transaction as could not be maintained, but that it did fall within the cases of young men, having estates in possession and in reversion, and dealing with a man of business, and of advantage taken of their distress, except that this case had the pre-eminence, as being the case where *confidence had been so much abused. It was also argued, that inadequacy of price was not a ground for set- [*125] ting aside the bargain, though it has been frequently decided that, where the inadequacy is very great, that has been a ground for rescinding the transaction: *Chesterfield* v. *Janssen*, 1 Atk. 301; 2 Ves. 125. The real value of the estate here was 50,500*l.*, and it is sold for 39,500*l.*: the inadequacy, therefore, proves the abuse of confidence; and, though it is undoubtedly true that every contract improperly made shall not be rescinded, yet a contract grossly inadequate and founded in breach of confidence, will surely be set aside: though the Court cannot affect the strict rule of morality, and can only enforce what Mr. *Madocks* called a technical morality, yet, in the case of a trustee or a person stand-ing in a situation of which he can avail himself, the Court will not suffer him to derive advantage from that circumstance. Here every art was used to impress Fox with the idea that Mackreth and Garforth were his friends, though the transactions with respect to the annuities show them very much otherwise. Mackreth certainly derived an advantage from his situation; Fox never was out of his debt. To deal with him at all was a fraud on the part of Mackreth: *Osmond* v. *Fitzroy*, 3 P. Wms. 129. There was nothing like the confidence, or the abuse of the confidence, in *Gwynne* v. *Heaton*, 1 Bro. C. C. 1, that there is in the present case; yet there the transaction was set aside. Here the confidence reposed in Mackreth is made use of to induce a confidence in Garforth. The same person being employed on both sides, has been considered, in the case of *Sir P. Jennings*

Clerke v. *Smith*, at the Rolls lately, as a sufficient badge of fraud to set aside a transaction. There, Sir Philip had bought an annuity of Smith; the same person was concerned as attorney on both sides, and had not taken proper care of the security; his Honor thought that a sufficient ground on which to direct an inquiry. Then with respect to the confirmations, none of the facts come within the cases which have been held to be confirmations; in order to be such they must amount to a release of action. The reason given in *Chesterfield* v. *Janssen*, for holding it a con-

[*126] firmation *was, that Spencer knew all the transaction, and that he was entitled to set it aside. In the present case the suffering the duplicates to be made of the deed is a mark of confidence, but by no means amounts to confirmation, as it was done without any knowledge in Fox that he could impeach the transaction. *Baugh* v. *Price*, 1 Wils. Exch. 320, was a case where all the acts were repeated, yet held no confirmation: *Taylor* v. *Rochford*, 2 Bro. P. C. 281. No act can be a confirmation of a preceding contract but what is done with full knowledge of that contract: *Cole* v. *Gibson*, 1 Ves. 503.

Mr. *Ambler*, Mr. *Madocks*, Mr. *Selwyn*,[1] Mr. *Ainge*, and Mr. *Hargrave*, for the defendant and appellant, Mackreth.—The Master of the Rolls has decreed 11,000*l*. to be paid by Mackreth to Fox. We shall submit to the Court, that his Honor has gone, in making the decree further than, from any of the cases, or from the reason of the thing, he ought to have done. It will be necessary, in order to shew this, to state the progress of the cause. The first bill was filed in the name of Fox, in June, 1781, three

---

[1] Mr. Selwyn read, as part of his speech, a note of what the Lord Chancellor (Thurlow) said on discharging the order for the injunction, to the following purpose : * *Lord Chancellor.*—It is impossible to observe, that one-fifth more has been paid for the estate, and not to wish that the first owner should have the advantage. I have tried, on the head of every one observation, whether I could decree that Mackreth should be a trustee for Fox, for the difference of value in the estate. I attended, with great care, to see whether I could find any surprise on Mr. Fox, but the whole case begins and ends with the circumstance of an advantage being made in point of price. If Mackreth had sold the estate to A. (being a trustee for Mackreth), the case could not have stood ; but Mackreth lost the character of a trustee when he became a purchaser of the estate. The rental was extended into particulars, for the purpose of calculating the true value of the estate. It is not argued, that the rental was unfair Jackman's calculation was pressed by Fox upon Mackreth ; deliberation was had, and the difference split between them. A slight memorandum was made by Mr. Garforth, who acted as agent for Fox ; and his memorandum was laid before Mr. Burton, at the bar. It is not on the 28th of January that the agreement is signed by Fox ; but it is a deliberate act by Fox at the distance of twenty-two days. The whole impeachment of the transaction, which is now opened, is upon the difference of price.† It does not appear to me, that, at the time of the purchase, a greater price could have been produced in the common course of business of sale of estates.

---

* This injunction was dissolved upon a clear mistake : Ex parte Lacey, 6 Ves. 627 ; vide note, post.

† The price given for the estate, according to the principle upon which the case was ultimately decided, was immaterial.

years after the purchase by Mackreth; another bill was filed in
February, 1782. In March, a motion was made for an injunction
to restrain Mackreth from proceeding on the annuity bond.
Mackreth's answer was read against that application; and your
Lordship was of opinion, that there should be no injunction,
there being *no surprise upon Fox, nor any fraud imputa-   [*127]
ble to Mackreth. Then, for the purpose of introducing
creditors into the cause, in May, 1782, an assignment is made by
Fox of his estate to four trustees, Mr. Pitt, Mr. Hoare, Mr.
Oliver, and Mr. James Farrer, in trust, to pay debts. In 1784,
Mr. O. Farrer releases himself, and in June in the same year a
bill is filed by the three trustees, to have the benefit of the suit
begun by Fox; this artifice was used in order to have the advantage of the plaintiffs appearing as creditors. The cause came
on to be heard in the same manner as if brought by Fox. The
decree is wrong, both in the declaration and in the direction.
We contend, first, that there was no confidence reposed by Fox
in Mackreth; secondly, whether there was a confidence reposed or
not, there was no abuse of it; thirdly, that neither the declaration, facts, nor circumstances support the directions. With respect to the first head, there is no circumstance by which a confidence can be shewn to have been reposed in Mackreth. He was
only a trustee as to the 28,403l. balance, to apply it in the payment of debts, for which sum he has accounted; certainly every
trust implies a confidence; but not such a confidence as is meant in
the decree, as a trust to be abused. If the trustee does not perform his trust, it is a breach of trust, not an undue advantage of
his situation. Where a person treats with another without the
power of inquiring into the value, and makes an improper bargain, that is taking an undue advantage; but that is not the case
of a trust. The declaration is, that Mackreth has taken an undue
advantage of his situation; and, therefore, is to be considered as a
trustee for the plaintiff; this could refer only to the purchase, not
to the loan or the annuity, and these cannot be said to be transactions of confidence; farther, can the purchase be so considered?
Two persons are dealing for an estate. Mr. Fox wants an extravagant price; Mr. Mackreth wants to purchase at a reasonable one;
both argued as to the value. Fox had a valuation as well as Mackreth, and a fair price was given. If so, the declaration cannot be
right. Secondly, the bill is filed to attack *every trans-   [*128]
action between the parties, and to make the whole appear
as one system of fraud, yet if they can succeed in the point of the
purchase, it is all they want; the other circumstances are thrown
in to give weight to the main point, that Mackreth shall account
for 11,000l. received from Page; that is, for 5500l. more than
Jackman's valuation. The true question is, whether Mackreth
is a fair purchaser of the estate at 39,500l.? There is no pretence
that he ever refused to let the annuities be redeemed—two of
them, in fact, were redeemed; nor is there any ground to quarrel
with the loan. Mackreth had no dealings with Mr. Fox during

his minority; he did not even know him at that time. The first application to Mackreth was from Garforth, to buy an annuity. Garforth was connected with Fox for the purpose of borrowing money. If none of the articles themselves are sufficient to impeach Mackreth, being taken together they will not do so. As to the annuities Fox sought Mackreth. In December, 1777, he granted him two annuities, amounting to 800*l.* a year; part of the 500*l.* a year annuity was the property of Mackreth, but the annuity was taken in the name of Dawes, and was at six years' purchase. Fox had been of age a month before Mackreth knew of his intention to suffer a recovery in the ensuing Michaelmas Term. It is said, Mackreth knowing this, should not have entered into this contract; but there is no reason why he should not. Fox had at that time only a life estate, and could make no security but a grant of an annuity. Six years' purchase was then allowed of as the common price. In a case of *Floyer* v. *Sherrard*,[1] before Lord Hardwicke, Hil., 1740, Floyer had bought of Sherrard an annuity at six years' purchase, secured upon money in the funds, in the names of trustees. He filed his bill against the trustees to pay the annuity; the objection was, that Sherrard was a man in distress, and that only six years' purchase was given for the annuity. Lord Hardwicke said, this case differed from that of young heirs, because Sir B. Sherrard, the father, was in possession of the estate. A sale of an annuity, not redeemable, was not an usurious transaction; *where they are made redeemable, the [*129] Court has thought it an evasion of the law. As to the price of an annuity, it is the most uncertain thing in the world; taking it upon the highest calculation, it is only one year's purchase under the value; and the Court will not set it aside on that account. Then as to the security; if he had taken it on the estate, it would have been good. It was done on bond and judgment, without insurance of the life. Every hardship which occurs in this case is such as must occur in every case of the kind. Then this annuity was not redeemable. Lord Hardwicke's opinion on this subject appears to have been, that a redeemable annuity is usurious.[2]

[*Lord Chancellor.*—I do not believe that has ever been decided. It is certainly a ground to suspect a shift; but there is no decided case, that the annuity being redeemable will make the transaction usurious.[3]]

With respect to consulting Farrer, that was not Mackreth's business, if Fox did not choose so to do. If it was anybody's business to advise Fox, it was rather Farrer's than Mackreth's. The next transaction is, the recovery suffered in Michaelmas, 1777; the legal estate was by it vested in Farrer, to protect it

---

[1] Amb. 18.   [2] See Floyer v. Sherrard, Amb. 19.
[3] It is now fully established that such a transaction is legal. See Irnham v. Child, 1 Bro. C. C. 92; Lord Portmore v. Morris, 2 Bro. C. C. 219, Amb. 244, note (3), Blunt's edit.

against the annuitants and creditors. He was mistaken with respect to this matter, for a judgment creditor could have taken out execution against the estate of the cestui que trust, the same as if it was a legal estate. As to the application for the loan of, first 2000*l*., then 3000*l*., what ground is there to quarrel with that? In that transaction Farrer was consulted; he was present at the execution of the mortgage deed, and proves the payment of the money. Two objections are made to it; first, that Mackreth took the legal estate out of Farrer; but Farrer thought it right that Mackreth should have the legal estate. Secondly, the other objection is, that it was part of the system, and having the legal estate would assist them in carrying it into execution; but, if it was wrong, Farrer ought not to have parted with the legal estate; no objection was made to Mackreth's being mortgagee in fee. Again, it is objected *that Mackreth did not then [*130] turn the annuity into a debt; but Fox wanted the 3000*l*. immediately, and it might not occur to Mackreth to turn the annuity into a debt. The next matter is, the transaction with respect to the trust. Mackreth did not propose himself; this was proved by Farrer, who says it was proposed either by himself or Fox. Mackreth says, in his answer, that he did not propose himself; Farrer declined being a trustee; and then Mackreth proposed Dawes, as being acquainted with annuity business. Farrer approved of Dawes, and Garforth took his instructions from Farrer. A copy of the particulars was delivered to Mackreth. On the 6th of January 1778, the draft of the conveyance was sent to Farrer, who returned it on the 7th, with this observation: that it was not as he expected; for the annuities were carried down to the time of the sale, whereas they were to be turned into loans; and that Mackreth and Dawes were to have the whole authority to sell without any consent of Fox. There had only been a conversation, in which it had been proposed to turn the annuities into a loan. Then as to the sale itself. On the 16th of January, Fox and Mackreth treat on the subject. Mackreth offered 37,000*l*., at last 39,500*l*. including the furniture, and securing Mrs. Fox (the mother's) jointure. This agreement was put into writing by Garforth; no objection is made to the form of the writing. On the 28th of January, the contract was signed by Fox and Mackreth. The conveyance was laid before Farrer, and executed on the 24th of April; so that it was incomplete from January to April. The objection now taken and relied upon is, that Mackreth was a trustee, and, therefore, could not contract for the purchase of the estate: but we deny that he was a trustee; and, even though he were so, he might purchase upon fair terms. They contend, on the other side, that the trust deed was executed, and Mackreth bound not to contract with his cestui que trust. It is true, it was executed by Fox; for, during the conversation about the purchase, Fox, not agreeing to sell at the price then offered by Mackreth, executed the trust deed, but

[*131] *continued the conversation relative to the purchase, the trust deed lying all the while upon the table. If the conversation had ceased, the deed would have had effect; as it was, it was a nullity. Then how can it operate as a trust? It was a trust intended, if they will—commenced, but at the same moment put an end to—never acted under, but broke off immediately. But, even supposing him to be a trustee, he might contract for the estate, so that he did but deal fairly. We admit that a trustee cannot purchase for his own benefit. If, as a trustee, he had conveyed to a third person as a trustee for himself, that would be void; but there is no case which has decided that the cestui que trust cannot sell to his trustee. On the contrary, it was done in the case of *Clarke* v. *Swaile*,[1] before Lord Northington, where Sir Samuel Clarke, by the advice of Swaile, conveyed the estate in question to him to sell for payment of debts. Swaile endeavoured to sell the estate, but could not meet with a purchaser. Swaile afterwards treated for and purchased the estate, which was conveyed to him at a fair price, and the money was applied in payment of Sir Samuel Clarke's debts. Another deed was afterwards executed on account of a variance in the description of the estate, and a third, occasioned by a variance of the boundaries. This last was executed by Sir Samuel Clarke and Robert, his brother. Sir Samuel died and, Robert (now Sir Robert) filed his bill, on the ground of a confidence being placed by Sir Samuel in Swaile as his attorney, and that his circumstances were such that he durst not quarrel with him. Lord Northington said, as to the cestui que trust dealing with the trustee, he did not much like it; but, upon the whole, he did not see any principle on which he could set the transaction aside. In the present case there is no species of fraud; it is not even attempted to be stated in the bill; but they argue, that, from the case itself, there is an implied fraud: the parties met for very different purpose; there is no colour to say it was to draw Fox into a sale at an under-value. In *Floyer* v. *Sherrard*, Lord Hardwicke relied on there being no [*132] proposal coming *from Floyer. Then as to the argument, that Fox was in distress: he was upon the eve of extricating himself from any distress he might have been in; he was of age, and there is nothing to prove any weakness of mind, or incapacity of any kind. He was perfectly competent to act. He asked 45,000*l.*, and for that purpose produced Jackman's valuation. Mackreth objected, that it was thirty-five years' purchase for houses and land, which was a monstrous price, and offered fourteen years' purchase for the cottages and thirty for the land, amounting to 37,000*l.* He afterwards advanced to 39,500*l.* Fox then insisted on 42,000*l.* Fox had a particular. It is said Mackreth had a valuation, but not a word of that is in proof. Farrer not being present at the final agreement, is the next head of objection. But if Mr. Fox did not choose to

---

[1] 2 Eden, 134. See also Coles v. Trecothick, 9 Ves. 234; Morse v. Royal, 12 Ves. 355.

have him present, it could not be incumbent on Mackreth to send for him: besides, the draft of the conveyance was sent to him; and if the price was not adequate to the value, or there was anything wrong in the contract, Farrer should have objected to it, and have advised Fox not to proceed; on the contrary, it appears by his letter of the 7th of April, 1788, that he approved of the conveyance, except that he objected, in some respects, to the mode, and to the money remaining in the hands of Mackreth for payment of Fox's debts; but to the purchase itself Farrer never objected. With respect to the money remaining in Mackreth's hands, that does not go to the merits of the case, though the gentlemen on the other side have treated it as a badge of fraud. Mackreth accounted for the application of every shilling of the money, with interest for the time it remained in his hands. We have no objection to an account being decreed with respect to the application of the money. Then with respect to the confirmations, they are very strong. We do not dispute the principle, that whilst the distress continues subsequent acts shall not be held to be confirmations. It appearing upon the sale to Page, that part of the estate which had been sold as freehold really was copyhold, Fox, on the 19th of August, 1779, executed a warrant of *attorney to surrender the same. This was not clandestinely, but openly applied for; it was a conveyance [*133] of part of the estate which was not conveyed before. He afterwards executed duplicates of the deeds. The purchasers from Page in parcels wishing to have original deeds, Farrer made no objection, if they would indorse upon the deeds that they were duplicates.

[*Lord Chancellor.*—He expressly stipulated that the execution of these deeds should not be a confirmation.]

The real cause of the suit is, that Mr. Page has given 50,500*l.* for the estate. Mr. Fox rested under the sale till 1781, when that sale was discovered; but an advanced price being afterwards obtained is no reason for setting aside a previous fair sale of lands. To assert that it is, would be too much, where there is no fraud. The price of 50,500*l.* paid by Page was, in fact, a *pretium affectionis*; it was 5500*l.* more than Jackman had valued it at, or Fox ever thought of getting for it. Having shewn, then, that Mackreth was no trustee, and that the separate acts are fair, there can be no fraud in them taken collectively; yet the argument, *juncta juvant*, is relied on in this case. There is only one case in which that argument has prevailed; indeed, it is only fit to have a popular effect, not to be used in a court of justice. It only applies to a case made use of in circumstances which all terminate in one point, and which cannot be accounted for any other way. It is said, the circumstances in this case are all linked in one chain—that they all tended to the making an unreasonable purchase; but the other side have not been able to connect them. The treaty for the annuities and the purchase are separate and unconnected; therefore it is to be hoped that the arguments used, viz., that, although the separate articles were not sufficient to set aside the transaction, yet that altogether they are sufficient, will meet the same fate here that it did in Parliament in the case alluded to,[1] and that this Court will reverse the attainder and restore Mr. Mackreth in blood.

Mr. *Mansfield* in reply.—It is not to be denied that the large price at which the estate has been sold to Mr. *Page is [*134] the cause of the present suit. It is that advance of price which affords the strongest evidence of the purchase by Mackreth being fraudulent. Mackreth and Garforth are to many intents one and the same. The decree against Mackreth is, that he shall deliver up all papers which are in his hands. The present case contains fewer contested facts than generally occur in similar matters; and the remedy which lies with the Court is a very evident one. It has been argued that the Court cannot enforce an absolute, but only a technical morality. I know of no such term as "technical morality," that has ever been applied in this or any other case; but where one person has obtained an unfair advantage over another, the province of a Court of equity is to give the latter redress. Lord *Coke*, in his First Institute, has very shortly defined the office of this Court to extend to cases of " covin, accident, and all deceit for which there is no remedy in a court of law." What, then, is the true question in the present case? The Master of the Rolls has founded his decree in a confidence reposed by Fox in Mackreth. The question is only as to the inference to be drawn from the facts. In order to make out the confidence reposed by Fox in Mackreth, a few circumstances are to be attended to. Mr. Fox came of age in August, 1777. Very soon after that (in September, 1777) the connexion between him and Mackreth began. The first step was the purchase of two annuities, at six years' purchase; then the loan of 3000*l.* on mortgage of the Surrey estate; then Mackreth engages to become a trustee to sell the estate for payment of debts, apparently with no other intention than to relieve Fox's necessities. On the 16th of January they met to execute the trust deed; but the meeting terminated in the agreement for the sale of the estate. On the 24th of April there is a conveyance of the estate, and Fox has nothing to show for the balance of 28,403*l.* but Mackreth's accountable receipt and charge of the money on the Surrey estate. On the 21st of March Mackreth had sold the estate to Page for 50,500*l.* Towards the close of 1778 he had lent Fox 1000*l.;* in June, 1779, *there was a treaty for an annuity, part of [*135] the consideration for which was to be the 1000*l.* The account made up in 1778 is agreed on all hands to be a false one. In June, 1779, another account was made up. Then Mackreth applied for duplicates of the conveyances, which Fox complied with. These are the material facts, from which it is impossible to doubt that the fullest confidence was reposed by Fox in Mackreth, and that Mackreth did, on the 16th of January, take an

---

[1] The case alluded to is that of Lord Strafford.

undue advantage of that confidence. Every transaction of that day shows that Mackreth represented himself as Fox's friend. The account given by Mackreth, in his answer, relative to the loan of 3000*l.* and the annuity, is contradicted by the evidence. A full confidence is not to be expected to an answer in general, which is proved false in any particular. Suppose it to be true that the proposal for the sale came on the 16th of January from Fox, how easy was it for Mackreth to suggest that an immediate sale would be better than entering into a trust deed, and to make the formal proposal come from Fox, though the suggestion was his own? But be this as it may, no just inference is to be drawn from it to the merits of the cause. Fox entered into the contract with Jackman's valuation in his hand, and at twelve o'clock at night drops his price to 39,000*l.* How is this to be accounted for but by his confidence in Mackreth? If the sale had been fair and open, I should be precluded from these observations; but there never was a contract which was more suspicious, from the characters of the parties concerned. The counsel on the other side have said, that, when they were treating for the sale, the confidence was over, and that they were in a market; but it is impossible a sale could be negotiated under circumstances more private. It is as near the case of a trustee selling to himself as can possibly be; but still it shows what opinion Fox had of Mackreth. It is highly probable that the latter had the sale in his contemplation when he made the appointment. This is rendered probable by his having a valuation. This observation has received no answer, except that it *was natural, that, [*136] in order to sell as a trustee, he should have a valuation; but no notice was given to Fox of that valuation by Hampton. Fox and his agents were kept in the dark as to that survey. Mr. Fox came to Garforth's to meet Mackreth as a friend, where Mackreth, having in his possession a valuation, and concealing that fact, induced Fox to sell for 5500*l.* less than the only valuation he had. If there was nothing more in the case, Mackreth ought not to retain the great advantage he has made. As a friend Mackreth should have let Fox know he had sold the estate to him for 11,000*l.* less than he (Mackreth) had contracted to sell it for to Page. Then Fox parts with the estate on a bare accountable receipt and a charge upon the estate. The money is not deposited in the hands of any banker, and the estate is conveyed to Page without any notice of the charge, which made an end of the charge. This plainly shows that Fox trusted entirely to Mackreth. The settlement of the account is another mark of the most implicit confidence, and the whole transaction as to the loan and the annuity proves the same; but the gentlemen on the other side say, that the accumulation of the facts is immaterial, and that the application of *juncta juvant* ought to have no weight. If it was proved that the transaction of the 16th of January was perfectly fair, I allow their argument would apply; but whilst the great question of evidence is with respect to the fairness of the transaction of the 16th of January, it is material to show the complexion of the whole transaction taken together, and especially the power Mackreth had over Fox. This has the more weight, because it is incumbent on Mackreth to prove that the transaction of the 16th of January was fair and honest. To whom is it to be imputed but to him, that there was no witness of the transaction? He ought not to have entered into such a treaty with a young man, without having a witness present. The whole transaction speaks the truth of the Master of the Rolls' declaration, that there was a confidence reposed in Mackreth; and it will need very little argument to prove that [*137] that confidence *was abused. Either Mackreth had a valuation at the time of the treaty, or not. If he had not, he induced Fox to sell at 5500l. less than his own valuation; if he had, he concealed that circumstance from Fox, and now conceals it from the Court. Another thing that is urged is, that Fox has confirmed the transaction. If he has confirmed it, I admit it cannot be rescinded; but the first preliminary to a confirmation is, that the party should be previously apprised what it is he confirms. When the present comes to be compared with the confirmations in the cases where they have been held to bind, it is very unlike them; for none of them, except the execution of the duplicates of the conveyances, have the least tendency to confirm. They are mere consequential acts. In *Chesterfield* v. *Janssen* and *Cole* v. *Gibson* there were clear acts of confirmation. Here they are only carrying the contracts into execution; and the execution of the duplicates only shows how much Fox was in the power of Mackreth. It was only done for the purpose of getting something which might be called an act of confirmation; and Farrer refused to consent to their execution but with the proviso that it should not be considered as a confirmation. If Mackreth had first informed Fox of the real value of the estate, and then he had affirmed the contract, it would have been final. On the contrary, he was in distress in 1779, and absolutely in the hands and power of Mackreth; and so he was at every period when the confirmations were obtained. No one act was done with a knowledge of the value of the estate. By his own admission, Mackreth cheated Fox out of 600l. or 700l. in his first account. In May, 1781, he sent him another account rectifying the mistake. In the meanwhile he had lent his money on bond, and bought an annuity of him. If not from friendship, from what principle did Mackreth act, but from the desire to get this estate, or as much as he could out of Fox? It is urged, that this transaction cannot be set aside, because, if it is, no man can purchase at a fair price, and sell at a greater without the fear of having the transaction rescinded. But was there ever a fair [*138] *case where such an advantage was taken as in the present? No man, acting fairly, would deal with a young man without witnesses; no man acting fairly, would conceal his having a valuation. It is to be hoped such a transaction will never exist again ; but no fear can arise to fair transactions from such a transaction as this being overturned.

LORD CHANCELLOR THURLOW.[1]—The great and only doubt which I have had from the beginning to the end of this case is, whether the ground upon which I must go, if I affirm this decree, will not by necessary implication extend to many other cases, in which I shall run the hazard of undoing all the common transactions of mankind, and of rendering all their dealings too insecure. I do not agree with those who say, that, wherever such an advantage has been taken in the course of a contract by one party over another, as a man of delicacy would refuse to take, such a contract shall be set aside. Let us put this case :—Suppose A., knowing of a mine on the estate of B., and knowing at the same time that B. was ignorant of it, should treat and contract with B. for the purchase of that estate at only half its real value, can a Court of equity set aside this bargain ? No; but why is it impossible ? Not because the one party is not aware of the unreasonable advantage taken by the other of this knowledge, but *because there is no contract existing between them by which the one party is bound to disclose to the other the circumstances which have come within his knowledge ;* for, if it were otherwise, such a principle must extend to every case in which the buyer of an estate happened to have a clearer discernment of its real value than the seller. It is therefore not only necessary that great advantage should be taken in such a contract, and that such an advantage should arise from a superiority of skill or information, *but it is also necessary to show some obligation binding the party to make such a disclosure.* Therefore the question is, not whether this transaction be such as a man of honour would disclaim and disdain, but it must fall within some settled definition of wrong recognized *by this Court; for, otherwise, the general [*139] transactions of mankind would be too much in hazard and uncertainty. In this view, and in this view only, I have entertained considerable doubts on this case.

The Master of the Rolls has referred a great variety of accounts, subsisting between the parties, to the Master ; and it is not quite a fair argument to consider this part of the case as altogether decided. If these points are material, the only consequence is, that, as to them, the judgment must be suspended.

In the present appeal I shall consider the case entirely on the transaction of the 16th of January. I shall also consider certain terms necessary to be found, in analogy to the finding of a jury. First, it is necessary to find the real value to be what Page gave for the estate, or much more at least than the price given by Mackreth ; for, unless there be great inadequacy of value, the case comes to nothing. The fraud or imposition of the one party affords no ground of relief, unless *damage* be sustained by the

[1] 2 Cox, 320.

other ;[1] and, on the other hand, it does not follow, though the real value should be found such as now represented on the part of the plaintiff, that it will put an end to the contract, unless such advantage has been obtained by some of those frauds which the policy of this Court has adopted as grounds on which to set contracts aside.

The Master of the Rolls has said that Mackreth shall be a trustee, and so he must be taken *consequentially ;* for, if it be true that Mackreth has cheated Fox in this bargain, he did get the estate at law, but he did not get the estate in equity, and then he is reduced to a trustee. It is *only* in consequence of his getting the estate by fraud, that he becomes a trustee. Suppose an estate to be of the value of 50,000*l.*, and Mackreth buys it for 40,000*l.*, committing great fraud in such purchase, but, from the calamities of war and other public distresses, landed property as well as stocks sink in value more than one-fifth, and Mackreth then sells the estate for 35,000*l.* or 30,000*l.* only, would it not be [*140] true that Mackreth would *be bound to pay the 10,000*l.* as a satisfaction for the fraud committed by him, although he had not made the money he actually gave for it? The money would be due, not in consequence of what Mackreth afterwards sold it for, but what Fox lost by it at the time. The only consequence, in a Court of equity, is, that what one party lost by the undue advantage taken by the other must be answered to him.

The Master of the Rolls went on the fact of the value of the estate being that for which it was sold to Page, and thought, that, this being the value, Mackreth had cheated Fox. Taking this for the present to be *so,* let us go over shortly the facts of the case.

Fox began to be distressed about three or four years before he came of age. He engaged other young men, with whom he was connected, to become securities for him for sums of money he had borrowed. He had involved himself in annuities. When he came of age he found himself under this imperfect obligation in point of law, but very strong obligation in point of honour, to relieve those who had pledged their names for him. A plan was formed to sell a part of his estate. His situation as to fortune when he came of age was this: his estate in Surrey was about 1200*l.* per annum. Of this he was tenant in tail. He had an estate in Yorkshire of 1100*l.* per annum, of which he was tenant for life. He had also an estate in Ireland, of which he was tenant for life in possession, of about 5000*l.* or 6000*l.* per annum. Such was his situation when he came of age. He had resorted to a man of character in his profession, Mr. Farrer, for the purpose of settling this business. The 23rd of August, 1777, came, and no step was taken towards taking any account of his debts and annuities, or negotiating with any of his creditors; yet it is most

---

[1] This opinion Lord Thurlow changed, for he refused an inquiry as to the value of the estate.

evident that the best time for settling these matters with his creditors was before he came of age.

However, he came of age on the 23rd of August; and on the 23rd of September, it seems, the first conversation was had upon this subject. He had then been introduced to Mackreth. At that time, certainly, there was nothing *confidential in [*141] their intercourse, or any close connection between them; but Fox applied to Mackreth for about 5000*l.* Mackreth naturally asked what security he had to offer. Fox thereupon told him his real situation, by which it appeared that Fox had no permanent security to offer till Michaelmas Term, when he could suffer a recovery of the Surrey estate. Mackreth then proposed to him, as the ordinary mode of raising money, to buy an annuity of him at six years' purchase, which is, in truth, about half the real value; and, therefore, whoever proposes to deal with another upon this sort of terms, quits at once all idea of delicacy or generosity or propriety of conduct. It is such as cannot be endured out of a Court of justice; and, if a Court does affirm such transactions, it cannot be the heart of a judge which affirms it, but it must be done from a fear of laying down such rules as may tend to make the general transactions of mankind too insecure. There were other modes which might have occurred to a man of different feelings. A contract to make a mortgage when the Term came would have been an effective lien on the estate; and then it would only have been necessary to have insured Fox's life to the end of Michaelmas Term. This would have been the just and honorable way of relieving him. On the other hand, it is observable, that, though Mackreth adopted the other mode of raising the money, it was done in the usual course of his business; for, by profession, he dealt in the distresses of mankind. What he did, he did in his way and business of an annuity-monger. I make neither better nor worse of his conduct than that of a common and professed annuity-monger.

In November the recovery was suffered. Still nothing was done by Fox's friends towards relieving him from the annuities, which were eating him up. On the 24th of December Fox sends word that he was in great distress, in confinement, and wanted money immediately. Mackreth came to him and lent him money on common terms, and took a mortgage for it. A judge cannot impute anything to this part of the transaction, either one way or *another. There was no generosity on one side, nor [*142] any plot of circumvention on the other. It would be a most extravagant conjecture to suppose that by this Mackreth had in view to get the legal estate in himself. When one once gets beyond the natural result of facts, there is no end to conjecture or its consequences. This was the situation on the 24th.

Mackreth was made acquainted with the plan of the trust deed, and it is certain that he industriously recommended himself and Dawes as trustees for this purpose. It has been said, that Mack-

reth's forcing himself into the trust was improper, and done for
some bad motive; and that taking the business out of the hands
of Mr. Farrer was calculated to give Fox a bad impression of
him. I do not agree to this. In whose room were Mackreth and
Dawes to be substituted? The two first were Lord Grantley and
Lord Ligonier, who were put in only because they were lords, I
believe; for it was not very probable that they should be active
or attentive in executing such a trust as this. As to Mr. Farrer
himself, it is only to be said that he had, in fact, done nothing in
the affairs, nor taken any step towards it. I therefore really believe that Mackreth meant what he said upon that occasion;
and, when he proposed himself and Dawes as trustees, he meant
to transact the business to the best advantage. In doing this he
undertook a very delicate trust: first, he was to make the most
of the estate; then to deal with the several annuitants. This
put him into very awkward circumstances, himself and Dawes
being both considerable annuitants; and, therefore, when he undertook to deal with annuitants at large, he undertook a very
nice charge, and it was incumbent on him to see with very great
attention that he did not show more favour to the annuitants
than he ought to do.

I certainly do not approve of Mackreth's conduct, when after
having recommended himself as a trustee for these purposes, he
allowed the several annuities to stand as far as they had then
gone, redeeming them only from that time. However, in fact,
[*143] he bought the annuities *on behalf of Fox, though with
his own money; but, instead of considering them as discharged on the 24th of December, when he bought them, he considered them as bought for his own use, and treated them as existing annuities. Here, therefore, he has gone beyond the line of
delicacy; for this is a transaction that a Court of equity will
never permit to stand. Here the Court will say he took an undue
advantage of his situation. Yet it seems as if he thought this a
fair mode of dealing in this sort of market.

In another instance he charged Fox more than he actually
gave for the redemption of an annuity; and this part of the
transaction must of necessity be rescinded, as Mackreth has
acted *unfairly* in it; and Fox has the advantage of finding that
Mackreth, after having recommended himself as a trustee, and
undertaken to act faithfully for his cestui que trust, has yet been
dealing unfairly in this very article.

On the 16th of January it is allowed that Mackreth was a
trustee of Fox, and whatever consequences arise from this character must belong to him. Considering him, therefore, as a
trustee, see what he has done! First, he sent down a surveyor to
the estate; but he has so managed this part of the case as to prevent the Court from seeing much into it. The Court will act
temperately in its conjectures on this, but at the same time will
impute all that it fairly can in point of suspicion. On one side
it is said that Hampton was sent down to survey the estate with

a view of enabling Mackreth to make the greatest advantage of
it for his private benefit; but I do not think so.   I think it
ought to be taken that he had the estate surveyed as a *trustee*, in
order that, in that character, he might know the real value of it,
and thereby be better qualified to sell it to advantage.   This,
then, I consider as a part execution of his trust.   But then
Hampton's knowledge ought to be Fox's knowledge; and upon
this arises a question which I think material—whether a trustee,
gaining a knowledge of the subject in the execution of his trust
and at the expense of the *cestui que trust* (for I suppose   [*144]
the expenses incurred by the trustee must fall ultimately
on Fox), and that knowledge consequently *belonging* to the cestui
que trust, whether a trustee may not in *this respect* have the
hand of justice laid upon him, if this knowledge is made use of
by him to circumvent his cestui que trust, so as to afford a distinct ground of fraud in a Court of equity?   I am rather at a
loss to find what the evidence affords to this point.   It appears,
however, that Hampton stayed on the estate till the 17th of
January.

In these circumstances Mackreth began to deal with Fox,
remaining in his character of a trustee.   Fox had a valuation of
the estate made by Jackman, which, though not very full or
particular, yet afforded the general terms for a treaty and agreement; and it went generally to show that the estate was capable
of being improved about 100*l.* per annum.   On this valuation,
lying in medio, one party says the estate is worth 47,000*l.*
Mackreth reasons on this survey, and says, first, that the houses
are valued too high; secondly, that thirty-two years' purchase
for the land is too much; next, that forty years' purchase for the
lord's rent is out of all sight.   Thus running down the valuation
made by Jackman, he argued down Fox either from conviction
or a sense of his distress, not indeed so low as 30,000*l.*, which
Mackreth first proposed, but to a medium price of 39,500*l.*

*The first question to be asked is, whether the character of a trustee
shall vary the consequence of this transaction from what it would be
in the case of a stranger?* for it has not been argued, I think, that,
in the case of a stranger, this bargain could be rescinded.   Now,
to what conclusion does the character of trustee go in this case?
*If a trustee, though strictly honest, buys an estate himself and then
sells it for more, yet, according to the rules of a Court of equity, from
general policy and not from any peculiar imputation of fraud, a trustee shall not be permitted to sell to himself, but shall remain a trustee
to all intents and purposes.*   It is not therefore, in that view, that
Mackreth, being called a trustee, can operate.   It *does   [*145]
not rest on the name of a trustee, or on the legal or equitable relation of trustee, but on the familiar intercourse between
him and Fox.   Now, can I, putting myself in the place of a
juryman, pronounce that Fox agreed to the price, *trusting that
Mackreth knew the price and represented it fairly to him?*   If A.
says to B., I know the value of the subject, and, if you will trust

me, I will fairly tell you what it is worth, and A. at the same
time knows the value to be double what he represents it to be,
this is such an abuse of confidence as shall be relieved against,
not because A. is a trustee, but because he stipulated with B. to
tell him fairly the value, and he broke that stipulation; and then,
to be sure, it makes full as strong a case as that of a trustee.
But was this the express or tacit understanding of the parties
here? I have no materials to affirm this fact upon; at least I
am considerably in doubt how to find any evidence of this,
where one party asserts one sum to be the value of the estate,
and the other another, and both try to make the best of the bargain. At the same time there are such circumstances respecting
the manner in which Mackreth undertook the trust, as make me
hesitate. All this makes the question of the real value of the
estate extremely material.[1] I do not think it could have been
sold at the time according to the rate of Jackman's valuation;
and Mackreth's observations upon this seem to me to be well
founded. No evidence has been adduced to show his valuation
to be correct.

Now, see what follows on the 16th of January. Garforth was
called up and desired to put their agreement into writing. I do
not see why it was necessary that this memorandum should be
signed by both parties. I at first thought it showed an eagerness
to get the bargain made; but it seems it was agreed that more
regular articles should be executed afterwards. The execution
of these articles carried the transaction one step farther in point
of form. Still, however, the conveyance was not executed. It
is asked, whether any man of honour would let Fox execute the
deeds, after he had actually sold the estate for a much larger
[*146] price? Many men, perhaps, would do it; *but I should
never allow it to be the transaction of an honest man.
Mackreth had forced himself into the confidence of Fox, and was
called upon by every tie of honour and honesty, to consider himself as a trustee; but my doubt is, whether this is not too general
a line to lay down in a court of justice.

As to the manner of Mackreth's paying Fox the purchase-
money, it has been much observed upon; but I do not see much
in it. He had not the money by him, which may readily be supposed, but he gave an accountable note, with 5l. per cent. interest;
and, to be sure, his note was just as good as a bond—very little
danger of losing the money from a man of Mackreth's fortune;
besides, it was a sort of lien on the estate. The manner in which
the accounts are made up by Mackreth is objected to, and it is
said that this shows a confidence reposed in Mackreth by Fox.
So it does; but the question is, whether this confidence is ad
idem—whether it shows a confidence on the part of Fox, *that
Mackreth would tell him the true value of the estate?*

---

[1] Not for the purpose of the decision in a case between a trustee and his cestui
que trust. See 8 Ves. 353; 9 Ves. 247.

It is then said, that he was called upon to do several subsequent acts ; but these are to be so naturally accounted for by other circumstances, that I do not see how fraud can be inferred from these. They are then spoken of as instances in which Fox has confirmed the original purchase. As to confirmation it has been considered by the Court in very different ways. In *Lord Chesterfield* v. *Janssen*, the Court did not go on confirmation as it is usually understood, but on this, that Mr. Spencer, with his eyes open, and after the death of the Duchess, and when his situation was totally changed, thought proper to confirm the former bargain. So, the judges assistant relied on this principally, and did not give much opinion on the former part of the case. I wish they had gone further ; for, as to the confirmation, he stood at that time under the former bonds. Another way in which confirmation operates is, by showing that the party then thinks himself to have been fairly dealt with. This occurs in the present case on the 28th of January. Again, on the 25th of April, Fox did not see he had had *any advantage taken of him. The [*147] use that I think is to be made of such confirmations is, as a proof that the party has seen no occasion to complain. In this view the present case is still stronger, for no complaint was made of this transaction till 1781 ; and, therefore, it is fair to infer that so notorious a disproportion of price as is now insisted upon was not within the suspicion of those who dealt for Mr. Fox ; and it certainly would have been better if this suit had been brought earlier, for when are the affairs of mankind to be at rest ? Nay, more than this, it is evident, and indeed not denied by the plaintiff's counsel, that the transaction never would have been impeached if Page had not given so large a price for the estate. This very much shakes my idea of the real value[1] of it. If this estate, situate near London, had really been sold at a great under-value, the friends of Mr. Fox must have known it by other means. Supposing the transaction with Page to be purely accidental and not springing out of the actual value, it never can affect this question. At the same time it is observable that Mackreth has produced no evidence of the value of the estate, to show that it is not worth more than what he gave Fox.

I have been desirous of stating my thoughts on this case, that the gentlemen concerned may be apprised of them, as it will very possibly be necessary to have this matter discussed further even before me. I have conversed with the Master of the Rolls and the judges, with a wish to find some rule of evidence on which I can go in this case, without running the hazard of shaking too much the contracts of mankind. It is of very little consequence to the public to law down *definite* rules of *law*, if you have *indefinite* rules of *evidence*. I shall therefore at present only direct an inquiry into the real value of this estate ; and if upon that inquiry the value should turn out to bear a considerable disproportion to

---

[1] The value, as before observed, was immaterial.

what Mackreth gave for it, I shall probably require some assistance in laying down such rules of decision as will set men at ease as to the disposition of their property.

His Lordship, however, did not direct any such inquiry, [*148] *but after a lapse of a considerable time affirmed the decree, saying only that he had considered the case very much, and that he could not see that his Honor's decree was wrong.

The defendant afterwards petitioned his Lordship for a rehearing of the appeal, but that petition was dismissed. See 2 Cox, 158. He then appealed to the House of Lords, assigning the reasons set forth in 2 Cox, 330; but, on the 14th of March, 1791, the appeal was dismissed with costs. Id. 339; 4 Bro. P. C. 258, Toml. ed.

The well-known and thoroughly discussed case of *Fox* v. *Mackreth* is usually referred to as having established the rule ever since recognised and acted on by Courts of equity, viz., that a purchase by a trustee for sale from his cestui que trust, although he may have given an adequate price, and gained no advantage, shall be set aside at the option of the cestui que trust, unless the connection between them most satisfactorily appears to have been dissolved, and unless all knowledge of the value of the property acquired by the trustee has been communicated to his cestui que trust. " It is founded," observes Lord Eldon, " upon this : that though you may see in a particular case that the trustee has not made advantage, it is utterly impossible to examine, upon satisfactory evidence, in the power of the Court (by which I mean in the power of the parties), in ninety-nine cases out of a hundred, whether he has made advantage or not. Suppose a trustee buys any estate, and, by the knowledge acquired in that character, discovers a valuable coal mine under it, and, locking that up in his own breast, enters into a contract with the cestui que trust; if he chooses to deny it, how can the Court try that against that denial? The probability is, that a trustee who has once conceived such a purpose will never disclose it, and the cestui que trust will be effectually defrauded:" *Ex Parte Lacey*, 6 Ves. 627. Lord Thurlow, indeed, in *Fox* v. *Mackreth*, when he dissolved the injunction granted by the Master of the Rolls (see ante, p. 123), and in his judgment, intimated an opinion that it was extremely material to ascertain the value of the estate purchased by Mackreth from Fox, his cestui que trust, and proposed to direct an inquiry for that purpose. Ultimately, however, he did not direct any such inquiry, and he afterwards admitted that he was wrong in dissolving the injunction. *Fox* v. *Mackreth*, therefore, was decided, [*149] not upon the ground that *Mackreth had purchased the estate at an under-value, but that he had purchased it from his cestui que trust while the relation of trustee and cestui que trust continued to

subsist between them, and without having communicated to Fox the
knowledge of the value of the estate which he had acquired as trustee;
for if the relation of trustee and cestui que trust had been clearly dissolved, and Mackreth had made Fox fully acquainted with the knowledge
which he had acquired of the value of the estate, the purchase would
not have been set aside. " In the case of *Fox* v. *Mackreth*," says Lord
Eldon, " so much referred to, and now become a *leading authority*, in
which I have now Lord Thurlow's own authority for saying he went
upon a clear mistake in dissolving the injunction, it was never contended that if Fox, in a transaction clear of suspicion (but which must
be looked at with the most attentive jealousy), had discharged Mackreth from the office of trustee, he would not have been able to hold the
purchase. Why? because, being no longer a trustee, he was not under
an obligation not to purchase. But we contended that it was not in the
power of Fox to dismiss him; that the trust was accepted under an express undertaking to the friends of Fox, that the trustee should not be
dismissed without their privity; that Fox himself had too much imbe-
cility of mind as to these transactions: and we contended, that between
the dates of Mackreth's taking upon himself the character of trustee
and purchasing, he had acquired a knowledge of the value of the estate,
by sending down a surveyor at the expense of the cestui que trust,
which was not communicated to the cestui que trust even at the moment of the supposed dissolution of the relation between them; and,
under these circumstances, we contended that Mackreth remained a
trustee. This was the principle upon which the cause was decided.
Either that cause ought to have been decided in favour of Mackreth, or
this Court originally, and the House of Lords finally, were right in
refusing an issue to try whether the estate was of the value Mackreth
gave, or of a greater value at that time. Upon this principle, that was
an immaterial fact: for, if the original transaction was right, it was of
no consequence at what price he sold it afterwards; if the original
transaction was wrong, Mackreth not having discharged himself from
the character of trustee, if an advantage was gained by the most for-
tuitous circumstances, still it was gained for the benefit of the cestui
que trust, not of the trustee:" *Ex parte Lacey*, 6 Ves. 627. Lord
Eldon, upon several other occasions, in commenting on *Fox* v. *Mackreth*, most strongly insisted that the injunction was dissolved by mistake, and that the inquiry or issue which *Lord Thurlow, [*150]
although he ultimately refused it, at one time seemed inclined
to grant, was pressed for by an argument based on a false principle,
viz., that a fair price having been given in the first instance by Mackreth, he was therefore entitled to the benefit of an accidental rise in the
value of the property when he sold it to Page. " I believe," says his
Lordship, " that a fair price was given in the first instance; that is, as
good a price as, according to what was then known, could be obtained.

But the purchaser had received his information as to the value from a surveyor employed at the expense of the trust. In the judgment of this Court and the House of Lords (certainly Lord Thurlow having doubt, to whose doubt the utmost respect is due), Mackreth had not shaken off the character of trustee, but remained a trustee after he sold to himself; and the second sale was in equity to be considered as made, not by the purchaser, but by the trustee buying from himself; and, therefore, though the advantage was righteously obtained, it was obtained for the cestui que trust:" *Ex parte Bennett*, 10 Ves. 394.

It has, indeed, been asserted, that in *Whichcote v. Lawrence*, 3 Ves. 750, Lord Rosslyn considered, that, in order to set aside a purchase by a trustee, it is necessary to prove that an advantage has been gained by him. His Lordship, however, merely said, that he did not recollect any case in which the mere abstract rule came distinctly to be tried, abstracted from the consideration of advantage made by the purchaser, and that it would be difficult for such a case to occur: for unless advantage was made, the act of purchasing would never be questioned: and Lord Eldon disavowed such an interpretation of Lord Rosslyn's doctrine: *Ex parte Lacey*, 6 Ves. 627. See also *Ex parte Bennett*, 10 Ves. 385; *Randall v. Errington*, 10 Ves. 423; *Kilbee v. Sneyd*, 2 Moll. 186; *Ex parte Badcock*, 1 Mont. & Mac. 239; the important case of *Hamilton v. Wright*, 9 C. & F. 111, 123, 124, 125.

That a trustee for sale cannot purchase for himself, whatever may be the nature of the property, real or personal, in addition to the cases already cited, see *Killick v. Flexney*, 4 Bro. C. C. 161: *Hall v. Hallet*, 1 Cox, 134; *Pike v. Vigors*, 2 Dru. & Walsh, 262; *Price v. Byrne*, cited 5 Ves. 681; *Ingle v. Richards*, 28 Beav. 361. Nor can a trustee for him, even at an auction: *Campbell v. Walker*, 5 Ves. 678; *S. C., Sanderson v. Walker*, 13 Ves. 601; *Randall v. Errington*, 10 Ves. 423; *Watson v. Toone*, 6 Madd. 153; *Baker v. Carter*, 1 Y. & C. Exch. Ca. 250. And a purchase from co-trustees is equally objectionable: *Hall v. Noyes*, cited 3 Ves. 748; *S. C.*, 3 Bro. C. C. 483; *Whichcote v. Lawrence*, 3 Ves. 940. Nor will a purchase by trustees at a public auction [*151] *be sustained; for if persons who are trustees to sell an estate are there professedly as bidders to buy, that is a discouragement to others to bid. The persons present, seeing the seller there to bid for the estate to or above its value, do not like to enter into that competition: *Ex parte Lacey*, 6 Ves. 629; *Ex parte James*, 8 Ves. 348; *Whichcote v. Lawrence*, 3 Ves. 740; *Attorney-General v. Lord Dudley*, Coop. 146. Nor can a trustee be allowed to purchase the trust property, by his retirement from the trust with that object in view: *Spring v. Pride*, 12 W. R. (V. C. W.), 510. Nor can a trustee purchase before the Master under a decree for sale. (See *Price v. Byrne*, cited 5 Ves. 681; *Cary v. Cary*, 2 S. & L. 173: but see *Wren v. Kirton*, 8 Ves. 402.) Nor can a trustee purchase from the assignees of his cestui que trust in bankruptcy under an agreement to divide the profits, more especially if the purchase-money consists of part of the trust funds: *Vaughton* v. *Noble*, 30 Beav. 34. Nor can a trustee purchase as agent for another person: *Ex parte Bennett*, 10 Ves. 381, 400; *Gregory* v. *Gregory*, Coop. 204.

Upon the same principle, a receiver (*Eyre* v. *M'Donnell*, 15 Ir. Ch. Rep. 534; *Boddington* v. *Langford*, Ib. 358) or an agent employed by a trustee in managing a sale cannot purchase: *Whitcomb* v. *Minchin*, 5 Madd. 91.

Directors of companies being trustees for the shareholders, they cannot purchase shares from the chairman of the company, who is in fact their co-trustee, unless authorized so to do by the constitution of the company or the deed of settlement: *Hodgkinson* v. *The National Live Stock Insurance Co.*, 26 Beav. 473, 4 De G. & Jo. 422; and see *The Imperial Mercantile Credit Association* v. *Coleman*, 6 L. R. Ch. App. 558.

So the director of a railway company being a trustee for the company, is as such precluded from dealing on behalf of the company with himself, or the firm of which he is a partner: *Aberdeen Railway Company* v. *Blakie*, 1 Macq. 461; *Flanagan* v. *Great Western Railway Co.*, 7 L. R. Eq. 116.

Where a trustee has fairly sold an estate, a subsequent *bonâ fide* purchase of the estate from the purchaser is unobjectionable: *Baker* v. *Peck*, 9 W. R. (L. C. & L. J.), 472, reversing the decision of Sir J. Stuart, V. C., Ib. 186; and see *Dover* v. *Buck*, 5 Giff. 57.

A mortgagee (*Downes* v. *Glazebrook*, 3 Mer. 200; *Waters* v. *Groom*, 11 C. & F. 684); or an annuitant (*In re Bloye's Trust*, 1 Mac. & G. 488, *S. C. nom.*; *Lewis* v. *Hillman*, 3 Ho. Lo. 607, 630), with power of sale, being in fact a trustee for sale, cannot, either directly or by means of his solicitor, except by the express authority of his cestui que trust, purchase the estate upon which the mortgage or annuity is a *charge. See also *Ingle* v. *Richards*, 28 Beav. 361. [*152]

Nor can the solicitor conducting the sale do so on his own account, at any rate without a full explanation to the parties interested, and putting them in full possession of the facts, and a knowledge that he was to become purchaser for himself. *Ib.* See also *Robertson* v. *Norris*, 1 Giff. 421, 428.

A mortgagee, however, does not ordinarily stand in a fiduciary position towards the mortgagor, so as to render a purchase of the equity of redemption by him from the mortgagor (*Knight* v. *Majoribanks*, 2 Mac. & G. 10; and see *Webb* v. *Rorke*, 2 S. & L. 661, 673; *Waters* v. *Groom*, 11 C. & F. 684; *Dobson* v. *Land*, 8 Hare, 220; *Rushbrook* v. *Lawrence*, 8 L. R. Eq. 25; 5 L. R. Ch. 3. See post, vol. 3, notes *Howard* v. *Harris*), or from a prior mortgagee selling under a power of sale (*Shaw* v. *Bunny*, 33 Beav. 494; 2 De G. Jo. & Sm. 468), impracticable, even, it seems, although the purchaser be a second mortgagee with a trust for sale: *Kirkwood* v. *Thompson*, 2 Hem. & Mill. 392; 2 De G. Jo. & Sm. 613. But see and consider *Parkinson* v. *Hanbury*, 1 Drew & Sm. 613, 2 De G. Jo. & Sm. 450.

Transactions, however, between mortgagor and mortgagee are viewed with considerable jealousy, and the sale of the equity of redemption will be set aside where, by the influence of his position, the mortgagee has purchased for less than others would have given, and where there are circumstances of misconduct in obtaining the purchase. *Ford* v. *Olden*, 3 L. R. Eq. 461; and see *Prees* v. *Coke*, 6 L. R. Ch. App. 645, 649. There a mortgagee, who was also a solicitor, obtained a conveyance from the mortgagor, a man in humble circumstances, and without a legal adviser; it was held, that the onus of justifying the transaction, and showing that it was right and fair, was thrown upon the mortgagee.

As to a lease from the mortgagor to the mortgagee, see *Ford* v. *Olden*, 3 L. R. Eq. 461; *Hickes* v. *Cooke*, 4 Dow, 16.

It seems that a trustee who has become mortgagee of the trust estate will not be allowed to foreclose. " It is the duty," says Lord Hatherley, C. (in *Tennant* v. *Trenchard*, 4 L. R. Ch. App. 544), " of every trustee to make the most he can of the trust property for the benefit of the cestui que trust, and the only possibility of saving the estate must be by selling some portion of it. As mortgagee, he is not at all interested in doing that, but is interested in foreclosing the estate; and when he has foreclosed he will become master of the estate, and the whole of the trust which he is bound to protect will be entirely frustrated. So again, if he were only cestui que trust and not mortgagee, or only trustee and not mortgagee, on a bill being filed for foreclosure, he would immediately try to sell all the property to the [*153] greatest advantage, in order *to realise sufficient to pay off the mortgage, and save the estate from destruction. But from the first moment that he becomes mortgagee, it is greatly to his interest that the estate should be at once foreclosed. This case must be put upon the broad principle, that the trustee is in a position in which it is impossible for him, if a foreclosure is granted, to make the performance of his duty coincide with his interest; and therefore this Court would be bound, even if the mortgage deed gave him the power of foreclosure to say that it was impossible to allow him to foreclose when his duty was to take every possible step for the saving of the estate. In that respect the other observations made by Lord Brougham in *Hamilton* v. *Wright* (9 C. & F. 123) are of very considerable force, though the doctrine is so well recognised in this Court that the authority of the House of Lords was scarcely required to affirm it."

There is no rule in equity which prevents a surviving partner from purchasing the share of a deceased partner from his representatives (*Chambers* v. *Howell*, 11 Beav. 6, 14), or which prevents one of several residuary legatees from buying the share of another, or purchasing for less than the amount a charge on the share of another. *Barwell* v. *Barwell*, 34 Beav. 371,

A trustee cannot take a lease from himself: *Attorney-General* v. *Earl of Clarendon*, 17 Ves. 500.   And with so great jealousy does the Court look upon a trustee becoming a lessee of the trust property, that even in a case where a testator had given a trustee power to become lessee, he was removed, principally upon the ground that he was placed in a position in which his interest necessarily came in conflict with his duty. *Passingham* v. *Sherborn*, 9 Beav. 424.

But although a trustee cannot purchase from himself, he can purchase from a cestui que trust, who is sui juris, and has discharged him from the obligation which attached upon him as trustee. " Although," observes Lord Eldon, " a trustee who is intrusted to sell and manage for others undertakes, at the same moment in which he becomes a trustee, not to manage for the benefit and advantage of himself, it does not preclude a new contract with those who have intrusted him.   It does not preclude him from bargaining that he will no longer act as trustee. The cestui que trust may, by a new contract, dismiss him from that character ; but even then that transaction, by which they dismiss him, must, according to the rules of the Court, be watched with infinite and most guarded jealousy ; and for this reason, that the law supposes him to have acquired all the knowledge a trustee may acquire, which may be very useful to him, but the communication of *which to the cestui que trust the Court can never be sure he has made, [*154] when entering into the new contract by which he is discharged : " *Ex parte Lacey*, 6 Ves. 626.   So, in the principal case, it was fully admitted that Mackreth might have dealt with Fox for the purchase of the trust estate, had he done so without taking an undue advantage of his position as trustee, and the knowledge he had acquired in that character. In *Coles* v. *Trecothick*, 9 Ves. 234, a purchase, by a trustee under a trust to sell for payment of debts, of the trust property, as agent of his father, both of whom were creditors and in partnership, was sustained, upon the ground that the trustees did not appear to have interfered in the business up to the sale, otherwise than that they sanctioned the acts of the cestui que trust, and that the cestui que trust had full information, and the sole management of the sale, making surveys, settling the particulars, and fixing the prices of the lots, and specific performance of the agreement to purchase was decreed by Lord Eldon in favour of the trustee for sale. " As to the objection," observed his lordship, " to a purchase by the trustee, the answer is, that a trustee may buy from the cestui que trust, provided there is a distinct and clear contract, ascertained to be such after a jealous and scrupulous examination of all the circumstances, that the cestui que trust intended the trustee should buy ; and there is no fraud, no concealment, no advantage taken by the trustee, of information acquired by him in the character of trustee. I admit, it is a difficult case to make out, wherever it is contended that the exception prevails. The principle was clearly recognised in *Fox* v. *Mackreth*, and was established long before. The principle upon which I ever held that case right stands upon this only: not that Mackreth might not have purchased from Fox, and would not have been entitled to the increase; but that he had not been placed in circumstances to make that contract. See also *Morse* v. *Royal*, 12 Ves. 355, and *Clarke* v. *Swaile*, 2 Eden, 134, in both which cases purchases by trustees were, though with some reluctance, sustained: and see the remarks of Sir J. Romilly, M. R., in *Denton* v. *Donner*, 23 Beav. 285; see too *In re M'Kenna's Estate*, 13 Ir. Ch. Rep. 239; *Beale* v. *Billing*, Id. 250; *Luff* v. *Lord*, 34 Beav. 220; *Franks* v. *Bollans*, 3 L. R. Ch. App. 717.

Merely nominal trustees, as for instance, a trustee who has disclaimed, without ever acting in the trust, may become a purchaser (*Stacey* v. *Elph*, 1 My. and K. 195; *Chambers* v. *Waters*, 3 Sim. 42), as may also a mere trustee to preserve contingent remainders: *Parkes* v. *White*, 11 Ves. 209, 226.

Under the statutes for the redemption of the land tax, the Lords [*155] Commissioners are placed in the *position of vendors; and therefore, if trustees should purchase the property of the trust under those acts, as they would not be purchasing from themselves but from the Lords Commissioners, the transaction would be valid: *Beaden* v. *King*, 9 Hare, 499.

A trustee for infants or persons under disability cannot purchase the trust estate, unless by leave of a Court of equity, because persons not sui juris cannot enter into any contract with him which would have the effect of removing him from the character of trustee, which, as we have already seen, can be done by cestui que trust, who are sui juris. The only terms upon which such trustees may purchase, "is a bill filed: and the trustee saying so much is bid, and that he will give more. The Court would examine into the circumstances; ask who had the conduct of the transaction; whether there is any reason to suppose the premises could be sold better; and, upon the result of that inquiry, would let another person prepare the particular and let the trustee bid:" per Lord Alvanley, M. R., *Campbell* v. *Walker*, 5 Ves. 682; *S. C.*, 13 Ves. 601. See also 1 Ball & B. 418, and *Farmer* v. *Dean*, 32 Beav. 327.

The circumstance that two parties stand towards each other in the relation of trustee and cestui que trust does not affect any dealing between them unconnected with the subject of the trust: *Knight* v. *Majoribanks*, 2 Mac. & G. 10.

The doctrine which is applicable to purchases by trustees applies also to purchases by persons acting in any fiduciary capacity, which imposes upon them the obligation of obtaining the best terms for the vendor, or which has enabled them to acquire a knowledge of the property.

An agent or solicitor employed to sell cannot purchase from his principal, unless he make it perfectly clear that he furnished his employer with all the knowledge which he himself possessed (*Lowther* v. *Lowther*, 13 Ves. 103; and see the great case of *The York Buildings Company* v. *Mackenzie*, 8 Bro. P. C. 42, Toml. ed.; and see *S. C.*, 3 Paton's Scotch App. Cas. 578, 579, where the judgments of Lord Thurlow and Lord Loughborough are given at length; *Watt* v. *Grove*, 2 S. & L. 492; *Whitcomb* v. *Minchen*, 5 Medd. 91; *Woodhouse* v. *Meredith*, 1 J. & W. 204; *Oliver* v. *Court*, 8 Price, 127); and the moment it appears in a transaction between principal and agent that there has been any underhand dealing by the agent,—that he has made use of another person's name as the purchaser, instead of his own,—however fair the transaction may be in other respects, from that moment it has no validity in equity: *Trevelyan* v. *Charter*, 9 Beav. 140; *Charter* v. *Trevelyan*, 11 C. & F. 714; *Lewis* v. *Hillman*, 3 H. L. Cas. 607; * *Walsham* v. *Stainton*, 1 De G. Jo. & Sm. 678. See also [*156] *Murphy* v. *O'Shea*, 2 J. & L. 420, in which case it was argued that there was no proof that lands were sold to an agent at an under-value. Sir Edward Sugden, L. C., however, observed, "It is perfectly well settled that it is not necessary to prove under-value. A principal selling to his agent is entitled to set aside the sale upon equitable grounds, whatever may have been the price obtained for the property." In *Crowe* v. *Ballard*, 3 Bro. C. C. 117, Lord Thurlow thought that the person employed to sell could not be permitted to buy, and even if that were done with the knowledge of the party selling, it could not be supported; and that the principle must prevail, even if he had bought fairly. Lord Thurlow, however, it is conceived, did not mean to lay down, as a general rule, that an agent could in no case purchase from his principal; he spoke probably with reference to the case he was deciding, which was one of gross fraud. At any rate, it is clear now, that an agent to sell can purchase from his employer, if he comply with the rule laid down in *Lowther* v. *Lowther*. "The rule of the Court," observes Sir Edward Sugden, L. C. of Ireland, "does not prevent an agent from purchasing from his principal, but only requires that he shall deal with him at arm's length, and after a full disclosure of all that he knows with respect to the property:" *Murphy* v. *O'Shea*, 2 J & L. 425.

If an agent employed to make a purchase purchases for himself, he will be held a trustee for his principal: *Lees* v. *Nuttall*, 1 Russ. & My. 53; *S. C.*, 1 Toml. 282. So, also, if he is employed to obtain a lease, he shall not take it for his own benefit (*Taylor* v. *Salmon*, 4 My. & Cr. 134); nor will an agent employed to settle a debt due from his principal be permitted to derive any benefit from it by purchasing it

himself; because it is his duty, on behalf of his employer, to settle the
debt upon the best terms he can obtain; and if he is enabled to procure
a settlement of the debt for anything less than the whole amount, it
would be a violation of his duty to his employer, or at least would hold
out a temptation to violate that duty, if he might take an assignment
of the debt he was employed to settle, and so make himself a creditor
of his employer to the full amount of the debt which he was employed
to settle: if, therefore, an agent obtained under these circumstances an
assignment of a debt due from his principal, he would be held a trustee
for his principal, and would only be entitled to the sum he actually
paid for the debt: *Reed* v. *Norris*, 2 My. & Cr. 374.

Nor will an agent employed to purchase be permitted, unless by the
plain and express consent of his principal, to make any profit by becom-
[*157] ing a seller to him.   This *doctrine is recognised by Lord Thurlow in *East India Company* v. *Henchman*, 1 Ves. jun., 289,
where he observes, " If, being a factor, a man buy up goods which he
ought to furnish as factor, and, instead of charging porterage duties,
or accepting a stipulated salary, he takes the profits, and deal with his
constitutent as a merchant, this is a fraud for which an account is due."

If an agent employed by his principal to obtain another to do work
for him, for instance, as a sub-contractor, it would be fraud cognizable
in equity if the agent entered into a contract at a preposterous price in
order that he and the sub-contractor might divide the profits to accrue
from it. *Holden* v. *Webber*, 29 Beav. 117, 120; in which case, however,
under peculiar circumstances, the Court refused to grant any relief.
There the plaintiff Holden, a contractor for works on a railway, employed Cowdy as his agent to get a sub-contractor to do a portion of
the works. Cowdy accordingly, as agent, entered into a contract with
Webber. An allowance of £5 per cent. was made by Webber to Cowdy.
After the work had been finished, Holden filed a bill against Webber
and Cowdy to set aside the contract between him and Webber, to restrain Webber from proceeding against him at law for the balance due
to him on the contract, and that Cowdy might be decreed to pay to
him the sums received or retained by him on account of such contract.
It appeared in evidence that Cowdy had been the means of obtaining
the contract for the plaintiff from Messrs. Peto and Betts, for which
he was to receive £5 per cent. from the plaintiff. It was admitted that
Webber had made to Cowdy an allowance of £5 per cent. on his contracts, that it was the ordinary practice of the trade to make such an
allowance to an agent obtaining a contract, and that the plaintiff had
been in the habit of doing so himself. Sir J. Romilly, M. R., dismissed the bill. " I am not," said his Honor, " at all satisfied as to
what was the situation of Cowdy with respect to Webber, whether, in
fact, the services which he performed, the inquiries which he made, and
the superintending various matters, were to be considered as acts of

agency done for the plaintiff; for if not, this might properly be paid for by Webber. The situation between the parties, and their relative rights and positions, are not clearly ascertained by the evidence in this case; and, in addition to these circumstances, there also appears to be, that which I cannot call a custom (a word which has a legal and a technical meaning), but rather a practice which prevails on the part of contractors of giving to the officers and servants of the railway companies who obtain these contracts for them, remuneration in the shape of commission *on the price of the work to be done. Now, whether it is a gift or calculated as commission is a mat- [*158] ter of very little importance; but that this practice prevailed, and that the plaintiff knew it prevailed, and was himself in the habit of acceding and conforming to it, is, in my opinion, established by the evidence in the case. I think he must have known what occurred in that respect, or must have had good reason to believe, if he had turned his attention to the subject, that such was the course adopted here." And after dismissing the bill as against Cowdy without costs, without prejudice to the plaintiff bringing any action against him, his Honor said, " I wish that no decree of mine should fetter the question, but I mean to express nothing that can be construed into an encouragement of the practice I have alluded to."

Upon the same principle, where one of several partners was employed to purchase goods for the firm, and he, unknown to his co-partners, purchased goods of his own at the market price, and made considerable profit thereby: It was held by Sir J. Romilly, M. R., that the transaction could not be sustained, and that he was accountable to the firm for the profit thus made: *Bentley* v. *Craven*, 18 Beav. 75; *Williams* v. *Trye*, Ib. 366, 371; *Perens* v. *Johnson*, 3 Sm. & G. 419; *Burton* v. *Wookey*, 6 Madd. 367. So in *Richie* v. *Couper*, 28 Beav. 344, it was held that one of several co-owners of a ship, who acted as ship's husband, was only entitled to charge the cost price of supplies to the ship furnished by him in the course of his business. See also *Beck* v. *Kantorowicz*, 3 K. & J. 230. So, also, in *Massey* v. *Davies*, 2 Ves. 317, an agent for a colliery, who it was stipulated was to have no emolument beyond his salary, was decreed to account for the profits made by selling to his principal timber belonging to himself and another person, with whom he had clandestinely entered into partnership, under the name of that person. In this case the partner was held to have no knowledge that the agent was acting contrary to his trust; otherwise he would have been held bound, for not only the agent acting contrary to his trust, but a man who, knowing the agent to be guilty of a breach of trust, entered into a transaction with him, will be answerable.

Upon the same principle where a person is employed as a stock-broker, if he himself purchase the stock of his employer, or sell his own stock to him, without his knowledge, such sales and purchases will be set aside. See *Brookman* v. *Rothschild*, 3 Sim. 153; 2 D. & C. 188; 5 Bligh. N. S., 165. So in *Gillett* v. *Peppercorne* (3 Beav. 78), the plaintiff employed the defendant, a stockbroker, to purchase some canal shares, and he bought them from a person who, though ostensibly owner, was *a mere trustee for himself: Lord Langdale, M. R., [*159] set aside the sale with costs. " It is said," observed his Lordship, " that this is every day's practice in the city. I certainly should be very sorry to have it proved to me that such a sort of dealing is usual; for nothing can be more open to the commission of fraud than transactions of this nature. Where a man employs another as his agent, it is on the faith that such agent will act in the matter purely and disinterestedly for the benefit of his employer, and assuredly not with the notion that the person whose assistance is required as agent has himself in the very transaction an interest directly opposed to that of his principal." See also, *The Bank of Bengal* v. *Macleod*, 7 Moore, P. C. C. 35, 46. See Sug. Prop. 662.

Upon the same principle a solicitor employed in making a purchase is accountable to his clients for the benefits which he may have derived clandestinely from a sale to them of his own property. See *The Bank of London* v. *Tyrrell*, 27 Beav. 273: there a solicitor was active in founding a banking company. Before its establishment he entered into a secret arrangement with a stranger, that the latter should purchase some property eligible for the banking house on a joint speculation. After its establishment the company purchased part of the premises for their banking-house, not knowing that their solicitor was interested in it. It was held by Sir John Romilly, M. R., whose decision was affirmed by the House of Lords (10 Ho. Lo. Ca. 26, *nom. Tyrrell* v. *The Bank of London*), that the solicitor ought to account to the company for all the profit made by him in the transaction, but that the stranger was under no such liability. See also *Chaplin* v. *Young*, 33 Beav. 414.

A solicitor having, under a decree, the conduct of a sale, is under an absolute incapacity to purchase at it: *Atkins* v. *Delmege*, 12 Ir. Eq. Rep. 1. And see *In re Ronayne's Estate*, 13 Ir. Ch. Rep. 444.

And the better opinion seems to be that, although a solicitor may not under a decree actually have the conduct of the sale, if he has intervened on behalf of parties interested in the sale so as to render it his duty towards them to assist in procuring the best price for the property offered for sale, he ought not to be allowed to purchase it for himself. See *Guest* v. *Smythe*, 5 L. R. Ch. App. 551. There B. Gibbons, a mortgagee for 8,000*l.*, and J. Guest, his sub-mortgagee, in 1863 instituted a suit against the persons interested in the equity of redemption of the mortgaged property. B. Gibbons died, and the suit was revived by Emily Gibbons, his personal representative. Mr. Wight was solicitor for the plaintiffs in the suits of *Gibbons* v. *Gibbons* and *Berry* v. *Gibbons*,

*instituted for the administration of the estate of B. Gibbons. [*160]
On the 23rd of January, 1865, a decree was made in *Guest* v.
Smythe, directing a sale in case of non-payment of what should be found
due on the mortgage. On the 19th of April, 1869, Mr. Wight applied
in *Gibbons* v. *Gibbons*, for leave to apply in *Guest* v. *Smythe*, for an
order enabling the plaintiff in *Gibbons* v. *Gibbons*, to attend the proceedings, which leave was given. On the 13th of July, 1869, Mr.
Wight got the consent of the solicitors to the plaintiff in *Guest* v.
Smythe to his obtaining an order for the plaintiff in *Gibbons* v. *Gibbons*,
to attend the proceedings in *Guest* v. *Smythe*, and on the 27th of July,
1869, a summons, returnable on the 30th, was taken out for the plaintiff
in *Gibbons* v. *Gibbons* to have liberty to attend the proceedings in
Guest v. *Smythe*, upon which the order was made, but was dated on the
4th of August in consequence of the delay in obtaining an affidavit of
service on some of the parties. No person attended any appointment
in *Guest* v. *Smythe* until after this order had been made.

In the meantime, on the 29th of July, the mortgaged property was
put up for sale. It does not appear that Mr. Wight in any way intervened in the preparations for the sale, or that he was consulted with
regard to the particulars or the reserved bidding, which was fixed at
5,600*l.* On the printed particulars and conditions of sale which were
issued was this notice : " Particulars and conditions of sale may be obtained in London, of the following solicitors . . . ., *and in the
country of Messrs. Caldicott & Canning, Dudley ; Mr. Wight, Dudley ;
Messrs. Hodgson & Son, Birmingham, and of the auctioneer.*"

Mr. Wight attended at the sale, and bid in person for Lot 1, which
was knocked down to him at 6,110*l.* The chief clerk certified the result of the sale on the 3rd of August, and the certificate was signed and
approved by the judge on the 9th. It was held by Lord Romilly, M.
R., upon a summons taken out by a person interested in the estate,
that Mr. Wight stood in such a fiduciary position as disqualified him
from becoming a purchaser of Lot 1, and directed it to be put up for
sale at 6,110*l.*, Mr. Wight to be the purchaser if no one bid more than
that sum. " First," said his lordship, " I have to consider what was
the position of Mr. Wight. He was the solicitor of certain creditors of
Mr. Gibbons, and in that character was employed to take steps for the
purpose of intervening in the suit, and having some management in the
suit, for which purpose he obtained an order, though not until a day or
two after the sale. That, however, was his character ; he, therefore,
was representing *the creditors in the cause. The sale was [*161]
clearly a sale on behalf of the persons interested in the mortgage. It was for the purpose of *all* the creditors, therefore, and they
were as much interested in its being a good sale, in order that there might
be sufficient to pay them, as any other person ; and Mr. Wight was
their solicitor, and only their solicitor . . . . Mr. Wight applied

to intervene in their behalf, and I consider that when his name was added as one of the solicitors for the vendor, he was to act on their behalf, and to make the sale as effective as it could be for them. That being his character, I do not think he was in a situation in which he was able to buy . . . . It was the duty of Mr. Wight to give all his assistance to obtaining the best possible price, and his name was put upon the list as one of the solicitors for that purpose . . . . Observe, what might in many cases be the effect of a bidding by a person in Mr. Wight's position. Upon seeing the person bid whose name was put on the particulars as one of the solicitors concerned in the sale, people might suppose that the property was bought in, and that it was not an effectual sale," 5 L. R. Ch. App. 553, 554, n. The decision of Lord Romilly was reversed by Lord Justice Giffard sitting alone, who was of opinion that the rule as laid down by Lord Romilly was not essential for the ends of justice, and not at all essential for the purpose of insuring a fair sale, but on the contrary, would tend to depreciate sales by the Court.

It appears, however, to be clear, that Lord Romilly's decision is in strict accordance with the principles laid down by Sir John Leach in *Grover* v. *Hugell*, 3 Russ. 428; by Lord Cottenham in *Re Bloye's Trusts*, 1 Mac. & G. 488; and by Lord Langdale, in *Greenlaw* v. *King*, 3 Beav. 49; viz., that where a person has put himself in such a position towards other parties, by which it becomes his duty to obtain the highest price for property in which they have an interest, he cannot be allowed by becoming a purchaser to put himself in a position antagonistic to the duties he has undertaken. The sub-mortgagee, Mr. Guest, appears to have been represented by Messrs. Caldicott & Canning, and they would, therefore, be only interested in obtaining from the sale sufficient to pay the sum due on the sub-mortgage (the amount of which is not stated in the report). The creditors, represented by Mr. Wight as their solicitor, and after them Emily Gibbons, the personal representative of Mr. Benjamin Gibbons, were deeply interested in the sale being conducted in such a way as that it should produce more than sufficient to pay the amount of the sub-mortgage. Mr. Wight, solicitor [*162] for the creditors, clearly *intervened for the purpose of protecting their interests, whereby it became his duty, as observed by Lord Romilly, " to make the sale as effective as possible."

The very difficulty of ascertaining whether this was done or not, necessitates the strict application of the rule so well laid down by Lord Romilly—which if carried out as it ought to be, with unvarying strictness, would not, it is believed, have, as supposed by Lord Justice Giffard, a tendency to depreciate sales by the Court, but would prevent solicitors wishing to become purchasers of property, from putting themselves into positions in which their interests conflicted with their duties.

An agent or steward may take a lease from his employer or principal; (*Lord Selsey* v. *Rhoades*, 2 S. & S. 41; 1 Bligh, N. S., 1); but it must always be difficult to sustain such a lease in a court of equity, as it must be proved that full information has been imparted, and that the agreement has been entered into with perfect good faith: *Molony* v. *Kernan*, 2 D. & W. 31.

Where a surety gets rid of, and discharges an obligation, at a less sum than its full amount, he will not be allowed, as against his principal, to make himself a creditor for the whole amount, but only for the amount which he has actually paid in discharge of the common obligation: *Reed* v. *Norris*, 2 My. & Cr. 361, 375; *Ex parte Rushforth*, 10 Ves. 420; *Butcher* v. *Churchill*, 14 Ves. 567.

Executors or administrators will not be permitted, either immediately or by means of a trustee, to purchase for themselves any part of the assets, but will be considered as trustees for the persons interested in the estate, and must account to the utmost extent of the advantage made by them of the subject so purchased: *Hall* v. *Hallet*, 1 Cox, 134; *Killick* v. *Flexney*, 4 Bro. C. C. 161; *Watson* v. *Toone*, 6 Madd. 153; *Kilbee* v. *Sneyd*, 2 Moll. 186; *Baker* v. *Carter*, 1 Y. & C. Exch. Ca. 250; *Naylor* v. *Winch*, 1 S. & S. 566; *Cook* v. *Collingridge*, Jac. 607; *Wedderburn* v. *Wedderburn*, 4 My. & Cr. 41. So, if they compound debts or mortgages, or buy them in for less than is due upon them, they will not be allowed to retain any benefit from the transaction for themselves, but for the estate. See *Anon.*, Salk. 155; *Ex parte James*, 8 Ves. 346; *Ex parte Lacey*, 6 Ves. 628.

Assignees of a bankrupt cannot in any case purchase his property. This may be laid down as a general rule, which will be more peculiarly applied with unrelenting jealousy, from the impossibility of reaching the transaction, and, moreover, because the assignee has the bankrupt and his property altogether under his own disposal; (see *Ex parte Chadwick*, cited in Montague and Ayrton's book on Bankruptcy, vol. 1, 329, 2nd ed.; *Ex parte *Lacey*, 6 Ves. 623; *Ex parte Hughes*, 6 Ves. 617; *Ex parte James*, 8 Ves. 337; *Ex parte Tanner; Ex parte Atwood; Owen* v. *Foulkes*, 6 Ves. 430, n.; *Ex parte Bage*, 4 Madd. 459; *Ex parte Badcock*, 1 Mont. & Mac. 231; *Turner* v. *Trelawny*, 12 Sim. 49; *Ex parte Thwaites*, 1 M. & A. 323; *Ex parte Alexander*, 2 M. & A. 492); nor can his partner buy: *Ex parte Burnell*, 7 Jur. 116. In *Whelpdale* v. *Cookson*, 1 Ves. 9, 5 Ves. 682, Lord Hardwicke, confirmed a sale of a bankrupt's estate to an assignee, in case the majority of the creditors should not dissent; but Lord Eldon, in *Ex parte Lacey*, 6 Ves. 628, doubted the authority of that case: "If," said his Lordship, " the trustee is a trustee for all the creditors, he is a trustee for them all in the article of selling to others; and if the jealousy of the Court arises from the difficulty of a cestui que trust duly informing himself which is most or least for his [*163] advantage, I have considerable doubt whether the majority in that article can bind the minority:" *Ex parte Thwaites*, 1 M. & A. 323. But in a recent case, on payment of costs, a purchase by an assignee on being found beneficial by the Court was confirmed; (*Ex parte Gore*, 6 Jur. 1118; 3 M. D. & De G. 77; 7 Jur. 136); and an assignee has been removed by the Court in order that he might bid at a sale of the bankrupt's estate; (*Ex parte Perks*, 3 M. D. & De G. 385); and in a case where the Court refused to allow an assignee to bid, he was allowed to name the price he would give if the property were not sold by auction, and afterwards to buy at that price; *Ex parte Holyman*, 8 Jur. 156.

The Court of Chancery will rarely allow persons conducting a sale to bid at it. Thus, when those who are interested in an estate insist that a trustee ought not to be allowed to bid, the court will give so much weight to their wishes, as to say, although the trustee may be also mortgagee, that until all other ways of selling be exhausted he shall not be allowed to buy. (*Tennant* v. *Trenchard*, 4 L. R. Ch. App. 547.) But if the court is satisfied that no purchaser at an adequate price can be found, then it is not impossible that he may be allowed to make proposals and become a purchaser. (*Ib.*) So where a sale is directed by the Court of Chancery of partnership property upon a dissolution of partnership, liberty to bid at the sale will only be given to such of the partners as have not the conduct of the sale: *Wild* v. *Milne*, 26 Beav. 506.

As to the purchase of debts due from the bankrupt by the assignee, it has been decided that, as the assignees cannot buy the estate of the bankrupt, so, also, they cannot for their own benefit buy an interest in [*164] the bankrupt's estate, because they are trustees *for the creditors. In that respect there is no difference between assignees and executors, who cannot for their own benefit buy the debts of the creditors; for although, in a moral point of view, such a transaction may not be blamable, still the court, considering that, unless the policy of the law made it impossible for them to do anything for their own benefit, it was impossible to see in what cases the transaction was morally right, and also the prodigious power of the assignees connected with solicitors under the commission, and bankers receiving the money, over the creditors and the bankrupt, has held the assignees trustees of the debts purchased by them for the benefit of those entitled to the interest in the residue, the creditors or the bankrupt, as the case may be: *Ex parte Lacey*, 6 Ves. 628. And see *Pooley* v. *Quilter*, 2 De G. & Jo. 327, reversing the decree of Sir R. T. Kindersley, V. C., reported 4 Drew. 184; and see *Adams* v. *Sworder*, 2 De G. Jo. & Sm. 44, reversing *S. C.*, 4 Giff. 287.

Solicitors to the commission (*Owen* v *Foulkes*, 6 Ves. 630; *Ex parte Linwood*, cited 8 Ves. 343; *Ex parte Town*, 2 M. & A. 29), or solicitors having conduct of a sale under a decree of the Court of Chancery (*Sidney* v. *Ranger*, 12 Sim. 118), cannot purchase.

The rule affecting assignees of bankrupts applies with equal force to a commissioner of bankrupts: *Ex parte Bennett*, 10 Ves. 381; *Ex parte Harrison*, 1 Buck. 17; *Ex parte Dumbell*, Mont. 33, cited in notes.

The Courts of Bankruptcy having jurisdiction over trustees of deeds executed in conformity with section 192 of the Bankruptcy Act, 1861 (24 & 25 Vict c. 134), repealed by 32 & 33 Vict. c. 83, the Court of Chancery, although its jurisdiction was not excluded by the former act, has refused to exercise it, except where the Court of Bankruptcy was unable to give adequate relief. See *Stone* v. *Thomas*, 5 L. Rep. Ch. App. 219; there a creditor filed a bill in Chancery against the trustees of a creditor's deed, alleging that one of the trustees had purchased some of the property at an undervalue, and praying that the sale might be set aside: it was held by Lord Hatherley, L. C., that as there was nothing in the case which would render the relief in Chancery more effectual than in Bankruptcy, the bill must be dismissed. See also *Martin* v. *Powning*, 4 L. R. Ch. App. 356.

A solicitor is not incapable of contracting with or purchasing from his client; but inasmuch as the parties stand in a relation which gives, or may give, the solicitor an advantage over the client, the onus lies on the solicitor to prove that the transaction was fair: *Montesquieu* v. *Sandys*, 18 Ves. 302; *Cane* v. *Lord Allen*, 2 Dow. 289; *Champion* v. *Rigby*, 1 *Russ. & M. 839; *Edwards* v. *Meyrick*, 2 Hare, 60; *Gibbs* v. *Daniel*, 4 Giff. 1; and the usual indorsement or acknowledg- [*165] ment in the deed of the receipt of the purchase-money will not be sufficient evidence of its payment by the solicitor to his client: *Gresley* v. *Mousley*, 3 De G. F. & Jo. 433. In the case of *Gibson* v. *Jeyes*, 6 Ves. 266, where Jeyes, an attorney, sold an annuity to his client, this subject was much considered by Lord Eldon: " An attorney," says his Lordship, " buying from his client, can never support it, unless he can prove that his diligence to do the best for the vendor has been as great as if he was only an attorney dealing for that vendor with a stranger. That must be the rule. If it appears that in that bargain he has got an advantage by his diligence being surprised, putting fraud and incapacity out of the question, which advantage, with due diligence, he would have prevented another person from getting, a contract under such circumstances shall not stand. The principle so stated may bear hard in a particular case; but I must lay down a general principle, that will apply to all cases; and I know of none short of that, if the attorney of the vendor is to be admitted to bargain for his own interest, where it is his duty to advise the vendor against himself." And in another part of his judgment his Lordship observes, " If he will mix with the character of attorney that of vendor, he shall, if the propriety of the contract comes in question, manifest that he has given his client all that reasonable advice against himself that he would have given against a third person. It is asked, where is that rule to be found? I answer, in that great rule of the Court, that he who bargains in matter of advantage with a person placing confidence in him, is bound to show that a reasonable use has been made of that confidence; a rule applying to trustees, attornies, or any one else." See also *Austin* v. *Chambers*, 6 C. & F. 1, 37; *Trevelyan* v. *Charter*, 9 Beav. 140; *S. C.*, 11 C. & F. 714; *King* v. *Savery*, 1 Sm. & G. 271; *S. C.*, nom. *Savery* v. *King*, 5 H. L. Cas. 627, 656, 665; *Bellamy* v. *Sabine*, 2 Ph. 425; *Holman* v. *Loynes*, 4 De G. Mac. & G. 270; *Salmon* v. *Cutts, Cutts* v. *Salmon*, 4 De G. & Sm. 125; *Barnard* v. *Hunter*, 2 Jur. N. S. 1213; *Waters* v. *Thorn*, 22 Beav. 547; *Spencer* v. *Topham, Ib.* 573; *Denton* v. *Donner*, 23 Beav. 285; *Pearson* v. *Newson*, 28 Beav. 598; *Popham* v. *Exham*, 10 Ir. Ch. Rep. 440; *Gresley* v. *Mousley*, 1 Giff. 450, 4 De G. & Jo. 78; 3 De G. F. & Jo. 433; *Beale* v. *Billing*, 13 Ir. Ch. Rep. 250.

But the rule laid down by Lord Eldon will not apply if the solicitor does not act in such capacity in hac re: (*Cane* v. *Lord Allen*, 2 Dow. 289; *Edwards* v. *Meyrick*, 2 Hare, 68; but see *Edwards* v. *Williams*, [*166] 11 W. R. (L. J.), 561; *unless it appears that he is aware, or takes advantage of a neglect of duty on the part of the new solicitor, or he withholds or suppresses any information of importance acquired when he acted as solicitor: *Gibbs* v. *Daniel*, 4 Giff. 1). In *Montesquieu* v. *Sandys*, 18 Ves. 302, the purchase of a reversionary interest, viz., a second presentation to a living, after the death of the then incumbent, by an attorney, from his client, though advantageous in the end, was sustained, no fraud or misrepresentation being proved, and the proposal coming from the client, both the attorney and client being ignorant of the real value. See *Hesse* v. *Briant*, 2 Jur. N. S. 922.

A solicitor, if a purchase from his client be a fair transaction, may file a bill for specific performance (*Cane* v. *Lord Allen*, 2 Dow. 289). And if a solicitor purchasing from his client institute a suit against third parties to enforce his right, the objection to the transaction on the ground of its being a purchase by a solicitor from his client, cannot be maintained by such third parties. *Knight* v. *Bowyer*, 23 Beav. 609.

Although a person may have ceased to act as attorney for another, if by means of former transactions, while holding that character, he had acquired at the expense of his client, a knowledge of the value of his property which the client had not, he will not be able to sustain any contract relative to such property, if he concealed from his former client the knowledge so obtained: *Cane* v. *Lord Allen*, 2 Dow. 294; *Montesquieu* v. *Sandys*, 18 Ves. 308; *Ex parte James*, 8 Ves. 352. See *Galbraith* v. *Elder*, 8 Watts, 81; *Henry* v. *Raineman*, 1 Casey, 354. If, however, such knowledge were communicated to the former client by the attorney, the parties would be placed upon an equality, and such communication being proved, the difficulty, quoad hoc, would be removed : *Edwards* v. *Meyrick*, 2 Hare, 69.

Although a beneficial purchase by a solicitor from his client pending that relation cannot be supported, the solicitor may insist on and obtain a mortgage from his client for what is justly due to him. *Johnson* v. *Fesenmeyer*, 25 Beav. 88, 3 De G. & Jo. 13; *Pearson* v. *Newson*, 28 Beav. 598.

The employment of counsel as confidential legal adviser disables him from purchasing for his own benefit charges on his client's estates, without his permission ; and although the confidential employment ceases, the disability continues as long as the reasons on which it is founded continue to operate. Thus in *Carter* v. *Palmer*, 1 Dru. & Walsh, 722, 8 C. & F. 657, C., a barrister, who had been for several years confidential and advising counsel to P., and had by reason of that relation acquired an intimate knowledge of his property and liabilities, and was particularly consulted as to a compromise of securities given *by P. for a debt which C. considered not to be recoverable to [*167] the full amount, purchased those securities for less than their nominal amount, without notice to P.; it was held by Lord Plunket, and by the House of Lords on appeal, that C.'s purchase, while the compromise proposed by P. was feasible, was in trust for P.; and that C. was entitled only to the sum he had paid, with interest. " The several cases," observes Lord Cottenham (8 C. & F. 707), " which have occurred in which solicitors have been restrained from acting against their former clients, or communicating information acquired in such employment, proceed upon a principle which governs this case; for it cannot be contended that they are at liberty to use for their own benefit, and to the prejudice of their former clients, information acquired whilst acting for them, which they are not permitted to communicate or to use for the benefit of others. I am therefore of opinion that Mr. C. had been incapacitated by the character of his employment from purchasing, for his own benefit, these securities upon his employer's property, and that such incapacity continued at the time of his purchase, and consequently that he is to be considered as having so purchased for the benefit of his former employer."

In *Greenfield* v. *Bates*, 5 Ir. Ch. Rep. 219, a solicitor purchased a leasehold interest from his client, and himself prepared the assignment, which contained no covenant to indemnify the vendor, but did contain the words " subject to rent and covenants," in the lease. It was held by Lord Chancellor Brady that the executor of the solicitor was bound to indemnify the vendor against the rent and covenants.

So in *Hobday* v. *Peters*, 28 Beav. 349, a mortgagor consulted a solicitor who turned her over to his clerk to assist her gratuitously. The clerk, by reason of information derived during such employment, bought up the mortgage for less than half the amount. It was held by Sir

John Romilly, M. R., that he was a trustee of the benefit for the mortgagor.

A person chosen as arbitrator cannot buy up the unascertained claims of any of the parties to the reference ; for, to use the words of Lord Manners, " that he should purchase an interest in those rights upon which he was to adjudicate, could not be endured. It would indeed be to corrupt the fountain, and contaminate the award : " *Blennerhassett* v. *Day*, 2 Ball. & B. 116.

Upon the same principle a judgment delivered by a judge, who has an interest in the subject-matter of the suit, will be set aside. See *Hoydenfeldt* v. *Towns*, 27 Alabama, 423, 430. See *Paddock* v. *Wells*, 2 Barber, Ch. 331 ; *Underhill* v. *Deaming*, Paige, 202. Such judgments, however, are voidable only not void, and will be binding on the parties until regularly set aside or reversed on error. *Hoydenfeldt* v. *Downs* ; *Dimes* v. *The Proprietors*. See *Dimes* v. *Proprietors of the Grand Junction Canal* (3 H. L. Cas. 759) ; there it was held that a judgment of Lord Cottenham, C., assisted by Lord Langdale, M. R. [*168] (*2 Mac & G. 285), in which, affirming the decision of the Court below, he had decided in favour of a company in which he was a shareholder to the amount of several thousand pounds, ought to be reversed. " No one," said Lord Campbell, " can suppose that Lord Cottenham could be in the remotest degree influenced by the interest he had in this concern ; but it is of the last importance that the maxim that no man is to be a judge in his own cause, should be held sacred. . . . . This will be a lesson to all inferior tribunals to take care not only that in their decrees they are not influenced by their personal interest, but to avoid the appearance of labouring under such an influence."

So, where an Act of Parliament empowered a rector, with the consent of the bishop, who was patron of the living, to raise money by annuity for building a new rectory-house, the plan and accounts of which were to be approved of by the bishop. The bishop advanced the necessary money, and obtained a grant of the annuity charged on the living. The bishop being placed in the position of a trustee to protect the interests of the rectory, it was held, by Lord Langdale, M. R., that he could not become the purchaser of the annuity ; and that the transaction, although there was no unfairness in it, could not stand, because it was a clear violation of those rules which have been established for the defence of those whose interests and property have been committed to the protection of persons placed in a fiduciary situation : *Greenlaw* v. *King*, 3 Beav. 49. See also *Grover* v. *Hugell*, 3 Russ. 428. But see *Boyd* v. *Barker*, 4 Drew. 582.

It may, however, be laid down as a general rule that a tenant for life may purchase or take in exchange lands from trustees, in whom they are vested with a power of sale and exchange, with his consent and direction (*Howard* v. *Ducane*, 1 T. & R. 81), but this case has been put entirely upon the practice of conveyancers (*Grover* v. *Hugell*, 3 Russ. 432); though probably it might be better rested upon the principle that as the trustees were the vendors, their intervention to check and control the transaction, was quite sufficient to take the case out of the operation of the rule preventing a person in a fiduciary position from purchasing from himself. See *Beaden* v. *King*, 9 Hare, 499.

In a recent case, Lord Justice James, says, that " the ground of the rule is, that the power of consenting to or requesting an exercise of a power of sale, is given to the tenant for life for his own benefit, and that he is not in a fiduciary position as to it. He has, therefore, the same right to buy from the trustees that any one else has." [*169] *Dicconson* v. * *Talbot*, 6 L. R. Ch. App. 32, 37.

A tenant for life, with power to lease, may at law grant a lease to a trustee for himself (*Wilson* v. *Sewell*, 4 Burr. 975; *Taylor* v. *Horde*, 1 Burr. 124; *Lord Cardigan* v. *Montague*, 2 Sugd. Pow., 7th ed., App., p. 551): so likewise where, under a mortgage, power was reserved to the mortgagor until entry by the mortgagee to grant building leases, it was held by Sir W. Page Wood, V. C., that a lease to a trustee for the mortgagor was good; *Bevan* v. *Habgood*, 1 J. & H. 222.

A power of sale given without restriction to a party having a limited interest only, may well be held to impart a negative upon the power of the same party to buy, for the power to sell is in the nature of a trust; but as the rule does not extend to prevent, in all cases, a party having a power to sell from becoming a purchaser; so neither, where there is a restriction upon the power of sale, is the party having the power to sell in all cases at liberty to become the purchaser. It must, in each case, depend upon the circumstances under which, and the purposes for which, the power was given, and upon the nature and extent of the restrictions which are put upon the exercise of the power. In the proportion in which the power is restricted, the danger incident to allowing the donee to purchase is diminished: per Sir G. Turner, V.-C., 9 Hare, 519.

A creditor taking out execution is not precluded from becoming the purchaser of the property seized under it. " The case of trustees," observed Sir Thomas Plumer, M. R., " is quite different; with respect to them, the principle is, that the same person shall not be buyer and seller; but here the sheriff is the seller:" *Stratford* v. *Twynam*, Jac. 421; and it has been held that a mere creditor, having his debt secured by an agreement from the debtor to convey an estate upon trust for the creditor to sell, and amongst others to pay his own debt, is not in such a fiduciary position as to be disabled from purchasing the estate from the agent of his debtor; *Chambers* v. *Waters*, 3 Sim. 42; Coop. Cas. temp. Brougham, 91; S. C., nom. *Waters* v. *Groom*, 11 C. & F. 684.

With regard to transactions between guardian and ward, Lord Hardwicke observed, in *Oldin* v. *Samborn*, 2 Atk. 15, that it was improper for a guardian to purchase his ward's estate immediately upon his coming of age. But although it has a suspicious look, yet if he be paid the full consideration, it is not voluntary, and cannot be set aside. See *Hylton* v. *Hylton*, 2 Ves. 549. In *Carey* v. *Carey*. 2 S. & L. 173, leaseholds belonging to an infant were sold under a decree of the Court, and [*170] purchased by his guardian in the *suit, who acted also as receiver. The sale was set aside, although the full value was given, and decreed fraudulent and void, it being wholly unnecessary, as there were funds sufficient for the purposes to which the purchase-money was to be applied; and the old lease having been surrendered, and a new one obtained, it was declared to be held in trust for the persons entitled to the former lease. See also *Dawson* v. *Massey*, 2 Ball & B. 219. And Lord St. Leonards says, with reference to Lord Hardwicke's observation in *Oldin* v. *Samborn*, that " it seems clear that such a purchase would now be set aside on general principles, without reference to the adequacy of consideration." Sugd. V. & P. 692, 14th ed.

In a recent case, a young lady, two years after she came of age, granted a mining lease as to part of the property in possession, and as to the rest in reversion, to her brother-in-law and uncle, at the suggestion and advice of her father's executor, and with no independent advice. Three months afterwards the executor was taken into partnership with the lessees. It appeared that applications of other persons to become lessees had been discountenanced, and concealed from the knowledge of the lady. It was held by Sir John Romilly, M. R., that, in order to support the lease in equity, the lessees were bound to show that no better terms could have been obtained; that the grantor had the fullest information on the subject; that she had separate, independent, and disinterested advice; and that she had deliberately and intentionally made the grant ; and, the lessees having failed in proving this, the lease was cancelled: *Grosvenor* v. *Sherratt*, 28 Beav. 659. See also *Low* v. *Holmes*, 8 Ir. Ch. Rep. 53.

If a guardian buys up incumbrances upon his ward's estate at an under-value, he will be held a trustee for his ward, and can only charge him with what he has actually paid : *Henley* v. ——, 2 Ch. Ca. 245.

The principle of these cases has been acted upon by the Legislature, which, under the General Inclosure Act, has rendered commissioners incapable of purchasing *any* estate in the parish in which an inclosure is made until five years after the date and execution of the award (41 Geo. 3, c. 109, s. 2). And under the Commons Inclosure Act, a similar prohibition prevents valuers from purchasing land until after seven years from the confirmation of the award (8 & 9 Vict. c. 118. s. 219).

See also in Joint Stock Companies Act, 7 & 8 Vict. c. 110, the 29th section of which enacts that if any contract or dealing (with certain exceptions) shall be entered into in which any director shall be interested, then the terms of such contract or dealing shall be submitted to the next general *or special meeting of the shareholders to be [*171] summoned for that purpose, and that no such contract shall have force until approved and confirmed by the majority of votes of the shareholders present at such meeting. "The object of the clause," observes Wood, V.-C., "is to prevent a person, who is a trustee, from entering into contracts on behalf of his cestuis que trust in which he is himself personally interested. The exception to the prohibition introduced by the words, 'no such contract shall have force until approved and confirmed,' is intended to afford an opportunity to the cestui que trust to consider whether he will ratify any such contract." *Re South Essex Gas, &c., Co.*, Johns. 483. See *Ernest v. Nicholls*, 6 Ho. Lo. Ca. 401; *Murray's Executors' Case*, 5 De G. Mac. & G. 746. A contract between a company and a person who acts as a director, whether legally or not, is within the prohibition of the statute; *Re South Essex Gas, &c., Co.*, Johns. 480. The exception in the 29th section of the statute, of contracts for articles or services the subject of the proper business of the company, refers to articles and services supplied or rendered by the company to a director, and not to those supplied by a director to the company. *Ib.*

Moreover, although there be no particular relation between the parties such as that of trustee and cestui que trust, principal and agent, solicitor and client, if there exist a confidence between them, of such a character as enables the person in whom confidence or trust is reposed to exert influence over the person trusting him, the Court will not allow any transaction between the parties to stand unless there have been the fullest and fairest explanation and communication of every particular resting in the breast of the one who seeks to establish a contract with the person so trusting him. See *Tate v. Williamson*, 2 L. R. Ch. App. 55. There Tate, a young man aged twenty-three, entitled to a moiety of a freehold estate, the entirety of which brought in about £440 a year, being pressed for payment of his college debts, amounting to about £1000, and being estranged from his father, wrote to his great uncle for advice and assistance as to the payment of the debts. The uncle deputed the defendant, his nephew, to see Tate on the subject. The defendant met Tate by appointment, and at this interview Tate refused to allow any attempt to compromise the debts, and said he would sell his moiety of the estate, upon which the defendant offered him £7000 for it, payable by instalments. Tate, next day, accepted the offer. Before an agreement had been signed, the defendant obtained a valuation by a surveyor, estimating the value of the mines under the entirety *at £20,000. The sale was completed with- [*172] out this valuation having ever been communicated to Tate.

Tate's heir filed a bill to impeach the sale, and it was held by Lord Chelmsford, C., affirming the decision of Sir W. Page Wood, V. C., (reported 1 Law Rep. Eq. 528), that the defendant had stood in a fiduciary relation to Tate, that made it his duty to communicate to him all material information which he acquired affecting the value of the property; and that as he had not communicated the valuation to Tate, the transaction must be set aside. See also *Hobday* v. *Peters*, 28 Beav. 349.

It may here be mentioned that where no fiduciary relation exists between the parties, in the absence of fraud, mere inadequacy of consideration, although the vendor may have no professional adviser, will not be a sufficient reason for setting aside a sale: (*Harrison* v. *Guest*, 6 De G. Mac. & G. 424, 8 Ho. Lo. Ca. 481; but inadequacy of price, the want of due protection and advice, precipitation in concluding and carrying out the bargain, especially when the vendor is poor and illiterate, may be held to be sufficient evidence of fraud on the part of the purchaser, so as to enable the vendor or his heir to set aside the sale. *Longmate* v. *Ledger*, 2 Giff. 157; *Clark* v. *Malpas*, 31 Beav. 80, 10 W. R. (L. J.) 677; *Douglas* v. *Culverwell*, 10 W. R. (V. C. S.) 189; *Baker* v. *Monk*, 33 Beav. 419; and see *Clarkson* v. *Hanway*, 2 P. Wms. 202; *Rees* v. *Coke*, 6 L. R. Ch. App. 645.

Where a person standing in a fiduciary position purchases at a sale, which takes place by order of the Court, although such sale has been absolutely confirmed, the statute 30 & 31 Vict. c. 48, s. 7, will not be a bar to its being set aside. *Guest* v. *Smythe*, 5 L. R. Ch. App. 551.

Nature of Relief granted by Courts of Equity.] It remains to consider the nature of the relief a Court of equity will grant against a trustee or other person who has made a purchase which is improper, according to the rules before laid down, and upon what terms that relief will be granted.

The cestui que trust, if he wishes it, can insist upon a reconveyance of the property from the trustee who purchased, if it remains in his hands unsold; (*York Buildings Company* v. *Mackenzie*, 8 Bro. P. C. 42 Toml. ed.; *Lord Hardwicke* v. *Vernon*, 4 Ves. 411; *Randall* v. *Errington*, 10 Ves. 423; *Hamilton* v. *Wright*, 9 C. & F. 123); or from a person who has purchased from him, with notice: *Attorney-General* v. *Lord Dudley*, Coop. 146; *Dunbar* v. *Tredennick*, 2 Ball & B. 304; *Pearson* v. *Benson*, 28 Beav. 598. But the re-conveyance will only be decreed upon the terms of his repaying the purchase-money, with [*173] interest at *4l. per cent., and all sums which may have been expended in repairs and improvements of a permanent and lasting nature, and also such as have a tendency to bring the estate to a better sale. On the other hand, there must be an allowance for acts that deteriorate the value of the estate, and the trustee must account for all rents received by him, and for all profits, such as money arising from the sale of timber; and he must also pay an occupation rent for such part of the estate as may have been in his actual possession: *Hall v. Hallet*, 1 Cox, 134; *Ex parte Hughes*, 6 Ves. 624, 625; *Campbell v. Walker*, 5 Ves. 682; *Ex parte Bennett*, 10 Ves. 400, 401; *Robinson v. Ridley*, 6 Madd. 2; *Ex parte James*, 8 Ves. 351; *Ex parte Lacey*, 6 Ves. 630; *Watson v. Toone*, 6 Madd. 153; *York Buildings Company v. Mackenzie*, 8 Bro. P. C., 42 Toml. ed.; *Mill v. Hill*, 3 H. L. Cas. 869; and see *Popham v. Exham*, 10 Ir. Ch. Rep. 440, and the form of decree given.

If the cestui que trust does not wish for a reconveyance of the property, an order will be made, that the expense of repairs and improvements not only substantial and lasting, but such as have a tendency to bring the estate to a better sale, after making an allowance for acts that deteriorate the value of the estate, shall be added to the purchase-money, and that the estate shall be put up at the accumulated sum; if any one makes an advance upon that sum, the trustee shall not have the estate; if no one does, he will be held to his purchase; (*Ex parte Reynolds*, 5 Ves. 707; *Ex parte Hughes*; *Ex parte Lacey*; *Lister v. Lister*, 6 Ves. 617, 625, 631; *Ex parte Bennett*, 10 Ves. 281; *Ex parte Hewitt*, 2 Mont. & Ayr. 477; *Stepney v. Biddulph*, 13 W. R. (V. C. W.) 576; *Tennant v. Trenchard*, 4 L. R. Ch. App. 546); but where the trustee has bought the estate in one lot, and the cestuis que trust are desirous of having it sold in several lots, the cestuis que trust must first repay him all the money he has advanced, with interest, he accounting for the rents received by him, or paying an occupation rent, if he actually occupied the estate: *Ex parte James*, 8 Ves. 351.

Although the purchaser has paid the purchase-money into Court and it has been invested in the funds, he will not be entitled to any benefit from any advance in the funds, but to his purchase-money and interest only; for, if the stock had fallen, instead of advancing, he could not have been compelled to take it: *Ex parte James*, 8 Ves. 351.

Where the trustee has *resold* the estate, the cestui que trust can, as in the principal case, make him account for what he has received over and above the purchase-money he himself paid, with interest at 4*l.* per cent.: *Ex parte *Reynolds*, 5 Ves. 707; *Hall v. Hallet*, 1 Cox, 134.   [*174]

The costs of the suit, where the sale is set aside, must be paid by the trustee; (*Sanderson v. Walker*, 13 Ves. 601; *Hall v. Hallet*, 1 Cox, 141; *Whichcote v. Lawrence*, 3 Ves. 740; *Dunbar v. Treddenick*, 2 Ball. & B. 304; see, however, *Baker v. Carter*, 1 Y. & C. Exch. Ca. 250); unless there has been great delay on the part of the cestui que trust; *Attorney-General v. Lord Dudley*, Coop. 146. And even if the cestui que trust fails to set aside the sale, on account of his own delay, the Court may refuse the trustee his costs: *Gregory v. Gregory*, Coop. 201; *Champion v. Rigby*, 1 Russ. & My. 539.

Acquiescence.]—Acquiescence for a long time in an improper sale
will disable a person from coming into a Court of equity to set it aside :
Morse v. *Royal*, 12 Ves. 355; *Price* v. *Byrne*, cited with approbation
by Lord Alvanley in *Campbell* v. *Walker*, 5 Ves. 681 ; *Champion* v.
Rigby, 1 Russ. & My. 539 ; *Roberts* v. *Tunstall*, 4 Hare, 257 ; *Beaden*
v. *King*, 9 Hare, 499, 532; *Baker* v. *Read*, 18 Beav. 398; *Marquis of
Clanricarde* v. *Henning*, 30 Beav. 175; *Wentworth* v. *Lloyd*, 32 Beav.
467; *In re M'Kenna's Estate*, 13 Ir. Ch. Rep. 239 ; *Barell* v. *Barwell*,
34 Beav. 371; and see *Seagram* v. *Knight*, 3 L. R. Eq. 398, varied on
appeal, 2 L. R. Ch. 628; *Bergen* v. *Bement*, 1 Caine's Cases in Error,
Slee v. *The Manhatten Co.* 1 Paige, 48, 55.

But "to fix acquiescence upon a party, it should unequivocally appear that he knew the fact upon which the supposed acquiescence is
founded, and to which it refers," per Sir William Grant, M. R., in
Randall v. *Errington*, 10 Ves. 428 : see also, *Chalmer* v. *Bradley*, 1 J.
& W. 51 ; *Trevelyan* v. *Charter*, 9 Beav. 140; *S. C.* 11 C. & F. 714 ; 4
L. J. (N. S.) Ch. 209 ; *Savery* v. *King*, 5. H. L. Cas. 624, 667 ; but see
and consider *Knight* v. *Majoribanks*, 11 Beav. 322, 2 Mac. & G. 10; and
the distress of the cestui que trust may be an excuse for acquiescence ;
(*Gregory* v. *Gregory*, Coop. 201 ; *Roche* v. *O'Brien*, 1 Ball & B. 342;
Gresley v. *Mousley*, 4 De G. & Jo. 78, 98, sed vide *Life Association of
Scotland* v. *Siddal*, 3 De G. F. & J. 58); but it has been held that
laches does not apply to a body of creditors, to whom relief will be
granted when it would be refused to an individual : see case in Exchequer, cited 6 Ves. 632; *Whichcote* v. *Lawrence*, 3 Ves. 740 ; *York
Buildings Company* v. *Mackenzie*, 8 Bro. P. C. 42, Toml. ed.

And in considering lapse of time it only commences to run from the
discovery of the circumstances giving the title to relief. *Trevelyan* v.
Charter, 9 Beav. 140; 11 C. & F. 714; 4 L. J. (N. S.) Ch. 209 ; *The
Marquis of Clanricarde* v. *Henning*, 30 Beav. 175. Nor will it in
[*175] general run against a party so long as his interest is *contingent
        or reversionary (*Gowland* v. *De Faria*, 17 Ves. 20 ; *Bennett* v.
Colley, 5 Sim. 191; *Duke of Leeds* v. *Lord Amherst*, 2 Ph. 117 ; *Browne*
v. *Cross*, 14 Beav. 105; *Hope* v. *Liddell*, 21 Beav. 183; *Life Association of Scotland* v. *Siddal*, 3 De G. F. & Jo. 58, 7 Jur. N. S. 785 ;
Bowen v. *Evans*, 1 Jo. & L. 178), or dependent on the will of the trustee making the purchase (*Roberts* v. *Tunstall*, 4 Hare, 257), but the
fact of the interest being reversionary does not prevent the party interested assenting to a breach of trust. *Life Association of Scotland*
v. *Siddal*, 3 De G. F. & Jo. 58.

Although acquiescence in an improper sale may have the effect of
not enabling a party to set it aside, it nevertheless will not be sufficient
to induce a Court of equity to exercise its discretionary power of compelling specific performance of the agreement to sell: *Salmon* v. *Cutts,
Cutts* v. *Salmon*, 4 De G. & Sm. 125.

Where a bill to set aside a purchase by a solicitor from his client is dismissed on the ground of lapse of time, the Court gives the solicitor no costs unless he proves the fairness of the transaction: *The Marquis of Clanricarde* v. *Henning*, 30 Beav. 175.

Confirmation.]—A cestui que trust may confirm an invalid sale, so that he cannot afterwards set it aside: *Morse* v. *Palmer*, 12 Ves. 353; *Roche* v. *O'Brien*, 1 Ball & B. 353; *Dover* v. *Buck*, 5 Giff. 57. But in order to constitute a valid confirmation, a person must be aware that the act he is doing will have the effect of confirming an impeachable transaction: *Murray* v. *Palmer*, 2 S. & L. 486; *Dunbar* v. *Tredennick*, 2 Ball & B. 317; *Malony* v. *L'Estranye*, 1 Beat. 413; *Adams* v. *Clifton*, 1 Russ. 297; *Cockerell* v. *Cholmeley*, 1 Russ. & My. 425; *Chalmer* v. *Bradley*, 1 J. W. 51; *De Montmorency* v. *Devereux*, 7 C. & F. 188; *Salmon* v. *Cutts*, 4 De G. & Sm. 129; *Stump* v. *Gaby*, 2 De Gex, Mac. & G. 623; *Waters* v. *Thorn*, 22 Beav. 547; *Lloyd* v. *Attwood*, 3 De G. & Jo. 650; and see *Lyddon* v. *Moss*, 4 De G. & Jo. 104. Nor will the act of confirmation be valid, if it be done in distress and difficulties, under the force, pressure, and influence of the former transaction (*Crowe* v. *Ballard*, 3 Bro. C. C. 139; *Wood* v. *Downes*, 18 Ves. 128; *Roche* v. *O'Brien*, 1 Ball & B. 330; *Roberts* v. *Tunstall*, 4 Hare, 257): and it must be an act separate and distinct from the impeachable transaction, and not, as in the principal case, a conveyance executed in consequence of a contract or covenant connected with it: *Morse* v. *Royal*, 12 Ves. 370; *Wood* v. *Downes*, 18 Ves. 124, 128; *Roche* v. *O'Brien*, 1 Ball & B. 338. A confirmation of an invalid sale, by the majority of the creditors of a bankrupt, *will not be binding upon the minority: see *Ex parte Lacey*, 6 Ves. 628; *Sir G. Colebrooke's* [*176] *case*, cited *Ex parte Hughes*, 6 Ves. 622, overruling *Whelpdale* v. *Cookson*, cited in *Campbell* v. *Walker*, 5 Ves. 682; *S. C.*, 1 Ves. 9; *Ex parte Thwaites*, 1 M. & A. 323; *Tommey* v. *White*, 3 H. L. Cas. 49

The equitable maxim that a trustee is disabled to purchase, for his own benefit, at a sale of the trust property, has two applications, which, though embraced under the same conception of duty and policy, are so far distinguished in their circumstances and appearance, that it is better to state them separately. (1.) One of them is derived from the general and fundamental principle in the doctrine of trusts, which was mentioned in the note to *Keech* v. *Sandford*, ante, that a person assuming a fiduciary relation towards another, in regard to property, is bound to exercise for the benefit of his *cestui que trust*, all the rights, powers, knowledge, and advantages of every description, which he derives from that position, or acquires by means of it; at least he is disabled from exert-

ing them for his own private benefit : *Michaud* v. *Girod*, 4 Howard,
503; *Keighler* v. *The Savage Man.
Co.*, 12 Maryland, 383, 416. (2.)
The other is the more specific and
positive rule, that an agent to sell
for others, though he have but a
mere ministerial power for that
single purpose, is disabled from
being a purchaser at the sale:
Michaud v. *Girod; Keighler* v
The Savage Man. Co. His duty,
as vendor for others, is to sell the
property for the highest price, and
his interest, as purchaser for himself, is to get it for the lowest;
and these two relations are so
essentially repugnant, that a court
of chancery never allows them to
be united in the same person:
Garthen v. *Myrick*, 9 Maryland,
143; *Ricketts* v. *Montgomery*, 15
Id. 46, 51. A sheriff or commissioner, or other judicial or ministerial officer, buying at the sale
which he is appointed to conduct,
is an instance under the latter
rule : where a general trustee purchases trust property at a sale
under adverse process with which
he has no connexion, we find an
illustration of the former principle, to which the other does not
extend: in the case of a trustee
purchasing at his own sale, the
two run together. But though,
for clearness and certainty in practice,
this distinction between the
larger and narrower application of
the maxim should be observed, the
equitable notion of a trust is so
comprehensive, that all of these
cases are embraced under the same
head in chancery, and all of them
are dealt with, in precisely the
same manner. The relief in equity
proceeds upon the same method :
without any reference to fraud,
and without any inquiry into circumstances, it touches with a trust,
alike, the office of the fiduciary
and the power of the agent: at
the option of the parties interested, it converts the purchase
into a trust for them, and gives
them the choice of confirming the
sale, or of having the property
resold for their benefit, upon terms
of the trustee's being compensated
for what he has expended. "There
is no magic in the terms *trust* and
trustee," said the counsel in the
case of *The York Buildings Company* v. *Mackenzie*, 8 Tomlin's
Brown's P. C. 42, 64 : " He is a
trustee, in technical style, who is
vested with property *in trust for
others ;* but every man has a *trust*,
to whom a business is committed
by another, or the charge and care
of any concern is confided or delegated by commission." *Beeson* v.
Beeson, 9 Barr, 279, 284.

Understanding, then, by a trustee, any one who acts representa-
tively, or whose office is to advise
or operate, not for himself, but for
others, the principle is general,
that a trustee, so far as the trust
extends, can never be a purchaser
of the property embraced under
the trust, without the consent of
all the persons interested : and
this principle applies to executors,
administrators, guardians, attorneys at law, general and special
agents, assignees, commissioners,
sheriffs, and all persons, judicial
or private, ministerial or counsel-
ling, who, in any respect, have a

concern in the sale of the property of others : *Beeson* v. *Beeson ;* it extends to sales by public auction, and to judicial sales, as well as to private ones; and applies to purchases direct and indirect, in person or through an agent, or by the medium of a person who subsequently re-conveys to the trustee: *Abbott* v. *The American Co.,* 33 Barb. 578; *Forbes* v. *Halsey,* 26 New York, 53; and to purchases made by the trustee as agent for a third person : *Brackenridge* v. *Holland,* 2 Blackford, 377; *Martin* v. *Wyncoop,* 12 Indiana, 266; and to purchases in which he is to have a partial interest as well as those in which he is exclusively concerned : *Roberts* v. *Butler,* 24 Illinois, 387; *Michoud* v. *Girod,* 4 Howard, 503; *Keighler* v. *The Savage Man. Co.,* 12 Maryland, 383, 416 ; *Collins* v. *Smith,* 1 Head. 251, 257 ; *Salle* v. *Graft,* 7 Richardson, Eq. 34 ; *Mulford* v. *Bowen,* 1 Stockton, 797; *Hoitt* v. *Webb,* 36 New Hampshire, 758. " No person," according to the expression approved in *Torrey* v. *Bank of Orleans,* 9 Paige, 650, 763, in *Van Epps* v. *Van Epps,* Id. 238, 241; in *Cram* v. *Mitchell and others,* 1 Sandford, 251, 256; in *Dobson* v. *Racey,* 3 Id. 61; and in *Voorhees* v. *The Presbyterian Church of Amsterdam,* 8 Barbour's S. Ct. 136, 142, " can become a purchaser of an interest in property, where he has a duty to perform which is inconsistent with the character of a purchaser :" or, in other words, wherever it is the duty or undertaking of a person to advise or act for the purpose of

obtaining the highest price for the property, there is an incapacity in that person to be a purchaser, under any form, or to any extent, except by consent of the *cestui que trust,* because the interest and effort of the purchaser is to obtain the property at the lowest price. This great pervading principle of equity was explained and vindicated with equal elegance and ability in *Davoue* v. *Fanning,* 2 Johnson's Chancery, 252; and has been again copiously illustrated in the late case of *Michoud et al.* v. *Girod et al.,* 4 Howard, 503, 553 ; and is recognized and adopted in every equitable jurisdiction in this country; see *Ames* v. *The Port Huron Co.,* 11 Michigan, 39 ; *Huston* v. *Cassidy,* 2 Beesely, 228 ; *Mulford* v. *Mench,* 3 Stockton, 16 ; *Calver* v. *Calver,* Ib. 215; *Fawcett* v. *Fawcett,* 1 Bush, 511 ; *Campbell* v. *Pennsylvania Life Ins. Co.,* 2 Wharton, 53, 63 ; *Leisenring* v. *Black,* 5 Watts, 303, 304 ; *Litchfield* v. *Cudworth,* 15 Pickering, 24, 31 ; *Shelton* v. *Homer and others,* 5 Metcalf, 462, 467 ; *Caldwell* v. *Sigourney,* 19 Connecticut, 37, 51 ; *Thorp et al.* v. *M'Cullem et al.,* 1 Gilman, 615, 625 ; *Brackenridge* v. *Holland,* 2 Blackford, 377 ; *Pitt* v. *Petrovy,* 12 Iredell, 69 ; *Boyd* v. *Hawkins,* 2 Devereux's Equity, 195, 207 ; *Wormley* v. *Wormley,* 8 Wheaton, 422, 441 ; &c. It matters not, that there was no fraud contemplated, and no injury done: the rule is not intended to be remedial of actual wrong, but preventive of the possibility of it : it is one of those processes, derived from the system of trusts, by which a court of chancery turns parties away from wrong, and from the power of doing wrong, by making their act instantly enure in equity to rightful purposes. The cases are uniform in declaring that it matters not how innocent and bona fide, and free from suggestion of fault, the transaction may be; *Shelton* v. *Homer and others; Dobson* v. *Racey*, 3 Sandford, 61; *Jewett* v. *Miller*, 10 New York, 402; *The Aberdeen Railway Co.* v. *Blaikie*, 1 Macqueen, 461, 479; *Johnson* v. *Bennett*, 39 Barb. 140; *Staats* v. *Bergen*, 2 C. E. Green, Ch. 297, 554; *Wade* v. *Harper*, 3 Yerger, 383, 385; *Scott et al.* v. *Freeland*, 7 Smedes & Marshall, 410; *Brothers* v. *Brothers*, 7 Iredell, Eq. 150; *Mason* v. *Martin*, 4 Maryland 124; *Zimmerman* v. *Marmon*, 4 Richardson's Eq. 165; nor how harmless or even beneficial the interference of the trustee may have been; *Leisenring* v. *Black*, 5 Watts, 303, 304; *Campbell* v. *Johnson and others*, 1 Sandford, 148, 152; *Saltmarsh* v. *Beene*, 4 Porter, 283, 293; the trustee can never, by his own act, shake off the equity of the *cestui que trust* to have the benefit of all that he does in the scope of the trust, and the *cestui que trust* may come into equity, as of course, and, without the imputation either of fraud or injury, ask for a resale of the property; and whether the property was or was not worth more than the amount of the trustee's bid, is a matter which is never inquired into; *Torry* v. *Bank of Orleans*, 9 Paige, 650, 664; *Van Epps* v.

Van Epps, Id. 238, 242; *Martin* v. *Martin*, 12 Indiana, 266, 269; *Brothers* v. *Brothers*, 7 Iredell, Eq. 156; *Patton* v. *Thompson*, 2 Jones, Eq. 285. In the pointed language of the court in *Brothers* v. *Brothers*, the sale is set aside, not because there is, but that there may not be fraud. In explaining the reasons and operation of this principle, successive judges have only been able to vary and impair the language of the counsellor for the appellants, (Messrs. R. Dundas, J. Mansfield and J. Mackintosh,) in the case of the *The York Buildings Company* v. *Mackenzie*, 8 Tomlins' Brown, 42, 63. "The ground on which the disability or disqualification rests," it was there argued, "is no other than that principle which dictates that a person cannot be both judge and party. No man can serve two masters. He that is entrusted with the interest of others, cannot be allowed to make the business an object of interest to himself; because from the frailty of nature, one who has the power, will be too readily seized with the inclination to use the opportunity for serving his own interest at the expense of those for whom he is entrusted. The danger of temptation, from the facility and advantages for doing wrong, which a particular situation affords, does, out of the mere necessity of the case, work a disqualification; nothing less than incapacity being able to shut the door against temptation where the *danger* is *imminent*, and the *security* against discovery *great*, as it must be where the difficulty of prevention or remedy is inherent to the very situation which creates the danger. The wise policy of the law has therefore put the sting of a disability into the temptation as a defensive weapon against the strength of the danger which lies in the situation." See *The Aberdeen Railway Co.* v. *Blakie*, 1 Macqueen, 461, 478, where Lord Brougham observed that the principle was as established in *The York Building Co.* v. *Mackenzie*, and had been followed throughout the subsequent course of decision. The practice established in chancery, of giving the *cestui que trust* an option to affirm the purchase, or to have the property resold, unites practical convenience with exact justice to both of the principal parties : if the property brought its full value, the *cestui que trust* will have no motive for disturbing the transaction; if less, it is just that the difference should enure to his benefit, and not to the trustee's ; and the trustee never suffers, for he is always allowed to hold his purchase as a security for what he has expended upon it : *Rogers* v. *Rogers*, 1 Hopkins, 515, 525 ; *Mulford* v. *Mench*, 3 Stockton, 16.

[The principle is the same, whether the trustee stands alone, or is one of many ; *The Aberdeen R. W. Co.* v. *Blakie*, 1 MacQueen, 461, 473 ; *The Cumberland Coal Co.* v. *Sherman*, 30 Barb. 553 ; *The Hoffman Coal Co.* v. *The Cumberland Coal Co. and Sherman*, 30 Id. 117 ; *Holcomb* v. *Holcomb*, 3 Stockton's Ch. 281. In the *Aberdeen R. W. Co.* v. *Blakie*,

Lord Cransworth said, "it made no difference that the appellant Blakie was only one of a body of directors, and not a sole trustee or manager. It was equally his duty to give to his co-directors, and through them to the company, the full benefit of all the knowledge, and all the skill which he could bring to bear on the subject. He was bound to assist them in getting the articles contracted for at the cheapest possible rate. In dealing with the company as a manufacturer and vendor, his interest came as much in conflict with his duty, as if he had been the sole director, instead of the member of a board."

So, where co-executors bought from one of their number under a trust to invest, the Court set aside the sale at the instance of the *cestui que trust* ; *Holcomb* v. *Holcomb*, 3 Stockton, 281. For a like reason, if a trustee unites with others in buying from himself, or sells to a company in which he is largely interested, the transaction will be as invalid as if he were the only party to the contract ; *Robbins* v. *Butler*, 24 Illinois, 387. So, where the directors of a railway company are the purchasers at a sale of the road under a mortgage on behalf of a new company which they have organized, the transaction will be fraudulent and void as it regards the stockholders and creditors, and may be set aside at their instance ; *James* v. *The Railroad Co.*, 6 Wallace, 752 ; and the result will be the same where they stipulate for an advantage to themselves, with the consent of the purchaser; *Drury* v. *Cross*, 7 Wallace, 299.

The principle was applied in a somewhat different form in *Goodwin* v. *The Cincinnati R. R. Co.*, 18 Ohio, N. S. 169, and a sale by the directors of a corporation to another corporation, in which they were largely interested as stockholders, held to be invalid as against any stockholder of the former company who did not assent to the sale. See *Ashurst's Appeal*, 10 P. F. Smith, 290.

As a man cannot sell as trustee and buy for himself, so he cannot sell on his own account, and buy as a trustee or agent; *Gould* v. *Gould*, 36 Barb. 370; *Staats* v. *Bergen*, 2 E. C. Green Ch. 297, 554; *Holcomb* v. *Holcomb;* nor can he make any contract in the conduct of the trust tending to place his interest in opposition to his duty, or that might tempt him to derive an undue advantage at the expense of the *cestui que trusts; Sloo* v. *Law*, 3 Blatchford, 459; *Gould* v. *Gould*, 36 Barb. 271; *Burton* v. *Wooley*, 6 Maddock, 367; *The Aberdeen Railway Co.* v. *Blakie*, 1 MacQueen, 461, 473. In the case last named, a manufacturing firm agreed to supply certain articles to a railway company. The transaction was admitted to be a fair one, untainted by actual fraud. But inasmuch as Blakie, a member of the firm, was also one of the directors of the railway company, the Court held that the contract came within the principle of *Mackenzie* v. *York Building Co., ante,* 240.

The person who effects the sale need not be clothed with the legal title; it is enough that he ex-

pressly or impliedly agreed to act for others, and ought not to bring his duty in conflict with his interests. A director of a bank, railway, or other body corporate, or joint stock company is accordingly under the disability which attends on every one who accepts a fiduciary position, *ante ;* and if he enters into a contract of sale or purchase with the company which he represents, it may be set aside at the instance of the stockholders, although for an adequate consideration and free from fraud; *The Aberdeen Railway Co.* v. *Blakie*, 1 MacQueen, 461, 473; *Bowen* v. *The City of Toronto*, 11 Moore, C. C. 465; *The Hoffman Coal Co.* v. *The Cumberland Coal Co.*, 16 Maryland, 456; *The York Midland Railway Co.* v. *Hudson*, 16 Bevan, 485; *The Cumberland Coal Co.* v. *Sherman*, 30 Bab. 553; 20 Maryland, 117; *The Madrid Bank* v. *Peltz*, 7 L. R. Eq. 442; *Turquand* v. *Marshall*, 6 Id. 112, 134; *The New Brunswick and Canada Railway Co.* v. *Muggridge*, 2 Drewry & Smale, 363, 367. This is a logical conclusion from the doctrine that an agent appointed to buy cannot sell, or *vice versa;* and *a fortiori* a contract between a director and the board, must be characterized by entire good faith and a scrupulous regard for the interest of the stockholders.

In *Koehler* v *The Black River Falls Co.*, 2 Black, 715, 720, the Court accordingly set aside a mortgage of the assets of the corporation, designed to secure the advances which had been made by three of the directors, to the exclusion of the other creditors. Instead, said Davis, J., " of honestly endeavoring to effect a loan of money advantageously for the benefit of the corporation, these directors, in violation of their duty, and in betrayal of their trust, secured their own debts to the injury of the stockholders and creditors. Directors cannot thus deal with the important interests entrusted to their management. They hold a place of trust, and by accepting the trust, are obliged to execute it with fidelity; not for their own benefit, but for the common benefit of the stockholders of the corporation. In executing this mortgage, and thereby securing to themselves advantages which were not common to all the stockholders, they were guilty of an unauthorized act, and violated a plain principle of equity applicable to trustees. The directors are the managing partners, and the stockholders are the *cestui que trust*, and have a joint interest in all the property and effects of the corporation; and no injury that the stockholders may sustain by a fraudulent breach of trust, can, upon the general principles of equity, be suffered to pass without a remedy;" Angell & Ames on Corporations, edition 1861, sec. 312; *The Charitable Corporation* v. *Sutton* (2 Atkyns, 404); *Robinson* v. *Smith* (3 Paige, 220); *Hodges* v. *New England Screw Co.*, 1 Rhode Island, 321.

The same disability attaches to the officers of a corporation, and in *The Bank of Orleans* v. *Torrey*, 9 Paige, 653; 7 Hill, 260, a purchase by the cashier of a bank

was set aside on this principle; as tending to fraud, if it was not actually fraudulent.

In *Turquand* v. *Marshall*, 6 Law R. Eq. 127, 4 Ch. Appeals, 36, it was held inter alia by the Lord Chancellor, reversing the decree of the Master of the Rolls that directors are not answerable for lending the funds of the company to a co-director, although he proves to be insolvent and the debt is lost; and in *Spering's Appeal*, 21 P. F. Smith, 11, where this decision was cited and relied on by the court, Sharswood, J., said that the directors of a banking company are not trustees, nor responsible as such for lending the money of the institution to themselves without security, or making hazardous investments that would be illegal in the case of a trust. " A director is but a gratuitous agent—scarcely that —and not held as agent to the same strict accountability as if he were acting for a private estate."

The point actually determined in *Spering's Appeal* was that directors are not answerable for mismanagement, unless it is wilful and corrupt, or the neglect gross. An agent should not any more than a trustee adopt a course that will operate as an inducement to postpone the principal's interest to his own, and where several persons are acting in the same agency, each should not only observe this rule but refrain from sanctioning a violation of it by the others. This is equally true of the directors of a body coporate or joint-stock association, because the stockholders are entitled to require that all the members of the board shall exercise an unbiased judgment, *ante;* and it may be thought that the rule should be more stringent as it regards one who is acting for a body of stockholders, than if he were the representative of an individual, because the injury may have a wider range, and it is not so easy for the parties whose interests are at stake to protect themselves.

The rule is not less applicable because the power is conferred primarily for the benefit of the donee, if it is also held in trust for another, who may be injured by a want of fidelity and diligence. A creditor who is intrusted with the control and disposition of the property of the debtor, as a means of security or payment, should obviously sell for the best price, and account for any surplus that may remain after satisfying the demand. He is, therefore, subject to the salutary rule laid down in *Fox* v. *Mackreth.*

Accordingly, where the mortgaged premises are sold by the mortgagee under a power to that effect, and bought in by him or for his benefit, the equity of re_ demption is not divested, and the mortgagor may tender the amount due, and call for a re-conveyance; *Hall* v. *Towne,* 45 Illinois, 493; *Griffin* v. *The Marine Ins. Co.,* 52 Id. 130; *Roberts* v. *Fleming,* 53 Id. 96; *Hindeman* v. *Hindeman,* 19 Vermont, 9; *Slee* v. *Manhattan Co.,* 1 Paige, 48; *Emerson* v. *Atwater,* 7 Michigan, 12; *Robin-*

son v. *Guillou,* 4 Alabama, 693; *Rowe* v. *Burnham,* 2 California, 387; *Thornton* v. *Irwin,* 43 Missouri, 153.

"It is a rule of universal application, that the officer or person charged with the sale of property at auction, whether by authority of law or under a power derived from the owner, is prohibited from becoming the purchaser;" *Mapps* v. *Sharpe,* 32 Illinois, 13. "A mortgagee acting under such a power is a mere trustee, so far as the interests of the mortgagor are concerned, and should be subjected to the disabilities incident to that character. It makes no difference that he is also a creditor. If he voluntarily assume a trust relation—if he is clothed with confidential powers, and opportunities are thus afforded him to speculate at the expense of his principal—his acts should be guarded with the same jealousy, and he should be equally removed from temptation, as though he were a mere trustee or agent;" *Thornton* v. *Irwin,* 43 Missouri, 153, 166.

The mortgagor may indeed dispense with the restraint, by authorizing the mortgagee to sell to himself, if he is the highest bidder. This results from the right of every man to waive a rule intended for his benefit. But such transactions will notwithstanding, be closely scrutinized, and may be set aside if the sale is not conducted with entire fairness, and in a way to obtain the market value; *Montague* v. *Duvals,* 14 Allen, 369; see *Hubbard* v. *James,* 23

Maryland, 66. Though a trustee may buy at his own sale with the sanction of his principal, or the leave of the Court, he is still in a position of much delicacy, and the inadequacy of the price may be a reason for surcharging him, or directing a re-sale to the highest bidder; *Dundas' Appeal*, 14 P. F. Smith, 325, 333; *Cadwalader's Appeal*, Id. 293. In the case first cited, the wife of the executor purchased with the permission of the proper court, at a public sale by her husband under an authority conferred by the will, and he was adjudged to pay the difference between what she gave and the value as ascertained by the testimony of experts, although the money came from her separate estate, and there was no proof of fraud, or that he did not use due diligence to obtain a full price.

It results from what has been said, that a creditor who sells the collaterals in his hands, although publicly, and purchases them himself, will hold them after the sale, as he did previously, as a mere security; and the debtor may redeem, or require the creditor to account for their market value as shown by a re-sale; *The Hestonville Railroad Co.* v. *Shields*, 3 Brewster, Penna. 237; *The Middlesex Bank* v. *Minot*, 4 Metcalf, 324; *The Bank* v. *The Dubuque & Pacific Railroad*, 8 Iowa, 277; *Hoyt* v. *Martinsee*, 16 New York, 231.

These decisions may be referred to the doctrine of the principal case, or to the rule once a mortgage always a mortgage, which is an equally well settled head of equity. The distinction is more material than would at first appear, because in the former aspect acquiescence is a bar, *ante*, while an equity of redemption cannot be defeated by anything short of the lapse of twenty years; see *Slee* v. *The Manhattan Co.; Robinson* v. *Collum*, 41 Alabama, 693; or a release for a full and valuable consideration, *post*, vol. 2, notes to *Thornborough* v. *Baker*.

In *Freeman* v. *Harwood*, 49 Maine, 195, fifty shares of stock in an incorporated company were transferred to one of the directors as security for a loan. He subsequently sold the stock at auction, under an order from the board, for the non-payment of dues, and became the purchaser. The court held, that his position was unchanged, and that he must account for the stock as if it had not been sold.

It is, notwithstanding, universally conceded, that a sale of the mortgaged premises under a decree of foreclosure, or other proceeding of a like kind, puts an end to the equity of redemption, and that the mortgagee is as much at liberty to buy as if he were a stranger; *Jackson* v. *Colden*, 4 Cowen, 266; *Roberts* v. *Fleming*, 53 Illinois, 196, 205; *Griffin* v. *The Ins. Co.*, 52 Id. 130; *Worthall* v. *Rives*, 34 Alabama, 92; *Woodlee* v. *Burch*, 43 Missouri, 231; *Eaton* v. *Tallmadge*, 22 Wisconsin, 526.

The case is obviously different where the holder of the equity is not a party, and the decree does not bind or pass his interest. If A. transfers a mortgage to B. to secure a debt, and B. sues it out, the mortgagor is barred, but A. has an equity as against B. This is manifest where a third person buys the land and B. receives the proceeds, and equally true when B. is the purchaser.

The assignment of a mortgage to a creditor as a collateral security, is in effect a mortgage of a mortgage; the assignee cannot by obtaining a decree of foreclosure get rid of his obligation to the assignor, and will, on the contrary, hold the premises in trust for the latter, subject to the lien of the debt which the assignment was designed to secure; *Slee* v. *The Manhattan Co.*, 1 Paige, 48; *Hoyt* v. *Martinsee*, 16 New York, 238; *Price* v. *Reeves*, 38 California, 457. A creditor who sells a mortgage or other collateral security, and buys it in, is a trustee for the debtor, and the principle is the same where he takes advantage of the mortgage to effect a sale of the land.

A sale by a trustee or executor to a near relative will be narrowly scrutinized, and set aside if it is not fair and adequate; *The Oberlin College* v. *Fowler*, 10 Allen, 545; and it has been said that a sale by a trustee to his wife is equivalent to a purchase by the trustee himself; *Leitch* v. *Wells*, 48 Barb. 637; *Dundas' Appeal*, 14 P. F. Smith, 325, 332; but it seems that as a trustee cannot prevent his wife from using her separate estate to buy at a public sale, such a purchase may be valid, if made in good faith, and for the best price obtainable under the circumstances.]

Executors and administrators are fully within the application of these principles; being considered in equity as trustees for creditors, legatees, distributees and heirs, and in that character disabled from purchasing at sales of either lands or chattels under a power in the will or a power derived from the court; for as they always have a power and duty to sell lands under authority of the court, so far as may be necessary for the payment of debts, their trust, in its nature, embraces an administration of both classes of property, and by virtue of their powers and duties in respect to both the lands and the personalty, they are, substantially, trustees, and therefore disabled from purchasing for their own benefit and to the loss of those for whom they are entrusted. A purchase, therefore, direct or indirect, entire or partial, by one or more executors or administrators, at their own sale, whether by a power in the will or under an order of court, will always be set aside on application of any of the heirs, or any of the unsatisfied creditors, or other persons interested; *Davoue* v. *Fanning; Rogers* v. *Rogers; Ward* v. *Smith*, 3 Sandford, 592, 596; *Michoud et al.* v. *Girod et al.*, 4 Howard, 504, 554; *Harrington* v. *Brown*, 5 Pickering, 519, 521; *Litchfield* v. *Cudworth*, 15 Id. 24, 31; *Shelton* v. *Homer and others*, 5 Metcalf, 462, 467; *Fleming* v. *Faron*, 12 Georgia, 544; *Lessee of Moody et al.* v. *Vandyke et al.*, 4 Binney, 31, 43; *Painter* v. *Henderson*, 7 Barr, 48, 50; *Musselman* v. *Eshelman*,

10 Id. 394; *Beeson* v. *Beeson*, 9 Barr, 279; *Green* v. *Blair*, 9 Wisconsin, 352; *Price* v. *Morris*, 5 M'Lean, 4; *Price* v. *Gamble*, 1 Stockton, 218; *Shuman's Appeal*, 3 Casey, 64; *Johnson* v. *Blackman*, 11 Conn. 343, 357; *Green* v. *Sergeant*, 23 Vermont, 466; *Arrowsmith & Wife* v. *Van Harlingen's Ex'ors*, Coxe, 26; *Den ex Dem. Obert* v. *Hammel*, 3 Harrison, 74, 81; *Den* v. *Wright*, 2 Halsted, 175; *Den* v. *M'Knight*, 6 Id. 385; *Davis* v. *Simpson*, 5 Harris & Johnson, 147; *Ryden* v. *Jones*, 1 Hawks, 497, 504; *Gordon* v. *Finlay*, 3 Id. 239, 242; *Brackenridge* v. *Holland*, 2 Blackford, 377, 380; *Cox's Heirs* v. *Cox and Talbert*, Peck, 443, 450; *Thorp et al.* v. *M'Cullum et al.*, 1 Gilman, 615, 625; *Scott* v. *Gamble*, 1 Stockton's Ch. 235; *Mulford* v. *Bowen*, Id. 797; *Doe* v. *Harvey*, 3 Indiana, 104; *Calloway* v. *Gilmer*, 36 Alabama, 354; *Joyner* v. *Congers*, 6 Jones, Eq. 78; *Howell* v. *Silving*, 1 M'Carter, 84; *Skillman* v. *Skillman*, 2 Ia. 388; *Remick* v. *Rutterfield*, 11 Foster, 70; *Hoitt* v. *Webb*, 36 New Hampshire, 158; and the same disability is applied to an agent of an administrator purchasing for himself at an administrator's sale; *Buckles* v. *Laferty's Legatees*, 2 Robinson, 294, 300.

Some earlier cases in Kentucky and Virginia, which threw doubts upon the application of the rule to executors and administrators, are now entirely overruled, at least in regard to sales of real estate; *Grider* v. *Payne*, 9 Dana, 188, 190; *Moore* v. *Hilton et al.*, 12 Leigh, 2, 28; *Bailey's Adm'r* v.

Robinson's, 1 Grattin, 4, 9. In South Carolina, however, after much variation in the cases, the latest decision of the Court of Appeals appears to be, that an executor or administrator is not, in regard to personal estate, to be regarded as a mere trustee to sell, and that a purchase of chattels by him at his own sale, if fairly made and for full value, is good; *Stallings and Wife* v. *Freeman*, *Adm'r*, 2 Hill's Chancery, 401, 409, where the cases are collected; but see also *Britton and Wife* v. *Johnson*, Id. 430, 434; and *Crispin* v. *Taylor*, Id. 434, *note*. And the rule is the same in North Carolina; *Lyon* v. *Lyon*, 8 Iredell, Eq. 201. In Alabama, also, it is held, that an executor or administrator may purchase at his own sale, provided it be fairly and for full value; *Brannon et al.* v. *Oliver*, 2 Stewart, 47; *Saltmarsh* v. *Beene* 4 Porter, 283, 295; *Julian et al.* v. *Reynolds et al.*, 8 Alabama, 680, 683; but this seems to have been applied only to personal estate. And the existence of this exception to the general rule, that a trustee cannot purchase at his own sale, is regretted, and declared to rest only on authority and precedent, in *M'Cartney et als.* v. *Calhoun et al.*, 17 Id. 301, 203. See, also, *Lovell* v. *Briggs*, 2 New Hampshire, 218, 221. An administrator may sell the goods of his intestate at private sale, and may repurchase them; but such a transaction would not be sustained unless obviously free from all suspicion of fraud; *Johnson et als.* v. *Kay, Adm'r*, 8 Humphreys, 142

" It is a well established principle of equity," said the court in that case, " that an executor or administrator, will not be permitted under any circumstances, to derive a personal benefit from the manner in which he transacts the business, or manages the assets of the estate. Any profit thus derived, is considered as so much increase of the trust fund in his hands, and as belonging to the estate."

[At common law the office of an executor or administrator was confined to the personal estate. In the United States his powers have been enlarged. Land is assets for the payment of debts, and may be levied on and sold under a judgment obtained during the lifetime of the testator, or against his personal representatives after his decease. It is nevertheless the duty of the executor to apply the personalty in exoneration of the real estate. If this were all, he would be entitled where there were no personal assets, to bid for the land at a sale under a writ issued by a third person, and which he could neither obviate nor control. The point arose in *Meanor* v. *Hamilton*, 3 Casey, 137, and was so decided. But he is now under a statutory obligation in most of the States, where the personal property proves insufficient, to apply to the appropriate tribunal for an authority to sell the real estate. Although not a trustee, he is consequently clothed with a power in the nature of a trust, and cannot make a profit out of the subject matter to which it relates. It is therefore very clear that he cannot buy under his own execution, although issued before the death of the testator. Such a transaction involves that conflict of duty and interest which it is the object of the rule under consideration to exclude. Under these circumstances, the executor is at once debtor and creditor, principal and agent, and vendor and vendee. As creditor and purchaser he is naturally prompted to sell at once and buy at the lowest price ; as executor he should apply to the Orphans' Court, or other like tribunal, for authority to effect a sale in the way best calculated to promote the interest of all concerned as distributees, legatees or creditors. If he buys under his own writ though the sale is not conducted by him, it may be set aside, or he may be sur-charged with the value in excess of what he gave. The law was so held in *Rogers* v. *Rogers*, 1 Hopkins, Ch. 515, 3 Wend. 504 ; and *Martin* v. *Wynkoop*, 12 Indiana, 266 ; and although *Meanor* v. *Hamilton*, 3 Casey, 137, may appear to follow a different doctrine, it is not at variance with that advanced above.

The argument is nearly, if not quite, as strong where the executor buys at Sheriff's sale, under a writ issued by a third person, which he might have obviated by satisfying the judgment, or applying to the proper Court for authority to sell for the payment of debts. Under these circumstances he is in default, and cannot take advantage of a sacrifice resulting from his own laches. The principle was enunciated with much clearness by Agnew, J., in *Meanor* v. *Hamilton*, although the circumstances did not call for its application.]

The same disabling rule applies to guardians ;· a purchase by a guardian at his own sale, made under an order of the Court, may be set aside by the ward on arriving at full age, as a matter of course, though perfectly fair and for a full price; *Scott et al.* v. *Freeland*, 7 Smedes & Marshall, 410, 418; *Patton* v. *Thompson*, 2 Jones, Eq. 285; *Beal* v. *Harmon*, 38 Missouri, 435. And it applies to all who hold a situation of trust or confidence in reference to the subject of the sale; see *Van Epps* v. *Van Epps*, 9 Paige, 238, 241; to the cashier of a bank, for example, attending a sale under a mortgage from which the bank was equitably bound to protect the complainant's property; in such a case the officer could not be allowed to purchase on his own account, and thereby leave the bank liable to indemnify the complainant; *Torrey* v. *Bank of Orleans*, 9 Paige, 650, 663; S. C., 7 Hill, 260. In like manner, if one who is employed as an agent to pay taxes on the lands of non-residents, suffer them to be sold for taxes, and buy them himself, he is a trustee for the owners; *Oldhams* v. *Jones, &c.*, 5 B. Monroe, 458, 467; *Morris* v. *Joseph*, 1 West Virginia, 256. And, in general, the rule extends to all cases in which confidence has been reposed, and applies as strongly to one who has gratuitously or officiously undertaken the management of another's property, as to one

who is engaged for that purpose and paid; *Rankin* v. *Porter*, 7 Watts, 387, 390; *Baker* v. *Whiting*, 3 Sumner, 475, 483; *Casey* v. *Casey*, 14 Illinois, 112; *Winn* v. *Dillon*, 27 Mississippi, 494.

An assignee, or trustee, in an assignment for the benefit of creditors, is also incapacitated from purchasing at his own sale; *Harrison, &c.*, v. *Mock et al.*, 10 Alabama, 185, 194; *Campbell* v. *McLain*, 1 P. F. Smith, 200; and an agent of the assignee is equally disabled; *Cram* v. *Mitchell*, 1 Sandford, 251, 256; *Hammond* v. *Stanton*, 4 Rhode Island, 65. In *Ex parte Wiggins*, 1 Hill's Chancery, 353, the assignees of a debtor filed a bill against his heirs and creditors to marshal the assets, and the court ordered a sale of real estate by a commissioner, under the superintendence of the assignees. One of the assignees bought, and filed this bill to have the sale confirmed : the commissioner reported that the sale was fairly conducted, and the purchase was *bona fide* and for an adequate consideration, and that the purchaser was a creditor of the assignor : but the court decided, that the trustee could not purchase, except subject to the option of the parties interested, without any inquiry into circumstances, to have a release, or to hold the trustee to his purchase; and it was accordingly ordered to be inquired if any creditor or other party interested desired a re-sale, and if so, that the property should be re-sold, but if not, that the sale should be confirmed. In *Wade* v. *Harper*, 3

Yerger, 383, where a deed of trust for the payment of a creditor was made, authorizing the trustee to sell at the request and option of the creditor, it was held that the creditor could not purchase. " We cannot distinguish the relation of (the creditor) to this transaction," said Catron, Ch. J., " from that of a commissioner of a bankrupt, where the trustee makes the sale of the assets. In such case, the commissioner has a duty to perform, to make the estate bring the best price, and cannot buy without being subject to have the sale set aside at the election of the creditors. In all cases where the property is vested in a trustee, with power to sell, or where there is a power in one to sell, the title remaining in the *cestui que trust*, or the aid of a solicitor is called in, or where there is an agent to aid in effecting the sale, such persons cannot be permitted to buy the property, denuded of the trust, and if any interested, especially the *cestui que trust*, calls in question the purchase, that it was fair, is no defence; the trust attends it." In *Saltmarsh* v. *Beene*, 4 Porter, 283, the rule was applied to a commissioner appointed by the Orphans' Court to sell lands, who was held incapable to buy directly or indirectly, in whole or in part; and a receiver is obviously within the scope of the same principle; *Jewett* v. *Miller*, 10 New York, 402.

It is equally settled, that an agent to sell cannot be the purchaser, nor an agent of the purchaser, because he is bound to act exclusively for the benefit of the vendor; *Cumberland* v. *Sherman*, 30 Barb. 553; *Remick* v. *Butterfield*, 11 Foster, 70; *The Cumberland Coal Co.* v. *Sherman*, 30 Barb. 553. A sale by an agent to himself is void in law, and if the transaction assumes such a form as to be valid in law, equity will make him a trustee for his principal; see *Teakle* v. *Bailey*, 2 Brockenbrough, 44, 51; *Banks* v. *Judah*, 8 Connecticut, 146, 157; *Church* v. *Marine Insurance Company*, 1 Mason, 341, 344; *Barker* v. *Marine Insurance Company*, 2 Id. 369; *Copeland* v. *Mercantile Ins. Co.*, 6 Pickering, 198, 204; *Pensoneace* v. *Bleakley*, 14 Illinois, 15. So, if a trustee or agent to sell, in a deed, makes a sale in which he is to be at all interested, the transaction may be set aside in equity by the *cestuis que trust; Armstrong* v. *Campbell*, 3 Yerger, 202, 236; *Hunt* v. *Bass*, 2 Devereux's Equity, 292, 295; and where a mortgagee with power to sell, makes a conveyance to a third person, and immediately takes a re-conveyance to himself, though the value of the premises is not greater than the mortgage debt, the heirs may set aside the sale, as of course; *Dobson* v. *Racey*, 3 Sandford, 61. And the same thing is applicable to judicial and legal officers. A sheriff selling land on execution cannot be a purchaser directly, or through the medium of a third person, who purchases in secret trust for him; *Lessee of Lazarus* v. *Bryson*, 3 Binney, 54, 58; *Carter, &c.* v. *Harris*, 4 Randolph, 199, 204; *Parkins* v. *Thompson*, 3 New

Hampshire, 144 ; and a purchase by a tax collector is within the scope of the principle, even after the expiration of the period fixed by the law for redemption ; *Chandler* v. *Moulton*, 33 Vermont, 245. An attorney in the execution is also incapable of purchasing for himself, without his client's consent, unless for a price sufficient to cover the client's demand ; *Moore* v. *Moore*, 4 Sandford's Ch. 37 ; 1 Selden, 256 ; and if an attorney acts for two or more clients, and buys for one, the others have an equity to claim the equal benefit of the purchase ; *Leisenring* v. *Black*, 5 Watts, 303, 305 ; *Hawley* v. *Cramer.* 4 Cowen, 719, 739 : and see *Howell* v. *Baker*, 4 Johnson's Chancery, 118, 120 ; and this disability reaches all who take part officially in the process of sale, or even in the preliminary steps that precede it ; and it has therefore been held that an appraiser of the property for an administrator's sale, cannot purchase at the sale ; *Armstrong* v. *Huston's Heirs*, 8 Ohio, 552. There is no objection, however, to a purchase by a mortgagee, or creditor, under an execution issued by him or others ; *Lyon* v. *Jones*, 6 Humphreys, 533 ; *Murdock's case*, 2 Bland. 461, 468.

[It will make no difference in the application of the principle that the agent is also a judgment creditor, and effects the sale through an execution issued on the judgment, and not in his character as agent, because the acceptance of the agency puts him under an obligation to postpone his interest to that of the principal, and do

nothing that can prejudice the latter ; *Jameson* v. *Glasscock*, 29 Missouri, 191 ; *Rogers* v. *Rogers*, Hopkins, Ch. n. 3, 3 Wend. 504 ; *Martin* v. *Wynkoop*, 12 Indiana, 266.

It seems that a trustee, agent, or other person acting in a fiduciary capacity, who is liable as a surety or guarantor for the debt on account of which the sale is made, may buy the property and hold it as a counter security, subject to the right of the principal or cestui que trust to redeem on tendering an indemnity against the obligation incurred for his benefit ; *Smith* v. *Lansing*, 22 New York, 520.

The rule is a general one, and will apply not merely where the trust or confidence is actually betrayed, but where the circumstances are such that there is a temptation to violate it : *Moore* v. *Moore*, 4 Sandford, Ch. 37 ; I Selden, 256 ; *Henry* v. *Raiman*, 12 Casey, 354, 359 ; *Statts* v. *Bergen*, 2 Green, Ch. 559. Hence, an agent or attorney employed to collect a debt, cannot buy the property of the debtor at a sale under an execution issued in the course of the agency, for less than the amount of the debt ; *Moore* v. *Moore ; Leisenring* v. *Black*, 5 Watts, 303 ; *Campbell* v. *M'Lain*, 1 P. F. Smith, 200 ; *Howell* v. *Baker*, 4 Johnson, Ch. 118 ; *Wade* v. *Pettibone*, 11 Ohio, 57 ; 14 Id. 557 : *Stockton* v. *Ward*, 11 Howard, 232, 248 ; because his interest as a buyer might induce him to force a sale to the injury of his principal : Ib. And the better opinion would seem to be, that an attorney cannot purchase any interest in the thing or property in litigation, to the prejudice of his client while the litigation still continues; *Hill* v. *Hallett*, 1 Cox, 134; nor until it is to all intents and purposes at an end : *Clinger* v. *Reimer*, 3 W. & S. 486. The same result will follow, where an agent, employed to obtain information with a view to a purchase, misapplies what he learns, by buying for his own benefit; *Reid* v. *Stanley*, 6 W. & S. 376; or when one duly authorized to make insurances, or to issue policies on behalf of an insurance company, insures his own property, without the express sanction of his principals, thus bringing his interest into conflict with theirs, in a way to influence his judgment; *Bentley* v. *The Columbia Ins. Co.*, 19 Barbour, 595.]

Where a person stands in the situation of a trustee for others, and bound as such to protect the general interests of those for whose benefit the trust was created, in regard to the subject of the sale, he is equally incapacitated from purchasing for his own benefit, at a sale under an adverse proceeding, and at a judicial sale, as at his own sale, under his powers as trustee; *Elliott* v. *Poole*, 3 Jones, Eq. 17; *Freeman* v. *Harwood*, 49 Maine, 195; *Ricketts* v. *Montgomery*, 15 Maryland, 46; *Jamison* v. *Glasscock*, 29 Missouri, 191; *Martin* v. *Wyncoop*, 12 Indiana, 266; *Hoitt* v. *Webb*, 36 N. H. 159; *Jewett* v. *Miller*, 10 New York, 402; *Chandler* v. *Moulton*,

33 Vermont, 245. The reason is obvious; as general trustee of the subject, it is his duty to make it bring as much as possible, at any sale that may take place; and therefore he cannot put himself in a situation where it becomes his interest that the property should bring the least sum. In *Chapin* v. *Weed and others*, 1 Clarke's Chancery, 464, the assignee of all a debtor's property under a general assignment in trust for the payment of debts, bought a part of the trust property at a master's sale under a previous mortgage : but it was decided that the creditors had a right to the purchase, the assignee being a trustee for them, and that although the sale was a judicial one, and there was no pretence of collusion or connivance by the assignee to procure the sale, and the sale was public, and there was no contrivance to prevent persons from bidding, still, without a special authority from the court, the trustee could not become a purchaser for his own benefit: " The rule in relation to all classes of trustees," said the court, " is well settled. A trustee cannot purchase or be interested in the purchase of the trust estate, or any part thereof. He cannot derive any private advantage from the sale of the trust property committed to his guardianship; and all the advantages which he does thus acquire, shall result to the benefit of the *cestui que trust*." In *Campbell* v. *Johnson and others*, 1 Sandford, 148, a testator appointed two persons his executors, and the guardians of his children,

and devised all his estate to them in trust to sell for the benefit of his heirs. The land was subject to mortgages given by the testator, and under one of them it was sold, and one of the executors purchased. The court held that the sale must be set aside on the application of the heirs, upon the ground that in both capacities, as trustees to sell and as guardians of the children, the executors had a duty to perform in regard to the property, which rendered it inequitable for either of them to become a purchaser.

In *M'Ginn* v. *Shaeffer*, 7 Watts, 412, 415, also, it was held that a trustee for an infant, suffering the property to be sold under incumbrances, and buying it in, is a trustee for the infant. In *Callis & Seems* v. *Ridout & Ringgold*, 7 Gill & Johnson, 2, 7, commissioners had been appointed to hold and sell lands for certain purposes, and one of them bought a part of the land under an adverse judgment; it was held that this could not enure to his own benefit, but must be applied to the objects of the trust, after reimbursing to him the amount of his purchase-money and all proper and necessary expenses. In *Bell et al.* v. *Webb & Mong*, 2 Gill, 164, 170, a trustee in a deed of trust to sell for the payment of debts, purchased through his agent, at a sheriff's sale, a part of the property. "One of the questions which arises in this case," said the court, "is, whether a trustee can be permitted to purchase the *cestui que trust's* property, levied upon and sold at

a sheriff's sale, without any instrumentality of his:" and upon the authority of the preceding case, it was decided that the *cestui que trust* was entitled to the benefit of the purchase, though the trustee had a just claim to be reimbursed for his expenditures in the purchase. In *Evertson* v. *Tappen*, 5 Johnson's Chancery, 498, 514, it was held that an executrix who was the widow of the testator and the natural guardian of his children, could not buy the property for herself at a sale under a mortgage given by the testator in his lifetime; *Torrey* v. *Bank of Orleans*, 9 Paige, 650, 653; S. C., affirmed, 7 Hill, 260, establishes the same point, which may also be found in *Martin* v. *Wyncoop*, 12 Indiana, 266. In *Van Epps* v. *Van Epps*, 9 Paige, 238, 241, a person who held a second mortgage in trust for third parties, bought in the premises for himself at a sale under the first mortgage, for a sum insufficient to satisfy both mortgages. "The defendant," said the Chancellor, "is wrong in supposing that he was authorized to become the purchaser of the farm, under the master's sale upon the prior mortgage, for his own exclusive benefit, to the prejudice of the subsequent mortgage, which he held in trust for others. The duty of the trustee, as the holder of the junior mortgage, was to make the mortgaged premises, if possible, produce upon the sale sufficient not only to pay off the prior incumbrance, and the costs of foreclosure, but also to satisfy the subsequent incumbrance which he held in his fiduciary character; and this duty came directly in conflict with his interest, as a purchaser for his own benefit, to bid in the property at the lowest sum for which he could obtain it; *Jewett* v. *Miller*, 10 New York, 402, 405.

Against this clear application of a safe and conservative principle of equity, two American cases stand opposed; *Prevost* v. *Gratz*, 1 Peters' C. C. 365, 378, where Washington, J., said that a purchase by a trustee or executor at a sheriff's sale was not prohibited; and *Fisk* v. *Sarber*, 6 Watts & Sergeant, 18, where it was held (Rogers, J., dissenting) that the assignee of an insolvent debtor might purchase at a sale under a mortgage existing previously to the mortgage. The reasoning of Kennedy, J., in this case, is wholly unsound, and proceeds upon the error of overlooking the former of the two principles stated in the beginning of this note, as distinguished from the latter of them: the accurate view of the law upon the subject then before the court is to be found in the dissenting opinion of Rogers, J. See *Cadbury* v. *Duval*, 10 Barr, 265, 272.

[In *Chorpenning's Appeal*, 8 Casey, 315, *Prevost* v. *Gratz* was, nevertheless, cited with approbation; and held to justify a purchase by a guardian at a sheriff's sale under a judgment against the ancestor from whom the land had descended to the ward. See *Hager* v. *Hager*, 9 Richardson, Eq. 217; *Elrod* v. *Lancaster*, 2 Head. 571; *Mercer* v. *Newsom*, 23 Georgia, 151. The

principle has been recognized in other instances, and would appear to be the established rule in Pennsylvania. *Moore's Appeal*, 10 Casey, 29. It does not, however, apply when the sale is brought about or procured by the trustee, as where he issues the execution or causes it to be issued by another. *Parshall's Appeal*, 15 P. F. Smith, 224, 235; *Campbell* v. *McLain*, 1 Id. 209. And the case is substantially the same where an executor suffers land to be sold by the sheriff, which he might have sold in person under an authority conferred by the appropriate tribunal, because one who permits that which it is his duty to prevent, is in fact the actor, and should not profit by his own laches. See *Mears* v. *Hamilton*, 5 Casey, 15.

In *Parshall's Appeal*, 15 P. F. Smith, 224, the heirs of an intestate entered into a contract of sale with one Parshall, who was their near relative and the administrator of the estate, conditioned that if Parshall did not pay the price on or before a certain day the contrac should be void, and he should proceed to sell the land for their benefit. Parshall failed to pay th money by the time prescribed, but resold the premises for his own account to the holder of an outstanding judgment, with a stipulation that the latter should issue an execution, buy in the land, and pay him the difference between the amount of his bid and the price agreed on. The court held this agreement fraudulent as against the heirs, and that they were entitled to the full amount received by Parshall from the purchaser, although exceeding the sum which he originally agreed to give.

An agent, trustee or other person, holding a fiduciary relation, who is under a disability to buy for himself, cannot buy for another: *Remick* v. *Butterfield*, 11 Foster, 70; *The Cumberland Coal Co.* v. *Sherman*, 30 Barb. 553; *Brackenridge* v. *Holland*, 2 Blackford, 377; *Martin* v. *Wyncoop*, 12 Indiana, 266; nor can he acquire title through a purchase made by another for his benefit. *Abbott* v. *The American Ins. Co.*, 33 Barb. 278; *Forbes* v. *Halsey*, 26 New York, 53.

Such an indirection darkens the blot which it is intended to conceal, as indicating collusion, and a conscious desire to obtain an undue advantage at the expense of the trust. Accordingly, where the purchaser at such a sale re-conveys the property at once, or within a brief period, to the executor or trustee, the presumption is that he was used as a tool or cover, and the transaction will be set aside as a constructive, if not actual fraud. *Obert* v. *Obert*, 2 Stockton's Ch. 98; 1 Beasley, 423; *Rosenberg's Appeal*, 2 Casey, 67. And as the defect is apparent on the face of the record or title papers, a third person buying subsequently will be affected with notice, and cannot hold the land; *Rosenberger's Appeal*. The presumption may, however, be repelled, and does not apply where it is made to appear with sufficient clearness that the purchaser

bought for himself, and that there was no concert between him and the trustee; *Waterman* v. *Skinner*, 1 Beasley, 423. In *Waterman* v. *Skinner*, the court refused to interfere, although the executor purchased the premises immediately after the sale, from a bidder who, as it would seem, had not paid. Such transactions should, nevertheless, be scrutinized with jealous care; and it is very clear that, the disability continues until the sale is consummated by payment and the delivery of the deed. Until then, the vendor is acting on behalf of the cestui que trusts, and cannot acquire an interest in the property confided to his care; *Rosenberger's Appeal*.]

It is admitted, in all the cases, that a trustee may purchase by consent of the Court of Chancery, to be obtained by his filing a bill and showing the circumstances, and making out a sufficient case; see *Davoue* v. *Fanning*, 2 Johnson's Chancery, 252, 261, 262; *Dobson* v. *Racey*, 3 Sandford, 61; *Brackenridge* v. *Holland*, 2 Blackford, 377, 381; but the court, upon such an application, will always require such facts to be shown as justify a departure from the general rule. Where it is made to appear that the trustee has a personal interest in procuring a fair price for the property, which interest would probably be sacrificed if he were not permitted to bid, it is very much a matter of course to give him leave to purchase; and if it be his own sale, a master or another trustee will be substituted for the execution of the trust: but even in these cases, the court must always be satisfied that the interest of the *cestui que trust* will not suffer by the permission, and if the trustee, from his connection with the property, has had better means of information as to its situation and value, so that he will not come to the sale on terms of equality with other bidders, the court will not put him in a position which will make it for his interest to keep that information to himself; but will require him to obtain the consent of all the *cestuis que trust; De Caters* v. *Le Ray De Chaumont*, 3 Paige, 178.

[A trustee who obtains such an order does not thereby cease to be responsible for the faithful administration of the trust. He is still as much a trustee as he was before, and should use the utmost care and diligence in view of the imputations to which he may conceivably be exposed. Every effort should, therefore be made to secure a full and free competition, and if it appears that the interest of the cestui que trusts was postponed to that of the trustee, although unintentionally, he will not be allowed to gain by their loss; *Cadwalader's Appeal*, 14 P. F. Smith, 293; *Dundas' Appeal*, Ib. 325. "A trustee," said Agnew, J., in *Cadwalader's Appeal*, "thus permitted to bid at his own sale, must act within the strictest line of his responsibility. His character as a bidder cannot be permitted to derogate from his duty as trustee." And so where the wife of an executor obtained leave from the court to bid at a public sale made by him under a power in the will, and the property was knocked down to her for less than it was worth, the court refused to set aside the conveyance, but sur-charged the executor with the excess of the market value beyond what she gave; *Dundas' Appeal, ante*, 244.

In like manner, a trustee or agent may buy at his own sale with the consent of the cestui que trust or principal, and such a permission is not unfrequently accorded where a creditor is empowered to sell property which has been pledged or mortgaged (*ante*). If one who is *sui juris* chooses to repose implicit confidence in the good faith of another, the law will not intervene unless the confidence is abused. Here, however, as in the cognate case of a purchase by the trustee with the leave of the court, the trustee must do all that he can to obtain a full price, and if there is reason to believe that he failed in the discharge of this duty, the sale will be declared invalid, or he may be charged with the difference. *Montague* v. *Dawes*, 14 Allen, 369.]

A purchase by a trustee is not absolutely void; it is voidable only by the *cestuis que trust*, in equity, and then only upon certain terms: it is valid in equity as well as at law, unless some of them choose thus to avoid it; *Thorp et al.* v. *Cullum et al.*, 1 Gilman, 615, 627; *Wilson* v. *Troup*, 2 Cowen, 238; *Baldwin* v. *Allison*, 4 Minnesota, 25; *Ives* v. *Ashley*, 97 Mass. 198. [Hence, the proper remedy is in chancery, which can bring all the parties before it, and do justice to all by a single decree: *Davoue* v. *Fanning*, 2 Johnson's Ch. 252; *Doe* v. *Henry*, 3 Indiana, 104; although a different view is taken in some of the States, and such sales held to be legally as well as equitably invalid: 1 Stockton, Ch. 218; *Remick* v. *Butterfield*, 11 Foster, 70, 89.] They will not, however, be set aside, either by law or equity, on the application of the trustee, or of an agent who bids for him, for the rule was not adopted in favor of trustees, but for the protection of the *cestui que trust: Richardson* v. *Jones*, 3 Gill and Johnson, 164, 184; and a decision in *Saltmarsh* v. *Beene*, 4 Porter, 283, that an agreement between a trustee and an agent that the latter shall purchase for him is so far unlawful that the trustee cannot enforce it, seems hardly to be correct. No one, but the *cestuis que trust*, that is, the persons interested in the property or in the sale of it, can apply to be relieved against the purchase by the trustee; and a stranger cannot avoid the sale; *Jackson* v. *Van Dalfsen*, 5 Johnson, 43, 48; *Jackson* v. *Walsh*, 14 Id. 407, 415; *Wilson* v. *Troup*, 2 Cowen, 196, 238; *Hawley* v. *Cramer*, 4 Id. 719, 744; *Rice* v. *Cleghorn*, 21 Indiana, 80; *Remick* v. *Butterfield*, 11 Foster, 70, 89. However gross the irregularities of a sale by an administrator, the only persons who can avoid it are the intestate's creditors and heirs, and the creditors of his heirs have no standing in court, or right to intervene; *Lathrop* v. *Wightman*, 5 Wright, 297. But any one of the

cestuis que trust may apply, though a majority are content with the sale; *Davoue* v. *Fanning*, 2 Johnson's Chancery, 252, 268. The equity of the *cestuis que trust* is, to have the option of confirming the purchase and holding the trustee to it, or of setting it aside, and having the property re-sold. *Jennison* v. *Hapgood*, 7 Pickering, 1; S. C., 10 Id. 79, 111; see *Prevost* v. *Gratz*, 1 Peter's C. C. 365, 368; *Hyndman* v. *Hyndman*, 19 Vermont, 10, 13. They may elect to confirm it, and if they do so, deliberately, with full knowledge, neither they themselves afterwards, nor their legal representatives, nor a stranger, can object to it; *Lessee of Lazarus* v. *Bryson*, 3 Binney, 54, 58; *Painter* v. *Henderson*, 7 Barr, 48, 50; *Beeson* v. *Beeson*, 9 Id. 279; *Jennison* v. *Hapgood*, 7 Pick. 1; 10 Id. 77; *Remick* v. *Butterfield*, 11 Foster, 70, 89; *Musselman* v. *Eshleman*, 10 Barr, 394; *Harrington* v. *Brown*, 5 Pickering, 519, 521; *Moore* v. *Hilton et al.*, 12 Leigh, 2, 28; *Williams' Ex'rs* v. *Marshall*, 4 Gill & Johnson, 377, 379; *Field* v. *Arrowsmith*, 3 Humphreys, 442, 446; *Scott et al.* v. *Freeland*, 7 Smedes & Marshall, 410, 419, 420; although the information must be full and complete to give validity to the election, and the intention to affirm unequivocal; *Hoffman* v. *The Cumberland Coal Co.*, 16 Maryland, 456; *Andrews* v. *Holson*, 25 Alabama, 219; *Ricketts* v. *Montgomery*, 15 Maryland, 46; *Minford* v. *Mench*, 3 Stockton, 15; see *Beeson* v. *Beeson*, 9 Barr, 279, 300. If the property has been re-sold by the trustee to a *bona fide* purchaser without notice, before the *cestui que trust* applies to the court, the original sale cannot be set aside, and the remedy will be only personal against the trustee for an account of the profit, if he made any; *Lessee of Lazarus* v. *Bryson; Jackson* v. *Walsh; Hawley* v. *Cramer; Robbins* v. *Bates*, 4 Cushing, 104; *Hoffman* v. *The Cumberland Coal Co.;* but if a conveyance is made by two administrators or other trustees, to one of themselves, the heirs may set aside the sale, even in the hands of a purchaser for value, for he has notice upon the face of the title; *Ward* v. *Smith*, 3 Sandford, 592, 596. And even where the property has not been alienated, the *cestui que trust* must apply to chancery, within a reasonable time after he has knowledge of the facts which impeach the sale, or he will be presumed to have acquiesced; and reasonable time depends upon the circumstances of the case, and the sound discretion of the court; *Wade* v. *Pettibone*, 11 Ohio, 57; 14 Id. 557; *Ashurst's Appeal*, 10 P. F. Smith, 290, 320; under some circumstances, sixteen years have been held to constitute *laches*, and under others, twenty-seven years have been held to be too long a delay; see *Bergen and another* v. *Bennett*, 1 Caines's Cases, 1, 20; *Hawley* v. *Cramer*, 4 Cowen, 719, 743; *Dobson* v. *Racey*, 3 Sandford, 61; *Ward* v. *Smith*, 3 Id. 592, 596; *Bell et al.* v. *Webb and Mong*, 2 Gill, 164, 170; *Johnson* v. *Bennett*, 39 Barb. 237. Independently of circumstances, equity usually

adopts as a bar to the assertion of such a trust the period which bars a title at law; see *Robinson* v. *Hook*, 4 Mason, 151; *Baker* v. *Whiting*, 3 Sumner, 486; *Bacon* v. *Chiles*, 10 Peters, 223; *Miller* v. *Mitchell*, 1 Bailey, 437; *Pipher* v. *Lodge*, 4 S. & R. 315; *Keeton* v. *Kenton*, 20 Missouri, 530.

[Hence, when the subject of the alleged trust is personalty, it cannot be enforced after the lapse of six years, unless the transaction was concealed from the injured parties; *Ashurst's Appeal*, 10 P. F. Smith, 290, 316. There may, said Strong, J., be cases where even six years cannot be allowed, as when a party having a right to set aside a transaction, or treat it as a trust, stands by and sees another dealing with the property in a manner inconsistent with any trust, and makes no objection; *Duke of Leeds* v. *Amherst*, 2 Phillips, 123; *Jordan* v. *Money*, 5 H. L. C. 185. Such acquiescence gives birth to a new equity which supersedes that already in existence.] There is, however, no absolute or unbending rule and circumstances may operate to shorten or extend the time; *Obert* v. *Obert*, 2 Stockton, Ch. 98; 1 Beasley, 423; *Lafferty* v. *Turley*, 179, 3 Sneed. 157. In the late case of *Michoud et al.* v. *Girod et al.*, 4 Howard, 504, 661, it was said that where there is actual fraud, no case can be found in the books in which a court of equity has refused to give relief within the lifetime of either of the parties upon whom the fraud is proved, or within thirty years after it has been discovered or becomes known to the party whose rights are affected by it. In the later case of *Bowen* v. *Evans*, House of Lords' Cases, 257, 282, the Lord Chancellor (Cottenham) stated the principle as follows, in regard to the setting aside of remote transactions on the ground of fraud : " When much time has elapsed since the transactions complained of, there having been parties who were competent to have complained, the court will not, upon doubtful or ambiguous evidence, assume a case of fraud: although upon fraud clearly established, no lapse of time will protect the parties to it, or those who claim through them, against the jurisdiction of equity depriving them of the effects of their plunder.

[In *Beeson* v. *Beeson*, 9 Barr, 279, the receipt of the purchase money by the cestui que trusts, or their consent that it should be applied to their use, was said to be an unequivocal act of acquiescence which precluded them from questioning the sale; but the soundness of this inference has been denied in other instances, and it has been said that accepting the proceeds of such a sale will not preclude the right to set it aside, because the trustee ought not to present such an alternative, or compel the complainants to choose between foregoing the power to challenge his conduct, and lying out of money that would have been theirs at once, if he had pursued the regular course of business; *Rosenberger's Appeal*, 2 Casey, 67 ; *Campbell* v. *M'Lain*, 1 P. F. Smith, 200.

To render an election to affirm the sale binding, it must be made with a full knowledge not only of the facts, but of the law, or in other words, of the way in which the facts would be dealt with by a court of equity, *ante; The Hoffman Iron Co.* v. *The Cumberland Coal and Iron Co.*, 16 Maryland, 456, 509.

In *Fellowsbee* v. *Killreth*, 17 Illinois, 522, the complainant was held to be precluded from impugning the conduct of his agent in purchasing the land for himself, which he had been employed to buy, by acquiescence for three years, during which the agent obtained a conveyance and paid the price. In this instance, however, the principal had been called upon by letter to say whether he would take the land, and his failure to reply operated as a ratification.]

When a cestui que trust objects to a purchase by a trustee, the trustee is not to be called upon to make up the difference between what he paid, and what was the true or probable value at the time ; the ordinary relief consists in ordering a re-sale upon such terms as fully secure to the trustee all that he has expended ; *Mason* v. *Martin*, 4 Maryland, 124. The court in ordering a re-sale will direct an account to be taken, in which the purchaser will be credited with the purchase-money which he has paid, and interest, and with the cost of all valuable improvements made upon the land since the purchase, and will be charged with the profits of the land, or a fair annual rent instead; the balance of this account with the commissions and charges of re-sale is to be the price at which the land is to be set up at the resale; if no more is bid than the upset price the former purchase stands confirmed; but if more is bid, the former purchase is vacated, and a new conveyance ordered to be made to the purchaser at the resale, and the proceeds are applied first to pay the expenses of the sale, and then to pay the trustee the balance expended by him for the purchase-money and improvements, and the surplus is decreed to the *cestuis que trust; Imboden* v. *Hunter,* 23 Arkansas, 622; *Buckles* v. *Lafferty's Legatees,* 2 Robertson's Virginia, 294, 391; *Bailey's Adm'x* v. *Robinson,* 1 Grattan, 4, 9; *Davoue* v. *Fanning,* 2 Johnson's Chancery, 252, 271; *Hawley* v. *Cramer,* 4 Cowen, 719, 744; *Ex parte Wiggins,* 1 Hill's Chancery, 353, 355; *Crispin* v. *Taylor,* 2 Id. 434, 436, *note; Scott et al.* v. *Freeland,* 7 Smedes and Marshall, 410; *Spuseler* v. *Atkinson,* 3 Maryland, 409; *Mason* v. *Martin,* 4 Id. 124; *The Aberdeen Railway Co.* v. *Macqueen,* 461, 480; *Minford* v. *Minch,* 3 Stockton, 15; but the court may in its discretion set aside the sale entirely, if necessary, and order the purchase-money to be refunded; *Scott et al.* v. *Freeland; Campbell* v. *Johnson and others,* 1 Sandford, 148, 152; *Mulford* v. *Minch.* Where there has been actual, conscious fraud, a trustee would probably .not be allowed for the value or cost of improvements; *McCaskey* v. *Griff,* 11 Harris, 321; *Sands* v. *Codwise,* 4 Johnson 536. If the trustee has sold the property before the bill is filed, he will be compelled to account for the profits, and if by his own conduct it has become impossible to ascertain with exactness what profit was made, he will be charged with the largest amount that the case will reasonably admit of; *Brackenridge* v. *Holland,* 2 Blackford, 377, 383; *Ringgold* v. *Ringgold,* 1 Harris & Gill, 70; *Ricketts* v. *Montgomery,* 15 Maryland, 46, 53.

A trustee is not under an absolute disability to purchase the trust property from his *cestui que trust: Spindler* v. *Atkinson,* 3 Maryland, 409; *Buell* v. *Buckingham,* 16 Iowa, 284; *Delamater's Estate,* 1 Wharton, 362, 375; but all such transactions are scanned in a court of equity with the most searching and questioning suspicion; and will not be sustained unless they fully appear to have been in all respects, fair and candid and reasonable. The trustee must show that he took no advantage whatever of his situation; that he gave to his *cestui que trust* all the information which he possessed or could obtain, upon the subject; that he advised him, as he would have done in relation to a third person offering to become a purchaser; and that the price was fair and adequate: and the onus of proving all this is upon the trustee; *Coffee* v. *Ruffin,* 4 Caldwell, 487; *Michoud* v. *Girod,* 4 Howard, 503; *Brook* v. *Berry,* 2 Gill, 99; *Keigler* v. *The Savage Man. Co.* 12 Maryland, 383, 417; *Puzey* v. *Siner,* 9 Wisconsin, 370. And these principles apply to all cases where confidence is reposed; to agents, attorneys, solicitors guardians, cashiers of banks, directors of corporations, promoters of industrial enterprise, &c.; *The Hoffman Steam Coal Co.* v. *The Cumberland Coal and Iron Co.* 16 Maryland, 456, *ante*; *Eberts* v. *Eberts*, 5 P. F. Smith, 510. See *Butler et al.* v. *Haskell*, 4 Desaussure, 652, 705; *M'Cants and wife* v. *Bee and others*, 1 M'Cord's Chancery, 383, 389; *Farr* v. *Farr*, *Ex'or*, 1 Hill's Chancery, 387, 390; *Hawley* v. *Cramer*, 4 Cowen, 719, 740; *Colton* v. *Gardner*, 3 Paige, 274, 279; *Poillon* v. *Martin*, 1 Sandford, 569, 572; *Stuart* v. *Kissam*, 2 Barbour, 494, 505; *Boyd* v. *Hawkins*, 2 Devereux's Equity, 195, 208, 329, 330; *Adm'r of Spence* v. *Whitaker et al.*, 3 Porter, 297, 325; *Kennedy's Heirs and Executors* v. *Kennedy's Heirs*, 2 Alabama, 574, 606; *Johnson* v. *Johnson*, 5 Id. 91, 95; *Farnham* v. *Brooks*, 9 Pickering, 214, 231; *Brook et al.* v. *Berry*, 2 Gill, 84; *Greenfield's Estate*, 2 Harris, 489, 506; [to every one, in short, who has entered into a fiduciary relation, or assumed an obligation by contract or otherwise towards another which it would be a breach of trust and confidence to violate; and hence, where A. agreed for a valuable consideration to furnish B. with the information necessary for the entering of public land in his own name, and afterwards took up the same land himself in fraud of the agreement, equity decreed a trust in favor of B.: *Winn* v. *Dillon*, 27 Mississippi, 494. A purchase by a factor of goods which have been sent to him for sale on commission, falls within

the same principle, and will be set aside unless there has been entire good faith and a full disclosure of all material facts and circumstances: *Keighler* v. *The Savage Man. Co.*, 12 Maryland, 413, *ante*, 250.

It has been said, and there is a great weight of authority for the position, that a purchase by an agent cannot, of itself, and without special circumstances, give rise to a trust in favor of the principal, consistently with the provisions of the Statute of Frauds, unless the agency is proved by written evidence, or admitted by the agent; *Bartlett* v. *Pickersgill*, 1 Eden, 515; 4 East, 577, note *b.*; *Peebles* v. *Reading*, 8 S. & R. 484, 492; *Kisler* v. *Kisler*, 2 Watts, 322; *Barnet* v. *Dougherty*, 8 Casey, 371; *Walker* v. *Bringard*, 13 Smedes & Marshall, 723, 765; *Schmidt* v. *Gatewood*, 2 Richardson's Eq. 162; *Wallace* v. *Brown*, 2 Stockton's Ch. 308; 2 Story's Eq. 1201; and the same rule has been held to apply where a person, who has agreed verbally to buy for the joint account of himself and another, effects the purchase, and takes a deed solely for his own benefit; *Atkins* v. *Rowe*, Mosely, 133; *Flagg* v. *Mann*, 2 Sumner, 488, 546; *Smith* v. *Burnham*, 3 Id. 435, 463. There can, however, be no doubt, that the law will raise a trust wherever one who is confessedly an agent, buys in fraud of the agency, or of the duty which it imposes, *ante*, 250; *Henry* v. *Raiman*, 1 Casey, 354; *Church* v. *Sterling*, 16 Conn. 388, 401; and the better opinion would seem to be, that a fact which would give rise to an implied or resulting trust, if it were admitted, may be proved orally, notwithstanding the Statute of frauds ; *Jenkins* v. *Eldridge*, 3 Story, 181, 290.

Implied trusts are excepted by the express words of the statute, and the exception would manifestly be inoperative, if it were necessary to give written evidence of the facts from which the trust is deduced. Hence, whenever the circumstances under which a purchase is made by an agent, are such that an implied trust would arise if they were established by a writing signed by the party to be charged, the means of proof will be immaterial, and the testimony of witnesses equally good with the most formal instrument.

There are, accordingly, a number of instances in which a trust has been decreed in favor of a principal, without adverting to whether the agency appeared from oral or written evidence; *Taylor* v. *Salmon*, 4 Mylne and Craig, 134 ; *Church* v. *Sterling*, 16 Conn. 388 ; *Morey* v. *Herrick*, 6 Harris, 125 ; *Rankin* v. *Porter*, 7 Watts, 387 ; *Parkist* v. *Alexander*, 1 Johnson's Ch. 394; *Rogers* v. *Ross*, 4 Id. 118 ; *Sweet* v. *Jacocks*, 6 Paige, 364 ; *The Bank of Orleans* v. *Torrey*, 9 Id. 653 ; 7 Hill, 360 ; *Safford* v. *Hynds*, 1 Barb. 625 ; *Piatt* v. *Oliver*, 3 Howard, 353 ; *Copeland* v. *The Mercantile Ins. Co.*, 6 Pick. 198 ; *Moore* v. *Moore*, 4 Sandford's Ch. 1 ; 1 Selden, 256 ; *Pennsonneau* v. *Bleakley*, 14 Illinois, 15 ; and such is clearly the rule where the conduct of the agent is marked by actual fraud : *Brown* v. *Lynch*, 1 Paige, 347 ; *Sweet* v. *Jacocks*, 6 Id. 364 ; *Lees* v. *Nuttall*, 1 Tamlyn, 282 ; 1 Russell ; 1 Mylne, 53 ; *Cloninger* v. *Summit*, 2 Jones' Eq. 513 ; *Hargrave* v. *Ring*, 5 Iredell Eq. 430 ; *Mosely* v. *Lane*, 27 Alabama, 62 ; *Edmonson* v. *Welsh*, Id. 578 ; *Reid* v. *Stanley*, 6 W. & S. 369 ; *Myers' Appeal*, 2 Barr, 463 ; *Baker* v. *Whiting*, 3 Sumner, 475, 483 ; *Brown* v. *Dysinger*, 1 Rawle, 408 ; *Willink* v. *Vanderveer*, 1 Barbour, 599 ; *Shields* v. *Trammell*, 19 Arkansas, 51 ; *M'Caskey* v. *Graff*, 11 Harris ; *Soggins* v. *Heard*, 31 Mississippi, 426, 427 ; *Stowey* v. *M'Murray*, 27 Missouri, 113, 118. An agent or sub-agent who uses the information which he has obtained in the course of the agency as a means of buying for himself, will be compelled to convey to the principal ; *M'Dowell* v. *Fithian*, 1 Gilman, 269, *ante ; Poillon* v. *Martin*, 1 Sandford Ch. 569 ; *Gardner* v. *Ogden*, 22 New York, 327, *ante*. So a man who agrees to buy or redeem land sold for taxes, or under a writ of execution on behalf of the owner, and takes the deed in his own name, is not the less a trustee *ex maleficio* for his principal, because his authority was merely oral, and there is no written proof of the confidence which he abused ; *Soggins* v. *Heard, Howell* v. *Baker*, 4 Johnson, Ch. 118, 121. And a trust will also be decreed where an agent, by professsing to bid for his principal, obtains the property for less than he would have had to give had he been known to be buying for himself; *Trapnall* v. *Brown*, 19 Arkansas, 39; *Kisler* v. *Kisler*, 2 Watts, 323; *M'Donald* v. *May*; *M'Caskey* v. *Graff*; *Peebles* v. *Reading*; *Brown* v. *Dysinger*; *Brown* v. *Lynch*; *Slowey* v. *M'Murray*. Some of the cases might convey the idea that this rule should be restricted to purchases at public sales, where a trust will, it has been said, arise from motives of public policy, and to prevent the repetition of a course injurious to the community; *Kennard* v. *Harris*, 3 Richardson's Eq. 423; *Cox* v. *Cox*, 5 Id. 365; *M'Donald* v. *May*, 1 Id. 91; *Lloyd* v. *Currin*, 3 Humphreys, 462. The better opinion, however, would seem to be, that the nature of the sale makes no difference, and that a trust will be implied wherever there has been a violation of confidence on one side, and an injury resulting from it on the other; *Winn* v. *Dillon*, 27 Mississippi, 494.

Whatever doubt may exist under other circumstances, it is clear that where one who is employed to negotiate for another takes advantage of the opportunity to obtain a conveyance to himself, there is a wrong against which relief may be had in equity: *Lees* v. *Nuttall*, 1 Tamlyn, 282; 1 Russell & Mylne, 53; *Taylor* v. *Salmon*, 4 Mylne & Craig, 134; *Jenkins* v. *Eldridge*, Story, 181, 293; *Cloninger* v. *Summit*, 2 Jones' Eq. 513; *Hargrave* v. *King*, 5 Iredell, Eq. 430. "When one," said the Court in *Hargrave* v. *King*, "by parol agrees to procure a lease for himself and others, and procures that

lease in his own name, he is a trustee for those for whom he agreed to act, and the statute has no application." The trust springs from the fraud, and the breach of an unwritten promise will not give rise to a trust; *Schmidt* v. *Gatewood*, 2 Richardson's Eq. 162; *Jackman* v. *Ringland*, 4 W. & S. 149; *Sharp* v. *Long*, 4 Casey, 434. The fraud must nevertheless be contemporaneous with the purchase: *Barnet* v. *Dougherty*, 8 Casey, 371; and consist in the fraudulent substitution of the name of the agent for that of the principal; for where the agent is expressly or impliedly authorized to take the deed in his own name, on the faith of an assurance that he will hold the premises for the principal, and convey to him when reimbursed, the latter must submit to the consequences of his ill-placed confidence, and no trust can be raised without disregarding the plain import of the Statute of Frauds; *Pennock* v. *Clough*, 16 Vermont, 507; *Lathrop* v. *Hoyt*, 7 Barbour, 69; *Blair* v. *Bass*, 4 Blackford, 539; *Wallace* v. *Brown*, 2 Stockton's Ch. 308; *Slowey* v. *M'Murray*, 27 Missouri, 113. The distinction is plain between getting a title in fraud of the agency, and keeping it contrary to an agreement that it shall be conveyed; and will, perhaps, serve to reconcile most if not all of the decisions in which written evidence of the agency has been treated as essential to the trust.

Trusts arising under the circumstances specified in this note, and in that to *Keech* v. *Sandford*, *ante*, and in general all trusts which are fastened by equity on the conscience of the holder of the legal title, to compel the surrender of that which he acquired or seeks to retain in his own wrong, have been described as constructive trusts, or trusts by construction of equity, while those which arise from the presumed meaning or intention of the parties, as where the consideration for the purchase is paid by one man, and the deed taken in the name of another, are ranged under the head of resulting or presumptive trusts ; Hill on Trustees, 91, 144, *post*, notes to *Dyer* v. *Dyer*. Both, are, however, due to a legal or rather equitable implication, and both fall, alike, under the proviso which excepts trusts arising or resulting " by implication or construction of law," from the operation of the statute : the word law being used in the general sense in which it includes equity.]

---

                    *LAKE v. GIBSON.

                    TRIN. TERM, 1729.

               REPORTED 1 EQ. CAS. AB. 294, PL. 3.

JOINT PURCHASERS.]—*Where several persons make a joint purchase for the purposes of a joint undertaking or partnership, either in trade or any other dealing, although they are joint-tenants at law, in equity they will be considered as tenants in common, and the survivors as trustees for those who are dead.*

THE Commissioners of Sewers had sold and conveyed lands to five persons and their heirs, who afterwards, in order to improve and cultivate those lands, entered into articles whereby they agreed to be equally concerned as to profit and loss, and to advance each of them such a sum to be laid out in the manurance and improvement of the land.

SIR JOSEPH JEKYLL, M. R., held that they were tenants in common, and not joint tenants, as to the *beneficial interest* or *right* in those lands, and that the survivor should not go away with the whole ; for then it might happen that some might have paid or laid out their share of the money, and others, who had laid out nothing, go away with the whole estate.

And his Honor held, that when two or more purchase lands, and advance the money in *equal* proportions, and take a conveyance to them and their heirs, that this is a joint-tenancy ; that is, a purchase by them jointly of the chance of survivorship, which may happen to the one of them as well as to the other ; but where the proportions of the money are *not equal*, and this appears in the deed itself, this makes them *in the nature of partners ;* and

*however the legal estate may survive, yet the survivor [*178]
shall be considered but as a trustee for the others, in
proportion to the sums advanced by each of them.

So, if two or more make a joint purchase and afterwards one
of them lays out a considerable sum of money in repairs or improvements, and dies, this shall be a lien on the land, and a trust
for the representative of him who advanced it; and that in all
other cases of a joint undertaking or partnership, either in trade
or any other dealing, they were to be considered as tenants in
common, or the survivors as trustees for those who were dead.

---

*LAKE v. CRADDOCK.'   [*179]

(On an Appeal from the Decree at the Rolls in LAKE v. GIBSON.)

DE TERM. S. MICHAELIS, 1732.

REPORTED 3 P. WMS. 158.

JOINT PURCHASERS.]—*Five persons purchased West Thorock Level
from the Commissioners of Sewers, and the purchase was to them
as joint tenants in fee ; but they contributed ratably to the purchase,
which was with an intent to drain the Level ; after which several of
them died.   They were held to be tenants in common in equity ; and
though one of these five undertakers deserted the partnership for
thirty years, yet he was let in afterwards, on terms.*

THE case was thus : Great part of the lands in West Thorock,
in Essex, having been overflowed by the river Thames, near
Dagenham, and the landowners not thinking it worth their while
to pay the assessments made on them by the Commissioners of
Sewers, the commissioners decreed the lands to be forfeited, and
conveyed them to three trustees in trust to sell, and raise money
for the draining of these overflowed lands.

The defendant Craddock's father, the plaintiff Lake, and three
others, five in all, having entered into an undertaking to drain
the level or overflowed lands of West Thorock, the trustees for
the sale, by the consent and direction of the Commissioners of
Sewers, did, by deed, indented and enrolled, dated the 8th of
February, 1695, in consideration of 5,145l. paid to the Commissioners by the five purchasers, convey this level to the defendant
Craddock's father, the plaintiff Lake, the three others, and their
heirs; upon which several sums of money were *expended [*180]
in carrying on the undertaking; and in 1699, the defendant Craddock's father paid his last contribution, which, with
what he had advanced before, came in all to 1025l.

Afterwards, it seeming to be an enterprise which would prove
very expensive, and there being some uncertainty as to the suc-

cess of it, the defendant Craddock's father wholly deserted it, and never more concerned himself therewith.

The four other undertakers were advised that some neighbouring lands would be of service to their design ; upon which, in April, 1703, they purchased the manor of Porretshalls, in West Thorock, of the Lady Smith, for 2550*l.*, and in February following purchased the moiety of the rectory and tithes of West Thorock, for 1400*l.* of Sir Charles Tyrrell ; which two purchases were thought useful in the undertaking, and were made in the names of the four undertakers, omitting Craddock ; nor did it appear that he was ever consulted therein, or desired to contribute to the purchase. Craddock, the father, died, leaving the defendant Craddock, the son, his *heir* and *executor.*

The plaintiff, Sir Bibye Lake, one of the original partners, brought this bill against the rest of the partners, or their representatives, for an account and division of the partnership estate. And on the first coming on of the cause, at the Rolls, his Honor referred it to the Master to state a case between the parties, for the judgment of the Court. And the Master having made his report, the cause was thereupon heard, when the principal or rather the only question was, whether these five purchasers having made this purchase jointly, so as to become in law joint tenants, the same should survive in equity ?

Sir Joseph Jekyll, M. R., on debate, decreed that the survivorship should not take place; for that the payment of money created a trust for the parties advancing the same ; and an undertaking upon the hazard of profit or loss was in the nature of merchandising,[1] when the jus accrescendi is never allowed ; that, supposing one of the partners had laid out the whole of the [*181] money, and had *happened to die first, according to the contrary construction, he must have lost all, which would have been most unjust.[2] Wherefore, it was decreed that these five purchasers were tenants in common, not only as to the level lands which were first purchased, but also with respect to the lands bought afterwards by the four undertakers of the Lady Smith and Sir Charles Tyrrell ; but that the defendant Craddock ought not to have the benefit of this tenancy in common, unless he would pay so much money as would make up what had been already advanced by his father equal to what had been contributed by each of the other partners, together with interest for the same from the respective times that Craddock, the father, ought to have made those payments; and on the defendant Craddock's paying the same, then all the said lands to be divided into five parts, the defendant Craddock to have one-fifth ; but on default of payment, the defendant Craddock to be excluded, and the lands to be divided and distributed into four parts among the four other partners.

[1] 1 Inst. 182 ; 1 Vern. 217 ; 2 Lev. 188, 228.
[2] See 9 Ves. 549 ; Dale v. Hamilton, 5 Hare, 385.

From this decree the defendant Craddock appealed to the Lord Chancellor King, insisting that he ought either to receive back the 1025*l.*, which it was admitted his father expended in this undertaking, or to be allowed to come in for a share of the level only, and not to be bound to contribute towards the two purchases made by the four other undertakers of the Lady Smith and Sir Charles Tyrrell: that the four other undertakers had chosen to make these two purchases in their own names only, by which they seemed to have excluded Craddock from all concern therein, and of which, had it proved never so beneficial, he would have had no means of forcing them to admit him to a share; and therefore, now that it had turned out a losing bargain, there could be no reason to compel him to bear a portion of the loss. Besides, there was nothing in the articles empowering the partners, or the major part of them, to buy lands; and, by the same reason that they would oblige Craddock to pay his share towards these purchases, they might, if they had fancied *buying [*182] half the country, have compelled him to contribute to that also. That it was difficult to conceive how the uplands thus purchased much less the tithes, could be of any use in the undertaking; though, as to the charge of draining the level, exclusive of the two purchases, the defendant Craddock was willing to advance his proportion.

It was, moreover, pretended that the decree was unreasonable, on account of its having directed that the defendant Craddock, in order to be admitted to one-fifth, should pay not only his proportion of these two purchases, but also of the interest of the purchase-money, from the time that his father ought to have made these payments; whereas the direction ought to have been, that an account should be taken of the profits of these two purchases, which profits might have amounted to as much as the interest, or, if not quite so much, yet that the defendant Craddock ought to pay no more towards such interest than the deficiency of the quantum of the profits would come to.

To which it was answered by Mr. Solicitor Talbot that, as the defendant Craddock's father and himself had for so long a time (near thirty years) relinquished and abandoned the partnership, and in regard the defendant Craddock had no manner of right thereto but through the indulgence of a court of equity (it being, by law, a joint-tenancy, and as such, belonging to the survivors), it was a favourable decree to let him in upon any terms; and surely the terms now offered him must appear reasonable, viz., that he should, upon his contributing to all the expenses that had been contracted and incurred by reason of any purchases or otherwise, in the prosecution of the undertaking, be admitted to one-fifth of the partnership; that had the defendant Craddock brought his bill for the benefit of such undertaking, he could not have hoped to succeed on any other conditions: that it was still stronger against him, in that he now seemed to decline meddling with the undertaking, so that here was rather great favour shown him than any hardship imposed : that he was not absolutely and [*183] at all events bound by this *decree to pay his proportion towards the new purchases, but had it in his election whether he would do it or no : that, as to the interest which was required of him previous to his being admitted into the partnership, it was reasonable he should pay it for his default in not having contributed his share of the principal before, which if he had done, he would not have been charged with the interest ; and this was some disadvantage to the other four partners, who had been deprived of their arrear of interest for near thirty five years : that, in truth, the design of the defendant Craddock appeared to be to delay matters, and to defer the bringing in of his money and interest till such time as this long account of the profits should be taken, which would require many years ; and that if the defendant's share of the profits of these two purchases should exceed his proportion of the interest, the surplus, on the making up of the accounts, must be paid him.

For these reasons, the decree of the Master of the Rolls was affirmed.

LORD CHANCELLOR KING [1] said, that this was plainly a tenancy in common *in equity*, though otherwise *at law ;* and the defendant Craddock having only a title in equity, that he must do equity, and that this was equitable in all its branches ; for he had his election to drop all claim, or to take it on the same foot with the rest of the partners ; and that it was not reasonable that he should be let into the account of the profits or loss of the undertaking until he had made his election.

It is an invariable rule at law, that, when purchasers take a conveyance to themselves and their heirs, they will be joint tenants : and, upon the death of one of them, the estate will go to the survivor. See Litt. s. 280.

The same rule prevails in equity, except where circumstances exist from which the rule of law is controlled by the presumed intention of the parties. Thus, as is laid down by Sir Joseph Jekyll in *Lake* v. [*184] *Gibson*, where two or more purchase *lands and advance the purchase-money in *equal* proportions, and take a conveyance to them and their heirs, they will be held joint tenants in equity as well as at law, upon this principle, that it may be presumed they intended to purchase jointly the chance of survivorship. The rule of law, therefore, not being repugnant to the presumed intention of the parties, will be followed in equity. See *Taylor* v. *Fleming*, cited in *York* v. *Eaton*, Freem. 23 ; *Rigden* v. *Vallier*, 3 Atk. 735 ; *S. C.*, 2 Ves. 258 ; *Rea* v.

[1] This judgment is from Sugd. V. & P. 903, 11th edit., and is there stated to have been taken from unprinted MS.

Williams, Sugd. V. & P., App. No. xxi., 11th ed. See *Rex* v. *Williams*, Bumb. 342; *Harris* v. *Fergusson*, 16 Sim. 308.

Upon the same principle, where persons have entered into a joint contract for the purchase of an estate to them and their heirs, and have paid or contracted to pay the purchase-money in *equal* proportions, a court of equity will not, upon the death of one of them, decree a conveyance to the survivor and the heirs of the deceased purchaser as tenants in common; for if both parties to the contract contribute *equally* towards the purchase-money, the surviving purchaser will be solely entitled to the benefit of the contract, and to have a conveyance of the estate decreed to himself alone. See *Aveling* v. *Knipe*, 19 Ves. 441, where Sir W. Grant, M. R., observed that a doubt had been suggested whether a court of equity would in any case execute such an agreement by a conveyance in joint-tenancy. "It would not," observed his Honor, "if there were any circumstances from which it could be collected that a joint-tenancy was not in contemplation; but I have no conception that it is of course upon a controversy between two purchasers to depart from the letter of the agreement, and decree them to be tenants in common. And see *Davis* v. *Symonds*, 1 Cox, 402.

In equity, however, there is a strong leaning against joint-tenancy; and whenever circumstances occur from which it can reasonably be implied that a tenancy in common was intended, a court of equity will hold the survivors of joint purchasers trustees of the legal estate for the representatives of the deceased purchaser.

In *Lake* v. *Gibson*, Sir Joseph Jekyll lays it down as a general rule, that, where two or more purchase lands and advance the purchase-money in *unequal* proportions, and this appears on the deed itself, this makes them *in the nature of partners*, and, however the legal estate may survive, yet the survivor will be considered in equity but as a trustee for the other, in proportion to the sums advanced by each of them. See also *Rigden* v. *Vallier*, 3 Atk. 735; *S. C.*, 2 Ves. 258. The soundness of the distinction between *equal* and *unequal* advances is doubted by Mr. *Vesey, in a note to *Jackson* v. *Jackson*, 9 Ves. 597. "If," [*185] he observes, "the advance of consideration, generally, will not prevent the legal right, the mere *inequality* of proportion, which may be naturally attributed to the relative value of the lives, ought not have that effect." Sir Edward Sugden, however, thought the distinction founded on rational grounds. " Where the parties," he observes, "advance the money *equally*, it may fairly be presumed that they purchased with the view to the benefit of survivorship: but where the money is advanced in *unequal* proportions, and no express intention appears to benefit the one advancing the smaller proportion, it is fair to presume that no such intention existed; the *inequality* of proportion can scarcely be attributed to the relative value of the lives, because neither of the parties can be supposed not to know that the other may, immediately after the purchase, compel a legal partition of the estate, or may even sever the joint-tenancy by a clandestine act:" Sugd. V. & P. 902, 11th ed.; see 14th edit. 698. Sed vide *Harris* v. *Fergusson*, 16 Sim. 308. Explained, however, in *Robinson* v. *Preston*, 4 K. & J. 515.

It will be observed, that Sir Joseph Jekyll qualifies the general rule laid down in the principal case of *Lake* v. *Gibson* by the words "and this appears upon the deed itself." Lord Hardwicke, however, lays down the same rule without this qualification, *Rigden* v. *Vallier*, 3 Atk. 735; 2 Ves. 258.

Again, where money is advanced by persons, either in *equal* or *unequal* shares, who take a mortgage to themselves jointly, although the debt and security will at law belong to the survivor, in equity there will be a tenancy in common, the survivor being a trustee for the personal representatives of the deceased mortgagees; (*Petty* v. *Styward*, 1 Ch. Rep. 31 Eq. Ca. Ab. 290; *Rigden* v. *Vallier*, 2 Ves. 258). For "equity says it could not be the intention that the interest should survive. Though they take a joint security, each means to lend his own and to take back his own:" Per Lord Alvanley, M. R., in *Morley* v. *Bird*, 3 Ves. 631; and see *Robinson* v. *Preston*, 4 K. & J. 505, 511.

The personal representatives of the deceased mortgagees are therefore necessary parties to a bill of foreclosure or redemption (*Vickers* v. *Cowell*, 1 Beav. 529); and although the entire legal estate is in the survivor, they are necessary parties to a reconveyance, in order that they may give a valid discharge for their share of the mortgage-money: Carth. 16. Hence it is usual, where trustees advance money on mortgage, to insert a declaration, that, if one of the mortgagees die before the money is paid off, the receipt of the survivor shall be a sufficient [*186] *discharge; and that the concurrence of the personal representative of the deceased mortgagee shall not be requisite. See *Matson* v. *Denis*, 12 W. R. (V. C. S.), 596.

If joint mortgagees purchase or foreclose the equity of redemption, they will be held, in equity, tenants in common, "because their intent is presumed to be so:" *Rigden* v. *Vallier*, 2 Ves. 258. Thus in *Edwards* v. *Fashion*, Prec. Ch. 332, where the two daughters of a mortgagee for a term of years, taking under his will the residue of his personal estate, including the mortgage, equally to be divided between them, afterwards purchased the equity of redemption to them and their heirs, it was held, that there was no survivorship, upon the ground that the purchase *was founded on the mortgage*, and the daughters being tenants in common of the mortgage, they were held to be tenants in common of the equity of redemption likewise. See *Aveling* v. *Knipe*, 19 Ves. 444; and the comments therein of Sir Wm. Grant, M. R., on *Edwards* v. *Fashion*.

The circumstances, however, attending a purchase in the names of two persons advancing the purchase-moneys in equal proportions, may show an intention that the parties should hold as tenants in common.

Thus, in *Robinson* v. *Preston*, 4 K. & J. 505, two ladies, about the same age, who lived together in a common establishment, were tenants in common of land, the rents of which were from time to time paid to their joint account at a bank, upon which they both drew drafts as they had occasion, and the bankers were in the habit of investing portions of the balances in their joint names; and, upon one occasion, part of the money drawn from their joint account in the bank was invested upon a mortgage to them as tenants in common, in which there was a declaration (perfectly unnecessary) that the two ladies should hold as tenants in common.   The surviving sister (who afterwards became a lunatic), by her will bequeathed to her sister her share of the stock standing in the joint names of herself and her sister.   It was held by Sir W. Page Wood, V. C., on the death of the other sister, that the two sisters held the stock purchased in their joint names, and the balance to their joint account at their bankers', as tenants in common.   " I am'not," said his Honor, " aware of any decision as to the effect of a payment of moneys in which two or more persons are interested as tenants in common, to their joint account at a banker's, whether such a payment would fall within the doctrine as to mortgages, or within that as to purchases; and perhaps I might be allowed to entertain some degree of doubt if the case rested simply there; but the bankers, from time to time, invested portions of these moneys, *and I must assume that they did so by the direction of both ladies in the purchase of [*187] stock in their joint names; which, no doubt, as it was argued, they might have invested in equal moieties, one in the name of each lady." And after referring to *Edwards* v. *Fashion*, Prec. Ch. 332 (ante, p. 186), where mortgagees purchasing the mortgaged estate were held to be tenants in common, his Honor, quoting Sir Wm. Grant, proceeds to observe : " That case proceeds on the ground that the purchase was founded on the mortgage; and the mortgagees being tenants in common of the mortgage were held to be tenants in common of the equity of redemption likewise.   That is a case that has some bearing upon the present, when one looks to what was the root of the property now in question, viz., rents of land held by the two ladies as tenants in common.

" But besides the first point, as to the root of the property, there is a second, viz., that where it was necessary for a deed to be executed, as in the case of the mortgage, there was actually a declaration that they would hold the money so invested as tenants in common.   With regard to the investments in the purchase of stock, in those transactions there was, of course, no necessity for a deed to be executed, or any memorandum signed.

" Then I find the third point,—perhaps the strongest of all,—viz., that the sister who proved to be the survivor, and against whom, of course, her own declaration may be read, by her will, executed in the lifetime of her sister, not only speaks of ' her share ' of the property in question, but affects to dispose of it in favour of her sister ; and further, in the assumption that her sister will survive her, she directs that, after her sister's decease, a legacy of 350*l.* stock should be paid out of a part of the stock in question, that part standing exactly in the same position as the rest.

" These three circumstances concurring, and the whole being a question of intention, to be ascertained from the circumstances of the case, it is not illogical to say, that the three combined have a force and carry a conviction, which perhaps any one of them taken alone would not produce." But see and consider *Bone* v. *Pollard*, 24 Beav. 283.

And it seems that parol evidence of subsequent dealings, as well as of surrounding circumstances, is admissible on a purchase by two persons contributing equally to the cost of it, to prove an intention to hold in severalty (*Harrison* v. *Barton*, 1 J. & H. 287); but it seems that parol evidence of statements of intention is not admissible.—*Ib.* But see *Devoy* v. *Devoy*, 3 Sm. & G.

[*188] Another rule laid down by the Master of the Rolls in *Lake* v. *Gibson* is, that, in all cases of a joint undertaking or partnership, either in trade or in any other dealing, two or more persons who make a joint purchase will be considered in equity as tenants in common, or the survivors as trustees for the representatives of those who are dead. This was the ground of the decision in *Lake* v. *Gibson*, or *Lake* v. *Craddock*, which shows that a joint speculation in improving land, on a hazard of profit and loss, is treated, in a court of equity, as in the nature of merchandise, and the *jus accrescendi* is not allowed. See *In re Thomas Ryan*, 3 I. R. Eq. 222, 232.

In favour of merchandise it is well known that an exception to the rule of survivorship has been long established. It is thus stated in Co. Litt. 182, a :—" An exception is to be made of two joint merchants: for the wares, merchandises, debts, or duties that they have as joint merchants or partners shall not survive, but shall go to the executors of him that deceaseth ; and this is per legem mercatoriam, which (as hath been said) is part of the laws of this realm, for the advancement and continuance of commerce and trade, which is pro bono publico ; for the rule is, that *jus accrescendi inter mercatores pro beneficio commercii locum non habet.*" And see *Nelson* v. *Bealby*, 30 Beav. 472.

The exception in favour of merchants was afterwards extended to all traders ; and courts of equity have extended it to the analogous cases of real property purchased for a joint undertaking or partnership in trade, or in any other dealing. It has been remarked by Sir James Wigram, V. C., that the consequences of the admission of the partnership contract were carried to a great length in *Lake* v. *Craddock* ; " for one of the five original contractors," observed his Honor, " who had retired for nearly thirty years, was held bound by a subsequent contract, made by the other four, for the purchase of other lands in aid of the original design;" 5 Hare, 384. In *Jeffereys* v. *Small*, 1 Vern. 217, where two persons having jointly stocked a farm, and occupied it as joint tenants, the bill was to be relieved against survivorship, one of them being dead, Lord Keeper North was clearly of opinion that the plaintiff ought to be relieved, and said that, if the farm had been taken jointly by them, and proved a good bargain, then the survivor should have the benefit of it; but as to a stock employed in the way of trade, that should in no case survive. That the custom of merchants was extended to all traders, to exclude survivorship; and though it was common for traders in articles of co-partnership to provide against survivorship, yet that was more than was necessary; and he said, *he took the distinction to be, where two became joint tenants, [*189] or jointly interested in a thing by way of gift or the like, there the same shall be subject to all the consequences of law; but as to a joint undertaking in the way of trade or the like, it is otherwise; and decreed for the plaintiff accordingly. Lord Eldon, in commenting upon this case, observed :—" *Jeffereys* v. *Small* has been approved, with some distinctions, in subsequent cases. It was held, in that case, that, if two take a lease of a farm jointly, the lease shall survive, but the stock on the farm, though occupied jointly, shall not survive. I have a note of my own of a case of *Elliot* v. *Brown*, upon the 25th of July, 1791, in which another distinction was made by Lord Thurlow, that the law, with reference to the stock, would be the same as to lease, *provided the lease was taken only upon the same purpose as the stock*, and the lease was only the substratum; and *Lake* v. *Gibson* was referred to. The observation upon that was, that the purchase of the land was made to the intent that they might become partners in the improvement; that it was only the substratum for an adventure, in the profits of which it was previously intended they should be concerned : *Jackson* v. *Jackson*, 9 Ves. 596. In *Elliot* v. *Brown* (since reported, 3 Swanst. 489), there was a lease of a farm to two partners; one partner dying, the other agreed to a division of stock with the representatives of the deceased partner, but insisted on holding the lease by survivorship; Lord Thurlow, however, thought the lease was accessory to the trade in which the parties were embarked, and granted an injunction to restrain the surviving partner from proceeding by ejectment to obtain possession of the farm. From Lord Colchester's MSS. See also 1 Vern. 217, n. (3).

So, likewise, in *Lyster* v. *Dolland*, 1 Ves. jun. 421, where two persons took a building lease, and laid out money in erecting houses, Lord Thurlow held them to be partners in respect to this property; and the survivor was decreed to be a trustee of a moiety for the representatives of the deceased partner. "Though," observed his Lordship, "if two persons take a farm, the lease will survive, yet has it not been determined that, if they lay out money jointly upon it, that turns round the estate at law, and makes it equitable? I allude to the case of a joint lease taken or a fee purchased to carry on a joint trade; the object being to carry on the trade, the Court thought it would convert the joint property for the purposes of trade, and making a common advantage. I am now clearly of opinion, that, if partners purchase leasehold [*190] or freehold to carry on trade, that will carry with it all those circumstances." *See also *Crawshay* v. *Maule*, 1 Swanst. 508.

A deceased partner, may, however, have so conducted himself by repudiating a contract, as for instance a lease of ground for a building speculation, as to preclude his executors from claiming a share in the lease: *Reilly* v. *Walsh*, 11 Ir. Eq. Rep. 22. And see *Norway* v. *Rowe*, 19 Ves. 143; *Clements* v. *Hall.* 24 Beav. 333.

And though the conveyance of real estate be taken in the name of one of the partners, having been purchased with partnership funds, it will be part of the partnership property: *Smith* v. *Smith*, 5 Ves. 193; *Clegg* v. *Fishwick*, 1 Mac. & G. 294. And see *Tibbits* v. *Phillips*, 10 Hare, 355.

The question whether property purchased with partnership assets is joint or separate property of the partners depends upon the circumstances under which and the purposes for which it was bought. Thus, in the *Bank of England Case*, 3 De G. F. & Jo. 645; one of two partners carrying on the business of leather factor bought lands for the purpose of erecting a residence on part of it, and selling the remainder to a railway company. He offered a share to his partner, who was also desirous of building a house out of town for his residence. The offer was accepted, and the purchase-money paid out of the partnership assets; but the conveyance was to the partners in separate moieties, each of which was conveyed to the usual uses to bar dower. The partners at their individual expense built houses upon portions of the land set apart for the purpose, but the other expenses relating to the land were paid out of the partnership assets. It was held by the Lords Justices that the whole of the land constituted joint estate. "Questions of this nature," said Lord Justice Turner, "depend, as I apprehend, generally, if not universally, upon the circumstances. It cannot, I think, be laid down as an universal rule, that when lands are bought by partners in trade, and are paid for out of the partnership assets, they of necessity become part of the joint estate of the partners. There are different purposes for which the lands may have been bought. They may have been bought for the purpose of being used and employed in the trade, but for the purpose of a mere speculation on account of the partnership, for I know nothing which can prevent partners from speculating in land, if they think proper to do so, as freely as they may speculate in mere articles of commerce, though foreign to their trade. Again, they may have been bought without reference to the purposes of the trade or the benefit of the partnership, with the intention of with-

drawing from the trade the amount employed in the *purchase, [*191]
and converting that amount into separate property of the partners, or they may have been bought on account of one or more of the
partners, he or they becoming debtors to the partnership for the amount
laid out in the purchase. The form of the conveyance in these cases
does not settle the question, for in whatever form the conveyance may
be, there may be a trust of the land which may follow the money,
liable, however, as other trusts are, to be rebutted by evidence. Where
land purchased is not merely paid for out of the partnership assets, but
is bought for the purpose of being used and employed in the partnership
trade, it is scarcely possible to conceive a case in which there could be
sufficient evidence to rebut the trust, and accordingly in these cases we
find the decisions almost if not entirely uniform—that the purchased
land forms part of the joint estate of the partnership; but where the
land is not purchased for those purposes, the question becomes more
open, and we have to consider whether the circumstances attending the
purchase show that it was made on account of the partnership, or of
any one or more of them individually, in whose name the land may have
been bought. . . . I am of opinion that, looking at the case with
reference to the whole of the estate, this purchase must be taken to
have been made by way of speculation on account of the partnership,
and that the petition of the Bank of England accordingly fails and
must be dismissed."

Where property is *not purchased* by persons for partnership purposes, but is *devised* to them as joint tenants, although they make use
of it for partnership purposes, they will not be held tenants in common
in equity, unless by express agreement, or by their course of dealing
with it for a long period, it may be inferred that they meant to sever
the joint tenancy. In *Jackson* v. *Jackson*, 9 Ves. 591, a testator left
leasehold and other personal estate embarked in trade to his two sons,
as joint tenants, who continued to carry on the trade for twelve years,
when one of them died. Lord Eldon, overruling the decision of Sir W.
Grant, M. R. (reported 7 Ves. 535), held, that, under all the circumstances of the case, the two sons of the testator were to be considered
as tenants in common of his property embarked in trade, from the time
they were let into possession, including as well the capital as the profits ;
for, though there might be cases of distinction between them, the course
of dealing for so many years ought to be taken as evidence that they
meant to sever the joint tenancy. See also *Brown* v. *Oakshot*, 24 Beav.
254. In the case, however, of *Morris* v. *Barrett*, 3 Y. & J. 384, in the
*Exchequer, a testator *devised and bequeathed* the residue of his [*192]
real and personal estate to his two sons, their heirs, executors,
and administrators. The two sons, after their father's death, during
the period of twenty years, carried on the business of farmers with such
estate, and kept the moneys arising therefrom in one common stock,

and, with part of such moneys, *purchased other estates* in the name of
one of them, but never in any manner entered into any agreement
respecting such farming business, or ever accounted with each other.
One of the brothers died; and, upon a bill being filed by the legatees
and persons beneficially entitled under his will, it was admitted, by the
counsel of the surviving brother, that the estates *purchased* with the
profits of the business and the partnership stock were held by the
brothers as tenants in common, but they contended that the leasehold
estates and the personal estate which the father *bequeathed* to them
were held by them as joint tenants; that where real estates, conveyed
to persons as joint tenants, had been adjudged to have been held by
them as tenants in common, the estates had been *purchased* expressly
for the purpose of a partnership, or for a joint speculation, as in *Lake*
v. *Craddock*, and that no case could be cited in which real estate *devised*
had been converted from an estate in joint tenancy to a tenancy in common: Alexander, C. B., held that the brothers remained joint tenants
of all the property that passed by the will of their father, but were
tenants in common of the after-purchased lands.

In *Dale* v. *Hamilton*, 5 Hare, 369, it was held by Sir J. Wigram, V.
C., that a partnership agreement between A. & B. that they should be
jointly interested in a speculation for buying, improving for sale, and
selling lands, might be proved without being evidenced by any writing
signed by, or by the authority of, the party to be charged therewith,
within the Statute of Frauds: and that such an agreement being proved,
A. or B. might establish his interest in the land, the subject of the partnership, without such interest being evidenced by any such writing.
See S. C., 2 Ph. 266; and *Darby* v. *Darby*, 3 Drew. 495; but see and
consider *Caddick* v. *Skidmore*, 2 De G. & Jo. 52; *Smith* v. *Matthews*,
3 De G. F. & Jo. 139, 151.

Where partners hold real estate for partnership purposes, a question
arises, which was not decided in *Lake* v. *Gibson*, and *Lake* v. *Craddock*
(in which case the defendant Craddock, it will be observed, was both
heir-at-law and executor of his father), whether the real estate is not,
even in the absence of any expressed intention of the partners, so abso-
[*193] lutely *converted into personalty as to be held by the surviving
partners, not in trust for the heir-at-law, but for the personal
representative, of the deceased partner.

It is clearly settled, that where real estate is purchased *with partnership capital*, for the *purposes of partnership trade*, it will, in the
absence of any express agreement, be considered as absolutely converted into personalty; and, upon the death of one of the partners,
his share will not go to his heir-at-law, nor be liable to dower, but will
belong to his personal representatives. See *Townsend* v. *Devaynes*,
1 Mont. on Partnership, Append. 97; 1 Rob. H. & W., Jac. ed. p. 346;
Selkrig v. *Davies*, 2 Dow. 231. So, in *Phillips* v. *Phillips*, 1 My. & K.

649, Sir J. Leach, M. R., held, that freehold and copyhold public-houses, purchased with partnership capital, and conveyed to the two partners and their heirs, for the purposes of the partnership trade, were to be considered as personal estate generally, and not only for the payment of the partnership debts. " I confess," observed his Honor, " I have for some years, notwithstanding older authorities, considered it to be settled that all property, whatever might be its nature, *purchased with partnership capital for the purposes of the partnership trade*, continued to be partnership capital, and to have, to every intent, the quality of personal estate ; and in the case of *Fereday* v. *Wightwick*, 1 Russ. & My. 45, I had no intention to confine the principle to the payment of the partnership demands. Lord Eldon has certainly, upon several occasions, expressed such an opinion. The case of *Townsend* v. *Devanes* is a clear decision to that effect, and general convenience requires that this principle should be adhered to." This decision has been followed in *Broom* v. *Broom*, 3 My. & K. 443 ; *Morris* v. *Kearsley*, 2 Y. & C. Excheq. Ca. 140 ; *Bligh* v. *Brent*, 2 Y. & C. Excheq. Ca. 268 ; *Houghton* v. *Houghton*, 11 Sim. 491. *In re Thomas Ryan*, 3 I. R. Eq. 232.

It seems, however, that where real estate belonged to the partners at the time of their entering into partnership, or has been subsequently acquired by them out of their own private moneys, or by gift, conversion will not, unless by express agreement, take place, although the real estate has been used for the partnership purposes in trade. In *Thornton* v. *Dixon*, 3 Bro. C. C. 199, three persons, *seised in fee* of some land called Broadmoor, entered into partnership for twenty-one years as papermakers, and mills were erected upon the land, and they declared the uses of the land to themselves in fee, as tenants in common. They afterwards entered into a new partnership for twenty-one years, by deed, taking in four new partners interested in different *proportions ; and in the partnership deed there was a covenant from the three original partners to stand seised of the land in trust for the co-partnership, in the proportions in which they were respectively interested therein ; and a proviso, that, in case any of the partners wished to dispose of his or their shares, he or they might do so, giving notice to the other partners, in order that they might have an opportunity of purchasing. The partnership term expired, and they went on afterwards without any new agreement. During the second partnership they bought a freehold messuage with a little land adjoining, called Low Meerbeck, for the better carrying on the trade, which was enjoyed by the partners as joint tenants. Upon the death of one of the partners, who by purchase from the others had acquired one-half of the whole concern, the question arose, whether his share was to be considered as real or personal property. Lord Thurlow, when the cause was first heard, said, he " had always understood [*194] that, where partners bought lands for the purpose of a partnership concern, it was to be considered as part of the partnership fund, and that, consequently, Broadmoor and Meerbeck must be considered as personal estate, and distributable as such." However, when the cause came on again, his Lordship said, he " thought that, had the agreement been that the mills should be valued and sold, it would have converted them into personalty of the partnership; but that the agreement in this case was not sufficient to vary the nature of the property; therefore, that, after the dissolution, the property would result according to its respective nature, the real as real, the personal as personal estate." It does not appear whether Low Meerbeck was purchased out of the partnership or private funds of the partners; if the former was the case, this part of the decision cannot be supported, as it is opposed to the doctrine laid down in *Phillips* v. *Phillips*. In *Balmain* v. *Shore*, 9 Ves. 500, three persons agreed to enter into partnership for ninety-nine years in the business of potters; and it was covenanted by the articles, that, in case of the decease of any of the co-partners, his share should belong to his widow for her life, and that, after her decease, her share of the joint trade should go to her children; and if there was no child, to her executors. Afterwards a china and pot manufactory, and other premises, were purchased by the partners, and conveyed to them as tenants in common in fee. The conveyance then recited the partnership, and declared that the premises should continue to be used in the partnership trade during the continuance of the partnership, and each of the partners covenanted that he would *not, during the continuance of the partnership, sell his share, or sue out a writ or file a bill of partition. Sir William Grant, M. R., observed, " Here the parties have limited and defined the extent of the interest the partnership was to have in the real property. Considering themselves as owners of the real estate, as tenants in common, they stipulate that the partnership shall have a certain ownership, notwithstanding that interest in them, as tenants in fee. The premises are to be continued to be used in the trade as long as the partnership lasts. They can claim nothing as partners, except through the covenants; subject to the covenants, it goes as real estate. Whether the heir can derive any benefit is another question. The question for my decision is only, whether I can declare this real estate to be personal property, to go as the shares of the partnership. That, I am of opinion, I cannot declare." It was stated in the answers, that the purchase-money of the freehold premises was paid, not out of the partnership effects, but out of *the separate property of each partner.*

[*195]

In *Cookson* v. *Cookson*, 8 Sim. 529, A. carried on trade upon land of which he was *seised in fee*. Afterwards he took one of his sons into partnership for twenty-four years, *and conveyed to him* in fee certain shares in the land; and, by their articles of partnership, they covenan-

ted that the land should at all times thereafter be held as partnership
property, and be considered and treated as part of the joint stock of
the trade; and it was provided that, if either partner died or retired
during the twenty-four years, his copartner might purchase his share,
at the sum stated to be its value in the last yearly accounts. In the
course of the twenty-four years 1700*l.* was expended out of the partnership funds in building on the land. After the expiration of the twenty-
four years, and until A.'s death, he and his son continued to carry on their
trade on the land, without entering into any new agreement. Sir L.
Shadwell, V. C., held, that A.'s share of the land retained its original
character, and descended to his heir. His Honor observed, that those
cases could hardly be said to bear upon the' subject, the foundation of
which was, in effect, that freehold tenements were purchased for the
benefit of the partnership out of the partnership assets, *for the father
was originally solely seised in fee of the freehold tenements in question,* and *the whole benefit which the son took proceeded from the father
by way of bounty exclusively, and there was no application of partnership assets to the purchase of the land in question for the purposes of
the partnership;* and his Honor thought that the covenant could not
be taken as showing that, for all intents and purposes and for all time,
the effect of the dealing between *the father and son was to [*196]
make the father's shares personal property; for his Honor understood that covenant as having a very distinct meaning, namely, that
during the partnership, and, if necessary for partnership purposes, after
the expiration of the partnership, the shares which the father and son
had respectively should be considered as personal estate; but that it
would be quite absurd to say that the covenant should be so extended
as that, though the land was not required to be sold for partnership
purposes, it should have the effect of making that which was unquestionably land in its own nature absolutely personal estate, not for any
beneficial purpose to the father or to the son, but for the purpose after
making a sort of unnatural and unnecessary conversion of real assets
into personal, as between the real and personal representatives of the
two partners respectively. "In the first place," observes his Honor, in
conclusion, "there was no purchase of the land out of the partnership
assets for partnership purposes; and there are no stipulations in the
articles of partnership, which, upon a fair construction, can be said to
have this effect, namely, as between the real and personal representatives of A., of converting the real estate into personalty; and it was not
necessary for any partnership purpose that there should be any conversion."

Mr. Bisset, in his work upon Partnership, states that it appears
from the MS. notes of Mr. Williamson, one of the counsel for the plaintiffs in *Phillips* v. *Phillips*, that the following important points were
determined in that cause: First, that public-houses, *devised* by the

uncle, who was a brewer, to the two nephews, who carried on the brewery as partners, were held not to be partnership property, although they were used exactly for the same purposes as other public-houses, which having been purchased out of the partnership capital, were held to be partnership property, and to be converted into personalty. Second that, where the uncle had mortgages of public-houses, whether in fee or for years, which he *devised* to his nephews, and the nephews *purchased* the equity of redemption out of the partnership funds, the equity of redemption was held to follow the mortgage, and not to become partnership property. See Bisset on Partnership, p. 50, and notes (*a*) and (*b*), where extracts from the decree as to these two points are given from the Reg. Lib. See Lindley, vol. i., p. 653, 2nd ed.

Where, however, real estate was purchased for the purposes of a partnership in trade, and paid for out of the partnership capital, but upon an agreement between the partners, that it was to be the separate property of one of them, who took a conveyance of it in his own name, [*197] Lord Eldon held, that *he was debtor to the partnership for so much money as he borrowed, and that the property not being partnership property, his wife was entitled to dower of the whole. *Smith* v. *Smith*, 5 Ves. 193.

Where real estate is purchased by partners out of the partnership capital, but not for the purposes of the partnership *in trade*, it will not be converted into personalty.

Thus, in *Bell* v. *Phyn*, 7 Ves. 453, three persons, carrying on business as merchants, in London, joined with another person in the purchase of a plantation in the Island of Grenada, two-thirds of which were to belong to the partners and the remaining third to another person. Part of the purchase-money for the two-thirds was paid out of the funds of the partnership, and the parties severally covenanted to pay the remainder. The accounts relative to the estate were kept in the partnership books. Further payments were made, from time to time, out of the partnership funds, till the death of one of the partners. Upon the death of one of the partners, the question arose, whether his share of the estate was real or personal. Sir William Grant, M. R., held that it was real. " Suppose," observed his Honor, " this was partnership property, I doubt whether the conveyance is a conversion : there was no occasion to call for it for any of the purposes of the partnership. It remains clear. Each might have entered into the enjoyment of his share. Then suppose all die. Why is it to be considered personal property—something different from what it really is, as between the real and personal representatives ? " On a subsequent day his Honor said, that he doubted whether there was quite enough admitted by the heir to show that the estate at Grenada could be considered, in a proper sense, partnership property, but that the authority of *Thornton* v. *Dixon* went the full length of the point for the heir; for, even if it was partnership property, there was nothing done by the partners to alter the nature of it.

In *Randall* v. *Randall*, 7 Sim. 271, Richard and William Randall, tenants in common of an estate, in 1792 agreed to carry on the business of farming together, including the growing of hops; and in 1794 they entered into the partnership of maltsters, and soon after as biscuit bakers. At that time, and during all the subsequent time, Richard Randall carried on his separate business of a land surveyor, and William Randall the business of a grocer. The farming and malting businesses were carried on upon the family estate, and the manufacture of biscuit partly on the family estate, and partly on Richard Randall's separate property. In 1802, Richard and William Randall purchased *one-fourth of the family estate from their brother James; in 1803 land from Miss Long; and in 1805 land from Joseph Tarver. No [*198] conveyance was executed of the lands so purchased, except those purchased of Tarver, which were conveyed, as to one moiety, to the use of Richard Randall in fee, and, as to the other moiety, to the use of William Randall, and a trustee, in the usual manner, to bar dower. All the lands so purchased were paid for out of the partnership moneys, and (excepting the family estate, where the malting and biscuit making were partly carried on) were used solely for farming and agricultural purposes. In 1820, Richard and William Randall purchased, with partnership moneys, two messuages and gardens in Portsea, which were conveyed in the same manner as the lands purchased from Tarver. This property was not used for any partnership purposes, but was let to tenants. In or before 1815, all the partnership *business in trade* had been given up, but the farming business was carried on in partnership up to August, 1827, when it was terminated by the death of Richard Randall. Sir L Shadwell, V. C., after an elaborate examination of the authorities, held, that the lands were not converted into personalty. "It does not," said his Honor, "appear that the parties purchased any part of the land for the purposes of their *partnership in trade*. Having in the first instance agreed to carry on the farming business in partnership, they subsequently agreed to become co-partners, first as maltsters, and afterwards as biscuit bakers. The first purchase that they made was of an undivided fourth part of an estate, of which they previously had a moiety as tenants in common. It would, however, be strong to say, that, because these parties, being partners in the farming business, *which is not a trade*, happen, collaterally to that business, to carry on a trade, therefore the nature of the property which they so purchased is to be changed; and, consequently, I do not think that it would be right to hold, that one-fourth of the family estates which Richard and William Randall purchased of their brother James is to be considered as partaking of the nature of personal estate.

" The next estate was purchased of Miss Long, but it was never used for any of the purposes of the partnership trade; and, as the judges who decided the cases to which I have alluded, have expressed their opinions to be, that land cannot become personal estate unless it is purchased for the purposes of the partnership trade, the land purchased of Miss Long, although it may have been paid for out of the partnership capital, cannot be considered as partaking of the nature of personal estate.

[*199]   *" With respect to the land purchased from Tarver, it was conveyed, as to one moiety, to the use of Richard Randall in fee; and, as to the other moiety, to the use of William Randall and his trustee, to the usual uses to bar dower. Therefore, there was no contract, either express or implied, that it should have any nature except that which was originally impressed upon it.

" The malting business ceased in 1807, and the biscuit baking in 1815. In 1820, the two brothers purchased two houses and gardens in Portsea, which of course were not used for farming purposes, but were let to tenants. These premises were conveyed in the same manner as the land purchased of Tarver; and if in those instances in which the lands purchased by the brothers were conveyed to them, it is to be inferred from the form of the conveyance that they intended to hold them as real estate, it is but fair to conclude that they intended to hold those lands which were not conveyed to them in like manner; for it would be unreasonable to suppose that they meant to hold part as land and part as impressed with the character of personal estate.

" The fair inference to be drawn from the facts of this case is, that the trade was collateral to, and arose out of, the principal business of farming; and there is no reason to conclude, from any of the decided cases, that any of the property to which this suit relates ought to be considered as personal estate." See also *Steward* v. *Blakeway*, 6 L. R. Eq. 479; 4 L. R. Ch. App. 603.

If, however, the owners of real estate, upon entering into partnership, direct or agree that it shall be sold upon the death of one of them, it will be held to be absolutely converted into personalty, and will go to the personal representative, and not to the heir of a deceased partner. See *Ripley* v. *Waterworth*, 7 Ves. 425; *Thornton* v. *Dixon*, 3 Bro. C. C. 199. In the recent case of *Essex* v. *Essex*, 20 Beav. 442, two persons seised of freeholds agreed to carry on business in partnership upon the premises for fourteen years, and that if either died during that term, the survivor should purchase the freeholds at a stated price. The fourteen years having expired, they by parol agreement continued the partnership " on the old terms;" one of them afterwards died intestate. It was held by Sir J. Romilly, M. R., that the stipulation as to purchase was binding, and that the freeholds were converted into personalty, and did not pass to the heir.

So, likewise, property purchased with partnership capital, for partner-

ship purposes in trade, and therefore converted into personality, may be
reconverted by the express or implied agreement of *the part- [*200]
ners. Thus, in *Rowley* v. *Adams*, 7 Beav. 548, A. & B. purchased realty out of their partnership assets, which was used for their
partnership purposes, and was in equity to be considered as personalty.
A new partnership was formed between A., B., and C. The realty continued to be used for partnership purposes, but A. and B. stipulated for
a rent to be paid them by the new partnership, composed of A., B., and
C. A. died. Lord Langdale, M. R., held, that the property was to be
considered as part of his real estate.

The share of a deceased partner in real estate purchased with partnership capital and used for partnership purposes in trade is now, it
seems, held to be converted into personalty, not only as between the
partners and the real and personal representatives of a deceased partner—but also for fiscal purposes, and that the Crown is entitled to the
benefit of such equitable conversion, and can claim legacy and probate
duty in respect of the property which at the death of the partner was
existing as real estate. See *Forbes* v. *Stevens*, 10 L. R. Eq. 178, 189,
where it was held, (overruling the law supposed to have been established in *Custance* v. *Bradshaw*, 4 Hare, 315,) that legacy duty was
payable upon a share of a deceased partner—a domiciled Englishman,
in the proceeds of freehold property in Bombay used for the purposes
of the partnership, and forming a partnership asset. See also *Attorney-
General* v. *Brunning*, 8 Ho. Lo. Ca. 243. And Hanson on the Prob.
Leg. and Succ. Duty Acts, pp. 190, 197.

But real estate, acquired by partners for the purposes of their business, may be dealt with by them in the conveyances in such a way as to
prevent this result, by showing that conversion into personalty was not
intended. *Custance* v. *Bradshaw*, 4 Hare, 315. See also the remarks
in Hanson on the Prob. Leg. and Succ. Duty Acts, pp. 7, 189.

The result of these authorities appears to be this, that, in the absence
of any agreement, and even for fiscal purposes, real estate purchased
with partnership capital for the purposes of partnership in trade will in
equity be converted into personalty; but, where real estate belongs to
the partners, or has been acquired by them out of their private moneys,
or by gift, although it is used for partnership purposes in trade, or if,
although paid for out of the partnership capital, it is not purchased for
the purposes of partnership in trade, it will, in the absence of any agreement or direction for its sale, retain the character of realty.

And it seems that conversion will take place not only where real
property is acquired for the purposes *of partnership in trade, [*201]
but also where it is acquired with partnership funds for the
purpose of re-sale upon a speculation not properly coming under the de-
nomination of trade. Thus, in *Darby* v. *Darby*, 3 Drew. 495, where
two persons on a joint speculation with their joint moneys, purchased

land for the purpose of laying it out in building lots, and re-selling it at
their joint profit or loss, it was held by Sir R. T. Kindersley, V. C.,
that the land was converted out and out, and that the share of a deceased partner in part of the unrealized real estate passed to his personal representatives. " I can have no difficulty," said his Honor, " in
coming to the conclusion, that whenever a partnership purchase real estate for the partnership purposes, and with the partnership funds, it is
as between the real and personal representatives of the partners personal estate. Now this is not the ordinary case, where persons carrying on the ordinary business of a commercial or manufacturing partnership have found it necessary to purchase real estate for partnership
purposes. That is not the case; here they bought land as stock in
trade, by the sale of which they were to make their profits;—the land
was not in the nature of plant, but was the very subject matter of their
trade. Does that make any difference? If it does, I think it is in
favour of treating it as converted; because the real estate is here clearly
put in the same position as ordinary stock in trade; and it appears to
me, that if I entertained more doubt than I do on the general question,
that doubt would in this case be very much diminished by the circumstance, that here the real estate is itself bought for the very purpose of
selling it again. The very intention of the partnership was to buy land
to re-sell it. That is their very contract; and, without selling the land
again there would be no partnership business,—the partnership was for
the purpose of buying land, to parcel it out in plots, and to sell them
again; and each partner had a right to say he would have that contract
carried out. We have here what Lord Thurlow wanted in *Thornton* v.
Dixon, (3 Bro. C. C. 199)—an actual contract that the land shall be
sold."

Where, as in the principal case, lands are held for partnership purposes, that is to say, for employment for some purposes which may produce a return in the shape of profits, so as to add to its value, the joint
property will be liable to repay the advances of the various partners
before any division can take place (21 Beav. 536); but this is not the
case where persons are mere joint owners of lands. Thus, in *Kay* v.
Johnston, 21 Beav. 536, the plaintiff and defendant were joint owners
of a house, and the *defendant had laid out, in improving and
decorating it, moneys he had obtained from the plaintiff, it was
held by Sir J. Romilly, M. R., that the plaintiff, in the absence of contract, had no lien on the share of the defendant in the house for the
amount so laid out.

[*202]

" There certainly are cases in
which equity will consider joint
tenants as tenants in common;
and one of those cases is, where a
purchase of land is made by two
persons, with a view to expending

large sums of money in the improvement of it;" per Tilghman, C. J., in *Duncan* v. *Forrer*, 6 Binney, 193, 196. See *Mayburry* v. *Brien et al.*, 15 Peters, 21, 36. In a case, in Pennsylvania, of a title under warrant and survey, where the purchase-money had been paid in equal portions by two persons, it was decided that the interest was not joint, but in common, chiefly upon the ground that the estate was not a complete legal one, but was only an inchoate interest, in the nature of an equitable estate. " If a patent had been issued to the two persons," said Tilghman, C. J., " I incline to think, that the circumstance of their having paid the purchase-money equally, would not have been sufficient to render the estate a tenancy in common in equity. Such is the opinion of Lord Hardwicke in [*Rigden* v. *Vallier*,] 3 Atk. 735, although the contrary seems to have been taken for granted, in the argument of counsel, in 1 Vern. 361. But there are cases, where in equity, an estate will be considered as in common, although at law it is a joint tenancy. In such cases, courts of equity proceed on the intention of the parties deduced from the nature of the transaction : as where several persons engage in an enterprise, which requires large advances besides the original purchase-money, the draining of marshes, for instance, or the erection of mills or manufactories. The case of *Lake* v. *Craddock et al.*, 3 P. Wms. 158, was a purchase of lands overflowed

with water, for the purpose of reclaiming them. This was considered as a tenancy in common, although the legal transfer was in joint tenancy. So if two advance money on a mortgage, though the estate is conveyed jointly, it shall be a tenancy in common." *Caines* v. *Lessee of Grant*, 5 Binney, 119, 120. See *Cuyler and others* v. *Bradt and others*, 2 Caines' Cases, 326; *Currie, &c.* v. *Tibb's Heirs*, 5 Monroe, 440, 443; *Overton* v. *Lacy, &c.*, 6 Id. 13, 15.

In regard to the case discussed in the preceding note, where a mortgage is made to two jointly as security for money advanced by both, there is a difference among the authorities in this country. In Massachusetts, although a statute provides that all conveyances to two or more grantees shall create a tenancy in common, unless an opposite intent be apparent, it is yet settled that a conveyance by mortgage to two persons in fee, to secure a joint debt, makes a joint tenancy, before foreclosure; upon the ground that as the remedy to recover the debt would survive upon the death of either, the intent of the parties must be that the collateral security of the mortgage should comport with the remedy by action, and therefore should survive; *Appleton* v. *Boyd*, 7 Massachusetts, 131, 134; but after foreclosure it becomes a tenancy in common in the land; *Woodwin* v. *Richardson*, *Adm.*, 11 Id. 469. And the decision in *Appleton* v. *Boyd*, has been followed in Maine; *Kinsley*

v. *Abbott*, 19 Maine, 430, 434; where it is spoken of as convenient, and as affording the most simple remedies with the least liability to inconvenience and loss. Under a similar statute of Rhode Island, however, this construction was disapproved of in the Circuit Court, and it was held that the tenancy was in common, and that upon the death of one, the legal title to a moiety of the estate vested in his heirs, though as a security, the benefit of it followed the debt; *Randall* v. *Phillips et al.*, 3 Mason, 378, 384.

[The question when and under what circumstances real estate shall be considered as partnership property, has been the subject of much discussion in this country, and the cases as a whole amply show, that land bought with the assets and for the purposes of a partnership, is partnership property in equity, although the deed is taken in the name of the partners as tenants in common, or of one partner only, and without anything on its face to show the existence or right of the firm; *Jarvis* v. *Brooks*, 7 Foster, 37; *Matlock* v. *Matlock*, 5 Indiana, 403; *Burnside* v. *Merrick*, 4 Metcalf, 537; *The Fall River Whaling Co.* v. *Borden*, 10 Cushing, 458; *Champlin* v. *Tillinghast*, 4 Rhode Island, 173, 208; *Jones* v. *Neale*, 2 Patton & Heath, 339; *Willis* v. *Freeman*, 35 Vermont, 44; *Dewey* v. *Dewey*, Ib. 555; *The Fall River Co.* v. *Borden*, 10 Cushing, 458; *Crooker* v. *Crooker*, 46 Maine, 250, 260; *Matlack* v. *James*, 2 Beasley, 126; *Peck* v. *Fisher*, 7 Cushing, 386; *Ludlow* v. *Cooper*, 4 Ohio, N. S. 1; *Moreau* v. *Saffaran*, 3 Sneed, 595; see 1 Am. Leading Cases, 595, 602, 5th Amer. ed. It is therefore subject to the equities of the partners as such, and of those claiming under them as creditors and purchasers, and the partnership debts, must consequently be satisfied, before any portion of the fund is applied to the separate debts of the partners; *Brooker* v. *Brooker*, 46 Maine, 250; *Buffum* v. *Buffum*, 49 Id. 108; *Matlack* v. *James*, 2 Beasley, 126; *Abbott's Appeal*, 14 Wright, 284; *Overholt's Appeal*, 2 Jones, 222; *Fowler* v. *Bailey*, 14 Wisconsin, 125; *The Bank* v. *Sprague*, 5 C. E. Greene, 13; *Robertson* v. *Baker*, 11 Florida, 19; *The Fall River Whaling Co.* v. *Borden*, 11 Cushing, 458. Hence, a judgment against one of the members of a firm, will be postponed to a subsequent mortgage by the partnership; *The Lancaster Bank* v. *Miley*, 1 Harris, 544, while a similar preference will be given to an execution issued for a demand against the firm, over a prior writ for the separate debt. of a partner; *Jarvis* v. *Brooks;* *Peck* v. *Fisher;* *Rice* v. *Barnard*, 20 Vermont, 479; *Brooker* v. *Brooker*, 46 Maine, 250, 260; although the lien of a separate creditor will extend as far as the interest of the debtor, and cannot, as it would seem, be a nullity, unless the latter is in debt to the firm, or the assets of the firm are not more than adequate to the satisfaction of the joint creditors; see *post*, vol. 2, notes to *Silk* v. *Prime*.

The principle applies *a fortiori*

to those claiming under the partners as volunteers, and the widow, heirs and devisees of a deceased partner consequently hold in trust for the payment of the partnership debts, and cannot have any beneficial interest until these are paid in full, and the equities of the partners adjusted among themselves: *Dyer* v. *Clark*, 5 Metcalf, 562; *Nicoll* v. *Ogden*, 29 Illinois, 323; *Uhler* v. *Semple*, 5 C. E. Greene, 288.

The right thus acquired by the partnership is, however, a mere equity, and will consequently be discharged by a transfer of the legal title to a purchaser for value, and without notice; *M'Dermot* v. *Lawrence*, 7 S. & R. 438; *Haile* v. *Henrie*, 2 Watts, 143; *Ridgway's Appeal*, 3 Harris, 177; *Coder* v. *Huling*, 3 Casey, 84; *Arnold* v. *Wainwright*, 6 Minnesota, 358; *Buchan* v. *Sumner*, 2 Barbour, Ch. 198; *Hale* v. *Plummer*, 6 Indiana, 121: *Tillinghast* v. *Champlin*, 4 Rhode Island, 173, 209; although notice will be implied in this as in other cases, if the circumstances are such as to justify the presumption that the purchaser either knew, or was wilfully ignorant; *Tillinghast* v. *Champlin*, 4 Rhode Island, 173, 209; *Jones* v. *Neale*, see *post*, vol. 2, note to *Le Neve* v. *Le Neve.* Some of the cases go further, and hold that the equity of the partners cannot be set up or enforced by or on behalf of the joint, against the separate creditors, unless the latter are shown to have had notice of its existence at or before the time when the debts came into ex-

istence; *Haile* v. *Henrie*; *Ridgway's Appeal*; but this would seem more questionable, and is contrary to the general rule that creditors are subject to all the equities of their debtors, and can take no right which the latter could not have enforced for their own benefit; *post*, vol. 2, notes to *Bassett* v. *Nosworthy.*

In *Crooker* v. *Crooker*, 46 Maine, 250, 263, the partnership creditors accordingly obtained a preference over a prior lien arising out of an attachment for the private debt of one of the partners, notwithstanding the objection that there was nothing on the face of the deed to indicate the equity of the firm, or that the partners were not tenants in common. The law was held the same way in *Matlack* v. *James*, 2 Beasley, 126, and a conveyance in consideration of a separate debt, postponed to a judgment against the firm.

A trust for the firm may, as it seems, arise out of, or be fastened upon a conveyance of land to one or more of the partners, in the absence of written evidence, on proof that the consideration moved from the partnership, or consisted of their funds or property, as in other cases where a purchase is made by one man, with the money of another; *Buchan* v. *Sumner*, 2 Barb. Ch. 165; *Columb* v. *Read*, 24 New York, 505; *post*, note to *Dyer* v. *Dyer*; or by a declaration or admission in writing, signed by the party to be charged; *Tillinghast* v. *Champlin*, 4 Rhode Island, 173, 209; *Delmonico* v. *Guillaume*, 2 Sandford's Ch. 366; *Philips* v.

Cramond, 2 W. C. C. R. 441; *The Fall River Whaling Co.* v. *Borden; Buchan* v. *Sumner; Jarvis* v. *Brooks*, 7 Foster, 37; but cannot, apparently grow out of an oral agreement, without facts and circumstances of a nature to satisfy the Statute of Frauds, which requires a writing where real estate ·is in question. When, moreover, the trust is sought to be deduced from the nature of the assets which formed the consideration for the purchase, it will be open to the whole range of parol evidence, and may be rebutted by every species of proof tending legitimately to show, that the equity is consistent with or should be subordinated to the legal title; *Phillips* v. *Cramond*, 1 American Leading Cases, 496, 4th ed. (See *Haile* v. *Henrie*, 2 Watts, 143, which restricts, and *Dale* v. *Hamilton*, 5 Hare, 369, *ante*, which goes as far the other way in extending, the right to raise a trust for the partnership by parol evidence.)

There can be little doubt that the purchase of land by a partner in his own name with the money of the firm, without the knowledge or consent of his co-partners, will give rise to a trust for the partnership as distinguished from the partners; *Phillips* v. *Cramond*, 2 W. C. C. R. 441, 445; *Lacey* v. *Hall*, 1 Wright, 360, 365; although a different view was taken in *Krug* v. *Hamilton*, 16 Illinois, 190. The trust in such cases arises from the fraud, and is constructive rather than resulting; *Lacey* v. *Hall*.

In *Danvers* v. *Smith*, 5 Sandford, 669, where a co-partnership

erected buildings and made other improvements on the land of one of the partners, it was held that a trust arose for the firm and it is clear that money so laid out may give birth to a lien, which equity will enforce; *Averill* v. *Loucks*, 6 Barb. 19; *Kendall* v. *Rider*, 35 Id. 100; *Lane* v. *Tyler*, 49 Maine, 252.

There can be little doubt that the purchase of land by the partners, for the purposes of the partnership, and subject to an express or implied agreement that it shall be held for the benefit of the firm, will render it partnership property, although the whole of the consideration is furnished by the partners individually, and no part of it comes from the assets of the partnership; *Roberts* v. *M'Carty*, 9 Indiana, 16, and the weight of authority in England seemingly is, that the investment of the funds of a firm in land, with their consent and approbation, will not render it partnership property, unless the purchase is made for partnership purposes, and will simply give rise to a resulting trust, for the partners individually, under which they will *prima facie*, take equal shares or moieties, unless shown to have been unequally interested in the consideration; *Coder* v. *Huling*, 3 Casey, 84; *Cox* v. *McBurney*, 2 Sandford, 561.

In New York, on the other hand, land bought with the assets of the partnership, or taken in payment of a partnership debt, belongs *prima facie* to the firm. *Buchan* v. *Sumner*, 2 Barb. Ch. 65; *Columb* v. *Read*, 24 New York, 505; although the presumption may be rebutted by parol; *post*, notes to *Dyer* v. *Dyer*. If the object of the parties is to withdraw so much capital from the firm, and distribute it as land among the partners, there will be no trust, and as this is a question of intention, recourse may be had to the partnership books, and the cotemporaneous declarations of the partners as a means of ascertaining their design; *Columb* v. *Read; Burd* v. *Morrison*, 12 Wisconsin, 138.

The courts of Pennsylvania hold, in conformity with the general course of decision, that where the partnership assets are surreptitiously invested in the purchase of real estate, a trust will arise for the firm: *Lacy* v. *Hall*, 1 Wright, 360; *Erwin's Appeal*, 3 Id. 535. The trust may, as Mr. Justice Strong remarked, in *Lacy* v. *Hall*, be regarded as resulting from the consideration, or as implied from the confidential relation existing between the parties.

A conveyance to the partners as individuals, or to one or more of them, with the knowledge and consent of the rest, will not, however, give rise to a trust for the firm, although the purchase is made with the money of the partnership, and with a view to the prosecution of its business, because the presumption arising from the nature of the consideration is rebutted by the form of the instrument, which indicates that the grantees are to take and hold as tenants in common: *Hale* v. *Henrie*, 2 Watts, 143; *Ridgway's Appeal*, 3 Harris, 177; *M'Dermott* v. *Lawrence*, 7

VOL. I.—19

S. & R. 438; *Lefevre's Appeal*, 19 P. F. Smith, 122.

Although such is the rule in Pennsylvania as it regards lien creditors and purchasers, it has, notwithstanding, been held that land bought with partnership assets, and for the purposes of the firm, is partnership property as between the parties, and must be so treated when the rights of strangers do not intervene: *Abbott's Appeal*, 14 Wright, 234. In *Abbott's Appeal*, the question arose between surviving members of an insolvent firm and the representatives of a deceased partner, and the latter were held to be entitled to the proceeds of the land, although 'it had been conveyed to the partners individually as tenants in common.

If this equity exists between the partners, it should be enforced against those claiming under them as creditors, and purchasers with notice, because the right of a creditor does not ordinarily transcend that of the debtor. In *Overholt's Appeal*, 2 Jones, 212, a judgment for a debt due by the firm was accordingly said to have priority over judgments for the debts of the partners individually, and the cases of *Abbott's Appeal*, 14 Wright, 234, and *Erwin's Appeal*, 3 Wright 535, point in the same direction. But these decisions were virtually overruled in *Lefevre's Appeal*, 19 P. F. Smith, 122, and *Ebbert's Appeal*, 20 Id. 79, which establish in accordance, in *M'Daraugh* v. *Lawrence*, 7 S. & R. 438, and *Hale* v. *Henrie*, that where the rights of third persons are involved, the court will not go beyond the legal title for the sake of giving effect to a doubtful equity. The rule as now settled in Pennsylvania, is that as between the partners themselves, a resulting trust may be inferred for the firm, and the land treated as partnership property, where it is clearly shown that they so regarded it, and that it was paid for with the money of the partnership; but that such a trust cannot be set up against creditors and purchasers where the title is taken and held by the partners in their individual capacity as tenants in common: *Ebert's Appeal*, 20 P. F. Smith, 79, 81.

Whatever difficulty may exist under other circumstances, it is clear, that unless the trust is established by written evidence, it must be cotemporaneous with the acquisition of the legal title. An oral agreement to bring land into a firm, or to share it with an incoming partner, is invalid under the Statute of Frauds, notwithstanding the payment of the consideration. The subject was carefully considered in *M'Cormick's Appeal*, 7 P. F. Smith, 54. Strong, J., said: "The land originally belonged to Martin Billmyer. In January, 1854, he ' agreed to sell one undivided half to Jacob M. and W. H. Follmer, for the sum of $6,700; and the three agree to become partners in the lumber business, and in the property. It was agreed, that of the purchase money, $2,000 should be paid in cash, and the balance out of the profits of the business.' The agreement was not in writing. On the 20th of February follow-

ing, the Follmers paid $2,000, to be credited as part payment on the property. The balance does not appear ever to have been paid. In the spring of that year, precisely at what date is not shown, they went into possession with Billmyer, and the three continued the lumbering business in the firm name of Billmyer, Follmer, & Co. Afterwards the firm built a saw mill on the tract with partnership funds, and made other improvements. These are the facts substantially as found, quite as strongly stated as they were proved by Chamberlain, the witness. Do they show a divesture of the title of Martin Billmyer, and an effective transfer of it to the firm of Billmyer, Follmer & Co.? And do they show such a transfer before the lien of the judgments of Porter, for the use of McCormick, the appellant attached?—These judgments were recovered on the 29th day of March, 1854.—Most clearly they do not. The contract to sell the land or to put it into the partnership stock, is as much within the operation of the Statute of Frauds as any other parol contract of sale would have been. If the title passed out of Billmyer, when was it? Not when the parol agreement was made, in the winter of 1854; nor when the $2,000 were paid on account, February 20th, 1854. This is not claimed. It must have been then in the spring, when the Follmers went into possession jointly with Billmyer. But that such a taking possession does not withdraw a parol contract from the operation of the Statute of

Frauds, is too clearly settled to admit of denial. The possession taken under such a contract must not only be notorious and distinct, but it must be exclusive of the vendor. Receiving a parol vendee into joint possession with his vendor, is not equivalent to the ancient feudal investiture, for which the Statute of Frauds intended to declare a writing should be the only substitute. The notoriety and significance of an entry into common possession, is much less than when an owner leaves, and another person takes the sole and exclusive enjoyment. Hence, it has been held, that a tenant in common in possession, cannot pass his title to his co-tenant in possession by parol, because there cannot be in such a case that distinct transfer of possession which equity regards equivalent to a written contract: *Hill* v. *Meyers*, 7 Wright, 170 ; *Workman* v. *Guthrie*, 5 Casey, 495. In *Frye* v. *Shepler*, 7 Barr, 91, it was said that "to constitute a valid parol sale under the Statute of Frauds, the possession must be exclusive of the donor." The same doctrine was asserted in *Haslet* v. *Haslet*, 6 Watts, 464 ; so, also, in *Chadwick* v. *Felt*, 11 Casey, 305. There is in the present case an additional reason for holding that the entry of the Follmers into joint possession with Billmyer did not take their purchase out of the Statute of Frauds. It is found in the fact that they became partners with him to prosecute the lumbering business. This business was to be conducted on the property. There was, there-

fore, a reason for their entry apart from any purchase. To the neighborhood the partnership was quite sufficient to account for the possession. The Court below thought these doctrines were inapplicable to the case, because there was no tenancy in common here. But the mischief against which the statute was designed as a guard, is greater in cases of parol transfers to partnerships than in any other cases."

"In *Hale* v. *Henrie*, 2 Watts, 143, Judge Sergeant expressed the opinion, that "when partners intend to bring real estate into the partnership stock, their intention must be manifested by deed or writing placed on record, that purchasers and creditors may not be deceived." He added, "that to permit a person, apparently owning property as an individual, to aver a different right in himself as a partner, by which his relation to creditors and others would be affected, would defeat the Statute of Frauds and Perjuries, by which no interests in real estate can vest, or be transferred without deed or writing." And in *Ridgway, Budd & Co.'s Appeal*, 3 Harris, 177, it was said, that "when partners intend to bring real estate into partnership, their intention must be manifested by deed or writing placed on record ; and it is not competent to show by parol evidence, that real estate, conveyed to two persons as tenants in common, was purchased and paid for by partners, and was partnership property." See, also, *Lancaster Bank* v. *Myley*, 1 Harris, 544. From these cases, it appears that proof by writing, and even record, is more rigidly required in conveyances to partnerships than in other sales."

"Undoubtedly a partnership may hold real estate, and they may have a resulting trust, where the partnership funds have paid for land. Such was the case of *Erwin's Appeal*, 3 Wright, 535. So, there may be a constructive trust in favor of a firm, as was held in *Lacey* v. *Hall*, 1 Wright, 360; but these come within the exceptions to the Statute of Frauds. In both these cases the lands were acquired after the partnerships had been formed, and while the joint business was in progress. But there is no resulting or constructive trust. The agreement, if there was any, to put the land into the joint stock, was made before the firm had any being, and the partnership funds did not pay for it. A parol agreement to put land into a firm, or to consider it as firm property, made before the firm exists, is wholly ineffectual to pass any title either in law or in equity."

The weight of authority seems to be in accordance with this decision, that the mere circumstance that the parties to such a transaction are partners, will not dispense with the necessity for written evidence, or take the case out of the Statute of Frauds; *Bird* v. *Morrison*, 12 Wisconsin, 138. The agreement need not, however, be reduced to writing, and may be collected from the books or letters of the firm, or of the partner whom it is sought to charge.

Although this appears to be the better view of the law, it is embarrassed with some practical difficulties, which the opposite theory avoids. A., B. & C. enter into a partnership on equal terms. Land is purchased with the assets of the firm and for its use. An arrangement is subsequently effected, under which A. is paid in full, and withdraws, but without signing any writing that will satisfy the requisitions of the statute of frauds. C. subsequently becomes a member of the firm. Does the ownership of the land vary with these changes? If it does not, the intention of the parties fails of effect; if it does, the trust is an implied or constructive, and not a resulting trust, because a resulting trust must be contemporaneous with the transfer or acquisition of the legal title; *M'Cormick's Appeal*, 7 P. F. Smith; *post*, notes to *Dyer* v. *Dyer*. See *Shearer* v. *Shearer*, 98 Mass. 107, 111; *Erwin's Appeal*, 1 Wright, 360, 365.

The better opinion would seem to be, that land does not lose the character of realty, or acquire that of personalty, by the mere fact of becoming partnership property; and that it still remains land, although charged with an equitable lien for the payment of the partnership debts, and the balance of the accounts between the partners; *Tillinghast* v. *Champlin*, 4 Rhode Island, 173, 207; *Dyer* v. *Clark*, 5 Metcalf, 580; *Buchan* v. *Sumner*, 2 Barb. Ch. 168, 201; *Buckley* v. *Buckley*, 11 Barbour, 43, 74; *Lacy* v. *Waring*, 25 Alabama, 625; 1 American Leading Cases, 608, 5th ed.; unless there is an agreement actually made between the partners, or implied from the nature of the partnership, that it shall be sold and distributed as money, when a conversion will result as in other cases, where such an agreement is entered into by persons competent to make it; *Kramer* v. *Arthur*, 7 Barr, 165; *post*, notes to *Fletcher* v. *Ashburner*. Dicta may be found the other way, and to the point that real estate owned by a partnership, is viewed by equity as personal property for all purposes, unless the rights of *bona fide* purchasers are in question; *Roberts* v. *M'Carty*, 9 Indiana, 16; *Coderwell* v. *Mullison*, 9 Harris, 257; *The Lancaster Bank* v. *Miley*, 1 Id. 544; *Pierce* v. *Trigg*, 10 Leigh, 406, 424; *Buchan* v. *Sumner; Collumb* v. *Read; Lawrence* v. *Taylor*, 5 Hill, 107, 111; *Black* v. *Black*, 15 Georgia, 445, and *Hoxie* v. *Barr*, 1 Sumner; but the point was not actually presented in these cases; and it would seem more reasonable to hold, with the Supreme Court of Massachusetts in *Dyer* v. *Dyer*, 5 Metcalf, 580, and with the High Court of Appeals of Maryland in *Goodburn* v. *Stevens*, 1 Md. Ch. 420; 5 Gill, 127; that land does not necessarily cease to be a corporeal hereditament, by being charged with a trust for the payment of the debts, and rendered subservient to the other purposes of a partnership, and that any portion of it which remains after such a trust is satisfied, will, in analogy to the rule laid down in *Ackroyd* v. *Smithson, post*, descend to heirs, and be subject to

the other incidents of realty, instead of vesting in the representatives of the parties as personalty; *Galbraith* v. *Gedge*, 16 B. Monroe, 631; *M'Cullough* v. *Somerville*, 8 Leigh, 415; *Hall* v. *Plummer*, 6 Indiana, 621; *Green* v. *Graham*, 5 Ohio, 163. Equity should, as it would seem under these circumstances, follow the law, except in so far as it may be necessary to depart from it, and leave the legal title free to follow the path which the law has marked out; unless a different course is requisite to protect the equities of the partners; *Lacy* v. *Waring*, 25 Alabama, 625. And the safer ground on which to put the case of *The Lancaster Bank* v. *Miley*, seem to be, that an execution for a liability of the firm is equally entitled to priority over an antecedent lien for the separate debt of one of the partners, whether real or personal estate is in question; *Buchan* v. *Sumner*, 2 Barbour's Ch. 178: a position which is undeniable when the partnership is insolvent, and which would appear to be thought applicable, in many of the States of this country, to solvent firms, *post*, vol. 2, note to *Silk* v. *Prime*. It was accordingly held in *Hale* v. *Plummer; Galbraith* v. *Gedge*, 16 B. Monroe, 631, and *Goodburn* v. *Stevens*, 1 Maryland Ch. 420, that land bought or held as partnership property, is subject to the dower of the widow of a deceased partner, unless it has been stamped with the character of personalty for all purposes, by an express or implied agreement, although her right is subordinate to the lien of the debts of the firm, and the state of the accounts between the individual partners. Hence, she will be precluded if the partnership is insolvent, and cannot recover until its solvency has been ascertained; *Goodburn* v. *Stevens;* while in *Goodburn* v. *Stevens*, the court went still further by denying her a proportionate share of the arrears of rent and profits, which had accrued while the sufficiency of the assets was under investigation. "It may be answered," said Gookins, J., in delivering the opinion of the court in *Hall* v. *Plummer*, "that the widow of a deceased partner is not entitled to dower in real estate, held for partnership purposes. It is true that real estate may be so held for partnership purposes as to exclude the widow's right of dower; but we think it may also be so held as not to exclude it. Mr. Story says, that 'so far as the partners and their creditors are concerned, real estate belonging to the partnership is, in equity, treated as mere personalty, and governed by the general doctrines of the latter. And so it will be deemed, in equity, to all intents and purposes, if the partners themselves have, by their agreement or otherwise, purposely impressed upon it the character of personalty;' Story on Partnership, s. 93. In the absence of any such agreement or act, the same writer says, 'there is a great diversity of judicial opinion, and of judicial decision, as to whether it is to be treated as real or personal property.' Upon looking into the authorities, English and American, it is quite evident that the effort to reconcile them would be a hopeless task, and we are left to adopt what seems to us the more reasonable rule upon the subject. In a late decision, in New York, Chancellor Walworth uses the following language: 'The American decisions in relation to real estate purchased with partnership funds, or for the use of the firm, are various and conflicting. But I think they may generally be considered as establishing these two principles. First, That such real estate is in equity chargeable with the debts of the co-partnership, and with any balance that may be due from one co-partner to another, upon the winding up of the affairs of the firm. Secondly, That as between the personal representatives and the heirs at law of the deceased partner, his share of the surplus of the real estate of the co-partnership, which remains after paying the debts of the co-partnership, and adjusting all the equitable claims of the different members of the firm, as between themselves, is to be considered and treated as real estate; *Buchan* v. *Sumner*, 2 Barb. Ch. R. 165. See also *Buckley* v. *Buckley*, 11 Barb. S. C. R. 44.

"The High Court of Chancery, in Maryland, has adopted the rule, as indicated by Judge Story, in the section quoted from his work on partnership. That court decided in the case of *Goodburn* v. *Stevens*, that real estate of a partnership, though regarded in a court of equity as personal estate for all partnership purposes, yet, in the absence of an express or implied agreement, indicating an intention to convert it into personal estate, it will, when the claims of the partnership have been satisfied and the partnership accounts adjusted, be treated in a court of equity as at law, as real estate, and be subject to the dower of a deceased partner; 1 Maryland Ch. Decisions, 420."

The principle is the same where a husband asserts his right as tenant by the curtesy to land held by his deceased wife as a co-partner; *Buckley* v. *Buckley*, 11 Barb. 43.

The main current of decision in the United States is in accordance with these authorities. Thus it has been held in Massachusetts that the purchase of land with partnership assets, and for the use of the firm, does not convert it into personalty. It will, therefore, descend to the heirs of a deceased partner, instead of being distributed among his next of kin or legatees; *Wilson* v. *Wilcox*, 13 Allen, 253; *Shearer* v. *Shearer*, 98 Mass. 107. It is subject to the lien of the partnership debts, and the advances made by the partners to the firm, but in all else it obeys the ordinary rule, that a trust arising from the conversion of money into land, is real estate. The same doctrine prevails in Alabama, 625, and in New York, *Buckley* v. *Buckley*, 11 Barb.; and, as it would seem, in Pennsylvania, even when the deed recites that the premises are to be held for the use and as the property of the firm; *Wood* v. *Witherow*, 8 Philada. 517.

The subject was elaborately examined in *Shearer* v. *Shearer*, where Wells, J., held the following language in delivering judgment: " The real estate of a firm is to be converted into personalty, only when such conversion is required for the payment of claims against which are in the nature of debt. Balances due to individual partners come within this definition. So also may capital, furnished by one partner, when by the terms upon which it was furnished, or from the nature and necessity of the case, it is to be repaid in specific amounts, in order to reach the net result, or body of the partnership interests, to which the proportional rights or shares of the several partners attach. In short, whatever is required to be paid or measured in precise sums must be so adjusted; and real estate, converted for that purpose, undoubtedly becomes personalty, and is to be distributed as such when paid over to the party entitled. But the shares in the body of the partnership, those interests which are not measured by precise amounts, but consist in a common proprietorship after all special claims are satisfied, stand upon different footing. These interests are determined by the proportions fixed by the articles or organic law of the partnership. When the beneficial interests and the legal title correspond, it has already been decided that the rights of the partners in real estate, so held, will be left to adjust themselves by the descent of the legal title, with its incidents, as real estate of the several partners, held in common; *Wilcox* v. *Wilcox*, *ubi supra*. When the legal title is otherwise held, it is held in trust; and the equitable title descends in like manner and with like incidents, except as to dower. The office of equity in such case is merely to declare the trusts, and compel the legal title to serve the equitable interests. This is accomplished by directing such conveyances, as will make the legal title of the several parties conform to their respective beneficial interests. By the rule above indicated, all partnership rights and obligations are secured, and all equities growing out of that relation are met and answered. To require equitable interference to go further, and convert all real estate into personalty, for the mere purpose of a division, seems to us to be an unnecessary invasion of the right of the co-partners, and when undertaken in the interests of one class of the representatives of a deceased partner, against another class of representatives of the same partner, it seems to be a departure from the legitimate sphere of equitable jurisdiction. It is not the province of equity to seek to counteract or modify the operation of the laws of descent and distribution.

There are no equities between heirs and distributees, under our laws, which can call into exercise or quicken the powers of the court, for the conversion of realty into personalty. We do not understand that, in the English courts, any such supposed equities have ever been made a ground for the doctrine of equitable conversion, as held there. In the case of *Cookson* v. *Cookson*, 8 Sim. 529, such a ground of interference was emphatically discarded. That case, however, is not one in which the full extent of the English doctrine was asserted. Conversion into personalty is not necessary to enable creditors of the individual partner to secure payment of their debts out of the share of their debtor in real estate held in co-partnership. By our laws, all property of a debtor, whether personal or real, is liable for payment of all his debts. Creditors, therefore, require no equitable interposition, except such as may be necessary for the assertion of the rights of the partner himself. Their rights are secured, in respect to real estate held in copartnership, through the equities which pertain to their debtor. In this particular the laws of England differ. The inheritance there being exempt from liability for debts by simple contract, it is only by conversion and payment of the proceeds to the personal representatives of a deceased partner, that his private creditors can receive payment out of such property. How far, if at all, this consideration may have been influential in determining the extent to which the doctrine of equitable conversion should be carried, and in establishing the right of the personal representative to require it to be made in his favor, we are unable to judge. The cases in which the personal representative of a deceased partner has been held entitled to enforce this right against the heir, do not indicate, so far as we have been able to examine them, whether it is done in behalf of creditors or of distributees. The doctrine, however, seems now to be fully established, without regard to the consideration whether there are private creditors or not; *Darby* v. *Darby*, 3 Drewry, 495. This may, perhaps, be regarded as the most natural result of the rule holding such property liable for the payment of all partnership obligations, when it is considered how far that liability deprived partnership real estate of the fixedness and permanency of ownership, which characterize the inheritance in realty there."

It is entirely consistent with these principles, that land purchased with an expressed or implied agreement in writing, or appearing from facts and circumstances, that it shall be sold, and the proceeds divided among the parties, should be the subject of an equitable conversion, entitling the administrators of a deceased partner as against his heirs; *Kramer* v. *Arthur*, 7 Barr, 165; *Nicoll* v. *Ogden*, 29 Illinois, 323; *Claggett* v. *Kilbourne*, 1 Black, 346. But this rule should be applied with caution, as tending to frustrate the intention of the deceased, unless he is cognizant of its existence. See *Nicoll* v. *Ogden*. There is no doubt, said Tilghman, Ch. J., in *M'Dermott* v. *Lawrence*, 7 S. & R. 491, " that by the agreement of the parties, land may be brought into the stock and considered as personal property, so far as it concerns the parties themselves, and

their heirs and personal representatives," and similar language was held in *Abbott's Appeal*, 14 Wright, 234, 238.

The question whether the real estate of a firm is personal property, does not arise unless the partnership is solvent, because all the authorities agree that if it be not, there is an undoubted equity to have the land applied to the payment of the partnership debts, and of the advances made by the members of the firm on partnership account, which is all that the authorities in the United States establish, when regarded as a whole. On the dissolution of an insolvent firm by death, the duty of working out this equity devolves on the surviving partners, who may consequently effect a sale of the real estate of the partnership, and file a bill against the heirs of the deceased partner, to compel a conveyance of the legal title; *Delmonico* v. *Guillaume*, 2 Sandford, Ch. 366; *Abbott's Appeal*, 14 Wright, 234; *Depuy* v. *Levenworth*, 17 California, 262; *Andrew* v. *Brown*, 21 Alabama, 437.

Another reason for not regarding the conversion as absolute is, that while the personal property of a partnership is subject to the control of each of its members, and a *bona fide* purchaser from one of the partners will have as good a title as if he had bought from the firm, its real estate is governed by different principles, and cannot be sold without the concurrence of all the members of the partnership; *Galbraith* v. *Gedge*, 16 B. Monroe, 631; *Ruffin*

v. *M'Connell*, 17 Illinois, 212, 217 ; *Arnold* v. *Stevenson*, 2 Nevada, 234; Story on Partnership, sect. 94 : a sale by one partner to a purchaser with notice, passing, as it would seem, nothing more than his interest as an individual, subject to the debts of the firm, and to an account with his co-partners, even when professing to be made for partnership purposes, and to be of the whole interest of the firm ; *Anderson* v. *Tompkins*, 1 Brockenbrough, 457 ; *Tapley* v. *Butterfield*, 1 Metcalf, 513 ; *Dyer* v. *Clark*, 5 Id. 580 ; *Tillinghast* v. *Champlin*, 4 Rhode Island, 173, 219 ; 1 Am. Lead. Cases, 609, 5th ed. *Jones* v. *Neale*, 2 Patton & Heath, 339, 352. He should, therefore, confine himself to selling that which he is really entitled to dispose of ; and an attempt on his part to use the legal title, as a means of transferring any greater interest, to the prejudice of his co-partners and the joint creditors of the firm, will be presumptive evidence, of fraud on his part, and of collusion on that of the purchaser if the latter is aware of the equity, which will vitiate the sale and prevent it from operating as a purchase for value and without notice, and thus barring the equity of the other partners ; *Hoxie* v. *Carr*, 1 Sumner, 193. The death of the other members of the firm will, however, as it would seem, invest the surviving partner with the absolute control, both of the real and personal property of the partnership, for the purpose of winding up its affairs and distributing the proceeds among all

concerned ; *Andrews* v. *Brown*, 21 Alabama, 437 ; and enable him to confer a good title on a purchaser, free from all liability, on the part of the latter, for the application of the purchase money ; *Tillinghast* v. *Champlin*, 4 Rhode Island, 173, 219. But as the power thus acquired, is in strict subordination to the trust for the partnership, it must be exercised in the way best calculated to obtain the full value of the property. Hence, the estate must be sold as a whole, and not in separate shares or moieties, and a surviving partner cannot sell or convey his legal right to the land as a tenant in common, without committing a fraud which will attach to, and invalidate the title of a purchaser with notice ; *Tillinghast* v. *Champlin*, 4 Rhode Island, 173, 219 ; *Lacy* v. *Waring*, 25 Alabama, 625 ; *ante*, note to *Elliot* v. *Merryman*. And in *Galbraith* v. *Gedge*, 16 B. Monroe, 631, 633, the right of a sole surviving partner to sell of his own motion, was denied, and the proper course said to be to procure the concurrence of the heirs of the deceased members of the firm, either *in pais*, or by a resort to the aid of equity.

In *Lawrence* v. *Taylor*, 5 Hill, 107, the court held that although an authority to convey land must be in writing under the statute of frauds, the rule was otherwise with regard to a contract to convey. In the latter case, the agent might be appointed by parol, or the existence of the authority deduced from the acts of the principal. A ratification would, moreover, relate back, and be equivalent to a command. If the principal adopted the act, though merely by silence or acquiescence, he would be bound. A recovery was accordingly had against the firm for money which had been paid to one of the partners, under a contract with him for the purchase of the real estate of the partnership, on proof that the title was defective, and that the other partners had said in the hearing of three persons, that they had an interest in the contract.

It has been decided in some instances that if a deed by one of several partners is sanctioned by the rest, it is immaterial whether their consent is given orally or in writing; *Gibson* v. *Warden*, 14 Wallace, 244; *Haynes* v. *Seechrist*, 13 Illinois, 496; *Wilson* v. *Hunter*, 14 Wisconsin, 173. In *Hunter* v. *Wilson*, a mortgage by a partner, acknowledged by him as his act and deed on behalf of the firm, and proved to have been authorized by his co-partners, was accordingly held valid against a subsequent purchaser with notice. The court cited and relied on Story on Partnership, 122, where it is said that an authority or ratification, express or implied, verbal or written, will render a deed by one of the members of a firm as effectual as if it had been executed by all. This may be true as a general proposition; *Gibson* v. *Warden; Greuter* v. *Williams*, 40 Alabama, 561; but it does not apply where land is concerned, nor in any case within the provisions of the statute of frauds. Whatever may be thought on this

point, it is clear that as the doctrine of relation is a legal fiction, devised for the purposes of justice, a ratification by the firm should not be allowed to defeat an intervening encumbrance; *Haynes* v. *Seachrist;* see 1 Smith's Leading Cases, 722, 7 Am. ed.; *Bird* v. *Brown*, 4 Exchequer, 786; *Buron* v. *Denman*, 2 Id. 166.

In *Tillinghast* v. *Champlin*, 4 Rhode Island, 173, 219, Ames, C. J., held the following language, in delivering the opinion of the court. " The counsel for the respondent is mistaken in supposing, under such a state of facts as this, that the fact that the deed of this lot runs to the individual members of the firm of Gardner & Brother, as tenants in common, without describing them as co-partners, raises a presumption, in the view of a court of equity, that the property, thus bought and used, is intended to be kept as the separate property of the respective partners, which stands, until some express and even written proof is given to show the contrary intention. A court of equity does not ordinarily, in relation to such a subject, base its presumptions upon mere forms, but rather upon facts which lead to the substantial truth and justice of the case. The well-settled presumption in equity is precisely the other way. As said by Chancellor Walworth, in *Buchan* v. *Sumner*, 2 Barbour's Ch. R. 198, 199, ' Where real estate is purchased with partnership funds for the use of the firm, and without any intention of withdrawing the funds from the firm for the use of all or any of the members thereof as individuals, it has never been doubted in England, that such real estate was in equity, to be considered and treated as the property of the members of the firm collectively; and as liable to all the equitable rights of the partners as between themselves. And for this purpose the holders of the legal title are considered, in equity, as the mere trustees of those beneficially interested in the fund, not only during the existence of the co-partnership, but also upon the dissolution thereof by the death of some of the co-partners or otherwise.' And see the cases cited by him, and to same effect. *Hoxie* v. *Carr*, 1 Summ. 181, per Story, J. In this last case, Mr. Justice Story says: ' But the circumstance that the payment has been made out of the partnership funds, especially if the property purchased be necessary to the operations of the partnership business, and be actually so employed, will afford a very cogent presumption that it was intended to be held as partnership property; and in the absence of all countervailing circumstances, it will be absolutely decisive.' ' In whosesoever hands the legal title may be placed, whether in one or all of the co-partners, and whether the deed describes them as co-partners or as tenants in common, if the property be purchased with the funds, and for the use of the firm, the decisive presumption in the absence of proof to the contrary, is that it was intended to be held as partnership property.'

Hunt v. *Benson*, 2 Humph. 459; *Buchan* v. *Sumner*, 2 Barb. Ch. R. 205; *Smith* v. *Tarlton*, Id. 336, 338; *Delmonico* v. *Guillaume*, 4 Sandf. Ch R. 366; *Dyer* v. *Clark*, 5 Metcf. 578, 581; *Howard* v. *Priest et al.* Id. 585; *Burnside et al.* v. *Merrick et al.*, 4 Id. 541; 1 Am. Lead. Cases, Hare & Wallace's notes, 604, and cases cited; Collyer on Partn., sect. 154, where see the result of all the authorities stated. The line of cases cited and relied on by the counsel for the respondent upon this subject will be found to refer to the question whether real estate of a co-partnership, upon the death of one of the co-partners, and *after the debts have been paid and the equities adjusted between the several members of the firm*, belongs, in equity, to the executor or administrator of the decedent as a part of his personal property; or whether the beneficial interest, as well as the legal title, in the decedent's share of such real estate, descends to his heirs at law. Upon this question of equitable conversion of real into personal estate as between the heir and personal representative of a deceased partner, Lord Eldon overruled the latest decision of Lord Thurlow and the decision of Sir William Grant, and held in *Devaynes* v. *Devaynes*, Montague on Partn. App. 97, in favor of the conversion, and consequently in favor of the title of the executor or administrator, to such surplus. His ruling upon this point seems to have been generally followed by the later chancery judges in England; although two or three recent cases, in which the circumstances were special, have been decided in favor of the heir. The American cases, on the other hand, generally adopt the conclusion that the deceased partner's share of the surplus of the real estate of the co-partnership, which remained after paying the debts of the co-partnership and adjusting all the equitable claims of the different members of the firm as between themselves, is, as between the heirs-at-law and personal representatives of the deceased partner, to be considered and treated as real estate. *Dyer* v. *Clark*, 5 Metcf. 578, 579; *Howard et al* v. *Priest et al.*, Id. 585, 586; *Burnside et al.* v. *Merrick et al.*, 4 Id. 541, 544; 1 Am. Lead. Cas., Hare & Wallace's notes, 491, 492, and cases cited. The whole subject is, however, so luminously treated by Chancellor Walworth, in *Buchan* v. *Sumner*, 2 Barb. Ch. R. 198, and onwards, with a full discussion of the cases, English and American, up to the time of his judgment, (1847,) that nothing need be added; and indeed the question of what shall become of any surplus of such property, after the equitable trust under which it is held is satisfied out of it, is so foreign to the case before us, that we should not have mentioned it, except in answer to the cases with regard to it, cited and relied upon by the counsel for the respondent.

" It was noticed, too, by the counsel for the respondent, that in *Dyer* v. *Clark*, *Howard et al.* v. *Priest et al.*, and *Hoxie* v. *Carr*, the respective deeds under which

the partners in those cases held the real estates there in question, described them as co-partners, as if that were the ground of decision in either of those cases. That the deed did describe the grantees as co-partners is true of the case of *Dyer* v. *Clark;* but it is true only of one of the *two* parcels of land in question in *Priest et al.* v. *Howard et al.*, which were conveyed by separate deeds; the land and store in Moon street, Boston, being conveyed to the two partners as tenants in common, and not describing them as co-partners; 5 Metcf. 583. In *Burnside et al.* v. *Merrick et al.*, 4 Id. 537, decided at the same time, the deed does not seem to have described the grantees as co-partners, as is shown by the mode in which the court state the question on page 541. It is evident, therefore, that the absence of such a description in the deeds was not deemed controlling in either of those decisions. In *Hoxie* v. *Carr*, Judge Story notices that one of the deeds from a former proprietor to the co-partners, Reynolds & Hoxie, of *his* interest in the thirty-seven acres of land thereby conveyed, bounds it, on one side, on a three-acre lot, stated to belong to the West Greenwich Manufacturing Co., and which formed part of premises in dispute, and that the deed from Reynolds to Carr spoke of the whole as *formerly* belonging to the same company. No doubt a chancellor would seize hold of such a feature in a case before him, for the purpose of strengthening the presumption raised by the substantial fact that the estate was purchased with the co-partnership funds, for the co-partnership use; but we have already seen that Judge Story put the latter as the main ground of presumption and not the former fact; liable to be rebutted, of course, by any controlling agreement or act of the co-partners. This feature,—deemed so controlling,—exists in very few of the American cases, and in none of the English cases that we recollect. In *Delmonico* v. *Guillaume*, 2 Sandf. Ch. R. 366, the deed of the farm adjudged by the chancellor to be co-partnership property, was originally executed to John Delmonico, who subsequently executed to Peter Delmonico a deed conveying to him an undivided half. But without taking more time in commenting on particular cases, all of which have, of course, their peculiar features more or less marked, and more or less controlling the judgment of the courts before which they were heard, it is clear from them, that the trust in favor of the firm is held to result from the fact that the consideration was paid by it, as in other cases of resulting trusts; and the implication of this trust is held to be confirmed by the fact that the property was bought for the use of the firm and actually used in its business, when no agreement, or conduct implying such an agreement, prior, or subsequent to, or at the time of the purchase, is proved, to indicate an intention on the part of the co-partners to hold the real estate thus purchased by them in undivided shares as their separate property.

"The other question involved in this cause, that is, whether the title to the property in question acquired by the respondent, Champlin, is, under the circumstances, held by him subject to, or exonerated from, the trust with which it was clothed in the hands of his grantor, remains to be considered.

"Beyond doubt, a *bona fide*, purchaser or mortgagee of partnership lands, who obtains the legal title from the person in whom it is vested without notice of the equitable rights of others in the property as a part of the funds of the co-partnership, is entitled to protection in courts of equity as well as in courts of law. Per Walworth, Chancellor, *Buchan* v. *Sumner*, 2 Barb. Ch. R. 198. To this extent, and no further, go the decisions in the cases of *M'Dermot* v. *Lawrence*, 7 Serg. & Rawle, 438; *Forde* v. *Herron*, 4 Munf. 416; *Haile* v. *Henrie*, 2 Watts, 143; *Ridgway's Appeal*, 3 Harris, (15 Penn.) 177, and the remark of the court in *Sigourney* v. *Mann*, 7 Conn. 11, relied upon by the counsel for the respondent. Holding, as we do, that this real estate was co-partnership property, the legal title to the undivided half was held by the surviving partner, according to every authority on this subject, English and American, cited on either side, in trust, for the payment of the debts of the firm, and of any balance that might be due to the estate of the deceased co-partner upon the settlement of the partnership accounts. For the purpose of executing this trust, though but half the *legal* title was vested in him, the surviving partner had the right in equity to sell the whole beneficial interest in the estate ; and a court of equity would assist the purchaser by contract, to get in the legal title to the other half from the heirs-at-law of the deceased co-partner, even though they were infants. *Delmonico* v. *Guillaume*, 2 Sandf. Ch. R. 366-368, and cases cited ; *Dyer* v. *Clark*, 5 Metcf. 576 ; *Howard et al.* v. *Priest et al.*, Id. 585 ; *Burnside et al.* v. *Merrick et al.*, 4 Id. 540, 541, 545 ; *Andrews* v. *Brown*, 21 Ala. 437 ; *M'Alister* v. *Montgomery*, 3 Hayw. 94. On the other hand, the surviving partner, though he may be clothed with the whole legal title, has no right or power to divert the trust property to his own private uses, in derogation of the rights of the creditors of the firm, or of those entitled to the estate of his deceased co-partner. If he were to attempt it, a court of equity would, upon proper application, restrain him from so doing, remove him from the trust he was violating, and appoint a receiver in his stead. If he convey the trust estate for such a purpose to any one cognizant of the trust with actual, or under such circumstances or in such form or mode as to give constructive, notice of his design to violate it, the person taking the conveyance, though a purchaser for full value, takes it subject to the same trust, though the consequence may be to deprive him of the whole benefit of his purchase. It is only the *bona fide* purchaser for value, who, as in the cases already cited, purchases it in ignorance that it is co-partnership or trust property, or, as in cases that might be supposed, knowing that it was co-partnership property, takes the title in such form and under such circumstances as to indicate to him that it is sold and conveyed for the purpose of applying the proceeds to the proper uses of the trust, that can hold the title exonerated from the trust. Such a purchaser does not stand in equity merely upon the derivative title of his grantor. Invested with the legal title, he securely rests upon his own equities as an honest purchaser, without notice and for value—always protected—always a favorite, so to speak, in a court of equity. We agree with the counsel for the respondent, that it will not do to say, as taking the language of the courts away from the connection in which it is used in some of the cases that have been cited, and especially in the case of *Hoxie* v. *Carr*, it has been said before us, that, under all circumstances, he who purchases the real estate of a co-partnership from the surviving partner, knowing it to be such, and knowing that there are co-partnership debts, will take the estate subject to those debts. Much less is it true, as it has been contended, that such an estate can be administered, and a title to it given, only through the intervention of a court of equity. Such a partner, certainly, and each partner of a dissolved firm, unless deprived of it by contract, has, in equity, precisely the same power to deal with the co-partnership property as during the continuance of the co-partnership, though liable in proper cases to be deprived of that power by the appointment of a receiver. Per Turner, Lord Justice, *Butchart* v. *Dresser*, 31 Eng. L. & Eq. R. 121. If the legal title in co-partnership lands be in him, he may dispose of and convey the whole beneficial interest in those lands for the purpose of realizing the proceeds of sale, and of applying them to the payment of the debts of the firm and of the final balance that may be due to him as co-partner; and a court of equity will not interfere most surely with this exercise, which duty imposes, or his said claims justify, of his *jus disponendi.* So far from it, it will, as we have seen, if the legal title be in part only vested in him, or be wholly vested in another, assist him in the exercise of his right, by compelling the conveyance of the legal title to himself, or to a purchaser from him, when such a conveyance is needed to enable him to perform his duty to others or to satisfy even the demands that *he* may have as co-partner upon such property of the firm. In such cases, the purchaser, though he know that he has purchased co-partnership property, and that there are co-partnership debts to be paid out of it, yet if he honestly buy the property of and pay for it to the surviving partner, with no knowledge of, and under circumstances from which a court of equity implies no notice of, an intended misapplication by the partner of the proceeds of sale, will not be liable, on account of any fraud, default, or miscarriage of the surviving partner with regard to them. It is a strict logical sequence, that the right to dispose of such property on the part of the surviving partner, implies and requires the right to buy it, on the part of an honest and careful purchaser; nor is this, as has been contended before us, one of that class of trusts, in which, notwithstanding the power of sale on the part of the trustee or surviving partner, the purchaser, knowing that he is purchasing trust property is bound to see to the application of the purchase-money; or, in this case, to see that it is applied to the payment of the co-partnership debts. We grant that such a notion is inferable from the language used by Mr. Justice Story, in *Hoxie* v. *Carr*, 1 Sumn. 192, if it be proper to disconnect his language from the case before him, or to suppose that he intended accurately to state all the conditions of the case in which, under all circumstances, a purchaser of the real estate of a partnership from a co-partner of a dissolved firm would take the estate subject to the burden of the trust. But such an inference would do great injustice to that learned judge, who to great acquisitions added a keen sense of justice. He was speaking in relation to the case before him, which we shall have occasion hereafter to compare with and apply to this. A surviving partner, in the sense in which he is a trustee of the real estate of the co-partnership, is certainly a trustee with as clear a power to give receipts for the purchase-money, upon sale, as to give receipts to the debtors of the firm, upon payment to him of the co-partnership debts. This results from his power and duty, so far as necessary, to convert the partnership property into money, and therewith to pay the co-partnership debts and to settle the final balance, if any, which may be due, upon settlement of the co-partnership accounts, to the representative of his deceased co-partner. It was never dreamed, in a court of chancery, that this fell within that class of trusts, in which, tested by the well-known distinctions of the leading case of *Elliot* v. *Merryman*, Barnardiston's Ch. R. 78, the purchaser was bound to see to the application of the purchase-money, provided he knew that he was purchasing a portion of the trust estate. Thus to limit his power of sale, would be to load the settlement of the co-partnership estate with an intolerable burden,—lessen it at once to one-half its value, as a subject of sale,—and, as contended by the counsel for the complainant, necessarily draw the settlement of every such estate into a court of chancery to be administered and sold under its orders, for the protection of purchasers and the consequent realization of the value of the property of the firm. How foreign all this would be to the course of chancery with regard to such a trust, may be

seen by the examination of the case above cited, and the admirably arranged collection of authorities, American as well as English, which, allowing for the difference of circumstances, have, in the main, followed it for upwards of an hundred years, found in 1 White & Tudor's Leading Cases in Equity, with Hare and Wallace's notes, *ante*, 101, 123. The only danger to a purchaser of the trust estate from a trustee of the class in which a surviving partner is to be ranked, can arise from his becoming a party to a breach of trust on the part of the trustee, or from his making his purchase under such circumstances as to visit him with constructive notice that a breach of trust, as to purchase-money, is designed; *Eland* v. *Eland*, 4 Mylne & Craig, 18 Eng. Cond. Ch. R. 427; *Hill* v. *Simpson*, 7 Ves. 152; *Champlin* v. *Haight*, 10 Paige, 275; and see *Rogers* v. *Skillicorne*, Amb. 189; *Walker* v. *Smalwood*, Id. 676; *Lloyd* v. *Baldwin*, 1 Ves. 173; *Watkins* v. *Cheek*, 2 Sim. & Stu. 1 Eng. Cond. Ch. R. 199.

" That a gross fraud has been perpetrated by the surviving partner in this case, by the sale of the undivided half of this real estate of the firm of Gardner & Brother, and absconding with the proceeds, is admitted on all hands; and the question which we are to decide, is, whether the consequences of this fraud are to fall upon the creditors of the firm and the estate of the deceased co-partner, or upon the respondent Champlin, who, as he alleges and proves, paid full value for his purchase. In the view in which the state of the proof compels us to regard this case, it will be a hard case which ever way we decide it; and the question simply is, whether, under the circumstances of his purchase, the respondent, Champlin, having obtained the legal title to an undivided half of the real estate of the firm in question, has an equal equity with the creditors and the estate of the deceased co-partner to the beneficial interest of the moiety purchased by him. If he has, he cannot be disturbed in the full enjoyment of his purchase by us, whatever may be the consequences to them; if he has not, our course and duty will be plain before us, whatever may be the consequences to him. This question, in our judgment, depends upon the solution of two other questions, mainly questions of fact.

" First. Did he know that he was purchasing the property of the firm of Gardner & Brother, needed for the payment of the debts of that firm, or to settle any balance of the co-partnership accounts due to the estate of the deceased co-partner? and

" Second. Are the circumstances under which he made his purchase, and the nature of the interest conveyed to him, such as in the view of a court of equity, give him notice of the breach of trust intended by Benjamin W. Gardner, from whom he took his deed?

" He has sworn in his answer that he did not know that this real estate was co-partnership prop-erty; but supposed that it was the separate property of the two co-partners, held by them as sepa-rate property, according to the form of the deed under which they held it, as equal tenants in common. Now this may be quite true in one sense; for he probably did not know how a court of equity regards real property held by the co-partners under a deed in that form, when bought with the money and credit, and held for the uses of the co-partnership; and indeed the whole manner in which this co-partnership was attempted to be settled, both by Benjamin W. Gardner and the administrator of William A. Gardner, shows a gross ignorance of the law relating to this whole subject. But such ignorance, though it might relieve him under some circumstances from the imputation of actual fraud, cannot aid him in the view of a court of equity, when called upon to determine whether he had legal notice of a fact, or to adjudge the legal effect of his acts. If, knowing the facts that this property was bought with the partnership funds for partnership use, and was exclusively used by the partnership during the whole term of its continuance, he took upon himself to determine, from the form of the deed under which it was held by the co-partners, that it was not co-partnership property, he took upon himself, in a matter of law, to be wiser than the law; and if mistaken, has no one to blame for his presumption but himself. The aid of the able counsellor who has argued his case, invoked before he made his purchase, might have been even more helpful to him in this particular than circumstances have allowed it to be.

" Now for us to doubt that the respondent, Champlin, knew these facts, which appear from the proof to have been notorious in the village of East Greenwich, and which the partners themselves, by their daily acts and repeated declarations, took pains, for the sake of obtaining credit for their firm, to make so, would suppose on our part a degree of skepticism quite unfitting us for an office which requires us, in matters of proof, to weigh and decide upon probabilities. Although, during a portion of the time, at least, of the continuance of this co-partnership, the respondent owned and occupied a farm a few miles off, in West Greenwich, yet the occasions of his business and pleasure, as proved, brought him frequently to the village of East Greenwich, where the firm did business, and where the works in question were situated, and where, also, the respondent's mother and family resided. His personal and business relations with both the members of this firm were intimate. His sister was the wife of William A. Gardner, and Benjamin W. Gardner boarded with his mother, and was thought to be attentive to an unmarried sister, and he was frequently with both the co-partners, and was advised with about their business. He bid off for William A. Gardner, at auction, the very lot upon which these

works were situated, when sold by the town of East Greenwich, and must have known the openly declared purpose for which it was bought. From the proof, no one could have been more cognizant of the credit and capital upon which the firm did business, and out of which they built up the property in question. This intimacy continued with Benjamin W. Gardner, after the decease of William A. His brother, Robert H. Champlin, was the original administrator appointed on the estate of William A. Gardner, and he himself took apparently a great interest in the affairs of the estate, frequently attending the courts of probate when questions concerning it were there agitated, and seeming to be a prominent actor in its affairs. He knew, or affected to know, the precise condition of the estate of his deceased brother-in-law ; and informed the witness, David W. Hunt, a creditor of the firm to the amount of $400, only some six weeks after the death of William A. Gardner, that he would get his whole debt, —that the debts of the estate were about $3,000, and that there would be property enough to pay them all ; though he declined the offer of the witness to guarantee the payment of his debt for a commission of five per cent. In his answer, he admits that both at the decease of William A. Gardner, and at the time of the taking of his deed, he knew that the firm owed debts, though not the amount ; and although he denies that he knew that the firm was insolvent, yet it is evident from the fact, and his means of knowledge concerning it, that he must have known that it was grossly so, and that nothing was done by the surviving partner, who still continued to use the property of the firm, to pay any of its debts. A purchase made of a surviving partner thus situated and thus conducting, to the knowledge of the purchaser, would be required by a court of chancery to be made under circumstances of openness, publicity, and consultation with all interested in the estate, and in a mode quite free from suspicion in all respects, before the purchaser could affect to stand before it upon as high a ground of equity as the creditors of the firm, or the representatives of the estate of the deceased co-partner.

" But what were the circumstances of this purchase, and the mode in which it was affected? Without communication, so far as the evidence shows, with the representative or heirs of the deceased co-partner, in the latter of whom the legal title to the other undivided moiety of this estate was vested, and in the disposition of which the former was interested in relief of the estate of his decedent, he is found with Benjamin W. Gardner one evening, as late as 9 o'clock, rousing up a justice of the peace to take the latter's acknowledgment of the deed in question, ostentatiously hands over to the justice $1,200 in the first place to count, as the consideration of the deed, and then hands over that, with $50 more, to make

the precise amount, to Benjamin W. Gardner, who delivers to him the deed. After this they are seen together in conversation coming from the house as late as 10 o'clock, and this is the last that we hear of this consideration money or of the surviving partner, Benjamin W. Gardner, who that same night, or early the next morning, absconded with the whole of it and probably much more, and has never been heard of by the creditors of the firm since.

" Now grant that, considering the denial of the answer, there is here no such proof of community of corrupt design and action between the seller and the purchaser, so pointedly charged in the bill, as will justify us in holding that the charge is proven; yet there are circumstances creating grave suspicion, which cannot be overlooked in a court called upon to weigh and balance the equities of such a purchaser with the undoubted equitable rights of the creditors of the firm. If this secrecy and cover of night in this transaction were sought at the suggestion of the seller, they should have excited the suspicion of the purchaser; if sought by the latter, considering the other facts attending the execution of the deed, they go somewhat farther, and certainly do not aid the case of the respondent.

" But further, and most especially, it is to be considered, that this was an insolvent firm, with a large amount of debts outstanding, whose existence was known to the respondent, and none of which he knew had been paid by the co-partner, whose duty it was to pay them, and with whom he was dealing. He was taking from this partner a conveyance of a portion of what he knew, or should have known, as a matter of law, was the property of the firm; and certainly knew, as a matter of common honesty, should be applied to the payment of its debts. This mill property should have been sold together, as a whole, if the purpose had been to realize the most from it for the benefit of the creditors; and no one could have known this better than a sharp, active man of business, such as the respondent is proved to be. To sell it in undivided shares was to sacrifice a large portion of its value; for no one would buy the other half except the respondent, and he could get it almost at his own price; and the proof is, as might have been foretold, and should have been foreseen, that, as the consequence of this transaction, neither half of this property is worth the nominal amount of the consideration paid by the respondent for the moiety thus purchased by him.

" We do not say that under no circumstances can the sale by a surviving partner of an undivided moiety of the real estate of a firm, the legal title of which is to that extent vested in him, be upheld in a court of equity. Such a sale may be made with such consent of all parties interested in it, with such publicity, and may even be so advantageous in some conceivable cases, as a mode of sale, as to be approved and even directed by a court of equity. But when, as in this case, a surviving partner in whom one half of the legal title of the real estate of the firm happens to be vested, affects privately to convey to one who knows that it is partnership property, precisely that undivided half, treating it as if it were beneficially his own, he thereby gives presage of an intent to convert the proceeds to his own use, instead of applying them to the uses of the firm whose property it is. The purchaser must know, if the property be co-partnership property, that the state of the legal title cannot represent in whom the beneficial interest in it is really vested; and in what proportion, if in any proportion, in him from whom he is taking the title. The very fact that he knows that it is co-partnership property, and especially, as in this case, that there were co-partnership debts outstanding to a large amount, gives him notice that others are interested in the estate than him with whom he is dealing, with whom he should in all fairness communicate, as entitled to know what disposition is about to be made of their own. But if he will privately and secretly contract with and pay his money to a surviving partner for his legal title, who by the form of the transaction is treating the matter as if he deemed the property as his own, and meant to appropriate the proceeds of sale as his own, to his own use, it is doing him no more than justice for a court of chancery to inform him, that he shall have precisely what in such a mode of purchase, and under such circumstances, he had a right to expect,—the legal title only; the beneficial interest to go to those to whom in equity it belongs. Though warned by the surroundings of the transaction, he chooses to rely solely upon the good faith and honesty in his trust, of the mere owner of the legal title, who may not, as he should know, have a *scintilla* of interest in the beneficial estate, and must abide by the result of his misplaced confidence, if such it turn out to be. If added to all this there be, as here, circumstances of suspicion hanging about the execution of the deed, looking at the time and mode of conducting it, and the sudden absconding at the close of the transaction of the surviving partner with the proceeds of sale, we cannot estimate the equities of the purchaser at so high a value as to allow them to counterbalance the clear and undoubted rights of the creditors of the firm in whose aid our jurisdiction is invoked by the equitable representative of the rights of the deceased co-partner. In *Hoxie* v. *Carr*, 1 Sumn. 193, the fact that the deed was executed by one copartner only, was alluded to by the learned judge who tried the cause, as showing 'that the purchasers should and ought to have known, that without a joint conveyance or release from all the partners, no absolute conveyance could be acquired by their grantee, Reynolds. They were put upon inquiry to ascertain whether any

such conveyance or release had been made; and they cannot now set up their ignorance of law to excuse their want of diligence;' and he then goes on to show that if the purchasers in that case had made inquiries, that they would have ascertained the very facts which the evidence convinces us that this respondent knew. Indeed, the learned and accurate commentators upon this and the class of cases to which it belongs, —Messrs. Hare & Wallace—say, that 'it is a consequence of the principle of land being affected with a trust as co-partnership property, that when one partner disposes of his separate interest in land held as co-partnership stock, to a purchaser having notice, he sells only his residuary interest, after the partnership debts and the share of the other partner are paid;' 1 Am. Lead. Cas. Hare & Wallace's notes, 492.[1] Such was evidently the idea of Mr. Justice Story, as expressed in his decision in the case of *Hoxie* v. *Carr et al.*; and such was the opinion expressed by the Supreme Court of Massachusetts, in *Dyer* v. *Clark*, 5 Metcalf, 580. 'But if,' says the learned chief justice of that court, in delivering its judgment in the latter case, 'a person knows that a particular real estate is the partnership property of two or more, and he attempts to acquire a title to any part of it from one alone, without the knowledge or consent of the

---

[1] The note cited above is from the pen of the late Mr. Wallace.

other, there seems to be no hardship in holding that he takes such title at his peril, and on the responsibility of the person with whom he deals.' It is true, as suggested by the counsel for the respondent, that in case of a dissolution by death of a firm consisting of but two co-partners, the sole power to dispose of the co-partnership property and apply it to the payment of debts and to close the co-partnership accounts, survives to the surviving partner; and thus, that he is the only person, as long as he is suffered to exercise the trust, to act in its administration. But the surviving partner is but a trustee; and if he from his secret and suspicious mode of dealing with the trust property, treating it by the very mode of his conveying it as if it were his own, and regardless of the interests of the creditors of the firm as to the residue, sells to a purchaser an undivided share of it, because the legal title to that share happens to be vested in himself, we deem that he thus apprises the purchaser of his design; and that, under such circumstances, his absconding with the proceeds of sale should be regarded as little more than the fulfilment of a reasonable expectation on the part of the purchaser."

Whatever the rule may be under ordinary circumstances, it is settled that the real estate of a partnership will be regarded as personalty, where the agreement between the parties, or the purpose for which it is purchased, shows that the intention was that it should be sold, and distributed as money; *Ludlow* v. *Cooper*, 1 Ohio, N. S. 1; *Kramer* v. *Arthurs*, 7 Barr, 165. Thus in *Kramer* v. *Arthurs*, the object of a joint stock association, formed for the purpose of buying and selling land, and dividing the profits which might accrue among the stockholders, was said to be obviously, to deal with the land as a mere commodity, and to look not to it, but to the proceeds for compensation. The interest of its members, as between themselves, and those claiming under them with notice, was consequently held to be a mere right to the amount, if any, which might remain after the winding up of the association, which partook of the nature of personalty and could not be bound by the lien of a judgment. " That an incorporated joint stock company," said Gibson, C. J., in delivering the opinion of the court, " is an ordinary partnership, and that there may be a partnership to deal in lands, are elementary principles that have not been disputed. The latter was expressly recognized by this court in *Brady* v. *Calhoun's Administrators*, 1 Penna. Rep. 147. 'Partnerships,' says Gow on Partnership, 6, ' are not necessarily confined to trades in commercial adventures. They may lawfully exist in cases unconnected with commercial speculations. For instance, a partnership may exist between attorneys or farmers, as well as between merchants or bankers.' It would be absurd to let the nature of the article dealt in change the nature of the contract; or not to let partners give to the land the attributes of a commodity, as between themselves and those standing in their place, especially in a country where it is a chattel for payment of debts, and not unfrequently a subject of speculation. Where it is brought into a concern as stock, it is, as between the partners and a person who has knowingly dealt with one of them for it, to be treated as personal estate belonging, not to the partners individually, but to the company collectively. The members of this company, being sharers of profit and loss, were partners to the world; but, between themselves, they had only a contingent interest in the profits to be derived from the lands when the concern should be wound up, not a vested estate as tenants in common of the lands themselves; and, to a purchaser with notice, or its equivalent, neither of them could part with more, either by a voluntary or an involuntary conveyance. As an agent entitled to a third of the profits in compensation of his services, it cannot be said that Havens had any property at all in the corpus of the stock: and as to him, or a purchaser from him with notice, or the means of it, the joint creditors would have been entitled to priority of satisfaction without aid from the special provisions in the articles. But even if his title as a shareholder had given him a several estate in the land, it would have given him no more than an undivided twentieth part of each tract, and no more could have

been sold on a judgment against him by a separate creditor; certainly not the entire tract, as was done here. But the lands constituted the stock, and, so far as Havens, or his alienees, with the means of notice, are concerned, they are to be treated as a commodity, as well by the express provisions of the articles as by the implied conditions of the contract. By these, it was stipulated that the estate on hand should be sold at the expiration of the partnership, and that the cash and securities, after payment of the debts, should be divided among the shareholders '*pro rata*, according to their respective shares of the stock.' Now, what was the nature of the shares in the meantime? Havens did not own even a twentieth part of the land jointly or severally. In *Allison* v. *Wilson's Executors*, 13 Serg. & Rawle, 330, and *Morrow* v. *Brenizer*, 2 Id. 188, it was ruled, that where a party is entitled merely to the proceeds of land when sold, he has no estate in the realty which can be bound by a judgment, or sold on an execution against him. The present is a stronger case; for so to interpret such a contract as to allow each member of the company to have a specific interest in the lands which might be clogged by the liens or attachment of his separate creditors, would defeat the very end of the association. I grant that a sale on a judgment against the company by a partnership creditor, would pass its lands, no matter whether as such or as chattels; but by no device can a separate creditor of a partner take any part of his share out of the capital stock and apply it to the satisfaction of his debt, or sell anything but his contingent share of the profits and stock at the settlement of the partnership account; and, as that is personalty, it cannot be bound by a judgment. A glance at the facts of the case will show an attempt by the plaintiffs to do so at the expense of a party standing in the place of the company; and it must not succeed."

A similar view was taken in *Ludlow* v. *Cooper*, 1 Ohio, N. S. 1, and the purchase of land by a firm, for the purpose of being resold on their joint account, held to render it personal property for the purposes of descent and distribution. There can be no doubt, that until the debts due by the firm, and the mutual claims of the partners, are satisfied, real estate may be treated by equity as if it were personal, but it does not follow, that this course should be pursued after the partnership equities are at an end, and when the question arises between the heirs or devisees of the individual partners; *Ludlow* v. *Cooper; Goodburn* v. *Stevens*, 1 Maryland, Ch.; *Pierce* v. *Trigg*, 10 Leigh, 406; *Hale* v. *Plummer*, 6 Indiana, 121. Most of the cases in this country, perhaps

all, may be reconciled by the aid of this distinction, and of that which exists between the effect of the purchase of land as partnership property, and of an express or implied agreement, that it shall be viewed as a commodity, and sold for the benefit of the partnership. Thus, in *Roberts* v. *M'Carty* 9 Indiana, 16, the court spoke of the land as if it were a mere chattel interest, but the decision was limited to treating its true character of realty, as subordinate to the equities of the firm.

It was held in *Patterson* v. *Brewster* 4 Edwards, Ch. 352, that the union of several persons in an association for the purchase and resale of land through a trustee, who gives his bond for the purchase-money, does not constitute a partnership, or render them answerable for the price. The decision was influenced by the doctrine of merger, and the true import of it seems to be that a purchase on the credit of a partner does not impose a liability on the firm. There can be little doubt that where an insolvent contractor has a right of action over against others for whom he acts, equity may give an immediate remedy against them although they are not legally answerable in consequence of the form of the obligation.

[*203]   *DYER *v.* DYER.

NOVEMBER 20, 21. AND 27, 1788. IN THE EXCHEQUER, BEFORE LORD
CHIEF BARON EYRE, BARON HOTHAM, BARON THOMPSON.

REPORTED 2 COX, 92.[1]

PURCHASE IN THE NAME OF A SON.—ADVANCEMENT.]—*Copyhold
granted to A. and B. his wife, and C. his younger son, to take in
succession for their lives and the life of the survivor. The purchase-
money was all paid by A. C. is not a trustee of his life-interest for
A.; but takes it beneficially as an advancement from his father.—
Resulting trust.*

IN 1737, certain copyhold premises, holden of the manor of
Heytesbury, in the county of Wilts, were granted by the lord,
according to the custom of that manor, to Simon Dyer (the
plaintiff's father) and Mary his wife, and the defendant William
his other son, to take in succession for their lives and to the
longest liver of them. The purchase-money was paid by Simon
Dyer, the father. He survived his wife, and lived until 1785,
and then died, having made his will, and thereby devised all his
interest in these copyhold premises (amongst others) to the plaintiff, his younger son.

The present bill stated these circumstances, and insisted that
the whole purchase-money being paid by the father, although by
the form of the grant, the wife and the defendant had the legal
interest in the premises for their lives in succession, yet in a
court of equity they were but trustees for the father, and the bill
therefore prayed that the plaintiff, as devisee of the father, might
be quieted in the possession of the premises during the life of the
defendant.

[*204]   The defendant insisted that the insertion of his name *in
the grant operated as an advancement to him from his
father to the extent of the legal interest thereby given to him.
And this was the whole question in the cause.

This case was very fully argued by Mr. Solicitor-General and
Ainge, for the plaintiff; and by Burton and Morris, for the defendant. The following cases were cited, and very particularly
commented on :—*Smith* v. *Baker*, 1 Atk. 385 ; *Taylor* v. *Taylor*,
1 Atk. 386 ; *Mumma* v. *Mumma*, 2 Vern. 19 ; *Howe* v. *Howe*, 1
Vern. 415 ; *Anon.*, 2 Freem. 123 ; *Benger* v. *Drew*, 1 P. Wms.
781 ; *Dickenson* v. *Shaw*, before the Lords Commissioners, in
1770 ; *Bedwell* v. *Froome*, before Sir T. Sewell, on the 10th of
May, 1778 ; *Row* v. *Bowden*, before Sir L. Kenyon, sitting for the
Lord Chancellor; *Crisp* v. *Pratt*, Cro. Car. 549 ; *Scroope* v. *Scroope*,

[1] S. C., 1 Watk. Cop. 216.

1 Ch. Ca. 27; *Elliot* v. *Elliot*, 2 Ch. Ca. 231; *Ebrand* v. *Dancer,* Ch. Ca. 26; *Kingdon* v. *Bridges*, 2 Vern. 67; *Beck* v. *Andrew*, 2 Vern. 120; *Rundle* v. *Rundle*, 2 Vern. 264; *Lamplugh* v. *Lamplugh*, 1 P. Wms. 111; *Stileman* v. *Ashdown*, 2 Atk. 477; *Pole* v. *Pole*, 1 Ves. 76.

LORD CHIEF BARON EYRE, after directing the cause to stand over for a few days, delivered the judgment of the Court.

The question between the parties in this cause is, whether the defendant is to be considered as a trustee for his father in respect of his succession to the legal interest of the copyhold premises in question, and whether the plaintiff, as representative of the father, is now entitled to the benefit of that trust. I intimated my opinion of the question on the hearing of the cause; and I then indeed entertained very little doubt upon the rule of a court of equity, as applied to this subject; but as so many cases have been cited, some of which are not in print, we thought it convenient to take an opportunity of looking more fully into them, in order that the ground of our decision may be put in as clear a light as possible, especially in a case in which so great a difference of opinion seems to have prevailed at the bar. And I have met *with a case, in addition to those cited, which is that of [*205] *Rumboll* v. *Rumboll,*[1] on the 20th of April, 1761.

The clear result of all the cases without a single exception, is that *the trust of a legal estate, whether freehold, copyhold, or leasehold ; whether taken in the names of the purchaser and others jointly, or in the names of others without that of the purchaser ; whether in one name or several ; whether jointly or successive, results to the man who advances the purchase-money.* This is a general proposition, supported by all the cases, and there is nothing to contradict it; and it goes on a strict analogy to the rule of the common law, that where a feoffment is made without consideration, the use results to the feoffor. It is the established doctrine of a court of equity, that this resulting trust may be rebutted by circumstances in evidence.

The cases go one step further, and prove that *the circumstance of one or more of the nominees being a child or children of the purchaser, is to operate by rebutting the resulting trust ;* and it has been determined in so many cases, that the nominee, being a child, shall have such operation as a circumstance of evidence, that we should be disturbing land-marks if we suffered either of these propositions to be called in question, namely, that such circumstance shall rebut the resulting trust, and that it shall do so as a circumstance of evidence. I think it would have been a more simple doctrine if the children had been considered as purchasers for a valuable consideration. Natural love and affection raised a use at common law. Surely, then, it will rebut a trust resulting to the father. This way of considering it would have shut out all the circumstances of evidence which have found their way into

[1] Since reported, 2 Eden, 15.

many of the cases, and would have prevented some very nice distinctions, and not very easy to be understood. Considering it as a circumstance of evidence, there must be of course evidence admitted on the other side. Thus, it was resolved into a question of intent, which was getting into a very wide sea, without very certain guides.

[*206] *In the most simple case of all. which is that of a father purchasing in the name of his son, it is said that this shows that the father intended an advancement; and, therefore, the resulting trust is rebutted; but then a circumstance is added to this namely, that the son happened to be provided for. Then the question is, did the father intend to advance a son already provided for? Lord Nottingham[1] could not get over this; and he ruled, that in such a case the resulting trust was not rebutted; and in *Pole* v. *Pole*, 1 Ves. 76, Lord Hardwicke thought so too; and yet the rule, in a court of equity, as recognised in other cases, is, that the father is the only judge as to the quantum of a son's provision; that distinction, therefore, of the son being provided for or not is not very solidly taken or uniformly adhered to.[2] It is then said, that *a purchase in the name of a son is a primâ facie* advancement (and, indeed, it seems difficult to put it in any other way). In some of the cases, some circumstances have appeared which go pretty much against that presumption : as where the father has entered and kept possession and taken the rents, or where he has surrendered or devised the estate, or where the son has given receipts in the name of the father; the answer given is, that the father took the rents as guardian of his son. Now, would the Court sustain a bill by the son against the father for these rents? I should think it pretty difficult to succeed in such a bill. As to the surrender and devise, it is answered, that these are subsequent acts; whereas the intention of the father in taking the purchase in the son's name must be prove by concomitant acts; yet these are pretty strong acts of ownership, and assert the right and coincide with the possession and enjoyment. As to the son's giving receipts in the name of the father, it is said that the son being under age, he could not give receipts in any other manner; but I own this reasoning does not satisfy me.

In the more complicated cases, where the life of the son is one of the lives to take in succession, other distinctions are taken.

[*207] If the custom of the manor be, that *the first taker might surrender the whole lease, that shall make the other lessees trustees for him; but this custom operates on the legal estate, not on the equitable interest; and therefore, this is not a very solid argument. When the lessees are to take *successive*, it is said, that, as the father cannot take the whole in his own name,

---

[1] Grey v. Grey, 2 Swanst. 600 ; S. C., Finch, 343 ; and see Elliot v. Elliot, 2 Ch. Ca. 231 ; Lloyd v. Read, 1 P. Wms. 608.

[2] See Redington v. Redington, 3 Ridg. 190 ; Sidmouth v. Sidmouth, 2 Beav. 456.

but must insert other names in the lease, then the children shall
be trustees for the father; and, to be sure, if the circumstance of
a child being the nominee is not decisive the other way, there is
a great deal of weight in this observation. There may be many
prudential reasons for putting in the life of a child in preference
to that of any other person; and if that case it is to be collected
from circumstances whether an advancement was meant, it will
be difficult to find such as will support that idea; to be sure,
taking the estate in the name of the child, which the father
might have taken in his own, affords a strong argument of such
an intent; but where the estate must necessarily be taken to lives
in succession, the inference is very different. These are difficulties which occur from considering the purchase in the son's
name as a circumstance of evidence only. Now, if it were once
laid down that the son was to be taken as a purchaser for a valuable consideration, all these matters of presumption would be
avoided.

It must be admitted, that the case of *Dickenson* v. *Shaw* is a
case very strong to support the present plaintiff's claim. That
came on in Chancery on the 22nd of May, 1770. A copyhold
was granted to three lives to take in succession, the father, son,
and daughter; the father paid the fine; there was no custom
stated; the question was, whether the daughter and her husband were trustees during the life of the son, who survived
the father. At the time of the purchase the son was nine, and
the daughter seven years old. It appeared that the father had
leased the premises from three years to three years to the extent
of nine years. On this case, Lords Commissioners Smythe and
Aston were of opinion that, as the father had paid the purchase-
money, the children were *trustees for him. To the note [*208]
I have of this case it is added, that this determination
was contrary to the general opinion of the bar, and also to a case
of *Taylor* v. *Alston* in this court. In *Dickenson* v. *Shaw* there
was some little evidence to assist the idea of its being a trust,
namely, that of the leases made by the father; if that made an
ingredient in the determination, then that case is not quite in
point to the present; but I rather think that the meaning of the
Court was, that the burthen of proof lay on the child; and that
the cases, which went the other way, were only those in which
the estate was entirely purchased in the names of the children;
if so, they certainly were not quite correct in that idea, for there
had been cases in which the estates had been taken in the names
of the father and son. I have been favoured with a note of
Rumboll v. *Rumboll*,[1] before Lord Keeper Henley on the 20th of
April, 1761, where a copyhold was taken for three lives in succession, the father and two sons; the father paid the fine; and
the custom was, that the first taker might dispose of the whole
estate (and his Lordship then stated that case fully). Now this

---

[1] 2 Eden, 15.

case does not amount to more than an opinion of Lord Keeper Henley; but he agreed with me in considering a child as a *purchaser* for good consideration of an estate bought by the father in his name, though a trust would result as against a stranger. It has been supposed that the case of *Taylor* v. *Alston* in this court denied the authority of *Dickenson* v. *Shaw*. That cause was heard before Lord Chief Baron Smythe, myself, and Mr. Baron Burland, and was the case of an uncle purchasing in the names of himself and a nephew and niece: it was decided in favour of the nephew and niece, not on any general idea of their taking as relations, but on the result of much parol evidence, which was admitted on both sides; and the equity on the side of the nominees was thought to preponderate. Lord Kenyon was in that cause, and his argument went solely on the weight of the parol evidence; indeed, as far as the circumstances of the first taker's right [*209] to surrender, it was a strong case in favour of a *trust; however, the Court determined the other way on the parol evidence; that case, therefore, is not material. Another case has been mentioned, which is not in print, and which was thought to be materially applicable to this (*Bedwell* v. *Froome*, before Sir T. Sewell); but that was materially distinguishable from the present: as far as the general doctrine went, it went against the opinion of the Lords Commissioners. His Honor there held, that the copyholds were part of the testator's personal estate, for that it was not a purchase in the name of the daughter; she was not to have the legal estate; it was only a contract to add the daughter's life in a new lease to be granted to the father himself; there could be no question about her being a trustee; for it was as a freehold in him for his daughter's life; but, in the course of the argument, his Honor stated the common principles as applied to the present case; and ended by saying that, *as between father and child, the natural presumption was that a provision was meant.* The anonymous case in 2 Freem. 123, corresponds very much with the doctrine laid down by Sir T. Sewell: and it observes that an advancement to a child is considered as done for valuable consideration, not only against the father, but against creditors. *Kingdon* v. *Bridges* is a strong case to this point: that is, the valuable nature of the consideration arising on a provision made for a wife or for a child; for there the question arose as against creditors.

I do not find that there are in print more than three cases which respect copyholds, where the grant is to take *successive: Rundle* v. *Rundle*, 2 Vern. 264, which was a case perfectly clear; *Benger* v. *Drew*, 1 P. Wms. 781, where the purchase was made partly with the wife's money; and *Smith* v. *Baker*, 1 Atk. 385, where the general doctrine, as applied to strangers, was recognised; but the case turned on the question, whether the interest was well devised. Therefore, as far as respects this particular case, *Dickenson* v. *Shaw* is the only case quite in point; and then the question is, whether that case is to be abided by? With

great reverence to the memory of *those two judges who [*210]
decided it, we think that case cannot be followed; that
it has not stood the test of time or the opinion of learned men;
and Lord Kenyon has certainly intimated his opinion against it.
On examination of its principles, they seem to rest on too narrow
a foundation, namely, that the inference of a provision being intended did not arise, because the purchase could not have been
taken wholly in the name of the purchaser. This, we think, is
not sufficient to turn the presumption against the child. If it is
meant to be a trust, the purchaser must show that intention by a
declaration of trust; and we do not think it right to doubt
whether an estate in succession is to be considered as an advancement when a moiety of an estate in possession certainly would be
so. If we were to enter into all the reasons that might possibly influence the mind of the purchaser, many might perhaps occur in
every case upon which it might be argued that an advancement
was not intended; and I own it is not a very prudent conduct of a
man just married to tie up his property for one child, and preclude himself from providing for the rest of his family; but this
applies equally in case of a purchase in the name of the child
only. Yet that case is admitted to be an advancement; indeed,
if anything, the latter case is rather the strongest, for there it
must be confined to one child only. We think, therefore, that
these reasons partake of too great a degree of refinement, and
should not prevail against a rule of property which is so well
established as to become a land-mark, and which, whether right
or wrong, should be carried throughout.

This bill must therefore be dismissed; but, after stating that
the only case in point on the subject is against our present
opinion, it certainly will be proper to dismiss it without costs.

Dyer v. *Dyer* is a leading case on the doctrine of resulting trusts
upon purchases made in the names of strangers, but more especially
on the very important exception to the doctrine where purchases
*are made, not in the names of strangers, but of children or [*211]
persons equally favored.

As to purchases made in the names of strangers, the Lord Chief
Baron Eyre in his judgment observes, " The clear result of all the
cases, without a single exception, is, that the trust of a legal estate,
whether freehold, copyhold, or leasehold; whether taken in the names
of the purchaser and others, jointly, or in the names of others without
that of the purchaser; whether in one name or several, whether jointly
or successive, results to the man who advances the purchase-money;
and it goes on a strict analogy to the rule of common law, that, where
a feoffment is made without consideration, the use results to the
feoffor."

To illustrate this statement of the doctrine, suppose A. advances the

purchase-money of a freehold, copyhold, or leasehold estate, and a conveyance, surrender, or assignment of the legal interest in it is made either
to B. or to B. and C., or to A., B., and C. jointly, or to A., B., and C.
successively. In all these cases, if B. and C. are strangers, a trust will
result in favor of A. That a trust results where the conveyance is
taken in one name or several jointly, see *Ex parte Houghton*, 17 Ves.
253; *Rider* v. *Kidder*, 10 Ves. 367; or successive, see *Howe* v. *Howe*,
1 Vern. 415; *Withers* v. *Withers*, Amb. 151; *Smith* v. *Baker*, 1 Atk.
385; and a custom of a manor that a nominee should take beneficially
will not hold good, as being unreasonable and contrary to the principles of resulting trusts: *Lewis* v. *Lane*, 2 My. & K. 449, overruling
Edwards v. *Fidel*, 3 Madd. 237; *Jeans* v. *Cooke*, 24 Beav. 513.

The doctrine is applicable to personal as well as to real estate; and
a trust will result for the person advancing the consideration-money
who takes a bond or a transfer of stock, or who purchases an annuity
or any other thing of a personal nature in the name of a stranger: see
Ebrand v. *Dancer*, 2 Ch. Ca. 26; *Mortimer* v. *Davies*, cited *Rider* v.
Kidder, 10 Ves. 365, 366; *Loyd* v. *Read*, 1 P. Wms. 607; *Ex parte
Houghton*, 17 Ves. 253; *Sidmouth* v. *Sidmouth*, 2 Beav. 454.

The doctrine of resulting trusts is applicable also to cases where two
or more persons advance the purchase-money jointly. Lord Hardwicke,
indeed, in *Crop* v. *Norton*, Barnard, C. Rep. 184, *S. C.*, 9 Mod. 235, is
said to have thought that it was confined to cases where the whole
consideration moved from one person. However, in *Wray* v. *Steele*, 2
V. & B. 388, Sir Thomas Plumer, V. C., upon the general principle, decided that there was a resulting trust upon a joint advance, where the
purchase was taken in the name of one. " Lord Hardwicke," observed
[*212] his Honor, " could not have used the language ascribed *to him.
What is there applicable to an advance by a single individual,
that is not equally applicable to a joint advance under similar circumstances?" See *In re Thomas Ryan*, 3 I. R. Eq. 237.

But no trust will result if the policy of an Act of Parliament would
be thereby defeated. Thus, no trust will result in favour of a person
advancing the purchase-money of a ship registered in the name of another; for the register, according to the policy of the Registry Acts, is
conclusive evidence of ownership, both at law and in equity. " The
Registry Acts," says Lord Eldon, " were drawn upon this policy; that
it is for the public interest to secure evidence of the title to a ship,
from her origin to the moment in which you look back to her history;
how far throughout her existence she has been British built and British
owned; and it is obvious, that, if where the title arises by act of the
parties, the doctrine of implied trust in this court is to be applied, the
whole policy of these acts may be defeated :" *Ex parte Yallop*, 15 Ves.
68; see also *Ex parte Houghton*, 17 Ves. 251; *Slater* v. *Willis*, 1 Beav.
354. See and consider *Armstrong* v. *Armstrong*, 21 Beav. 71, 78. See

the Merchant Shipping Act, 1854 (17 & 18 Vict. c. 104, amended by 25 & 26 Vict. c. 63), whereby, after enacting that not more than thirty-two individuals shall be entitled to be registered at the same time as owners of any one ship, it is provided, " but this rule shall not affect the beneficial title of any numbers of persons or of any company represented by or claiming under or through any registered owner or joint owner." Sect. 37 (2).

Where, however, a person having no title to a ship procures it to be registered in his name, the Court of Chancery will compel him to retransfer it to the rightful owner, and account for the earnings, even though there have been no fraud, and notwithstanding the Merchant Shipping Act, 1854 (17 & 18 Vict. c. 104): *Holderness* v. *Lamport*, 29 Beav. 129.

The principle upon which these cases proceed seems to have been lost sight of in the case of *Field* v. *Lonsdale* (13 Beav. 78). There a person having deposited moneys in his own name in a savings bank to the full extent allowed by Act of Parliament (9 Geo. 4, c. 92), made further deposits to an account in his own name " in trust for " his sister, but no notice of the investment was given to her. By the terms of the Act he retained a control over the whole fund. It was held by Lord Langdale, M. R., on the death of the depositor, that his sister was not entitled. " I think," said his Lordship, " that the only intention was to *evade* the provisions of the Act of Parliament, and not to create a trust. The declaration is therefore ineffectual, and the claim must be dismissed."

*A trust will not, it seems, result in favour of a person who has purchased an estate in the name of another in order to give [*213] him a vote in electing a member of Parliament: *Groves* v. *Groves*, 3 Y. & J. 163, 175.

If the advance of the purchase-money by the real purchaser does not appear on the face of the deed, and even if it is stated to have been made by the nominal purchaser, parol evidence is admissible to prove by whom it was actually made. Thus, in *Sir John Peachey's case*, Rolls, E. T. 1759, MS., Sugd. V. & P. 910, 11th edit., Sir Thomas Clarke, M. R., laid it down, that if A. sold an estate to C., and *the consideration was expressed to be paid by B.*, and the conveyance made to B., the Court would allow parol evidence to prove the money paid by C.; see also *Ryall* v. *Ryall*, 1 Atk. 59; *S. C.*, Amb. 413; *Willis* v. *Willis*, 2 Atk. 71; *Bartlett* v. *Pickersgill*, 1 Eden, 516; *Lane* v. *Dighton*, Amb. 409; *Groves* v. *Groves*, 3 Y. & J. 163. We may, therefore, consider that these authorities overrule *Kirk* v. *Webb*, Prec. Ch. 84; *Heron* v. *Heron*, Prec. Ch. 163, and other older cases in which it was held that parol evidence could not be admitted to prove payment of purchase-money so as to raise a resulting trust, on the ground, that the admission of such evidence would be contrary to the Statute of

Frauds: for the trust, which results to the person paying the purchase-money and taking a conveyance in the name of another, is a trust resulting by operation of law, and trusts of that nature are expressly excepted from the statute. See 29 Car. 2, c. 3, s. 8.

Where the trust does not arise on the face of the deed itself, the parol evidence must prove the fact of the advance of the purchase-money very clearly: *Newton* v. *Preston*, Prec. Ch. 103; *Gascoigne* v. *Thwing*, 1 Vern. 366; *Willis* v. *Willis*, 2 Atk. 71; *Goodright* v. *Hodges*, 1 Watk. Cop. 229; *Groves* v. *Groves*, 3 Y. & J. 163. Lord Hardwicke, however, in *Willis* v. *Willis*, 2 Atk. 72, thought that parol evidence might be admitted to show the trust from the mean circumstances of the pretended owner of the real estate or inheritance, which made it impossible for him to be purchaser. See, also, *Lench* v. *Lench*, 10 Ves. 518; *Heard* v. *Pilley*, 4 L. R. Ch. App. 552.

It is said by Mr. Sanders, in his Treatise on Uses and Trusts, Vol. I., p. 354, 5th edit., "that, after the death of the supposed nominal purchaser, parol proof can in no instance be admitted against the express declaration of the deed." The same opinion is expressed by another author. See Roberts on Frauds, 99, and *Chalk* v. *Danvers*, 1 Ch. Ca. 310. It does not, however, appear that the Statute of Frauds is violated [*214] by admitting parol proof of the advance of the *purchase-money after the death of the nominal purchaser, any more than it is by allowing such proof in his lifetime. See *Lench* v. *Lench*, 10 Ves. 511, 517; Sugd. V. & P. 910, 11th edit.

If the nominal purchaser admits the payment of the purchase-money by the real purchaser, a trust will doubtless result: *Ryall* v. *Ryall*, 1 Atk. 58; *Lane* v. *Dighton*, Amb. 413; and even although he, by answer to a bill, denies such payment, parol evidence is, it appears, admissible in contradiction to it. See *Gascoigne* v. *Thwing*, 1 Vern. 366; *Newton* v. *Preston*, Prec. Ch. 103; *Bartlett* v. *Pickersgill*, 1 Eden, 515, 516; *Edwards* v. *Pike*, 1 Eden, 267; sed vide *Skett* v. *Whitmore*, 2 Freem. 280.

But parol evidence has been held not admissible to prove a verbal agreement of an agent to purchase an estate for his principal, where the agent having purchased the estate for himself, *with his own money*, had, by his answer, denied the agreement. See *Bartlett* v. *Pickersgill*, 1 Eden, 515, where Lord Keeper Henley, clearly drawing the distinction between the admission of evidence to prove the advance of purchase-money, where the trusts result by operation of the law, and are exempted from the Statute of Frauds, and the admission of parol evidence to prove an agreement, said, that to allow parol evidence in the latter case would be to overturn the statute. "The statute," observes his Lordship, "says that there shall be no trust of land unless by memorandum in writing, *except such trusts as arise by operation of law*. Where money is actually paid, there the trust arises from the payment of the money, and *not from any agreement of the parties.* But this is not like the case of money paid by one man, and the conveyance taken in the name of another; in that case, the bill charges that the estate was bought with the plaintiff's money. If the defendant says he borrowed it of the plaintiff, then the proof will be whether the money was lent or not; if it was not lent, the plaintiff bought the land: but as *here the trust depends on the agreement,* if I establish the one by parol, I establish the other also. . . . *If the plaintiff had paid any part of the purchase-money, it would have been a reason for me to admit the evidence.*" The defendant in this case was afterwards convicted of perjury for having denied the trust; but the record of the conviction was held not to be evidence of the agreement: *Bartlett* v. *Pickersgill,* 1 Eden, 517; see *Chadwick* v. *Maden,* 9 Hare, 188.

In the recent case of *Heard* v. *Pilley,* 4 L. R. Ch. App. 548, doubts were thrown upon *Bartlett* v. *Pickersgill,* by Lords Justices Selwyn and Giffard, the latter of whom observes, " that as regards *the case of *Bartlett* v. *Pickersgill,* it seems to be inconsistent with [*215] all the authorities of the Court, which proceed on the footing that it will not allow the Statute of Frauds to be made an instrument of fraud." See *Nicholson* v. *Mulligan,* 3 I. R. Eq. 308.

Parol evidence is admissible to prove that a purchase has been made with trust-money; and upon that being proved, a trust will result in favour of the cestui que trust, the real owner of the money. Thus, Sir William Grant, M. R., in *Lench* v. *Lench,* 10 Ves. 517, speaking of a purchase alleged to have been made with trust-money, says, " all depends upon the proof of the facts; for, whatever doubts may have been formerly entertained upon this subject, it is now settled that money may, in this manner, be followed into the land in which it is invested; and a claim of this sort may be supported by parol evidence." See also *Anon.,* Sel. Ch. Ca. 57; *Ryall* v. *Ryall,* 1 Atk. 59; *S. C.,* Amb. 413; *Lane* v. *Dighton,* Amb. 409; *Balgney* v. *Hamilton,* cited Amb. 414; *Hughes* v. *Wells,* 9 Hare, 749; *Harford* v. *Lloyd,* 20 Beav. 310; *Bridgman* v. *Gill,* 24 Beav. 302; *Birds* v. *Askey,* 24 Beav. 618; *Pennell* v. *Deffell,* 4 De G. Mac. & G. 372; *Trench* v. *Harrison,* 17 Sim. 111; *Wadham* v. *Rigg,* 1 Drew. & Sm. 216; *Williams* v. *Thomas,* Il. (V. C. K.) 417; *Rolfe* v. *Gregory,* 13 W. R. (L. C.) 355; *Frith* v. *Cartland,* 2 Hem. & Mill. 417; *Hopper* v. *Conyers,* 2 L. Rep. Eq. 549.

No trust will result for a person who advances the purchase-money merely as a loan: *Bartlett* v. *Pickersgill,* 1 Eden, 516; *Crop* v. *Norton,* 9 Mod. 233, 235; *Aveling* v. *Knipe,* 19 Ves. 445.

Resulting trusts, however, as they arise from equitable presumption, may be rebutted by parol evidence, shewing it was the intention of the person who advanced the purchase-money that the person to whom the property was transferred, either solely or jointly with such person, should take for his own benefit (*Goodright* v. *Hodges,* 1 Watk. Cop.

227; *S. C.*, Lofft, 230; *Rider* v. *Kidder*, 10 Ves. 364; *Rundle* v. *Rundle*, 2 Vern. 252; see Order, n. (1) Ib.; *Redington* v. *Redington*, 3 Ridg. P. C. 178; *Deacon* v. *Colquhoun*, 2 Drew. 21; *Garrick* v. *Taylor*, 29 Beav. 79, 10 W. R. (L. J.) 49; *Wheeler* v. *Smith*, 1 Giff. 300; *Nicholson* v. *Mulligan*, 3 I. R. Eq. 308); and they may be rebutted as to part, and prevail as to the remainder. Thus, where a person has advanced the purchase-money, and has taken a transfer of stock, or the conveyance of an estate in the name of a stranger, upon proof of the intention of the person advancing the money to confer upon the nominee a life interest in the stock or estate, the resulting trust will be rebutted [*216] as to the life interest, but will prevail *as to the remainder: *Lane* v. *Dighton*, Amb. 409; *Rider* v. *Kidder*, 10 Ves. 368; *Benbow* v. *Townsend*, 1 My. & K. 501.

But it seems that statements on the part of the person making the purchase, evidencing an intention to confer some undefined benefit not shown to be acted on, and a fortiori if they are inconsistent with the acts of enjoyment of the property, will not be sufficient to rebut a resulting trust: *Nicholson* v. *Mulligan*, 3 I. R. Eq. 308, 323. " Where, however, a person purchased stock in the names of four trustees, who already held stock under a marriage settlement upon trust for him and his wife successively for life, with remainder to their children, it was held that it must be presumed that he intended the stock so purchased to be held upon the trusts of the settlement: *In re Curteis' Trusts*, 14 L. R. Eq. 217."

Where there is an express trust declared, though but by parol, there can be no resulting trust; for resulting trusts, though saved by the Statute of Frauds, are only saved and left as they were before the act; and a bare declaration by parol, before the act, would prevent any resulting trust. See *Bellasis* v. *Compton*, 2 Vern. 294.

Where a person in order to defraud his creditors had transferred stock to a fictitious person, upon proof of the fact, a transfer was ordered to be made to the personal representatives of the transferor (*Arthur* v. *Midland Railway Co.*, 3 K. & J. 204); and in a case where a person had made a similar transfer with the same object, and afterwards became bankrupt, a re-transfer at the suit of his assignees was ordered to be made into his own name: *Green* v. *The Bank of England*, 3 Y. & C. 722.

Advancement.]—As to purchases made in the names of children, or of persons equally favoured, it may be laid down as a general rule that where a purchase is made by a parent in the name of a child, there will prima facie be no resulting trust for the parent, but on the contrary, *a presumption arises that an advancement was intended.* " I remember," says Lord Eldon, " the case of *Dyer* v. *Dyer*, which was very fully considered; and the Court meant to establish this principle, viz., admitting the clear rule that, where A. purchases in the name of B., A.

paying the consideration, B. is a trustee, notwithstanding the Statute of Frauds; that rule does not obtain where the purchase is in the name of a son; that purchase is an advancement prima facie; and in this sense, that this principle of law and presumption is not to be frittered away by nice refinements. Therefore, if the purchase was of a fee simple immediately, prima facie the son would take; so, if it was the purchase of a reversion; and it is very difficult, upon the mere circumstance of the proximity or possible remoteness of possession, to do that away. Nothing could be stronger than the circumstance in *Dyer* v. *Dyer*, that the purchaser had actually devised it. He certainly took it to be his own; but he happened to mistake the rule;" *Finch* v. *Finch*, 15 Ves. 50; see also *Franklin* v. *Franklin*, 1 Swanst. 17, 18; *Grey* v. *Grey*, 2 Swanst. 597; *S. C.*, Finch, 340; *Sidmouth* v. [*217] *Sidmouth*, 2 Beav. 454; *Christy* v. *Courtenay*, 13 Beav. 96; *Williams* v. *Williams*, 32 Beav. 370; *Tucker* v. *Burrow*, 2 Hem. & Mill. 515, 524; and see *Keates* v. *Hewer*, 13 W. R. (L. J.) 34, where, however, it was held that there was an express trust for the purchaser.

The presumption may also arise in favour of any person in regard to whom the person advancing the money has placed himself in loco parentis: thus in *Beckford* v. *Beckford*, Lofft, 490, an illegitimate son; in *Ebrand* v. *Dancer*, 2 Ch. Ca. 26, a grandchild; and in *Currant* v. *Jago*, 1 Coll. 261, the nephew of a wife, were held entitled to property purchased in their names, from the presumption of *advancement* being intended.

But it has been held in a recent case that the mere fact that a grandfather has placed himself in loco parentis towards his illegitimate grandson during the life of his father, will not of itself alone raise a presumption that a purchase in the name of such illegitimate grandson was intended for his advancement; *Tucker* v. *Burrow*, 2 Hem. & Mill. 515; and see *Forrest* v. *Forrest*, 13 W. R. (V.-C. S.) 380.

The presumption also arises in favour of a wife: (*Kingdon* v. *Bridges*, 2 Vern. 67; *Christ's Hospital* v. *Budgin*, 2 Vern. 683; *Back* v. *Andrew*, 2 Vern. 120; *Glaister* v. *Glaister*, 8 Ves. 199; *Rider* v. *Kidder*, 10 Ves. 367; and *Lorimer* v. *Lorimer*, 10 Ves. 367, n.; *Low* v. *Carter*, 1 Beav. 426; and see *Gosling* v. *Gosling*, 3 Drew, 335; *Re Gadbury*, 11 W. R. (V.-C. K.) 395; and where there is a purchase by a person in the joint names of himself and his wife and child: *Devoy* v. *Devoy*, 3 Sm. & Giff. 403.

But the presumption does not arise when the purchaser makes the purchase in the names of himself and a woman with whom he was cohabiting or with whom he had gone through the mere form of marriage, as in the case of a marriage with a deceased wife's sister after the passing of 5 & 6 Will. 4, c. 54; *Soar* v. *Foster*, 4 K. & J. 152.

It seems the presumption of advancement will not arise from the mere purchase by a married woman out of her separate estate in the names of her children, because a married woman is under no legal obligation to provide for her children: *Re De Visme*, 2 De G. Jo. & Sm. 17. But it has been held upon proof of the intention to advance by a married woman making a purchase out of her separate estate in the name of her niece, that the latter was absolutely entitled to the property so purchased: *Beecher* v. *Major*, 2 Drew. & Sm. 431, 13 W. R. (L. C.) 1054.

[*218] *A widowed mother is, it seems, a person standing in such a relation to her child as to raise the presumption in favour of her child. See *Sayre* v. *Hughes*, 5 L. R. Eq. 576; there Susannah Barling, widow, after making her will in favour of her two daughters, transferred East India Stock, which had stood in her own name, into the names of herself and her unmarried daughter, and died. It was held by Sir John Stuart, V. C., that there was a presumption of intended benefit to the unmarried daughter, which was unrebutted, and that the stock belonged absolutely to her. "It has been argued," said his Honor, "that a mother is not a person bound to make an advancement to her child, and that a widowed mother is not a person standing in such a relation to her child as to raise a presumption that in a transaction of this kind a benefit was intended for the child. But the case of a stranger who stands *in loco parentis* seems not so strong as that of a mother. In the case *Re De Visme* (2 De G. Jo. & S. 17), it was said that a mother does not stand in such a relationship to a child as to raise a presumption of benefit for the child. The question in that case arose on a petition in lunacy, and it seems to have been taken for granted that no presumption of benefit arises in the case of a mother. But maternal affection, as a motive of bounty, is, perhaps, the strongest of all, although the duty is not so strong as in the case of a father, inasmuch as it is the duty of a father to advance his child. That, however, is a moral obligation and not a legal one. In *Dyer* v. *Dyer*, Eyre, C. B., shewed that the relationship between parent and child is only a circumstance of evidence . . . . The word 'father' does not occur in Lord Chief Baron Eyre's judgment, and it is not easy to understand why a mother should be presumed to be less disposed to benefit her child in a transaction of this kind than a father."

Where a contract is entered into to purchase real property in the name of a wife or child, although the wife or child as volunteers could not file a Bill for specific performance of the contract, nevertheless if the vendor enforces, or is entitled to payment out of the husband's estate, the conveyance must be made to the wife or child. *Redington* v. *Redington*, 3 Ridg. P. C. 106; *Skidmore* v. *Bradford*, 8 L. R. Eq. 134; and see *Drew* v. *Martin*, 2 Hem. & Mill. 130. There an agreement for the purchase of land was entered into in the names of the husband and wife, and the husband died before the whole of the purchase-money was paid. Upon an inquiry in an administration suit as to the real property of the husband, it was held by Sir W. Page Wood, V.-C., that it did not inclnde the purchased estate, *that the purchase enured for the benefit of the widow, and that the unpaid pur- [*219] chase-money was payable out of the husband's personal estate. But see now 30 & 31 Vict. c. 69.

A binding contract to purchase in the joint names of a man and his wife, has been held to entitle the wife to the benefit of the purchase as survivor: thus in *Vance* v. *Vance*, 1 Beav. 605, A. B. gave directions to his bankers to invest a sum of money in the joint names of himself and his wife, and their brokers accordingly made the purchase. A. B. died after the contract, but before the transfer had been completed. It was held by Lord Langdale, M. R., that the wife was entitled to the stock by survivorship. See also *Bailey* v. *Collett*, 18 Beav. 181; *Harrison* v. *Asher*, 12 Jur. 834, 2 De G. & Sm. 436.

The presumption of advancement also arises in the case of personal as well as of real property. As, for instance, where a person purchases stock, and causes it to be transferred into the name of his son or wife: *Crabb* v. *Crabb*, 1 My. & K. 511; *Sidmouth* v. *Sidmouth*, 2 Beav. 447; *Lorimer* v. *Lorimer*, 10 Ves. 367, n.; *Hepworth* v. *Hepworth*, 11 L. R. Eq. 10. So, also, in *Ebrand* v. *Dancer*, 2 Ch. Ca. 26, a grandfather took bonds in the names of his infant grandchildren. The Lord Chancellor, considering that the grandfather was in loco parentis (the father being dead), said, " The grandchildren are in the immediate care of the grandfather; and if he take bonds in their names, or make leases to them, it shall not be judged a trust, but a provision for the grandchildren, unless it be otherwise declared at the same time ;" and decreed accordingly on that reason, though there were other matters.

Many circumstances of evidence have been taken into consideration by different equity Judges, as rebutting the presumption of advancement, which have given rise to many nice distinctions, not very easy to be understood; most of them, however, are now disregarded. Thus, at one time, it was thought that the *infancy* of a child, in whose name a purchase was made, was a circumstance against its being considered an advancement; it is now, however, considered a strong circumstance in favour of advancement being intended; as in *Lamplugh* v. *Lamplugh*, 1 P. Wms. 111, where a father made a purchase in the name of an infant eight years old, Lord Cowper held, that, " the son, being but eight years old, was unfit for a trustee, and must be intended to be named for his own benefit." See also *Mumma* v. *Mumma*, 2 Vern. 19; *Finch* v. *Finch*, 15 Ves. 43. And it is clear, that the argument against advancement being intended, from the circumstance of the property purchased by the parent being *reversionary, and therefore not [*220] a proper provision for the child, will not prevail, although it has formerly been entertained: *Rumboll* v. *Rumboll* 2 Eden, 17; *Finch* v. *Finch*, 15 Ves. 43; *Murless* v. *Franklin*, 1 Swanst. 13; *Wil-*

liams v. *Williams*, 32 Beav. 378 ; and see *Pilsworth* v. *Mosse*, 14 Ir. Ch. Rep. 163.

The purchase by a parent in the *joint names* of himself and his son, has been objected to by Lord Hardwicke, as a weaker case for advancement than a purchase in the name of the son alone : *Pole* v. *Pole*, 1 Ves. 76 ; and in *Stileman* v. *Ashdown*, 2 Atk. 480, he said that it did not answer the purposes of advancement, as it entitled the father to the possession of the whole till a division, besides the father taking a chance to himself of being a survivor of the other moiety ; nay, if the son had died during his minority, the father would have been entitled to the whole, by virtue of the survivorship ; and the son could not have prevented it by severance, he being an infant. And, moreover, that the father might have other reasons for purchasing in joint-tenancy, namely, to prevent dower upon the estate, and other charges. It seems, however, clear, that, at the present day, the objections of Lord Hardwicke would have little or no weight ; for it has been repeatedly held, both in the old and modern cases, that a purchase by a parent in the joint names of himself and his child, as well as a purchase in the joint names of the child and a stranger, will be held an advancement for the child to the extent of the interest vested in him. See *Scroope* v. *Scroope*, 1 Ch. Ca. 27 ; *Back* v. *Andrew*, 2 Vern. 120 ; *Grey* v. *Grey*, 2 Swanst. 599 ; *Lamplugh* v. *Lamplugh*, 1 P. Wms. 111 ; *Crabb* v. *Crabb*, 1 My. & K. 511 ; *Fox* v. *Fox*, 15 Ir. Ch. Rep. 89. A stranger, however, taking jointly with the child, must hold the estate vested in him in trust for the parent : *Kingdon* v. *Bridges*, 2 Vern. 67 ; *Rumboll* v. *Rumboll*, 1 Eden, 17.

The principal case, overruling *Shaw* v. *Dickenson*, decides that a grant of copyholds, taken by a father in the names of himself and his sons, will be an advancement for the sons, although, according to the custom of the manor, grants were made for lives successive. See *Murless* v. *Franklin*, 1 Swanst. 13 ; *Finch* v. *Finch*, 15 Ves. 43 ; *Skeats* v. *Skeats*. 2 Y. & C. C. C. 9 ; *Jeans* v. *Cooke*, 24 Beav. 513, decided upon the authority of the principal case.

Another circumstance, which has been considered as an objection against the presumption of advancement, is, that the child has been already *fully advanced* : in that case he *may*, it seems, be held a trustee for the father. See *Elliot* v. *Elliot*, 2 Ch. Ca. 231 ; *Pole* v. *Pole*, [*221] 1 Ves. 76 ; *Grey* v. *Grey*, 2 Swanst. 600 ; *Loyd* v. **Read*, 1 P. Wms. 608 ; *Redington* v. *Redington*, 3 Ridg. P. C. 190. The observation, however, of the Lord Chief Baron, in the principal case, would, at the present day, probably be considered a sufficient answer to such an objection to the presumption of advancement. " The rule of equity," observes his Lordship, " as recognised in other cases, is, that the father is the only judge on the question of a son's provision ; and therefore the distinction of the son's being provided for or not, is not very solidly taken." See *Redington* v. *Redington*, 3 Ridg. P. C. 190. And in *Sidmouth* v. *Sidmouth*, 2 Beav. 456, where it was argued that, as the son was adult, he ought to be considered as provided for, and therefore a trustee for his father, Lord Langdale held that circumstance to be of no weight. " The circumstance," said his Lordship, " that the son was adult, does not appear to me to be material. It is said that no establishment was in contemplation, and that no necessity or occasion for advancing the son had occurred; but, in the relation between parent and child, it does not appear to me that any observation of this kind can have any weight. The parent may judge for himself when it suits his own convenience, or when it will be best for his son, to secure him any benefit which he voluntarily thinks fit to bestow upon him ; and it does not follow, that, because the reason for doing it is not known, there was no intention to advance at all." See also *Hepworth* v. *Hepworth*, 11 L. R. Eq. 10.

If a child is advanced but *in part* no implication against advancement arises : *Redington* v. *Redington*, 3 Ridg. P. C. 106. And a child will not be considered as advanced who has only a reversionary estate : *Lamplugh* v. *Lamplugh*, 1 P. Wms. 111.

Another circumstance is mentioned in the principal case, as going against the presumption of advancement, viz., the father's entering into, and keeping possession, and taking the rents and profits of the purchased property, or the son's giving receipts in the name of the father : in such case, if the son is an *infant*, the presumption of advancement will not be rebutted, as the acts of the father, it is said, may be referable to his duty as guardian of his son, and not to an assumption of ownership : *Loyd* v. *Read*, 1 P. Wms. 608 ; *Mumma* v. *Mumma*, 2 Vern. 19 ; *Alleyne* v. *Alleyne*, 2 J. & L. 544 ; *Lamplugh* v. *Lamplugh*, 1 P. Wms. 111 ; *Stileman* v. *Ashdown*, 2 Atk. 480 ; *Taylor* v. *Taylor*, 1 Atk. 386 ; *George's case*, cited 2 Swanst. 600 ; and see *Devoy* v. *Devoy*, 3 Sm. & Giff. 403 ; *Fox* v. *Fox*, 15 Ir. Ch. Rep. 89.

The Lord Chief Baron, however, in the principal case, expresses himself dissatisfied with *the reasoning which refers those acts [*222] of the father to his guardianship; and in *Grey* v. *Grey*, 2 Swanst. 600, Lord Nottingham observed, that " plainly, the reason of the resolution stands not upon the guardianship, but upon the presumptive advancement."

Even where the son is *adult*, it seems that similar acts of ownership by the father will not prevent the presumption of advancement from arising, especially where the son is *advanced but in part*. A leading authority on this subject is *Grey* v. *Grey*, 2 Swanst. 299 ; *S. C.*, Finch, 338. In that case the father received the profits of the estate purchased in the name of his son for twenty years, made leases, took fines, inclosed part of the estate in a park, built much, and provided materials for more buildings, gave directions for a settlement, and treated for a sale of the estate, yet, after all this, it was decided by Lord Nottingham, after much consideration, that the purchase by the father in the son's name was an advancement. " In all cases whatsoever," said his Lordship, " where a trust shall be between father and son contrary to the consideration and operation of law, the same ought to appear upon very plain, and coherent, and binding evidence, and not by any argument or inference from the father's continuing in possession and receiving the profits, which sometimes the son may not in good manners contradict, especially where he is *advanced but in part;* and if such inference shall not be made from the father's perception of profits, it shall never be made from any words between them in common discourse; for, in those, there may be great variety and sometimes apparent contradiction. Therefore, where the proof is not clear and manifest, the Court ought to follow the law, and it is very safe so to do :" Finch, 340 ; see, however, *Murless* v. *Franklin*, 1 Swanst. 171. Upon the same principle, in *Sidmouth* v. *Sidmouth*, 2 Beav. 447, where moneys were invested in the funds by a father in the name of the son, the dividends of which were received by the father during his life, under a power of attorney from his son, it was held, after his death, that this was an advancement, and that the funds belonged to the son.

Where, however, a son is *fully advanced*, the father's entering into possession, and into the receipt of the rents or profits of property purchased in his son's name, *may* be considered as evidence of a trust. See *Grey* v. *Grey*, 2 Swanst. 600.

It seems, however, that where evidence contemporaneous with the transaction shows that the father had an intention of reserving a life interest in the property to himself, or that he had an intention of qualifying the absolute right purported to be given to his son, the presumption of advancement will be rebutted : *Dumper* v. *Dumper*, 3 Giff. 583 ; *Down* v. *Ellis*, 35 Beav. 578.

[*223]

The presumption of advancement may be rebutted by evidence of facts showing the father's intention that the son should take property, purchased in his name, as a trustee, and not for his own benefit. Such facts, however, must have taken place antecedently to, or contemporaneously with, the purchase, or else immediately after it, so as to form, in fact, part of the same transaction (*Grey* v. *Grey*, 2 Swanst. 594 ; *Redington* v. *Redington*, 3 Ridg. P. C. 106, 177, 194 ; *Murless* v. *Franklin*, 1 Swanst. 17, 19 ; *Sidmouth* v. *Sidmouth*, 2 Beav. 447 ; *Scawin* v. *Scawin*, 1 Y. & C. C. C. 65 ; *Prankerd* v. *Prankerd*, 1 S. & S. 1 ; *Christy* v. *Courtenay*, 13 Beav. 26 ; *Collinson* v. *Collinson*, 3 De G. Mac. & G. 409 ; *Bone* v. *Pollard*, 24 Beav. 283 ; *Childers* v. *Childers*, 1 De G. & Jo. 482) ; but subsequent facts will not be admissible in evidence to show the intention of the father against the presumption of advancement. Thus, a devise of the property, as in the principal case (*Mumma* v. *Mumma*, 2 Vern. 19 ; *Crabb* v. *Crabb*, 1 My.

& K. 511; *Skeats* v. *Skeats*, 2 Y. & C. C. C. 9; *Jeans* v. *Cooke*, 24 Beav. 513; *Dumper* v. *Dumper*, 3 Giff. 583; *Williams* v. *Williams*, 32 Beav. 370), or a mortgage (*Back* v. *Andrew*, 2 Vern. 110), or a demise of copyholds by a licence obtained *subsequently* to the purchase in the name of the child (*Murless* v. *Franklin*, 1 Swanst. 13), will be ineffectual: secus, where the licence to lease is obtained, or a surrender to the use of a will is made at the same Court as the grant: *Swift* v. *Davis*, 8 East, 354, n.; *Prankerd* v. *Prankerd*, 1 S. & S. 1.

The presumption of advancement may also be rebutted by evidence of parol declarations of the father contemporaneous with, but not by any of his declarations made subsequent to, the purchase: *Elliot* v. *Elliot*, 2 Ch. Ca. 231; *Woodman* v. *Morrell*, 2 Freem. 33; *Birch* v. *Blagrave*, Amb. 266; *Finch* v. *Finch*, 15 Ves. 51; *Redington* v. *Redington*, 3 Ridg. P. C. 106; *Sidmouth* v. *Sidmouth*, 2 Beav. 456. But where a person had transferred stock into the joint names of himself, wife, and child, and had regularly received the dividends, Sir J. Stuart, V.-C., some years after the transfer, received the evidence of the husband and wife as to his intention at the time of the transfer, in order to repel the presumption of advancement: *Devoy* v. *Devoy*, 3 Sm. & Giff. 403; *Forrest* v. *Forrest*, 13 W. R. (V.-C. S.) 380; see also *Stone* v. *Stone*, 3 Jur. N. S. 708.

A fortiori, parol evidence may be given by the son to show the intention of the father to advance him; for such evidence is in support both of the legal interest of the son and of the equitable presumption: *Lamplugh* v. *Lamplugh*, *1 P. Wms. 113; *Redington* v. *Redington*, 3 Ridg. P. C. 182, 195; *Taylor* v. *Taylor*, 1 Atk. 386. [*224]

The acts and declarations of the father *subsequent* to the purchase may be used in evidence *against* him by the son, although they could not, as we have before seen, be used by the father against the son: (*Redington* v. *Redington*, 3 Ridg. P. C. 195, 197; *Sidmouth* v. *Sidmouth*, 2 Beav. 455;) and the better opinion seems to be, that the subsequent acts and declarations of the son can be used against him by the father where there is nothing showing the intention of the father, at the time of the purchase, sufficient to counteract the effect of those declarations: *Sidmouth* v. *Sidmouth*, 2 Beav. 455; *Scawin* v. *Scawin*, 1 Y. & C. C. C. 65; *Pole* v. *Pole*, 1 Ves. 76; *Jeans* v. *Cooke*, 24 Beav. 521; see, however, *Murless* v. *Franklin*, 1 Swanst. 20.

Evidence, however, it seems, will not be admissible to rebut the presumption of advancement where the object of the evidence is to show that the person who made the transfer intended it to take effect in fraud of the law. See *Childers* v. *Childers*, 3 K. & J. 310; there a father conveyed by registered deed 900 acres of land in the Bedford Level to his son, in order to make him eligible as a bailiff. The son shortly afterwards died, without being aware of the conveyance, and without having been elected bailiff. It was held by Sir W. Page Wood, V.-C., that the gift was irrevocable, and that the heir of the son was entitled to it for his own benefit. "I cannot," said his Honor, "allow the plaintiff to say, 'I intended this deed to operate in fraud of the law.'" Upon the discovery of fresh evidence in this case—a letter to the Registrar of the Level—the order of the Vice-Chancellor was discharged, and leave was given to amend the bill. Whereupon it was held by the Lords Justices, upon the evidence, that neither the father nor the Registrar intended or considered the transaction to have the effect of making the son beneficial owner; that, moreover, on the construction of the Bedford Level Act, a dry legal estate was a sufficient qualification. And that, therfeore, as there was nothing illegal in the father's design, and no intention to represent the son as beneficial owner, the father was entitled on the ground of trust or mistake or both to have a reconveyance from the heir of the son. See *Childers* v. *Childers*, 1 De G. & Jo. 482. In *May* v. *May*, 33 Beav. 81, a conveyance of property by a father to his son to give him a qualification to vote was held not invalid but a bounty. In *Davies* v. *Otty*, 35 Beav. 208, the plaintiff, believing that his wife, who had deserted him ten years previously, was dead, married a second time, and having afterwards heard that his first [*225] wife was living, and *thinking that he was liable to be convicted for bigamy, absolutely conveyed his real estate to the defendant in consideration of 20*l*. It was proved by parol evidence that the deed was executed in pursuance of an arrangement that the defendant should hold the property at the disposal of the plaintiff. The plaintiff's alarm was groundless; the consideration was never paid. The plaintiff remained in possession, and paid certain sums due to a building society in respect of the property. The defendant denied the trust, and claimed the benefit of the Statute of Frauds. It was held by Sir John Romilly, M. R., that "the operation of the Statute of Frauds was excluded by the fraud of the defendant in refusing to reconvey. And also by reason of a resulting trust within the 8th section of the Statute, his Honor said he was clearly of opinion that there was no illegality in the transaction, and that the plaintiff was quite justified, morally and legally, in marrying the second wife, although the effect of it may have been, that she did not become his wife: The long absence of his first wife was sufficient to justify the plaintiff in coming to the conclusion that she was dead." See also *Manning* v. *Gill*, 13 L. R. Eq. 485; *Haigh* v. *Kaye*, 7 L. R. Ch. App. 469.

As to the presumption of advancement of a wife being rebutted on a purchase by a husband of stock in the joint names of himself and his wife, see *Smith* v. *Warde*, 15 Sim. 56, and *Hoyes* v. *Kimbersley*, 2 Sm. & Giff. 195.

Where part of the money invested in stock by a husband in the name of himself and his wife is sold out by them, it becomes his property.

Thus, in *Re Gadbury*, 11 W. R. (V.-C. K.) 895, a sum of money was invested in the funds in the joint names of a husband and wife, and she, by power of attorney from him, sold out a portion, and with his knowledge kept it locked up in her own special custody until his death. It was held by Sir R. T. Kindersley, V.-C., that the portion which remained in the funds in the joint names of the husband and wife survived to the wife, but that the other portion, which was sold out by her and kept in her custody, formed, on the husband's death, a part of his general personal estate.

In the case of an advancement, where part of the purchase-money remains unpaid, it will be a debt payable by the assets of the father: *Redington* v. *Redington*, 3 Ridg. P. C. 106, 201.

Where an advancement is made by a person largely indebted at the time, it will be void under the 13 Eliz. c. 5, as against his creditors: (*Christy* v. *Courtenay*, 13 Beav. 96, 101; *Barrack* v. *M'Culloch*, 3 K. & J. 110; sed vide *Drew* v. *Martin*, 2 Hem. & Mill. 133), but *it [*226] is not within 27 Eliz. c. 4: *Drew* v. *Martin*, 2 Hem. & Mill. 130, 133.

And where the relation of client and solicitor subsists between the parent and child, the ordinary presumption in favour of the transaction being a gift, will be excluded, and the burden of proof, as to its validity, will be thrown upon the son acting as solicitor: *Garrett* v. *Wilkinson*, 2 De G. & Sm. 244.

Where a father transfers shares in an incorporated company to his infant son, although the son might claim the shares as an advancement, nevertheless the Court will, on the part of the infant, repudiate the shares, if the company be wound up, and the father will be a contributory (*Reid's Case*, 24 Beav. 318); but where the father has applied for shares in the name of his son, and although he has paid a deposit, if the company have refused to allow him to execute the deed on behalf of his son, he will not be a contributory: *Maxwell's Case*, 24 Beav. 321.

It is well settled in this country, as it is in England, that if a person purchases an estate with his own money, and the deed is taken in the name of another, the trust of the land results, by presumption or implication of law, and without any agreement, to him who advances the money; and the case is the same where the contract of purchase is made by the *cestui que trust* personally, and where it is made through the nominal grantee as his agent: such trusts are not within the statute of frauds, and may be established by parol, notwithstanding the deed acknowledges the consideration to have been paid by the nominal grantee; *Jackson* v. *Sternbergh*, 1 Johnson's Cases, 153, 155; S. C., 1 Johnson, 45, n.; *Foote* v. *Colvin*, 3 Id. 216, 221; *Jackson* v. *Matsdorf*, 11 Id. 91,

96; *Jackson* v. *Mills*, 13 Id. 463; *Jackson* v. *Seelye*, 16 Id. 107, 199; *Forsyth* v. *Clark*, 3 Wendell, 638, 650; *Guthrie* v. *Gardner*, 19 Id. 414; *Boyd* v. *M'Lean*, 1 Johnson's Chancery, 582, 586; *Botsford* v. *Burr*, 2 Id. 405, 409; *White* v. *Carpenter*, 2 Paige, 218, 238; *Kellogg* v. *Wood*, 4 Id. 579, 580; *Partridge* v. *Havens*, 10 Id. 618, 626; *Lowersbury* v. *Purdy*, 16 Barbour, 376; *Farunger* v. *Ramsay*, 2 Maryland, 365; *Williams* v. *Brown*, 14 Illinois, 200; *Nichols* v. *Thornton*, 16 Id. 113; *Gass* v. *Gass*, 1 Hieshell, 113; *Lloyd* v. *Carter*, 5 Harris, 216; *Curd* v. *The Lancaster Bank*, Ohio State R. 1; *Williams* v. *Van Tuyl*, 2 Ohio, N. S. 336; *Barron* v. *Barron*, 24 Vermont, 375; *Peabody* v. *Tarbill*, 2 Cushing, 236; *Lynch* v. *Cox*, 11 Id. 265; *Caple* v. *M'Callum*, 27 Alabama, 461; *Beck* v. *Graybill*, 4 Casey, 66; *Kisler* v. *Kisler*, 2 Watts, 323, 324; *Jackman* v. *Ringland*, 4 Watts & Sergeant, 149, 150; *Page* v. *Page*, 8 New Hampshire, 187, 195; *Buck* v. *Pike*, 2 Fairfield, 9, 23; *Baker* v. *Vining*, 30 Maine, 121, 125; *Dorsey et al.* v. *Clarke et al.*, 4 Harris & Johnson, 551, 556; *Neale* v. *Hagthrop*, 3 Bland, 551, 584; *Perry et al.* v. *Head et al.*, 1 Marshall, 46, 47; *Chapline's Adm'r* v. *M'Afee, &c.*, 3 J. J. Marshall, 513, 515; *Letcher* v. *Letcher's Heirs*, 4 Id. 590, 592; *Jenison* v. *Graves*, 2 Blackford, 441, 447; *Elliott* v. *Armstrong*, Id. 199, 207; *Runnels* v. *Jackson*, 1 Howard's Mississippi, 358; *Powell* v. *Powell*, 1 Freeman, 134; *Talliaferro* v.

The Heirs of Talliaferro, 6 Alabama, 404, 406; *Anderson & Bro's* v. *Jones et al.*, 10 Id. 401, 420; *Caple* v. *M'Callum*, 27 Id. 461; *Smitheal* v. *Gray*, 1 Humphreys, 491, 496; *Ensley et als.* v. *Balentine et als.*, 4 Id. 233, 234; *Thomas* v. *Walker*, 6 Id. 93, 95; *Peabody & Another* v. *Tarbill*, 2 Cushing, 227, 232; *Long* v. *Steiger*, Texas, 460; *Shepherd* v. *White*, 10 Id. 72. "The substance of the cases on this subject," said the court in *Newells* v. *Morgan et al.*, 2 Harrington, 225, 230, in the language of the principal case, "appears to be, that the trust of a legal estate, whether freehold, copyhold, or leasehold; whether taken in the names of the purchasers and others jointly, or in the name of others without that of the purchaser; whether in one name or several; whether jointly or successively, results to the man who advances the purchase-money; and this in analogy to the rule of the common law, that where a feoffment is made without consideration, the use results to the feoffor." The trust will revert to the source and origin of the consideration, whatever may be its character or nature; and hence land set off or taken in payment of a judgment, held in trust for another, will belong in equity to the latter, and not to the person by whom the judgment is recovered, or who appears on the record as its owner; *Peabody* v. *Tarbill*, 2 Cushing, 236. A trust arises *a fortiori* where a trustee or guardian takes a conveyance in his own name, and gives the assets of the estate in payment, because there is, under these circumstances, a breach of confidence beside the principle that the right of property, should result to the source of the consideration; *Blauvelt* v. *Ackerman*, 5 C. E. Green, 141; *Durling* v. *Harmar*, Ib. 220; *Snell* v. *Elam*, 2 Heiskell, 82. But there is this difference, that the *cestui que trusts* may, under these circumstances, elect whether they will take the land, or charge the trustee with the sum wrongfully diverted from the proper channel.

It may be considered also as settled in this country, that a resulting trust may be established upon parol evidence against the answer of the grantee denying the trust; but the evidence must be full, clear, and satisfactory; *Boyd* v. *M'Lean*, 1 Johnson's Chancery, 582, 586; *Elliott* v. *Armstrong*, 2 Blackford, 199, 209; *Jenison* v. *Graves*, Id. 441, 447; *Blair* v. *Bass*, 4 Id. 540, 545; *Snelling* v. *Utterback*, *&c.*, 1 Bibb, 609, 610; *Larkins* v. *Rhodes*, 5 Porter, 196, 207; *Enos et al.* v. *Hunter*, 4 Gilman, 211, 218; *Smith et al.* v. *Sackett et al.*, 5 Gilman, 544; *Page* v. *Page*, 8 New Hampshire, 187, 195; *Buck* v. *Pike*, 2 Fairfield, 9, 24; *Baker* v. *Vining*, 30 Maine, 121, 126; *M'Cannon* v. *Pettitt*, 3 Sneed, 242. There is no doubt, also, that, here, such a trust may be set up after the death of the nominal purchaser: see *Freeman* v. *Kelly*, 1 Hoffman, 90, 98. A resulting trust may be established upon the parol declarations or acknowledgments of the person in whose name the conveyance is

taken, that another paid the purchase-money, which will be evidence against himself, and against those claiming under him by descent, or otherwise than as *bona fide* purchasers for value; and though such evidence is admitted to be most unsatisfactory, on account of the facility with which it may be fabricated, and the impossibility of contradicting it, and the total alteration of the effect which the slightest mistake or failure of recollection may cause, yet, under strict caution, it is competent ground for a decree, and if plain and consistent, and especially if corroborated by circumstances, may be sufficient; *Malin* v. *Malin*, 1 Wendell, 626, 648, 649, 652, 653; *Harder* v. *Harder*, 2 Sandford, 17, 21, 22; and see *Smith* v. *Burnham*, 3 Sumner, 435, 438. See *Botsford* v. *Burr*, 2 Johnson's Chancery, 405, 411, 412; *Snelling* v. *Utterback*, *&c.*, 1 Bibb, 609, 611. The doctrine of resulting trusts from payment of the purchase-money is admitted to be a very questionable one, and is acted upon, only with great caution, and the circumstances from which such a trust is to be raised, must be clearly proved; *Faringger* v. *Ramsay*, 4 Maryland Ch. 33; especially if much time has elapsed; *Botsford* v. *Burr*, 409, 415; *Freeman* v. *Kelly*, 1 Hoffman, 90, 93, 98; *Jackson* v. *Moore*, 6 Cowen, 706, 726; *Jackson* v. *Bateman*, 2 Wendell, 570, 573; *Carey* v. *Callan's Ex'r*, *&c.*, 6 B. Monroe, 44, 45; *Baker* v. *Vining*, 30 Maine, 121, 126. In *Strimpfler* v. *Roberts*, 6 Harris, 283, the lapse of fifty-one years was held to be a bar; and the opinion expressed by the court that the same result ought to follow, in every case where the claimant lies by during the period fixed by the Statute of Limitations as a bar to the assertion of a title to land by ejectment, unless there are circumstances which explain and excuse his inaction, has been adopted and confirmed in the subsequent course of decisions : *Langelfelter* v. *Richey*, 8 P. F. Smith, 128; *Collier* v. *Collier*, 30 Indiana, 32.

It has been said that the evidence must not only be distinct and credible, but preponderate, and that if it does not, the presumption is in favor of the party who has the deed; *Johnson* v. *Quarles*, 46 Missouri, 423; *Nixon's Appeal*, 13 P. F. Smith, 279, and the case of *Faringger* v. *Ramsay*, 2 Maryland, 365; would seem to show, that the payment must be proved explicitly, and not be a mere inference or deduction from the facts and circumstances.

The whole foundation of a resulting trust of this nature, is the payment of the money by the *cestui que trust*, or by the trustee, with funds which are, in equity, the funds of the *cestui que trust;* *Russell* v. *Allen*, 10 Paige, 249; *The Harrisburg Bank* v. *Tyler*, 3 W. & S. 373; *Kirkpatrick* v. *M'Donald*, 1 Jones, 393; *Smith* v. *Burnham*, 3 Sumner, 435. A parol agreement that another shall be interested in the purchase of lands, or a parol declaration by the purchaser that he buys for another, without an advance of money by

that other, comes directly within the provisions of the Statute of Frauds, and cannot give birth to a resulting trust, nor in the absence of fraud to a trust of any other description : *Irwin* v. *Ivers*, 7 Indiana, 308. An allegation that a purchaser at a sheriff's sale agreed orally to hold the premises for the benefit of the defendant in the execution, will not therefore render him a trustee, unless sustained by evidence in writing, and signed by the party to be charged, *Mincot* v. *Mitchell*, 30 Indiana, 228; *Kisler* v. *Kisler*, 2 Watts, 323. If a person takes a conveyance of lands in his own name, and pays for them with his own money, parol evidence that he was employed to do this as agent for another, whatever other equity it may raise, will not create a resulting trust of the land by implication of law;[1] *Barnet* v.

---

[1] The exception which withdraws trusts arising by implication or construction of law, from the operation of the statute, extends far enough to embrace every trust growing out of a breach of duty aside from contract. *Seichrist's Appeal*, 16 P. F. Smith, 237, 241. Thus, a purchase by an executo , trustee, or agent, in fraud of his office, or of the confidence reposed by the principal, will give rise to a trust, whether (as the better opinion would seem to be) the transaction is proved by the testimony of witnesses or by written evidence, *ante*, 221; for, under these circumstances, the trust is deduced from the *res gestæ*, which may always be proved by oral testimony, because, from the nature of things, they can seldom be established in any other way. And it is, perhaps, hardly too much to say, that wherever

Dougherty, 8 Casey, 272; and therefore, if the party who sets up a resulting trust, made no payment, he cannot show by parol proof that the purchase was made for his benefit, or on his account; *Botsford* v. *Burr; Freeman* v. *Kelly; Lathrop* v. *Hoyt*, 7 Barbour's S. C. 60, 63; *Smith* v. *Burnham*, 3 Sumner, 435, 462; *Pinnock* v. *Clough*, 16 Vermont, 501, 506, 509; *Dorsey et al.* v. *Clarke et al.*, 4 Harris & Johnson, 551, 557; *Fischli* v. *Dumaresly*, 3 Marshall, 23; *Thompson* v. *Branch*, Meigs, 390, 394; *Ensley et als.* v. *Balentine et als.*, 4 Humphreys, 233, 235; *Peebles* v. *Reading*, 8 Sergeant & Rawle, 484, 492; *Lynn* v. *Lynn et al.*, 5 Gilman, 602, 620; or, as it has been frequently declared, unless there is something more in

the transaction than is implied from the violation of a parol agreement, there is no resulting trust; see *Jackman* v. *Ringland*, 4 Watts & Sergeant, 149, 150; *Smith* v. *Smith*, 3 Casey, 180; *Sharp* v. *Long*, 4 Id. 434; *Green* v. *Drummond*, 31 Maryland, 71; *Walker* v. *Brenagerd*, 13 Smedes & Marshall, 723, 765, where the cases are collected; and see *Sample* v. *Coulson*, 9 Watts & Sergeant, 62, 66. Payment or advance of the purchase-money *before*, or *at the time of* the purchase, is indispensable; a *subsequent* payment will not, by relation, attach a trust to the original purchase; *Nixon's Appeal*, 13 P. F. Smith, 279; because the trust arises out of the circumstance that the money of the real, and not of the nominal purchaser, formed, at the time, the consideration of the purchase, and became converted into land; *Botsford* v. *Burr; Steere* v. *Steere*, 5 Johnson's Chancery, 1, 19, 20; *Jackson* v. *Moore*, 6 Cowen, 706, 726; *Freeman* v. *Kelly*, 1 Hoffman, 90, 93; *White* v. *Carpenter*, 2 Paige, 218, 238; *Pennock* v. *Clough*, 16 Vermont, 501, 506; *Page* v. *Page*, 8 New Hampshire, 187, 196; *Buck* v. *Pike*, 2 Fairfield 9, 24; *Conner* v. *Lewis*, 16 Maine, 268, 274; *Graves* v. *Dugan*, 6 Dana, 331, 332; *Foster* v. *The Trustees of the Athenæum*, 3 Alabama, 302, 309; *Wallaces* v. *Marshall*, &c., 9 B. Monroe, 148, 155; *Gee* v. *Gee*, 2 Sneed, 395. "The trust, said Chancellor Kent, in *Botsford* v. *Burr*, 2 Johnson's Chancery, 405, 414, 415, "must have been coeval with the deeds, or it cannot exist

---

one obtains or withholds land in fraud of another, equity will decree a trust, the statute being meant to suppress, and not to encourage fraud; *Jenkins* v. *Eldridge*, 3 Story, 181, 291; *Morey* v. *Herrick*, 6 Harris, 125, 128; *Brown* v. *Dysinger*, 1 Rawle, 408; *Hoge* v. *Hoge*, Id. 163, 214. See *Lingelfelter* v. *Richey*, 8 P. F. Smith, 415; *Seichrist's Appeal*, 16 Id. 237; *Foust* v. *Haas*, 23 Id. 235; 2 Story's Equity Jurisprudence, 68; Hill on Trustees, 91; *post*, notes to *Woollam* v. *Hearn*, vol. 2.

Trusts thus deduced from facts and circumstances, or from the relation which the parties bear to each other, are more accurately described as constructive trusts than as trusts by operation of law; Hill on Trustees, 144; although the latter name has also been applied to them by judges of great authority; *Church* v. *Sterling*, 16 Conn. 388, 401. In either aspect. they are independent of agreement, and may be established by parol evidence.

at all. After a party has made a purchase with his own moneys or credit, a subsequent tender, or even re-imbursement, may be evidence of some other contract, or the ground of some other relief, but it cannot, by any retrospective effect, produce the trust of which we are speaking. There never was an instance of such a trust so created, and there never ought to be, for it would destroy all the certainty and security of conveyances of real estate. The resulting trust, not within the Statute of Frauds, and which may be shown without writing, is *when the purchase is made* with the proper moneys of the *cestui que trust*, and the deed not taken in his name. The trust results from the *original transaction*, at the time it takes place, and at no other time, and it is founded on the *actual payment of money*, and on no other ground. It cannot be mingled or confounded with any subsequent dealings whatever. They are governed by different principles, and the doctrine of a resulting trust would be mischievous and dangerous, if we once departed from the simplicity of this rule." See *Latham* v. *Henderson*, 47 Illinois, 185. "After the legal title has once passed to the grantee by deed," said another Chancellor, in *Rogers* v. *Murray*, 3 Paige, 390, 398, "it is impossible to raise a resulting trust so as to divest that legal estate, by the subsequent application of the funds of a third person to the improvement of the property, or to satisfy the unpaid purchase-money. The resulting trust must arise, if

at all, at the time of the execution of the conveyance." Accordingly, it has been held that if one of two partners buys in his own name, and gives his own bond and mortgage, and afterwards pays out of partnership funds, a resulting trust will not thereby be created, unless it be unequivocally shown that there was an agreement at the time of the purchase that the funds should be so appropriated; *Forsyth* v. *Clarke*, 3 Wendell, 638, 651. [Where, however, two persons make a joint purchase and one pays at the time, a subsequent payment by the other in pursuance of the original agreement, may relate back to the execution of the deed and give rise to a resulting trust; *Nixon's Appeal*, 13 P. F. Smith, 279, 282. A note or other security given by a third party for, and paid afterwards out of the funds of the *cestui que trust*, may, moreover, be a sufficient payment; *Morey* v. *Herrick*, 6 Harris, 123; *Lounsbury* v. *Purdy*, 16 Barbour, 380; and this is equally true of money advanced or loaned to him by a third person; *Gomez* v. *The Tradesmen's Bank*, 4 Sandford's S. C. 106; *Smith* v. *Sacket*, 5 Gilman, 534, or even by the person sought to be charged with the trust, because he will be equally entitled to repayment, whether the land rises or falls in value; *Paige* v. *Paige*, 8 New Hampshire, 187; *Boyd* v. *M'Lean*, 1 Johns. Ch. 582; *Deyden* v. *Hanway*, 31 Maryland, 254; *Runnels* v. *Jackson*, 1 Howard, Miss. 358; *Bragg* v. *Panck*, 42 Maine, 502; and may, by an express or implied agreement, have an equitable lien for reimbursement; *Reeve* v. *Strawn*, 14 Illinois, 94; *Ferguson* v. *Sutphen*, 3 Gilman, 547; *Coates* v. *Woodsworth*, 13 Illinois, 634; *post*, notes to *Woollam* v. *Hearn*, vol. 2. Hence, proof that part of the consideration of a deed to a father, consisted of money belonging to his daughter, and that the rest was paid by him for her benefit as an advancement, will create a trust in the whole land for the daughter; *Beck* v. *Graybill*, 4 Casey, 66. See *Fleming* v. *M'Hale*, 47 Illinois, 282.]

There is no doubt that payment of part of the purchase-money will create a resulting trust to the extent of that payment; *Botsford* v. *Burr*, 2 Johnson's Chancery, 405, 410; *Purdy* v. *Purdy*, 3 Maryland, Ch. Decisions, 547; *Bank* v. *Swazey*, 35 Maine, 81; *Shoemaker* v. *Smith*, 11 Humph. 81; *Pierce* v. *Pierce*, 7 B. Monroe, 433; *Duffield* v. *Wallace*, S. & R. 521; *Morey* v. *Herrick*, 6 Harris, 123; *Smith* v. *Wright*, 47 Illinois, 185; *Car* v. *Codding*, 38 California, 91; and a joint advance of money for a purchase, raises a corresponding resulting trust; *Ross* v. *Hegeman*, 2 Edwards, 373, 375; *Larkins* v. *Rhodes*, 5 Porter, 196, 200. If a joint deed be made to several who pay unequally, a trust in the land results to each *pro tanto* of the amount paid by each; *King* v. *Hamilton*, 16 Illinois, 190, 196; *Fleming* v *M'Hale*, 47 Illinois, 282; and where an executory contract of joint purchase was entered into, and separate notes executed to the vendor for the amounts to be paid

by each, it was held that an equitable trust arose in favor of each, *pro tanto* of the consideration promised to be paid by each, which chancery, upon full payment, would specifically enforce by decreeing a conveyance accordingly; *Brothers* v. *Porter et al.*, 6 B. Monroe, 106, 107, 108. See *Bogert* v. *Perry*, 17 Johnson, 351; *Jackson* v. *Bateman*, 2 Wendell, 570, 573. But the amounts paid by the different parties must be shown with certainty; and no case, it was recently said, has been found where a resulting trust has been held to arise upon payments made in common by the one asserting his claim, and the grantee in the deed, where the consideration is set forth in the deed as moving solely from the latter, where the amount belonging to one and the other is uncertain, and unknown even to those who make the payment, and no satisfactory evidence is offered of the portion, which was really the property of each; *Baker* v. *Vining*, 30 Maine, 121, 127.

The trust which results by implication and operation of law, from the payment of the purchase-money or of a part of it, and without any agreement, is a pure and simple trust of the ownership of the land; it is not an interest in the proceeds of the land, nor a lien upon it for the advance, nor an equity or right to a sum of money to be raised out of it, or upon the security of it. Such rights arise from special agreements, and are the subjects of express trusts; or where implied, it is from other circumstances than the mere ownership of the purchase-money. There can be no resulting trust of an estate to a particular extent of its value, leaving the residue of its value in the grantee; nor can an estate result to one who pays the consideration, as a pledge or security for its payment: such interests may be created or secured by mortgage, lien, or express trusts. What is known as a resulting trust is a complete trust of original ownership, and it is nothing else. Therefore, to make a partial payment create a resulting trust at all, the money must be paid as a definite aliquot part of the *consideration* of the purchase, and then the trust will be of an aliquot part of the whole estate in the property: but unless the payment or advance be of a definite part of the *consideration* money, as such, no trust will result by implication of law, and without agreement; *White* v. *Carpenter*, 2 Paige, 218, 238, 239, 240, 241; *Sayre* v. *Townsend*, 15 Wendell, 647, 650; *Freeman* v. *Kelly*, 1 Hoffman, 90, 96; *Evans' Estate*, 2 Ashmead, 470, 482; *Smith* v. *Burnham*, 3 Sumner, 435, 462, 463; *Green* v. *Drummond*, 31 Maryland, 71; *Baker* v. *Vining*, 30 Maine, 121; *Cutler* v. *Tuttle*, 4 C. E. Greene, 549, 562; *M'Gowan* v. *M'Gowan*, 14 Gray, 119. [It has, nevertheless, been said, that where a purchase is made with funds furnished jointly, and there is no sufficient proof the amount advanced by each, the presumption should be, that the same amount was contributed by all; *Shoemaker*

v. *Smith*, 11 Humphreys, 81; and it would seem that when the doubt or uncertainty arises from the failure of a buyer who has been acting on behalf of others, to keep an accurate account, or from his having confused the funds of his principals with his own, it should be solved by making every reasonable inference against him, and in favor of those whose remedy is embarrassed by his negligence; *Seaman* v. *Cook*, 14 Illinois, 501.

There can be little doubt that when the means through which a purchase is to be effected, come from the alleged *cestui que trust*, and go into the hands of one who agrees to act as his agent, but takes the deed in his own name, a trust will result, although the agent uses his own money and suffers the principal's to lie idle, or employs it in some other way; *Melloy* v. *Melloy*, 5 Bush. 464; *Langerfelter* v. *Rickey*, 2 P. F. Smith; *Rann County* v. *Harrington*, 50 Illinois, 252; *Frank's Appeal*, 9 P. F. Smith, 190, 195, 196. Under these circumstances the trust is deduced not from contract or agreement, but from the transaction as a whole, and although the very money may not be traced into the land, still the case is one where equity, for the sake of the remedy, regards that which ought to be done as done, and will not allow the agent to rely on his disregard of his duty as a reason why he should be in a better position than if it had been fulfilled; *Frank's Appeal*, see *Sandford* v. *Jones*, 35 California, 422; *Price* v.

Reeves, 38 Id. 457 ; *Squire's Appeal*, 20 P. F. Smith, 266.

It is immaterial whether the price is paid in money, or by giving value in any other form; *Clark* v. *Clark*, 43 Vermont, 685; *Blauvelt* v. *Akerman*, 5 C. E. Greene, 41 ; *Peabody* v. *Tarbill*, 2 Cushing, 346. Accordingly where a mortgage which has been transferred to secure a loan, is sued out by the assignee who buys at the sale, and exchanges receipts with the sheriff, or pays the money and receives it back, the transaction may be regarded as a purchase with the funds of the lender, and a trust decreed for his benefit; *Slee* v. *The Manhattan Co.*, 1 Paige, 48; *Hoyt* v. *Martense*, 16 New York, 231, *ante*. And such will clearly be the effect if the lender stays away from the sale in consequence of a promise that the title shall be held on the same trust as the mortgage, and with a right to redeem on repaying the amount due; *Price* v. *Reeves*, 38 California, 457.

A trust will be decreed under these decisions in favor of him who is the source of the consideration, whether it be land, goods, money, securities, or credit. " The exact time and form," said Wells, J., in *Blodgett* v. *Hildreth*, 103 Mass. 484, " in which the consideration was rendered, are immaterial, provided they were in pursuance of the contract of purchase. He who purchases at the time and pays afterwards, is as much a purchaser as if he had bought for cash."]

If a trustee, or agent of any description, lay out the money which he holds in his fiduciary character, in the purchase of land, and take the conveyance to himself, the person entitled to the money, may, at his election, charge the trustee personally, or follow the money into the land, and claim the purchase as made in trust for him, and he may establish such a trust by parol evidence; *Wallace* v. *Duffield*, 2 S. & R. 521 ; *Kisler* v. *Kisler*, 2 Watts, 323 ; *The Harrisburg Bank* v. *Tyler*, 3 W. & S. 373; *Wilhelm* v. *Folmer*, 6 Barr, 296; *Kirkpatrick* v. *M'Donald*, 1 Jones, 393; *Oliver* v. *Pitt*, 3 Howard, 401; *Seaman* v. *Cook*, 14 Illinois, 501; *Williams* v. *Hollingsworth*, 1 Strobhart's Eq. 103; *Garrett* v. *Garrett*, Id. 96 ; *The Methodist Church* v. *Jaques*, 1 Johnson, 450; *Moffit* v. *M'Donald*, 11 Humphreys, 437 ; Hill on Trustees, 142, note 1 ; *Valle* v. *Bryan*, 19 Missouri, 423 ; *Neill* v. *Keese*, 13 Texas, 187. In like manner, a purchase by one partner with partnership funds, will create a resulting trust in the firm ; *Freeman* v. *Kelly*, 1 Hoffman, 90, 94 ; *Smith* v. *Burnham*, 3 Sumner, 435, 462 ; *Philips et al.* v. *Cramond et al.*, 2 Washington's C. C. 441, 445 ; *Turner* v. *Petigrew et als.*, 6 Humphreys, 438, 439 ; *Harrisburg Bank* v. *Tyler*, 3 Watts & Sergeant, 373, 378, *ante ;* [and in *King* v. *Hamilton*, 16 Illinois, 190, a purchase of land by a partner with the funds of the firm, without the consent and in fraud of his copartners, was held to give rise to a resulting trust in their favor, in the ratio of their interest in the assets of the partnership. Under these circumstances, the principal, or *cestui que trust*, is entitled to the money or the land, at his option, and may use his hold on the land as the means of getting the money, which distinguishes such cases from those where the money of one man is invested in the purchase of land, with his consent and approbation, and a deed taken in the name of another, which may give a right to the land, but necessarily precludes all claim to the money; *Lench* v. *Lench*, 10 Vesey, 511; 17 Id. 58; *Wallace* v. *Duffield*, 2 S. & R. 521, 529.

A similar result will follow from a purchase by a husband with the proceeds or accumulations of the separate estate of his wife, or with money bequeathed in trust for her benefit, whether the deed is made in his own name or in that of a third person; *The Methodist Church* v. *Jaques*, 1 Johnson's Ch. 450; 3 Id. 77; *Dickenson* v. *Codwise*, 1 Sandford's Ch. 214; *Pinney* v. *Fellows*, 15 Vermont, 325; *Barron* v. *Barron*, 24 Id. 375; *Lathrop* v. *Gilbert*, 2 Stockton's Ch. 345; *Lench* v. *Lench*, 10 Vesey, 511; but not, as it would seem, from a purchase out of the wife's savings, from money given to her by her husband, or acquired by her own industry after marriage, unless the fund would have been her property if it had not been converted into land; *Raybold* v. *Raybold*, 8 Harris, 308; *Merrill* v. *Smith*, 37 Maine, 394; *Henderson* v. *Warmack*, 27 Mississippi, 830; although a trust may be raised in favor of the wife, by proof that her husband paid the purchase-money for her benefit, out of his own funds; *Raybold* v. *Raybold; Pinney* v. *Fellows; Farley* v. *Blood*, 10 Foster, 354.

If the property which goes to pay for the land belongs to the wife, it is not requisite that it should have been conveyed or settled for her separate use. But the sale of the wife's estate, and the receipt of the proceeds by the husband, did not, formerly render him her debtor, or fasten a resulting trust for her on land in which they are subsequently invested; *Chester* v. *Greer*, 5 Humphreys, 34; *Powel* v. *Powel*, 9 Idem. 476; *Ex parte M'Donough*, 1 Swan. 202; unless she was induced to join in the deed by a promise that the proceeds should be hers, when a trust will attach to any species of property into which the money is subsequently converted; *Pritchard* v. *Wallace*, 4 Sneed. 405.]

A resulting trust may, in all cases, be rebutted; and it is well settled, that it may be rebutted by parol evidence, or circumstances. The rule is general, that an equity founded on parol, may be rebutted, put down, or discharged by parol proof; *Myers* v. *Myers*, 1 Casey, 100; *Livermore* v. *Aldrich*, 5 Cushing, 431, 436. A resulting trust is a mere creature of equity, founded upon presumptive intention, and designed to carry that intention into effect, not to defeat it. It will not attach in the person paying the purchase-money, if it was not the intention of either party that the estate should vest in him. It will therefore not be raised in opposition to the declaration of the person who advances the money, nor in opposition to the agreement of the parties on which the conveyance is founded, or to the obvious purpose and design of the transaction; *Botsford* v. *Burr*, 2 Johnson's Chancery, 405, 416; *Steere* v. *Steere*, 5 Id. 1, 18, 19; *Squire* v. *Harder*, 1 Paige, 494, 495; *White* v. *Carpenter*, 2 Id. 218, 265; *Philips et al.* v. *Cramond et al.*, 2 Washington's C. C. 441, 445; *M'Guire et al.* v. *M'Gowen et al.*, 4 Dessaussure, 487, 491; *Page* v. *Page*, 8 New Hampshire, 187, 195; *Elliott* v. *Armstrong*, 2 Blackford, 199, 213; *Sedge* v. *Morse*, 16 Johnson, 199; nor, if the purpose was a fraudulent one, will it be raised in favor of the person committing the fraud; *Proseus* v. *M'Intyre*, 5 Barbour's S. Ct. 425, 434; *Ford's Ex'rs, &c.* v. *Lewis*, 10 B. Monroe, 127. [Proof that a resulting trust was intended to defraud or delay creditors, will, therefore, be sufficient to prevent a decree in favor of the complainant; *Baldwin* v. *Campfield*, 4 Halsted's Ch. 891; *Vanzant* v. *Davies*, 6 Ohio, N. S. 52; both law and equity refusing to interfere as between wrong-doers, and leaving each in the position in which his own acts and those of his accomplices have placed him; *Murphy* v. *Hubert*, 4 Harris, 50; *Brantley* v. *West*, 27 Alabama, 542. And the case of *Baldwin* v. *Campfield* would seem to show that the court will take notice of the fraud, when disclosed by the evidence, although not appearing on the face of the pleadings, nor set up by the respondent. But it is hardly necessary to say, that the creditors may prove the real nature of the transaction, and have a decree for their benefit, as they might in any other case of the fraudulent or voluntary disposition of the property of a debtor; *Kennard* v. *M'Right*, 2 Barr, 38; *Guthrie* v. *Gardner*, 19 Wend. 414; *Jackson* v. *Forrest*, 2 Barbour's Ch. 576; *Newitt* v. *Morgan*, 2 Harrington, 225; *Watson* v. *Le Row*, 6 Barbour, 487; *Rucker* v. *Abell*, 8 B. Monroe, 566; *Bauskett* v. *Holsenback*, 2 Richardson, 624; *Vansant* v. *Davies*, 6 Ohio, N. S. 52.]

Moreover a resulting trust will not be raised in opposition to the law of the land, and, therefore, not in favor of an alien incapable of holding. The law never casts a legal or equitable estate upon one who has no right or capacity to hold it; therefore, where an alien purchases land and takes an absolute conveyance in the name of a citizen, without any agreement or declaration of a trust, a resulting trust will not be raised by operation of law, in favor of the alien who cannot hold the land; *Leggett* v. *Dubois*, 5 Paige, 114, 117; *Philips* v. *Cramond*, 2 W. C. C. R. 441. In like manner, no resulting trust can arise in contravention of the language or policy of a statute, as when the purpose is to do that through the medium of a trustee which the *cestui que trust* could not do in his own person; *Alsworth* v. *Cordty*, 31 Mississippi, 32.

The presumption of a resulting trust is fully rebutted, or no such presumption arises, where a parent advances the purchase-money, and takes the conveyance in the name of his child. A purchase by a father in the name of his son who is not provided for, is presumptively an advancement of the son, and no trust results to the parent; although this presumption may be rebutted; *Partridge* v. *Havens*, 10 Paige, 618, 626; *Proseus* v. *M'Intyre*, 5 Barbour's S. Ct. 425, 432; *Tremper* v. *Barton, Jr.*, 18 Ohio, 418, 423; *Butler* v. *M. Ins. Co. et al.*, 14 Alabama, 777; *Stanley* v. *Brannon*, 6 Blackford, 194, 195; *Dennison* v. *Goehring*, 7 Barr, 180, 182, note; *Douglass* v. *Brien*, 4 Richardson's Eq. 322; *Cartwright* v. *West*, 4 Illinois, 417; *Shepherd* v. *White*, 10 Texas, 72; *Alexander* v. *Warrance*, 17 Missouri, 230; *Dudley* v. *Bosworth*, 10 Humphreys, 12; *Walton* v. *Divine*, 20 Barbour, 9; *Dyer* v. *Dyer*, 2 Cox, 92; *Pinney* v. *Fellows*, 15 Vermont, 525; *Vanzant* v. *Davies*, 6 Ohio, N. S. 52. The same rule was followed in *Baker* v. *Leathers*, 3 Indiana, 557, and applied to a case where land bought by a father, was conveyed, with his assent, to his daughters. And if an obligation to convey to the father and son is entered into, and the money is paid by the father, this is, presumptively, an advancement of the son to the extent of one-half the estate; the equitable estate to that extent accordingly vests in him and descends to his heirs, and if the deed be made to the father, instead of the father and son jointly, the grantee becomes a trustee as to one-half, and may be compelled to

convey; *Thompson's Heirs* v. *Thompson's Devisees*, 1 Yerger, 97, 99. A purchase by a husband in the name of his wife is, in like manner, in the first instance, taken to be an advancement of the wife, and not a resulting trust; *Guthrie* v. *Gardner*, 19 Wendell, 414; *Whitten & others* v. *Whitten*, 3 Cushing, 194, 197; *Walton* v. *Divine*, 20 Barbour, 9; *Alexander* v. *Warram*, 17 Missouri, 228; *Fatheree* v. *Fletcher*, 31 Mississippi, 265; *Cotton* v. *Wood*, 25 Iowa, 30. And the same rule applies in relation to one towards whom the party stands *in loco parentis*, as a son-in-law; *Baker* v. *Leathers*, 3 Porter, Indiana, 558; or a nephew who has lived with the uncle as a member of his family. In *Jackson* v. *Feller*, 2 Wendell, 465, 469, an uncle bought a farm and paid the purchase-money, and took the conveyance in the name of his nephew, who had lived with him and worked for him for a long time without other recompense than his clothing; Southerland, J., said that as a resulting trust may be proved, so it may be rebutted by parol evidence, and he held that declarations by the uncle that he had given the farm to his nephew, and intended it as a provision for him, were sufficient to show that the purchase was a gift and advancement to the nephew.

The rule does not apply as between more distant relatives. That the person who pays the money is the brother of him who takes the deed, will not alone rebut the presumption of a resulting trust; *Edwards* v. *Edwards*, 3

Wright, 369; although it is a circumstance which may have that effect in connection with other circumstances.

The presumption of an advancement, from the grantee's being the child or wife of the person who pays the purchase-money, may be rebutted by evidence which shows that the intention of the latter was to secure a trust for himself; *Jackson* v. *Matsdorf*, 11 Johnson, 91, 96; *Shepherd* v. *White*, 10 Texas, 72; the question, in such cases, is one entirely of intention; *Proseus* v. *M'Intyre*, 5 Barbour, 425, 432; *Butler* v. *M. Insurance Co. et al.*, 14 Alabama, 777, 788; *Cotton* v. *Wood*, 25 Iowa, 30; *Hodgson* v. *Macy*, 8 Indiana, 121; and hence proof is seemingly admissible that a conveyance of land bought and paid for by a husband, was made to his wife under the mistaken impression that it would vest a title in, or operate for the joint use and benefit of both of them; 2 Williams, 638. And if a person indebted, purchases lands with his own money, and takes the conveyance in the name of another, for the purpose of defrauding his creditors, the trust in the land results to him for the benefit of his creditors and may be taken by them; *Guthrie* v. *Gardner*, 19 Wendell, 414; *Brown and others* v. *M'Donald*, 1 Hill's Chancery, 297, 306; *Demaree* v. *Driskill*, 3 Blackford, 115; *Doyle, &c.* v. *Sleeper, &c.*, 1 Dana, 531, 537; *Hunt and Tucker* v. *Booth, Edwards and Hunt*, 1 Freeman, 215, 217; *Bell* v. *Hallenback et al.*, Wright, 751; *Newells* v. *Morgan et al.*, 2 Harrington, 225, 229; *Dewey* v. *Long*, 25 Vermont, 564; but it seems that a trust will not result for the benefit of the party who has thus attempted a fraud; *Proseus* v. *M'Intyre*, 5 Barbour, 425, 434, *ante.*

[In *Edwards* v. *Edwards*, 3 Wright, 377, where the question arose between brothers, Woodward, C. J., held the following language in delivering judgment: "The plaintiff's case does not rest upon any declaration of trust by the defendant, either written or parol, but entirely upon that implication which the law makes in favor of a purchaser, who buys real estate with his own money, and takes the title in the name of another. This is a well recognized mode of making title to real estate. Indeed, most of the text writers, and many of the adjudged cases, define a resulting trust by the instance of the very case made by the plaintiff's bill; a purchase by one in the name of another. The nominee in the title deeds becomes trustee for him who paid the money. The ownership of the money which purchased, draws to itself the beneficial or equitable interest in the estate."

"And such equitable title, though resting generally in parol proof, is expressly exempted from the Statute of Frauds and Perjuries. Still, it is a mere implication or presumption, as it has sometimes been called, but a reasonable one, founded in the general experience and observation of men. At common law, before the Statute of

Uses, a feoffment made without consideration was presumed to be made for the use of the feoffor, and it is upon parity of reason and in strict analogy to this, that equity regards the owner of the money which is paid for land as the owner of the land. But being a mere *prima facie* presumption, it may be rebutted. If the nominee in the title be a wife, or child, or grandchild, or one to whom the purchaser stands in *loco parentis*, the moral obligation to provide for a such party is at once recognized, and an advancement is presumed. But brothers are not within this rule; *Maddison v. Andrew*, 1 Vesey, Sr. 58; *Benbow v. Townsend*, 1 Mylne & Keene, 506. The presumption may be rebutted also by the declarations of the purchaser, made at the time of and in such immediate connection with the purchaser as to be part of the *res gestæ*. It is important that this rule in regard to declarations be received with the limitation here stated. And so received, it will be apparent that much of the evidence in the large volume of proofs we have before us, is either wholly irrelevant or of small consequence. If a purchaser declare that he pays his money for the benefit of the nominee in the deed, though that party do not stand in such relationship as would of itself, without any declaration, raise a presumption against the purchaser, let it tell against him. The legal effect of his act, without the declaration, would have been to give him an equity; but any man of com-

mon sense may qualify the legal effect of his conduct by an accompanying declaration. But what do declarations before or after the purchase signify? If before, they can import no more than an intention, which, because it is a mere mental purposes, may be changed. If after, they operate to divest an equitable estate, and therefore, are unworthy to be received. In *Bailey v. Boutcott*, 4 Russ. 345, it was held that the expression of a mother's inchoate intention to settle the property, was not such a declaration of trust as the court could act upon; and generally loose and indefinite expressions, and such as indicate only an incomplete executory intention, are insufficient either to fasten a trust upon property, or to loosen it where it has once attached. The expressions must be used contemporaneously with or in contemplation of the act of disposition; *Kilpin v. Kilpin*, 1 Mylne & Keene, 537; *Tritt v. Crotzer*, 1 Harris, 457; Hill on Trustees, 97; 2 Sug. on Vend. 131."

A subsequent declaration will, like a subsequent promise, be inoperative from the want of consideration, if from no other cause; *Williard v. Williard*, 6 P. F. Smith, 119, 124; 2 Am. Lead. Cases, 186, 5 ed. It may, notwithstanding, like a subsequent promise, be evidence from which a jury or chancellor may infer the nature of the original transaction, and thus establish or disprove the equity which the complainant is seeking to enforce; *Williard v. Williard*. Where the effect of what passes at the time is to confer an equity, nothing that is said afterwards can defeat the interest thus acquired. But a declaration by the alleged *cestui que trust*, that the land does not belong to him, is a reason for inferring that he did not pay the purchase-money, or that if he did, it was as a gift or loan. An admission against interest is ordinarily a safe guide as against the person making it.]

The admissibility of parol evidence of intention, in cases where the purchase-money has been paid by another person than the legal grantee, has, undoubtedly, in the American cases, taken a very general and very dangerous range. But the evil seems to be inherent in the practical administration of the original principle of equity, that a trust results presumptively from payment of the purchase-money: and so long as that doctrine is acted upon, it is almost impossible to lay down any general restriction upon the reception of parol evidence, without incurring a risk of doing in some cases great injustice. Lord Chancellor Sugden, indeed, in *Hall* v. *Hill*, 1 Connor & Lawson, 120, 139, has endeavored to establish a difference between the admission of such evidence to rebut, and to fortify, an equitable presumption; he suggests that the true general principle of equity is, that parol evidence of intention is admissible to rebut a presumption arising against the apparent intention of the instrument, but not to fortify such a presumption; that is to say, not to fortify

it in the first instance, because, if parol evidence be given to rebut the presumption, no doubt that may be counteracted by other parol evidence in support of the presumption. But it is very difficult to apply that distinction, supposing it to be sound ; because, in many instances, it is scarcely possible to say whether the conclusion that would be arrived at upon particular circumstances, is a presumption, or the rebuttal of a presumption. For example, when a purchase is made by a father in the name of a son who has not received any advancement, it is not easy to say whether the inference which would be made upon those facts, of a trust for the son, is the presumption of an advancement, or the rebuttal of a resulting trust. If it is the latter, parol evidence of intention that the son should be a trustee for the father, would, upon Sir E. Sugden's rule, be objectionable, as opposing the deed ; and parol evidence the other way would be still more so, as cumulative upon both the legal construction and the equitable presumption: yet upon the English cases, it is admissible both ways. But the distinction, at least in reference to resulting trusts, seems not to be sound in principle. When the doctrine is once taken up, that the intention of the parties is not to be found in the legal construction of an instrument, and that you are to infer it from extrinsic circumstances, nothing short of a general admission of all parol evidence that throws light on the intention, and is in its nature competent, can be adopted. The rule in equity certainly is, that until the *fact* of the payment of the purchase-money by another is proved, the interests vest according to the legal operation of the deed: but when that fact is proved, the deed is no longer, in equity, absolutely, the legal determination of the intention of the parties, and that intention must be sought for elsewhere, and, of course, from circumstances in parol. In seeking it, elsewhere, why should the written instrument be suffered to thwart the discovery of that intention, from parol, when it is admitted that that instrument is not the absolute expression of the intention of the parties to the contract? The ground of a resulting trust is, that payment of the purchase-money is an equity to have the land; but evidence of intention must often enter into the fact whether that payment is such an equity, under the circumstances. The mere fact of payment may, in some cases, not be sufficient to show a clear presumption of a trust, yet explained by parol evidence of intention, it might be; or the mere fact of payment may, in the evidence of it, be inseparately connected with some other circumstances which tend to rebut the presumption: and in such a case, parol evidence of intention would only be counteracting this rebutting evidence. The original doctrine is probably one of the mistakes of equity: but being admitted, it becomes necessary, both by logical consequence, and in practical justice, to give complete and consistent scope to the evidence which the doctrine sanctions and introduces: and an attempt to narrow the use of such evidence by arbitrary little rules which are applied out of place, only increases the mischief. When it is once settled that payment of the purchase-money raises an equity and a trust, which overrides the deed, the practice, in reason and conscience, ought to be, to admit all legal evidence that can explain, define, and determine the equity. See *Baker* v. *Leathers*, 5 Indiana, 558.

In New York, by the revised statutes, (vol. 1, p. 728, pt. 2, ch. 1, sec. 51,) resulting trusts from payment of the purchase-money are abolished; except (sec. 52) that where a conveyance is taken in the name of another person, it shall be presumed fraudulent as against the creditors at the time of the person paying the consideration; and where a fraudulent intent is not disproved, a trust results in favor of such creditors, to an extent sufficient to satisfy their demands; and except also (sec. 53) where the grantee has taken the conveyance in his own name without the consent or knowledge of the person paying the consideration, or has purchased the lands in violation of some trust, with moneys belonging to another person; *Turcks* v. *Alexander*, 11 Paige, 619; *Watson* v. *Le Row*, 6 Barbour, 481. The creditors of the person furnishing the consideration money can therefore reach the land only by charging fraud; *Bodine* v. *Edwards*, 10 Paige, 504; and none but creditors existing at the time can avail themselves of such fraud; *Brewster* v. *Power*, Id. 563, 568: but if a case of such fraud be established, the trust in the land results to the debtor in favor of his creditors, and they may proceed against it at law as an estate in him; *Wait* v. *Day*, 4 Denio, 439; controlling the dictum in *Brewster* v. *Power*, 10 Paige, 562, to the contrary. But in the recent case of *Gorfield* v. *Hatmaker*, 15 New York, R. 475, *Wait* v. *Day* was overruled, and the only remedy of the creditors, under such circumstances, held to be in equity. A misapplication of trust funds by a purchase in the trustee's name, will, however, give rise to a resulting trust, under these statutes, as it did before; *Russell* v. *Allen*, 10 Paige, 250.

[Resulting trusts, arising from the payment of the purchase-money, have also been abrogated in Kentucky, Minnesota and Indiana; *Durfee* v. *Pasitt*, 14 Minnesota, 424; *Hodson* v. *Macy*, 8 Indiana, 122; *Martin* v. *Martin*, 5 Bush, 47. The hardship of the restriction has led the courts to engraft exceptions and limitations which were not contemplated by the legislature. Thus it has been decided in New York, that where it does not appear that the person who paid the money knew that the conveyance was absolute on its face, the presumption is that it was so drawn in through mistake or fraud, and a trust will be decreed accordingly; *Day* v. *Roth*, 18 New York, 448; *Siemon* v. *Schrack*, 29 Id. 558. It was also intimated that if A. supplies the funds and the deed is made to B, the intention being that it shall enure for the benefit of C., the case is not within the statute, and C. may enforce the trust. It was held with more reason in *Hodson* v. *Macy*, 8 Indiana, 122, that where the party who is the source of the consideration, enters upon and occupies the premises with the acquiescence of the grantee, a trust will be decreed, as in other instances where possession is given and received in part performance of an oral contract.

The general rule, where a resulting trust is sought to be established, and indeed in all cases where aid is sought either from law or equity, is, that the *allegata* and *probata* must agree; and the complainant cannot set forth one case in the pleadings and recover on another as ultimately established by the proofs; *Andrew* v. *Farnham*, 2 Stockton's Ch. 91; although it seems that the court may, at their discretion, enforce an equity disclosed by the answer, differing from that alleged in the bill.

A resulting trust arose at common law on a feoffment without consideration, and it has been said, that the same rule should apply to all conveyances which appear on their face to be voluntary, or for a merely nominal consideration; Story's Equity Jurisprudence, sect. 1197; Cruise's Digest, 402, sect. 37; although the better opinion is, that such a trust will not arise from the absence of a consideration.

without corroborating circumstances, (such as the retention of the deed, the long continued and exclusive possession of the grantor, the absence of the grantee at the time of its execution, and his failure to exercise or act upon the rights which it purports to confer,) tending to show that there was no intention to make a gift, or pass the beneficial interest in the property conveyed; Hill on Trustees, 106; *Cecil* v. *Butcher*, 2 J. & W. 573; *Sowerbye* v. *Arden*, 1 Johnson's Ch. 240; *Tolar* v. *Tolar*, 1 Dev. Eq. 456. And however this may be, it would seem well settled, that a deed which purports to be made for a full and valuable consideration, cannot be shown to be merely voluntary, in order to raise a trust in favor of the grantor; because such evidence is directly at variance not only with the Statute of Frauds, but with the rule that a written instrument cannot be varied by parol evidence; *ante*, *Leman* v. *Whitley*, 4 Russell, 323; *Harper* v. *Harper*, 5 Bush, 137; *Porter* v. *Mayfield*, 9 Harris, 264; *Wilkinson* v. *Wilkinson*, 2 Devereux, Eq. 376; *Rathbone* v. *Rathbone*, 6 Barb. 93; *Philbrook* v. *Delano*, 29 Maine, 410; *Squire* v. *Harder*, 1 Paige, 494; *Graves* v. *Graves*, 9 Foster, 129. This view of the law is somewhat at variance with the language held by Story, in his Treatise on Equity Jurisprudence, (2 Equity Jurisprudence, 1199,) and in *Jenkins* v. *Eldridge*, 3 Story, 181, 290, where the case of *Leman* v. *Whitley* is questioned, and an opinion intimated, that procuring a convey-

ance for one purpose, and then using it for another, is a fraud, against which equity will relieve, whether the evidence is written or oral, but would seem essential to the certainty and stability of the assurances on which the title to real property depends, and is sustained by the recent case of *Balbeck* v. *Donaldson*, 6 Law Register, 148, where the retention of the conveyance, and of the possession of the property which it purported to convey, coupled with other circumstances which raised a strong presumption that the grantees had really paid nothing, and that it was not intended that they should have the beneficial interest, were held insufficient to raise a resulting trust in opposition to the express words of the deed, which purported to have been made for a full and valuable consideration. It has, notwithstanding, been held in Pennsylvania, that the oral declarations of the grantee are admissible in evidence, to show that a deed is voluntary, and subject to a trust for the grantor, in opposition not only to the words of the deed itself, but of a bond executed at the same time, for the full amount of the consideration expressed in the deed; *Murphy* v. *Hubert*, 7 Barr, 420; the ground of the decision being, that as the seventh section of the Statute of Frauds was not in force in that State, a trust might be declared orally, and proved by the testimony of witnesses. The court, however, seems to have omitted to inquire how there could be a trust, if the consideration was valuable, and how the deed could be shown to be merely voluntary, in opposition to its language, and that of the bond which the grantee executed for the purchase-money, without violating rules of evidence, which were anterior to the Statute of Frauds, and would be binding if it were repealed ; vol. 2, *post*, note to *Woollam* v. *Hearn*.

Murphy v. *Hubert* was virtually overruled in *Porter* v. *Mayfield*, 9 Harris, 264, but the question seems to be again at large under *Lingelfelter* v. *Ritchey*, 8 P. F. Smith, 485.

A trust may be engrafted on an absolute conveyance, by showing that the consideration was such as to give rise to the trust. Proof that the consideration was a loan will convert a deed into a mortgage. If the consideration moves from a third person, the inference is that the land belongs to him who paid for it; *Morris* v. *Nixon*, 17 Peters, 109 ; 1 Howard, 118; and the same result will follow where a deed, absolute on its face, is shown to have been given as security for a loan, or the payment of an antecedent debt. In cases of this description the parol evidence does not contradict the writing or set up an oral agreement dehors the instrument. It establishes the existence of a collateral fact, from which an equity arises to control the deed. This is the true explanation of *Morris* v. *Nixon*, which seems to have been differently interpreted in *Jenkins* v. *Eldredge*, 3 Story, 181, 219. In the absence of such evidence, it is well established that a trust

cannot arise except on the ground of fraud, as distinguished from a breach of contract; *Gillin* v. *Drummond*, 31 Maryland, 71 ; *Sheldon* v. *Harding*, 44 Illinois; *Holmes* v. *Holmes*, Ib. 168 ; *Dorsey* v. *Clark*, 4 Harris, 556; *post*, vol. 2, notes to *Woollam* v. *Hearn*. What will constitute such a fraud has not been accurately defined; but it is clear that there must be something more than the bad faith implied in every wilful breach of an agreement on which others have acted. It is not enough that the grantee made a promise, which he subsequently refused to fulfil, unless there are other circumstances which in the aggregate amount to fraud ; *Jackman* v. *Ringland*, 6 W. & S. ; *Barnet* v. *Dougherty*, 8 Casey, 371; *Hoge* v. *Hoge*, 1 Watts, 163, 214.

The defendant may admit that he sold the land and received the purchase-money, and yet allege the statute as a reason why he should not be required to convey. No stronger case can be presented short of fraud. The reason is because a purchaser who chooses to go outside of the law and trust to the honor of the vendor, must take the consequences of his mistaken confidence. The case is obviously different where artifice is employed to conceal the real nature of the transaction or throw the other party off his guard. It is no more possible to be secure at all times against fraud than against violence. But it must appear that the deceit was the inducement to the conveyance, without which it would not have been made; and unless the evidence goes to this extent, a court of equity can no more dispense with the statute than a court of common law; *Kisler* v. *Kisler*, 2 Watts, 323 ; *Hoge* v. *Hoge*, 1 Id 163.

The decisions may be ranged under three heads : 1st. Where the conveyance is gratuitous, as in the case of a will or deed, for a merely nominal consideration. 2d. Where it purports to be for a full and valuable consideration, but is in fact gratuitous. 3d. Where the consideration is valuable, and paid in whole or in part by the grantee.

It is established under the first head that where one obtains a gift of property, on the faith of a parol assurance that he will dispose of it, either wholly, or in part, in a particular way, equity will enforce the performance of the agreement; Hill on Trustees, 59 ; *Jenkins* v. *Eldridge*, 3 Story, 182. This is well settled, as it regards wills; *Devenish* v. *Baines*, Pue in Chancery, 3 ; *Whynn* v. *Whynn*, 1 Vernon, 296; *Hoge* v. *Hoge*, 1 Watts, 163; *Church* v. *Ruland*, 14 P. F. Smith, 432; *Jones* v. *M'Kee*, 3 Barr, 496; 6 Id. 425; *Barrell* v. *Hanrick*, 42 Alabama, 60; and the case is substantially the same where the gift is made by a deed reciting a consideration, which is not really paid; *Onson* v. *Cown*, 22 Wisconsin, 529; *Miller* v. *Pearce*, 6 W. & S. 97; *Kennedy* v. *Kennedy*, 2 Alabama, 571; *Thomson* v. *White*, 1 Dallas, 447; *Dixon* v. *Olmius*, 1 Cox, Ch. Cases, 414; *Chamberlain* v. *Chamberlain*, 2 Freeman, 34; *Oldham* v. *Litchfield*, 2 Vermont,

506 ; *Hoge* v. *Hoge*, 1 Watts, 163, 214; *Sheriff* v. *Neal*, 6 Id. 534. So a trust may arise where an owner is fraudulently induced not to exercise the *jus disponendi* by one who will inherit at his death. In *Strickland* v. *Aldridge*, 9 Vesey, 516, Lord Eldon treated it as indisputable, that an heir who induces the ancestor to refrain from making a will by a promise, must make it good if the estate descends to him; and the principle is the same where a will is allowed to stand in consequence of the assurances of the devisee that he will provide for one to whom the testator would otherwise have left a legacy. *Jorden* v. *Money*, 5 House of Lords, 185. See *post*, vol. 2, notes to *Woollam* v. *Hearn*, 250. In like manner where one who will succeed to personal property, if the person to whom it belongs dies intestate, promises the latter to dispose of it in a particular way after his death, a trust will arise *ex maleficio* if the promise is not fulfilled ; see *Parker* v. *Urie*, 9 Harris, 305 ; *Pringle* v. *Pringle*, 9 P. F. Smith, 281 ; *Williams* v. *Fitch*, 18, New York, 548.

The fraud consists in the diversion of the donor's bounty from its intended channel, by a promise which is not kept, and it has been contended that a devise, made without solicitation or undue influence, cannot be charged with a trust by a promise to hold it for the benefit of a third person. But the weight of authority is, that whether the execution of a will is procured by a fraudulent assurance, or the alteration of it prevented, the fraud and consequent injury are the same. A devisee may be declared a trustee *ex maleficio*, on this ground for the heir-at-law, or the heir-at-law for an intended devisee. So the complainant may show that the testator would have executed a codicil in his favor, if the residuary legatee had not promised that his wishes should be observed.

The principle is clearly stated by Lord Westbury in *M'Cormick v. Grogan*, 4 Law R., House of Lords, 97. "The Court of Equity has, from a very early period, decided that even an Act of Parliament shall not be used as an instrument of fraud; and if in the machinery of perpetrating a fraud an Act of Parliament intervenes, the Court of Equity, it is true, does not set aside the Act of Parliament, but it fastens on the individual who gets a title under that Act, and imposes upon him a personal obligation, because he applies the Act as an instrument for accomplishing a fraud. In this way the Court of Equity has dealt with the Statute of Frauds, and in this manner, also, it deals with the Statute of Wills. And if an individual on his death-bed, or at any other time, is persuaded by his heir-at-law, or his next of kin, to abstain from making a will, or if the same individual, having made a will, communicates the disposition to the person on the face of the will benefited by that disposition, but, at the same time, says to that individual that he has a purpose to answer, which he has not expressed in the will, but which he depends on the disponee to

carry into effect, and the disponee assents to it, either expressly or by any mode of action which the disponee knows must give to the testator the impression and belief that he fully assents to the request, then, undoubtedly, the heir-at-law in the one case, and the disponee in the other, will be converted into trustees, simply on the principle that an individual shall not be benefited by his own personal fraud. You are obliged, therefore, to show most clearly and distinctly that the person you wish to convert into a trustee acted malo animo. You must show distinctly that he knew that the testator, or the intestate, was beguiled and deceived by his conduct. If you are not in a condition to affirm that, without any misgiving or possibility of mistake, you are not warranted in affixing on the individual the delictum of fraud, which you must do before you convert him into a trustee."

It has been held repeatedly that proof that a testator was prevented from revoking his will by fraud, violence, or undue influence, does not invalidate the instrument, unless, perhaps where the devisee is *particeps criminis*. See *Boyd v. Cook*, 3 Leigh, 32; *Hise v. Pincher*, 10 Iredell, 137; *Clingman v. Micheltree*, 7 Casey, 25; *Kent v. Mehaffey*, 10 Ohio, N. S. 204; 2 American Leading Cases, 494, 5th ed. So evidence that a will was executed on the faith of a promise, is only admissible as against the promisor. Yet it has been held, that a will procured by undue influence is invalid, even as it regards one who took no part in procuring the will; *Hugnenin* v. *Bazzley*, 14 Vesey, 273; *post*, vol. 2. And it seems to have been thought, in *Williams' Appeal*, 23 P. F. Smith, 249, 284, that a promise by an executor to the testator, may control the exercise of a testamentary power conferred by the will.

It results from what has been said, that a grant cannot be affected with an oral trust for a third person, merely on the ground of contract, nor unless the evidence goes far enough to establish fraud. *A fortiori* such a trust cannot be sustained in favor of the grantor. It seems that a trust resulted *prime facie* from a feoffment without consideration where no services were reserved, although the presumption might be rebutted by parol; 1 Cruise Title, 12, ch. 1, sect. 52; *The Duke of Norfolk* v. *Brown*, Prec. in Ch. 88. No such inference is possible in the case of a bargain and sale, although for a nominal consideration, or of a release " *habendum* " to the use of the releasee, because the intention of the parties as expressed in the instrument is to vest the right of property in the grantee: *Philbrook* v. *Delano*, 29 Maine, 410; *Rathbun* v. *Rathbun*, 6 Barb. 98; *Graves* v. *Graves*, 9 Foster, 129; Hill on Trustees, 106; Story's Eq. Jurisprudence, sect. 1199; 4 Kent's Com. 306. It cannot, therefore, be shown that he gave no consideration, or agreed to hold for the grantor, because the evidence is irrelevant, and tends to contradict the deed. This results from the doctrines of the

common law, aside from the restraint imposed by the statute of frauds, *ante*. See *Blodgett* v. *Hildreth*, 103 Mass. 350; *Hogan* v. *Jaques*, 4 C. E. Green, 123. It was indeed said in *Porter* v. *Mayfield*, 9 Harris, 263, that evidence that the grantee agreed to hold the title in trust for the grantor, is a flat contradiction of the deed, but that the deed is not contradicted by showing that the vendee purchased in trust for a third person, for such evidence only establishes a new and consistent relation. This distinction can hardly be sustained. A grant is a contract executed, and whatever impairs the grant, impairs the obligation of the contract: *Fletcher* v. *Peck*, 6 Cranch, 87. Evidence that the intention was to vest the beneficial interest in a third person, is, therefore, not less inadmissible than evidence that it was to revert to the grantor.

The second head is also capable of subdivision. The trust may be set up between the original parties, or in favor of a third person. In the former instance, the objection is two-fold, under the provisions of the Statute of Frauds, and that the evidence contradicts a writing under a seal. See *Porter* v. *Mayfield*, 9 Harris, 264. The trust cannot be alleged consistently with the deed, because it is impossible to believe that the grantee gave a full and valuable consideration for the privilege of holding the land for the use of the grantor. A deed may be regarded in two aspects. In one it is the means by which the title is conveyed; in the other, a memorandum of the terms and conditions of the transfer. If a man deliberately executes a sealed instrument, reciting that he has transferred the right of ownership for value received, he should not be permitted to put the grantee to the proof of that which has been established with the utmost solemnity known to the law. This is the more true, because such a disguise is generally adopted for some sinister purpose, to defraud creditors, or deprive a wife of dower. See *Murphy* v. *Hubert*, 4 Harris, 50. If there be any instance to the contrary, it is better that the grantee should suffer for his folly in putting the transaction in a form contrary to the truth, than that the stability of titles should be endangered by rendering it impossible to frame a conveyance that shall be secure from attack; *Leman* v. *Whetley*, 4 Russell, 323; *Porter* v. *Mayfield*, 9 Harris, 264, *post*; *Hogan* v. *Jaques*, 4 C. E. Green, 123. If it be proved that the deed was misdrawn through accident or fraud; or that it was procured through undue influence—*Lingenfelter* v. *Richey*, 8 P. F. Smith, 485—a trust may arise *dehors* the instrument; but this depends on other principles.

The law was so held in *Blodgett* v. *Hildreth*, 103 Mass. 484, where Wells, J., used the following language in delivering judgment: "As to the share of Lucinda, conveyed by her to Sophronia, without consideration, and upon an agreement to reconvey or hold it

for the benefit of Lucinda, no valid trust arises from that transaction; *Walker* v. *Locke*, 5 Cushing, 90. A voluntary deed is valid between the parties as a gift, and does not raise any trust in favor of the grantor. It is otherwise with a feoffment, and perhaps in other conveyances, wherever there is no declaration of the uses, or the consideration is open to inquiry in determining the effect of the deed between the parties and their privies: Cruise Dig. (Greenleaf ed.), tit. 11, c. 4, § 16, and tit. 32, c. 2, § 38. In this commonwealth, the consideration is not open to such inquiry. Supposing the deed in question to have been in the common form, the recital of a consideration, and the declaration of the use to the grantee and her heirs in the habendum, are both conclusive between the parties, and exclude any resulting trust to the grantor; *Squire* v. *Harder*, 1 Paige, 494; Hill on Trustees, 112, 2 Story's Eq. § 1197; *Philbroke* v. *Delano*, 29 Maine, 410; *Farrington* v. *Barr*, 36 N. H. 86; *Graves* v. *Graves*, 9 Foster, 129." See *Haigh* v. *Reye*, 4 L. R. Ch. Appeals, 473.

It was held in like manner in *Wilkinson* v. *Wilkinson*, 2 Devereux Eq. 378, that the recital of a valuable consideration is conclusive on the parties and those claiming under them, unless it is shown to have been introduced by mistake or fraud. Gaston, J., said: "The plaintiffs here allege, that the defendant caused this consideration of value to be untruly inserted in the deed, either without the knowledge of the grantor, or by availing himself of the misconception of the grantor, that it was a necessary form to give the instrument validity. The parol evidence is admissible to support this charge, for if it be made out, then the instrument must be considered as if it had truly been what the contracting parties intended it to be. But it is admissible for this purpose only."

The main current of decision is in this direction, and establishes that a trust cannot be fastened on an absolute deed by evidence that the grantee paid no consideration, or that he agreed to take and hold the premises for the grantor; *Hutchinson* v. *Tindall*, 2 Green. Ch. 357; *Robson* v. *Harwell*, 6 Georgia, 589; *Squire* v. *Harder*, 1 Paige, 494; *Rathbun* v. *Rathbun*, 6 Barb. 98; *Philbrooke* v. *Delano*, 29 Maine, 410; *Graves* v. *Graves*, 9 Foster, 129; *Leman* v. *Whetley*, 4 Russell, 423. In *Squire* v. *Harder*, the complainants sought to establish a resulting trust in land which they had conveyed with warranty, and were held to be estopped from showing that the grantee had only a life interest in the purchase-money, and that upon her death it would have belonged to them.

The recital in a deed of bargain and sale is conclusive that the grant is for a valuable consideration, but not that it was paid. It is not, therefore, conclusive on the latter point in an action of assumpsit for the price, or bill filed, to establish the vendor's lien; and

the plaintiff may consequently recover on proof that the debt is due, notwithstanding an admission to the contrary in the deed or accompanying receipt. See *Leman* v. *Whetley*, 4 Russell, 423; *Jorden* v. *Money*, 5 House of Lords, 185, 234; *Thomas* v. *M'Cormick*, 9 Danas, 108.

In *Walker* v. *Locke*, 5 Cushing, 90, the plaintiffs being desirous of raising money on an estate which was already encumbered, applied to the defendant, a broker. The latter said that he would endeavor to find a lender, but feared that he could not succeed unless the plaintiffs would convey the property to him. Such a deed was accordingly executed, but the defendant refused to carry out the agreement or reconvey the premises. The bill also averred that the plaintiffs were induced by the fraudulent representations of Locke, one of the defendants, to convey the real estate described in the bill to him, for the purpose of raising money to pay off certain mortgages and attachments thereon, and then to reconvey the estate to the plaintiff, The Court held, that the only material allegation was that Locke informed the plaintiffs that the deed was a mere matter of form, to enable him to obtain the money and pay off the attachments and mortgages, and that he would raise the money and pay the same, and then reconvey the estate to the plaintiffs. The inference from the whole bill was that there was no agreement in writing or declaration of trust by Locke to hold the estate in trust, and any parol agreement or declaration to that effect was void by the Statute of Frauds. And as this appeared on the face of the bill, it was dismissed with costs. This case cannot be reconciled with *Jenkins* v. *Eldridge*, 3 Story, and may be thought to err as much in one direction as that does in another, because every one who, like a broker, holds himself out to the world as acting in a fiduciary capacity, owes entire good faith to those whom he undertakes to represent or advise. If he buys from one who relies on his superior skill and knowledge, the transaction should be narrowly scanned, and the sale set aside if there is reason to suspect misrepresentation, concealment, or undue influence.

The decisions in Pennsylvania go to the opposite extreme, and it is there held, that if a man who is in possession under an equitable or imperfect title, conveys to another on the faith of an assurance that the grantee will take the necessary steps to make it good by obtaining a patent from the Commonwealth, and then reconvey, equity will compel a specific performance of the promise, or decree a trust; *McCullough* v. *Cowher*, 5 W. & S. 427; *Church* v. *Church*, 1 Casey, 278; *Plumer* v. *Reed*, 2 Wright, 46; *Lingenfelter* v. *Ritchey*, 8 P. F. Smith, 485. In *Murphy* v. *Hubert*, 7 Barr, 420; 4 Harris, 50, the court went still further, and to the extent of founding a trust on the oral admissions of the grantee, that she gave nothing for the land, and had agreed to hold it for the grantor and his children, although

the deed was absolute and recited valuable consideration paid in full. These decisions proceed on the ground that obtaining a gift by a promise to use it in a particular way is a fraud, if the promise be not fulfilled, which is indisputable, but they omit to inquire how such a promise can be shown consistently with the common and statute law, when the gift is of land and under seal. The only answer that can be given is, that by a rule peculiar to Pennsylvania, a written instrument may be controlled or modified by what passes before and at the time of execution, and that the legislature saw fit to omit the seventh section in re-enacting the statute of frauds. Thus, Gibson, C. J., said that, only the three first sections of the English Statute of Frauds were in force in Pennsylvania. The seventh section had been designedly omitted, and there was consequently nothing to prevent the declaration or reservation of a trust by parol.

There is another consideration which the court would seem to have overlooked. One who seeks to affect the terms or operation of a deed by oral evidence, is encountered, not only by the statute of fraud, but by the common law rule that a written contract shall not be varied by parol. The seventh section is now a part of the law of that State, under the provisions of a recent act of Assembly, and will probably have a marked influence on the future course of decision. Accordingly, when the question arose in *Porter* v. *Mayfield*, 9 Harris, 263, Lowrie, J., said, that " evidence that at the time of the conveyance the vendee agreed to hold the title in trust for the vendor, is flat contradiction of the written instrument. Oral testimony could have no such power. As between vendor and vendee, it was inadmissible to change a title, absolute on its face, into a trust."

The doctrine that obtaining an absolute conveyance by a promise to hold or use it for the grantor may give rise to a trust, is also sustained by *Jenkins* v. *Eldredge*, 3 Story, 181, and *Foote* v. *Foote*, 58 Barb. 258, which go very far towards substituting the more or less arbitrary discretion of the chancellor for the rule prescribed by the statute of frauds.

It has been said in vindication of these decisions that to obtain a deed by a promise which the grantee does not intend to fulfil, is a trick against which equity should relieve. This is no doubt true where the promise is one that can be proved consistently with legal policy, but the difficulty lies in the proof. It is a rule alike of the common law and of equity, that where a contract is embodied in a written instrument, which is duly executed, the writing shall be presumed to contain the contract. This presumption is irrefragable, because the writing being the act of both parties, is better evidence of what both designed than any evidence that can be adduced by one. See *Lord Irnham* v. *Child*, 1 Brown, Ch. 92 ; *Howard* v. *Thomas*, 12 Ohio, N. S. 201 ; *The Bank of Westminster* v. *White*, 1 Maryland, Ch. 539 ; *Artz* v. *Grove*, 21 Maryland, 456. Moreover, where real estate is in question, the legislature have enacted that a promise shall not be valid unless it is reduced to writing, and signed by the party to be charged. This does not mean that facts may not be proved orally from which a trust will arise, but that where such facts do not exist, a trust shall not be founded on an oral promise. To make this rule effectual, it must be not only general, but universal. If any case can be taken out of it by showing that a promise accompanied the deed, every case may be. It is, as long experience has shown, admirably calculated to diminish litigation, prevent perjury, and banish fraud ; and if there be any instance where it operates harshly on an individual, it is better that he should be postponed, than that the community should lose the advantage of having a path marked out in which every one may be secure. No one can suffer from its operation, who does not rely on a verbal assurance where law and usage require a writing, and a man who is so unwise as to take this course ought to suffer, unless he has been misled by falsehood or undue influence. Above all, it is the rule prescribed by the legislature, and if the wisdom of it were doubtful, the courts ought not to be wiser than the law. In the cognate case, where goods are sold on the faith of an unwritten guaranty, it has never been held, or even contended, that relief should be given on the ground of fraud, although the inference may be strong, if not irresistible, that the design of the guarantor was to induce the vendor to part with the goods, and then escape under cover of the statute.

It was held in *Collins* v. *Tillou*, 26 Conn. 368, that a deed ceases to be conclusive when the land is sold and conveyed by the grantee, and that the grantor may then prove the trust and recover the proceeds in assumpsit. But this distinction can hardly be regarded as consistent with the rules of evidence or the object of the statute of frauds, which was to provide against the uncertainty of oral testimony. But such a trust may be established by the parol declarations of the grantee after the land has been converted into money; *Maffit* v. *Rynd*, 19 P. F. Smith, 383.

It has been said that the rule which forbids the introduction of parol evidence to controvert a deed, does not apply where the trust is alleged by a third person, who not being a party to the instrument, may show that it was not made for a full or valuable consideration, or contradict any other recital or averment which it contains; *Porter* v. *Mayfield*, 9 Harris, 263; *Blodgett* v. *Aldrich*, 103 Mass. 484. Hence the question is not so much as to the admissibility of the evidence as whether it goes far enough to sustain a trust. It is accordingly established under the decision in the principal case, that if it be shown, though orally, that the consideration moved from the complainant, a trust will result in his favor, although the deed was made to another. So it may be shown that a deed purporting to be made for a full and valuable consideration was in truth voluntary, and that the grantee induced the grantor to execute it by promising to hold the land in trust for the complainant; *Miller* v. *Pearce*, 6 W. & S. 97.

We may now turn to the third head, that where the party to be affected with the trust confessedly gave value for the land. Here the consideration is consistent with and supports the deed, and a recovery cannot be had, except on the ground of fraud. It is therefore necessary to distinguish between the cases where the acquisition of the title is a breach of trust, and those where it is acquired with the knowledge of the complainant. A promise by A. to buy land and convey it to B., is not legally distinguishable from a promise to convey land which A. already holds; *Kisler* v. *Kisler*, 2 Watts, 323, 326; *Sheldon* v. *Harding*, 44 Illinois, 68; *Holmes* v. *Holmes*, Id. 168; *Jackman* v. *Ringland*, 4 W. & S. 149; *Dorsey* v. *Clarke*, 4 Harris, 2 Johnson, 551; *Green* v. *Drummond*, 31 Maryland, 71; *Barnet* v. *Dougherty*, 8 Casey, 371. " An agreement to convey a title to be acquired and paid for hereafter, may be specifically enforced, if the externals of the contract be such as the statute of frauds allows of, but is no more a trust than is an agreement to pay a stipulated price for a title acquired already;" *Kisler* v. *Kisler*, 2 Watts, 323, 326. The violation of such an agreement may be a signal breach of faith, but it is one against which relief cannot be given consistently with the statute. There is a material difference where one agrees to procure the title for another, and takes the deed in his own name. Such an act is a manifest abuse of confidence, against which equity ought to relieve. It is intolerable that a man should go forward as the agent, confidential adviser, or attorney of another, and then take advantage of the opportunity to supplant him with the vendor. Such a case is clearly within the rule laid down in *Keech* v. *Sandford*, that a party holding a fiduciary relation, shall not gain an advantage by indirect means at the expense of his principal. The trust results from the dereliction of duty on the part of the agent, and if that is established to the satisfaction of a chancellor, it is immaterial whether the evidence is written or oral. The strongest case is that of an attorney who purchases for himself in a matter where he has been consulted professionally; *Galbraith* v. *Elder*, 8 Watts, 94; *Cleavenger* v. *Reimar*, 3 W. & S. 486; *Henry* v. *Raiman*, 1 Casey, 354; *Smith* v. *Brotherline*, 12 P. F. Smith, 461, 469. Here the trust is universally conceded; and this is conclusive of the principle, because every one who assumes to advise or act for another, is as much bound to good faith as if he were an attorney. Accordingly, where an agent employed to procure a lease, took it in his own name, he was compelled to assign the term; *Lees* v. *Nuttal*, 1 Tamlyn, 282; 1 Russell &

Mylne, 53; and the same rule was applied in *Taylor* v. *Salmon*, 4 Mylne & Craig, 134.

It has indeed been said that a trust will not arise unless the agency is proved by written evidence, *ante*, *Bartlett* v. *Pickersgill*, 1 Eden, 517; *Barnet* v. *Dougherty*, 8 Casey, 371, 373; but the case is essentially different where one who is employed to effect a purchase, buys for himself in fraud of the principal.

These decisions do not warrant the inference that a promise to buy for another, and hold the title until he is ready to pay for it, can give birth to a trust; *Barnet* v. *Dougherty*, 8 Casey, 371. Strong, J., said, "It is fraud in the purchase which makes the holder of the title a trustee. Subsequent fraud, if any exists, no more raises a trust than does subsequent payment of the purchase-money. Setting up the sheriff's deed as an absolute conveyance of both the legal and the equitable interest was not a fraud from which the law implies a trust. It was nothing more than the violation of a promise, implied or express, which is of no avail to induce a chancellor to decree the purchaser to be a trustee."

Fraud is, nevertheless, infinite in its variety; and it has been said that one reason why it should not be defined is, that if it were, new methods would be found beyond the line. See *Hoge* v. *Hoge*, 1 Watts, 163, 211. See *Stillman* v. *Ashdown*, 2 Atkyns, 481; *Webb* v. *Rorke*, 2 Schoales & Lefroy, 666. Where a gross abuse of confidence is apparent, equity will not be deterred by a regard for forms ; *Seichrist's Appeal*. 16 P. F. Smith, 237, 241. See *Hidden* v. *Jordan*, 21 California, 92 ; *Sandfoss* v. *Jones*, 35 Id. 482 ; *Price* v. *Reeves*, 38 Id. 457 ; *Sogen* v. *Heard*, 3 Mississippi, 428. A man who pays for land and takes the deed in his own name, may, therefore, be charged as a trustee for another who was not only a stranger to the conveyance and the consideration, but authorized or sanctioned what was done, and, although the presumption is strong against such a trust, it may still be overcome by clear proof that the transaction was marked by fraud. " Where," said Agnew, J., in *Seichrist's Appeal*, " one procures a title, which he could not have obtained except by a confidence reposed in him, and abuses that confidence, he becomes a trustee *ex maleficio*." The case of *Jenkins* v. *Eldredge*, 3 Story, went on this ground, and the principle is clear, although it seems to have been misapplied. It not unfrequently happens that land is exposed for sale under an execution, and bought in by some one who promises to convey it to the judgment debtor. If this is all, it is a mere contract, and invalid, unless reduced to writing ; *Jackman* v. *Ringland*, 4 W. & S. 149 ; *Fox* v. *Hefner*, 1 Id. 372 ; *Kisler* v. *Kisler*, 2 Watts, 323. *Kistler's Appeal*, 2 P. F. Smith, 393. But there is at times something more. The promise is used to induce the debtor and his friends to refrain from satisfying the writ, or bidding the land up

to its real value, and ignored or disregarded after the purpose is accomplished. " Had the ward," said Gibson, Ch. J., in *Kisler* v. *Kisler*, " reposed on the guardian's promise to purchase the land for him, the case might have gone in his favor on another ground. There would then have been a trust *ex maleficio* from the conduct of the guardian in keeping the ward back as a bidder, and perhaps getting the land at a cheaper rate by seeming to buy for him. Such a trust seems to be recognized in *Lloyd* v. *Spillett*, 2 Atkyns, 148 ; and *Peebles* v. *Reading*, 8 S. & R. 492 ; and was actually enforced in *Brown* v. *Dysinger*, 5 Rawle, 408. It arises from the artifice of the party to be affected, and not from the contract. *Cook* v. *Cook*, 19 P. F. Smith, 443.

A trust was decreed on this ground in *Sogins* v. *Heard*, 31 Mississippi, 426 ; *Combs* v. *Little*, 3 Green's Ch. 310, and *Marlatt* v. *Warwick*, 3 C. E. Green, 108 ; and the cases of *Brown* v. *Dysinger*, 5 Rawle, 408, and *Brown* v. *Lynch*, 1 Paige, 147, proceed on the same principle. It is, notwithstanding, a questionable branch of equity, inviting the fraud and perjury which the statute was intended to prevent. " It would," said Rogers, J., in *Jackman* v. *Ringland*, 4 W. & S. 149, " be of the most mischievous consequence if a purchase at a judicial sale could, at any distance of time, have an absolute turned into a defeasible conveyance by parol evidence." It may be added that if the defendant in the judgment has the means, he should pay his creditors; if he has not, a secret trust in his favor is a wrong done to them. Such a purchase may, notwithstanding, be attended with circumstances, which point unequivocally to a fraud that should not be allowed to succeed. A purchaser at a sheriff's sale sometimes disarms competition by declaring publicly that he is buying for the person whose property has been seized, and will convey to him on being reimbursed. This is a manifest fraud on the judgment creditors of the latter, for which they may seek redress by bill; but the equity of the defendant in the judgment is much more questionable. If A. procures a deed from B., by falsely representing that he is buying for C., a trust will arise in favor of the latter, because B., being entitled to give or withold, may prescribe the conditions, but this cannot be said where land is sold by the sheriff under legal process. It is, notwithstanding, established in Pennsylvania and some of the other States.

A different view prevails in South Carolina, where it has been held that an oral promise to buy land at a judicial sale, and hold it for the owner's use, cannot be enforced as a trust, although a trust may be deduced where such a purpose is declared as a means of inducing bidders to stand aloof, and the land obtained for less than it is worth; *McDonald* v. *May*, 1 Richardson's Eq. 91; *Schmidt* v. *Gatwood*, 2 Id. 162; *Johnston* v. *LaMotte*, 6 Id. 347. In *Schmidt* v. *Gatwood*, the court said: " It is

alleged that this purchase was made at a sacrifice, under an agreement on the part of the plaintiff, that the family should have the benefit of it. The evidence rests in parol. It is argued that the family, trusting to the agreement, permitted the plaintiff to purchase at a sacrifice ; that to allow him to retain the property under such circumstances, would encourage fraud ; and that, upon this distinct ground, independently of the Statute of Frauds, a trust should be decreed. Undoubtedly there are cases, (such as *M'Donald* v. *May*, 1 Rich. Eq. 91,) where a party, who enables himself to purchase at an under rate, by representing that he is buying for another, is liable to have his purchase set aside for fraud. These are cases where competition is fraudulently reduced or destroyed. In such cases, it matters not whether there was an agreement or not.

" Indeed, in the latter case, where, of course, the representation is wholly false, that circumstance serves only to enhance the fraud complained of. Such cases as these, steer entirely clear of the Statute of Frauds. The evidence of the purchaser's representations is received, not for the purpose of substantiating the supposed agreement, but for the purpose of showing the means by which he effected his fraudulent design, and when received, it is employed not for the purpose of enforcing the contract, but for that of setting it aside.

" But no such circumstances have been developed in this case. The fraud insisted on, consists merely in the non-fulfilment of the alleged agreement, and depends, of course, entirely on the question, whether there was in fact an agreement to be performed, and that preliminary fact, the statute will not allow to be established by parol;" See *Peebles* v. *Reading*, 8 S. & R. 484; *Brown* v. *Dysinger*, 5 Rawle, 408; *Brown* v. *Lynch*, 1 Paige, 147; *Ryan* v. *Dox*, 34 New York, 307; *Cox* v. *Cox*, 5 Richardson, Eq. 492; *Langhorne* v. *Payne*, 14 B. Monroe; *Creutcher* v. *Lord*, 4 Bush, 380; *Trapnall* v. *Brown*, 19 Arkansas, 39.

It is immaterial under these decisions that the purchaser is not acting for, or authorized by the owner of the land, if he declares that he is buying for his use, and thus obtains the property at a lower figure. So one who induces another whose property is going to be sold, to stay away by promising to bid for him, may be affected with a trust, although he does not announce his intention publicly or at the sale; *Baugh* v. *Wentz*, 5 P. F. Smith, 360; *Boynton* v. *Housler*, 23 Id. 453.

In *Sheriff* v. *Neal*, 6 Watts, 534, the defendant agreed to redeem land which had been sold for taxes, and hold the title for the former owner, and so informed the tax commissioners, and it was held that the execution of a deed by them on the faith of the assurance, gave birth to a trust which might be enforced, although the evidence was merely oral.

The principle is the same where one foregoes an estate or interest in land for the purpose of enabling another to become the purchaser, on the faith of the latter's promise to hold the property for his benefit, or give a deed. In *Plumer* v. *Reed*, 3 Wright, 46, the defendant entered into possession of a tract under a written contract of sale, and built a house on one of the lots. It was subsequently agreed between him, the vendor, and the plaintiff, that the contract should be rescinded, and that the plaintiff should buy the tract and convey the house and lot to the defendant. The vendor thereupon conveyed the tract to the plaintiff, and it was held that a resulting trust arose in favor of the defendant, who had contributed his estate in the land, and was as much entitled to protection as if he had parted with value in any other form.

In *Hidden* v. *Jordan*, 21 California, 92, the complainant, Hidden, was in possession of a farm which he had improved and cultivated, but the legal title was outstanding in the hands of one Bissell, who was willing to part with it for $6,000. The complainant, who had only $2,000, gave it to the defendant on the faith of a promise that he would furnish the remaining $4,000, and obtain a conveyance from Bissell, in trust to execute a deed to the plaintiff, when the latter should be able to repay the amount advanced. Bissell accordingly conveyed to the defendant, who subsequently repudiated his contract with the plaintiff, and claimed to hold the land as his own. It was contended under these circumstances that if a trust arose it could only be in the ratio of the sum which the plaintiff had actually paid, and that all beyond was an oral contract which could not be enforced consistently with the statute. Judgment was, notwithstanding, given for the whole of the land. "What the defendant undertook to do," said Cope, J., "was to purchase the land; not a part of it, but the whole; not for himself, but for the plaintiff. What he is attempting to do is to deprive the plaintiff of benefit of the purchase. This, according to the doctrine of *Bartlett* v. *Pickersgill*, 1 Eden, 515, 4 East, 577, note b., *ante*, he might succeed in doing, if the whole of the purchase-money had been paid by himself, but as the plaintiff paid a portion of it, he is entitled to insist on the agreement. The money was paid with the understanding that he was to have the entire estate, and the defendant agreed that he should have it, became his agent for the purchase, and bought the land. The plaintiff cannot be required to take less than the whole, for that was his bargain; to force him into the position of a judg-ment purchaser would be to legalize a fraud."

The question may be viewed in another aspect. Where an agent who has received a sum, which proves to be insufficient, to be employed in buying land, agrees to advance the residue, and hold the title until he is repaid, the transaction is virtually a loan to the principal, and the whole consideration may consequently be regarded as moving from him. That the agent pays the price in full out of his own funds, does not necessarily exclude the operation of this principle. *Sheriff* v. *Neal*, 6 Watts, 534, 542. The defendant, said Kennedy, J., proposed " to the plaintiffs to advance the money, and take a deed from the commissioners of the county, in his own name, as a security that they would make the amount good, so that the real transaction upon which the commissioners conveyed the land to him would appear to have been as much like a loan of money to the plaintiffs, as anything else, and the deed taken merely as a security for the repayment of it."

*TOLLET *v.* TOLLET. [*227]

DE TERM S. MICHAELIS, 1728.

[REPORTED 2 P. WMS. 489.[1]]

DEFECTIVE EXECUTION OF A POWER AIDED.]—*Husband has a power to make a jointure to his wife by deed: he does it by will, and she has no other provision; equity will make this good. Equity will supply the want of a surrender of a copyhold, in case it be devised for payment of debts, or for a wife, or for younger children; so also will it help a defective execution of a power; but not a non-execution.*

THE husband, by virtue of a settlement made upon him by an ancestor, was tenant for life, with remainder to his first and other sons in tail male, with a power to the husband to make a jointure on his wife by *deed* under his hand and seal.

The husband having a wife, for whom he had made no provision, and being in the *Isle of Man*, by his last *will*, under his hand and seal, devised part of his lands within his power to his wife for her life.

Objection.—This conveyance, being by a will, is not warranted by the power, which directs that it should be by *deed;* and a will is a voluntary conveyance, and, therefore, not to be aided in a Court of Equity.

SIR JOSEPH JEKYLL, M. R.—This is a provision for a wife who had none before, and within the same reason as a provision for a child not before provided for;[2] and as a Court of Equity would, had this been the case of a copyhold *devised*, have supplied the want of a surrender; so where there is a defective execution of the power, be *it either for payment of debts or provision [*228] for a wife or children unprovided for, I shall equally supply any defect of this nature.

The difference is betwixt a *non-execution* and a *defective execution of a power;* the latter will always be aided in equity, under the circumstances mentioned, it being the duty of every man to pay his debts, and a husband or father to provide for his wife or child. But this Court will not help the *non-execution* of a power, since it is against the nature of a power, which is left to the free will and election of the party whether to execute or not; for which reason equity will not say he shall execute it, or do that for him which he does not think fit to do himself.

[1] S. C., Mos. 46; 2 Eq Ca. Ab. 233, pl. 16; 633, pl. 10.
[2] Equitable relief will be granted, although the wife or child seeking it is provided for. Vide Kettle v. Townsend, 1 Salk. 187; Smith v. Baker, 1 Atk. 385; Hervey v. Hervey, 1 Atk. 568; Chapman v. Gibson, 3 Bro. C. C. 229.

And in this case, the legal estate being in trustees, they were decreed to convey an estate to the widow for life in the lands devised to her by her husband's will.

Wherever the formalities required by a power are not strictly complied with, the appointment will, at law (unless made valid by statute, see post, pp. 239, 240), be void, and the property which is the subject of the power will consequently go as in default of appointment. Courts of Equity, however, although not holding the power to be well executed, will, in favour of certain parties, aid the defective execution of a power by compelling, as in the principal case, the person having the legal interest to transfer it in the manner pointed out by the defective appointment. The principle upon which Courts of Equity act in these cases is thus stated by Lord Alvanley, M. R., in the case of *Chapman* v. *Gibson*, 3 Bro. C. C. 229: "I have looked," said his Lordship, " at all the cases I can, to find on what principle this Court goes in supplying a defect, and altering the legal right; it is this: Whenever a man, having power over an estate, whether ownership or not, in discharge of moral or natural obligations, shows an intention to execute such power, the Court will operate upon the conscience of the heir, to make him perfect this intention." In the same case his Lordship remarked, " that the execution of a power, and a surrender of a copyhold, go hand in hand, precisely on the same ground." It may, therefore, be considered as a settled rule, that the Court interposes its aid upon the same principles and under *similar circumstances in cases of a want of a surrender of copyholds, and a defective execution of a power. See also *Rodgers* v. *Marshall*, 17 Ves. 297.

[*229]

Surrenders of copyholds to the use of wills were rendered unnecessary for the future by 55 Geo. 3, c. 192, repealed by 1 Vict. c. 26, which, however, substitutes similar provisions. See sects. 3, 4, and 5.

Although there are decisions leading to an opposite conclusion (*Rodgers* v. *Marshall*, 17 Ves. 295; *Ellis* v. *Nimmo*, L. G., temp. Sugd. 333), it is now clearly settled, in accordance with the inference which may be drawn from the remark of the Master of the Rolls in the principal case, that equity will not supply a surrender in the case of a *deed* at the instance of persons having merely a *meritorious* consideration, any more than it will carry into execution a voluntary contract at the instance of the same persons (*Jefferys* v. *Jefferys*, Cr. & Ph. 138; *Tatham* v. *Vernon*, 29 Beav. 604); secus, where the consideration is valuable: *Nandike* v. *Wilkes*, Gilb. Eq. Rep. 114; *Jennings* v. *Moore*, 2 Vern. 609; *Cotter* v. *Layer*, 2 P. Wms. 623. See *Price* v. *Price*, 14 Beav. 604.

Although, however, the jurisdiction of equity to supply surrenders of copyholds is now seldom exercised (see *Freeman* v. *Freeman*, Kay, 479), nevertheless, since equity aids defective executions of powers upon precisely the same principles, and for and against the same persons, it will still be useful to consider the cases upon supplying the surrenders of copyholds. See *Sayer* v. *Sayer, Innes* v. *Sayer*, 7 Hare, 387.

As to the classes in whose favour equity will aid a defective execution of a power or supply a surrender.]—First, equity will aid purchasers (*Fothergill* v. *Fothergill*, 2 Freem. 257 ; *Jackson* v. *Jackson*, 4 Bro. C. C. 462; *Sergeson* v. *Sealey*, 2 Atk. 414; 9 Mod. 390 ; *Wade* v. *Paget*, 1 Bro. C. C. 363 ; *Burrell* v. *Crutchley*, 15 Ves. 544 ; *Affleck* v. *Affleck*, 3 Sm. & Giff. 394 ; *In re Dykes' Estate*, 7 L. R. Eq. 337) ; and mortgagees (*Taylor* v. *Wheeler*, 2 Vern. 564 ; *Jennings* v. *Moore*, 2 Vern. 609); and lessees (*Campbell* v. *Leach*, Amb. 740; *Shannon* v. *Bradstreet*, 1 S. & L. 52; *Doe* v. *Weller*, 7 T. R. 478; *Willes*, 176; *Dowell* v. *Dew*, 1 Y. & C. C. C. 345; *King* v. *Roney*, 5 Ir. Ch. Rep. 64, 72); mortgagees and lessees being purchasers pro tanto. And it has been laid down, "That in order to constitute a purchaser in whose favour a defective execution of a power can be aided, there must be a consideration and an intention to purchase, either proved or to be presumed," per Sir George Turner, V. C., 9 Hare, 769.

Secondly, equity will aid creditors. Thus, where a person directed his copyhold estate to be sold for payment of debts, and *died without having surrendered it to the use of his will, equity decreed the surrender to be supplied, and the copyhold estate to be sold. [*230] See *Bixby* v. *Eley*, 2 Bro. C. C. 325; *S. C.*, 2 Dick. 698; *Ithell* v. *Beane*, 1 Ves. 215; *Tudor* v. *Anson*, 2 Ves. 582; *Fothergill* v. *Fothergill*, 2 Freem. 257. In *Wilkes* v. *Holmes*, 9 Mod. 485, power was given, in a marriage settlement, to the husband and wife to raise 2000l. out of certain lands of the wife's ; and if no part should be raised in the life of the husband and wife, then it should be lawful for the survivor of them by will *duly* executed, to raise that sum, for the purpose of paying the debts of the husband and wife, or either of them, or making a provision for younger children. The wife, upon the death of her husband, defectively executed the power ; it was objected, that the debts which were to be paid by means of the power were the debts of the husband, whereas the estate was originally the wife's. However, Lord Hardwicke supplied the defect, observing that the debts were expressly provided for by the deed of settlement.

Where, moreover, a person has a general power of appointment over property, which in default of appointment is given over, if he exercises such appointment in favour of volunteers by deed, or by will, equity will interfere and intercept such property in aid of the assets of the appointer for the benefit of his creditors, but if he does not exercise his power equity cannot interfere, and the persons entitled in default of appointment will be entitled to the property. See *Thompson* v. *Towne*, 2 Vern. 319; *Holmes* v. *Coghill*, 7 Ves. 499, 12 Ves. 206; *Fleming* v. *Buchanan*, 3 De G. Mac. & G. 976; and the note to *Silk* v. *Prime*, 2 Lead. Cas. Eq., and the cases there cited.

Thirdly, charities will be aided. "I take," says Lord Northington, "the uniform rule of this Court, both before, at, and after the Statute of Elizabeth, to have been, that where the uses are charitable, and the person has in himself full power to convey, the Court will aid a defective conveyance to such uses:" *Attorney-General* v. *Tancred*, 1 Eden. 14: see also *Piggot* v. *Penrice*, Prec. Ch. 471; Com. Rep. 250; *Attorney-General* v. *Sibthorpe*, 2 Russ. & My. 111 n. In *Innes* v. *Sayer* (7 Hare, 377), a testatrix had power to dispose of certain sums of stock by her last will and testament, or any writing purporting to be her last will and testament, to be by her signed and published in the presence of, and attested by, two or more credible witnesses. The testatrix by her will, dated in January, 1833, unattested, and not referring to the power, gave certain sums of stocks to charities. She afterwards made eight other unattested testamentary papers, giving legacies, or revoking legacies, previously inserted, the last of which papers was dated [*231] the 1st *of September, 1836; and at the foot of it she had written as follows:—"This will has not been witnessed, as I intend, if I am spared, to write it out fair." The testatrix died in June, 1844. It was held by Sir James Wigram, V. C., that the defect in the execution of the power ought to be supplied in equity in favour of the charities. "The principle," said his Honor, "upon which the Court appears to go is this, that if a person has power, by his own act, to give property, and has, by some paper or instrument, clearly shown that he intended to give it, although that paper, by reason of some informality, is ineffectual for the purpose, yet the party having the power of doing it by an effectual instrument, and having shown his intention to do it, the Court will, in the case of a charity, by its decree make the instrument effectual to do that which was intended to be done. It is not for me to give any opinion, whether the principle is right or not. There appears to be very high authority for the application of the principle, independently of the Statute of Elizabeth; and it has been applied since the Statute." See *S. C.*, affirmed on appeal, 3 Mac. & G. 606, Tudor on Charitable Trusts, p. 37, 255, 2nd edit.

Fourthly, equity will aid a wife and a legitimate child, although they claim merely as volunteers, upon a meritorious consideration; as, for instance, upon a provision made for them after marriage: *Fothergill* v. *Fothergill*, 2 Freem. 257; *Sarth* v. *Blanfrey*, Gilb. Eq. Rep. 166; *Sneed* v. *Sneed*, Amb. 64; *Churchman* v. *Hervey*, Amb. 335; *Medwin* v. *Sandham*, 3 Swanst. 686; *Affleck* v. *Affleck*, 3 Sm. & Giff. 394; *Proby* v. *Landor*, 28 Beav. 504. "In cases," says Lord Hardwicke, "of aiding the defective execution of a power, either for a wife or a child, whether the provision has been for a valuable consideration has never entered into the view of the Court, but being intended for a provision, whether voluntary or not, has been always held to entitle this Court to give aid to a wife or child to carry it into execution, though defectively made:" *Hervey* v. *Hervey*, 1 Atk. 567 ; *Barron* v. *Constabile*, 7 Ir. Ch. Rep. 467.

Although an inference to the contrary might be drawn from the principal case, it is now clearly established that a wife or child, although provided for, will be entitled to the aid of equity. " I am of opinion," says Lord Hardwicke, in *Hervey* v. *Hervey*, " that the rule as laid down by the defendant's counsel, that a wife or child, who comes for the aid of this Court to supply a defective execution of a power, must be entirely unprovided for, is not the right rule of the Court. I think the general rule, that the husband or a father are the proper judges what is a reasonable provision for a wife or child, is a good and invariable* rule: 1 Atk. 568; see also *Kettle* v. *Townsend*, 1 Salk. 187; *Smith* v. *Baker*, 1 Atk, 385; *Chapman* v. *Gibson*, 3 Bro. C. C. 229. [*232]

To no other persons, except a wife or legitimate child, will the aid of the Court be granted, upon the ground of the provision being for a meritorious consideration; neither to a husband (*Watt* v. *Watt*, 3 Ves. 244; *Moodie* v. *Reid*, 1 Madd. 516; *Hughes* v. *Wells*, 9 Hare, 749, 769); nor to a natural child (*Fursaker* v. *Robinson*, Prec. Ch. 475; *Tudor* v. *Anson*, 2 Ves. 582); nor to a grandchild (*Bland* v. *Bland*, 2 Cox, 349; *Perry* v. *Whitehead*, 6 Ves. 544; and 1 Watk. Copyh. 136, 138); nor to a father (*Sloane* v. *Lord Cadogan*, App. to Sug. on Powers, No. 9, 7th edit.); nor to a mother, brother, or sister (*Goodwyn* v. *Goodwyn*, 1 Ves. 228; *Goring* v. *Nash*, 3 Atk. 189, overruling *Watts* v. *Bellas*, 1 P. Wms. 60); nor to a nephew or niece (*Strode* v. *Russell*, 2 Vern. 621, 625; *Marston* v. *Gowan*, 3 Bro. C. C. 170); nor to a cousin (*Tudor* v. *Anson*, 2 Ves. 582); not to a settlor defectively executing a power in his own favour (*Ward* v. *Booth*, cited 3 Ch. Ca. 69, 92; *Ellison* v. *Ellison*, post, 245, 6 Ves. 656). A fortiori equity will not afford its aid to a mere volunteer, in no way related to the person defectively executing a power: *Smith* v. *Ashton*, 2 Freem. 309; *Sergeson* v. *Sealey*, 2 Atk. 415; *Godwin* v. *Kilsha*, Amb. 684. It is clearly settled that a defective appointment by a married woman will be aided (*Pollard* v. *Grenvil*, 1 Ch. Ca. 10; *Dowell* v. *Dew*, 1 Y. & C. C. C. 345; *Doe* v. *Weller*, 7 T. R. 480; *Stead* v. *Nelson*, 2 Beav. 245); although, by some extra-judicial observations of Sir Thomas Plumer, in *Martin* v. *Mitchell*, 2 J. & W. 424, this appears to have been doubted. See also *Dillon* v. *Grace*, 2 S. & L. 456. It seems that in the United States Chancery will not distinguish between children and grandchildren in the exercise of its jurisdiction to correct an oversight or mistake in the

execution of a power for their benefit. See *Huss* v. *Norris*, 13 P. F.
Smith, 372 ; *Watts* v. *Bellas*, 1 Pearce, 60.

*Next, as against whom equity will aid a defective execution of a
power, or supply a surrender.*]—It is clear from the principal case,
that aid will be granted as against the remainderman who takes,
although by purchase, subject to the power (*Coventry* v. *Coventry*, 2 P.
Wms. 222 ; *Shannon* v. *Bradstreet*, 1 S. & L. 52 ; *Howard* v. *Carpenter*, 11 Md. 202, 259) ; and also in general as against an heir-at-law
or customary heir ; *Smith* v. *Ashton*, 1 Ch. Ca. 263, 264.

A defective execution of a power has been aided in equity in favour
of a sister as against her brothers who were provided for, and who in
default of appointment would have participated in the property : *Morse*
v. *Martin*, 34 Beav. 500.

It has, however, been a question of much difficulty, whether equity
will afford its aid as against an heir totally unprovided for. In *Chapman* v. *Gibson*, 3 Bro. C. C. 229, Lord Alvanley thought that the heir,
being a *son* of the testator unprovided for, could not be relieved
[*233]   *against. " The principle," said his Lordship " must be this,
that the testator being under an obligation to do an act, we will
compel the heir to perfect it ; but we will not compel him to fulfil an
obligation at the expense of another ; and if the testator has totally
forgot to make any provision for his eldest son, this shall be an answer
to the claim of the wife, or other children." Lord Rosslyn thought
that the Court ought never to enter into the consideration of the heir
being or not being provided for. " I confess," observes his Lordship,
" it appears to me there is no rule at all, unless the Court takes it upon
the relation in which they stand. Otherwise, it is all loose and arbitrary. It never entered into the mind of the Court to consider that
argument, where the want of a surrender was to be supplied for creditors : but the same sort of argument might be used there—that the heir
was starving, the creditors opulent and severe. Those circumstances
are not fit to be considered by the Court. The Court must go upon a
certain line, which is very obvious—that, where the will expresses an
intention to do that which legally and morally the testator ought to do,
so simple a form as supplying the want of a surrender shall not im-
pede the performance of that duty :" *Hills* v. *Downton*, 5 Ves. 564.
But, it was unnecessary to decide that point in *Hills* v. *Downton*, for
the heiresses-at-law, against whom the want of a surrender was supplied,
were married, and, therefore, in Lord Rosslyn's opinion, provided for.
Lord Alvanley, nevertheless, still retained the opinion he expressed
in *Chapman* v. *Gibson*. See his observations on *Hills* v. *Downton*,
Sugd. Pow. vol. ii., App. No. xxiv., 7th ed. In *Braddick* v. *Mattock*,
6 Madd. 363, Sir J. Leach, V. C., said, " This Court will not supply a
surrender against the heir-at-law unprovided for ; but it considers the
parent as the best judge of the provision of that heir, and will not ex-

amine the sufficiency of the provision, unless, perhaps in a case in which it may be challenged as illusory." In *Rodgers* v. *Marshall*, 17 Ves 294, Sir W. Grant, M. R., seemed inclined to think, that, as against a grandchild, being the heir-at-law, and unprovided for, the want of sur render ought not to be supplied, and directed an inquiry as to whether he was provided for. But see *Hills* v. *Downton*, 5 Ves. 565.

It is clear, however, that a surrender will be supplied as against a collateral heir, whether provided for or not; as a person is not sup posed under any obligation to provide for a collateral heir; *Fielding* v. *Winwood*, 16 Ves. 90; see also *Chapman* v. *Gibson*, 3 Bro. C. C. 229; *Snith* v. *Baker*, 1 Atk. 385.

As to the nature of a defect which will be aided.] It may be laid *down as a general rule, that were the intention to execute a power is sufficiently declared, but the act declaring the inten- [*234] tion is not an execution of the power in the form prescribed, there the defect will be supplied in equity: *Shannon* v. *Bradstreet*, 1 S. & L 63.

Thus equity will aid a defect which arises from the instrument itself being informal or inappropriate, if the intention to execute the power appear clearly in writing; *Lover* v. *The Sierra Nevada Mining Co.*, 32 California, 653, where, for instance, a donee of a power covenants to execute it (*Fothergill* v. *Fothergill*, 2 Freem. 256; *Coventry* v. *Coventry*, Franc. Max., the last case; *S. C.*, 2 P. Wms. 222; *Sergeson* v. *Sealey*, 2 Atk. 414; *Sarth* v. *Lord Branfrey*, Gilb. Eq. Rep. 166);— or when, by his will, he desires the remaindermen to create the estate authorized by the power (*Vernon* v. *Vernon*, Amb. 1);—or if he enters into an agreement to execute it (*Shannon* v. *Bradstreet*, 1 S. & L. 52; *Mortlock* v. *Buller*, 10 Ves. 292; *Coventry* v. *Coventry*, Franc. Max., the last case; *Lowry* v. *Dufferin*, 1 Ir. Eq. Rep. 281; *Dowell* v. *Dew*, 1 Y. & C. C. C. 345);—even although he keep the agreement in his own possession (*King* v. *Roney*, 5 Ir. Ch. Rep. 64, 77);—or if he promises by letters to grant an estate, which he could only do by the exercise of his power: *Campbell* v. *Leach*, Amb. 740; Sugd. on Powers, App. No. xxv., 7th ed.; and see *Blake* v. *French*, 5 Ir. Ch. Rep. 246. So an agreement to sell land to a Railway Company at a sum to be fixed by arbitrators, will be aided in equity as an informal execution of a gen eral power of appointment: *In re Dykes' Estate*, 7 L. R. Eq. 337. A recital by the donee of a power, in the marriage settlement of one of his daughters, who was one of the objects of the power, that she was entitled to a share of a sum to which she could only be entitled by his appointment, has been held sufficient evidence of his intention to exe cute the power, and was therefore aided as a defective execution of a power: *Wilson* v. *Piggott*, 2 Ves. jun. 351; *Poulson* v. *Wellington*, 2 P. Wms. 533. So also where a donee of a power, in an answer to a bill in Chancery, states that he " appoints, and intends, by writing in due form, to appoint:" *Carter* v. *Carter*, Mos. 365; and see *Fortescue* v. *Gregor*, 5 Ves. 553.

A parol contract, however, to execute a power, is void, *as against a remainderman*, although, in the case of a parol contract to grant a lease under a power, the lessee may have expended money in improvements, on the faith of the parol contract (*Carter* v. *Carter*, Mos. 370; *Shannon* v. *Bradstreet*, 1 S. & L. 72; *Blore* v. *Sutton*, 3 Mer. 237; *Lowry* v. *Lord Dufferin*, 1 Ir. Eq. Rep. 281; and see *Morgan* v. *Milman*, 10 Hare, 279; 3 De G. Mac. & G. 24, 32, 33); *O'Fay* v. *Burke*, [*235] 8 Ir. Ch. *Rep. 225; unless, after the death of the tenant for life, the remainderman lie by and suffer the lessee to continue to improve the estate: *Stiles* v. *Cowper*, 3 Atk. 692.

Equity will afford its aid, where there has been a defective execution by a formal or appropriate instrument: thus, if the instrument, whether it be a deed or will, is by the power required to be executed in the presence of a certain number of witnesses, and it is executed in the presence of a smaller number; or if it is required to be signed and sealed, and sealing is omitted, equity will supply the defect: *Wade* v. *Paget*, 1 Bro. C. C. 363; *Cockerell* v. *Cholmeley*, 1 Russ. & My. 424; 1 C. & F. 60. And in wills not coming within the operation of the late Wills Act, an appointment of personalty, required to be attested by two witnesses, has been aided, though attested by no witness: *Lucena* v. *Lucena*, 5 Beav. 146. So, also, where a power of appointment over land was required to be exercised by will *duly executed*, and a will was made in exercise of the power, attested by *two* witnesses only, Lord Hardwicke was of opinion that the will was not duly executed within the meaning of the power, but that the Court ought to aid the defective execution in favour of the creditors and younger children, considering their claim as under the settlement, and the mode of executing the power as depending on the settlement, and not on the Statute of Frauds, except as the words, "duly executed" were construed by reference to that statute. If this had been a voluntary execution of the power, and not for the payment of debts, or for valuable or meritorious consideration, it must have stood on its own ground, and would not have been supported; *Wilkie* v. *Holmes*, 1 S. & L. 60, n.; *S. C.* reported under the name of *Wilkie* v. *Holme*, 1 Dick. 165; *S. C.*, 9 Mod. 485; and see *Smith* v. *Ashton*, 1 Ch. Ca. 263; *Morse* v. *Martin*, 34 Beav. 500. See, however, now, 1 Vict. c. 26, ss. 9, 10, whereby it is enacted, "that no will shall be valid unless it shall be in writing and executed in manner thereinafter mentioned; that is to say, it shall be signed at the foot or end thereof, by the testator, or by some other person in his presence and by his direction; and such signature shall be made or acknowledged by the testator, in the presence of two or more witnesses present at the same time, and such witnesses shall attest and shall subscribe the will, in the presence of the testator, but no form of attestation shall be necessary;" and "that no appointment made by will in exercise of any power shall be valid, unless the same be executed in manner thereinbefore required; and every will executed in manner thereinbefore required shall, so far as respects the execution and attestation thereof, be a valid execution *of a power of appointment by will, notwithstanding it shall have been expressly required that a will made in exercise of such power shall be executed with some additional or other form of execution or solemnity." [*236]

A power will, as in the principal case, be aided, if it has been executed by a *will*, when it ought strictly to have been executed by deed: *Sneed* v. *Sneed*, Amb. 64; *Mills* v. *Mills*, 8 Ir. Eq. Rep. 192.

In *Hervey* v. *Hervey*, 1 Atk. 561, Barnard, 103, a power was given to the husband to make a jointure of *such* of the lands in a deed as he thought proper, not exceeding 600*l.* a year. The husband by successive deeds charged all the lands with rent-charges exceeding 600*l.* a year. Lord Hardwicke supplied in favour of the wife the defect occasioned by the excessive execution of the power. Upon the same principle in *Baron* v. *Constabile*, 7 Ir. Ch. Rep. 467, where the power was to *charge* a jointure not exceeding 600*l.* a year by deed or will, and the donee of the power *devised* instead of charging a jointure, the devise was upheld as a valid execution of the power.

So in *Bruce* v. *Bruce*, 11 L. R. Eq. 371, by articles on the marriage of Ann Bruce (then Ann Daniel) followed by a disentailing assurance, an estate was conveyed in trust for the children of the marriage as Ann Bruce should by *deed* appoint, and in default of appointment for such children equally. By a subsequent assurance, which was inoperative, Ann Bruce purported to put an end to the former power and to confer upon herself a general power of appointment over the same estate. She married a second time, and died leaving three children by the first marriage and two by the second, and having made *her will*, whereby without any reference to the power in the marriage articles, pursuant to the alleged general power, and *in exercise of every other power enabling her*, she purported to appoint the said estate to her eldest son by the first marriage, charged with a sum of 3000*l.* in favour of all the children by both marriages other than the eldest son. It was held by Lord Romilly, M. R., that the will operated as a valid exercise of the power in the articles, and that the eldest son was entitled to the estate, subject to raising the sum of 3000*l.* for the other two children of the first marriage.

But equity will not aid a defective execution of a power, if the intention of the author of the power would be thereby defeated. Thus, although there is no doubt that a Court of equity will aid the defective execution of a power in favour of a creditor or purchaser, although the donee be a married woman (*ante*, p. 232), the Court, in such cases,

[*237] must be satisfied that the formalities which *have not been observed, are no more than matters of form; and that the donee of the power has not by their non-observance been deprived of any of the protection which the due exercise of the power would have afforded her. For instance in *Reed* v. *Shergold*, 10 Ves. 370, where a lady, entitled under a devise to copyholds for life, with a power to appoint them *by will*, sold and surrendered them to a purchaser, Lord Eldon, held, that the purchaser could not be aided in equity. " The testator," said his Lordship, " did not mean that she should so execute her power—he intended that she should give by will, or not at all ; and it is impossible to hold, that the execution of an instrument or deed, which, if it availed to any purpose, must avail to the destruction of that power the testator meant to remain capable of execution to the moment of her death, can be considered in equity an attempt in or towards the execution of the power."

And the Courts look with especial jealousy on any such transaction, in which the wife may have acted under the influence of her husband. Thus in *Hopkins* v. *Myall* (2 Russ. & My. 86), on a marriage, a settlement had been made of the wife's property to herself for life to her separate use, with remainder as she should appoint by any writing under her hand, attested by two witnesses, and for default of appointment to the children of the marriage. The trustees upon the joint application of the husband and wife, by a letter not attested by any witnesses, parted with the trust fund; it was held by Sir John Leach, M. R., that the trustees were bound, after the death of the wife, to make good the trust fund for the children. " The ceremonies," said his Honor, " required by the settlement were introduced for the express purposes of protecting the wife against the influence of her husband, and are matters of substance and not of form; and without an adherence to those ceremonies, the interests of the children could not be defeated." See, also, *Thackwell* v. *Gardiner*, 5 De G. & Sm. 58 ; and *Majoribanks* v. *Hovenden*, 6 Ir. Eq. Rep. 238.

So an appointment not made within the time prescribed by the donor of the power will not be aided in Equity, where the time within which the appointment was to be made, was not a mere matter of form, but of the substance and essence of the power. See *Cooper* v. *Martin*, 3 L. R. Ch. App. 47.

Moreover the Court will not aid a defective instrument, where there does not appear thereby to have been on the part of the donee of the power a distinct intention to execute it. See *Garth* v. *Townsend*, 7 L. R. Eq. 220 ; there Mrs. Garth having power to appoint funds amongst [*238] her children by deed, or by her last *will in writing, or any writing purporting to be or being in the nature of her last will, or any codicil thereto, to be signed and published in the presence of, and to be attested by, two credible witnesses, died intestate; but left ·

in an envelope, addressed to her son, an unattested memorandum (signed by herself and dated eight years before her death), "for my sons and daughters. Not having made a will, I leave this memorandum, and hope my children will be guided by it, though it is not a legal document. The funds I wish divided as follows" (and after apportioning the funds among her children, and making a bequest to them out of another fund, and a gift of the residue, she thus ends the memorandum) :—"this paper contains my last wishes and blessings upon my dear children, and thanks for their love to me." It was held by Sir W. M. James, V. C., that the Court could not aid any defects in the execution of the memorandum, so as to give it validity as an appointment. "The true test," said his Honor, "is that mentioned by Mr. Osborne Morgan: is there a distinct intention to execute the power? Now, here the persons to take and the amount to be taken, are sufficiently pointed out, but where the instrument fails is in *intention to execute the power*. Mrs. Garth purposely abstained from executing it. She simply wished her children to be quite unfettered, saying, 'I tell you my wishes, but I do not mean to tie you up by any legal document. I know I have power to appoint these funds, but I do not exercise that power.' The jurisdiction of the Court is to *supply defects occasioned by mistakes or inadvertence: not to supply omissions intentionally made.*"

Formerly when trustees under a common power of sale and exchange sold an estate without the timber, such exercise of the power was held not only to be invalid at law but also in equity, where the defect in the execution could not be aided. Thus, in *Cockerell* v. *Cholmeley*, 1 Russ. & My. 418, where an estate was devised to a trustee and his heirs, to the use of A. for life, without impeachment of waste, and a power of sale, with the consent of the tenant for life, was given to the trustee, the trustee, with the consent of the tenant for life, sold the estate under the power, without the timber, which was to be taken at a valuation; at law the power was held to be badly executed; and, upon a bill being filed in equity for relief by the purchasers of the estate, Sir J. Leach, M. R., held, that they were entitled to none. "The plaintiffs," said his Honor, "call upon this Court to supply the defect in the execution of the power. A Court of equity will, in favour of persons standing in the situation of the plaintiffs, supply a defect in the execution of a power which consists in the *want of some circumstance required in the manner of execution, as the want of a seal, or of a [*239] sufficient number of witnesses, or where it has been exercised by will instead of a deed. But here it is at law decided, that there was no power in the trustees to sell the land without the growing timber; and there is no execution by the trustees of the power to sell the land with the growing timber; and I find no authority which applies to the case." This case was, on appeal to the House of Lords, affirmed: 2 Russ. &

My. 751; 6 Bligh, N. S. 120; 1 C. & F. 60; *Cholmeley* v. *Paxton*, 3 Bing. 207; *S. C.* nom. *Cockerell* v. *Cholmeley*, 10 B. & C. 564; *Cholmeley* v. *Paxton*, 5 Bing. 48, and see Sugd. Prop. 491. See, also, *Adney* v. *Field*, Amb. 654; *Stratford* v. *Lord Aldborough*, 1 Ridg. 281; *Scott* v. *Davis*, 4 My. & Cr. 87.

Upon the same principle, the sale of the surface of land under the ordinary power of sale, reserving the minerals, has been held to be invalid: *Buckley* v. *Howell*, 29 Beav. 546, and see Article 7, Jur. N. S., part 2, 235.

However, by 22 & 23 Vict. c. 35, s. 13, where under a power of sale a bonâ fide sale shall have been made of *an estate with the timber thereon, or any other articles attached thereto*, and the tenant for life, or any other party to the transaction, shall by mistake be allowed to receive for his own benefit a portion of the purchase-money as the value of the timber or other articles, the Court of Chancery, upon payment of the full value of the timber or other articles, at the time of the sale, with interest, and the settlement thereof, may declare the sale valid, and thereupon the legal estate is to vest as if the power had been duly executed.

Under the Settled Estates Act, 19 & 20 Vict. c. 120, the Court may authorize a sale of timber or mines apart from the surface (*In re Mallin's Settled Estate*, 9 W. R. (V. C. S.) 588; *Re Law*, 7 Jur. N. S. 511, see sect. 11); and on a sale of mines apart from the surface, with rights of using the surface for the workings, may reserve a rent in respect of the surface damage from time to time; *In re Milward's Estate*, 6 L. R. Eq. 248; moreover, on the sale of any land under the Act, " any earth, coal, stone, or mineral, may be accepted," sect. 13.

By the Confirmation of Sales Act (25 & 26 Vict. c. 108); no sale, exchange, partition, or enfranchisement made in exercise of a trust or power not forbidding the exception or reservation of minerals, is to be invalid (unless already declared to be so, or there is a suit pending), on the ground only that the trust or power did not expressly authorise an exception or reservation of minerals which has been made (sect. 1), [*240] *and hereafter such exception or reservation may be made by trustees and others, with the sanction of the Court of Chancery, to be obtained on petition (sect. 2). The Act does not, however, extend to Ireland or Scotland (sect. 3).

Mortgagees are within the confirmation of Sales Act, and may have liberty to sell under their power of sale, with a reservation of the mines and minerals in the land sold, and incidental powers of working them; and it is not necessary for mortgagees, in order to exercise the power of selling with such a reservation, to serve the petition on any subsequent incumbrancer: *In re Beaumont's Mortgage Trusts*, 12 L. R. Eq. 86; *In re Wilkinson's Mortgaged Estates*, 13 L. R. Eq. 634.

Cestuis que trust ought to be made parties to any application under

25 & 26 Vict. c. 108, s. 2, for sale of the surface, apart from the minerals : *In re Palmer's Will*, 13 L. R. Eq. 408 ; and see *In re Brown's
Trust Estate*, 9 Jur. (N. S.) 349 ; 11 W. R. 19. But it has been held
that where trustees of settled land with power of sale, exerciseable
with consent of the tenant for life, present a petition under the Confirmation of Sales Act, for leave to sell the land and minerals separately,
it need not be served on the beneficiaries entitled in remainder : *In re
Pryse's Estates*, 10 L. R. Eq. 531.

Lastly, as to what powers will be aided.]—There is no doubt that
powers of jointuring, of raising portions, of sale, of revoking uses and
generally appointing an estate, will, if defectively executed, be aided.
It was, however, at one time doubted whether defective appointments
under powers of leasing would be aided as against the remainderman.
See Powell on Powers, 389. Lord Redesdale, however, in *Shannon* v.
Bradstreet, 1 S. & L. 52, held a contract to grant a lease by a tenant
for life, according to a power, binding upon a remainderman, although
it was objected that a leasing power differs from other powers, inasmuch
as in other powers the remainderman has no interest in the mode in
which the power is executed, as he claims nothing under it, but that
under the leasing power he claims the rent reserved. " On what
ground," said his Lordship, " can it be contended that that which is a
mere charge upon a remainderman is to receive a more liberal construction than what is not a mere charge upon him, but may be much for his
benefit ? In the case of powers to make leases at the best rent that can
be obtained, it is evident that the author of the power looks to the
benefit of the estate, and that the power is given for the benefit both of
the tenant for life and of all persons claiming after him ; for where the
tenant for life can give no permanent interest, and his tenant is liable
every day to be turned out of possession by the accident of *his
death, it is hard to procure substantial tenants ; and therefore [*241]
it is beneficial to all parties that the tenant for life should have a power
to grant such leases. . . . . This, therefore, is a power which is
calculated for the benefit of the estate. Other powers, generally speaking, such as jointuring powers, and powers to make provisions for
younger children are calculated for the benefit of the family ; they may
be indirectly beneficial to the remainderman, in some respects, but they
are no direct benefit to him ; nor can I conceive why these powers
should be construed more liberally than powers to make leases, except
where it is evident that such power is abused ; and in case of letting
leases, the power is certainly more liable to be abused than in making
provisions for wife or children. In these latter cases, the sum to be
raised is generally limited, and cannot be exceeded ; but a power of
leasing is, to a certain extent, a power of charging ; if a fine is taken,
it is unquestionably so ; and even where no fine can be taken, it is, to
a certain degree, a charge, and for the benefit of tenant for life as well

as the remainderman, for tenant for life will get a better rent than if he had no such power. I cannot conceive, therefore, what distinction there is between a leasing power and the other powers before noticed; they are all powers given to the tenant for life for his benefit, to enable him to charge the estate; and in case of a rack-rent, the power of leasing is also a benefit to the remainderman. Now, in case of a jointuring power, and in all the other cases, a contract has been held sufficient to enable a party to have the power executed in equity." See, also, *Doe* v. *Weller*, 7 Term. Rep. 478; Willes, 176; and *Dowell* v. *Dew*, 1 Y. & C. C. C. 345, where an agreement to grant a lease was held binding as against a feme covert, as being a defective execution of her power of leasing.

The legislature has also extended the remedies of lessees by the act for granting relief against defects in leases made under powers of leasing in certain cases, see 12 & 13 Vict. c. 26, suspended in its operation by a subsequent act in the same session until the 1st of June, 1850 (12 & 13 Vict. c. 110), and amended by 13 & 14 Vict. c. 17.

But equity will not aid a defect even in favour of purchasers, if the execution of the power would involve a breach of trust (*Mortlock* v. *Buller*, 10 Ves. 292; *Stratford* v. *Lord Aldborough*. 1 Ridg. 281);— or would be a fraud upon the power: *Harnett* v. *Yielding*, 2 S. & L. 549.

And a power of leasing will not be aided where the best rent has not been reserved, or a fine has been paid, contrary to the requisitions [*242] of the power; or where there has been an agreement or *covenant to grant a lease, commencing in futuro, where the power authorises only leases in possession, and the donee has died before the estate fell into possession (*Campbell* v. *Leach*, Amb. 740; *Shannon* v. *Bradstreet*, 1 S. & L. 52; *Doe* v. *Weller*, 7 Term Rep. 478; Willes, 176; *Dowell* v. *Dew*, 1 Y. & C. C. C. 345, 356; *Temple* v. *Baltinglass*, Rep. t. Finch, 275). But it seems that when the question is raised whether the rent reserved is adequate or not, Courts of equity will not decline to aid the imperfect execution of the power of leasing, unless the rent be so low, as to afford evidence of fraud: *King* v. *Roney*, 5 Ir. Ch. Rep. 64, 77.

In *Sandham* v. *Medwin*, 3 Swanst. 685, where unusual and unheard of covenants were introduced into the lease, "usual and reasonable covenants" being required by the power, a Court of equity would not interfere.

If a tenant for life has power to lease, with the consent of trustees or others, an agreement by the tenant for life alone to lease will not be aided: *Lawrenson* v. *Butler*, 1 S. & L. 13. In *Shannon* v. *Bradstreet*, 1 S. & L. 52, where a tenant for life, with power to grant leases "in possession, and not in reversion," entered into an agreement to grant a lease a day or two before the lease was to commence, the tenant for life having survived that time, no objection arose, and the agreement

was held by Lord Redesdale to be binding upon the remainderman.
See, also, *Dowell* v. *Dew*, 2 Y. & C. C. C. 345.

A Court of equity will not grant its aid where there is a defect in
the execution of a power under an act of Parliament, which must
always be taken strictly; thus, where a tenant in tail made a lease for
years, not authorized by 32 Hen. 8, c. 28 (repealed by 19 & 20 Vict. c.
120, s. 35), equity would not make good the defect: *Rosswell's Case*,
per Hutton Ro. Abr. 379, fol. 6. See, also, Cowp. 267; 2 Burr. 1146;
Anon., 2 Freem. 224.

Non-execution of a power.—We must, however, distinguish between
the defective execution and the non-execution of a power, for a non-
execution of a power will not be aided: *Howard* v. *Carpenter*, 11
Md. 259, 282; a person, for instance, is not entitled to the aid of
the Court on the ground of the execution of the power having been
prevented by the sudden death of the donee: *Piggott* v. *Penrice*, Com.
250; Gilb. Eq. Rep. 138. So, disability to sign from gout has not
been aided: *Blockvill* v. *Ascott*, 2 Eq. Ca. Abr. 659, n.; and see
Buckell v. *Blenkhorn*, 5 Hare, 131. We may, however, except those
cases in which the execution of a power has been prevented by fraud,
as where the deed creating the power has been fraudulently retained
by *the person interested in its non-execution, for then it seems [*243]
equity will afford its aid; 3 Ch. Ca. 83, 84, 122: *Ward* v. *Booth*,
cited 3 Ch. Ca. 69. See, also, *Piggott* v. *Penrice*, Prec. Ch. 471; *Vane*
v. *Fletcher*, 1 P. Wms. 354; *Luttrell* v. *Olmius*, cited 11 Ves. 683;
Seagrave v. *Kirwan*, 1 Beat. 157; *Bulkley* v. *Wilford*, 2 C. & F. 102;
Middleton v. *Middleton*, 1 J. & W. 94.

Defects in the execution of powers cured by statute.]—It may here
be mentioned that if a will is in other respects properly executed, probate cannot be refused upon the ground that the power under which it
has been made has not been properly followed. See *Barnes* v. *Vincent*,
(5 Moore, P. C. C. 201), where a decision of the Prerogative Court refusing probate to the will of a feme covert, on the face of it not executed according to the requisites of the power, was reversed by the
Judicial Committee of the Privy Council. " It is certain," said Lord
Brougham, " that there is a considerable class of cases, in which equity
will relieve against a defective execution of a power. Thus in favour
of a purchaser; of a creditor; of a child; equity will relieve. But if
probate shall have been refused by the Ecclesiastical Court, on the
ground of the execution being defective, no such relief can ever be extended in any case; because the Court, which alone can relieve, never
can know if the instrument had existed, nor can see the defect in the
execution; and the Court of Probate is bound by the fact of the defective execution, and cannot remedy it. Thus a feme covert having made
a will in favour of a child, and imperfectly executed it, the child must
be excluded, by probate being refused; when, had a Court of equity

been put in possession of the instrument, it would have held the defective execution relievable in the child's behalf." See and consider *Este* v. *Este*, 15 Jur. 159; *De Chatelain* v. *De Pontigny*, 1 Swab. & Tr. 411.

The will in *Barnes* v. *Vincent* was made prior to the passing of the Wills Act (1 Vict. c. 26), and it must be remembered, that by that Act, no appointment made by will, in exercise of any power, will be valid, unless the same be executed with the solemnities required by the Act; but if those are complied with, the appointment will be valid, although some additional or other form of execution or solemnity may have been required by the power. See sects. 9 and 10, *ante*, p. 235.

An appointment by deed is now rendered valid in many cases, although not executed and attested by all the solemnities required by the instrument creating the power. See the Property and Trustees' Relief Amendment Act (22 & 23 Vict. c. 35, s. 12), which enacts that " a deed [*244] hereafter executed *in the presence of, and attested by, two or more witnesses in the manner in which deeds are ordinarily executed and attested shall, so far as respects the execution and attestation thereof, be a valid execution of a power of appointment by deed or by any instrument in writing not testamentary, notwithstanding it shall have been expressly required that a deed or instrument in writing made in exercise of such power should be executed or attested with some additional or other form of execution, or attestation, or solemnity: provided always, that this provision shall not operate to defeat any direction in the instrument creating the power, that the consent of any particular person shall be necessary to a valid execution, or that any act shall be performed in order to give validity to any appointment having no relation to the mode of executing and attesting the instrument, and nothing herein contained shall prevent the donee of a power from executing it conformably to the power by writing or otherwise than by an instrument executed and attested as an ordinary deed, and to any such execution of a power this provision shall not extend."

Where forms are imposed on the execution of a power, the circumstances must be strictly adhered to; and however arbitrary and unessential to the validity of the appointing instrument, they must be strictly pursued, in order to constitute a good execution in law; *Pepper's Will*, 1 Parson's Eq. 436, 446; *Porter* v. *Turner*, 3 S. & R. 108; *Slifer and others* v. *Beates and another*, 9 Id. 166, 181; *Ford* et al. v. *Russell et al.*, 1 Freeman, 42, 50; *Marshall* v. *Stephens et als.*, 8 Humphreys, 159, 173; *Bakewell* v. *Ogden*, 2 Bush, 265. But " whenever the intention to execute a power is sufficiently manifest, but the execution is defective, or it has not been executed according to the terms, or in the form prescribed, equity will correct the mistake or supply the defect. When nothing has been done, or attempted to be done, toward the execution of a power, equity, in general, will not interfere, unless the instrument creating the power shall have vested, or recognized in third persons, rights, to secure which the execution of the power is necessary. If the attorney or agent has attempted to execute the power, but has done it defectively, the party claiming under it, cannot avail himself of it, at law, but equity interposes its aid, upon the broad principle of relieving against accident or mistake;" *Barr* v. *Hatch and others*, 3 Ohio, 527, 529. Equity will aid the defective execution of a power in favor of purchasers for a valuable consideration; *Schenck* v. *Ellingwood*, 3 Edwards, 175, 176 ; *Thorp et al.* v. *M'Cullum et al.*, 1 Gilman, 615, 629; *Beatty* v. *Clark*, 29 California, 11 ; *Love* v. *The Sierra Nevada Mining Co.*, 32 California, 653 ; in favor of a charity; *Pepper's Will*, 1 Parson's Eq. 436, 446 ; and in favor of creditors, and of a wife or a legitimate child; *Porter and others* v. *Turner and others*, 3 Sergeant & Rawle, 108, 111, 114 ; *Dennison* v. *Goehring*, 7 Barr, 175, 180; *Beatty* v. *Clark*, 20 California, 12 ; see also, *Bradish* v. *Gibbs*, 3 Johnson's Chancery, 523, 550; but not in favor of grand-children, where in default of appointment, the estate would go to grand-children ; *Porter and others* v. *Turner and others*.

But relief will not be given in equity, where the act which may have been done about the property cannot reasonably be referred to an intention to execute the power;

Ford et al. v. *Russell et al.*, 1 Freeman, 42, 51. Nor can that court give aid in the case of a defective power ; it cannot, therefore, give validity to a conveyance where an attorney conveying by a sealed instrument, has not been appointed under seal ; *The Heirs of Piatt and others* v. *The Heirs of M'Cullough*, 1 M'Lean, 69, 82. In *Roberts' Widow and Heirs* v. *Stanton*, 2 Munford, 129, 138, 139, where one trustee, only, had conveyed under a power which was required to be executed by all jointly, Tucker, J., was of opinion, that as there was a want of competency in the person acting, to execute the power, except in conjunction with others, it was not a case in which chancery would relieve on the ground of aiding a defective execution of a power; but Fleming, J., considered, that it was a case in which a power had been imperfectly executed, and that in favor of a valuable consideration, equity would supply the defect; and the latter view appears to be correct. See *Thorp et al.* v. *M'Cullum et al.*, 1 Gilman, 615, 629. Though equity will never supply a non-execution of a bare power; *Johnson* v. *Cushing*, 15 New Hampshire, 178 ; *Howard* v. *Carpenter*, 11 Maryland, 259, 282 ; *Wilkinson* v. *Getty*, 13 Iowa, 157 ; yet if a trust has been imposed in connection with the power, upon a person who was to execute it, equity will not allow the person intended to be benefited, to suffer from the negligence, mistake or ignorance of the trustee, or other circumstances ; *Withers* v. *Yeadon*,

1 Richardson's Equity, 325, 229; *Gibbs* v. *Marsh*, 2 Metcalf, 243, 251; *Thorp et al.* v. *M'Cullum et al.*, 1 Gilman, 615, 625, 630. Thus in *Norcum* v. *D'Deuch*, 17 Missouri, 98, a power given to a widow, who took a life estate under the will, to sell for the benefit of children, with the consent of the executor, was held to be a trust for the children, coupled with an interest in herself; and the court, consequently, upheld the title of a purchaser under the power, notwithstanding the refusal of the executor to concur in the sale.

The remedy, in cases of aiding an imperfect execution, is, in chancery, only, where it proceeds upon the ground of compelling parties, in respect of the consideration, to supply a defect in their acts: the transaction remains defective and inoperative in law; *Sinclair* v. *Jackson*, 8 Cowen, 544, 588.

[*245]   *ELLISON v. ELLISON.

FEBRUARY 24, 1802.

REPORTED 6 VES. 656.

VOLUNTARY TRUSTS.]—*Distinction as to volunteers. The assistance of the Court cannot be had without consideration, to constitute a party cestui que trust, as upon a voluntary covenant to transfer stock, &c.; but if the legal conveyance is actually made, constituting the relation of trustee and cestui que trust, as if the stock is actually transferred, &c., though without consideration, the equitable interest will be enforced.*

Settlement of leasehold estates not revoked by a subsequent assignment by the trustee to the settlor entitled for life, or by the will of the latter; no intention to revoke appearing; and the terms of a power of revocation not being complied with.

BY indenture, dated the 1st of July, 1791, reciting a lease, dated the 6th of June preceding, of collieries at Hebburn and Jarrowwood, in the county of Durham, for thirty-one years, to Charles Wren and others; and that the name of Wren was used in trust for Nathaniel Ellison and Wren, in equal shares; it was declared, that Wren, his executors and administrators, would stand possessed of the lease, in trust, as to one moiety, for Ellison, his executors, &c.

By another indenture, dated the 18th of June, 1796, reciting, that Ellison was interested in and entitled to one undivided eighth part of certain collieries at Hebburn and Jarrow, held by two separate leases for terms of thirty-one years, and that he was desirous of settling his interest, he assigned and transferred all his interest in the said collieries, and all the stock, &c., to Wren,

his executors, *administrators, and assigns, in trust for [*246]
Nathaniel Ellison and his assigns during his life; and,
after his decease, in trust to manage and carry on the same, in
like manner as Wren should carry on his own share; and upon
further trust, out of the profits, to pay to Margaret Clavering,
during the remainder of the term, in case she should so long live,
the yearly sum of 103l. 2s. 8d., which sum is thereby mentioned
to be secured to her by an indenture, dated the 14th of May last;
and, subject thereto, in trust to pay thereout to Jane Ellison, in
case she should survive Nathaniel Ellison, during the remainder
of the term, during the joint lives of Jane Ellison and Anne
Furye, the clear yearly sum of 180l.; and after the decease of
Anne Furye, then the yearly sum of 90l., during the remainder
of the term, in case Jane Ellison should so long live; and, subject
as aforesaid, upon trust to pay thereout, to each of the children
of Nathaniel Ellison that should be living at his decease, during
the remainder of the term, during the joint lives of Jane Ellison
and Anne Furye, and the life of the survivor, the yearly sum of
30l. apiece; and after the decease of the survivor the yearly sum
of 15l.; and upon further trust to pay the residue of the profits
arising from the collieries to the eldest son of Nathaniel Ellison,
who should attain the age of twenty-one; and upon the death of
Margaret Clavering, then upon trust to pay to each of the children of Nathaniel Ellison the further yearly sum of 10l.; with
survivorship, in case any of the children should die before twenty-
one, or marriage of daughters, provided none except the eldest
should be entitled to a greater annuity than 50l.; and upon
further trust to pay the residue to the eldest son; provided
further, in case all the children die before twenty-one, or the
marriage of daughters, upon trust to pay the whole to such only
child at twenty-one, or marriage of a daughter; provided further,
in case the profits to arise from the collieries should not be sufficient to pay all the annuities, the annuitants, except Margaret
Clavering, should abate, to be made up whenever the profits
should be sufficient; *and upon further trust, in case [*247]
Wren, his executors or administrators, should think it
more beneficial for the family to sell and dispose of the collieries,
upon trust to sell and dispose of the same for the most money
that could reasonably be got, and to apply the money, in the first
place, in payment of all debts due from the collieries, in respect of
the share of Ellison; and, subject thereto, to place out the residue
on real securities, and apply the interest, in the first place, in payment of the annuity of 103l. 2s. 8d. to Margaret Clavering; then
to the annuities of 180l., or 90l.; then to pay all the children of
Ellison, during the life of Margaret Clavering, the yearly sum of
22l. 10s., and to pay the residue of the dividends and interest to
the eldest son of Ellison, in manner aforesaid; and if the dividends, &c., should not be sufficient for the annuities, the two
annuitants, except Margaret Clavering, to abate; and, after her
death, to pay to each of the children of Nathaniel Ellison the

further yearly sum of 2*l.* 10*s.* for their lives ; and, after the decease of Margaret Clavering and Jane Ellison, upon trust to pay to each of the children of Nathaniel Ellison the sum of 500*l.*, in case the money arising from the sale should be sufficient ; then upon trust to divide the same equally among all the children, share and share alike ; and, subject as aforesaid, to pay over the residue to the eldest son on his attaining twenty-one ; and it was declared, that the portions of the children should be paid to the sons at twenty-one, to the daughters at twenty-one or marriage : and in case of the death of any before such period, to pay that share to the eldest son at twenty-one ; and if only one child should survive, to pay the whole to such one at twenty-one or marriage, if a daughter ; and in case all die before twenty-one, &c., then the said Charles Wren, his executors and administrators, shall stand possessed of the said collieries, and the money to arise by sale thereof, subject as aforesaid, in trust for Nathaniel Ellison, his executors, administrators, and assigns. It was further declared, that the annuities should be paid half-yearly ; and that, upon any [*248] such sale, the receipt of Wren, his *executors or administrators, should be a sufficient discharge to purchasers. Then followed this proviso :—" Provided always and it is hereby further declared, that it shall and may be lawful for the said Nathaniel Ellison, by any deed or deeds, writing or writings, to be by him signed, sealed, and delivered in the presence of and *attested by two or more credible witnesses*, to revoke, determine, and make void all and every the uses, trusts, limitations, and powers hereinbefore limited and created, of and concerning the said collieries and coal mines ; and by the same deed or deeds, or by any other deed to be by him executed in like manner, to limit any new or other uses of the said collieries and coal mines, as he, the said Nathaniel Ellison shall think fit."

By another indenture, dated the 3rd of July, 1797, *but not attested by two witnesses*, reciting the leases of the collieries, and that the name of Charles Wren was used in trust for Nathaniel Ellison and himself, in equal shares, and that Ellison had advanced an equal share of the monies supplied for carrying on the collieries, amounting to 9037*l.* 10*s.*, it was witnessed, that, in consideration of 4518*l.* 15*s.*, Wren assigned to Nathaniel Ellison one undivided moiety or half part of all the said collieries, demised to him by the said several leases, with a like share of the stock ; to have and to hold the said collieries to Ellison, his executors, administrators, and assigns, for the residue of the said terms, subject to the rents, covenants, and agreements in the said leases ; and to have and to hold the stock unto Ellison, his executors, administrators and assigns, to and for his and their own proper use for ever, with the usual covenants from Wren as to his title to assign, &c., and from Ellison to indemnify Wren, his executors, &c.

Nathaniel Ellison, by his will, dated the 22nd June, 1796, after several specific and pecuniary legacies, gave all the rest and residue of his personal estate and effects, of what nature or kind soever, not before disposed of, to his wife, and Wren, and the survivor, and the executors and administrators of such survivor, upon trust to call in *and place the same out in the funds, [*249] or on real securities ; and he directed that all sums of money which should come to the hands of his wife and Wren, or of the executors, &c., of either of them, under the said trusts, should be equally divided between all his children, sons and daughters, born and to be born, share and share alike ; the shares to become vested and be payable upon marriage, with consent of their guardians, and not otherwise, until the age of twenty-one ; such part of the interest in the meantime, as the guardians shall think proper, to be applied for maintenance ; the residue to accumulate ; with a direction for payment of part of the principal for advancement, and survivorship upon the death of any before the respective shares should be payable ; and, in case of the death of all under age and unmarried, he gave the dividends and interest to his wife for life ; and, upon her death, he gave the principal and a sum of 3000*l*., charged upon her estates, to his sister, Margaret Clavering, and his nephew. Then, after some further dispositions of stock in favour of his children, he gave a legacy of twenty guineas to Wren, and appointed his wife and Wren executors and guardians.

The testator died in 1798, leaving his widow and ten children surviving ; one of whom, Charles Ellison, died in 1799, an infant. Wren also died in that year.

The bill was filed by the testator's widow and Margaret Clavering, praying, that the trusts of the deed of June, 1796, may be established, and that new trustees may be appointed.

The younger children, by their answer, submitted whether the trusts of that deed were not varied or revoked by the deed of July, 1797.

Mr. *Romilly* and Mr. *Bell*, for the plaintiffs, insisted, that the subsequent deed, not reciting or taking any notice of the prior settlement, could not revoke it ; that it was not the object of the latter deed to revoke the former ; and that it was not attested by two witnesses, as, in order to effect a revocation, it ought to be.

*Mr. *Richards*, for the eldest son, defendant, claiming [*250] also under the deed of 1796, declined to argue the case.

Mr. *Steele* and Mr. *W. Agar*, for the other defendants, the younger children.—Though the expression in the clause of revocation is " deed or writing," a will with two witnesses would do, according to the case[1] from Ireland, cited in *Lord Darlington* v. *Pulteney*.[2] No intention, however, can be found in the will to revoke this settlement ; but the subsequent deed is an implied revocation. What use could there be in that deed but to give Ellison the absolute estate, which is quite inconsistent with the trusts of the former deed, which are very special, and give a large

---

[1] Roscommon v. Fowke, 6 Bro. P. C., Toml. ed., 158.   [2] Cowp. 268.

discretion ?   An instrument may be revoked by another, though
not taking notice of the former, but only making a disposition
inconsistent with it : *Lord Fauconberge* v. *Fitzgerald*,[1] *Arnold* v.
Arnold.[2]   And though the latter of these cases was upon a will,
there is no difference upon a voluntary settlement.   There is no
instance in which a voluntary deed, defective, and not effectual
at law, has been aided in this court ; and though this is, in some
respects, in favour of a wife and children, one of the parties claiming under it is a volunteer ; and it is opposed by nine out of ten
children.   This deed, like that in *Colman* v. *Sarrel*,[3] cannot be
proceeded upon at law.   But if the trust was originally well
created, yet if the subject gets back, and is vested in the author
of the trust, the objection lies.

Mr. *Romilly*, in reply.—Can it be stated as a question here,
whether a settlement for a wife and children can be enforced
against the representative of the father or the husband ?   *Colman*
v. *Sarrel* has not the most remote application ; the parties claiming under the deed being mere strangers, except by a connection
illegal and immoral.   It is not necessary to consider the case of
a mere volunteer.   Mrs. Clavering was a creditor by an annuity
secured by a prior deed.   Supposing Ellison had an intention to
revoke this settlement, he had prescribed to himself certain forms,
the attestation of two witnesses.   There is no instance of an im-
[*251] plied revocation of trusts, *which are only to be revoked
expressly, by a particular certain form.   But there is not
the least pretence upon these instruments, either the deed or the
will, of any such intention.   The will was executed only four
days after the settlement, which is not noticed in either instrument.   It is no more than consenting that the trustee, having
the legal interest, shall assign to another person, and taking it
himself.   Notwithstanding the length the Court have gone upon
wills,[4] this would not be a revocation even of a will, merely taking
the legal interest, having disposed of the equitable.   The intention that these trusts should not prevail would have been expressly declared.   As far as Wren was a trustee, the deed is
revoked ; but it was the act of Wren, Ellison being passive.

Lord Chancellor Eldon.—I had no doubt, that, from the
moment of executing the first deed, supposing it not to have
been for a wife and children, but for pure volunteers, those volunteers might have filed a bill in equity, on the ground of their
interest in that instrument, making the trustees and the author
of the deed parties.   *I take the distinction to be, that, if you want the
assistance of the Court to constitute you cestui que trust, and the instrument is voluntary, you shall not have that assistance for the purpose
of constituting you cestui que trust: as, upon a covenant to transfer
stock, &c., if it rests in covenant, and is purely voluntary, this Court*

---

[1] 6 Bro. P. C. 295, Toml. ed.   [2] 1 Bro. C. C. 401.
[3] 1 Ves. Jun. 50 ; S. C., 3 Bro. C. C. 12. .
[4] See Harmood v. Oglander, 6 Ves. 199, and note.

will not execute that voluntary covenant. But if the party has completely transferred stock, &c., though it is voluntary, yet the legal conveyance being effectually made, the equitable interest will be enforced by this Court. That distinction was clearly taken in *Colman* v. *Sarrel*,[1] independent of the vicious consideration. I stated the objection, that the deed was voluntary; and the Lord Chancellor[2] went with me so far as to consider it a good objection to executing what remained in covenant. But if the actual transfer is made, that constitutes the relation between trustee and cestui que trust, though voluntary, and without good or *meritorious*[3] consideration; and it is clear, in that case, that, if the stock had been *actually transferred, unless the transaction was [*252] affected by the turpitude of the consideration, the Court would have executed it against the trustee and the author of the trust.

In this case, therefore, the person claiming under the settlement might maintain a suit, notwithstanding any objection made to it as being voluntary, if that could apply to the case of a wife and children; considering, also, that Mrs. Clavering was an annuitant, and not a mere volunteer. But it was put for the defendant thus—that though the instrument would have been executed originally, if the subject got back by accident into the author of the trust, and was vested in him, then the objection would lie in the same manner as if the instrument was voluntary. I doubt that, for many reasons—the trust being once well created, and whether it would apply at all where the trust was originally well created, and did not rest merely in engagement to create it. Suppose Wren had died, and had made Ellison his executor, it would be extraordinary to hold, that though an execution would be decreed against him as executor, yet, happening to be also author of the trust, therefore an end was to be put to the interest of the cestui que trust. But it does not rest there; for Ellison clothes the legal estate remaining in Wren with the equitable interests declared by the first deed, making him, therefore, a trustee for Ellison himself first, and, after his death, for several other persons; and he has said, he puts that restraint upon his own power, not only that he shall not have a power of revocation whenever he changes his intention, but that he shall not execute that power, nor be supposed to have that change of intention, unless manifested by an instrument executed with certain given ceremonies. My opinion is, that if there is nothing more in this transaction than taking out of Wren the estate clothed with a trust for others with present interests, though future in enjoyment, and that was done by an instrument with no witness, or only one witness, it is hardly possible to contend that such an

---

[1] 1 Ves. jun. 50; S. C., 3 Bro. C. C. 12.   [2] Thurlow.

[3] That meritorious consideration merely will not entitle a volunteer to the aid of equity. See Jefferys v. Jefferys, 1 Cr. & Ph. 138; Dillon v. Coppin, 4 My. & Cr. 647, overruling Ellis v. Nimmo, L. & G. 333, t. Sugd.

[*253] instrument would be a revocation *according to the intention of the party, the evidence of whose intention is made subject to restrictions that are not complied with. The only difficulty is, that the declaration of the trusts in the first instrument could not be executed, the second instrument being allowed to have effect. It is said, a power was placed in Wren, his executors and administrators, not his assigns, if in sound discretion thought fit, to sell and to give a larger interest to the younger children than they otherwise would take. If Wren had not, after the re-assignment, that discretion still vested in him, I think it would not be in the executors of Ellison, and it could not be exercised by the Court, though, *in general cases, trusts will not fail by the failure of the trustee.* But, though the effect would be to destroy the power of Wren, which I strongly doubt, attending to the requisition of two witnesses, I do not know that it would destroy the other interests. I think, therefore, upon the whole, this trust does remain, notwithstanding this re-assignment of the legal estate to Ellison. I do not think, consistently with the intention expressed in the first instrument, and the necessity imposed upon himself of declaring a different intention under certain restrictions, that, if a different intention appeared clearly upon the face of the instrument, the latter would have controlled the former. But I do not think his acts do manifest a different intention. Supposing one witness sufficient, the second deed does not sufficiently manifest an intention to revoke all the benefits given by the first deed to the children; and it is not inconsistent that he might intend to revoke some, and not all.

As to the will, it is impossible to maintain that the will is a writing within the meaning of the power, considering how the subject is described. The word " residue " there means, that estate of which he had the power of disposing, not engaged by contracts, declarations of trusts, &c. It was necessary for him to describe the subject in such a way that there could be no doubt he meant to embrace that property. Upon the whole, therefore, [*254] this relief *must be granted ; *though I agree, that, if it rested in covenant, the personal representative might have put them to their legal remedies,* he cannot, where the character of trust attached upon the estate while in Wren ; which character of trust, therefore, should adhere to the estate in Ellison, unless a contrary intention was declared ; and the circumstance of one witness only, when the power reserved required two witnesses, is also a circumstance of evidence that he had not the intention of destroying those trusts which had attached, and were then vested in the person of Wren.

The ordering part of the decree, extracted from the Registrar's Book, is thus :[1] " Whereupon, and upon debate of the matter, and hearing the deed of trust dated the 18th June, 1796, read,

---

[1] Taken from the judgment of Lord Justice Knight Bruce, in Kekewich v. Manning, 1 De G. Mac. & G. 191.

and what was alleged by the counsel on both sides, his lordship
doth declare that the trust of the said deed, bearing date 18th
June, 1796, ought to be performed and carried into execution,
and doth order and decree the same accordingly. And it is
further ordered and decreed, that it be referred to Mr. Ord, one
of the Masters of this Court, to appoint a new trustee or trustees
of the premises comprised in the said trust deed, and that the
share of the said Nathaniel Ellison of and in the said collieries,
and the stock and effects belonging thereto comprised in the said
deed, be assigned to such new trustee or trustees so to be appointed, upon the trusts and upon and for the intents and purposes declared by the said deed concerning the same, and such
new trustee or trustees is or are to declare the trust thereof accordingly, and the said Master is to settle such assignment; and
it is ordered that the said Master do tax all parties their costs in
this suit, and that such costs, when taxed, be paid out of the
estate of the said testator, and any of the parties are to be at
liberty to apply to this Court as there shall be occasion."

In the leading case of *Ellison* v. *Ellison*, Lord Eldon lays down and
acts upon the well-known rule, that, where a trust is actually created,
*and the relation of trustee and cestui que trust established, a [*255]
Court of equity will, in favour of a volunteer, enforce the execution of the trust against the person creating the trust, and all subsequent volunteers; although it will not create a trust or establish the
relationship of trustee and cestui que trust, by enforcing the performance of an agreement, or by giving effect to an imperfect conveyance
or assignment in favour of volunteers. The application, however, of
this rule, is by no means free from difficulty, as it is frequently a question of much nicety to determine whether the relation of trustee and
cestui que trust has or not been established. It is intended, therefore,
in this note to examine the cases in which equity interposes or refuses
its aid in favour of volunteers.

Where there has been an actual bonâ fide transfer of the legal interest in real or personal property by the settlor or his trustees to trustees
upon trusts declared in favour of volunteers, these trusts, it is clear,
will be enforced in equity against the settlor or his representatives or
subsequent volunteers (*Colman* v. *Sarrel*, 3 Bro. C. C. 12, 14; *S. C.*
1 Ves. jun. 50; *Pulvertoft* v. *Pulvertoft*, 18 Ves. 84, 99; *Bill* v. *Cureton*, 2 My. & K. 503; *Jefferys* v. *Jefferys*, Cr. & Ph. 138, 141; *Den-
ning* v. *Ware*, 22 Beav. 184; *Muggeridge* v. *Stanton*, 7 W. R. (V. C.
K.) 638; *Dilrow* v. *Bone*, 3 Giff. 538); even although, as in the principal case, the trust property by accident gets back into the hands of the
donor (*Smith* v. *Lyne*, 2 Y. & C. C. C. 345; *Browne* v. *Cavendish*, 1
J. & L. 637; *Newton* v. *Askew*, 11 Beav. 145; and see *Page* v. *Horne*,
11 Beav. 227; *Lanham* v. *Pirie*, 2 Jur. N. S. 753, 3 Jur. N. S. 704;

Gilbert v. *Overton*, 2 Hem. & Mill. 117); to whom, if it were transferred by the trustees, they would commit a breach of trust: *M'Donnell* v. *Hesilrige*, 16 Beav. 346.

Where, although there has been an intended transfer to trustees, the trusts have not been finally determined upon by the settlor, he has a locus pœnitentiæ, and may call for a re-transfer: *Re Sykes' Trusts*, 2 J. & H. 415.

Where, however, a legal transfer of property has been made to trustees, for payment *of the debts* of the owner without the knowledge or concurrence of his creditors, such a transaction, it has been repeatedly held, does not invest creditors with the character of cestuis que trust, but amounts merely to a direction to the trustees as to the method in which they are to apply the property vested in them for the benefit of the *owner* of the property, who alone stands towards them in the relation of cestui que trust, and can vary or revoke the trusts at pleasure. Courts of equity, therefore, will not, at the instance of the creditors, who are looked upon as mere strangers, compel the trustees to execute the trusts for *payment of debts. Thus, in *Walwyn* v. *Coutts*, 3 Mer. 707, S. C., 3 Sim. 14, where estates were conveyed to trustees upon trust for the payment of the debts of certain scheduled creditors, who were *neither parties nor privies to the deed*, Lord Eldon held, that the trust was voluntary, and that it could not be enforced against the owners of the estates, who might vary it as they pleased. So, also, in *Garrard* v. *Lord Lauderdale*, 3 Sim. 1, where an assignment of personal property was made to trustees for payment of certain scheduled creditors *who were parties to, but who neither executed nor were privy to the execution of the deed*, Sir L. Shadwell, V. C., *although the execution of the deed had been communicated to the creditors*, upon the authority of *Walwyn* v. *Coutts*, held, that they had no right to enforce the trusts of the deed, and he considered that the principle of the two decisions of *Ellison* v. *Ellison* and *Walwyn* v. *Coutts* were reconcilable with each other; "because," said his Honor, "I apprehend that Lord Eldon must have considered that where a person does, without the privity of any one, without receiving consideration, and without notice to any creditor, himself make a disposition, as between himself and trustees, for the payment of his debts, he is merely directing the mode in which his own property shall be applied for his own benefit, and that the general creditors, or the creditors named in the schedule, are merely persons named there for the purpose of showing how the trust property under the voluntary deed shall be applied for the benefit of the volunteers." This case was, on appeal, affirmed by Lord Brougham: 2 Russ. & My. 451. So, likewise, Sir J. Leach, M. R., in *Acton* v. *Woodgate*, 2 My. & K. 495, held, that a conveyance to trustees for the benefit of creditors, who were neither parties nor privies to it, was revoked by a second conveyance,

[*256]

executed by several creditors, not privy to the first. In *Page* v. *Broom*, 4 Russ. 6, a debtor had by deed poll directed the receiver of his estate to pay the interest of a particular debt: it was held by Sir J. Leach, M. R., that, as the deed was executed without consideration, and without the privity of the creditor, no trust was created in his favour. This case was affirmed on appeal by Lord Brougham. See 2 Russ. & My. 214. In *Bill* v. *Cureton*, 2 My. & K. 511, Lord Cottenham, then Master of the Rolls, with reference to the cases of *Walwyn* v. *Coutts* and *Garrard* v. *Lord Lauderdale*, observes, " that these two cases, so far from deciding that a cestui que trust becoming entitled under a voluntary settlement had not a good title against the settlor, proceeded upon this, that the character of trustee and cestui que trust never existed between the creditor and the trustees of the trust deeds, but *that the settlor himself was the only cestui que trust, and therefore that he was entitled to direct the application of his own trust fund." In *Gibbs* v. *Glamis*, 11 Sim. 584, a [*257] suit was instituted by A. against B. and C. respecting a sum of £4000. D. was also made a party to the suit; but having no interest, he disclaimed. A., B., and C. afterwards came to a compromise; in pursuance of which they executed a deed, assigning the £4000 to trustees in trust to pay D. his costs of the suit, and to divide the rest of the fund amongst A., B., and C. D., though he was not a party either to the compromise or to the deed, filed a bill against A., B., and C., and the trustees, to compel a performance of the trusts and payment of his costs. Lord Cottenham, reversing the decision of Sir L. Shadwell, V. C., allowed the demurrer of C. for want of equity, observing, " that the question was, whether the provision for payment of costs gave the party whose costs were so provided for a right to institute a suit as cestui que trust, he having no interest in the fund, not having been a party to the arrangement, and the arrangement having been made between the parties interested in the fund, for their own benefit or convenience; that the present case was not distinguishable from *Garrard* v. *Lord Lauderdale*, and the other cases which had been cited, in each of which the plaintiff was as much a cestui que trust as the plaintiff in that case was. See also *Ravenshaw* v. *Hollier*, 7 Sim. 3; *Wilding* v. *Richards*, 1 Coll. 655; *Law* v. *Bagwell*, 4 D. & W. 398; *Browne* v. *Cavendish*, 1 J. & L. 635; *Simmons* v. *Palles*, 2 J. & L. 489; and the observations of Sir Edward Sugden in the last case on *Gibbs* v. *Glamis; Smith* v. *Hurst*, 10 Hare, 30; *Steele* v. *Murphy*, 3 Moore, P. C. C. 445; *Smith* v. *Keating*, 6 C. B. 136, 158; *Thayer* v. *Lister*, 9 W. R. (V. C. W.) 360; *Henriques* v. *Bensusan*, 20 W. R. (V. C. M.) 350.

It is clear also, that, in other cases in which creditors are not concerned, a person not intending to give or part with the dominion over his property, may retain such dominion, notwithstanding he may have vested the property in trustees, and declared a trust upon it in favour of third persons. Thus, in *Hughes* v. *Stubbs*, 1 Hare, 476, a testatrix drew a cheque on her bankers for £150 in favour of A., and she verbally directed A. to apply that sum, or so much of it as might be necessary, to make up to a legatee the difference in value between a legacy of £100, which the testatrix, by her will, had given to the legatee, and the price of a £100 share in a certain railway : the testatrix informing A. that she intended to give the share instead of the legacy, but she did not think it necessary to alter her will. The bankers gave credit to A. for [*258] the £150. The testatrix afterwards *died. In a suit for the administration of her estate, Sir J. Wigram, V. C., held, that no trust was created for the benefit of the legatee in respect of the £150. " The cases," observed his Honor, " on this subject are necessarily of difficulty ; but the conclusion to which I feel bound to come is, that the testatrix did not part with her property in the sum in question, or create any trust for the legatee." See also *Gaskell* v. *Gaskell*, 2 Y. & J. 502; *Paterson* v. *Murphy*, 11 Hare, 88; and the remarks of Wood, V. C., in *Vandenberg* v. *Palmer*, 4 K. & J. 214, 218; *Pedder* v. *Mosely*, 31 Beav. 159.

Where however a trust in favour of creditors has been acted upon (*Cosser* v. *Radford*, 1 De G. Jo. & Sm. 585), or has been communicated to the creditors, it can no longer be revoked by the settlor. This was laid down in *Acton* v. *Woodgate*, 2 My. & K. 495, by Sir John Leach, M. R., who said, that, in the case of *Garrard* v. *Lord Lauderdale*, it seemed to have been considered that a communication by the trustees to creditors of the fact of such a trust would not defeat the power of revocation by the debtor, but that it appeared to him that such a doctrine was questionable, because the creditors, being aware of such a trust, might be thereby induced to a forbearance in respect of their claims, which they would not otherwise have exercised. Other judges have taken the same view as Sir J. Leach, as to the effect of the communication of the deed to the creditors, (see *Browne* v. *Cavendish*, 1 J. & L. 635; *Simmonds* v. *Palles*, 2 J. & L. 504; *Kirwan* v. *Daniel*, 5 Hare, 499; *Harland* v. *Binks*, 15 Q. B. 713,) which it would seem must be clearly proved (*Cornthwaite* v. *Frith*, 4 De G. & Sm. 552), but where an assignment is made to a creditor in trust for himself and other creditors, it cannot be revoked by the assignor after it has been communicated to the assignee, unless he has done something to show his dissent: *Siggers* v. *Evans*, 5 Ell. & B. 367, 380, 381; *Lawrence* v. *Campbell*, 7 W. R. (V. C. K.) 170; *Hobson* v. *Thelluson*, 2 L. R. Q. B. 642. And it seems to be doubtful whether, after the trust has been communicated to some of the creditors, it can after satisfying them be revoked by the settlor as to the other creditors. See *Griffith* v. *Ricketts*, 7 Hare, 307.

The execution, however, of a trust deed for (amongst other things) the payment of creditors does not constitute one of the creditors, who becomes so after the execution of the deed, and was not a party to it, a cestui que trust, entitled to call on the trustee to execute the trusts of the deed: *La Touche* v. *Earl of Lucan*, 7 C. & F. 772.

Where a creditor is party to a deed whereby his debtor conveys property to a trustee to be *applied in liquidation of the debt due to that creditor, the deed is, as to that creditor, irrevocable. [*259]
A valid trust is created in his favour, and the relation between the debtor and trustee is no longer that of mere principal and agent (per Lord Cranworth, V. C., in *Mackinnon* v. *Stewart*, 1 Sim. N. S. 88, and see *Glegg* v. *Rees*, 7 L. R. Ch. App. 71). And that which is true where a single creditor is the cestui que trust, is at least equally so where there are many creditors. Nor does the creditor executing the deed become less a cestui que trust, because he gives nothing to the debtor, as a consideration for the trust created in his favour, or because it was the voluntary, unsolicited act of the debtor to create the trust: (per Lord Cranworth, V. C., in *Mackinnon* v. *Stewart*, 1 Sim. N. S. 88; see, also, *Field* v. *Lord Donoughmore*, 2 Dru. & Walsh. 630, 1 Dru. & War. 227; *Gurney* v. *Lord Oranmore*, 4 Ir. Ch. Rep. 470; 5 Ir. Ch. Rep. 436; or because he was party to the deed in another right. *Montefiore* v. *Browne*, 7 Ho. Lo. Ca. 241, 266).

And though there is a time limited in the deed within which creditors must execute it, if by accident any of them fail to do so, they will not necessarily, in equity at any rate, should they act under the deed (*Spottiswoode* v. *Stockdale*, Sir G. Coop. Rep. 102; *Raworth* v. *Parker*, 2 K. & J. 163), or upon the faith of it (*Nicholson* v. *Tutin*, 2 K. & J. 18), or acquiesce in it (*In re Baber's Trusts*, 10 L. R. Eq. 554), be excluded from the benefit of the trusts (*Dunch* v. *Kent*, 1 Vern. 260; *Field* v. *Lord Donoughmore*, 1 Dru. & War. 227; and see *Lane* v. *Husband*, 14 Sim. 661; *Whitmore* v. *Turquand*, 1 J. & H. 444; 3 De G. F. & Jo. 107; *Biron* v. *Mount*, 24 Beav. 642), though they might not be allowed to disturb any dividend already made amongst the creditors (*Broadbent* v. *Thornton*, 4 De Gex & Sm. 65; *Field* v. *Cook*, 23 Beav. 600); but the Court, before it permits a creditor, who has not executed to take a benefit under a deed, is bound to see that he has performed all the fair conditions of such deed, and if he has taken any step inconsistent with its provisions, he will be deprived of all advantage therefrom (*Field* v. *Lord Donoughmore*, 1 Dru. & War. 227; *Drever* v. *Mawdesley*, 16 Sim. 511; *Forbes* v. *Limond*, 4 De G. M. & G. 298).

A creditor who for a long time delays (*Gould* v. *Robertson*, 4 De G. & Sm. 509), or if he refuses, to execute such deed within the time limited, and does not retract his refusal within such time (*Johnson* v. *Kershaw*, 1 De G. & Sm. 260), and a fortiori if he has set up a title adverse to the deed (*Watson* v. *Knight*, 19 Beav. 369; *Brandling* v. *Plummer*, 6 W. R. (V. C. K.) 117), will not be allowed to claim the benefit of its provisions.

The principle according to which property vested in trustees [*260] *for the purpose of distribution among creditors, is revocable on the ground of its being a mere arrangement for the benefit of the settlor and which he can therefore at any time revoke, will not, it seems, be applied as between the settlor and persons who are purely the objects of his bounty, the former having appointed an agent to administer the bounty, and declared for whom it was intended. (*Paterson* v. *Murphy*, 11 Hare, 88) ; nor to a case where the trust is to come into operation only on the death of its author, and where, subject to the trust for payment of debts, the lands charged are conveyed by way of bounty to a third person, inasmuch as in such a case the settlor must *prima facie* be understood to be dealing with his property as if he were disposing of it by will, and therefore as contemplating bounty throughout. *Synnot* v. *Simpson*, 5 H. L. Cas. 121, 139, 141. But see *Montefiore* v. *Browne*, 7 Ho. Lo. Ca. 241, 266 ; *Burrowes* v. *Gore*, 6 Ho. Lo. Ca. 907.

Where a debtor assigns property for the benefit of his creditors, although no creditor may be aware of the assignment, the assignee may, nevertheless, take proceedings in equity to recover the property (*Glegg* v. *Rees*, 7 L. R. Ch. App. 70).

Trust deeds for the benefit of creditors, in default of registration, either under the 192nd or 194th sections of the Bankruptcy Act, 1861 (24 & 25 Vict. c. 134, repealed by 32 & 33 Vict. c. 83, except as to its past operation), cannot be received in evidence.

In order to pass property in chattels verbally by way of gift, it has been laid down in some cases that there must also be a delivery from the donor to the donee. Hence, where there were words of gift, but the chattels remained in the possession of the donor (*Irons* v. *Smallpiece*, 2 B. & Ald. 551), or even when they were in the possession of the donee at the time of the gift, so that no delivery was made (*Shower* v. *Pilck*, 4 Exch. 478), it was held that no property passed therein to the donee. In other cases it has been held, that a donatio inter vivos as distinguished from a donatio mortis causa does not require actual delivery, and it is sufficient to complete a gift inter vivos that the conduct of the parties should show that the ownership in the chattels has been changed. *Flory* v. *Denny*, 7 Exch. 583 ; *Ward* v. *Audland*, 16 M. & W. 862 ; *Winter* v. *Winter*, 9 W. R. (Q. B.) 747.

In *Farington* v. *Parker*, 4 L. R. Eq. 116, under a settlement certain jewels were assigned upon trust for such person as Mrs. Glegg should by writing direct or appoint, and in default of such appointment, upon trust for her during her life for her separate use, and to be at her absolute disposal, *and her receipt, or that of the person to whom [*261] she should direct the jewels to be delivered, to be a good discharge. Mrs. Glegg, without any direction in writing, delivered the jewels as an absolute gift to her daughter, Lady St. Vincent, who retained them in her possession. It was held by Lord Romilly, M. R., that under the gift and manual delivery Lady St. Vincent was absolutely entitled to the jewels.

The delivery by the donor to the donee of securities transferable by delivery, will, with words of gift, constitute a valid donation (*M'Culloch* v. *Bland*, 2 Giff. 428).

In *Bromley* v. *Brunton*, 6 L. R. Eq. 275, a cheque was given by **A.** to B., and presented without delay. The bankers had sufficient assets of A., but refused payment, because they doubted the signature. The next day A. died, the cheque not having been paid. It was held by Sir John Stuart, V. C., to be a complete gift *inter vivos* of the amount of the cheque, and ordered its payment, with interest, by the executors of the donor.

[It was said in *Rhodes* v. *Childs*, 14 P. F. Smith, 18, 24, on the authority of *Gourley* v. *Linselbigler*, 1 P. F. Smith, 345, that bills or checks drawn by the deceased on his banker, will pass by delivery and become an executed gift. The point was not before the court in these instances. The weight of authority in the United States is the othey way ; *Cowperthwaite* v. *Shuffield*, 3 Comstock, 243; *Harris* v. *Clark*, Ib. 93 ; *Winters* v. *Drury*, 1 Selden, 325 ; *Chapman* v. *Whity*, 3 Id. 412. But a check drawn by a third person may clearly be the subject of a gift *inter vivos* or *causa mortis ; Rhodes* v. *Childs, post,* notes to *Ward* v. *Turner*.]

In order to establish the fact of a gift of chattels from a husband to his wife, there must be clear and distinct evidence corroborative of the wife's testimony. It is not necessary that he should deliver them to a trustee for his wife. It is sufficient if he constitutes himself a trustee for her by making the gift in the presence of a witness, or by subsequent statements to a witness that he has made the gift ; but a mere declaration of intention to give is not sufficient (*Grant* v. *Grant*, 34 Beav. 623).

And it seems that presents made by a husband to his wife, whether in contemplation of, or subsequent to, their marriage, are the separate property of the wife, and do not form part of the husband's personal estate (Ib.).

Although there has been no actual transfer of the legal interest in property to trustees, if the settlor has constituted himself a trustee for volunteers, a Court of equity will enforce the trusts. This is well illustrated in *Ex parte Pye, Ex parte Dubost*, 18 Ves. 140, 145. In that case M. had, by letter, directed an agent in Paris to purchase an annuity for a lady, which was accordingly purchased, but in the name of M., the lady being at that time married, and also deranged. M. afterwards sent to his agent a power of attorney authorizing him to transfer the annuity into the lady's name, but died before the transfer was made. Lord Eldon held, that, although the legal interest remained in M., he had constituted himself a trustee for the lady. "The question," says his Lordship, "involves the point, whether the power of attorney amounts here to a declaration of trust? It is clear that this Court will not assist a volunteer; yet, if the act is completed, though voluntary, the Court will act upon *it. It has been decided, that, upon an [*262] agreement to transfer stock, this Court will not interpose; but, if the party had declared himself to be the trustee of that stock, it becomes the property of the cestui que trust without more, and the Court will act upon it. Upon the *documents* befor me, it does appear, that, though in one sense this may be represented as the testator's personal estate, yet he has committed to writing what *seems to me a sufficient declaration that he held this part of the estate in trust for the* annuitant." And see and consider *Airey* v. *Hall*, 2 Sm. & G. 315; *Parnell* v. *Hingston*, 3 Sm. & G. 337; and *Kiddell* v. *Farnell*, 3 Sm. & G. 428, appealed and compromised, 5 W. R. (L. J.) 793. In *Wheatley* v. *Purr*, 1 Kee. 551, H. O. directed her bankers to place £2,000 in the joint names of her children, J. R. W., M. W., and H. W., and her own as trustee for her children. That sum was accordingly entered in the books of the bankers to the account of H. O. as trustee for J. R. W., M. W., and H. W. The bankers gave H. O. as trustee for J. R. W., M. W., and H. W., a promissory note for the amount, with interest at $2\frac{1}{2}$ per cent., and she gave the bankers a receipt for the promissory note. Lord Langdale, M. R., was of opinion that she had constituted herself a trustee for the plaintiffs, her children, and that a trust was completely declared, so as to give them a title to relief. See, also, *Vandenberg* v. *Palmer*, 4 K. & J. 204; *Evans* v. *Jennings*, 6 W. R. (V. C. S.) 616.

A trust relating to lands must, under the 7th section of the Statute of Frauds, be manifested and proved by some writing (*Foster* v. *Hall*, 3 Ves. 696; *Smith* v. *Matthews*, 9 W. R. (L. J.) 644). But a declaration by parol of the trusts of personal property will be sufficient to create a trust. Thus in *M'Fadden* v. *Jenkyns*, 1 Ph. 153, A. had sent a verbal direction to B., who owed him £500, to hold the debt in trust for C., a volunteer; B. assented to and acted upon the direction, by paying C. £10, as part of the trust money. Lord Lyndhurst, affirming the decision of Sir J. Wigram, V. C., reported 1 Hare, 458, held, that a *declaration by parol was sufficient* to create a trust of personal property, and that, as the debtor had assented to and acted upon the direction, a complete and irrevocable trust was impressed upon the money. And see *Peckham* v. *Taylor*, 31 Beav. 250.

Where, however, there is a declaration of trust by parol, if the case be one of doubt or difficulty upon the words which have been supposed to have been used, the Court will give weight to the consideration that the words, not being committed to writing in any definite and unquestionable form, may not be the deliberately expressed sentiments of the

party : *Dipple* v. *Corles*, 11 Hare, 183 ; *and see *Paterson* v. [*263]
Murphy, Ib. 91, 92.

In the following cases it will be seen what will be considered to amount to a declaration of trust, and it may be observed, notwithstanding the remarks of Lord Justice Turner in *Milroy* v. *Lord*, 31 L. J. Ch. 798, 803, that there is an inclination on the part of the Court to hold that to amount to a declaration of trust, which according to a strict construction would amount only to an imperfect assignment : *Framp‑ton* v. *Frampton*, 4 Beav. 287 ; *James* v. *Bydder*, 4 Beav. 605 ; *Thorpe* v. *Owen*, 5 Beav. 224 ; *Stapleton* v. *Stapleton*, 14 Sim. 186 ; *Wilcocks* v. *Hanyngton*, 5 Ir. Ch. Rep. 38 ; *Donaldson* v. *Donaldson*, Kay, 711, 717 ; *Woodroffe* v. *Johnston*, 4 Ir. Ch. Rep. 319 ; *Gray* v. *Gray*, 2 Sim. N. S. 273 ; *Ouseley* v. *Anstruther*, 10 Beav. 461 ; *Moore* v. *Darton*, 4 De G. & Sm. 517 ; *Paterson* v. *Murphy*, 11 Hare, 88 ; *Lloyd* v. *Chune*, 2 Giff. 441 ; *Steele* v. *Waller*, 28 Beav. 466 ; *Maguire* v. *Modd*, 9 Ir. Ch. Rep. 452 ; *Arthur* v. *Clarkson*, 35 Beav. 458 ; *Gee* v. *Liddell*, Ib. 621 ; *Richardson* v. *Richardson*, 3 L. R. Eq. 686 ; *Morgan* v. *Dalleson*, 10 L. R. Eq. 475 ; *Miller* v. *Harrison*, 5 I. R. Eq. 324 ; and see the remarks of Sir John Romilly, M. R., in *Price* v. *Price*, 14 Beav. 602.

The dictum attributed to Lord Cranworth, C., in *Scales* v. *Maude*, 6 De Gex, Mac. & C. 51, to the effect that a mere declaration of trust by the owner of property in favour of a volunteer is inoperative, and that the Court of Chancery will not interfere in such a case, seems to be un‑supported by the authorities, and is said by his Lordship in *Jones* v. *Lock*, 1 Law Rep. Ch. Ap. 28, to be "clearly wrong as a general state‑ment of the law."

The consent of a married woman, given before commissioners, for the transfer and payment to her husband of sums of stock and cash stand‑ing in Court to her separate account, has been held not to amount to a declaration of trust, and that it was competent to her, at any time before the transfer had been completed, to retract her consent : *Penfold* v. *Mould*, 4 L. R. Eq. 562.

A mere expression of an intention to divide property with, or to leave it to, others will not, it seems, be held to amount to a declaration of trust, and, like a mere promise to give, will not be enforced in equity ; *Dipple* v. *Corles*, 11 Hare, 183 ; *Re Glover*, 2 J. & H. 186 ; and see *In re Mills's Estate*, 7 W. R. (V. C. K.) 372 ; *Forbes* v. *Forbes*, 6 W. R. (V. C. W.) 92.

A declaration of trust by the equitable owner of a chose in action vested in trustees will be supported. Thus, in *Collinson* v. *Patrick*, 2 Kee. 123, a bond, and all sums of money recoverable in respect thereof, had been assigned to trustees, in trust for such intents *and [*264] purposes, and such person or persons, as E. P., a married woman, should direct or appoint ; and, in default of appointment, for her separate use. E. P. afterwards appointed her interest in the bond to certain persons, in order to indemnify them, in case they should not be able to recover the whole of a sum appropriated by her husband, who was their solicitor, and for no other consideration appearing upon the deed. It was objected, that the deed being voluntary, and something requiring to be done by the party creating the trust, it was a trust which could not be executed by the Court. However, Lord Langdale, M. R., held, that a binding trust had been created. " It seems to me," said his Lordship, " that, so far as depended upon the party executing this deed, everything has been done to constitute an executed trust. It is certainly a matter well worthy of consideration how far the peculiar situation of a married woman, entering into such an engagement as the present, by which she binds her separate estate, is not entitled, in a court of equity, to the same species of protection which the law gives to persons entering into a legal obligation, and whether a contract of indemnity so entered into should not, in this court, be supported by a valuable consideration. A declaration of trust is considered, in a court of equity, as equivalent to a transfer of the legal interest in a court of law ; and, if the transaction by which the trust is created is complete, it will not be disturbed for want of consideration. If this had been a transaction resting on an agreement not conferring the legal interest— if it had been an executory contract, this court, in the absence of consideration, would not have given effect to it ; but, *if what has been done is equivalent to a transfer of the legal interest*, the parties in whose favour the trust is created are entitled to have the benefit of it in this court; and I am of opinion that this deed gives an interest to the plaintiffs which does so entitle them : " see also *Tierney* v. *Wood*, 19 Beav. 330.

Upon the same principle, if the equitable owner of property vested in trustees, as in *Ellison* v. *Ellison*, assigns it to them, or directs them to apply it upon trusts declared in favour of volunteers, and the trustees accept and act upon the trusts, they will be enforced in equity. In *Rycroft* v. *Christie*, 3 Beav. 238, Mrs. Rycroft, the cestui que trust of money in the hands of a trustee, by deed without consideration, directed part of the dividends to be paid by him for the maintenance of an infant, a stranger to Mrs. Rycroft, and covenanted to indemnify the trustee, and agreed to allow the same out of the dividends of the trust fund. The trustee accepted the new trust and acted upon the deed. Lord Langdale *M. R., held, that, as there was no further instrument or formality to be executed, from the moment when the direction was signed and accepted by the trustee a valid and executed trust was created, which Mrs. Rycroft could not revoke. So in *Meek* v. *Kettlewell*, 1 Hare, 471, Sir James Wigram, V. C., observes, that, if the equitable owner of the property, the legal interest of which is in a trustee, should execute a voluntary assignment of the property, and authorise the assignee to sue for and recover the property from that

[*265]

trustee, and the assignee should give notice thereof to the trustee, and the trustee should accept the notice and act upon it, by paying the dividends or interest of the trust property to the assignee during the life of the assignor, and with his consent, it might be difficult for the executor or administrator of the assignor afterwards to contend that the gift of the property was not perfect in equity. See also *Bentley* v. *Mackay*, 15 Beav. 12; *Bridge* v. *Bridge*, 16 Beav. 322; *Donaldson* v. *Donaldson*, Kay, 711; *Gilbert* v. *Overton*, 2 Hem. & Mill. 110.

It does not, however, seem now to be considered essential to the validity of the creation of a trust by the beneficial owner of property, that there should be an acceptance or declaration of the trusts by the trustees in whom the legal interest is vested. Thus, in *Tierney* v. *Wood*, 19 Beav. 330, where land and stock were vested in the plaintiff, Tierney, in trust for Wood, the latter signed a document addressed to Tierney, directing that the land and stock should after his death be held for the benefit of certain persons. The document was not attested. It was held by Sir J. Romilly, M. R., that an effectual trust within the meaning of the Statute of Frauds had been declared by the beneficial owner, and that the document was not testamentary. " The authorities," said his Honor, " show that the proper person to create the trust in personal property, is the person in whom the beneficial interest of the property is vested; and the trust being created by the beneficial owner, the trustee is bound, and if disposed to refuse may be compelled to obey it. I am at a loss to find any reason which should cause this document to be effectual as a declaration of trust, so far as the stock is concerned, and not so, so far as the land is concerned. It is obvious, that in both cases the person enabled by law to declare the trusts is the same. In the case before me, there can be no doubt that if Mr. Tierney had, in pursuance of this paper, signed a document to the same effect, stating that he held the property on the trusts therein mentioned, the trusts would, apart from any question on the construction of the document, have been fully and completely declared; and it is also clear, that if the trustee had declared that he *held the property on [*266] any trusts not recognised or sanctioned by Wood, the beneficial owner, such declaration of trust would have been insufficient and unavailing, and would have given no interest to the supposed cestui que trust. A declaration of trust in writing, by Tierney, following that of Wood, would therefore have been merely formal, and would have been valid only so far as it followed his instructions, and would have been void to the extent, if any, that it departed from his directions. I think that the fair conclusion to be drawn from these considerations is, that the person to create the trust, and the person who is by law enabled to declare the trust) are one and the same, and that, consequently, the beneficial owner is the person, by law, enabled to declare the trust."

Nor is notice of the declaration of trust to the cestui que trust necessary: *Tate* v. *Leithead*, Kay, 658. And as between volunteers, notice to the debtor of an assignment of a debt, will not affect priorities: *Justice* v. *Wynne*, 12 I. Ch. R. 289.

If a testator *by will* gives personal property upon trusts to be afterwards declared, he cannot, either by any instrument not duly executed as a will or codicil, or by parol, make any valid declaration of trust; and the property will go either to the next of kin or the residuary legatees: *Johnson* v. *Ball*, 5 De. G. & Sm. 85.

We must, however, carefully distinguish that class of cases in which the settlor constitutes himself a trustee for volunteers, from another class of cases in which a person has ineffectually attempted, by an imperfect gift, to confer the whole interest upon volunteers or trustees for their benefit; for it has been repeatedly determined, that the most clear intention to confer an interest will not be sufficient to create a trust in favor of a volunteer. The leading case on this point is *Antrobus* v. *Smith*, 12 Ves. 39. There Gibbs Crawford made the following indorsement upon a receipt for one of the subscriptions in the Forth and Clyde navigation: " I do hereby assign to my daughter, Anna Crawford, all my right, title, and interest of and in the inclosed call, and all other calls, of my subscription in the Clyde and Forth Navigation." This not being a legal assignment, Sir S. Romilly argued, " that the father meant to make himself a trustee for his daughter of these shares." But Sir W. Grant, M. R., observed, " Mr. Crawford was not otherwise a trustee than as any man may be called so who professes to give property by an instrument incapable of conveying it. He was not in form declared a trustee; nor was that mode of doing what he proposed in his contemplation. He meant a gift. He says, he assigns the property. But it was a gift not complete. The property was not transferred by the *act. Could he himself have been compelled to give effect to the gift by making an assignment ? There is no case, in which a party has been compelled to perfect a gift, which, in the mode of making it, he has left imperfect. There is locus pœnitentiæ as long as it is incomplete." So, in *Edward* v. *Jones*, 1 My. & Cr. 226, where the obligee of a bond signed a memorandum, not under seal, which was endorsed upon the bond, and which purported to be an assignment of the bond, without consideration, to the person to whom the bond was at the same time delivered, Lord Cottenham, upon the authority of the doctrine laid down in *Antrobus* v. *Smith*, which he said it was impossible to question, held, that the gift was incomplete, and that, as it was without consideration, the Court could not give effect to it. So, also, in *Dillon* v. *Coppin*, 4 My. & Cr. 647, a voluntary assignment of East India Stock and shares in the Globe Insurance Company, by a deed poll, incapable of passing such property, was held, by Lord Cottenham, not to affect the settlor's interest in the East

[*267]

India Stock and the Globe shares. In *Searle* v. *Law*, 15 Sim. 95, A. made a voluntary assignment of turnpike road bonds and shares in an insurance and in a banking company to B., in trust for himself for life, and after his death for his nephew. He delivered the bonds and shares to B., but did not observe the formalities required by the Turnpike Act, and the deeds by which the companies were formed, to make the assignment effectual. Sir L. Shadwell, V. C., held, that on A.'s death no interest in either the bonds or the shares passed by the assignment, and that B. ought to deliver them to the executor of A. " If that gentleman," observed his Honor, " had not attempted to make an assignment of either the bonds or the shares, but had simply declared, in writing, that he would hold them upon the same trusts as are expressed in the deed, that declaration would have been binding upon him ; and whatever bound him, would have bound his personal representative. But it is evident that he had no intention whatever of being himself a trustee for any one, and that he meant all the persons named in the deed as cestuis que trust to take the provisions intended for them through the operation of that deed. He omitted, however, to take the proper steps to make that deed an effectual assignment ; and, therefore, both the legal and the beneficial interest in the bonds and shares vested in him at his death." In *Woodford* v. *Charnley*, 28 Beav. 96, Alice Fisher was mortgagee in fee of land conveyed to her to secure 5000*l.* and interest, but the mortgage deed contained no covenant for payment of the 5000*l.* The mortgagor died intestate. Alice Fisher afterwards *executed a voluntary settlement by which she assigned the [*268] sum of 5000*l.* to trustees, and gave them a power of attorney to recover it. *The legal estate was never conveyed by Alice Fisher to the trustees.* It was held by Sir John Romilly, M. R., that the voluntary settlement was incomplete and could not be enforced against the settlor or any person claiming under her. See also *Coningham* v. *Plunkett*, 2 Y. & C. C. C. 245 ; *Price* v. *Price*, 14 Beav. 598 ; *Scales* v. *Maude*, 6 De Gex, Mac. & G. 43 ; *Weale* v. *Olive*, 17 Beav. 252 ; *Peckham* v. *Taylor*, 31 Beav. 250 ; *Lambert* v. *Overton*, 13 W. R. (V. C. S.) 227.

However, assignments both of equitable and legal choses in action, although nothing passes thereby at law, have been held binding in favour of volunteers, where the assignor has done all in his power to make the assignment complete. Thus, in *Sloane* v. *Cadogan*, Sugd. V. and P., App. No. xxiv., 11th ed., Mr. W. Cadogan, having an equitable reversionary interest in a fund vested in trustees, assigned it to other trustees upon trust for volunteers. It was contended by Sir Edward Sugden, in his argument, that, in order to constitute an actual settlement, so as to enable a volunteer to claim the benefit of it, it is absolutely necessary that the relation of trustee and cestui que trust should be established ; that Mr. W. Cadogan did all he

could; but that is not enough: that he could not make an actual
transfer; that the trustees in whom it was vested would not have
been authorized in transferring it of their own authority to the trustees of Mr. W. Cadogan's settlement. "If," he says, "a man is
seised of the legal estate, and agree to make a voluntary settlement, it
cannot be enforced. Can it make any difference that the legal estate
happens to be outstanding? Certainly not. As the settlement, therefore, was not completely perfected, the Earl could not enforce it." Sir
W. Grant, M. R., however, held, that the equitable assignment created
a perfect trust. "The Court," observed his Honor, "will not interfere
to give perfection to the instrument, but you may constitute one a
trustee for a volunteer. Here *the fund was vested in trustees:* Mr. W.
Cadogan had an equitable reversionary interest in that fund, and he assigned it to certain trustees, and then the first trustees are trustees for
his assigns, and they may come here; for when the trust is created, no
consideration is essential, and the Court will execute it though voluntary."

In *Fortescue* v. *Barnett*, 3 My. & K. 36, J. B. made a voluntary assignment by deed of a policy of assurance effected upon his own life
and in his own name for 1000*l.*, to trustees, upon trust for the benefit
[*269] of his sister and her children. The deed was delivered *to one
of the trustees, and the grantor kept the policy in his own possession. *No notice of the assignment was given to the assurance office*
and J. B. afterwards surrendered, for a valuable consideration, the policy
and a bonus declared upon it to the assurance office. A bill was filed
by the surviving trustee of the deed against J. B. to have the value
of the policy replaced. It was argued by Mr. Pemberton, for the defendant upon the distinction laid down by Lord Eldon in the principal
case, between an actual transfer and a mere covenant to transfer stock,
that the assignment of stock by deed, no actual transfer of the
stock having been made, and an assignment of a policy of assurance
by deed, the policy remaining in the hands of the grantor, stood
upon exactly the same footing. But Sir J. Leach, M. R., held, that
J. B. was bound to give security to the amount of the value of the
policy assigned by the deed. "In the case," observed his Honor,
"of a voluntary assignment of a bond, where the bond is not delivered, but kept in the possession of the assignor, the Court would undoubtedly, in the administration of the assets of the assignor, consider
the bond as a debt to the assignee. There is a plain distinction between an assignment of stock, where the stock has not been transferred,
and an assignment of a bond. In the former case, the material act remains to be done by the grantor, and nothing is in fact done which will
entitle the assignee to the aid of this Court until the stock is transferred,
whereas the Court will admit the assignee of a bond as a creditor.

"In the present case, the gift of the policy appears to me to have been perfectly complete without delivery. Nothing remained to be done by the grantor; nor could he have done what he afterwards did to defeat his own grant, if the trustees had given notice of the assignment to the assurance office. The question here does not turn upon any distinction between a legal and an equitable title, *but simply upon whether any act remained to be done by the grantor which, to assist a volunteer, this Court would not compel him to do.* I am of opinion, that no act remained to be done to complete the title of the trustees. The trustees ought to have given notice of the assignment; but their omission to give notice cannot affect the cestui que trust." See, also, *Godsal* v *Webb*, 2 Kee. 99; *Pearson* v. *The Amicable Assurance Office*, 27 Beav. 229; *Pedder* v. *Mosely*, 31 Beav. 159.

Lord Cottenham, in *Edwards* v. *Jones*, 1 My. & C. 238, in commenting upon *Sloane* v. *Cadogan*, and *Fortescue* v. *Barnett*, observes, "that in neither of them was any intention expressed by the learned judge to depart from the established *rule, but that, in both, the decision [*270] turned upon the question of fact, whether or not the relation of trustee and cestui que trust was actually constituted. In neither was it attempted to make an imperfect a perfect gift. In *Sloane* v. *Cadogan*, the *claim was not against the donor or his representatives*, for the purpose of making that complete which had been left imperfect, but against the persons who had the legal custody of the fund; and the question was, whether the transaction constituted them trustees of the fund for the cestui que trusts. Sir W. Grant came to the conclusion that it did, and the consequence was that they were bound to account. That case has been considered by Sir Edward Sugden as going a great way; but upon the principle stated by Sir W. Grant, it is free from all possible question, for there was no attempt in that case to call in aid the jurisdiction of this court.

" *Fortescue* v. *Barnett* falls precisely within the same observation, although there are some expressions in it, especially where the learned judge speaks of a bond which has been voluntarily assigned being considered a debt to the assignee, which probably were not intended to convey the meaning they do . . . . . There a party had insured a life, and the contract of the office was to pay to the party insuring, his executors, administrators, and assigns, but the practice of the office was stated to be, that, upon an assignment, the office recognised the assignee; and the policy was, therefore, an assignable instrument. The policy *was not assignable at law, but it was a title which, by contract, was assignable as between the parties;* and the party in that case assigned, but the assignee did not give notice to the office, and consequently, the original insurer dealt with the office, received a bonus, and then surrendered the policy. The Master of the Rolls in that case considered, as he naturally would, whether this transaction was not a gift — whether it did not, in fact, confer a title on the assignee; and if it did, then, consistently with all the authorities, he considered that he was bound to give the assignment its full effect; and he put his decision expressly upon the fact, that the transaction was complete; that there was nothing further for the donor or the donee to do; that the latter had nothing to ask further from the donor." His Lordship then adds, " Whether, upon the circumstances of that case, it was right or wrong to come to that conclusion, is a question with which I have nothing to do. The principle of the decision is quite consistent with the other cases; for it proceeds upon the same ground, namely, that, if the transaction is complete, the Court will give it effect."

[*271] *Upon the authority of *Sloane* v. *Cadogan* and *Fortescue* v. *Barnett*, it has been held that the assignment of a debt to a volunteer was binding, although nothing passed at law. Thus in *Blakely* v. *Brady*, 2 Dru. & Walsh. 311, A. made a voluntary assignment to B. of a note or memorandum in writing, being the acknowledgment of a sum of 1,620*l*. then due to him from K., and all interest then due, or which might thereafter accrue due on the foot thereof, upon trust to pay the interest thereof unto A., his executors, administrators, and assigns, for his life, and a period of fourteen months afterwards, and, at the expiration of the said fourteen months, to pay out of the principal some small sums to and amongst certain persons and relations in the deed particularly mentioned; and as to the residue, in trust for B., his executors, administrators, and assigns, for his and their own benefit. The deed also contained a provision, whereby B., his executors, administrators, and assigns, were irrevocably appointed the attorneys of the said A., for the purpose of suing for and recovering the said debts. A. soon afterwards died, without having made any will or other disposition of the property. The administrator of A. refused to allow his name to be used to enable B. to recover the said sum, having actually himself commenced an action for that purpose. Upon a bill filed by B. to restrain proceedings in the action, and to carry the trusts of the deed into execution, it was held by Lord Plunket, that, as the transaction between A. and B. was complete, the deed, though voluntary, should be carried into execution. " In this case," observed his Lordship, " as between the assignor and assignees, the gift is absolute; and the difference between the cases where something remains to be done, and those in which nothing remains to be done, is so fully established by the authorities, which have been cited on both sides in the argument, that it is unnecessary for me to enter into any enumeration of them. The case of *Fortescue* v. *Barnett*, besides recognizing the general distinction which I have just adverted to, bears directly on the present point. There the assignment of a policy of insurance was held valid and complete, though the instrument itself was never delivered.

" It is said, but in my opinion, most erroneously, that the authority of that case is shaken by the case of *Jones* v. *Edwards*, before the present Lord Chancellor of England. It seems to me, that he expressly recognizes its authority, and on this principle, that, if the transaction is complete, the Court will give it effect. It is true Lord Cottenham says, that the observation of Sir J. Leach, in *Fortescue* v. *Barnett*, 'that a *bond voluntarily assigned was considered as a debt to the assignee,' was probably not intended to convey the [*272] meaning the words might bear; but this observation of Lord Cottenham must, in my opinion, be merely understood as a guard against the supposition, that the mere assignment of a bond, unaccompanied by delivery, or by any other circumstances, would be considered as a debt to the assignee. In the case before Lord Cottenham there was no assignment, but a mere memorandum entered on a bond, attached to another bond, which clearly was never intended to be given to the plaintiff; and he there dismissed the bill, on the ground of the transaction not being complete, and that a further act remained to be done by the donor.

" The case of *Uniacke* v. *Giles*, 2 Moll. 257, does not resemble this. There the person entitled to a chose in action executed an assignment of it, to the defendant in trust for the plaintiff, and did not deliver the deed, but kept it in her possession until her death ; and it was held that the retention of the deed in the custody of the donor made it revocable, and that it had been revoked.

" The decision in *Antrobus* v. *Smith* cannot be drawn in aid of the defendant's case. There the conveyance was imperfect, never delivered : it was simply an indorsement on a receipt for subscription, and found among the papers of the executrix.

" The present case differs from all these. The assignment as between the donor and donee is perfect; and the only objection is, that the chose in action is not legally assignable. Besides, it is admitted that the original security was, at some time during the life of the assignor, delivered to the assignee ; and, in addition to this, the assignment contains a full power of attorney to the assignee, which alone, in my opinion, ought to govern the case.

"It is asked, why does the plaintiff come into this Court, if the assignment is imperfect ? The answer is obvious : he comes here because the property is in the defendant, to whom the ecclesiastical court has granted administration, and he is an administrator in trust. Now you may constitute a trustee for a volunteer; and the case of *Sloane* v. *Cadogan* is directly in point as to that. The only difference is, that, in the present case, the law has created the trust; and in *Sloane* v. *Cadogan* the trust was created by the act of the donor. See also *Parnell* v. *Hingston*, 3 Sm. & G. 337 ; *Gannon* v. *White*, 2 Ir. Eq. Rep. 207 ; *Roberts* v. *Lloyd*, 2 Beav. 376 ; sed vide *Sewell* v. *Moxsy*, 2 Sim. N. S. 189."

The remarks however of Lord Langdale in *Ward* v. *Audland*, 8

Beav. 201, seem to be scarcely consistent with the cases of *Sloane*
[*273]   *v. Cadogan, Fortescue* v. *Barnett,* and *Blakely* v. *Brady,* for
there his Lordship appears to be of opinion that the mere
voluntary assignment of a chose in action is not binding, upon the
ground that nothing thereby passes at law, and the transaction is, therefore, incomplete. This seems to have been the opinion of Sir L.
Shadwell, V. C., in *Beatson* v. *Beatson,* 12 Sim. 291.

In *Ward* v. *Audland,* W. W., who was possessed of and entitled to
certain household goods, and effects, a sum of 546*l.* 2*s.* 6*d.* (the payment of which was secured by a mortgage in fee of certain customary
lands), and a policy of assurance for the sum of 1000*l.* payable after
his death, by a voluntary deed assigned to the plaintiff all his household goods, and all sums of money then owing to him, with all policies
of assurance and other securities for the same, and all other his personal estate, together with the mortgage deeds and writings relating to
the premises, upon trust for W. W., for life, and, after his death, for
others ; and he gave the plaintiff a power of attorney to get in any
sum of money secured on mortgage ; and he also covenanted for further
assurance.   On the execution of the deed by W. W., it was delivered to
the plaintiff; but W. W. continued in possession of the furniture thereby
assigned, and in receipt of the income arising from the mortgage, and
no notice of the assignment was given, either to the mortgagor or to
the grantors of the policy of assurance.   Lord Langdale, M. R., said:
"Supposing the assignment to have been a complete and effectual
assignment, there is not only no conflict, but no question nor any difficulty as to the trusts which the plaintiff had to perform. If the
property was *legally* vested in the plaintiff, he might have recovered it
at law, and applied it on the trusts ; if the property was not *legally and
effectually* vested in the plaintiff, then, as the deed was voluntary, this
Court could afford no assistance to the plaintiff in recovering it ; and,
under these circumstances, the only question between the parties is,
what is the *legal* effect of the assignment ? . . . . . . The debt and
policy of assurance are choses in action *not assignable at law,* and it is
plain that the whole estate and interest of the assignor did not and
could not pass to an assignee ; and I apprehend, that, in the case of a
voluntary deed, neither the assignor nor his executor could have been
compelled to permit the assignee to use his name for the recovery of
the debt.   The assignment was deficient, because it did not vest in the
assignee all that the assignor professed, and intended to pass ; and no
instance, except the case of *Fortescue* v. *Barnett,* has been produced,
[*274]   in which this Court has given effect to such an assignment. *It
does not appear by the report what were the grounds on which
Lord Cottenham, in deciding the case of *Edwards* v. *Jones,* gave the
interpretation he did to *Fortescue* v. *Barnett ;* but it is certainly clear,
that Sir John Leach did not in that case intend to alter the rule of the

Court which was previously established; and it is also clear that the circumstances, by which Lord Cottenham seemed to think *Fortescue* v. *Barnett* might be explained, are not found in the present case. It appears to me, that neither a voluntary assignment by deed of a mortgage debt, accompanied by a grant, not specifying the particular estate, but of all estates held in mortgage, and by a covenant for further assurance, without delivery of the mortgage deed or notice to the mortgagor, nor the voluntary assignment of a policy of assurance retained in the hands of the assignor, and without notice given to the grantor, though accompanied by a covenant for further assurance, can be considered as a complete and effectual assignment, to be acted upon and enforced by the assignee, without any further or other act to be done by the assignor. With respect to the furniture, the bill claims the legal right to it for the plaintiff; and if he had it, I am of opinion that he ought to have proceeded at law to recover it. With respect to the mortgage, the bill alleges the legal estate to be in the defendants, or some of them, and prays for a conveyance in aid of the voluntary gift. On the whole, I think that the plaintiff is not entitled to any relief, and that the bill must be dismissed but with costs."

Sir J. Wigram, V. C., also (1 Hare, 474), was clearly of opinion, that an assignment under seal of that which did not pass at law by the operation of the assignment itself, unaccompanied by other acts, was no better than a covenant or agreement to assign : see *Meek* v. *Kettlewell*, 1 Hare, 464. There M., who in the event of surviving her daughter, and of the death of her daughter without issue, would, as next of kin, be entitled to a fund which was vested in trustees, executed a voluntary assignment of her interest in the fund to the husband of the daughter, and declared the trusts of the assignment as to part for the benefit of M. herself, and as to another part for the daughter's husband absolutely. No notice of the assignment was given to the trustees. The daughter afterwards died without issue, and the husband filed his bill against the trustees and M., to compel the performance of the trust. Sir J. Wigram was of opinion, upon the authority of the cases of *Colman* v. *Sarrel*, 3 Bro. C. C. 12, and *Holloway* v. *Headington*, 8 Sim. 324, that an assignment under seal of that which did not pass at law by the operation of the assignment, *itself, stood upon no bet- [*275] ter ground than a covenant or agreement to assign : and that a voluntary assignment, unaccompanied by any other acts, was not to be regarded as effectual to pass an equitable interest. His Honor therefore held, that the voluntary assignment did not create a trust which equity would enforce; observing, however, that he decided only that a voluntary assignment of a mere expectancy, not communicated to those in whom the legal interest was, did not create a trust in equity, within the principle of the cases relied upon by the plaintiff. This decision, on appeal, was affirmed by Lord Lyndhurst : 1 Ph. 342. See also *Beat-*

son v. *Beatson*, 12 Sim. 281; *Ward* v. *Audland*, 8 Sim. 571; *S. C.*, C. P. Coop. Rep. 146; 8 Beav. 201.

The leading case, however, of *Kekewich* v. *Manning* (1 De Gex, Mac. & G. 176) must be considered in effect, though perhaps not expressly, as overruling *Holloway* v. *Headington*, (8 Sim. 324); *Ward* v. *Audland*, (8 Beav. 201); *S. C.*, C. P. Coop. Rep. 146; 8 Beav. 201, and even *Meek* v. *Kettlewell*, unless that case can be supported upon the ground that it was the assignment of a mere expectancy. The case of *Kekewick* v. *Manning* is as follows: A lady entitled absolutely to the reversion in stock, *subject to the life interest of her mother* therein, and which stock was standing in the joint names of herself and her mother, assigned her interest in this stock on her marriage, to trustees in trust for herself for, remainder to her husband for, life, and after their decease, in trust for a niece, and for the issue of the marriage and the issue of the niece according to appointment; and in default of issue of the marriage, in trust for the niece of the settlor. No transfer of the fund took place, but the mother had notice of the settlement. There was no issue of the marriage. It was held by the Lords Justices Knight Bruce and Lord Cranworth, that even if the settlement were voluntary as regarded the niece and not supported by the marriage consideration (which point, however, the Court did not decide), the assignment being complete would be enforced by the Court. "Suppose," said Lord Justice Knight Bruce, "stock or money to be legally vested in A. as trustee for B. for life; and subject to B.'s life interest, for C. absolutely; surely it must be competent to C. in B.'s lifetime, with or without the consent of A., to make an effectual gift of C.'s interest to D. by way of mere bounty, leaving the legal interest and legal title unchanged and untouched. Surely it would not be consistent with natural equity or with reason or expediency to hold the contrary, C. being sui juris, and acting freely, fairly, and with sufficient advice [*276] *and knowledge. If so, can C. do this better or more effectually than by executing an assignment to D.? It may possibly be thought necessary to the complete validity of such a transaction, that notice should be given to A.: upon that we do not express an opinion.

"Suppose the case only varied by the fact that A. and C. are the trustees jointly, instead of A. being so alone? Does that make any substantial difference as to C.'s power, the mode of making the gift, or the effect of the act, C. not severing nor affecting the legal joint tenancy? C. would necessarily have notice. Possibly it may be thought material that B. should have notice likewise, but upon that we avoid saying anything, beyond referring to *Meux* v. *Bell* (1 Hare, 73), and to *Smith* v. *Smith*, mentioned in *Meux* v. *Bell*." See also the elaborate judgment of Sir J. Stuart, V. C., in *Voyle* v. *Hughes*, 2 Sm.

& Giff. 18; *Re Way's Trusts*, 2 De G. Jo. & Sm. 365; *Richardson* v. *Richardson*, 3 L. R. Eq. 686.

It has, however, been held by Lord Romilly, M. R., that the transfer of an equitable estate in real property to volunteers was invalid; *Bridge* v. *Bridge*, 16 Beav. 315, 327, 328; but Lord St. Leonards, with reference to this decision, says, it "seems open to reconsideration." Sugd. V. & P. 719, 14th ed.; and see *Gilbert* v. *Overton*, 2 Hem. & Mill. 117: where Sir W. Page Wood, V. C., observes, "I do not wish to say more as to *Bridge* v. *Bridge* than this: that the points there dealt with will require much consideration. A man who conveys his equitable interest may well be considered to do all that can be required, and it would be a great extension of the established doctrine on these subjects to hold that if a legal estate is discovered, perhaps many years afterwards, to have been outstanding at the date of a voluntary settlement, the settlement itself is to be deprived of effect. Where a settlor by a voluntary instrument conveys all his interest, it may well be held that if that interest proves to be merely equitable, the assignee becomes entitled to claim a conveyance of the legal estate from the person in whom it may be vested."

And it has been decided that it is not essential to the validity of an equitable voluntary assignment, at any rate where it has been acted upon by all parties, that it should be by deed. *Lambe* v. *Orton*, 1 Drew. & Sm. 202.

A distinction has been taken in recent cases by the Master of the Rolls to this effect, that although it is clear that an assignment by deed of reversionary personal property vested in trustees in favour of volunteers will be enforced in equity, yet, if, although property be vested in *trustees, it is entirely in the power of the assignor, so that he could compel a transfer from them, should he neglect to do so, [*277] a mere assignment will, in the same manner as if the property had been legally vested in himself, be imperfect, that is to say, not so complete as he could have made it, and will consequently not be enforced by a Court of equity. Thus in *Bridge* v. *Bridge*, 16 Beav. 315, where it appears that a sum of stock was standing in the name of four trustees of a will by the terms of which they were to apply the dividends for the benefit of the plaintiff until he was twenty-five, at which age it was to be paid over to him. On the 10th of February, 1846, the plaintiff attained his age of twenty-one. On the 9th of April, 1847, he executed a voluntary deed, by which he directed (amongst other things) that the personal estate to which he was entitled under the will, should thenceforth be considered as vested in the plaintiff and two new trustees, upon certain trusts therein mentioned. The deed also contained a covenant for further assurance. No transfer of the stock was made to the new trustees. The plaintiff having filed a bill, seeking a declaration that the settlement of 1847 was not binding upon him, it was held by Sir John

Romilly, M. R., that as there had been no legal transfer made, and no recognition of the trust by the original trustees, there was no complete trust constituted, and the plaintiff was therefore entitled to a transfer of the stock. "In my view of this particular case," said his Honor, "the question must be regarded in exactly the same manner, whether the plaintiff or a stranger had been the third trustee. This being so, there being four trustees of the will in whom the legal interest was vested, and the beneficial owner having assigned over the funds to these persons, in trust for certain persons as volunteers, no transfer is made to the new trustee so appointed, *nor is there any reason as in Keke-wick* v. *Manning, why the transfer should not have been made.* In *Kekewick* v. *Manning,* the original trusts were not exhausted, but the life-estate of the mother continued in the stock, *and until her death no transfer could have been made. The assignor had done all she could do.* That is not so in this case. The trustees of the deed of settlement did not do anything inconsistent with the trusts which remained to be performed under the testator's will, and the trustees of the will seem not to have been advised to resist making any transfer to the trustees of the deed, until the settlor had attained his age of twenty-five years." So likewise in *Beech* v. *Keep*, 18 Beav. 285, A., subject to the life-interest of B., was absolutely entitled to a sum of stock, which [*278] was standing in the names of two deceased trustees, to the *survivor of whom A. was sole executor. Under these circumstances, A. by deed voluntarily assigned all her interest in the stock to B., "to the intent that he might be and become present and absolute owner thereof." A. having refused to execute a power of attorney to B., for a transfer of the stock, it was held by Sir John Romilly, M. R., that A. could not be declared by the Court to be a trustee of the fund, nor compelled to transfer it. His Honor distinguishing the case from *Kekewick* v. *Manning* (1 De G. Mac. & G. 176), considered that it fell within the principle of his own decision in *Bridge* v. *Bridge*, 16 Beav. 315). "In the present instance," said his Honor, "it is obvious, there was no outstanding interest except the plaintiff's, and *the transfer of the stock ought to have been made, if both parties had been willing to complete the transaction, and if the transfer had been made, the plaintiff's title would have been complete.* The argument employed by the plaintiff, that having himself the life estate, no transfer could be made without his consent, clearly does not apply, because he would be the absolute owner if this assignment was perfect, and it was throughout his expressed desire to get the transfer completed. The transfer of the stock is, in fact, what the defendant has refused to make, and it is that transfer which the plaintiff has all along been trying to get, and which is now asked, to make the transaction complete."

Notice of the voluntary assignment of an equitable interest or of a chose in action, to the trustees or debtor, according to the recent authorities is not essential to its validity, but if the trustees or debtor, before notice of the deed, transferred the property or paid the debt, the donee would have no remedy against them. Thus in *Donaldson* v. *Donaldson*, Kay, 711, the settlor having assigned stock standing in the names of trustees, to other trustees in favour of volunteers, it was held by Sir W. Page Wood, V. C., that as between the donees under the assignment, and the representatives of the assignor, the title of the former was complete, although no notice of the assignment had been given to the trustees in whose names the stock was standing. " The question," said his Honor, " is, whether, notice not having been given to the trustee, the gift could be enforced. As to that, it has been said in some cases that the gift is complete when no further act is required to be done by the donor or donee : and that seems to imply a doubt, whether, if there were any act to be done by the donee, the gift could be treated as complete, but the assignment has completely passed the interest of the donor. It is true, that if no notice of it were given to the trustees, they would be justified *in transferring the stock to the origi- [*279] nal cestui que trust for whom they held it ; and if they did so, there would be no remedy against them ; and it is possible that the donee might not be able to recover the stock ; but all that the donee has to do is, at any time he thinks fit, to give notice to the trustees before the stock is transferred ; and when he has given such notice his title is complete : and unless the donor or his executors actually obtain possession of the fund, the donee does not require the aid of the Court against them." See *Roberts* v. *Lloyd*, 2 Beav. 376 ; *Re Way's Trusts*, 2 De G. Jo. & Sm. 365.

Although a conveyance in favour of a volunteer be complete, if it were executed under the influence of mistake (*Manning* v. *Gill*, 13 L. R. Eq. 485 ; 20 W. R. 357), or fraud (*Chesterfield* v. *Janssen*, post and note : *Huguenin* v. *Baseley*, vol. 2, post and note), it will not be carried into effect by a Court of equity, but will ordinarily be rescinded.

That Courts of equity, as is laid down in the principal case, will not carry into effect a mere voluntary agreement, contract, or covenant to transfer property, see *Cotteen* v. *Missing*, 1 Madd. 176 ; *Colyear* v. *Mulgrave*, 2 Kee. 81 ; *Jeffreys* v. *Jeffreys*, Cr. & Ph. 138 ; *Dening* v. *Ware*, 22 Beav. 184 ; *Cheale* v. *Kerwood*, 6 W. R., M. R., 494 ; *Tatham* v. *Vernon*, 29 Beav. 604. In *Coningham* v. *Plunkett*, 2 Y. & C. C. C. 245, a person who was entitled to stock, standing in the names of two trustees, gave instructions to his attorney to prepare a settlement of it for the benefit of A., B., and C., and to procure from the trustees a transfer for the purposes of settlement. The settlement was prepared and a power of attorney for the transfer of the stock executed by both the trustees ; but the intended settlor died without having seen the settlement, and before the stock was actually transferred. Sir J. L.

Knight Bruce, V. C., held, that no trust of the stock was constituted for A., B., and C. See also *Pownall* v. *Anderson*, 2 Jur. N. S. 857.

Where, however, a person entered into a voluntary covenant to surrender copyholds, and in the meanwhile to stand possessed of them for trustees for the volunteers, though the covenant to surrender *per se* cannot be enforced, yet a valid trust is constituted for the volunteers; *Steel* v. *Waller*, 28 Beav. 466.

A merely meritorious consideration, as a provision for a wife or children, after marriage, will not be a sufficient inducement for a Court of equity to lend its aid in enforcing a voluntary agreement or covenant, or in giving effect to an imperfect gift. It might, perhaps, be inferred from an expression of Lord Eldon's, in the principal case, that a meritorious consideration is sufficient; and *Sir Edward Sugden, in [*280] the case of *Ellis* v. *Nimmo*, 1 L. & G., t. Sugd. 333, held, that, a post-nuptial agreement, in writing, by which a father undertook to make a provision for a child, ought to be specifically performed, although founded only on a meritorious consideration. The decision, however, of Sir Edward Sugden must be considered now as distinctly overruled by Lord Cottenham, in *Jefferys* v. *Jefferys*, Cr. & Ph. 138, and *Dillon* v. *Coppin*, 4 My. & Cr. 647. See also *Holloway* v. *Headington*, 8 Sim. 324, per Sir L. Shadwell, V. C.

Sir J. Wigram, V. C., in commenting upon the different classes of cases on voluntary trusts, has observed, that "they are perhaps to be reconciled and explained upon the principle that a declaration of trust purports to be, and is in form and substance, a complete transaction, and the court need not look beyond the declaration of trust itself, or inquire into its origin, in order that it may be in a position to uphold and enforce it; whereas, an agreement or attempt to assign, is, in form and nature, incomplete, and the origin of the transaction must be inquired into by the Court; and, where there is no consideration, the Court, upon its general principles, cannot complete what it finds imperfect: and there is a close analogy for this reasoning in the case of suits to enforce demands arising out of illicit dealings between parties. If, in such cases, the Court finds an account rendered, or other act done by one of the parties, upon which account or act, the Court can proceed without investigating the origin of the demand, it will do so. But it will not so proceed where the form of the transaction is such as to oblige the Court to go into the original illegal transaction, out of which the demand arises:" *M'Fadden* v. *Jenkyns*, 1 Hare, 462. See also *Davenport* v. *Whitmore*, 2 My. & Cr. 177, and the cases there cited.

Where a voluntary instrument, although effecting no transfer of property, creates a valid legal obligation, equity will give effect to it. Thus, where a person executes a bond (*Hall* v. *Palmer*, 3 Hare, 532), or even a promissory note (*Dawson* v. *Kearton*, 3 Sm. & Giff. 186), in favour of a volunteer, he may prove the debt against the assets of the debtor; but it will be postponed in equity to debts by simple contract; *Ramsden* v. *Jackson*, 1 Atk. 294. A voluntary bond, however, will be preferred to interest upon debts not by law carrying interest payable under the 46th order of August, 1841: (Consol. ord. xlii., 10) *Garrard* v. *Lord Dinorben*, 5 Hare, 213. And if it be doubtful whether a bond be voluntary or for valuable consideration, an issue may be directed: *Hepworth* v. *Heslop*, 6 Hare, 561.

But an assignee for value of an *equitable interest in money payable under a voluntary bond has been held entitled to rank [*281] as a specialty creditor for value against the assets of the obligor, *Payne* v. *Mortimer*, 4 De G. & Jo. 447; 1 Giff. 118.

Where a person without consideration covenants to pay a sum of money, if the covenant is complete, and the Court is not called upon to do any act to make it perfect, it will give effect to a trust declared upon the covenant. Thus, in *Clough* v. *Lambert*, 10 Sim. 174, where a person, by a voluntary deed, for himself, his heirs, executors, and administrators, covenanted to pay an annuity to trustees, upon trust for his wife for her life, Sir Lancelot Shadwell, V. C., was of opinion that the covenant might be enforced by the wife against the executors of her husband, though not as against his creditors, and that the mere intervention of a trustee made no difference. See also *Fletcher* v. *Fletcher*, 4 Hare, 67, which shows, that, in the event of the trustee refusing or declining to sue on the covenant, equity will assist the cestui que trust, by enabling him to use the deed either at law or in equity. " My opinion," said Sir J. Wigram, V. C., " is, that the plaintiff would be entitled to use the name of the trustee at law, or to recover the money in this Court, if it were unnecessary to have the right decided at law, and, where the legal right is clear, to have the use of the deed, if that use is material." In another part of his judgment, his Honor observes, " The rule against relief to volunteers cannot, I conceive, in a case like that before me, be stated higher than this—that a Court of equity will not, in favour of a volunteer, give to a deed any effect beyond what the law will give to it. But, if the author of the deed has subjected himself to a liability at law, and the legal liability comes regularly to be enforced in equity, the observation that the claimant is a volunteer is of no value in favour of those who represent the author of the deed; " and his Honor, therefore, in that case, thought that, as there was no reason for trying the case at law, the decree ought to be for the payment of the money due upon the admission of the assets of the covenantor. See also *Williamson* v. *Codrington*, 1 Ves. 511; *Watson* v. *Parker*, 6 Beav. 283; *Lomas* v. *Wright*, 2 My. & K. 769; *Alexander* v. *Bramo*, 19 Beav. 436; *Hales* v. *Cox*, 32 Beav. 118; *Bonfield* v. *Hassell*, Ib. 217; and the observations of Sir John Romilly, M. R., in *Bridge* v. *Bridge*, 16 Beav. 321.

In *Hervey* v. *Audland*, 14 Sim. 531, the executors of a person who had entered into a covenant for further assurance in a voluntary settlement having refused to perform it, the Court, in a suit instituted by a [*282] third party for the *administration of the covenantor's estate, would not permit the covenantee to prove as a creditor under the decree in the administration suit, but gave him leave to bring such action as he should be advised. In the case, however, of *Cox* v. *Barnard*, 8 Hare, 310, a testator had assigned annuities, mortgage debts, and policies of assurance to volunteers, and entered into the usual covenant for further assurance. No notice of the deed was given in the lifetime of the testator to the mortgagors or grantors of the annuities. It was held, however, by Sir J. L. Knight Bruce, V. C., in a suit to administer the assets of the testator, that the covenant could be enforced against them without recourse to a Court of law. "The Court of Chancery," said his Honor, "undertook to administer the estates of deceased persons, and it was the duty of this Court to do so, if practicable, without sending parties to Courts of law ; and there was no reason for sending this case to a Court of law. He did not say the Court would specifically perform the covenant; but all the covenantee required was damages, and those damages the Court of Chancery could in such a case estimate and give better than a Court of law. His Honor said that it was not necessary for him to decide, and he did not decide, whether, without the covenant for further assurance, the voluntary instrument would prevail ; but the covenant being there, the Court would fasten upon it, and hold that the assignment operated to bind the estate." See also *Ward* v. *Audland*, 16 M. & W. 682 ; *Aulton* v. *Atkins*, 18 C. B. 249 ; *Patch* v. *Shore*, 11 W. R. (V. C. K.) 142.

And where a person settled property by a voluntary deed with a trust for payment of debts due at his decease, voluntary bonds subsequently given have been held to be debts payable out of the trust property, *Markwell* v. *Markwell*, 34 Beav. 12.

Although a Court of equity will not upon a bill filed by a volunteer, give him any assistance, yet, upon a bill filed by any of the parties to a deed from whom any valuable consideration moved, all the trusts will be carried into effect, even those in favour of volunteers : *Davenport* v. *Bishopp*, 2 Y. & C. C. C. 451, 1 Ph. 698 ; *Touche* v. *Metropolitan Railway Warehousing Co.*, 6 L. R. Ch. App. 671. And where two persons for valuable consideration, as between themselves, covenant to do some act for the benefit of a mere stranger, that stranger cannot enforce the covenant against the two, although either of the two might do so against the other : *Coleyear* v. *Mulgrave*, 2 Kee. 81 ; *Hill* v. *Gomme*, 1 Beav. 540, 5 My. & Cr. 250 ; *Cramer* v. *Moore*, 3 Sm. & Giff. 141 ; *Joyce* v. *Hutton*, 11 Ir. Ch. Rep. 123 ; and see and consider [*283] *Kekewich* v. *Manning*, *1 De G. Mac. & G. 176 ; *Heap* v. *Tonge*, 8 Hare, 90, 103, 104 ; *Page* v. *Cox*, 10 Hare, 163, 169 ;

Harman v. *Richards,* 10 Hare, 81, 88; *Westbury* v. *Clapp,* 12 W. R. (V. C. W.) 511.

When once an instrument creating a valid and complete trust is duly sealed and delivered, the obligation is complete; the detention of the instrument by the grantor does not render it inoperative: *Doe* d. *Garnons* v. *Knight,* 5 B. & C. 671; *Exton* v. *Scott,* 6 Sim. 31; *Hall* v. *Palmer,* 3 Hare, 532; *Re Way's Settlement,* 13 W. R. (L. J.) 149; *Bonfield* v. *Hassell,* 32 Beav. 217.

Statute 27 Eliz. c. 4.] A voluntary settlement of real estate, whether freehold, copyhold, or leasehold, unless it be in favour of a charity (*Attorney General* v. *The Corporation of New Castle*), 5 Beav. 307, 12 C. & F. 402, will, under 27 Eliz. c. 4, be held fraudulent and void, as against subsequent purchasers for a valuable consideration from the settlor, including mortgagees (*Dolphin* v. *Aylward,* 4 L. R. Ho. Lo. 486), *even with notice* of the settlement, and although it is a fair provision for a wife and children; and the settlor will not be restrained from selling the settled estates; but, if the trust is complete, the volunteers will be entitled to the execution of it until the sale. (See *Pulvertoft* v. *Pulvertoft,* 18 Ves. 84, 91, 93; *Buckle* v. *Mitchell,* 18 Ves. 100; *Metcalf* v. *Pulvertoft,* 1 V. & B. 180; *Willats* v. *Busby,* 5 Beav. 193; *Stackpoole* v. *Stackpoole,* 4 D. & W. 320; *Clarke* v. *Wright,* 6 H. & N. 849.) And the law is the same when the voluntary settlement is made by a married woman: *Butterfield* v. *Heath,* 15 Beav. 408.

A voluntary settlement, however, will be defeated by a conveyance or settlement for value to the extent only necessary to give effect to the conveyance or settlement for value: *Croker* v. *Martin,* 1 Bligh., N. S. 573; 1 D. & C. 15. See also *Dolphin* v. *Aylward,* 4 L. R. Ho. Lo. 486, but it cannot be defeated by a subsequent judgment creditor, who can only have resort against such interest, if any, as remained in the settlor by virtue of, or unaffected by, the voluntary settlement. *Ib.*

A bona fide settlement although voluntary, cannot be defeated by the conveyance for value of the heir or devisee of the settlor. See *Lewis* v. *Rees,* 3 K. & J. 132, and *Doe* d. *Newman* v. *Rusham,* 17 Q. B. 721; overruling *Jones, Lessee of Moffett,* v. *Whitaker,* Longfield & Townsend's Ir. Exch. Rep. 141. And it should be remembered that a deed, apparently voluntary, may be supported by collateral evidence, showing a contract for value: *Pott* v. *Todhunter,* 2 Coll. 76. And see *Ford* v. *Stuart,* 14 Beav. 493; *Kelson* v. *Kelson,* 10 Hare, *385; *Townsend* v. *Toker,* 1 L. R. Ch. App. 446. [*284]

The settlor himself cannot come into a Court of equity to enforce the specific performance of a contract for the sale of the estate entered into by him after the settlement (*Smith* v. *Garland,* 2 Mer. 123; *Johnson* v. *Legard,* T. & R. 294; *Clarke* v. *Willott,* 7 L. R. Ex. 313; except as against a purchaser willing to complete upon a good title being shown:

Peter v. *Nicolls*, 11 L. R. Eq. 391; but a purchaser from the settlor can: *Currie* v. *Nind*, 5 My. & C. 17; *Daking* v. *Whimper*, 26 Beav. 568.

Where a voluntary settlement of land is avoided by a subsequent sale for valuable consideration, the volunteers have no equity against the purchase-money payable to the settlor. *Daking* v. *Whimper*, 26 Beav. 568.

Chattels personal do not come within the stat. 27 Eliz. c. 4; a settlement, therefore, of chattels personal cannot be defeated by a subsequent sale: *Sloane* v. *Cadogan*, 2 Sugd. V. & P., App. xxiv. ed. 11; *Jones* v. *Croucher*, 4 S. & S. 315.

It may be here mentioned, that the Courts considering the law under the statute 27 Eliz. c. 4, by which a person can indirectly get rid of a settlement, to be unsatisfactory, have held that a small and inadequate consideration is sufficient to support such a settlement: *Bayspoole* v. *Collins*, 6 L. R. Ch. App. 228, 232; and see *Thompson* v. *Webster*, 4 De G. & J. 600; *Ford* v. *Stuart*, 15 Beav. 493; *Roe* v. *Mitton*, 2 Wils. 356; *Townend* v. *Toker*, 1 L. R. Ch. App. 446.

Statute, 13 *Eliz. c.* 5.] By the statute, 13 Eliz. c. 5, a voluntary settlement of real or personal estate will be void, and may be set aside by a creditor of the settlor upon his showing an intent on the part of the settlor to delay hinder, or defraud creditors. This intent may be actual and express (*Spirett* v. *Willows*, 3 De G. Jo. & Sm. 293), or it may be inferred in different ways, as, for instance, by the creditor showing that the settlor was indebted to the extent of insolvency, or even that he was largely indebted at the time of making the settlement: (*Fletcher* v. *Sedley*, 2 Vern. 490, and note; *Taylor* v. *Jones*, 2 Atk. 600; *Townsend* v. *Westmacott*, 2 Beav. 340; *Skarf* v. *Soulby*, 1 Mac. & G. 364; *Jenkyn* v. *Vaughan*, 3 Drew. 419; *Re Magawley's Trust*, 5 De G. & Sm. 1; *Holmes* v. *Penney*, 3 K. & J. 90; *Barton* v. *Vanheythysen*, 11 Hare, 126; *French* v. *French*, 6 De G. Mac. & G. 95; *Clements* v. *Eccles*, 11 Ir. Eq. Rep. 229; *Neale* v. *Day*, 7 W. R. (V. C. W.) 45; *Christy* v. *Courtenay*, 26 Beav. 140; *Penhall* v. *Elwin*, 1 Sm. & Giff. 258; *Acraman* v. *Corbett*, 1 J. & H. 410; *Elsey* v. *Cox*, 26 Beav. 95; *Thompson* v. *Webster*, 4 Drew. 628, 4 De G. & Jo. 600, 7 Jur. *N. S., Ho. [*285] Lo. 531; *Murphy* v. *Abraham*, 15 Ir. Ch. Rep. 371; *Graham* v. *O'Keeffe*, 16 Ir. Ch. Rep. 1; *Crossley* v. *Elworthy*, 12 L. R. Eq. 158; *Cornish* v. *Clarke*, 14 L. R. Eq. 184; or that after deducting the property which was the subject of the settlement, sufficient available assets were not left for payment of the settlor's debts (*Freeman* v. *Pope*, 5 L. R. Ch. App. 538, 641), a fortiori, if by putting everything into settlement, the effect was to render the settlor absolutely insolvent, and to deprive him of the means of paying his debts: *Smith* v. *Cherrill*, 4 L. R. Eq. 390, 396; *Freeman* v. *Pope*, 5 L. R. Ch. App. 538; 9 L. R. Eq.

206; because in such cases the intention to defeat, hinder, or delay creditors within the meaning of the statute, would necessarily be inferred. See the remarks in the last two cases on *Spirett* v. *Willows*, 3 De G. Jo. & Sm. 293.

A creditor under a voluntary post obit bond, is as much entitled to the benefit of the statute of 13 Eliz. c. 5, as any other creditor. Where, therefore, a testator having executed a voluntary post obit bond for securing an annuity of 100*l.* to his daughter-in-law for her life, afterwards made a voluntary settlement, from and after his decease, in favour of his widow and child, comprising all his property (except about 300*l.*), and before his death acquired only about 1000*l.* more, it was held by Sir G. M. Giffard, V.-C., that the settlement was void under the statute as against the bond creditor: *Adames* v. *Hallett*, 6 L. R. Eq. 468.

A creditor, however, may by his concurrence with or acquiescence in a deed voidable under 13 Eliz. c. 5, preclude himself and his representatives from impeaching such deed (*Olliver* v. *King*, 8 De G. Mac. & G. 110), especially if he has been a party with the donees to instruments and transactions proceeding on the assumption of its validity. *Ib.* And an inquiry may be directed whether any and which of the creditors of the settlor had acquiesced in a voluntary deed. *Freeman* v. *Pope*, 9 L. R. Eq. 212.

The statute of 13 Eliz. c. 5, extends to future as well as existing debts, and a deed having for its object to defraud future creditors is void under that statute: as for instance, where a person settles all his present and future property (*Ware* v. *Gardner*, 7 L. R. Eq. 317, 321), or all his property with some small exception; *Reese River Silver Mining Company* v. *Atwell*, 7 L. R. Eq. 347; *Barling* v. *Bishop*, 29 Beav. 417: especially when he is about to engage in trade; *Mackay* v. *Douglass*, 14 L. R. Eq. 106.

If there be a creditor whose debt was incurred subsequently to the voluntary deed, and there is also at the time of filing the bill an unpaid creditor whose debt was incurred prior to the deed, the subsequent creditor has exactly the same right to file a bill as the *prior creditor has: *Jenkyn* v. *Vaughan*, 3 Drew, 419; *Freeman* v *Pope*, 9 L. R. Eq. 206; 5 L. R. Ch. App. 538. [*286]

"But a subsequent creditor files a bill, and it can be shown that the person who executed the deed, though indebted at the time he made it, has since paid every debt, it is very difficult to say that he executed the settlement with an intention to defeat or delay creditors, since his subsequent payment shows that he had not such an intention." Per Kindersley, V.-C., in *Jenkyn* v. *Vaughan*, 3 Drew. 425. "An din the absence of actual intent to defeat creditors, a voluntary settlement made by a settlor in embarrassed circumstances, but having property, not included in the settlement, ample for the payment of the debts owing by him at the time of making it, may be supported against creditors, although debts due at the date of the settlement may to a considerable amount remain unpaid: *Kent* v. *Riley*, 14 L. R. Eq. 190."

It may be here mentioned that a purchaser from a volunteer under a deed void by the statute of 13 Eliz. c. 5, will be preferred to the general creditors of the settlor having no specific charge. *George* v. *Milbanke*, 9 Ves. 190.

A voluntary deed executed, pendente lite, for the purpose of defeating any process in the nature of execution, will be set aside in equity: *Blenkinsopp* v. *Blenkinsopp*, 12 Beav. 568, 1 De Gex, Mac. & G. 495, or where a man knows that a decision is about to be pronounced against him: *Barling* v. *Bishop*, 29 Beav. 417; *Reese River Silver Mining Company* v. *Atwell*, 7 L. R. Eq. 347.

Choses in action, having, since the 1 & 2 Vict. c. 110, become available for the payment of debts under an execution, are within the statute against fraudulent conveyances. See *Stokoe* v. *Cowan*, 29 Beav. 637, where an assignment of a policy on his life by a person in extremis was set aside as fraudulent against his creditors. See also *Law* v. *The Indisputable Life Policy Company*, 1 K. & J. 223; *Robson* v. *M'Creight*, 25 Beav. 272.

The statute 13 Eliz. c. 5, s. 3, enacts that every party to a fraudulent conveyance "shall incur the penalty and forfeiture of one year's value of the said land," "and the whole of the value of the said goods," and "also being thereof lawfully convicted, shall suffer imprisonment for one half-year without bail or mainprise;" and with respect to this enactment, it has been held that a defendant may refuse to answer interrogatories which would render him liable thereunder. *Wich* v. *Parker*, 22 Beav. 59.

In the recent case, however, of *Bunn* v. *Bunn*, 4 De G. Jo. & S. 316; 12 W. R. (L. J.) 561, where the defendants objected to make the usual affidavit as to documents, on the ground that the discovery would expose them to pains and penalties under the 13 Eliz. c. 5, the Lords Justices of the Court of Appeal, affirming the decision of Sir John Stuart, V.-C., held that the discovery must be made.

There is a similar clause in 27 Eliz. c. 4. See sect. 3.

The Bankruptcy Act, 1869, (32 & 33 Vict. c. 71, contains a clause [*287] more stringent in some respects *as against voluntary deeds executed by traders, than the statute of 13 Eliz. c. 5; it enacts that "Any settlement of property made by a trader not being a settlement made before and in consideration of marriage, or made in favour of a purchaser or incumbrancer in good faith and for valuable consideration, or a settlement made on or for the wife or children of the settlor, of property which has accrued to the settlor after marriage in right of his wife, shall, if the settlor becomes bankrupt within two years after the date of such settlement, be void as against the trustee of the bankrupt appointed under this act, and shall, if the settlor becomes bankrupt at any subsequent time within ten years after the date of such settlement, unless the parties claiming under such settlement can prove that the settlor was at the time of making the settlement able to pay all his debts without the aid of the property comprised in such settlement, be void as against such trustee . . . . 'Settlement' shall for the purposes of this section include any conveyance or transfer of property." Sect 91.

It seems that in order to enable a creditor of a living debtor to set aside a fraudulent conveyance under the 13 Eliz. c. 5, it is not necessary that the creditor should have any lien or charging order on the property comprised in the conveyance, but in the absence of such lien, the Court will not apply the property in satisfaction of the creditor's claim. *Reese Silver Mining Company* v. *Atwell*, 7 L. R. Eq. 347. It seems, also, that a bill to set aside such a conveyance ought to be filed on behalf of all the creditors of the debtor. *Ib.*

A voluntary settlement, though void as against creditors, subsists for all other purposes. Suppose, for instance, a man by a voluntary deed, void as against his creditors, conveys real estate for the benefit of his wife and children, and afterwards becomes bankrupt, any surplus of the estate so settled will be bound by the trusts of the settlement. *Ex parte Bell*, 1 G. & J. 282 ; *French* v. *French*, 6 De G. M. & G. 95.

So in *Smith* v. *Cherrill*, 4 L. R. Eq. 390, a lady being indebted to the plaintiff at the time of her marriage in the sum of 350*l*. settled all her real and personal property, (with the exception of jewels and furniture, exceeding in value the amount of her debt,) upon failure of issue of the marriage, in favour of certain collateral relatives, including a niece whom she had adopted as her daughter. The lady survived her husband, and died without issue, leaving no assets. It was held by Sir R. Malins, V. C., first that the consideration of marriage not extending to collaterals, the ulterior limitations to them upon the authority of *Johnson* v. *Legard*, *3 Madd. 283; and *Cotterell* v. *Homer*, [*288] 13 Sim. 506, were voluntary. Secondly, that so far only as the sum of 350*l*. was concerned, the settlement was void, and ought to be set aside, and the debt being a charge upon her property, ought, if necessary, to be raised with interest.

A Court of equity will not set aside a voluntary deed or agreement not obtained by fraud, by mistake, or against public policy, even if it be such as, according to the principles before laid down, it will not carry into effect. Equity stands neutral and invariably follows the rule thus quaintly laid down in an old case, " that if a man will improvidently bind himself up by a voluntary deed, and not reserve a liberty to himself by a power of revocation, a Court of equity will not loose the fetters he hath put upon himself, but he must lie down under his own folly :" *Villers* v. *Beaumont*, 1 Vern. 101; *Bill* v. *Cureton*, 2 My. &

K. 503; *Petre* v. *Espinasse*, 2 My. & K. 496; *Page* v. *Horne*, 9 Beav. 570; 11 Beav. 227; *M'Donnell* v. *Hesilrige*, 16 Beav. 346; *De Hough-ton* v. *Money*, 1 L. R. Eq. 154; 35 Beav. 98; 2 L. R. Ch. 164. And the rule is the same whether the interference of equity is invoked by the settlor himself, or through the medium of a person, not a purchaser for value, claiming only through the settlor: *Dolphin* v. *Aylward*, 6 L. R. Ho. Lo. 486.

As we have before seen, a deed for valuable consideration not carry-ing out the intention of the parties may be so modified and rectified as to carry them out. (See note to *Lord Glenorchy* v. *Bosville*, ante, p. 33.) But in the case of a voluntary executory gift this is impossible. The instrument is either good or bad; it cannot be modified to suit for-mer intentions, unless the donor consent to make a new and distinct instrument. *Phillipson* v. *Kerry*, 32 Beav. 628, 638. Secus it seems, if the trust be executed (*Thompson* v. *Whitmore*, 1 J. & H. 268), or if it be shown clearly after the settlor's death that the instrument was not prepared as he intended. *Lister* v. *Hodgson*, 4 L. R. Eq. 30, 34.

A person who receives a gift takes it subject to the conditions im-posed by the donor. *Seale* v. *Hayne*, 12 W. R. (V. C. S.) 239.

The principle is well established in this country, that an executory agreement, or an imperfect con-veyance, upon a merely voluntary consideration, will not be enforced or aided in equity; *Caldwell* v. *Williams*, 1 Bailey's Equity, 175, 176; *Crompton* v. *Vessee*, 19 Ala. 259; *Hayes* v. *Kershaw*, 1 Sand-ford's Ch. 258; *Reid* v. *Vanars-dale*, 2 Leigh, 560; *Evans* v. *Bat-tle*, 19 Alabama, 398; *Pinkard* v. *Pinkard*, 23 Id. 649; *Holland* v. *Hensley*, 4 Clarke, 222; and hence, a gift of real or personal estate will be void, unless so far executed as to pass the legal title, or attended with some peculiar circumstance which give rise to a special equity; *Pringle* v. *Pringle*, 9 P. F. Smith, 281. "It is a clear, general rule," said Chancellor Kent, in *Minturn* v. *Seymour*, 4 Johnson's Chancery, 98, 500, "that a bill does not lie to enforce a mere voluntary agree-ment. The language of the books, from the earliest to the latest cases, is uniform in support of the doc-trine, that a voluntary defective conveyance, which cannot operate at law, is not helped in equity, in favor of a volunteer, where there is no consideration, nor any acci-dent or fraud in the case. To en-title the party to the aid of this court, the instrument must be sup-ported by a valuable consideration, or, at least, by what a court of equity considers a meritorious con-sideration, as payment of debts, or making a provision for a wife or child." To the same effect is *Acker* v. *Phœnix*, 4 Paige, 305, 308. "Voluntary executory agree-ments," said Henderson, J., in *Dawson* v. *Dawson*, 1 Devereux, Equity, 93, 99, "receive no aid, either from courts of law or of equity. The parties stand upon their rights, such as they are, and hence it is a maxim, that defective voluntary agreements will not be aided in equity; any reformation of a conveyance being an execution of the original agreement, so far as the conveyance is varied. The same motive, which induces a court to refrain from enforcing an agreement, no part of which is executed, prevents it from enforcing any *part* of it. The want of a consideration is therefore universally a good defence to a bill for rectifying a voluntary conveyance, or enforcing a voluntary agreement." See also, *Banks* v. *May's Heirs et al.*, 3 Marshall, 435, 436; *Bibb* v. *Smith, &c.*, 1 Dana, 580, 582; *Darlington* v. *M'Coole*, 1 Leigh, 36, 42; *Tiernan* v. *Poor et ux.*, 1 Gill & Johnson, 217, 228; *Forward et al.* v. *Armstead*, 12 Alabama, 124, 127; *Shaw, Guardian, &c.* v. *Burney et al.*, 1 Iredell's Equity, 148, 150; *Pinkard* v. *Pinkard*, 14 Texas, 331; *Bozelius* v. *Dyer, post*, note to *Lester* v. *Foxcraft*.

That trusts when created and declared, though by a voluntary conveyance or settlement, will be sustained or enforced in equity, is equally well settled; *Wright* v. *Miller*, 4 Selden, 9; *Andrews v. Holson*, 23 Alabama, 219; *Greenfield's Estate*, 2 Harris, 489; *Riese* v. *Ruke*, 13 S. & R. 434; *Delamater's Estate*, 1 Wharton, 362; and it has been repeatedly held, that from the moment that such a conveyance is executed, the property vests in equity, in the *cestui que trust*, and cannot be taken away

from him, even by the concurrent action of the grantor and the trustee. In *Gault* v. *Trumbull*, 17 B. Monroe, 672; a provision in a deed, that the purchase-money should be paid to a grandson of the vendor, was said to be within this principle; and it was held, that he acquired a vested right to the money which the vendor could not defeat by releasing the vendee, or accepting a reconveyance. In *Bunn* v. *Winthrop*, 1 Johnson's Chancery, 329, a party made a voluntary settlement by deed on his mistress and her child, and retained the deed by him until his death; but the court held that as there was an actual creation of the trust and transfer of the interest, the transaction was valid in equity, although the grantor retained the instrument in his possession. "It will be sufficient," said Chancellor Kent, in delivering judgment, " on this subject of aiding voluntary agreements, to recur to the distinction declared by Lord Eldon, in *Ellison* v. *Ellison* (6 Ves. 662), as being one which reduces this point to something like established rule. If you want, according to that distinction, the assistance of chancery to raise an interest by way of trust, on a covenant, or executory agreement, you must have a valuable or meritorious consideration; for the court will not constitute you *cestui que trust*, when you are a mere volunteer, and the claim rests in covenant, as a covenant to transfer stock. But if the actual transfer be made, the equitable interest will be enforced; for the transfer constitutes the relation between trustee and *cestui que trust*, though voluntary and without consideration. To the same effect was the observation of Sir Joseph Jekyll, in *Lechmere* v. *Earl of Carlisle*, (3 P..Wms. 222,) that every *cestui que trust*, though a volunteer, and the limitation without consideration, was entitled to the aid of a court of equity." And this is approved in *Minturn* v. *Seymour*, 4 Id. 498, 500. See, however, *Perine* v. *Dunn*, 3 Id. 508, 517. The same principle is placed in a very clear light in the opinion of Gibson, C. J., in *Dennison* v. *Goehring*, 7 Barr, 175, 178. In that case, a conveyance had been made to a person who himself paid the purchase-money, but the trust was declared for his children; and it was held that the trust, though voluntary, was enforceable. "Equity," said the Chief Justice, "will not enforce a contract *to create* a trust, though it were under hand and seal; and in this respect it carries the doctrine of *nudum pactum* further than even the law does; but the difference between a covenant to create a trust, and a trust created, is as wide as the difference between a covenant to convey and a conveyance executed. It enforces no contract which does not rest on a valuable, or at least a meritorious consideration; but it enforces an executed contract with as much alacrity as the law would enforce it. The reason of the difference in regard to the effect of a seal is, that the interposition of a chancellor is matter of favor; but that

the interposition of a court of law, with whom a seal stands for a consideration, is matter of right. While a contract for a trust, therefore, is executory, the trust itself is held to be executory; and it stands on the footing of any other executory contract, in respect to which a chancellor is guided by his apprehension of the justice of the contract in applying or refusing his power to the execution of it; but when the legal estate has passed by a conveyance in which a trust is distinctly declared, the trustee will not be allowed to set up want of consideration to defeat it." In *Tolar* v. *Tolar*, 1 Devereux, Equity, 456, a voluntary deed to a child, had been destroyed by the donor before registration; and a court of equity compelled the grantor to convey the same property by another deed.—The application of this distinction is, certainly, in some cases, a matter of nicety; see *Dawson* v. *Dawson*, Id. 93; S. C. 396.

[It results from the same principle that the deposit of money in a bank for the use of a third person is a valid gift to him, if it appears from the evidence that the donor, though reserving a discretionary right to say in what way the money should be expended, intended the transfer to be irrevocable. So where A. gave B. $300, and took from him a written promise to repay the money to her, if it was called for, and if she did not demand it, then to pay it on her death to M., the transaction enured as a trust for M., which he might enforce if A. died without demanding the money; *Blanchard* v. *Sheldon*, 43 Vermont, 512.]

There can be no doubt, that, in this country, under a voluntary assignment for the benefit of creditors, although the assignee, before the creditors have assented to it, is rather the trustee of the debtor than of the creditors; *Brooks* v. *Marbury*, 11 Wheaton, 79, 87; yet the latter may claim the benefit of such an assignment, and may enforce it in equity, even if they are not parties to the conveyance, and had no knowledge of it at the time it was made. This was settled in *Moses* v. *Murgatroyd*, 1 Johnson's Chancery, 119, 129; *Shepherd* v. *M'Evers*, 4 Id. 136, 138; *Nicoll* v. *Mumford*, Id. 523, 529: and has been recognized and adopted in other states; *Ward et al.* v. *Lewis et al.*, 4 Pickering, 518, 523; *New Eng. Bank* v. *Lewis et al.*, 8 Id. 113, 118; *Pingree* v. *Comstock*, 18 Id. 46, 50, 51; *Ingram* v. *Kirkpatrick*, 6 Iredell, Equity, 463; *Stimpson* v. *Fries*, 1 Jones, Eq. 156. In *Weir and others* v. *Taneyhill and others*, 2 Yerger, 57. The complainants filed a bill setting forth that they were creditors of T., who had conveyed personal estate to trustees, to be distributed by them among his creditors, and that the trustees would not pay them, nor show them the trust deed, and they feared the parties to the deed would cancel it, or otherwise deprive the complainants of the benefit of it; and to this there was a demurrer. " It struck me at first," said Haywood, J., in delivering an opinion, that the de-

murrer should be overruled; "that as these complainants were not parties to the deed of assignment, and were not concluded by it, and might still sue the debtor and recover at law, and as they had acquired no lien on the estate, as judgment-creditors who had taken out execution, that therefore, they had no right to this fund, and that the trustee was answerable for a breach of trust only to the maker of the deed of assignment. But I am now satisfied from the authorities (from Johnson's Chancery Reports,) shown to me by the counsel, that those creditors have a lien upon the fund, though no parties to the deed." An assignment of this kind is not revocable after it has been communicated to the creditors: *Galt* v. *Dibrell*, 10 Id. 147, 158; and see *Robertson et als.* v. *Sublett et al.*, 6 Humphreys, 313, 316; nor, as it would seem, after it has been delivered or placed on record for their benefit; *Wilt* v. *Franklin*, 1 Binney, 502; *Stimpson* v. *Fries*, 1 Jones, Eq. 156; unless they are shown to have dissented; assent being, in general, presumed to be that which confers a benefit; *M'Kinney* v. *Rhoads*, 5 Watts, 343. In *Read* v. *Robinson*, 6 W. & S. 329, executed an assignment for the benefit of his creditors, and sent it by a messenger to the grantee, who refused to accept the instrument. It was held that the beneficial interest vested in the creditors immediately on the execution of the instrument, and that equity would not suffer the trust to be frustrated by the dissent of the trustee. The subject is ex-

amined with some care by Johnston, Ch., in *Tennant* v. *Stoney*, 1
Richardson's Equity, 223, 253, and
a view taken of the English cases
which appears to be satisfactory.
" It is impossible," said the Chancellor there, " to put a deed, made
with the motive of securing creditors, upon precisely the same footing with one creating a trust for
pure volunteers. But taking them
as such, the case of *Ellison* v.
Ellison sustains the position, that
wherever the instrument effectually
constitutes a trust, even for volunteers, they may enforce it. The
same doctrine was held by the
same great Chancellor in *Pulvertorft* v. *Pulvertorft*. . . . The
difficulty, in subsequent cases, has
been to discover upon what principles, consistent with his own decisions in *Ellison* v. *Ellison*, and
Pulvertorft v. *Pulvertorft*, the
authority of which has been con-
stantly acknowledged, Lord Eldon
could have rested his judgment (in
Walwyn v. *Coutts*). Sir Lancelot
Shadwell, in commenting upon it
in *Garrard* v. *Lauderdale*, supposes that the principle of the case
is, that where a debtor, for his own
convenience, makes a disposition
between himself and a third person,
constituting him trustee as between
themselves for the payment of his
debts, and this without concert
with or notice to his creditors, he
may countermand it. Lord Brougham, before whom the last mentioned case afterwards came, says
of the instrument in *Walwyn* v.
Coutts, that it was not so much a
conveyance, vesting a trust in A.
for the benefit of the creditors of

the grantor, but rather an arrangement made by a debtor for his own
personal convenience and accommodation, (for the payment of his
own debts, in an order prescribed
by himself,) over which he retains
power and control. Upon these
views the authority of *Walwyn* v.
Coutts was sustained in *Garrard*
v. *Lauderdale;* and upon the same
principle the latter case was also
itself decided. It will be seen at
once, that the application of the
principle depends upon the construction of the instrument, and
the intention with which it was
executed. If it appear that the
trustee was not intended to be the
trustee of the creditors, but of the
grantor, his mere agent, and that
the conveyance was executed simply with a view to enable him to
perform the acts directed, these
cases say the deed is revocable;
though it is not clear that it could
be revoked after the transaction
has come to the knowledge of the
creditors, and against their wish,
expressed before the revocation.
This is the interpretation put upon
these cases, by Sir C. Pepys, in
Bill v. *Cureton*. . . . I have
thus brought together the two decisions of Lord Eldon, in which
the rule is firmly laid down on the
one hand, and the cases, one of
them decided by himself, which
have been supposed to oppose it
on the other, and I have shown
that the rule was not intended to
be shaken by these cases." See
also the view taken of *Walwyn* v.
Coutts, and *Garrard* v. *Lauderdale*, in *Cunningham* v. *Free-
born*, 3 Paige, 557, 560. (See 1

American Leading Cases, 72, 5th ed.)

It is stated in the preceding note of the English editor, that "a merely meritorious consideration, as a provision for a wife or children, after marriage, will not be a sufficient inducement for a court of equity to lend its aid in enforcing a voluntary agreement or covenant, or in giving effect to an imperfect gift." But this is believed to be a hasty inference from the decisions there referred to, and not to be entirely correct. The state of the authorities on the subject, is thus: In *Ellis* v. *Nimmo*, Lloyd & Goold, t. Sugden, 333, Lord Chancellor Sugden, after a careful review of the authorities, decided that the meritorious consideration of providing for a child, was sufficient to lead to the enforcement, in equity, of an executory contract, as against the person contracting. At the end of the case, p. 349, the reporter adds, " The decree in this case was affirmed by Lord Plunket on rehearing, but upon other grounds." *Holloway* v. *Headington*, 8 Simon, 324, was wholly unlike this case, and went upon other grounds, but it contains the following remark by Vice-Chancellor Shadwell: " However high the authority may be of the Lord Chancellor who decided *Ellis* v. *Nimmo*, that cause was reheard by his successor, who rejected the grounds of the former decision and decided in the same way, but on different grounds. Therefore, there is the authority of one Lord Chancellor in its favor, and the authority of another Lord Chancellor against it. Consequently, it is not a decision that binds." But this is obviously an extreme and inaccurate statement of the Vice-Chancellor. The mere fact that Lord Plunket, on a rehearing, affirmed the decree on other grounds than those on which Sir Edward Sugden had placed it, affords no inference that Lord Plunket's authority was thereby given against the principle which Sir Edward Sugden had established. This supposed rejection by Lord Plunket, and this mistaken observation in *Holloway* v. *Headington*, may, therefore, be set aside as not in the least degree impairing the force of the well-considered and direct decision of Lord Chancellor Sugden. The next case is *Dillon* v. *Coppin*, 4 Mylne & Craig, 646, 671, before Lord Cottenham. There, a father had executed a deed, imperfectly assigning certain shares of stock for the benefit of his daughter, but had retained the deed in his possession during his life, and had indorsed upon an envelope on the deed that it was to be given to his daughter at his death. Now, the difficulty in the way of enforcing this settlement, was the same as in *Antrobus* v. *Smith*, 12 Ves. 39 ; that the case did not show an absolute intention or agreement of the parent to make the transfer. It was an imperfect transfer, but under circumstances which did not indicate an attempt or design to make a present transfer, and which, therefore, equity could not turn into a contract to transfer. " It is not necessary," said the Lord Chancellor, "to look further than the case of *Antrobus* v. *Smith*. There, the gift was in favor of a child, but it was voluntary and imperfect, and *the instrument was found in the father's possession*. I believe that case to have been well decided, and nothing which has since occurred affords any reason for departing from the principle upon which it is founded. It is also to be observed in this case, that the envelope proves that the father did not intend that the instrument should operate till after his death, though it professes to be an immediate assignment: it is not, therefore, to be presumed that he even parted with the possession of it." It must be observed, also, that this case was between one child and other children of the same testator, so that the meritorious consideration operated on both sides, and was evenly balanced. Lord Cottenham must have conceived that he was not overruling *Ellis* v. *Nimmo*, for he does not allude to that decision, in delivering judgment. Moreover he expresses his entire approbation of *Ellison* v. *Ellison*, and *Pulvertoft* v. *Pulvertoft*, in both of which Lord Eldon recognizes, or inclines to recognize, the principle, that equity will give aid in the case of a meritorious consideration in favor of a wife or child. The remaining case is *Jefferys* v. *Jefferys*, 1 Craig & Phillips, 138, 141, where a father had covenanted to surrender certain copyholds to the use of his daughter, and had afterwards devised a part of them to his wife, who, after his death,

was admitted. This bill was brought by the daughters to have the settlement decreed against the widow. "I have no doubt," said Lord Cottenham, "that the court will not execute a voluntary contract, and my impression is, that the principle of the court to withhold its assistance from a volunteer applies equally, whether he seeks to have the benefit of a contract, a covenant, or a settlement. As, however, the decision in *Ellis* v. *Nimmo* is entitled to the highest consideration, I will not dispose of this case absolutely, without looking at a former case, in which I had occasion to refer to that decision." On another day, he said that he had looked at the case alluded to, (*Dillon* v. *Coppin*,) and that he saw no reason for altering the opinion he had before expressed. Now, here, the case was between two classes equally meritorious in respect to consideration; daughters on one hand, and a widow on the other. The case of *Ellis* v. *Nimmo*, was between a daughter and the father who made the contract. Considering then, that the direct decision of Lord Chancellor Sugden stands supported by Lord Eldon's recognition of the same principle, and not opposed by any decision whatever, it may be stated as the result of the English authorities, that equity will aid a defective transfer which was intended and meant to be a complete present transfer, and probably will enforce an executory agreement, upon the inducement of a meritorious consideration, that is to say, in favor of a wife or child, and against one not standing in one of those relations, such as a brother, or other collateral connection, or against the person himself contracting: but it will not interfere between persons standing upon the same meritorious consideration, that is, being the children, or children and widow, of the person whose estate is in question: *Holland* v. *Hensley*, 4 Clarke, 222. The former part of this rule may be considered as established by *Ellis* v. *Nimmo;* and the latter part is the just result of *Jefferys* v. *Jefferys*.

In this country, it may be considered as the prevailing, and probably the settled, doctrine, that a provision for a wife or child is a sufficient meritorious consideration to lead to the enforcement of an executory agreement or trust, at least where the instrument is under seal; *Shepherd* v. *Bowie*, 4 Maryland, Ch. 133; 9 Gill, 32; *Harris* v. *Haines*, 6 Maryland, 435. This point was decided in *M'Intire* v. *Hughes*, 4 Bibb. 186, in the case of an agreement under seal by a father to convey land to his son; and in that State, (Kentucky,) since a statute has placed sealed and unsealed instruments of an executory character upon the same footing, the same principle has been established in relation to agreements not under seal; *Mahan, &c.* v. *Mahan*, 7 B. Monroe, 579, 582. See, also, *Bright's Ex'rs* v. *Bright*, 8 Id. 194, 197. In *Dennison* v. *Goehring*, 7 Barr, 175, 179, it was thought that an executory agreement to create a trust in favor of the children of the grantor, was upon a consideration that would be recognized in equity as against the grantee. " Natural affection," said Gibson, C. J., in that case, " though not a valuable, is a meritorious consideration ; on the foot of which, an agreement by a father to secure a provision for his child has been enforced in equity, by reason of the obligation of parents to provide for their offspring. Thus, a covenant with a son to renew a lease, was enforced in *Husband* v. *Pollard*, cited 2 P. W. 467 ; and in *Goring* v *Nash*, 3 Atk. 186, a father's covenant to settle an estate on his son was specifically decreed. In such a case, a legitimate child is not held to be a volunteer, though it was held in *Fursaker* v. *Robinson*, Prec. in Chan. 475, that a bastard is so. In corroboration of the principle, may be mentioned those cases in which equity has supplied the surrender of a copyhold, and a defective execution of a power in favor of a legitimate child."

But this principle of a meritorious consideration reaches only to the cases of a wife and a child; it does not extend to any collateral kin, nor, probably, to a descendant more remote than a child. In *Buford's Heirs* v. *M'Kee, &c.*, 1 Dana, 107, a bill was filed to have specific performance of a voluntary covenant by an uncle to convey land to his nephew ; but it was dismissed for want of a sufficient equitable consideration. " In exercising the discretion, which a chancellor retains to himself, over applications for the specific performance of contracts," said the court in that case, "it has always been deemed an essential pre-requisite, that the contract he is called upon thus to enforce, should be based upon, either a valuable, or what is termed a meritorious consideration. The moral obligation to provide for a wife or a child, constitutes such a meritorious consideration as will induce a specific performance of an agreement in their favor, and some of the cases have declared, that grandchildren come within the rule; but we have been able to find no authoritative case where a voluntary agreement has been specifically enforced in favor of a collateral relation, such as a nephew, unless there was some other controlling circumstance besides the mere affinity. The cases where relief has been extended in favor of collaterals, either expressly recognize the doctrine, that some additional circumstance is necessary to call forth the interposition of the chancellor in their behalf, or by the stress laid upon such additional and controlling circumstance, indicate clearly that such is the rule of the court. . . . In an analogous class of cases, it seems to be well established, that a defective surrender will be supplied only in favor of three descriptions of persons, viz., creditors, wife, and children." In *Hayes* v. *Kershaw*, 1 Sandford, Ch. 258, also, it was decided that a covenant for a future conveyance, without a valuable consideration, in favor of the issue of a nephew and niece, could not be enforced in equity. "In the exercise of the discretion which courts of equity still have in decreeing specific performance of agreements," said the Assistant Vice Chancellor, "they uniformly decline to enforce voluntary covenants. . . . Covenants and agreements founded upon a good consideration, or as oftentimes expressed, on a *meritorious* consideration, are, however, upheld and enforced specifically in this court. And it has been a mooted question whether collateral consanguinity, as that of a brother, nephew, niece, &c., was not a meritorious consideration. I think it is now settled upon authority that it is not. . . . In the case before me, there was no moral obligation to provide for a wife and children, or a parent; and there was therefore no such good or meritorious consideration, as will induce this court to decree the performance of the covenant in the sealed instrument in question."

[This distinction is of comparatively recent growth; and it was long the established rule in chancery to enforce a covenant to stand seised to the use of any one who was connected with the donor by blood or marriage. By a singular anomaly this rule now prevails at law, and a grant to a relative, however remote, in consideration of natural love and affection, raises a use which the statue executes. And it seems that a voluntary grant will be enforced in Pennsylvania in favor of a grandchild wherever it would be valid if made to a child. The observation of Chancellor Kent, in *Bunn* v. *Winthrop*, 1 Johnson's Ch. 329, 337, that the duty of providing for a mistress and illegitimate child formed a consideration, must be understood of the case then before the court, and as meaning a consideration to support an executed trust.]

It seems, also, that, in the case of an executory agreement, equity will not decree a specific performance, even in favor of a wife or child, where there is not a valuable consideration, unless the instrument is under seal; *Kennedy* v. *Ware*, 1 Barr, 445. The doctrine appears to be, that there must exist a valid and obligatory contract at law, as a preliminary basis to any equitable interference, and then that equity grants its extraordinary aid only where there is an actual consideration, valuable or meritorious. In *M'Intyre* v. *Hughes*, 4 Bibb, 186, 188, the court said, "Whether, if the contract was not by deed, a court of equity would, where there was no other consideration than that of blood, decree its specific execution, is not material to be decided; nor is the court to be understood as having given any opinion upon that point." But, as before remarked, since the distinction in executory agreements between sealed and unsealed has been abolished, unsealed agreements, where the consideration appears in the agreement, will be enforced; *Mahan, &c.* v. *Mahan*, 7 B. Monroe, 579. In *Caldwell* v. *Williams*, 1 Bailey's Equity, 175, 176, it is declared, that although some agreements which are termed voluntary, are executed by a court of equity, when made in favor of a

wife or children, yet this is only where the agreement is under seal, which imports a consideration and renders it valid at law; and that there is no instance of an agreement being enforced, which is not only voluntary in the equity sense of the word, but is also *nudum pactum* at law. See, also, *Pennington, Adm'r of Patterson*, v. *Gitting's Ex'or*, 2 Gill & Johnson, 209, 218; *post*, vol. 2, note to *Row* v. *Dawson*.

[It is proper to observe that as marriage is a valuable consideration, equity will enforce a gift made in contemplation of, and followed by marriage; *Duval* v. *Getting*, Gill, 38; *Gough* v. *Crane*, 3 Maryland Ch. 119; 4 Id. 316; and the same course will be pursued where a gift of land, which fails to pass the legal title, is followed by expenditures induced by and made on the faith of the gift; *post*, notes to *Lester* v. *Foxcroft*. In regard to the subject of voluntary conveyances, as against creditors and purchasers, and the subject of assignments for the benefit of creditors, see the notes to *Sexton* v. *Wheaton*, and *Thomas* v. *Jenks*, in 1 American Leading Cases, 37, 71, 5th ed.

The view taken above, was cited and followed in *Jones* v. *Obenchain*, 10 Grattan, 259; where it was said that equity will lend its aid to support a transfer which has its origin in a desire to provide for a man's wife or children, and is consequently founded upon a meritorious consideration. In this case, however, the gift was as complete as the grantor could make it, a deed having been executed, which would have passed the estate but for the technical rule which forbids a conveyance by a husband to his wife; and the court expressed no opinion as to what the result would have been, had the instrument been executory; had there been a want of a meritorious consideration; or in the absence of a seal.

Chancery held a seal unnecessary to raise a use in land where value was given, and esteemed blood or an antecedent marriage insufficient without a seal; *Denison* v. *Goehring*, 7 Barr, 175; 2 Am. Lead. Cases, 168, 5th ed.; Williams on Real Property, 150: although any tie of blood, however remote, might give force and effect to a covenant to stand seised; Cornish on Uses, 65: Sheppard's Touchstone, 512. A similar view has been taken in some instances, with regard to the equitable assignment of *choses in action*, and a seal held essential, unless the consideration is valuable; *Cox* v. *Sprigg; Kennedy* v. *Ware*, 1 Barr, 445. But the modern decisions tend to qualify and enlarge the ancient doctrine, by holding that a seal may be dispensed with, where the consideration is meritorious, and that blood will not operate as a meritorious consideration, unless it flows in the veins of the donor's children, or at furthest of his grand-children or other direct descendants, *ante; Hayes* v. *Kershaw*, 1 Sandford's Ch. 258; while the English authorities take the ground, that the consideration for an agreement to assign, must be valuable, and

not merely good, although an executed gift or transfer may be upheld in equity, notwithstanding its insufficiency to pass the title at law, *ante*, 401, 412. An attempt to reconcile the cases on this point, *ante*, 408, would obviously be fruitless; but common sense would seem to indicate, that if chancery will interfere to sustain gifts of *choses in action* in any case in the absence of a consideration, it should do so whenever the intention to make a present gift is plain, without regard to the period at which the right will vest in possession, and whether the gift is put in the form of a declaration of trust or of an assignment, *Boyle* v. *Hughes; ante, Henderson* v. *Henderson*, 21 Missouri, 379, 384; *Gilchrist* v. *Stevenson*, 9 Barbour, 9. To say, as did the Vice-Chancellor, in *Searle* v. *Law, ante*, 401, that an assignment of a *chose in action* in trust was void, although a declaration of trust would have been valid, is to fetter the course of equity by a technical distinction. If, as may well be the case, justice and right require that the owner of a debt should have the power of bestowing it on any one whom he desires to aid or favor, the inquiry should be, has he done enough to manifest his intention? and if this question is answered affirmatively, equity should sustain the gift.

What evidence of intention should be deemed requisite and sufficient, is not easy to determine; but we may doubt whether a chancellor should be satisfied with any thing short of a transfer of the legal title, when such a transfer is feasible; the mode which the law has provided for making a grant, being, as it would seem, the only one which should be recognized by equity when the question is whether a grant has been made, and not whether there is an obligation to make it. Thus, the most express words of gift would, probably, be held insufficient to confer an interest in land, in the absence of a consideration, unless the proper and usual means were taken to pass the title; and the same rule should, seemingly, be applied to stocks, promissory notes, and other securities which are in their nature negotiable, and, therefore, susceptible of being transferred at law, without the aid of equity *Pennington* v. *Getting*, 2 Gill & Johnson, 688. When, however, the law neither prescribes nor provides the means of giving, as in the case of debts not negotiable, equity may well supply the want of a power, which every man should have over his property, of whatever kind.

Although a voluntary covenant to give or settle a chose in action will not be specifically enforced, it is a good cause of suit, and the whole value of the property may be recovered as damages; *Mark's Appeal*, 18 P. F. Smith, 231 ; *Yard* v. *Patton*, 1 Harris, 279, 285.

By a curious anomaly, if the donor uses words of gift instead of covenanting to give, the transfer will fail at law, but may be enforced in equity as a declaration of trust, *ante*, 402. Whether a debt can be assigned without a consideration by a writing not under seal, is a dis-

puted question, which was decided in the affirmative in *Morgan* v. *Millison*, 10 L. R. Eq. 475, and negatively in *Kennedy* v. *Ware*, 1 Barr, 445 ; see *Hatch* v. *Davis*, 3 Maryland, Ch. 266. There is little doubt that such a gift may be effectual, if executed by the delivery of the note, bond or other security which represents the debt; *Crump's Appeal*, 36 Conn. 88 ; *Cox* v. *Sprigg*, 6 Maryland, 274. But a parol promise to give is invalid in both jurisdictions, although reduced to writing, if not upheld by a consideration. See *Carpenter* v. *Dodge*, 20 Vermont, 425 : *Henderson* v. *Henderson*, 20 Missouri, 379, 384.

There can be no doubt that the delivery of chattels or securities for the use of a third person, may vest the beneficial interest in the latter, but it is not always easy to determine whether the intermediary is a trustee for the beneficiary, or the donor's agent or bailee. The delivery of a note to one man, with instructions to collect it and apply the proceeds for the benefit of another, has been held to confer a mere authority, which will not operate as a gift until executed, and may be revoked at any moment before final execution ; *Thomson* v. *Dorsey*, 4 Maryland, Ch. 149 ; but the assignment of a mortgage by a writing duly indorsed, in trust for the children of the assignee, accompanied by a delivery of the instrument, will operate as an irrevocable gift, which cannot be annulled by a re-delivery to the assignor without the consent of the children ; *Gilchrist* v. *Stevenson*, 9 Barbour,

9. In *Withers* v. *Weaver*, 10 Barr, 391, however, the effect of a delivery of a certificate of deposit to a third person, in trust for the donor's son, was held to be invalidated by a cotemporaneous declaration, that if the donor wanted money at any time, the trustee should pay him what he required, and deduct the amount, after his death, in settling with his son; and the court would seem to have thought that a gift cannot be valid, unless the thing given is handed over directly to the donee, or, to some one who receives it as his agent, free from the control and authority of the donor.

The question when equity will intervene on behalf of a volunteer to sustain a grant or trust, is one of the most perplexing in jurisprudence. This is due in a great measure to the inherent difficulty of the subject. In general, instruments will be so construed as to give effect to the intention of the parties. But the clearest manifestation of intention will not supply the want of the forms which the law requires. It is not universally, or even generally true, that one can give by simply declaring that such is his design. The most explicit words of gift will not pass the title to land, unless the estate lies in grant, nor without a seal. So, delivery is essential to a gift of chattels. Equity follows the law unless there is a sufficient reason for departing from it. It is only where there are no appropriate legal means of conveyance that a chancellor will intervene to support a gratuitous transfer. A chose in action is an instance of this kind, and another may exist where property is held in trust. There the *cestui que trust* cannot convey the legal estate, and may consequently be entitled to make an equitable transfer; *Turner* v. *Wood*, 19 Beavan, 330, *ante*, 401. Where real estate is conveyed, with an express or implied agreement that it shall be held for the use of a third person, equity will fasten a trust on the conscience of the grantee. The trust arises from the breach of confidence on the part of the grantee, and a declaration of it in writing and under his hand, is evidence which he will not be permitted to contravene. But a declaration that one holds his land in trust for a volunteer to whom he is under no obligation, is as inefficacious in equity as it is at law. Such an instrument may be prima facie evidence but it will not confer a right where none existed previously, unless it is under seal and so worded as to operate as a grant or covenant to stand seised. And such is also the rule in the case of personal property, unless the transaction operates as a gift. See *Read* v. *Robinson*, 6 W. & S. 329.

The question may be considered under two heads: one, where the instrument purports to confer a present interest; the other, where it is a mere promise to convey. The first head admits of subdivision. The title to be affected with the trust may pass from the donor, or may remain in him; *Read* v. *Robinson*, 6 W. & S. 329,

331. It is well settled that a grant to one in trust for another will vest the beneficial interest in the latter, although he be a mere volunteer. This was established at an early period with regard to land, and is equally true of personalty; *Stone* v. *Hackett*, 12 Gray, 247. The transfer of the title is a sufficient consideration for the trust, and it would obviously be inequitable to permit the grantee to withhold the estate from him for whose benefit it was given, *ante*, 387. The same principle was laid down in *Dennison* v. *Goehring*, 7 Barr, 175. Such a trust may be enforced, although the grantee is a purchaser, and the *cestui que trust* a mere volunteer, because it may well be that the grantor would not have parted with the right of property on any other terms; 2 Smith's Leading Cases, 476 7 Am. ed. A bargain and sale to A. in trust for B. will consequently vest the beneficial interest in the latter; *Dennison* v. *Goehring*, *Sprague* v. *Woods*, 4 W. & S. 192. In *Sprague* v. *Woods* the trust was for the children of the bargainee, but it might equally well have been declared in favor of a stranger; *Stearns* v. *Palmer*, 10 Metcalf, 32. In like manner the actual or constructive delivery of personal property in trust for a volunteer, will give rise to an obligation to him which chancery will enforce; *ante*, *Stone* v. *Hacket*, 12 Gray, 227; *Blanchard* v. *Sheldon*, 34 Vermont, 512. It is certainly true, said Bigelow, J., in *Stone* v. *Hacket*, that a court of equity will lend no assistance towards perfecting a

voluntary contract or agreement for the creation of a trust, nor regard it as binding so long as it remains executory. But it is equally true that if such an agreement or contract be executed by a conveyance of property in trust, so that nothing remains to be done by the grantor or donor to complete the transfer or title, the relation of trustee and *cestui que trust* is deemed to be established, and the equitable rights and interests arising out of the conveyance, though made without consideration, will be enforced in chancery. The principle was declared by Lord Eldon, in the leading case of *Ellison* v. *Ellison*, and is sustained by the subsequent course of decision." The delivery of a certificate of stock with a blank assignment endorsed thereon, for the following purposes and uses declared in writing by the recipient, " to pay the income to the donor for life, and at his death to transfer the stock to the M'Lean Asylum, the donor reserving the right to modify the uses or revoke the gift," was accordingly held to create a valid trust, which would be upheld in equity against the donor's widow. It results from the same principle that a deposit in bank for the use of a third person may give rise to a valid trust; and it does not necessarily vary the case, that the donor reserves the right to control and supervise the expenditure of the fund; *Gardner* v. *Merrett*, 32 Maryland, 78. So, a gift in trust may be valid notwithstanding a power of revocation. In *Blanchard* v.

Sheldon, 43 Vermont, 512, Aurilla Ballou delivered $300 to Henry L. Sheldon, and took the following writing: "For value received, I promise to pay Aurilla Ballou the sum of $300 with annual interest, on demand, if she calls for it before she dies, if not to be paid to Daniel M. Blanchard by her order. (Signed) HENRY L. SHELDON." It was held that this was a gift to Blanchard, subject to the contingency of the donor's calling for it before her death.

The case is essentially different where the legal title remains in the donor. Under these circumstances the gift is incomplete, and it was held at one period that a chancellor should not intervene on behalf of a volunteer, *ante*, 420, *Kennedy* v. *Ware*, 1 Barr, 445; but it is now established that if the donor has done all that is in his power to complete the transfer, it will be carried into effect by equity, *ante*, 401. A husband cannot contract with his wife; *Benedict* v. *Montgomery*, 7 W. & S. 242; *McKeenan* v. *Phillips*, 6 Wharton, 571; nor can he execute any conveyance to her that will be valid; *Sheppard* v. *Sheppard*, 7 Johnson's Ch. 60; *Stickney* v. *Borman*, 2 Barr, 66. If, however, the deed be executed with the meritorious purpose of providing for the wife, and does not exceed a just proportion of his estate, it will be upheld as a post nuptial settlement, notwithstanding the want of a trustee; *Lobourette* v. *Williams*, 1 Barb. 9; *Nevfille* v. *Thompson*, 3 Edwards, 92; *Ker* v. *Vasser*, 2 Iredell, Ch. 553; *Stanwood* v. *Stanwood*, 7 Mass. 57; *Phillips* v. *Phillips*, 20 Pick. 536.

It was said in *Huntly* v. *Huntly*, 8 Iredell, Eq., that although such a deed did not pass the title, it amounted to a declaration of trust. But as specific performance is discretionary, such a gift will not be sustained if it is excessive or inequitable; *Benedict* v. *Montgomery; Halloway* v. *Headington*, 8 Simons, 324; nor if there is reason to suppose that it was made with a fraudulent design; *Stickney* v. *Borman*. It is well settled that the parties to a corrupt or dishonest transaction have no standing in a court of justice, which will neither lend its aid to enforce the contract while executory, nor to set it aside when executed. In *Stickney* v. *Borman*, relief was accordingly refused to the wife's assignee, on the ground that the object of the conveyance was to hinder and delay the husband's creditors. Where, however, the wife agreed to live separate and apart from her husband, in consideration of an annuity from him, the court held, that although equity would not have intervened to enforce the contract, the money actually paid under it became hers, and could not be recovered back by the husband from one, to whom she had given it as a *donatio causa mortis; M'Kenan* v. *Phillips*, 6 Wharton, 571.

The maxim " *nemo allegans turpidetudenem suem audiendus est*" precludes a party from impeaching his contract as fraudulent on grounds which do not appear in the instrument, unless such proof is requisite for the protection of a third person who is injured by the fraud, or when the contract cannot be enforced consistently with the common or statute law. *Montefiore* v. *Montefiore*, 1 W. Blackstone, 364; *Shirk* v. *Endress*, 3 W. & S. 256; *Hubert* v. *Murphy*, 10 Barr, 58. True policy requires that a fraudulent grantor or obligor should not escape from the natural and legal consequences of his act on the ground that the instrument is voluntary, or subject to a resulting trust; *Murphy* v. *Hubert*, 1 Smith's Lead. Cases, 708, 7 Am. ed. It has, notwithstanding, been decided in Massachusetts, that the maker of a note or other parol contract in fraud of creditors, may rely on the want of consideration as a defence; *Weaver* v. *Pierce*, 24 Pick. 14. In every such case the court should look beyond the parties, and consider what course will tend most effectually to prevent a repetition of the fraud, and there can be little doubt that this end is best attained by refusing to extricate the fraudulent debtor from the toils which he has set for his creditors.

In like manner, equity will not allow a trust to fail in consequence of the dissent or renunciation of the trustee. In *Read* v. *Robinson*, 6 W. & S. 329, an assignment for the benefit of creditors was accordingly sustained, although the assignees had refused to accept the deed when tendered.

The difficulty arose in these instances from the dissent or incapacity of the grantee, but the principle is the same where the transfer fails from the nature of the subject-matter. It is accordingly established, that a gift of a *chose in action* may be sustained or enforced by a chancellor. The equity grows out of two considerations: first, that the owner of property should have the power of disposing of it as he thinks fit; and next, that where a *chose in action* is in question, the law does not afford the means of carrying his purpose into effect—reasons which apply equally—whether the assignment is for value, or gratuitous—for the benefit of a wife or child, or to one who is not connected with the donor by blood or marriage.

The courts were, notwithstanding, slow in reaching this conclusion, and it was long held, that when the legal title did not pass, equity would not intervene in favor of one who had not given value, *ante*, 400; see *Voyle* v. *Hughes*, 2 Smale & Giffard, 18. The question arose, and was decided in *Kennedy* v. *Ware*, 1 Barr, 445. Kennedy assigned a judgment gratuitously to Ware, the object being to advance his daughter, who was Ware's wife. Gibson, Ch. J., said that "consanguinity would sustain a covenant to stand seised, but it was not a consideration for a parol contract, even when coupled with the duty of providing for one's offspring. Lord Mansfield's doctrine in *Hawkes* v. *Saunders*, Cowper, 289, and *Freeman* v. *Fenton*, Ib. 544, that a promise might be upheld by a moral obligation, had been narrowed, if not overthrown, by the subsequent course of decision. (See 2 Am. Lead. Cases, 190, 5 ed.) What gave validity to an equitable assignment, was the implied agreement that the assignee might sue in the assignor's name. It was, therefore, executory, and would fail unless value was given in some form for its support." The case of *Pennington* v. *Getting*, 2 Gill & Johnson, turns on the same principle, and that of *Cox* v. *Sprigg*, 6 Maryland, 286 may be cited as looking in the same direc- ton, although the reasons assigned are not clear or precise.

So in *Meek* v. *Kettlewell*, 1 Hare, 474, *ante*, 407, the Vice Chancellor was clearly of opinion, that an as- signment under seal of that which does not pass at law by the opera- tion of the assignment itself, unac- companied by other acts, is no bet- ter than a covenant or agreement to assign. It was by treating a deed which failed of effect as a cove- nant, that chancery was enabled to give relief through a decree for specific performance. (See *Chew* v. *Barnett*, 11 S. & R. 389 ; *Baylis* v. *The Commonwealth*, 4 Wright, 37.) Hence it followed, that where the grantor receives no considera- tion, and the obligation is merely gratuitous, the grantee should be left to find such remedy as he can at law.

This course of decision seems to have been well founded in the peculiar doctrines of equity and the relation which they bear to the common law, *ante*, 286. It can hardly be vindicated on the broad principles of jurisprudence. It is a general rule, that one who owns shall have the power to dispose.

The *jus disponendi* should not be withheld except for some sufficient cause, and on special grounds. What, if anything, the grantor re- ceives as an equivalent, concerns him, and not society at large. The right to give is consequently as clearly incident to the right of property as the right to sell. *Choses in action* are as much within the scope of this principle as lands or chattels ; and yet as they cannot be legally assigned, the refusal of equity to aid volun- tary transfers rendered it imprac- ticable to give a *chose in action*. The effect was to impose an arbi- trary restraint on alienation, which was not unfrequently attended with injurious consequences. A large amount of property is locked up at the present day, in bonds, stocks, and other evidences of debt. A capitalist might count his wealth in these by thousands, and yet find it difficult to provide for a friend or relative. It was easy to give a house or chattel, but if he attempted to bestow a debt, there was an unexpected obstacle. A demand might be sold, or pledged, or released, but it could not be the subject of a voluntary transfer. If the donor was versed in the law, he might obviate the difficulty by collecting the money, and invest- ing it in the name of the benefi- ciary. But this required time and more knowledge than is ordinarily possessed. It was, moreover, im- practicable, where, as in the case of a policy of insurance, the debt was contingent and payable at a future day.

The evil was so obvious, that

there was a constant effort to escape from it. A *chose in action* could not be assigned without a valuable consideration, but where a trust existed, it might be enforced, though in favor of a volunteer. Hence an inference, that where a man declared that he held assets which belonged to him in trust for a volunteer, it was a valid gift. If, said Lord Cranworth, " I say expressly or impliedly that I constitute myself a trustee of personalty; that is, a trust executed and capable of being enforced without consideration;" and the doctrine was applied in numerous instances to *choses in action, ante,* 396.

It is not easy to find any sufficient ground for this distinction.

It was established at an early period, that the transfer of the legal title in trust for a third person, would vest the beneficial interest in the latter. Such was the origin of uses, and subsequently of trusts. A declaration of trust under these circumstances, substantiates the existence of a duty which would be obligatory independently of the declaration. But it does not follow, that an admission can give rise to a fiduciary obligation where none exists. " The ordinary power of a chancellor," said Gibson, C. J., in *Read* v. *Robinson,* 6 W. & S. 329, " extends no further than the execution of a trust sufficiently framed to put the title out of the grantor, or to the execution of an agreement for a trust founded on a valuable consideration," and the language of the same judge in *Morrison* v. *Bierer,* 2 W. & S.

86, shows that he regarded a declaration of trust as inoperative where it does not rest on an antecedent obligation.

In this uncertainty, we may revert to principles. A declaration of trust by the owner of property in favor of a volunteer, has no peculiar efficacy. It is simply a gift which derives its force from the will of the donor. As applied to land, it is consequently invalid, if not under seal; and perhaps even then, unless the estate lies in grant. Where the law prescribes the mode of conveyance, it must be followed. Where, however, there are no legal means of transfer, any words expressing an intention to confer a present interest, may be effectual in equity.

In *Kennedy* v. *Ware,* 1 Barr, 445, 450, an equitable assignment was defined by C. J. Gibson, on the authority of Mr. Butler (Coke Lit. 222, b. *ante,* 435), as a declaration of trust with an agreement to permit the assignee to sue in the assignor's name. It follows that if a consideration may be dispensed with when the transaction takes the form of a declaration of trust, it cannot be essential to the validity of an assignment. The notion that a benefaction which would be valid if made through a declaration of trust, will fail if put in the shape of an assignment, has accordingly been replaced by the more intelligible rule, that a gift may be made by any form of words expressing such an intent. Whether the donor says that he " assigns " a chose in action to another, that he " bestows " it on him, or that

he "holds it in trust for his benefit," the intention is equally plain
and should not be allowed to fail,
because it is differently expressed.
It was said in *Kekewich* v. *Manning, ante,* 408, that if one who is
sui juris, thinks fit to dispose of
his property in the stocks, or of
any other chose in action, though
merely by way of benefaction, the
gift is valid, and that there is no
more effectual way in making such
a transfer than by executing an
assignment to the donee. This
doctrine was cited and confirmed
in *Voyle* v. *Hughes,* 2 Smale &
Giffard, 18. The Vice Chancellor
said, it had been erroneously contended that because the transfer of
a chose in action does not pass the
legal title, it is to be regarded
as a contract, which cannot be
enforced in the absence of a valuable consideration. If an actual
assignment had been assimilated
to an agreement to assign, in some
of the earlier decisions, it was in
order to get rid of the legal
doctrine that no possibility, right,
title or thing in action shall be
granted or assigned to a stranger.
The object was to sustain the title
of the assignee and not to defeat it.
It had been said as far back as
Lord Cathcart v. *Pascal,* 3 Peere
Wms. 97, that if a man is entitled
to a bond or other chose in action,
he may assign it without any consideration. In the subsequent decisions, a consideration was treated
as essential to the validity of an
equitable assignment. The more
recent case of *Kekewich* v. *Manning,* where such an assignment had
been upheld, notwithstanding the

want of a consideration, had a
sufficient basis of authority, and
rested on a sound and intelligible
principle. The instrument before
the Court should be viewed as
being what it really was, a present
and immediate transfer of a vested
interest.

In *Richardson* v. *Richardson,* 3
L. R. Eq. 686, the question was,
whether the beneficial interest in
certain promissory notes passed
by a voluntary assignment of all
the donor's personal estate. She
did not endorse the notes, and the
legal title consequently remained
in her. The chancellor said that
it could not be contended since the
decision in *Kekewich* v. *Manning,*
1 De Gex, Mac. & G. 176, that the
beneficial interest did not pass by
the assignment, because "the decision in that case was not merely
that a person who being entitled
to a reversionary interest or to
stock standing in another's name,
assigns it by a voluntary deed,
the interest thereby passes, notwithstanding that he does not in
formal terms declare himself to be
a trustee of the property; but it
amounts to this, that an instrument executed as a present and
complete assignment, is equivalent to a declaration of trust."

"It was impossible to read the
argument in that case, and the
judgment of Lord Justice Knight
Bruce, without seeing that his
mind was directed to *Meek* v. *Kettlewell,* and that class of causes,
where it had been held (such was
the nicety upon which the decisions
turned) that an actual assignment
is nothing more than an agreement

to assign in equity, because it merely passes such equitable interest as the assignor may have, and some further step must be taken by the assignee to acquire the legal interest. That further step being necessary, the assignment was held to be in truth, nothing but an agreement to assign; and being so, was not enforceable in this court, the court having often decided that it will not enforce a mere voluntary agreement."

"The distinction, undoubtedly, is very fine between that and a declaration of trust, and the good sense of the decision in *Kekewich* v. *Manning*, I think, lies in this: that the real distinction should be made between an agreement to do something when called upon—something distinctly expressed to be future in the instrument—and an instrument which affects to pass everything, independently of the legal estate. It was held in *Kekewich* v. *Manning* that such an instrument operates as an out and out assignment, disposing of the whole of the assignor's equitable interest, and that such a declaration of trust is as good a form as any that can be devised. The expression used by the Lords Justices, is this: "A declaration of trust is not confined to any express form of words, but may be indicated by the character of the instrument."

"In that case, reference was made in the argument principally to the case of *Ex parte Pye*, which was a decision of Lord Eldon to the same effect. Reliance is often placed on the circumstance that the assignor has done all he could;

that there is nothing remaining for him to do; and it is contended that he must in that case only be taken to have made a complete and effectual assignment. But that is not the sound doctrine on which the case rests; for if there be an actual declaration of trust, although the assignor has not done all he could do—for example, although he has not given notice to the assignee—yet the interest is held to have effectually passed as between the donor and donee. The difference must be rested simply on this: aye or no has he constituted himself a trustee." * * * * * * *

"Following, therefore, *Kekewich* v. *Manning*, I must regard this instrument as having effectually assigned the promissory notes, although they were not indorsed. The instrument is an actual assignment, with a power immediately vested in the assignee to make himself master of the property."

Here, as in *Kekewich* v. *Manning*, the instrument was under seal, but the *ratio decidendi* was broad enough to include an assignment by parol. Where a seal does not operate to confer a legal right, it is merely formal, and should be so regarded by a chancellor, *ante*, 407; *Dennison* v. *Goehring*, 7 Barr, 175, 178. In *Morgan* v. *Mullison*, 10 L. R. Eq. 475, the donor signed and delivered the following memorandum to his physician: "I hereby give and make over to Dr. Morris an India bond, numbered 506, value £1000, as some token for his kind attention to me during illness;" (signed) "John Saunders." The signature was attested by two witnesses, and the memorandum was handed over to Dr. Morris; but the bond, which was transferable by delivery, remained with the donor, and was found among his paper at his death. It was conceded that the transfer was gratuitous and not in payment of an antecedent debt, or for value received at the time. Lord Romilly said, "The writing is equivalent to a declaration of trust. If the donor had said: 'I undertake to hold the bond for you,' that would have been a declaration of trust, though there had been no delivery. This amounts to the same thing, and Dr. Morris is entitled to the bond."

It results from this decision, that a writing signed and delivered by an obligee, may operate as an equitable transfer, notwithstanding the want of a consideration, and although the bond is not handed over to the donee.

It is equally well settled that the delivery of the securities for a debt may be effectual as a gift, although the intention is not expressed in writing, and has to be collected from the acts and declarations of the donor, *ante*, 395. In *Crump's Appeal*, 36 Conn. 88, a depositor in a saving fund handed his bank book to the appellant, with the remark that he intended it as a present. Carpenter, J., said the question was whether such a delivery was sufficient in the absence of an order for the money, or other written indication of the intention of the donor. It was well settled under the modern authorities that choses in action and negotiable paper not endorsed, might be the subject of a gift, and that a delivery which did not pass the legal title, might confer a beneficial interest; *Grover* v. *Grover*, 24 Pick. 261; *Champney* v. *Blackhead*, 39 New York, 111; *Penfield* v. *Thayer*, 2 E. D. Smith, 305. The question had been virtually determined in *Brown* v. *Brown*, 18 Conn. 410; and although that was a *donatio causa mortis*, the principle was the same, because there was no difference, as it regarded delivery, between such a gift, and one *inter vivos;* *Session* v. *Moseley*, 4 Cushing, 87; *Westals* v. *De Witt*, 36 New York, 340. It is established in like manner in New York that shares of stock may be given by an assignment in writing and under seal, or by delivering the certificates to the donee, although the shares are not transferred to him on the books of the corporation; *Grymes* v. *Horie*, 49 New York, 17. Such, at least, are the decisions with regard to donations *causa mortis*, and it does not appear that gifts *inter vivos* obey a different rule.

In Massachusetts, as in New York, the delivery of a certificate of stock, with a power of transfer, passes the legal title, and the stock need not be actually transferred on the books; *Stone* v. *Hackett*, 12 Gray, 227; *Eames* v. *Wheeler*, 19 Pick. 144; *M'Neil* v. *The National Bank*, 43 New York. It was, notwithstanding, held in *Pennington* v. *Getting*, 2 Gill & John.

209, that as a power not based on a consideration is essentially revocable, a gift so made was imperfect, and chancery would not afford its aid to a volunteer.

Some of the decisions take the intermediate position, that although a consideration is requisite, it need not be valuable. Agreeably to this view, the claims of a wife or child are a meritorious ground, which may uphold a gift, although equity will not intervene on behalf of a stranger, or even of a grandson or collateral relative, *ante*, 427. See *Hayes* v. *Kershaw*, 1 Sand. Ch. 258; *Buford* v. *M'Kee*, 1 Denio, 107; *Jones* v. *Obenchain*, 10 Gratton, 259. This distinction can hardly be sustained. It abandons the logical rule laid down in *Kennedy* v. *Ware*, without substituting any principle sufficiently comprehensive to meet the requirements of policy and justice. A parent is not under any legal or moral obligation to settle any part of his estate on his children, and it may be proper to make such a gift to a stranger. What he ought to do in any particular case depends on circumstances, of which he is the best judge. There is, consequently, no sufficient reason why the power of giving should be limited to the immediate family of the donor. He may have none, or there may be fitter recipients of his bounty. It is well settled that a man may dispose by will of his property to any one whom he desires to benefit, and the power of making a gift *inter vivos* should not be circumscribed by narrower bounds. In *Kekewich* v. *Manning*, the court

sustained a settlement of a reversionary interest in stock on the niece of the settlor, although there was no actual transfer of the fund; and it is established in accordance with this decision, that the bounty of the donor is sufficient to uphold a gift to any one whom he desires to aid, *ante*, 404, 408.

A chancellor should, notwithstanding, be slow to deduce a trust in favor of one who had no antecedent right and is a mere volunteer. It is not enough that what the alleged donor said or did indicates that he entertained a purpose or design of giving; it must appear that he meant to pass the right of property. If this is doubtful on the evidence as a whole, the interpretation should be in his favor, and that of those claiming under him in the due course of law and against the gift, *ante*, 396. This is especially true of language used in the confidence of friendship, or to a near relative, because resolves are not unfrequently uttered in the effusion of kindly and social intercourse, which the speaker does not mean to bind himself to execute. To construe such expressions as an irrevocable grant or contract, would defeat rather than effectuate intention. The question is one of fact, where the circumstances of each case are not less to be considered than general rules. In *Bright* v. *Bright*, 8 B. Monroe, 194, a letter from one brother to another, containing an assurance that if the writer could not repay a loan which had been made to his son, in any other way, he would convey the farm on which he lived, was held to express a hope or expectation which should not be read as a declaration of trust.

Although tradition is a circumstance of much moment in determining whether a gift has been perfected, it is not conclusive, especially where possession is soon afterwards resumed. Handing over is not necessarily delivery, and may consist with an intention to retain the right of property; *Jones* v. *Locke*, 1 Law Rep. Eq. 251. The converse of this proposition is also true, and the delivery of a written transfer or assignment may confer an equitable right, notwithstanding the retention of the instrument by which the debt was secured, *ante*, 402; *Morgan* v. *Mullison*, 10 Law R. Eq. 475.

The failure to make an actual or symbolical delivery may, nevertheless, justify the inference that a writing purporting to convey a present interest is the expression of a purpose which the donor entertains, but is not prepared to carry into effect; *Lonsdale's Estate*, 5 Casey, 406. In *Cox* v. *Sprigg*, 6 Maryland, 286, Mrs. Lonsdale signed and delivered the following intrument: " From natural affection for my daughter, Eliza Cox, wife of Wm. F. Cox, and in consideration of one dollar, I hereby give, grant, assign and make over to her a certain debt of $3500, due to me by Clement Hill, and represented by his note, reserving to myself the interest as it falls due, or so much thereof as I may receive during my natural life, it being my intention to secure said debt to my said daughter Eliza Cox." A copy of this assignment was delivered to Hill, who subsequently gave his bond to the assignor in exchange for the note which she had retained. Eliza Cox died not long afterwards, and her mother thereupon assigned and delivered the bond to another daughter, Violet Sprigg. A bill of interpleader having been filed by Hill, it was held that the first gift must be postponed to the second, which had been perfected by delivery. Aside from this the contest lay between the husband of the deceased, and a living child, and as the claim of the latter was at least equally meritorious, there was no reason why equity should interpose.

It is notwithstanding entirely possible to confer a vested right while postponing the period of possession and enjoyment, and there is consequently nothing to preclude the gift of a reversionary interest in a chose in action to take effect on the death of the donor; *Cox* v. *Sprigg*, 6 Maryland, 286; *Hope* v. *Hawkins*, 9 Gill & J. 77; *Harrow* v. *The State*, 9 Gill, 440, *ante*. This distinction seems to have escaped the auditors in Lonsdale's Estate.

Where the aid of a chancellor is asked to sustain a gift which is legally invalid, he may consider the circumstances of the donor, and whether the effect of the decree will be to leave him without the means of support. Such, at least, is the rule as between husband and wife; *Coates* v. *Gerlach*, 8 Wright, 45; and there can be little doubt that it applies wherever the alleged equity has its foundation in the respondent's bounty. " A court of equity," said Strong, J., in *Coates* v. *Gerlach*, "will not enforce a voluntary conveyance, if it be of more than a reasonable provision; *Beard* v. *Beard*, 3 Atk. 72; Story's Eq., § 1374. Upon this branch of the case it is conclusive against the wife, that the deed was for all the husband's real estate, and indeed for all his property, so far as appears, except some farming stock, subsequently sold by him for $500."

" A conveyance that denudes a husband of all, or the greater part of his property, is much more than a reasonable provision for a wife; for in considering what is and what is not a reasonable provision, the circumstances of the husband are to be regarded, his probable necessities as well as his debts. Equity will not assist a wife to impoverish her husband. Accordingly, it has always been held, that a conveyance to a wife of all or the greater part of a husband's estate, is an unreasonable provision, which, if voluntary, a court of equity will not sustain. Section 1, Fonblanque's Eq., book 1, ch. 4, § 12, note *a*, where the author remarks, that 'if a conveyance be of the whole, or the greater part of a grantor's property, such conveyance or gift would be fraudulent; for no man can voluntarily divest himself of all, or the most of what he has, without being aware that future creditors, will probable suffer by it;' 2 Story's Eq., § 1374, where the principle is clearly stated with

a reference to authorities. It is recognised also, in *Benedict* v. *Montgomery*, and in *Stickney* v. *Borman*, 2 Barr, 67." For a like reason in determining whether a gift by a father to a child shall be enforced, regard should be had to the father's circumstances, and those of his other children.

If we now turn to the case where the contract is in terms executory —to give or convey at a future period—the weight of authority is that chancery will not enforce such an agreement without a consideration, which may, however, be found in natural love and affection, *ante*, 427; *Mahan* v. *Mahan*, 7 B. Monroe, 579. It has been held that equity will enforce a voluntary covenant for the benefit of a wife or child, and that it will not enforce such a covenant where the beneficiary is a grandchild or collateral relative. See *Read* v. *Robinson*, 6 W. & S. 329; *Buford* v. *M'Kay*, 1 Dana, 107; *Jones* v. *Obenchain; Dennison* v. *Goehring*, 10 Grattan, 259; *Hayes* v. *Kershaw*, 1 Sand. Ch. 258. The ground of this distinction is not altogether clear. A promise reduced to writing and under seal, differs widely from the expression of a hope, expectation or design, and when sustained by the consideration of blood or marriage, may be a sufficient ground for the intervention of a chancellor on behalf of the grantee; *Watts* v. *Bullas*, 1 Peere Wms. 60; *Huss* v. *Morris*, 13 P. F. Smith, 372. In *Huss* v. *Morris*, the distinction which has been taken in some instances between children and grandchildren was disapproved, and it was held that as both had a claim on the affections of the ancestor, so both were entitled to the aid of a Chancellor to sustain any gift which he ought to make in their favor.

Want of consideration is not a defence to a bond or covenant to pay a sum certain in either jurisdiction; *Mack's Appeal*, 18 P. F. Smith, 231; *Yard* v. *Patton*, 1 Harris, 278, 285, *ante*, 412; and the compensation for a breach is the same in both, to wit, the amount due, with interest. In other words, the contract is specifically enforced; *Mack's Appeal, ante; Spark* v. *Endress*, 3 W. & S. 256. Chief Justice Gibson said, that a voluntary bond was a gift of the money both in law and equity; and it is certain, that if a chancellor will not decree the performance of such a contract, he will not stay the arm of the law. Such a covenant, and a covenant to settle land or stocks, are viewed with equal favor by the courts of law; and as the measure of damage in the latter case is the value of the property, there would seem to be no reason why a court of equity should not award a conveyance of the property itself.

In applying the distinction, it must be remembered that intention is to be gathered from the instrument as a whole, and not from any particular clause; *Krider* v. *Lafferty*, 1 Wharton, 303, 305. Words of grant may enure as a covenant, and words of covenant as a grant, in order to effectuate the object; *Roe* v. *Trumner*, Willes, 632; 2 Smith's Lead. Cases,

466, 472, 7 Am. ed. A covenant to stand seised was a customary mode of settling land before the statute of uses, and until the introduction of the present system of conveyancing; 2 Bl. Com. 338. The requisites to such a conveyance are "words sufficient to make a covenant," "that the grantor be seised at the time," and "that there be a proper consideration to raise the use;" and if these are present, the title will pass, notwithstanding any want of form; *Hayes* v. *Kershaw*, 1 Sand. Ch.

In *Hays* v. *Kershaw*, the grantor executed two deeds on the same day. By one of them, the title to certain premises was vested in fee in A. and D., to hold to the use of A. during her life, and after her death to the use of her children during their lives, and that of the survivor of them, with remainder to the grantor, his heirs and assigns. The second recited the first in full, and the desire of the grantor to convey the premises to the lawful issue of the children of A. absolutely; and then in consideration of love and affection for A. and her offspring and of one dollar, covenanted for himself and his heirs, with A. and D., to convey the premises to the lawful issue of the children. It was held that "the deeds were as one instrument, and took effect as a conveyance in præsenti. The principal object of the grant and covenant must fail, unless this construction be adopted. By adopting it, I do no violence to the words used. I make the covenant to operate as an executed, instead of an executory agreement. I do what equity is called upon to hold every day, by considering as done that which is agreed to be done, in order the better to carry out the object of the contract. This construction accomplishes what the parties to these deeds thereby declared, in the most solemn terms, it was their aim to effect by the execution of the instruments."

In like manner, where a mother agreed under seal to appropriate the assets which had devolved upon her from a deceased son, exclusively to the support of another child who was in feeble health, the instrument was sustained as conferring a present interest, although executory in form; *Cressman's Appeal*, 6 Wright, 147. The case of *Yard* v. *Patton*, 1 Harris, 278, may be referred to the same principles.

The doctrine in *Kekkewich* v. *Manning*, "that a person acting freely, fairly and with sufficient knowledge, ought to have and has it in his power to make a voluntary gift of any part of his property," implies that when the donor is ignorant of his right, or unduly influenced, the gift will fail, *ante*, 413; *In re Painter's Est.*, 6 Wright, 156. But there is a marked distinction in this regard between executed and executory contracts, and a Chancellor may refuse to set aside a perfected gift, although the circumstances are such that he would not enforce it if still inchoate; *Delamater's Est.*, 1 Wharton, 362, 374; *Yard* v. *Patton*, 1 Harris, 278, 282. In the language of Ch.

J. Gibson, "though equity will refuse to execute wherever the circumstances are such that it would revoke, it may refuse to revoke where it would decline to execute."

It has been said that an imperfect gift or voluntary covenant will not be enforced against the donor, and that his heirs and distributees succeed prima facie to his rights in this as in other respects; *Garner* v. *Garner*, 1 Busbee's Eq. 1; *Cox* v. *Sprigg*, 6 Maryland, 286, *ante*, 426. It follows that when the contest is between the children of the giver, equity will not lend its aid to either side, unless some reason can be assigned of sufficient moment to turn the scale; *Holland* v. *Husley*, 4 Clarke, 222, 225; *Cox* v. *Sprigg*. Where, however, the respondents had been advanced by their father in his lifetime, and the complainant was without any such provision, it was held that the latter had a preponderating equity; *Garner* v. *Garner*. In *Cox* v. *Sprigg*, a mother assigned a debt in writing to a married daughter, reserving the interest to herself as long as she lived. The daughter died, and the mother thereupon delivered the bond by which the debt was secured to another child. The Court held that the second gift was equally meritorious, and having been perfected by delivery, should be preferred. Every such case must, to a great extent, depend on its own circumstances, and if there be any general rule, it is, that equity will not enforce an imperfect gift at the cost of impoverishing the donor or his heirs.

If natural love and affection may give effect to a deed, it will not sustain a parol agreement. A naked promise to make a gift is invalid, whatever be its object, or the circumstances under which it is made : *Phelps* v. *Pond*, 23 New York, 69, 78; *Frost* v. *Frost*, 36 Vermont, 639; and it will make no difference that the promise is put in the form of a draft or promissory note; *Harris* v. *Clark*, 3 Comstock, 93 ; *Pierson* v. *Pierson*, 7 Johnson, 26. In *Fink* v. *Cox* (18 John. 145), a father gave a note to his son for $1,000, payable in sixty days. It was a gift founded on the consideration of natural love and affection only. After the father's death, the son brought his action against his father's executors. It was held that although such a consideration is sufficient in a deed against all persons except creditors and bona fide purchasers, it is not so in a personal action on an executory contract. The same point was decided in *Haliday* v. *Atkinson*, 5 Barn. & Cress. 501; and the rule applies a fortiori where such an instrument is made to one who is a stranger in blood ; *Swain* v. *Ettling*, 8 Casey, 486. In *Phelps* v. *Pond*, the testator shortly before his death executed and delivered a promissory note for $100,000, and at the same time gave written directions that the interest on that amount should be paid to the Bible Society and the Board of Foreign Missions during his son's life, and the principal when he died. The Court held that, notwithstanding the charitable object of the benefaction, it was not valid either as a trust or a contract. See *Dawson* v. *Rearton*, 1 Giffard, 186, *ante*, 412.

It has been held that a mistake in a voluntary grant or assignment which does not pass the legal title, will not be rectified as against the donor, or during his life, between those claiming under him; because if he is satisfied with the result there is no ground for the intervention of a chancellor; and if he is not, he can cure the defect by executing another instrument in accordance with his original design. This argument is of questionable validity, and does not apply where the grant, though erroneous in some of its details or limitations, divests the donor's estate, and with it the power of reformation; nor where his control over the estate has ceased by death. Under these circumstances, the question is whether the fund shall go as the giver intended, or to one whom he did no design or benefit ; and the mistake may be rectified as against a volunteer, or, as it would seem, a purchaser with notice; *Lister* v. *Hodgson*, L. R. 4 Eq. 30, *ante*. See notes to *Lord Glenorchy* v. *Bosville*, *ante ; Mattingly* v. *Speak*, 4 Bush, 316; *Mitchell* v. *Mitchell*, 40 Georgia, 11 ; *Larkins* v. *Biddle*, 21 Alabama, 252, 256; *Stewart* v. *Brand*, 25 Iowa, 477 ; *Hart* v. *Hart*, Ib. 599. Such relief may be afforded at the instance of one who is not connected with the giver by blood or marriage, and *a fortiori* to his lineal descendants. See *Morris* v. *Stephens*, 10 Wright,

200; *Huss* v. *Stephens*, 4 P. F. Smith, 282; *Huss* v. *Morris*, 13 P. F. Smith, 367; *ante*, 420, 421.

In *Huss* v. *Morris* the grant was to the heirs of the donor's son, who was still alive. It therefore failed for uncertainty, and the Court remedied the defect by substituting "grandchildren" for "heirs," on proof that such was the donor's intention, as communicated to the conveyancer who drew the deed. Sharswood, J., said: "In *Watts* v. *Bullas*, 1 P. Wms. 60, where J. S. made a voluntary conveyance to his brother by the half blood, which was void and defective at law, Lord Keeper Wright was of opinion that as the consideration of blood would at common law raise an use, so would this imperfect conveyance raise a trust in respect of the consideration of blood, and consequently ought to be made good in equity. And in the same case the Master of the Rolls is reported to have said

that a devise of a copyhold without a surrender, ought to be made good for grandchildren as well as children, an opinion concurred in by Lord Harcourt, in *Freestone* v. *Kant*, 1 P. Wms. 61, n. Some doubts have been thrown upon the authority of this case, because later equity cases have confined the interference of that court in supplying defects in the execution of powers to creditors, wife and children. But Chancellor Kent cites *Watts* v. *Bullas*, with apparent approbation, 2 Johns. Ch. 599; and our courts certainly will not distinguish between children and grandchildren in the exercise of the equitable power of correcting a plain mistake in a conveyance intended for their benefit, especially when it is for the purpose of rendering valid and effectual what would otherwise be void for informality. The natural affection of grandparents is generally as strong as that of parents."

---

*MACKRETH v. SYMMONS. [*289]

MAY 13, 14, NOV. 26, 1808.

REPORTED 15 VES. 329.

VENDOR'S LIEN FOR UNPAID PURCHASE-MONEY.]—*Vendor's lien for purchase-money unpaid, against the vendee, volunteers, and purchasers with notice, or having equitable interests only, claiming under him, unless clearly relinquished, of which another security taken and relied on may be evidence, according to the circumstances, the nature of the security, &c.: the proof being upon the purchaser: and, failing in part upon the circumstances, another security being relied on, may prevail as to the residue.*

As to marshalling the assets of the vendee by throwing the lien upon the estate, quære.

THE bill stated, that, in the years 1783 and 1784, the plaintiff was indebted to John Manners in several sums, amounting in the whole to 43,500*l.*; for which sums John Martindale, as surety, joined the plaintiff in bonds. In 1790, Martindale, having, upon a settlement of accounts with the plaintiff in 1785, *taken credit for payment to Manners of* 3000*l.*, *undertook to discharge the remaining* 10,500*l.*; and they settled an account accordingly. Other accounts were afterwards settled between them—the last in February, 1792; upon which a balance of 54,000*l.* was due to Martindale, including 10,393*l.* 17*s.*, *the value of annuities* granted by the plaintiff; against which Martindale agreed to indemnify the plaintiff, in consideration of the plaintiff's agreeing to pay him the amount. *A bond for* 20,000*l. was given accordingly;* and a mortgage in fee was executed by the plaintiff to Martindale for the balance of 54,000*l.*

By indentures of lease and release, dated the 30th and [*290] *31st of October, 1793, reciting an agreement by the plaintiff to sell the reversion of the mortgaged estates to Martindale, which was valued at 60,000*l.*, composed of the principal and interest due upon the mortgage, those estates were conveyed to Henry Martindale, and his heirs, to the use of the plaintiff for life, with remainder to John Martindale in fee.

The bill further stated, that John Martindale *did not, according to his undertaking, pay the sum of* 13,500*l. to Manners,* nor *the value of the annuities;* which sums constituted part of the consideration for his purchase of the reversion of the estate. In September, 1797, a commission of bankruptcy issued against him, under which Manners' representatives proved the debt upon the bonds, and received dividends; the plaintiff being obliged to pay the remainder of the debt on account of those bonds, being 14,128*l.* 3*s.* 9*d.*, besides costs, and several sums on account of the annuities.

John Martindale, before his bankruptcy, had contracted to execute a mortgage to the defendant of the reversion comprised in the indentures of 1793; and the plaintiff, claiming a lien upon the estate for the payments he had made in consequence of Martindale's failure to fulfil his engagements, gave notice to the assignees under the commission. In 1798, Symmons obtained a decree, that the assignees should execute a mortgage of the reversion to him, expressly without prejudice to the plaintiff's claim; and afterwards filed a bill of foreclosure against the assignees, and obtained a decree; Mackreth not being a party to that suit. *The legal estate was vested in Coutts,* as a trustee, under a conveyance by Mackreth and Martindale in 1793, to secure annuities of 200*l.*

The bill, filed by Mackreth, prayed a declaration, that the plaintiff has a lien upon the reversion of the estates, sold to Martindale and mortgaged to Symmons, for the payments he had been obliged to make, and those sums which he may hereafter pay in respect of annuities, &c.

The defendant, Symmons, by his answer, denied that he had

any notice, prior to his entering into the agreement *with Martindale, that the plaintiff had not received full consideration ; and submitted that he had no lien. [*291]

Sir Samuel Romilly and Mr. Wriottesley, for the plaintiff.— The equitable lien of a vendor upon the estate sold for the purchase-money, as against the vendee, and even though a bond was taken, is established by a great number of cases, from *Chapman* v. *Tanner*,[1] to *Nairn* v. *Prowse*.[2] In *Austin* v. *Halsey*,[3] your Lordship considered it as clearly settled, except where upon the contract evidently the lien by implication was not intended ; and the case of *Hughes* v. *Kearney*,[4] is another direct authority ; Lord Redesdale laying down, as a very clear rule, that in all cases the vendor has the lien, and that it lies upon the purchaser to show a special agreement excluding it ; that case being decided upon that ground. It cannot be admitted, certainly, against a purchaser for a valuable consideration without notice ; but this defendant has not that character, having merely an equitable agreement for a security, not performed, when Martindale became a bankrupt, the plaintiff giving notice to the assignees, and the decree, obtained by the defendant Symmons, for a mortgage to him, expressing, that it was without prejudice to the claim of this plaintiff. Certainly, a former debt is sufficient to sustain a purchase as for a valuable consideration ; but it is necessary that a party taking a conveyance for such a consideration should not have had notice of the claim when he took the conveyance. There are but two periods to which the point of notice can apply : first, the time when the consideration was advanced ; secondly, when the conveyance was executed ; and even where a consideration has actually passed, it is necessary to state, in pleading, that there was no notice at either period, otherwise the purchaser cannot protect himself ; *Wigg* v. *Wigg*.[5] In this case it is essential that there should not have been notice at the later period, before which notice is clearly established. The estate was never properly out of the hands of the plaintiff. He had not taken a security carved out by *himself, which might preclude the equitable lien he once had, which therefore still remains. [*292] From the nature of this transaction, the consideration, being a former debt, no money actually passing, no such harship can arise from enforcing the lien, as in the case of a purchaser for valuable consideration actually paid in that transaction, who is affected by notice.

If, however, this defendant is to be considered as a purchaser for valuable consideration without notice, so that the lien cannot prevail against him, the plaintiff is entitled to consider him only as a mortgagee, having contracted with Martindale, as against whom the lien is good, for a mortgage. This plaintiff, therefore,

---

[1] 1 Vern. 267. [2] 6 Ves. 752. [3] 6 Ves. 475 ; see 483.
[4] 1 S. & L. 132. [5] 1 Atk. 382.

cannot be affected by the decree for a foreclosure obtained by this defendant, who, having notice of the plaintiff's claim, did not make him a party.

Mr. *Richards* Mr. *Alexander*, and Mr. *William Agar*, for the defendant.—There is nothing in the circumstances of this case depriving this defendant of the protection due to a purchaser for valuable consideration without notice, his transaction with Martindale being perfectly fair; the vendor claiming a preference by way of lien for the purchase-money remaining unpaid, as an equitable charge, prior in time, though he took the security of Martindale to that extent. Under such circumstances the lien has never been established; nor can the inference necessary to maintain it be collected, either upon principle or authority. The general case of lien as between vendor and vendee, is admitted, where there is no special agreement, no security taken in respect of the purchase-money; but this equity has not been carried beyond that simple case of vendor and vendee. In the case of *Chapman* v. *Tanner*,[1] there was a special agreement: the title-deeds were kept by the vendor, a deposit of the title-deeds of itself amounting to an equitable charge. Other cases, besides those which have been mentioned, in which this point arose, either directly or incidentally, are *Bond* v. *Kent*[2]—the case of a mortgage of the purchased estate for part of the money, and a [*293] note for the remainder: *Pollexfen* v. *Moore*[3]—a *very perplexed case often cited; *Fawell* v. *Heelis;*[4] *Blackburn* v. *Gregson*[5]—which is merely the opinion of Lord Loughborough, who desired to have the point further considered; *Trimmer* v. *Bayne*.[6] The result of all of them is, that, where a security is given, there is no place for this equity, the purchaser certainly having to show that it does not exist. Here, a bond was given by Martindale; the security stipulated between the parties; and, therefore, the lien, substituted by equity, where there is no stipulation for a particular security, cannot be raised.

Sir *Samuel Romilly*, in reply.—The plaintiff being called upon, and obliged to pay the debt, against which Martindale undertook to indemnify him, that undertaking forming the consideration of Martindale's purchase, he cannot, upon the ground of fraud, be permitted to retain the estate. The lien, therefore, is clear in respect of the 10,500*l.* The distinction as to the annuities rests upon the single circumstance, that a security by a bond of indemnity was taken, which is confined to the annuities. If this plaintiff had filed a bill against Martindale while in possession, he would have been compelled to pay the annuities out of the purchased estate, and a receiver would have been appointed. No stronger instance of bad faith, no act more unconscientious, can be stated, than taking an estate in consideration of making pay-

---

[1] 1 Vern. 267.　　　[2] 2 Vern. 281.　　　[3] 3 Atk. 272.
[4] Amb. 724; 1 Bro. C. C. 422, n., 3rd ed; 2 Dick. 485.
[5] 1 Bro. C. C. 420.　　　[6] 9 Ves. 209.

ments, and, by a direct violation of the contract, permitting those payments to fall upon the vendor.

As to this defendant, if, from the passage, appearing in the report of *Pollexfen* v. *Moore*, it is supposed that the lien cannot be extended to a purchaser from the original vendee, it would be perfectly ineffectual; but that proposition is contradicted by many authorities. In *Walker* v. *Preswick*[1] it is distinctly laid down, that the lien prevails against a purchaser with notice. Upon what principle can such a distinction between this and any other equity be maintained? The point is expressly decided in the same way in *Gibbons* v. *Baddall*,[2] viz., if A. sells an estate, taking a promissory note for part of the purchase-money, and then the purchaser sells to B., who has notice *that A. [*294] had not received all the money, the land is in equity chargeable with the money due on the note. The defendant cannot be represented as a purchaser without notice, merely as not having notice when he advanced his money. It is true, not then having this estate in contemplation, he could not have notice at that time; but, to sustain a purchase as for valuable consideration without notice, it is essential that there should not have been notice either when the money was advanced, or when the conveyance was executed. That doctrine has been always held from the earliest period, in *More* v. *Mayhow*,[3] to the time of Lord Hardwicke, in *Wigg* v. *Wigg*;[4] and the reason is, that some suspicion arises from not taking the legal estate, when the money is advanced. The defendant, having the means, by acquiring the legal estate, of placing himself in a situation, in which the want of notice would avail, merely took an agreement; and having only an equitable title, cannot maintain the plea of purchaser for valuable consideration without notice. The doctrine that certainly prevails between mortgagees, that, the equities being equal, a subsequent mortgagee, having got in the legal estate, may exclude a prior incumbrance, applies only where the money was advanced upon the credit of the estate; not where the estate was not in contemplation, and other securities were looked to, which is the case of this defendant, when he advanced his money; and upon that ground a judgment creditor, taking in a prior mortgage, cannot tack.[5]

[The *Lord Chancellor* (Eldon).—With regard to the doctrine to which you are now alluding, is there any case where a third mortgagee has excluded the second, if the first mortgagee, when he conveyed to the third, knew of the second? When the case of *Maundrell* v. *Maundrell*[6] was before me, I looked for, but could not find, such a case—that, where there was bad faith on the part of the first mortgagee, that equity was applied.[7]]

[1] 2 Ves. 622. [2] 2 Eq. Ca. Abr. 682, n. [3] 1 Ch. Ca. 34.
[4] 1 Atk. 382; Tourville v. Naish, 3 P. Wms. 307, where the notice was before payment of the money.
[5] Brace v. Duchess of Marlborough, 2 P. Wms. 491. [6] 10 Ves. 246.
[7] See Peacock v. Burt, Coote, Mort. 693, where a third mortgagee without

Sir *Samuel Romilly*, in reply.—I do not believe that was ever decided ; and there would be great difficulty in deciding it in [*295] favour of the third mortgagee, who puts *himself in the place of the first. The result of the authorities, and of the circumstances to which they are to be applied, is, that a part of the money, which was the consideration of the original purchase, remaining unpaid, the Court will raise the lien, and will enforce it against a second purchaser with notice; that universally the time of the conveyance, as well as the time of the advance, is material with regard to notice ; and that this defendant clearly had notice before the conveyance.

LORD CHANCELLOR ELDON.—Upon the special circumstances of this case I shall postpone my judgment.; I should be very unwilling to leave some of the doctrine, that has been brought into controversy, with as much doubt upon it, as would be the consequence of deferring the judgment without taking some notice of it.

The settled doctrine, notwithstanding the case of *Fawell* v. *Heelis*,[1] is, that unless there are circumstances such as we have been reasoning upon, *where the vendor conveys, without more, though the consideration is upon the face of the instrument expressed to be paid, and by a receipt indorsed upon the back, if it is the simple case of a conveyance, the money, or part of it, not being paid, as between the vendor and the vendee, and persons claiming as volunteers, upon the doctrine of this Court, which, when it is settled, has the effect of contract, though perhaps no actual contract has taken place, a lien shall prevail; in the one case, for the whole consideration; in the other, for that part of the money which was not paid.* I take that to have been the settled doctrine at the time of the decision of *Blackburn* v. *Gregson*,[2] which case so far shook the authority of *Fawell* v. *Heelis* as to relieve me from any apprehension, that Lord Bathurst's doctrine can be considered as affording the rule to be applied as between the vendor and vendee themselves, and persons claiming under them.

There is a case, *Smith* v. *Hibbard*,[3] reported nowhere but in Dickens, which seems to decide that point. There is also another [*296] case, besides those which have been mentioned, *showing the opinion of Lord Hardwicke, that the lien prevails: *Harrison* v. *Southcote*,[4] the case of a Papist vendor, for whom, Lord Hardwicke says, the lien would not be raised, as that would be giving an interest in land to a Papist; the specialty of that proving, that the lien prevails in general cases. In the case of *Elliott* v. *Edwards*,[5] Lord Alvanley was very strong upon it. There was a covenant for payment of the money upon the first pur-

notice, taking a transfer from the first mortagee who had notice of the second, was not affected by it.
[1] Amb. 724 ; 1 Bro. C. C. 422, n., 3rd ed. ; 2 Dick. 485.
[2] 1 Bro. C. C. 420.   [3] 2 Dick. 730.
[4] 2 Ves. 389 ; see 393.   [5] 3 B. & P. 181 ; see 193.

chase, and also an undertaking by a surety—strong circumstances to show, that, as between the vendor and vendee, there is no intention to rely upon the lien. The point was not decided in that case; but Lord Alvanley lays down the doctrine as I have stated it, that even in the hands of another person, with notice, the lien remains. In *Gibbons* v. *Baddall*,[1] the lien was held to be clear against a second purchaser, with notice. There is a very old case in Cary,[2] which I have heard cited as one of this class; but I have some doubt whether it is not a case of equitable inter-position upon another ground. The circumstance leading me to that doubt is, that there was a lost bond; and the modern doctrine of dispensing with *profert*,[3] was not at that time known. The Lord Chancellor might, therefore, consider himself as having jurisdiction in that case to direct payment of the money due upon that bond out of the estate. In *Austin* v. *Halsey*,[4] what I stated upon this subject was not said without much consideration. I had not at that time, nor have I now, the least doubt that it is the doctrine.

I have some doubt upon another point: taking the vendor to have the lien, whether the Court will, in case of the death of the vendee, marshal the assets, so as to throw the lien upon the purchased estate. It has often been said, and the case of *Coppin* v. *Coppin*[5] stated as an authority, that the Court will not do that. The Lord Chancellor, in his judgment, takes no notice of that point. In that case the vendor happened to be the heir of the vendee, so that the estate was at home; and it was held, that, being also the executor, he was entitled to retain the purchase-money out of the personal assets. That *decision requires a good deal of consideration. If the estate had been in a [*297] third person, the general doctrine, as to a person having two funds to resort to, might be thought to have an immediate appli-cation; and the express terms of the decree in *Polexfen* v. *Moore*[6] might be found very inconsistent with it.

It is not, however, necessary to decide that point; as this is an equity, that in ordinary cases will affect a purchaser. Upon principle, without authority, I cannot doubt that it goes upon this, that *a person having got the estate of another, shall not, as between them, keep it, and not pay the consideration; and there is no doubt that a third person, having full knowledge that the other got the estate without payment, cannot maintain, that though a court of equity will not permit him to keep it, he may give it to another person without payment.* It is not, however, necessary to discuss that upon general principles, as it has been repeatedly stated by authorities that ought, at this time, to bind upon that point.

[1] 2 Eq. Ca Abr. 682, n.   [2] Hearle v. Botelers, Cary, 35.
[3] Profert dispensed with, where a bond is lost; see 5 Ves. 238, n., 2d edit.
[4] 6 Ves. 475.
[5] 2 P. Wms. 291; Sel Ca. Ch. 28. See, however, Trimmer v. Bayne, 9 Ves. 209; Sproule v. Prior, 8 Sim. 189; Selby v. Selby, 4 Russ. 336; Wythe v. Hen-niker, 2 My. & K. 635.
[6] 3 Atk. 272.

Another principle, as matter of general law, is involved in this case ; what shall be sufficient to make a case in which the lien can be said not to exist. It has always struck me, considering this subject, that it would have been better at once to have held that the lien should exist in no case, and the vendor should suffer the consequences of his want of caution ; or to have laid down the rule the other way so distinctly, that a purchaser might be able to know, without the judgment of a court, in what cases it would, and in what it would not, exist. Lord Bathurst seems to have thought a note would put an end to it. Other judges, of very high authority, dissented from that ; as appears by the cases of *Gibbons* v. *Baddall* [1] and *Hughes* v. *Kearney.* [2] It does not necessarily follow from a written contract, giving another remedy, that the lien was not intended to exist. It is very difficult, then, to distinguish the case where a note or bond is given for part of the money. In the case of *Bond* v. *Kent,* [3] where the estate sold was mortgaged for part of the money, and a note [*298] taken for the rest, there was strong *negative evidence, that the vendor was not intended to be a mortgagee for the rest. The case put by the Master of the Rolls, in *Nairn* v. *Prowse,* [4] of a mortgage upon another estate, also afforded strong, perhaps not quite conclusive, evidence against the lien, considering the value of the mortgaged estate—in general much more than the amount of the money. It does not, however, appear to me a violent conclusion, as between vendor and vendee, that notwithstanding a mortgage, the lien should subsist. The principle has been carried this length : *that the lien exists, unless an intention, and a manifest intention, that it shall not exist appears.*

This case remains to be considered upon its own circumstances with reference to the points I have stated. The questions are, first, supposing the lien would have existed as to the gross sum, the debt to Manners and the annuities, or their value, whether the circumstances of silence as to the debt, and the indemnity taken against the annuities, which is very important, amount in equity to evidence of a manifest intention to abandon the lien ; if they do, another very considerable point is, whether, the lien having been abandoned, the plaintiff can set himself up as a mortgagee, claiming to redeem the defendant. If the lien is to be considered as not abandoned, the question will be, not whether a purchaser, with notice, would be affected by the lien—which, as general doctrine, I admit,—but whether, under the circumstances attending the contract with, and conveyance to, this defendant, it shall prevail against him. Upon the particular circumstances, the case must stand for judgment.

LORD CHANCELLOR ELDON,[5] having stated the case very particularly, and observing that the legal estate in the premises was,

---

[1] 2 Eq. Ca. Abr. 682, n.   [2] 1 S. & L. 132.   [3] 2 Vern. 281.
[4] 6 Ves. 752; see 760.   [5] Nov. 26th, 1808.

before the assignees of Martindale executed the agreement for a mortgage to Symmons, vested, under a former conveyance by Mackreth, in a trustee to secure annuities granted by him, pronounced the following judgment:

This case, when it was argued, and since, has appeared *to me to involve a question of very great importance, [*299] with regard to which I am not able to find any rule which is satisfactory to my mind. If I had found, laid down in distinct and inflexible terms, that, where the vendor of an estate takes a security for the consideration, he has no lien, that would be satisfactory; as, when a rule, so plain, is once communicated, the vendor, not taking an adequate security, loses the lien by his own fault. If, on the other hand, a rule has prevailed, as it seems to be, that it is to depend, not upon the circumstances of taking a security, but upon the nature of the security, as amounting to evidence, as it is sometimes called, or to declaration plain, or manifest intention, the expressions used upon other occasions, of a purpose to rely, not any longer upon the estate, but upon the personal credit of the individual, it is obvious that a vendor, taking a security, unless by evidence, manifest intention, or declaration plain, he shows his purpose, cannot know the situation in which he stands, without the judgment of a court, how far that security does contain the evidence, manifest intention, or declaration plain, upon that point. That observation is justified by a review of the authorities: from which it is clear that different judges would have determined the same case differently; and, if some of the cases that have been determined had come before me, I should not have been satisfied that the conclusion was right.

This bill insists upon a lien in respect of these annuities; to be paid all that the plaintiff himself has paid: and either as to the original value, or the present value, or the future payments. I state that claim in these different terms, as, to determine what is the lien, it is necessary to point out the amount of it, and how it is to be calculated. Some doubt was thrown in the argument upon the question of lien between the vendor and vendee; but it was not carried far; and it is too late to raise a doubt upon it: but it is insisted, that the lien does not prevail against third persons, even with notice of the situation of the vendor and vendee. It may be of use to state the cases upon this subject in the order of time.

*The earliest case, not very applicable, is in Cary,[1] and [*300] most of the Abridgments, which imperfectly collect the authorities upon this head. According to my own understanding, that case is to be classed rather among those of relief in equity upon a security that has been lost,[2] than under this head: but the fact of its existence is a circumstance of evidence that this doctrine has obtained in professional practice. There is no other case between that and *Chapman* v. *Tanner*,[3] which is very

---

[1] Hearle v. Botelers, Cary, 35.   [2] See 5 Ves. 238, n.   [3] 1 Vern. 267.

imperfectly reported; and its authority is weakened by the observation in subsequent cases, that there was a special agreement that the vendor should keep the writings; and it is stated as a fact, that he had not taken any security. Taking it to be a decision in favour of the lien under those circumstances, the declaration of the Court, which was the natural equity, shows strongly how the law upon this subject was understood; and that case, therefore, has considerable weight. The doctrine is probably derived from the civil law as to goods, which goes further than our law, by which, though the right of stoppage in transitu is founded upon natural justice and equity, yet if possession, either actual or constructive, was taken by the vendee, the lien is gone. That is not so by the civil law. The digest states:[1] "quod vendidi non aliter fit accipientas quam si aut pretium nobis solutum sit, aut satis eo nomine factum, vel etiam fidem habuerimus emptori sine ullâ satisfactione;" which points at this article of security; but with those excepted cases, the lien, according to the civil law, is so strong, that the goods may be taken out of the possession of the individual who had obtained actual or constructive possession of them.

The next case is *Bond* v. *Kent*,[2] the circumstances of which are special—a mortgage for part of the money, and a note for the residue. It was urged with considerable, perhaps not conclusive, weight, that the express charge of a part gave a ground for the inference, that a lien for the residue was not intended. The case, however, goes to prove, that, in equity, this lien was supposed to [*301] exist; *amounting to an admission, that, without those special circumstances, there would have been a lien.

The next case is *Coppin* v. *Coppin*,[3] where the doctrine of *Pollexfen* v. *Moore*,[4] as to marshalling, was practically, though I doubt whether it ought to have been, admitted. I should mention *Gibbons* v. *Baddall*,[5] where it is expressly stated, that the lien remained, though a note was given for part of the purchase-money; but I cannot ascertain the date of that decision. In *Pollexfen* v. *Moore*, Lord Hardwicke affirms the lien of the vendor upon the estate for the remainder of the purchase-money, considering the vendee from the time of the agreement a trustee as to the money for the vendor; but adds, that " this equity will not extend to a third person."

If that is to be understood, that this equity would not extend to a third person, who had notice that the money was not paid, Lord Hardwicke's subsequent decisions contradict that: if the meaning is, that he would follow the case of *Coppin* v. *Coppin*, and that, if the vendor exhausted the personal assets, the legatee of the purchaser should not come upon the estate, there is great difficulty in applying the principle; as it would then be in the power of the vendor to administer the assets as he pleases, having

---

[1] Dig., lib. 18, tit. 1, l. 11; Inst., lib. 2, tit. 2, § 41. [2] 2 Vern. 281.
[3] 2 P. Wms. 291   [4] 3 Atk. 272.   [5] 2 Eq. Ca. Abr. 682, n.

a lien upon the real estate to exhaust the personal assets, and disappoint all the creditors, who, if he had resorted to his lien, would have been satisfied ; and in that respect, with reference to the principle, the case is anomalous.

The next case in which the doctrine was admitted is *Harrison* v. *Southcote*,[1] followed by *Walker* v. *Preswick;*[2] which case, it is remarkable, was not cited in *Fawell* v. *Heelis;*[3] and in *Burgess* v. *Wheate*,[4] Sir Thomas Clarke lays down the rule, both as to vendor and vendee, thus:—Where conveyance is made prematurely, before money paid, the money is considered as a lien on that estate in the hands of the vendee. So, where money is paid prematurely, the money would be considered as a lien on the estate in the hands of the vendor for the personal representatives of the purchaser." *Tardiffe* v. **Scrughan*[5] is [*302] very material upon this point, as it is represented[6] as a case in which the lien was held to attach upon the two moieties of the estate ; but it has been also considered[7] a case, whether of lien upon the land or not, for contribution upon the circumstances between the sisters : giving the one sister a right to call upon the husband of the other to pay a moiety of the annuity. In another case, also, *Powell* v. ———, whether accurate or not I cannot trace, Lord Camden determined in favour of the lien.

In *Fawell* v. *Heelis*,[8] Lord Bathurst's opinion certainly was, for reasons best stated in the case of *Nairn* v. *Prowse*,[9] by Sir Samuel Romilly, that the bonds taken by the vendor furnished evidence, that credit was not given to the land ; and therefore there was no lien. In *Beckett* v. *Cordley*,[10] Lord Thurlow says, it was compared to a person selling an estate, and not receiving the money ; and, therefore, there is a lien : asserting the general doctrine as familiar, but distinguishing that case upon the nature of the transaction : younger children joining the eldest in a mortgage ; discharging the estate from their portions ; and by their consent the whole money being paid to the eldest son : the lien being discharged by that transaction.

In the argument of *Blackburn* v. *Gregson*,[11] Lord Kenyon took the doctrine to be perfectly clear ; and it is not possible to state a stronger judicial opinion than Lord Loughborough expressed, that the lien does exist, though it is not a decision. In *Smith* v. *Hibberd*,[12] it was insisted that the delivery of possession, upon payment of a small part of the money, was evidence that he meant to trust to the personal security ; but it was held clear, that the money contracted to be paid was a specific lien upon the premises. The contract for payment of the money is itself, in a sense,

---

[1] 2 Ves. 389 ; see 393. [2] 2 Ves. 622.
[3] Amb. 724 ; 1 Bro. C. C. 422, n., 3d edit. ; 2 Dick. 485.
[4] 1 Black 123 ; see 150. [5] Cited Amb. 725 ; 1 Bro. C. C. 423.
[6] 1 Bro C. C. 423., in Blackburn v. Gregson.
[7] Amb. 726, in Fawell v. Heelis.
[8] Amb. 724 ; 1 Bro. C. C. 422, n.. 3d ed. ; 2 Dick. 485. [9] 6 Ves. 752.
[10] 1 Bro. C. C. 353 ; see 358. [11] 1 Bro. C. C. 420. [12] 2 Dick. 730.

a security full as good as a note. I do not state, as an authority,
what appears upon this subject in *Austen* v. *Halsey*,[1] as it is a
mere dictum, and a dictum that fell from me; but, endeavouring
to state this doctrine as accurately as I could, I see I expressed it
[*303] in *these words:[2] "That the vendor has a lien for the
purchase-money, while the estate is in the hands of the
vendee. I except the case where upon the contract evidently
that lien by implication was not intended to be reserved."

In the case of *Elliott* v. *Edwards*,[3] this is the doctrine of Lord
Alvanley, a very experienced judge in equity, with reference to
whom I may say, his judgments will be read and valued as producing great information and instruction to those who may
practise in Courts of equity in future times. He there states,
that, if a man, having purchased an estate, conveys it before the
purchase-money has been paid, a Court of equity will compel the
person to whom the estate was conveyed to pay that money, provided he knew at the time he took the conveyance that it had
not been paid.

The next case in equity is *Nairn* v. *Prowse*,[4] before the Master
of the Rolls, in which it was contended that there was no lien;
the vendor had taken a security for the money, payable at a
future time, and during the interval the vendee might have sold
the stock. The Master of the Rolls, in his judgment, admitting
the general doctrine as to the vendor's lien, observes upon the
question, whether a security taken will be a waiver, that by conveying the estate without payment a degree of credit is given to
the vendee, which may be given upon the confidence of the existence of such lien ; and it may be argued, that taking a note or a
bond cannot materially vary the case ; a credit is still given to
him, and may be given from the same motive, not to supersede
the lien, but for the purpose of ascertaining the debt, and countervailing the receipt indorsed upon the conveyance. There is great
difficulty to conceive how it should have been reasoned, almost in
any case, that the circumstance of taking a security was evidence
that the lien was given up, as in most cases there is a contract
under seal for payment of the money. The Master of the Rolls,
having before observed that there may be a security, which will
[*304] have the effect of a waiver, proceeds to express his *opinion, that, if the security be totally distinct and independent, it will then become a case of substitution for the lien,
instead of a credit given on account of the lien ; meaning that,
not a security, but the nature of the security, may amount to
satisfactory evidence that a lien was not intended to be reserved,
and puts the case of a mortgage of another estate, or any other
pledge, as evidence of an intention that the estate sold shall remain free and unencumbered. It must not, however be understood that a mortgage taken is to be considered as a conclusive

[1] 6 Ves. 475.   [2] 6 Ves. 483.
[3] 3 B. & P. 181 ; see 183.   [4] 6 Ves. 752.

ground for the inference that a lien was not intended, as I could put many instances that a mortgage of another estate for the purchase-money would not be decisive evidence of an intention to give up the lien, though, in the ordinary case, a man has always greater security for his money upon a mortgage than value for his money upon a purchase; and the question must be, whether, under the circumstances of that particular case, attending to the worth of that very mortgage, the inference arises. In the instance of a pledge of stock, does it necessarily follow that the vendor, consulting the convenience of the purchaser by permitting him to have the chance of the benefit, therefore gives up the lien which he has? Under all the circumstances of that case the judgment of the Master of the Rolls was satisfied that the conclusion did follow; but the doctrine as to taking a mortgage or a pledge, would be carried too far if it is understood, as applicable to all cases, that a man taking one pledge therefore necessarily gives up another; which must, I think, be laid down upon the circumstances of each case, rather than universally. In the case of *Hughes* v. *Kearney*[1] Lord Redesdale states the doctrine; and the proposition is, not merely that the vendor might have security, but that he relied upon it: and a note or bills are considered not as a security, but as a mode of payment.

From all these authorities the inference is, *first, that, generally speaking, there is such a lien; secondly, that in those general cases in which there would be the lien, as *between vendor and vendee,* [*305] *the vendor will have the lien against a third person, who had notice that the money was not paid.* Those two points seem to be clearly settled. I do not hesitate to say, that, if I had found no authority that the lien would attach upon a third person, having notice, I should have no difficulty in deciding that upon principle, as I cannot perceive the difference between this species of lien, and other equities, by which third persons, having notice, are bound. In the case of a conveyance to B., the money being paid by A., B. is a trustee; and C. taking from him, and having notice of the payment by A., would also be a trustee, and many other instances may be put.

The more modern authorities upon this subject have brought it to this inconvenient state—that the question is not a dry question upon the fact, whether a security was taken, but it depends upon the circumstances of each case whether the Court is to infer that the lien was intended to be reserved, or that credit was given, and exclusively given, to the person from whom the other security was taken.

In this case, having, as other judges have had, to determine this question of intention upon circumstances, I may mistake the fair result of the circumstances which I have endeavoured to collect. I must say, I have felt from the first, that there is, upon the part of the plaintiff, that natural justice and equity, which

[1] 1 S. & L. 132.

excite a wish, that I could enforce the lien throughout ; but, first, as to the annuities, I am persuaded, that, with reference to that part of the case involving the question of lien as to the consideration, or any part of it, or any sum of money, the quantum of which is to be estimated with reference to the present value, or the past or future payments, this is a case in which the plaintiff intended to rely entirely upon the personal security, the bond for 20,000l.; and that was the conception of Martindale also ; by whose default of payment, therefore, the estate is not now subject to the lien in respect of the consideration of the annuities, or [*306] any allowance in respect of it. See how it *stands. In 1790, the plaintiff, as principal, and Martindale, as surety, being engaged in an obligation, which I understand to be a personal one, for these annuities, agree to change situations ; Martindale to be the principal, and the plaintiff to be surety ; in consideration of which the plaintiff agrees to give 9000l., secured by a mortgage. It rests upon that until 1793, when the transaction takes this course: that Martindale shall be no longer a mortgagee, but owner of the reversion in fee, and, which is material, of the reversion, expectant upon the plaintiff's life estate. The annuities remain upon the old footing ; that is, some payments were made, or arrears accrued, between 1792 and 1793, and payments were to arise from time to time. The value given to Martindale, in 1792, by the mortgage of 9000l., for taking the liability upon himself, was a value which merely, by the lapse of time, between 1792 and 1793, must have varied. If the annuities had been paid there must have been a difference in the estimation ; also, de anno in annum, the value was decreasing, not only as the annuities were wearing out, but also as the number of the annuitants was decreasing by death. It is impossible, it is not natural, to suppose, that parties dealing for the consideration of annuities and the purchase of a reversion, which might not take effect in possession until all the annuitants were dead, relied on that reversion as security, in addition to the indemnity by the bond for 20,000l.; in the original transaction the estate being pledged for the sum of 9000l., as if actually paid.

Then, as to the lien, for what is it ? Is it for the original sum ? That it cannot in justice be. Is it for future payments—that, one sum being paid, it does not attach ? another sum not being paid, it does attach ? a charge upon the reversion arising from time to time, accordingly as these payments are, or are not, made ? And is that inference to be drawn where a conveyance was executed without the least notice of such an intention—a security taken, not of itself sufficient to exclude the purpose of such a [*307] lien ? but the nature of the subject, connected *with the fact of that security taken, is decisive proof against such an intention ; and it appears accordingly in the other cause, *Symmons* v. *Rankin*, that Mackreth and Martindale joined in the conveyance to Coutts, to secure an annuity of 2000*l.*, without the least reference to such an intention.

I admit that the opinion of Lord Loughborough,[1] that the case, before Lord Camden,[2] went upon the ground of lien, is an authority very considerably against my opinion ; and I cannot say upon what the case did proceed, if not upon that ground ; as the estate, given by the wife to her husband for his life, after her own death, if not affected by the lien, could not be bound to pay the annuity. If that case is accurately represented, Lord Camden's opinion seems to have been that the mere circumstance of an estate given in consideration of an annuity, with a bond, would not prevent the lien attaching from time to time ; and, so understanding it, I cannot bring my mind to the conclusion that it is an authority which ought to lead me to determine, that, with reference to these annuities, there is a lien, either for the original value, the present value, or the future payment, which may or may not become due.

As to the other part of the case, I have considered long, whether the conclusion is just, that, not meaning to have a lien, as I think this party did not, with regard to the annuities, he should mean to have a lien as to the sum of money due to Manners. My individual opinion is, that the intention was the same as to both ; but, with regard to the latter, the cases authorise the lien ; unless it is destroyed by particular circumstances, which do not exist here. That sum is precisely in the condition of a part of the consideration, not paid ; and then the inference in equity, unless there are strong circumstances, getting over it, is, that a lien was intended. This comes very near the doctrine of Sir Thomas Clarke,[3] which is very sensible ; that, where the conveyance, or the payment, has been made by surprise, there shall be a lien. This plaintiff understood at the time of the conveyance, *that this money was to be paid on his account to Manners ; which is the same as if it was to have been [*308] paid to himself, and was not paid ; and then the only question is, whether, as, from the special circumstances as to the value and nature of the annuities, I am to infer that a lien was not intended as to them, I must make the same inference with respect to this gross sum ; as to which, if the annuities were not mixed with the transaction, the doctrine of equity is, that the lien would attach. As to that sum, my judgment is, that the plaintiff has a lien.

It is contended that there are other circumstances in this case ; that the defendant, Symmons, has a conveyance of the estate without notice, or, rather, a contract ; as he had notice at the time of the conveyance. It is not necessary to go into the doctrine as to the effect of notice at the time of the contract, or at the time of payment of the money ; though there is no doubt the defendant, when he took his conveyance, had notice from the

1 See Blackburn v. Gregson, 1 Bro. C. C. 420.
2 Tardiffe v. Scrughan, stated 1 Bro. C. C. 423.
3 Burgess v. Wheate, 1 Black, 150.

recitals in his title-deed of Mackreth's rights and Martindale's obligations, as vendor and vendee. Neither is it necessary to go into the consideration of another argument; that the defendant's money was not originally lent upon the faith of the land. There is a great difference between the effect of a judgment, as attaching upon the land, and a special agreement by a creditor for a security upon the land. It is not, however, necessary to determine such questions; as neither the plaintiff nor the defendant Symmons has the legal estate, which appears in the other cause, *Symmons* v. *Rankin*, to be in Coutts, under the *conveyance* of 1793, in which Martindale and Mackreth joined; and then, between equities, the rule " Qui prior est tempore potior est jure,"[1] applies.

The result of this case is, that the bill must be dismissed as it regards the annuities, and is right as to the other part of the claim; and, being right in one point, and wrong in the other, the decree must be without costs.

[*309]   *This case was mentioned by way of motion to vary the minutes, upon a misunderstanding as to the costs.

LORD CHANCELLOR ELDON, having repeated the ground upon which no costs were given, made the following additional observations :—

Since the judgment was pronounced, I have met with a case which was not cited in the argument, but is referred to in Mr. Sugden's work,[2] which seems to me to be a book of considerable merit,[3] in which this subject is considered with much attention, and he comes to a conclusion different from mine. I looked into the Registrar's Book for that case, the name of which I do not recollect; and it does seem to me that his inference is not the necessary inference, arising from the circumstances of that case, as I find it in the Registrar's Book. I mention this, to show that I have not withdrawn from the opinion I have expressed upon this subject; as to which, conceiving it to be of great importance, I should, if convinced, be very ready to retract ; but, having endeavoured to collect all the doctrine of the Court upon it, I am sure I am right in that. I wish I was as sure in the application of the evidence.

In the important and leading case of *Mackreth* v. *Symmons*, Lord Eldon, in his elaborate and learned judgment, very fully examines the authorities upon the doctrine of the vendor's equitable lien for unpaid purchase-money. The doctrine itself, which at the present day is

----

[1] This rule only applies when the equities are equal. See Rice v. Rice, 2 Drew. 1.

[2] The case alluded to by the Lord Chancellor appears to be Comer v. Walkley, stated 356, 2nd edit. ; 465, 866, 11th edit., Sugd. V. & P.

[3] The work on Vendors and Purchasers, the 14th edition of which appeared in the year 1862.

seldom, if ever, brought into dispute, is thus stated by Lord Eldon in
the principal case:—" Where," observes his Lordship, "the vendor
conveys, without more, though the consideration is upon the face of the
instrument expressed to be paid, and by a receipt indorsed upon the back,
if it is the simple case of a conveyance, the money, or part of it, not
being paid, as between the vendor and the vendee, and persons claiming
as volunteers, upon the doctrine of this Court, which when it is settled
has the effect of a contract, though perhaps no actual contract has taken
place, a lien shall prevail ; in the one case, for the whole consideration ;
in the other, for that part of the money which was not paid." See also
Chapman v. *Tanner*, 1 Vern. 267 ; *Austen* v. *Halsey*, 6 Ves. 475 ; and
the vendor of land to a railway company has been held to have a lien in
respect of unpaid *compensation as well as purchase-money
(*Walker* v. *The Ware, Hadham, and Buntingford Railway* [*310]
Company*, 1 L. R. Eq. 195, 35 Beav. 52), unless such compensation is
the subject of a separate agreement between him and the Company (Ib.),
and he is not deprived of such lien by a deposit and bond under the 85th
section of the Lands Clauses Consolidation Act, 1845 (8 & 9 Vict. c. 18,)
(Ib.), or by accepting a deposit in the names of trustees in lieu of the
statutory deposit, if the purchase and compensation moneys exceed the
deposited sum, (Ib.) ; and also as against another Company, lessee of
the Company which made the purchase (*Bishop of Winchester* v. *Mid-
Hants Railway Company*, 5 L. R. Eq. 17 ; *Cosens* v. *Bognor Railway
Company*, 1 L. R. Ch. App. 594) ; and the Court of Equity will, although
the railway may have been made over the land, and opened for public
use, enforce the lien by sale (1b.), (*Wing* v *Tottenham and Hampstead
Junction Railway Co.*, 3 L. Rep. Ch. App. 740), and will in the meantime appoint a receiver ; but it is now ultimately settled, overruling on
that point the cases of *Cosens* v. *Bognor Railway Company*, 1 L. R. Ch.
App. 594, (where, however, Turner, L. J., was in favour of a receiver)
and (*Earl St. Germains* v. *Crystal Palace Railway Company*, 11 L. R.
Eq. 568), that the Court will not grant an injunction to restrain the Company from running trains or engines over the land until the sale of the land
agreed to be taken (*Pell* v. *Northampton and Banbury Junction Railway Company*, 2 L. R. Ch. App. 100; *Munns* v. *Isle of Wight Railway
Company*, 5 L. R. Ch. App. 414 ; reversing the decision of Sir W. M.
James, V. C., reported, 8 L. R. Eq. 653. *Lycett* v. *Stafford and Uttoxeter Railway Company*, 13 L. R. Eq. 261). "But the vendor of land to a
railway company will not, after payment of the purchase-money, be entitled to a lien on the land sold for the costs of arbitration under the
'Lands Clauses Act, 1845,' payable to him by the Company : *Earl,
Ferrers* v. *Stafford and Uttoxeter Railway Company*, 13 L. R. Eq.
524."

Where a decree had been obtained by a vendor against a Railway
Company for specific performance of a contract for sale, in which in-

quiries were directed to ascertain the amount due for damages and costs, and the amount, when found due, together with the purchase-money, was ordered to be paid, but was not declared to be a charge on the land, it was held by Lord Romilly, M. R., that the vendor was not entitled, under the liberty to apply, to enforce by petition a lien on the land for the sums due, especially as there were incumbrances not parties to the suit, whose rights would be affected by such lien, (*Attorney-General* v. *Sittingbourne and Sheerness Railway Company,* 1 L. R. Eq. 636; 35 Beav. 268).

The lien also attaches if possession of the estate has been delivered to the purchaser, although there has been no conveyance of it to him [*311] (*Smith* v. *Hibbard,* 2 Dick. 730; *Charles* v. *Andrews,* 9 *Mod. 153; *Topham* v. *Constantine,* Taml. 135; *Evans* v. *Tweedy,* 1 Beav. 55; *Andrew* v. *Andrew,* 8 De G. Mac. & G. 336; *Langstaff* v. *Nicholson,* 25 Beav. 160); and upon copyholds and leaseholds, as well as freeholds (*Winter* v. *Lord Anson,* 3 Russ. 492; *Matthew* v. *Bowler,* 6 Hare, 110; *Wrout* v. *Dawes,* 25 Beav. 369).

When, however, the vendor has taken from the purchaser a security for the unpaid purchase-money, the question arises, whether that amounts to an abandonment of the lien; for its existence must be decided, not as a dry question of fact, whether a security was taken, for the mere taking of a security is not a waiver of the lien, but it depends upon the circumstance of each case, whether the Court is to infer that the lien *was intended to be reserved, or that credit was given, and exclusively given, to the person from whom the security was taken.*

The inconvenience of such a doctrine, so unsatisfactory and productive of litigation, may well have caused Lord Eldon to observe, in the principal case, " that it would have been better at once to have held, that the lien should exist in no case, and the vendor should suffer the consequences of his want of caution; or to have laid down the rule the other way so distinctly, that a purchaser might be able to know, without the judgment of a Court, in what cases it would, and in what cases it would not, exist."

It is now settled, that a mere personal security for the purchase-money, as a bond (*Hearle* v. *Botelers,* Cary, 35, and *Winter* v. *Anson,* 3 Russ. 488, reversing the decision of Sir J. Leach, V. C., 1 S. & S. 434; *Collins* v. *Collins,* 31 Beav. 346,) a bill of exchange (*Hughes* v. *Kearney,* 1 S. & L. 136; *Teed* v. *Caruthers,* 2 Y. & C. C. C. 31; *Grant* v. *Mills,* 2 V. & B. 306), or a promissory note (*Gibbons* v. *Baddall,* 2 Eq. Ca. Abr. 682, n.; *Hughes* v. *Kearney,* 1 S. & L. 132; *Ex parte Peake,* 1 Madd. 346; *Ex parte Loaring,* 2 Rose, 79), will not, without more, be sufficient evidence of the intention of the vendor to give credit exclusively to the purchaser, or to his security, so as to take away the lien.

In *Winter* v. *Lord Anson,* 1 S. & S. 434, there was an agreement for

the sale of an estate, by which it was, amongst other things, agreed that
the amount of the consideration-money should be secured by the bond
of the purchaser to the vendor, with interest at 4*l.* per cent., and should
remain so secured, *during the life of the vendor,* on the regular payment of interest. A conveyance was executed, *in pursuance of the
agreement, and in consideration of the purchase-money therein expressed to have been paid,* and the vendor's receipt was indorsed upon
it. Part only of the purchase-money had, in fact, been paid, and the
residue was secured by bond conditioned *to be void on payment [*312]
by the vendee, to the executors, administrators, or assigns of
the vendor of the residue of the purchase-money within twelve months
next after the decease of the vendor, with interest at 4*l.* per cent. Sir
J. Leach, M. R., although he at first decided in favour of the lien,
afterwards decided against it, upon the ground that the case was,
in principle, the same as if the conveyance had stated the real
contract of the parties; and that by the effect of that contract, the
vendor agreed to part with his estate *in consideration of the bond for
the future* payment of the price; and that, when such bond was executed, the estate passed to the vendee in equity, as well as at law. " Suppose," observed his Honor, " it had been expressed in this conveyance,
that the price was not to be paid until the death of the vendor, and
there had been a covenant on the part of the purchaser then to pay the
amount, and to pay the interest in the meantime; could it then have
been said that it appeared by this deed that the vendor had contracted
not to part with his estate until the actual payment of the price?
Would it not rather have been the true effect of the language of the
conveyance in such case, that the vendor had contracted to part with
his estate presently, and not in consideration of the actual immediate payment of the price, *but in consideration of the covenant for the
future payment of that sum,* with interim interest: and that having,
therefore, the covenant, which was the consideration bargained for, the
estate must pass by the conveyance in equity, as well as at law?" This
decision was reversed by Lord Lyndhurst, who held, that the circumstance, that the money was secured to be paid at a future day, did not
affect the lien. " I do not think," said his Lordship, " that the lien is
affected by the fact of the period of payment being dependent on the
life of the vendor. That circumstance does not appear to me to afford
such clear and convincing evidence of the intention of the vendor to
rely, not upon the security of the estate, but solely upon the personal
credit of the vendee, as would be necessary in order to get rid of the
lien. It would not be inconsistent with an express pledge; and I do
not perceive why it is at variance with the lien resulting from the rules
of a Court of Equity;" 3 Russ. 488. An appeal was lodged in the
House of Lords against this decision, but it was afterwards withdrawn:
Sugd. V. & P. 258, 11th edit.

Where an estate is conveyed, in consideration of an annuity, the vendor will have a lien upon the land for the annuity, although a bond or covenant is given to secure the payment of the annuity. See *Tardiffe* v. *Scrughan*, 1 Bro. C. C. 423, where Lord Camden's opinion [*313] seems to have been that the mere *circumstance of an estate being given in consideration of an annuity, with a bond, would not prevent the lien attaching from time to time: *Blackburn* v. *Greyson*, 1 Bro. C. C. 420. In *Clarke* v. *Royle*, 3 Sim. 502, Sir L. Shadwell, V. C., is reported to have said, that it appeared to him that Lord Eldon, in *Mackreth* v. *Symmons*, had expressly overruled the decision of Lord Camden, in *Tardiffe* v. *Scrughan*. However, in *Buckland* v. *Pocknell*, 13 Sim. 412, his Honor, in allusion to what he was reported to have said in *Clarke* v. *Royle*, observes : " I think that, if that were said in those very terms, it was said too strongly ; because it cannot be said that my Lord Eldon did overrule *Tardiffe* v. *Scrughan;* although I think that it may be fairly inferred from the remarks that he made upon that case, in his judgment in *Mackreth* v. *Symmons*, that he was not satisfied with the decision in all its parts. He shows, as it strikes me, an inclination to criticise it, and to escape from it, if the circumstances of the case before him would allow him to do so. But I do not wish it to be understood to be my opinion, that he overruled it point blank." In the case of *Matthew* v. *Bowler*, 6 Hare, 110, where there was a sale and assignment of a life interest in leaseholds in *consideration of a weekly sum*, to be paid to the vendor during her life, with *a covenant by* the purchaser, for himself, his heirs, executors, and administrators, to make the weekly payment to the vendor, and to repair and insure the premises, and otherwise perform the covenants in the lease; it was held by Sir James Wigram, V. C., that the vendor was entitled to a lien on the life interest in the leaseholds, which was the subject of the assignment for the weekly payment. His Honor said, " That, if the case of *Tardiffe* v. *Scrughan* was not approved, it certainly was not overruled by Lord Eldon. The case had been much considered by Sir Edward Sugden ; and it was clear that his opinion was, that the lien in such a case ought to be sustained. He should be most reluctant to come to a different conclusion. He was of opinion, in this case, that the plaintiff was entitled to the lien claimed by her bill. The purpose of the covenants in the deed to uphold the property could scarcely be understood, unless the property was intended to constitute a security."

Upon examining carefully that branch of the principal case which relates to the lien claimed for the annuities, it will be found, notwithstanding the ambiguity of Lord Eldon's language, that it may be reconciled with *Tardiffe* v. *Scrughan* and *Matthew* v. *Bowler ;* for Lord Eldon did not, as a bare abstract point of law, decide that there is no lien where an estate is sold in consideration of an annuity secured by

a bond or *covenant; but he considered that the *special cir-* [*314]
cumstances of the case showed that the vendor *intended to*
rely upon the personal security, viz., the bond for 20,000*l.,* and that
such was the conception also of the vendee. The principle, therefore,
upon which that branch of *Mackreth* v. *Symmons* was decided, is certainly correct; but it has been doubted by an eminent writer, whether
the circumstances of the case were such as justified Lord Eldon in
coming to the conclusion, that it was the intention of the vendor to
rely upon the personal security, and thus discharge the lien for the
annuities. See Sugd. V. & P. 869, 11th edit.

In *Clarke* v. *Royle,* 3 Sim. 499, the conveyance was made in *consid-*
eration of the vendee entering into covenants therein contained for pay-
ment of an annuity to the vendor, and 3,000l. to certain persons in the
event of the vendee's marrying. Sir L. Shadwell, V. C., distinguishing
the case from *Tardiffe* v. *Scrughan,* held, that there was no lien, on
the ground that the deed plainly marked out, that the *consideration on*
the one side, was the conveyance of the estate, and, on the other the
entering into the covenants. " Why," he asked, " am I to declare, that,
in respect of this annuity, and of the sum which is payable on a contingency, and which, therefore, never may be payable, there is to be a
lien on the purchased estates? Why should I go further than any of
the cases that have been hitherto decided upon the subject of lien on
purchased estates, and do that which appears to be contrary to the intention of the parties? I consider that this case is decided by the
authority of *Winter* v. *Lord Anson."* It may be here remarked, that
the Vice-Chancellor does not appear to have been aware that the decision of Sir J. Leach had been reversed by Lord Lyndhurst. However, it is presumed that *Clarke* v. *Royle* is still a binding authority,
because there a case actually arose similar to that which Sir J. Leach
assumed, though wrongly, to exist in *Winter* v. *Lord Anson.* In that
case, the conveyance, though expressed to be made in pursuance of the
agreement (which, however, was to take a bond, and not a covenant),
did not otherwise refer to it, and was expressed to be made, not in consideration of the agreement, but *in consideration of a sum of money.*
In *Clarke* v. *Royle,* the conveyance was *in consideration of certain*
covenants being entered into by the purchaser; the covenants, therefore, plainly formed the consideration, and the lien was gone.

Upon the same principle it has been held, that, where a receipt was
given by the vendor for a bond, as the consideration for an estate, the
lien was gone; thus, in *Parrott* v. *Sweetland,* 3 My. & K. 655, a daughter conveyed her *remainder in fee in an estate to her father, [*315]
who was tenant for life, subject to a mortgage, in consideration
of his entering into a covenant to indemnify her against the mortgage,
and in consideration of 3000*l.* advanced, or agreed to be advanced or
secured to her, in contemplation of her intended marriage, *upon the*

terms expressed in a bond bearing even date therewith. On the indenture of release was indorsed a receipt signed by the daughter, as follows:—" Received on the day and year first written, of and from the within-named J. P., *a bond for the sum of* 3000*l.*, *being the full consideration within expressed to be given by him ;*" and the condition for making void the bond was, upon payment to his daughter and her intended husband of an annuity for their lives, and of 3000*l.* in certain events. Sir J. Leach, M. R., decided against the lien, observing that it was plain that it was not a case of a security, but a substitution for the price which the vendor had agreed to accept, and that the lien for the purchase-money was consequently discharged. This decision was affirmed by the Lords Commissioners, Sir L. Shadwell and Mr. Justice Bosanquet. Sir L. Shadwell thought that, although the appeal had been argued as if it were a naked case of vendor and purchaser, it appeared to be a sort of family arrangement between a father, daughter, and her intended husband, utterly inconsistent with the notion of a payment of purchase-money ; and that it was obvious that the parties did not treat the consideration as a mere sum of 3000*l.* ; that the receipt was for the bond, and not for the 3000*l.* ; and it appeared, therefore, that the parties were bargaining for a security, and not a stipulated sum, and consequently no lien arose, because the vendor had actually received the consideration.

So, likewise, in *Buckland* v. *Pocknell*, 13 Sim. 406, where A. agreed to sell an estate to B. for the annuity of 200*l.*, to be paid to him for his life, and an annuity of 92*l.*, to be paid after his decease to his son, and B. was to pay off a mortgage to which the estate was subject. Accordingly B. executed a deed, by which he granted the annuities to A. and his son, and covenanted to pay them ; and by a conveyance of even date, but executed after the annuity deed, after reciting the annuity deed, A. and the mortgagee, in pursuance of the agreement, and in *consideration of the premises and of the annuities having been so granted as thereinbefore recited,* and of the payment of the mortgage-money, conveyed the estate to B. Upon the death of A., his son's annuity, which had been assigned to the plaintiff, became in arrear. Sir L. Shadwell, V. C., held that there was no lien for the annuity. " The [*316] *question," observes his Honor, " is whether it does not appear, on the face of the deeds, that the party who contracted to sell the land has got *that which he contracted to have.* Adverting to the mode in which the conveyances are made, my opinion is, that it would be quite wrong, because it would be contrary to what appears to have been the agreement of the parties, to hold, that, after the deeds were executed, any lien remained for the annuities. As there was a separate instrument, which was executed first, which contained a distinct grant of the two annuities, and covenants for payment of them ; and *as the conveyance was made expressly in consideration of that deed;* and as it was part of the express stipulation that the mortgage-money should be paid off, and, consequently, that the mortgagee should convey his legal estate to the purchaser, it would be quite inconsistent with the mode in which the parties have dealt, to say that there is still an ulterior latent equity, for the purpose of securing the annuity in a manner in which neither party ever thought that it was to be secured; and it is evident that they did not think that it was to be so secured, from their having taken a specific security for it. In the case of *Parrott* v. *Sweetland*, which came before me and Mr. Justice Bosanquet, when we had the honour of being Commissioners of the Great Seal, we affirmed the judgment of Sir J. Leach, in a case where the course of the transaction showed that the party had got that for which he bargained."

So, likewise, in *Dixon* v. *Gayfere*, (17 Beav. 421; 21 Beav. 118), where the purchaser contracted to buy an estate from the vendor, and upon an assignment being made to grant to the vendor an annuity of £50 per annum, during three lives, "*to be secured by bond*," Sir John Romilly, M. R., held, that the vendor had no lien on the estate for payment of the annuity. "The case of *Buckland* v. *Pocknell*," said his Honor, "appeals to me to be very near the present. . . . It appears to me the mode of carrying the contract in the present case into effect is this:—By a separate and independent instrument the vendor should convey the land, and, in consideration of that conveyance, the purchaser should secure the annuity by his bond. . . . . This result does not appear to me to militate with the case of *Winter* v. *Lord Anson* (3 Russ. 488), nor do I dispute the authority of that case. In fact, both the cases of *Clarke* v. *Royle*, (3 Sim. 499), and *Buckland* v. *Pocknell*, are distinguished from that; and one of the grounds on which the Vice-Chancellor of England went, in *Buckland* v. *Pocknell*, was, that it would be quite inconsistent with the mode in which the parties had dealt, to say that there should be *a lien for the purchase- [*317] money during the lives of the annuitants." The decree of his Honor in this case was varied by Lord Cranworth, C., who, agreeing with his Honor that the vendor had no lien on the estate for payment of the annuity, held that he was entitled (the purchaser being dead, and there having been no conveyance) to have the annuity secured by a valid and effectual bond before he could be called upon to convey the estate. 1 De G. & Jo. 655. See also *Dyke* v. *Rendall*, 2 De G. Mac. & G. 209; *Stuart* v. *Ferguson*, Hayes, Ir. Exch. Rep. 452.

Upon the same principle it has been held, that the vendor to a railway company in consideration of a rent-charge, has no lien for it if unpaid. See *Earl of Jersey* v. *Briton Ferry Floating Dock Co.*, 7 L. R. Eq. 409. There, by an agreement dated in 1851, a company under powers conferred by the Lands Clauses Act, in consideration of the payment of a yearly rent-charge and royalties, agreed to purchase land for the construction of docks. It was agreed, by the 14th clause of the agreement, that "the above mentioned rents and royalties should be *charged and secured by the conveyance*, according to the provisions of the 11th section of the Lands Clauses Consolidation Act, 1845." The company entered and completed the construction of the docks, but had not made any payment in respect of the rent-charge. It was held by Sir W. M. James, V. C., upon the authority of *Winter* v. *Lord Anson*, 1 S. & S. 434, which he considered to be unaffected by Lord Lyndhurst's decision, that the vendors were not entitled to a lien for the unpaid arrears of the rent-charge; and, after referring to Lord Lyndhurst's judgment (3 Russ. 488), his Honor observed, "Let us consider what the effect of these doctrines is, as applied to this case. A man conveys a piece of land for the construction of a public work, in consideration of an annual payment. It appears to me it would be quite contrary to the intention of the parties to suppose the vendor was reserving to himself a right, at some future time, to enter and destroy the public work, if the annual rent should fall into arrear. Hence, in my opinion, there is no lien in such a case for unpaid purchase-money. The question of receiver stands on a very different footing, but that question does not arise till the conveyance is settled." See further as to remedies of the owner of a rent-charge against a railway company, *Eyton* v. *Denbigh, Ruthin, and Corwen Railway Company*, 6 L. R. Eq. 14.

From the foregoing cases we may conclude, that, although the mere giving of a bond, bill of exchange, promissory note, or covenant, [*318] *for the purchase-money, or the granting of an annuity secured by a bond or a covenant, will not be sufficient to discharge the equitable lien, yet where it appears that the note, bond, covenant, or annuity was *substituted* for the consideration-money, and was, in fact, the thing bargained for, the lien will be lost. See *In re Albert Life Assurance Company*, 11 L. R. Eq. 178.

An actual agreement, though by parol, to accept a security, and rely upon it alone, will, it seems, discharge the vendor's lien for unpaid purchase-money. See 1 S. & S. 445, where Sir John Leach observes, "That it is the vendor who in the first place attempts to raise an equity against the allegation of the deed; and if the vendor be permitted to repel the effect of the deed, by showing that the price was not paid, it must necessarily follow, that the vendee must be at liberty to disclose the whole truth, and to explain the reason why that payment was not made."

Although the lien of a vendor for unpaid purchase-money may be discharged by his accepting the solicitors employed in the sale as his debtors in the place of the purchaser, on the supposition that the purchase-money had been paid to them, this was held not to be the case where in fact no payment of the purchase-money was made by the vendor to the solicitors, but they were simply directed by the purchaser to pay the purchase-money out of monies due by them to the purchaser on an unsettled account. See *Wrout* v. *Dawes*, 25 Beav. 369.

If a vendor who knows the purchase-money is trust-money, suffers one of the trustees to retain part of it, without the knowledge of the co-trustees or the cestuis que trust, he has no lien on the estate for the part so retained: *White* v. *Wakefield*, 7 Sim. 401; and see *Price* v. *Blakemore*, 6 Beav. 507.

Upon the same principle in *Muir* v. *Jolly*, 26 Beav. 143, a trustee having purchased an estate on behalf of the trust, the vendor executed a conveyance to the trustee, which recited the trust, and that the trustee had called in trust-monies sufficient to pay the purchase-money, and it contained a receipt for the whole purchase-money. In fact, only a part was paid, and the trustee gave his bond and a memorandum of deposit for the deficiency, the latter reciting that the vendor had lent the trustee that sum to enable him to complete. It was held by Sir John Romilly, M. R., that the vendor had no lien on the title-deeds in his possession for the unpaid purchase-money.

Where there was a stipulation that the purchase-money should be paid *within two years after a re-sale*, it was held that the vendor's *lien was gone: *Ex parte Parkes*, 1 G. & J. 228. [*319]

It has been held, that, if a vendor take a totally distinct and independent security for the unpaid purchase-money, it will then become a case of substitution for the lien, instead of a credit given. Thus, in *Nairn* v. *Prowse*, 6 Ves. 752, Sir William Grant, M. R., held, that a vendor's equitable lien upon an estate, for the purchase-money, was lost by his taking, as a special security, a Long Annuity of £100 a-year, by way of a pledge. "Suppose," said his Honor, "a mortgage was made upon another estate of the vendee, will equity, at the same time, give him what is in effect a mortgage upon the estate he sold; the obvious intention of burthening one estate being, that the other shall remain free and unencumbered? Though in that case the vendee would be a creditor, if the mortgage proved deficient, yet he would not be a creditor by lien upon the estate he had conveyed away. The same rule must hold with regard to any other pledge for the purchase-money. In this case the vendor trusts to no personal security of the vendee, but gets possession of a Long Annuity of £100 a-year, which, according to the rise or fall of stock, might or might not be sufficient for the purchase-money. He has, therefore, an absolute security in his hands, not the personal security of the vendee. Could the vendee have any motive for parting with his stock, but to have the absolute dominion over the land?"

The case put by Sir William Grant, that a mortgage of another estate will be a substitution for the lien, must, it seems, be qualified in the manner laid down by Lord Eldon in the principal case: as the question will be, whether, from the circumstances attending the mortgage, the intention of the vendor to give up the lien can be clearly and satisfactorily implied. See *Cowell* v. *Simpson*, 16 Ves. 278; 2 Ball & B. 515. But, where a bond was given for the unpaid purchase-money, and a mortgage *on part* of the purchased estate, the intention, that the lien should not extend over the rest of the estate, was held to be sufficiently clear: *Capper* v. *Spottiswoode*, Taml. 21. So, likewise, in *Bond* v. *Kent*, 2 Vern. 281, where the vendor took a mortgage of the estate for part of the purchase-money, and a note for the remainder, it was held that he had no lien for the money due on the note; "because," as observed by Lord Redesdale, in commenting on that case, "it was manifestly the intention of the parties that the amount of the note should not be a lien on the lands, else they would have had a mortgage for the whole; the seller took the estate for his debtor for part of the purchase-money, and was content with the note for the remaining part."

[*320] *See *Hughes* v. *Kearney*, 1 S. & L. 135; *Eyre* v. *Sadleir*, 14 Ir. Ch. Rep. 119, 15 *Ib* 1.

In *Cood* v. *Pollard*, 9 Price, 544; 10 Price, 109, the purchaser, with the concurrence of the vendor, mortgaged the estate for a sum which the vendor received in part payment of the purchase-money, taking bills, which were ultimately dishonoured, for the remainder: it was held, that the vendor had no lien on the purchase-money arising from a second sale, in preference to the mortgagee.

Where the vendor, without receiving the purchase-money, executes a conveyance for the purpose of enabling the purchaser to execute a mortgage, he will lose his lien on the estate as against mortgagee: *Smith* v. *Evans*, 28 Beav. 59.

There will be no lien upon land in favour of a legatee, who has conveyed it away pursuant to the directions of a will, as a condition precedent to the receipt of the legacy, and which the executor (who had lost the assets of his testator) did not pay. See *Barker* v. *Barker*, 10 L. R. Eq. 438. There a testator gave a legacy to each of his daughters on condition that she should convey her share of certain real estate, to which the daughters were entitled, to the sons of the testator; and in case of any daughter refusing or being unable to comply with the condition, the legacy bequeathed to her was to be forfeited, and to form part of the testator's residuary personal estate. The testator gave his residuary personal estate to his sons; and he appointed one of them, and two other persons, executors. The daughters conveyed their shares of the real estate to their brothers, but did not obtain payment of the legacies. It was held by Lord Romilly, M. R., that they were not entitled to any lien, in the nature of a vendor's lien, on the real estate conveyed by them for their legacies. "Unquestionably," said his Lordship, "they had an election in the first instance; they might have given up their legacies and retained the property, but till they conveyed it there was no right to the legacies. They did not then convey, making any terms as to the payment of the legacies, but they performed the condition absolutely. They might unquestionably have done this—have bargained with their brothers that the legacies should remain a charge upon the shares until the legacies were paid; but there was no contract of that description: and the question, which is a somewhat novel one I think, and which was fully argued before me, is this: whether, on the construction of the will, this express condition that each daughter shall, at the request and costs of the sons, convey her estate, does create a charge upon the property *conveyed. I [*321] think this is a mere personal obligation, and that it does not create a charge."

Marshalling for Lien. In the principal case, Lord Eldon expressed some doubt, although it was not necessary to decide the point, whether, on the death of the vendee, without having paid his purchase-money, a Court of Equity would marshal his assets in favor of *third parties*, by allowing them, in case the vendor, having a lien on the real estate, should exhaust the personalty, to stand in his place on the real estate to the extent of his lien. In *Coppin* v. *Coppin*, Sel. Ch. Ca. 28, Lord King held that the ordinary rule of marshalling would not apply to such a case; and in *Pollexfen* v. *Moore*, 3 Atk. 273, Lord Hardwicke said, " That this equity (*i. e.* the lien for unpaid purchase-money) will not extend to a third person, but is confined to the vendor and vendee." It has, however, been repeatedly decided, overruling *Coppin* v. *Coppin*, and the dictum in *Pollexfen* v. *Moore*, that the lien of a vendor must be subjected to the ordinary rule of marshalling assets, and that, consequently, when the purchased estate *descends*, the estate and personal assets will, as against the heir, be marshalled in favour of simple contract creditors and legatees (*Trimmer* v. *Bayne*, 9 Ves. 209; *Sproule* v. *Prior*, 8 Sim. 189); and where the purchased estate is *devised*, as against the devisees, in favour of simple contract creditors (*Selby* v. *Selby*, 4 Russ. 336; *Emuss* v. *Smith*, 2 De G. & Sm. 722), but not in favour of legatees (*Wythe* v. *Henniker*, 2 My. & K. 635; but see *Birds* v. *Askey*, 24 Beav. 618, 621; Lord *Lilford* v. *Powys-Keck*, 1 L. R. Eq. 347; but now, freehold and copyhold estates are, under the statute 3 & 4 Will. 4, c. 104, assets for the payment of debts by simple contract, in all cases coming within the operation of the statute, the doctrine of marshalling is inapplicable and such debts will be satisfied when necessary out of those estates.

The doctrine of marshalling will form the subject of another note, and is only mentioned here on account of the doubt thrown out by Lord Eldon in the principal case, as to its being extended to the vendor's lien for unpaid purchase-money.

The vendor's lien is assignable even by parol (*Dryden* v *Frost*, 3 My. & Cr. 640); but the assignee will take it subject to any prior incumbrances created by the vendor: *Lacey* v. *Ingle*, 2 Ph. 413 ; *Mangles* v. *Dixon*, 1 Mac. & G. 437, 3 Ho. Lo. Ca. 702.

Vendee's Lien for prematurely paid Purchase-Money.]—If the purchase-money, or part of it, has been paid prematurely, before a convey-[*322] ance, the vendee will have a lien upon the estate in the hands *of the vendor, even it seems although he may have taken a security for his money. This doctrine has been laid down in various cases, and it has been the subject of great consideration in the leading case of *Wythes* v. *Lee*, 3 Drew. 396: there the defendant, a mortgagee, who held the mortgage, as to the greater part, in trust for several persons; as to a part, as mortgagee for himself, selling under a power of sale, contracted to sell the mortgaged estate for 380,000*l.*, and the plaintiff paid 38,000*l.*, part of the purchase-money, by way of deposit. A bill having been filed by the purchaser, claiming a lien on the estate for his deposit, a demurrer to the bill was overruled by Sir R. T. Kindersley. V. C. " The point," said his Honor, " most discussed, and the most important, is this abstract question. Suppose a person, absolute beneficial owner in fee of an estate, contracts to sell it, and the purchaser pays a deposit in part payment of the purchase-money, and by reason of the vendor being unable to make a title, or from any other reason, not being misconduct on either side, the contract goes off, and cannot be completed ; has the purchaser a lien on the estate for his deposit? That is the most important question. If there is a right of lien, as that is a right in equity, it follows that it must be capable of being enforced by bill.

" Now, that question I have looked at in three different points of view:— 1. With reference to natural justice, irrespectively of any specific rule of law ; and it does appear to me that it is consistent with natural justice, that if a purchaser, on the faith of the contract being completed, and the estate becoming his, has advanced money in payment, or part payment, for the purchase, he has advanced it under circumstances which entitle him to say, ' If you cannot complete, not only are you bound to give me back my money, but I have a right to a lien on the estate.' 2. With reference to the general law of this Court, I do not mean with reference to decided cases, but to the general law and principles of this Court. This is clear, that the *vendor*, if he has parted with the estate to the purchaser before he has got his money, has a lien for it on the estate ; that is unquestionable. Now, does the right of the *purchaser*, if the contract goes off, stand in principle on the same footing as that of the vendor? The only distinction that occurs to me is this:—the vendor, when he contracts to sell his estate, is owner ; he has the estate in his own possession, at least under his own control ; and when he contracts to sell, his right is to say, ' I will convey the estate when the purchase-money is paid, but till that is done, I will

not convey it.' That right creates a lien of itself, *very analo- [*323]
gous to the common law lien; and that lien, which exists before
conveyance, still continues; it is not a new, but the same lien. But
with regard to the purchaser, he has not the estate in his possession,
and his lien is not in its origin the same sort of lien as that of the
vendor. But when a contract is made and then goes off, it appears to
me, that, in principle and justice, the equity of the purchaser to a lien
on the estate ought to stand on as good a footing as the lien of the vendor after conveyance. A difficulty has been suggested, that with
regard to a vendor, by taking an additional security for the purchase-
money, as a general rule, he loses his right to his lien, and a purchaser
does not. The ground of the distinction I am at a loss to understand,
But, however that may be, it appears to me that, on principles of equity
and justice, the purchaser, when the contract goes off, has a lien." His
Honor then examining this subject in a third point of view, viz., as to
the authorities, after noticing the dictum in *Burgess* v. *Wheate*, referred
to in the principal case (*ante*, p. 301); and the opinion of Lord St.
Leonards, in his work on Vendors and Purchasers (see vol. ii. p. 857,
11th ed.), and observing, that "there is no single case in which any
such claim has been made by a purchaser," added: "But I do not see
any inconvenience in establishing the rule; I do not see any hardship
in it. It is true, that in some cases the Court has refused to order the
deposit to be returned; but those have all been cases in which the bill
was for other purposes, and the return of the deposit was collateral. I
do not see what mischief could result from entertaining a bill for the
single purpose of establishing the right to a lien for the deposit; and,
if it were necessary for me now to determine the question of the right
to a lien, I should feel great difficulty in getting over the authorities
on the subject, the dictum in *Burgess* v. *Wheate*, the observations of
Lord Eldon in *Mackreth* v. *Symmons*, and the opinion of Lord St.
Leonards, especially as I think natural justice is strongly in favour of
the doctrine." But his Honor did not decide whether, in the peculiar
circumstances of the case, the vendee would have a lien for the purchase-money as against the mortgagor or the persons for whom the
mortgagee was trustee.

The vendee will have a lien for prematurely paid purchase-money not
only as against the vendor, but as against a subsequent mortgagee who
had notice of the payments having been made: (*Watson* v. *Rose*, 10 W.
R. (V.-C. K.), 755, S. C. nom. *Rose* v. *Watson*, 10 H. L. Ca. 672,) even
although some of the payments are in pursuance of the contract made
after the mortgage, at any rate if the mortgagee gives no notice [*324]
of any *intention to interfere with the contract.—*Ib.*

It seems, however, that where a purchaser prematurely pays part of
the purchase-money to a mortgagee selling under a power of sale, he
would have a lien upon the interest of the mortgagee. "There is," said

Kindersley, V. C., "certainly a ground of equity for that; for though that which was the subject of sale was a fee-simple, there is justice in saying, if the vendor is entitled to some lesser interest, to the extent of that interest, the purchaser is entitled to the lien." See *Wythes* v. *Lee*, 3 Drew, 406; *Burgess* v. *Wheate*, 1 Eden, 211; *Lacon* v. *Mertins*, 3 Atk. 1; *Oxenham* v. *Esdaile*, 2 Y. & J. 493; 3 Y. & J. 262.

In the event of a sale by the first purchaser of an estate having a lien upon it for prematurely paid purchase-money, the second purchaser who has also paid his *purchase-money* or part of it prematurely will, in case the first purchase is rescinded, have a lien upon the sum in respect of which the first purchaser had a lien upon the estate. See *Aberaman Iron Works* v. *Wickens*, 4 L. R. Ch. App. 101. There Bailey, the owner of on estate, agreed to sell it to Wickens for 250,000*l*., representing it to contain 1530 acres. Wickens paid Bailey 50,000*l*., part of the purchase-money. Wickens agreed to sell the Aberaman estate to the Aberamen Iron Works Company for 350,000*l*., of which 150,000*l*. was paid to him, 75,000*l*. in cash, and bonds for 75,000*l*. Wickens having brought an action against Bailey (in consequence of the estate containing 430 acres less than it was represented to contain), the action was compromised by Baily repaying the 50,000*l*., 25,000*l*. in cash and 25,000*l*. in bills of 5000*l*. each, and by the agreement being abandoned. The company then filed a bill against Wickens for a return of the 75,000*l*. and the bonds. Wickens received the proceeds of four of the bills of exchange for 5000*l*.; but the fifth bill for 5000*l*. remaining unpaid, the proceeds were brought into Court in the suit. It was held by Lord Cairns, L. C., reversing the decision of Sir R. Malins, V. C. (reported 5 L. R. Eq. 485), that the company were entitled to repayment of what they had paid, and to a return of the bonds, and that they had a lien on that portion of the 50,000*l*. repaid to the purchaser which had been paid into court. "Adverting," said his lordship, "to the demand which is made on the part of the plaintiffs for a lien in respect of the purchase-money which has been paid, that question stands thus:— 50,000*l*. was paid by Wickens to Bailey on account of the purchase of the estate. According to the decisions which were referred to—the case of *Wythes* v. *Lee* (3 Drew. 396) and the case of *Rose* v. *Watson* (10 Ho. Lo. C. 672), Wickens, *in the event of the purchase going off, would have a lien for this 50,000*l*. upon the Aberaman estate belonging to Bailey. In like manner the company, in their turn, for the purchase-money which they paid Wickens, would, in the event of their contract going off, have lien upon any interest which Wickens might possess in the Aberaman estate; and, according to the decisions to which I have referred, Wickens to the extent of the 50,000*l*. he paid, had become the owner, by way of incumbrance, of a corresponding amount in value on the Aberaman estate. It appears to me, therefore, upon the authority of those decisions, to be clear that the company,

[*325]

supposing the 50,000*l.* had not been repaid by Bailey to Wickens, would have been entitled to maintain a bill against Wickens and Bailey to prevent the money getting back into the hands of Wickens. In point of fact, when the bill was filed, the 50,000*l.* had, in part, been repaid to Wickens; but part of the amount remained in *specie* in the form of a bill of exchange of Bailey's, which had not been paid. This bill of exchange was intercepted by the injunction of the Court; and, in respect of it, I find 6,232*l.* is now in court. Upon that sum it appears to me the plaintiffs in this suit have established their right to a lien. The decree of the Vice Chancellor, therefore, must, in my opinion, be reversed; and a decree must be made directing an account of the purchase-money paid by the company to Wickens, and repayment of it with interest at 4*l.* per cent. from the time of payment. A time must be fixed for that repayment. The bonds remaining in the possession of Wickens must be delivered up; and he must be ordered to concur in the delivery up of some which are with the London and County Bank."

Where it turns out that another person is, under the contract of sale, entitled to the estate, the person taking the conveyance to himself, or his assignees, will have a lien for the purchase-money that he has paid: *Neeson* v. *Clarkson*, 4 Hare, 97. But the lien will not exist where the purchaser has by his own default abandoned the contract (*Dinn* v. *Grant*, 5 De G. & Sm. 451), nor where the contract is by statute illegal (1 *Ewing* v. *Osbaldiston*, 2 My. & Cr. 88). *Secus*, if the purchaser repudiates the contract where the vendor cannot make a good title, or where the sale constitutes a breach of trust (*Wythes* v. *Lee*, 3 Drew. 396).

Where, in a suit by a vendor for specific performance, a good title is not deduced, the Court will order a return of deposit-money with interest at 4*l.* per cent., declaring also that the purchaser has a lien on the estate for the same, and also for the costs of the suit; *Turner* v. *Marriott*, 3 L. R. Eq. 744; *Middleton* v. *Magnay*, 2 H. & M. 233; "and it will make the same order where a contract has [*326] been rescinded on the ground of fraud, surprise, misrepresentation, or anything of the kind; *Torrance* v. *Bolton*, 14 L. R. Eq. 124, 135."

Upon the same principle, a person who pursuant to an agreement expends money upon property agreed to be leased to him, and which the proposed lessor agrees to repay on his failure to grant a lease, will have a lien on the interest of the proposed lessor in the property, upon his being unable to grant a lease for want of title: *Middleton* v. *Magnay*, 2 Hem. & Mill. 233.

Estate in the hands of Third Parties when Bound by Lien.]—The equitable lien for unpaid purchase-money will, as is laid down in *Mackreth* v. *Symmons*, bind the estate not only in the hands of the purchaser and his heirs, and persons taking from them as volunteers, but also in the hands of purchasers for valuable consideration, who bought with notice that the purchase-money remained unpaid (*Hearle* v. *Bote-lers*, Cary's Ch. Rep. 35; *Walker* v. *Preswick*, 2 Ves. 622; *Hughes* v. *Kearney*, 1 S. & L. 135; *Winter* v. *Lord Anson*, 3 Russ. 488; *S. C.*, 1 S. & S. 434; *Frail* v. *Ellis*, 16 Beav. 350, 354); but the lien will not prevail against a bonâ fide purchaser who bought without notice that the purchase-money remained unpaid (*Cator* v. *Earl of Pembroke*, 1 Bro. C. C. 302); and, although the title is deduced from the first vendor, in recital, still that will not be sufficient to affect the purchaser with notice, if the recital does not show that the estate was not paid for: *Cator* v. *Earl of Pembroke*, 1 Bro. C. C. 302; *Eyre* v. *Sadleir*, 14 Ir. Ch. Rep. 119; 15 *Ib.* 1. See, however, *Davies* v. *Thomas*, 2 Y. & C. Exch. Ca. 234; in which case a reference, in the conveyance of the second purchasers to the will under which the sale was made, was held to be sufficient notice of a lien not appearing upon the face of the will, upon the ground that notice of the will ought to have put the purchasers upon inquiries which would have led to the discovery of the lien. The authority of this case, as to what is deemed sufficient notice, seems doubtful. See Sugd. V. & P. 819, 11th ed.

The fact of the vendor remaining in possession of the estate as lessee, where he has acknowledged the receipt of the purchase-money in the body of the deed and by indorsement, will not be notice of the purchase-money remaining unpaid, so as to cause the lien to attach: *White* v. *Wakefield*, 7 Sim. 401.

But where the vendor claiming a lien retains the conveyance and the title-deeds, a subsequent purchaser or mortgagee may be affected with notice of the lien; *Worthington* v. *Morgan*, 16 Sim. 547; *Peto* v. *Hammond*, 30 Beav. 495; and see *Hewitt* v. *Loosemore*, 9 Hare, 449; *Finch* v. *Shaw*, 18 Jur. 937.

[*327] *If the legal estate is outstanding, then, as the second purchaser has only an equitable interest, subsequent to that of the equitable lien, the maxim, " Qui prior est tempore potior est jure," may, as in the principal case, apply; and the equitable lien will have precedence.

Where, however, the equity of a second purchaser or mortgagee having only an equitable interest is better than that of the vendor claiming a lien for unpaid purchase-money, such purchaser or mortgagee will be entitled to priority over the lien.

This subject has been much discussed in the important and leading case of *Rice* v. *Rice*, 2 Drew. 73. There certain leasehold property was assigned to a purchaser, *by a deed which recited the payment of the whole purchase-money, and had the usual receipt indorsed on it*, and the *title-deeds were delivered up to the purchaser*. Some of the vendors received no part of their share of the purchase-money, having allowed the payment to stand over for a few days, on the promise of the purchaser then to pay. The day after the execution of the deed, the purchaser depos-

ited the assignment and title-deeds with the defendants, with the memorandum of deposit to secure an advance, and then absconding, without
paying either the vendors or the equitable mortgagees. It was held by
Sir R. T. Kindersley, V. C., that the defendants, the equitable mortgagees, having the better equity, were entitled to payment out of the
estate in priority to the claim of the vendors for their lien. " In a contest," said his Honor, " between persons having only equitable interests,
priority of time is the ground of preference *last resorted to ; i. e.*, a
Court of equity will not prefer the one to the other, on the mere ground
of priority of time, until it finds, upon an examination of their relative
merits, that there is no other sufficient ground of preference between
them ; or, in other words, that their equities are *in all other respects
equal ;* and that if one has, on other grounds, a better equity than the
other, priority of time is immaterial. . . . . So far as relates to the nature and quality of the two equitable interests, abstractedly considered,
they seem to me to stand on an equal footing ; and this I conceive to
have been the ground of Lord Eldon's decision in *Mackreth* v. *Symmons*, where, in a contest between the vendor's lien for unpaid purchase-
money, and the right of a person who had subsequently obtained from
the purchasers a mere contract for a mortgage, and nothing more, he
decided in favour of the former, as being prior in point of time. . . . . .
If, then, the vendor's lien for unpaid purchase-money, and the right of
an equitable mortgagee by mere contract for a *mortgage, are [*328]
equitable interests of equal worth in respect of their abstract
nature and quality, is there anything in the special circumstances of the
present case to give to the one a better equity than the other ? One
special circumstance that occurs is this, that the equitable mortgagee
has the possession of the title-deeds." . . . . . And his Honor, after referring to *Foster* v. *Blackstone* (1 My. & K. 307) ; *Stanhope* v. *Verney*
(Butler's Co. Litt. 290, b, note (1), sect. 15 ; 2 Eden, 81) ; 3 Sudg. & V.
P. 218 ; and *Maundrell* v. *Maundrell* (10 Ves. 271), adds : " We have
here ample authority for the proposition, or rule of equity, that as between two persons, whose equitable interests are precisely of the same
nature and quality, and in that respect precisely equal, the possession
of the deeds gives the better equity. And applying this rule to the
present case, it appears to me that the equitable interests of the two
parties being, in their nature and quality, of equal worth, the defendant,
having possession of the deeds, has the better equity ; and that there is,
therefore, in this case, no room for the application of the maxim, ' Qui
prior est tempore potior est jure,' which is only applicable where the
equities of the two parties are, in all other respects, equal. I feel all the
more confidence in arriving at this conclusion, inasmuch as it is in accordance with the opinion expressed by Lord St. Leonards in his work
on Vendors and Purchasers. And I have no doubt that, in *Mackreth* v.
Symmons, if the equitable mortgagee had, in addition to his contract

for a mortgage, obtained the title-deeds from his mortgagor, Lord Eldon
would have decided in his favour." And his Honor, after guarding
against the supposition that he meant to express an opinion that the
possession of the title-deeds would, in all cases, and under all circumstances, give the better equity, and after referring to *Allen* v. *Knight*
(5 Hare, 272, 11 Jur. 527), says: "It appears to me that in all cases of
contest between persons having equitable interests, *the conduct of the
parties, and all the circumstances*, must be taken into consideration, in
order to determine which has the better equity. And if we take that
course in the present case, everything seems in favour of the defendant,
the equitable mortgagee. The vendors, when they sold the estate, chose
to leave part of the purchase-money unpaid, and yet executed and delivered to the purchaser a conveyance, by which they declared, in the
most solemn and deliberate manner, both in the body, and by a receipt
indorsed, that the whole purchase-money had been duly paid. They
might still have required that the title-deeds should remain in their custody, with a memorandum, by way of equitable mortgage, as a security
[*329]　for the unpaid purchase-money; *and if they had done so, they
　　　　would have been secure against any subsequent equitable incumbrance; but that they did not choose to do, and the deeds were delivered
to the purchaser. Thus they voluntarily armed the purchaser with the
means of dealing with the estate as the absolute, legal, and equitable
owner, free from every shadow of incumbrance or adverse equity. In
truth, it cannot be said that the purchaser, in mortgaging the estate by
the deposit of the deeds, has done the vendors any wrong, for he has
only done that which the vendors authorised and enabled him to do.
The defendant, who afterwards took a mortgage, was in effect invited
and encouraged by the vendors to rely on the purchaser's title. They
had in effect, by their acts, assured the mortgagee that, as far as they
(the vendors) were concerned, the mortgagor had an absolute indefeasi-
ble title both at law and in equity." See also, *Wilson* v. *Keating*, 4 De
G. & Jo. 588.

A person taking a conveyance with notice of a purchaser's lien for
upaid purchase-money, would, it seems, take subject to it. Thus, if a
man sell an estate to B., and receive part of the purchase-money, and
then repudiate the contract and sell the estate to C., who has notice of
the first contract and the payment of part of the purchase-money by B.,
B. will, in that case, have a lien on the estate in the hands of C. for the
money paid to the original owner (see 29 Beav. 254); but semble that if
the property the subject of the contract were situated abroad, no decree
enforcing the lien would be made, at any rate in the absence of any
special circumstances: *Morris* v. *Chambers*, 29 Beav. 246; see also,
Watson v. *Rose*, 10 W. K. (V. C. K.) 745; 10 H. L. Ca. 672.

The assignees of a bankrupt will be affected by the equitable lien,
although they may have had no notice of it; for it is a clear principle

that assignees in bankruptcy take subject to all the equities attaching to the bankrupt: *Bowles* v. *Rogers*, 6 Ves. 95, cited in note (*a*); *Ex parte Hanson*, 12 Ves. 349; *Mitford* v. *Mitford*, 9 Ves. 99; *Grant* v. *Mills*, 2 V. & B. 306; *Ex parte Peake*, 1 Madd. 346. So, also, will the assignees under a general assignment for the benefit of creditors: *Fawell* v. *Heelis*, Amb. 724; and see 1 Bro. C. C. 302.

Where a vendor takes a security for his purchase-money, as, for instance, a bond, he will not be permitted to sue at law and in equity at the same time, but must elect in which court he will proceed: *Barker* v. *Smark*, 3 Beav. 64.

A vendor's lien for unpaid purchase-money not being an express trust, his right to recover it may be barred by the 40th section of the Statute of Limitations, 3 & 4 *Will. 4, c. 27 (*Toft* v. *Stephenson*, 7 Hare, 1); but a case may be taken out of the operation of the [*330] statute by a sufficient acknowledgment (*S. C.*, 1 De G. Mac. & G. 28; 5 De G. Mac. & G. 735); and thereupon, payment of the purchase-money remaining unpaid, and arrears of interest, may be enforced in equity: *Ib.*

The vendor's lien for unpaid purchase-money has been held not to be a "charge by way of mortgage," within the meaning of 17 & 18 Vict. c. 113; hence the personal estate of the deceased purchaser under that act remained primarily liable for its payment: *Hood* v. *Hood*, 5 W. R. (N. S.) 747; 3 Jur. N. S. 684, and *Barnewell* v. *Iremonger*, 1 Drew. & Sm. 255, 9 W. R. (V. C. K.) 88, but now, by 30 & 31 Vict. c. 69, the word "mortgage," in the construction of these statutes, has been extended to any lien for unpaid purchase-money upon any lands or hereditaments purchased by a *testator*.

As the enlarged meaning of the word "mortgage" is only given in the case of lands purchased by a *testator*, when lands have been purchased by an *intestate*, his personal estate will remain primarily liable to discharge the lien for unpaid purchase-money. *Harding* v. *Harding*, 13 L. R. Eq. 493; *Hudson* v. *Cook*, 26 L. T. Rep. (N. S.) 181, overruling *Evans* v. *Poole*, 49 L. T. (N. S.) 50.

The English chancery doctrine of the vendor's equitable lien for unpaid purchase-money, upon an absolute conveyance of land, is adopted in several of the States of this country, viz., New York, Maryland, New Jersey, California, Virginia, Tennessee, Mississippi, Georgia, Alabama, Missouri, Illinois, Indiana, Ohio, Kentucky, Vermont, and Texas; *Delassus* v. *Poston*, 19 Missouri, 425; *Herbert* v. *Scofield*, 1 Stockton's Ch. 492; *Pincham* v. *Collard*, 13 Texas, 333; *Salmon* v. *Hoffman*, 2 California, 138; *Burt* v. *Wilson*, 28 Id. 682; *M'Candlish* v. *Keen*, 13 Grattan, 615; *Carr* v. *Hobbs*,

11 Maryland, 285; *Dodge* v. *Evans*, 43 Mississippi, 570; and has been recognized in the Circuit and Supreme Courts of the United States; *Gilman* v. *Brown et al.*, 1 Mason, 192, 212; S. C., 4 Wheaton, 256; *Bailey* v. *Greenleaf*, 7 Id. 46; *English* v. *Russell*, 1 Hempstead, 35; *Chilton* v. *Branden*, 2 Black, 458. In *Richardson* v. *Bowman*, 40 Mississippi, 782, it was held that the vendor of a leasehold had a lien for the unpaid purchase-money, and the same point has been decided in Maryland. In the recent case of *Manly et al.* v. *Slason et al.*, 21 Vermont, 271, the doctrine was, after full consideration, approved and adopted: see also *Weed* v. *Beebe et al.*, Id. 496, 501; *Pinney* v. *Fellows*, 15 Vermont, 525; while in *Burns* v. *Taylor*, 23 Alabama, 255, it was said to apply with as much force to an exchange, as to a sale for money. In some other States, it has been condemned and abandoned. In Pennsylvania, the whole principle has been rejected; a vendor, after an absolute conveyance of the legal title, has no implied lien for the purchase-money; *Kauffelt* v. *Bower*, 7 Sergeant & Rawle, 64; *Semple* v. *Burd*, Id. 286; *Mergargel* v. *Saul*, 3 Wharton, 19; *Hepburn* v. *Snyder*, 3 Barr, 72, 78: though there may be a conditional conveyance of the title, that will give the claim for purchase-money a priority over all claiming through the vendee; *Bear* v. *Whisler*, 7 Watts, 144; see *Cook* v. *Trimble*, 9 Id. 15; *Zentmyer* v. *Mittower*, 5 Barr, 403, 408. In North Carolina, after some fluctuation of opinion, (*Wynne* v. *Alston*, 1 Devereux's Equity, 163; *Johnson* v. *Cawthorn*, 1 Devereux & Battle's Equity, 32; *Crawley* v. *Timberlake*, 1 Iredell's Equity, 346, 348;) the doctrine of an implied lien after an absolute conveyance is now entirely expelled; *Womble* v. *Battle*, 3 Iredell's Equity, 182, (A. D. 1844.) In South Carolina, also, it appears to be completely rejected; *Wragg's Representatives* v. *Comp. Gen. and others*, 2 Dessaussure, 509, 520. In Massachusetts, Maine and Kansas, it has no existence : per Story, J., in *Gilman* v. *Brown et al.*, 1 Mason, 192, 219; *Philbrook* v. *Delano*, 29 Maine, 410, 415; *Simpson* v. *Kundee*, 3 Kansas, 172; *Brown* v. *Simpson*, 4 Id. 76. In New Hampshire, Connecticut and Delaware, its existence remains undecided and doubtful; *Atwood* v. *Vincent*, 17 Connecticut, 576, 583; *Budd et al.* v. *Busti and Vanderkemp*, 1 Harrington, 69, 74; *Avlin* v. *Brown*, 44 New Hampshire, 10. In some of the courts, in which its existence has been recognized, it has been considered as a dangerous principle, and one opposed to the prevailing policy of this country which discourages secret liens, and tends to make all matters of title the subject of record evidence. See the remarks of Marshall, C. J., in *Bayley* v. *Greenleaf*, 7 Wheaton, 46, 51; of Carr, J., in *Moore et al.* v. *Holcombe et al.*, 3 Leigh, 597, 600, 601; of Tucker, P., in *Brawley* v. *Catron, &c.*, 8 Id. 522, 527; and of Treat, J., in *Conover* v. *War-*

ren et al., 1 Gilman, 498, 502; *M'Candlish* v. *Keen*, 13 Grattan, 615, 621.

The doctrine, in its general statement, is, that the vendor of land, if he has taken no security, although he has made an absolute conveyance by deed, with a formal acknowledgment in the deed or on the back of it, that the consideration has been paid, yet retains an equitable lien for the purchase-money, unless there be an express or implied waiver and discharge of it; and this lien will be enforced in equity against the vendee, volunteers, and all others claiming under him with notice; that is, against all persons except *bona fide* purchasers without notice; *Stafford* v. *Van Rensselaer*, 9 Cowen, 316, 318; *Tompkins* v. *Mitchell*, 2 Rand. 428, 429; *Cox* v. *Fenwick*, 3 Bibb, 183, 184; *Sedford* v. *Smith*, 6 Bush, 129; *Thornton, &c.* v. *Knox's Ex'r*, 6 B. Monroe, 74, 75; *Williams* v. *Roberts et al.*, 5 Ohio, 35, 39; *Ross* v. *Whitson*, 6 Yerger, 50; *Deibler* v. *Barwick*, 4 Blackford, 339, 340; *Dyer* v. *Martin et al.*, 4 Scammon, 148, 151; *Hall's Ex'rs* v. *Click et al.*, 5 Alabama, 363, 364; *Stewart et al.* v. *Ives et al.*, 1 Smedes & Marshall, 197, 206; *Upshaw et ux.* v. *Hargrove*, 6 Id. 286, 291; *Walton* v. *Hargraves*, 42 Mississippi, 18; *Fonda* v. *Jones*, Ib. 792; *Marsh* v. *Turner and Lisle*, 4 Missouri, 253; *Manley et al.* v. *Slason et al.*, 21 Vermont, 271; *Briscoe* v. *Bronaugh*, 1 Texas, 326, 330; *Pintard* v. *Goodloe*, 1 Hempstead, 502; *Tiernan* v. *Thurman*, 14 B. Monroe,

277. It applies *a fortiori* where the purchaser is a *feme covert*, because the vendor might otherwise be without remedy; *Chilton* v. *Branden*, 2 Black. 45; *Armstrong* v. *Ross*, 5 C. E. Greene, 107; and taking an invalid mortgage from her as a security, does not waive the vendor's lien; *Armstrong* v. *Ross*. In like manner a judgment confessed by a married woman for the purchase-money of land binds the land itself in Pennsylvania, although invalid for every other purpose. This lien is recognized, to the same extent, in case of a sale of an equitable title as of a legal one; *Stewart* v. *Hutton*, 3 J. J. Marshall. 178; *Ligon* v. *Alexander, &c.*, 7 Id. 288, 289; *Galloway* v. *Hamilton's Heirs, &c.*, 1 Dana, 576; *Iglehart* v. *Armiger*, 1 Bland, 519, 526, 527; though the point was left undecided in the Court of Appeals in Maryland; *Schnebly & Lewis* v. *Ragan*, 7 Gill & Johnson, 120, 124; and some difference of opinion existed upon it in the Supreme Court of the United States, in *Bayley* v. *Greenleaf*, 7 Wheaton, 46, 50. The principle is, that this lien exists in equity, presumptively, when the purchase-money, or any part of it, remains unpaid; and it is for the vendee to show such circumstances as repel the presumption or rebut the equity; *Garson* v. *Green*, 1 Johnson's Chancery, 308, 309; *Gilman* v. *Brown et al.*, 1 Mason, 192, 213; *Schnebly and Lewis* v. *Ragan*, 7 Gill & Johnson, 120, 125; *Tompkins* v. *Mitchell*, 2 Randolph, 428, 429; *Allen et al.* v. *Bennett*, 8 Smedes & Marshall, 672, 681;

Campbell v. *Baldwin et als.*, 2 Humphreys, 248, 258; *Marshall* v. *Christmas et als.*, 3 Id. 616, 617; *Tinsbody* v. *Jacobson*, 2 California, 269. An acknowledgment, in the body of the deed, or on the back of it, of the receipt of the whole purchase-money, if the money has in fact not been paid, will not be a waiver or discharge of this lien; *Gilman* v. *Brown et al.*, 1 Mason, 192, 214; *Redford* v. *Gibson*, 12 Leigh, 332, 344; *Eubank* v. *Poston, &c.*, 5 Monroe, 285, 287; *Tribble, &c.* v. *Oldham*, 5 J. J. Marshall, 137, 144; *Sheratz* v. *Nicodemus*, 7 Yerger, 9; *Sestt* v. *Robison*, 21 Arkansas, 202; nor will a recital in the deed that the consideration is " paid or secured to be paid ;" *Thornton, &c.* v. *Knox's Ex'r*, 6 B. Monroe, 74, 76; nor will the circumstance that the money is not to be payable till after the death of a particular person, and then only contingently, as where a part of the consideration is retained as an indemnity against a possible claim of dower; *Redford* v. *Gibson*, 12 Leigh, 332, 347; but this lien will not be given by a court of equity as a security for unliquidated and uncertain damages; *Payne* v. *Avery*, 21 Michigan, 524; and will therefore not exist when the consideration of the sale is an engagement to support the vendor during his life; *Brawley* v. *Catron, &c.*, 8 Leigh, 522, 558; *Avlin* v. *Brown*, 44 New Hampshire.

In regard to the effect upon this equitable lien of the vendor's taking a security, the American cases agree in establishing and applying the following simple and satisfactory rule:—that the implied lien will be sustained wherever the vendor has taken the personal security of the vendee only, by whatever kind of instrument it be manifested, and therefore that any bond, note or covenant, given by the vendee alone will be considered as intended only to countervail the receipt for the purchase-money contained in the deed, or to show the time and manner in which the payment is to be made, unless there is an express agreement between the parties to waive the equitable lien: and on the other hand, that the lien will be considered as waived whenever any distinct and independent security is taken, whether by mortgage on other land, or pledge of goods, or personal responsibility of a third person, and also when a security is taken upon the land, either for the whole or a part of the unpaid purchase-money; unless there is an express agreement that the implied lien shall be retained. See this distinction recognized in *Gilman* v. *Brown et al.*, 1 Mason, 192, 214, &c.; *Louis* v. *Covilland*, 21 California, 178; *Williams* v. *Young*, Ib. 227; *Silby* v. *Stanley*, 4 Minnesota, 65; *Fish* v. *Howland*, 1 Paige, 20, 30; *Warner* v. *Van Alstyne*, 3 Id. 513, 514; *Shirley* v. *Sugar Refinery*, 2 Edwards, 505, 507; *Lagow* v. *Badollet*, 1 Blackford, 417, 419; *Boon* v. *Murphy*, 6 Id. 273, 276; *Conover* v. *Warren et al.*, 1 Gilman, 498, 501; *Williams* v. *Roberts et al.*, 5 Ohio, 35, 40; *Eskridge* v. *M'Clure and Walker*,

2 Yerger, 84, 85; *Marshall* v. *Christmas et als.*, 3 Humphreys, 616; *Foster* v. *The Trustees of the Athenæum*, 3 Alabama, 302, 306; *Dodge* v. *Evans*, 4 Mississippi, 574; *Palmer and others, Appellants*, 1 Douglas, 422, 427; *Mims* v. *Macon & Western R. R. Co.*, 3 Kelley, 333, 343; *Manly et al.* v. *Slason et al.*, 21 Verm. 271; *M'-Candlish* v. *Keen*, 13 Grattan, 615, 625; *Denny* v. *Steakly*, 1 Heiskell, 156. It may, accordingly, be considered as settled by the unanimous concurrence of the cases in this country, that, wherever this lien is recognized at all, it will not be affected by the vendor's taking the bond, or bill single, of the vendee; *Evans* v. *Goodlet*, 1 Blackford, 246; *Cox* v. *Fenwicke*, 3 Bibb, 183, 184, 185; *Taylor* v. *Hunter and Searcy*, 5 Humphreys, 569; or his negotiable promissory note; *Garson* v. *Green*, 1 Johnson's Chancery, 308, 309; *White* v. *Williams*, 1 Paige, 502; *Tompkins* v. *Mitchell*, 2 Randolph, 428; *Clark* v. *Hunt*, 3 J. J. Marshall, 553, 558; *Thornton, &c.* v. *Knox's Ex'rs*, 6 B. Monroe, 74, 75; *Aldridge* v. *Dunn*, 7 Blackford, 249, 250; *Ross* v. *Whitson*, 6 Yerger, 50; *Sheratz* v. *Nicodemus*, 7 Id. 9; *Manley et al.* v. *Slason et al.*, 21 Vermont, 271; *Pinchain* v. *Collard*, 13 Texas, 333; *Trubody* v. *Jacobson*, 2 California, 269; or a check drawn on a bank by the vendee, which is not presented or paid; *Honore's Ex'r* v. *Bakewell et al.*, 6 B. Monroe, 67, 72; or by accepting a new or substituted security for one previously given, unless there is an agreement that it shall be received

as payment; *Bradford* v. *Harper*, 25 Alabama, 337; or by any instrument whatever, involving merely the personal liability of the vendee; *Mims* v. *Macon and Western R. R. Co.*, 3 Kelly, 333, 343: but, that taking a mortgage of other property; *White* v. *Dougherty et al.*, Martin & Yerger, 309, 323; (see also, *Richardson* v. *Ridgely et al.*, 8 Gill & Johnson, 87, 91;) or the bond or note of the vendee with a surety; *Wilson, &c.* v. *Graham's Executor*, 5 Munford, 297; *Francis* v. *Hazlerigg's Ex'rs*, Hardin, 48; *Williams* v. *Roberts et al.*, 5 Ohio, 35; *Mayham* v. *Coombs, Parker & others*, 14 Id. 428, 435; *Boon* v. *Murphy*, 6 Blackford, 273, 276; *Way* v. *Petty*, 1 Carter, 102; *Canico* v. *The Farmer's Bank*, 33 Maryland, 235; *M'Gonigal* v. *Plummer*, 30 Id. 422; or a negotiable note drawn by the vendee and indorsed by a third person, or drawn by a third person and indorsed by the vendee; or a draft on a third person and accepted by the drawee; *Bogerton* v. *Champlin*, 42 Illinois, 57; *Gilman* v. *Brown et al.*, 1 Mason, 192, 218, 219; S. C., 4 Wheaton, 256, 291; *Conover* v. *Warren et al.*, 1 Gilman, 498, 501; *Campbell* v. *Baldwin et al.*, 2 Humphreys, 248; *Marshall* v. *Christmas et als.*, 3 Id. 616; *Baum* v. *Gregsby*, 21 California, 172; *Burke et al.* v. *Gray et al.*, 6 Howard's Mississippi, 527; *Foster* v. *The Trustees of the Athenæum*, 3 Alabama, 302; *Sanders* v. *M'Affee*, 41 Georgia, 684; *Fonda* v. *Jones*, 47 Mississippi, 792; *Durett* v. *Briggs*, 47 Missouri, 356; *Simerz* v. *Stein*, 29

Maryland, 112; *Yargan* v. *Shriner*, 26 Indiana, 364; will repel the lien, presumptively: and in like manner, an express security on the land itself for the whole amount unpaid, as by mortgage or deed of trust, will merge the implied lien; *Little and Telford* v. *Brown*, 2 Leigh, 353, 355; *Mattix* v. *Weeand*, 19 Ind. 151; (though the contrary was held in *Boos* v. *Ewing et al.*, 17 Ohio, 500, 520;) and an express security, or an express contract for a lien, on the land conveyed, as to part of the amount remaining unpaid, will be an implied waiver of the lien to any greater extent; *Brown* v. *Gilman*, 4 Wheaton, 256, 290, 291; *Fish* v. *Howland*, 1 Paige, 30, 31; *Phillips* v. *Saunderson et al.*, 1 Smedes & Marshall's Chan. 462, 465. In *Griffin* v. *Blanchard*, 17 California, 70, this result was held to follow from taking the note of a husband and wife for the price of land sold to the wife. But though the mere taking of the vendee's personal security will not be a discharge of this equity or lien, yet any conduct which shows an intention to give up the lien, or which makes it inequitable for the vendor to insist upon it, as against the vendee or third persons, will, as against such persons, be a bar to its assertion; *Redford* v. *Gibson*, 12 Leigh, 332, 343; *The Elysville Man. Co.* v. *The Ohio Ins. Co.*, 5 Maryland, 152; *Carter* v. *The Bank of Georgia*, 24 Alabama, 37; *Fowler* v. *Rust's Heirs*, 2 Marshall, 294; *Clark* v. *Hunt*, 3 J. J. Marshall, 553, 558; *Phillips* v. *Saunderson and others; M'Cown* v. *Jones*, 14

Texas, 682; *Scott* v. *Orbison*, 21 Arkansas, 202; and, on the other hand, the waiver arising from the acceptance of collateral security, is said to be only presumptive, and may be rebutted by evidence from other circumstances, of an intention not to rely exclusively upon it, but to retain the equitable lien; *Campbell* v. *Baldwin et als.*, 2 Humphreys, 248, 258; *Marshall* v. *Christmas et als.*, 3 Id. 616, 617; *Mims* v. *Macon and Western Railroad Company*, 3 Kelly, 333, 342; *Kyles* v. *Tait's Admr's*, 6 Grattan, 44, 48; see *Tiernan* v. *Thurman*, 14 B. Monroe, 277; *Fonda* v. *Jones*, 42 Missouri, 42 Mississippi, 792; *Canico* v. *The Farmer's Bank*, 33 Maryland, 235; *Durette* v. *Briggs*, 43 Missouri, 356.

[It follows that taking a mortgage or other collateral security will not extinguish the lien where there is an express agreement that it shall survive; *Daughaday* v. *Paine*, 6 Minnesota, 443.

It has been held that taking a mortgage for the purchase-money, excludes the lien, although the security is defective or inadequate; *Camden* v. *Vail*, 23 California, 633; but this rule does not apply where the vendor is misled by the fraudulent representations of the vendee; See *Cort* v. *Fougeray*, 36 Barb. 195, 199; nor where, as in the case of a *feme covert*, the mortgage is merely void; *Armstrong* v. *Ross*, 5 C. E. Greene, 107.

The lien exists only as between the vendor and vendee, and perhaps their privies in estate or law; and then only for the unpaid purchase-money. If an obligation to maintain the vendor and a third person, be substituted for the purchase-money, such an obligation will not be a lien; *M'Killip* v. *M'Killip*, 8 Barbour, 553. And a lien cannot, it has been said, be reserved orally to a third person who pays the purchase-money and takes the note of the vendee as a security; *Skeggs* v. *Nelson*, 25 Mississippi, 88; although as a surety of the vendee is entitled to subrogation to the lien of the vendor, on payment, it would seem immaterial whether the payment is made at the time or subsequently, if the circumstances are such as to render it a purchase and not an extinguishment ; *ante*, notes to *Dering* v. *Winchelsea*.

It has been said that equity will not give a specific remedy against the land to a stranger to the compact; nor unless the sale results in a definite pecuniary obligation to the vendor; *Chapman* v. *Beardsley*, 31 Conn, 115. A lien will not, therefore, arise from the exchange of land for chattels, or for other land ; *Cort* v. *Fougeray*, 36 Barb. 195, 199; nor where the consideration is an agreement to support the grantor; *Meggs* v. *Delmock*, 6 Conn. 438 ; or pay his debt; *Chapman* v. *Beardsley*. A somewhat different view prevails in Kentucky and Tennessee, and the vendor will not necessarily lose his lien by stipulating that the price shall be paid to a third person; *Gault* v. *Trumbo*, 17 B. Monroe, 682 ; *Hamilton* v. *Gillett*, 2 Heiskell, 681; while it was said in *Burns* v. *Taylor*, 23 Alabama, 225, that there is nothing to distinguish an

exchange of lands, so far as respects the application of this principle of lien for the purchase-money, from a sale of lands; *Bradley* v. *Bosler*, 1 Barb. Ch. 125. Whatever the rule may be on these points, it is clear that the sale of land for a sum certain, payable in goods or land, is not inconsistent with the lien, because the vendor may maintain indebitatus assumpsit if the buyer makes default. In like manner, a vendor who is fraudulently induced to take land instead of the money, for which he originally agreed, may treat the payment as a nullity and enforce his lien : *Bradley* v. *Bosler*. The lien for the price of chattels ceases on delivery ; *James* v. *Bird*, 8 Leigh, 51 ; and hence where real and personal property, are sold under an entire contract for a gross sum, there will be no lien, even as it regards the land ; *M'Candless* v. *Keen*, 13 Grattan, 605; but this argument does not apply where it appears on the face of the instrument or from extrinsic evidence, that the land and chattels were valued separately, though conveyed by the same deed ; *Russell* v. *M'Cormick*, 45 Alabama, 587. On principle, a person having got the estate of another, shall not as between them keep it and not pay the consideration. While this is the rule, it will yield to circumstances. If it appears from the transaction as a whole, or the terms of the deed, that the vendor relied exclusively on the personal responsibility of the vendor, and did not look to the land, a lien will not be implied

contrary to the intention of the
parties. Thus, where land, slaves,
stock and farming implements,
were sold and conveyed by the
same instrument, it was held that
as there could be no lien on the
slaves and stock, so the land was
also presumably exempt; *M'Candlish* v. *Keen*, 13 Grattan, 616, 628.
In like manner the execution of a
deed in consideration of a covenant to pay by instalments, to
pay at a future day, to maintain
the grantor, or to pay him an annuity, affords ground for an inference that the land is not to be tied
up during the interval that must
elapse before the fulfilment of the
covenant, which will be conclusive
if it appears that the covenant was
substituted for the purchase-money,
and was in fact the thing bargained
for; *M'Candlish* v. *Keen*, 13 Grattan, 615, 625. The subject was
elaborately examined in *M'Candlish* v. *Keen*, where Lee, J., held
the following language in delivering the opinion of the court :

" From the English cases, it
would seem to be deduced that
in general this lien is presumed
to exist, and that it will follow
the subject into the hands of a
purchaser with notice from the
vendee: *Hughes* v. *Kearney*, 1
Sch. & Lef. 132; *Mackreth* v.
Symmons, 15 Ves. R. 329, and the
cases cited and reviewed by Lord
Eldon: *Saunders* v. *Leslie*, 2 Ball
& Beat. 509; *Winter* v. *Anson*, 3
Russ. 488 (3 Cond. Eng. Ch. R.
495); *Grant* v. *Mills*, 2 Ves. &
Beame, 306. Nor will the mere
taking of a note or covenant for
the payment of the purchase-money

suffice to extinguish the lien: *Gibbons* v. *Baddall*, 2 Equ. Cas. Abr.
682, n. (*b*.); *Ex parte Peake*, 1
Madd. R. 344; Cary's Ch. R. 25,
cited 3 Sug. Vend. [192], [193];
Winter v. *Anson*, ubi sup.; *Hughes*
v. *Kearney*, ubi sup.; *Teed* v. *Car-
ruthers*, 2 Younge & Coll. 31; 21
Eng. Ch. R. 31. Nor will it make
any difference that the purchase-
money claimed is in the form of
an annuity, and not a gross sum :
Blackburn v. *Gregson*, 1 Bro. C. C.
420; *Tardiffe* v. *Scrughan*, cited
1 Bro. C. C. 423. So in case of a
covenant for payment of purchase-
money in weekly sums, the vendor
was held entitled to the lien, by
Wigram, V. C., in *Matthew* v.
Bowler, 6 Hare's R. 110 (31 Eng.
Ch. R. 110.) It is true, that Lord
Camden's decision in *Tardiffe* v.
Scrugan, would appear to have
been criticised and questioned by
Lord Eldon, in *Mackreth* v. *Symmons ;* and in *Clarke* v. *Royle*, 3
Simons' R. 499, 502, the Vice
Chancellor (Sir Lancelot Shadwell) is reported to have said,
that it appeared to him that Lord
Eldon had, in *Mackreth* v. *Symmons*, expressly overruled Lord
Camden's decision in *Tardiffe* v.
Scrugan ; and Tucker, P., in
Brawley v. *Catron*, 8 Leigh, 522,
530, speaks of the latter case as
overruled. He says, " it certainly
was." However, in *Buckland* v.
Pocknell, 13 Simons' R. 406, 412
(36 Eng. Ch. R. 406), Sir. L. Shadwell, alluding to what he had been
reported as having said in *Clarke*
v. *Royle*, observed, that if that had
been said in those very terms, it
was said too strongly ; because al-

though Lord Eldon was not satisfied with the decision in *Tardiffe* v. *Scrugan*, in all its parts, yet it could not be said, that he had overruled it. The decision, too, is supported by that of *Matthew* v. *Bowler*, above cited, and the case of *Winter* v. *Lord Anson;* and is fully sustained by the opinion of Sir Edward Sugden, who thinks that it is still an authority, and that in such a case the lien will be raised : 3 Sug. Vend., Ch. 18, §§ 32, 38, p. 127, 131 (ed. of 1843). But in every case, whether of an entire gross sum or a sum payable in instalments, or in the form of an annuity for lives, the question of lien depends on the particular circumstances; and although, generally speaking, the lien exists, yet it may be waived or repelled by the character of the case. " The rule," says Judge Story, " is manifestly founded on a supposed conformity " with the intention of the parties, upon which the law raises an implied contract ; and, therefore, it is not inflexible, but ceases to act where the circumstances of the case do not justify such a conclusion." *Gilman* v. *Brown*, 1 Mason's R. 191. What are the circumstances which shall decide whether lien or no lien, is a matter of some difficulty and obscurity, and many doubts and nice distinctions will be found in the authorities. As the lien is generally presumed, it would seem that the burden is upon the purchaser to show that it was waived : *Hughes* v. *Kearney*, above cited ; *Mackreth* v. *Symmons*, 15 Ves. R. 329 ; *Garson* v. *Green*, 1 John. Ch.

R. 308. But this the purchaser may do, not only by showing an express agreement to that effect, but also by the reasonable inference and implication from the circumstances. Now it would seem settled, that the mere taking a bond, promissory note, bill of exchange, or a simple covenant of the vendee himself will not repel the lien, because, as said by Lord Eldon, it may have been given, not to supersede the lien, but for the purpose of ascertaining the debt, and countervailing the receipt indorsed upon the conveyance. But it is equally clear, that where a distinct and independent security is taken, either of other property, or the responsibility of a third person, the party having carved out his own security, the law will not come to his aid by creating another, and the equitable lien will be gone : *Bond* v. *Kent*, 2 Vern. R. 281 ; *Fawell* v. *Heelis*, Amb. R. 724 ; *Nairn* v. *Prowse*, 6 Ves. R. 752 ; *Cole* v. *Scot*, 2 Wash. 141 ; *Fish* v. *Howland*, 1 Paige's R. 20 ; *Wilson* v. *Graham's Ex'or*, 5 Munf. 297 ; *Gilman* v. *Brown*, 1 Mason's R. 191 ; S. C. Wheat. R. 255. In such cases, the waiver of the lien is placed upon the ground of intention, deduced from the party's taking a special security."

"See 3 Sugd.Vend.191; 4 Kent's Comm. 153. So where, although the responsibility of a third person be not taken, if it appear that the note, bond or covenant was substituted for the consideration money, and was in fact the thing bargained for, the lien will not exist. There it may be inferred that credit was given exclusively to the person on whom the security was taken. Thus in *Clarke* v. *Royle*, 3 Sim. R. 499 (5 Cond. Eng. Ch. R. 218), the conveyance was in consideration of the vendee entering into covenants therein contained, for an annuity to the vendor, and three thousand pounds to certain persons, in the event of the vendee's marrying. The Vice Chancellor distinguished the case of *Tardiffe* v. *Scrugan*. He considered that the deed plainly marked out that the consideration on the one side was the conveyance of the estate, and on the other, the entering into the covenants."

" He said that to declare a lien in such a case would be to go further than any of the cases that had been previously decided upon the subject of lien on purchased estates, and to do that which appeared to be contrary to the intention of the parties. He accordingly pronounced against the lien."

" This case is cited as authority, and with apparent approbation, by Tucker, P., in *Brawley* v. *Catron*, 8 Leigh. 522, 530; and although the Vice Chancellor said that he considered it decided by the case of *Winter* v. *Lord Anson*, 1 Sim. & Stu. 434 (1 Cond. Eng. Ch. R. 221), in apparent ignorance of the fact that the opinion of Sir J. Leach in that case had been overruled by Lord Chancellor Lyndhurst (3 Russ. R. 488, 3 Cond. Eng. Ch. R. 495), yet its weight as authority is not on that account lessened; because the difference between Sir J. Leach and Lord

Lyndhurst was not in the principle applicable to the case, but as to the exact state of the case. The former, when he decided against the lien (for he had at first decided in favor of it), thought that the case was in principle the same as if the conveyance had stated the real contract of the parties; and that by the effect of that contract, the vendor agreed to part with his estate on consideration of the bond for the future payment of the price, and that upon the execution of such bond, the estate passed to the vendee in equity as well as at law."

"Lord Lyndhurst, however, held that the lien was not affected by the circumstance that the period of payment was dependent on the life of the vendor."

"He did not think it afforded such evidence of intention to rely on the personal credit of the vendee as would waive the lien. The fault in the reasoning of Sir John Leach, as stated by Sugden (3 Sug. Vend. 187, § 6), was that he placed the case on grounds that did not exist. He assumed that it was a case in which, in effect, the conveyance was, in consideration of a covenant, in a deed to pay the price at the future period. But though the conveyance was in pursuance of the agreement, but in consideration of the purchase-money. In *Clarke* v. *Royle*, however, the very case was presented which was erroneously assumed to exist in *Winter* v. *Lord Anson*. The conveyance was, in fact, in consideration of covenants entered into by the same deed for payment of the price. " There is a marked difference," says Sir Edward Sugden, " between a conveyance as for money paid with a separate security for the price, whether by covenant, bond, or note, and a conveyance expressed to be in consideration of covenants which the purchaser enters into by the deed itself. It may be considered against the bearing of such a security for the purchase-money to raise another upon the estate itself by implication from the very transaction." He concludes, therefore, that *Clarke* v. *Royle* is not shaken by Lord Lyndhurst's decision in *Winter* v. *Lord Anson.*"

" The principle of the case of *Clarke* v. *Royle*, was applied in the case of *Parrott* v. *Sweetland*, 3 Mylne & Keene, 655 (10 Cond. Eng. Ch. R. 348). There a receipt was indorsed on the conveyance for the bond of the vendee, conditioned for the payment of three thousand pounds to one Orlebar, with whom the vendor was about to be united in marriage, and expressed to be the full consideration to be given by the vendee. Sir John Leach, Master of the Rolls, held that it was a case of substitution for the price, and not security, and pronounced against the heir. The cause was reheard before the V. C. Sir L. Shadwell and Mr. Justice Bosanquet, sitting as Lords Commissioners, and the decree of the Master of the Rolls was affirmed. So in *Buckland* v. *Pocknell*, 13 Sim. R. 406 (36 Eng. Ch. R. 406), which was the case of a conveyance in consideration of certain annuities granted by the ven-

dee, also being bound to pay off a mortgage debt to which the estate was subject : Held by Sir L. Shadwell, V. C., referring to *Parrott* v. *Sweetland*, that there was no lien for the annuity. And the same principle may be traced in other cases. Now the case before us seems plainly to fall within the class of which *Clarke* v. *Royle* is the leading case. It differs from that case in no material particular. Here the consideration of the conveyance of the sum of five thousand three hundred and sixty-five dollars, and the covenants of Coke to maintain Mrs. Byrd during her life, for the payment of the annuity, in case she should survive him ; of three hundred dollars if she chose to board out of his family, or if she should continue in his family after his death, of one hundred and fifty dollars ; and in the latter case, that she was to have a room and furniture, &c., and in either case a maid servant to wait upon her."

" These covenants of the vendee, and the conveyance to him, were by the same deed, and upon the principle of the above cases, the covenants were the thing contracted for, and no lien can be held to exist."]

The vendor, having this equitable lien, may file a bill in equity to have satisfaction of it, and the court will order the land, or so much of it as may be necessary, to be sold for the discharge of the debt ; *Mullikin* v. *Mullikin*, 1 Bland, 538, 541 ; *Wilson, &c.*, v. *Davisson*, 2 Robinson's Virginia, 385, 404 ; *Wade's Heirs* v. *Green-*

wood, Id. 475, 484 ; *M'Gee* v. *Beall,* 3 Littell, 190, 192 ; *Outton* v. *Mitchell,* 4 Bibb, 239. But a lien of this kind is not an original, specific, and absolute charge on the land, but only an equity to resort to it upon the failure of the personal estate. The personal estate of the purchaser is the primary fund for the payment of the vendor's claim, and the real estate is liable only secondarily.

Therefore, a bill in equity, to enforce the vendor's lien, must show that the complainant has exhausted his remedy at law against the personal estate, or must aver such facts as show that the complainant cannot have a full, complete, and adequate remedy at law ; *Eyler* v. *Crabbs,* 2 Maryland, 137 ; *Stevens* v. *Hurt,* 17 Indiana, 141 ; but a court of equity will not compel him to proceed at law against the particular land in question ; *Pratt* v. *Van Wyck's Ex'rs,* 6 Gill & Johnson, 495, 498 ; *Hall* v. *Maccubin,* Id. 107, 110 ; *Richardson* v. *Stillinger,* 12 Id. 478, 482 ; *Bottorf* v. *Cohner,* 1 Blackford, 287 ; *Russell* v. *Todd,* 7 Id. 239 ; *Roper* v. *M'Cook & Robinson's Adm'r,* 7 Alabama, 319, 324. A different view of the nature of this lien, however, prevails in some of the courts ; which consider it as in the nature of a mortgage, and hold that the vendor may enforce his claim in equity without having obtained a judgment, or taken any steps whatever at law ; *High & Wife* v. *Batte,* 10 Yerger, 186 ; *Richardson, &c.* v. *Baker,* 5 J. J. Marshall, 323 ; *Galloway* v. *Hamil-*

ton's Heirs, 1 Dana, 576 ; *Sparks* v. *Hess,* 15 California, 186.

If there be an unexecuted contract of sale, the vendor may file a bill to have a specific performance, and then have the land sold for satisfaction of this lien ; *Clark* v. *Hall,* 7 Paige, 382, 385 ; *Brush & Stanbury* v. *Kinsley, Adams & Stillwell,* 14 Ohio, 20.

In the distribution of a decedent's, or an insolvent's estate, equity will marshal the assets, so as to put the vendor altogether upon his equitable lien, for the benefit of other creditors ; *Iglehart* v. *Armiger,* 1 Bland, 519, 524 ; and perhaps of legatees ; see *Schnebly & Lewis* v. *Ragan,* 7 Gill & Johnson, 120, 126 ; *Hamilton* v. *Rakestram,* 14 Iowa, 147.

In regard to the question, whether the benefit of the vendor's lien accompanies an assignment of the vendee's note or bond for the purchase-money, the cases are in direct conflict. It seems to be settled, that if a debt is secured by an express lien, as, where there is a mortgage, or an agreement for a lien, which creates an equitable mortgage, or where the vendor has not parted with the legal title, an assignment of the debt entitles the assignee to the benefit of the pledge ; *Graham* v. *M'Campbell,* Meigs, 52, 55 ; *Eskridge* v. *M'Clure and Walker,* 2 Yerger, 84, 87 ; *Tanner* v. *Hicks et al.,* 4 Smedes & Marshall, 294, 300 ; see, also, *Norvell* v. *Johnson et als.,* 5 Humphreys, 489, 491 ; *Williams* v. *Young,* 21 California, 172 ; *Lewis* v. *Covelland* (Ib.), 227 ; but a vendor's equity, or implied lien, is not necessarily governed by the same principle. In Kentucky, Iowa, and Indiana, indeed, it appears to be settled that there is no distinction between the vendor's implied lien and any express lien, as to transferability, and that an assignment of the note or bond for the purchase-money carries the lien with it; *Kenny* v. *Collins*, 4 Littell, 289; *Johnston* v. *Gwathmey*, &c., Id. 317; *Eubank* v. *Poston*, &c., 5 Monroe, 285, 287; *Edwards* v. *Bohannon*, 2 Dana, 98; *Honore's Ex'r* v. *Bakewell et al.*, 6 B. Monroe, 67, 71, 72; *Ripperdon* v. *Cozine*, &c., 8 Id. 465, 466; *Lagow* v. *Badollet*, 1 Blackford, 417, 419, 420; *Brumfield* v. *Palmer*, 7 Id. 227, 230; *Fisher* v. *Johnson*, 5 Indiana, 492; and in Alabama, though an assignment of a note, expressly, "without recourse," does not transfer the lien; *Hall's Ex'rs* v. *Click et al.*, 5 Alabama, 363, 364; *Grigsby* v. *Hare*, 25 Alabama, 327; yet an endorsement not thus restricted, does transfer the lien; *Roper* v. *M'Cook and Robertson's Adm'r*, 7 Id. 319; *White* v. *Stover et al.*, 10 Id. 441; *Plowman and M'Lean* v. *Riddle*, 14 Id. 169, 171; *Grigsby* v. *Hare*, 25 Alabama, 327; *Wells* v. *Morrow*, 38 Id. 125. Elsewhere, however, the decisions have been different; and the weight of authority is decidedly against this lien's accompanying a transfer of the debt; *Webb* v. *Robinson*, 14 Georgia, 216; *Ross* v. *Huntzen*, 36 California, 331; *Williams* v. *Covelland*, 21 Id. 178. In Ohio and Tennessee it is well settled, that this lien is

merely a personal and equitable right, not passing with the assignment of the vendee's obligation, but extinguished when an assignment takes place; *Jackman* v. *Hallock & others*, 1 Ohio, 318; *Tiernan* v. *Beam & others*, 2 Id. 383; *Brush & Stanbury* v. *Kinsley, Adams & Stillwell*, 14 Id. 20, 24; *Horton* v. *Horner*, Id. 437, 443; *Simpson* v. *Montgomery*, 25 Arkansas, 565; *Claiborne* v. *Crockett*, 3 Yerger, 27, 35; *Gann* v. *Chester*, 5 Id. 205, 207; *Sheratz* v. *Nicodemus*, 7 Id. 9, 13; and the same thing had been held in North Carolina, before the whole doctrine was rejected from that State; *Green et al.* v. *Crockett et al.*, 2 Devereux & Battle's Equity, 390, 392. In New York and in Mississippi, also, it has been decided that an endorsement of the vendee's negotiable note, where the assignor has not been made liable upon his endorsement, does not carry the lien by implied assignment, it being left undetermined, in these cases, whether the lien is transferable by a special conveyance; *White* v. *Williams*, 1 Paige, 502, 506; *Briggs et al.* v. *Hill*, 6 Howard's Mississippi, 362, 364; *Lindsey* v. *Bates*, 42 Mississippi, 397; see *Briggs, Lacoste & Co.* v. *The Planters' Bank*, 1 Freeman's Chancery, 574, 584. In Maryland, also, it was settled in the Court of Appeals, that an assignment, with an express agreement that the assignor should in no case be made liable, extinguished the lien, it neither passing to the assignee, nor remaining operative in favor of the assignor: "The lien," the Court said, "was intended to secure the payment of the purchase-money to the vendor;" and the assignment of the notes without responsibility for their ultimate payment, amounted, as far as the vendor was concerned, to absolute payment and satisfaction of his claim; *Schnebly & Lewis* v. *Ragan*, 7 Gill & Johnson, 120, 126. And in the Court of Chancery, in that State, it has been decided that this lien is, in its nature, unassignable, and that an assignment of the note or bond extinguishes the lien; *Iglehart* v. *Armiger*, 1 Bland, 519, 524, 525; *Hayden* v. *Stuart*, 4 Maryland, Ch. 280; *Welsh* v. *Boyle*, 30 Maryland, 262; see, however, *Hall* v. *Maccubin*, 6 Gill & Johnson, 107, 109. The cases which hold that an indorsement or assignment, upon which the assignor is not made liable, does not transfer, but extinguishes the lien, but that if the endorser is made liable, the lien is not extinguished, do in fact adjudge this lien to be not assignable; the view which they take is, that the endorsee or assignee, in a suit against the vendee, cannot enforce the lien, but that if he recovers against the endorser, the latter, getting the note back, may enforce his original lien against his vendee. This is deciding, in the clearest manner, that the lien is not assignable. But though the balance of authorities is thus, altogether, against the transferability of this equity, there seems to be no doubt, that a surety for the payment of the purchase-money, may, after discharging it, claim to be subrogated to the vendor's rights in respect to it; *ante*,

150; *Tompkins* v. *Mitchell*, 2 Randolph, 428; *Mellery* v. *Cooper*, 2 Bland, 199, note.

[It is not easy to comprehend how a surety can be subrogated to that which cannot be assigned, or how any one can be entitled to use a right for himself, and yet unable to exercise it for the benefit of another. Subrogation is, in effect, an assignment or transfer by implication or operation of law, as deduced from the act or contract of the parties; and every equitable assignment is carried into effect by subrogating the assignee to the rights and remedies of the assignor. Rights which do not admit of subrogation, may therefore be unassignable, but those which do, may always be made the subject of an assignment under proper circumstances. If a vendor, who negotiates a note given for the purchase-money, can recur to the lien for his own protection, if the note be thrown back upon him, he may obviously enforce it for the protection of the endorsee. *Dixon* v. *Dixon*, 1 Maryland, Ch. 220; *Watson* v. *Bane*, 7 Maryland, 117; *Fisher* v. *Johnson*, 5 Indiana, 492.

The better opinion consequently seems to be that where, as in the case of the indorsement of a note, the nature of the transfer is such that the assignor is interested in the recovery of the debt, and will be a loser if it is not paid, the lien will survive for his security, and may consequently be enforced for that of the assignee; *Griggs* v. *Hair*, 25 Alabama, 327; *Lindsay* v. *Bates*, 42 Mississippi, 397; *Stratton* v. *Gould*, 40 Id. 778.

The same result will follow when the debt is guaranteed or transferred as a collateral security. But an absolute transfer or indorsement, without recourse, extinguishes the lien ; See *Williams* v. *Christian*, 23 Arkansas, 255 ; although equity may still enforce an agreement that it shall enure to the assignee ; *Crawley* v. *Riggs*, 24 Arkansas, 563 ; *Willis* v. *Bryant*, 22 Maryland, 373. A covenant to collect the debt for his benefit, and enforce the lien as a means to that end, would obviously be obligatory, and an assignment which cannot operate directly, may be construed as a covenant for the purpose of carrying it into effect.

In *Watson* v. *Bauer*, 7 Maryland, 117, the union of the vendor and vendee in a mortgage to a third person, was held to extinguish the vendor's lien, without transferring it to the mortgagee, and the mortgage was consequently postponed to a judgment which had been obtained against the vendee since the sale, thus defeating the end which it was the object of the transaction to secure. In this instance, the sale was not consummated by a deed, and the court overlooked the distinction between such a case and the equitable lien of an unpaid vendor who has not conveyed. Where the vendor retains the title, he is legally the owner, and a conveyance by him for value, and without notice, will defeat the equity of the vendee and of those claiming under him as creditors and purchasers ; *Smith* v. *Scheeder*, 23 Missouri, 447. If the grantee has notice, he will take subject to their equity, which is to have a deed on tendering the price. It will make no difference in the application of the principle that the vendee joins in the deed. Such an instrument operates as the grant of the vendor, confirmed by the vendee, and if the confirmation does not strengthen the grant, it does not detract from it. And the better opinion is, that where a vendor conveys to the vendee for the purpose of enabling him to give a mortgage, which is executed on the same day, the mortgagee will have priority to the extent of the unpaid purchase-money, over the judgment creditors of the vendor. The whole is in effect one transaction, and the seisin of the vendee being transitory and instantaneous, does not vary the legal aspect of the case ; *Holbrook* v. *Kenney*, 4 Mass. 569 ; *Chickering* v. *Lovejoy*, 13 Mass. 51 ; *Stow* v. *Tift*, 15 Johnson, 458. The mortgagee succeeds to the right of the vendor to be paid before parting with the title, and although the judgment creditors have all the equity of the vendee, they have no more. It is conceded that the vendor may execute a deed and take a mortgage for the purchase-money, without letting in the incumbrances that have attached to the equitable estate of the vendee ; and the case is the same in principle where the mortgage is given to a third person, at his instance. Under these circumstances, the vendor's hold on the land is clearly gone ; *Clover* v. *Rawlings*, 9 Smedes & Marshall, 122 ; but it is as clearly transferred to the mortgagee. The point was decided the other way in *Lynch* v. *Dearth*, 2 Penna. R. 101, on grounds which are not easily reconcilable with principle. The error is the more obvious, because the agreement under which the vendee's equity arose, not being recorded, it was not incumbent on the mortgagee to carry the search for incumbrances against him behind the time at which he acquired the legal title.

The vendor's lien is assignable in New York. If he assign the debt absolutely, without providing for the transfer of the lien, it will be extinguished; *Smith* v. *Smith*, 9 Abbott, 420. But this result will not follow from an assignment for the benefit of creditors; *Holbrook* v. *Smith*, 3 Barb. 267; nor, as it seems, where the debt is transferred as collateral security.]

In *Moreton* v. *Harrison*, 1 Bland, 491, and *Lingan* v. *Henderson*, Id. 236, 281, Mr. Chancellor Bland, upon the ground that this lien was a trust in the land, held that it was not barred when the personal security or debt was barred; but that it would continue till the presumption of payment accrued; and that, though it would be presumed to be at an end after twenty years, yet that presumption might be rebutted by circumstances, and the lien might be enforced after a still longer period But this appears to be altogether erroneous. Even if it is a trust, it is not a direct trust for the payment of a debt, (as in *Alexander* v. *M'Murry*, 8 Watts, 504, and *Addams* v. *Heffernan*, 9 Id. 530;)

but only a collateral trust for the security of the debt, and must be inoperative when the debt is barred. See the remarks of Catron, C. J., in *Sheratz* v. *Nicodemus*, 7 Yerger, 9, 12. And the better opinion would seem to be, that as it is a remedy or security, not a right of property, and does not vary the nature of the debt, or take it out of the operation of the Statute of Limitations, it cannot be enforced after the bar of the statute has attached to the debt; *Borst* v. *Corey*, 15 New York R. 505; *Trotter* v. *Erwin*, 27 Mississippi, 772.

This equity of a vendor, as has already been said, will be enforced against the vendee, and all standing in his position: against his heirs; *Garson* v. *Green*, 1 Johnson's Chancery, 308, 309; *Wade's Heirs* v. *Greenwood*, 2 Robinson's Virginia, 475, 484; and as against them it will attach upon improvements made on the land by the vendee in his lifetime; *Warner* v. *Van Alstyne*, 3 Paige, 513, 514; *Phyfe* v. *Wardell*, 5 Paige, 268; *Cook* v. *Craft*, 41 Howard, New York, 279; and upon a sale of the land for debts, after the vendee's death, the purchase-money is first to be paid out of the proceeds; *White* v. *Casanave*, 1 Harris & Johnson, 106: against his widow's right of dower, as that estate is cast upon her by act of law, and not as a purchaser; *Warner* v. *Van Alstyne*; *Wilson*, &c. v. *Davisson*, 2 Robinson's Virginia, 385, 404; *Ellicott* v. *Welch*, 2 Bland, 243, 244; see also *Nazareth Lit. & Benevo. Inst.* v. *Lowe &*

Wife, 1 B. Monroe, 257, 258: against a voluntary donee; *Upshaw et ux.* v. *Hargrove,* 6 Smedes & Marshall, 286, 292: and against a purchaser for value, *with notice,* actual or constructive, on the face of the deed, or *aliunde,* that the purchase-money is unpaid; *Wilcox* v. *Calloway,* 1 Washington's Virginia, 38; *Graves* v. *M'Call,* 1 Call, 414; *Redford* v. *Gibson,* 12 Leigh, 332, 347; *Pierce* v. *Gates,* 7 Blackford, 162; *Brumfield* v. *Palmer,* Id. 227, 230; *Mounce* v. *Byers,* 11 Georgia, 180; *Thornton, &c.* v. *Knox's Ex'r,* 6 B. Monroe, 74; *Honore's Ex'r* v. *Bakewell,* Id. 67; *Tiernan* v. *Thurman,* 14 Id. 279; *Grapingether* v. *Fegervary,* 9 Iowa, 163; *Murett* v. *Wells,* 18 Indiana, 171; *Eskridge* v. *M'Clure & Walker,* 2 Yerger, 84, 86; *Sheratz* v. *Nicodemus,* 7 Id. 9, 11; *M'Knight & Brady* v. *Bright,* 2 Missouri, 110; *Briscoe* v. *Bronaugh,* 1 Texas, 326, 330, 332; *Croskey* v. *Chapman,* 26, Indiana, 333; *Wright* v. *Woodland and Wife et al.,* 10 Gill & Johnson, 388; (see also, *Ghiselin & Worthington* v. *Ferguson,* 4 Harris & Johnson, 522, 525;) and, in general, against all not appearing clearly to be purchasers for value without notice; *High & Wife* v. *Batte,* 10 Yerger, 186, 335; *Mounce* v. *Byers,* 16 Georgia, 469; *Burlingame* v. *Robbins,* 21 Barbour, 327; who have actually paid the purchase-money; *Ripperdon* v. *Cozine, &c.,* 8 B. Monroe, 465, 466; *Gault* v. *Tirmbo,* 17 Id. 682; but not against those who are *bona fide* purchasers without notice; *Blight's Heirs* v.

Banks, &c., 6 Monroe, 192, 198; *Taylor* v. *Hunter & Searcy,* 5 Humphreys, 569, 570; *Stewart et al.* v. *Ives et al.,* 1 Smedes & Marshall, 197, 206; *Carnes* v. *Hubbard et al.,* 2 Id. 108, 113; *Dunlap* v. *Burnett et al.,* 5 Id. 702, 710; *Parker* v. *Foy,* 43 Mississippi, 260; *Gooch* v. *Baxter,* 2 Duval, 389; *Work* v. *Brayton,* 5 Indiana, 396; *Coster* v. *The Bank of Georgia,* 24 Alabama, 37; *Bradford* v. *Harper,* 25 Id. 337; *Burch* v. *Carter,* 44 Id. 115; *Selby* v. *Stanley,* 4 Minnesota, 65; *Webb* v. *Robinson,* 14 Georgia, 216; dictum in *Bayley* v. *Greenleaf,* 7 Wheaton, 46, 50. Notice to the agent of the purchaser, will, as in other cases, operate as notice to the principal; *Mounce* v. *Byers,* 11 Georgia, 180; and in *Ringgold* v. *Bryan,* 3 Maryland Ch. 488, the possession of the vendor was said to be notice of his lien to a subsequent purchaser from the vendee.

The right to protection as a bona fide purchaser does not exist, unless the deed is executed and the price paid before notice. If part only is paid, the vendor's lien will attach as to the residue, which will be due to him and not to the vendor; *Parker* v. *Foy; Perkins* v. *Swank,* 4 Mississippi, 349. See *Bassett* v. *Nosworthy,* vol. 2 notes.

In regard to the existence of this lien as regards creditors, the cases are somewhat at variance. It appears to be agreed that it does not prevail against a *bona fide* mortgagee *without* notice, who in fact is regarded in equity as a purchaser; *Duval* v. *Bibb,* 4 Henning & Munford, 113, 120; *Wood* v. *Bank of*

Kentucky, &c., 5 Monroe, 194, 195; *Clark* v. *Hunt,* 3 J. J. Marshall, 553, 557; *Growning & Co.* v. *Behn, &c.,* 10 B. Monroe, 383, 385; *Shirley* v. *The Steam Sugar Refinery,* 2 Edwards, 505; *Schwarz* v. *Stein,* 29 Maryland, 112; though it was held that it would prevail against a mortgagee with notice, (Bibb, C. J., dissenting in *Eubank* v. *Poston, &c.,* 5 Monroe, 285, 291, 313. In *Bayley* v. *Greenleaf,* 7 Wheaton, 46; it was decided, that it will not be enforced against a conveyance to creditors in consideration of antecedent debts; and strong considerations were presented in opposition to its prevailing against judgment creditors, or creditors under any circumstances. In *Moore et al.* v. *Holcombe et al.,* 3 Leigh, 597, 600, these views were approved, and it was decided that if one sold land without payment or security, and the vendee resold, and took bonds, and assigned those bonds for value and without notice, the first vendor's lien would be postponed to the assignee of the bonds. In Georgia, creditors will not be postponed to a lien for unpaid purchase-money, unless they become such with notice of its existence; *Webb* v. *Robinson,* 14 Georgia, 216. In Mississippi, it has been held, that it cannot prevail against creditors claiming under a deed of trust made for their benefit, or under a mortgage, for they have more than an equity or lien, they have the legal title; *Dunlap* v. *Burnett et al.,* 5 Smedes & Marshall, 702, 710. In North Carolina, before the lien was rejected entirely, it had been decided that it was subordinate to the rights of judgment creditors, and purchasers at their sale; *Johnson* v. *Cawthorn,* 1 Devereux & Battle, 32, 35; *Harper* v. *Williams,* Id. 379: "If a vendor claiming such a lien," said Gaston, J., in the former of these cases, "will not reduce it to a legal form, and give it the notoriety of registration, which our laws require for the validity of legal liens, it cannot prevail against creditors." In Tennessee, it is settled, that the vendor's lien will not be sustained against judgment creditors or purchasers at their sale; *Roberts* v. *Rose et al.,* 2 Humphreys, 145, 147; nor against creditors who receive a mortgage to indemnify them against previous liabilities, and Catron, C. J., said, of *Bayley* v. *Greenfield,* "this decision meets the most decided and unanimous approbation of this court;" *Gann* v. *Chester,* 5 Yerger, 205, 209; but that it will prevail against a voluntary assignment for the benefit of creditors, where a bill is filed by the vendor, before the trust is executed; *Brown* v. *Vanlier et als.,* 7 Humphreys, 239, 249. In New York, also it was held by the Vice Chancellor that the vendor's lien will prevail against a voluntary assignment to a trustee for the benefit of antecedent creditors; *Shirley* v. *Sugar Refinery,* 2 Edwards, 505, 508; see also *Repp et al.* v. *Repp, Warfield & Fox,* 12 Gill & Johnson, 341, 352: and in Mississippi, Indiana and Maryland, *Ringgold* v. *Bryan,* 3 Maryland Ch. 488, the lien prevails against judgment creditors and assignees in bankruptcy; *Aldridge* v. *Dunn*, 7 Blackford, 249, 250; *Walton* v. *Hargreaves*, 42 Mississippi, 18. But in *Hallett* v. *Whipple*, 58 Barb. 224, a judgment creditor who had made advances without notice of the lien was held to be a quasi purchaser, and as such entitled to priority. The decisions are, therefore, in conflict; but in respect to the justice and policy of postponing this equitable lien to the rights of creditors, the reasoning of Marshall, C. J., in *Bayley* v. *Greenleaf*, is unanswerable. "To the world," says the Chief Justice, "the vendee appears to hold the estate, divested of any trust whatever; and credit is given to him in the confidence that the property is his own in equity, as well as at law. A vendor relying upon this lien, ought to reduce it to a mortgage, so as to give notice of it to the world. If he does not, he is, in some degree, accessory to the fraud committed on the public, by an act which exhibits the vendee as the complete owner of an estate on which he claims a secret lien. It would seem inconsistent with the principles of equity, and with the general spirit of our laws, that such a lien should be set up in a court of chancery, to the exclusion of *bona fide* creditors. The lien of the vendor, if in the nature of a trust, is a secret trust; and, although to be preferred to any other subsequent equal equity, unconnected with a legal advantage, or equitable advantage which gives a superior claim to the legal estate, will be postponed to a subsequent

equal equity connected with such advantage. . . . In the United States, the claims of creditors stand on high ground. There is not perhaps a State in the Union, the laws of which do not make all conveyances not recorded, and all secret trusts, void as to creditors as well as subsequent purchasers without notice."

In order to determine whether a vendor's claim for unpaid purchase-money is of a character to prevail over the rights of subsequent creditors, it is necessary to examine, somewhat more closely, the origin and nature of this, so called, "equitable lien." It is difficult, from the American authorities, to derive a satisfactory notion upon the subject. The neglect in many of the courts to distinguish, carefully, between the implied equity, where the title has been absolutely conveyed, and the lien existing where the title is retained by the vendor, and only a title-bond given to the purchaser, has increased the confusion, and led to much inaccuracy, See *Anthony* v. *Smith*, 9 Humphreys, 508, 511. In some of the States, the "vendor's lien" has come to be considered as in the nature of an equitable mortgage: see the Kentucky decisions, and the remarks of Baldwin, J., in *Wilson, &c.* v. *Davisson*, 2 Robinson's Virginia, 385, 404, who speaks of it, "as a kind of equitable mortgage, inherent in the contract of sale, and qualifying the ownership of the vendee:" by other tribunals, it has been regarded as a trust, incident, uniformly and necessarily, in equity, to all conveyances where the purchase-money is not paid: *Ringgold* v. *Bryan*, 3 Maryland, Ch. 488: see the views of Bland, C., in *Moreton* v. *Harrison*, 1 Bland, 491, and in *Inglehart* v. *Armiger*, Id. 519, 524, 525. It is believed that both of these theories are unsound, and that this claim is neither an equitable mortgage nor a trust. An equitable mortgage springs from an agreement, express or implied, of the parties, that there shall be a lien: but this claim, though the question of its waiver may be a matter in agreement and intention, is in its inception and essence, a simple equity, raised and given by the court, and not created by the intion or contract of the vendor and vendee. It seems to be equally clear that it is not a trust. Upon a ready money sale, if a conveyance be made in advance of payment, there is no doubt that the vendee is a trustee for the purchase-money; but whether, when credit is expressly given for the purchase-money, and a note payable *in futuro*, is taken upon the conveyance, the land, in the hands of the vendee, is affected with a trust for the satisfaction of that debt, is a different question. There are but two grounds upon which equity raises a trust; one, the agreement or intention of the parties; the other, the fraud, or breach of faith or duty of the person who thereby is made a trustee. No agreement for a security on the land can be inferred when the parties expressly decline making such an agreement; and it is admitted that this claim does not arise from agreement. Where it is a part of the contract that a note or bond is to be given for the purchase-money, no trust, *ex maleficio*, can arise at the time of the conveyance, for the vendee is acting strictly within his duty; and none can be created from the mere non-payment of the debt, when it becomes due, for that is not such a fraud as equity makes the ground of a trust. The case presents none of the elements of a trust in land. The circumstances, that the vendor's claim is not such an interest as he can assign, and that he cannot charge the land until he has exhausted his legal remedies against the personal estate, which the best authorities agree in, indicate, unmistakably, that this is neither an equitable mortgage, nor a trust. The true nature of the claim appears to be this: It had its origin in a country where lands were not liable, both during and after the life of the debtor, for all personal obligations, indiscriminately, including debts by simple contract: and it seems to be an original and natural equity, that the creditor whose debt was the consideration of the land, should, by virtue of that consideration, be allowed to charge the land upon failure of the personal assets. It is not a lien until a bill has been filed to assert it: before that is done, it is a mere equity or capacity to acquire a lien, and to have a satisfaction of it. When a bill is filed, it becomes a specific lien. This equity no doubt dates back to the time of the conveyance, and to the origin of the debt. As soon as the debt for purchase-money exists, though to be paid *in futuro*, the equity to come upon the land attaches to it. Therefore, it prevails against dower, and all other estates which the law considers as in privity with that of the vendee ; it prevails against all who take with notice, actual or legal, for all such persons are considered as standing in the situation of the vendee. In such cases the dispute is between the vendor, on the one hand, and the vendee and his representatives on the other. But when subsequent lien creditors intervene, the contest is no longer between the vendor and vendee ; it is between third persons contending for his estate. It depends no longer on the equity of one party as against the vendee and those in privity with him ; it depends upon the relative equities and rights of the disputants, in comparison with one another. If this be a correct view of the nature of the vendor's claim, the question is at an end. Lien creditors will supplant one who, though he had a right in equity to charge the land, through his own laches and default, failed to secure a lien. Lien creditors are entitled to the whole estate of their debtor, subject only to prior specific liens, legal or equitable ; if the vendor's equity be neither a specific lien, nor a trust qualifying the estate in equity, the right of lien creditors is paramount to it. The principle then is, that the vendor's equity, though prevailing against the vendee and all

claiming through him, is subordinate to the rights of subsequent lien creditors, with or without notice. It then only remains to determine who are lien creditors. Judgment creditors, mortgagees with or without notice, creditors receiving a conveyance directly to themselves, of course, are : in the case of a voluntary assignment to a trustee for the benefit of creditors, the difficulty is to determine when the creditors become lien creditors by virtue of the assignment. Before they have elected to take under the deed, the assignee is rather the trustee for the debtor than for them ; when they have accepted the assignment, by claiming or taking a benefit under it, the assignee becomes their trustee, and they assume, by virtue of the assignment, the character of lien creditors. The decision in Tennessee, above referred to, that the vendor's equity will override a voluntary assignment to a trustee, if asserted before anything has been done in execution of the trust, appears, therefore, to be strictly correct : but there can be little doubt, that if the creditors have filed a bill to have the trust under the assignment executed, or have otherwise made themselves parties to the assignment by claiming or receiving a benefit under it, they would prevail over the tardy claim of the vendor.

If there be a difficulty in defining, with precision, the nature of this creditor's equity, there seems to be little doubt, that it is something less firm, distinct, and positive, than the lien of a creditor by

mortgage, judgment, or bill filed;
Trotter v. *Erwin*, 27 Miss. 772.
" The lien of a vendor for the purchase money," says Story, J., in
Gilman v. *Brown et al.*, 1 Mason,
192, 221, " is not of so high and
stringent a nature, as that of a
judgment creditor, for the latter
binds the land according to the
course of the common law : whereas
the former is the mere creature of
a court of equity, which it moulds
and fashions according to its own
purposes. It is, in short, a right
which has no existence, until it is
established by the decree of a
court in the particular case, and is
then made subservient to all the
other equities between the parties,
and enforced in its own peculiar
manner, and upon its own peculiar
principles. It is not, therefore,
an equitable estate in the land itself, although sometimes that ap-
pellation is loosely applied to it."
Whatever may be its name or nature, it seems to be reasonable,
that when a man claims an equity,
not under an agreement, but in
direct opposition to his own express and solemn acknowledgment,

intended to be put on record and
made known to all the world, he
ought not to be allowed to enforce
it against persons who may have
given credit and incurred risk on
the faith of that acknowledgment.

If the views above stated be
sound, there can be little doubt
that this principle, of an implied
lien for purchase-money, has no
just application in a country
where every debt may be at once
made a lien by a judgment, and
where debts generally are a lien
on the lands of decedents; and
that the courts of those states,
which have wholly expelled the
doctrine, have exhibited a more
accurate appreciation of its nature
and purpose, than those which have
retained it.

The vendor of personal property has no implied or equitable
lien for the purchase-money, after
parting with the possession, but
must look to the personal responsibility, only, of the vendee;
James v. *Bird's Adm'r*, 8 Leigh,
510, 513; *Beam* v. *Blanton*, 3 Iredell's Equity, 59, 62, *Lupin* v.
Marie, 6 Wendell, 77, 82.

*NOYS v. MORDAUNT. [*331]

DE TERM. S. HIL., FEB. 4th, 1706.

REPORTED 2 VERN. 581.[1]

ELECTION.]—*A. having two daughters, B. and C., devises fee-simple lands to B., and lands which were settled upon him in tail to C. If B. will claim a share of the entailed lands under the settlement, she must quit the fee-simple lands ; for the testator having disposed of the whole of his estate amongst his children, what he gave them was upon the implied condition they should release to each other.*

JOHN EVERARD, having two daughters, in 1686 makes his will, and devises to Margaret, his eldest daughter, his lands in Beeston, and 800*l.* in money ; to Mary, his second daughter, his lands in Stanborn and Broom, and 1300*l.* in money, provided and on condition she released, conveyed, and assured Beeston lands to her sister Margaret ; and devised to his said second daughter 1300*l.* in money.[2] Provided, if he should have a son, what was devised to his daughters to be void ; and, in such case, gave to Margaret 1200*l.*, and to Mary 1000*l.* Provided, if he should have another daughter, then he gave the 800*l.* devised to Margaret to such after-born daughter ; and the lands at Stanborn and Broom, and the 1300*l.* devised to Mary, the second daughter, to the said Mary and such after-born daughter, equally between them.

He shortly afterwards died, and left his wife enceinte of a daughter, Elizabeth. Mary married Higgs, and died without issue, not having given any release to Margaret, her sister, according to the will.

Elizabeth claimed not only the lands devised to her by *the will, and a moiety of what was devised to her sister [*332] Mary, but also a moiety of the Beeston lands, devised to Margaret: the same, on the testator's marriage, being settled on himself for life, and his wife for her jointure, and to the first and other sons, and, in default of issue male, to the heirs of his body.

Question was, whether she should be at liberty so to do, or ought not to acquiesce in the will, or renounce any benefit thereby.

LORD KEEPER COWPER.—In all cases of this kind, where a man is disposing of his estate amongst his children, and gives to one fee-simple lands, and to another lands entailed or under settlement,[3] it is upon an *implied condition* that each party acquit and

[1] That is to say entailed or settled upon the one to whom the fee-simple lands are given, or upon such one jointly with the other.
[2] S. C., Eq. Ca. Ab. 273, pl. 3 ; Prec. Ch. 265 ; Gilb. Eq. Rep. 2.
[3] This last bequest of £1300 in money seems to be a repetition of the first bequest of that sum with the lands in Stanborn and Broom.

release the other ; especially as in this case, where, plainly, he had
the distribution of his whole estate under his consideration, and
has given much more to Elizabeth than what belonged to her by
the settlement, and had it in his power to cut off the entail.

[*333]   *STREATFIELD v. STREATFIELD.

DE TERM. S. HIL., 1735.

REPORTED CAS. TEMP. TALB. 176.

ELECTION.]—*The ancestor, by articles previous to his marriage, agrees
to settle certain lands to the use of himself and his intended wife,
remainder to the issue of the marriage in the usual manner. After
marriage he makes a deed, not pursuant to the articles, and has a
son and two daughters; and upon the marriage of his son, settles
other lands, in consideration of this last marriage, in the usual
manner, and levies a fine of the former lands to the use of himself
in fee; and then makes his will, and devises part of the former
lands to his two daughters, and the rest of his real estate to trustees,
to the use of his grandson for life, with usual remainders; and with
direction, out of the profits to educate the grandson, and to place out
the rest of the profits to be paid to the grandson at twenty-one years
of age; and if he does not attain that age, to be paid to his said
daughters, their executors, &c. The grandson is not to be bound by
the deed, which did not pursue the articles, but then he shall make
his election when he comes of age, and if he chooses to take lands
which ought to have been settled, the daughters (his aunts) shall be
reprised out of the lands devised to him.*

THOMAS STREATFIELD, the plaintiff's grandfather, by articles
previous to his marriage, May 31st, 1677, agreed to settle lands
in Sevenoake [in the county of Kent] to the use of himself and
Martha, his intended wife, for their lives and the life of the survivor ; and after the survivor's decease, to the use of the heirs of
the body of him the said Thomas on his wife begotten, with other
remainders over.

[*334]   *The marriage soon after took effect, and by deed,
dated April 5th, 1698, reciting the foresaid articles, he
settled his lands at Sevenoake to the use of himself and his wife
for their lives, and the life of the longest liver of them without
impeachment of waste during the life of Thomas, and after their
decease, to the use of the heirs of the body of the said Thomas,
on the said Martha to be begotten ; and for want of such issue,
remainder to the right heirs of Thomas. They had issue, Thomas
(their only son), and two daughters, Margaret and Martha.
    In the year 1716, upon the marriage of Thomas, the son, the
father settled other lands (of which he was seised in fee), of the

yearly value of 355*l.*, to the use of his son for life, remainder to the daughters of the marriage, remainder in fee to the son, with a power to raise 2000*l.* for younger children.

After the son's death, [leaving a son called Thomas], Thomas, the father, in the year 1723, levied a fine of the lands comprised in the deed of 1698 to the use of himself in fee, and in the year 1725 made his will, and thereby devised part of those lands[1] to his two daughters, Margaret and Martha; " And also all other his manors, messuages, lands, tenements, and hereditaments whatsoever, either in possession, reversion, or remainder, not thereinbefore given or disposed of, situate in the counties of Kent, Surrey, or elsewhere, to trustees in trust for the plaintiff Thomas, his grandson, for life; remainder to his first and other sons in tail male; remainder to his daughters in tail; remainder to Margaret and Martha, with several remainders over." Then comes this clause: " And my will and meaning farther is, and I do hereby authorize and appoint the trustees, and the survivor of them, to receive the rents and profits of the said estates to them devised, and out of the same to allow and expend, for the education of my grandson Thomas, so much as they shall think fit during his minority; and that the trustees shall place out at interest such monies arising out of the rents and profits of the said estates; which said monies, with interest arising therefrom, my will is, *be paid to my grandson Thomas at his age of twenty-one years, if he so long live; or, in case he dies before [*335] that age, then that the same shall be paid to my two daughters, Margaret and Martha, their executors," &c.

The testator died in the year 1730.

The question was, whether the settlement in 1698 was a proper execution of the articles of 1677? and if not, whether the general devise to the plaintiff should be taken as a satisfaction for what he was entitled to under the articles of 1677?

Mr. Solicitor-General, Mr. *Browne*, Mr. *Fazakerley*, and Mr. *Noel* argued, for the plaintiff, that, although in a will or articles executed, Thomas the grandfather would have been tenant in tail, yet the articles of 1677 being but executory, this Court would interpose, by carrying them into execution in the strictest manner, and not leaving it in his power to destroy the uses as soon as raised. That, according to that rule, the deed of 1698 was certainly no execution of the articles in equity; for, though it was in the very words, yet did it not at all answer the intent of the articles, and came, therefore, within the rules of *Trevor* and *Trevor's case*, 1 Eq. Ca Abr. 387.[2]

That the settlement in 1716, upon Thomas the son's marriage (although it was of lands of greater value than those contained in the articles), could never be thought a satisfaction for them, there being no reference at all in it to the articles, and it being made only in consideration of the son's marriage, and for settling a joint-

---

[1] i. e. viz., the lands at Sevenoake in Kent.   [2] P. Wms. 622, S. C.

ure upon his wife, and making a competent provision for the issue; all which are new considerations, no way relative to the articles: and where there is an express consideration mentioned in a deed, there can be no averment of another not contained therein.[1]

That nothing could be taken for a satisfaction but what was in its nature agreeable to the thing which was to be done, was held in *Lechmere* and *Lady Lechmere's case*.[2] But, in this case, Thomas the son was, by the articles, to have been tenant in tail; but, by the settlement in 1716, he was to be but tenant for life: which [*336] was giving him a *less estate for a greater, and consequently not to be deemed a satisfaction without a special acceptance of it as such, according to the rule in *Pinnel's case*, 5 Co. 117, where it is held that payment of a lesser sum can never be a satisfaction for a greater, unless upon a special circumstance showing the intent, as payment at an earlier day, &c. That the will could no more be taken for a satisfaction than the settlement, and upon the same reasons; for, by it, the plaintiff is no more than tenant for life, and even that not absolutely, the profits being directed by the testator to be accumulated until the plaintiff attains his age of twenty-one, and then to be paid to him; but if he dies before that age, they are given away to the testator's daughters; and when he does arrive to that age, he is to be but barely tenant for life, and even not that without impeachment of waste; besides, if the will be construed a satisfaction, as against the plaintiff, so it must likewise be as to all the others claiming under the articles; whereas, the plaintiff's sisters, who were entitled under the articles, can never take anything under this will, but are wholly excluded.

The general devise of all his manors, lands, &c., *in possession, reversion, or remainder,* will not alter the case; for where the testator hath estate sufficient to satisfy such general words, he shall never be construed to have intended to pass that which he had no right to dispose of, and the giving of which would work a wrong. That he had no right to dispose of the lands contained in the articles, is evident from what hath been already said; and had not this been upon his own marriage, but in any other settlement, he had been a trustee for his son, and then had made his will in the same words that he hath done here, surely that trust estate would never have passed; and there is no difference, whether the trust be expressed, or whether it arises by implication of equity. It would be an absurdity to construe these words to pass away a third person's estate. *A grant of all one's goods* will not pass those which he hath in auter droit: So, if he had [*337] had a mortgage in fee, such general words would *not have passed it from the devisee of the personal estate to the devisee of the land. In *Rose and Bartlett's case*, Cro. Car.

[1] Dyer, 146, p. 71
[2] Lechmere v. Lechmere, Ca. t. Talb. 80; S. C., 3 P. Wms. 211.

292, a general devise of *all his lands and tenements*, having both freehold and leasehold, was held to pass the freehold lands only.[1] And, in *Harwood and Child's case*, heard by the present Lord Chancellor, March 18, 1734, a devise of all his lands for payment of debts, having both freehold and copyhold, but no surrender made of the copyhold to the use of his will, was held not to pass the copyhold. Nor can the cases of *Duffield* v. *Smith*, 2 Vern. 250; *Noys* v. *Mordaunt*, 2 Vern. 581; be objected: for, in the former, the decree was reserved, upon account of the sister's being heir-at-law, and disinherited, which is the present case; (for here they would take a beneficial interest from the plaintiff, who was heir-at-law to his grandfather, and give him but a very small one in its room;) and, in the latter case, the father, being tenant in tail of part, had power to bar it by fine; in which respect he might well be looked upon as a proprietor of the whole; but, if he be decreed to make his election, it must be done presently, for then it is that he is to take; whereas, he cannot by law make his election, being but an infant; and if so, the Court must compel him to that which the law disables him from doing.

Mr. Attorney-General, Mr. *Strange*, and Mr. *Peere Williams*, argued for the defendant, that this Court will not, in all cases whatever, decree a specific performance; but would, in some particular cases, leave the party to his remedy at law upon the covenant; that these articles were made so long ago as in 1677, and Thomas, the son, who was the person entitled to have them carried into execution, lived until 1722, forty-five years after, without ever desiring to have them executed; and that the intent of those articles did not seem to go any further than the settling the jointure on the wife, and the making Thomas, the grandfather, tenant in tail, the words being *to provide for the wife*, but no mention made of the issue; but, *whoever comes into equity must do equity;* and therefore, if the plaintiff would take ad- [*338] vantage of those articles, he must make a compensation for it out of the will, which gives him an estate upon a plain supposal that he shall take nothing by the articles; but shall never be at liberty to take a great benefit under the will, and waive that part which makes against him to the prejudice of a third person. The whole will must be acquiesced under, or no part of it at all, according to the resolution in *Noys and Mordaunt's case;*[2] which went upon the reason of an entire compliance with the testator's intent in taking entirely under the will, and not upon the supposed reason of his being proprietor by having it in his power to levy a fine. The like resolution was in the case of *Hearne* v. *Hearne*, 2 Vern. 555, in that of *Cowper* v. *Cotton*, February 16, 1731,[3] at the Rolls: where a freeman of London devised his estate to trustees for the raising 6000*l.* for his four daughters, and made

---

[1] See now, 1 Vict. c. 26, s. 6.   [2] Ante.
[3] Cowper v. Scott, 3 P. Wms. 123.

a disposition of the surplus, it was held that they should stand
either by the will or by the custom ; and if by the former, that
they should not defeat the devise over. That, in cases where
general words in a will had been restrained from passing all
which the testator had, it hath been upon the testator's intention
manifestly appearing in the will itself, not to pass so much as the
generality of his words would comprehend ; but, in the present
case, his intent plainly appears to pass all : nor will that intent
be satisfied by saying, that he had a reversion of the lands comprised in the articles, since he would have been tenant in tail
under the articles, and only for life under the will.

LORD CHANCELLOR TALBOT.—It cannot be doubted but that,
upon application to this Court for the carrying into execution
the articles of 1677, the Court would have decreed it to be done
in the strictest manner, and would never leave it in the husband's
power to defeat and annul everything he had been doing : and
the nature of the provision is strong enough for this purpose,
without any express words, and I must, therefore, consider what
[*339] was the *operation of the deed of 1698, which is declared
to be in performance of the true intent and meaning of
the articles. If it be so, all is well ; but if it be not, it only shows
that the parties intended it so, but were mistaken. So was the
case of *West* v. *Errissey*,[1] where the articles were, by the House
of Lords, decreed to be made good ; and the same must be done
in this case, if nothing intervenes to prevent it.

The settlement, in 1716, whereby the grandfather settled other
lands upon his son's marriage, has been called a satisfaction for
those articles ; but to me it appears neither an actual satisfaction
nor to have been intended as such. The grandfather had done
that in 1698, which he apprehended to be a satisfaction for the
articles ; but this deed proceeds upon considerations quite different
from those of the articles, the persons claiming under this being
purchasers for a consideration entirely new, the limitations being
entirely different ; and, therefore, it would be absurd to call this
a satisfaction for another thing it hath nothing to do with, and
to which it is no way relative.

The next thing to be considered is, the fine levied of the lands
in question in the year 1723, by the grandfather ; the intent
whereof was to have the absolute ownership of those lands in
him. And one reason why no application hath been made till
now to have those articles carried into execution, might be that
during the grandfather's life nobody was entitled to anything in
possession under them.

Then comes the will in 1725, whereby he gives part of those
lands, settled in 1698, to his daughters ; thereby showing his apprehension to be, that, by a fine, he had given himself a power
of disposing of them ; and it would be a very strained construc-

[1] 2 P. Wms. 349 ; 1 Bro. P. C. 225 ; Toml. edit.

tion to say that he intended this, not as a present devise to his daughters, but to take effect out of the reversion of the lands comprised in the articles.

The next thing is the devise to the trustees for his grandson the plaintiff, upon his attaining the age of twenty-one; and the question here is, whether the general *words shall ever pass lands not capable of the limitation in the will? And [*340] to that have been cited *Rose and Bartlett's case*, Cro. Car. 292, and other cases; but they cannot influence the present case: for, the testator had legally a power to dispose of those lands; and though they might be affected with a trust in equity, yet that cannot be supposed to lie in his connusance, he having done an act to enable himself to dispose of these lands. And it differs from the case that was put of an express trust, and the trustee devises *all his lands;* for there the trustee cannot be ignorant that the lands which he holds in trust are not his own. But what makes his intent clear is, that he hath devised part of these lands to his daughters, and he must have looked upon himself as master of the one part as well as the other; I, therefore, *think his intent was clear to pass these lands by the will;* and if so, we must now consider what will be the effect of this will.

If the plaintiff has a lien upon the lands of the articles, then he may stand to them if he pleases; *but when a man takes upon him to devise what he had no power over, upon a supposition that his will will be acquiesced under, this Court compels the devisee, if he will take advantage of the will, to take entirely, but not partially under it; as was done in* Noys and Mordaunt's case; *there being a tacit condition annexed to all devises of this nature, that the devisee do not disturb the disposition which the devisor hath made.* So are the several cases that have been decreed upon the custom of London.

The only difficulty in the present case is, that what is given to the plaintiff is precarious, nothing being given to him if he dies before twenty-one, and if after, then but an estate for life; and that he appears before the Court in the favourable light of being heir-at-law; but this will not alter the case. The estates which the testator has given him were undoubtedly in his power; he hath given them to trustees until his grandson attain twenty-one, and has disposed of them in such a manner as that there can never be any undisposed residue to go *to the plaintiff as [*341] heir-at-law; and surely it is as much in the power of the Court to make this bequest, thus limited, to be a satisfaction, if the party will stand to the will, as in the other cases. Indeed; if he takes by the will, there is nothing to make satisfaction to his sisters for their general chance under the articles; but that is because nothing is left them by the will; and they cannot be said to be quite destitute of provision, since it is just and reasonable that they should be maintained by their mother, who is entitled to a large and ample provision by her marriage settlement: nor can what is devised to the plaintiff be looked upon as intended by the testator to go towards the maintenance of younger children ; for, if the plaintiff dies before twenty-one, then all the profits already received are to go to his aunts ; and so by that construction I must take the maintenance out of their estate, and oblige them to contribute to the maintenance of distant relations, viz., nieces, at the same time that the mother (who hath an ample provision) would be left at large, and under no tie of maintaining her own children.

And so decreed[1] the plaintiff to have six months after he comes of age, to make his election, whether he will stand to the will or the articles ? And if he makes his election to stand to the latter, then so much of the other lands devised to him as will amount to the value of the lands comprised in the articles, and which were devised to Margaret and Martha, to be conveyed to them in fee.

Noys v. *Mordaunt*, and *Streatfield* v. *Streatfield*, are printed together, since they are usually cited as having conclusively established the doctrine of election, which is founded upon the principle, that there is an implied condition, that he who accepts a benefit under an instrument must adopt the whole of it, conforming with all its provisions, and renouncing every right inconsistent with them. See *Walpole* v. *Conway*, Barnard, Ch. Rep. 159; *Kirkham* v. *Smith*, 1 Ves. 258; *Macnamara* v. *Jones*, 1 Bro. C. C. 411; *Frank* v. *Standish*, 1 Bro. C. C. 588, n.; *Blake* v. *Bunbury*, 4 Bro. C. C. 21 : *Swan* v. *Holmes*, 19 Beav. 471; [*342] *Wintour* v. *Clifton*, *21 Beav. 447, 8 De G. Mac N. & G. 641; *Crosby* v. *Lord Ashtown*, 10 Ir. Ch. Rep. 219; *Heazle* v. *Fitzmaurice*, 13 Ir. Ch. Rep. 481, and *Dillon* v. *Parker*, 1 Swanst. 359; and *Gretton* v. *Haward*, 1 Swanst. 409, and Mr. Swanston's learned and elaborate notes to those cases. To illustrate the doctrine of election, suppose A., by will or deed, gives to B. property belonging to C., and by the same instrument gives other property belonging to himself to C , a Court of equity will hold C. to be entitled to the gift made to him by A. only, upon the implied condition of his conforming with all the provisions of the instrument, by renouncing the right to his own property in favour of B.; he must, consequently, make his choice, or, as it is technically termed, he is put to his election, to take either under or against the instrument ; if C. elects to take under, and consequently to conform with all the provisions of, the instrument, no difficulty arises, as B. will take C.'s property, and C. will take the property given to him by A.; but if C. elects to take against the instrument, that is to say, retains his own property and at the same time sets up a claim to the property given to him by A., an important question arises whether he thereupon incurs a forfeiture of the whole of the benefit conferred upon him by the instrument, or is merely bound to make compensation out

---

[1] See the decree, 1 Swanst, 447; Reg. Lib. B., 1735, fol. 205.

of it to the person who is disappointed by his election. There are
many dicta in favour of the doctrine of forfeiture. See *Cowper* v. *Scott*,
3 P. Wms. 124 ; *Cookes* v. *Hellier*, 1 Ves. 235 ; *Morris* v. *Burroughs*, 1
Atk. 404 ; *Pugh* v. *Smith*, 2 Atk. 43 ; *Wilson* v. *Mount*, 3 Ves. 194 ;
Wilson v. *Townsend*, 2 Ves. jun. 697 ; *Broome* v. *Monck*, 10 Ves. 609 ;
Thellusson v. *Woodford*, 13 Ves. 220 ; *Villareal* v. *Lord Galway*, 1
Bro. C. C. 292, n. ; *Green* v. *Green*, 2 Mer. 86 ; and see the decision of
Lord Langdale, M. R., in *Greenwood* v. *Penny*, 12 Beav. 406 ; and the
late Mr. Jacob, in a note to 1 Roper on Husband and Wife, 566, sup-
ports the doctrine of forfeiture. The same view is also taken by Sir
Edward Sugden. See 2 Sugd. Pow. 145, 7th edit. The principal case
of *Streatfield* v. *Streatfield*, is a distinct authority for the doctrine of
compensation. See also *Webster* v. *Milford*, 2 Eq. Ca. Ab. 363, marg.;
Bor v. *Bor*, 3 Bro. P. C. Toml. Ed. 167 ; *Ardesoife* v. *Bennet*, 2 Dick.
465 ; *Lewis* v. *King*, 2 Bro. C. C. 600 ; *Freke* v. *Barrington*, 3 Bro. C.
C. 284 ; *Whistler* v. *Webster*, 2 Ves. jun. 372 ; *Ward* v. *Baugh*, 4 Ves.
627 ; *Lady Caven* v. *Pulteney*, 2 Ves. jun. 560 ; *Blake* v. *Bunbury*, 1
Ves. jun. 523 ; *Welby* v. *Welby*, 2 V. & B. 190, 191 ; and Lord Eldon,
in *Dashwood* v. *Peyton*, 18 Ves. 49 ; *Tibbits* v. *Tibbits*, Jac. 317 : *Lord
Rancliffe* v. *Parkyns*, 6 Dow. 179 ; and *Ker* v. *Wauchope*, *1 [*343]
Bligh. 25, clearly recognises the principle of compensation, as
applied to the doctrine of election. " In our Courts," observes his
Lordship, in the latter case, " we have engrafted upon this primary
doctrine of election, the equity, as it may be termed, of *compensation*.
Suppose a testator gives his estate to A., and directs that the estate of
A., or any part of it, should be given to B. If the devisee will not comply with the provision of the will, the Courts of equity hold that another
condition is to be implied as arising out of the will and the conduct of
the devisee ; that inasmuch as the testator meant that his heir-at-law
should not take his estate which he gives A., in consideration of his
giving his estate to B. ; if A. refuses to comply with the will, B. shall
be compensated by taking the property, or the value of the property,
which the testator meant for him, out of the estate devised, though he
cannot have it out of the estate intended for him." Nearly all these
authorities are stated in Mr. Swanston's learned note to *Gretton* v.
Haward, 1 Swanst. 433, and in his opinion they establish two propositions : " 1st. That, in the event of election to take against the instrument, Courts of equity assume jurisdiction to sequester the benefit intended for the refractory donee, in order to secure compensation to those
whom his election disappoints. 2nd. That the surplus after compensation does not devolve as undisposed of, but is restored to the donee,
the purpose being satisfied for which alone the Court controlled his
legal right." See also *Padbury* v. *Clark*, 2 Mac. & G. 298 ; *Greenwood*

v. Penny, 12 Beav. 403; *Howells* v. *Jenkins*, 1 De G. Jo. & Sm. 617; *Grissell* v. *Swinhoe*, 7 L. R. Eq. 291.

As the doctrine of election depends then upon compensation, it follows that it will not be applicable unless there be a fund from which compensation can be made. Thus it was held, by Lord Loughborough, C., in *Bristowe* v. *Warde*, 2 Ves. jun. 336, that where, under a power to appoint to children, the father made an appointment improperly, any child entitled in default of appointment might set it aside, although a specific share was appointed to him. " The doctrine of election," said his Lordship, " never can be applied, but where, if an election is made contrary to the will, the interest that would pass by the will can be laid hold of, to compensate for what is taken away ; therefore in all cases there must be some free disposable property given to the person, which can be made a compensation for what the testator takes away. That cannot apply to this case, where no part of his property is comprised in the will but that which he had power to distribute." So in *Box* v. *Bar-*
[*344] *rett*, 3 L. R. Eq. 244, under a settlement *the four daughters of a testator took equal shares subject to his life interest. The testator, by his will, recited that under the settlement his *two daughters, Ellen and Emily, would become entitled to certain hereditaments,* and that in making his will he had taken that into consideration, and had not devised them so large a share under his will, as he would have done had they not been so entitled. He then devised to his daughters, Ellen and Emily, certain estates, and to his other daughters, Edith and Eliza, certain other estates of much larger value. *The will did not purport to dispose of or affect the settled estates.* It was held by Lord Romilly, M. R., that as the will did not purport to make any disposition of the settled estates, and was only made under a mistaken impression, Edith and Eliza were not put to their election. "I am of opinion," said his Lordship, "that no case of election arises here. There must be some disposition of property which the testator had no right to dispose of to make it one. I assent to the observations that have been cited to me from the judgments in the cases of *Langslow* v. *Langslow* (21 Beav. 552), and *Blacket* v. *Lamb* (14 Beav. 482), which cases were decided by myself. In the present case there is nothing more than a recital of an intention under a belief which was erroneous, and thereupon the testator gives certain property in a particular way. If I were to hold that a case of election arises here, the most serious and yet strange results would follow : for suppose a man recited in his will that his nephew would have a large fortune from his father, and that, therefore, he left all his property to his other nephew, and that recital turned out to be incorrect, would any question of election arise upon that, because the supposed intention of the testator was that the property should be divided equally ? The most that can be said of the recital in the case before me now is, that it is an erroneous one; but, be-

cause the testator has made a mistake, you cannot afterwards remodel the will and make it that which you suppose he intended, and as he would have drawn it if he had known the incorrectness of his supposition." See also *Banks* v. *Banks*, 17 Beav. 352; *In re Fowler's Trust*, 27 Beav. 362, Lead. Cas. R. P. 352, 2nd ed.

It seems to be doubtful whether the doctrine of election applies to grants from the Crown, for the Crown is always in existence and can always be applied to, to set right the grant: per Sir T. Plumer, M. R., 2 J. & W. 345. Where, however, two persons, A. and B. joined in a petition to the Crown, representing an estate to have escheated, and procured a grant of it, to be made to them, *it was held by Sir T. Plumer, M. R., that the assignees of A. could not afterwards set [*345] up a claim to one part under a prior title in himself, while taking the benefit of the grant as to the rest; *Cummings* v. *Forrester*, 2 J. & W. 334.

The doctrine of election is applicable to deeds as well as to wills (*Llevellyn* v. *Mackworth*, Barnard Ch. Rep. 445; *Bigland* v. *Huddleston*, 3 Bro. C. C. 286, n.; *Moore* v. *Butler*, 2 S. & L. 266; *Birmingham* v. *Kirwan*, 2 S. & L. 450; *Green* v. *Green*, 2 Mer. 86; *Bacon* v. *Cosby*, 4 De G. & Sm. 261; *Cumming* v. *Forrester*, 2 J. & W. 345; *Anderson* v. *Abbott*, 23 Beav. 457; *Mosley* v. *Ward*, 29 Beav. 407): although by the civil law, from which it appears to have been borrowed by our courts of equity, it was confined to wills. See Mr. Swanston's note to *Dillon* v. *Parker*, 1 Swanst. 394. And notwithstanding the opinion of Lord Hardwicke, in *Bor* v. *Bor*, 3 Bro. P. C. 178, n., Toml. Ed., and the decision in *Stewart* v. *Henry*, Vern. & Scriv. 49, the doctrine of election is applicable to interests remote, contingent, or of small value, as well as to those which are immediate or of great value: *Webb* v. *Earl of Shaftesbury*, 7 Ves. 480; *Greaves* v. *Forman*, cited 3 Ves. 67; *Highway* v. *Banner*, 1 Bro. C. C. 584; *Wilson* v. *Townsend*, 2 Ves. jun. 697; *Morgan* v. *Morgan*, 4 Ir. Ch. Rep. 606; *Sadlier* v. *Butler*, 1 I. R. Eq. 415; *Henry* v. *Henry*, 6 I. R. Eq. 286.

In order to raise a case of election, there must appear in the will or instrument itself a clear intention, on the part of the author of it, to dispose of that which is not his own (*Forrester* v. *Cotton*, 1 Eden, 531; *Judd* v. *Pratt*, 13 Ves. 168; 15 Ves. 390; *Dashwood* v. *Peyton*, 18 Ves. 27; *Blake* v *Bunbury*, 4 Bro. C. C. 21; *S. C.*, 1 Ves. jun. 514; *Rancliffe* v. *Lady Parkyns*, 6 Dow. 149, 179; *Dillon* v. *Parker*, 1 Swanst. 359; *S. C.*, Wils. 253; Jac. 505; 7 Bligh, N. S. 325; 1 C. & F. 303; Sugd. Prop. 450; *Jervoise* v. *Jervoise*, 17 Beav. 566; *Padbury* v. *Clark*, 2 Mac. & G. 298; *Lee* v. *Egremont*, 5 De G. & Sm. 348; *Wintour* v. *Clifton*, 21 Beav. 447, 8 De G. Mac. & G. 641; and *Stephens* v. *Stephens*, 3 Drew. 697; 1 De G. & Jo. 62; *Poole* v. *Olding*, 10 W. R. (V. C. K.) 337 (L. J.) 591; *Fox* v. *Charlton*, 10 W. R. (V. C. K.)

506; *Thornton* v. *Thornton*, 11 Ir. Ch. Rep. 474; *Box* v. *Barrett*, 3 L. R. Eq. 244; *Sadlier* v. *Butler*, 1 I. R. Eq. 415): and it is immaterial whether he knew the property or not to be his own, or by mistake conceived it to be his own; for, in either case, if the intention to dispose of it appears clearly, his disposition will be sufficient to raise a case of election; *Whistler* v. *Webster*, 2 Ves. jun. 370; *Thellusson* v. *Woodford*, 13 Ves. 221; *Welby* v. *Welby*, 2 V. & B. 199, overruling *Cull* v. *Showell*, Amb. 727; *Whitley* v. *Whitley*, 31 Beav. 173; *Coutts* v. *Ackworth*, 9 L. R. Eq. 519.

[*346]

The difficulty of sustaining a case of erection is always much greater where the testator has a partial interest in the property dealt with, than where he purports to devise an estate in which he has no interest at all (*Lord Rancliffe* v. *Lady Parkyns*, 6 Dow. 185).

Where the testator has some interest, the Court will lean as far as possible to a construction which would make him deal only with that to which he is entitled: *Maddison* v. *Chapman*, 1 J. & H. 470; *Re Bidwell's Settlement*, 11 W. R. (V. C. K.), 161.

Where, however, a testator entitled only to part of an estate, uses words in devising it which show clearly that he intended to pass the entirety, if the owner of the other part takes other benefits by the will, he will be put to his election: *Padbury* v. *Clark*, 2 Mac. & G. 298; *Wintour* v. *Clifton*, 21 Beav. 447; 8 De G. Mac & G. 644; *Grosvenor* v. *Durston*, 25 Beav. 97; *Usticke* v. *Peters*, 4 K. & J. 437; *Fitzsimons* v. *Fitzsimons*, 28 Beav. 417; *Howells* v. *Jenkins*, 2 J. & H. 706; 1 De G. Jo. & Sm. 617; *Miller* v. *Thurgood*, 33 Beav. 496; *Wilkinson* v. *Dent*, 6 L. R. Ch. App. 339; but see *Chave* v. *Chave*, 2 J. & H. 713, n.

A mere general devise will only comprehend property of which the devisor is owner, and although at one time a different opinion prevailed, it is now clearly settled that parol evidence, dehors the will, is not admissible for the purpose of showing that a testator considering property to be his own, which did not actually belong to him, intended to comprise it in a general devise or bequest. See *Pulteney* v. *Lord Darlington*, referred to in 2 Ves. jun. 544; 3 Ves. 384, 521, 529; 6 Ves. 314, 322, 391, 399, 402, in which case rent-rolls and steward's accounts, agreements of solicitors, cases and opinions of counsel, and all sorts of papers, were admitted to be read, to prove that the testator dealt with property of which he was tenant in tail, as absolute owner, and that he intended to comprise it in a general devise; so that the heir in tail, who took other benefits under the will, was compelled to elect, although the testator had large real estates to satisfy the words of the devise. See also, *Finch* v. *Finch*, 4 Bro. C. C. 38; *S. C.*, 1 Ves. jun. 534; *Hinchcliffe* v. *Hinchcliffe*, 3 Ves. 516; *Rutter* v. *Maclean*, 4 Ves. 531; *Pole* v. *Lord Somers*, 6 Ves. 309; *Druce* v. *Denison*, 6 Ves. 385. Lord Commissioner Eyre, however, in *Blake* v. *Bunbury*, 1 Ves. jun. 523, says, "that the intent of the testator to dispose of that which is not his, ought to appear upon the will;" and in *Stratton* v. *Best*, 1 Ves. jun. 285, *where a testator suffered a recovery of the whole of [*347] a manor, though he was only entitled to part of it, and after- wards devised in general words all his real and personal estate to trus- tees, Lord Thurlow refused to admit evidence to show that the testator supposed himself entitled to the whole manor. "I admit," observed his Lordship, "you have proved, that in 1764, when the recovery was suffered, he took himself to be master of the whole. I have no doubt but that, if he had been asked, when he made his will, whether he did not mean the whole, he would have said yes; and if desired to put in a description of it he would have done so: that I believe, upon the evidence you have brought. But to do this I must say that evidence, dehors the will, of the testator's opinion at any time, may be produced: and I do not think that is the law of the Court. All the argument in *Noys* v. *Mordaunt*, and the whole suite of cases upon this subject, have turned upon the expressions of the will. If I was to receive evidence of the testator's fancy, I should introduce a very desperate rule of property in this Court." Lord Rosslyn, in the case of *Rutter* v. *Mac- lean*, 4 Ves. 537, expressed himself dissatisfied with *Pulteney* v. *Dar- lington*, as did also Lord Eldon, in *Pole* v. *Somers*, 6 Ves. 322 ; and in *Druce* v. *Denison*, 6 Ves. 402, where he observed that he agreed with Lord Rosslyn, and that he could not see upon what principle the evi- dence was admitted in that case. See also *Doe* v. *Chichester*, 4 Dow. 76, 89, 90, and the case of *Clementson* v. *Gandy*, 1 Kee. 309, where parol evidence was tendered for the purpose of showing that the testa- trix intended to pass, under a general bequest, certain property in which she had only a life interest, supposing it to be her own abso- lutely, so as to put a legatee who had an interest in the property to his election. However, Lord Langdale, M. R., refused to admit the evi- dence. "I am of opinion," observed his Lordship, "that this evidence cannot be admitted. It is tendered for the purpose of showing that the testatrix bequeathed property as her own which did not belong to her, and that she intended to leave a considerable residue for charitable purposes, which by reason of that mistake, turns out to be much less than she intended ; and it is argued that this raises a case of election. The intention to dispose must in all cases appear by the will alone. In cases which require it, the Court may look at external circum- stances, and consequently, receive evidence of such circumstances for the purpose of ascertaining the meaning of the terms used by the tes- tator. But parol evidence is not to be resorted to except for the pur- pose of proving facts which make intelligible something *in the [*348] will which, without the aid of extrinsic evidence, cannot be understood." See also *Blonmart* v. *Player*, 2 S. & S. 597; *Drummer* v. *Pitcher*, 2 My. & K. 262 ; *Crabb* v. *Crabb*, 1 My. & K. 511; 5 Sim.

35 ; *Smith* v. *Lyne*, 2 Y. & C. C. C. 345 ; *Allen* v. *Anderson*, 5 Hare, 163 ; *Seaman* v. *Woods*, 24 Beav. 372.

But a testator may in his will itself show an intention under a general devise to dispose of property which is not absolutely his own, for instance of which he is only tenant in tail (even when he has other property which might satisfy the words of the devise), so as to put the heir in tail to his election between the estate and benefits conferred upon him by the will. See *Honywood* v. *Forster*, 30 Beav. 14. There a testator had freeholds in fee, and was tenant in tail of copyholds. They were intermixed ; part of the copyholds were in his own occupation, and part, with parts of the freeholds, in the occupation of tenants upon leases at one rent. By his will he devised " all his real estates " to the defendants, and gave all the lands occupied by him to his wife for life, and confirmed the tenants in their occupations for twenty-one years. He likewise gave benefits to the heir in tail of the copyholds. It was held, by Sir John Romilly, M. R., that the heir must be put to his election. " If," said his Honor, " a testator says, ' I give all the property I have in the world to A. B.,' and he leaves a large legacy to his heir in tail, that will not raise a case of election against such heir, because the testator only gives what he has. It occurred to me at first that such was the character of the present will ; but on the facts of the case being brought to my attention, it became plain that such was not the case. . . . . It was a just observation made to me, that the scope of the will is to dispose of two sorts of properties—the property he occupied himself, and the property which was occupied by his tenants. The property occupied by himself he left to his wife for her life, and as to the property occupied by his tenants, he directed that his executors should confirm their occupation by leases for a period of twenty-one years. The property occupied by himself included some of the copyholds in question ; and it is therefore clear that he intended to give them to his wife for life ; the land in the occupation of his tenants included the remainder of the copyholds, and he directs the executors to confirm to them for twenty-one years, the leases of the property they held, which are part of the copyholds in question. I think that in this state of circumstances, coupled with the fact of the nature and holding of the property, [*349] there *is an intention shown on the face of the will* to dispose *of these copyholds away from the heir in tail. I am of opinion, therefore, that the plaintiff must elect either to take the copyholds in question, and give up the benefits bequeathed to him by the will, or to take under the will and give up the copyholds."

The rule of election, the subject of this note, which depends, as before observed, upon an implied condition, will not be excluded by the parties being expressly put to their election, as between the benefits conferred upon them, and sums due to them from the person conferring such benefits. See *Wilkinson* v. *Dent*, 6 L. R. Ch. App. 339.

There a testatrix devised "all and singular the estate and mines of Aroa," to trustees in trust for sale, and gave to T. Dent 10,000*l.*, which was to be taken in full satisfaction of any sums which she might owe him at her decease, and to W. Dent 3000*l.*, which she declared was to be taken in satisfaction of any rent-charge out of a certain part of her real estate. Her will contained the usual devise of trust and mortgage estates. She was in possession of the entirety of the Aroa estate, but was owner only of one moiety, being in possession of the other moiety by virtue of a mortgage, the money due upon which was subject to trusts, under which T. Dent and W. Dent on her death became entitled, each to one-fifth. It was held by the Lords Justices, affirming the decision of Lord Romilly, M. R., that T. Dent and W. Dent were put to their election between the benefits they took under the will, and their shares in the mortgage money. "The question," said Lord Justice James, "is, whether there is testamentary bounty to persons whose estates and rights are, under another part of the will, interfered with. It appears to me clear, that this question must be answered in the affirmative, though, before the amount of the bounty can be ascertained, the amount of the claims which the legatees had against the testatrix must be ascertained."

But the ordinary doctrine of election may be excluded by an apparent expression of intention by a testator that only one of the gifts, to an object of his bounty, is conditional on his giving up what the testator purports to take away from him. For instance, if a testator had an eldest son, owner of a bit of property, and it would be convenient that this bit of property should go along with a property which the testator is devising to his second son. So, the testator devises this bit of property to the second son ; and amongst other gifts to his eldest son, he gives him a piece of property which he states in his will to be in lieu of his bit of property which the testator purported to take away from him. In such case, the eldest son would merely *be put to his choice [*350] between those two bits of property : *East* v. *Cook*, 2 Ves. 30, as explained by Lord Justice James, in *Wilkinson* v. *Dent*, 6 L. R. Ch. App. 341.

The question has been raised whether, where a testator makes two or more separate devises or bequests, the devisee is bound to elect to take all or none of the gifts, or whether he may accept what is beneficial and reject what is burdensome. These cases, though at first sight similar, are in reality different from cases of election, properly so called, which, as we have before seen, arise where a person disposes of that which is *not his own* (*ante*, p. 342), and confers upon the real owner of the property other benefits, in which case it is at once implied independently of any intention expressed upon the face of the instrument, that the party upon whom such benefits are conferred must elect between his own property and such benefits. But where the gifts, whether beneficial or onerous, are all the property of the testator, the devisee may take what is beneficial and reject what is onerous (*Andrew* v. *Trinity Hall*, 9 Ves. 525; *Moffett* v. *Bates*, 3 Sm. & G. 468; *Warren* v. *Rudall*, 1 J. & H. 1). But where it appears upon the will that it was the intention of the testator to make the acceptance of the burden a condition of the benefit, the result will be different: *Talbot* v. *Lord Radnor*, 3 My. & K. 252; *Warren* v. *Rudall*, 1 J. & H. 13; and see *Long* v. *Kent*, 13 W. R. (V. C. S.) 961.

Although, under the old law, a devise to the heir was in a certain sense inoperative, as he took by *descent* as heir, and not by purchase as devisee, it has been held, ever since the decision of *Noys* v. *Mordaunt*, to be a sufficient gift to him of the testator's property to raise a case of election, should the testator devise or bequeath to another, property belonging to the heir. "That an heir," observes Sir W. Grant, M. R., "to whom an estate is devised in fee, may be put to an election, although, by the rule of law, a devise in fee to an heir is inoperative, I should have thought perfectly clear, independently of Lord Cowper's decision in the case of Gilbert; for if the will is in other respects so framed as to raise a case of election, then not only is the estate given to the heir under an implied condition, that he shall conform the whole of the will, but in contemplation of equity, the testator means, in case the condition shall not be complied with, to give the disappointed devisees out of the estate, over which he had a power, a benefit correspondent to that of which they are deprived by such non-compliance. So that the devise is read as if it were to the heir absolutely, if he confirm the will; if not, then in trust for the disappointed devisees as to so much of the [*351] estate, given to him, as *shall be equal in value to the estates intended for them:" *Welby* v. *Welby*, 2 V. & B. 190; *Anon.*, Gilb. 15; *Thellusson* v. *Woodford*, 13 Ves. 209; *S. C.*, 1 Dow. 249, nom. *Rendlesham* v. *Woodford; a fortori* will the heir now be put to his election, since, by a recent statute, where lands are devised by the will of a testator dying after the 31st of December, 1833, to the heir, he will take as devisee by purchase, and not by descent; see 3 & 4 Will. 4, c. 106, s. 3; and *Schroder* v. *Schroder*, Kay, 578.

Where an express appointment is made to a stranger to the power, which is therefore void, and a benefit is conferred by the same instrument upon a person entitled in default of appointment, the latter will be put to his election. Thus, "where a man having a power to appoint to A. a fund, which in default of appointment is given to B., exercises the power in favour of C., and gives other benefits to B., although the execution is merely void, yet if B. will accept the gifts to him, he must convey the estate to C. according to the appointment," Sug. Pow. 578, 8th ed.; *Whistler* v. *Webster*, 2 Ves. jun. 367; *Reid* v. *Reid*, 25 Beav. 469; *Ex parte Barnard*, 6 Ir. Ch. Rep. 133; *Tomkyns* v. *Blane*, 28 Beav. 422. "So where a person has power to appoint to two, and he appoints to one only, and gives a legacy to the other, that is a case of election:" Sug. Pow. 589, 8th ed.; *Wollen* v. *Tanner*, 5 Ves. 218; *Vane* v. *Lord Dungannon*, 2 S. & L. 118. So where a person having a power to appoint, delegates the power (which he has really no right to do) to another, and by the same instrument confers benefits upon the objects of the power, they cannot retain the benefits given to them by the will and also claim the property against the execution of the power so improperly delegated : *Ingram* v. *Ingram*, cited 1 Ves. 259.

Merely precatory words, requesting appointees, objects of the power, to leave the fund appointed to others, not objects of the power, will not raise a case of election ; *Blackett* v. *Lamb*, 14 Beav. 482; *Kampf* v. *Jones*, 2 Keen, 756; *Carver* v. *Bowles*, 2 Russ. & My. 301.

Where a person appoints simply to objects of the power, and gives them property of his own, subsequently directing them to settle the property so appointed on persons not objects of the power, such direction will not raise a case of election (*King* v. *King*, 15 Ir. Ch. Rep. 479, overruling *Moriarty* v. *Martin*, 3 Ir. Ch. Rep. 26). Secus where there is a clause of forfeiture of the legacies on non-compliance with such direction (Ib.).

And it has been recently decided that where there is an absolute appointment by will in favour of a proper object of the power, and that appointment is *followed by attempts to modify the interest so appointed in a manner which the law will not allow, the will [*352] must be read as if all the passages in which such attempts are made were swept out of it, not only so far as they attempt to regulate the quantum of interest to be enjoyed by the appointee in the settled property, but also so far as they might otherwise have been relied upon as raising a case of election : *Woolridge* v. *Woolridge*, 1 Johns. 63. See, also, *Churchill* v. *Churchill*, 5 L. R. Eq. 44.

And in no instance has a case of election been raised where a testator gave no property absolutely his own to an object of the power out of which, in the event of his not acquiescing in an appointment by the donee to a person not an object of the power, the latter could be compensated. *In re Fowler's Trust*, 27 Beav. 362. Neither will the non-execution of a power upon an erroneous impression stated in the will, that by its non-execution one person who is a legatee will divide the fund equally with another: *Langslow* v. *Langslow*, 21 Beav. 552.

But where the donee of a power by the same instruments appoints to a stranger, and confers benefits out of property *absolutely his own* upon an object of the power, the latter will be put to his election, and if he takes the benefits conferred upon him, he must comply with the directions, or if he declines to do so he must give up the benefits so far as may be necessary for compensating the person disappointed by his election. See *Blacket* v. *Lamb*, 14 Beav. 482.

In a recent case, A. had power to appoint by will a fund to any one or more of his children. He had under a distinct instrument power to appoint another fund amongst his children, but not exclusively to any one of them, and they were to take equally in default of appointment. He had five children. By his will he exercised the first power in favour of S., one of his children, and the second in favour of two others of his children. The second power was accordingly badly exercised, and S. took a share in default of appointment. It was held by Sir W. Page Wood, V. C., that no case of election was raised against S.: *Re Aplin's Trust*, 13 W. R. (V. C. W.) 1062.

So where an appointment was made of the interest of a fund to a person for life, irrevocably, and after his decease the fund was appointed to others, with power to the appointor, by deed or will, to revoke the appointments subsequent to the life interest, and the appointor afterwards, supposing he had complete dominion over the fund, revoked all the appointments before made, giving the person entitled to the interest of the fund for life part of it absolutely, and the remainder of the [*353] *fund to others, the person to whom, under the first appointment, a life interest was given in the whole fund, was compelled to elect between the life interest in the whole fund, and his interest in part of the fund given to him absolutely, under the second appointment. *Coutts* v. *Acworth*, 9 L. R. Eq. 519.

It seems that when there is an attempt to create a power in violation of the rules of law, as for instance, the rule against perpetuities, the Court will not aid such an attempt, by the application of the doctrine of election: *Wollaston* v. *King*, 8 L. R. Eq. 165, 175.

The rule as to election is to be applied, as between a gift under a will, and a claim dehors the will, and adverse to it, and is not to be applied as between one clause in a will and another clause in the same will. See *Wollaston* v. *King*, 8 L. R. Eq. 165. There, Mrs. King, having under her marriage settlement, power to appoint a fund in favour of the children of the marriage, by her will, in execution of the power, appointed a portion of the fund to her son, J. E. King, for life, with remainder to such persons *as he should by will appoint*. There was also a general residuary appointment of the settled fund (subject to all other appointments made thereof), to Mrs. King's three daughters, to whom benefits out of Mrs. King's own property were also given by the will. The appointment in favour of J. E. King's appointees being void for remoteness, the property comprised therein, upon the death of J. E. King, went to the three daughters of Mrs. King under the residuary appointment in her will. It was held by Sir W. M. James, V. C., that the daughters were not put to their election between the benefits which they took under the will in the testatrix's own property, and the settled property which they took under the residuary appointment in the will. "The ordinary principle," said his Honor, "is clear, that if a testator gives property, by design or by mistake, which is not his to give, and gives at the same time to the real owner of it other property, such real owner cannot take both. And the principle has been applied where the first gift is made, purporting to be in execution of a power; so that, if under a power to appoint to children, the donee of the power appoints to grandchildren, which is bad, and the children who are entitled to claim by reason of the badness of the appointment, also take under the will other property, the grandchildren are entitled to put them to an election. But to this rule, so far as regards appointments, a notable exception is taken; viz., that when there is an appointment to an object of the power, with directions that the same shall be *settled, or upon any trust, or subject to any condition, then the appoint- [*354] ment is held to be a valid appointment, and the superadded direction, trust, or condition is void, and not only void, but inoperative to raise any case of election.

" This rule has not been followed in the Irish case of *Moriarty* v. *Martin* (3 Ir. Ch. Rep. 26), which is said to have received the approval of Lord St. Leonards. Notwithstanding that case, and that approval, I feel bound by the current English authorities. I have endeavoured to extract from these cases a principle which I can apply to the decision of the case before me. The rule laid down by the Master of the Rolls in *Whistler* v. *Webster* (2 Russ. & My. 301) is, in general terms, that no man shall claim any benefit under a will without conforming, so far as he is able, and giving effect to everything contained in it, whereby any disposition is made, showing an intention that such a thing shall take place."

" This rule, expressed in these terms, was certainly not applied in the case of *Carver* v. *Bowles* (2 Russ. & My. 301), and the cases which followed it. There, it was clear, that certain persons were intended to take benefits under the will, and other persons were allowed to take other benefits, without conforming to, and giving effect to, the first dispositions and, in fact, after defeating them. But why? The only intelligible principle which I can find is, that it was held, that the failure of the first dispositions, so far as they failed, did, under the will itself, enure for the benefit of the legatees: that the legatees were allowed to retain both benefits, because they took both as legatees under the will itself, without calling in aid any other instrument or adverse title. It results in this, that *the rule as to election is to be applied as between a gift under a will, and a claim dehors the will, and adverse to it, and is not to be applied as between one clause in a will, and another clause in the same will.*" See *Wallinger* v. *Wallinger*, 9 L. R. Eq. 301.

No case of election will be raised where there is a want of capacity to devise real estate by reason of infancy. Thus, under the old law, where an infant, whose will was valid as to personal, but invalid as to real estate, gave a legacy to his heir-at-law, and devised real estate to another person, the heir-at-law would not have been obliged to elect between the legacy and the real estate, which descended to him in consequence of the invalidity of the devise ; he might take both : *Hearle* v. *Greenbank*, 3 Atk. 695, 715 ; 1 Ves. 298.

Nor will a case of election be raised if there is a want of capacity to bequeath arising from coverture. Thus, where a feme covert made [*355] *a valid appointment by will to her husband, under a power, and also bequeathed to another personal estate, to which the power did not extend, the husband was not put to his election; but was held to be entitled to the benefit conferred upon him by the power, and also to the property bequeathed by his wife, to which he was entitled jure mariti : *Rich* v. *Cockell*, 9 Ves. 369. See also *Blaiklock* v. *Grindle*, 7 L. R. Eq. 215.

With regard to infants, however, it must be remembered, that the Wills Act, 1 Vict. c. 26, s. 7, renders them incapable of making a will even of personalty.

Previous to the Wills Act, 1 Vict. c. 26, where a testator by a will, not properly attested for the devise of freeholds, but sufficient to pass personal estate, devised freehold estates away from his heir, and gave him a legacy, the question has arisen, whether the heir-at-law was not obliged to elect between the freehold estate which descended to him in consequence of the devise being inoperative, and the legacy ; it is clearly settled that he would not be obliged to elect (*Sheddon* v. *Goodrich*, 8 Ves. 481 ; *Gardiner* v. *Fell*, 1 J. & W. 22 ; *Wilson* v. *Wilson*, 1 De G. & Sm. 152 ; and see *Middlebrook* v. *Bromley*, 11 W. R. (V. C. K.) 712) ; unless the legacy was given to him with an express condition, that if he disputed or did not comply with the whole of the will, he should forfeit all benefit under it : *Boughton* v. *Boughton*, 2 Ves. 12. " Lord Kenyon said, the distinction was settled, and not to be unsettled, that if a pecuniary legacy was bequeathed by an unattested will, under an express condition to give up a real estate by that unattested will attempted to be disposed of, such condition being expressed in the body of the will, it was a case of election, as he could not take the legacy without complying with the express condition. But Lord Kenyon also took it to be settled, as Lord Hardwicke has adjudged, that if there was nothing in the will but a mere devise of real estate, the will was not capable of being read as to that part ; and unless, according to an express condition, the legacy was given, so that the testator said expressly the legatee should not take unless that condition were complied with, it was not a case of election. The reason of that distinction, if it were res integra, is questionable." Per Lord Eldon, in *Sheddon* v. *Goodrich*, 8 Ves. 496. See also *Brodie* v. *Brady*, 2 V. & B. 130.

These questions will not arise under wills coming within the Wills Act, because if they are sufficiently attested for the bequest of a personal legacy, they will also pass freehold estates.

Previous to the Wills Act a testator could not devise after-acquired lands, for although by his will he devised lands of which he should be seised at the time of *his decease, they would descend to his heir: *Bunker* v. *Coke*, 1 Bro. P. C. 199; *S. C.*, 1 Salk. 234; [*356] *Holt's Rep.* 248; *Fitzger.* 228: the reason being that the Statute of Wills, 32 Hen. 8, gives the power of disposition by will of lands only to persons *having* lands, but does not give power to persons *not having lands*, to make any disposition of such as they *shall have*.

This act also puts an end (as far as regards wills coming within its operation) to questions which sometimes arose upon the testator attempting to dispose of real estate to which he might become entitled subsequent to the making of his will. When therefore a testator devised after-acquired lands away from his heir, he nevertheless took such lands by descent, subject however to the application of the doctrine of election; for the rule in such cases was, that if the testator showed a clear intention of disposing of after-acquired estates, the heir was obliged to elect between the after-acquired estates which would descend to him, and any benefits given him by the will (*Thellusson* v. *Woodford*, 13 Ves. 209; *S. C.*, *Rendlesham* v. *Woodford*, 1 Dow. 249; *Churchman* v. *Ireland*, 4 Sim. 520; 1 Russ. & My. 250; *Greenwood* v. *Penny*, 12 Beav. 403; *Schroder* v. *Schroder*, Kay, 578, *S. C.*, on appeal, 24 L. J. Ch. N. S. 510; *Hance* v. *Truwhitt*, 2 J. & H. 216); but not if the intention of the testator to dispose of the after-acquired estates was equivocal: *Back* v. *Kett*, Jac. 534. But here, again, the law has been altered by 1 Vict. c. 26, s. 24, which enacts, " That every will shall be construed with reference to the real and personal estate comprised in it, to speak and take effect as if it had been executed immediately before the death of the testator, unless a contrary intention shall appear by the will."

Previous to 55 Geo. 3, c. 192 (which rendered a surrender of copyholds to the use of wills unnecessary for the future), it was held, that the heir to whom copyholds descended, in consequence of their not having been surrendered to the use of a will, was obliged to elect between the copyholds and any benefit he may have taken under the will. See *Unett* v. *Wilkes*, Amb. 430; 2 Eden, 187; *Rumbold* v. *Rumbold*, 3 Ves. 65; *Pettiward* v. *Prescott*, 7 Ves. 541; but in *Judd* v. *Pratt*, 13 Ves. 168, 15 Ves. 390, the heir was not compelled to elect, because the testator, having freeholds as well as copyholds, was held not to have sufficiently indicated his intention to pass the copyholds by a mere general devise of all his real estate.

The heir of heritable property in Scotland, becoming entitled to it in consequence of the will, by which it is devised to another, not being conformable to the solemnities required by the law of Scotland, and taking also under the same will real or personal property in this country, will be compelled to elect between the heritable property which has descended to him as heir, and the benefits given to him by the will: *Bro-*

[*357] *die* v. *Barry*, 2 *V. & B. 127; *Orrell* v. *Orrell*, 6 L. R. Ch. App. 302; *Dewar* v. *Maitland*, 2 L. R. Eq. 834, as to lands in St. Kitt's; *M'Call* v. *M'Call*, Dru. Ca. to Sugd. 283; *secus*, if it does not appear clearly that the testator intended to pass his Scotch estates: *Johnson* v. *Telfourd*, 1 Russ. & My. 244; *Allen* v. *Anderson*, 5 Hare, 163, *Maxwell* v. *Maxwell*, 16 Beav. 106; 2 De G. Mac. & G. 705; *Lamb* v. *Lamb*, 5 W. R. (V. C. K.) 720; *Maxwell* v. *Hyslop*, 4 L. R. Eq. 407.

A widow may at law be put to her election by express words between her dower and a gift conferred upon her (*Gosling* v. *Warburton*, Cro. Eliz. 128; *Lacy* v. *Anderson*, Choice Cases in Chancery, 155; *Boynton* v. *Boynton*, 1 Bro. C. C. 445; see *Dyke* v. *Rendall*, 2 De G. Mac. & G. 209; *Nottley* v. *Palmer*, 2 Drew. 93), in equity she may be put to her election between dower, and a gift conferred upon her, by manifest implication, demonstrating the intention of the donor to exclude her from her legal right to dower. " If," observes Lord Redesdale, " there be anything ambiguous or doubtful,—if the Court cannot say that it was clearly the intention to exclude,—then the averment that the gift was made in lieu of dower cannot be supported : and, to make a case of election, that is necessary ; for a gift is to be taken as pure, until a condition appear. . . . The only question made in all the cases is, whether an intention, not expressed by apt words, could be collected from the terms of the instrument. The result of all the cases of implied intention seems to be, that the instrument must contain some provision inconsistent with the assertion of a right to demand a third of the lands, to be set out by metes and bounds." *Birmingham* v. *Kirwan*, 2 S. & L. 452.

Where the widow is not in express terms excluded from her right to dower, a question arises, and it is one by no means free from difficulty, what is a gift inconsistent with her assertion of that right? It has been long since settled in cases previous to the Dower Act (3 & 4 Will. 4, c. 105) coming into operation, that a devise by a testator to his widow of *part of* the lands of which she is dowable, is not inconsistent with her claim to dower in the remainder; this was decided in the leading case of *Lawrence* v. *Lawrence*. There the testator devised part of his real estate to his wife during her widowhood, and devised the residue to trustees, in trust for other persons ; and he bequeathed to his widow several specific and pecuniary legacies. It was held by Lord Keeper Wright, on appeal, reversing the decision of Lord Somers, and afterwards by Lord Cowper and the House of Lords, affirming the decision of Lord Keeper Wright, that the widow was not obliged to elect between her dower and the benefits derived under the will, and that she was *entitled to both : 2 Vern. 365 ; 2 Freem. 234, 235 ;

[*358] 3 Bro. P. C. 483, Toml. Ed. See also *Lemon* v. *Lemon*, 8 Vin. Abr. " Devise," p. 366, pl. 45 ; *French* v. *Davies*, 2 Ves. jun. 572 ; *Strahan* v. *Sutton*, 3 Ves. 249 ; *Lord Dorchester* v. *Earl of Effingham*,

Coop. 319; *Brown* v. *Parry*, 2 Dick. 685; *Incledon* v. *Northcote*, 3 Atk. 430, 436; and *Gibson* v. *Gibson*, 1 Drew. 42.

A devise of lands, out of which the widow is dowable, upon *trust for sale*, is not inconsistent with her claim to dower out of those lands, even although the interest of a part of the proceeds of the sale is given to her. Thus, in *Ellis* v. *Lewis*, 3 Hare, 310, a testator devised all his real estate to a trustee upon trust for sale, with power to convey the same to purchasers, without the concurrence of any person or persons beneficially claiming under his will; and he directed the trustee to stand possessed of the proceeds of such sale, together with the residue of his personal estate, upon trust to pay one moiety of the interest and dividends thereof to his wife during her widowhood, and the other moiety of such interest and dividends (and the whole after his wife's decease or second marriage) to his sister for her life, with remainder as to the whole of the trust-funds to the children of the testator's sister for their lives and the life of the survivor; remainder over. It was held by Sir James Wigram, V. C., that the widow was entitled both to her dower and to the benefit given to her by the will. " I take the law," observed his Honor, "to be clearly settled at this day, that a devise of lands eo nomine upon trust for sale, or a devise of lands eo nomine to a devisee beneficially, does not, per se, express any intention to devise the lands otherwise than subject to its legal incidents, that of dower included. There must be something more in the will, something inconsistent with the enjoyment by the widow of her dower by metes and bounds, or the devise standing alone will be construed as I have stated. The case of *French* v. *Davies*, 2 Ves. jun. 572, is a direct authority for this proposition; and the current of the authorities which are collected in the last edition of Roper's Husband and Wife, vol. i., p. 577, beginning with the leading case of *Lawrence* v. *Lawrence*, down to *Dowson* v. *Bell*, 1 Kee. 761, confirm it. If that be so, it is impossible, in the case of a devise of lands upon trust for sale, that any direction for the application of the proceeds of such sale can affect the case. The devise is of land subject to dower. The trust to sell is a trust to sell subject to dower; and the proceeds of the sale will represent the gross value of the estate, minus the value of the dower. Whatever direction, therefore, for the mere distribution of the proceeds the will may contain, that direction *must leave the widow's right to [*359] dower untouched. . . . I found myself upon these two propositions: first, that a devise of land upon trusts for sale does not, per se, import an intention to pass the land otherwise than subject to the legal incident of dower; and, secondly, that the direction to divide the proceeds of the sale cannot decide what the subject of sale is; and there is no circumstance affecting the proposition in its application to the present case." See *Gibson* v. *Gibson*, 1 Drew. 42.

It is immaterial, when there is a trust for sale, that there is a direction that the rents and profits are in the meantime to be applied in the same way as the income to arise from the produce of the sale: *Ib.* 57. See also *Bending* v. *Bending*, 3 K. & J. 257.

The gift by the husband of an annuity or rent-charge to the widow, charged upon the property out of which she is at law entitled to dower, is not inconsistent with her claim to dower, and will not consequently of itself alone put her to her election between the annuity or rent-charge and dower. See *Pitts* v. *Snowden*, 1 Bro. C. C. 292, n.; *Pearson* v. *Pearson*, 1 Bro. C. C. 291; *Foster* v. *Cook*, 3 Bro. C. C. 347; *Dowson* v. *Bell*, 1 Kee. 761; *Harrison* v. *Harrison*, 1 Kee. 765; and *Holdich* v. *Holdich*, 2 Y. & C. C. C. 18; *Norcott* v. *Gordon*, 14 Sim. 258, overruling *Arnold* v. *Kempstead*, Amb. 466; *S. C.*, 2 Eden, 236; *Jones* v. *Collier*, Amb. 730; and *Wake* v. *Wake*, 3 Bro. C. C. 255; *S. C.*, 1 Ves. jun. 335. The case of *Villa Real* v. *Lord Galway*, 1 Bro. C. C. 292, n., though sometimes cited as an authority for the proposition, that a widow will be put to her election by the mere gift of a rent-charge or annuity out of the lands of which she is dowable, was decided, it seems, upon the ground that certain directions in the will as to the management of the whole estate, the payment of the annuity, and the accumulation during the minority of a child, were inconsistent with the setting out a third part of the estate by metes and bounds. See *Birmingham* v. *Kirwan*, 2 S. & L. 453; *Roadley* v. *Dixon*, 3 Russ. 202; *Hall* v. *Hill*, 1 D. & W. 103; *S. C.*, 1 C. & L. 129. In *Holdich* v. *Holdich*, 2 Y. & C. C. C. 18, an important case on this subject, Sir J. L. Knight Bruce, V. C., after having fully considered all these cases, observes, " I feel bound by the present state of the authorities to say, that a mere gift of an annuity to the testator's widow, although charged on all the testator's property, is not sufficient to put her to her election. I consider myself equally bound by the authorities to say, that a mere gift to the widow of an annuity so charged, and a gift of the whole of the testator's real estate, though specified by name, to some other person, *are not together of themselves sufficient to put the widow to her election; and, moreover, that a gift of a portion of the real estate to the widow, whether for life or during widowhood, is not sufficient, as to the residue of the estate, to put the widow to her election in respect of dower." In *Dowson* v. *Bell*, 1 Kee. 761, where a testator gives " all and singular his freehold lands" to trustees upon certain trusts for his children, subject to an annuity, or rent-charge for his wife during widowhood, with power of distress, and he also gives to his wife specific legacies and the residue of his personal estate; it was contended, that the gift of " all" the testator's estates, for the purposes of his will, was inconsistent with the abstraction of one-third of those estates for dower, in addition to the benefits given by the will to the widow, and that the remedy by distress for enforcing payment of the annuity applied to all the testator's lands, and was consequently

[*360]

inconsistent with an intention to devise two-thirds of them.   However, Lord Langdale, M. R., said, that in the consideration of this question, when a testator speaks of " all his estates," he must be held to mean all his estates subject to the legal rights against them, and amongst them is the wife's right to dower; and that the widow should, therefore, be declared to be entitled both to the annuity and other benefits given to her by the will and to her dower.   See also *Thompson* v. *Nelson*, 1 Cox, 447; *Harrison* v. *Harrison*, 1 Kee. 765.

A testator's dealings in his lifetime cannot, it seems, be taken into consideration in construing his will, with reference to the question whether he intended to exclude his wife from her dower, when the will contains no reference to those dealings.   Thus, in *Gibson* v. *Gibson*, 1 Drew. 42, where a testator had, before making his will (under which it was argued a case of election arose), sold part of his freehold estate, his wife joining to bar her dower, and previously and subsequently to the making of his will he had contracted to lease part thereof, and after the date of his will to sell part to the lessee, and after his will he entered into an agreement to let another part of his freeholds, with liberty to the lessee to pull down the buildings and erect others, which agreement after the death of the testator' the lessee acted upon, it was held by Sir R. T. Kindersley, V. C., that these dealings with the property by the testator could not be taken into consideration by the Court.   " The intention," said his Honor, " to exclude the widow's dower, must be collected from the will itself; and the Court cannot, in my opinion, look at the evidence of acts done in the testator's lifetime which are not noticed in the will."

*The provisions which have generally been held inconsistent with the widow's legal right to dower, are those which prescribe [*361] to the devisees a certain mode of enjoyment, which shows the testator's intention that they should have the entirety of the property.   Thus, in *Birmingham* v. *Kirwan*, 2 S. & L. 444, the testator devised his house and demesne to trustees upon trust to permit his wife to enjoy the same for life, she paying 13s. yearly for every acre, to keep the house in repair, and not to let, except to the person who should be in possession of the remainder; and he devised the residue of his lands, subject to debts and legacies, to A. for life, remainder to B. in fee.   The question was as to the wife's right of dower: first, in the part devised to her; secondly, in the residue.   " The result," said Lord Redesdale, " of all the cases of implied intention seems to be, that the instrument must contain some provision inconsistent with the assertion of a right to demand a third of the land to be set out by metes and bounds. . . . . Now, in the present case, it is clear the assertion of a right of dower as to the house and demesne would be inconsistent with the dispositions of the house and demesne contained in the will; and therefore the widow cannot have both.   The house and demesne are devised with the rest of the estate to trustees. That devise taken simply might be subject to the widow's right of dower, but it is coupled with a direction that she shall have the enjoyment of the house and demesne, paying a rent of 13s. an acre, which must be out of the whole. Then follow directions that she shall keep the house and demesne in repair, that she shall not alien, except to the persons in remainder; directions which apply to the whole of the house and demesne, and could not be considered obligations on a person claiming by dower. It was clearly, therefore, the intention of the testator, that the wife should enjoy the whole of the house and demesne under a right created by the will; and not a part of it under a right which she previously had, and part under the will. . . . . Then comes the question, whether the implication extends to the rest of the estate? I cannot, on the whole of the case, think the testator has sufficiently manifested an intent that this beneficial interest in the house and demesne, given upon a reserved rent, and under certain conditions, should be considered as a bar of dower out of the rest of the estate. The will may be perfectly executed as to all other purposes without injury to the claim of dower, with respect to the rest of the estate; it may be mortgaged or sold, subject to that claim."

[*362] And see *Goodfellow* v. *Goodfellow*, 18 Beav. 356; see, *however, *Strahan* v. *Sutton*, 3 Ves. 249.

In *Miall* v. *Brain*, 4 Madd. 119, a testator devised all his real and personal estate to trustees upon trust, as to a certain freehold messuage, for his wife during her widowhood, and to pay her, out of the rents and profits, an annuity for life; and upon further trust *to permit his daughter to use, occupy, and enjoy* a certain messuage for her life, and after her decease to raise 2000*l.* for her children; and after giving legacies to his other children, the testator gave the residue of his real and personal estate amongst his children, and gave the usual power of sale to the trustees. Sir J. Leach, M. R., held, that the widow was put to her election. " The testator," observes his Honor, " directs the trustees to whom he devises his estates to permit his daughter to use, occupy, and enjoy a certain freehold house for her life. I think the testator contemplated for his daughter the personal use, occupation, and enjoyment of his house; and such personal use, occupation, and enjoyment is inconsistent with the widow's right to dower out of that house. . . . . This house is part of a general devise to the trustees of all his real estate, and the testator has not given this house to the trustees free from the widow's dower, unless he has so given his whole real estate. I think the testator has shown a plain intent that the trustees should take an interest in this house which would exclude the widow's dower; and the same intention must necessarily be applied to the whole estate which passes by the same devise." In *Butcher* v. *Kemp*, 5 Madd. 61, where the testator, having devised a freehold farm, containing about 136 acres, to trustees and their heirs, during the minority of his daughter, directed them *to carry on the business of the farm, or let it on lease, during the daughter's minority*, and the testator devised some lands to his widow for her life, and also gave her several specific and pecuniary legacies, Sir John Leach, V. C., held, that the widow was put to her election. " The question," said his Honor, " is, whether the testator can be considered as speaking here of his interest in the farm, subject to his widow's claim of dower ? His plain intention is that the trustees should, for the benefit of his daughter, have authority to continue his business in the entire farm which he himself occupied, consisting of about 136 acres ; and this intention must be disappointed if the widow could have assigned to her a third part of this land. This case is within the principle of *Miall* v. *Brain*, which was lately before me, in which I held the claim of dower necessarily excluded by the gift of a house for the personal occupation and enjoyment of the testator's daughter." In *Roadley* v. *Dixon*, *3 [*363] Russ. 192, where a testator, after bequeathing to his wife an annuity charged on his estate at S., with power of entry and distress, if it should be in arrear for thirty days, and after giving other legacies and annuities, which he charged on his lands at S., in aid of his personal estate, gave and devised all his real and personal property to trustees upon certain trusts ; and he directed them *to occupy and manage, during the minority of his son*, a farm, constituting the greater part of his estate at S., and *to let and manage* the residue of the real estates, and to *receive the rents of the whole* of his real estates, Lord Lyndhurst held, that the widow was put to her election between her dower and the benefits given to her by the will. " Without meaning to say," observed his Lordship, " that a mere charge of an annuity in favour of the widow, with a clause of entry and distress, would be sufficient to put her to her election ; but considering the particular dispositions which the testator has made of his property,—the charge of the annuity, the clause of entry and distress, the express direction for the occupation of part of the estate by the trustees, the trusts declared with respect to the rents, profits, and issues of the whole of the real estate ;—taking all these circumstances together, I think it was the manifest intention of the testator that the whole of his property should be free of dower ; and that intention is so clear and distinct as to authorise me to say that the widow must be put to her election." In this case the Lord Chancellor acts upon and approves of the rule laid down in *Miall* v. *Brain*, viz., *that where a testator devises the whole of the property together in general terms, and it is manifest that it was his intention that one part of the property should not be subject to dower, it follows that no part of the property should be considered as so subject.* See *Hall* v. *Hill*, 1 D. & W. 94 ; 1 C. & L. 120 ; decided, in a great measure, on the ground of a power of leasing, which applied to the whole property. See also *Reynard* v. *Spence*, 4 Beav. 103 ; *Taylor* v.

Taylor, 1 Y. & C. C. C. 727; *O'Hara* v. *Chaine,* 1 J. & L. 662; *Holdich* v. *Holdich,* 2 Y. & C. 22; *Lowes* v. *Lowes,* 5 Hare, 501; *Robinson* v. *Wilson,* 13 Ir. Eq. Rep. 168, 183; *Pepper* v. *Dixon,* 17 Sim. 200; *Grayson* v. *Deakin,* 3 De Gex & Sm. 298; *Parker* v. *Sowerby,* 1 Drew. 488; 4 De Gex, Mac. & G. 321; *Taylor* v. *Linley,* 5 Jur. N. S. (V. C. S.) 701; and a direction to cut down timber on any part of the estate would, it seems, be entirely inconsistent with the wife's right to dower. *Ib.* It must be considered that *Warbutton* v. *Warbutton,* 2 Sm. & Giff. 163 (which seems to proceed upon a misapprehension of the judgment [*364] of Lord St. Leonards in *Hall v. *Hill,* 1 Dru. & War. 94), is overruled.

There is another class of cases in which much discussion has arisen, where a testator has devised lands, of which his widow is dowable, to herself and others in equal shares. The first case is that of *Chalmers* v. *Storil,* 2 V. & B. 222. There the words of the will were, " I give to my dear wife A., and my two children B. & C., all my estates whatsoever, to be equally divided amongst them, whether real or personal." And the testator specified the property bequeathed by him as consisting of freehold ground-rents, money on mortgage, American bank stock, an estate in America, &c. Sir W. Grant, M. R., held, that it was a case of election, the claim of dower being directly inconsistent with the disposition of the will. " The testator," observed his Honor, " directing all his real and personal estate to be equally divided, the same equality is intended to take place in the division of the real as of the personal estate, which connot be if the widow first takes out of it her dower, and then a third of the remaining two-thirds. Further, by describing his English estates he excludes the ambiguity which Lord Thurlow in *Foster* v. *Cook,* 3 Bro. C. C. 347, imputes to the word 'my estate,' as not necessarily extending to the wife's dower." As to the last remark being one ground for his Honor's decision, it is clear at the present day, if not in the time of Lord Thurlow, that such a devise, as " all my English estates" would merely mean and pass the testator's English estates, subject to dower. See *Read* v. *Crop,* 1 Bro. C. C. 492; *Dowson* v. *Bell,* 1 Kee. 761; *Gibson* v. *Gibson,* 1 Drew. 50. The other and principal ground upon which *Chalmers* v. *Storil* was decided—viz., that equality, which was intended, would be destroyed by letting in claim to the dower—has been followed by subsequent judges. Thus, in *Dickson* v. *Robinson,* Jac. 503, the testator gave his real and personal estate to his wife in trust for the equal benefit of herself and her two daughters. Sir Thomas Plumer, M. R., said that he could not distinguish the case from *Chalmers* v. *Storil.* " The substance of the will," said his Honor, " is, that there should be an equal division of the property, which cannot take place if the widow is to have a third. The real and personal estate are united together; the personal estate is not subject to any antecedent claim; and is not the real estate intended to be given in the same manner? The principle certainly is, that the Court will go as far as it can, not to exclude the claim of dower; but here it would be inconsistent with the will." In *Roberts* v. *Smith*, 1 S. & S. 513, the testator, after giving his wife an estate in fee, and certain legacies, devised gavelkind lands, and *all other his property of what nature or kind soever, to his wife and two other per- [*365] sons in trust, as to one moiety, for the maintenance of herself and her children by a former marriage, and as to the other moiety, for his children. Sir J. Leach, V. C., held, that the widow was put to her election. "The principle," said his Honor, "referred to in *Chalmers* v. *Storil* decides this case. The plain intention of the testator was, that the wife should have half the income of his property, for the maintenance of herself and her children by her former husband, and that the other half of the income should be applied to the maintenance and education of the testator's own children. That intended equality would be disappointed if the wife were in the first place to take her dower." See also *Reynolds* v. *Torin*, 1 Russ. 129.

Although *Chalmers* v. *Storil*, has been so often recognised and followed as an authority, it scarcely seems to have been decided upon correct principles; because, when a person devises all his " estates " to his widow and children, " equally to be divided among them," he, according to the ordinary rules of construction, would be held to devise only what belonged to him—viz., the estate subject to the widow's right to dower; and an equal division of the estate after the assignment of the widow's dower by metes and bounds would fully satisfy the words of the will. See 1 Jarm. on Devises, 402; *Ellis* v. *Lewis*, 3 Hare, 315. In a recent case, Sir W. Page Wood, V. C., stated that *Chalmers* v. *Storil* is imperfectly reported; see *Bending* v. *Bending*, 3 K. & J. 261.

If a man devises his real estate from his heir after giving his widow a provision in lieu, satisfaction and bar of dower, and the devisee dies in the lifetime of the devisor, the heir will take the estate, but the widow will be obliged to elect. See *Pickering* v. *Lord Stamford*, 3 Ves. 337. But a gift by a testator to his widow in lieu of thirds of his personal property, does not preclude her from claiming her share of the personalty under the Statute of Distributions, in the event of the failure of a bequest of that property. Thus, in *Pickering* v. *Lord Stamford*, 3 Ves. 492, where a testator gave part of his real and personal property to his wife in lieu of dower or thirds, which she could claim out of his real or personal estate, or either of them, and bequeathed the residue of his personal estate (part of which consisted of real securities) to his executors, for charitable purposes, which bequest was of course void as to the real securities; it was held by Lord Loughborough, affirming the decision of Lord Alvanley, M. R. (3 Ves. 332), that the widow was not barred by the clauses in the will. His Lordship observed,—

[*366] *" Neither an heir-at-law, nor by parity of reasoning next of kin, can be barred by anything but a disposition of the heritable subject or personal estate to some person capable of taking. Notwithstanding all the words of anger and dislike applied to the heir, he will take what is not disposed of. It is impossible to make a different rule as to personal estate, with regard to what is not disposed of. Here is a legal intestacy, for the gift to the charity is void at law. Being a legal intestacy, I am to control the Statute of Distributions. How can the Court possibly do that? I must close the will, and cannot look at it." See *Sympson* v. *Hornby*, cited 3 Ves. 335; *Wetherell* v. *Wetherell* 4 Giff. 1. But it seems that the principle of the decision in *Pickering* v. *Stamford* will not apply to a case where, on the face of the will, there is an intestacy as to a great part of the estate: *Lett* v. *Randall*, 3 Sm. & G. 83, 91, n.

A provision made for a wife, by a rent-charge " for her jointure, and in lieu of dower and thirds at common law," does not extend to her share of the personal estate under the Statute of Distributions: *Colleton* v. *Garth*, 6 Sim. 19. But the addition of the words " out of any real or personal estate " has been held to do so (*Gurly* v. *Gurly*, 8 C. & F. 743; and see *Thompson* v. *Watts*, 2 J. & H. 291; and the words " in lieu of dower or thirds at common law, or *otherwise*," have been held to extend to a wife's freebench in copyholds: *Nottley* v. *Palmer*, 2 Drew. 93.

With regard to widows married since the 1st January, 1834, questions of election will less frequently arise, as dower may now be much more readily barred by the husband. See 3 & 4 Will. 4, c. 105, ss. 4, 5, 6, 7, and 8.

And a devise of land by a man married after the 3 & 4 Will. 4, c. 105, came into operation, will, in the absence of a contrary intention declared by the will, deprive her of dower. See Sect. 9, which enacts, " that where a husband shall devise any land out of which his widow would be entitled to dower if the same were not so devised, or any estate or interest therein to or for the benefit of his widow, such widow shall not be entitled to dower out of or in any land of her said husband, unless a contrary intention shall be declared by his will." In *Rowland* v. *Cuthbertson*, 8 L. R. 466, a testator after directing his debts to be paid by his executors, devised his real and personal estate, subject as aforesaid, to trustees upon certain trusts, being partly for the benefit of his widow. It was held by Lord Romilly, M. R., that the widow was deprived of her dower by Sect. 9, of the Dower Act. " I thought it desirable," said his Lordship, " to reserve my judgment in order that I might refer to some of the *cases decided before the Act (of which *Lawrence* v. *Lawrence*, 3 Bro. P. C. 483, may be taken as an example), by which it was settled that were a man devises all his estate, that does not dispose of the wife's dower, but means the estate subject

[*367]

to dower. I think, however, that the Act was intended to make a difference in that respect. . . . Certainly there is no indication of a contrary intention, and I am of opinion that there is no dower."

By the 10th section of 3 & 4 Will. 4, c. 105, it is enacted, " that no gift or bequest made by any husband to or for the benefit of his widow, of or out of his personal estate, or of or out of any of his land not liable to dower, shall defeat or prejudice her right to dower, unless a contrary intention shall be declared by his will."

If a testator, having an undivided interest in a particular property, devises that property *specifically* to his co-owner, a case of election arises, and the devisee must elect between his own interest in the property and the interest he takes under the will. But if the testator does not dispose of it specifically, but by general words, such as " all my lands and hereditaments," or the like, no case for election arises, because there is other property of the testator's sufficient to satisfy the devise itself. Thus in *Miller* v. *Thurgood*, 33 Beav. 496, a testator had a freehold in Potter Street and a freehold in South Street, and he was entitled to two-thirds of a house and eighteen freehold cottages in South Street, the other one-third belonging to his wife. By his will he devised all his freehold messuages, cottages, &c., in the two streets, to his wife for life, she keeping them in tenantable repair, and after her decease upon trusts to sell and divide the proceeds amongst his children. It was held by Sir John Romilly, M. R., that the wife was bound to elect between her one-third of the house and cottages and the other benefits given to her by the will. " If," said his Honor, " the testator had devised his property in these terms, 'all and every my freeholds in Potter Street and South Street and elsewhere, with the appurtenances,' I should be of opinion that no case for election arose. But he specifically points to his ' cottages ' in South Street, and that being so, I am of opinion that these words can only refer to the messuage and eighteen cottages of which he had only two-thirds, and consequently I am of opinion that a case for election arises."

If a person comes in directly under a settlement, and asks to have the benefit of such of its provisions as give him an advantage, and at the same time claims adversely to what was intended to be the rest of the settlement, because it was not binding, then *a case of election arises. Thus, in *Brown* v. *Brown*, 2 L. R. Eq. 481, mar- [*368] riage articles executed when the lady was a minor, contained a covenant by the husband to settle her interest in real and personal estate, including after-acquired property, on the usual trusts ; and she died without having confirmed the articles, leaving her husband surviving, and an only child, her heiress-at-law, who claimed an interest under the articles in the personal estate, and also claimed the real estate attempted to be settled as heiress-at-law of her mother. It was held by Lord Romilly, M. R., that the heiress-at-law was put to her election whether she would take under or against the settlement. "In the present case," said his Lordship, "the plaintiff comes in and claims directly under the limitation of the personal estate for her benefit under the settlement, and claims the real estate adversely to the settlement, on the ground that in the event the settlement did not bind it. I think, therefore, that she claims beneficially under the settlement directly, and that consequently she must elect whether she will take adversely to it or under it; if the latter, she must give effect to the whole of it as far as she can." And see also *Anderson* v. *Abbott*, 23 Beav. 457; *Willoughby* v. *Middleton*, 2 J. & H. 344.

Where, however, a person, as, for instance, an heir-at-law of an infant, claims property as not being bound by a settlement made by the infant, if he has no benefit, and claims none under the settlement, he may assert his right, there being no case of election (*Campbell* v. *Ingilby*, 21 Beav. 567; 1 De G. & Jo. 393); and he is entitled to do this, though it may be from extraneous circumstances, and by some separate and independent cause, he has obtained some benefit under the settlement. Per Lord Romilly, M. R., in *Brown* v. *Brown*, 2 L. R. Eq. 485.

The doctrine of election is not applicable to creditors taking the benefit of a devise for the payment of debts, and also enforcing their legal right against other funds disposed of by the will: *Kidney* v. *Coussmaker*, 12 Ves. 136. See also *Clark* v. *Guise*, 2 Ves. 617. In *Deg* v. *Deg*, 2 P. Wms. 412, 418, where a father devised his own estate and an estate of his son's for the payment of debts, the son was allowed as a creditor of his father to share with the other creditors in the benefit conferred upon them by the provision for payment of debts, without being obliged to give up his own estate. But these questions will not arise often now, as real estates are liable to the payment of debts by simple contract as well as specialty. See 3 & 4 Will. 4, c. 104.

A devise of an estate does not, per se, import an intention to [*369] *devise it free from incumbrances to the devisee, so as to put the incumbrancers taking benefits under the will to their election (*Stephens* v. *Stephens*, 1 De G. & Jo. 62; 3 Drew. 697); the intention to do so must appear conclusively from the words of the will: *Sadlier* v. *Butler*, 1 I. R. Eq. 415, 423.

A person will not be obliged to elect between benefits conferred upon him by an instrument, and an interest which he takes derivatively from another, who has elected to take in opposition to the instrument. Thus it was held, that a husband might be tenant by the courtesy of an estate-tail, which his wife had elected to take in opposition to a will, under which he had accepted benefits: *Lady Cavan* v. *Pulteney*, 2 Ves. jun. 544; 3 Ves. 384.

Nor will a person be compelled to elect between a benefit conferred upon him by an instrument and an interest which he took adversely to the instrument, and derivatively from the real owner who took no benefit thereunder. Thus, in *Grissell* v. *Swinhoe*, 7 L. R. Eq. 291, a testator being entitled under a settlement, subject to a life interest, to a moiety of a fund of 25,300 rupees, by his will, after reciting erroneously that he was under the settlement, " subject to the trusts therein contained," entitled to the said sum of 25,300 rupees, he bequeathed the whole of the said sum of rupees in equal moieties, viz., one moiety to H. Swinhoe, whose wife was really entitled under the settlement to one moiety, and the other moiety to his daughter, Charlotte. Mrs. H. Swinhoe died, and her husband took out letters of administration to her estate and effects. It was held by Sir W. M. James, V. C., that H. Swinhoe was not bound to elect between the legacy and the moiety of the fund which he took as administrator of his wife. " I am of opinion," said his Honour, " that no case of election arises, because the gift is to H. Swinhoe in his own right, and the claim is by him as the representative of Mrs. Swinhoe. True it is that the representative of Mrs. Swinhoe, being her husband, would be entitled to the ultimate surplus, whatever that may be, of that which he took as her personal estate. But that is a mere incident to her estate. The result will be that the fund is divisible in fourths; three-fourths going to Henry Swinhoe, and the remaining fourth to the plaintiff." See the remarks on this case in *Cooper* v. *Cooper*, 6 L. R. Ch. App. 21. Now it is presumed that if in this case, before the death of the testator, H. Swinhoe, had, by his wife's death, and by taking out letters of administration to her, become the real owner of her share in the 25,300 rupees before the death of the testator, he would have been compelled to *elect, and would consequently only have been entitled to a moiety. This it seems is the effect of the recent [*370] decision of *Cooper* v. *Cooper*, 6 L. R. Ch. App. 15; there a lady having a power of appointment during a limited time in favour of any of her issue over (amongst other property) the proceeds of an estate, called Pain's Hill, directed to be sold, made within that time an appointment by deed which included such proceeds, in favour of all her three children, reserving a power of revocation and new appointment. The lady survived the time during which she could exercise the power; and after her death, it appeared, that by her last will and testament in writing " she gave and appointed " Pain's Hill to her eldest son absolutely, and by a subsequent codicil she gave her residuary property to her three sons equally; and afterwards, upon the death of Roland Edward, one of her sons, by another codicil, she gave to his children two-thirds of the share of the residuary estate, intended for him, and the other one-third of that share to her two surviving sons. The gift and appointment by her will of the Pain's Hill estate being held inoperative, the proceeds of Pain's Hill belonged, under the appointment by deed, to the two surviving sons, and the children of the deceased son. Upon a bill, filed by the eldest son, it was held by the Lords Justices, reversing the decision of Sir John Stuart, V. C., that not only the surviving younger son, but also the children of his deceased brother, Roland Edward, were put to their election to take, either under or against the will and codicils, that is, that they were bound, either to allow the whole of the proceeds of Pain's Hill to go according to the will to the eldest brother, or to give up to the extent of compensating him the other benefits provided for them by the will and codicils. " What was pressed upon us," said Lord Justice James, " was this : that the children of Roland Edward were not the owners of one-third of Pain's Hill, within the meaning of the rule ; but what they were entitled to was not Pain's Hill or any part of Pain's Hill in specie, but a share of the ultimate residue, whatever that might be, of the entire personal estate of the intestate, in a due course of administration ; that it vested not in them, but in Roland Edward's estate, and that their share was an incident to that estate. In support of that contention, a decision of mine, when Vice Chancellor, was much pressed upon us : *Grissell* v. *Swinhoe* (7 L. R. Eq. 291 ; but the decision there, whether right or wrong, proceeded on the assumption that the legatee's title to the property did not exist at the death, but was a derivative title, through the title of another person [*371] who was *the true owner at the death ; just as if in this case the children of Roland Edward had been the objects of the testatrix's bounty, and Roland Edward had survived the testatrix, and afterwards the children had succeeded beneficially to his estate, including his share of the proceeds of Pain's Hill." See also *Brodie* v. *Barry*, 2 V. & B. 127.

A person entitled in remainder, to an interest in property is not bound by the election of a person having a prior interest : *Ward* v. *Baugh*, 4 Ves. 623 ; *Long* v. *Long*, 5 Ves. 445. See also *Hutchison* v. *Skelton*, 2 Macq. H. L. Cas. 492, 495. So, likewise, every member of a class, as, for instance, next of kin, has a distinct right to elect, and will not be bound by the election of the majority : *Fytche* v. *Fytche*, 7 L. R. Eq. 494.

Privileges of persons compelled to elect.]—Persons compelled to elect are entitled previously to ascertain the relative value of their own property, and that conferred upon them : *Newman* v. *Newman*, 1 Bro. C. C. 186 ; *Wake* v. *Wake*, 3 Bro. C. C. 255 ; 1 Ves. jun. 335 ; *Chalmers* v. *Storil*, 2 V. & B. 222 ; *Hender* v. *Rose*, 3 P. Wms. 124, n. ; *Whistler* v. *Whistler*, 2 Ves. jun. 367, 371. In *Boynton* v. *Boynton*, 1 Bro. C. C. 445, although Lady Boynton had by her answer elected to take her dower, instead of the benefit given to her by her husband's will, Sir Thomas Sewell, M. R., declared on the hearing, that as no account of the testator's personal estate and of his debts had been taken, she was not obliged to make any election until the account should be taken, and it should appear out of what real estate she was dowable at the time of the testator's decease; and it was referred to the Master to take an account of the personal estate, and also to state out of what estate she was dowable.

As to the apportionment of debts upon different funds, see *Cooper* v. *Cooper*, 6 L. R. Ch. App. 15.

A person compelled to elect may in general file a bill to have all necessary accounts taken (*Butricke* v. *Brodhurst*, 3 Bro. C. C. 88; 1 Ves. jun. 171; *Pusey* v. *Desbouvrie*, 3 P. Wms. 315); but a bill is not always necessary for this purpose, as the Court may, when there is a cause in existence relating to the same matter, direct such inquiries as may be necessary to guide the person put to his election in exercising it: *Douglas* v. *Douglas*, 12 L. R. Eq. 617.   And an election made under a mistaken impression will not be binding, for in all cases of election the Court, while it enforces the rule of equity, that the party shall not avail himself of both his claims, is anxious to secure to him the option of either, and not to hold him concluded by equivocal acts, performed, perhaps, in ignorance of the value of the funds: *Pusey* v. *Desbouvrie*, 3 P. Wms. 315; *Wake* v. *Wake*, 3 Bro. C. C. 255; *Kidney* v. *Coussmaker*, 12 Ves. 136; *Dillon* v. *Parker*, 1 Swanst. 381, [*372] and note.

What will be considered as an election.]—Election is either *express* (about which it is unnecessary to say anything) or *implied*.   And here considerable difficulty often arises in deciding what acts of acceptance or acquiescence amount to an implied election; and this question, it seems, must be determined more upon the circumstance of each particular case, than upon any general principle; *Whitridge* v. *Parkhurst*, 20 Maryland, 62, 72.

On a question of election by a party bound to elect between two properties, it is necessary to inquire into the circumstances of the property against which the election is supposed to have been made; for if a party so situated, not being called on to elect, continues in the receipt of the rents and profits of both properties, such receipt cannot be construed into an election to take the one and reject the other; *Whitridge* v. *Parkhurst;* and in like manner, if one of the properties does not yield rent to be received, and the party liable to elect deals with it as his own,—as, for instance, by mortgaging it (particularly if this be done with the knowledge and concurrence of the party entitled to call for an election),—such dealing will be unavailable to prove an actual election as against the receipt of the rent of the other property: *Padbury* v. *Clark*, 2 Mac. & G. 298; and see *Morgan* v. *Morgan*, 4 Ir. Ch. Rep. 606, 614.   As we have before seen, any acts, to be binding upon a person, must be done with a knowledge of his rights.   They must also be done with the knowledge of the right to elect: *Briscoe* v. *Briscoe*, 7 Ir. Eq. R. 123: 1 Jo. & L. 334: *Sweetman* v. *Sweetman*, 2 I. R. Eq. 141, and with the intention of electing: *Stratford* v. *Powell*, 1 Ball & B. 1; *Dillon* v. *Parker*, 1 Swanst.

380, 387; *Edwards* v. *Morgan*, M'Clell. 541; 13 Price, 782; 1 Bli. N. S. 401; *Worthington* v. *Wiginton*, 20 Beav. 67; *Wintour* v. *Clifton*, 21 Beav. 447, 468; 8 De G. Mac. & G. 641; *Campbell* v. *Ingilby*, 21 Beav. 582.

It is difficult to lay down any rule as to what length of time, after acts done by which election is usually implied, will be binding upon a party, and prevent him from setting up the plea of ignorance of his rights. In *Wake* v. *Wake*, 1 Ves. jun. 335, it was held that three years' receipt of a legacy and annuity, under a will by a widow in ignorance of her rights, did not preclude her from making her election; in *Reynard* v. *Spence*, 4 Beav. 103, where a widow had received an annuity for five years, it was held, she had not elected. See also *Butricke* v. *Brodhurst*, 3 Bro. C. C. 90; *S. C.*, 1 Ves. jun. 172; *Dillon* v. *Parker*, 1 Swanst. 386; and in *Sopwith* v. *Maugham*, 30 Beav. 235, where a widow had *for sixteen years enjoyed a provision under a will in ignorance of her right to dower, in express satisfaction of which the provision was made for her, she was held not to have elected.

[*373]

But a person may by his acts suffer specific enjoyment by others until it becomes inequitable to disturb it; *Tibbits* v. *Tibbits*, 19 Ves. 663; *Dewar* v. *Maitland*, 2 L. R. Eq. 834.

Acts of implied election which will bind a party will also bind his representatives; (*Earl of Northumberland* v. *Earl of Aylesford*, Amb. 540, 657; *Dewar* v. *Maitland*, 2 L. R. Eq. 834. See also 2 Ves. 525; *Stratford* v. *Powell*, 1 Ball & B. 1; *Ardesoife* v. *Bennet*, 2 Dick. 463;) and some acts, which it appears would not be binding upon him if insisted upon in his lifetime, will bind his representatives "upon that principle only," as observed by Lord Hardwicke, "not to disturb things long acquiesced in in families, upon the foot of rights which those, in whose place they stand, never called in question:" *Tomkyns* v. *Ladbroke*, 2 Ves. 593; *Worthington* v. *Wiginton*, 20 Beav. 67; *Sopwith* v. *Maugham*, 30 Beav. 235, 239; *Whitley* v. *Whitley*, 31 Beav. 173.

If election be doubtful it may be sent to a jury to determine that fact: *Roundell* v. *Currer*, 2 Bro. C. C. 73; 1 Swanst. 383, n.

But if the representative of those who were bound to elect, and who have accepted benefits under the instrument imposing the obligation of election, but without explicitly electing, can offer compensation, and place the other party in the same situation as if those benefits had not been accepted, they may renounce them and determine for themselves: *Dillon* v. *Parker*, 1 Swanst. 385; *Moore* v. *Butler*, 2 S. & L. 268; *Tysson* v. *Benyon*, 2 Bro. C. C. 5.

If election be doubtful it may be sent to a jury to determine that fact: *Roundell* v. *Currer*, 2 Bro. C. C. 73; 1 Swanst. 383, n.

The case of *Harris* v. *Watkins*, 2 K. & J. 473, seems to have been decided scarcely in accordance with the principles deducible from the authorities. There a testator devised his residuary, real, and personal estate to his wife "in lieu and discharge of all money which he had borrowed out of and forming part of the trust moneys mentioned in the settlement made on his marriage with her," and he made his wife executrix. She died three days after the testator, and without having possessed herself of any of his real or personal estate. On the testator's death the widow became entitled to the trust moneys under the settlement absolutely. The evidence as to the relative value of the property given to the widow by the will, and the money which she would be entitled to out of her husband's estate in payment of the trust moneys borrowed by him, seems to have been involved in much obscurity. It was held by Sir W. P. Wood, V. C., that the Court could not presume a disclaimer by the widow, *and consequently that her heir was entitled to the devised estate, and the debts claimed by her administrator as due to her from the testator were discharged. His Honor thought it was not so much whether the Court would presume election, as whether it would presume a rejection of the devise. That there was no evidence as to any disclaimer, and that the only question was whether, having regard to the circumstances of the devisee's death, and to the relative values of the estate devised and of the debts to be discharged, the Court was called upon to presume a disclaimer. "Whether," his Honor added, "circumstances might not exist under which the Court would be justified in presuming a disclaimer, is a question of some nicety. I am not aware of any authority upon the point; but I apprehend that in a strong case,—for instance, if a testator devised real estate worth 10,000*l.* only, and declared that it should be taken in lieu and discharge of debts to the amount of 20,000*l.*, in such a case, it being manifest that it would be to the disadvantage of the devisee to retain the estate upon the terms mentioned in the will, the Court, in the event of the devisee dying under circumstances like the present, would, as between his real and personal representatives, struggle hard to presume a disclaimer; but where it is not manifest that it would be for the advantage of the devisee to retain the estate upon the terms proposed by the testator, the ground of that presumption fails, and the presumption does not arise." [*374]

Where an infant is bound to elect, in some instances, as in *Streatfield* v. *Streatfield*, the period of election is deferred until after the infant comes of age. See *Boughton* v. *Boughton*, 2 Ves. 12; *Bor* v. *Bor*, 2 Bro. P. C. 473, Toml. Ed. In other cases there has been a reference to inquire what would be most beneficial to the infant: *Chetwynd* v. *Fleetwood*, 1 Bro. P. C. 300, Toml. Ed.; 2 S. & L. 266; *Goodwyn* v. *Goodwyn*, 1 Ves. 228; *Bigland* v. *Huddleston*, 3 Bro. C. C. 285, n.; *Gretton* v. *Haward*, 1 Sawnst. 413; *Ebrington* v. *Ebrington*, 5 Madd. 117; *Ashburnham* v. *Ashburnham*, 13 Jur. 1111; *Prole* v. *Soady*, 8 W. R. (V. C. S.) 131; *Brown* v. *Brown*, 2 L. R. Eq. 481; and see *Griggs* v. *Gibson*, 1 L. R. Eq. 685; Scton, 495, 3rd ed. In others an order has been made for an infant to elect without a reference to Chambers: *Blunt* v. *Lack*, 26 L. J. Ch. 148; *Lamb* v. *Lamb*, 5 W. R. (V. C. K.) 772: Seton, 260, 261, 3rd ed.

The practice as to election by married women in the Court of Chancery also varies; see Mr. Swanston's note to *Gretton* v. *Haward*, 1 Swanst. 413; but in general there will be an inquiry what is most beneficial for them, and they will be required to elect within a limited time.

[*375] See *Pulteney* v. *Darlington*, 7 Bro. P. C. 546, 547, *Toml. Ed. 2 Ves. jun. 560; 3 Ves. 385; *Vane* v. *Lord Dungannon*, 2 S. & L. 133; *Davis* v. *Page*, 9 Ves. 350. In *Wilson* v. *Lord John Townsend*, 2 Ves. jun. 693, Lord Rosslyn, although he admitted that to be the general practice, dismissed the bill without a reference, as the married woman " had manifestly a much better interest than the testatrix intended." See also *Parsons* v. *Dunne*, 2 Ves. 60, Belt's Suppl. 276.

A married woman may elect so as to affect her interest in real property; and where she has once so elected, though without deed acknowledged, the Court can order a conveyance accordingly; the ground of such order being that no married woman shall avail herself of a fraud. Having elected, she is bound, and the transaction will be enforced against the heir: *Ardesoife* v. *Bennet*, 2 Dick. 463; *Barrow* v. *Barrow*, 4 K. & J. 409; *Willoughby* v. *Middleton*, 2 J. & H. 344; *Sisson* v. *Giles*, 11 W. R. (V. C. S.) 558; *Savill* v. *Savill*, 2 Coll. 721; *Anderson* v. *Abbott*, 23 Beav. 457; *sed vide Campbell* v. *Ingilby*, 21 Beav. 567, which may be considered as contrary to the current of authorities on this point. Lord Cottenham, however, was of opinion in the case of *Frank* v. *Frank*, 3 My. & Cr. 171, that a feme covert was not competent during the coverture to elect between a jointure made to her after her marriage and her dower at common law, because there is an express provision in 27 Hen. 8, c. 10, that her election shall be made at the time when the right is claimed, that is to say, after her husband's death. See also *Anon.*, Dyer, 358, b.

Ordinarily a married woman cannot elect to relinquish a reversionary chose in action: *Robinson* v. *Wheelwright*, 6 De G. Mac. & G. 535, 546; *Whittle* v. *Henning*, 2 Ph. 731; *Williams* v. *Mayne*, 1 I. R. Eq. 549, overruling *Wall* v. *Wall*, 15 Sim. 513. But see now 20 & 21 Vict. c. 57, fully noticed in the note to *Ryall* v. *Rowles*, vol. ii. *post*.

It would seem however that upon principle a married woman, in the case of a reversionary interest in personalty, equally as in the case of real property (at any rate where under the act 20 & 21 Vict. c. 57, she has power to dispose, in manner therein mentioned, of such reversionary interest), would not be allowed to avail herself of a fraud, and might therefore be held to have made her election even when such reversionary interest in personalty was thereby affected. See, however, *Williams* v. *Mayne*, 1 I. R. Eq. 519.

A person who does not elect within the time limited will be considered as having elected to take against the instrument putting him to his election. See the decree in *Streatfield* v. *Streatfield*, 1 Swanst. 447.

Parties disappointed by the election of the heir to take against a *will, by requiring the executors to complete a contract for an estate entered into by the testator, have no lien on the estate [*376] for the amount of the benefits the heir has taken under the will, but after his death they are entitled to prove against his estate for the amount which he has so received: *Greenwood* v. *Penny*, 12 Beav. 402.

It may be here mentioned that under 36 Geo. c. 52, and 45 Geo. 3, c. 28, no legacy duty is payable on the value of personal estate given up by one legatee to another under the doctrine of election ; but where a testator devises his own real estate to one person, and bequeaths such person's personal estate to a third party, legacy duty will be payable on the value of the personal estate so charged on the testator's real estate: *Laurie* v. *Clutten*, 15 Beav. 131.

The principle of election, treated in the preceding note, is recognized and established in this country, almost exactly as in England. It rests upon the equitable ground, that no man can be permitted to claim inconsistent rights with regard to the same subject, and that any one who claims an interest under an instrument, is bound to give full effect to that instrument as far as he can : a person cannot accept and reject the same instrument, or, having availed himself of it as to a part, defeat its provisions in any other part: and this applies to deeds, wills, and all other instruments whatsoever. See *ante*, *Wilbanks* v. *Wilbanks*, 18 Illinois, 19 ; *Waters* v. *Howard*, 1 Maryland, Ch. 112 ; *M'Elfresh, Adm'r*, v. *Schley and Barrs*, 2 Gill, 181; 201, 202 ; *Field* v. *Eaton*, 1 Devereux, Equity, 283, 286, 287 ; *Ex'rs of Cogdell* v. *Widow, &c.*, 3 Dessaussure, 346, 387 ; *Whilldin* v. *Whilldin*, Riley's Chancery, 205, 207 ; *Cauffman* v. *Cauffman*, 17 Sergeant & Rawle, 16, 24, 25 ; *Stump and others* v. *Findlay and others*, 2 Rawle, 168, 174 ; *Preston* v. *Jones*, 9 Barr, 456 ; *George* v. *Bassing*, 15 B. Monroe, 558 ; *Tiernan et al.* v. *Roland and Blackstone*, 3 Harris, 430, 450 ; *Smith* v. *Gould*, 7 W. & S. 238 ; *Palton* v. *Moore*, 1 Casey, 468 ; *Smith* v. *Gould*, 34 Maine, 442 ; *Glen* v. *Fisher*, 6 Johnson's Chancery, 33, 35 ; see 2 Smith's Leading Cases, 141, 7th Am. ed.

[The principle has been applied under a great variety of circumstances. In *Wilbanks* v. *Wilbanks*, 18 Illinois, 17, the testator devised land belonging to another, and in the same will bequeathed a moneyed legacy to the owner of the land, and it was held that the latter must relinquish his own estate to the devisee, or forego the legacy, at least to an extent equivalent to the value of the estate ; *Brown et al. Ex'rs, &c.*, v. *Pitney*, 39 Illinois, 473. The same point was decided in *O'Kelly* v. *Nicholson*,

45 Missouri, 159; and *Pemberton* v. *Pemberton*, 29 Id. 409. In *Reaves* v. *Garrett*, 34 Alabama, 558, a husband devised land and slaves to his wife during life or widowhood. The slaves were her separate property, and it was held that if she had elected to take the land she would not only have forfeited it, but the slaves, on her marriage. In like manner a widow must choose between a benefit conferred upon her by will and her right of dower, if the testator's intention clearly is that she should not have both; *Pemberton* v. *Pemberton*, 29 Missouri, 413, *Brown* v. *Pitney*, 39 Illinois, 475. "If, as decided by this Court in *Wilbanks* v. *Wilbanks*, 18 Illinois, 17, a testator can compel a devisee to give up his own land to another as a condition of his bounty, *a fortiori*, can a testator compel a widow to relinquish her right to land not her own, but the title of which is to come through the testator, as a condition to her enjoyment of a bequest which the law does not require him to make; " *Brown* v. *Pitney*. So where the testator gave the complainant a slave belonging to his children by a former marriage, and at the same time made them his residuary legatees, it was held that the acceptance of the bequest precluded them from asserting their title to the slave, *Pemberton* v. *Pemberton*.]

It has been said, very justly, that "the cases arising under the doctrine of election are susceptible of being divided into two classes; first, those of election proper, where something is given by the will to one who is entitled to some other thing disposed of by the said will to another, in which case the devisee is put to choose whether he will take that which is given, or that to which he has a claim; and secondly, those cases in which there is an express condition annexed to a devise, with which the devisee must comply, or not take the property; in which case he is to elect whether he will comply with the condition or give up the property; but in which, if he does not comply with the condition, he violates none of the provisions of the will as to any other person than himself; " *Hall* v. *Hall*, 2 M'Cord's Chancery, 269, 306. This distinction undoubtedly exists, and, in some parts of this subject, is important. Wherever there is in the will a clear intention that a legatee or devisee shall not take but upon terms of giving up something else, there is a condition, affecting the title of the party to the legacy or devise; but election in equity, depends upon the inconsistency of holding both interests, even though the testator may not have been aware. that his will would give rise to any such inconsistency, and therefore may not have contemplated that the party should be put to an election.

In all cases, the intention to create an election, or the intention to make such dispositions as raise an election,—that is to say, the construction upon which the party is put to an election, must be clear upon the face of the will: a party will never be put to an election upon a doubtful construction; *M'Elfresh, Adm'r,* v. *Schley and Barr,* 2 Gill, 182, 201, 202; *Jones* v. *Jones,* 8 Id. 139; *Havens* v. *Sackett,* 5 New York Reports, 365; *Watson* v. *Howard,* 1 Maryland, Ch. 112; *Penna. L. Ins. Co.* v. *Stokes,* 11 P. F. Smith, 136; and the intention must be derived from the will itself, and not from evidence *dehors; City of Philadelphia* v. *Davis,* 1 Wharton, 490, 502; *Timberlake* v. *Parish's Ex'or,* 5 Dana, 345. [The bar of an election is, in fact, in the nature of an estoppel, and, like every estoppel tending to defeat rights which would otherwise be valid, and consequently operating as a forfeiture, should be certain in every material particular, both as it regards the duty or obligation to elect, and the act by which the election is alleged to have been made; *Jones* v. *Jones; Fitts* v. *Cook,* Cushing, 596; see 2 Smith's Leading Cases, 453, 739, 7th Am. ed. And the inconsistency which puts a party to an election, must arise out of the same instrument; and therefore, if one devises certain land to A. and certain other land to B., and afterwards by deed, conveys to B. the land formerly devised to A., B. is not put to an election, but may hold both the land devised, and that conveyed; *Thompson* v. *Thompson,* 2 Strobhart, 48.

It results from a cognate principle that one who accepts the benefit of a transaction cannot set it aside. If A. sells B.'s land, and B. accepts the purchase-money, he is as much bound as if he had set his hand to the deed; 2 Smith's Lead. Cases, 742, 7 Am. ed. The case is substantially the same where the money comes to B. indirectly through a residuary bequest from the vendor. In *Gable* v. *Daub,* 4 Wright, 217, the testator devised "all the remainder of my real estate that I may die possessed of," to his wife. He subsequently acquired lands which did not pass by his will. These were sold by her after his death for $1,500. The purchaser paid part in cash and gave a bond for the residue. The widow died not long afterwards, having bequeathed her personal estate to the heirs of the testator, and it was held that their election to accept the bequest confirmed the title of the purchaser.

"A general devise of the testator's real estate has always been held to show an intention to give what strictly belongs to him and nothing more, even if the testator had no real estate of his own on which the devise could otherwise operate; Jarman on Wills, 393. It will not, therefore, constitute a case of election, although the testator had no title or pretence of title to any other than the land in question; *Miller* v. *Springer,* 20 P. F. Smith, 269; and evidence, *dehors* the will, is not admissible to show that he considered the estate as his, and intended to bestow it on his devisee."]

It is universally agreed in this country, that the principle upon which equity enforces an election, in a case where there is not a condition, is compensation, not forfeiture. If a benefit is given by a will, and some property or interest of the legatee is given to a third person, if the first legatee elect to retain his property, he does not forfeit all benefits given him by the will, but is only bound to make compensation to the disappointed party according to the value of the interest given; *Key* v. *Griffin*, 1 Richardson's Eq. 67, 68; *Stump and others* v. *Findlay and others*, 2 Rawle, 168, 174; *Cauffman* v. *Cauffman*, 17 Sergeant and Rawle, 16, 24, 25; *City of Philadelphia* v. *Davis*, 1 Wharton, 490, 502. See *Tiernan et al.* v. *Roland & Blackstone*, 3 Harris, 430, 451; *Wilbanks* v. *Wilbanks*, 18 Illinois, 17. [The equity is worked out by sequestering so much of the benefit intended for the refractory devisee, as may be requisite to compensate those who are prejudiced by his election to take against the will; *Mascall* v. *Goodall*, 2 Disney, 202; Sauder's Appeal, 4 P. F. Smith, 314.

Lapse of time, and still more, the introduction of third parties as purchasers, on the faith of the acquiescence in the validity of a will implied in accepting a benefit under its provisions, may, nevertheless, render an election absolute, and preclude the right to avoid it by a tender of compensation; *Fulton* v. *Moore*, 1 Casey, 468, 476.

The ordinary method of procedure is to sequestrate the gift intended for the recalcitrant devisee, until the rents, issues, and profits compensate the beneficiary whom he has disappointed by electing to take against the will. Where, however, the rejected estate is manifestly inferior in value, the delay incident to sequestration would be prejudicial to one party without any corresponding advantage to the other, and equity will decree a conveyance, or a recovery may be had in an equitable ejectment under the mixed jurisprudence of Pennsylvania. In *Lewis* v. *Lewis*, 1 Harris, 79, the testator devised land belonging to himself to the defendant, and other land to which the defendant was entitled as tenant in tail, to the plaintiff. The defendant entered into possession of the latter tract, and it was held that the plaintiff might maintain ejectment for the former, which was not worth nearly so much as the other. Gibson, C. J., said: " Though where the land elected is of inferior value to the land rejected, compensation may be the rule in equity, which compensation our Orphans' Court, under the acts of the 29th March, 1832, and of 16th June, 1836, may enforce by sequestration, or other process; yet where the value of the land rejected is inferior to the land taken, the land rejected is forfeited by the act of election, and may be recovered in ejectment. All the authorities show that equity relieves, in a case of the kind, on the ground of trust. The devise passes the legal title; but a chancellor holds the recusant devisee bound, as a trustee, to compensate the devisee he has disappointed. Being seized of the legal estate, he is, in the words of the statute last quoted, a trustee, possessed of and accountable for the real estate of a decedent; and were this purely a case for compensation, the remedy would, undoubtedly, be by sequestration. But the estate of the refractory devisee, in this instance, is found in the special verdict, to be worth twice as much as the estate he rejected; and it is impossible to conceive that the disappointed devisee could get more than compensation from it. As a general principle, the weight of authority decisively inclines to the side of compensation, and not forfeiture; and the writ of sequestration is used to prevent the disappointed devisee from being in reality a gainer by what was apparently his loss. After compensation is made, pursuant to it, the surplus remains to the devisee; but why employ it, when there cannot, by any possibility, be a surplus? Where the disappointed devisee must be a loser, in any event, it would be useless to keep the property locked up in the hands of a sequestrator, who must be paid for his services. The profits from it would not be equal to the profits of the estate, of which the complainant had been deprived; and the property would remain sequestered forever. I confess that I have found no precedent for such a case; but it appears to me to be one, not of compensation, but of forfeiture. Even Lord Eldon, who maintained the principle of compensation as a general one, admitted in *Tibbets* v. *Tibbets*, 10 Vesey, 666; and *Green* v. *Green*, 1b. 668, that there are cases to which it is inapplicable. There would often be no

other remedy than a decree to convey."

An election between legal rights, or by compulsion of law, as where a widow is bound by statute to choose between her dower at common law in the land, and the right conferred upon her by act of assembly, is, as it would seem, irrevocable, except on the ground of fraud or undue influence; *Buist* v. *Somers*, 1 Richardson's Eq. 281.]

Equitable election usually arises when a testator gives to A. certain property, real or personal, and in the same will gives a third party certain property belonging to A.; in this case, A. must elect between the two; if he accepts the legacy or devise to himself, he must confirm and carry out the gift of his own property to the third party; and if he file a bill for the legacy, equity will compel him to make his election within a certain time, and to execute such conveyances as will give effect to the gift of his property which the testator has made: and this applies equally to the case where a testator disposes of property belonging to his wife in her separate right; *Field* v. *Eaton*, 1 Devereux's Equity, 283, 286; *Wilson* v. *Arny*, 1 Devereux and Battle's Equity, 376; *M'Queen* v. *M'Queen*, 2 Jones's Equity, 16; *Upshaw* v. *Upshaw and others*, 2 Hening & Munford, 381; *Kinnaird, Ex'r, &c.* v. *Williams's Adm'r et. al.*, 8 Leigh, 400; *Brown* v. *Ricketts*, 3 Johnson's Chancery, 553, 556; *Allen* v. *Getz*, 2 Penrose and Watts, 311, 323; *Preston* v. *Jones*, 9 Barr, 457; *Hall* v. *Hall*, 1 Bland, 130, 134; *Craig* v. *Craig and Hart,* 7 Dana, 1, 5; *Ex'rs of Cogdell* v. *The Widow, &c.,* 3 Dessaussure, 346, 388; *M'Ginnis et al.* v. *M'Ginnis,* 1 Kelly, 496. " Ever since the case of *Noys* v. *Mordaunt,*" said Gaston, J., in *Melchor* v. *Burger,* 1 Devereux and Battle's Equity, 634, " it has been holden for an established principle of equity, that where a testator by his will confers a bounty on one person, and makes a disposition in favor of another *prejudicial* to the former, the person thus prejudiced shall not insist upon his old right, and at the same time enjoy the bounty conferred by the will. The intention of the testator is apparent that both dispositions shall take effect, and the conscience of the donee is affected by the condition thus *implied*, that he shall not defraud the design of the donor by accepting the benefit, and disclaiming the burthen—giving effect to the disposition in his favor, and defeating that to his prejudice. The donee is therefore put to his election, either to take the thing given, and confirm the will; or retaining what is his independently of the will, to surrender to the disappointed devisees or legatees, so much of what the testator has given him, as will compensate them for the disappointment." It makes no difference, in regard to election, whether the testator knew that the property he attempted to dispose of, belonged to another, or whether he mistakenly supposed that it was his own; *M'Ginnis et al.* v. *M'Ginnis,* 1 Kelly, 496, 503; *Stump and others* v. *Findlay and others,* 2 Rawle, 168, 174. But

the intention to dispose of property which calls for an election, must be clear and unequivocal, both in respect to the particular property which is the supposed subject of disposal, and in respect to the design and attempt to dispose of it. " To put the legatee to his election," said Ruffin, C. J., in *Wilson* v. *Arny,* 1 Devereux and Battle's Equity, 376, 377, " it is necessary that the instrument should clearly ascertain the property given, and that the gifts themselves should be in such terms, as are inconsistent with the notion that the donee can keep his own estate, and also take, under the will, without defeating the intention of the testator. It is, in other words, in the nature of a condition, and generally speaking, that condition is implied from the nature of the several dispositions; and where the implication is not plain thereform, and almost necessary, such a condition cannot be implied, because no one in a doubtful case, is to be taken as intending to give away what belongs to another." " The intention of the testator, that such devisee should be put to an election," said Bland, C., in *Hall* v. *Hall,* 1 Bland, 130, 135, " must be either distinctly expressed, or very strongly manifested by facts and circumstances; for, no one can be stripped of his ⁻rights by guessing or conjecture. It must distinctly appear, that the claim is irreconcilable and incompatible with the devise; or that to sustain the claim, would throw the testator's estate into a channel entirely different from that in which he had placed it by his will. To prevent such a perversion, or disappointment of the express, or clearly manifested intention of the testator, a court of equity will, by a strong operation of its powers, put the devisee to an election. But there is no instance of a devisee being made to· elect upon slight presumptions or inferences; or where the will might have its full effect without impairing the obligation of the claim; or where the testator has property, which is absolutely his own, answering fully to the description of that spoken of in his will, and by which all its expressions may be satisfied." Accordingly, it was held in that case, that a devise of all the testator's " estate, real and personal," would not be considered as including an estate tail, so as to put the heir in tail to an election, though the testator might have disposed of the estate tail in his lifetime.

[It is accordingly well settled, that to call the doctrine of election into operation, the gift to one party must be irreconcilable with the right or title which the other is asked to relinquish, and that an election need not be made if both can, in any way, stand together; *Havens* v. *Sackett*, 15 New York Reports, 365. Thus, a devise to a wife, for life, of certain leaseholds, and " of all my funded property and estate whatsoever," followed by a bequest of " the sum of £300, 4 per cent.," to a third person, was held not to render it incumbent on the wife to elect between resigning the leaseholds and giving effect to the bequest of the stock, although it appeared that the only stock owned by the testator became the property of his wife by survivorship upon his death; because the bequest did not refer with sufficient clearness to the funded property which the testator then had, and might have had reference to such stock as he might subsequently acquire; *Dammer* v. *Pitcher*, 2 Mylne & Keene, 262; 5 Simons, 35. In like manner, where land was devised to A., and stock which belonged to him, bequeathed by the same will to B., A. was permitted to retain both the land and the stock, on the ground that the testator had a contingent interest in the stock, and might have meant to give the stock, only in case the contingency happened; *Havens* v. *Sackett*.]

As election depends upon the apparent intent of the testator, at the same time that he gives to one legatee a portion of his own property, to give to another certain property, which, in fact, then belongs to the former legatee; it can never arise where the legatee had not at the time of the execution of the will, any interest or right in the latter property; for, though a will, in respect of its legal operation, takes effect only at the death of the testator, yet, in arriving at intention, regard must be had to the state of things existing at the time the will is made, and not to subsequent circumstances, unless they are expressly referred to and provided for; accordingly, where a testator bequeathed a legacy to his daughter, and a certain slave to another person, and afterwards, during his life, gave the slave to his daughter, it was held that the daughter was not obliged to elect between accepting the legacy and retaining the slave, but was entitled to both; it was a mere ademption of the legacy of the slave in his will; *Long* v. *Weir*, 2 Richardson's Equity, 283; see also *Hall* v. *Hall*, 2 M'Cord's Chancery, 269, 300.

The principle of election, by implication, in equity, depends upon the circumstance that the same instrument which transfers or conveys certain property of the testator's to one legatee or devisee, transfers or conveys certain other property to another legatee or devisee, and that the former beneficiary, availing himself of the instrument in one particular, must not defeat its operation in another. But if the latter devise or bequest be invalid—if the instrument in respect to it be legally inoperative and void—the former beneficiary's retaining his own property does not defeat the operation of the instrument. If it be a will, it does not defeat the intention of the testator legally declared. Retaining the subject of a transfer does not disappoint the instrument, if the law has already avoided and nullified the transfer. This occurs in the case of a devise of lands by a feme covert, or an infant, or under a will not executed so as to pass lands; *Kearney* v. *Macomb*, 1 C. E. Greene, 189; *Tongue* v. *Nutwell*, 17 Maryland, 212, 229; *Jones* v. *Jones*, 8 Gill, 197. The rule as above given, was cited and approved in *Tongue* v. *Nutwell*, 17

Maryland, 212, 219; and it was said to follow that where a testator after giving a legacy to A., proceeded to bequeath land to him with a limitation over to B. which was too remote, A. might accept the legacy without losing the right to contest the validity of the gift to B. In like manner, accepting a benefit in one state under a will will not preclude the devisee from disputing its operation in another, where it does not accord with the forms prescribed by law; *Jones* v. *Jones*, 8 Gill, 197. Thus in *Jones* v. *Jones*, the respondent was permitted to take an estate in Pennsylvania under the will, and retain his own estate in Maryland against it; the instrument being so executed as to pass land in the former state, but not in the latter.

In cases of this description, the intention that the devisee shall not have both estates, is not so expressed as to be a subject of legal cognizance. There is consequently no obligation to elect. Such an obligation may, notwithstanding, result from a declared purpose qualifying the gift which takes effect.

And this brings up the distinction mentioned at the beginning of this note, between an election based upon a condition, and an election enforced by a court of equity upon mere implication; a distinction, plain enough, abstractly, but of infinite difficulty in the application. It may, perhaps, be said, in general, that if it be expressly declared in the will, or if the dispositions in the will are such that it is plainly apparent, that the testator did not intend one devise or bequest to take effect unless in the case of another's taking effect—if the several devises or bequests are so connected together and dependent upon one another, that one cannot take effect according to the testator's intention without the other—then, it is a condition, and the legatee or devisee accepting a benefit under such an arrangement must give effect to other devises forming an inseparable part of such an arrangement, even though these other dispositions are not valid and legal as devises. A case of mere equitable election arises where only the *instrument*, or the operation of it, would be disappointed in part; if the purpose, object, and actual intention of the testator in regard to making a particular devise or legacy would be violated and defeated, without the devisee's or legatee's carrying out such object and intention, it is a condition. This subject was discussed in *Melchor* v. *Burger*, 1 Deverenx and Battle's Equity, 634. The distinction is there stated between a devise or bequest to the heir, on condition of giving up the land to which he would be otherwise entitled, and a case of election proper, arising from equitable implication. If a condition of giving up the lands to another be annexed to a legacy to the heir-at-law, though in a will not executed so as to pass lands, the heir cannot claim the legacy without complying with the condition; but if the two things be not thus connected by a condition, but there be

merely a bequest to the heir, and a devise of real estate to some other person, by one not having legal capacity to make such a disposition, or in a will not sufficiently executed for the purpose, though the instrument be operative in regard to personalty, there is no obligation on the heir to elect between his right as heir, and the personal benefit bequeathed by the will; the attempted devise being nought, affords, it is said, no legal evidence of an intention to devise away. "If no more appears," says Gaston, J., in that case, "than a devise from the heir, and a bequest of personalty to him, in a will sufficiently executed to pass personal, but not sufficiently executed to pass real estate, it is a good-will of the personalty; it is no will as to the lands; there is no implied condition of election; and the heir may keep the lands descended, and also take his legacy. In *Snelgrove et al* v. *Snelgrove et al.*, 4 Dessaussure, 274, 300, the same principle was decided. The law was held the same way in *Kearney* v. *Malcomb*, 1 C. E. Greene, 189; and *Jones* v. *Jones*, 8 Gill, 197.

[In *Jones* v. *Jones*, a bill was filed in Maryland to enforce a devise which was invalid in consequence of not having been executed in the presence of three witnesses as the laws of that State require. It is not surprising that the court refused to go so far. The question whether the devise in Pennsylvania was subject to an implied condition that the devisee should comply with the provisions of the will,

was not directly under consideration. It is one thing to sustain an
invalid gift, and another to mould
a valid gift in accordance with the
wishes of the testator, as deduced
from the whole instrument. Although a chancellor cannot arbitrarily dispose of property on
which the will does not operate,
he may affect that on which it
does with a trust for the person who is prejudiced by the
election of the devisee to take
against the will. Such a case does
not really present a conflict of
laws. It is rather one where an
intention which is not so expressed as to be effectual under
the laws of one State, may, notwithstanding, operate under those
of another. In *Vandyke's Appeal*, 10 P. F. Smith, 481, 489, the
testator gave legacies to his daughters, which absorbed the bulk of
his estate in Pennsylvania, and by
the same will, gave his real estate
in New Jersey to his sons. The
will was not so executed as to pass
real estate in New Jersey. A bill
was filed in Pennsylvania to compel the legatees to execute conveyances in conformity with the
wishes of the testator, or else that
so much should be withheld from
the amount bequeathed to them,
and appropriated to the devisees, as
would compensate the latter for the
loss of the land. Sharswood, J.,
said: " This is not a proceeding to
recover a legacy charged on land,
nor to compel a settlement or distribution, but falls within the admitted scope of the authority of a
court of equity in cases of trust.
The legal title being in the defend-

ants, as heirs-at-law, that court,
if it is a case of election, holds
them bound as trustees to compensate the devisees disappointed
of the bounty intended for them
by the testator. It may certainly
be considered as settled in England, that if a will, purporting to
devise real estate, but ineffectually,
because not attested according to
the statute of frauds, gives a
legacy to the heir-at-law, he cannot be put to his election ; *Hearle*
v. *Greenbank*, 3 Atk. 695 ; *Thellusson* v. *Woodford*, 13 Ves. 209 ;
Breckinbridge v. *Ingram*, 2 Ves.
Jr. 652 ; *Sheddon* v. *Goodrich*, 8
Id. 482."

" These cases have been recognized and followed in this country : *Melchor* v. *Burger*, 1 Dev. &
Batt. 634 ; *M'Elfresh* v. *Schley*,
1 Gill. 181 ; *Jones* v. *Jones*, 8 Gill,
197 ; *Kearney* v. *Macomb*, 1 C. E.
Greene, 189. Yet, it is equally
well established, that if the testator annexes an express condition
to the bequest of the personalty,
the duty of election will be enforced ; *Boughton* v. *Boughton*, 2
Ves. Sen. 12 ; *Whistle* v. *Webster*,
2 Ves. Jr. 367 ; *Rex* v. *Wauchop*,
1 Bligh, 1 ; *M'Elfresh* v. *Schley*,
1 Gill, 181. That this distinction
rests upon no sufficient reason,
has been admitted by almost every
judge before whom the question
has arisen. Why an express condition should prevail, and one,
however clearly implied, should
not, has never been, and cannot
be satisfactorily explained. It is
said, that a disposition absolutely
void is no disposition at all, and
being incapable of effect as such

it cannot be read to ascertain the intent of the testator. But an express condition annexed to the bequest of the personalty does not render the disposition of the realty valid; it would be a repeal of the statute of frauds so to hold."

"How, then, can it operate any more than an implied condition to open the eyes of the court, so as to enable them to read those parts of the will which relate to the realty, and without a knowledge of what they are, how can the condition be enforced?"

"As to the question of election," said Lord Kenyon, while Master of the Rolls, "the cases which have been cited are certainly great authorities, but I must confess I should have great difficulty in making the same distinctions, if they had come before me. They have said you shall not look into a will unattested, so as to raise the condition which would be implied from the devise, if it had appeared; but if you give a legacy on condition that the legatee shall give the lands, then he must elect. However, I am bound by the force of authorities to take no notice whatever of the unattested will, as far as relates to the freehold estate: *Carey* v. *Askew*, 1 Cox, 241."

"I do not understand," said Sir William Grant, "why a will, though not executed so as to pass real estate, should not be read for the purpose of discovering in it an implied condition, concerning real estate annexed to a gift of personal property, as it is admitted it must be read, when such condition is expressly annexed to such gift. For if by a sound construction such condition is rightly inferred from the whole instrument, the effect seems to be the same as if it was expressed in words:" *Brodie* v. *Barry*, 2 Ves. & Beams, 127. So Lord Eldon declared, that "the distinctions upon this head of the law appear to be rather unsubstantial," and that "there are, undoubtedly, these distinctions, and a judge, having to deal with them, finds a difficulty in stating to his own mind satisfactory principles on which they may be grounded:" *Rex* v. *Wauchop*, 1 Bligh. 1. And in another place: "The reason of that distinction, if it was *res integra*, is questionable." "With Lord Kenyon, I think the distinction such as the mind cannot well fasten upon:" *Sheddon* v. *Goodrich*, 8 Ves. Jr. 482.

"Mr. Justice Kennedy has expressed the same opinion: "When a condition is necessarily implied by a construction in regard to which there can be but one opinion, there can be no good reason why the result or decision of the court should not be the same as in the case of an express condition, and the donee bound to make an election in one case as well as the other:" *City of Philadelphia* v. *Davis*, 1 Whart. 510. There is another class of cases in England wholly irreconcilable with this shadowy distinction; for the heir at law of a copyhold was formerly put to his election, though there had been no surrender to the use of the will. This was previous to 55 Geo. III., c. 192, 1 White & Tudor's Leading Cases, 239, note;

yet as Sir William Grant has remarked, "a will, however executed, was as inoperative for the conveyance of freehold estates :" *Brodie* v. *Barry*, 2 Ves. & Beames, 130.

"The precise point can never arise in this State, for happily our Statute of Wills of April 8th, 1833, Pamph. L. 249, wisely provides that the forms and solemnities of execution and proof shall be the same in all wills, whether realty or personalty."

"The case before us is of a will duly executed according to the laws of Pennsylvania, devising lands in New Jersey, where, however, it is invalid as to the realty by not having two subscribing witnesses."

"A court of New Jersey might hold themselves on these authorities, bound to shut their eyes on the devise of the realty, and consider it as though it were not written, and so they have held; *Kearney* v. *Macomb*, 1 C. E. Greene, 189. They might feel themselves compelled to say, with Lord Alvanley, however absurdly it sounds: "I canot read the will without the word ' real' in it, but I can say, for the statute enables me, and I am bound to say, that if a man by a will unattested, gives both real and personal estate, he never meant to give the real estate ;" *Buckeridge* v. *Ingram*, 2 Ves. Jr. 652. But a statute of New Jersey has no such moral power over the conscience of a court of Pennsylvania, to prevent it from reading the whole will upon the construction of a

bequest of personalty within its rightful jurisdiction. If a question could arise directly upon the title of the heirs-at-law to the New Jersey land, doubtless the court of any other State upon the well settled principle of the comity of nations, must decide it according to the *lex rei sitæ*."

"We are dealing only with the bequests of personalty, and the simple question is, whether the testator intended to annex to them a condition. If, without making any disposition whatever of the New Jersey estates, dying intestate as to them, he had annexed an express proviso to the legacies to his daughters, that they should release to their brothers all their right and title as heirs-at-law to these lands, it is of course indubitable that such a condition would have been effectual. We are precluded by no statute, to which we owe obedience, from reading the whole will; and, if we see plainly that such was the intention of the testator, from carrying it into effect. Some cases have arisen in England upon wills disposing of English and Scotch estates, in which the judgments have not been harmonious; nor can any general principle be extracted from them bearing upon this question. In *Brodie* v. *Barry*, 2 Ves. & Beames, 127, an heir-at-law of heritable property in Scotland, being also a legatee under a will not conforming to the law in Scotland as to heritable property, was put to his election. By that law, a previous conveyance by deed was necessary, according to the proper

NOYS V. MORDAUNT.—STREATFIELD V. STREATFIELD. 553

feudal forms, upon which the uses declared by the will might operate. As by the law of Scotland, the heir-at-law in such a case was put to his approbate or reprobate (the Scotch law term for election), and it was very similar to a will of copyhold; Sir William Grant considering the law of both countries to be the same, felt himself relieved from the necessity of determining by which law the decision should be made. *Dundas* v. *Dundas*, 2 Dow & Clark, 349, was a case in the House of Lords from Scotland."

"The will was formal according to the Scotch laws, but was invalid as to real estate in England under the Statute of Frauds. Yet the decision of the Court of Sessions, putting the English heir-at-law to his approbate or reprobate, was affirmed. This case is certainly in point, in favor of the position taken in this opinion. It is true, that in the judgment pronounced by Lord Chancellor Brougham, then but recently raised to the wool sack, it is not put on that ground. He assumes, that in England while a court of law would be precluded by the statute from looking at the disposition made of the realty, it was competent for a court of equity to do so, and that the Court of Sessions in Scotland had only done what a chancellor in England had a right to do; a distinction, it must be allowed, not adverted to in any of the previous cases, which were all in courts of equity."

"In *M'Call* v. *M'Call*, Drury, 283, Lord Chancellor Sugden, held,

that an heir-at-law of heritable property in Scotland, who was also the devisee of real estate in Ireland, under a will duly executed as to the Irish, but ineffectual as to the Scotch estate, was bound to make his election. In the later case of *Maxwell* v. *Maxwell*, 13 Eng. L. & Eq. 443, which arose in England, the heir-at-law in Scotland was not put to his election, but distinctly on the ground that the will, in the alleged disposition of the Scotch estate, had used only general words." If the will had mentioned Scotland in terms," said Sir Knight Bruce, Lord Justice, " or the testator had not any real estate except real estate in Scotland, that might have been a ground for putting the heir to his election. The matter, however, standing as it does, we are bound to hold that the will does not exhibit an intention to give or affect any property which it is not adapted to pass," and Lord Cranworth concurred in this view. In this state of the authorities, we are clear in holding that we are not precluded by force of the New Jersey Statute of Frauds, from reading the whole will of the testator, in order to ascertain his intention in reference to the bequest of personalty now in question. We are equally clear that it is a case of election. The intention of the testator does not rest merely upon the implication arising from his careful division of his property, among his children, in different classes, but he has indicated it in words by the clause: "I direct and enjoin on my heirs, that no exception be taken to this will, or any part thereof, on any legal or technical account." It is true, that for want of a bequest over, this provision would be regarded as *in terrorem* only, and would not induce a forfeiture; *Chew's Appeal*, 9 Wright, 228. But, as has been often said, the equitable doctrine of election is grounded upon the ascertained intention of the testator, and we can resort to every part of the will to arrive at it. "The intention of the donor or testator ought doubtless to be the polar star in such cases," says Mr. Justice Kennedy, "and wherever it appears from the instrument itself conferring the benefit, with a certainty that will admit of no doubt, either by express declaration, or by words that are susceptible of no other meaning, that it was the intention of the donor or testator that the object of his bounty should not participate in it, without giving his assent to everything contained in the instrument, the donees ought not to be permitted to claim the gift, unless they will abide by the intention and wishes of its author; *City of Philadelphia* v. *Davis*, 1 Whart. 510."

"This, however, is not the only mode in which the equity of the case can be reached."

"The doctrine of equitable election rests upon the principle of compensation, and not of forfeiture, which applies only to the non-performance of an express condition; 2 Madd. Ch. 49. Besides, no decree of this court could authorize the guardians of the minors to execute releases of their right and title to the New Jersey lands, which would be effectual in that State. The alternative relief prayed for in the bill is that which is most appropriate to the case."

It was accordingly decreed that the executors should deduct such an amount from the legacies as would suffice to compensate the complainants, for the value of the shares of the legatees, in the real estate in New Jersey which would have vested in the complainants under the will if it had been duly executed.

That the legacy, may be so inseparably connected with the devise, and dependent upon it, as to be in effect conditional, is also shown by *Nutt* v. *Nutt et al.*, 1 Freeman's Chancery, 128. There a devise of the testator's whole real and personal estate was made to one who was not the heir-at-law, by a will executed so as to pass personalty, but not so as to pass real estate, and legacies were charged on it payable to the heirs-at-law and others. It was held, that as the devise was of the fund, out of which, in part, the legacies were to be paid, the legacy was clearly upon an implied condition that the devise should take effect, and equity would give effect to it, and put the heir to an election.

How far the doctrine, that a void devise does not put a party to an election applies to a devise of after-acquired lands, which independently of special legislation, is an inoperative disposition, has been discussed in some of the

American cases. In *Hall* v. *Hall*, 2 M'Cord's Chancery, 269, 299, 306, a testator, having made a provision for his wife in his will, expressly declared that it " should be taken in lieu and bar of all claim of dower, inheritance, or any other claim on her part," and the question arose whether she was bound to elect in reference to her title as distributee of the after-acquired lands. The case, however, was decided against the necessity of election, on the ground that it did not sufficiently appear, that the testator had reference to after-acquired lands, when he inserted that clause; the presumption, in fact, being that he referred only to the estate which he then had. The *City of Philadelphia* v. *Davis*, 1 Wharton, 490, 503, went upon the same ground, that it did not clearly appear that the testator was intending to dispose of after-acquired lands : but Kennedy, J., declared his own opinion, and that of a majority of the court, to be, that if the testator had intended to dispose of after-acquired lands, a legacy to the heir-at-law would not have made a case for election. He said, that where there is a devise or bequest on a condition, express, or implied from a construction that admits of no doubt or uncertainty, the devisee or legatee cannot take the benefit except upon the condition : but where the election arises only impliedly, from a legacy being given to one, and lands which would descend on him being disposed of to another, a devise that is inoperative and invalid, as of after-acquired lands,

will not create an election. This doctrine, however, is entirely contradicted by *M'Elfresh, Adm'r*, v. *Schley and Barr*, 2 Gill, 182. There, a testator devised and bequeathed to one of his sisters, A., all his real and personal estate, " of which he was then possessed, or of which he might be possessed at the time of his death ;" and to another sister, B., he gave certain real and personal estate. The question was, whether B. could claim this devise and bequest, and also her share as heir-at-law, in a certain farm purchased by the testator after the execution of his will. The Court of Appeals held, that though the principle of election did not apply in the case of void wills, such as a will of lands of a feme covert or an infant, or one not executed so as to pass lands, those not being wills, and not capable of being read in evidence, and therefore not adequate to demonstrate intention ; yet, that it did apply wherever the will was properly in evidence, and the intention clearly indicated, though the devise was ineffective, as in case of a disposition of after-acquired lands. They said, that there might be an implied condition in a devise or bequest to an heir-at-law, if the intent was plain and clear, as well as an express condition : and accordingly they held that B. was put to her election in respect to her claim upon the after-acquired lands. This last decision appears to put the subject upon its true footing. An election will not be enforced unless the intent to dispose of after-acquired lands be clear and undeniable: but if such an intent clearly appear, the matter stands exactly upon the same ground with every other disposition of property which the testator does not own. The opinion of Mr. Justice Kennedy in *City of Philadelphia* v. *Davis*, 1 Wharton, 490, 509, that a devise of after-acquired lands is " void, invalid, and in effect no will with respect to those lands," seems to be an entire misconception. The *devise* of after-acquired lands is not *void ;* it is, legally, a valid devise; the only difficulty is, that the testator has no power over the *subject* of the devise. It is simply a devise of property which the testator does not own and over which he he has no control. It is then exactly on the footing of every other attempt to dispose of property belonging to others. All such devises are inoperative , and yet they raise a case of election. The case where the instrument, or some particular part of it, is insufficient and legally void as â declaration of intention, and as a transfer of such rights as the testator may have, is totally different from the case where the instrument is in all respects unexceptionable in law, but a part of it finds no subject upon which it can operate effectively.

The remarks of Sir W. Grant, M. R., in *Kidney* v. *Coussmaker*, 12 Vesey, 136, 154, referred to in the preceding note, that the doctrine of election is inapplicable to creditors, if it is to be regarded as the announcement of a general principle, is opposed by decisions in this country, and seems not to be well founded. It has been decided in Pennsylvania, that creditors taking a benefit under an instrument making provision for them, cannot object to any of the conditions or terms of the instrument, nor to any provisions which it makes to other persons. In one case, a debtor mortgaged property to three distinct creditors, two of whom (including the plaintiff) had advanced, at the date of the mortgage, the amounts secured thereby, but the third had not then done so, but afterwards made up the deficiency by further advances. The plaintiff, after having joined in suing out the mortgage, claimed to appropriate the proceeds to the exclusion of the third creditor, who had been secured in the mortgage for advances not then made, on the ground that the plaintiff, by seeing the land apparently protected by this mortgage, might have been prevented from proceeding against it by other methods. " It must, perhaps, be conceded," said Gibson, C. J., in delivering the opinion of the Court, " that a mortgage to secure future advances, which does not contain notice of the agreement, is void against creditors generally, because the land is apparently covered for more than it actually owes, and pursuit might thus be eluded, when a knowledge of a true state of the facts would invigorate exertion, and render success certain. Had the plaintiff claimed as a general creditor, the mortgage might not have entitled the others to a preference. But, so far is he from having treated it as fraudulent, that *he has elected to claim under it.* Now, there is no rule of equity more universal in its application, nor more just in its consequences, than that a party shall not claim in repugnant rights, and that he who takes the benefit shall also bear the burden. The books are full of cases which show, that a party shall not contest the validity of an instrument from which he draws a benefit, or affirm it in part and disaffirm it in part. Here the plaintiff might have repudiated the whole transaction, and stood on his former rights: but, claiming to participate in the benefit, he can be admitted only on the terms prescribed by the mortgagor. It cannot be believed that the mortgagor would have preferred the plaintiff at the expense of the general creditors, on any other terms than having his assent to the mortgage as a security for those future advances; to withhold it now, would be a fraud on him." *Irwin* v. *Tabb*, 17 Sergeant & Rawle, 419, 423. The same principle was enforced in *Adlum* v. *Yard*, 1 Rawle, 163, 171. In that case, the plaintiff, having taken a dividend under a voluntary general assignment of his debtor, sought to attach a certain interest as being the debtor's and not vested in the assignees, on the ground that the assignment was fraudulent for restraining the assignee from selling for three years. That restriction, said Gibson, C. J., undoubtedly brought the deed within the purview of the st. 13 Eliz.; and "the plaintiff might originally

have repudiated this assignment, but having taken a dividend under it, he shall not now question its validity. Where money is actually received, and on an implied condition that the receiver shall not question the title, every principle of natural justice requires that the condition should be performed. But it is supposed that the doctrine of election is inapplicable to creditors. There is no adjudication in support of this, but *Kidney* v. *Coussmaker*, from which, in the broad terms in which the principle is predicated, I entirely dissent. That was the case of a devise of part of the estate to trustees for payment of debts; and it was held that the creditors having obtained from the trust fund, satisfaction only in part, were not precluded from recourse to other parts of the estate which passed by the same will. To this I entirely assent, because the creditors could not be viewed as legatees, and the setting apart of a portion of the estate for the sake of convenience, indicated no intention that the creditors should not be paid in the event of its falling short. The law, therefore, would not imply a condition that the creditors should relinquish their right on the rest of the estate. But the unqualified assertion of the Master of the Rolls, that the doctrine of election is utterly inapplicable to creditors, seems to be received with many grains of allowance, even in England. (1 Hovenden's notes to Vesey, 172.) In *Irwin* v. *Tabb*, we applied it to creditors claiming different debts, under the same mortgage. In the case at bar, the debtor might prescribe the terms; and the plaintiff, having received his dividend on an inherent condition to permit the whole arrangement to take effect, it seems clear, that, subsequent to the period of acceptance, the debt attached as due to the assignor, was, to every intent, vested in his assignees." See 2 Smith's Lead. Cases, 141, 7th Am. ed.

The application of the doctrine of election to the case where a devise or bequest is made to the widow of the testator, and the estate of which she would be dowable, is disposed of to others, has been much discussed; and though the general principle belonging to the subject is settled and unquestioned, the bearing of it in particular instances has led to some conflict in the decisions. The general rule is agreed to be, that as dower is a legal interest vested in the wife by the act of the law, paramount to the will of the husband and beyond his control, of which matters he is presumed to be cognizant, and as every devise or bequest imports a bounty, and does not naturally imply satisfaction of a pre-existing encumbrance, a gift to the wife in the will, is to be taken as a cumulative provision, unless the intent that it shall be in lieu and exclusion of dower, be demonstrated by express declaration, or by clear and manifest implication arising from the instrument's containing some provision incompatible with the right of dower; *Higginbotham* v. *Cornwell*, 8 Grattan, 83; *Lasher* v. *Lasher*,

13 Barbour, 106; *Tobias* v. *Ketchum*, 32 New York, 319; *Tooke* v. *Hardeman*, 7 Georgia, 20. To establish such implied intention, the claim of dower must be inconsistent with the will and repugnant to its dispositions, or some of them. It must, in fact, disturb or disappoint the will. It is not enough that the matter is doubtful, or that the testator did not contemplate that his wife should take both estates: she will not be put to an election, unless it be clear that he distinctly contemplated and designed that she should not enjoy both provisions, or unless he has made such a disposition of his estate, that the assertion of dower would do violence to his will. This is, in substance, the principle established after a careful review of the cases, by Chancellor Kent, in *Adsit* v. *Adsit*, 2 Johnson's Chancery, 448; and however variously it may have been enforced, it is accepted in the subsequent cases, as the true and sound rule upon the subject. See *Smith* v. *Kinskern*, 4 Id. 9; *Wood* v. *Wood*, 5 Paige, 597, 601; *Fuller* v. *Yates*, 8 Id. 325; *Sanford* v. *Jackson*, 10 Id. 266; *Havens* v. *Havens and others*, 1 Sandford, 325, 330; *Bull* v. *Church*, 5 Hill, 206; S. C., 2 Denio, 430; *Sheldon* v. *Bliss*, 4 Selden, 31; *Lewis* v. *Smith*, 5 Id. 503; *Van Arsdale* v. *Van Arsdale*, 2 Dutcher, 404, 417; *Gordon, Adm'r*, v. *Stevens*, 2 Hill's Chancery, 46; *Whilden* v. *Whilden*, Riley's Chancery, 205; *Brown* v. *Caldwell*, 1 Spears' Equity, 322; *Timberlake* v. *Parish's Ex'or*, 5 Dana, 345; *Stark et al.* v. *Hunton*

et al., Saxton's Chancery, 217, 224, 225; *Kinsey et al.* v. *Woodward*, 3 Harrington, 459, 464. See also, *Ambler and Wife* v. *Norton*, 4 Hening & Munford, 23, 44; *Snelgrove et al.* v. *Snelgrove et al.*, 4 Dessaussure, 274, 294; *Webb* v. *Evans*, 1 Binney, 565, 572; *Kennedy* v. *Nedrow*, 1 Dallas, 415, 418; *Hamilton* v. *Buckwalter*, 2 Yeates, 389, 392, 395; *M' Cullough and Wife*, 3 Id. 10, 12; *Clark* v. *Griffith*, 4 Clarke, Iowa, 405. Accordingly, in Missouri and Illinois, a bequest of personalty will not preclude the right to dower, unless there is something more than the bare existence of the gift to indicate that such was the design; *Pemberton* v. *Pemberton*, 29 Missouri, 408; *Brown* v. *Pitney*, 39 Illinois, 468. And the same rule applies where the testator aliens part of his land during marriage, and gives all his estate, real and personal, to his widow, by devise, at his death; *Braxton* v. *Freeman*, 6 Richardson's Eq. 35. "The right of dower," said Johnson, Ch., in *Brown* v. *Caldwell*, 1 Spears' Eq. 322, 325, " is amongst the most favored by the law. It is put on the footing of life and liberty, and in looking through the cases, one is led almost to conclude, that common sense and sound reasoning have been violated in giving it effect. But there is less apparent impropriety in it, when it is recollected with what facility the husband may put his intention beyond all dispute, by declaring that the provision made for the wife was intended to bar her right of dower." This presumption in favor of the testamentary provision being additional to the legal estate of dower, has been carried to the greatest extent in the New York cases. It should be remarked that previously to the case of *Adsit* v. *Adsit*, the rule as to exclusion of dower had been laid down by Marshall, C. J., in *Herbert and others* v. *Wren and others*, 7 Cranch, 370, 378, in a much more moderate form, and made to depend rather upon a fair construction of the whole will, than upon any decided leaning in favor of the two provisions being concurrent; and a similar view was taken in the recent case of *Lord* v. *Lord*, 23 Conn. 327.

" It is," said Chief Justice Marshall, in *Herbert and others* v. *Wren and others*, 7 Cranch, 378, " a maxim of a court of equity, not to permit the same person to hold under and against a will. If, therefore, it be manifest from the face of the will, that the testator did not intend the provision it contains for his widow to be in addition to dower, but to be in lieu of it; if his intention, discovered in other parts of the will, must be defeated by the allotment of dower to the widow, she must renounce either her dower, or the benefit she claims under the will. But if the two provisions may stand well together; if it may fairly be presumed that the testator intended the devise or bequest to his wife as additional to her dower, then she may hold both." See *Pemberton* v. *Pemberton*, 29 Missouri, 413.

Under the general principle

above stated, as to the necessity of election by the wife, between the testamentary provision and dower, some of the applications which have occurred may be stated.

It appears to be agreed, in all the cases, that if a legacy or annuity be given to the wife, and the lands be devised to trustees to be sold, or directed to be sold by executors, for any purpose whatever, the lands continue subject to dower, both in the hands of the trustees, executors or heirs, and in those of a purchaser ; *Hall* v. *Hall,* 8 Richardson, 407 ; and this, whether the legacy be charged upon the fund arising from the sale of the lands, or be given from some wholly distinct property. This may be considered as established by *Adsit* v. *Adsit.* There, a testator directed his personal estate and his farm to be sold ; and gave his wife a pecuniary legacy to be left in the hands of his executors, to be paid to her, for her support, at any time, or at all times, as her need might require ; and gave her also, what household goods she might need, and gave certain legacies to his grand-children, and directed the residue also to be divided among his children and grand-children ; and it was decided, that the lands sold were subject to dower in the purchaser's hands; *Adsit* v. *Adsit,* 2 Johnson's Chancery, 448. The same point was again decided in *Wood* v. *Wood.* In that case, a testator had devised all his estate, real and personal, to a trustee to be sold, and directed, that after certain ex-

penses were paid, the interest on one-third of the whole fund should be paid to the widow during her widowhood ; and in case of her marriage, one-third of that third. The Chancellor said, " Although the testator directs all his estate to be sold, and one-third of the proceeds to be invested for the use of his wife during her widowhood, it does not appear, by any necessary implication from the will itself, that he intended this provision to be in lieu of dower in the real estate of which he died seised. The widow is not therefore obliged to elect between that provision and her dower. I am satisfied, from the examination of the American, as well as the English cases, that a devise of all the testator's real and personal estate to trustees, to be converted into money, without any particular designation of the real property to be sold, and giving to the widow an annuity or other provision out of such mixed fund, is not, of itself, sufficient to show that the testator intended her interest in the land, as tenant in dower, should be sold as part of the estate ; so as to make it necessary for the widow to elect between such dower and the provision contained in the will. The widow in the present case is therefore entitled to both." *Wood* v. *Wood,* 5 Paige, 597, 601. These were cases in which the legacy was chargeable upon the lands sold, or was payable out of the proceeds of them. Several cases have decided the same point, where real estate was directed to be sold, and a legacy, or even a devise, unconnected with the estate to be sold, was given to the wife. In *Timberlake* v. *Parish's Ex'or*, 5 Dana, 345, a legacy to the wife, and an order to sell all the residue of the estate, real and personal, and distribute it equally among the testator's children, were held not to be a bar to dower in the lands; and the court declared that a provision by will for the wife is not presumed to be in lieu of dower, " unless the intention that it should so operate be expressed, or can be *plainly* inferred, or unless any other interpretation would be inconsistent with the will;" and that " a mere devise of the whole of the testator's remaining estate to others, or to be sold for their benefit, and even for that of the wife also, is not so inconsistent with her legal right to dower," as to make it a provision in lieu of it. In *Whilden* v. *Whilden*, Riley's Chancery, 205, a testator bequeathed one thousand dollars to his wife, and then directed the whole of his real and personal estate to be sold, and the fund invested for the support of his children during minority, and then divided among them. The legacy was held not to be a bar of dower. " The dower," said Chancellor Dessaussure, " is a provision made by law, for the support of the widow. A legacy is a provision made by affection, for the better support of the wife. There is scarcely any man owning real estate, who does not know, in fact, that his wife is entitled to dower in that estate; and the law implies the knowledge. The presumption, therefore, is,

that when a testator bequeaths a legacy to his wife, he intends it as an addition to the legal provision of dower, unless he declares it to be in bar of dower; and she shall be entitled to both. In some of the books it is said, that where the wife has two provisions, such as a legacy under her husband's will, and her dower, she shall be, in most cases, put to her election. But this is putting it quite too broadly—and I apprehend the true rule to be, that a widow cannot be put to her election, unless by express declaration or necessary inference, arising from the inconsistency of her claim with the provisions of her husband's will. It is not that there is an additional provision made for the wife, by the will of the husband, which deprives her of dower, or puts her to her election, for, in many cases, she is entitled to both. . . . There being no express declaration in the will, we must examine whether the legacy of one thousand dollars to the widow shows such an intent to exclude dower by plain and manifest intent. And, certainly, taken by itself, it does not show such a manifest intent; else, in every case, any legacy to a wife might be said to raise the same implication. But it was urged, that the claim of dower would defeat the other provisions of the will, which direct the sale of the real and personal estate, and the investment of the proceeds, for the support of the children of the testator. It will, certainly, lessen the amount to be invested, so as to form that fund, but it will not defeat the arrangements and dispositions made by the testator. They may, and will, all be carried into effect, diminished only by a small amount which he, himself, carved for his wife. For this direction to sell and invest, is after the legacy of one thousand dollars to the wife, showing that he intended that amount to be first withdrawn from the fund, before investment. It is not clear of difficulties, but to the best of my judgment, the widow is entitled to her dower and the legacy." On appeal, these views were sustained. See also, to the same effect, *Gordon, Adm'r,* v. *Stevens,* 2 Hill's Chancery, 46. In *Kinsey et al.* v. *Woodward,* 3 Harrington, 459, the testator bequeathed an annuity to his wife, and directed his executors to sell all his real and personal estate, and divide the proceeds among his daughters, and added, "I do authorize and empower them, (the executors,) to convey to the purchaser of said real estate, a good and sufficient fee simple title or titles, being of equal tenor with those by which I now hold the same;" and it was decided that the intention that the lands should be sold free of dower was not sufficiently clear to put the widow to an election. A strong case, to the same purport, is *Fuller* v. *Yates,* 8 Paige, 325. There, a testator left his whole real and personal estate to three persons, (of whom his wife, during widowhood, was to be one,) as trustees and executors for the purposes of his will, and directed that they should lay out certain lands into

village lots, and sell them, as from time to time might be required; and he directed that an annuity should be paid to the wife during life, and that she should have the possession and direction of certain other real estate, and for the purpose of keeping it in repair, should receive an additional annual sum; and besides all this, gave her sundry other bequests. "The right of dower," said the Chancellor, "being a legal right, the wife cannot be deprived of it by a testamentary disposition in her favor, so as to put her to an election, unless the testator has manifested his intention to deprive her of dower, either by express words or necessary implication. It is not pretended in this case that the language of the will in respect to the provisions for the wife is at all inconsistent with her claim to dower in the residue of the testator's real estate. The cases on the subject of implied manifestation of intention to exclude the right of dower appear to establish this principle, that to put the wife to her election, the will must contain provisions which are wholly inconsistent with her claim of dower, in the particular portion of the estate to which the claim of dower is made. . . . In the present case, although the testator has expressly directed village lots to be laid out and sold, as they may be wanted, it is not necessary that each lot should be sold subject to the widow's right of dower. For a portion of the lots thus laid out may be assigned to her for her dower in the whole, and the rest may be sold free from any claim of dower. Or she may be endowed of other portions of the real estate, leaving all that is wanted for village lots during her life entirely free and unincumbered. I therefore conclude that, upon the settled principles of law on this subject, the widow is entitled to dower in the testator's real estate, notwithstanding the bequests and devises in her favor in the will. Taking the whole disposition which the testator has made of his property into consideration, it can hardly be said he intended to give her dower in addition to the testamentary dispositions in her favor; and probably if the question of dower had occurred to him, he would have inserted a provision in the will declaring that the dispositions in her favor should be in lieu of dower in the residue of his estate. But it is not sufficient to bar her dower that he did not think on the subject; as that would only indicate a want of intention either one way or the other. To exclude her right to dower, which is given to her by law, the will itself must show that he probably did contemplate the subject, and intended that the testamentary provisions for the wife should exclude her from all claim to dower, if she elected to take them." In like manner, a devise of the residue of the real and personal estate of the testator to his widow, will not bar her dower in land mortgaged in his lifetime, nor compel her to resign the rights which she would have independently of the devise, as the price

of claiming under it. *Lewis* v. *Smith*, 5 Selden, 503. See, also, *Sample* v. *Sample et al.*, 2 Yeates, 433. From these cases, the principle may be deduced, that if a legacy or devise, of whatever amount be given to the wife, and subject to this, the whole real estate, or the residue of the real estate, be directed to be sold, for any purpose, the legacy or devise will not be taken to be in lieu of dower.

See, however, the remark of Marshall, C. J., in *Herbert and others* v. *Wren and others*, 7 Cranch, 370, 379, as to the presumption afforded in such a case, by a direction to sell the residue for the payment of debts. [This remark was cited and relied on in *Norris* v. *Clark*, 2 Stockton's Ch. 51, and a devise of all the testator's real estate to his executor, with a direction that it should be sold and the proceeds distributed as provided for in the will, held to show that a declaration that the acceptance of a legacy bequeathed to the wife, should debar her from any further demand on the estate, meant the estate generally, and not merely that portion of it which consisted of personal property.]

If there be a devise or bequest to the widow, and a devise of a general residue of real estate, not to be sold, but to be enjoyed by the devisee, an intent that the provision for the wife shall be in lieu of dower, cannot be implied; *Brown* v. *Caldwell*, 1 Spears' Equity, 322, 325; *Havens* v. *Havens and others*, 1 Sandford, 325, 329. "I have not been able to find any case," said Johnson,

Ch., in *Brown* v. *Caldwell*, "in which it has been held, that any general disposition of the estate would raise the implication." And even if the devise is specific, though that naturally imports that the devisee is to take the whole estate, yet, in an ordinary case, as where the devisee is a brother or sister merely, or a child otherwise provided for in the will, the intention to exclude dower will not be inferred; *Straham* v. *Sutton*, 3 Vesey, 249; *Kennedy* v. *Nedrow*, 1 Dallas, 415, 418; though there is an intimation to the contrary in *Brown* v. *Caldwell*. Where, however, after a provision for the wife, there is a specific devise of real estate to a person whom the testator is bound to provide for, and who is obviously intended to be a principal object of the bounty of the will, as where the devise is for the support of an infant child, otherwise unprovided for, and is not more than sufficient for that purpose, the intention that the bounty to the child should not be invaded and impaired by a claim of dower may very fairly and reasonably be implied. And the case of *Herbert and others* v. *Wren and others*, 7 Cranch, 370, 378, appears to be an authority for that principle. There, a testator devised to his wife certain real estate for life, with remainder to his three daughters, and also bequeathed to her personal estate; he then devised to his two sons the premises in which dower was claimed, which were then under lease at an annual rent of £140, and directed this rent to be appro-

priated to the education and maintenance of his children; and other lands he ordered to be sold for the payment of debts. "The only fund provided for the maintenance and education of his five children," said Marshall, C. J., in delivering judgment, "is the rent of £140 per annum. Since he has made a distinct provision for his wife, the presumption is much against his intending that this fund should be diminished by being charged with her dower." Upon this, and some other less important grounds, a majority of the Court were of opinion that the testator intended the provision for the wife to be in lieu of dower.

Another case, under this perplexing subject, is where real estate is devised to a particular person, charged with an annuity in favor of the widow. Something may depend upon the extent to which the devisee is apparently the object of the testator's bounty, and in connection with that, upon the apparent sufficiency of the devised estate, in the view of the testator, to raise the annuity and dower, and also leave a beneficial interest in the devisee. But the distinction upon which, really, the cases have gone, both in England and in this country, is, between a rent-charge, or an annuity in the nature of a rent-charge, issuing out of the specific land in which dower is claimed, and chargeable upon no other fund, and an annuity, which, though chargeable on the land, is primarily payable out of some other fund. The English cases are to be reconciled upon this difference: that a rent-charge, or an annual sum payable to the wife out of the particular land, and out of nothing else, is necessarily repugnant to the enjoyment of dower in that land, upon the ground stated by Lord Camden in his very able judgment in *Villa Real* v. *Lord Galway*, 1 Bro. C. C. 292, n., that an entry upon the land, as dowress, necessarily extinguishes the rent-charge, at least *pro tanto;* but if the annuity, though chargeable on the dower land, is payable also out of other funds, and especially if it is payable also out of personal estate, which then becomes the primary fund—in other words, if it be not a rent-charge, but properly an annuity—there is no such inherent and necessary repugnancy between the enjoyment of that annuity and the assertion of dower, as to put the widow to an election. All the cases in which the annuity has been held to be in lieu of dower, were cases in which it was, in fact, a rent-charge, and payable out of no other fund than that land in which dower was claimed. Those cases are *Arnold* v. *Kempstead*, Ambler, 466; S. C, 2 Eden, 236; *Villa Real* v. *Lord Galway*, 1 Bro. C. C., 292, n.; S. C., Ambler, 682; *Jones* v. *Collin*, Ambler, 730; *Wake* v. *Wake*, 3 Bro. C. C. 255. On the other hand, where the provision for the wife is payable out of other funds also, especially if out of personal estate, in which case it is strictly an annuity, and not a rent-charge, the cases have held that dower is not barred. The first case is *Pitts* v. *Snowden;* of which the only report is the following note in

1 Bro. C. C. 292, n.—" Devise to his wife of an annuity of £50 a year, payable out of his *copyhold* and his freehold messuages, with clause of entry and distress, *to be made good out of his personal estate.* And, subject to the annuity, he gave his freehold messuages to his three children." Lord Hardwicke, determined the widow to be entitled to both the dower and the annuity. Here, not only were the copyholds liable, in addition to the freeholds, and perhaps primarily liable, but the annuity was chargeable also on the personal estate ; so that the reasoning of Lord Camden, in *Mr. Villa Real's case* had no application, since if the widow's entry on the freeholds had interrupted her dower, it would have been *made good out of the personal estate.* In *Foster* v. *Cook*, 3 Bro. C. C. 347, the annuity was payable out of real and personal estate, devised to trustees, so that the personal estate was liable in the first instance. In *French* v. *Davis*, 2 Vesey, Jr., 572, the annuity was payable out of a fund composed of the produce of the real and personal estates mixed together. *Greatorex* v. *Cary*, 6 Id. 615, is the same case as *Foster* v. *Cook*, and decided upon it. In *Strahan* v. *Sutton*, 3 Id. 249, the annuity was payable only out of personalty. There is, therefore; perhaps, no such contradiction between Lord Hardwicke's and Lord Thurlow's decisions on the one hand, and those of Lord Camden, Lord Northington and Mr. Justice Buller on the other, as is supposed by Chancellor Kent in *Adsit* v. *Adsit*, and by some other writers.

The late English cases carry out
the same distinction. On the one
hand, in *Holdich* v. *Holdich*, 2
Young & Collier's C. C. 18, the
bequest was of an annuity charged
generally with other legacies upon
both real and personal estate, and
therefore payable primarily out of
the personalty. In *Dowson* v. *Bell*,
1 Keen, 761, though the freeholds
were devised subject to the annuity, copyholds were clearly intended to be the primary fund for
its payment. On the other hand,
in *Roadley* v. *Dixon*, 3 Russell,
192, the annuity was '' to be issuing
out of the estate at S.,'' and was
therefore a rent-charge strictly,
payable out of that land only : and
the remarks of Lord Lyndhurst in
that case tend decidedly to sustain
Lord Camden's view in *Villa Real*
v. *Lord Galway*. *Norcott* v. *Gordon*, 14 Simon, 258, does not overrule *Arnold* v. *Kempstead*, nor
concern the same point. *Harrison*
v. *Harrison*, 1 Keen, 765, belongs
to a different class of cases; there,
the provision for the wife was
neither a rent-charge, nor an annuity charged on land; lands were
devised to trustees to pay an annuity out of the rents and profits ;
and of course the considerations in
Villa Real's case did not apply.
The cases in this country support
the distinction above mentioned ;
that an annual provision for the
widow, payable out of personal
and real estate, is not a bar to
dower, in that real estate, but such
a provision issuing out of the real
estate only, is : see *Lord* v. *Lord*,
23 Conn. 327. The former point is
decided in *Smith* v. *Kniskern*, 4

Johnson's Chancery, 9. There, a
testator possessed of real and personal estate, gave his wife several
legacies, '' and her comfortable
support and maintenance out of his
estate, to be, from time to time,
rendered and paid to her by his
executors, and the privilege and use
of one room in his dwelling-house
during all such time as she should
continue to be his widow, and no
longer ;'' and after giving other
legacies, left the residue of his
estate to his two daughters. '' The
charge of a 'comfortable support
and maintenance' falls, probably,
upon the real estate as well as the
personal,'' said the Chancellor.
'' But the latter ought to be first
applied ; and as the executors were
directed to render the maintenance
from time to time, and as no authority is given to them over the
real estate, it would seem that the
testator had a particular reference
to the personal estate, in making
that provision for his wife. I do
not perceive, however, that the
provision destroys the right to
dower. There is no inconsistency
between the two claims, even supposing the charge for maintenance
to rest upon the real estate. From
the large and valuable real estate
set forth in the pleadings, and admitted, it is quite apparent that
the real estate is much more than
adequate to furnish the support
and the dower. There is nothing
repugnant in the operation of the
two claims; and the assertion of
the right of dower will not disturb
or defeat any provision in the will.
. . . The rule is, that the
widow takes both provisions, un-

less the estate is insufficient to support both, or such an inconsistency appears between the provisions in the will and the dower, as to make the intention clear and indubitable, that both provisions were not to be taken." The other branch of the distinction is established in *White* v. *White*, 1 Harrison, 202, 211. The testator, in that case, bequeathed to his wife all the property which she had before marriage, and further ordered that she should have one room in his dwelling-house, " and a comfortable maintenance *out of his real estate*, during her natural life or widowhood:" and then devised his real estate to his two sons. It was decided that the maintenance was intended to be in lieu of dower. " If the demandant shall be allowed to recover dower in the real estate," said Ford, J., in delivering the opinion of the court, " it will disturb and prevent the testator's own provisions from being carried into effect. He has provided for her a comfortable maintenance, and has made it a charge upon his whole real estate, so that it goes with the estate as a burden, into the hands of his two sons : they are to furnish the maintenance, and in consideration of it they are to have the *whole* estate. Now, if the widow takes one-third of it for her dower, and they obtain only *two-thirds* of it during her lifetime, it wholly deranges the testator's settlement, which was that they should have the whole estate, and be liable in respect of it, for the whole of her maintenance. The will can never be executed according to his

intent, for the sons will have only two-thirds of what the testator intended ; and the uttermost for the widow would be only two-thirds of the maintenance provided and intended for her. The testator's settlement would be broken up, and some other would have to be substituted in the place of it. Either the widow must lose her whole maintenance, or it must be apportioned on the sons according to the proportional part of the lands they obtain. If she, by an act of her own, takes one-third of the land away from her sons, does she not discharge them from any maintenance ?" If a man having a rent-charge, purchases *part of the land*, out of which the rent issues, the whole rent is thereby extinguished, because wilfully and by his own act, he has prevented the operation of the charge on the land, *according to the original grant.*" Litt. sec. 222 ; Gilb. on Rents, 152. If so, her claim of dower contravenes the will by defeating the very maintenance the testator has provided for her. If it be said that dower accrues by operation of law, not by her own act, and therefore that the charge shall not be entirely lost, but apportioned on the sons, according to the estate they actually receive, even this will defeat the disposition made by the testator, according to which the sons were to have all the land, and to furnish the whole of the maintenance. This is quite the reasoning of Lord Camden, in his judgment in *Villa Real's case*. In *Addams* v. *Heffernan*, 9 Watts, 530, 541, it was decided that if a rent-charge or rent-seck, or annuity payable out of land, be given to one upon whom in common with others the land descends as heirs-at-law, the rent or annuity is extinguished *pro tanto* as the annuitant took as heir-at-law. In further support of this principle, the case of *Duncan* v. *Duncan's Ex'rs*, 2 Yeates, 302, may be referred to. Here a testator directed that all his estate, both real and personal, should be sold to the be t advantage, as soon as convenient, and gave to his wife the interest of one-third part of the price of his real estate when sold, for her support during her natural life; and it was held that the widow was put to her election. The court said, " Though the devise to the widow is not expressed ' to be in lieu and satisfaction of dower,' yet it is absolutely inconsistent with and repugnant to such claim. Ambl. 467, 682, 730. She could not possibly have the interest of one-third of the amount of *sales* of the *whole* land during her life, and at the same time hold one-third part *of* it *unsold* for her benefit." In like manner a devise of all the testator's real and personal property to trustees, with directions to pay two-thirds of the rents and profits to his children, and the remaining third to his widow during her life, followed by a direction that the real estate should be sold after her demise, was held, in *Savage* v. *Burnham*, 17 New York R. 562, to debar the right of dower.

A devise to the widow, of an estate for life in certain property,

and of the residue of the real estate to others, will not, by implication, exclude her from dower in the residue; *Havens* v. *Havens and others*, 1 Sandford, 325. But upon the question whether a devise to her for life, or during widowhood, in particular lands, or in all the testator's real estate, will exclude dower in the same lands in which she has the devise for life or during widowhood, the decisions are in conflict. In New York it has been decided that a devise of all the testator's property, real and personal, during widowhood, or during widowhood and the minority of her children, and then to be divided among the children, is not a devise in lieu of dower, so clearly as to put the wife to an election: *Sandford* v. *Jackson*, 10 Paige, 266; *Bull* v. *Church*, 5 Hill, 206; S. C., affirmed on error; *Church* v. *Bull*, 2 Denio, 430. In some other States, however, the decisions have been the other way: and it is held that a devise to the wife during widowhood, or during life, is an implied exclusion of dower in the same lands, because the two estates cannot exist together; especially if coupled with a direction that upon her re-marriage, all her interest in the testator's estate shall cease; *Wilson, Ex'r,* v. *Hayne et ux.*, Cheves' Equity, 37, 40; *Caston* v. *Caston*, 2 Richardson's Equity, 1, 2; *Cunningham* v. *Shannon*, 4 Id. 135; *Stark et al.* v. *Hunton et al.*, Saxton's Chancery, 217, 224, 225; *Hamilton* v. *Buckwalter*, 2 Yeates, 389, 392; *Creacraft and Wife* v. *Dille*, 3 Id. 79; sec, however,

Evans v. *Webb*, 1 Yeates, 424; 1 Binney, 565; *M'Cullough and Wife* v. *Allen and Wife*, 3 Yeates, 10; *Chappel* v. *Avery*, 6 Connecticut, 31; *Smith* v. *Bone*, 7 Bush. 367.

The principles relating to a testamentary provision being in lieu of dower, and to the widow's election between such a provision and dower, appear to be in all respects the same at law as in equity. See *Van Orden* v. *Van Orden*, 10 Johnson, 30, 32; *Jackson* v. *Churchill*, 7 Cowen, 287; *Bull* v. *Church*, 5 Hill, 206; S. C., affirmed on error, 2 Denio, 430; *Pickett* v. *Peay*, 3 Brevard, 545. It was said, indeed, by Thompson, J., in *Larrabee and Wife* v. *Van Alstyne*, 1 Johnson, 307, 308, that to render a provision for the wife by will, a *legal bar* of dower, it must consist of lands given or assured to her for life, and that a sum of money or other chattel interest, given by will, in lieu of dower, will, if accepted, be only an equitable bar: see also *Jones* v. *Powell*, 6 Johnson's Chancery, 194, 200; but this distinction is now exploded, and it is held that any testamentary provision, clearly intended to be in lieu of dower, if accepted deliberately, and understandingly, will be a bar, at law, to claim for dower; *Kennedy* v. *Mills*, 13 Wendell, 553; *Tobias* v. *Ketchum*, 32 New York, 319; *Worthen* v. *Pearson*, 33 Georgia, 385; *Davison* v. *Davison*, 3 Green, 235. Statutory provisions in respect to the relation between dower and a testamentary devise or bequest to the widow, have been introduced into the law of several

of the States. In North Carolina, and Tennessee, any provision for the widow in the will bars her of dower, unless within a certain time she dissents from the will; see *Craven* v. *Craven*, 2 Devereaux, Equity, 338; *Bray* v. *Lamb*, Id. 372; *Reid* v. *Campbell*, Meigs, 378; *M'Daniel* v. *Douglas*, 6 Humphries, 220. In Massachusetts, Maine, Ohio, and Alabama, any testamentary provision is a bar to dower, unless the widow elect within six months after probate to waive it and be endowed, or unless it plainly appear by the will that the testator intended that she should have both; see *Reid* v. *Dickerman*, 12 Pickering, 146; *Crane* v. *Crane*, 17 Id. 422; *Delay* v. *Vinal*, 1 Metcalf, 57; *Adams* v. *Adams and others*, 5 Id. 277; *Pratt* v. *Fulton*, 4 Cushing, 174; *Atherton* v. *Corliss*, 101 Mass. 40; see *Smith* v. *Bone*, 7 Bush, 367; *Allen* v. *Pray*, 3 Fairfield, 138; *Hastings* v. *Clifford*, 32 Maine, 132; *Stilley et ux.* v. *Folger et al.*, 14 Ohio, 610, 646; *Lingard* v. *Ripley*, 19 Ohio, N. S. 324; *Baxter* v. *Bowger*, Id. 490; *Hilliard* v. *Binford*, 10 Alabama, 977. In New Jersey, any devise of real estate to the widow, without a declaration as to whether it is in lieu of dower, or not, is made a bar, unless dissented from within six months after probate; see *Thompson* v. *Egbert*, 2 Harrison, 460; *Stark et al.* v. *Hunton et al.*, Saxtons Chancery, 217, 228; see *Bray* v. *Neill*, 21 New Jersey, Eq. 343. In Delaware, any devise, and in Pennsylvania and Maryland, any devise or bequest, will be taken to be in lieu of dower, unless the testator declare otherwise, the widow still having her election; Penna. Act of 8th April, 1833, sect. 11, (Purd. 1169;) and of March 29th, 1832, sect. 35, (Purd. 892;) *Reed* v. *Reed*, 9 Watts, 263; *Chandler* v. *Woodward*, 3 Harrington, 428: *Collins* v. *Carman*, 5 Maryland, 503; *Gough* v. *Manning*, 26 Id. 47. In New York, by the revised statutes, if any provision, real or personal, is made for a widow by will, in lieu of dower, she must elect; and will be taken to have elected against dower, unless within one year she enter on the lands to be assigned for dower, or commence proceedings for the recovery of assignment thereof. 1 R. S. 741, ss. 13, 14; see *Hawly* v. *James*, 5 Paige, 323, 445.

A bequest in lieu of dower, accepted by election, is so far based upon a valuable consideration, that, though subject to the demands of creditors; *Leavenworth* v. *Cooney*, 48 Barb. 570; *Brant's Will*, 40 Missouri, 266, it has priority over other legacies, and will not abate with them; *Isenhart* v. *Brown*, 1 Edwards, 411; *Reed* v. *Reed*, 9 Watts, 263; *Lord* v. *Lord*, 23 Conn. 327; *Bard's Estate*, 8 P. F. Smith, 393; 15 Id. 314; *Durham* v. *Rhodes*, 23 Maryland, 233; see *Mitchener* v. *Atkinson*, Phillip's Eq. 23.

It was said in *Sandoe's Appeal*, 14 P. F. Smith, 314, that where a woman elects to takes her dower, or as a distributee and against the will, and other bequests or devises are thereby frustrated, the legacy or devise which she thus renounces will be charged with a trust for the compensation of the disappointed claimants.

An election may be determined by matter *in pais* as well as by matter of record; but it can only be by plain and unequivocal acts, under a full knowledge of all the circumstances, and of the party's rights; and a bare acquiescence, without a deliberate and intelligent choice, will not be an election; *Duncan* v. *Duncan's Executors*, 2 Yeates, 302, 305; *Cauffman* v. *Cauffman*, 17 Sergeant and Rawle, 16, 25; *Heron* v. *Hoffner and others*, 3 Rawle, 393, 396; *Adlum* v. *Yard*, 1 Id. 163, 171; *Bradford* v. *Kent*, 7 Wright, 474, 484; *Anderson's Appeal*, 12 Casey, 476; *O'Driscoll* v. *Koger*, 2 Dessaussure, 295, 299; *Snelgrove et al.* v. *Snelgrove et al.*, 4 Id. 274, 300. It is a general rule, that one is not bound to elect, until he is fully informed of the relative value of the things between which he is to choose, and an election before the circumstances necessary to a judicious and discriminating choice are ascertained, is not obligatory; *Pinckney* v. *Pinckney*, 2 Richardson's Equity, 219, 237; *Upshaw* v. *Upshaw and others*, 2 Henning and Munford, 381, 390, 393; *Reaves* v. *Garrett*, 34 Alabama, 563. "The cases have gone so far," said the Chancellor, in *Hall* v. *Hall*, 2 M'Cord's Chancery, 269, 280, "that after the wife has made her election, and has received benefits under the will, she has been allowed to retract and resort to her legal rights, when the estate has turned out differently from what it was believed and stated to be at the time of the election prematurely made ; " and this was held to be allowable in *Adsit* v. *Adsit*, 2 Johnson's Chancery, 448, 451. Taking possession of property under a will or other instrument, and exercising unequivocal acts of ownership over it, for a long period of time, will amount to a binding election to confirm the instrument; *Bradford* v. *Kents*, 7 Wright, 474, 484; *Upshaw* v. *Upshaw and others; Wilson, Ex'r,* v. *Hayne et ux.,* Cheves' Equity, 37, 42 ; *Caston* v. *Caston*, 2 Richardson's Equity, 1, 2; *Stark et al.* v. *Hunton et al.,* Saxton's Chancery, 217, 227 ; *Clay and Craig* v. *Hart*, 7 Dana, 1, 6. In like manner, if a legatee's real estate is devised away, his recovering that estate, by proceedings in law or equity, by title paramount to the will, would be an election not to take under the will; *Kinnaird, Ex'or, &c.,* v. *William's Adm'r et al.*, 8 Leigh, 400. If a party has once made an election he is bound to abide by his determination, unless he can restore the property to its original situation; *Leonard* v. *Crommelin,* 1 Edwards, 206, 210.

In *Bradford* v. *Kents*, 7 Wright, 474. Strong, J., held the following language in delivering the judgment of the court. " That an election may be evidenced by matter *in pais* as well as by matter of record is certain, and it was conceded in the court below. It is true, nothing less than unequivocal acts will prove an election, and they must be acts done with the knowl-

edge of the parties' rights, as well as the circumstances of the case. Nothing less than an act of choice intelligently done will suffice. When the question is as it was in this case, whether a widow has elected to take a devise or a bequest under her husband's will, in lieu of dower at law, it is not sufficient to prove that she had been merely passive, or even that she has received the property given to her by the will, unless she knew the situation of her husband's estate, and the relative value of the properties between which she was empowered to choose. All this must be conceded. And so, even when a widow has the requisite knowledge, where an act done by her is equivocal, the intention with which the act was done is material to be considered. But a widow who, after having become acquainted with all that is necessary for her to know in order to make a binding election, receives the gift conferred by her husband's will, and uses it as her own, is not at liberty to say she did not intend to relinquish dower. Her acts are inconsistent with any other intention. They are not equivocal ; she has no right to the gift except as a legatee or devisee, and her taking and using it is an admission that she chooses to take under the will. It necessarily involves an election, and in the case supposed, a case where there is full knowledge, it bars her dower. There are undoubtedly decisions that a widow may elect dower even after she has claimed and received the legacy or devise made to her, but she may not receive and hold the benefits conferred by the will of her husband, after the extent of her rights has become known to her, and then retract her election."

" In the case before us, the widow was an executrix, and acted as such. She took out letters testamentary. It was her duty to inform herself of the situation, circumstances and value of her husband's estate. She must, therefore, be presumed to have known. All the personalty was spread before her, and she took a large portion of it. To no part of it had she any right except as legatee. She took it expressly under the will, used it as her own, and never afterwards until this suit was brought, retracted this act of choice. Not even yet has she returned or offered to return all that she claimed and received. She continued on the farm as long as the will gave her a right to continue, and left when her estate under the will terminated. Her continued possession was rightful if she held as devisee; it was wrongful if she had made no election to take under the will. * * * * * The true question to be answered was, not what her motives were, or her purposes in regard to the property, but whether she had elected to take what her husband had given her by his will."

It seems that where land is given to A. by an instrument which assumes to bestow other land belonging to him on B., A.'s entering into or continuing in possession of both tracts will not amount to an election, or preclude him from determining, subsequently, which he will have. Although under an obligation to choose, he need not do so until formally required by some one duly authorized to that end. " To constitute an election," said Price, J., in *Whitredge* v. *Parkhurst*, 20 Maryland, 62, " there must be a choosing between the two; the taking of the one and the rejection of the other. The taking of both is no election; *Marriott* v. *Badger*, 5 Maryland, 311. * * * * Acts of ownership over both properties cannot evidence an election; a choosing between the two; whether those acts of ownership are the taking possession of both, or receiving the rents of one, and the mortgaging or leasing of the other. Such and similar acts show that both were claimed, therefore that neither was abandoned, and consequently instead of establishing an election they negative it." In this instance the testatrix had a life estate in certain land, in which her daughter had the fee, and owned another tract absolutely. She devised both tracts to the daughter, with the remainder over to her children. The daughter proved the will and went into possession of both tracts, and subsequently united with the remaindermen in mortgaging that which she held in her own right, and it was decided that these acts did not constitute an election. It was further held to be immaterial that the will was made in pursuance of an oral agreement that if the mother would leave all she had to her daughter for life, the latter would give effect to the bequest over to her children. The court were also of opinion, that a declaration by the daughter of her intention to carry out the will, came too late after she had incurred debts, which could not be paid without a sale of the property, which belonged to her in fee.

There are cases of election in other departments of equity, where infants and *femes covert* cannot make a binding decision; but they may be enforced to elect, in cases of the present nature, where the choice lies between two inc nsistent rights, and there is a clear intention on the part of him under whom one of them is derived, that both shall not be enjoyed, and it is therefore against conscience to retain both; *Robertson* v. *Stephens*, 1 Iredell's Equity, 247, 251; *M'Queen* v. *M'Queen*, 2 Jones' Eq. 16; see *Tiernan et al.* v. *Ro-*

land and Blackstone, 3 Harris, 430, 452. The acceptance by a married woman of a benefit under a. will, may be as conclusive on her, and those claiming under her as if she were sole; *Tiernan* v. *Roland; Robinson* v. *Buck*, 21 P. F. Smith, 386 ; 2 Smith's Leading Cases, 742, 7 Am. ed. The court will make election for infants; and, in doing so, will be guided altogether by a view to the benefit of the infant, on a consideration of all the circumstances ; *Addison* v. *Bowie*, 2 Bland, 606. 623. The proper course, therefore, under such circumstances, lies in a reference to a Master, to ascertain the value of both interests, followed by a decree that the infant shall retain that which will, on the whole, be most for his advantage, and resign all claim to the other. *Grattan* v. *Howard*, 1 Swan. 409 ; *M'Queen* v. *M'Queen*, 2 Jones' Eq. 16.

---

*ALEYN v. BELCHIER. [*377]

JULY 5, 1758.

REPORTED 1 EDEN, 132.[1]

FRAUD UPON A POWER.]—*Power of jointuring executed in favour of a wife, but with an agreement that the wife should only receive a part as an annuity for her own benefit, and that the residue should be applied to the payment of the husband's debts : held a fraud upon the power, and the execution set aside, except so far as related to the annuity; the bill containing a submission to pay it, and only seeking relief against the other objects of the appointment.*

THE Rev. Thomas Aleyn being seised of a real estate in Essex, of the yearly value of 540*l.*, subject to a mortgage for a term of 500 years to Sir Charles Palmer for 500*l.*, and having a nephew,

[1] S. C. Sugd. on Pow. App. Amb. MSS. Reg. Lib. A. 1757, fol. 432.

Edmund Aleyn, and two brothers, the plaintiff, Giles Aleyn, and William, who was a defendant, by his will bearing date the 28th of May, 1746, devised the same to Eyre and Bragg in trust by sale or mortgage to raise money, and pay his debts and legacies, and to permit his wife to receive the rents and profits of the residue for her life, and after her death in trust to convey to his nephew Edmund for life, with remainder to his first and other sons in tail male, with proper limitations to support contingent remainders, with *a power to his nephew to make a jointure on any woman he should then after marry, for her life in bar of dower*, with powers to provide for younger children, and to make leases, with remainder to the testator's brother Giles for life; remainder to his first and other sons in tail male; remainder to his brother William for life; remainder to his first and other sons in tail [*378] male; remainder to his *own right heirs: he gave his brother, the plaintiff, an annuity of £30 a year for his life, to be paid out of his estate, to be increased to 50*l.* a year in case his nephew should survive his, the testator's, wife.

A bill was filed soon after the testator's death by the widow, and on the 14th of February, 1749, a decree made to establish the will, and for payment of debts and legacies by mortgage or sale in the usual way. The master reported, there was due for debts and legacies 1516*l.* 1*s.* 10*d.* which he approved to be raised by mortgage. The widow died in April, 1750, and Edmund became entitled to the possession of the estate. The defendant William Belchier, having advanced money to pay off the incumbrances, a mortgage, bearing date the 26th and 27th of June, 1750, was made of the estate to him in fee, and the term for years was assigned to John Belchier in trust for W. Belchier.

Edmund was very extravagant, and became indebted to William Belchier in the sum of 1760*l.*

On the 4th of June, 1750, Edmund married the defendant Jane, who was a low woman without fortune, and no provision for her was either made or agreed to be made; but soon after the marriage, by articles of agreement, bearing date the 1st of August, 1750, and made between Edmund Aleyn and his wife of the one part, and William Belchier of the other, reciting the will of Thomas Aleyn, giving Edmund power of jointuring, and that he and Jane were lately married, and that he was indebted to William Belchier in the sum of £1760, besides the mortgage, Edmund Aleyn, in satisfaction and discharge of the said sum of 1760*l.*, and in consideration of the several annuities and money thereinafter agreed to be paid, covenanted within six months to procure an effectual conveyance and settlement to be made by the trustees in Thomas Aleyn's will, and immediately after such settlement should be made, to appoint the whole estate to his wife for her life, in case she should survive him, for her jointure; and that he and his wife, as soon as they should become respec- [*379] tively seised of the legal estate of freehold, *would, by fine and conveyances, convey and assure all the said premises by the said will devised and intended to be settled, unto and to the use of William Belchier, his heirs and assigns, during the lives of Edmund Aleyn and Jane his wife, and the longer liver of them; and in consideration thereof, William Belchier covenanted that, in case the said settlement should be perfected, whereby the estate should become well vested in him and his heirs, for the lives of Edmund and Jane his wife, and the longer liver of them, to pay the several annuities after mentioned, namely: to Jane Aleyn, during the joint lives of her and Edmund her husband, 60*l.* a year, clear of all deductions, for her separate use; to Edmund Aleyn, for his life, in case he should survive Jane his wife, £60 a year, clear of all deductions; and to Jane, in case she should survive Edmund her husband, for her life, £100 a year, clear of all deductions; and to pay to John Miles, son of Jane by a former husband, 105*l.* at the age of twenty-one years; and also to pay Jane 5*l.* yearly towards his maintenance and education, till the 105*l.* should become payable.

The estate was conveyed by lease and release of 6th and 7th of August, 1750, to the uses of Thomas Aleyn's will, pursuant to the decree: and by deed, dated 8th August, 1750, reciting the conveyance and power to jointure, Edmund Aleyn, in consideration of the marriage, and in order to make a provision for Jane, his wife, appointed the whole estate to Jane, his wife, for a jointure, subject to the payment of the annuities given by the will of Thomas Aleyn, and of the mortgage of 1516*l.* 1*s.* 10*d.* and interest.

On the 10th of August, 1750, Edmund Aleyn and Jane, his wife, executed a deed, by which Edmund covenanted with George Townsend, that he and his wife would levy a fine of the premises to Townsend and his heirs, for and during the lives of Edmund and his wife and the longer liver of them, in trust for William Belchier and his heirs, which was levied accordingly.

William Belchier took possession of the estate, and *re- [*380] ceived the rents and profits, and paid the plaintiff, during Edmund's life, two sums of 25*l.* and 21*l.* 5*s.*, in part of the annuity he was entitled to under Thomas Aleyn's will.

Edmund died in June, 1755.

On 26th November, 1756, the plaintiff filed the present bill to redeem the estate, on payment of 1516*l.* 1*s.* 10*d.*, the mortgage money borrowed under the decree, and to be let into the possession of the estate; for an account of the rents and profits from the death of Edmund, submitting to pay Jane 100*l.* a year for her life, and to have the deeds and writings of the estate delivered up.

Jane Aleyn and William Belchier admitted, in their several answers, the facts as before stated. Jane Aleyn said that the settlement was intended to make a reasonable provision for her, and to save Edmund from ruin; and that if Edmund had not been in debt at the time of their marriage, he would have settled the whole estate on her for her jointure. William Belchier said, that the consideration of the settlement and conveyance was truly and bona fide advanced, part before the execution of the settlement, and the remainder at or about the time of the execution of the settlement and conveyance to Townsend ; and they both admitted that Edmund was, at the time of the settlement, in distressed circumstances, and in want of money.

Mr. *Perrot* and Mr. *Ambler*, for the plaintiff:—This is an improper execution of the power, which was to bar dower by giving a jointure ; but even supposing it well executed, the fraud will vitiate it. The appointment and conveyance were a deceit upon the testator, and a fraud upon the remainder-man. The power given to the nephew, who was only tenant for life, was to make a fair jointure, to encourage him to marry, not to pay his debts. The remainder-man was only to be kept out of the estate in case a fair and honest jointure were made. It must not be colourable, and for other purposes. This was an artful contrivance of Belchier and the defendant Jane ; a low, mean woman, of no fortune. There is no settlement, nor agreement for one, at the time of the [*381] marriage, nor *till Belchier put it into Edmund's head, with a view to secure his own debt by taking an absolute interest in the estate for two lives instead of a mortgage for Edmund's life only. It is at best an unreasonable bargain. The articles of the 1st August discover the whole scheme. Upon the face of them it appears it was not the intention to jointure, but to pay debts. The only jointure averred is 100*l*. a year ; Edmund is stripped of everything during the joint lives of himself and his wife ; only 60*l*. a year to be paid during their joint lives, and that to the separate use of the wife. Suppose a power to make a jointure of so much for every thousand pounds fortune : it has been repeatedly held, that if the husband or others advance a sum of money, colourably to authorise the husband to settle largely, a Court of Equity will set aside all above the proportion of the real value of the fortune.[1] So, if a father, having a power to appoint amongst his children, bargains with one for a share, equity will set it aside. Though it may be honest in Edmund to pay his debts, it must be done with his own money ; this is a method of doing it with other persons' money, contrary to the intention of the testator. Even admitting the estate had been fairly and bona fide appointed as a jointure, and the wife had afterwards parted with her jointure, or part of it to pay her husband's debts, it would have been good to bind the remainder-man ; yet in this case the whole is one transaction, a collusion between the husband and wife and Belchier. The case of *Lane* v. *Page*, determined by Lord Hardwicke, is precisely in point.

The Attorney-General, Sir *Charles Pratt*, and the Solicitor General, the Hon. *Charles Yorke*, for the defendant Belchier ; *Clark*, for the jointress :—

The first question is, as to the extent of the power given by the will. The objection that the power is only to bar dower,

---

[1] Lane v. Page, Amb. 233 ; Lord Tyrconnel v. Duke of Ancaster, Amb. 237.

and consequently can only comprehend jointures made before marriage, is too extensive, as it will comprehend every jointure, though made bona fide. The devise is to a nephew, having no estate of his own, for life, without impeachment of waste; he had no estate to *which dower could attach, which shows [*382] that the words were put in by the scrivener currente calamo.

As to the execution, the power was substantially executed; the husband and wife agreed to sell their interest to Belchier. If an appointment had been made of the whole estate, and the wife had afterwards joined with the husband and sold her interest, it would have been good if only a day had intervened. This is the same thing. Suppose the wife had made a stand after the power was executed, the Court would not have compelled her to levy a fine. It was in her power to do it or not. In the case put, of a father appointing to a child, making himself a partaker, the appointment would only be avoided as against other children, not against a remainder-man.

The LORD KEEPER HENLEY.[1]—The question is whether Edmund Aleyn has properly executed the power as a jointure, and has properly conveyed to the defendant, Belchier, or whether the transaction is void in toto, or in part. I am inclined to think the power was not well executed in point of law.[2] It ought to have been before marriage. The power is given under restrictions. It must be a jointure in bar of dower, which can only be before marriage. Dower is not barrable by a jointure after marriage. But, I build my opinion upon the next question.

The whole transaction is on agreement between the husband and wife. No point is better established than that *a person having a power must execute it bona fide for the end designed, otherwise it is corrupt and void.* The power here was intended for a jointure, not to pay the husband's debts. The motive that induced Edmund to execute it was not a provision for his wife. This case is not distinguishable from the cases alluded to, nor from *Lane* v. *Page.* If a father has a power to appoint amongst children, and agrees with one of them, for a sum of money to appoint to him, such appointment would be void. It was admitted the execution share of the property subjected to such power; provided that nothing would be void, but it was said to be only so amongst the children. In that case the money is to go to the children; no other person has any *interest in it; here the remainder-man has an immedi- [*383] ate right to the estate after the death of Edmund, if there is no appointment. It was said to differ from the case of parent and children; and that, if the husband had fairly executed the power, the wife might have immediately afterwards joined in a fine to pay his debts. The reason is plain: she would then have had a first interest, and the husband would have had no control

---

[1] Afterwards Lord Chancellor and Earl of Northington.
[2] Sed vide 2 Sugd. Pow. 321.

over it; but it does not from thence follow that they might make
an agreement to divide the money between them. It cannot be
supposed he would have settled the whole on her without some
such view. She was of no family and had no fortune. It would
have kept the children, if they had any, entirely out of the
estate till her death. It is like the case put of parents and
children; and I think *Lane* v. *Page* is in point, and ought to
govern my decision in the present case.

Declare the appointment good as to the 100*l*. only for the
benefit of Jane. The plaintiff to redeem, on payment of principal
and interest of the mortgage and costs, so far as relates to the
mortgage. ● Account of rents and profits from the death of
Edmund: and Belchier to pay the rest of the costs.

Aleyn v. *Belchier*, was decided upon the well-established principle
that a person having a power. *must execute it bona fide for the end designed*, otherwise the appointment, although unimpeachable at law, will
be held corrupt and void in equity; for, although the Lord Keeper
seemed inclined to think, that the power was not well executed, even
at law, he founded his decision expressly upon the ground that the
appointment was a fraud upon the donor of the power, and therefore
void in equity. See *Topham* v. *The Duke of Portland*, 31 Beav. 525;
1 De G. Jo. & Sm. 517; *S. C.*, nom. *Duke of Portland* v. *Topham*, 11
H. L. Ca. 32. *Topham* v. *Duke of Portland*, 5 L. R. Ch. App. 40;
D'Abbadie v. *Bizion*, 5 I. R. Eq. 205. The recent case, however, of *In
re Huish's Charity*, 10 L. R. Eq. 5, seems to have departed from the
doctrines above laid down. The principle, somewhat concisely stated
by the Lord Keeper in *Aleyn* v. *Belchier*, has been recently more fully
and forcibly enunciated in the House of Lords. " The donee, the ap-
[*384] pointer *under the power," observes Lord Westbury, C. " must,
the time of the exercise of that power, and for any purpose for
which it is used, act with good faith and sincerity, and with an entire
and single view to the real purpose and object of the power, and not
for the purpose of accomplishing or carrying into effect any bye or
sinister object (I mean sinister in the sense of its being beyond the
purpose and intent of the power), which he may desire to effect in the
exercise of the power," 11 H. L. Ca. 54; and to the same effect Lord
St. Leonards observes : " A party having a power like this (to appoint
amongst children) must fairly and honestly execute it, without having
any ulterior object to be accomplished. He cannot carry into execution any indirect object, or acquire any benefit for himself, either directly or indirectly. It may be subject to limitations and directions ;
but it must be a pure, straightforward, honest dedication of the property, as property, to the person to whom he affects, or attempts to give
it in that character." *Ib.* 55.

Upon the same grounds as the decision in the principal case, where
a man has a power to make a jointure under restrictions, as 100*l.* a-year
for every 1000*l.* of the wife's portion, and he has himself advanced a
sum of money, in order colourably to enable him to make the jointure
larger, the Court will reject such part as is more than proportionate to
the real fortune : *Lane* v. *Page*, Amb. 234, per Lord Hardwicke; *Lord
Tyrconnel* v. *Duke of Ancaster*, Amb. 237 ; *S. C.*, 2 Ves. 500 ; where
the judgment is more fully reported ; and see *Weir* v. *Chamley*, 1 Ir.
Ch. Rep. 295, 317.   In *Lane* v. *Page*, Amb. 233, a tenant for life, with
power of jointuring, being greatly in debt, and actually arrested, executed his power of jointuring to its full extent, having previously
entered into an agreement with the woman whom he afterwards married, that she was to join in levying a fine, the use of which was to pay
her 20*l.* a-year only for her benefit ; 50*l.* a-year was to be applied in
payment of his debts, and then to his wife for life ; and the residue of
the profits during her life should, after his death, be paid as he should
appoint, or, in default of appointment, should go to his executors, administrators, and assigns.   The husband died soon after the marriage,
no fine having been levied ; but the widow, by indentures of lease and
release, conveyed the premises, in trust to pay 20*l.* a-year to herself for
life, the overplus of the rents in discharge of her husband's debts, and
then in trust for herself for life.   Upon a bill being filed by the remainder-man to set aside this execution of the power, Lord Hardwicke
held, that it was a fraud on the property of a third person, the remainder-man, but *that it ought to be supported as to the 20*l.* a-year.   [*385]
" Fraud," he observed, " will affect only so far as it extends ; and
this Court will not say that *participes criminis* shall have no benefit of
the agreement in any part."   And, accordingly, it was declared that the
agreement and conveyance ought to be considered as one transaction,
and set aside, except as to the 20*l.* to the wife.

So an appointment to a child by a father in consideration of his wife
postponing her jointure to some mortgages which he proposed to effect,
was held by Sir W. Page Wood, V. C., to be void.   " I think," said
his Honor, " it would be impossible to contend if a direct bribe were
given to the appointor, though out of a separate fund, that the appointment could be upheld in favour of the party to whom the fund subject
to the appointment was given :" *Rowley* v. *Rowley*, Kay, 242.

Upon the same principle also, if a parent, having a power of appointment amongst his children, appoints to one or more of them, to the exclusion of the others, upon a bargain for his own advantage, equity will
relieve against the appointment as a fraud upon the power, as where
there was a secret understanding that the child should assign a part of
the fund to a stranger (*Daubeny* v. *Cockburn*, 1 Mer. 626 ; *In re Marsden's Trusts*, 4 Drew. 594) ; where an appointment was made to one of
the children in consideration of her having agreed, out of part of the

sum appointed, to pay her father's debts (*Farmer* v. *Martin*, 2 Sim.
502; and see *Thomson* v. *Simpson*, 2 D. & W. 459; 8 Ir. Eq. Rep. 55,
59; *Askham* v. *Barker*, 12 Beav. 499; *Conolly* v. *M'Dermott*, Beat.
601; Sugd. Prop. 513; *Jackson* v. *Jackson*, Dru. 91; 7 C. & F. 977;
Carver v. *Richards*, 27 Beav. 488; 1 De G. F. & Jo. 548), or where
the appointment is expressed to be made in payment of a debt: *Reid*
v. *Reid*, 25 Beav. 469. In *Arnold* v. *Hardwick*, 7 Sim. 343, Sir L.
Shadwell, V. C., even held that an antecedent bargain between a father
and two of his children, that if the appointment were made in their
favour they would lend the fund to their father, would vitiate the appointment.

An appointment to a child, although not for the advantage of the
appointor, will be invalid, if it be not made bona fide. Thus, in *Salmon*
v. *Gibbs* (3 De G. & Sm. 343), the dónee of a power of appointment
among his children, to whom it was given in default of appointment,
had only two daughters, and appointed nearly the whole of the fund to
one of them, who was unmarried, on an understanding, but without
any positive agreement, that the appointee would re-settle one moiety
of it on trust for the separate use of the other daughter, who was married, exclusively of her husband, *and after her death on trust
for her children. A re-settlement was accordingly made without
the privity of the married daughter, who did not hear of the transaction until several years after. It was held by Sir J. L. Knight Brnce,
V. C., on the suit of her husband, that the appointment was invalid,
and a settlement was directed to be made of his wife's share.

[*386]

Moreover, where an appointment is exercised with the view of defeating the object of the power, it will be invalid, although the objectionable arrangement has not been made known to the appointee, if the
appointment was made by the appointor relying upon the moral influence which his wishes, when made known to the appointee, would exercise over him, in carrying out such arrangement. See in *Re Marsden's
Trusts*, 4 Drew. 594. There a married woman having power to appoint
a fund (of which she received the income for her life), among her
children, appointed the whole fund at her death to her eldest daughter.
It appeared in evidence that the married woman, considering that her
husband was unjustly excluded from any interest under the settlement,
intended to exercise her power by appointing the whole property to
her eldest daughter, upon condition that upon attaining her majority
she should give certain interests to her father: but when advised that
such an appointment would on the face of it be invalid, she exercised
her power by giving the whole of the property to her eldest daughter,
under an arrangement with her husband that on her death the daughter
should be informed by her father of the intention with which the appointment was made, and so be induced to carry out the intention. Sir
R. T. Kindersley, V. C., held the appointment bad, as a fraud on the

power. "In some of the cases which have been cited," said his Honor, "there has been a direct bargain between the donee of the power and the person in whose favour it is exercised, under which the donee of the power was himself to derive a benefit; and certainly there has been nothing of that kind in this case. In my opinion, however, it is not necessary that the appointee should be privy to the transaction, because the design to defeat the purpose for which the power was created will stand just the same, whether the appointee was aware of it or not; and the case of *Wellesley* v. *Mornington* (2 K. & J. 143) shows that it is not necessary, in order to bring the case within the scope of the jurisdiction on which this Court acts, that the appointee should be aware of the intentions of the appointment, or of its being actually made. Neither is it necessary that the object should be the personal benefit of the *donee of the power. If the design of the donee in exercising the power is to confer a benefit, not upon himself [*387] actually, but upon some other person not being an object of the power, that motive just as much interferes with and defeats the purpose for which the trust was created, as if it had been for the personal benefit of the donee himself." See also *Ranking* v. *Barnes*, 12 W. R. (V. C. K.) 565; *Topham* v. *The Duke of Portland*, 31 Beav. 525; 1 De G. Jo. & Sm. 517: 11 Ho. Lo. 32, nom. *The Duke of Portland* v. *Topham; Topham* v. *Duke of Portland*, 5 L. R. Ch. App. 40. But see *Proby* v. *Landor*, 28 Beav. 504.

Although questions of this nature generally arise upon a fraudulent arrangement between husband and wife, or between parent and child, the interference of equity is by no means confined to cases in which the donee and object of the power stand in that relation towards each other; for an arrangement between any person having a power, even although he may have been by a voluntary deed the original donor of the power, and any of the objects of it, in fraud of the original intention with which the power was created, will render an appointment void in equity. Thus, in *Lee* v. *Fernie*, 1 Beav. 483, A. B., being desirous of settling property on the female descendants then in existence of C. D., by a voluntary deed reciting this desire, and that certain persons therein named were the only descendants then living of C. D., settled a part of the property on the persons so named, and reserved to himself a power of appointing the remaining part of the property amongst such several persons before named, which, in default of appointment, was given to those several persons. A. B. afterwards discovered that there were other descendants in existence, of C. D., who had been omitted, and to remedy the omission, he appointed a part of the fund to an object of the power, upon his executing bonds for the payment to the persons newly discovered of the amount when received. Lord Langdale, M. R., held, that the appointment was void. "It certainly seems," said his Lordship, " a hard thing that he, the author of this gift, and the owner of this property, could not do this; but he had declared a trust—he had said that it should belong to certain persons—that the power he had reserved should be exercised for the benefit of certain persons only; and I quite agree with those who advised him, that it was not competent for him, of his own authority, to alter that destination of his property." And see *Topham* v. *The Duke of Portland*, 1 De. G. Jo. & Sm. 517.

As in all other cases imputing fraud, the burden of proof lies on the person who seeks to set aside *an appointment as fraudulent. [*388] Thus in *Campbell* v. *Home*, 1 Y. & C. C. C. 664, where a lady who had a life interest in a fund, with power to appoint to one or more of her children, exclusively of the others, appointed the whole to one child, who had attained the age of twenty-one, and assigned her life interest to such child, one of the trustees refused to join in the transfer to the daughter. Sir J. L. Knight Bruce, V. C., upon a bill being filed against the trustee by the daughter, held that he was bound to join in the transfer. " What may be the intention," said his Honor, " of this lady in regard to the disposition of her money, is not a question with which the Court has to deal. If it can even be shown that this deed was executed from improper motives, those who are interested in doing so can apply to set it aside." So in *Askham* v. *Barker*, 17 Beav. 37, a tenant for life had the power of appointing the settled property amongst such of his children as he should think fit. The trustees had in breach of trust lent him part of the trust monies, without taking any security. Afterwards the tenant for life appointed to his daughters the money so lent, and 500*l.* in exclusion of his son. Contemporaneously the daughters exchanged the sum so appointed for an estate of the father, and then the old trustee retired. Sir John Romilly, M. R., held that there was no fraud on the power, as the estate was worth the amount given in exchange. See also *M'Queen* v. *Farquhar*, 11 Ves. 467; *Green* v. *Pulsford*, 2 Beav. 70; *Mills* v. *Spear*, 3 Ir. Ch. Rep. 304; *Pickles* v. *Pickles*, 9 W. R. (V. C. K.) 396; *Ib.* (L. J.) 763; *Pares* v. *Pares*, 33 L. J. (N. S.) Ch. 215.

A question sometimes arises, whether a fraudulent arrangement as to part of the property appointed vitiates the appointment in toto of such part merely to which the fraud extends. In *Daubney* v. *Cockburn*, 1 Mer. 626, this question was fully considered. In that case there was a voluntary settlement of personal property, in trust for such one or more of his children as the settlor should appoint. He appointed to one child exclusively, upon a secret understanding that she should assign a part of the fund to, or in favor of a stranger. It was contended upon the authority of *Lane* v. *Page*, and the principal case, that the appointment was only void as to the part of the fund agreed by the daughter to be assigned. However, Sir W. Grant, M. R., held the appointment void in toto. " Upon principle," said his Honor, " I do not see how any part of a fraudulent agreement can be supported, except where some consideration has been given that cannot be restored, and it has consequently become impossible to rescind the transaction in toto, and to replace the parties in the same situation."

But where the fair inference from the facts is, that the appointor *before* the execution of an appointment intended to derive to himself a benefit therefrom, the burden rests on those who support the transaction to show that the intention had been abandoned at the time of the execution of the deed: *Humphrey* v. *Olver*, 7 W. R. (L. J.) 334; 28 L. J. (N. S.) Ch. 406.

Where the donee of a power intends to appoint, and the appointee intends to settle the property, the appointment will be valid, although the appointee by a deed executed soon after, or even by the same deed, settles the property upon persons who are not objects of the power. This often takes place when a parent, on the marriage of a child, makes an appointment in favour of the child, who is the object of the power, and the child either by the same or a subsequent deed, settles the property upon (amongst others) her intended husband and the children of the marriage, who are no objects of the power. See *Routledge* v. *Dorril*, 2 Ves. jun. 357; *Langstone* v. *Blackmore*, Amb. *289; *West* v. *Berney*, 1 Russ. & My. 431; *White* v. *St. Barbe*, 1 V. & B. 399; *Wade* v. *Paget*, 1 Bro. C. C. 363; *Irwin* v. *Irwin*, 10 Ir. Ch. Rep. 29; *Sed vide Trollope* v. *Routledge*, 1 De G. & Sm. 662; *Salmon* v. *Gibbs*, 3 De G. & Sm. 343; *In re Gosset's Settlement*, 19 Beav. 529, 537; *Fitzroy* v. *The Duke of Richmond*, 27 Beav. 190. [*389].

And where, after an appointment made by a father to his daughter previous to marriage, the intended husband in the marriage settlement gave up to the father an interest in the sum appointed, to which otherwise he (the husband) would be entitled, by his marital right, the appointment has been held not to be thereby invalidated; at any rate, where the father was not, on making it, influenced by what the husband gave up to him. See *Cooper* v. *Cooper*, 5 L. R. Ch. App. 203. There by a settlement made on the marriage of Mr. Thomas Daniell and Mrs. Daniell, funds were settled after the death of the survivor of them in trust for all and every of the children of the marriage, as they should jointly or as the survivor should appoint; and in default of appointment, in trust for all the children in equal shares. Upon the marriage, in 1834, of Sophia, one of their daughters, then under age, to Captain England, Mr. and Mrs. Daniell appointed a portion of the funds in her favour, and Mr. Daniell executed a bond for payment of an equal sum to her trustees in or before 1842, with interest in the meantime. Subsequently a settlement was executed, the trusts of which were to pay the income of the trust funds to Mr. and Mrs. England successively for life; after the death of the survivor, the principal to go among the children of the marriage; and the ultimate limitation in default of children

of the marriage was " for *Mr. Thomas Daniell, his executors, adminis-*
trators, and assigns." There were children of this marriage, to some
of whom, on their marriage, appointments had been made by Mr. and
Mrs. England. Upon a bill being filed by the second husband of one
of Mr. and Mrs. Daniell's daughters, praying, amongst other things,
that the appointment to Mrs. England might be declared a fraud upon
the power, and that the fund might be divided as in default of appointment, it was held by Lord Hatherley, L. C., affirming the decision of
Sir W. M. James, V. C. (reported 8 L. R. Eq. 312), that the appointment to Mrs. England, who was an infant at the time of her marriage,
was not corrupt or improper, so as to render the appointment invalid,
inasmuch as the bargain under which Mr. Thomas Daniell reserved to
himself an ultimate interest in the appointed fund, was a bargain between himself and Mr. England, *the intended husband. "It
[*390] is said," observed his Lordship, " that this case falls within
that class of authorities which have decided that a donee of a power
cannot stipulate for any benefit for himself with reference to the exercise of the power; and that if he does so the whole appointment is
vitiated by the consideration that he has not made it with the simple
intention of providing for the children, and that you cannot separate
such part of the transaction as has been done under the influence of
the corrupt bargain from the other part, but the whole appointment
must be held to be void in favour of all those who take in default of
appointment. I should be extremely sorry to say a word that would
tend to break in on a rule so well and so justly established. Undoubtedly there would be considerable difficulty in dealing with a deed of
this description if any such bargain were proved, notwithstanding the
father's making a provision which is said to be equal to or greater in
value than the ultimate reversion which he takes, because it is obvious
that in the event of the husband and wife dying early without issue,
the father might take an interest far greater than anything he has provided. It seems to me, therefore, an exceedingly doubtful transaction
in any way to support. But in the case of Mrs. England's settlement,
the bargain was not to take anything out of the daughter's share; but
the husband says to the father, ' I will settle the fund in this way ; but
in the event of my wife dying, and there being no issue, and any right
accruing to me, except under the settlement, I waive altogether my
marital right, and the fund shall go back to you or the family of my
wife.' I have not found any case which goes *to the extent of over-
throwing a bargain which was not a bargain with the daughter, not a
bargain to induce the father to make the appointment.* In the present
case the deeds are all put before me, and nothing else, without a word
of evidence or explanation, and I am entitled to construe them in a reasonable way, taking into consideration the whole transaction. I find
no authority for saying that this is such a bargain as can be supposed

to have influenced the father's mind in making the appointment, and without which it would not have been made. I put the question as Lord Justice Knight Bruce put it in the course of the argument in *Topham* v. *The Duke of Portland* (1 De G. J. & Sm. 555), 'Would the appointment have been made but for the condition?' The answer is 'Yes.' The appointment is made of a reasonable and proper share, and it is settled reasonably and properly, and the whole result of the settlement takes nothing from the daughter. All that comes to the father is such a claim as he *may have against the husband, so that it shall not go to the husband's family." [*391]

Where, however, the reason of an appointment being made to the appointee arises from a previous contract by him with the donee of the power to settle the property upon persons who are not objects of the power, then the appointment is invalid, as being a fraud upon the power: *Birley* v. *Birley*, 25 Beav. 299; *Pryor* v. *Pryor*, 32 L. J. (N. S.) 731; 33 L. J. (N. S.) 441; 2 De G. J. & S. 33.

The question in all these cases is this, In what character did the appointee take the property? If he took absolutely, he might do with it as he pleased; but if in trust for the donee of the power, and to effect that which it was not within the authority of the donee to effect under the terms of the power, then it is illegal, and amounts to nothing: per Sir J. Romilly, M. R., in *Birley* v. *Birley*, 25 Beav. 308.

As to the costs of trustees declining to make a transfer to a father and child who has just attained his majority, and to whom his father has made an appointment in exclusion of other objects, see *King* v. *King*, 3 Jur. (N. S.) 608; 5 W. R. (V. C. S.) 699; 1 De G. & Jo. 663.

A question sometimes arises, whether a fraudulent arrangement as to part of the property appointed vitiates the appointment in toto, or such part merely to which the fraud extends.

Where a fraudulent appointment has been made in pursuance of a power of jointuring, the wife, in whose favour the power is exercised, being the sole object of the power, it appears to be now settled that the appointment may be severed, and held good to the extent to which the jointress is entitled, but bad with reference to the corrupt and improper use that may be made of the surplus. *Lane* v. *Page*, Amb. 233; *Aleyn* v. *Belchier*, 1 Eden, 138; and *ante*, p. 377; and the remarks of Sir W. Page Wood, V. C., in *Rowley* v. *Rowley*, Kay, 259.

Where, however, the power is to appoint to several objects, an appointment to one of them, fraudulent in part, will ordinarily be set aside in toto. See *Daubeny* v. *Cockburn*, 1 Mer. 626, where this question was fully considered. In that case there was a voluntary settlement of personal property, in trust for such one or more of his children as the settlor should appoint. He appointed to one child exclusively, upon a secret understanding that she should assign a part of the fund to or in favour of a stranger. It was contended, upon the authority of

Lane v. *Page*, and the principal ease, that the appointment was only void as to the part of the fund agreed by the daughter to be assigned.

[*392] However, Sir W. Grant, M. R., held the appointment void *in toto. " Upon principle," said his Honor, " I do not see how any part of a fraudulent agreement can be supported, *except where some consideration has been given that cannot be restored ; and it has, consequently, become impossible to rescind the transaction in toto, and to replace the parties in the same situation.*"

" In the ease of *Lane* v. *Page*, the subsequent marriage formed such a eonsideration on the part of the wife. In the case of *Aleyn* v. *Belchier*, where the appointment was subsequent to the marriage, it can hardly be said to have been deeided that the appointment was good in any part. For it appears, by the registrar's book, that the bill eontained a submission to pay the annuity to the wife, and only sought relief against the other objeets of the appointment."

" In ordinary eases of fraud the whole transaction is undone, and the parties are restored to their original situation. If a partially valuable consideration has been given, its return is seeured as the condition on which equity relieves against the fraud. But in sueh a ease as the present, the appointment of any particular proportion to any particular child, is a purely voluntary aet on the part of the parent; and, although as good, if fairly made, as if the eonsideration were valuable, yet what is there that a Court ean treat as a consideration, whieh must be restored if a fraudulent appointment be set aside, or as incapable of restitution, and, therefore, support the appointment, so far as it is for the ehild's benefit ? To say it is to be supported to that extent, would be to say that the ehild shall have the full benefit of the fraudulent agreement. . . . Either, then, you must hold that a child giving a consideratiou for an appointment in its favour, is guilty of no fraud on the power, or you must wholly set aside the appointment proeured by the fraud. Now, although the father in proposing sueh a bargain is mueh more to blame than the child in acceding to it, still it is impossible to say that an appointment obtained by means of such an agreement is fairly obtained. It is a fraud upon the other objects of the power, who might not, and in all probability would not have been exeluded but for this agreement. It is more particularly a fraud upon those who are entitled in default of appointment ; for non eonstat that the father would have appointed at all, if the ehild had not agreed to the proposed terms." See *Beddoes* v. *Pugh*, 26 Beav. 407, 412.

The distinetion taken by Sir W. Grant seems to be sound in principle ; and appointments to children, in part fraudulent, have ever since, notwithstanding the dieta attributed to Lord *Hardwicke*, in *Lane* v. *Page*, Amb. 235, been set aside in toto. See *Farmer* v. *Martin*, 2 Sim. [*393] 502 ; *Arnold* *v. *Hardwicke*, 7 Sim. 343 ; aud see *Lee* v. *Fernie*, Beav 483.

The general rule, however, laid down in *Daubeny* v. *Cockburn* (1 Mer. 626), that where an appointment is made for a bad purpose, the bad purpose affects the whole appointment, does not, it seems, apply to cases in which the evidence enables the Court to distinguish what is attributable to an authorised from what is attributable to an unauthorized purpose: *Topham* v. *The Duke of Portland*, 1 De G. Jo. & Sm. 517 : *Carver* v. *Richards*, 1 De G. F. & Jo. 548 ; *Rankin* v. *Barnes*, 12 W. R. (V. C. K.) 565 ; and see *Sadler* v. *Pratt*, 5 Sim. 632.

So, where there is a sum of money to be appointed among children, although an appointment to one child may be void on account of a corrupt agreement, an appointment to another child, although by a contemporaneous deed, if it can be severed from the previous appointment, so as not to form part of the same transaction, will be valid: *Rowley* v. *Rowley*, Kay, 242 ; and see *Harrison* v. *Randall*, 9 Hare, 397.

A fraudulent execution of a power will be set aside as against a purchaser for valuable consideration, *with notice* of the fraud: *Palmer* v. *Wheeler*, 2 Ball. & B. 18 ; or even if he had *not notice* of the fraud, if he has not got the legal estate, for then there are only equities to deal with ; and, as observed by Sir W. Grant, " The payment of a money consideration cannot make a stranger become the object of a power created in favour of children ; he can only claim under a valid appointment executed in favour of some or one of the children :" *Daubeny* v. *Cockburn*, 1 Mer. 626, 638.

But a purchaser must, it seems, have actual notice of a fraud upon a power, in order to be affected by it ; circumstances which may give rise to mere grounds of suspicion or probability of fraud are not sufficient. Thus in *McQueen* v. *Farquhar*, 11 Ves. 467, where A. was tenant for life, remainder to his wife for life, with power to appoint to one or more of his children by her, A. entered into a contract with T. for the sale of the estate to him, and afterwards appointed (subject to the life-interest of himself and his wife) the fee simple of their estate to R., the eldest son, who had attained the age of twenty-one; and then A. and his wife, and R. and their son, conveyed the estate to T. in consideration of a sum of money, expressed to be paid to all of them. This appearing upon an abstract, an objection was taken to the title that the appointment by A. in favour of his son R. appeared to have been made under a previous agreement between them ; and that if A. derived any benefit from that agreement, which seemed probable, or even made any previous stipulation that his *son should join [*394] him in a sale, which there appeared the strongest reason to apprehend, it would have been a fraudulent execution of the power. Lord Eldon, however, overruled the objection. " It does not appear," said his Lordship, " that the estate sold for less than its value—that the son got less than the value of his reversionary interest. But the estate becoming his absolutely by the appointment, he by an instrument, affected by nothing but the contents of it, as the owner of the reversion, accedes to the purchase, conveys with his father and mother, in consideration of 8000*l.*, and the parties taking the conveyance pay the money to the father, the mother and the son, to be dealt with according to their respective interests; that is, according to their rights in the land: and, though the contract with T. was only to substitute money for the estate, there was nothing to show that the son was not to receive a due proportion of the money, when the contract was afterwards executed by the deed, in which he joins, and, with his father and mother, receives all the money. Upon the question, therefore, whether those possibilities and probabilities are sufficiently evidenced by anything to show that this is not a good title, my opinion is, that it is a good title:" see also *Cockcroft* v. *Sutcliffe*, 2 Jur. N. S. 333, 25 L. J. Ch. 313; *Laurie* v. *Bankes*, 4 K. & J. 142.

And it seems that the Court would be less disposed to impeach an appointment as fraudulent, after a great lapse of time, and where there have been subsequent dealings with the funds, such, for instance, as subsequent appointments thereof on the marriage of daughters or the establishment of sons in the world: *Cooper* v. *Cooper*, 5 L. R. Ch. App. 203, 212, 213; *S. C.*, 8 L. R. Eq. 312.

Where there is an arrangement for settling the interests of *all* the branches of a family, children may contract *with each other* to give a parent, who had a power to distribute property among them, some advantage, which the parent, without their contract with each other, could not have. Thus, in *Davis* v. *Uphill*, 1 Swanst. 130, an estate being limited, under her marriage settlement, to A. *for life*, with remainder to her children by her deceased husband, in such manner as she should appoint, remainder, in default of appointment, to all the children as tenants in common; an agreement by the children, that on her joining in suffering a recovery, the first use to which the recovery should enure, should be to A. for life, *without impeachment of waste*, is it seems valid in equity; and the Court, therefore, refused to continue an injunction to restrain her from cutting timber. See also *Rhodes* v. *Cook*, 2 S. & S. 488; *Skelton* v. *Flanagan*, 1 Ir. Eq. Rep. 362.

[*395] *But if any such transaction taken as a whole appears not to be a bonâ fide family arrangement, but that it has been entered into in fraud of the power, for the purpose of giving a benefit to a person who was by the donor excluded from being an appointee, or from deriving any advantage from the exercise of the power, it will be held wholly void: *Agassiz* v. *Squire*, 18 Beav. 431.

Where there is no fraud, equity will not advert to the circumstances of anger and resentment, under which it may be alleged that an appointment has been made. See *Vane* v. *Lord Dungannon*, 2 S. & L. 130, where Lord Redesdale said, he did not think it safe to advert to

such objections, as there would be no end of them, if they were admitted as grounds for questioning appointments, since in almost all these
cases, where there has been an inequality in the appointment, something
of that kind has existed. See, also, *Supple* v. *Lowson*, Amb. 729.

If under a power of appointment and selection among children, an
appointment be made upon a condition to be performed by the appointee, not authorised by the power, the appointment will be good, but the
condition void: *Stroud* v. *Norman*, Kay, 313; *Re Lord Sondes' Will*,
2 Sm. & Giff. 416; *Watt* v. *Creke*, 3 Jur. N. S. 56, 3 Sm. & Giff. 362,
and see *Stuart* v. *Lord Castlestuart*, 8 Ir. Ch. Rep. 408.

The principle laid down in *Aleyn* v. *Belchier*, viz., *that a power must
be executed bonâ fide, and for the end designed*, is applicable also to
another class of cases where parents having power to raise portions for
children, and even to fix the time when they are to be raised, will not
be allowed by a Court of equity, as personal representatives of a deceased child, to derive any advantage from an appointment made to the
child during infancy, and while not in want of a portion, especially if
the death of the child, at the time of the appointment was expected.
Thus in *Hinchinbroke* v. *Seymour*, 1 Bro. C. C. 394, a father, under a
power, in a settlement to raise portions to be paid at *such time* as he
should appoint, directed the trustees to raise 10,000*l.* *immediately* for
his daughter, then fourteen years of age, who soon afterwards died; he,
as her administrator, filed a bill against the trustees to have the 10,000*l.*
raised for his own use, but Lord Thurlow dismissed the bill, observing,
" The meaning of a charge for children is that it shall take place when
it shall be wanted; it is contrary to the nature of such a charge to have
it raised before that time. And although the power is, in this case, to
raise it when the parent shall think proper, yet that is only to enable
him to raise it in his own life, if it should be necessary. It would have
been very proper so to do upon the daughter's marriage, *or [*396]
for several other purposes; but this is against the nature of the
power." So, also where a fund was limited to a father for life, with remainder to his children, in such shares as he should appoint, and in default of appointment to the children equally, the father released the
power as to a portion of the funds so as to vest a share of it in himself
as executor of a deceased son, who, in default of appointment, took a
vested interest, the court refused to order the transfer of the share to
the father; *Conyngham* v. *Thurlow*, 1 Russ. & My. 436.

" *The case of Lord Sandwich*," observes Lord Chancellor Sugden,
" where a father, who had a power of appointment among his children,
thinking one of them was in a consumption, appointed to that child, in
order that he might take as the child's administrator, decides that if a
father, having such a power, charges a portion for a child, not because
the child wants it, but because it is sickly and likely to die, the Court
has power to defeat it: " *Keily* v. *Keily*, 5 Ir. Eq. Rep. 442; 4 D. &

W. 55; *S. C.*, cited 11 Ves. 479. See also, *Lord Pawlet's case*, 2 Vent. 366; *Edgeworth* v. *Edgeworth*, Beat. 328; *Gee* v. *Gurney*, 2 Coll. 486; *Wellesley* v. *Earl of Mornington*, 2 K. & J. 143.

An appointment however to an infant child before he wants it, of a sum already set apart, will not be as invalid, merely because the appointor may, in the event of the child's death, derive some benefit from it to the disappointment of those entitled in default of appointment: (*Butcher* v. *Jackson*, 14 Sim. 444 : *Hamilton* v. *Kirwan*, 2 J. & L. 393; *Beere* v. *Hoffmister*, 23 Beav. 101;) à fortiori will the appointment be good if the parent himself can derive no benefit from it, although upon the death of the child the mother takes as his representative to the exclusion of the persons who would have been entitled in default of appointment. Thus in *Fearon* v. *Desbrisay* (14 Beav. 641) a father had power of appointing a fund amongst his children, their shares to vest at such ages as he should appoint, and if he made no appointment, it was to vest in them equally at twenty-one or marriage, and there was a gift over, if there should be no child entitled under the trusts or power: on the birth of a son, the father executed the power by giving the whole to such son, but afterwards upon an expected addition to his family, he, being in a weak state of health, revoked the former appointment and executed the power in favour of *all* his children *who should be living at his death*, equally. The father then died. It was held by Sir John Romilly, M. R., that the appointment was good, as not being a fraud on the power, and that upon the death of one of the children the mother was entitled to her share as administratrix. "To say," observed his Honor, "that because the settlement specifies the manner in which the fund is to go if unappointed, the power must necessarily be partially cut down, so as to prevent the donee from disappointing those to whom the property is to go in default of appointment, does not appear to me a fair conclusion . . . . In the present case it is manifest that the appointor could *gain no personal advantage for himself*, by [*397] *the mode in which he has executed the power; for the persons in whose favour the appointment is to take effect could not be ascertained until his own death. All the cases therefore in which the donee obtained an advantage by the execution of the power may be excluded from my consideration. I cannot speculate on what other objects he might have had, if I find that he had the absolute power of appointment amongst his children, and that he exercised it in such a manner that he could not obtain any personal advantage from it."

Although it would doubtless be a fraud upon the trusts if trustees having power of advancing moneys to an infant under powers of maintenance and advancement, laid out money, for instance, in the purchase of a commission in the army, with the intention that the infant should by sale of the commission obtain the money for other purposes, that will not be the case where the advance has been bona fide made, al-

though the infant is soon afterwards obliged to sell his commission in
consequence of his debts, and he or his assignees for value, if without
notice of any impropriety in the sale, will be entitled to the proceeds
thereof: *Lawrie* v. *Bankes*, 4 K. & J. 142.

A tenant for life may clearly release a power to appoint amongst
children (*West* v. *Berney*, 1 Russ. & My. 434; *Horner* v. *Swann*, T. &
R. 430; *Smith* v. *Death*, 2 Madd. 371; *Bickley* v. *Guest*, 1 Russ. & My.
446; 1 Bligh, 15; *Davies* v. *Huguenin*, 1 Hem. & Miller, 730), or may
covenant with a mortgagee of his life interest not to exercise a power
of charging the estate with portions for younger children (*Hurst* v.
Hurst, 16 Beav. 372, and see *Miles* v. *Knight*, 17 L. J. (N. S.) Ch. 458;
12 Jur. 666), or with creditors to make a certain appointment by will
in favour of a child an object of the power: *Coffin* v. *Cooper*, 13 W. R.
(V. C. K.) 571.

But no effect will be given to a release of a power by a father, so as
to vest property in himself, which was intended for his children; or in
other words, a power given for a particular purpose will not be allowed
by a fraudulent circuity to be exercised for a different purpose. Thus,
in *Cuninghame* v. *Thurlow*, 1 Russ. & My. 436, where a fund was limited to a father for life, with remainder to his children, in such shares
as he should appoint, and in default of appointment to the children
equally, the father released the power as to a portion of the fund, so as
to vest a share of it in himself as executor of a deceased son, who, in
default of appointment, took a vested interest. Sir L. Shadwell, V. C.,
although he was of opinion that the power was extinguished by the release, nevertheless decided that the Court ought not to give effect to
the release, so far as it operated *to vest a share of the fund in
the father, who was the donee of the power. In the case, how- [*398]
ever, of *Smith* v. *Houblon*, 26 Beav. 482, a father had an exclusive
power of appointment in favour of his children over a fund, which in
default of appointment was limited to them equally, and as representative of a deceased son he was, in default of appointment, beneficially
entitled to one-third of the fund. The father released the power to his
mortgagees. A bill was filed by the mortgagees, praying, amongst
other things, for a declaration that the deceased son's share, on the
release of the power, became vested in the mortgagees. Counsel for
the mortgagees distinguished the case from *Cuninghame* v. *Thurlow*,
inasmuch as there the donee of the power, by the deed releasing it,
obtained for himself a personal benefit, to which he would not otherwise have been entitled; whereas in the case under consideration, the
release was to the mortgagees, as against whom the mortgagor could
not execute the power in derogation of his own grant. It was held by
Sir John Romilly, M. R., that the power had been effectually released,
and he declared the rights of the parties consequent thereon.

If the consent of another person to the exercise of a power is requisite, and that consent is obtained by misrepresentation, the appointment will be set aside. Thus, in *Scroggs* v. *Scroggs*, Amb. Blunt's ed. 272, and App. 812, a case which falls entirely within the principle of *Aleyn* v. *Belchier*, a father was tenant for life, with remainder to the use of such of his son and sons as he, with *the consent* of the trustees, or the survivor of them, should appoint, and, in default of appointment, to his first son in tail male. The father, by misrepresenting his eldest son to the surviving trustee as extravagant and undutiful, *prevailed upon him to consent* to an appointment to a younger son. Upon a bill being filed by the eldest son, it was proved that the son was dutiful and not extravagant, and that the father, from improper motives, had misrepresented him to the trustee. The appointment was set aside by Lord Hardwicke, who observed, that if the trustee and father had met fairly, and without imposition, and considered the family circumstances, and had executed the power for such reasons as biased their judgment, the Court would not interfere; but that, upon the whole, he was of opinion that it was a power accompanied with a trust, and that it was executed by an imposition on the trustee, who was designed to be a check on the father.

It seems that where in a marriage settlement there is a power of revocation and new appointment, with the consent of the trustees, [*399] *it will be presumed that it was the intention of the parties that such consent was only to be given for the benefit of the objects of the settlement, and that if it be given merely for the purpose of putting money into the hands of the father, the revocation and new appointment will be considered as a fraud upon the power, and consequently void. See *Eland* v. *Baker*, 29 Beav. 137; there, by a marriage settlement, land was settled by the father of the lady to the wife for life, remainder to the husband for life, remainder to the children of the marriage. And there was a power to the father of the lady and the husband and wife, with the consent of the trustees in writing, by deed absolutely to revoke and make void all or any of the uses or trusts, and also by the same or any other deed to limit and declare new uses and trusts in substitution for those revoked. The father of the lady, and the husband and wife, with the consent of the trustees, revoked the settlement so far as was necessary, and appointed the property to one of the trustees in fee to secure a sum of money advanced to the husband. The estate was afterwards sold under a power contained in the mortgage deed. It was held by Sir John Romilly, M. R., that a good title could not be made under it. " I do not," said his Honor, " dispute the proposition, that a person may in a marriage settlement introduce a proviso which shall simply put an end to the deed. . . . . But I consider this power of revocation to be for the purpose of re-limiting the estate, and re-limiting the estate to any new trusts and declarations. How must the estate be re-limited? To what trusts and with what declarations? The answer is, to trusts for the benefit of the persons who are the cestuis que trust of the instrument according to the true scope and intent of the deed itself. . . . . How could it be said that this is a fair exercise of the discretion of the trustees in favour of their cestuis que trust, if they exercise it in such a manner so as totally to defeat the whole beneficial interest of those persons whom, as trustees, they are bound to protect?" And after observing in addition to this upon the objection that the mortgage was to one of the trustees who became thereby pro tanto a purchaser of the estate, his Honor said it was impossible to force the title upon a purchaser.

Where a person makes an appointment which is afterwards set aside as being in fraud of a power, the question is undetermined whether in the event of his not having reserved a right of revocation and new appointment he can again exercise his power. *The Duke of Portland* v. *Topham*, 11 Ho. Lo. Ca. 32.

It is, however, clear that where an appointment has been set *aside by reason of what has taken place between the donee of a power and an appointee, a second appointment by the [*400] same donee to the same appointee cannot be sustained, otherwise than by clear proof on the part of the appointee that the second appointment is perfectly free from the original taint which attached to the first : *Topham* v. *The Duke of Portland*, 5 L. R. Ch. App. 40.

It has been intimated in a recent case, where a person was donee of a power to be exercised only by a will, in favour of children, that a covenant on the marriage of a child to exercise the power by appointing a certain share in favour of such child, may be illegal and void— upon the ground that the power is fiduciary, to be exercised by will only ; so that up to the last moment of his life, the donee was to have the power of dealing with the fund as he should think it his duty to deal with it, having regard to the then wants, position, merits, and necessities of his children : per Sir W. M. James, V. C., in *Thacker* v. *Key*, 8 L. R. Eq. 414, 415; where, however, it was not necessary to decide the point. In the subsequent case of *Bulteel* v. *Plummer*, 6 L. R. Ch. App. 169, Lord Hatherley, C., said, that to hold an appointment made pursuant to such a covenant " bad as a device, would be to strain the doctrine as to improper appointments too far."

There is another class of cases to be noticed, in which Courts of equity have interposed, upon the same principle, but not with the same beneficial results as in *Aleyn* v. *Belchier ;* viz., where a person having a power of appointing property amongst a class, although with full discretion as to the amount of their shares, has exercised it by appointing to one or more of the objects a merely nominal share ; such an appointment, although valid at law, will, if executed previous to the passing of 1 Will. 4, c. 46, be set aside as *illusory*, not being exercised bona fide for the end designed by the donor. To illustrate the doctrine of illusory appointments, suppose A. had a power to distribute 100,000*l*. amongst a class in such shares and proportions as he should appoint, and he gave one of the class five shillings only, that would be at law a good execution of the power: *Morgan* v. *Surman*, 1 Taunt. 289. But such an appointment, or an appointment of ten guineas, or of any sum merely nominal, taking into consideration the amount to be distributed, and the number of persons amongst whom it is distributable, will, if executed previous to the passing of 1 Will. 4, c. 46, be held void in equity as illusory. It would, indeed, be perfectly competent to the donee of a power to make a very unequal distribution of the fund, provided that the inequality was [*401] not so great as to lay the *appointment open to the objection of its being merely nominal and illusory, and, consequently, a fraud upon the donor of the power, who, it would be presumed, intended that each of the objects of the power should take a substantial share. Amongst the earlier cases on this subject, see *Gibson* v. *Kinven*, 1 Vern. 66; *Wall* v. *Thurborne*, 1 Vern. 355, 414, and *Cragrave* v. *Perrost* there cited; *Astry* v. *Astry*, Prec. Ch. 256; *Maddison* v. *Andrew*, 1 Ves. 57; *Coleman* v. *Seymour*, 1 Ves. 211; *Vanderzee* v. *Aclom*, 4 Ves. 771; *Spencer* v. *Spencer*, 5 Ves. 362. The doctrine applies to appointments of real as well as of personal estate: *Pocklington* v. *Bayne*, 1 Bro. C. C. 450.

Much litigation arose in consequence of the great difficulty of deciding what was a substantial, and not merely an illusory share; and great dissatisfaction with the doctrine was expressed by the most eminent judges, who endeavoured, in many cases, to narrow it. In *Wilson* v. *Piggott*, 2 Ves. jun. 351, where there was a sum of 4000*l*. to be appointed amongst four persons, Lord Alvanley said, that an appointment of 250*l*. to one of them would have been good. In *Kemp* v. *Kemp*, 5 Ves. 849, a person having a power of appointing nearly 1900*l*. among three children, appointed 10*l*. to one child, 50*l*. to another, and the remainder to the third. Lord Alvanley, M. R., in his judgment, observed, " I should hardly have conceived that 50*l*. could be considered a substantial part; but the sum of 10*l*. to the daughter was evidently meant to be no gift, the mother merely supposing herself to be under the necessity of giving something to each. . . . I am bound to say the bequest of 10*l*. was clearly meant as an illusion, and not as an execution; therefore the execution is void. It is vain now to lament, as I have in many other cases, that this Court did not follow the rule of law; but now this is so settled, that no judge will, and certainly I will not, presume to go against it. The Court must decide whether the share is substantial or not." In the celebrated case of *Butcher* v. *Butcher*, 9 Ves. 382, the objects of the power were nine in number, and the fund to be appointed amongst them about 17,000*l*. To some of the objects of the power shares of 200*l*. Three per Cents. only were given. Sir W. Grant, M. R., held the appointment not to be illusory, but, like Lord Alvanley, strongly disapproved of this doctrine of equity. " To say," observed his Honor, " that under such a power an illusory share must not be given, or that a substantial share must be given, is rather to raise a question than to establish a rule. What is an illusory share, and what is a substantial share? Is it to be judged of upon a mere statement of the sum given, without reference to the amount of the fortune which is the *subject of the power? If so, what is the sum that must be given, [402] to exclude the inference of the Court? What is the limit of the amount at which it ceases to be illusory, and begins to be substantial? If it is to be considered with reference to the amount of the fortune, what is the proportion, either of the whole or of the share that would belong to each upon an equal division? In terms, the power, though limited as to objects, is discretionary as to shares. A Court of law says, no object can be excluded, but there it stops; it does not attempt to correct any, the extremest, inequality in the distribution. . . . As no case has been found, in which a sum of this amount has been declared illusory, there is no ground upon which I think myself justified in determining that this is an invalid appointment." So in *Bax* v. *Whitbread*, 16 Ves. 15, where the fund to be appointed between two children, objects of the power, was 2500*l.* Old South Sea Annuities, and 100*l.* stock was given to one child, and 2400*l.* to the other, Sir W. Grant, M. R., referring to his decision in *Butcher* v. *Butcher*, held that the appointment was not illusory. So, also, in *Mocatta* v. *Lousada*, 12 Ves. 123, the fund was 2500*l.;* the objects of the power were five in number: to some he gave only a share of 33*l.* 6*s.* 8*d.* Sir W. Grant, M. R., held the appointment not illusory. " I adhere," said his Honor, " to the rule I laid down in *Butcher* v. *Butcher*, that I will go as far as I am bound by authority, but no farther. Show me a case in which a specific sum, or an equal proportion of what would be the share of each object of the appointment upon an equal division, has been held to be illusory, and I will in the same case make the same decision. But, where I am deprived of the guidance, or freed from the compulsion, of authority, I will not hold any appointment to be invalid upon that ground of objection. The case of *Kemp* v. *Kemp* is not an authority for this case; for the discussion of that turned not upon the 50*l.*, but upon the 10*l.* All that is decided in that case is, that the appointment of 10*l.* was, under the circumstances, illusory, therefore I must hold this appointment to be good, adhering to the rule I laid down in *Butcher* v. *Butcher ;* for this sum of 33*l.* 6*s.* 8*d.* is not the same specific sum, or the same proportion of the share of each child, upon an equal division, that has been, in any former instance, held to be illusory." See, also, *Duke* v. *Sylvester*, 12 Ves. 126, where his Honor adhered to the same rule.

Lord Eldon, however, although he affirmed the decision of the Master of the Rolls, in *Bax* v. *Whitbread* and *Butcher* v. *Butcher* (see 16 Ves. 15, and 1 V. & B. 79), disapproved of the rule there laid down by the

[*403] Master of the Rolls. *In the former of these cases his Lordship observes, " I should pause on giving judgment, if bound to decide upon those authorities with reference to the principle stated in these late cases, now before me, which, in effect (and it would be better to do it in words), destroys all the authorities, as no two cases will probably ever be the same. The sum of 50l. being given in one family, and by one will, it is difficult to imagine that the identity of the sum or the proportion, can afford the ground of determination in another family and upon another will. The motives, also, must be furnished by the same circumstances, whether good conduct or misconduct; a provision by a parent or by a third person; circumstances, if the Court is at liberty to regard them, of utility; for instance, in the case of a power to appoint between two children, and the situation in life of one of them, the effect of the appointment may enable him to do more for the other, than if he had an equal share. If, therefore, it is established that the Court has this authority to consider, whether the execution of such a trust, or power coupled with a trust, is reasonable, it seems to me better to deny the doctrine at once, than to lay down a rule that will destroy it in effect; looking only to sums and figures; excluding circumstances, unless in the same case; and considering in each case, merely, whether the motives and circumstances by which the judgment was so regulated, as among the different objects, were the same. . . . . The result is, that from the time of Lord Nottingham the Court has taken upon itself the duty of exercising this discretion; and I should feel great embarrassment, if, on account of the difficulty and the apprehension of not well exercising it, I should step aside from the path of my predecessors, and be deterred from doing it as well as I can; confining myself to the inquiry, whether a case precisely the same had ever occurred; taking as my rule of acting, that circumstance, instead of the principle decided by former cases."

If a share not illusory comes to one of the objects in default of appointment, it will be considered as an appointment, and no question of illusion will arise: *Wilson* v. *Piggott*, 2 Ves. jun. 351.

An appointment to some only of the objects of a power which does not authorize an exclusive appointment may be rendered valid, by the partial failure of the appointment in consequence of its being, to the extent of which it fails, a fraud upon the power: *Ranking* v. *Barnes*, 12 W. R (V. C. K.) 565. If, under a power to appoint amongst all the children, a part is well appointed to some, leaving a share not illusory, which is afterwards appointed, so as entirely to exclude one, the last [*404] *appointment only will be void: *Wilson* v. *Piggott*, 2 Ves. jun. 355.

Formerly, an illusory appointment might be justified, and equity would not give relief against it when misbehaviour was shown in the child to whom such illusory share was given: *Maddison* v. *Andrew*, 1

Ves. 57 ; but this doctrine was overruled in *Kemp* v. *Kemp*, 5 Ves. 855 ; 1 V. & B. 97.

Where, however, gross inequality is accounted for by the situation of the children, and is humane and wise and discreet, the Court will not call it illusory : *Boyle* v. *The Bishop of Peterborough*, 1 Ves. jun. 310, per Lord Thurlow. Thus, an appointment of a very small share to a son, who is an uncertificated bankrupt, would not be looked upon as illusory : *Bax* v. *Whitbread*, 16 Ves. 15. So, if a parent has made a provision for a child, an appointment of a very small share to that child would not be held illusory : *Bristowe* v. *Ward*, 2 Ves. jun. 336 ; *Smith* v. *Lord Camelford*, 2 Ves. jun. 698 ; *Long* v. *Long*, 5 Ves. 445 ; *Spencer* v. *Spencer*, 5 Ves. 367. The provision, it seems, must have been made by the donee of the power : *Mocatta* v. *Lousada*, 12 Ves. 123 ; though Lord Alvanley thought that the same result would follow if the provision was made aliunde : *Vanderzee* v. *Aclom*, 4 Ves. 785 ; and see 16 Ves. 25 ; *Lysaght* v. *Royse*, 2 S. & L. 151, and 1 V. & B. 97. It is clear, however, that a provision moving from the donor of the power will not be sufficient : *Kemp* v. *Kemp*, 5 Ves. 861.

The interference of Courts of equity, in cases of illusory appointments, was so unsatisfactory in its results, that the Legislature at length interferred, and by stat. 1 Will. 4, c. 46, passed June 16, 1830, it was enacted that no appointment, which from and after the passing of the Act should be made in exercise of any power or authority to appoint any property, real or personal, amongst several objects, should be invalid, or impeached in equity, on the ground that an unsubstantial, illusory, or nominal share only should be thereby appointed to, or left unappointed to, devolve upon any one or more of the objects of such power ; but that every such appointment should be valid and effectual in equity, as well as at law, notwithstanding that any one or more of the objects should not thereunder, or in default of such appointment take more than an unsubstantial, illusory, or nominal share of the property subjected to such power ; provided that nothing in the Act contained should prejudice or affect any provision in any deed, will, or other instrument creating any such power as aforesaid, which should declare the amount of the share or shares from which no object of the power should be excluded ; and provided also *that [*405] nothing in the Act contained should be construed, deemed or taken at law or in equity to give any other validity, force, or effect to any appointment than such appointment would have had if a substantial share of the property affected by the power had been thereby appointed to, or left unappointed to, devolve upon any object of such power. See *In re Stone's Estate*, 3 I. R. Eq. 621.

Lord St. Leonards has observed, with reference to this Act, that, " where it is intended that a party shall have a power to divide a fund among several objects in *substantial* proportions, according to his discretion, but shall not be at liberty to give a merely nominal share to any, the smallest sum which the person creating the power should wish each of the objects in any events to have, should be named, and it should be declared that the donee of the power shall not be at liberty to appoint a less sum to any of the objects.'' (1 Pow. 545.)

The statute as to illusory appointments (1 W. 4, c. 46) has a retrospective operation on any power of appointment in esse at the time of the passing of the Act, but executed afterwards (*Reid* v. *Reid*, 25 Beav. 469, 480); it does not, however, make valid an appointment which previous to the Act would have been invalid, in consequence of the exclusion of certain objects of a power, not authorizing an exclusive appointment: *Minchin* v. *Minchin*, 3 Ir. Ch. Rep. 167.

[In the exercise of powers of appointment and dismissal, it is generally more prudent to state the conclusions arrived at, without giving the reasoning which led to them, for if the power be honestly exercised, the court will not interfere, while if the reason does not justify the conclusion, the court may correct it; *Rex* v. *Archbishop of Canterbury*, 15 East, 117; *Re Beloved Wilkes Charity*, 3 Mac. & Gor. 440; *S. C.*, more fully reported, 7 Eng. Law & Eq. Rep. 85. Thus in the very recent case of *Hayman* v. *The Governors of Rugby School*, Law Rep., 18 Equity, 28, which attracted much attention, the plaintiff, while acting as head master of Rugby School, received a notification from the defendants, its governing body, that they had resolved to dismiss him by virtue of their powers under the Public Schools Act of 31 & 32 Vict. c. 118, whose 13th section provided, that " The head master of every school to which this act applies shall be appointed by, and hold his office at the pleasure of the governing body." The plaintiff thereupon filed his bill to restrain the defendants from removing him, or electing any one as his successor, alleging that his dismissal was due to the influence of certain members of the board, who, being hostile to him, had formed a scheme to dismiss him. The defendants having demurred for want of equity, the demurrer was, after extended argument, sustained, the court (Malins, V. C.) holding t at, by the terms of the act, the plaintiff held his office at the mere pleasure of the defendants, and that " The clear result of the numerous authorities cited on both sides of the argument is, that all arbitrary powers, such as the power of dismissal, by exercising their pleasure, which is given to this governing body, may be exercised without assigning any reason, provided they are fairly and honestly exercised, which they always will be presumed to have been until the contrary is shown, and that the burden of showing the contrary lies upon those who object to the manner in which the power has been exercised. No reasons need be given, but if they are given, the court will look at their sufficiency."]

" The general rule of law is, that the execution of a power must be according to the substantial intention and purpose of the party creating the power; not restraining or lessening it by a narrow and rigid construction; nor by a loose and extended interpretation, dispensing with the substance of what was meant to be performed. Powers are to be construed equitably in a court of law as well as in a court of equity. And the general intention must be carried into effect, though it may defeat a particular intent." Per Thompson, C. J., in *Jackson* v. *Veeder*, 11 Johnson, 169, 171. But where a power is discretionary a court of law can grant no relief, and impose no penalty, in case of an unreasonable exercise of the discretion; the remedy is only in equity. In *Cloud* v. *Martin*, 1 Devereux & Battle's Law R. 397, a testator had directed that his grandson should be "raised and taken care of at the direction and care of his son, J. M.," and should be instructed in the English, Latin, and Greek languages; and he appointed J. M. one of his administrators. An action on behalf of the grandson was brought upon the administration bond, for failing to supply the grandson with funds for his support and education according to the will; but the Court held that the provision to be made for the grandson was entirely discretionary with J. M., and that

his determination was binding at law. " Courts of equity," said Ruffin, C. J., " relieve against conditions, and prevent advantage being unconscientiously taken of their breach or non-performance; and also control the unreasonable exercise by one, of a power or discretion which may affect the interest of another person. The propriety of assuming to review and reverse the determination of one to whom a testator has given a discretion, absolute in terms, upon the ground that it was not a reasonable and just determination, though arrived at after fair inquiry, and full deliberation, has not escaped animadversion; since it makes the instrument read so as to confer on the Chancellor the discretion which the maker of it declares he reposes exclusively in the individual selected by himself. But the jurisdiction is established; and upon the facts now appearing, relief would certainly be granted in equity, there being no cause whatever assigned for the neglect to provide for the testator's grandson; and such neglect or refusal without cause, is, by itself, unreasonable; and it does not appear that any fund was in fact provided. But a court of law is bound by the terms of the will; and the acts, right or wrong, of him to whom the testator gives the authority to decide, must stand as parts of the will. It is the testator's bounty, and must be taken subject to the restrictions by him imposed. If he puts it upon the will and judgment of another person, that will, however vicious, and that judgment, however erroneous and unreasonable, cannot be controverted at law. If the law itself confers an authority or discretion, it means a reasonable, and not an arbitrary one; and guards its faithful exercise, by giving damages for its malicious abuse; but a court and jury cannot limit a discretion, which parties for themselves declare shall be unlimited, or to which they have affixed no limit. Damages cannot be given for the neglect to exercise it, for there is no legal obligation to do so. Nor can its exercise upon mistaken, unreasonable or dishonest motives, be set at nought as not being, for those reasons, obligatory; because the motives do not impeach the legal power but only affect the conscience of the party. The Court is unable to find a case of such jurisdiction at law, and knows of no principle on which to base it." And this controlling power in a court of equity was further recognized, in *Haynesworth* v. *Cox*, Harper's Equity, 117, 119, where a testator gave to his niece four shares, " or in lieu thereof one thousand dollars, as his brother (the executor) might think best." It was decided by Dessaussure, Ch., that the testator must be considered as meaning " best " for the legatee. "This reasonable construction," he added, " seems also to be in accordance with a rule of equity, which has long prevailed and is of considerable extent and application. It is, that where the power of electing is given to a trustee, as to the rights of a third person, the trustee is bound to exercise that power most beneficially for the *cestui que use*. Now an executor invested with such a power, is trustee for the legatee, and is bound to follow this rule of equity; and he shall not exercise it illusorily. This principle is illustrated by many decided cases which are familiar. See 5 Ves. 848; *Kemp* v. *Kemp*, 16 Ves. 15; *Bax* v. *Whitbread*, 11 Ves. 479; *M'Queen* v. *Farquhar*." [Hence, when a power to appoint among brothers and sisters and their children, in such proportions as the donee of the power should think fit, was exercised by appointing the whole to one, the appointment was held void and effect given to the purpose of the testator by a distribution among all; *Lippincott* v. *Ridgway*, 2 Stockton's Chancery, 164; and the same course would probably have been pursued had the appointment, although professedly to all, been so grossly unequal as to be in fact a provision only for one; *Melvin* v. *Melvin*, 6 Maryland, 530.]

But the equitable jurisdiction to control the exercise of discretionary power of appointment among several persons, has been viewed with strong disfavor, if not entirely condemned, in some of the courts of this country. In *Cowles et al.* v. *Brown et al.*, 4 Call, 477, where there was a power, after a life estate, to give among the nephews of the testator, "in such manner and proportion as he (the donee of the power) shall think proper," it was decided that a gift of unequal proportions was not objectionable:

"It was left to him," said Lyons, J., "to make the appointments according to his own discretion; and then, what right has the court to control the execution? The latitude which has been sometimes taken by chancellors in England, has been reprobated, a different course is beginning to manifest itself there, 2 Fonb. Eq. 201; which meets my own approbation." A similar condemnation is passed upon this judicial authority in *Fronty* v. *Fronty*, 1 Bailey's Equity, 518, 529. "Powers may be general, or limited," says O'Neall, J., in delivering the opinion of the court in that case. "In the execution of a general power, there can be no rule but the discretion of the party to whom it is confided. In a limited one, the limitations contained in it constitute the rule by which it is to be executed. In the former, no court can undertake to control that, which the party creating the power intended to leave to the honesty, good faith, and discretion of the person to whom he confided it. In the latter the courts do no more than execute the intention of the party by whom it is created, by declaring the execution of the power contrary to the limitations contained in it, void."

"The doctrine of illusory appointments, which, in England, has been carried to a most unwarrantable length, and is reprobated by the wisest judges, is, nevertheless, predicated on the ground, that the power given has not been executed according to the intention of the testator. This, if it had been con-fined to plain and palpable violations of the intention, as indicated by the words of the power, could have produced no conflict between law and equity. But when it is attempted to control a discretionary power of distribution among children, by saying that each must receive a substantial part, it is to substitute the discretion of the court for the discretion of the person to whom the power is confided. It is creating an equity against, and above the law, when it is our duty to follow, and obey the law; to declare it, not to make it."

[In *Graeff* v. *De Turk*, 8 Wright, 527, the English rule that a power of appointment among several distributees, must be so exercised as to give each distributee a substantial share of the fund, was held not to prevail in Pennsylvania.

It is well settled that a person having a power of appointment for the benefit of others, cannot use it for his own benefit, and if he does, the exercise of the power will be invalid; *Pratt* v. *Hogan*, 5 Jones, Eq. 92. But the court will not interfere on a mere suspicion that the appointment was corrupt; *Budington* v. *Munson*, 33 Conn. 481; nor, as it seems, after the lapse of the period prescribed by the statute of limitations as a bar at law.

In the recent case of *Williams' Appeal*, 23 P. F. Smith, 249, a testator left the residue of a large estate to the defendant, his executor, in trust to purchase a lot of ground of such size, and in such location, as the latter should, "upon a broad and thoughtful foresight," deem most expedient, and thereupon to erect a suitable building for a public library, which, when completed, was to be conveyed to the complainants, "The Library Company of Philadelphia," an institution of old standing. During his last illness, and shortly before his death, the testator caused a lot to be purchased, and asked his executor to ascertain whether the Library Company "would make any objection to it as a site." The executor had a conversation with a Director of the Library Company, and having, as he supposed, ascertained his views, made a favorable report to the testator. The latter was "greatly pleased," and without altering his will, obtained an oral promise from his executor that he would build the library on the lot, and nowhere else. After the testator's death, the complainants, representing to the defendant that the erection of the building on the proposed site would, by reason of its remote and inconvenient location, be destructive of the usefulness of the library, begged him to consult with them as to its change to a more central location, and he was also informed that any increased outlay incident to the purchase of another lot, would be met by voluntary contributions. The defendant having refused this request, partly on the ground that considering the proposed site to be the best, he himself, in exercise of his power, chose it for a site, and chiefly because of his promise to the testator, which he regarded "as sacred as an oath," the complainants thereupon filed a bill setting forth that the trust confided to the defendant was in the nature of property of the complainants, to be exercised for their benefit; that the verbal directions of the testator varying the nature of the trust reposed in the defendant, were void by reason of not being in writing, and signed in accordance with the statute of wills; that although the defendant might conscientiously believe that he did himself select the site, yet by reason of his solemn promise and pledge to the testator, it was not possible for him to make a voluntary selection of that, or any other site, because he had bound the discretion given him by the will by undertaking to build the library on that site, and nowhere else. The bill, therefore, prayed that it might be declared, 1. That the power conferred on the defendant by the will was a trust, to be administered by him only in the manner in which all trusts ought of right to be administered; 2. That the defendant being before and when the trust vested in him, under an obligation which bound his discretion as to the selection of a site, was disqualified from exercising the trust confided to him, and that it be referred to a master to report what would be a fit location for the building, to the end that the intent of the testator, *as contained in his will*, might be carried into full effect. In his answer, the defendant among other things, averred that, notwithstanding his sacred pledge to the testator, he deemed himself quite as free to exercise his judgment as though it had never been made, and gave his reasons for considering the site he had chosen to be the best under all the circumstances. After testimony taken, and a reference of the cause to a master, the latter reported, amongst other things, that the defendant had, by his promise to the testator, so crippled his discretion as to make it impossible to say how much his preference for the proposed site was due to his unbiased opinion, and how much to his promise, and that the trust under the will should, according to its true intent and meaning, be exercised under the supervision of the court according to the course and practice of chancery. Exceptions h ving been filed to this report, it was contended on behalf of the complainants, that the testator's intention must be sought in the will, and not *dehors ;* That the intention there indicated, was that his executor should with a " broad and *thoughtful* foresight select a lot in any situation he may deem most expedient ;" That the power thus conferred did not vest in the executor until the testator's death, and could not legally be exercised before ; That when the testator died, it became the executor's duty to make a " thoughtful " choice in view of existing circumstances; That a material circumstance, which was not anticipated by the testator, and as to which he had been misinformed, then became

known, to wit, the unwillingness of the Library Company to occupy the lot which the executor had by anticipation selected for their use ; That if the executor had been free to choose, he would have been influenced by their wishes in this regard, when taken in connection with the proposal to subscribe the difference between the lot which he had chosen, and one in a central situation ; That the promise assigned by the executor as a reason for the rejection of this offer, was in effect a promise not to exercise the discretion conferred by the will at the proper time, to wit, after he became executor, and not less in derogation of the will, than if he had promised to select a lot outside of the city limits ; That having thus bound himself to act in a particular way, it was impossible for him to say what he would have done if he had been free, because no one can certainly say what his mind would be under circumstances which have not occurred. It followed, that the alleged choice was no choice, because the executor had no power under the will to choose while the testator lived, and had by a promise " not less sacred than an oath," precluded himself from choosing, when the proper time arrived after the testator's death. The testator being dead, the Library Company had neither the benefit of his judgment, nor of that of the executor, whose promise obliged him to act without regard to circumstances which could not be known to the testator. The executor's course sacrificed the testator's main object to a secondary purpose, of which there was no legal evidence, because, by the terms of the will, the available funds of the estate were to be employed in the erection of a building to be used as a receptacle for the books of the Library Company, and if the edifice was not occupied by the Company, it might remain for years with empty shelves.

The report was confirmed by the judge before whom the cause was heard, but upon appeal to the Court in Banc, this decision was reversed, and the bill ordered (two of the five judges dissenting) to be dismissed. The court (per Agnew, J.) considered that the defendant's averment in his answer, that, notwithstanding his promise to the testator, he was quite unbiassed, was conclusive as to this, and that even if influenced by it, it was " a proper influence, and does not show a man void of discretion, and so bound by conscience, that his judgment is lost in the obligation of a foolish pledge;" that even although a court cannot regard a verbal direction of a testator, which is in conflict with a power contained in his written will, yet that it was the province of equity to follow the mind of the testator, and to give effect to the solemn act of a testator who had involved his estate in the obligation of a contract in the line of a will, and to carry out its very intent, and hence equity could not regard the promise of the executor to follow the wishes of the testator, as a constructive fraud on the power.

Of this decision it may be remarked, that the fallacy of the argument that the court, by looking at what the testator said he desired, and what the executor promised to do, gave full effect to the wishes of the former, is demonstrated by the fact that it practically repeals the Statute of Wills, and it is, of course, immaterial whether the verbal wishes of a testator are in accordance with, or opposed to, his written will. A remarkable instance occurred in the same court in the unreported case, shortly before decided, of *Alter's Appeal*, in which a husband and wife having made mutual wills, each in favor of the other, each, by mistake, signed the other's will ; and though the evidence was conclusive, yet, the court correctly held, even in the face of an act of the Legislature, passed to help the difficulty, that the wife, who died first, died intestate. If a testator were verbally to direct his executor to bestow his bounty in a quarter other than that named in his will, such a direction would not in any court be suffered to prevail, and it seems difficult to distinguish such a case from one where the testator having in his will left to his executor an uncontrolled discretion, then directs him verbally to execute it in a particular manner, and no other. Subject to certain well known exceptions, it is to the will alone, and not to any outside words or acts of the testator, or of his executor, or of any one, that a court can afford to listen.

As respects the conclusiveness

of the defendant's averment in his answer, that his judgment was unbiassed, we may refer to the case cited *supra* of *Wellesly* v. *Mornington*, where the defendant having sworn that he exercised a power of appointment for purposes other than his own ulterior benefit, his answer, necessarily uncontradicted, was said by the court to be " monstrous and incredible ;" and to the case of *Topham* v. *Duke of Portland, supra,* where the defendant swore that his making the appointment complained of was uninfluenced by obedience to his father's well-known wishes, and it was considered either that he had sworn incorrectly, or was incapable, from his bias, of knowing whether he was or was not influenced.]

COUNTESS OF STRATHMORE *v.* BOWES.   [*405]

MARCH 2 AND 3, 1789.

REPORTED 1 VES. JUN. 22.[1]

FRAUD ON MARITAL RIGHTS.]—*A woman pending a treaty of marriage with A., settled all her property to her separate use, with his approbation; a few days after, B., by stratagem, induced her to marry him, the day after she first thought of it; B. had no notice of the settlement. The settlement was established, and a deed of revocation obtained by duress set aside.*

The burthens, to which a husband is liable, are a consideration for his marital rights, upon which, therefore, fraud may be committed.

Conveyance by a woman under any circumstances, and even the moment before marriage, is good, prima facie: is bad only if fraudulent, as where it is made pending the treaty, without notice to the intended husband.

LADY STRATHMORE being seised and possessed of great property, both real and personal, pending a treaty of marriage with Mr. Grey, conveyed all her real, and assigned all her personal, estate to trustees for her sole and separate use, nothwithstanding any future coverture. This settlement was prepared with the approbation of Grey.

A few days after the execution, hearing that Mr. Bowes had fought a duel on her account with the editor of a newspaper, who had traduced her character, she determined to marry him, and the marriage took place the next day. Bowes had no notice of the settlement.

There were two bills: an original bill by Lady Strathmore, to set aside a deed revoking the settlement, as having been obtained

---

[1] S. C., on the first hearing, 2 Bro. C. C. 345 ; 2 Cox, 28, affirmed on appeal, 6 Bro. P. C. 427, Toml. ed.

[*407] by duress; and a cross bill by Mr. *Bowes, to set aside the settlement, as against the rights of marriage, and a fraud upon him, and to establish the deed of revocation.

An issue was directed, to try whether the deed of revocation had been obtained by duress; and the verdict in the Common Pleas was against the deed. The cause coming on upon the equity reserved, Mr. Justice Buller, sitting for the Lord Chancellor, decreed in favour of Lady Strathmore, and dismissed the cross bill with costs.

It came on again, upon the petition of Mr. Bowes, for a rehearing, and reversal of that decree so far as it dismissed the cross bill.

Mr. *Richards*, for Mr. Bowes.—The question is, whether this settlement made before marriage, is valid or not, as being in derogation of the common rights of marriage. A wife, by the marriage contract, becomes extinct, from the nature of it, for several civil purposes with regard to which she merges in the husband. He becomes liable to all her debts, and answerable for all her acts that do not amount to felony; and even for that, if committed in his presence; because her mind is supposed to be under his coercion. In order to enable him to answer this, he has by the law all her property. It is absurd to say, the wife shall by her own act deprive the husband of what the law has given him. It was not decided till lately, that a legacy to a wife for her sole and separate use would have been good without the interposition of trustees; and this case is much stronger, because to be construed more strictly than a devise; nor can the interposition of trustees make any difference, because it cannot alter the nature of the thing. As to his not having made any settlement on her, many marriages are made without any: and in this case it could not be necessary; for she had 10,000*l.* or 12,000 a year, a great estate for life, and much personal property. There is another principle very material: marriage, by the law of England, gives the husband the whole dominion over the property, and [*408] also over the person of his wife, except as *to murder; for, by the old law, he could not be punished for cruelty towards her. The civil existence of the wife merged in that of the husband; he is the head of the family: to make another, would be against the policy of the law. If the wife can by her own act, against the consent of the husband, make herself independent of him, it will destroy that subordination so necessary in families, which is analogous to that in the state, and tends to support it; for if Lady Strathmore is right in this, the husband is become a cipher in his own house; for he cannot educate his children, or do any other act, which by law he has a right to do. The deed was executed on the 10th or 11th of January, and the marriage took place on the 17th. If the deed had been meant fairly in contemplation of marriage, the husband would have been a party to it: there is no instance to the contrary; and it is necessary, in order to testify the consent of the husband. In *Howard* v. *Hooker*, 2 Ch. Rep. 81, a settlement by the wife, before marriage, without notice to the husband, was set aside. In *Lance* v. *Norman*, 2 Ch. Rep. 79, a bargain entered into by the wife, before marriage, was set aside, because the husband was not a party; and this case is stronger: because there, the wife was only made poorer; but here she is made quite independent of the husband. In *Carleton* v. *Dorset*, 2 Vern. 17, the estate was made over, before marriage, to trustees without privity of the husband; and a conveyance was decreed to the six-clerk, and the personal property to be paid into Court for the husband, because in derogation of the rights of marriage; and in *Edmonds* v. *Dennington*, cited in the foregoing case, a deed of settlement made before marriage, without notice to the husband, was set aside. In *Poulson* v. *Wellington*, 2 P. Wms. 535, Lord King said, that if a woman before marriage settled her property, without giving notice to the intended husband, it would, as to him, be fraudulent and void. In *Cotton* v. *King*, 2 P. Wms. 353, 674, Lady Cotton, widow, had ten children by her first husband, and before the second marriage, by indenture settled part of her fortune in their favour *(reserving, however, a considerable portion), without notice [*409] to the husband. King filed a bill to have this deed delivered up to him: but as the transaction of making the deed had been public: as she had so many children by her first husband, for whom it was reasonable to provide before she entered into a second marriage; and as the second husband was a person in mean circumstances, and had received a good fortune with her; and as she had reserved something to herself, King's bill was, for these reasons, dismissed. This decision shows, that if it had not been for the benefit of the children of the first marriage, and on account of these several circumstances, it would not have been good. Upon these cases, and the principle of the thing, this settlement is void, as being in derogation of common right. It is to be observed, that in all these cases something was reserved; here there is nothing; for Lady Strathmore has conveyed all her real and assigned all her personal, property to trustees, for her own use; and the circumstance of appointing trustees will not alter the nature of the thing, though it drives us into a Court of equity.

Mr. *Mansfield*, Mr. *Hardinge*, Mr. *Law*, and Mr. *King*, for Lady Strathmore.—Lady Strathmore is in possession by a deed to trustees, giving her own property to her use. It was done in contemplation of marriage with another person; therefore not fraudulent as to Mr. Bowes, unless any deed by a feme sole, by which she disposes of her property, shall be construed to be fraudulent, if not communicated to any future husband. Want of communication is the only circumstance that can be alleged; but that is very different from concealment, for which there can be no pretence here. It is true, a man by marrying a woman gains a dominion over her property, and in a great degree over her person, though perhaps not in the extent contended; but he had nothing to do with this property, for it was not in her at the time of the marriage, having been previously vested in trustees: and as every man knows that a woman may settle her property so that a future husband shall not be able to [*410] *touch it, Mr. Bowes ought to have inquired about it beforehand. There is no pretence of actual imposition upon him, nor even upon Grey. The deed was prepared by a gentleman of the first credit; she had several children by Lord Strathmore; she was going to marry Mr. Grey, and make this previous settlement for her children; and she acted meritoriously and honourably in so doing. The deed was with Grey's knowledge and under his direction; his approbation of it appeared by his having called to know when it would be ready, and to hasten it; and it was prepared, though not executed. a month before the time of the marriage, therefore not fraudulent as to Mr. Grey; and there is no authority for vacating a settlement made by a woman for the protection of her children without fraud. Mr. Bowes made no settlement on Lady Strathmore; neither did King upon Lady Cotton, in the case cited (which was one of the grounds of the decision in that case), though Bowes had some fortune by a former wife. He took Lady Strathmore as she then was, with what she then had; therefore there is nothing fraudulent, or that can entitle him to relief in this Court. Knowing that she was a woman subject to sudden and violent impulses of generosity, he made use of a vile artifice to obtain her by means of a sham duel (for it is in every stage of the cause admitted to have been so) with the proprietor of a newspaper, who had traduced her; and the emotion and precipitation which he caused by this artifice, was the cause which prevented the communication of the actual situation of her fortune. After this Mr. Bowes made use of the most reproachful means to set aside this deed: and the verdict was, that the revocation was obtained by violence. He would not have done this, had he not thought the deed a good one. The reason of the case is (nor is there a dictum to the contrary), that where a woman about to marry, represents herself as possessed of a fortune which she had previously disposed of, this Court will not permit the husband to be cheated. *Howard* v. *Hooker*, to which all the cases refer, was of that kind, [*411] being a specific fraud *upon the husband. The marriage had been broken off, and was brought on again by the interposition of friends, upon the idea of the husband that he was to enjoy the wife's fortune, in consideration of which he made a settlement on her of 500*l*. a year. In *Lance* v. *Norman*, the wife before marriage entered into a recognizance, concealed from the intended husband, and the object of it was to enable the creditor, who was her own brother, to distress the husband; and they had made an attempt to defraud him before, by getting him to sign a deed which was in Latin, that he might not understand it, telling him it was only a memorandum. In *Carleton* v. *Dorset*, the wife conveyed all her fortune to trustees for her own use, with permission to herself to appoint, and in default of appointment, to her own right heirs, and afterwards married: here the case was, that the husband had assurance that he was to enjoy the estate of his wife; and the decree was upon the ground that it was a trust for her, with power to appoint; and as she made no appointment, it was resolved to be a trust for her husband. Besides, in that case the fortune was paid into court, and a reasonable allowance was to be made to her. It has been remarked, that the foundation of the decree in *King* v. *Cotton* was, that it was to provide for children, which has been said to be the only case in which this can be good: but the settlement on children, or on any one else, will not make any difference; the question is, what right the husband has; if he has any right, notwithstanding any voluntary disposition without notice to him, because he was deceived, the manner in which that deceit was practised will make no difference with respect to him; for the ground for relief must be, that he was cheated, because the settlement was not communicated to him. *King* v. *Cotton* is for Lady Strathmore; for Lady Cotton had disposed of her fortune so as to put it quite out of the power of her husband; and yet the settlement was established. As to *Edmonds* v. *Dennington*,[1] Mr. Justice Buller suspected that it was misreported in Vernon, where it is only a loose note cited at the bar; and, on inspecting the *register, the decree turns out to be quite different from that report; for the deed was established upon the [*412] ground of distinct notice to the husband; and, in that case, as in this, the settlement was all her property. These cases, therefore, only go on the ground of fraud of the husband, of which there is no suggestion here. But this is not a question upon a deed executed by a future wife pending a treaty of marriage with a future husband; nor upon a deed made in prejudice generally of marital rights; nor of a settlement by a husband, by which he pays for his future power over the fortune of his wife. Suppose a husband to say he is indifferent as to the fortune of his wife, in order to appear disinterested; suppose, having a fortune, he makes no settlement; and suppose the marriage instantaneous, no time being given for communication or concealment, is it enough for the husband to say, his secret hope was disappointed? The only pretence here is, that he expected her fortune would have been greater than it proved, which expectation he did not disclose. To make this deed valid, is only to put a safeguard in her hands against the consequences of an improvident marriage; and she had a right, while sui juris, to baffle, for so much, what would otherwise have been the marital power of her husband. It is enough for us to say, Mr. Bowes was not cheated.

LORD CHANCELLOR THURLOW.—The mere question seems to be, what is the true foundation for setting aside an instrument prima

[1] And see 1 My. & K. 621.

facie good ? Can less be imputed to it than fraud ? Or can it be
void upon the notion of general policy, as has been urged for Mr.
Bowes ? If not, must not fraud be imputed ? and, if so, will the
circumstances of its being made in contemplation of marriage
affect it with fraud ? Suppose a relation had given 10,000*l.* for
her sole and separate use ; if she had represented it as her own
absolutely, so that upon a marriage, it would have gone to her
husband, this Court would have compelled the trustees to give it
to the husband, but not otherwise ;[1] nor is there any difference
[*413] between a *fortune so circumstanced by an act of her own
or of the donor. Consider what will be the effect of this
void deed of revocation ? If he had joined with her to revoke
that settlement and appoint new uses, he could not have rescinded
that afterwards ; because he had affirmed the deed by acting
upon it. If he had acted honestly upon it, as in the case I have
put, he could not have set that aside ; his counsel are to show
that he may, because he has acted dishonestly upon it, which at
present I think rather a vain attempt.

Mr. *Partridge* was to have argued for Mr. Bowes, by way of
reply, at his own request, but could not attend.

Lord Chancellor Thurlow.—I never had a doubt about this
case. If it is to be considered upon the ground of its being
against a rule of judicial policy, the arguments for Mr. Bowes
would have had great weight. The law conveys the marital
rights to the husband, because it charges him with all the burthens, which are the consideration he pays for them ; therefore,
it is a right upon which fraud may be committed. Out of this
right arises a rule of law that the husband shall not be cheated
on account of his consideration.

A case of this kind came before me a few days ago.[2] A woman
adult, about to marry an infant, made a settlement, in contemplation of that marriage, in which he joined, though an infant,
for the purpose of expressing his consent. As it was upon fair
consideration, and no fraud to draw him in as an infant, I thought
the circumstance of its being fair would bind him, though as an
infant, not capable of consenting ; according to which I held the
settlement good, as she was capable of conveying ; and as it
was a public and open transaction, with the consent of the family,
and consequently no fraud, though his being privy to it would
not have concluded him from any rights as being an infant.

A conveyance by a wife, whatsoever may be the circumstances, and
[*414] *even the moment before the marriage, is primâ *facie good,*
and becomes bad only upon the imputation of fraud. If a
woman, during the course of a treaty of marriage with her, makes,
without notice to the intended husband, a conveyance of any part of her

----

[1] See Ashton v. M'Dougall, 5 Beav. 66.
[2] Slocombe v. Glubb, 2 Bro. C. C. 545.

property, I should set it aside, though good primâ facie, because affected with that fraud.

As to the morality of the transaction, I shall say nothing to that. They seem to have been pretty well matched. Marriage in general seems to have been Lady Strathmore's object ; she was disposed to marry anybody, but not to part with her fortune. This settlement is to be considered as the effect of a lucid interval, and, if there can be reason in madness, by doing this she discovered a spark of understanding.

The question which arises upon all the cases is, whether the evidence is sufficient to raise fraud. Even if there had been a fraud upon Grey, I would not have permitted Bowes to come here to complain of it. But there was no fraud, even upon Grey, for it was with his consent ; and so I cannot distinguish it from a good limitation to her separate use. Being about to marry Grey, she made this settlement with his knowledge ; and the imputation of fraud is, that having suddenly changed her mind and married Mr. Bowes, in the hurry of that improvident transaction she did not communicate it to him ; but there was no time, and could be no fraud, which consists of a number of circumstances. It is impossible for a man marrying in the manner Bowes did, to come into equity and talk of fraud. Therefore the decree must be affirmed with costs ; but let him have all just allowances as to what he paid when in receipt of the profits, and as to the annuities, which are declared not to be disturbed by the decree.

In the well-known case of *Strathmore* v. *Bowes*, the rule upon which Courts of equity act in setting aside a settlement made by a woman of her own property previous to marriage, in violation or fraud of the marital rights of her intended husband, is well laid *down by Lord Thurlow. " A conveyance by a wife," observes his Lordship, " whatsoever may be the circumstances, and even the moment before the marriage, is prima facie good, and becomes bad only upon the *imputation of fraud.* If a woman, *during the course of a treaty of marriage* with her, makes, without notice to the intended husband, a conveyance of any part of her property, I should set it aside, though good prima facie, because affected with that fraud." [*415]

The case, however, of *Strathmore* v. *Bowes*, does not come within the principle of those cases in which, according to the rule as laid down by Lord Thurlow, a Court of equity will set aside a settlement of a woman's property, made by her previous to marriage ; for it will be observed, that the settlement was made by Lady Strathmore with the consent of Grey, her then intended husband, and not during the course of a treaty of marriage with Bowes, whom she afterwards married, and it was, therefore, not a fraud upon him. The settlement, to use Lord Thurlow's words, was prima facie good, and there was no imputation of fraud to render it bad. " *Strathmore* v. *Bowes*," observes Lord Loughborough, " went upon this, that the deed was honest and proper, being made in contemplation of a marriage with another person, and with the consent of that person: " *Ball* v. *Montgomery*, 2 Ves. jun. 194 ; see, also *M'Donnell* v. *Hesilridge*, 16 Beav. 346. It is necessary, therefore, for a person impeaching a settlement, to prove that, at the time of its execution, he was *the then intended husband*, otherwise it will not be set aside : *England* v. *Downs*, 2 Beav. 522.

It is clearly settled, that if a woman, during a treaty for marriage, holds herself out to her intended husband as entitled to property, which will become his upon the marriage, and then makes a settlement of it without his knowledge or concurrence, actual fraud will be imputed to her, and the settlement will be set aside in a Court of equity. " If," observes Lord Langdale, M. R., " a woman entitled to property enters into a treaty for marriage, and, during the treaty, represents to her intended husband that she is so entitled, that, upon the marriage, he will become entitled jure mariti ; and if, during the same treaty, she clandestinely conveys away the property, in such manner as to defeat his marital right and secure to herself the separate use of it, and the concealment continues till the marriage takes place, there can be no doubt but that a fraud is thus practised on the husband, and he is entitled to relief. The equity which arises in cases of this nature depends upon the pecu-[*416]　liar circumstances *of each case, as bearing upon the question, whether the facts proved do or do not amount to sufficient evidence of fraud practised on the husband. It is not doubted that proof of direct misrepresentations, or of wilful concealment, with intent to deceive the husband, would entitle him to relief : " *England* v. *Downs*, 2 Beav. 528 ; see also *Howard* v. *Hooker*, 2 Ch. Rep. 81 ; *Carleton* v. *The Earl of Dorset*, 2 Vern. 17 ; *S. C.*, 2 Cox, 33.

It was observed by Mr. Justice Buller, when *Strathmore* v. *Bowes* was before him, that " Fraud consists in falsely holding out that a woman has an estate unfettered, and that the husband will be of course entitled to it. No case has yet established, that all conveyances by a wife before marriage are void, merely because not communicated to the husband : " 2 Bro. C. C. 350 ; 2 Cox, 29. And again, he says, " It is necessary to show other facts, and that the husband is actually deceived and misled ; and that the bare concealment is not sufficient : " 2 Cox, 30. These dicta, however, of Mr. Justice Buller can scarcely be supported, although there have been some cases in which, under peculiar circumstances, it has been held that a bare concealment by a woman from her intended husband, of a gift or a settlement of part of her property made during the treaty for a marriage, was not sufficient evidence of fraud, so as to render the settlement void as against the husband. Thus, in *Thomas* v. *Williams*, Mos. 177, a woman, during a treaty of marriage, released a legacy to which she was entitled, without the knowledge of her husband. Lord King, however, refused to set aside the release because it did not appear that he ever inquired after the legacy. So also in *De Mandeville* v. *Crompton*, 1 V. & B. 354, a daughter, after instructions were given for her marriage settlement, by which she assigned all monies, debts, bills, bonds, *notes*, and other securities for money, and chattels real, and other chattels, and personal estate, to trustees, upon trusts under which her intended husband took only a partial and contingent interest, without his knowledge cancelled a promissory note for 2000*l.*, which had been given to her, without consideration, about seventeen years before, by her mother, then a widow, as a provision in case she should marry again ; Lord Eldon held, that the husband was entitled to no relief with regard to the note. " My opinion," observed his Lordship, " is that the marriage was not upon any representation as to the amount of the property, that it should be *in no way diminished*, or that this note should make part of the settlement ; and I should go beyond any precedent by holding that here was a misrepresentation leading to marriage, which was either *fraudulently or substantially defeated by what took place afterwards [*417] with reference to this note."

However, in *Goddard* v. *Snow*, 1 Russ. 485, a woman, ten months before marriage, but after the commencement of that intimate acquaintance with her future husband which ended in marriage, made a settlement of a sum of money which he did not know her to be possessed of. The marriage took place, she concealing from him both her right to the money and the existence of the settlement. Ten years afterwards she died, and after her death the husband filed a bill to have the money paid to him. It was argued, on behalf of the defendants, that, as the husband did not know of the existence of the sum of money, and was, therefore, not induced to contract the marriage on the notion that it would be subject to his marital rights, no fraud, such as the authorities held to be necessary, had been committed ; that there was, at the utmost only concealment, and that concealment alone was not sufficient to avoid a settlement confessedly valid at law. Lord Gifford, M. R., however, held that the settlement was void against the husband, as a fraud upon his marital rights ; and his Lordship said, that the opinion of Lord Thurlow, in *Strathmore* v. *Bowes*, was, that if a woman, contemplating marriage with an individual, made a settlement of her property on herself, reserving to herself the dominion over it, and *concealed* that settlement from her husband, the settlement was a fraud on his marital rights, which he was entitled to avoid. See *St. George* v. *Wake*, 1 My. & K. 622, where Lord Brougham says, that the principle was carried further in *Goddard* v. *Snow* than in any other case. See also *Downes* v. *Jennings*, 32 Beav. 290 ; *Prideaux* v. *Lonsdale*, 4 Giff. 159 ; 1 De G. Jo. & Sm. 433 ; *Chambers* v. *Crabbe*, 34 Beav. 457.

It has been supposed that a settlement by a widow upon her children by a former marriage, even if made during the treaty for a second mar-

riage, without the knowledge of her intended husband, is valid, because
the object of the settlement, it has been said, is meritorious. *Hunt* v.
Matthews, 1 Vern. 408, and *King* v. *Cotton*, 2 P. Wms. 674, Mos. 259,
have been cited as supporting the proposition; it appears, however, by
an extract from the decree in Mr. Raithby's edition of Vernon, that the
husband, in *Hunt* v. *Matthews, consented* to the settlement being made
by his intended wife upon her children by a former marriage; and in
King v. *Cotton*, the settlement was made by Lady Cotton upon the
children of a former marriage, *previous to her entering upon a treaty
for a second marriage.*

These cases, therefore, only decide that a settlement is valid
[*418]   *if made by a woman upon her children by her former marriage,
either with the consent of the intended husband, or without his
consent or knowledge, if made *previous to the treaty for* marriage;
but it is conceived that a provision for children would not render a settlement valid which without it would be fraudulent; for, although in
the execution of a settlement, so far as it makes provision for her children, a woman may perform a moral duty towards her children, she has
no right to act fraudulently towards her husband; and she can, in such
circumstances, only reconcile all her moral duties by making a proper
settlement on herself and her children, with the knowledge of her intended husband; see *England* v. *Downs*, 2 Beav. 528, 529; in which
case, however, the settlement made by a widow upon herself and the
children of a former marriage was held not to be fraudulent, because it
was not proved that the person she afterwards married was, at the time
of the execution of the settlement, " *her then intended husband.*"

In *Taylor* v. *Pugh*, 1 Hare, 608, where a husband filed a bill to set
aside a settlement made, as he alleged, in fraud of his marital rights, it
was argued, that, as he was ignorant that his wife had any property, and
as she had practised no actual deception upon him, a Court of equity
ought not to interfere; but Sir James Wigram, V. C., although he decided against the husband upon other grounds, clearly intimated his
opinion that those arguments were unsound. " It was argued," observed his Honor, " for the defendants, who resist this claim, that the
plaintiff was ignorant, until after the marriage, that the wife was possessed of the property in question; and I was referred to cases, in which
the Court had apparently laid some stress on that circumstance, as a
ground for refusing relief to the husband."

" In *De Mandeville* v. *Crompton*, Lord Eldon made the important
observation, that, in the absence of any representation having been
made as to specific property, no implied contract is raised on the part
of the lady, during the treaty of marriage, that her property, as it
existed at the time of the commencement of the treaty, shall be *in no
way diminished.* This undoubtedly shews Lord Eldon's opinion to be,
that it is not every alienation of the wife's property, during the treaty,

which can be regarded as fraudulent, only because the husband was not a party to it. But I should certainly have great difficulty in applying the proposition so laid down by Lord Eldon to a case in which every farthing of the wife's property was, without the knowledge of the husband, wholly withdrawn from his control and settled on herself, her children, or her appointees, to the total exclusion of the husband. A very *special [*419] case must be made out before the Court would carry the proposition so far. I think Lord Eldon meant only to decide, that, there being no implied contract on the part of the lady, that her property should not be in any way diminished, it is for the Court to determine, whether having regard to the condition in life of the parties, and the other circumstances of the case, a transaction complained of by the husband should be treated as fraudulent or not."

" I think another argument on behalf of the defendants was also carried beyond its just limits, in contending that actual fraud or deception on the husband must be proved. Notwithstanding there are some dicta which may at first be considered as implying the contrary, (but which may, I think, be explained,) I take the rule of the Court to be correctly stated in Mr. Roper's Treatise, vol. 2, p. 162: ' Deception will be inferred if, after the commencement of the treaty for marriage, the wife should attempt to make any disposition of her property without her intended husband's knowledge or concurrence.' This way of stating the law does not exclude inquiry into the circumstances by which the apparent deception may be explained; nor does it conflict with the modern cases to which I was referred. I shall, as I understand those cases, content myself with referring to the valuable note of the learned editor (Rop. Hus. & Wife, vol. 2, p. 166, n.), in support of the general proposition I have cited.

" Several circumstances would certainly appear to have been sometimes thought material as negativing the imputed fraud; such as the poverty of the husband—the fact that he has made no settlement upon the wife—the reasonable character of the settlement, as in the case of a settlement upon the children of a former marriage—and the ignorance of the husband that his wife possessed the property. . . . I could not give my individual assent to the sufficiency of any of the reasons I have mentioned. The poverty of the husband—the absence of any settlement upon the wife—the reasonable manner in which she desires to deal with her property, may be very material considerations for the guidance of the parties in determining in what manner the wife's fortune should be settled; but why they should constitute a reason for concealing the arrangement from the husband, I cannot comprehend. It might be very proper to bring these considerations to the attention of the intended husband. He might be told that the lady has a certain fortune, but regard being had to the claims upon her, and to his circumstances, the settlement ought to be made in a particular way ; but I cannot compre-

hend the reasoning, which says, that any one of the reasons suggested
[*420] is a sufficient ground for *practising concealment upon the husband, or treats such concealment as immaterial.   So, also, with
respect to ignorance of the husband of the property of the wife—that,
no doubt, materially lessens his disappointment at finding the wife's
fortune has been withdrawn from his control; but the equity is not
founded upon his disappointment; for, if that were so, it would follow
that his ignorance of the existence of the property would always be an
answer, however that ignorance was produced; the equity would never
arise where the wife had contrived to conceal her property from the
husband ; but this is not so, for the cases clearly show that practised
concealment by the wife will be treated as a fraud on the husband."

But a gift or settlement, by a woman, of her property, during the
treaty for marriage, will not be set aside, if the husband knew of the
gift or settlement before the marriage.   Thus, in *St. George* v. *Wake*,
1 My. & K. 610, where a lady, during a treaty for a marriage which afterwards took effect, made a voluntary assignment of part of her property to her sister, her husband filed a bill to set it aside; but he did not
allege that the transaction was concealed from him, or that he was ignorant of the assignment having been made, at the time of the marriage.
Sir J. Leach, M. R., held that the husband, who was, under the circumstances, presumed to have had notice of the assignment before his
marriage, was not entitled to set it aside on the ground of fraud.   And
his Honor stated, that he had looked into the authorities, and had
not found any case which went the length of establishing the proposition, that if a person, who had entered into a treaty of marriage with a
lady, knew of a gift made by the lady, pending such treaty, and nevertheless thought fit to marry her, the gifts could be considered as void in
this court.   At law, if a lady secretly disposed of a part of her property, after the contract of marriage, the contract was thereby avoided;
and proof of this secret disposition was a valid defence, if an action were
brought against the intended husband for breach of the promise of marriage.   This decision, on appeal, was affirmed by Lord Brougham.
See also *Ashton* v. *M'Dougall*, 5 Beav. 56; *Griggs* v. *Staplee*, 2 De G.
& Sm. 472; *Wrigley* v. *Swainson*, 3 De G. & Sm. 458. See 1 My. & K.
619.

The seduction by a man of his intended wife, may be a reason why a
Court of equity should not set aside a settlement made by her before
marriage.   Thus, in *Taylor* v. *Pugh*, 1 Hare, 608, where a man had induced his intended wife to cohabit with him previous to marriage, Sir
J. Wigram, V. C., refused to set aside a settlement of her property, al-
[*421] though executed without his knowledge, *during the treaty for
the marriage, because the husband, before the marriage, had put
it out of the power of the wife effectually to make any stipulation for
the settlement of her property, by his conduct towards her.   " Retire-

ment," said his Honor, "from the marriage on her part was impossible. She must have submitted to a marriage with her seducer, even although he should have insisted on receiving and spending the whole of her fortune." But see *Downes* v. *Jennings*, 32 Beav. 290.

The concurrence or acquiescence of the husband in the settlement, even though he be a minor, will preclude him from taking any objections to it: *Slocombe* v. *Glubb*, 2 Bro. C. C. 545; but see *Nelson* v. *Stocker*, 4 De G. & Jo. 458. In a recent case, however, a settlement made by a woman of her personal property after her engagement to be married, was set aside at the suit of the husband, although he was told before the marriage that she had executed a settlement affecting her property, it appearing that neither she nor her husband was accurately informed of the nature and effect of the trusts of the settlement. *Prideaux* v. *Lonsdale*, 4 Giff. 159, 1 De G. Jo. & Sm. 433. If a husband acquiesces in, or confirms, a settlement, he will not afterwards be allowed to dispute it: *Maber* v. *Hobbes*, 2 Y. & C. Exch. Ca. 317; *England* v. *Downs*, 2 Beav. 535; *Ashton* v. *M'Dougall*, 5 Beav. 56; *Grazebrook* v. *Percival*, 14 Jur. 1103; *Loader* v. *Clarke*, 2 Mac. & G. 382. In *Downes* v. *Jennings*, 32 Beav. 290, 523, it was held that delay in instituting a suit for two and a half years after the discovery by the husband of the settlement did not operate as a bar to the relief sought.

If a woman gives a security to a *volunteer*, prior to marriage, without the consent of the intended husband, it may be set aside by him. Thus, in *Lance* v. *Norman*, 2 Ch. Rep. 79, the wife of Lance, the plaintiff, the day before her marriage, was persuaded to enter into a recognizance of 2000*l.* without defeasance, to her brother, the defendant, without the privity or consent of the plaintiff. The Court, being assisted by the judges, held, that the recognizance was entered into whereby to defraud the plaintiff; and decreed it to be set aside and vacated on the record thereof, and granted a perpetual injunction against it.

But where a woman, about to marry, gave a bond for *valuable consideration*, although without her intended husband's knowledge, it was held by Lord Hardwicke, that the husband could not be relieved against it. "If," observed his Lordship, "a woman about to marry parts with part of her property, or gives a security or assignment, they are relievable against in this court; but where a debt is contracted for *valuable consideration*, *though concealed from the husband, it is no fraud [*422] on the marriage. But concealment of such securities or debts is not to be encouraged:" *Blanchet* v. *Foster*, 2 Ves. 264: see also *Llewellin* v. *Cobbold*, 1 Sm. & Giff. 376.

It is presumed that a woman about to be married, availing herself of the powers conferred upon her by the Married Woman's Property Act, 1870 (33 & 34 Vict. c. 93) ss. 3, 4, 5, to invest in the funds, joint stock or other companies, or in societies duly registered, certified or enrolled, will still come within the rule laid down in *Strathmore* v. *Bowes*, if she does not obtain the concurrence of her intended husband.

A secret settlement made by a woman whilst under a treaty for marriage, though liable to be set aside in equity, is not necessarily void in a court of law. Thus, in *Doe d. Richards* v. *Lewis*, 11 C. B. 1035, A., pending a treaty of marriage between herself and B., without B.'s knowledge made a settlement of certain leaseholds to herself for life, remainder to C. her son by a former marriage, remainder over to D. It was held by the Court of Common Pleas that this deed was not avoided by the marriage under the statute of Eliz. 27, c. 4, the husband not taking as a purchaser.

It seems to be doubtful how far Courts of equity will interfere in favour of women, against secret acts of the husband immediately before marriage to deprive them of their right to dower. It is, however, said by Lord C. B. Gilbert, that a conveyance in trust privately made by the husband on the eve of marriage, for the purpose of barring dower, would be decreed fraudulent, as being designed to deprive the wife of the provision given her by the Common law : Lex. Præt. 267 ; 1 Bright, H. & W. 356 ; and see *Drury* v. *Drury*, Wilmot's Opinions, 177, 4 Bro. C. C. 506, n. Lord Hardwicke however treats it as clear, " that if a man, before marriage, conveys his estate privately, without the knowledge of his wife, to trustees, in trust for himself and his heirs in fee, that will prevent dower : " *Swannock* v. *Lyford*, Co. Litt. 108, n. 1, and see *Banks* v. *Sutton*, 2 P. Wms. 700.

It has also been observed that the reasons for which it has been held that a conveyance privately made by a woman during a treaty of marriage is *prima facie* fraudulent and void, do not apply with equal force to a conveyance made under similar circumstances by the intended husband ; because estates are now most commonly conveyed or settled so as to prevent dower from attaching, it is not necessarily to be presumed that the marriage was contracted by the woman in the expectation of becoming entitled to that provision, unless it appears that representa-[*423] tions to that effect were *made to her (1 Bright, H. & W. 357) ; and perhaps these reasons would apply more forcibly in the case of women married since the Dower Act, 3 & 4 Will. 4, c. 105 (which puts dower entirely in the power of the husband), came into operation. See also *M'Keogh* v. *M'Keogh*, 4 I. Eq. 338.

It has been frequently decided in this country, that a secret voluntary settlement or conveyance of her property by a woman, pending a treaty of marriage, and in contemplation of marriage, without the knowledge of her intended husband, is fraudulent and void against her husband, as being in derogation of his marital rights and just expectations ; *Duncan's Appeal*, 7 Wright, 67 ; *Belt* v.

Ferguson, 3 Grant's Cases, 259; *Robinson* v. *Buck*, 21 P. F. Smith, 386; *Freeman* v. *Hartman*, 45 Illinois, 57; *Tucker* v. *Andrews*, 13 Maine, 124, 128; *Waller* v. *Armistead's Adm'rs*, 2 Leigh, 11, 14; *Linker* v. *Smith*, 4 Washington, 224, 225; *Manes* v. *Durant*, 2 Richardson's Equity, 404, 406 *Ramsay* v. *Joyce*, 1 M'Mullen's Equity, 237, 249; *Logan* v. *Simmons*, 3 Iredell's Equity, 487, 494; *M'Afee* v. *Ferguson*, &c., 9 B. Monroe, 475, 477, 478; *Williams* v. *Carle*, 2 Stockton's Chancery, 543. "The fortune of the intended wife," said Johnson, J., in *Terry, Adm'r*, v. *Hopkins and others*, 1 Hill's Chancery, 1, 4, "is most frequently a weighty consideration and a strong inducement to the marriage contract, and the happiness of both the parties may, in a great degree, depend on the observance of good faith, with respect to it : and the general rule, very clearly, is, that if pending a treaty of marriage, the intended wife makes a secret voluntary disposition of her property, and the marriage is had, it is a fraud upon the marital rights of the husband, and is void."

The fraud is not the less because the Legislature has exempted the property of married women from the control of their husbands, and conferred it absolutely on them, because a man is still entitled to look to the fortune of his intended wife as a fund for the maintenance and education of the offspring of the marriage; *Duncan's Appeal*, 7 Wright, 67. And it has been held that the burden is on those claiming under such an instrument, to show that it was made known to the intended husband; *Robinson* v. *Buck*, 21 P. F. Smith, 386.

It is universally agreed, that the ground of the invalidity of such transactions as against the husband is fraud. There is no doubt, of course, that if the husband has been actually and intentionally deceived and misled by the conduct of the wife, the transaction is void; *Logan* v. *Simmans*, 3 Iredell's Equity, 487, 497; and the sounder view, and the one prevailing generally in the courts of this country, is, that mere concealment,—*suppressio veri*,—the suppression of truth which the party was bound to disclose, constitutes, or evinces, fraud upon the rights of the husband, who is a purchaser in law of all the property of the wife. "If one should sell to another," said Harper, Ch., in *Manes* v. *Durant*, 2 Richardson's Equity, 404, 406, "for a valuable money consideration, property, of part of which he had a few days before made a voluntary conveyance to a third person, it could hardly be doubted that this amounted to actual fraud." The subject was discussed at some length, in *Logan* v. *Simmons*, 3 Iredell's Equity, 487, 494, and while it was admitted, "that it is a point yet open, and on which respectable opinions are much divided, whether concealment by the wife, merely, where there is no active expedient adopted to keep the husband in ignorance, and he makes no inquiry, is, *per se*, a fraud," yet a strong view in favor of that principle was presented in the opinion of the court, delivered by Ruffin, C. J. "A husband," he remarks, "being bound to pay his wife's debts and to maintain her during coverture, and being chargeable by the law with the support of the issue of the marriage, and bound by the ties of natural affection also to make provision for the issue, it is in the nature of things, as a matter of common discretion, that a woman's apparent property should enter materially, if not essentially, into his inducements for contracting the marriage, and incurring those onerous obligations. It is also to be assumed by a man proposing this relation to a woman, that she too has a view to their means of livelihood after marriage, and feels an interest in the provision that, between their joint stocks, can be made for a family. Every woman, therefore, must suppose, that the man, who is about to marry her, expects that she will not put away her fortune, at least the visible part of it, and thereby diminish his ability to discharge his duties and legal obligations to herself, her creditors, and her future family. And if she, after allowing him to form such expectations, deliberately defeats them by a conveyance of her property, and draws him into a marriage by a deception on that point, it would seem, that it could be nothing less than a fraud on the husband. He is disappointed of what the law promised him, and of what she had held out to him he would get. In such a case, it may be well argued, that a concealment of the conveyance would amount to a fraud, upon the principle of *suppressio veri* being in bad faith, when a person, towards whom it is practised, has an interest in knowing the truth, and has no ground to suspect anything that has not been avowed." And this, it is added, should be particularly the case in this country, where settlements are rare, and where the husband expects to get all that the wife has—that is, expects that she will allow him to receive by the marriage, all that she would keep for herself and within her own power if she had not contracted the marriage. "It is certain," said Johnston, Ch., in *Ramsay* v. *Joyce*, 1 M'Mullan's Equity, 237, 242, "that all the cases rank the husband as a purchaser of the property, held by the wife, during the treaty of marriage. I do not suppose that he has ever been regarded as a mere vendee, so as to be entitled to unravel trifling alterations in the wife's property, if made without his concurrence. But any material alteration, if voluntary, would, without explanatory circumstances, be regarded as evidence of fraudulent intention, and be liable to just exception on his part."

The fraud, however, is of a nature to be relieved against only in a court of equity; the conveyance or settlement cannot be treated as void at law; *Logan* v. *Simmons*, 1 Devereux and Battle's Law R. 13, 16.

It is agreed, that if the husband has notice or knowledge of the settlement, before the marriage, the transaction cannot be impeached; *Terry, Adm'r,* v. *Hopkins and others,* 1 Hill's Chancery, 1, 5; *M'Clure* v. *Miller,* 1 Bailey's Equity, 108, 109; *Cheshire* v. *Payne,* 16 B. Monroe, 618. See *Fletcher and Wife* v. *Ashley et als.,* 6 Grattan, 332, 339; and if the husband is a party to the settlement, though a minor, it will be valid, for it is evidence of his privity and consent, to repel the presumption of fraud, though he may be incompetent to convey any right or interest; *Kottman et ux.* v. *Peyton et al.,* 1 Spear's Eq. 46. "The only circumstances relied upon in this case," said Simpson, J., in *Cheshire* v. *Payne,* "to render the deed fraudulent against the husband, are its execution after the marriage contract was entered into, and his ignorance that it had been executed until a few moments before he was married. To render a disposition made by the wife of her property before marriage, fraudulent against her husband, as being in derogation of his marital rights and just expectations, it must be made pending a treaty, and in contemplation of marriage, and without the knowledge of her intended husband. Both of these elements must enter into the transaction, to constitute it a fraud against the rights of the husband."

"If the husband be apprized before his marriage of the disposition which his intended wife has made of the property, he cannot, in any just sense of the term, be said to be deceived by it. If, not-withstanding such knowledge, he deems it proper to consummate the marriage contract, the act is voluntary on his part, and he cannot afterwards complain that the disposition which his wife made of her property, is a fraud upon his marital rights. If the intended wife should secretly and without the consent of the man she had contracted to marry, dispose of a part of her property, the marriage contract would be thereby avoided; and proof of such a secret disposition of her property would be a valid defence, if an action were brought against the intended husband for breach of the promise of marriage; (*Ashton* v. *M'Dougal,* 5 Beav. 56; *Griggs* v. *Staplee,* 13 Jur. 32; see also My. & K. 619, referred to 1st vol. White's Leading Cases in Equity, Hare & Wallace's Notes, p. 448.)"

"It is true that it was held by this court, in the case of *Hobbs* v. *Blandford,* 7 Monroe, 469, that a conveyance of the wife's estate, between the time of the engagement and the marriage, was a fraud upon the marital rights of the husband, although he had notice of the conveyance before the marriage took place. But that decision cannot be sustained either upon principle or authority."

"Ignorance of certain facts, known to the other party, but concealed or misrepresented, is an essential ingredient to constitute fraud. If all the facts are known, there can be no deception; and if there be no imposition or deception, there cannot be any fraud. In conformity with this view it has been repeatedly decided, and seems to be the settled doctrine of the courts, both in England and in this country, that if the husband has notice or knowledge of the settlement or alienation, before the marriage, the transaction cannot be impeached; (*Terry, Adm'r,* v. *Hopkins, &c.,* 1 Hill's Ch. 15 ; *M'Clure* v. *Miller,* 1 Bailey's Eq. 108 ; *Fletcher and Wife* v. *Askley, &c.,* 6 Grattan, 322 ; *St. George* v. *Wake,* 1 My. & Keene, 610 ; 7 Con. Eng. C. R. 188.)"

" In the last named case the Chancellor said, ' it might perhaps be affirmed, that excepting *Goddard* v. *Snow,* no case exists of a conveyance by the wife, though without consideration, being set aside simply because made during a treaty of marriage, and without the knowledge of the intended husband. Yet, it is certain that all the cases in which the subject is approached, treat the principle as one of undoubted acceptance in this court; and it must be held to be the rule of the court to be gathered from an uniform current of dicta, though resting upon a very slender foundation of actual decision touching the simple point. As, however, everything depends upon the fraud supposed to be practised upon the husband, it is clearly essential to the application of the principle, that the husband should, up to the moment of the marriage, have been kept in ignorance of the transaction.' "

" But the question still arises, in this case, whether the husband should be regarded as having been kept in ignorance of the transaction or whether the knowledge of it at the time it was imputed to him, should be deemed sufficient to repel the legal presumption of fraud."

" As it is essential to constitute fraud, that the husband should remain ignorant of the transaction until the marriage ceremony takes place, it follows, as a necessary consequence, that his knowledge of it at any time previous to that period, will operate to prevent him from impeaching the conveyance on the ground of fraud. In reference to his knowledge, the law fixes but one period, and is the time of the marriage; it does not draw any nice distinctions with respect to the length of the time before that period, but considers any previous time as sufficient, and leaves the husband to act for himself, according to his own sense of justice and propriety. Until the marriage actually takes place, he is at liberty to retract, and the law justifies him in so doing, if he be notified that his intended wife has, without his assent, made a settlement of her estate that will be prejudicial to his marital rights. But if with this knowledge acquired at any time before the marriage actually takes place, he voluntarily complies with his previous engagement, he cannot complain that he was deceived, nor will the transaction be deemed to be a fraud on his rights as a husband."

Knowledge after the marriage, and mere acquiescence, will not give validity to a settlement, otherwise fraudulent ; *Logan* v. *Sim-*

mons, 3 Iredell's Equity, 487, 500; nothing, after marriage, will be a confirmation, but such acts by the husband as are intended to confirm the arrangement, and are done under full knowledge that the original transaction could be set aside by him; *Manes* v. *Durant*, 2 Richardson's Equity, 404, 406.

There are some dicta, that a reasonable provision for children of a former marriage, if made *bona fide*, or under circumstances of good faith, would not be fraudulent and voidable by the intended husband; *Tucker* v. *Andrews*, 13 Maine, 124, 128; but it is certain that such a settlement, to be sustained, must be reasonable and fair; *Logan* v. *Simmons*, 3 Iredell's Equity, 487; *Ramsay* v. *Joyce*, 1 M'Mullan's Eq. 237. And the better opinion, and one that has been repeatedly expressed in South Carolina, is, that if the settlement is without the knowledge of the husband, it makes no difference, whatever, in respect to its invalidity as against him, that it is upon a child by a former marriage; it is not the less deceptive, nor does it the less defeat his just claims and expectations, see per Johnson, J., in *Terry, Adm'r,* v. *Hopkins and others,* 1 Hill's Chancery, 1, 5; per Johnson, Ch., and Harper, Ch., in *Ramsay* v. *Joyce*, 1 M'Mullan's Equity, 237, 242, 251; per Harper, Ch., again, in *Manes* v. *Durant*, 2 Richardson's Equity, 404, 406.

---

*LADY ELIBANK *v.* MONTOLIEU. [*424]

APRIL 16, 19, 1799. February 19, 1801.

REPORTED 5 VES. 737.

WIFE'S EQUITY TO A SETTLEMENT.]— *Upon the bill of a married woman, entitled to a share of the personal estate as one of the next of kin of the intestate, against her husband and the administrator, the latter claiming to retain towards satisfaction of a debt by bond from the plaintiff's husband to him, it was declared he was not entitled to retain: but that the plaintiff's share was subject to a further provision in favour of her and her children, the settlement on her marriage being inadequate to the fortune she then possessed; and it was referred to the Master to see a proper settlement made on her and her children, regard being had to the extent of her fortune and settlement already made upon her.*

IN 1795, Lady Cranstown died intestate, possessed of large personal property, leaving two brothers and two sisters her next of kin. Lewis Montolieu, one of her brothers, took out letters of administration to her.

The bill was filed by Lady Elibank, one of the sisters, against her husband Lord Elibank and against Montolieu, *praying an account of the plaintiff's share, and that it may be settled on her and her family.*

The defendant Montolieu, by his answer claimed to retain Lady Elibank's share, towards satisfaction of the debt due to him from Lord Elibank by two bonds—one dated the 31st of May, 1783, for 12,217*l.* 9*s.* 9*d.* ; the other, dated the 14th November, 1794, [*425] for 1000*l.*—upon *the ground of the *provision made for the plaintiff by the settlement previous to her marriage with the defendant Lord Elibank,* in 1776. By that settlement, the sum of 12,000*l.* and 5000*l.* New South Sea Annuities were settled in trust for Lord Elibank for life; and after his decease, for Lady Elibank for life, as a jointure, and in lieu of dower or thirds; and after the decease of both, in trust for the children. The sum of 4000*l.* New South Sea annuities was settled in trust for her separate use for life; and after her death, for her children: and 2000*l.* 5*l.* per cent. Bank Annuities for her separate use for life; and after her death, for her children, as she should by will appoint. All these sums were her property before marriage. The settlement also gave her some contingent interests.

In the entail of Lord Elibank's estate, a power was reserved to charge 200*l.* a year jointure, and 50*l.* a year to each of his younger children, not exceeding in the whole 200*l.* a year, under a condition, that the estate should be chargeable with only one jointure at a time; and that, if the power of charging for children had been exercised by a preceding heir in tail, the heir in possession should not charge for his younger children. The defendant Lord Elibank, by his answer, stated that a former Lord Elibank did charge to the full extent of that power.

The Solicitor-General, Mr. *Grant,* and Mr. *Alexander,* for the plaintiff.—The plaintiff desires an account of the personal estate of Lady Cranstown, and that a provision may be made for her. The defendant Montolieu insists, that is not to be done, because he is a creditor of her husband; contending that this case is out of the usual rule upon which the Court acts for a wife; and that there is no necessity to come to this Court, the fortune not being in Court nor under the control of the Court. In *Jewson* v. *Moulson,*[1] Lord Hardwicke held, that is not a necessary ingredient to enable the Court to act upon the property; and that this Court would interfere to prevent the husband from obtaining it through a Court of concurrent jurisdiction, as the Ecclesiastical Court; [*426] because that *Court cannot give the wife a remedy ; though he doubted where it could be got at without the aid of this Court, or a Court of concurrent jurisdiction; and he states that the rule is as old as the time of King Charles I., and cites a case from Tothill.[2] There have been many instances of an injunc-

---

[1] 2 Atk. 417.
[2] Tanfield v. Davenport, Tothill, 179 ; Mealis v. Mealis, Hil. 1764 ; 5 Ves. 517, note to Blount v. Bestland.

tion to restrain the husband from proceeding in the Ecclesiastical Court, refusing to make any provision for his wife; and that Court having no power to compel him. The cases upon this subject are collected in Mr. Cox's note to *Bosvil* v. *Brander*;[1] and the result is, that, where the property is a subject of equitable cognizance, it is not material whether the wife, or the husband, or his representatives or general assignees, come for the aid of the Court. A wife in the situation of this plaintiff, therefore, may come to this Court for the purpose of having that to which she is entitled secured to her and her family, and part settled to her separate use. She is entitled to the same reference as w.ıs directed in *Worrall* v. *Marlar*, and *Bushman* v. *Pell*,[2] for the purpose of receiving a proposal for the settlement. In *Wright* v. *Rutter*,[3] the Master of the Rolls observes, that it is now determined, that an action will not lie against the executor for property bequeathed to a married woman; and one of the reasons is, that the husband would get it free from the condition a Court of equity imposes. It is not necessary, therefore, that the property should be in this Court, or in the hands of trustees; for, if it was in the Ecclesiastical Court, or in the hands of an executor or an administrator, the interest of the wife is protected. That case related to a residue of personal estate in the hands of an administrator, for which it was not necessary to come here; but that was held not to make any difference. But, suppose the husband could sue at law, this defendant could not make this defence, that he will not pay, but will keep this fund in satisfaction of the husband's debt to him; for it is clear, at law, a creditor of the husband cannot set off the husband's debt against the demand of the husband and wife, and being entitled in her right he must sue with her. Still less should he be permitted to retain in equity *upon that ground; for, where he is permitted to avail himself of [*427] the legal right, the right must be clear. There have been several other cases, in which the Court has acted upon a residue, just as if the property was in the hands of trustees. The accident, that Montolieu is the administrator, cannot alter the right of the wife. In *Atherton* v. *Knowell*, a husband, entitled in right of his wife to an income, being unable to maintain her, the Court referred it to the Master to see what it would be proper to allow her out of that fund; *Sleech* v. *Thorington*;[4] *Watkyns* v. *Watkyns*, there cited;[5] *Milner* v. *Colmer*;[6] *Oglander* v. *Baston*.[7]

The only ground that can be taken against this bill is, that Lord Elibank became the purchaser of what might in future accrue to Lady Elibank; but there is no stipulation of that sort in the settlement, nor any indication of that intention. On the contrary, all the funds settled are her own, and a very scanty provision is made for her out of his estate. In *Burton* v. *Blaster*,

---

[1] 1 P. Wms. 458.   [2] 1 Cox, 153; 1 P. Wms. 459; Mr. Cox's note
[3] 2 Ves. jun. 676.   [4] 2 Ves. 560.   [5] 2 Atk. 96.
[6] 2 P. Wms. 639.   [7] 1 Vern. 396.

in 1775, the husband having become a bankrupt, the question arose between the assignees and the wife. The bill was filed by the assignees; and, though an objection was raised on account of the settlement, the wife obtained her equity. In *Pawlet* v. *Delavel*[1] it is laid down that though the Court will make a decree, where the husband and wife are parties, where the wife has a proper settlement, to pay to the husband and wife, where the wife has not had a sufficient settlement the Court will not. As to the form of this suit, the wife sues alone, it is true, not with her husband; but that was the case in *Worrall* v. *Marlar;* if she has the equity against her husband, she must be entitled to sue.

The Attorney-General, Mr. *Mansfield*, and Mr. *W. Agar*, for the defendant Montolieu.—The objection to the form of the suit would merely occasion delay; and a bill would be filed in their joint names.

There is no case in which the Court has decreed against a trustee who had paid the husband without suit, that the wife had 428] an equity to charge the trustee. The husband *suing in the Ecclesiasticial Court is suing persons unwilling to pay him; and the trustee or executor, so sued, has come into this Court to restrain him. That is quite a different case. Suppose the husband institutes a suit in the Ecclesiastical Court, and the trustee submits to pay, could the wife come here and say, it was in fraud of her equity? Lord Hardwicke, in *Jewson* v. *Moulson*, supposes a case, where the husband can come at the property without the aid of the Court. All the instances are, where the person has refused to pay, unless compelled by a Court of equity. That gives the jurisdiction; and none can be produced, where the executor has been prevented from paying to the husband, if he chose to do so; or where, having paid to the husband, he has been charged as upon a breach of duty by reason of that payment, and made to refund. The case of *Worrall* v. *Marlar*, is a singular one, and was influenced by the insolvency of the husband; but this plaintiff has a competent provision.

This case is certainly new, in the circumstances that the husband is debtor to the other defendant; but if he could have paid the husband, and the Court would not have made him refund, there can be no difference from his retaining against the husband. Suppose Lord Elibank had sued, and the equity of the wife, having a very large provision, was out of the question, this Court would never compel the administrator to pay that share to his debtor, unless the latter would allow the debt. This Court goes infinitely beyond Courts of law, as to set off. It would be strange to permit the wife to intervene against the administrator retaining, where she could not intervene to prevent his paying her husband, and the husband paying his debt out of that. *Burdan* v. *Blaster, Jewson* v. *Moulson*, and all the other cases, go upon the same ground; that the property was in the Court, and the husband, or his assignees, could not have it without the assistance of the Court. In this case the plaintiff comes to get it from the administrator, contrary to the plainest equity between him and her husband. There is no instance of a bill, by the wife against her husband, to have *the property settled to her separate use; which is the object of this bill. This property, though subject to the equity of the wife, is the property of the husband: *Packer* v. *Wyndham*.[1] [*429]

The *Solicitor-General*, in reply.—*Packer* v. *Wyndham* has nothing to do with this case. The wife being dead, and without issue, the question arose between the assignees of Mr. Packer. and the next of kin of Mrs. Packer; and it was insisted that, if the agreement had been carried into execution, Mr. Packer would have been entitled to the money: and she having been provid d for during her life, and being dead, and not having left any children, the purpose for which the Court laid its hand upon the property, to secure a settlement, was at an end. The rule is clearly laid down in *March* v. *Head*,[2] and it is now a settled rule, that if a husband, in right of his wife, becomes entitled to any sum exceeding 200*l.*, this Court will not permit him to have it without a reference to the Master, for the purpose of a settlement, unless the wife consents that it shall be paid to her husband. The rule is clear, that, wherever the husband becomes entitled to sue in right of his wife, she must consent that he shall have it, or he is under the necessity of making a settlement, unless the Master is of opinion that the settlement already made by the husband is such as to answer all the purposes of the wife. *Packer* v. *Wyndham*, is mentioned by Lord Hardwicke in *Bates* v. *Dandy*,[3] as consisting of many particular circumstances. *Worrall* v. *Marlar* has determined, that the wife may file the bill by her next friend; and there can be no doubt, that this plaintiff has an interest that will enable her to file such a bill for the purpose of having her property ascertained. Lord Elibank is passive. It is true, if he had assigned this to Montolieu, that might have bound the plaintiff; but he has not done so. This administrator stands in the character of trustee, and has no right to object, merely for his own advantage. If this bill should be dismissed the defendant would not be discharged, but on the death of Lord Elibank the right would survive, and she might file *a new bill. [*430] It is not like a release. If a proper settlement has not been made, there must be a proposal laid before the Court, as in *Worrall* v. *Marlar*. That must be made by the husband, not by Montolieu, who has no more right than any other creditor.

LORD CHANCELLOR LOUGHBOROUGH.[4]—I wish to consider this case.

[1] Prec Ch. 412.   [2] 3 Atk. 720.
[3] 2 Atk. 207. See statement of Bates v. Dandy, from Reg. Lib. 1 Russ. 33, n., and a note of Lord Hardwicke's judgment, 3 Russ. 72, n.
[4] Afterwards Earl of Rosslyn.

LORD CHANCELLOR LOUGHBOROUGH.—The only difficulty I had in this cause was upon the form of the suit: whether a married woman, by her next friend, could be the plaintiff in this court.

With respect to the point made by the answer of Montolieu, that he had a right to retain against the debt of the husband, being possessed of the fund as administrator, and the wife being one of the next of kin, I am very clearly of opinion the defendant had no right to retain.[1] The administrator is trustee for the next of kin: the plaintiff being one of them, if she has any equity against her husband with regard to this money, that equity will clearly bar any right of retainer he can set up to the property, of which he became administrator.

With respect to the only difficulty I had upon the point of form, if she is entitled, and there is no way of asserting her right against her husband, except by a bill, that objection, I think, does not weigh much. If the defendant Montolieu had done what would have been the natural thing and the right thing, and what he certainly would have done but for his own interest, he would have been the plaintiff, desiring the Court to dispose of the fund, and for her benefit, to protect her interest in it. Then, upon all the circumstances, it is very clear, if it had come before the Court, it would have been matter of course to have pronounced upon her equity upon the bill of the administrator, praying that the money in his hands might be properly disposed of; and I would not have suffered this money to be paid to Lord Elibank, without making a provision for her, for the provision [*431] upon her marriage *was clearly not adequate to her fortune; and it is clear that provision was made upon the expectation, that, by circumstances to occur in his family, there would be an opportunity to do better for her at a future period. The difficulty was, that it was very unusual in point of form—the bill coming on the part of the wife instead of the husband.

Declare that the defendant Montolieu is not entitled to retain, in satisfaction of the debt due from the defendant Lord Elibank to him, but that the distributive share of Lady Cranstown's fortune, accruing to the plaintiff, as one of her next of kin, is subject to a farther provision in favour of the plaintiff and her children, the settlement made upon her marriage being inadequate to the fortune she then possessed. Refer it to the Master to take the accounts, and to see a proper settlement made upon the plaintiff and her children, regard being had to the extent of her fortune and the settlement already made upon her.

---

[1] See also Carr v. Taylor, 10 Ves. 574; Ex parte Blagden, 2 Rose, 294; Ex parte O'Farrell, 1 G. & J. 347.

Lightning Source UK Ltd.
Milton Keynes UK
UKHW011824231219
355935UK00001B/124/P